GHOSTS

TRUE ENCOUNTERS
WITH THE WORLD BEYOND

GHOSTS

TRUE ENCOUNTERS
WITH THE WORLD BEYOND

HANS HOLZER

By the author of
Great American Ghost Stories,
Ghost Hunter, and *Life Beyond.*

BLACK DOG
& LEVENTHAL
PUBLISHERS

Published by
Black Dog & Leventhal Publishers, Inc.
151 West 19th Street
New York, NY 10011

Distributed by
Workman Publishing Company
708 Broadway
New York, NY 10003

Designed by Martin Lubin Graphic Design

Typesetting by Brad Walrod / High Text Graphics

Manufactured in the United States of America

h g f e d

Holzer, Hans, 1920–
    Ghosts / by Hans Holzer.
        p.   cm.
    Includes bibliographical references.
    ISBN 1-884822-64-9
    1. Ghosts. 2. Supernatural. I. Title.
    GR580.H56   1997   96-52613
    133.1—dc21   CIP

CONTENTS

INTRODUCTION   11

CHAPTER ONE   **The Nature of Life and Death**   13

CHAPTER TWO   **What Every Would-be Ghost Hunter Should Know**   23

CHAPTER THREE   **Ghosts and the World of the Living**   29

CHAPTER FOUR   **What Exactly *Is* a Ghost?**   45

CHAPTER FIVE   **Famous Ghosts**   57

   1   The Conference House Ghost
   2   The Stranger at the Door
   3   A Visit with Alexander Hamilton's Ghost
   4   The Fifth Avenue Ghost
   5   The Case of the Murdered Financier
   6   The Rockland County Ghost
   7   A Revolutionary Corollary: Patrick Henry, Nathan Hale, et al.
   8   The Vindication of Aaron Burr
   9   Assassination of a President: Lincoln, Booth, and the Traitors Within
 10   A Visit with Woodrow Wilson
 11   Ring Around the White House
 12   The Ill-Fated Kennedys: From Visions to Ghosts
 13   Michie Tavern, Jefferson, and the Boys
 14   A Visit with the Spirited Jefferson
 15   Major André and the Question of Loyalty
 16   Benedict Arnold's Friend
 17   The Haverstraw Ferry Case
 18   "Ship of Destiny": The U.S.F. Constellation
 19   The Truth About Camelot
 20   Her Name Was Trouble: The Secret Adventure of Nell Gwyn
 21   Ghosts Around Vienna
 22   The Secret of Mayerling
 23   Royalty and Ghosts
 24   A Visit with Robert Louis Stevenson
 25   Bloody Mary's Ghost
 26   Spectral Mary, Queen of Scots
 27   Renvyle
 28   Is This You, Jean Harlow?
 29   Do The Barrymores Still Live Here?
 30   The Latest Adventures of the Late Clifton Webb
 31   The Haunted Rocking Chair at Ash Lawn
 32   A Visit with Carole Lombard's Ghost
 33   Mrs. Surratt's Ghost at Fort McNair

34 The Bank Street Ghost
35 The Whistling Ghost
36 The Metuchen Ghost
37 A Greenwich Village Ghost
38 The Hauntings at Seven Oaks
39 The Central Park West Ghost
40 The Ghosts at St. Mark's
41 The Clinton Court Ghosts
42 Hungry Lucy
43 The House Ghost of Bergenville
44 The Riverside Ghost
45 Ocean-Born Mary
46 The Ghosts of Stamford Hill
47 The "Spy House" Ghosts of New Jersey
48 The Strange Case of the Colonial Soldier
49 The House on Plant Avenue
50 The Whaley House Ghosts
51 The Ghost at the Altar
52 A Ghost's Last Refuge
53 The Octagon Ghosts
54 The Octagon Revisited
55 The Integration Ghost
56 The Ardmore Boulevard Ghosts
57 The Ghost Who Refused to Leave
58 The Haunted Motorcycle Workshop
59 Encountering the Ghostly Monks
60 The Somerset Scent (Pennsylvania)
61 The House of Evil (New York)
62 The Specter in the Hallway (Long Island)
63 The Bayberry Perfume Ghost (Philadelphia)
64 The Headless Grandfather (Georgia)
65 The Old Merchant's House Ghost (New York City)
66 The House on Fifth Street (New Jersey)
67 Morgan Hall (Long Island)
68 The Guardian of the Adobe (California)
69 The Mynah Bird (Canada)
70 The Terror on the Farm (Connecticut)
71 A California Ghost Story
72 The Ghostly Usher of Minneapolis
73 The Ghostly Adventures of a North Carolina Family
74 Reba's Ghost
75 Henny from Brooklyn
76 Longleat's Ghosts
77 The Ghosts at Blanchard
78 The Ghosts of Edinburgh
79 The Ghostly Monk of Monkton
80 Scottish Country Ghosts
81 The Ghost on the Kerry Coast
82 Haunted Kilkea Castle, Kildare

Contents

83 The Ghosts at Skryne Castle
84 Ghost Hunting in County Mayo
85 The Ghost at La Tour Malakoff, Paris
86 Haunted Wolfsegg Fortress, Bavaria
87 A Haunted Former Hospital in Zurich
88 The Lady from Long Island
89 The Ghost of the Olympia Theatre
90 The Haunted Rectory
91 The Haunted Seminary
92 The Ghostly Sailor of Alameda
93 The Ghost Clock
94 The Ghost of Gay Street
95 The Ship Chandler's Ghost
96 The Ghost-Servant Problem at Ringwood Manor
97 The Phantom Admiral
98 The Ghosts in the Basement
99 Miss Boyd of Charles Street, Manhattan
100 The Haunted Ranch at Newbury Park, California
101 The Narrowsburgh Ghost
102 The Ghost in the Pink Bedroom
103 The Poughkeepsie Rectory Ghost
104 The Ghost at West Point
105 The Stenton House, Cincinnati
106 The Ghost at El Centro
107 The Ghostly Stagecoach Inn
108 Mrs. Dickey's Ghostly Companions
109 The "Presence" on the Second-Floor Landing
110 The Oakton Haunt
111 The Restless Ghost of the Sea Captain
112 The Confused Ghost of the Trailer Park
113 The Ghost Who Would Not Leave
114 The Ghost at Port Clyde
115 A Plymouth Ghost
116 The Ghosts at the Morris-Jumel Mansion

CHAPTER SEVEN   **Haunted Places**   541

117 The Case of the Lost Head
118 The Woman on the Train (Switzerland)
119 The Lady of the Garden (California)
120 The Ghost Car (Kansas)
121 The Ghostly Monks of Aetna Springs
122 Who Landed First in America?
123 The Haunted Organ at Yale
124 The Ghost on Television
125 The Gray Man of Pawley's Island (South Carolina)
126 Haunted Westover (Virginia)
127 The Case of the I.R.A. Ghosts
128 The Last Ride
129 The San Francisco Ghost Bride

CHAPTER EIGHT   **Haunted People**   593

130   The Strange Death of Valerie K.
131   The Warning Ghost
132   Jacqueline
133   The Wurmbrand Curse
134   Dick Turpin, My Love
135   The Restless Dead
136   The Devil in the Flesh (Kansas)
137   The Case of the Buried Miners
138   The Ghostly Lover
139   The Vineland Ghost
140   Amityville, America's Best-Known Haunted House

CHAPTER NINE   **Stay-Behinds**   631

141   When The Dead Stay On
142   Alabama Stay-Behinds
143   Arkansas Stay-Behinds
144   Georgia Stay-Behinds
145   A Tucker Ghost
146   The Howard Mansion Ghost
147   The Stay-Behinds: Not Ready to Go
148   Rose Hall, Home of the "White Witch" of Jamaica
149   There Is Nothing Like a Scottish Ghost
150   The Strange Case of Mrs. C's Late but Lively Husband
151   The Ghost of the Little White Flower
152   Raynham Hall
153   The Ghost of the Pennsylvania Boatsman

CHAPTER TEN   **Poltergeists**   667

154   The Devil in Texas
155   Diary of a Poltergeist
156   The Millbrae Poltergeist Case
157   The Ghosts of Barbery Lane
158   The Garrick's Head Inn, Bath

CHAPTER ELEVEN   **Ghosts That Aren't**   707

     Contacts and Visits by Spirits
     When the Dead Reach Out to the Living
     Unfinished Business
     When the Dead Help the Living
159   Vivien Leigh's Post-Mortem Photograph
160   How the Dead Teacher Said Good-bye
     Bilocation or the Etheric Double of a Living Person
     Astral Projections or Out-of-Body Experiences
     Psychic Imprints of the Past
161   The Monks of Winchester Cathedral
162   The Secret of Ballinguile

Contents

CHAPTER TWELVE   **Psychic Photography—The Visual Proof**   741

    Communications from Beyond through Photography:
        Track Record and Test Conditions
    The Mediumship of John Myers
    Authentic "Spirit Pictures" Taken at Séances
    Spirit Photography at a Camp
    Some Unexpected Spirit Faces
    Photographing Materializations
    The Physician, Catherine the Great, and Polaroid Spirit Photography
    Mae Burrow's Ghostly Family Picture
    A Ghostly Apparition in the Sky
    The Parish House Ghosts

BOOKS PREVIOUSLY PUBLISHED BY HANS HOLZER   759

HANS HOLZER IS THE AUTHOR of 119 books, including *Life Beyond, The Directory of Psychics, America's Mysterious Places*, and *Windows to the Past.*

He has written, produced and hosted a number of television programs, notably "Ghost in the House," "Beyond the Five Senses," and the NBC series, "In Search of...," and has appeared on numerous national television programs, and lectured widely. He has written for national magazines, such as *Mademoiselle, Penthouse, Longevity,* and columns in national weeklies.

Hans Holzer studied at Vienna University, Austria, Columbia University, New York, and holds a Ph.D. from the London College of Applied Science. Professor Holzer taught parapsychology for eight years at the New York Institute of Technology, is a member of the Authors Guild, Writers Guild of America, Dramatists' Guild, the New York Academy of Science, and the Archaeological Institute of America; he is listed in *Who's Who in America*, and lives in New York City.

Introduction

AS WE APPROACH WHAT IS PERCEIVED to be the millennium, people's interests are veering toward the cosmic. Even ordinary Joes and Janes who normally wouldn't be caught dead reading an astrology column are suddenly wondering what the year 2000 will mean for them and this world of ours.

To begin with, the millennium has already come and gone. Jesus was born not in the year zero but in 7 B.C., on October 9, to be exact, as I proved quite a while ago after fifteen years of archeological research. This business of the millennium is strictly hype, a promotion that's suppose to make people think something very special is going to happen in the year 2000. The psychological effects of the impending "millennium," however, are already upon us—casting a shadow in terms of a renewed great interest in things paranormal, for instance.

Several new TV talk shows and documentaries dealing with psychic phenomena and the exploration of the frontiers of human consciousness have sprung up, filling the television screens with tabloid tidbits often lacking in depth and validating research. Fictional forays into worlds beyond are also currently hugely successful both in film and television, and in books and even Websites.

As a purveyor of genuine information regarding psychic phenomena, I welcome this resurgence of curiosity in worlds beyond the physical because contemplating these matters tends to make people think about themselves, their ultimate fate, and the nature of humankind itself.

When it comes to dealing with the hard evidence of life after death, there are three classes of people—and this may remain the case for a long time to come, considering how resistant humans are to embracing radically new or different concepts.

There are those who ridicule the idea of anything beyond the grave. This category includes anybody from hard-line scientists to people who are only comfortable with the familiar, material world and really do not wish to examine any evidence that might change their minds. The will to disbelieve is far stronger than the will to believe—though neither leads to proof and hard evidence.

Then there are those who have already accepted the evidence of a continued existence beyond physical death, including people who have arrived at this conclusion through an examination of hard evidence, either personal in nature or from scientifically valid sources. They are the group I respect the most, because they are not blind believers. They rightfully question the evidence, but they have no problem accepting it when it is valid. Included in this group are the religious-metaphysical folks, although they require no hard proof to validate their convictions, which emanate from a belief system that involves a world beyond this one.

The third group is often thrown offtrack when trying to get at the truth by the folks in the metaphysical camp. This makes it more difficult for them to arrive at a proper conviction regarding the psychic. The thing for this third group is to stick to its principles and not become blind believers.

The vast majority of people belong to the third group. They are aware of the existence of psychical phenomena and the evidence for such phenomena, including case histories and scientific investigations by open-minded individuals. But they may be skeptical. They hesitate to join the second group only because of their own inner resistance to such fundamental changes in their philosophical attitudes toward life and death. For them, therefore, the need to be specific when presenting evidence or case histories, which must be fully verifiable, is paramount, as is an acceptable explanation for their occurrence.

It is hoped that those in the second group will embrace the position of the last group: that there are no boundaries around possibilities, provided that the evidence bears it out.

Prof. Hans Holzer, Ph.D.
New York, New York, November 1996

CHAPTER ONE

The Nature of Life and Death

WHAT IS MAN? WHY IS MAN? HOW IS MAN?

To fully understand the existence of ghosts, one needs to come to grips with the nature of life—and death. Ghosts, apparitions, messages from beyond, and psychic experiences involving a loved one or friend who has passed away all presuppose that the receiver or observer accept the reality of another dimension into which we all pass at one time or another. A die-hard (if you pardon the pun) committed to pure material reality, even atheism, will not be comfortable with the subject of this book. But the subject of ghosts just won't go away. They have always been with us, under one designation or another, depending on the time period, culture, or religious orientation of the people to whom the experiences have occurred.

This is certainly not a matter of *belief* "in" a reality other than the ordinary three-dimensional one. It is, to the contrary, an *awareness* that we all have within us another component that passes on to the next stage of life fully intact in most cases, and somewhat disturbed in some. For everyone, except the skeptic, the evidence of this is overwhelming. For the skeptic all of this will always be unacceptable, no matter how concrete the grounds for believing. Above all, the nature of life and death requires a full understanding of the nature of man. One must come to this from an unbiased point of view, unafraid of the philosophical consequences of making adjustments in one's attitude toward life and death.

Although humans have walked on the moon and will soon reach for the stars, we have yet to learn what we are. After millions of years of existence on this planet, we are still unable to come to grips with the most important question of all: What is man? Why is man? How is man?

To toss the problem of man into the lap of religion by judging it to be the whim of an omnipotent creator is merely to beg the question. Even if we were to accept uncritically the notion of instantaneous creation by a superior force, it would leave unanswered the questions that would immediately arise from such a notion: Who created the creator?

To go the other end of the scale and ascribe our existence to a slow process of natural evolution in which particles of matter—chemicals—were mixed in certain ways to form larger pieces of matter and ultimately reached the stage where life began sounds like a more sensible approach to the puzzle of our existence. But only on the surface. For if we were to accept the theory of evolution—and there is good enough evidence that is valid—we would still be faced with the very problem religion leaves us: Who arranged things in this way, so that infinitesimal bits of matter would join to create life and follow what is obviously an orderly pattern of development?

Whether we are theistic or atheistic, materialistic or idealistic, the end result, as I see it, seems to lead to the same door. That door, however, is closed. Behind it lies the one big answer man has searched for, consciously or unconsciously, since the dawn of time.

Is man an animal, derived from the primates, as Dr. Desmond Morris asserted in The *Naked Ape*? Is he merely an accidental development, whereby at one point in time a large ape became a primitive man?

To this day, this hypothesis is unacceptable to large segments of the population. The revulsion against such a hypothesis stems largely from strongly entrenched fundamentalist religious feelings rather than from any enlightened understanding that knows better than Darwin. When religion goes against science, even imperfect science, it is bound to lose out.

On the other hand, the less violent but much more effective resistance, by scientists, doctors, and intellectuals, to the hypothesis that supports man's spontaneous creation by a superior being is so widespread today that it has made heavy inroads in church attendance and forced the religious denominations to think of new approaches to lure large segments of the population back into the fold, or at least to interest them in the nonreligious aspects of the church. But the professionals and intellectuals are by no means alone in their rejection of traditional views. A large majority of students, on both college and high school levels, are nonbelievers or outright cynics. They don't always cherish that position, but they have not found an alternative. At least they had not until ESP (extrasensory perception) came along to offer them a glimpse at a kind of immorality that their scientific training *could* let them accept.

To the average person, then, the problem of what man is remains unsolved and as puzzling as ever. But this is not true of the psychic or esoteric person.

An increasing number of people throughout the world have at one time or another encountered personal proof of man's immortality. To them, their own experiences are sufficient to assure them that we are part of a greater scheme of things, with some sort of superior law operating for the benefit of all. They do not always agree on what form this superior force takes, and they generally reject the traditional concepts of a personal God, but they acknowledge the existence of an orderly scheme of things and the continuance of life as we know it beyond the barriers of death and time.

Many of those who accept in varying degrees spiritual concepts of life after death do so uncritically. They believe from a personal, emotional point of view. They merely replace a formal religion with an informal one. They replace a dogma they find outmoded, and not borne out by the facts as they know them, with a flexible, seemingly sensible system to which they can relate enthusiastically.

It seems to me that somewhere in between these orthodox and heterodox elements lies the answer to the problem. If we are ever to find the human solution and know what man is, why he is, and how he is, we must take into account all the elements, strip them of their fallacies, and retain the hard-core facts. In correlating the facts we find, we can then construct an edifice of thought that may solve the problem and give us the ultimate answers we are seeking.

What is life? From birth, life is an evolution through gradual, successive stages of development, that differ in detail with each and every human being. Materialistic science likes to ascribe these unique tendencies to environment and parental heritage alone. Astrology, a very respectable craft when properly used, claims that the radiation from the planets, the sun, and the moon influences the body of the newly born from birth or, according to some astrological schools, even from the moment of conception. One should not reject the astrological theory out of hand. After all, the radiation of man-made atom bombs affected the children of Hiroshima, and the radiation from the cosmos is far greater and of far longer duration. We know very little about radiation effects as yet.

That man is essentially a dual creature is no longer denied even by medical science. Psychiatry could not exist were it not for the acknowledgment that man has a mind, though the mind is invisible. Esoteric teaching goes even further: man has a soul, and it is inserted into the body of the newborn at the moment of birth. Now if the soul joins the body only at or just before the moment of birth, then a fetus has no personality, according to this view, and abortion is not a "sin." Some orthodox religions do not hold this view and consider even an unborn child a full person. It is pretty difficult to prove objectively either assertion, but it is not impossible to prove scientifically and rationally that man *after* birth has a nonphysical component, variously called soul, psyche, psi, or personality.

What is death, then? The ceasing of bodily functions due to illness or malfunction of a vital organ reverses the order of what occurred at birth. Now the two components of man are separated again and go in different directions. The body, deprived of its operating force, is nothing more than a shell and subject to ordinary laws affecting matter. Under the influence of the atmosphere, it will rapidly decompose and is therefore quickly disposed of in all cultures. It returns to the earth in various forms and contributes its basic chemicals to the soil or water.

The soul, on the other hand, continues its journey into what the late Dr. Joseph Rhine of Duke University called "the world of mind." That is, to those who believe there is a soul, it enters the world of the mind; to those who reject the very notion of a soul factor, the decomposing body represents all the remains of man at death. It is this concept that breeds fear of death, fosters nihilistic attitudes toward life while one lives it, and favors the entire syndrome of expressions such as "death is the end," "fear the cemetery," and "funerals are solemn occasions."

Death takes on different powers in different cultures. To primitive man it was a vengeful god who took loved ones away when they were still needed.

To the devout Christian of the Middle Ages, death was the punishment one had to fear all one's life, for after death came the reckoning.

West Africans and their distant cousins, the Haitians, worship death in a cult called the "Papa Nebo" cult.

Spanish and Irish Catholics celebrate the occasions of death with elaborate festivities, because they wish to help the departed receive a good reception in the afterlife.

Only in the East does death play a benign role. In the spiritually advanced beliefs of the Chinese, the Indians, and the ancient Egyptians, death was the beginning, not the end. Death marked the gate to a higher consciousness, and it is because of this philosophy that the dreary aspects of funerals as we know them in the West are totally absent from eastern rites. They mark their funerals, of course, but not with the sense of finality and sadness that pervade the western concept. Perhaps this benigness has some connection with the strong belief in a hereafter that the people of the East hold, as opposed to the Western world, which offers, aside from a minority of fundamentalists to whom the Bible has spelled out everything without further need of clarification, faith in an afterlife but has no real conviction that it exists.

There is scarcely a religion that does not accept the continuance of life beyond death in one form or another. There are some forms of "reform" Judaism and some extremely liberal Christian denominations that stress the morality aspects of their religions rather than basic belief in a soul and its survival after death in a vaguely defined heaven or hell. Communism in its pure Marxist form, which is of course *a kind of religion*, goes out of its way to denounce the soul concept.

Not a single religious faith tries to rationalize its tenets of immortality in scientifically valid terms. Orthodox Catholicism rejects the inquiry *itself* as unwanted or at the very least proper only for those inside the professional hierarchy of the church. Some Protestant denominations, especially fundamentalists, find solace in biblical passages that they interpret as speaking out against any traffic with death or inquiry into areas dealing with psychic phenomena. The vast majority of faiths, however, neither encourage nor forbid the search for objective proof that what the church preaches on faith may have a basis in objective fact.

It is clear that one step begets another. If we accept the reality of the soul, we must also ask ourselves, where does the soul go after death? Thus interest concerning the nature of man quite easily extends to a curiosity about the world that the soul inhabits once it leaves its former abode.

Again, religion has given us descriptions galore of the afterlife, many embroidered in human fashion with elements of man-made justice but possessing very little factuality.

Inquiring persons will have to wait until they themselves get to the nonphysical world, or they will have to use one of several channels to find out what the nonphysical world is like.

When experience is firsthand, one has only one's own status or state of being to consider; waiting for or taking the ultimate step in order to find out about the next world is certainly a direct approach.

Desire to communicate with the dead is as old as humanity itself. As soon as primitive man realized that death could separate him from a loved one and that he could not prevent that person's departure, he thought of the next best thing: once gone, how could he communicate with the dead person? Could he bring him back? Would he join him eventually?

These are the original elements, along with certain observed forces in nature, that have contributed to the structure of early religions.

But primitive man had little or no understanding of nature around him and therefore personified all forces he could not understand or emulate. Death became a person of great and sinister power who ruled in a kingdom of darkness somewhere far away. To communicate with a departed loved one, one would have to have Death's permission or would have to outsmart him. Getting Death's permission to see a loved one was rare (e.g., the story of Orpheus and Eurydice).

Outsmarting Death was even more difficult. Everyman never succeeded, nor did the wealthy Persian merchant who ran away to Samara only to find Death there waiting for him. In these examples Death was waiting for the man himself, and it was not a question of getting past him into his kingdom to see the departed one. But it shows how all-knowing the personified Death of primitive and ancient man was.

The West African form of contact with the dead, which the people of Haiti still practice to this day, is speaking through the water; again it is a question of either avoiding the voodoo gods or bribing them. Communication with the dead is never easy in primitive society.

In the East, where ancestor worship is part of the religious morality, communication is possible through the established channel of the priest, but the occasion has to warrant it. Here too we have unquestioned adherence to the orders given to the living by their forebears, as a matter of respect. As we dig deeper into the religious concepts of eastern origin, we find such a constant interplay between the living and the dead that one understands why some Asians are not afraid to die or do not take the kind of precautions western people would take under similar circumstances. Death to them is not a stranger or a punishment or a fearful avenger of sins committed in the flesh.

In modern times, only spiritualism has approached the subject of the dead with a degree of rationalism, although it tends to build its edifice of believability occasionally on very shaky ground. The proof of survival of the human personality is certainly not wanting, yet spiritualism ignores the elements in man that are mortal but nonphysical, and gives credit to the dead for everything that transcends the five senses. But research on ESP has shown that some of these experiences need not be due to the spirit intervention, although they may not be explicable in terms of orthodox science. We do have ESP in our incarnate state and rarely use the wondrous faculties of our minds to the fullest.

Nevertheless, the majority of spiritualist beliefs are capable of verification. I have worked with some of the best spiritualist mediums to learn about trafficking with the "other world." For the heart of spiritualist belief *is* communication with the dead. If it exists, then obviously spiritualism has a very good claim to be a first-class religion, if not more. If the claim is fraudulent, then spiritualism would be as cruel a fraud as ever existed, deceiving man's deepest emotions.

Assuming that the dead exist and live on in a world beyond our physical world, it would be of the greatest interest to learn the nature of the secondary world and the laws that govern it. It would be important to understand "the art of dying," as the medieval esoterics called it, and come to a better understanding also the nature of this transition called death.

Having accepted the existence of a nonphysical world populated by the dead, we next should examine the continuing contacts between the two worlds and the two-way nature of these communications: those initiated by the living, and those undertaken by the dead.

Observation of so-called spontaneous phenomena will be just as important as induced experiments or attempts at contact. In all this we must keep a weather eye open for deceit, misinterpretation, or self-delusion. So long as there is a human faculty involved in this inquiry, we must allow for our weaknesses and limitations. By accepting safeguards, we do not close our minds to the astonishing facts that may be revealed just because those facts seem contrary to current thinking. If we proceed with caution, we may

contribute something that will give beleaguered humankind new hope, new values, and new directions.

RETURN FROM THE DEAD

Nothing could be more convincing than the testimony of those people who have actually *been* to that other world and returned "to tell the tale." This material substantiates much of the phenomena that has made itself known to many in personal encounters, and also with the help of competent psychics and mediums.

While evidence of communication with the dead will provide the bulk of the evidential material that supports the conditions and decrees existing in that other world, we have also a number of testimonies from people who have entered the next world but not stayed in it. The cases involve people who were temporarily separated from their physical reality—without, however, being cut off from it permanently—and catapulted into the state we call death. These are mainly accident victims who recovered and those who underwent surgery and during the state of anesthesia became separated from their physical bodies and were able to observe from a new vantage point what was happening to them. Also, some people have traveled to the next world in a kind of dream state and observed conditions there that they remembered upon returning to the full state of wakefulness.

I hesitate to call these cases dreams since, as I have already pointed out in another work on the psychic side of dreams, the dream state covers a multitude of conditions, some of which at least are not actual dreams but states of limited consciousness and receptivity to external inputs. Out-of-body experiences, formerly known as astral projections, are also frequently classed with dreams, while in fact they are a form of projection in which the individual is traveling outside the physical body.

The case I am about to present are, to the best of my knowledge, true experiences by average, ordinary individuals. I have always shied away from accepting material from anyone undergoing psychiatric treatment, not because I necessarily discount such testimony, but because some of my readers might.

As Dr. Raymond Moody noted in his work, there is a definite pattern to these near misses, so to speak, the experiences of people who have gone over and then returned. What they relate about conditions on the "other side of life" is frequently similar to what other people have said about these conditions, yet the witnesses have no way of knowing each other's experiences, have never met, and have not read a common source from which they could draw such material if they were inclined to deceive the investigator, which they certainly are not. In fact, many of these testimonies are reluctantly given, out of fear of ridicule or perhaps because the individuals themselves are not sure of what to make of it. Far from the fanatical fervor of a religious purveyor, those whose cases have been brought to my attention do not wish to convince anyone of anything but merely want to report what has occurred in their lives. In publishing these reports, I am making the information available to those who might have had similar experiences and have wondered about them.

I cannot emphasize strongly enough that the cases I am reporting in the following pages do not fall into the category of what many doctors like to call hallucinations, mental aberrations, or fantasies. The clarity of the experiences, the full remembrance of them afterward, the many parallels between individual experiences reported by people in widely scattered areas, and finally the physical condition of the percipients at the time of the experience all weigh heavily against the dismissal of such experiences as being of hallucinatory origin.

Mrs. Virginia S., a resident in one of the western states, had in the past held various responsible jobs in management and business. On March 13, 1960, she underwent surgery for, as she put it, repair to her muscles. During the operation, she lost so much blood she was declared clinically dead. Nevertheless, the surgeons worked feverishly to bring her back, and she recovered. This is what Mrs. S. experienced during the period when the medical team was unable to detect any sign of life in her:

"I was climbing a rock wall and was standing straight in the air. Nothing else was around it; it seemed flat. At the top of this wall was another stone railing about two feet high. I grabbed for the edge to pull myself over the wall, and my father, who is deceased, appeared and looked down at me. He said, 'You cannot come up yet; go back, you have something left to do.' I looked down and started to go down and the next thing I heard were the words 'She's coming back.'"

Mrs. J. L. H., a resident in her middle thirties living in British Columbia, had an amazing experience on her way back from the funeral of her stepfather, George H. She was driving with a friend, Clarence G., and there was a serious accident. Clarence was killed instantly, and Mrs. H. was seriously hurt. "I don't remember anything except seeing car lights coming at me, for I had been sleeping," Mrs. H. explained. "I first remember seeing my stepdad, George, step forward out of a cloudy mist and touch me on my left shoulder. He said, 'Go back, June, it's not time yet.' I woke up with the weight of his hand still on my shoulder."

The curious thing about this case is that two people were in the same accident, yet one of them was evidently marked for death while the other was not. After Mrs. H. had recovered from her injuries and returned home, she woke up one night to see a figure at the end of her bed holding out his hand toward her as if wanting her to come with him. When she turned her light on, the figure disappeared, but it always returned when she turned the light off again. During subsequent appearances, the entity tried to lift Mrs. H. out of her bed, pulling all the covers off her, thereafter forcing her to sleep with the lights on. It

would appear that Clarence could not understand why he was on the other side of life without his friend.

Mrs. Phyllis G., also from Canada, had a most remarkable experience in March 1949. She had just given birth to twin boys at her home, and the confinement seemed normal and natural. By late evening, however, she began to suffer from a very severe headache. By morning she was unconscious and was rushed to the hospital with a cerebral hemorrhage. She was unconscious for three days during which the doctors did their best to save her life. It was during this time that she had a most remarkable experience.

"My husband's grandmother had died the previous August, but she came to me during my unconscious state, dressed in the whitest white robe, and there was light shining around her. She seemed to me to be in a lovely, quiet meadow. Her arms were held out to me and she called my name. 'Phyllis, come with me.' I told her this was not possible as I had my children to take care of. Again she said, 'Phyllis, come with me, you will love it here.' Once again, I told her it wasn't possible, I said, 'Gran, I can't. I must look after my children.' With this she said, 'I must take someone. I will take Jeffrey.' I didn't object to this, and Gran just faded away." Mrs. G. recovered, and her son Jeffrey, the first of the two twins, wasn't taken either and at twenty-eight years old was doing fine. His mother, however, was plagued by a nagging feeling in the back of her mind that perhaps his life may not be as long as it ought to be. During the moments when her grandmother appeared, Mrs. G. had been considered clinically dead.

There are many cases on record in which a person begins to become part of another dimension even when there is still hope for recovery, but at a time when the ties between consciousness and body are already beginning to loosen. An interesting case was reported to me by Mrs. J. P. of California. While still a teenager, Mrs. P. had been very ill with influenza but was just beginning to recover when she had a most unusual experience.

One morning her father and mother came into her bedroom to see how she was feeling. "After a few minutes I asked them if they could hear the beautiful music. I still remember that my father looked at my mother and said, 'She's delirious.' I vehemently denied that. Soon they left. As I glanced out my second-floor bedroom window towards the wooded hills I love, I saw a sight that literally took my breath away. There, superimposed on the trees, was a beautiful cathedral-type structure from which that beautiful music was emanating. Then I seemed to be looking down on the people. Everyone was singing, but it was the background music that thrilled my soul. Someone dressed in white was leading the singing. The interior of the church seemed strange to me. It was only in later years, after I had attended services at an Episcopal church and also at a Catholic church, that I realized the front of the church I had seen was more in the Catholic style, with the beautiful altar. The vision faded. Two years later, when I was ill again, the scene and music returned."

On January 5, 1964, Mr. R. J. I. of Pittsburgh, Pennsylvania, was rushed to the hospital with a bleeding ulcer. On admittance he received a shot and became unconscious. Attempts were immediately made to stop the bleeding, and finally he was operated on. During the operation, Mr. I. lost fifteen pints of blood, suffered convulsions, and had a temperature of 106 degrees. He was as close to death as one could come and was given the last rites of his church. However, during the period of his unconsciousness he had a remarkable experience. "On the day my doctor told my wife I had only an hour to live, I saw, while unconscious, a man with black hair and a white robe with a gold belt come from behind the altar, look at me, and shake his head. I was taken to a long hall, and purple robes were laid out for me. There were many candles lit in this hall."

Many cases of this kind occur when the subject is being prepared for surgery or undergoing surgery; sometimes the anesthetic allows disassociation to occur more easily. This is not to say that people necessarily hallucinate under the influence of anesthetic drugs or due to the lack of blood or from any other physical cause. If death is the dissolution of the link between physical body and etheric body, it stands to reason that any loosening of this link is likely to allow the etheric body to move away from its physical shell, although still tied to it either by an invisible silver cord or by some form of invisible tie that we do not as yet fully understand. Otherwise those who have returned from the great beyond would not have done so.

Mrs. J. M., a resident of Canada, was expecting her fourth child in October 1956.

"Something went wrong, and when I had a contraction I went unconscious. My doctor was called, and I remember him telling me he couldn't give any anesthetic as he might have to operate. Then I passed out, but I could still hear him talking and myself talking back to him. Then I couldn't hear him any longer, and I found myself on the banks of a river with green grass and white buildings on the other side. I knew if I could get across I'd never be tired again, but there was no bridge and the water was very rough. I looked back and I saw myself lying there, back in the hospital, with nurses and doctors around me, and Dr. M. had his hand on the back of my neck and he was calling me, and he looked so worried that I knew I had to go back. I had the baby, and then I was back in the room and the doctor explained to my husband what happened. I asked him why he had his hand on my neck, and he replied that it was the only place on my body where he could find a pulse and for over a minute he couldn't even feel one there. Was this the time when I was standing on the riverbank?"

Deborah B. is a young lady living in California with a long record of psychic experiences. At times, when she's intensely involved in an emotional situation, she undergoes what we parapsychologists call a disassociation of personality. For a moment, she is able to look into another dimension, partake of visionary experiences not seen or felt by others in her vicinity. One such incident occurred to Deborah during a theater arts class at school. She looked up from her script and saw "a man standing there in a flowing white robe, staring at me, with golden or blond hair down to his shoulders; a misty fog surrounded him. I couldn't make out his face, but I knew he was staring at me. During this time I had a very peaceful and secure feeling. He then faded away."

Later that year, after an emotional dispute between Deborah and her mother, another visionary experience took place. "I saw a woman dressed in a long, blue flowing robe, with a white shawl or veil over her head, beckoning to a group of three or four women dressed in rose-colored robes and white veils. The lady in blue was on the steps of a church or temple with very large pillars. Then it faded out."

One might argue that Deborah's imagination was creating visionary scenes within her, if it weren't for the fact that what she describes has been described by others, especially people who have found themselves on the threshold of death and have returned. The beckoning figure in the flowing robe has been reported by many, sometimes identified as Jesus, sometimes simply as master. The identification of the figure depends, of course, on the religious or metaphysical attitude of the subject, but the feeling caused by his appearance seems to be universally the same: a sense of peace and complete contentment.

Mrs. C. B. of Connecticut has had a heart problem for over 25 years. The condition is under control so long as she takes the tablets prescribed for her by her physician. Whenever her blood pressure passes the two hundred mark, she reaches for them. When her pulse rate does not respond to the medication, she asks to be taken to the hospital for further treatment. There drugs are injected into her intravenously, a procedure that is unpleasant and that she tries to avoid at all costs. But she has lived with this condition for a long time and knows what she must do to survive. On one occasion she had been reading in bed and was still awake around five o'clock in the morning. Her heart had been acting up again for an hour or so. She even applied pressure to various pressure points she knew about, in the hope that her home remedies would slow down her pulse rate, but to no avail. Since she did not wish to awaken her husband, she was waiting to see whether the condition would abate itself. At that moment Mrs. B. had a most remarkable experience.

"Into my window flew, or glided, a woman. She was large, beautiful, and clothed in a multicolored garment with either arms or wings close to her sides. She stopped and hovered at the foot of my bed to the right and simply stayed there. I was so shocked, and yet I knew that I was seeing her as a physical being. She turned neither to the right nor to the left but remained absolutely stone-faced and said not a word. Then I seemed to become aware of four cherubs playing around and in front of her. Yet I sensed somehow that these were seen with my mind's eye rather than with the material eyes. I don't know how to explain from any reasonable standpoint what I said or did; I only knew what happened. I thought, 'This is the angel of death. My time has come.' I said audibly, 'If you are from God, I will go with you.' As I reached out my hand to her, she simply vanished in midair. Needless to say, the cherubs vanished too. I was stunned, but my heart beat had returned to normal."

Mrs. L. L. of Michigan dreamed in July 1968 that she and her husband had been killed in an automobile accident. In November of that year, the feeling that death was all around her became stronger. Around the middle of the month, the feeling was so overwhelming she telephoned her husband, who was then on a hunting trip, and informed him of her death fears. She discussed her apprehensions with a neighbor, but nothing helped allay her uneasiness. On December 17, Mrs. L. had still another dream, again about imminent death. In this dream she knew that her husband would die and that she could not save him, no matter what she did. Two days later, Mrs. L. and her husband were indeed in an automobile accident. He was killed, and Mrs. L. nearly died. According to the attending physician, Dr. S., she should have been a dead woman, considering her injuries. But during the stay in the hospital, when she had been given up and was visited by her sister, she spoke freely about a place she was seeing and the dead relatives she was in contact with at the time. Although she was unconscious, she knew that her husband was dead, but she also knew that her time had not come, that she had a purpose to achieve in life and therefore could not stay on the "plane" on which she temporarily was. The sister, who did not understand any of this, asked whether Mrs. L. had seen God and whether she had visited heaven. The unconscious subject replied that she had not seen God nor was she in heaven, but on a certain plane of existence. The sister thought that all this was nonsense and that her dying sister was delirious, and left.

Mrs. L. herself remembers quite clearly how life returned to her after her visit to the other plane. "I felt life coming to my body, from the tip of my toes to the tip of my head. I knew I couldn't die. Something came back into my body; I think it was my soul. I was at complete peace about everything and could not grieve about the death of my husband. I had complete forgiveness for the man who hit us; I felt no bitterness toward him at all."

Do some people get an advance glimpse of their own demise? It would be easy to dismiss some of the precognitive or seemingly precognitive dreams as anxiety-caused, perhaps due to the dreamer's fantasies. However, many of these dreams parallel each other and differ from ordinary

anxiety dreams in their intensity and the fact that they are remembered so very clearly upon awakening.

A good case in point is a vivid dream reported to me by Mrs. Peggy C., who lives in a New York suburb. The reason for her contacting me was the fact that she had developed a heart condition and was wondering whether a dream she had had twenty years before was an indication that her life was nearing its end. In the dream that had so unnerved her through the years, she was walking past a theater where she met a dead brother-in-law. "I said to him, 'Hi, Charlie, what are you doing here?' He just smiled, and then in my dream it dawned on me that the dead come for the living. I said to him 'Did you come for me?' He said, 'Yes.' I said to him, 'Did I die?' He said, 'Yes.' I said, 'I wasn't sick. Was it my heart?' He nodded, and I said, 'I'm scared.' He said, 'There is nothing to be scared of, just hold onto me.' I put my arms around him, and we sailed through the air of darkness. It was not a frightening feeling but a pleasant sensation. I could see the buildings beneath us. Then we came to a room where a woman was sitting at a desk. In the room were my brother-in-law, an old lady, and a mailman. She called me to her desk. I said, 'Do we have to work here too?' She said, 'We are all assigned to duties. What is your name?' I was christened Bernadine, but my mother never used the name. I was called Peggy. I told her 'Peggy.' She said, 'No, your name is Bernadine.' Then, my brother-in-law took me by the arms and we were going upstairs when I awakened. I saw my husband standing over me with his eyes wide open, but I could not move. I was thinking to myself, 'Please shake me, I'm alive,' but I could not move or talk. After a few minutes, my body jerked in bed, and I opened my eyes and began to cry." The question is, did Mrs. C. have a near-death experience and return from it, or was her dream truly precognitive, indicative perhaps of things yet to come?

Doctor Karlis Osis published his findings concerning many deathbed experiences, wherein the dying recognize dead relatives in the room who have seemingly come to help them across the threshold into the next world. A lady in South Carolina, Mrs. M. C., reported one particularly interesting case to me. She herself has a fair degree of mediumship, which is a factor in the present case. "I stood behind my mother as she lay dying at the age of some seventy years. She had suffered a cerebral stroke, and was unable to speak. Her attendants claimed they had had no communication with her for over a week. As I let my mind go into her, she spoke clearly and flawlessly, 'If only you could see how beautiful and perfect it all is,' she said, then called out to her dead father, saying 'Papa, Papa.' I then spoke directly to her and asked her, did she see Papa? She answered as if she had come home, so to speak. 'Yes, I see Papa.' She passed over onto the other side shortly, in a matter of days. It was as if her father had indeed come after her, as if we saw him, and she spoke to me clearly, with paralyzed mouth and throat muscles."

Sometimes the dead want the living to know how wonderful their newfound world is. Whether this is out of a need to make up for ignorance in one's earth life, where such knowledge is either outside one's ken or ignored, or whether this is in order to acquaint the surviving relative with what lies ahead, cases involving such excursions into the next world tend to confirm the near-death experiences of those who have gone into it on their own, propelled by accidents or unusual states of consciousness. One of the most remarkable reports of this kind came to me through the kindness of two sisters living in England. Mrs. Doreen B., a senior nursing administrator, had witnessed death on numerous occasions. Here is her report.

"In May 1968 my dear mother died. I had nursed her at home, during which time we had become extremely close. My mother was a quiet, shy woman who always wished to remain in the background. Her last weeks were ones of agony; she had terminal cancer with growths in many parts of her body. Towards the end of her life I had to heavily sedate her to alleviate the pain, and after saying good-bye to my daughter on the morning of the seventh of May, she lapsed into semiconsciousness and finally died in a coma, approximately 2:15 A.M. on the eighth of May 1968. A few nights after her death I was gently awakened. I opened my eyes and saw Mother.

"Before I relate what happened, I should like to say that I dream vividly every night, and this fact made me more aware that I was not dreaming. I had not taken any drinks or drugs, although of course my mind and emotions revolved around my mother. After Mother woke me, I arose from my bed; my hand instinctively reached out for my dressing gown, but I do not remember putting it on. Mother said that she would take me to where she was. I reacted by saying that I would get the car out, but she said that I would not need it. We traveled quickly, I do not know how, but I was aware that we were in the Durking Leatherhead area and entering another dimension.

"The first thing I saw was a large archway. I knew I had seen it before, although it means nothing to me now. Inside the entrance a beautiful sight met my eyes. There was glorious parkland, with shrubbery and flowers of many colors. We traveled across the parkland and came to a low-built white building. It seemed to have the appearance of a convalescent home. There was a veranda, but no windows or doors as we know them. Inside everything was white, and Mother showed me a bed that she said was hers. I was aware of other people, but they were only shadowy white figures. Mother was very worried about some of them and told me that they did not know that they were dead. However, I was aware that one of a group of three was a man.

"Mother had always been very frugal in dress, possibly due to her hardships in earlier years. Therefore her wardrobe was small but neat, and she spent very little on clothing if she could alter and mend. Because of this I was surprised when she said she wished that she had more clothes. In life Mother was the kindest of women, never saying or thinking ill of anyone. Therefore I found it hard to understand her resentment of a woman in a long, flowing robe who appeared on a bridge in the grounds. The bridge looked beautiful, but Mother never took me near it. I now had to return, but to my question, 'Are you happy?' I was extremely distressed to know that she did not want to leave her family. Before Mother left me she said a gentle 'Good-bye dear.' It was said with a quiet finality, and I knew that I would never see her again.

"It was only afterward when I related it to my sister that I realized that Mother had been much more youthful than when she died and that her back, which in life had been rounded, was straight. Also I realized that we had not spoken through our lips but as if by thought, except when she said, 'Good-bye, dear.' It is now three-and-a-half years since this happening, and I have had no further experience. I now realize that I must have seen Mother during her transition period, when she was still earthbound, possibly from the effects of the drugs I administered under medical supervision, and when her tie to her family, particularly her grandchild, was still very strong."

Don McI., a professional astrologer living in Richland, Washington, has no particular interest in psychic phenomena, is in his early seventies, and worked most of his life as a security patrolman. His last employment was at an atomic plant in Washington state. After retirement, he took up astrology full-time. Nevertheless, he had a remarkable experience that convinced him of the reality of afterlife existence.

"On November 15, 1971, at about 6:30 A.M., I was beginning to awaken when I clearly saw the face of my cousin beside and near the foot of my bed. He said, 'Don, I have died.' Then his face disappeared, but the voice was definitely his own distinctive voice. As far as I knew at that time, he was alive and well. The thought of telling my wife made me feel uncomfortable, so I did not tell her of the incident. At 11:00 A.M., about four-and-a-half hours after my psychic experience, the mail arrived. In it was a letter from my cousin's widow, informing us that he had a heart failure and was pronounced dead upon arrival at the hospital. She stated that his death occurred at 9:30 P.M., November 8, 1971, at Ventura, California. My home, where my psychic experience took place, is at least a thousand miles from Ventura, California. The incident is the only psychic experience I've ever had."

William W. lives and works in Washington, D.C. Because of some remarkable psychic incidents in his life, he began to wonder about the survival of human personality. One evening he had a dream in which he saw himself walking up a flight of stairs where he was met by a woman whom he immediately recognized as his elderly great-aunt. She had died in 1936. "However she was dressed in a long gray dress of about the turn-of-the-century style, her hair was black, and she looked vibrantly young. I asked her in the dream where the others were, and she referred me to a large room at the top of the stairs. The surroundings were not familiar. I entered the room and was amazed to see about fifteen people in various types of dress, both male and female and all looking like mature adults, some about the age of thirty. I was able to recognize nearly all of these people although most I had seen when they were quite old. All appeared jovial and happy. I awakened from the dream with the feeling that somebody had been trying to tell me something."

There are repeated reports indicating that the dead revert to their best years, which lie around the age of thirty in most cases, because they are able to project a thought-form of themselves as they wish. On the other hand, where apparitions of the dead are intended to prove survival of an individual, they usually appear as they looked prior to death, frequently wearing the clothes they wore at the time of their passing.

Not all temporary separations of the body and etheric self include a visit to the next world. Sometimes the liberated self merely hangs around to observe what is being done with the body. Mrs. Elaine L. of Washington state reported an experience that happened to her at the age of sixteen. "I had suffered several days from an infected back tooth, and since my face was badly swollen, our dentist refused to remove the tooth until the swelling subsided. When it did, and shortly after the novocaine was administrated, I found myself floating close to an open window. I saw my body in the dental chair and the dentist working feverishly. Our landlady, Mrs. E., who had brought me to the dentist, stood close by, shaking me and looking quite flabbergasted and unbelieving. My feeling at the time was of complete peace and freedom. There was no pain, no anxiety, not even an interest in what was happening close to that chair.

"Soon I was back to the pain and remember as I left the office that I felt a little resentful. The dentist phoned frequently during the next few days for assurance that I was alright."

According to one report, a Trappist monk who had suffered a cardiac arrest for a period of ten minutes remembered a visit to a world far different from that which his religion had taught him. Brother G. spoke of seeing fluffy white clouds and experiencing a sense of great joy. As a result of his amazing experience, the monk now helps people on the terminal list of a local hospital face death more adequately. He can tell them that there nothing to fear.

A New Jersey physician, Dr. Joseph G., admitted publicly that he had "died" after a severe attack of pneumonia in 1934 and could actually see himself lying on the deathbed. At the time, worrying how his mother would feel if he died, he heard a voice tell him that it was entirely up to him whether wanted to stay on the physical plane or go across. Because of his own experience, Dr. G. later paid serious attention to the accounts of several patients who had similar experiences.

The number of cases involving near-death experiences—reports from people who were clinically dead for varying lengths of time and who then recovered and remembered what they experienced while unconscious—is considerable. If we assume that universal law covers all contingencies, there should be no exceptions to it. Why then are some people allowed to glimpse what lies ahead for them in the next dimension without actually entering that dimension at the time of the experience? After investigating large numbers of such cases, I can only surmise that there are two reasons. First of all, there must be a degree of self-determination involved, allowing the subject to go forward to the next dimension or return to the body. As a matter of fact, in many cases, though not in all, the person is being given that choice and elects to return to earth. Secondly, by the dissemination of these witnesses' reports among those in the physical world, knowledge is put at our disposal, or rather at the disposal of those who wish to listen. It is a little like a congressional leak—short of an official announcement, but much more than a mere rumor. In the final analysis, those who are ready to understand the nature of life will derive benefits from this information, and those who are not ready, will not.

CHAPTER TWO

What Every Would-be Ghost Hunter Should Know

EVER SINCE I WROTE my first book, entitled *Ghost Hunter*, in 1965, that epithet has stuck to me like glue even when it was clearly not politic, such as when I started to teach parapsychology at the New York Institute of Technology and received a professorship. As more and more of my true ghost stories appeared in my books, a new vogue—amateur ghost hunting—sprang up. Some of these ghost hunters were genuinely interested in research, but many were strictly looking for a thrill or just curious. Foolish assumptions accompany every fad, as well as some dangers. Often a lack of understanding of the aspects of ghost hunting, of what the phenomena mean, is harmless; on the more serious side, this lack of knowledge can cause problems at times, especially when the possibility exists of making contact with a negative person for whom death has changed very little.

However, readers should keep in mind when looking at these pages the need to forget a popular notion about ghosts: that they are always dangerous, fearful, and hurt people. Nothing could be further from the truth. Nor are ghosts figments of the imagination, or the product of motion picture writers. Ghostly experiences are neither supernatural nor unnatural; they fit into the general pattern of the universe we live in, although the majority of conventional scientists don't yet understand what exactly ghosts are. Some do, however—those who have studied parapsychology have come to understand that human life does continue beyond what we commonly call death. Once in a while, there are extraordinary circumstances surrounding a death, and these exceptional circumstances create what we popularly call ghosts and haunted houses.

Ever since the dawn of humankind, people have believed in ghosts. The fear of the unknown, the certainty that there was something somewhere out there, bigger than life, beyond its pale, and more powerful than anything walking the earth, has persisted throughout the ages, and had its origins in primitive man's thinking. To him, there were good and evil forces at work in nature, which were ruled over by supernatural beings, and were to some degree capable of being influenced by the attitudes and prayers of humans. Fear of death was, of course, one of the strongest human emotions. It still is. Although some belief in survival after physical death has existed from the beginning of time, no one has ever cherished the notion of leaving this earth.

Then what are ghosts—if indeed there *are* such things? To the materialist and the professional skeptic—that is to say, people who do not wish their belief that death is the end of life as we know it to be disturbed—the notion of ghosts is unacceptable. No matter how much evidence is presented to support the reality of the phenomena, these people will argue against it and ascribe it to any of several "natural" causes. Delusion or hallucination must be the explanation, or perhaps a mirage, if not outright trickery. Entire professional groups that deal in the manufacturing of illusions have taken it upon themselves to label anything that defies their ability to reproduce it artificially through trickery or manipulation as false or nonexistent. Especially among photographers and magicians, the notion that ghosts exist has never been popular. But authentic reports of psychic phenomena along ghostly lines keep coming into reputable report centers such as societies for psychic research, or to parapsychologists like myself.

Granted, a certain number of these reports may be inaccurate due to self-delusion or other errors of fact. Still an impressive number of cases remains that cannot be explained by any other means than that of extrasensory perception.

According to psychic research, a ghost appears to be a surviving emotional memory of someone who has died traumatically, and usually tragically, but is unaware of his or her death. A few ghosts may realize that they are dead but may be confused as to where they are, or why they do not feel quite the way they used to feel. When death occurs unexpectedly or unacceptably, or when a person has lived in a place for a very long time, acquiring certain routine habits and becoming very attached to the premises, sudden, unexpected death may come as a shock. Unwilling to part with the physical world, such human personalities continue to stay on in the very spot where their tragedy or their emotional attachment had existed prior to physical death.

Ghosts do not travel; they do not follow people home; nor do they appear at more than one place. Nevertheless, there are reliable reports of apparitions of the dead having indeed traveled and appeared to several people in various locations. These, however, are not ghosts in the sense that I understand the term. They are free spirits, or discarnate entities, who are inhabiting what Dr. Joseph B. Rhine of Duke University has called the "world of the mind." They may be attracted for emotional reasons to one place or another at a given moment in order to communicate with someone on the earth plane. But a true ghost is unable to make such moves freely. Ghosts by their very nature are not unlike psychotics in the flesh; they are quite unable to fully understand their own predicament. They are kept in place, both in time and space, *by* their emotional ties to the spot. Nothing can pry them loose from it so long as they are reliving over and over again in their minds the events leading to their unhappy deaths.

Sometimes this is difficult for the ghost, as he may be too strongly attached to feelings of guilt or revenge to "let go." But eventually a combination of informative remarks by the parapsychologist and suggestions to call upon the deceased person's family will pry him loose and send him out into the free world of the spirit.

Ghosts have never harmed anyone except through fear found within the witness, of his own doing and because of his own ignorance as to what ghosts represent. The few cases where ghosts have attacked people of flesh and blood, such as the ghostly abbot of Trondheim, are simply a matter of mistaken identity, where extreme violence at the time of death has left a strong residue of memory in the individual ghost. By and large, it is entirely safe to be a ghost hunter or to become a witness to phenomena of this kind.

In his chapter on ghosts, in *Man, Myth, and Magic*, Douglas Hill presents alternate hypotheses one by one and examines them. Having done so, he states, "None of these explanations is wholly satisfactory, for none seems applicable to the whole range of ghost lore." Try as man might, ghosts can't be explained away, nor will they disappear. They continue to appear frequently all over the world, to young and old, rich and poor, in old houses and in new houses, on airports and in streets, and wherever tragedy strikes man. For ghosts are indeed nothing more or nothing less than a human being trapped by special circumstances in this world while already being of the next. Or, to put it another way, a human being whose spirit is unable to leave the earthy surroundings because of unfinished business or emotional entanglements.

It is important not to be influenced by popular renditions of ghostly phenomena. This holds true with most movies, with the lone exception of the recent picture *Ghost*, which was quite accurate. Television, where distortions and outright inventions abound, is especially troublesome. The so-called "reality" shows such as "Sightings" and some of its imitators like to present as much visual evidence of ghosts as they can—all within a span of seven minutes, the obligatory length for a story in such programs.

To capture the attention of an eager audience, these shows present "authorities" as allegedly renowned parapsychologists who chase after supposed ghosts with all sorts of technical equipment, from Geiger counters to oscilloscopes to plain flashlights. No professional investigator who has had academic training uses any of this stuff, but the programs don't really care.

Another difficult aspect of the quest for ghosts is that not everything that appears to fit the category does indeed belong in it.

Phenomena, encounters, and experiences are either visual, auditory, or olfactory—they are manufactured through sight, sound, or smell. In addition, there are poltergeist phenomena, which are nothing more than products of the phase of a haunting when the entity is capable of producing physical effects, such as the movement of objects.

Even an experienced investigator can't always tell to which class of phenomena an event belongs—only after further investigation over an extended period of time is an explanation forthcoming.

All three types of the phenomena (except for poltergeists) can be caused by the following:

1. A bona fide ghost—that is, a person who has passed out of the physical body but remains in the etheric body (aura, soul) at or near the place of the passing due to emotional ties or trauma. Such entities are people in trouble, who are seeking to understand their predicament and are usually not aware of their own passing.

The proof that the ghost is "real" lies in the behavior of the phenomena. If different witnesses have seen or heard different things, or at different times of the day, then we are dealing with a ghost.

In the mind of the casual observer, of course, ghosts and spirits are the same thing. Not so to the trained parapsychologist: ghosts are similar to psychotic human beings, incapable of reasoning for themselves or taking much action. Spirits, on the other hand, are the surviving personalities of all of us who pass through the door of death in a relatively normal fashion. A spirit is capable of continuing a full existence in the next dimension, and can think, reason, feel, and act, while his unfortunate colleague, the ghost, can do none of these things. All he can do is repeat the final moments of his passing, the unfinished business, as it were, over and over again until it becomes an obsession. In this benighted state, ghosts are incapable of much action and therefore are almost always harmless. In the handful of cases where ghosts seem to have caused people suffering, a relationship existed between the person and the ghost. Someone slept in a bed in which someone else had been murdered and was mistaken by the murderer for the same individual, or the murderer returned to the scene of his crime and was attacked by the person he had killed. But by and large, ghosts do not attack people, and there is no danger in observing them or having contact with them, *if* one is able to.

The majority of ghostly manifestations draw upon energy from the living in order to penetrate our three-dimensional world. Other manifestations are subjective, especially when the receiver is psychic. In this case, the psychic person hears or sees the departed individual in his mind's eye only, while others cannot so observe the ghost.

Where an objective manifestation takes place, and everyone present is capable of hearing or seeing it, energy drawn from the living is used by the entity to cause certain phenomena, such as an apparition, a voice phenomenon, or perhaps the movement of objects, the sound of footsteps, or doors opening by themselves, and other signs of a presence. When the manifestations become physical in nature and are capable of being observed by several individuals or recorded by machines, they are called poltergeist phenomena, or noisy phenomena. Not every ghostly manifestation leads to that stage, but many do. Frequently, the presence in the household of young children or of mentally handicapped older people lends itself to physical manifestations of this kind, since the unused or untapped sexual energies are free to be used for that purpose.

Ghosts—that is, individuals unaware of their own passing or incapable of accepting the transition because of unfinished business—will make themselves known to living people at infrequent intervals. There is no sure way of knowing when or why some individuals make a post-mortem appearance and others do not. It seems to depend on the intensity of feeling, the residue of unresolved problems, that they have within their system at the time of death. Consequently, not everyone dying a violent death becomes a ghost; far from it. If this were so, our battlefields and such horror-laden places as concentration camps or prisons would indeed be swarming with ghosts, but they are not. It depends on the individual attitude of the person at the time of death, whether he or she accepts the passing and proceeds to the next stage of existence, or whether he or she is incapable of realizing that a change is taking place and consequently clings to the familiar physical environment, the earth sphere.

A common misconception concerning ghosts is that they appear only at midnight, or, at any rate, only at night; or that they eventually fade away as time goes on. To begin with, ghosts are split-off parts of a personality and are incapable of realizing the difference between day and night. They are always in residence, so to speak, and can be contacted by properly equipped mediums at all times. They may put in an appearance only at certain hours of the day or night, depending upon the atmosphere; for the fewer physical disturbances there are, the easier it is for them to communicate themselves to the outer world. They are dimly aware that there is something out there that is different from themselves, but their diminished reality does not permit them to grasp the situation fully. Consequently, a quiet moment, such as is more likely to be found at night than in the daytime, is the period when the majority of sightings are reported.

Some manifestations occur on the exact moment of the anniversary, because it is then that the memory of the unhappy event is strongest. But that does not mean that the ghost is absent at other times—merely less capable of manifesting itself. Since ghosts are not only expressions of human personality left behind in the physical atmosphere but are, in terms of physical science, electromagnetic fields uniquely impressed by the personality and memories of the departed one, they represent a certain energy imprint in the atmosphere and, as such, cannot simply fade into nothingness. Albert Einstein demonstrated that energy never dissipates, it only transmutes into other forms. Thus ghosts do not fade away over the centuries; they are, in effect, present for all eternity unless someone makes contact with them through a trance medium and brings reality to them, allowing them to understand their predicament and thus free themselves from their self-imposed prison. The moment the mirror of truth is held up to a ghost, and he or she realizes that the problems that seem insoluble are no longer important, he or she will be able to leave.

Frequently, rescuers have to explain that the only way a ghost can leave is by calling out to someone close to her in life—a loved one or a friend who will then come and take her away with them into the next stage of existence, where she should have gone long before. This is called the rescue circle and is a rather delicate operation requiring the services of a trained psychical researcher and a good trance medium. Amateurs are warned not to attempt it, especially not alone.

2. No more than 10–15% of all sightings or other phenomena are "real" ghosts. The larger portion of all sightings or sound phenomena is caused by a replaying of a past emotional event, one that has somehow been left behind, impressed into the atmosphere of the place or house. Any sensitive person—and that means a large segment of the population—can re-experience such events to varying degrees. To them these replays may seem no different from true ghostly phenomena, except that they occur exactly in the same place and at the same time of day to all those who witness them.

These phenomena are called psychic impressions, and they are in a way like photographs of past events, usually those with high emotional connotations.

3. There are cases in which sightings or sounds of this kind are caused by the living who are far away, not in time but geographically. "Phantoms of the living" is one name given the phenomenon, which is essentially telepathic. Usually these apparitions or sounds occur when it is urgent that a person reach someone who is at a distance, such as in family crises, emergencies, or on occasion, between lovers or people who are romantically linked.

These projections of the inner body are involuntary, and cannot be controlled. A variant of these phenomena, however, deliberate projections, which occur when a person puts all her emotional strength into reaching someone who is far away. Instances of this are quite rare, however.

4. Finally, we should keep in mind that though apparitions may appear to be identical, whether as earthbound spirits called ghosts, or free spirits in full possession of all mental and emotional faculties and memories—just visiting, so to speak, to convey a message—ghosts and spirits are not the same.

Compare a ghostly apparition or a spirit visit to a precious stone: a diamond and a zircon look practically the same, but they are totally different in their value. Spirits are people like you and I who have passed on to the next world without too much difficulty or too many problems; they are not bound to anything left behind in the physical world. They do, however, have ties and emotional interests in the family or friends they left behind, and they might need to let people in this world know that they are all right "over there," or they may have some business in the living world that needs to be taken care of in an orderly fashion. Ghosts, too, may have unfinished business, but are generally unable to convey their requests clearly.

Spirits, people who have died and are *living* in their duplicate "inner body," the etheric body or aura, are different from physical living people in respect to certain limitations and the time element, but spirits are simply people who have passed on to the next world with their memories and interests intact.

The only thing these four categories of phenomena have indeed in common is their density: they *seem* three-dimensional and quite solid most of the time (though not always), but try to touch one, and your hand will go right through.

Only materializations are truly three-dimensional and physical, and they do occur when there is enough energy present to "clothe" the etheric body with an albumin substance called ectoplasm or teleplasm, drawn from the glands of the medium and/or assistants (known as sitters) during a séance, and sometimes even spontaneously site where something very powerfully traumatic has occurred in the past.

Such materializations look and even feel like physical bodies, but touching them may dissolve them or hurt the principal medium, as does bright light. In any event, the ectoplasm must be returned whence it came to avoid shock and illness.

The temptation to reproduce that rarest of all psychic phenomena, the full materialization, is of course always present, but also easy to spot. When I unmasked a group of such fakers as part of an investigation into one of the Spiritualist camps in Pennsylvania, I presented the evidence on television in a program I helped produce and appeared in with Mike Wallace, who remarked, "You mean these are only ghostly actors?" to which I replied spontaneously, "No, just ghastly actors, because I caught them in the act."

Séances, which are nothing fancier than a group of people getting together for a "sitting" *in the hope* that a departed spirit might be able to communicate through her or his principal medium or one of the sitters, have fallen out of favor these days. But if someone asks you to a séance *promising* you that someone on the other side of life will be contacted, or "called"—beware. The folks on the other side are the ones who decide that they want contact with us, not the other way around.

Ouija Boards, crystal balls, and tarot cards are all useful in helping a psychic focus his or her natural gift, but they have no powers of their own. Using a board can bring trouble if those using it are potential deep-trance mediums, because an unscrupulous person on the other side might want to come in and take over the players, which would result in possession.

Communication with ghosts or spirits does sometimes occur, however, when one of the persons operating the board is psychic enough to supply the energy for a communication to take place. But the majority of what comes through a Ouija board is just stuff from the sitter's own unconscious mind, and often it is just gibberish.

A word about the dreams of ghosts or departed loved ones. We are either awake or asleep. In my view, however, if we are asleep we are "adream," for we dream *all the time* even if we don't always remember it or are not aware of it.

Some psychic experiences involving ghosts and spirits occur during sleep in the form of quasi-dreams. These are not really bona fide dreams. It is just that in the sleep-dream state, when our conscious mind is at rest, the communicator finds it easier to "get through" to us than when we are fully awake and our conscious mind and rational attitude make it harder for the communicator's emanations to penetrate our consciousness.

Many who have had such dream visitations think that they "just dreamt" the whole thing, and the medical establishment encourages this by and large, classifying such events as quasi-fantasies or nightmares, as the case may be. But in reality, they are nothing of the kind. These dreams are just as real and as meaningful in their purpose as are encounters with ghosts or spirits when one is fully awake, either at night or in plain daylight.

In the dream state, visitors do not cast objective shadows, as they often do in the waking condition, but they *are* actual people, existing in etheric bodies, who are making contact with our own etheric bodies. The message, if any, is often much clearer than it is with ordinary dreams.

We should pay attention to such incursions from the world next door, and the people who continue their existence therein, whether the event occurs while one is awake or asleep. Most important of all, do not fear either ghosts or spirits. They will not harm you—only your own fear can do that. And fear is only the absence of information. By reading these lines, you are taking an important step toward the understanding of what ghosts and spirits really are.

The cases in this book are taken from my files, which are bulging with interesting experiences of ordinary people in all walks of life, and from all corners of the globe. The majority of the witnesses knew nothing about ghosts, nor did they seek out such phenomena. When they experienced the happenings described in these pages, they were taken by surprise; sometimes shocked, sometimes worried. They came to me for advice because they could not obtain satisfactory counsel from ordinary sources such as psychologists, psychiatrists, or ministers.

Small wonder, for such professionals are rarely equipped to deal with phenomena involving parapsychology. Perhaps in years to come they will be able to do so, but not now. In all the cases, I advised the individuals not to be afraid of what might transpire in their presence, to take the phenomenon as part of human existence and to deal with it in a friendly, quiet way. The worst reaction is to become panicky in the presence of a ghost, since it will not help the ghost and will cause the observer unnecessary anxiety. Never forget that those who are "hung up" between two phases of existence are in trouble and not troublemakers, and a compassionate gesture toward them may very well relieve their anxieties.

The people whose cases I tell of in these pages seek no publicity or notoriety; they have come to terms with the hauntings to which they were witness. In some cases, a haunting has changed a person's outlook on life by showing him the reality of another world next door. In other cases, what was once fear has turned into a better understanding of the nature of humans; still other instances have permitted witnesses to the phenomena a better understanding of the situation of departed loved ones, and a reassuring feeling that they will meet again in a short time on the other side of the curtain.

Remember that any of the phenomena described here could have happened to *you*, that there is nothing *supernatural* about any of this, and that in years to come you will deal with apparitions as ordinary events, part and parcel of human experience.

Lastly, I would suggest to my readers that they do not get into arguments about the existence or nonexistence of ghosts and haunted houses. Everyone must find their own explanations for what they experience, and *belief* has nothing to do with it.

Indeed, one of the most troubling aspects of today's world is this matter of beliefs. The power of one's beliefs is a frightening thing. People often believe in things and events whether they have actually happened or not. Because of beliefs people are murdered, wars are fought, crimes are committed. Disbelief, too, contributes its share of tragedies.

Beliefs—and disbeliefs—are emotional in nature, not rational. The reasoning behind certain beliefs may *sound* rational, but it may be completely untrue, exaggerated, taken out of context, or distorted.

Once belief or disbelief by one person becomes public knowledge and spreads to large numbers of people, some very serious problems arise: love and compassion go out the window, and emotionally tinged beliefs (or disbeliefs) take over, inevitably leading to action, and usually to some kind of violence—physical, material, emotional, or moral.

In this world of spiritual uncertainty, an ever-increasing contingent of people of all ages and backgrounds want a better, safer world free of fanaticism, a world where discussion and mutual tolerance takes the place of violent confrontation.

It is sad but true that religion, far from pacifying the destructive emotions, frequently contributes to them, and sometimes is found at the very heart of the problem itself. For religion today has drifted so far from spirituality that it no longer represents the link to the deity that it originally stood for, when the world was young and smaller.

When people kill one another because their alleged paths to the deity differ, they may need a signpost indicating where to turn to regain what has been patently lost. I think this signpost is the evidence for humankind's survival of physical death, as shown in these pages, the eternal link between those who have gone on into the next phase of life and those who have been left behind, at least temporarily.

Belief is uncritical acceptance of something you cannot prove one way or another. But the evidence for ghosts and hauntings is so overwhelming, so large and so well documented, that arguing over the existence of the evidence would be a foolish thing indeed.

It is not a matter for speculation and in need of further proofs: those who look for evidence of the afterlife can easily find it, not only in these pages but also in many other works and in the records of groups investigating psychic phenomena through scientific research.

Once we realize how the "system" works, and that we pass on to another stage of existence, our perspective on life is bound to change. I consider it part of my work and mission to contribute knowledge to this end, to clarify the confusion, the doubts, the negativity so common in people today, and to replace these unfortunate attitudes with a wider expectation of an ongoing existence where everything one does in one lifetime counts toward the next phase, and toward the return to another lifetime in the physical world.

Those who fear the proof of the continued existence beyond the dissolution of the physical, outer body and would rather not know about it are short-changing themselves, for surely they will eventually discover the truth about the situation first-hand anyway.

And while there may be various explanations for what people experience in haunted houses, no explanation will ever be sufficient to negate the experiences themselves. If you are one of the many who enter a haunted house and have a genuine experience in it, be assured that you are a perfectly normal human being, who uses a natural gift that is neither harmful nor dangerous and may in the long run be informative and even useful.

CHAPTER THREE

Ghosts and the World of the Living

I HASTEN TO STATE that those who are in the next dimension, the world of the spirit, are indeed "alive"—in some ways more so than we who inhabit the three-dimensional, physical world with its limitations and problems.

This book is about ghosts in relation to us, however, for it is the living in this world who come in contact with the dead. Since ghosts don't necessarily seek us out, ghosts just *are* because of the circumstances of their deaths.

For us to be able to see or hear a ghost requires a gift known as psychic ability or ESP—extra-sensory perception. Professor Joseph Banks Rhine of Duke University thinks of ESP as an extra sense. Some have referred to it as "the sixth sense," although I rather think the gift of ESP is merely an extension of the ordinary senses beyond their usual limitations.

If you don't have ESP, you're not likely to encounter a ghost or connect with the spirit of a loved one. Take heart, however: ESP is very common, in varying degrees, and about half of all people are capable of it. It is, in my view, a *normal* gift that has in many instances been neglected or suppressed for various reasons, chiefly ignorance or fear.

Psychic ability is being recognized and used today worldwide in many practical applications. Scientific research, business, and criminal investigations have utilized this medium to extend the range of ordinary research.

The problems of acknowledging this extra faculty are many. Prior to the nineteenth century, anything bordering on the occult was considered religious heresy and had to be suppressed or at least kept quiet. In the nineteenth century, with social and economic revolution came an overbearing insistence on things material, and science was made a new god. This god of tangible evidence leaped into our present century invigorated by new technological discoveries and improvements. Central to all this is the belief that only what is available to the ordinary five senses is real, and that everything else is not merely questionable but outright fantasy. Fantasy itself is not long for this world, as it does not seem to fill any useful purpose in the realm of computers and computerized humans.

Laboring under these difficult conditions, Dr. Rhine developed a new scientific approach to the phenomena of the sixth sense some thirty years ago when he brought together and formalized many diffused research approaches in his laboratory at Duke University. But pure materialism dies hard—in fact, dies not at all. Even while Rhine was offering proof for the "psi factor" in human personality— fancy talk for the sixth sense—he was attacked by exponents of the physical sciences as being a dreamer or worse. Nevertheless, Rhine continued his work and others came to his aid, and new organizations came into being to investigate and, if possible, explain the workings of extrasensory perception.

To define the extra sense is simple enough. When knowledge of events or facts is gained without recourse to the normal five senses—sight, hearing, smell, touch, and taste—or when this knowledge is obtained with apparent disregard to the limitations of time and space, we speak of *extrasensory* perception.

It is essential, of course, that the person experiencing the sixth-sense phenomena has had no access to knowledge, either conscious or unconscious, of the facts or events, and that her impressions are subsequently corroborated by witnesses or otherwise proved correct by the usual methods of exact science.

It is also desirable, at least from an experimental point of view, that a person having an extrasensory dealing with events in the so-called future should make this impression known at once to impartial witnesses so that it can be verified later when the event does transpire. This, of course, is rarely possible because of the very nature of this sixth sense: it cannot be turned on at will, but functions best during emergencies, when a genuine need for it exists. When ordinary communications fail, something within men and women reaches out and removes the barriers of time and space to allow for communication *beyond the five senses.*

There is no doubt in my mind that extrasensory phenomena are governed by emotional impulses and therefore present problems far different from those of the physical sciences. Despite the successful experiments with cards and dice conducted for years at the Duke University parapsychology laboratory, an ESP experience is not capable of exact duplication at will.

Parapsychology, that is, the science investigating the phenomena of this kind, has frequently been attacked on these grounds. And yet normal psychology, which also deals with human emotions, does not require an exact duplication of phenomena under laboratory conditions. Of course, psychology and psychiatry themselves were under attack in the past, and have found a comfortable niche of respectability only recently. It is human nature to attack all that is new and revolutionary, because man tends to hold onto his old gods. Fifty years from now, parapsychology will no doubt be one of the *older* sciences, and hence accepted.

It is just as scientific to collect data from "spontaneous phenomena," that is, in the field, as it is to produce them in a laboratory. In fact, some of the natural sciences could not exist if it were not for *in situ* observation. Try and reconstruct an earthquake in the lab, or a collision of galaxies, or the birth of a new island in the ocean.

The crux, of course, is the presence of competent observers and the frequency with which similar, but unrelated, events occur. For example, if a hundred cases involving a poltergeist, or noisy ghost, are reported in widely scattered areas, involving witnesses who could not possibly know of each other, could have communicated with each other, or have had access to the same information about the event, it is proper scientific procedure to accept these reports as genuine and to draw certain conclusions from them.

Extrasensory perception research does not rely entirely on spontaneous cases in the field, but without them it would be meaningless. The laboratory experiments are an important adjunct, particularly when we deal with the less complicated elements of ESP, such as telepathy, intuition beyond chance, and psychic concentration—but they cannot replace the tremendous impact of genuine precognition (the ability to foresee events before they occur) and other one-time events in human experience.

The nature of ESP is spontaneous and unexpected. You don't know when you will have an experience, you can't make it happen, and you can't foretell when and how it will happen. Conditions beyond your knowledge make the experience possible, and you have no control over it. The sole exception is the art of proper thinking—the training toward a wider use of your own ESP powers—which we will discuss later.

The ESP experience can take the form of a hunch, an uncanny feeling, or an intuitive impression. Or it can be stronger and more definite, such as a flash, an image or auditory signal, a warning voice, or a vision, depending on who you are and your inborn talents as a receiver.

The first impulse with all but the trained and knowledgeable is to suppress the "message" or to explain it away, sometimes taking grotesque paths in order to avoid admitting the possibility of having had an extrasensory experience. Frequently, such negative attitudes toward what is a natural part of human personality can lead to tragedy, or, at the very least, to annoyance; for the ESP impulse is never in vain. It may be a warning of disaster or only an advance notice to look out for good opportunities ahead, but it always has significance, even though you may miss the meaning or choose to ignore the content. I call this substance of the ESP message *cognizance*, since it represents instant knowledge without logical factors or components indicating time and effort spent in obtaining it.

The strange thing about ESP is that it is really far more than an extra, sixth sense, equal in status to the other five. It is actually a *supersense* that operates through the other five to get its messages across.

Thus a sixth-sense experience many come through the sense of sight as a vision, a flash, or an impression; the sense of hearing as a voice or a sound effect duplicating an event to be; the sense of smell as strange scents indicating climates other than the present one or smells associated with certain people or places; the sense of touch—a hand on the shoulder, the furtive kiss, or fingering by unseen hands; and the sense of taste—stimulation of the palate not caused by actual food or drink.

Of these, the senses of smell and taste are rarely used for ESP communication, while by far the majority of cases involve either sight or sound or both. This must be so because these two senses have the prime function of informing the conscious mind of the world around us.

What has struck me, after investigating extrasensory phenomena for some twenty-odd years, is the thought that we are not really dealing with an additional dimension as such, an additional sense like touch or smell, but a sense that is nonphysical—the psychic, which, in order to make itself known, must manifest itself through the physical senses. Rather than an extra sense, we really have here an extension of the normal five senses into an area where logical thinking is absent and other laws govern. We can compare it to the part of the spectrum that is invisible to the naked eye. We make full use of infrared and ultraviolet and nobody doubts the existence of these "colors," which are merely extensions of ordinary red and violet.

Thus it is with extrasensory perception, and yet we are at once at war with the physical sciences, which want us to accept only that which is readily accessible to the five senses, preferably in laboratories. Until radio waves were discovered, such an idea was held to be fantastic under modern science, and yet today we use radio to contact distant heavenly bodies.

It all adds up to this: Our normal human perception, even with instruments extending it a little, is far from complete. To assert that there is no more around us than the little we can measure is preposterous. It is also dangerous, for in teaching this doctrine to our children, we prevent them from allowing their potential psychic abilities to develop unhampered. In a field where thought is a force to be reckoned with, false thinking can be destructive.

Sometimes a well-meaning but otherwise unfamiliar reporter will ask me, "How does science feel about ESP?" That is a little like asking how mathematics teachers feel about Albert Einstein. ESP is part of science. Some scientists in other fields may have doubts about its validity or its potentials, just as scientists in one area frequently doubt scientists in other areas. For example, some chemists doubt what some medical science say about the efficiency of cer-

tain drugs, or some underwater explorers differ with the opinions expressed by space explorers, and the beliefs of some medical doctors differ greatly from what other medical doctors believe. A definition of science is in order. Contrary to what some people think, science is not knowledge or even comparable to the idea of knowledge; science is merely the process of gathering knowledge by reliable and recognized means. These means, however, may change as time goes on, and the means considered reliable in the past may fail the test in the future, while, conversely, new methods not used in the past may come into prominence and be found useful. To consider the edifice of science an immovable object, a wall against which one may safely lean with confidence in the knowledge that nearly everything worth knowing is already known, is a most unrealistic concept. Just as a living thing changes from day to day, so does science and that which makes up scientific evidence.

* * *

There are, however, forces within science representing the conservative or establishment point of view. These forces are vested in certain powerful individuals who are not so much unconvinced of the reality of controversial phenomena and the advisability of including these phenomena in the scientific process as they are unwilling to change their established concept of science. They are, in short, unwilling to learn new and startling facts, many of which conflict with that which they have learned in the past, that which forms the very basis and foundation of their scientific beliefs. Science derives from *scire*, meaning "to know." *Scientia*, the Latin noun upon which our English term "science" is based, is best translated as "the ability to know," or perhaps, "understanding." Knowledge as an absolute is another matter. I doubt very much that absolute knowledge is possible even within the confines of human comprehension. What we are dealing with in science is a method of reaching toward it, not attaining it. In the end, the veil of secrecy will hide the ultimate truth from us, very likely because we are incapable of grasping it due to insufficient spiritual awareness. This insufficiency expresses itself, among other ways, through a determined reliance upon terminology and frames of reference derived from materialistic concepts that have little bearing upon the higher strata of information. Every form of research requires its own set of tools and its own criteria. Applying the purely materialistic empiric concepts of evidence to nonmaterialistic areas is not likely to yield satisfactory results. An entirely different set of criteria must be established first before we can hope to grasp the significance of those nonmaterial concepts and forces around us that have been with us since the beginning of time. These are both within us and without us. They form the innermost layer of human consciousness as well as the outer reaches of the existing universe.

* * *

By and large, the average scientist who is not directly concerned with the field of ESP and parapsychology does not venture into it, either pro or con. He is usually too much concerned with his own field and with the insufficiencies found in his own bailiwick. Occasionally, people in areas that are peripheral to ESP and parapsychology will venture into it, partly because they are attracted by it and sense a growing importance in the study of those areas that have so long been neglected by most scientists, and partly because they feel that in attacking the findings of parapsychology they are in some psychologically understandable way validating their own failures. When Professor Joseph B. Rhine first started measuring what he called the "psi" factor in man, critics were quick to point out the hazards of a system relying so heavily on contrived, artificial conditions and statistics. Whatever Professor Rhine was able to prove in the way of significant data has since been largely obscured by criticism, some of it valid and some of it not, and of course by the far greater importance of observing spontaneous phenomena in the field when and if they occur. In the beginning, however, Professor Rhine represented a milestone in scientific thinking. It was the first time that the area, formerly left solely to the occultist, had been explored by a trained scientist in the modern sense of the term. Even then, no one took the field of parapsychology very seriously; Rhine and his closest associate, Dr. Hornell Hart, were considered part of the Department of Sociology, as there had not as yet been a distinct Department of Parapsychology or a degree in that new science. Even today there is no doctorate in it, and those working in the field usually must have other credits as well. But the picture is changing. A few years ago, Dr. Jules Eisenbud of the University of Colorado at Denver startled the world with his disclosures of the peculiar talents of a certain Ted Serios, a Chicago bellhop gifted with psychic photography talents. This man could project images into a camera or television tube, some of which were from the so-called future. Others were from distant places Mr. Serios had never been to. The experiments were undertaken under the most rigid test conditions. They were repeated, which was something the old-line scientists in parapsychology stressed over and over again. Despite the abundant amount of evidence, produced in the glaring limelight of public attention and under strictest scientific test conditions, some of Dr. Eisenbud's colleagues at the University of Colorado turned away from him whenever he asked them to witness the experiments he was then conducting. So great was the prejudice against anything Eisenbud and his associates might find that might oppose existing concepts that men of science couldn't bear to find out for themselves. They were afraid they would have to unlearn a great deal. Today,

even orthodox scientists are willing to listen more than they used to. There is a greater willingness to evaluate the evidence fairly, and without prejudice, on the part of those who represent the bulk of the scientific establishment. Still, this is a far cry from establishing an actual institute of parapsychology, independent of any existing facilities— something I have been advocating for many years.

Most big corporate decisions are made illogically, according to John Mihalasky, Associate Professor of Management Engineering at the Newark College of Engineering. The professor contends that logical people can understand a scientific explanation of an illogical process. "Experiments conducted by Professor Mihalasky demonstrate a correlation between superior management ability and an executive's extrasensory perception, or ESP." According to *The New York Times* of August 31, 1969, "research in ESP had been conducted at the college since 1962 to determine if there was a correlation between managerial talent and ESP. There are tests in extrasensory perception and also in precognition, the ability to foretell events before they happen. The same precognition tests may also be of use in selecting a person of superior creative ability."

But the business side of the research establishment was by no means alone in recognizing the validity and value of ESP. According to an interview in the *Los Angeles Times* of August 30, 1970, psychiatrist Dr. George Sjolund of Baltimore, Maryland, has concluded, "All the evidence does indicate that ESP exists." Dr. Sjolund works with people suspected of having ESP talents and puts them through various tests in specially built laboratories. Scientific experiments designed to test for the existence of ESP are rare. Dr. Sjolund knows of only one other like it in the United States —in Seattle. Sjolund does ESP work only one day a week. His main job is acting director of research at Spring Grove State Hospital.

* * *

According to Evelyn de Wolfe, *Los Angeles Times* staff writer, "The phenomenon of ESP remains inconclusive, ephemeral and mystifying but for the first time in the realm of science, no one is ashamed to say they believe there is such a thing." The writer had been talking to Dr. Thelma S. Moss, assistant professor of medical psychology at UCLA School of Medicine, who had been conducting experiments in parapsychology for several years. In a report dated June 12, 1969, Wolfe also says, "In a weekend symposium on ESP more than six hundred persons in the audience learned that science is dealing seriously with the subject of haunted houses, clairvoyance, telepathy, and psychokinesis and is attempting to harness the unconscious mind."

* * *

It is not surprising that some more liberally inclined and enlightened scientists are coming around to thinking that there is something to ESP after all. Back in 1957, *Life* magazine editorialized on "A Crisis in Science":

New enigmas in physics revive quests in meta-physics. From the present chaos of science's conceptual universe two facts might strike the layman as significant. One is that the old-fashioned materialism is now even more old-fashioned. Its basic assumption—that the only 'reality' is that which occupies space and has a mass—is irrelevant to an age that has proved that matter is inter-changeable with energy. The second conclusion is that old-fashioned metaphysics, so far from being irrelevant to an age of science, is science's indispensable comple-ment for a full view of life.

Physicists acknowledge as much; a current Martin advertisement says that their rocket men's shop-talk includes 'the physics (and metaphysics) of their work.' Metaphysical speculation is becoming fashionable again. Set free of materialism, metaphysics could well become man's chief preoccupation of the next century and may even yield a world-wide consensus on the nature of life and the universe.

* * *

By 1971, this prophetic view of *Life* magazine took on new dimensions of reality. According to the *Los Angeles Times* of February 11, 1971, Apollo 14 astronaut Edgar D. Mitchell attempted to send mental messages to a Chicago engineer whose hobby was extrasensory perception. Using ESP cards, which he had taken aboard with him to transfer messages to Chicago psychic Olaf Olsen, Mitchell managed to prove beyond any doubt that telepathy works even from the outer reaches of space. The Mitchell-Olsen experiment has since become part of the history of parapsychology. Not only did it add significantly to the knowledge of how telepathy really works, it made a change in the life of the astronaut, Mitchell. According to an UPI dispatch dated September 27, 1971, Mitchell became convinced that life existed away from earth and more than likely in our own galaxy. But he doubted that physical space travel held all the answers. "If the phenomenon of astral projection has any validity, it might be perfectly valid to use it in inter-galactic travel"; Mitchell indicated that he was paying additional attention to ESP for future use. Since that time, of course, Mr. Mitchell has become an active experimenter in ESP.

* * *

A few years ago I appeared at the University of Bridgeport (Connecticut). I was lecturing on scientific evi-dence of the existence of ghosts. My lecture included some slides taken under test conditions and attracted some 1,200 students and faculty members. As a result of this particular demonstration, I met Robert Jeffries, Professor of Mechan-ical Engineering at the university and an avid parapsychol-ogist. During the years of our friendship Professor Jeffries and I have tried very hard to set up an independent insti-tute of parapsychology. We had thought that Bob Jeffries,

who had been at one time president of his own data-processing company, would be particularly acceptable to the business community. But the executives he saw were not the least bit interested in giving any money to such a project. They failed to see the practical implications of studying ESP. Perhaps they were merely not in tune with the trend, even among the business executives.

In an article dated October 23, 1969, *The Wall Street Journal* headline was "Strange Doings. Americans Show Burst of Interest in Witches, Other Occult Matters." The piece, purporting to be a survey of the occult scene and written by Stephen J. Sansweet, presents the usual hodge-podge of information and misinformation, lumping witches and werewolves together with parapsychologists and researchers. He quotes Mortimer R. Feinberg, a psychology professor at City University of New York, as saying, "The closer we get to a controlled, totally predictable society, the more man becomes fearful of the consequences." Sansweet then goes on to say that occult supplies, books, and even such peripheral things as jewelry are being gobbled up by an interested public, a sure sign that the occult is "in." Although the "survey" is on the level of a Sunday supple-ment piece and really quite worthless, it does indicate the seriousness with which the business community regards the occult field, appearing, as it did, on the front page of *The Wall Street Journal*.

More realistic and respectable is an article in the magazine *Nation's Business* of April 1971 entitled "Dollars May Flow from the Sixth Sense. Is There a Link between Business Success and Extrasensory Perception?"

We think the role of precognition deserves special consideration in sales forecasting. Wittingly or unwit-tingly, it is probably already used there. Much more research needs to be done on the presence and use of precognition among executives but the evidence we have obtained indicates that such research will be well worth-while.

As far back as 1955 the Anderson Laboratories of Brookline, Massachusetts, were in the business of forecast-ing the future. Its president, Frank Anderson, stated, "Anderson Laboratories is in a position to furnish weekly charts showing what, in all probability, the stock market will do in each coming week." Anderson's concept, or, as he calls it, the Anderson Law, involves predictions based upon the study of many things, from the moon tides to human behavior to elements of parapsychology. He had done this type of work for at least twenty-five years prior to setting up the laboratories. Most of his predictions are based upon calculated trends and deal in finances and poli-tics. Anderson claimed that his accuracy rate was 86 per-cent accurate with airplane accidents because they come in cycles, 92.6 percent accurate in the case of major fires, 84 percent accurate with automobile accidents, and that his evaluations could be used for many business purposes, from advertising campaigns to executive changes to new product launchings and even to the planning of entertainment. In politics, Anderson proposed to help chart, ahead of time, the possible outcome of political campaigns. He even dealt with hunting and fishing forecasts, and since the latter two occupations are particularly dear to the heart of the business community, it would appear that Anderson had it wrapped up in one neat little package.

* * *

Professor R. A. McConnell, Department of Biophysics and Microbiology, University of Pittsburgh, Pennsylvania, wrote in an article published by the *American Psychologist* in May 1968 that in discussing ESP before psychology students, it was not unusual to speak of the credulity of the public. He felt it more necessary, however, to examine the credibility of scientists, including both those for ESP and those against it. Referring to an article on ESP by the British researcher G. R. Price, published by *Science* in 1955, Professor McConnell points to Price's contention that proof of ESP is conclusive only if one is to accept the good faith and sanity of the experimenters, but that ESP can easily be explained away if one assumes that the experimenters, working in collaboration with their witnesses, have intentionally faked the results. McConnell goes on to point out that this unsubstantiated suggestion of fraud by Price, a chemist by profession, was being published on the first page of the most influential scientific journal in America.

A lot of time has passed since 1955: the American Association for the Advancement of Science has recently voted the Parapsychology Association a member. The latter, one of several bodies of scientific investigators in the field of parapsychology, had sought entrance into the association for many years but had been barred by the alleged prejudices of those in control. The Parapsychology Association itself, due to a fine irony, had also barred some reputable researchers from membership in its own ranks for the very same reasons. But the dam burst, and parapsychology became an accepted subject within the American Association for the Advancement of Science. The researchers were also invited to join. My own New York Committee for the Investigation of Paranormal Occurrences, founded in 1962 under the sponsorship of Eileen Garrett, president of the Parapsychology Foundation, Inc., is also a member of the American Association for the Advancement of Science.

In his article, Professor McConnell points out the fallibility of certain textbooks considered to be bulwarks of scientific knowledge. He reminds his audience that until the year 1800 the highest scientific authorities thought that there were no such things as meteorites. Then the leaders

of science found out that meteorites came from outer space, and the textbooks were rewritten accordingly. What disturbs Professor McConnell is that the revised textbooks did not mention that there had been an argument about the matter. He wonders how many arguments are still going on in science and how many serious mistakes are in the textbooks we use for study. In his opinion, we ought to believe only one half of the ideas expressed in the works on biological sciences, although he is not sure *which* half. In his view, ESP belongs in psychology, one of the biological sciences. He feels that when it comes to ESP, so-called authorities are in error. McConnell points out that most psychology textbooks omit the subject entirely as unworthy of serious consideration. But in his opinion, the books are wrong, for ESP is a real psychological phenomenon. He also shows that the majority of those doing serious research in ESP are not psychologists, and deduces from this and the usual textbook treatment of the subject as well as from his own sources that psychologists are simply not interested in ESP.

* * *

L. C. Kling, M.D., is a psychiatrist living in Strasbourg, France. He writes in German and has published occasional papers dealing with his profession. Most psychiatrists and psychoanalysts who base their work upon the findings of Sigmund Freud, balk at the idea that Dr. Freud had any interest in psychic phenomena or ESP. But the fact is—and Dr. Kling points this out in an article published in 1966—that Freud had many encounters with paranormal phenomena. When he was sixty-five years old he wrote to American researcher Herewood Carrington: "If I had to start my life over again I would rather be a parapsychologist than a psychoanalyst." And toward the end of his life he confessed to his biographer E. Jones that he would not hesitate to bring upon himself the hostility of the professional world in order to champion an unpopular point of view. What made him say this was a particularly convincing case of telepathy that he had come across.

* * *

In June of 1966 the German physicist Dr. Werner Schiebeler gave a lecture concerning his findings on the subject of physical research methods applicable to parapsychology. The occasion was the conference on parapsychology held at the city of Constance in Germany. Dr. Schiebeler, who is as well versed in atomic physics as he is in parapsychology, suggested that memory banks from deceased entities could be established independently of physical brain matter. "If during séances entities, phantoms, or spirits of the deceased appear that have been identified beyond a shadow of a doubt to be the people they pretend to be, they must be regarded as something more than images of the dead. Otherwise we would have to consider people in the physical life whom we have not seen for some time and encounter again today as merely copies of a former existence." Dr. Schiebeler goes on to say that in his opinion parapsychology has furnished definite proof for the continuance of life beyond physical death.

This detailed and very important paper was presented in written form to the eminent German parapsychologist Dr. Hans Bender, head of the Institute of Borderline Sciences at the University of Freiburg, Germany. Since it contained strong evidence of a survivalist nature, and since Dr. Bender has declared himself categorically opposed to the concept of personal survival after death, the paper remains unanswered, and Dr. Schiebeler was unable to get any response from the institute.

* * *

Despite the fact that several leading universities are doing around-the-clock research on ESP, there are still those who wish it weren't so. Dr. Walter Alvarez writes in the *Los Angeles Times* of January 23, 1972, "In a recent issue of the medical journal *M.D.*, there was an interesting article on a subject that interests many physicians and patients. Do mediums really make contact with a dead person at a séance?" He then goes on to quote an accusation of fraudulence against the famous Fox sisters, who first brought spirit rappings to public attention in 1848. "Curiously, a number of very able persons have accepted the reality of spiritualism and some have been very much interested in what goes on in séances," Dr. Alvarez reports. Carefully, he points out the few and better-known cases of alleged fraud among world-famous mediums, such as Eusepia Palladino, omitting the fact that the Italian medium had been highly authentic to the very end and that fakery had never been conclusively proven in her case. There isn't a single word about Professor Rhine or any research in the field of parapsychology in this article.

Perhaps not on the same level, but certainly with even greater popular appeal, is a "Dear Abby" reply printed by the same *Los Angeles Times* in November 5, 1969, concerning an inquiry from a reader on how to find a reputable medium to help her get in touch with her dead husband. To this "Dear Abby" replied, "Many have claimed they can communicate with the dead, but so far no one has been able to prove it."

* * *

Perhaps one can forgive such uninformed people for their negative attitude toward psychic phenomena if one looks at some of the less desirable practices that have been multiplying in the field lately. Take, for instance, the publisher of *Penthouse* magazine, an English competitor to our own *Playboy*. A prize of £25,000 was to be paid to anyone producing paranormal phenomena under test conditions. A panel consisting of Sir George Joy, Society for Psychical Research, Professor H. H. Price, Canon John Pearce-Higgins, and leading psychical researcher Mrs. Kathleen Goldney resigned in protest when they took a good look at the pages of the magazine and discovered that it was more concerned with bodies than with spirits.

The *Psychic Register International*, of Phoenix, Arizona, proclaims its willingness to list everyone in the field so that they may present to the world a *Who's Who in the Psychic World*. A parapsychology guidance institute in St. Petersburg, Florida, advised me that it is preparing a bibliography of technical books in the field of parapsychology. The Institute of Psychic Studies of Parkersburg, West Virginia, claimed that "for the first time in the United States a college of psychic studies entirely dedicated to parapsychology offering a two-year course leading to a doctorate in psychic sciences is being opened and will be centrally located in West Virginia." The list of courses of study sounded very impressive and included three credits for the mind (study of the brain), background of parapsychology (three credits), and such fascinating things as magic in speech (three credits), explaining superstitions attributed to magic; and the secrets of prestidigitation. The list of courses was heavily studded with grammatical errors and misspellings. Psychic Dimensions Incorporated of New York City, according to an article in *The New York Times*, no less, on December 4, 1970, "has got it all together," the "all" meaning individual astrologists, graphologists, occasional palmists, psychometrists, and those astute in the reading of tarot cards. According to Lisa Hammel, writer of the article, the founder of the booking agency, William J. Danielle, has "about 150 metaphysical personalities under his wing and is ready to book for a variety of occasions." The master of this enterprise explains, "I had to create an entertainment situation because people will not listen to facts." Mr. Danielle originally started with a memorable event called "Breakfast with a Witch" starring none other than Witch Hazel, a pretty young waitress from New Jersey who has established her claim to witchcraft on various public occasions.

* * *

"Six leading authorities on mental telepathy, psychic experiences and metaphysics will conduct a panel discussion on extrasensory perception," said the *New York Daily News* on January 24, 1971. The meeting was being held under the auspices of the Society for the Study of Parapsychology and Metaphysics. As if that name were not impressive enough, there is even a subdivision entitled the National Committee for the Study of Metaphysical Sciences. It turned out that the experts were indeed authorities in their respective fields. They included Dr. Gertrude Schmeidler of City College, New York, and well-known psychic Ron Warmoth. A colleague of mine, Raymond Van Over of Hofstra University, was also aboard. Although I heard nothing further of the Society for the Study of Parapsychology and Metaphysics, it seemed like a reputable organization, or rather attempt at an organization.

Until then about the only reputable organization known to most individuals interested in the study of ESP was, and is, of course, the American Society for Psychical Research located at 5 West Seventy-third Street in New York City. But the society, originally founded by Dr. J. Hislop, has become rather conservative. It rarely publishes any controversial findings any more. Its magazine is extremely technical and likely to discourage the beginning student. Fortunately, however, it also publishes the ASPR *Newsletter*, which is somewhat more democratic and popularly styled. The society still ignores parapsychologists who do not conform to their standards, especially people like myself, who frequently appear on television and make definite statements on psychic matters that the society would rather leave in balance. Many of the legacies that help support the American Society for Psychical Research were given in the hope that the society might establish some definite proof for survival of human personality after death and for answers to other important scientific questions. If researchers such as I proclaim such matters to be already proven, there would seem to be little left for the society to prove in the future. But individual leaders of the society are more outspoken in their views. Dr. Gardner Murphy, long-time president of the society and formerly connected with the Menninger Foundation, observed, "If there was one tenth of the evidence in any other field of science than there is in parapsychology, it would be accepted beyond question." Dr. Lawrence L. Le Shan, Ph.D., writer and investigator, says:

Parapsychology is far more than it appears to be on first glance. In the most profound sense it is the study of the basic nature of man....There is more to man, more to him and his relationship with the cosmos than we have accepted. Further, this 'more' is of a different kind and order from the parts we know about. We have the data and they are strong and clear but they could not exist if man were only what we have believed him to be. If he were only flesh and bone, if he worked on the same type of principles as a machine, if he were really as separated from other men as we have thought, it would be impossible for him to do the things we know he sometimes does. The 'impossible facts' of ESP tell us of a part of man long hidden in the mists of legend, art, dream, myth and mysticism, which our explorers of reality in the last ninety years have demonstrated to be scientifically valid, to be real.

* * *

While the bickering between those accepting the reality of ESP phenomena and those categorically rejecting it was still occurring in the United States, the Russians came up with a startling coup: They went into the field wholesale. At this time there are at least eight major universities in Eastern Europe with full-time, full-staffed research cen-

ters in parapsychology. What is more, there are no restrictions placed upon those working in this field, and they are free to publish anything they like. This came as rather a shock to the American scientific establishment. In her review of the amazing book by Sheila Ostrander and Lynn Schroeder, *Psychic Discoveries Behind the Iron Curtain*, Dr. Thelma Moss said, "If the validity of their statements is proved, then the American scientist is faced with the magnificent irony that in 1970 Soviet materialistic science has pulled off a coup in the field of occult phenomena equal to that of Sputnik rising into space in 1957."

It would appear that the Russians are years ahead of us in applying techniques of ESP to practical use. Allegedly, they have learned to use hypnosis at a distance, they have shown us photographs of experiments in psychokinesis, the moving of objects by mental powers alone, and even in Kirilian photography, which shows the life-force fields around living things. Nat Freedland, reviewing the book for the *Los Angeles Times*, said:

Scientists in Eastern Europe have been succeeding with astonishingly far-reaching parapsychology experiments for years. The scope of what countries like Russia, Czechoslovakia, and even little Bulgaria have accomplished in controlled scientific psychokinesis (PSI) experiments makes the western brand of ESP look namby-pamby indeed. Instead of piddling around endlessly with decks of cards and dice like Dr. J. B. Rhine of Duke University, Soviet scientists put one telepathically talented experimenter in Moscow and another in Siberia twelve hundred miles away."

Shortly afterward, the newspapers were filled with articles dealing with the Russians and their telepaths or experimenters. Word had it that in Russia there was a woman who was possessed of bioplasmic energy and who could move objects by mental concentration. This woman, Nina Kulagina, was photographed doing just that. William Rice, science writer for the *Daily News*, asked his readers, "Do you have ESP? It's hard to prove, but hard to deny." The piece itself is the usual hodgepodge of information and conjecture, but it shows how much the interest in ESP had grown in the United States. Of course, in going behind the Iron Curtain to explore the realms of parapsychology, Sheila Ostrander and Lynn Schroeder did not exactly tread on virgin territory. Those active in the field of parapsychology in the United States had long been familiar with the work of Professor L. Vasiliev. The Russian scientist's books are standard fare in this field. Dr. I. M. Kogan, chairman of the Investigation Commission of Russian Scientists dealing with ESP, is quoted as saying that he believes "many people have the ability to receive and transmit telepathic information, but the faculty is undeveloped."

* * *

And what was being done on the American side during the time the Russians were developing their parapsychology laboratories and their teams of observers? Mae West gave a magnificent party at her palatial estate in Hollywood during which her favorite psychic, "Dr." Richard Ireland, the psychic from Phoenix, performed what the guests referred to as amazing feats. Make no mistake about it, Mae West is serious about her interest in parapsychology. She even lectured on the subject some time ago at a university. But predicting the future for invited guests and charming them at the same time is a far cry from setting up a sober institute for parapsychology where the subject can be dealt with objectively and around the clock.

On a more practical level, controversial Dutchman Peter Hurkos, who fell off a ladder and discovered his telepathic abilities some years back, was called in to help the police to find clues when the Tate murder was in the headlines. Hurkos did describe one of the raiders as bearded and felt that there were overtones of witchcraft in the assault. About that time, also, Bishop James Pike told the world in headline-making news conferences that he had spoken to his dead son through various mediums. "There is enough scientific evidence to give plausible affirmation that the human personality survives the grave. It is the most plausible explanation of the phenomena that occurred," Bishop Pike is quoted.

Over in Britain, Rosemary Brown was getting messages from dead composers, including such kingpins as Beethoven, Chopin, Schubert, and Debussy. Her symphonies, attributed to her ESP capabilities, have even been recorded. When I first heard about the amazing Miss Brown, I was inclined to dismiss the matter unless some private, as yet unpublished, information about the personal lives of the dead composers was also brought out by the medium. Apparently, this is what happened in the course of time and continued investigations. I have never met Miss Brown, but one of the investigators sent to Britain to look into the case was a man whom I knew well, Stewart Robb, who had the advantage of being both a parapsychologist and a music expert. It is his opinion that the Rosemary Brown phenomenon is indeed genuine, but Miss Brown is by no means the only musical medium. According to the *National Enquirer*, British medium Leslie Flint, together with two friends, Sydney Woods and Mrs. Betty Greene, claimed to have captured on tape the voices of more than two hundred famous personalities, including Frédéric Chopin and Oscar Wilde.

A RIFT EMERGES

Gradually, however, the cleavage between an occult, or mystical, emotionally tinged form of inquiry into psychic phenomena, and the purely scientific, clinically oriented way becomes more apparent. That is not to say that both methods will not eventually merge into one single quest for truth.

Only by using all avenues of approach to a problem can we truly accomplish its solution. However, it seems to me that at a time when so many people are becoming acquainted with the occult and parapsychology in general, that it is very necessary that one make a clear distinction between a tea-room reader and a professor of parapsychology, between a person who has studied psychical phenomena for twenty-five years and has all the necessary academic credits and a Johnny-come-lately who has crept out of the woodwork of opportunism to start his own "research" center or society.

Those who sincerely seek information in this field should question the credentials of those who give answers; well-known names are always preferable to names one has never heard before. Researchers with academic credentials or affiliations are more likely to be trusted than those who offer merely paper doctorates fresh from the printing press. Lastly, psychic readers purporting to be great prophets must be examined at face value—on the basis of their accomplishments in each individual case, not upon their self-proclaimed reputation. With all that in mind and with due caution, it is still heartwarming to find so many sincere and serious people dedicating themselves more and more to the field parapsychology and making scientific inquiry into what seems to me one of the most fascinating areas of human endeavor. Ever since the late Sir Oliver Lodge proclaimed, "Psychic research is the most important field in the world today, by far the most important," I have felt quite the same way.

PSYCHIC PHOTOGRAPHY

At Washington University, St. Louis, Missouri, a dedicated group of researchers with no funds to speak of has been trying to delve into the mystery of psychic photography. Following in the footsteps of Dr. Jules Eisenbud of the University of Colorado, and my own work *Psychic Photography—Threshold of a New Science?*, this group, under the aegis of the Department of Physics at the university, is attempting to "produce psychic photographs with some regularity under many kinds of situations." The group feels that since Ted Serios discovered his ability in this field by accident, others might have similar abilities. "Only when we have found a good subject can the real work of investigating the nature of psychic photography begin," they explain. The fact that people associated with a department of physics at a major American university even speak of investigating psychic photography scientifically is so much of a novelty, considering the slurs heaped upon this subject for so many years by the majority of establishment scientists, that one can only hope that a new age of unbiased science is indeed dawning upon us.

MIND CONTROL & THE ALPHA STATE

Stanley Korn of Maryland has a degree in physics and has done graduate work in mathematics, statistics, and psychology; he works in the Navy as an operations research analyst. Through newspaper advertisements he discovered the Silva Mind Control Course and took it, becoming acquainted with Silva's approach, including the awareness of the alpha state of brain-wave activity, which is associated with increased problem-solving ability and, of course, ESP. "What induced me to take the course was the rather astonishing claim made by the lecturer that everyone taking the course would be able to function psychically to his own satisfaction or get his money back. This I had to see," Mr. Korn explained. Describing the Silva Method, which incorporates some of the elements of diagnosis developed by the late Edgar Cayce but combines it with newer techniques and what, for want of a better term, we call traveling clairvoyance, Mr. Korn learned that psychic activities are not necessarily limited to diagnosing health cases, but can also be employed in psychometry, the location of missing objects and persons, even the location of malfunctions in automobiles. "After seeing convincing evidence for the existence of psi, and experiencing the phenomenon myself, I naturally wanted to know the underlying principles governing its operation. To date, I have been unable to account for the psychic transmission of information by any of the known forms of energy, such as radio waves. The phenomena can be demonstrated at will, making controlled experiments feasible."

THE APPARATUS

But the mind-control approach is by no means the only new thing in the search for awareness and full use of ESP powers in man. People working in the field of physics are used to apparatus, to test equipment, to physical tools. Some of these people have become interested in the marginal areas of parapsychology and ESP research, and hope to contribute some new mechanical gadget to the field. According to the magazine *Purchasing Week*, new devices utilizing infrared light to pinpoint the location of an otherwise unseen intruder by the heat radiating from his body have been developed. On August 17, 1970, *Time* magazine, in its science section headlines, "Thermography: Coloring with Heat." The magazine explained that

> [I]nfrared detectors are providing stunning images that were once totally invisible to the naked eye. The new medium is called color thermography, the technique of translating heat rays into color. Unlike ordinary color photographs, which depend on reflected visible light, thermograms or heat pictures respond only to the temperature of the subject. Thus the thermographic camera

can work with equal facility in the dark or light. The camera's extraordinary capability is built around a characteristic of all objects, living or inanimate. Because their atoms are constantly in motion, they give off some degree of heat or infrared radiation. If the temperature rises high enough, the radiation may become visible to the human eye, as in the red glow of a blast furnace. Ordinarily, the heat emissions remain locked in the invisible range of infrared light.

It is clear that such equipment can be of great help in examining so-called haunted houses, psychically active areas, or psychometric objects; in other words, it can be called upon to step in where the naked eye cannot help, or where ordinary photography discloses nothing unusual. The magazine *Electronics World* of April 1970, in an article by L. George Lawrence entitled "Electronics and Parapsychology," says,

> One of the most intriguing things to emerge in that area is the now famous *Backster Effect*. Since living plants seem to react bioelectrically to thought images directed to their over-all well-being, New Jersey cytologist Dr. H. Miller thinks that the phenomenon is based upon a type of cellular consciousness. These and related considerations lead to the idea that psi is but a part of a so-called paranormal matrix—a unique communications grid that binds all life together. Its phenomena apparently work on a multi-input basis which operates beyond the known physical laws.

Lanston Monotype Company of Philadelphia, Pennsylvania, manufactures photomechanical apparatus and has done some work in the ESP field. The company attempted to develop testing equipment of use to parapsychologists. Superior Vending Company of Brockton, Massachusetts, through its design engineer, R. K. Golka, offered me a look into the matter of a newly developed image intensifier tube developed for possible use in a portable television camera capable of picking up the fine imprints left behind in the atmosphere of haunted areas. "The basic function of this tube is to intensify and pick up weak images picked up by the television camera. These are images that would otherwise not be seen or that would go unnoticed," the engineer explained. Two years later, Mr. Golka, who had by then set up his own company of electronic consultants, suggested experiments with spontaneous ionization. "If energy put into the atmosphere could be coupled properly with the surrounding medium, air, then huge amounts of ionization could result. If there were a combination of frequency and wave length that would remove many of the electron shells of the common elements of our atmosphere, that too would be of great scientific value. Of course, the electrons would fall back at random so there would be shells producing white light or fluorescence. This may be similar to the flashes of light seen by people in a so-called haunted house. In any event, if this could be done by the output of very small energies such as those coming from the human brain of microvolt and microamp range, it would be quite significant." Mr. Golka responded to my suggestion that ionization of the air accompanied many of the psychic phenomena where visual manifestations had been observed. I have held that a change occurs in the atmosphere when psychic energies are present, and that the change includes ionization of the surrounding air or ether. "Some of the things you have mentioned over the years seem to fit into this puzzle. I don't know if science has all the pieces yet, but I feel we have a good handful to work with," Mr. Golka concluded in his suggestions to me. Since that time some progress has been made in the exploration of perception by plants, and the influence of human emotions on the growth of plants. Those seeking scientific data on these experiments may wish to examine Cleve Backster's report "Evidence of a Primary Perception in Plant Life" in the *International Journal of Parapsychology*, Volume X, 1968. Backster maintains a research foundation at 165 West Forty-sixth Street in New York City.

* * *

Dr. Harry E. Stockman is head of Sercolab in Arlington, Massachusetts, specializing in apparatus in the fields of physics, electronics, and the medical profession. The company issues regular catalogues of their various devices, which range from simple classroom equipment to highly sophisticated research apparatus. The company, located at P.O. Box 78, Arlington, Massachusetts, has been in business for over twenty years. One prospectus of their laboratory states:

> In the case of mind-over-matter parapsychology psychokinetic apparatus, our guarantee applies only in that the apparatus will operate as stated in the hands of an accomplished sensitive. Sercolab would not gamble its scientific reputation for the good reason that mind-over-matter is a proven scientific fact. It is so today thanks to the amazing breakthrough by Georgia State University; this breakthrough does not merely consist of the stunning performance of some students to be able to move a magnetic needle at a distance. The breakthrough is far greater than that. It consists of Georgia State University having devised a systematic teaching technique, enabling some students in the class to operate a magnetic needle by psychokinesis force.

Obviously, science and ESP are merely casual acquaintances at the present time. Many members of the family are still looking askance at this new member of the community. They wish it would simply go away and not bother them. But parapsychology, the study of ESP, is here to stay. ESP research may be contrary to many established scientific laws and its methodology differs greatly from established practices. But it is a valid force; it exists in every sense of the term; and it must be studied fully in order to make science an honest field in the coming age. Anything less will lead scientific inquiry back to medieval thinking, back into the narrow channels of prejudice and

severely limited fields of study. In the future, only a thorough re-examination of the scientific position on ESP in general will yield greater knowledge on the subject.

The notion still persists among large segments of the population that ESP is a subject suitable only for very special people: the weird fringe, some far-out scientists perhaps, or those young people who are "into" the occult. Under no circumstances is it something respectable average citizens get involved with. An interest in ESP simply does not stand up alongside such interests as music, sports, or the arts. Anyone professing an interest in ESP is automatically classified as an oddball. This attitude is more pronounced in small towns than it is in sophisticated cities like New York, but until recently, at least, the notion that ESP might be a subject for average people on a broad basis was alien to the public mind.

During that last few years, however, this attitude has shifted remarkably. More and more, people discussing the subject of extrasensory perception are welcomed in social circles as unusual people; and they become centers of attraction. Especially among the young, bringing up the subject of ESP almost guarantees one immediate friends. True, eyebrows are still raised among older people, especially business people or those in government, when ESP is mentioned as a serious subject matter. Occasionally one still hears the comment "You don't really believe in that stuff?" Occasionally, too, people will give you an argument trying to prove that it is still all a fraud and has "long been proved to be without substance." It is remarkable how some of those avid scoffers quote "authoritative" sources, which they never identify by name or place. Even Professor Rhine is frequently pictured as a man who tried to prove the reality of ESP and failed miserably.

Of course, we must realize that people believe what they want to believe. If a person is uncomfortable with a concept, reasons for disbelief will be found even if they are dragged in out of left field. A well-known way of dismissing evidence for ESP is to quote only the sources that espouse a negative point of view. Several authors who thrive on writing "debunking books," undoubtedly the result of the current popularity of the occult subjects, make it their business to select bibliographies of source material that contain only the sort of proof they want in light of their own prejudiced purpose. A balanced bibliography would, of course, yield different results and would thwart their efforts to debunk the subject of ESP. Sometimes people in official positions will deny the existence of factual material so as not to be confronted with the evidence, if that evidence tends to create a public image different from the one they wish to project.

A good case in point is an incident that occurred on the Chicago television broadcast emceed by columnist Irving Kupcinet. Among the guests appearing with me was Colonel "Shorty" Powers of NASA. I had just remarked that tests had been conducted among astronauts to determine whether they were capable of telepathy once the reaches of outer space had been entered, in case radio communications should prove to be inadequate. Colonel Powers rose indignantly, denouncing my statement as false, saying, in effect, that no tests had been undertaken among astronauts and that such a program lacked a basis of fact. Fortunately, however, I had upon me a letter on official NASA stationery, signed by Dr. M. Koneci, who was at the time head of that very project.

* * *

The kinds of people who are interested in ESP include some very strange bedfellows: on the one hand, there are increasing numbers of scientists delving into the area with newly designed tools and new methods; on the other hand, there are lay people in various fields who find ESP a fascinating subject and do not hesitate to admit their interest, nor do they disguise their belief that it works. Scientists have had to swallow their pride and discard many cherished theories about life. Those who have been able to do so, adjusting to the ever-changing pattern of what constitutes scientific proof, have found their studies in ESP the most rewarding. The late heart specialist Dr. Alexis Carrel became interested in psychic phenomena, according to Monroe Fry in an article on ESP that appeared in *Esquire* magazine, during his famous experiment that established the immortality of individual cells in a fragment of chicken heart.

After he had been working on the problem for years somebody asked him about his conclusions. "The work of a scientist is to observe facts," he said, "what I have observed are facts troublesome to science. But they are facts." Science still knows very little about the human mind, but researchers are now certain that the mind is much more powerful and complicated than they have ever thought it was.

* * *

People accept theories, philosophies, or beliefs largely on the basis of who supports them, not necessarily on the facts alone. If a highly regarded individual supports a new belief, people are likely to follow him. Thus it was something of a shock to learn, several years after his passing, that Franklin Delano Roosevelt had frequently sat in séances during which his late mother, Sarah Delano, had appeared to him and given him advice in matters of state. It has quite definitely been established that King George V of England also attended séances. To this day, the English royal family is partial to psychical research, although very little of this is ever published. Less secret is the case of Canada's late Prime Minister William Mackenzie King. According to *Life* magazine, which devoted several pages to

King, he "was an ardent spiritualist who used mediums, the ouija board and a crystal ball for guidance in his private life." It is debatable whether this marks King as a spiritualist or whether he was merely exercising his natural gift of ESP and an interest in psychical research.

* * *

I myself receive continual testimony that ESP is a fascinating subject to people who would not have thought of it so a few years ago. Carlton R. Adams, Rear Admiral, U.S. Navy retired, having read one of my books, contacted me to discuss my views on reincarnation. John D. Grayson, associate professor of linguistics at Sir George Williams University, Montreal, Canada, said, "If I lived in New York, I should like nothing better than to enroll in your eight-lecture course on parapsychology." Gerald S. O'Morrow has a doctorate in education and is at Indiana State University: "I belong to a small development group which meets weekly and has been doing such for the last two years." A lady initialed S. D. writes from California, "I have been successful in working a ouija board for eight years on a serious basis and have tried automatic writing with a small but significant amount of success. I have a great desire to develop my latent powers but until now I haven't known who to go to that I could trust." The lady's profession is that of a police matron with a local police department.

A. P. gives a remarkable account of ESP experiences over the past twenty years. His talents include both visual and auditory phenomena. In reporting his incidents to me, he asked for an appraisal of his abilities with ESP. By profession A. P. is a physician, a native of Cuba.

S. B. Barris contacted me for an appraisal of his ESP development in light of a number of incidents in which he found himself capable of foretelling the result of a race, whether or not a customer would conclude the sale he was hoping for, and several incidents of clairvoyance. Mr. Barris, in addition to being a salesman in mutual funds, is an active member of the United States Army Reserves with the rank of Major.

Stanley R. Dean, M.D., clinical professor of psychiatry at the University of Florida, is a member of the American Psychiatric Association Task Force on transcultural psychiatry and the recent coordinator of a symposium at which a number of parapsychologists spoke.

Curiously enough, the number of people who will accept the existence of ESP is much larger than the number of people who believe in spirit survival or the more advanced forms of occult beliefs. ESP has the aura of the scientific about it, while, to the average mind at least, subjects including spirit survival, ghosts, reincarnation, and such seemingly require facets of human acceptance other than those that are purely scientific. This, at least, is a widely held conviction. At the basis of this distinction lies the unquestionable fact that there is a very pronounced difference between ESP and the more advanced forms of occult scientific belief. For ESP to work, one need not accept survival of human personality beyond bodily death. ESP between the living is as valid as ESP between the living and the so-called dead. Telepathy works whether one partner is in the great beyond or not. In fact, a large segment of the reported phenomena involving clairvoyance can probably be explained on the basis of simple ESP and need not involve the intercession of spirits at all. It has always been debatable whether a medium obtains information about a client from a spirit source standing by, as it were, in the wings, or whether the medium obtains this information from his own unconscious mind, drawing upon extraordinary powers dormant within it. Since the results are the main concern of the client, it is generally of little importance whence the information originates. It is, of course, comforting to think that ESP is merely an extension of the ordinary five senses as we know them, and can be accepted without the need for overhauling one's greater philosophy of life. The same cannot be said about the acceptance of spirit communication, reincarnation, and other occult phenomena. Accepting them as realities requires a profound alteration of the way average people look at life. With ESP, a scientifically oriented person need only extend the limits of believability a little, comparing the ESP faculty to radio waves and himself to a receiving instrument.

So widespread is the interest in ESP research and so many are the published cases indicating its reality that the number of out-and-out debunkers has shrunk considerably during the past years. Some years ago, H. H. Pierce, a chemist, seriously challenged the findings of Dr. Joseph Rhine on the grounds that his statistics were false, if not fraudulent, and that the material proved nothing. No scientist of similar stature has come forth in recent years to challenge the acceptance of ESP; to the contrary, more and more universities are devoting entire departments or special projects to inquiry into the field of ESP. The little debunking that goes on still is done by inept amateurs trying to hang on to the coattails of the current occult vogue.

It is only natural to assume that extrasensory perception has great practical value in crime detection. Though some law enforcement agencies have used it and are using it in increasing instances, this does not mean that the courts will openly admit evidence obtained by psychic means. However, a psychic may help the authorities solve a crime by leading them to a criminal or to the missing person. It is then up to the police or other agency to establish the facts by conventional means that will stand up in a court of law. Without guidance from the psychic, however, the authorities might still be in the dark.

One of the best-known psychic persons to help the police and the FBI was the late Florence Sternfels, the great psychometrist. Her other talent, however, was police work. She would pick up a trail from such meager clues as an object belonging to the missing person, or even merely by being asked whatever happened to so-and-so. Of course, she had no access to any information about the case, nor

was she ever told afterwards how the case ended. The police like to come to psychics for help, but once they have gotten what they've come for, they are reluctant to keep the psychic informed of the progress they have made because of the leads provided. They are even more reluctant to admit that a psychic has helped them. This can take on preposterous proportions.

The Dutch psychic Peter Hurkos, whose help was sought by the Boston police in the case of the Boston Strangler, was indeed able to describe in great detail what the killer looked like.

Hurkos came to Boston to help the authorities but soon found himself in the middle of a power play between the Boston police and the Massachusetts Attorney General. The police had close ties to Boston's Democratic machine, and the Attorney General was a Republican. Hurkos, even worse, was a foreigner.

When the newspapers splashed the psychic's successful tracing of the killer all over the front pages, something within the police department snapped. Hurkos, sure he had picked the right suspect, returned to New York, his job done. The following morning he was arrested on the charge of having impersonated an FBI man several months before. He had allegedly said as much to a gas station attendant and shown him some credentials. This happened when the gas station man noticed some rifles in Hurkos's car. The "credentials" were honorary police cards which many grateful police chiefs had given the psychic for his aid. Hurkos, whose English was fragmentary—for that matter, his Dutch might not be good, since he was only a house painter before he turned psychic—said something to the effect that he worked with the FBI, which was perfectly true. To a foreigner, the difference between such a statement and an assertion of being an FBI man is negligible and perhaps even unimportant.

Those in the know realized that Hurkos was being framed, and some papers said so immediately. Then the Attorney General's office picked up another suspect, who practically matched the first one in appearance, weight, height. Which man did the killing? But Hurkos had done his job well. He had pointed out the places where victims had been found and he had described the killer. And what did it bring him for his troubles, beyond a modest fee of $1,000? Only trouble and embarrassment.

Florence Sternfels was more fortunate in her police contacts. One of her best cases concerns the FBI. During the early part of World War II, she strongly felt that the Iona Island powder depot would be blown up by saboteurs. She had trouble getting to the right person, of course, but eventually she succeeded, and the detonation was headed off just in the nick of time. During the ten years I knew and sometimes worked with her, Sternfels was consulted in dozens of cases of mysterious disappearances and missing persons. In one instance, she was flown to Colorado to help local law officers track down a murderer. Never frightened, she saw the captured man a day or two later. Incidentally, she never charged a penny for this work with the authorities.

The well-known Dutch clairvoyant Gerard Croiset has worked with the police in Holland on a number of cases of murder or disappearance. In the United States, Croiset attempted to solve the almost legendary disappearance of Judge Crater with the help of his biographer, Jack Harrison Pollack. Although Croiset succeeded in adding new material, Pollack was not able to actually find the bones in the spot indicated by Croiset through the use of clairvoyance. However, Croiset was of considerable help in the case of three murdered civil rights workers. He supplied, again through Jack Pollack, a number of clues and pieces of information as to where the bodies would be found, who the murderers were, and how the crime had been committed, at a time when the question of whether they were even dead or not had not yet been resolved!

Croiset sees in pictures rather than words or sentences. He need not be present at the scene of a crime to get impressions, but holding an object belonging to the person whose fate he is to fathom helps him.

What do the police think of this kind of help?

Officially, they do not like to say they use it, but unofficially, why that's another matter. When I worked on the Serge Rubinstein case a year after the financier's murder—when it was as much a mystery as it is, at least officially, today—I naturally turned over to the New York police every scrap of information I obtained. The medium in this case was Mrs. Ethel Meyers, and the evidence was indeed remarkable. Rubinstein's mother was present during the trance session, and readily identified the voice coming from the entranced psychic's lips as that of her murdered son. Moreover, certain peculiar turns of language were used that were characteristic of the deceased. None of this was known to the medium or to myself at the time.

As we sat in the very spot where the tragic event had taken place, the restless spirit of Serge Rubinstein requested revenge, of course, and named names and circumstances of his demise. In subsequent sittings, additional information was given, safe deposit box numbers were named, and all sorts of detailed business, obtained; but, for reasons unknown, the police did not act on this, perhaps because it hardly stands up in a court of law. The guilty parties were well known, partly as a result of ordinary police work, and partly from our memos and transcriptions, but to make the accusation stick would prove difficult. Then, after Rubinstein's mother died, the case slid back into the gray world of forgotten, unsolved crimes.

* * *

Some police officers, at least, do not hesitate to speak up, however, and freely admit the importance of ESP in their work. On October 9, 1964, Lieutenant John J. Cronin gave an interview to the *New York Journal-American's* William McFadden, in which he made his experiences with ESP known. This is what the reporter wrote:

In the not too distant future, every police department in the land will have extra-sensory perception consultants, perhaps even extra-sensory perception bureaus, New York Police Lt. John J. Cronin said today.

For 18 years—longer than any other man in the history of the department—he headed the Missing Persons Bureau.

"After I retire, I might write a book on ESP," he said. "It has provided much information on police cases that is accurate."

One of the fantastic cases he cited was that of a 10-year-old Baltimore girl who was missing last July.

A Baltimore police sergeant visited Mrs. Florence Sternfels of Edgewater, N.J., who calls herself a psychometrist. On her advice, when he got back to Baltimore he dug in a neighbor's cellar. The body of the girl was found two feet under the dirt floor.

Lt. Cronin also noted that Gerard Croiset, the Dutch clairvoyant, is credited with finding 400 missing children.

"Right now, ESP is a hit and miss proposition. It's in an elementary stage, the stage electricity was in when Ben Franklin flew his kite," Lt. Cronin said.

"But it does exist. It is a kind of sixth sense that primitive man possessed but has been lost through the ages. It's not supernatural, mind you. And it will be the method of the future.

"Once it is gotten into scientific shape, it will help law enforcement agencies solve certain crimes that have been baffling them."

Stressing that ESP will grow in police use, he said:

"In Europe some of the ESP people have been qualified to give testimony in court. It will come here, too."

More specific and illustrative of the methods used by psychics in helping solve crimes is a column devoted to a case in Washington State, written by Michael MacDougall for the *Long Island Press* of May 3, 1964, in which he suggests that someone with ESP should be on the staff of every police department in order to help solve difficult crimes. MacDougall makes a very strong case for his conviction in his report on a case that took place a month earlier.

DeMille, the famous mentalist currently touring for the Associated Executives Clubs, checked into the Chinook Hotel in Yakima, Wash., at 2 P.M. on Friday, April 3. He was tired, and intended to shower and sleep before that evening's lecture. But hardly had he turned the key in the lock when the phone rang.

It was a woman calling. "My friend has had her wallet stolen," the feminine voice said. "It contained several articles of sentimental value which she would like to recover. Can you help her find it?"

"Perhaps," said DeMille. "I'll do my best. But you'll have to wait until after my speech. Call me about ten-thirty."

DeMille hung up, tumbled into bed. But he couldn't sleep. The thought of that stolen wallet kept intruding. Then, just on the edge of unconsciousness, when one is neither asleep nor awake, he envisioned the crime.

Two teen-age boys, one wearing a red sweater, stole up behind a woman shopper. One stepped in front, diverting her attention, while his partner gently unfastened her handbag, removed the wallet, and scampered around the corner, to be joined later by his confederate.

DeMille saw more. The boys got into a beat-up Ford. They drove away, parked briefly in front of a used car lot. Opening the wallet, they took out a roll of bills, which were divided evenly. DeMille wasn't sure of the count but thought it was $46. Then the boys examined a checkbook. DeMille saw the number 2798301, and the legend: First National Bank of Washington. He also received an impression that it was some kind of a meat-packing firm.

Now fully awake, DeMille phoned K. Gordon Smith, secretary of the Knife and Fork Club, the organization for which DeMille was speaking that night. The secretary came up to DeMille's room, listened to the story, and advised calling the police.

Soon DeMille had callers. One introduced himself as Frank Gayman, a reporter for the Yakima Herald. The other was Sergeant Walt Dutcher, of the Yakima Police. Again DeMille told his story. Gayman was skeptical but willing to be convinced. The sergeant was totally disbelieving and openly hostile.

DeMille suggested they call the First National Bank and find out if a meat-packing company had a checking account numbered 2798301. Then it would be easy to call the company and discover whether or not any female employee had been robbed.

The report was negative. Account #2798301 was not a meat-picking company. In fact, the bank had no meat packers as customers. Fruit packers, yes; meat packers, no.

Sergeant Dutcher, after threatening DeMille with arrest for turning in a false crime report, stamped out of the room. Frank Gayman, still willing to be convinced, remained. The phone rang again. It was for Gayman; the bank was calling.

There was an account numbered 2798001 carried by Club Scout Pack #3. Could this be the one? Immediately, DeMille knew that it was.

The president of the Knife and Fork Club, one Karl Steinhilb, volunteered to drive DeMille about the city. Following the mentalist's directions, Steinhilb drove to an outlying section, parked in front of a used car lot. And sure enough, in the bushes fronting a nearby house they found the discarded wallet.

The Yakima Police Department was not quite the same after that.

The cases of cooperation between psychics or psychic researchers and police departments are becoming more numerous as time goes on and less prejudice remains toward the use of such persons in law enforcement.

In July, 1965, the Austin, Texas, police used the services of a Dallas psychic in the case of two missing University of Texas girls, who were much later found murdered. At the time of the consultation, however, one week after the girls had disappeared, she predicted that the girls would be found within twenty-four hours, which they weren't, and that three men were involved, which proved true.

But then the time element is often a risky thing with predictions. Time is one of the dimensions that is least capable of being read correctly by many psychics. This of course may be due to the fact that time is an arbitrary and perhaps even artificial element introduced by man to make life more livable; in the nonphysical world, it simply does not exist. Thus when a psychic looks into the world of the mind and then tries to interpret the conditions he or she is impressed with, the time element is often wrong. It is based mainly on the psychic's own interpretation, not on a solid image, as is the case with facts, names, and places that he or she might describe.

One of the institutes of learning specializing in work with clairvoyants that cooperate with police authorities is the University of Utrecht, Netherlands, where Dr. W. H. C. Tenhaeff is the head of the Parapsychology Institute. Between 1950 and 1960 alone, the Institute studied over 40 psychics, including 26 men and 21 women, according to author-researcher Jack Harrison Pollack, who visited the Institute in 1960 and wrote a glowing report on its activities.

Pollack wrote a popular book about Croiset, who was the Institute's star psychic and who started out as an ordinary grocer until he discovered his unusual gift and put it to professional use, especially after he met Dr. Tenhaeff in 1964.

But Croiset is only one of the people who was tested in the Dutch research center. Others are Warner Tholen, whose specialty is locating missing objects, and Pierre van Delzen, who can put his hands on a globe and predict conditions in that part of the world.

The University of Utrecht is, in this respect, far ahead of other places of learning. In the United States, Dr. Joseph B. Rhine has made a brilliant initial effort, but today Duke University's parapsychology laboratory is doing little to advance research in ESP beyond repeat experiments and cautious, very cautious, theorizing on the nature of man. There is practically no field work being done outside the laboratory, and no American university is in the position, either financially or in terms of staff, to work with such brilliant psychics as does Dr. Tenhaeff in Holland.

For a country that has more per-capita crime than any other, one would expect that the police would welcome all the help they could get.

In the following pages you will read about true cases of hauntings, encounters with ghosts and apparitions of spirits, all of which have been fully documented and witnessed by responsible people. To experience these phenomena, you need not be a true "medium," though the line between merely having ESP or being psychic with full mediumship, which involves clairvoyance (seeing things), clairaudience (hearing things), and/or clairsentience (smelling or feeling things), is rather vague at times. It is all a matter of degree, and some people partake of more than one "phase" or form of psychic ability. Regardless of which sensitivity applies to your situation, they are natural and need not be feared.

CHAPTER FOUR

What Exactly *Is* a Ghost?

FROM CLOSED-MINDED SKEPTICS to uninformed would-be believers, from Hollywood horror movies to Caspar the Ghost, there is a great deal of misinformation and foolish fantasy floating around as to what ghosts are and, of course, whether they do in fact exist.

I was one of the first people with a background not only in science, but also in investigative journalism to say to the general public, in books and in the media, Yes, ghosts are for real. Nobody laughed, because I followed through with evidence and with authentic photographic material taken under test conditions.

What exactly is a ghost? Something people dream up in their cups or on a sickbed? Something you read about in juvenile fiction? Far from it. Ghosts—apparitions of "dead" people or sounds associated with invisible human beings—are the surviving emotional memories of people who have not been able to make the transition from their physical state into the world of the spirit—or as Dr. Joseph Rhine of Duke University has called it, the world of the *mind*. Their state is one of emotional shock induced by sudden death or great suffering, and because of it the individuals involved cannot understand what is happening to them. They are unable to see beyond their own immediate environment or problem, and so they are forced to continually relive those final moments of agony until someone breaks through and explains things to them. In this respect they are like psychotics being helped by the psychoanalyst, except that the patient is not on the couch, but rather in the atmosphere of destiny. Man's electromagnetic nature makes this perfectly plausible; that is, since our individual personality is really nothing more than a personal energy field encased in a denser outer layer called the physical body, the personality can store emotional stimuli and memories indefinitely without much dimming, very much like a tape recording that can be played over and over without losing clarity or volume.

Those who die normally under conditions of adjustment need not go through this agony, and they seem to pass on rapidly into that next state of consciousness that may be a "heaven" or a "hell," according to what the individual's mental state at death might have been. Neither state is an objective place, but is a subjective state of being. The sum total of similar states of being may, however, create a quasi-objective state approaching a condition or "place" along more orthodox religious lines. My contact with the confused individuals unable to depart from the earth's sphere, those who are commonly called "ghosts" or earth-bound spirits, is through a trance medium who will lend her physical body temporarily to the entities in difficulty so that they can speak through the medium and detail their problems, frustrations, or unfinished business. Here again, the parallel with psychoanalysis becomes apparent: in telling their tales of woe, the restless ones relieve themselves of their pressures and anxieties and thus may free themselves of their bonds. If fear is the absence of information, as I have always held, then knowledge is indeed the presence of understanding. Or view it the other way round, if you prefer. Because of my books, people often call on me to help them understand problems of this nature. Whenever someone has seen a ghost or heard noises of a human kind that do not seem to go with a body, and feel it might be something I ought to look into, I usually do.

To be sure, I don't always find a ghost. But frequently I do find one, and moreover, I find that many of those who have had the uncanny experiences are themselves mediumistic, and are therefore capable of being communications vehicles for the discarnates. Ghosts are more common than most people realize, and, really quite natural and harmless. Though, at times, they are sad and shocking, as all human suffering is, for man is his worst enemy, whether in the flesh or outside of it. But there is nothing mystical about the powers of ESP or the ability to experience ghostly phenomena.

Scoffers like to dismiss all ghostly encounters by cutting the witnesses down to size—their size. The witnesses are probably mentally unbalanced, they say, or sick people who hallucinate a lot, or they were tired that day, or it must have been the reflection from (pick your light source), or finally, in desperation, they may say yes, something probably happened to them, but in the telling they blew it all up so you can't be sure any more what really happened.

I love the way many people who cannot accept the possibility of ghosts being real toss out their views on what happened to strangers. They say, "Probably this or that," and from "probably" for them, it is only a short step to "certainly." The human mind is as clever at inventing away as it is at hallucinating. The advantage in being a scientifically trained reporter, as I am, is the ability to dismiss people's interpretations and find the facts. I talked of the *Ghosts I've Met* in a book a few years ago that bore that title. Even more fascinating are the people I've met who encounter ghosts. Are they sick, unbalanced, crackpots or other unrealistic individuals whose testimony is worthless?

Far from it.

Those who fall into that category never get to me in the first place. They don't stand up under my methods of scrutiny. Crackpots, beware! I call a spade a spade, as I proved when I exposed the fake spiritualist camp practices in print some years ago.

The people who come across ghostly manifestations are people like you.

Take the couple from Springfield, Illinois, for instance. Their names are Gertrude and Russell Meyers and they were married in 1935. He worked as a stereotyper on the local newspaper, and she was a high-school teacher. Both of them were in their late twenties and couldn't care less about such things as ghosts.

At the time of their marriage, they had rented a five-room cottage which had stood empty for some time. It had no particular distinction but a modest price, and was located in Bloomington where the Meyerses then lived.

Gertrude Meyers came from a farm background and had studied at Illinois Wesleyan as well as the University of Chicago. For a while she worked as a newspaperwoman in Detroit, later taught school, and as a sideline has written a number of children's books. Her husband Russell, also of farm background, attended Illinois State Normal University at Normal, Illinois, and later took his apprenticeship at the *Bloomington Pantograph*.

The house they had rented in Bloomington was exactly like the house next to it; the current owners had converted what was formerly *one* large house into two separate units, laying a driveway between them.

In the summer, after they had moved into their house, they went about the business of settling down to a routine. Since her husband worked the night shift on the newspaper, Mrs. Meyers was often left alone in the house. At first, it did not bother her at all. Sounds from the street penetrated into the house and gave her a feeling of people nearby. But when the chill of autumn set in and the windows had to be closed to keep it out, she became aware, gradually, that she was not really alone.

One particular night early in their occupancy of the house, she had gone to bed leaving her bedroom door ajar. It was 10:30 and she was just about ready to go to sleep when she heard rapid, firm footsteps starting at the front door, inside the house, and coming through the living room, the dining room, and finally coming down the hall leading to her bedroom door.

She leapt out of bed and locked the door. Then she went back into bed and sat there, wondering with sheer terror what the intruder would do. But nobody came.

More to calm herself than because she really believed it, Mrs. Meyers convinced herself that she must have been mistaken about those footsteps.

It was probably someone in the street. With this reassuring thought on her mind, she managed to fall asleep.

The next morning, she did not tell her new husband about the nocturnal event. After all, she did not want him to think he had married a strange woman!

But the footsteps returned, night after night, always at the same time and always stopping abruptly at her bedroom door, which, needless to say, she kept locked.

Rather than facing her husband with the allegation that they had rented a haunted house, she bravely decided to face the intruder and find out what this was all about. One night she deliberately waited for the now familiar brisk footfalls. The clock struck 10:00, then 10:30. In the quiet of the night, she could hear her heart pounding in her chest.

Then the footsteps came, closer and closer, until they got to her bedroom door. At this moment, Mrs. Meyers jumped out of bed, snapped on the light, and tore the door wide open.

There was nobody there, and no retreating footsteps could be heard.

She tried it again and again, but the invisible intruder never showed himself once the door was opened.

The winter was bitterly cold, and Russell was in the habit of building up a fire in the furnace in the basement when he came home from work at 3:30 A.M. Mrs. Meyers always heard him come in, but did not get up. One night he left the basement, came into the bedroom and said, "Why are you walking around this freezing house in the middle of the night?"

Of course she had not been out of bed all night, and told him as much. Then they discovered that he, too, had heard footsteps, but had thought it was his wife walking restlessly about the house. Meyers had heard the steps whenever he was fixing the furnace in the basement, but by the time he got upstairs they had ceased.

When Mrs. Meyers had to get up early to go to her classes, her husband would stay in the house sleeping late. On many days he would hear someone walking about the house and investigate, only to find himself quite alone.

He would wake up in the middle of the night thinking his wife and gotten up, and was immediately reassured that she was sleeping peacefully next to him. Yet there was *someone* out there in the empty house!

Since everything was securely locked, and countless attempts to trap the ghost had failed, the Meyerses shrugged and learned to live with their peculiar boarder. Gradually the steps became part of the atmosphere of the old house, and the terror began to fade into the darkness of night.

In May of the following year, they decided to work in the garden and, as they did so, they met their next-door neighbors for the first time. Since they lived in identical houses, they had something in common, and conversation between them and the neighbors—a young man of twenty-five and his grandmother—sprang up.

Eventually, the discussion got around to the footsteps. They, too, kept hearing them, it seemed. After they had compared notes on their experiences, the Meyerses asked more questions. They were told that before the house was divided, it belonged to a single owner who had committed suicide in the house. No wonder he liked to walk in *both* halves of what was once his home!

* * *

You'd never think of Kokomo, Indiana as particularly haunted ground, but one of the most touching cases I know of occurred there some time ago. A young woman by the name of Mary Elizabeth Hamilton was in the habit of spending many of her summer vacations in her grandmother's house. The house dates back to 1834 and is a handsome place, meticulously kept up.

Miss Hamilton had never had the slightest interest in the supernatural, and the events that transpired that summer, when she spent four weeks at the house, came as a complete surprise to her. One evening she was walking down the front staircase when she was met by a lovely young lady coming up the stairs. Miss Hamilton noticed that she wore a particularly beautiful evening gown. There was nothing the least bit ghostly about the woman, and she passed Miss Hamilton closely, in fact so closely that she could have touched her had she wanted to.

But she did notice that the gown was of a filmy pink material, and her hair and eyes were dark brown, and the latter, full of tears. When the two women met, the girl in the evening gown smiled at Miss Hamilton and passed by.

Since she knew that there was no other visitor in the house, and that no one was expected at this time, Miss Hamilton was puzzled. She turned her head to follow her up the stairs. The lady in pink reached the top of the stairs and vanished—into thin air.

As soon as she could, she reported the matter to her grandmother, who shook her head and would not believe her account. She would not even discuss it, so Miss Hamilton let the matter drop out of deference to her grandmother. But the dress design had been so unusual, she decided to check it out in a library. She found, to her amazement, that the lady in pink had worn a dress that was from the late 1840s.

In September of the next year, her grandmother decided to redecorate the house. In this endeavor she used many old pieces of furniture, some of which had come from the attic of the house. When Miss Hamilton arrived and saw the changes, she was suddenly stopped by a portrait hung in the hall.

It was a portrait of her lady of the stairs. She was not wearing the pink gown in this picture but, other than that, she was the same person.

Miss Hamilton's curiosity about the whole matter was again aroused and, since she could not get any cooperation from her grandmother, she turned to her great aunt for help. This was particularly fortunate since the aunt was a specialist in family genealogy.

Finally the lady of the stairs was identified. She turned out to be a distant cousin of Miss Hamilton's, and had once lived in that very house.

She had fallen in love with a ne'er-do-well, and after he died in a brawl, she threw herself down the stairs to her death.

Why had the family ghost picked her to appear before, Miss Hamilton wondered.

Then she realized that she bore a strong facial resemblance to the ghost. Moreover, their names were almost identical—Mary Elizabeth was Miss Hamilton's, and Elizabeth Mary, the pink lady's. Both women even had the same nickname, Libby.

Perhaps the ghost had looked for a little recognition from her family and, having gotten none from the grandmother, had seized upon the opportunity to manifest herself to a more amenable relative?

Miss Hamilton is happy that she was able to see the sad smile on the unfortunate girl's face, for to her it is proof that communication, though silent, had taken place between them across the years.

* * *

Mrs. Jane Eidson is a housewife in suburban Minneapolis. She is middle-aged and her five children range in age from nine to twenty. Her husband Bill travels four days each week. They live in a cottage-type brick house that is twenty-eight years old, and they've lived there for the past eight years.

The first time the Eidsons noticed that there was something odd about their otherwise ordinary-looking home was after they had been in the house for a short time. Mrs. Eidson was in the basement sewing, when all of a sudden she felt that she was not alone and wanted to run upstairs. She suppressed this strong urge but felt very uncomfortable. Another evening, her husband was down there practicing a speech when he also felt the presence of another. His self-control was not as strong as hers, and he came upstairs. In discussing their strange feelings with their next-door neighbor, they discovered that the previous tenant had also complained about the basement. Their daughter, Rita, had never wanted to go to the basement by herself and, when pressed for a reason, finally admitted that there was a man down there. She described him as dark-haired and wearing a plaid shirt.

Sometimes he would stand by her bed at night and she would become frightened, but the moment she thought of calling her mother, the image disappeared. Another spot where she felt his presence was the little playhouse at the other end of their yard.

The following spring, Mrs. Eidson noticed a bouncing light at the top of the stairs as she was about to go to

bed in an upstairs room, which she was occupying while convalescing from surgery.

The light followed her to her room as if it had a mind of its own!

When she entered her room the light left, but the room felt icy. She was disturbed by this, but nevertheless went to bed and soon had forgotten all about it as sleep came to her. Suddenly, in the middle of the night, she woke and sat up in bed.

Something had awakened her. At the foot of her bed she saw a man who was "beige-colored," as she put it. As she stared at the apparition it went away, again leaving the room very chilly.

About that same time, the Eidsons noticed that their electric appliances were playing tricks on them. There was the time at 5 A.M. when their washing machine went on by itself, as did the television set in the basement, which could only be turned on by plugging it into the wall socket. When they had gone to bed, the set was off and there was no one around to plug it in.

Who was so fond of electrical gadgets that they were turning them on in the small hours of the morning?

Finally Mrs. Eidson found out. In May of 1949, a young man who was just out of the service had occupied the house. His hobby had been electrical wiring, it seems, for he had installed a strand of heavy wires from the basement underground through the yard to the other end of the property. When he attempted to hook them up to the utility pole belonging to the electric company, he was killed instantly. It happened near the place where Mrs. Eidson's girl had seen the apparition. Since the wires are still in her garden, Mrs. Eidson is not at all surprised that the dead man likes to hang around.

And what better way for an electronics buff to manifest himself as a ghost than by appearing as a bright, bouncy light? As of this writing, the dead electrician is still playing tricks in the Eidson home, and Mrs. Eidson is looking for a new home—one a little less unusual than their present one.

* * *

Eileen Courtis is forty-seven years old, a native of London, and a well-balanced individual who now resides on the West coast but who lived previously in New York City. Although she has never gone to college, she has a good grasp of things, an analytical mind, and is not given to hysterics. When she arrived in New York at age thirty-four, she decided to look for a quiet hotel and then search for a job.

The job turned out to be an average office position, and the hotel she decided upon was the Martha Washington, which was a hotel for women only on Twenty-Ninth Street. Eileen was essentially shy and a loner who only made friends slowly.

She was given a room on the twelfth floor and, immediately on crossing the threshold, she was struck by a foul odor coming from the room. Her first impulse was to ask for another room, but she was in no mood to create a fuss so she stayed.

"I can stand it a night or two," she thought, but did not unpack. It turned out that she stayed in that room for six long months, and yet she never really unpacked.

Now all her life, Eileen had been having various experiences that involved extrasensory perception, and her first impression of her new "home" was that someone had died in it. She examined the walls inch by inch. There was a spot where a crucifix must have hung for a long time, judging by the color of the surrounding wall. Evidently it had been removed when someone moved out...permanently.

That first night, after she had gone to bed, her sleep was interrupted by what sounded like the turning of a newspaper page. It sounded exactly as if someone were sitting in the chair at the foot of her bed reading a newspaper. Quickly she switched on the light and she was, of course, quite alone. Were her nerves playing tricks on her? It was a strange city, a strange room. She decided to go back to sleep. Immediately, the rustling started up again, and then someone began walking across the floor, starting from the chair and heading toward the door.

Eileen turned on every light in the room and it stopped. Exhausted, she dozed off again. The next morning she looked over the room carefully. Perhaps mice had caused the strange rustling. The strange odor remained, so she requested that the room be fumigated. The manager smiled wryly, and nobody came to fumigate her room. The rustling noise continued, night after night, and Eileen slept with the lights on for the next three weeks.

Somehow her ESP told her this presence was a strong-willed, vicious old woman who resented others occupying what she still considered "her" room. Eileen decided to fight her. Night after night, she braved it out in the dark, only to find herself totally exhausted in the morning. Her appearance at the office gave rise to talk. But she was not going to give in to a ghost. Side by side, the living and the dead now occupied the same room without sharing it.

Then one night, something prevented her from going off to sleep. She lay in bed quietly, waiting.

Suddenly she became aware of two skinny but very strong arms extended over her head, holding a large downy pillow as though to suffocate her!

It took every ounce of her strength to force the pillow off her face.

Next morning, she tried to pass it off as a hallucination. But was it? She was quite sure that she had not been asleep.

But still she did not move out, and one evening when she arrived home from the office with a friend, she felt a sudden pain in her back, as if she had been stabbed. During the night, she awoke to find herself in a state of utter paralysis. She could not move her limbs or head. Finally, after a long time, she managed to work her way to the tele-

phone receiver and call for a doctor. Nobody came. But her control started to come back and she called her friend, who rushed over only to find Eileen in a state of shock.

During the next few days she had a thorough examination by the company physician which included the taking of X-rays to determine if there was anything physically wrong with her that could have caused this condition. She was given a clean bill of health and her strength had by then returned, so she decided to quit while she was ahead.

She went to Florida for an extended rest, but eventually came back to New York and the hotel. This time she was given another room, where she lived very happily and without incident for over a year.

One day a neighbor who knew her from the time she had occupied the room on the twelfth floor saw her in the lobby and insisted on having a visit with her. Reluctantly, for she is not fond of socializing, Eileen agreed. The conversation covered various topics until suddenly the neighbor came out with "the time you were living in that haunted room across the hall."

Since Eileen had never told anyone of her fearsome experiences there, she was puzzled. The neighbor confessed that she had meant to warn her while she was occupying that room, but somehow never had mustered enough courage. "Warn me of what?" Eileen insisted.

"The woman who had the room just before you moved in," the neighbor explained haltingly, "well, she was found dead in the chair, and the woman who had it before her also was found dead in the bathtub."

Eileen swallowed quickly and left. Suddenly she knew that the pillowcase had not been a hallucination.

* * *

The Buxhoeveden family is one of the oldest noble families of Europe, related to a number of royal houses and —since the eighteenth century, when one of the counts married the daughter of Catherine the Great of Russia— also to the Russian Imperial family. The family seat was Lode Castle on the island of Eesel, off the coast of Estonia. The castle, which is still standing, is a very ancient building with a round tower set somewhat apart from the main building. Its Soviet occupants have since turned it into a museum.

The Buxhoevedens acquired it when Frederick William Buxhoeveden married Natalie of Russia; it was a gift from mother-in-law Catherine.

Thus it was handed down from first-born son to first-born son, until it came to be in the hands of an earlier Count Anatol Buxhoeveden. The time was the beginning of this century, and all was right with the world.

Estonia was a Russian province, so it was not out of the ordinary that Russian regiments should hold war games in the area. On one occasion, when the maneuvers were in full swing, the regimental commander requested that his officers be put up at the castle. The soldiers were located in the nearby town, but five of the staff officers came to stay at Lode Castle. Grandfather Buxhoeveden was the perfect host, but was unhappy that he could not accommodate all five in the main house. The fifth man would have to be satisfied with quarters in the tower. Since the tower had by then acquired a reputation of being haunted, he asked for a volunteer to stay in that particular room.

There was a great deal of teasing about the haunted room before the youngest of the officers volunteered and left for his quarters.

The room seemed cozy enough, and the young officer congratulated himself for having chosen so quiet and pleasant a place to spend the night after a hard day's maneuvers.

He was tired and got into bed right away. But he was too tired to fall asleep quickly, so he took a book from one of the shelves lining the walls, lit the candle on his night table, and began to read.

As he did so, he suddenly became aware of a greenish light on the opposite side of the room. As he looked at the light with astonishment, it changed before his eyes into the shape of a woman. She seemed solid enough. To his horror, she came over to his bed, took him by the hand, and demanded that he follow her. Somehow he could not resist her commands, even though not a single word was spoken. He followed her down the stairs into the library of the castle itself. There she made signs indicating that he was to remove the carpet. Without questioning her, he flipped back the rug. She then pointed at a trap door that was underneath the carpet. He opened the door and followed the figure down a flight of stairs until they came to a big iron door that barred their progress. The figure pointed to a corner of the floor, and he dug into it. There he found a key, perhaps ten inches long, and with it he opened the iron gate. He now found himself in a long corridor that led to a circular room. From there another corridor led on and again he followed eagerly, wondering what this was all about.

This latter corridor suddenly opened onto another circular room that seemed familiar—he was back in his own room. The apparition was gone.

What did it all mean? He sat up trying to figure it out, and when he finally dozed off it was already dawn. Consequently, he overslept and came down to breakfast last. His state of excitement immediately drew the attention of the count and his fellow officers. "You won't believe this," he began and told them what had happened to him.

He was right. Nobody believed him.

But his insistence that he was telling the truth was so convincing that the count finally agreed, more to humor him than because he believed him, to follow the young officer to the library to look for the alleged trap door.

"But," he added, "I must tell you that on top of that carpet are some heavy bookshelves filled with books which have not been moved or touched in over a hundred years. It is quite impossible for any one man to flip back that carpet."

They went to the library, and just as the count had said, the carpet could not be moved. But Grandfather Buxhoeveden decided to follow through anyway and called in some of his men. Together, ten men were able to move the shelves and turn the carpet back. Underneath the carpet was a dust layer an inch thick, but it did not stop the intrepid young officer from looking for the ring of the trap door. After a long search for it, he finally located it. A hush fell over the group when he pulled the trap door open. There was the secret passage and the iron gate. And there, next to it, was a rusty iron key. The key fit the lock. The gate, which had not moved for centuries perhaps, slowly and painfully swung open, and the little group continued its exploration of the musty passages. With the officer leading, the men went through the corridors and came out in the tower room, just as the officer had done during the night.

But what did it mean? Everyone knew there were secret passages—lots of old castles had them as a hedge in times of war.

The matter gradually faded from memory, and life at Lode went on. The iron key, however, was preserved and remained in the Buxhoeveden family until some years ago, when it was stolen from Count Alexander's Paris apartment.

Ten years went by, until, after a small fire in the castle, Count Buxhoeveden decided to combine the necessary repairs with the useful installation of central heating, something old castles always need. The contractor doing the job brought in twenty men who worked hard to restore and improve the appointments at Lode. Then one day, the entire crew vanished—like ghosts. Count Buxhoeveden reported this to the police, who were already besieged by the wives and families of the men who had disappeared without leaving a trace.

Newspapers of the period had a field day with the case of the vanishing workmen, but the publicity did not help to bring them back, and the puzzle remained.

Then came the revolution and the Buxhoevedens lost their ancestral home, Count Alexander and the present Count Anatol, my brother-in-law, went to live in Switzerland. The year was 1923. One day the two men were walking down a street in Lausanne when a stranger approached them, calling Count Alexander by name.

"I am the brother of the major domo of your castle," the man explained. "I was a plumber on that job of restoring it after the fire."

So much time had passed and so many political events had changed the map of Europe that the man was ready at last to lift the veil of secrecy from the case of the vanishing workmen.

This is the story he told: when the men were digging trenches for the central heating system, they accidentally came across an iron kettle of the kind used in the Middle Ages to pour boiling oil or water on the enemies besieging a castle. Yet this pot was not full of water, but rather of gold. They had stumbled onto the long-missing Buxhoeveden treasure, a hoard reputed to have existed for centuries, which never had been found. Now, with this stroke of good fortune, the workmen became larcenous. They opted for distributing the find among themselves, even though it meant leaving everything behind—their families, their homes, their work—and striking out fresh somewhere else. But the treasure was large enough to make this a pleasure rather than a problem, and they never missed their wives, it would seem, finding ample replacements in the gentler climes of western Europe, where most of them went to live under assumed names.

At last the apparition that had appeared to the young officer made sense: it had been an ancestor who wanted to let her descendants know where the family gold had been secreted. What a frustration for a ghost to see her efforts come to naught, and worse yet, to see the fortune squandered by thieves while the legal heirs had to go into exile. Who knows how things might have tuned out for the Buxhoevedens if *they* had gotten to the treasure in time.

At any rate there is a silver lining to this account: since there is nothing further to find at Lode Castle, the ghost does not have to put in appearances under that new regime. But Russian aristocrats and English lords of the manor have no corner on uncanny phenomena. Nor are all of the haunted settings I have encountered romantic or forbidding. Certainly there are more genuine ghostly manifestations in the American Midwest and South than anywhere else in the world. This may be due to the fact that a great deal of violence occurred there during the nineteenth and early twentieth centuries. Also, the American public's attitude toward such phenomena is different from that of Europeans. In Europe, people are inclined to reserve their accounts of bona fide ghosts for those people they can trust. Being ridiculed is not a favorite pastime of most Europeans.

Americans, by contrast, are more independent. They couldn't care less what others think of them in the long run, so long as their own people believe them. I have approached individuals in many cases with an assurance of scientific inquiry and respect for their stories. I am not a skeptic. I am a searcher for the truth, regardless of what this truth looks or sounds like.

Some time ago, a well-known TV personality took issue with me concerning my conviction that ESP and ghosts are real. Since he was not well informed on the subject, he should not have ventured forth into an area I know so well. He proudly proclaimed himself a skeptic.

Irritated, I finally asked him if he knew what being a skeptic meant. He shook his head.

"The term skeptic," I lectured him patiently, "is derived from the Greek word *skepsis*, which was the name of a small town in Asia Minor in antiquity. It was known for its lack of knowledge, and people from skepsis were called skeptics."

The TV personality didn't like it at all, but the next time we met on camera, he was a lot more human and his humanity finally showed.

* * *

I once received a curious letter from a Mrs. Stewart living in Chicago, Illinois, in which she explained that she was living with a ghost and didn't mind, except that she had lost two children at birth and this ghost was following not only her but also her little girl. This she didn't like, so could I please come and look into the situation?

I could and did. On July 4, I celebrated Independence Day by trying to free a hung-up lady ghost on Chicago's South Side. The house itself was an old one, built around the late 1800s, and not exactly a monument of architectural beauty. But its functional sturdiness suited its present purpose—to house a number of young couples and their children, people who found the house both convenient and economical.

In its heyday, it had been a wealthy home, complete with servants and a set of backstairs for the servants to go up and down on. The three stories are even now connected by an elaborate buzzer system which hasn't worked for years.

I did not wish to discuss the phenomena at the house with Mrs. Stewart until after Sybil Leek, who was with me, had had a chance to explore the situation. My good friend Carl Subak, a stamp dealer, had come along to see how I worked. He and I had known each other thirty years ago when we were both students, and because of that he had overcome his own—ah—skepticism—and decided to accompany me. Immediately upon arrival, Sybil ascended the stairs to the second floor as if she knew where to go! Of course she didn't; I had not discussed the matter with her at all. But despite this promising beginning, she drew a complete blank when we arrived at the upstairs apartment. "I feel absolutely nothing," she confided and looked at me doubtfully. Had I made a mistake? She seemed to ask. On a hot July day, had we come all the way to the South Side of Chicago on a wild ghost chase?

We gathered in a bedroom that contained a comfortable chair and had windows on both sides that looked out onto an old-fashioned garden; there was a porch on one side and a parkway on the other. The furniture, in keeping with the modest economic circumstances of the owners, was old and worn, but it was functional and the inhabitants did not seem to mind.

In a moment, Sybil Leek had slipped into trance. But instead of a ghost's personality, the next voice we heard was Sybil's own, although it sounded strange. Sybil was "out" of her own body, but able to observe the place and report back to us while still in trance.

The first thing she saw were maps, in a large round building somehow connected with the house we were in.

"Is there anyone around?" I asked.

"Yes," Sybil intoned, "James Dugan."

"What does he do here?"

"Come back to live."

"When was that?"

"1912."

"Is there anyone with him?"

"There is another man. McCloud."

"Anyone else?"

"Lots of people."

"Do they live in this house?"

"Three, four people…McCloud…maps…"

"All men?"

"No…girl…Judith…maidservant…"

"Is there an unhappy presence here?"

"Judith…she had no one here, no family…that man went away…Dugan went away…"

"How is she connected with this Dugan?"

"Loved him?"

"Were they married?"

"No. Lovers."

"Did they have any children?"

There was a momentary silence, then Sybil continued in a drab, monotonous voice.

"The baby's dead."

"Does she know the baby's dead?"

"*She cries…baby cries…*neglected…by Judith…guilty…"

"Does Judith know this?"

"Yes."

"How old was the baby when it died?"

"A few weeks old."

Strange, I thought, that Mrs. Stewart had fears for her own child from this source. She, too, had lost children at a tender age.

"What happened to the baby?"

"She put it down the steps."

"What happened to the body then?"

"I don't know."

"Is Judith still here?"

"She's here."

"Where?"

"This room…and up and down the steps. She's sorry for her baby."

"Can you talk to her?"

"No. She cannot leave here until she finds—You see if she could get Dugan—"

"Where is Dugan?"

"With the maps."

"What is Dugan's work?"

"Has to do with roads."

"Is he dead?"

"Yes. She wants him here, but he is not here."

"How did she die?"

"She ran away to the water…died by the water…but is here where she lived…baby died on the steps…downstairs…"

"What is she doing here, I mean how does she let people know she is around?"

"She pulls things…*she cries…*"

"And her Christian name?"

"Judith Vincent, I think. Twenty-one. Darkish, not white. From an island."

"And the man? Is he white?"

"Yes."

"Can you see her?"

"Yes."

"Speak to her?"

"She doesn't want to, but perhaps…"

"What year does she think this is?"

"1913."

"Tell her this is the year 1965."

Sybil informed the spirit in a low voice that this was 1965 and she need not stay here any longer, that Dugan was dead, too.

"She has to find him," Sybil explained and I directed her to explain that she need only call out for her lover in order to be reunited with him "Over There."

"She's gone…" Sybil finally said, and breathed deeply.

A moment later she woke up and looked with astonishment at the strange room, having completely forgotten how we got here, or where we were.

There was no time for explanations now, as I still wanted to check out some of this material. The first one to sit down with me was the owner of the flat, Mrs. Alexander Stewart. A graduate of the University of Iowa, twenty-five years old, Alexandra Stewart works as a personnel director. She had witnessed the trance session and seemed visibly shaken. There was a good reason for this. Mrs. Stewart, you see, had met the ghost Sybil had described.

The Stewarts had moved into the second-floor apartment in the winter of 1964. The room we were now sitting in had been hers. Shortly after they moved in, Mrs. Stewart happened to be glancing up toward the French doors, when she saw a woman looking at her. The figure was about five feet three or four, and wore a blue-gray dress with a shawl, and a hood over her head, so that Mr. Stewart could not make out the woman's features. The head seemed strangely bowed to her, almost as if the woman were doing penance.

I questioned Mrs. Stewart on the woman's color in view of Sybil's description of Judith. But Mrs. Stewart could not be sure; the woman could have been white or black. At the time, Mrs. Stewart had assumed it to be a reflection from the mirror, but when she glanced at the mirror, she did not see the figure in it.

When she turned her attention back to the figure, it had disappeared. It was toward evening and Mrs. Stewart was a little tired, yet the figure was very real to her. Her doubts were completely dispelled when the ghost returned about a month later. In the meantime she had moved the dresser that formerly stood in the line of sight farther down, so that the explanation of the reflection would simply not hold water. Again the figure appeared at the French doors. She looked very unhappy to Mrs. Stewart, who felt herself strangely drawn to the woman, almost as if she should help her in some way as yet unknown.

But the visual visitations were not all that disturbed the Stewarts. Soon they were hearing strange noises, too. Above all, there was the crying of a baby, which seemed to come from the second-floor rear bedroom. It could also be heard in the kitchen, though it was less loud there, and seemed to come from the walls. Several people had heard it and there was no natural cause to account for it. Then there were the footsteps. It sounded like someone walking down the back-stairs, the servant's stairs, step by step, hesitatingly, and not returning, but just fading away!

They dubbed their ghostly guest "Elizabeth," for want of a better name. Mrs. Stewart did not consider herself psychic, nor did she have any interest in such matters. But occasionally things had happened to her that defied natural explanations, such as the time just after she had lost a baby. She awoke form a heavy sleep to the intangible feeling of a presence in her room. She looked up and there, in the rocking chair across the room, she saw a woman, now dead, who had taken care of her when she herself was a child. Rocking gently in the chair, as if to reassure her, the Nanny held Mrs. Stewart's baby in her arms. In a moment the vision was gone, but it had left Alexandra Stewart with a sense of peace. She knew her little one was well looked after.

The phenomena continued, however, and soon they were no longer restricted to the upstairs. On the first floor, in the living room, Mrs. Stewart heard the noise of someone breathing close to her. This had happened only recently, again in the presence of her husband and a friend. She asked them to hold their breath for a moment, and still she heard the strange breathing continuing as before. Neither of the men could hear it, or so they said. But the following day the guest came back with another man. He wanted to be sure of his observation before admitting that he too had heard the invisible person breathing close to him.

The corner of the living room where the breathing had been heard was also the focal point for strange knockings that faulty pipes could not explain. On one occasion they heard the breaking of glass, and yet there was no evidence that any glass had been broken. There was a feeling that someone other than those visible was present at times

in their living room, and it made them a little nervous even though they did not fear their "Elizabeth."

Alexandra's young husband had grown up in the building trade, and now works as a photographer. He too has heard the footsteps on many occasions, and he knows the difference between footsteps and a house settling or timbers creaking. These were definitely human noises.

Mrs. Martha Vaughn is a bookkeeper who had been living in the building for two years. Hers is the apartment in the rear portion of the second floor, and it includes the back porch. Around Christmas of 1964 she heard a baby crying on the porch. It was a particularly cold night, so she went to investigate immediately. It was a weird, unearthly sound—to her it seemed right near the porch, but there was nobody around. The yard was deserted. The sound to her was the crying of a small child, not a baby, but perhaps a child of between one and three years of age. The various families shared the downstairs living room "like a kibbutz," as Mrs. Stewart put it, so it was not out of the ordinary for several people to be in the downstairs area. On one such occasion Mrs. Vaughn also heard the breaking of the *invisible* glass.

Richard Vaughn is a laboratory technician. He too has heard the baby cry and the invisible glass break; he has heard pounding on the wall, as have the others. A skeptic at first, he tried to blame these noises on the steam pipes that heat the house. But when he listened to the pipes when they were acting up, he realized at once that the noises he had heard before were completely different.

"What about a man named Dugan? Or someone having to do with maps?" I asked.

"Well," Vaughn said, and thought back, "I used to get mail here for people who once lived here, and of course I sent it all back to the post office. But I don't recall the name Dugan. What I do recall was some mail from a Washington Bureau. You see, this house belongs to the University of Chicago and a lot of professors used to live here."

"Professors?" I said with renewed interest.

Was Dugan one of them?

Several other people who lived in the house experienced strange phenomena. Barbara Madonna, who works three days a week as a secretary, used to live there too. But in May of that year she moved out. She had moved into the house in November of the previous year. She and her husband much admired the back porch when they first moved in, and had visions of sitting out there drinking a beer on warm evenings. But soon their hopes were dashed by the uncanny feeling that they were not alone, that another presence was in their apartment, and especially out on the porch. Soon, instead of using the porch, they studiously avoided it, even if it meant walking downstairs to shake out a mop. Theirs was the third-floor apartment, directly above the Stewart apartment.

A girl by the name of Lolita Krol also had heard the baby crying. She lived in the building for a time and bitterly complained about the strange noises on the porch.

Douglas McConnor is a magazine editor, and he and his wife moved into the building in November of the year Barbara Madonna moved out, first to the second floor and later to the third. From the very first, when McConnor was still alone—his wife joined him in the flat after their marriage a little later—he felt extremely uncomfortable in the place. Doors and windows would fly open by themselves when there wasn't any strong wind.

When he moved upstairs to the next floor, things were much quieter, except for Sunday nights, when noisy activities would greatly increase toward midnight. Footsteps, the sounds of people rushing about, and of doors opening and closing would disturb Mr. McConnor's rest. The stairs were particularly noisy. But when he checked, he found that everybody was accounted for, and that no living person had caused the commotion.

It got to be so bad he started to hate Sunday nights.

I recounted Sybil's trance to Mr. McConnor and the fact that a woman named Judith had been the central figure of it.

"Strange," he observed, "but the story also fits that of my ex-wife, who deserted her children. She is of course very much alive now. Her name is Judith."

Had Sybil intermingled the impression a dead maidservant with the imprint left behind by an unfit mother? Or were there two Judiths? At any rate the Stewarts did not complain further about uncanny noises, and the girl in the blue-gray dress never came back.

As he drove as out to the airport Carl Subak seemed unusually silent. What he had witnessed seemed to have left an impression on him and his philosophy of life.

"What I find so particularly upsetting," he finally said, "is Sybil's talking about a woman and a dead baby—all of it borne out afterwards by the people in the house. But Sybil did not know this. She couldn't have."

No, she couldn't.

In September, three years later, a group consisting of a local television reporter, a would-be psychic student, and an assortment of clairvoyants descended on the building in search of psychic excitement. All they got out of it were mechanical difficulties with their cameras. The ghosts were long gone.

* * *

Ghosts are not just for the thrill seekers, nor are they the hallucinations of disturbed people. Nothing is as democratic as seeing or hearing a ghost, for it happens all the time, to just about every conceivable type of person. Neither age nor race nor religion seem to stay these spectral people in their predetermined haunts.

Naturally I treat each case on an individual basis. Some I reject on the face of the report, and others only after I have undertaken a long and careful investigation. But other reports have a ring of truth about them and are worthy of belief, even though sometimes they are no longer capable of verification because witnesses have died or sites have been destroyed.

A good example is the case reported to me recently by a Mrs. Edward Needs, Jr., of Canton, Ohio. In a small town by the name of Homeworth, there is a stretch of land near the highway that is today nothing more than a neglected farm with a boarded-up old barn that's still standing. The spot is actually on a dirt road, and the nearest house is half a mile away, with wooded territory in between. This is important, you see, for the spot is isolated and a man might die before help could arrive. On rainy days, the dirt road is impassable. Mrs. Needs has passed the spot a number of times, and does not particularly care to go there. Somehow it always gives her an uneasy feeling. Once, the Need's car got stuck in the mud on a rainy day, and they had to drive through open fields to get out.

It was on that adventure-filled ride that Mr. Needs confided for the first time what had happened to him at that spot on prior occasions. Edward Needs and a friend were on a joy ride after dark. At that time Needs had not yet married his present wife, and the two men had been drinking a little, but were far from drunk. It was then that they discovered the dirt road for the first time.

On the spur of the moment, they followed it. A moment later they came to the old barn. But just as they were approaching it, a man jumped out of nowhere in front of them. What was even more sobering was the condition this man was in: he was engulfed in flames from head to toe!

Quickly Needs put his bright headlights on the scene, to see better. The man then ran into the woods across the road, and just disappeared.

Two men never became cold sober more quickly. They turned around and went back to the main highway fast. But the first chance they had, they returned with two carloads full of other fellows. They were equipped with strong lights, guns, and absolutely no whiskey. When the first of the cars was within 20 feet of the spot where Needs had seen the apparition, they all saw the same thing: there before them was the horrible spectacle of a human being blazing from top to bottom, and evidently suffering terribly as he tried to run away from his doom. Needs emptied his gun at the figure: it never moved or acknowledged that it had been hit by the bullets. A few seconds later, the figure ran into the woods—exactly as it had when Needs had first encountered it.

Now the ghost posse went into the barn, which they found abandoned, although not in very bad condition. The only strange thing was a cluster of spots showing evidence of fire: evidently someone or something had burned inside the barn without setting fire to the barn as a whole. Or had the fiery man run outside to save his barn from the fire?

* * *

Betty Ann Tylaska lives in a seaport in Connecticut. Her family is a prominent one going back to Colonial days, and they still occupy a house built by her great-great-great-grandfather for his daughter and her husband back in 1807.

Mrs. Tylaska and her husband, a Navy officer, were in the process of restoring the venerable old house to its former glory. Neither of them had the slightest interest in the supernatural, and to them such things as ghosts simply did not exist except in children's tales.

The first time Mrs. Tylaska noticed anything unusual was one night when she was washing dishes in the kitchen.

Suddenly she had the strong feeling that she was being watched. She turned around and caught a glimpse of a man standing in the doorway between the kitchen and the living room of the downstairs part of the house. She saw him only for a moment, but long enough to notice his dark blue suit and silver buttons. Her first impression was that it must be her husband, who of course wore a navy blue uniform. But on checking she found him upstairs, wearing entirely different clothes.

She shrugged the matter off as a hallucination due to her tiredness, but the man in blue kept returning. On several occasions, the same uncanny feeling of being watched came over her, and when she turned around, there was the man in the dark blue suit.

It came as a relief to her when her mother confessed that she too had seen the ghostly visitor—always at the same spot, between the living room and kitchen. Finally she informed her husband, and to her surprise, he did not laugh at her. But he suggested that if it were a ghost, perhaps one of her ancestors was checking up on them.

Perhaps he wanted to make sure they restored the house properly and did not make any unwanted changes. They were doing a great deal of painting in the process of restoring the house, and whatever paint was left they would spill against an old stone wall at the back of the house.

Gradually the old stones were covered with paint of various hues.

One day Mr. Tylaska found himself in front of these stones. For want of anything better to do at the moment, he started to study them. To his amazement, he discovered that one of the stones was different from the others: it was long and flat. He called his wife and they investigated the strange stone; upon freeing it from the wall, they saw to their horror that it was a gravestone—her great-great-great-grandfather's tombstone, to be exact.

Inquiry at the local church cleared up the mystery of how the tombstone had gotten out of the cemetery. It seems that all the family members had been buried in a small cemetery nearby. But when it had filled up, a larger cemetery was started. The bodies were moved over to the new cemetery and a larger monument was erected over the great-great-great-grandfather's tomb. Since the original stone was of no use any longer, it was left behind. Some- how the stone got used when the old wall was being built. But evidently great-great-great-grandfather did not like the idea. Was that the reason for his visits? After all, who likes having paint splashed on one's precious tombstone? I ask you.

The Tylaska family held a meeting to decide what to do about it. They could not very well put two tombstones on granddad's grave. What would the other ancestors think? Everybody would want to have two tombstones then; and while it might be good news to the stonecutter, it would not be a thing to do in practical New England.

So they stood the old tombstone upright in their own backyard. It was nice having granddad with them that way, and if he felt like a visit, why, that was all right with them too.

From the moment they gave the tombstone a place of honor, the gentleman in the dark blue suit and the silver buttons never came back. But Mrs. Tylaska does not particularly mind. Two Navy men in the house might have been too much of a distraction anyway.

* * *

Give ghosts their due, and they'll be happy. Happy ghosts don't stay around: in fact, they turn into normal spirits, free to come and go (mostly go) at will. But until people come to recognize that the denizens of the Other World are real people like you and me, and not benighted devils or condemned souls in a purgatory created for the benefit of a political church, people will be frightened of them quite needlessly. Sometimes even highly intelligent people shudder when they have a brush with the uncanny.

Take young Mr. Bentine, for instance, the son of my dear friend Michael Bentine, the British TV star. He, like his father, is very much interested in the psychic. But young Bentine never bargained for firsthand experiences.

It happened at school, Harrow, one of the finest British "public schools" (in America they are called private schools), one spring. Young Bentine lived in a dormitory known as The Knoll. One night around 2 A.M., he awoke from sound sleep. The silence of the night was broken by the sound of footsteps coming from the headmaster's room. The footsteps went from the room to a nearby bathroom, and then suddenly came to a halt. Bentine thought nothing of it, but why had it awakened him? Perhaps he had been studying too hard and it was merely a case of nerves. At any rate, he decided not to pay any attention to the strange footsteps. After all, if the headmaster wished to walk at that ungodly hour, it was his business and privilege.

But the following night the same thing happened. Again, at 2 A.M. he found himself awake, to the sound of ominous footsteps. Again they stopped abruptly when they reached the bathroom. Coincidence? Cautious, young Bentine made some inquiries. Was the headmaster given to nocturnal walks, perhaps? He was not.

The third night, Bentine decided that if it happened again, he would be brave and look into it. He fortified himself with some tea and then went to bed. It was not easy falling asleep, but eventually his fatigue got the upper hand and our young man was asleep in his room.

Promptly at 2, however, he was awake again. And quicker than you could say "Ghost across the hall," there were the familiar footsteps!

Quickly, our intrepid friend got up and stuck his head out of his door, facing the headmaster's room and the bathroom directly across the corridor.

The steps were now very loud and clear. Although he did not see anyone, he heard someone move along the passage.

He was petrified. As soon as the footsteps had come to the usual abrupt halt in front of the bathroom door, he crept back into his own room and bed. But sleep was out of the question. The hours were like months, until finally morning came and a very tired Bentine went down to breakfast, glad the ordeal of the night had come to an end.

He had to know what this was all about, no matter what the consequences. To go through another night like that was out of the question.

He made some cautious inquiries about that room. There had been a headmaster fourteen years ago who had died in that room. It had been suicide, and he had hanged himself in the shower. Bentine turned white as a ghost himself when he heard the story. He immediately tried to arrange to have his room changed. But that could not be done as quickly as he had hoped, so it was only after another two-and-a-half weeks that he was able to banish the steps of the ghostly headmaster from his mind.

His father had lent him a copy of my book, *Ghost Hunter*, and he had looked forward to reading it when exams eased up a bit. But now, even though he was in another room that had not the slightest trace of a ghost, he could not bring himself to touch my book. Instead, he concentrated on reading humor.

Unfortunately nobody did anything about the ghostly headmaster, so it must be that he keeps coming back down that passage to his old room, only to find his body still hanging in the shower.

You might ask, "What shall I do if I think I have a ghost in the house? Shall I run? Shall I stay? Do I talk to it or ignore it? Is there a rule book for people having ghosts?" Some of the questions I get are like that. Others merely wish to report a case because they feel it is something I might be interested in. Still others want help: free them from the ghost and vice versa.

But so many people have ghosts—almost as many as have termites, not that there is any connection—that I cannot personally go after each and every case brought to my attention by mail, telephone, e-mail, or television.

In the most urgent cases, I try to come and help the people involved. Usually I do this in connection with a TV show or lecture at the local university, for *someone* has to pay my expenses. The airlines don't accept ghost money, nor do the innkeepers. And thus far I have been on my own, financially speaking, with no institute or research foundation to take up the slack. For destruction and bombs there is always money, but for research involving the psychic, hardly ever.

Granted, I can visit a number of people with haunted-house problems every year, but what do the others do when I can't see them myself? Can I send them to a local ghost hunter, the way a doctor sends patients to a colleague if he can't or does not wish to treat them?

Even if I could, I wouldn't do it. When they ask for my help, they want my approach to their peculiar problems and not someone else's. In this field each researcher sees things a little differently from the next one. I am probably the only parapsychologist who is unhesitatingly pro-ghost. Some will admit they exist, but spend a lot of time trying to find "alternate" explanations if they cannot discredit the witnesses.

I have long, and for good scientific reasons, been convinced that ghosts exist. Ghosts are ghosts. Not hallucinations, necessarily, and not the mistakes of casual observers. With that sort of practical base to start from, I go after the cases by concentrating on the situation and the problems, rather than, as some researchers will do, trying hard to change the basic stories reported to me. I don't work on my witnesses; I've come to help them. To try and shake them with the sophisticated apparatus of a trained parapsychologist is not only unfair, but also foolish. The original reports are straight reports of average people telling what has happened in their own environment. If you try to shake their testimony, you may get a different story—but it won't be the truth, necessarily. The more you confuse the witnesses, the less they will recall firsthand information.

My job begins after the witnesses have told their stories.

In the majority of the cases I have handled, I have found a basis of fact for the ghostly "complaint." Once in a while, a person may have thought something was supernormal when it was not, and on rare occasions I have come across mentally unbalanced people living in a fantasy world of their own. But there just aren't that many kooks who want my help: evidently my scientific method, even though I am convinced of the veracity of ghostly phenomena, is not the kind of searchlight they wish to have turned on their strange stories.

What to do until the Ghost Hunter arrives? Relax, if you can. Be a good observer even if you're scared stiff. And remember, please—ghosts are also people.

There, but for the grace of God, goes someone like you.

Famous Ghosts

HERE WE DEAL WITH the ghosts of famous people, whose names nearly everyone will recognize. This category includes historical celebrities, national figures, heroes, leaders, and also celebrities of Hollywood, the theatre, people who once made headlines, and people who had some measure of fame, which is usually a lot more than the proverbial fifteen minutes that, according to the late Andy Warhol, *everyone* can find.

There are many houses or places where famous ghosts have appeared that are open to the public. These include national monuments, local museums, historical houses and mansions. But are the famous ghosts still there when you visit? Well, now, that depends: many ghostly experiences are, as I have pointed out, impressions from the past, and you get to sort of relive the events that involved them in the past. It is a little difficult to sort this out, tell which is a bona fide resident ghost still hanging around the old premises and which is a scene from the past. But if you are the one who is doing the exploring, the ghost hunter as it were, it is for you to experience and decide for yourself. Good hunting!

GHOSTS IN FICTION

Ghosts, phantoms and spirits have always been a staple for novelists and dramatists. Mysterious and worrisome ghosts are both part of the human experience yet outside the mainstream of that world. Many of the false notions people have about ghosts come from fiction. Only in fictional ghost stories do ghosts threaten or cause harm: in the real afterlife, they are too busy trying to understand their situation to worry about those in the physical world.

From Chaucer's Canterville ghost with his rattling chain to Shakespeare's ghost of Hamlet's father, who restlessly walked the ramparts of his castle because of unresolved matters (such as his murder), in literature, ghosts seem frightening and undesirable. No Caspars there.

The masters of the macabre, from E. T. A. Hoffman to Edgar Allan Poe, have presented their ghosts as sorrowful, unfortunate creatures who are best avoided.

The Flying Dutchman is a man, punished by God for transgressions (though they are never quite explained), who cannot stop being a ghost until true love comes his way. Not likely, among the real kind.

* * *

Edith Wharton's novels offer us far more realistic ghosts, perhaps because she is nearer to our time and was aware of psychical research in these matters.

There is a pair of ghostly dancing feet in one of Rudyard Kipling's Indian tales that used to keep me up nights when I was a boy. Today, they would merely interest me because of my desire to see the rest of the dancer, too.

Arthur Conan Doyle presents us with a colorful but very believable ghost story in "The Law of the Ghost." Lastly, the ghosts of Dickens' *A Christmas Carol* are not really ghosts but messengers from beyond, symbolic at best.

Please don't rush to Elsinore Castle in Denmark in search of the unfortunate king who was murdered by his brother because, alas, both the murdered king and his brother Claudius are as much figments of Shakespeare's imagination as is the melancholy Dane, Hamlet, himself.

Television ghosts tend to be much less frightening, even pleasant. The ghosts in "The Ghost and Mrs. Muir," starring Rex Harrison, were sarcastic, almost lovable. The ghostly couple the banker Topper had to contend with was full of mischief, at worst, and helpful, at best.

And they did all sorts of things real ghosts don't do, but special effects will have their say.

✳ 1

The Conference House Ghost

ONLY AN HOUR OR SO by ferry boat from bustling Manhattan lies the remote charm of Staten Island, where many old houses and even farms still exist in their original form within the boundaries of New York City.

One of these old houses, and a major sight-seeing attraction, is the so-called "Conference House," where the British Commander, Lord Howe, received the American Conference delegation consisting of Benjamin Franklin, John Adams, and Edward Rutledge, on September 11, 1776. The purpose of the meeting was to convince the Americans that a peaceful solution should be found for the difficulties between England and the Colonies. The meeting proved unsuccessful, of course, and the Revolutionary War ensued.

The house itself is a sturdy white two-story building, erected along typical English manorhouse lines, in 1688, on a site known then as Bentley Manor in what is today Tottenville. There are two large rooms on the ground floor, and a staircase leading to an upper story, also divided into two rooms; a basement contains the kitchen and a vaultlike enclosure. The original owner of the house was Captain Billopp of the British Navy, and his descendants lived in the house until the close of the Revolutionary period.

Local legends have had the house "haunted" for many years. The story was that Billopp, a hard man, jilted his fiancee, and that she died of a broken heart in this very house. For several generations back, reports of noises, murmurs, sighs, moans, and pleas have been received and the old Staten Island *Transcript*, a local newspaper, has mentioned these strange goings-on over the years. When the house was being rebuilt, after having been taken over as a museum by the city, the workers are said to have heard the strange noises, too.

It was against this background that I decided to investigate the house in the company of Mrs. Meyers, who was to be our sensitive, and two friends, Rose de Simone and Pearl Winder, who were to be the "sitters," or assistants to the medium.

After we had reached Staten Island, and were about half an hour's drive from the house, Mrs. Meyers volunteered her impressions of the house which she was yet to see! She spoke of it as being white, the ground floor divided into two rooms, a brown table and eight chairs in the east room; the room on the west side of the house is the larger one, and lighter colored than the other room, and some silverware was on display in the room to the left.

Upon arriving at the house, I checked these statements; they were correct, except that the number of chairs was now only seven, not eight, and the silver display had been removed from its spot eight years before!

Mrs. Meyers' very first impression was the name "Butler"; later I found that the estate next door belonged to the Butler family, unknown, of course, to the medium.

We ascended the stairs; Mrs. Meyers sat down on the floor of the second-story room to the left. She described a woman named Jane, stout, white-haired, wearing a dark green dress and a fringed shawl, then mentioned the name *Howe*. It must be understood that the connection of Lord Howe with the house was totally unknown to all of us until *after* checking up on the history of the Conference House, later on.

Next Mrs. Meyers described a man with white hair, or a wig, wearing a dark coat with embroidery at the neck, tan breeches, dark shoes, and possessed of a wide, square face, a thick nose, and looking "Dutch." "The man died in this room," she added.

She then spoke of the presence of a small boy, about six, dressed in pantaloons and with his hair in bangs. The child born in this room was specially honored later, Mrs. Meyers felt. This might apply to Christopher Billopp, born at the house in 1737, who later became Richmond County representative in the Colonial Assembly. Also, Mrs. Meyers felt the "presence" of a big man in a fur hat, rather fat, wearing a skin coat and high boots, brass-buckle belt and black trousers; around him she felt boats, nets, sailing boats, and she heard a foreign, broad accent, also saw him in a four-masted ship of the square-rigger type. The initial T was given. Later, I learned that the Billopp family were prominent Tory leaders up to and during the Revolution.

This man, Mrs. Meyers felt, had a loud voice, broad forehead, high cheekbones, was a vigorous man, tall, with shaggy hair, and possibly Dutch. His name was Van B., she thought. She did not know that Billopp (or Van Billopp) was the builder of the house.

"I feel as if I'm being dragged somewhere by Indians," Mrs. Meyers suddenly said. "There is violence, somebody dies on a pyre of wood, two men, one white, one Indian; and on two sticks nearby are their scalps."

Later, I ascertained that Indian attacks were frequent here during the seventeenth and eighteenth centuries and that, in fact, a tunnel once existed as an escape route to the nearby waterfront, in case of hostile Indian sieges. Large numbers of arrowheads have been unearthed around the house.

Down in the cellar, Mrs. Meyers felt sure six people had been buried near the front wall during the Revolutionary War, all British soldiers; she thought eight more were buried elsewhere on the grounds and sensed the basement full of wounded "like a hospital." On investigation, I found that some members of Billopp's family were indeed buried on the grounds near the road; as for the British soldiers, there were frequent skirmishes around the house between Americans infiltrating from the nearby New Jersey shore and the British, who held Staten Island since July 4, 1776.

At one time, Captain Billopp, a British subject, was kidnapped by armed bandits in his own house, and taken to New Jersey a prisoner of the Americans!

We returned to the upper part of the house once more. Suddenly, Mrs. Meyers felt impelled to turn her attention to the winding staircase. I followed with mounting excitement.

Descending the stairs, our medium suddenly halted her steps and pointed to a spot near the landing of the second story. "Someone was killed here with a crooked knife, a woman!" she said. There was horror on her face as if she were reliving the murder. On questioning the custodian, Mrs. Early, I discovered that Captain Billopp, in a rage, had indeed killed a female slave on that very spot!

✳ 2

The Stranger at the Door

I HAVE FOUND THAT there are ghosts in all sorts of places, in ancient castles, modern apartment houses, farms and ships—but it is somewhat of a jolt to find out you've lived in a house for a few years and didn't even know it was haunted. But that is exactly what happened to me.

For three years I was a resident of a beautiful twenty-nine-story apartment building on Riverside Drive. I lived on the nineteenth floor, and seldom worried about what transpired below me. But I was aware of the existence of a theater and a museum on the ground floor of the building. I was also keenly aware of numerous inspired paintings, some Tibetan, some Occidental, adorning the corridors of this building. The museum is nowadays known as the Riverside Museum, and the paintings were largely the work of the great Rohrach, a painter who sought his inspirations mainly in the mysticism of Tibet, where he spent many years. On his return from the East, his many admirers decided to chip in a few million and build him a monument worthy of his name. Thus, in 1930, was raised the Rohrach building as a center of the then flourishing cult of Eastern mysticism, of which Rohrach was the high priest. After his death, a schism appeared among his followers, and an exodus took place. A new "Rohrach Museum" was established by Seena Fosdick, and is still in existence a few blocks away from the imposing twenty-nine-story structure originally known by that name. In turn, the building where I lived changed its name to that of the Master Institute, a combination apartment building and school, and, of course, art gallery.

It was in February of 1960 when I met at a tea party —yes, there are such things in this day and age—a young actress and producer, Mrs. Roland, who had an interesting experience at "my" building some years ago. She was not sure whether it was 1952 or 1953, but she was quite sure that it happened exactly the way she told it to me that winter afternoon in the apartment of famed author Claudia de Lys.

A lecture-meeting dealing with Eastern philosophy had drawn her to the Rohrach building. Ralph Huston, the eminent philosopher, presided over the affair, and a full turnout it was. As the speaker held the attention of the crowd, Mrs. Roland's eyes wandered off to the rear of the room. Her interest was invited by a tall stranger standing near the door, listening quietly and with rapt attention. Mrs. Roland didn't know too many of the active members, and the stranger, whom she had never seen before, fascinated her. His dress, for one thing, was most peculiar. He wore a gray cotton robe with a high-necked collar, the kind one sees in Oriental paintings, and on his head he had a round black cap. He appeared to be a fairly young man, certainly in the prime of life, and his very dark eyes in particular attracted her.

For a moment she turned her attention to the speaker; when she returned to the door, the young man was gone.

"Peculiar," she thought; "why should he leave in the middle of the lecture? He seemed so interested in it all."

As the devotees of mysticism slowly filed out of the room, the actress sauntered over to Mrs. Fosdick whom she knew to be the "boss lady" of the group.

"Tell me," she inquired, "who was that handsome dark-eyed young man at the door?"

Mrs. Fosdick was puzzled. She did not recall any such person. The actress then described the stranger in every detail. When she had finished, Mrs. Fosdick seemed a bit pale.

But this was an esoteric forum, so she did not hesitate to tell Mrs. Roland that she had apparently seen an apparition. What was more, the description fitted the great Rohrach—in his earlier years—to a T. Mrs. Roland had never seen Rohrach in the flesh.

At this point, Mrs. Roland confessed that she had psychic abilities, and was often given to "hunches." There was much head shaking, followed by some hand shaking, and then the matter was forgotten.

I was of course interested, for what would be nicer than to have a house ghost, so to speak?

The next morning, I contacted Mrs. Fosdick. Unfortunately, this was one of the occasions when truth did not conquer. When I had finished telling her what I wanted her to confirm, she tightened up, especially when she found out I was living at the "enemy camp," so to speak. Emphatically, Mrs. Fosdick denied the incident, but admitted knowing Mrs. Roland.

With this, I returned to my informant, who reaffirmed the entire matter. Again I approached Mrs. Fosdick with the courage of an unwelcome suitor advancing on the castle of his beloved, fully aware of the dragons lurking in the moat.

While I explained my scientific reasons for wanting her to remember the incident, she launched into a tirade concerning her withdrawal from the "original" Rohrach group, which was fascinating, but not to me.

I have no reason to doubt Mrs. Roland's account, especially as I found her extremely well poised, balanced, and indeed, psychic.

I only wondered if Mr. Rohrach would sometime honor me with a visit, or vice versa, now that we were neighbors?

✳ 3

A Visit with Alexander Hamilton's Ghost

THERE STANDS AT Number 27, Jane Street, in New York's picturesque artists' quarters, Greenwich Village, a mostly wooden house dating back to pre-Revolutionary days. In this house Alexander Hamilton was treated in his final moments. Actually, he died a few houses away, at 80 Jane Street, but No. 27 was the home of John Francis, his doctor, who attended him after the fatal duel with Aaron Burr.

However, the Hamilton house no longer exists, and the wreckers are now after the one of his doctor, now occupied by a writer and artist, Jean Karsavina, who has lived there since 1939.

The facts of Hamilton's untimely passing are well known; D. S. Alexander (in his *Political History of the State of New York*) reports that, because of political enmity, "Burr seems to have deliberately determined to kill him." A letter written by Hamilton calling Burr "despicable" and "not to be trusted with the reins of government" found its way into the press, and Burr demanded an explanation. Hamilton declined, and on June 11, 1804, at Weehawken, New Jersey, Burr took careful aim, and his first shot mortally wounded Hamilton. In the boat back to the city, Hamilton regained consciousness, but knew his end was near. He was taken to Dr. Francis' house and treated, but died within a few days at his own home, across the street.

Ever since moving into 27 Jane Street, Miss Karsavina has been aware of footsteps, creaking stairs, and the opening and closing of doors; and even the unexplained flushing of a toilet. On one occasion, she found the toilet chain still swinging, when there was no one around! "I suppose a toilet that flushes *would* be a novelty to someone from the eighteenth century," she is quoted in a brief newspaper account in June of 1957.*

She also has seen a blurred "shape," without being able to give details of the apparition; her upstairs tenant, however, reports that one night not so long ago, "a man in eighteenth-century clothes, with his hair in a queue" walked into her room, looked at her and walked out again.

Miss Karsavina turned out to be a well-read and charming lady who had accepted the possibility of living with a ghost under the same roof. Mrs. Meyers and I went to see her in March 1960. The medium had no idea where we were going.

At first, Mrs. Meyers, still in waking condition, noticed a "shadow" of a man, old, with a broad face and bulbous nose; a woman with a black shawl whose name she thought was Deborah, and she thought "someone had a case"; she then described an altar of white lilies, a bridal couple, and a small coffin covered with flowers; then a very old woman in a coffin that was richly adorned, with relatives including a young boy and girl looking into the open coffin. She got the name of Mrs. Patterson, and the girl's as Miss Lucy. In another "impression" of the same premises, Mrs. Meyers described "an empty coffin, people weeping, talking, milling around, *and the American Flag atop the coffin*; in the coffin a man's hat, shoes with silver buckles, gold epaulettes...." She then got close to the man and thought his lungs were filling with liquid and he died with a pain in his side.

Lapsing into semitrance at this point, Mrs. Meyers described a party of men in a small boat on the water, then a man wearing white pants and a blue coat with blood spilled over the pants. "Two boats were involved, and it is dusk," she added.

Switching apparently to another period, Mrs. Meyers felt that "something is going on in the cellar, they try to keep attention from what happens downstairs; there is a woman here, being stopped by two men in uniforms with short jackets and round hats with wide brims, and pistols. There is the sound of shrieking, the woman is pushed back violently, men are marching, someone who had been harbored here has to be given up, an old man in a nightshirt and red socks is being dragged out of the house into the snow."

In still another impression, Mrs. Meyers felt herself drawn up toward the rear of the house where "someone died in childbirth"; in fact, this type of death occurred

Fate, June, 1957.

"several times" in this house. Police were involved, too, but this event or chain of events is of a later period than the initial impressions, she felt. The name Henry Oliver or Oliver Henry came to her mind.

After her return to full consciousness, Mrs. Meyers remarked that there was a chilly area near the center of the downstairs room. There is; I feel it too. Mrs. Meyers "sees" the figure of a slender man, well-formed, over average height, in white trousers, black boots, dark blue coat and tails, white lace in front; *he is associated with George Washington and Lafayette*, and their faces appear to her, too; she feels Washington may have been in this house. The man she "sees" is a *general*, she can see his epaulettes. The old woman and the children seen earlier are somehow connected with this, too. He died young, and there "was fighting in a boat." Now Mrs. Meyers gets the name "W. Lawrence." She has a warm feeling about the owner of the house; he took in numbers of people, like refugees.

A "General Mills" stored supplies here—shoes, coats, almost like a military post; food is being handed out. The name Bradley is given. Then Mrs. Meyers sees an old man playing a cornet; two men in white trousers "seen" seated at a long table, bent over papers, with a crystal chandelier above.

After the séance, Miss Karsavina confirmed that the house belonged to Hamilton's physician, and as late as

1825 was owned by a doctor, who happened to be the doctor for the Metropolitan Opera House. The cornet player might have been one of his patients.

In pre-Revolutionary days, the house may have been used as headquarters of an "underground railroad," around 1730, when the police tried to pick up the alleged instigators of the so-called "Slave Plot," evidently being sheltered here.

"Lawrence" may refer to the portrait of Washington by Lawrence which *used* to hang over the fireplace in the house. On the other hand, I found a T. Lawrence, M. D., at 146 Greenwich Street, in *Elliot's Improved Directory for New York* (1812); and a "Widow Patterson" is listed by Longworth (1803) at 177 William Street; a William Lawrence, druggist, at 80 John Street. According to Charles Burr Todd's *Story of New York*, two of Hamilton's pallbearers were Oliver Wolcott and John L. Lawrence. The other names mentioned could not be found. The description of the man in white trousers is of course the perfect image of Hamilton, and the goings-on at the house with its many coffins, and women dying in childbirth, are indeed understandable for a doctor's residence.

It does not seem surprising that Alexander Hamilton's shade should wish to roam about the house of the man who tried, vainly, to save his life.

✳ **4**

The Fifth Avenue Ghost

SOME CASES OF haunted houses require but a single visit to obtain information and evidence, others require two or three. But very few cases in the annals of psychic research can equal or better the record set by the case I shall call The Fifth Avenue Ghost. Seventeen sessions, stretching over a period of five months, were needed to complete this most unusual case. I am presenting it here just as it unfolded for us. I am quoting from our transcripts, our records taken during each and every session; and because so much evidence was obtained in this instance that could only be obtained from the person these events actually happened to, it is to my mind a very strong case for the truth about the nature of hauntings.

* * *

It isn't very often that one finds a haunted apartment listed in the leading evening paper.

Occasionally, an enterprising real-estate agent will add the epithet "looks haunted" to a cottage in the country to attract the romanticist from the big city.

But the haunted apartment I found listed in the *New York Daily News* one day in July 1953 was the real McCoy. Danton Walker, the late Broadway columnist, had this item—

One for the books: an explorer, advertising his Fifth Avenue Studio for sublet, includes among the attractions 'attic dark room with ghost.'...

The enterprising gentleman thus advertising his apartment for rent turned out to be Captain Davis, a celebrated explorer and author of many books, including, here and there, some ghost lore. Captain Davis was no skeptic. To the contrary, I found him sincere and well aware of the existence of psychical research. Within hours, I had discussed the case with the study group which met weekly at the headquarters of the Association for Research and Enlightenment, the Edgar Cayce Foundation. A team was organized, consisting of Bernard Axelrod, Nelson Welsh, Stanley Goldberg, and myself, and, of course, Mrs. Meyers as the medium. Bernard Axelrod and I knew that there was some kind of "ghost" at the Fifth Avenue address, but little more. The medium knew nothing whatever. Two days *after* the initial session, a somewhat fictional piece appeared in the *New York Times* (July 13, 1953) by the late Meyer Berger, who had evidently interviewed the *host*, but not the *ghost.* Mr. Berger quoted Captain Davis as saying there was a green ghost who had hanged himself from the studio gallery, and allegedly sticks an equally green hand out of the attic window now and then.

Captain Davis had no idea who the ghost was. This piece, it must be re-emphasized, appeared two days *after* the initial sitting at the Fifth Avenue house, and its contents were of course unknown to all concerned at the time.

* * *

In order to shake hands with the good Captain, we had to climb six flights of stairs to the very top of 226 Fifth Avenue. The building itself is one of those big old town houses popular in the mid-Victorian age, somber, sturdy, and well up to keeping its dark secrets behind its thickset stone walls. Captain Davis volunteered the information that previous tenants had included Richard Harding Davis, actor Richard Mansfield, and a lady magazine editor. Only the lady was still around and, when interviewed, was found to be totally ignorant of the entire ghost tradition, nor had she ever been disturbed. Captain Davis also told of guests in the house having seen the ghost at various times, though he himself had not. His home is one of the those fantastic and colorful apartments only an explorer or collector would own—a mixture of comfortable studio and museum, full of excitement and personality, and offering more than a touch of the Unseen. Two wild jungle cats completed the atmospheric picture, somewhat anticlimaxed by the host's tape recorder set up on the floor. The apartment is a kind of duplex, with a gallery or balcony jutting out into the main room. In the middle of this balcony was the window referred to in the *Times* interview. Present were the host, Captain Davis, Mr. and Mrs. Bertram Long, the Countess de Sales, all friends of the host's, and the group of researchers previously mentioned —a total of eight people, and, if you wish, two cats. As with most sittings, tape recordings were made of the proceedings from beginning to end, in addition to which written notes were taken.

MEETING A GHOST

Like a well-rehearsed television thriller, the big clock in the tower across the square struck nine, and the lights were doused, except for one medium-bright electric lamp. This was sufficient light, however, to distinguish the outlines of most of the sitters, and particularly the center of the room around the medium.

A comfortable chair was placed under the gallery, in which the medium took her place; around her, forming a circle, sat the others, with the host operating the recorder and facing the medium. It was very still, and the atmosphere seemed tense. The medium had hardly touched the chair when she grabbed her own neck in the unmistakable manner of someone being choked to death, and nervously told of being "hung by the neck until dead." She then sat

in the chair and Bernard Axelrod, an experienced hypnotist, conditioned her into her usual trance condition, which came within a few minutes.

With bated breath, we awaited the arrival of whatever personality might be the "ghost" referred to. We expected some violence and, as will be seen shortly, we got it. This is quite normal with such cases, especially at the first contact. It appears that a "disturbed personality" continuously relives his or her "passing condition," or cause of death, and it is this last agony that so frequently makes ghostly visitations matters of horror. If emotional anxiety is the cause of death, or was present at death, then the "disturbed personality," or entity, will keep reliving that final agony, much like a phonograph needle stuck in the last groove of a record. But here is what happened on that first occasion.

Sitting of July 11th, 1953, at 226 Fifth Avenue

The medium, now possessed by unknown entity, has difficulty in speaking. Entity breaks into mad laughter full of hatred.

Entity: . . . curry the horse . . . they're coming . . . curry the horse! Where is Mignon? WHERE IS SHE?

Question: We wish to help you. Who is Mignon?

Entity: She should be here . . . where is she . . . you've got her! Where is she? Where is the baby?

Question: What baby?

Entity: What did they do with her?

Question: We're your friends.

Entity: (in tears) Oh, an enemy . . . an enemy. . . .

Question: What is your name?

Entity: Guychone . . . Guychone. . . . (expresses pain at the neck; hands feeling around are apparently puzzled by finding a woman's body)

Question: You are using someone else's body. (Entity clutches throat.) Does it hurt you there?

Entity: Not any more . . . it's whole again . . . I can't see. . . . All is so different, all is very strange . . . nothing is the same.

I asked how he died. This excited him immediately.

Entity: (hysterical) I didn't do it . . . I tell you I didn't do it, no . . . Mignon, Mignon . . . where is she? They took the baby . . . she put me away . . . they took her. . . . (Why did she put you away?) So no one could find me (Where?) I stay there (meaning upstairs) all the time.

The Fifth Avenue ghost house—New York

At this point, tapes were changed. *Entity*, asked where he came from, says Charleston, and that he lived in a white house.

Question: Do you find it difficult to use this body?

Entity: WHAT?? WHAT?? I'm HERE... I'm here.... This is my house... what are YOU doing here?

Question: Tell me about the little room upstairs.

Entity: (crying) Can I go... away... from the room?

At this point, the entity left, and the medium's *control*, Albert, took over her body.

Albert: There is a very strong force here, and it has been a little difficult. This individual here suffered violence at the hands of several people. He was a Confederate and he was given up, hidden here, while they made their escape.

Question: What rank did he hold?

Albert: I believe that he had some rank. It is a little dubious as to what he was.

Question: What was his name?

Albert: It is not as he says. That is an assumed name, that he likes to take. He is not as yet willing to give full particulars. He is a violent soul underneath when he has opportunity to come, but he hasn't done damage to anyone, and we are going to work with him, if possible, from this side.

Question: What about Mignon and the baby?

Albert: Well, they of course are a long time *on this side*, but he never knew that, what became of them. They were separated cruelly. She did *not* do anything to him.

Question: How did he leave this world?

Albert: By violence. (Was he hanged?) Yes. (In the little room?) Yes. (Was it suicide or murder?) He says it was murder.

* * *

The *control* then suggests to end the trance, and try for results in "open" sitting. We slowly awaken the medium.

While the medium is resting, sitter Stanley Goldberg remarks that he has the impression that Guychone's father came from Scotland.

Captain Davis observes that at the exact moment of "frequency change" in the medium, that is, when Guychone left and Albert took over, the control light of the recording apparatus suddenly blazed up of *its own accord*, and had to be turned down by him.

A standing circle was then formed by all present, holding hands, and taking the center of the room. Soon the medium started swinging forward and back like a suspended body. She remarked feeling very stiff "from hanging and surprised to find that I'm whole, having been cut open in the middle."

Both Axelrod and I observed a luminescent white and greenish glow covering the medium, creating the impression of an older man without hair, with high cheekbones and thin arms. This was during the period when Guychone was speaking through the medium.

The séance ended at 12:30. The medium reported feeling exhausted, with continued discomfort in the throat and stomach.

THE INVESTIGATION CONTINUES

Captain Davis, unfortunately, left on a worldwide trip the same week, and the new tenant was uncooperative. I felt we should continue the investigation. Once you pry a "ghost" loose from his place of unhappy memories, he can sometimes be contacted elsewhere.

Thus, a second sitting took place at the headquarters of the study group, on West 16th Street. This was a small, normally-furnished room free of any particular atmosphere, and throughout this and all following sittings, subdued light was used, bright enough to see all facial expressions quite clearly. There was smoking and occasional talking in low voices, none of which ever disturbed the work. Before the second sitting, Mrs. Meyers remarked that Guychone had "followed her home" from the Fifth Avenue place, and twice appeared to her at night in a kind of "whitish halo," with an expression of frantic appeal in his eyes. Upon her admonition to be patient until the sitting, the apparition had vanished.

Sitting of July 14th, 1953, at 125 West 16th Street

Question: Do you know what year this is?

Guychone: 1873.

Question: No, it is 1953. Eighty years have gone by. You are no longer alive. Do you understand?

Guychone: Eighty years? EIGHTY YEARS? I'm not a hundred-ten years?

Question: No, you're not. You're forever young. Mignon is on your side, too. We have come to help you understand yourself. What happened in 1873?

Guychone: Nobody's goddamn business…mine…mine!

Question: All right, keep your secret then, but don't you want to see Mignon? Don't you want justice done? (mad, bitter laughter) Don't you believe in God? (more laughter) The fact you are here and are able to speak, doesn't that prove that there is hope for you? What happened in 1873? Remember the house on Fifth Avenue, the room upstairs, the horse to be curried?

Guychone: Riding, riding…find her…they took her away.

Question: Who took her away?

Guychone: YOU! (threatens to strike interrogator)

Question: No, we're your friends. Where can we find a record of your Army service? Is it true you were on a dangerous mission?

Guychone: Yes.

Question: In what capacity?

Guychone: That is my affair! I do not divulge my secrets. I am a gentleman, and my secrets die with me.

Question: Give us your rank.

Guychone: I was a Colonel.

Question: In what regiment?

Guychone: Two hundred and sixth.

Question: Were you infantry or cavalry?

Guychone: Cavalry.

Question: In the War Between the States?

Guychone: Yes.

Question: Where did you make your home before you came to New York?

Guychone: Charleston…Elm Street.

Question: What is your family name, Colonel?

Guychone: (crying) As a gentleman, I am yet not ready to give you that information…it's no use, I won't name it.

Question: You make it hard for us, but we will abide by your wishes.

Guychone: (relieved) I am very much obliged to you…for giving me the information that it is EIGHTY YEARS. Eighty years!

I explain about the house on Fifth Avenue, and that Guychone's "presence" had been felt from time to time. Again, I ask for his name.

(Apparently fumbling for paper, he is given paper and fountain pen; the latter seems to puzzle him at first, but he then writes in the artistic, stylized manner of the mid-Victorian age—"Edouard Guychone.")

Question: Is your family of French extraction?

Guychone: Yes.

Question: Are you yourself French or were you born in this country?

Guychone: In this country…Charleston.

Question: Do you speak French?

Guychone: No.

Question: Is there anything you want us to do for you? Any unfinished business?

Guychone: Eighty years makes a difference…I am a broken man…God bless you…Mignon…it is so dark, so dark….

I explain the reason for his finding himself temporarily in a woman's body, and how his hatred had brought him back to the house on Fifth Avenue, instead of passing over to the "other side."

Guychone: (calmer) There IS a God?

I ask when was he born.

Guychone: (unsure) 1840…42 years old….

This was the most dramatic of the sittings. The transcript cannot fully convey the tense situation existing between a violent, hate-inspired and God-denying personality fresh from the abyss of perennial darkness, and an interrogator trying calmly to bring light into a disturbed mind. Toward the end of the session, Guychone understood about God, and began to realize that much time had passed since his personal tragedy had befallen him. Actually, the method of "liberating" a ghost is no different from that used by a psychiatrist to free a flesh-and-blood person from obsessions or other personality disturbances. Both deal with the mind.

It became clear to me that many more sessions would be needed to clear up the case, since the entity was reluctant to tell all. This is not the case with most "ghosts," who generally welcome a chance to "spill" emotions pent up for long years of personal hell. Here, however, the return of reason also brought back the critical faculty of reasoning, and evaluating information. We had begun to liberate Guychone's soul, but we had not yet penetrated to his conscience. Much hatred, fear, and pride remained, and had to be removed, before the true personality could emerge.

Sitting of July 21st, 1953

Albert, the medium's control, spoke first.

Question: Have you found any information about his wife and child?

Albert: You understand that this is our moral code, that that which comes from the individual within voluntarily is his sacred development. That which he wishes to divulge makes his soul what it should eventually be.

I asked that he describe Guychone's appearance to us.

Albert: At the moment he is little developed from the moment of passing. He is still like his latter moments in life. But his figure was of slight build, tall...five feet nine or ten...his face is round, narrow at the chin, high at the cheekbones, the nose is rather prominent, the mouth rather wide...the forehead high, at the moment of death and for many years previous very little hair. The eyes set close to the nose.

Question: Have you learned his *real* name?

Albert: It is not his wish as yet. He will tell you, he will develop his soul through his confession. Here he is!

Guychone: (at first grimacing in pain) It is nice to come, but it is hell...I have seen the light. It was so dark.

Question: Your name, sir?

Guychone: I was a gentleman...my name was defiled. I cannot see it, I cannot hear it, let me take it, when it is going to be right. I have had to pay for it; she has paid her price. I have been so happy. I have moved about. I have learned to right wrongs. I have seen the light.

Question: I am going to open your eyes now. Look at the calendar before you, and tell me what is the date on it? (placing calendar)

Guychone: 1953....(pointing at the tape recorder in motion) Wagon wheels!

Question: Give us the name of one of your fellow officers in the war. Write it down.

Guychone: I am a poor soul....(writes: Mignon my wife...Guychone) Oh, my feet, oh my feet...they hurt me so now...they bleed...I have to always go backwards, backwards. What shall I do with my feet? They had no shoes...we walked over burning weed...they burned the weed...(Who?) The Damyankees...I wake up, I see the

burning weed....(Where? When?) I have to reach out, I have so much to reach for, have patience with me, I can only reach so far—I'll forget. I will tell you everything.... (Where?) Georgia! Georgia! (Did you fight under General Lee?) I fell under him. (Did you die under him?) No, no.

Question: Who was with you in the regiment?

Guychone: Johnny Greenly...it is like another world...Jerome Harvey. (Who was the surgeon?) I did not see him. Horse doctors. (Who was your orderly?) Walter...my boy...I can't tell the truth, and I try so hard.... I will come with the truth when it comes, you see the burning weeds came to me...I will think of happier things to tell...I'd like to tell you about the house in Charleston, on Elm Street. I think it is 320, I was born in it.

Question: Any others in the family?

Guychone: Two brothers. They died. They were in the war with me. I was the eldest. William, and Paul. (And you're Edward?) Yes. (Your mother?) Mary. (Your father?) Frederick. (Where was he born?) Charleston. (Your mother's maiden name?) Ah...! (Where did you go to college?) William...William and...a white house with green grass. (When did you graduate?) Fifty-three...ONE HUNDRED YEARS....It is hard to get into those corners where I can't think any more.

"I never had my eyes open before, in trance," observed Mrs. Meyers afterwards. "While I could look at you and you looked like yourself, I could almost look through you. That never happened before. I could only see what I focused on. This machine...it seemed the wheels were going much, much *faster* than they are going now."

* * *

On July 25th, 1953, a "planchette" session was held at the home of Mrs. Meyers, with herself and the late Mrs. Zoe Britton present, during which Guychone made himself known, and stated that he had a living son, 89 years old, now living in a place called Seymour, West Virginia.

EVIDENTIAL MATERIAL BEGINS TO PILE UP

By now we knew we had an unusual case. I went through all the available material on this period (and there is a lot), without turning up anyone named Guychone.

These were extremely hot afternoons, but the quest went on. Rarely has any psychic researcher undertaken a similarly protracted project to hunt down psychic evidence.

Sitting of July 28th, 1953

Finding a St. Michael's medal around my neck, Guychone says it reminds him of a medal of St. Anne, which his "Huguenot mother," Marie Guychone, had given him.

Question: Do you remember the name of your college?

Guychone: Two colleges. St. Anne's in Charleston, South Carolina.... Only one thought around another, that's all I had—curry the horses. Why? I know now. I remember. I want to say my mother is here, I saw her, she says God bless you. I understand more now. Thank you. Pray for me.

Sitting of August 4th, 1953

This sitting repeated previous information and consisted in a cat-and-mouse game between Guychone and myself. However, toward the end, Guychone began to speak of his son Gregory, naming him for the first time. He asked us to find him. We asked, "What name does Gregory use?" Guychone casually answered: "I don't know...Guychone...maybe McGowan...." The name McGowan came very quietly, but sufficiently distinct to be heard by all present. At the time, we were not overwhelmed. Only when research started to yield results did we realize that it was his real name at last. But I was not immediately successful in locating McGowan on the regimental rosters, far from it! I was misled by his statement of having served in the cavalry, and naturally gave the cavalry rosters my special attention, but he wasn't in them. Late in August I went through the city records of Charleston, West Virginia, on a futile search for the Guychone family, assuming still that they were his in-laws. Here I found mention of a "McGowan's Brigade."

Sitting of August 18th, 1953

Question: Please identify yourself, Colonel.

McGowan: Yes... Edward... I can stay? I can stay?

Question: Why do you want so much to stay? Are you not happy where you are?

McGowan: Oh yes. But I like to talk very much... how happy I am.

Question: What was your mother's name?

McGowan: Marie Guychone.

Question: What is your name?

McGowan: Guychone.

Question: Yes; that is the name you *used*, but you really are...?

McGowan: Edward Mac...Mac...curry the horses! (excited, is calmed by me) Yes, I see...Mac...McGowan! I remember more now, but I can only tell what I know...it is like a wall...I remember a dark night, I was crazy...war on one hand, fighting, bullets...and then, flying away, chasing, chasing, chasing....

Question: What regiment were you with?

McGowan: Six...two...sometimes horse...oh, in that fire....

Question: Who was your commanding general?

McGowan: But—Butler.

He then speaks of his service in two regiments, one of which was the Sixth South Carolina Regiment, and he mentions a stand on a hill, which was hell, with the Damyankees on all sides. He says it was at Chattanooga.

* * *

Question: The house on Fifth Avenue, New York...do you remember the name of your landlord?

McGowan: A woman...Elsie (or L. C.)...stout....

Actually, he says, a man collected the rent, which he had trouble paying at times. He knew a man named Pat Duffy in New York. He was the man who worked for his landlady, collecting the rent, coming to his door.

During the interrogation about his landlord, McGowan suddenly returns to his war experiences. "There was a Griffin," he says, referring to an officer he knew.

Sitting of August 25th, 1953

"The Colonel," as we now called him, came through very clearly. He introduced himself by his true name. Asked again about the landlady in New York, he now adds that she was a *widow*. Again, he speaks of "Griff...Griff...." Asked what school he went to, he says "St. Anne's College in Charleston, South Carolina, and also William and Mary College in Virginia, the latter in 1850, 51, 52, 53, 54." What was his birthday? He says "February 10, 1830." Did he write any official letters during the war? He says, "I wrote to General Robert E. Lee." What about? When? "January, 1864. Atlanta.... I needed horses, horses, wheels to run the things on." Did you get them? "No." What regiment was he with then? "The Sixth from South Carolina." But wasn't he from West Virginia? Amazed, McGowan says, "No, from South Carolina."

I then inquired about his family in New York.

McGowan explained that his mother did live with him there, and died there, but after his own death "they" went away, including his sister-in-law Gertrude and brother William. Again, he asks that we tell his son Gregory "that his father did *not* do away with himself."

I asked, "Where is there a true picture of you?" McGowan replied, "There is one in the courthouse in Charleston, South Carolina." What kind of a picture? "Etch...etch...*tintype!*"

All through these sittings it was clear that McGowan's memory was best when "pictures" or scenes were asked for, and worst when precise names or dates were being requested. He was never sure when he gave a figure, but was very sure of his facts when he spoke of situations or relationships. Thus, he gave varying dates for his own birthday, making it clear that he was hazy about it, not even aware of having given discrepant information within a brief period.

But then, if a living person undergoes a severe shock, is he not extremely hazy about such familiar details as his name or address? Yet, most shock victims can *describe* their house, or their loved ones. The human memory, apparently, is more reliable in terms of associations, when under stress, than in terms of factual information, like names and figures.

By now research was in full swing, and it is fortunate that so much prima facie evidence was obtained before the disclosure of McGowan's true name started the material flowing. Thus, the old and somewhat tiring argument of "mental telepathy" being responsible for some of the information can only be applied, if at all, to a part of the sittings. No one can read facts in a mind *before* they get into that mind!

The sittings continued in weekly sessions, with Colonel McGowan rapidly becoming our "star" visitor.

Sitting of September 1st, 1953

Question: What was your rank at the end of the war?

McGowan: That was on paper...made to serve.

Question: Did you become a general?

McGowan: Naw...honors...I take empty honors....

Question: When you went to school, what did you study?

McGowan: The law of the land.

Question: What happened at Manassas?

McGowan: Oh...defeat. Defeat.

Question: What happened to you personally at Manassas?

McGowan: Ah, cut, cut. Bayonets. Ah. Blood, blood.

Question: What happened at Malvern Hill?

McGowan: Success. We took the house. Low brick building. We wait. They come up and we see right in the mouth of a cannon. 1864. They burned the house around our ears. But we didn't move.

Question: What was under your command at that time?

McGowan: Two divisions.

Question: How many regiments?

McGowan: Four...forty...(Four?) TEEN!

Question: What did you command?

McGowan: My commander was shot down, I take over. (Who for?) John...Major....

Question: Listen, Colonel, your name is not Edward. Is there any other first or middle name you used? (Silence)

Did anyone of high rank serve from South Carolina? (My brother William) Anyone else? (Paul)

McGowan: Do you think of Charles McGowan? That was no relation of mine. He was on the waterfront. He was...exporter.

Question: Were you at Gettysburg, Colonel? (Yes.) What regiments were under your command then?

McGowan: I had a wound at Gettysburg. I was very torn. (Where did you get the wound?) Atlanta...change of rank. Empty honors (About his son Gregory) Seymour...many years Lowell, Massachusetts, and then he went back down South, Seymour, South Carolina, and sometimes West Virginia...he was in a store, he left and then he came into property, mother also had property, down there near Charleston in West Virginia...that is where he is, yes.

Question: You say your father was Frederick? (Yes.) Who was William. (My brother.) Who was Samuel? (Long pause, stunned, then: I wrote that name!) Why didn't you tell us? (Crying: I didn't want to tell....) Tell us your true rank, too. (I don't care what it was). Please don't evade us. What was your rank? (Brigadier...General). Then you are General Samuel McGowan?

McGowan: You made me very unhappy...such a name (crying)...blood, empty honors....

Question: Who was James Johnson? (My commander.) What happened to him? (Indicates he was shot.) Who took over for Johnson? (I did.) What regiment was it?

McGowan: I don't know the figures...I don't know.

Question: Your relative in New York, what was his name?

McGowan: Peter Paul.

Question: What was his profession?

McGowan: A doctor. (Any particular kind of doctor?) Cuts. (What kind?) (McGowan points to face.) (Nose doctor?) (McGowan points to mouth and shakes head.) (Mouth doctor?) (McGowan violently grabs his teeth and shakes them.) (Oh, teeth? A dentist) (McGowan nods assent.)

Question: I will name some regiments, tell me if any of them mean anything to you. The 10th...the 34th...the 14th...(McGowan reacts?) The 14th? Does it mean anything to you?

McGowan: I don't know, figures don't mean anything on this side....

SOME INTERESTING FACTS BROUGHT OUT BY RESEARCH

In the sitting of August 18th, McGowan stated his landlord was a woman and that her name was "Elsie" or L. C. *The Hall of Records* of New York City lists the owner of 226 Fifth Avenue as "Isabella S. Clarke, from 1853 to (at least) March 1, 1871." In the same sitting, McGowan stated that Pat Duffy was the man who actually came to

collect the rent, working for the landlady. Several days *after* this information was voluntarily received from the entity, I found in *Trow's New York Directory for 1869/70:*

Page 195: "Clark, Isabella, wid. Constantine h. (house) 45 Cherry."

Page 309: "Duffy, Patrick, laborer, 45 Cherry."

This could be known only to someone who actually knew these people, 80 years ago; it proved our ghost was there in 1873!

The sitting of September 1st also proved fruitful.

A "Peter McGowan, dentist, 253 W. 13 St." appears in *Trow's New York City Directory for 1870/71.*

J. F. J. Caldwell, in his *"History of a Brigade of South Carolinians known first as Gregg's, and subsequently as McGowan's Brigade,"* (Philadelphia, 1866) reports:

Page 10: "The 14th Regiment South Carolina Volunteers selected for field officers...Col. James Jones, *Lt. Col. Samuel McGowan*...(1861)."

Page 12: "Colonel Samuel McGowan commands the 14th Regiment."

Page 18: "McGowan arrives from the Chickahominy river (under Lee)."

Page 24: "Conspicuous gallantry in the battle of Malvern Hill."

Page 37: "...of the 11 field officers of our brigade, seven were wounded: Col. McGowan, etc. (in the 2nd battle of Manassas)."

Page 53: "Col. Samuel McGowan of the 14th Regiment (at Fredericksburg)."

Page 60: "The 13th and 14th regiments under McGowan...."

Page 61: "Gen. Gregg's death Dec. 14, 1862. McGowan succeeds to command."

Page 66: "Biography: Born Laurens district, S.C. 1820. Graduated 1841 South Carolina College, Law; in Mexican War, then settled as lawyer in Abbeville, S.C. Became a Brig. Gen. January 20, 1863, assists in taking Ft. Sumter April 1861; but lapsing commission as General in State Militia, he becomes Lt. Col. in the Confederate Army, takes part at Bull Run, Manassas Plains, under Gen. Bonham. Then elected Lt. Col. of 14th Regiment, S.C.; Spring 1862, made full Col. *succeeding Col. Jones who was killed.* McGowan is *wounded* in battle of Manassas." Biographer Caldwell, who was McGowan's aide as a lieutenant, says (in 1866) "he still lives."

Page 79: "April 29, 1863, McGowan's *Brigade* gets orders to be ready to march. Gen. McGowan commands the brigade."

Page 80: "Wounded again (Fredericksburg)."

Page 89: "Gen. Lee reviews troops including McGowan's. Brigade now consists of 1st, 12th, 13th, 14th Regiments and Orr's Rifles. Also known as 'McGowan's Sharpshooters.'"

Page 91: "McGowan takes part in battle of Chancellorsville."

Page 96: "Battle of Gettysburg: McGowan commands 13th, 12th, 14th, and 1st."

Page 110: "McGowan near Culpepper Courthouse."

Page 122: "Gen. McGowan returned to us in February (1864). He had not sufficiently recovered from the wound received at Chancellorsville to walk well, but remained with us and discharged all the duties of his office."

Page 125: *About Butler:* "Butler to lead column (against McGowan) from the Eastern coast." Another Butler (Col.) commanded the Confederate 1st Regt. (Battle of Chickamauga)

Page 126sq.: "Battle of Spottsylvania, May 1864."

Page 133: "Gen. Lee and Gen. Hill were there (defeat)."

Page 142: "McGowan wounded by a 'minie ball,' in the right arm, quits field."

But to continue with our sittings, and with McGowan's personal recollections—

Sitting of September 8th, 1953

McGowan: (speaking again of his death) It was in the forties...they killed me on the top floor. They dragged me up, that 'man of color' named Walter. He was a giant of a man. She was a virtuous woman, I tell you she was. But they would not believe it.

I wanted to get his reaction to a name I had found in the records, so I asked, "Have you ever met a McWilliams?"

McGowan: You have the knowledge of the devil with you. Her family name.

Question: Did you stay in New York until your passing?

McGowan: 1869, 1873. Back and forth. I have written to Lee, Jackson, James, and Beaufort. 1862-63, March.

Question: What did you do at the end of the war?

McGowan: Back and forth, always on the go. Property was gone, ruined. Plantations burned. I did not work. I could not. Three or four bad years. I quit. My wits, my wits. My uncle. The house was burned in Charleston. Sometimes Columbia. (Then, of Mignon, his wife, he says) She died in 1892...Francois Guychone...he was so good to little boys, he made excursions in the Bay of Charleston—we sailed in boats. He was my uncle.

Sitting of September 15th, 1953

I asked, what did he look like in his prime.

McGowan: I wasn't too bad to look at, very good brow, face to the long, and at one time I indulged in the whiskers...not so long, for the chin...colonial...I liked to see my chin a good deal, sometimes I cover (indicates mustache)....

Question: What can you tell us about the cemetery in Abbeville?

McGowan: There is a monument, the family cemetery... nobody cared...my father was born the fifth of January.... (What was on your tombstone?) Samuel Edward McGowan, born...32?...died 1883? 1873? 1-8-7 hard to read, so dirty...age 40...41...gray-brown stars...battered....I go between the bushes, I look at the monument, it's defaced....

Question: What news did your family give out of your death?

McGowan: Foul play. (What happened to the body?) Cremated I guess, I think in this city. The remains were destroyed: not in the grave, a monument to a memory.... (What did they tell the public?) Lost forever...I could have been at sea...house was destroyed by fire.... (Do you mean there is no official record of your death?) No. *Not identical to passing,* they never told the exact month or day...I see...1879...very blurred...September 4th....

Question: Were you ever injured in an argument?

McGowan: I spent much time on my back because of a wound...on my head. (An argument?) Yes. (With whom?) A man. Hand to hand. Rapier....Glen, Glen...Ardmore.

Sitting of September 22nd, 1953

"Mother" Marie Guychone spoke briefly in French and was followed by McGowan. He said he was at one time "an associate Justice" in the city of Columbia.

Here again do I wish to report some more research information bearing on this part of the investigation. Evans, in his *Confederate Military History*, 1899* has a picture of the General which became available to us after the September 22nd sitting. His biography, on page 414, mentions the fact that "he was associate Justice of the (State) Supreme Court." Curiously, this author also states that McGowan died in "December 1893." Careful scrutiny of two major New York dailies then existing (*Post* and *Times*) brought to light that the author of the *Confederate Military History* made a mistake, albeit an understandable one. A certain Ned McGowan, described as a "notorious character, aged 80" had died in San Francisco on December 9, 1893. This man was also a Confederate hero. (*The New York Times,* XII/9). However, the same source (*The New York Times,* August 13, 1897) reports General McGowan's death as having occurred on the 9th of August, *1897.* The obituary contains the facts already noted in the biography quoted earlier, plus one interesting additional detail, that McGowan *received a cut across the scalp in a duel.*

Another good source, *The Dictionary of American Biography,* says of our subject: "*McGowan, Samuel.* Son of William and Jeannie McGowan, law partner of William H. Parker. Died August 9, 1897 in Abbeville. Buried in Long

*Vol. V., p. 409.

Cane Cemetery in Abbeville. Born Oct. 9, 1819 in Crosshill section of Laurens district, S. C. *Mother's name was McWilliams*. Law partner of *Perrin* in Abbeville. Representative in State House of South Carolina. Elected to Congress, *but not seated*."

A Colonel at Gettysburg, by Varina Brown, about her late husband Colonel Brown, contains the following: "In the battle of Jericho Mills, '*Griffin's Division*' of Federals wrought havoc against McGowan's Brigade."

Correspondence with Mrs. William Gaynes, a resident of Abbeville, revealed on October 1st, 1953—"The old general was a *victim of the failing mind* but he was doctored up until the date of his death. He was attended by his cousin *Dr. F. E. Harrison*."

Eminent & Representative Men of South Carolina by Brant & Fuller (Madison, Wisconsin, 1892) gives this picture:

Samuel McGowan was born of *Scotch* Irish parents in Laurens County, S. C. on October 9th, 1819. Graduated with distinction from the South Carolina College in 1841. Read law at Abbeville with T. C. Perrin who offered him a partnership. He entered the service as a private and went to Mexico with the Palmetto Regiment. He was appointed on the general Quartermaster's Staff with the rank of Captain. After the war he returned to Abbeville and resumed the practice of law with T. C. Perrin. He married Susan Caroline, eldest daughter of Judge David Lewis Wardlaw and they lived in Abbeville until some years after the death of Gen. McGowan in 1897. The home of Gen. McGowan still stands in Abbeville and was sold some time ago to the Baptist Church for 50,000 dollars. . . . After the war he entered law practice with William H. Parker (1869/1879) in Abbeville. He took an interest in political affairs . . . member of the Convention that met in Columbia in September, 1865. Elected to Congress but not allowed to take his seat. Counted out on the second election two years later. In 1878 he was a member of the State Legislature and in 1879 he was elected Associate Justice of the State Supreme Court.

General McGowan lived a long and honorable life in Abbeville. He was a contributing member of the Episcopal Church, Trinity, and became a member later in life. At his death the following appeared in the *Abbeville Medium*, edited by Gen. R. R. Hemphill who had served in McGowan's Brigade. "General Samuel McGowan *died at his home in this city* at 8:35 o'clock last Monday morning August 8th. Full of years and honors he passed away surrounded by his family and friends. He had been in declining health for some time and suffered intense pain, though his final sickness was for a few days only and at the end all was Peace. Impressive services were held in *Trinity Church* Tuesday afternoon, at four o'clock, the procession starting from the residence. At the Church, the procession . . . preceded by Dr. Wm. M. Grier and Bishop Ellison Capers who read the solemn service . . . directly behind the coffin old Daddy Willis Marshall, a colored man who had served him well, bore a laurel wreath. Gen. McGowan was buried at *Long Lane*, cemetery and there is a handsome stone on the plot."

Mrs. William Gaynes further reports:

Gen. McGowan had a 'fine line of profanity' and used it frequently in Court. He was engaged in a duel once with Col. John *Cunningham* and was wounded behind one ear and came near passing out. Col. Cunningham challenged Col. *Perrin who refused* the challenge on the ground that he did not approve of dueling, and Gen. McGowan took up the challenge and the duel took place at Sand Bar Ferry, near Augusta, with McGowan being wounded.

As far as I know, there was never any difficulty between Mrs. McGowan and the old General. His father-in-law, Judge Wardlaw, married *Sarah* Rebecca Allen, and *her* mother was Mary Lucia *Garvey*.

In other words, Judge Wardlaw married *Sarah Garvey*.

Mrs. Gaynes continues: "I have seen him frequently on his way to his law office, for he had to pass right by *our* office. If he ever was out of town for any length of time, Abbeville *did not know it*."

The inscription on Samuel McGowan's tombstone in Long Cane Graveyard reads as follows:

"Samuel McGowan, born Laurens County 9 October 1819. Died in Abbeville 9 August 1897. Go soldier to thy honored rest, thy trust and honor valor bearing. The brave are the tenderest, the loving are the daring."

Side 2: "From humble birth he rose to the highest honor in Civic and military life. A patriot and a leader of men. In peace his country called him, he waited not to her call in war. A man's strength, a woman's tenderness, a child's simplicity were his and his a heart of charity fulfilling the law of love. He did good and not evil all the days of his life and at its end his country his children and his children's children rise up and call him blessed. In Mexican War 1846-1848. A Captain in United States Army. The Confederate War 1861–1865. A Brigadier General C.S.A. Member of the Legislature 1848-1850. Elected to Congress 1866. Associate Justice of Supreme Court of South Carolina 1878–1894. A hero in two wars. Seven times wounded. A leader at the Bar, a wise law giver, a righteous judge. He rests from his labors and his works do follow him."

McGOWAN BECOMES A "REGULAR" OF THE WEEKLY SITTINGS

General McGowan had by now become an always impatient weekly "guest" at our sittings, and he never liked the idea of leaving. Whenever it was suggested that time was running short, McGowan tried to prolong his stay by becoming suddenly very talkative.

Sitting of September 29th, 1953

A prepared list of eight names, all fictitious but one (the sixth is that of Susan Wardlaw, McGowan's wife) is read to him several times. McGowan reacts to two of the nonexistent names, but not to the one of his wife. One of the fictitious names is John D. Sumter, to which McGowan mumbles, "Colonel." Fact is, there *was* a Colonel Sumter in the Confederate Army!

McGowan also described in detail the farm where his son Gregory now lives. Asked about the name Guychone, he says it comes from Louisiana; Mignon, on her mother's side, had it. He identifies his hometown newspapers as "Star-Press." ("*Star-Press*, paper, picture, Judge, Columbia, picture in paper....")

Question: Who was Dr. Harrison?

McGowan: Family doctor.

Question: Is your home in Abbeville still standing?

McGowan: It isn't *what it was*. Strange pictures and things. (Anyone live in it?) No. Strange things, guns and cannons.

Sitting of October 14th, 1953

McGowan says he had two daughters. Trying again to read his tombstone, he says, "1887, or is it 97?" As to his birth year, he reads, "1821....31?"

Sitting of October 20th, 1953

When the control introduces McGowan, there is for several moments intense panic and fear brought on by a metal necklace worn by the medium. When McGowan is assured that there is no longer any "rope around his neck," he calms down, and excuses himself for his regression.

Question: Who was the Susan you mentioned the last time?

McGowan: The mother of my children.

Question: What was her other name?

McGowan: Cornelia.

Question: Were you elected to Congress?

McGowan: What kind of Congress? (The U. S. Congress.) I lost. Such a business, everybody grabs, everybody steals.... Somebody always buys the votes and it's such a mess.

Question: Are Mignon and Susan one and the same person or not?

McGowan: I don't wish to commit myself. (I insist.) They are not!

Question: Let us talk about Susan. What profession did your father-in-law follow?

McGowan: Big man...in the law.

Question: What was your mother-in-law's first name?

McGowan: Sarah.

Question: Did she have another name?

McGowan: Garfey....

Question: Coffee? Spell it.

McGowan: Not coffee. Garvey!

At a sitting on October 28th, 1953, at the home of Mrs. Meyers, McGowan's alleged grandson, Billy, manifested himself as follows:

"My name is William, I passed in 1949, at Charleston. I'm a grandson of General McGowan. I was born in Abbeville, January 2nd, 1894. Gregory is half-brother, son of the French bitch. He (McGowan) would have married her, but he had a boss, grandfather, who held the purse strings. Susan's father of Dutch blood, hard-headed."

Sitting of October 29th, 1953

McGowan: You must find Gregory. He may be surprised about his father, but I must let him know I wanted for him, and they took for *them*...all. And they gave him nothing. Nothing! I had made other plans. (Was there a will?) There was...but I had a Judge in the family that made other plans...THEY WERE NOT MINE! You must tell Gregory I provided....I tell you only the truth because I was an honest man...I did the best for my family, for my people, for those I considered my countrymen, that what you now call posterity...I suffer my own sins....For you maybe it means nothing, for me, for those who remember me, pity...they are now aware of the truth, only now is my son unaware of the truth. Sir, you are my best friend. And I go into hell for you. I tell you always the truth, sir, but there are things that would not concern you or anybody. But I will give you those names yet!

Question: I ask again for the name of McGowan's father-in-law.

McGowan: Wida...Wider.

THE "GHOST" IS FREED

One of the functions of a "rescue circle" is to make sure a disturbed entity does not return to the scene of his unhappiness. This mission was accomplished here.

Sitting of November 3rd, 1953

McGowan: I see the house where I lived, you know, where you found me. *I go there now, but I am not anymore disturbed.* I found my mother and my father. They could not touch me, but *now*, we touch hands. I live over my life, come back to many things. Herman! He was a good soul, he helped me when I was down in Atlanta. He bathed my feet, my legs were scorched, and he was good to me, and he is over here. I thank him. I thanked him then, but I was the big man, and he was nothing, but now I see he is a fine gentleman, he polished my boots, he put my uniform in order.

Sitting of November 6th, 1953

I was alone with the medium, Mrs. Meyers, at her home, when I had a chance to question McGowan about his apparent murder, and the "conspiracy of silence" concerning it.

McGowan: The Judge protected them, did not report my death. They had devised the kidnapping. I was murdered downstairs, strangled by the kidnapper Walter. He took her (Mignon) all the way to Boston. I wore the uniform of Damyankees (during the war), rode a horse *every night* to Boston...no, I made a mistake. I came to my Uncle Peter Paul in New York, I had a letter from Marie Guychone, she was in New York. Begged me to find Mignon and Gregory. I come to New York. I can't find her, she was in Boston then, but I didn't know that until later. Marie Guychone remained with my uncle, and I gave up the chase, and like a thief crawled back to Confederate grounds. That was in 1863. After the war, there was a struggle, property was worthless, finally the Union granted that we withdraw our holdings, and with that I came to New York. My mother and father came also, until rehabilitation was sufficient for their return.

I continued to live with my wife, Susan, and the children, and I found Mignon. She had escaped, and came to her mother in New York. I made a place for them to live with my uncle and when my wife returned to stay with her father (the Judge), I had Mignon, but she was pregnant and she didn't know it, and there was a black child—there was unpleasantness between us, I didn't know if it were mine and Mignon was black, but it was not so, it was his child (Walter's), and he came for it and for her, he traced her to my house (on Fifth Avenue); my father-in-law (the Judge) was the informer, and he (Walter) strangled me, he was a big man.

And when I was not dead yet, he dragged me up the stairs. Mignon was not present, not guilty. I think...it was in January 1874. But I may be mistaken about time. Gregory had two sons, William and Edward. William died on a boat in the English Channel in 1918. Gregory used the

name *Fogarty*, not McGowan. The little black boy died, they say. It was just as well for him.

McGowan then left peacefully, promising more information about the time lag between his given date and that officially recorded. I told him the difference was "about twenty years." For the first time, McGowan had stated his story reasonably, although some details of it would be hard to check. No murder or suicide was reported in the newspapers of the period, similar to this case. But of course anyone planning a crime like this might have succeeded in keeping it out of the public eye. We decided to continue our sittings.

Sitting of November 10th, 1953

McGowan talked about the duel he fought, which cost him his hair, due to a wound on the left side, back and top of his head. It was over a woman and against a certain Colonel C., something like "Collins," but a longer name. He said that Perry or Perrin *did so* make a stand, as if someone had doubted it!

MORE PROOF TURNS UP!

Leading away from personal subjects, the questioning now proceeded toward matters of general interest about New York at the time of McGowan's residence here. The advantage of this line of questioning is its neutral value for research purposes; and as no research was undertaken until after the sittings of November 17th, mental telepathy must be excluded as an alternate explanation!

Sitting of November 17th, 1953

McGowan: You don't have a beard. They called them milksops in my days, the beardless boys!

Question: What did they call a man who was a nice dresser and liked ladies?

McGowan: A Beau Brummel.

Question: What did they call a gentleman who dressed too well, too fancifully?

McGowan: A fop.

Question: What was your favorite sport?

McGowan: Billiards (He explains he was good at it, and the balls were *made of cloth*.)

Question: What was the favorite game of your day?

McGowan: They played a *Cricket* kind of game....

Question: Who was mayor of New York?

McGowan: Oh...Grace. Grace...*Edmond*...Grace... something like it.

William R. Grace was mayor of New York, 1881–1882, and Franklin Edson (not Edmond) followed, 1883–1884. Also, plastic billiard balls as we know them today are a comparatively recent invention, and billiard balls in the Victorian era were indeed made of cloth. The cricket kind of game must be baseball. Beau Brummel, fop, milksop are all authentic Victorian expressions.

Sitting of November 26th, 1953

I asked the General about trains in New York in his time.

McGowan: They were smoke stacks, up in the air, smoke got in your eyes, they went down to the Globe Building near City Hall. The Globe building was near Broadway and Nassau. The train went up to Harlem. It was a nice neighborhood. I took many strolls in the park.

Question: Where was the Hotel Waldorf-Astoria?

McGowan: Near Fifth Avenue and 33rd, near my house...and the Hotel Prince George. Restaurants were Ye Olde Southern, Hotel Brevoort. You crack my brain, you are worse than that boss in the Big House, Mr. Tammany and Mr. Tweed. (I discussed his house, and he mentioned doing business with—) Somebody named *Costi*...I paid $128.50 a month for the entire house. A suit of clothes cost $100.00.

Question: Who lived next door to you?

McGowan: Herman... *was a carriage smith.* He had a business where he made carriages. He lived next door, but his business was not there, the shop was on Third Avenue, Third Street, near the river.

Question: Any other neighbors?

McGowan: Corrigan Brown, *a lawyer*...lived three houses down. The editor of the *Globe* was White...Stone... White...the editor of the *Globe* was not good friends with the man in the Big House. They broke his house down when he lived on Fifth Avenue. *He was a neighbor.* Herman the carriage maker made good carriages. I bought one with fringes and two seats, a cabrio....

Question: Did you have a janitor?

McGowan: There was a black boy named Ted, mainly colored servants, we had a gardener, white, named Patrick. He collects the rent, he lives with the Old Crow on Cherry Street. Herman lives next door. He had a long mustache and square beard. He wore a frock coat, a diamond tie pin, and spectacles. I never called him Herman...(trying to remember his true name)...Gray...I never called him Herman. He had a wife named Birdie. His wife had a sister named Finny who lived there too...Mrs. Finny...she was a young widow with two children...she was a good friend to my Susan.

McGowan then reluctantly signs his name as requested.

* * *

Research, undertaken *after* the sitting, again excluded mental telepathy. The facts were of a kind not likely to be found in the records, *unless* one were specifically looking for them!

The *New York Globe* building, which McGowan remembers "near Broadway and Nassau," was then (1873) at 7 Square Street and apparently also at 162 Nassau Street.* The *Globe* is on Spruce, and *Globe and Evening Press* on Nassau, around the corner.

McGowan describes the steam-powered elevated railroad that went from City Hall to Harlem. Steam cars started in 1867 and ran until 1906, according to the New York Historical Society, and there were two lines fitting his description, "Harlem, From Park Row to...E. 86th Street" and "Third Avenue, from Ann Street through Park Row to...Harlem Bridge."[†] McGowan was right in describing Harlem as a nice neighborhood in his day.

McGowan also acknowledged at once that he had been to the Waldorf-Astoria, and correctly identified its position at Fifth Avenue and 33rd Street. The Waldorf-Astoria came into being on March 14th, 1893. Consequently, McGowan *was alive then*, and evidently sane, if he could visit such places as the Waldorf, Brevoort, and others.

McGowan refers to a (later) landlord as Costi. In 1895, a real-estate firm by the name of George and John Coster was situated at 173 Fifth Avenue, a few houses down the street from McGowan's place.[‡]

As for the carriage smith named Herman, a little later referred to as Herman Gray, there was a carriage maker named William H. Gray from 1872 or earlier, and existing beyond the turn of the century, whose shop was at first at 20 Wooster Street,[**] and who lived at 258 West Fourth Street, until at least 1882. In 1895 he is listed as living at 275 West 94th Street. Not all Troy volumes in between are available, so that residence in McGowan's neighborhood can neither be confirmed nor denied. At one time, Gray's shops were on West Broadway. As for Corrigan Brown, the lawyer neighbor, McGowan's mispronouncing of names almost tripped me up. There was no such lawyer. There was, however, one Edmond Congar Brown, lawyer, listed for the first time as such in 1886, and before that only as a clerk. No home is, unfortunately, listed for his later years.[††] McGowan stated that the editor of the *Globe* was

---

**Trow's New York City Directory for 1872/73*, p. 448 regular section and p. 38 City Register section.

[†]*Ibid*, City Register, p. 18, under "City Railroads."

[‡]*Trow*, 1895/96, p. 550.

[**]*Trow*, 1872/73, City Register, p. 27.

[††]*Trow*, 1895/96, p. 174, lists his office as 132 Nassau.

named White-and-something, and that he lived near his (McGowan's) house on Fifth Avenue.

Well, one Horace P. Whitney, editor, business, 128 Fulton Street, home, 287 Fifth Avenue, is listed in *Trow*.* And 128 Fulton Street is the place of the *Globe's* competitor, the *New York Mercury*, published by Cauldwell and Whitney.†

*1872, p. 1287, regular section.
†*Trow*, 1872, City Register section, p. 39.

* * *

That McGowan did not die in 1873 seems certain to me, as the above information proves. But if he did not die in 1873, something very traumatic must have been done to him at that time. Or perhaps the murder, if such it was, took place in 1897?

It could well be that General McGowan will take this ultimate secret with him into the Great Land where he now dwells safely forever.

✳ 5

The Case of the Murdered Financier

I REMEMBER THE NIGHT we went to visit the house where financier Serge Rubinstein was killed. It was a year after his death but only I, among the group, had knowledge of the exact date of the anniversary. John Latouche, my much-too-soon departed friend, and I picked up Mrs. Meyers at her Westside home and rode in a taxi to Fifth Avenue and 60th Street. As a precaution, so as not to give away the address which we were headed for, we left the taxi two blocks south of the Rubinstein residence.

Our minds were careful blanks, and the conversation was about music. But we didn't fool our medium. "What's the pianist doing here?" she demanded to know. What pianist, I countered. "Rubinstein," said she. For to our medium, a professional singing teacher, that name could only stand for the great pianist. It showed that our medium was, so to speak, on-the-beam, and already entering into the "vibration," or electrically charged atmosphere of the haunting.

Latouche and I looked at each other in amazement. Mrs. Meyers was puzzled by our sudden excitement. Without further delay, we rang the bell at the stone mansion, hoping the door would open quickly so that we would not be exposed to curiosity-seekers who were then still hanging around the house where one of the most publicized murders had taken place just a year before, to the hour.

It was now near midnight, and my intention had been to try and make contact with the spirit of the departed. I assumed, from the manner in which he died, that Serge Rubinstein might still be around his house, and I had gotten his mother's permission to attempt the contact.

The seconds on the doorstep seemed like hours, as Mrs. Meyers questioned me about the nature of tonight's "case." I asked her to be patient, but when the butler came and finally opened the heavy gate, Mrs. Meyers suddenly realized where we were. "It isn't the pianist, then!" she mumbled, somewhat dazed. "It's the *other* Rubinstein!"

With these words we entered the forbidding-looking building for an evening of horror and ominous tension.

The murder is still officially unsolved, and as much an enigma to the world as it was on that cold winter night, in 1955, when the newspaper headlines screamed of "bad boy" financier Serge Rubinstein's untimely demise. That night, after business conferences and a night on the town with a brunette, Rubinstein had some unexpected visitors. Even the District Attorney couldn't name them for sure, but there were suspects galore, and the investigation never ran out of possibilities.

Evidently Serge had a falling-out with the brunette, Estelle Gardner, and decided the evening was still young, so he felt like continuing it with a change of cast. Another woman, Pat Wray, later testified that Rubinstein telephoned her to join him after he had gotten rid of Estelle, *and that she refused.*

The following morning, the butler, William Morter, found Rubinstein dead in his third-floor bedroom. He was wearing pajamas, and evidently the victim of some form of torture—for his arms and feet were tied, and his mouth and throat thickly covered by adhesive tape. The medical examiner dryly ruled death by strangulation.

The police found themselves with a first-rate puzzle on their hands. Lots of people wanted to kill Rubinstein, lots of people had said so publicly without meaning it—but who actually did? The financier's reputation was not the best, although it must be said that he did no more nor less than many others; but his manipulations were neither elegant nor quiet, and consequently, the glaring light of publicity and exposure created a public image of a monster that did not really fit the Napoleonic-looking young man from Paris.

Rubinstein was a possessive and jealous man. A tiny microphone was placed by him in the apartment of Pat Wray, sending sound into a tape recorder hidden in a car parked outside the building. Thus, Rubinstein was able to monitor her every word!

Obviously, his dealings were worldwide, and there were some 2,000 names in his private files.

The usual sensational news accounts had been seen in the press the week prior to our séance, but none of them contained anything new or definite. Mrs. Meyers' knowledge of the case was as specific as that of any ordinary newspaper reader.

* * *

We were received by Serge's seventy-nine-year-old mother, Stella Rubinstein; her sister, Eugenia Forrester; the Rubinstein attorney, Ennis; a female secretary; a guard named Walter, and a newspaper reporter from a White Russian paper, Jack Zwieback. After a few moments of polite talk downstairs—that is, on the second floor where the library of the sumptuous mansion was located—I suggested we go to the location of the crime itself.

We all rose, when Mrs. Meyers suddenly stopped in her tracks. "I feel someone's grip on my arm," she commented.

We went upstairs without further incident.

The bedroom of the slain financier was a medium-size room in the rear of the house, connected with the front sitting room through a large bathroom. We formed a circle around the bed, occupying the center of the room. The light was subdued, but the room was far from dark. Mrs. Meyers insisted on sitting in a chair close to the bed, and remarked that she "was directed there."

Gradually her body relaxed, her eyes closed, and the heavy, rhythmic breathing of onsetting trance was heard in the silence of the room, heavily tensed with fear and apprehension of what was to come.

Several times, the medium placed her arm before her face, as if warding off attacks; symptoms of choking distorted her face and a struggle seemed to take place before our eyes!

Within a few minutes, this was over, and a new, strange voice came from the lips of the medium. "I can speak...over there, they're coming!" The arm pointed toward the bathroom.

I asked who "they" were.

"They're no friends...Joe, Stan...cheap girl...in the door, they—" The hand went to the throat, indicating choking.

Then, suddenly, the person in command of the medium added: "The woman should be left out. There was a calendar with serial numbers...box numbers, but they can't get it! Freddie was here, too!"

"What was in the box?"

"Fourteen letters. Nothing for the public."

"Give me more information."

"Baby-Face...I don't want to talk too much...they'll pin it on Joe."

"How many were there?"

"Joe, Stan, and Freddie...stooges. Her bosses' stooges! London...let me go, let me go...I'm too frantic here...not up here...I'll come again."

With a jolt, the medium awoke from her trance. Perspiration stood on her forehead, although the room was cold. Not a word was said by the people in the room. Mrs. Meyers leaned back and thought for a moment.

"I feel a small, stocky man here, perverted minds, and there is fighting all over the room. He is being surprised by the bathroom door. They were hiding in the next room, came through this window and fire escape."

We descended again to the library, where we had originally assembled. The conversation continued quietly, when suddenly Mrs. Meyers found herself rapidly slipping into trance again.

"Three men, one wiry and tall, one short and very stocky, and one tall and stout—the shorter one is in charge. Then there is Baby-Face...she has a Mona Lisa-like face. Stan is protected. I had the goods on them.... Mama's right, it's getting hot...."

"Give us the name!" I almost shouted. Tension gripped us all.

The medium struggled with an unfamiliar sound. "Kapoich...?" Then she added, "The girl here...poker face."

"But what is her name?"

"Ha ha...tyrant."

When Mrs. Meyers came out of her trance, I questioned Rubinstein's mother about the séance. She readily agreed that the voice had indeed sounded much like her late son's. Moreover, there was that girl—named in the investigation—who had a "baby face." She never showed emotion, and was, in fact, poker-faced all the time. Her name?

"My son often called her his tyrant," the mother said, visibly shaken.

"What about the other names?"

"My son used a hired limousine frequently. The chauffeur was a stocky man, and his name was Joe or Joey. Stan? I have heard that name many times in business conversations." One of the men involved in the investigation was named Kubitschek. Had the deceased tried to pronounce that name?

A wallet once belonging to Serge had been handed to Mrs. Meyers a few minutes before, to help her maintain contact with the deceased. Suddenly, without warning, the wallet literally *flew out of her hands* and hit the high ceiling of the library with tremendous impact.

Mrs. Meyers' voice again sounded strange, as the late financier spoke through her in anger. "Do you know how much it costs to sell a man down the river?"

Nobody cared to answer. We had all had quite enough for one evening!

We all left in different directions, and I sent a duplicate of the séance transcript to the police, something I have done with every subsequent séance as well. Mrs. Meyers and I were never the only ones to know what transpired in trance. The police knew, too, and if they did not choose to arrest anyone, that was their business.

We were sure our séance had not attracted attention, and Mrs. Rubinstein herself, and her people, certainly would not spread the word of the unusual goings-on in the Fifth Avenue mansion on the anniversary of the murder.

But on February 1, Cholly Knickerbocker headlined —"Serge's Mother Holds A Séance"!

Not entirely accurate in his details—his source turned out to be one of the guards—Mr. Cassini, nevertheless, came to the point in stating: "To the awe of all present, no less than four people were named by the medium. If this doesn't give the killers the chills, it certainly does us."

We thought we had done our bit toward the solution of this baffling murder, and were quite prepared to forget the excitement of that evening. Unfortunately, the wraith of Rubinstein did not let it rest at that.

During a routine séance then held at my house on West 70th Street, he took over the medium's personality, and elaborated on his statements. He talked of his offices in London and Paris, his staff, and his enemies. One of his lawyers, Rubinstein averred, knew more than he *dared* disclose!

I called Mrs. Rubinstein and arranged for another, less public sitting at the Fifth Avenue house. This time only the four of us, the two elderly ladies, Mrs. Meyers and I, were present. Rubinstein's voice was again recognized by his mother.

"It was at 2:45 on the nose. 2:45!" he said, speaking of the time of his death. "Pa took my hand, it wasn't so bad. I want to tell the little angel woman here, I don't always listen like a son should—she told me always, 'You go too far, don't take chances!'"

Then his voice grew shrill with anger. "Justice will be done. I have paid for that."

I asked, what did this fellow Joey, whom he mentioned the first time, do for a living?

"Limousines. He knew how to come. He brought them here, they were not invited."

He then added something about Houston, Texas, and insisted that a man from that city was involved. He was sure "the girl" would eventually talk and break the case.

There were a number of other sittings, at my house, where the late Serge put his appearance into evidence. Gradually, his hatred and thirst for revenge gave way to a calmer acceptance of his untimely death. He kept us informed of "poker face's moves"—whenever "the girl" moved, Serge was there to tell us. Sometimes his language was rough, sometimes he held back.

"They'll get Mona Lisa," he assured me on March 30th, 1956. I faithfully turned the records of our séances over to the police. They always acknowledged them, but were not eager to talk about this help from so odd a source as a psychical researcher!

Rubinstein kept talking about a Crown Street Headquarters in London, but we never were able to locate this address. At one time, he practically insisted in taking his medium with him into the street, to look for his murderers! It took strength and persuasion for me to calm the restless one, for I did not want Mrs. Meyers to leave the safety of the big armchair by the fireplace, which she usually occupied at our séances.

"Stan is on this side now," he commented on April 13th.

I could never fathom whether Stan was his friend of his enemy, or perhaps both at various times. Financier Stanley died a short time after our initial séance at the Fifth Avenue mansion.

Safe deposit boxes were mentioned, and numbers given, but somehow Mrs. Rubinstein never managed to find them.

On April 26th, we held another sitting at my house. This time the spirit of the slain financier was particularly restless.

"Vorovsky," he mumbled, "yellow cab, he was paid good for helping her get away from the house. Doug paid him, he's a friend of Charley's. Tell mother to hire a private detective."

I tried to calm him. He flared up at me. "Who're you talking to? The Pope?"

The next day, I checked these names with his mother. Mrs. Rubinstein also assured me that the expression "who do you think I am—the Pope?" was one of his favorite phrases in life!

"Take your nose down to Texas and you'll find a long line to London and Paris," he advised us on May 10th.

Meanwhile, Mrs. Rubinstein increased the reward for the capture of the murderer to $50,000. Still, no one was arrested, and the people the police had originally questioned had all been let go. Strangely enough, the estate was much smaller than at first anticipated. Was much money still in hiding, perhaps in some unnamed safe deposit box? We'll never know. Rubinstein's mother has gone on to join him on the other side of the veil, too.

My last contact with the case was in November of 1961, when columnist Hy Gardner asked me to appear on his television program. We talked about the Rubinstein séances, and he showed once more the eerie bit of film he called "a collector's item"—the only existing television interview with Rubinstein, made shortly before his death in 1955.

The inquisitive reporter's questions are finally parried by the wily Rubinstein with an impatient—"Why, that's like asking a man about his own death!"

Could it be that Serge Rubinstein, in addition to all his other "talents," also had the gift of prophecy?

❋ 6

The Rockland County Ghost*

IN NOVEMBER 1951 the writer heard for the first time of the haunted house belonging to the New York home of the late Danton Walker, the well-known newspaper man.

Over a dinner table in a Manhattan restaurant, the strange goings-on in the Rockland County house were discussed with me for the first time, although they had been observed over the ten years preceding our meeting. The manifestations had come to a point where they had forced Mr. Walker to leave his house to the ghost and build himself a studio on the other end of his estate, where he was able to live unmolested.

A meeting with Mrs. Garrett, the medium, was soon arranged, but due to her indisposition, it had to be postponed. Despite her illness, Mrs. Garrett, in a kind of "traveling clairvoyance," did obtain a clairvoyant impression of the entity. His name was "Andreas," and she felt him to be rather attached to the present owner of the house. These findings Mrs. Garrett communicated to Mr. Walker, but nothing further was done on the case until the fall of 1952. A "rescue circle" operation was finally organized on November 22, 1952, and successfully concluded the case, putting the disturbed soul to rest and allowing Mr. Walker to return to the main house without further fear of manifestations.

Before noting the strange phenomena that have been observed in the house, it will be necessary to describe this house a bit, as the nature of the building itself has a great deal to do with the occurrences.

Mr. Walker's house is a fine example of colonial architecture, of the kind that was built in the country during the second half of the eighteenth century. Although Walker was sure only of the first deed to the property, dated 1813 and naming the Abrams family, of pre-Revolutionary origin in the country, the house itself is unquestionably much older.

When Mr. Walker bought the house in the spring of 1942, it was in the dismal state of disrepair typical of some dwellings in the surrounding Ramapo Mountains. It took the new owner several years and a great deal of money to rebuild the house to its former state and to refurbish it with the furniture, pewter, and other implements of the period. I am mentioning this point because in its present state the house is a completely livable and authentic colonial building of the kind that would be an entirely familiar and a welcome sight to a man living toward the end of the eighteenth century, were he to set foot into it today.

The house stands on a hill which was once part of a farm. During the War for Independence, this location was

*Courtesy of *Tomorrow*, Vol. I, No. 3.

the headquarters of a colonial army. In fact, "Mad" Anthony Wayne's own headquarters stood near this site, and the Battle of Stony Point (1779) was fought a few miles away. Most likely, the building restored by Mr. Walker was then in use as a fortified roadhouse, used both for storage of arms, ammunitions, and food supplies, and for the temporary lodging of prisoners.

After the house passed from the hands of the Abrams family in the earlier part of the last century, a banker named Dixon restored the farm and the hill, but paid scant attention to the house itself. By and by, the house gave in to the ravages of time and weather. A succession of mountain people made it their living quarters around the turn of the century, but did nothing to improve its sad state of disrepair. When Mr. Walker took over, only the kitchen and a small adjoining room were in use; the rest of the house was filled with discarded furniture and other objects. The upstairs was divided into three tiny rooms and a small attic, which contained bonnets, hoop skirts, and crudely carved wooden shoe molds and toys, dating from about the Civil War period.

While the house was being reconstructed, Mr. Walker was obliged to spend nights at a nearby inn, but would frequently take naps during the day on an army cot upstairs. On these occasions he received distinct impressions of "a Revolutionary soldier" being in the room.

Mr. Walker's moving in, in the spring of 1942, touched off the usual country gossip, some of which later reached his ears. It seemed that the house was haunted. One woman who had lived in the place told of an "old man" who frightened the children, mysterious knocks at the front door, and other mysterious happenings. But none of these reports could be followed up. For all practical purposes, we may say that the phenomena started with the arrival of Mr. Walker.

Though Mr. Walker was acutely sensitive to the atmosphere of the place from the time he took over, it was not until 1944 that the manifestations resulted in both visible and audible phenomena. That year, during an afternoon when he was resting in the front room downstairs, he was roused by a violent summons to the front door, which has a heavy iron knocker. Irritated by the intrusion when no guest was expected, he called "Come in!," then went to the front door and found no one there.

About this time, Mr. Walker's butler, Johnny, remarked to his employer that the house was a nice place to stay in "if they would let you alone." Questioning revealed that Johnny, spending the night in the house alone, had gone downstairs three times during the night to answer knocks at the front door. An Italian workman named Pietro, who did some repairs on the house, reported sounds of someone walking up the stairs in midafternoon "with heavy boots on," at a time when there definitely was no one else in the place. Two occasional guests of the owner also were disturbed, while reading in the living room, by the sound of heavy footsteps overhead.

In 1950 Mr. Walker and his secretary were eating dinner in the kitchen, which is quite close to the front door. There was a sharp rap at the door. The secretary opened it and found nobody there. In the summer of 1952, when there were guests downstairs but no one upstairs, sounds of heavy thumping were heard from upstairs, as if someone had taken a bad fall.

Though Mr. Walker, his butler, and his guests never saw or fancied they saw any ghostly figures, the manifestations did not restrict themselves to audible phenomena. Unexplainable dents in pewter pieces occurred from time to time. A piece of glass in a door pane, the same front door of the house, was cracked but remained solidly in place for some years. One day it was missing and could not be located in the hall indoors, nor outside on the porch. A week later this four-by-four piece of glass was accidentally found resting on a plate rail eight feet above the kitchen floor. How it got there is as much of a mystery now as it was then.

On one occasion, when Johnny was cleaning the stairs to the bedroom, a picture that had hung at the top of the stairs for at least two years tumbled down, almost striking him. A woman guest who had spent the night on a daybed in the living room, while making up the bed next morning, was almost struck by a heavy pewter pitcher which fell ("almost as if thrown at her") from a bookshelf hanging behind the bed. There were no unusual vibrations of the house to account for these things.

On the white kitchen wall there are heavy semicircular black marks where a pewter salt box, used for holding keys, had been violently swung back and forth. A large pewter pitcher, which came into the house in perfect condition, now bears five heavy imprints, four on one side, one on the other. A West Pointer with unusually large hands fitted his own four fingers and thumb into the dents!

Other phenomena included gripping chills felt from time to time by Mr. Walker and his more sensitive guests. These chills, not to be confused with drafts, were also felt in all parts of the house by Mr. Walker when alone. They took the form of a sudden paralyzing cold, as distinct as a cramp. Such a chill once seized him when he had been ill and gone to bed early. Exasperated by the phenomenon, he unthinkingly called out aloud, "Oh, for God's sake, let me alone!" The chill abruptly stopped.

But perhaps the most astounding incident took place in November 1952, only a few days before the rescue circle met at the house.

Two of Mr. Walker's friends, down-to-earth men with no belief in the so-called supernatural, were weekend guests. Though Walker suggested that they both spend the night in the commodious studio about three-hundred feet from the main house, one of them insisted on staying upstairs in the "haunted" room. Walker persuaded him to leave the lights on.

An hour later, the pajama-clad man came rushing down to the studio, demanding that Mr. Walker put an end "to his pranks." The light beside his bed was blinking on and off. All other lights in the house were burning steadily!

Assured that this might be caused by erratic power supply and that no one was playing practical jokes, the guest returned to the main house. But an hour or so later, he came back to the studio and spent the rest of the night there. In the morning he somewhat sheepishly told that he had been awakened from a sound sleep by the sensation of someone slapping him violently in the face. Sitting bolt upright in bed, he noticed that the shirt he had hung on the back of a rocking chair was being agitated by the "breeze." Though admitting that this much might have been pure imagination, he also seemed to notice the chair gently rocking. Since all upstairs windows were closed, there definitely was no "breeze."

"The sensation described by my guest," Mr. Walker remarked, "reminded me of a quotation from one of Edith Wharton's ghost stories. Here is the exact quote:

"'Medford sat up in bed with a jerk which resembles no other. Someone was in his room. The fact reached him not by sight or sound...but by a peculiar faint disturbance of the invisible currents that enclose us.'

"Many people in real life have experienced this sensation. I myself had not spent a night alone in the main house in four years. It got so that I just couldn't take it. In fact, I built the studio specifically to get away from staying there. When people have kidded me about my 'haunted house,' my reply is, would I have spent so much time and money restoring the house, and then built another house to spend the night in, if there had not been some valid reason?"

On many previous occasions, Mr. Walker had remarked that he had a feeling that someone was trying "desperately" to get into the house, as if for refuge. The children of an earlier tenant had mentioned some agitation "by the lilac bush" at the corner of the house. The original crude walk from the road to the house, made of flat native stones, passed this lilac bush and went to the well, which, according to local legend, was used by soldiers in Revolutionary times.

"When I first took over the place," Mr. Walker observed, "I used to look out of the kitchen window twenty times a day to see who was at the well. Since the old walk has been replaced by a stone walk and driveway, no one could now come into the place without being visible for at least sixty-five feet. Following the reconstruction, the stone wall blocking the road was torn down several times at the exact spot where the original walk reached the road."

In all the disturbances which led to the efforts of the rescue circle, I detected one common denominator. Someone was attempting to get into the house, and to call attention to something. Playing pranks, puzzling people, or even frightening them, were not part of the ghost's purpose;

they were merely his desperate devices for getting attention, attention for something he very much wanted to say.

On a bleak and foreboding day in November 1952, the little group comprising the rescue circle drove out into the country for the sitting. They were accompanied by Dr. L., a prominent Park Avenue psychiatrist and psychoanalyst, and of course by Mr. Walker, the owner of the property.

The investigation was sponsored by Parapsychology Foundation, Inc., of New York City. Participants included Mrs. Eileen J. Garrett; Dr. L., whose work in psychiatry and analysis is well known; Miss Lenore Davidson, assistant to Mrs. Garrett, who was responsible for most of the notes taken; Dr. Michael Pobers, then Secretary General of the Parapsychology Foundation; and myself.

The trip to the Rockland County home of Mr. Walker took a little over an hour. The house stands atop a wide hill, not within easy earshot of the next inhabited house, but not too far from his own "cabin" and two other small houses belonging to Mr. Walker's estate. The main house, small and compact, represents a perfect restoration of colonial American architecture.

A plaque in the ground at the entrance gate calls attention to the historical fact that General Wayne's headquarters at the time of the Battle of Stony Point, 1779, occupied the very same site. Mr. Walker's house was possibly part of the fortification system protecting the hill, and no doubt served as a stronghold in the war of 1779 and in earlier wars and campaigns fought around this part of the country. One feels the history of many generations clinging to the place.

We took our places in the upstairs bedroom, grouping ourselves so as to form an imperfect circle around Mrs. Garrett, who sat in a heavy, solid wooden chair with her back to the wall and her face toward us.

The time was 2:45 P.M. and the room was fully lit by ample daylight coming in through the windows.

After a moment, Mrs. Garrett placed herself in full trance by means of autohypnosis. Quite suddenly her own personality vanished, and the medium sank back into her chair completely lifeless, very much like an unused garment discarded for the time being by its owner. But not for long. A few seconds later, another personality "got into" the medium's body, precisely the way one dons a shirt or coat. It was Uvani, one of Mrs. Garrett's two spirit guides who act as her control personalities in all of her experiments. Uvani, in his own lifetime, was an East Indian of considerable knowledge and dignity, and as such he now appeared before us.

As "he" sat up—I shall refer to the distinct personalities now using the "instrument" (the medium's body) as "he" or "him"—it was obvious that we had before us a gentleman from India. Facial expression, eyes, color of skin, movements, the folded arms, and the finger movements that accompanied many of his words were all those of a native of India. As Uvani addressed us, he spoke in perfect English, except for a faltering word now and then or an occasional failure of idiom, but his accent was typical.

At this point, the tape recorder faithfully took down every word spoken. The transcript given here is believed to be complete, and is certainly so where we deal with Uvani, who spoke clearly and slowly. In the case of the ghost, much of the speech was garbled because of the ghost's unfortunate condition; some of the phrases were repeated several times, and a few words were so badly uttered that they could not be made out by any of us. In order to present only verifiable evidence, I have eliminated all such words and report here nothing which was not completely understandable and clear. But at least 70% of the words uttered by the ghost, and of course all of the words of Uvani, are on record. The tape recording is supplemented by Miss Davidson's exacting transcript, and in the final moments her notes replace it entirely.

Uvani: It is I, Uvani. I give you greeting, friends. Peace be with you, and in your lives, and in this house!

Dr. L.: And our greetings to you, Uvani. We welcome you.

Uvani: I am very happy to speak with you, my good friend. (Bows to Dr. L.) You are out of your native element.

Dr. L.: Very much so. We have not spoken in this environment at all before....

Uvani: What is it what you would have of me today, please?

Dr. L.: We are met here as friends of Mr. Walker, whose house this is, to investigate strange occurrences which have taken place in this house from time to time, which lead us to feel that they partake of the nature of this field of interest of ours. We would be guided by you, Uvani, as to the method of approach which we should use this afternoon. Our good friend and instrument (Mrs. Garrett) has the feeling that there was a personality connected with this house whose influence is still to be felt here.

Uvani: Yes, I would think so. I am confronted myself with a rather restless personality. In fact, a very strange personality, and one that might appear to be in his own life perhaps not quite of the right mind—I think you would call it.

I have a great sense of agitation. I would like to tell you about this personality, and at the same time draw your attention to the remarkable—what you might call—atmospherics that he is able to bring into our environment. You, who are my friend and have worked with me very much, know that when I am in control, we are very calm—yes? Yet it is as much as I can do to maintain the control, as you see—for such is the atmosphere produced by this personality, that you will note my own difficulty to retain and constrain the instrument. (The medium's hand shakes in rapid palsy. Uvani's voice tremble.) This one, in spite of me, by virtue of his being with us brings into the process of our field of work a classical palsy. Do you see this?

Dr. L.: I do.

Uvani: This was his condition, and that is why it may be for me perhaps necessary (terrific shaking of medium at this point) to ask you to—deal—with this—personality yourself—while I withdraw—to create a little more quietude around the instrument. Our atmosphere, as you notice, is charged.... You will not be worried by anything that may happen, please. You will speak, if you can, with this one—and you will eventually return the instrument to my control.

Dr. L.: I will.

Uvani: Will you please to remember that you are dealing with a personality very young, tired, who has been very much hurt in life, and who was, for many years prior to his passing, unable—how you say—to think for himself. Now will you please take charge, so that I permit the complete control to take place....

Uvani left the body of the medium at this point. For a moment, all life seemed gone from it as it lay still in the chair. Then, suddenly, another personality seemed to possess it. Slowly, the new personality sat up, hands violently vibrating in palsy, face distorted in extreme pain, eyes blinking, staring, unable to see anything at first, looking straight through us all without any sign of recognition. All this was accompanied by increasing inarticulate outcries, leading later into halting, deeply emotional weeping.

For about ten seconds, the new personality maintained its position in the chair, but as the movements of the hands accelerated, it suddenly leaned over and crashed to the floor, narrowly missing a wooden chest nearby. Stretched out on the floor before us, "he" kept uttering inarticulate sounds for perhaps one or two minutes, while vainly trying to raise himself from the floor.

One of Dr. L.'s crutches, which he uses when walking about, was on the floor next to his chair. The entity seized the crutch and tried to raise himself with its help, but without success. Throughout the next seconds, he tried again to use the crutch, only to fall back onto the floor. One of his legs, the left one, continued to execute rapid convulsive movements typical of palsy. It was quite visible that the leg had been badly damaged. Now and again he threw his left hand to his head, touching it as if to indicate that his head hurt also.

Dr. L.: We are friends, and you may speak with us. Let us help you in any way we can. We are friends.

Entity: Mhh—mhh—mhh—(inarticulate sounds of sobbing and pain).

Dr. L.: Speak with us. Speak with us. Can we help you? (More crying from the entity) You will be able to speak with us. Now you are quieter. You will be able to talk to us. (The entity crawls along the floor to Mr. Walker, seems to have eyes only for him, and remains at Walker's knee throughout the interrogation. The crying becomes softer.) Do you understand English?

Entity: Friend... friend. Mercy... mercy... mercy.... (The English has a marked Polish accent, the voice is rough, uncouth, bragging, emotional.) I know... I know... I know.... (pointing at Mr. Walker)

Dr. L.: When did you know him before?

Entity: Stones... stones.... Don't let them take me!

Dr. L.: No, we won't let them take you.

Entity: (More crying) Talk....

Mr. Walker: You want to talk to me? Yes, I'll talk to you.

Entity: Can't talk....

Mr. Walker: Can't talk? It is hard for you to talk?

Entity: (Nods) Yes.

Dr. L.: You want water? Food? Water?

Entity: (Shakes head) Talk! Talk! (To Mr. Walker) Friend? You?

Mr. Walker: Yes, friend. We're all friends.

Entity: (Points to his head, then to his tongue.) Stones... no?

Dr. L.: No stones. You will not be stoned.

Entity: No beatin'?

Dr. L.: No, you won't be stoned, you won't be beaten.

Entity: Don't go!

Mr. Walker: No, we are staying right here.

Entity: Can't talk....

Mr. Walker: You can talk. We are all friends.

Dr. L.: It is difficult with this illness that you have, but you can talk. Your friend there is Mr. Walker. And what is your name?

Entity: He calls me. I have to get out. I cannot go any further. In God's name I cannot go any further. (Touches Mr. Walker)

Mr. Walker: I will protect you. (At the word "protect" the entity sits up, profoundly struck by it.) What do you fear?

Entity: Stones....

Mr. Walker: Stones thrown at you?

Dr. L.: That will not happen again.

Entity: Friends! Wild men... you know....

Mr. Walker: Indians?

Entity: No.

Dr. L.: White man?

Entity: Mh...teeth gone—(shows graphically how his teeth were kicked in)

Mr. Walker: Teeth gone.

Dr. L.: They knocked your teeth out?

Entity: See? I can't....Protect me!

Mr. Walker: Yes, yes. We will protect you. No more beatings, no more stones.

Dr. L.: You live here? This is your house?

Entity: (Violent gesture, loud voice) No, oh no! I hide here.

Mr. Walker: In the woods?

Entity: Cannot leave here.

Dr. L.: Whom do you hide from?

Entity: Big, big, strong...big, big, strong....

Dr. L.: Is he the one that beat you?

Entity: (Shouts) All...I know...I know...I know....

Dr. L.: You know the names?

Entity: (Hands on Mr. Walker's shoulders) Know the plans....

Dr. L.: They tried to find the plans, to make you tell, but you did not tell? And your head hurts?

Entity: (Just nods to this) Ah...ah....

Dr. L.: And you've been kicked, and beaten and stoned. (The entity nods violently.)

Mr. Walker: Where are the plans?

Entity: I hid them...far, far....

Mr. Walker: Where did you hide the plans? We are friends, you can tell us.

Entity: Give me map.

(The entity is handed note pad and pen, which he uses in the stiff manner of a quill. The drawing, showing the unsteady and vacillating lines of a palsy sufferer, is on hand.)

Entity: In your measure...Andreas Hid....(drawing)

Mr. Walker: Where the wagon house lies?

Entity: A house...not in the house...timber house...log....

Mr. Walker: Log house?

Entity: (Nods) Plans...log house...under...under... stones...fifteen...log...fifteen stones...door...plans— for whole shifting of....

Mr. Walker: Of ammunitions?

Entity: No...men and ammunitions...plans—I have for French....I have plans for French...plans I have to deliver to log house...right where sun strikes window....

Dr. L.: Fifteen stones from the door?

Entity: Where sun strikes the window....Fifteen stones... under...in log house....There I have put away... plans....(agitated) Not take again!

Mr. Walker: No, no, we will not let them take you again. We will protect you from the English.

Entity: (Obviously touched) No one ever say—no one ever say—I will protect you....

Mr. Walker: Yes, we will protect you. You are protected now for always.

Entity: Don't send me away, no?

Dr. L.: No, we won't send you away.

Entity: Protect...protect...protect....

Dr. L.: You were not born in this country?

Entity: No.

Dr. L.: You are a foreigner?

Entity: (Hurt and angry, shouts) Yeah...dog! They call me dog. Beasts!

Dr. L.: Are you German? (The entity makes a disdainful negative gesture.) Polish?

Entity: Yes.

Dr. L.: You came here when you were young?

Entity: (His voice is loud and robust with the joy of meeting a countryman.) Das...das...das! Yes...brother? Friends? Pole? Polski, yeah?

Mr. Walker: Yes, yes.

Entity: (Throws arms around Walker) I hear...I see... like...like brother...like brother...Jilitze...Jilitze....

Mr. Walker: What is your name?

Entity: Gospodin! Gospodin! (Polish for "master")

Mr. Walker: What's the name? (in Polish) *Zo dje lat?*

Entity: (Touching Mr. Walker's face and hands as he speaks) Hans? Brother...like Hans...like Hans...me Andre—you Hans.

Mr. Walker: I'm Hans?

Entity: My brother...he killed too...I die...I die... die...die....

Mr. Walker: Where? At Tappan? Stony Point?

Entity: Big field, battle. Noise, noise. Big field. Hans like you.

Mr. Walker: How long ago was this battle?

Entity: Like yesterday...like yesterday...I lie here in dark night...bleed...call Hans...call Hans...Polski?

Mr. Walker: Did you die here?

Entity: Out here.... (pointing down) Say again... protect, friend.... (points at himself) Me, me... you... Andreas? You like Hans... friend, brother... you... Andreas?

Dr. L.: Do you know anything about dates?

Entity: Like yesterday. English all over. Cannot... they are terrible.... (hits his head)

Dr. L.: You were with the Americans?

Entity: No, no.

Dr. L.: Yankees?

Entity: No, no. Big word... Re... Re... Republic... Republic.... (drops back to the floor with an outcry of pain)

Dr. L.: You are still with friends. You are resting. You are safe.

Entity: Protection... protection... the stars in the flag... the stars in the flag... Republic... they sing....

Dr. L.: How long have you been hiding in this house?

Entity: I go to talk with brother later.... Big man say, you go away, he talk now.... I go away a little, he stays... he talk... he here part of the time....

By "big man" the entity was referring to his guide, Uvani. The entity rested quietly, becoming more and more lifeless on the floor. Soon all life appeared to be gone from the medium's body. Then Uvani returned, took control, sat up, got back up into the chair without trouble, and addressed us in his learned and quiet manner as before.

Uvani: (Greeting us with bended arms, bowing) You will permit me. You do not very often find me in such surroundings. I beg your pardon. Now let me tell to you a little of what I have been able to ascertain. You have here obviously a poor soul who is unhappily caught in the memory of perhaps days or weeks or years of confusion. I permit him to take control in order to let him play out the fantasy... in order to play out the fears, the difficulties.... I am able thus to relax this one. It is then that I will give you what I see of this story.

He was obviously kept a prisoner of... a hired army. There had been different kinds of soldiers from Europe brought to this country. He tells me that he had been in other parts of this country with French troops, but they were friendly. He was a friend for a time with one who was friendly not only with your own people, but with Revolutionary troops. He seems, therefore, a man who serves a man... a mercenary.

He became a jackboot for all types of men who have fought, a good servant. He is now here, now there.

He does not understand for whom he works. He refers to an Andre, with whom he is for some time in contact, and he likes this Andre very much because of the similar name... because he is Andre(w)ski. There is this similarity to Andre. It is therefore he has been used, as far as I can see, as a cover-up for this man. Here then is the confusion.

He is caught two or three times by different people because of his appearance—he is a "dead ringer"... a double. His friend Andre disappears, and he is lost and does what he can with this one and that one, and eventually he finds himself in the hands of the British troops. He is known to have letters and plans, and these he wants me to tell you were hidden by him due east of where you now find yourselves, in what he says was a temporary building of sorts in which were housed different caissons. In this there is also a rest house for guards. In this type kitchen he... he will not reveal the plans and is beaten mercilessly. His limbs are broken and he passes out, no longer in the right mind, but with a curious break on one side of the body, and his leg is damaged.

It would appear that he is from time to time like one in a coma—he wakes, dreams, and loses himself again, and I gather from the story that he is not always aware of people. Sometimes he says it is a long dream. Could it therefore be that these fantasies are irregular? Does he come and go? You get the kind of disturbance—"Am I dreaming? What is this? A feeling that there is a tempest inside of me...." So I think he goes into these states, suspecting them himself. This is his own foolishness... lost between two states of being.

(To Mr. Walker who is tall and blue-eyed)

He has a very strong feeling that you are like his brother, Sahib. This may account for his desire to be near you. He tells me, "I had a brother and left him very young, tall, blue-eyed," and he misses him in a battlefield in this country.

Now I propose with your prayers and help to try to find his brother for him. And I say to him, "I have asked for your protection, where you will not be outcast, degraded, nor debased, where you will come and go in freedom. Do as your friends here ask. In the name of that God and that faith in which you were brought up, seek salvation and mercy for your restlessness. Go in peace. Go to a kindlier dream. Go out where there is a greater life. Come with us—you are not with your kind. In mercy let us go hand in hand."

Now he looks at me and asks, "If I should return, would he like unto my brother welcome me?" I do not think he will return, but if you sense him or his wildness of the past, I would say unto you, Sahib, address him as we have here. Say to him, "You who have found the God of your childhood need not return." Give him your love and please with a prayer send him away.

May there be no illness, nor discord, nor unhappiness in this house because he once felt it was his only resting place. Let there indeed be peace in your hearts and let there be understanding between here and there. It is such a little way, although it looks so far. Let us then in our daily life not wait for this grim experience, but let us help in every moment of our life.

Mr. Walker was softly repeating the closing prayer. Uvani relinquished control, saying, "Peace be unto you...until we meet again." The medium fell back in the chair, unconscious for a few moments. Then her own personality returned.

Mrs. Garrett rose from the chair, blinked her eyes, and seemed none the worse for the highly dramatic and exciting incidents which had taken place around her—none of which she was aware of. Every detail of what had happened had to be told to Mrs. Garrett later, as the trance state is complete and no memory whatsoever is retained.

It was 2:45 P.M. when Mrs. Garrett went into trance, and 4 P.M. when the operation came to an end. After some discussion of the events of the preceding hour and a quarter, mainly to iron out differing impressions received by the participants, we left Mr. Walker's house and drove back to New York.

On December 2, 1952, Mr. Walker informed me that "the atmosphere about the place does seem much calmer." It seems reasonable to assume that the restless ghost has at last found that "sweeter dream" of which Uvani spoke.

In cases of this nature, where historical names and facts are part of the proceedings, it is always highly desirable to have them corroborated by research in the available reference works. In the case of "The Ghost of Ash Manor" (*Tomorrow*, Autumn 1952) this was comparatively easy, as we were dealing with a personality of some rank and importance in his own lifetime. In this case, however, we were dealing with an obscure immigrant servant, whose name is not likely to appear in any of the regimental records available for the year and place in question. In fact, extensive perusal of such records shows no one who might be our man. There were many enlisted men with the name Andreas serving in the right year and in the right regiment for our investigation, but none of them seems to fit.

And why should it? After all, our Andrewski was a very young man of no particular eminence who served as ordinary jackboot to a succession of colonial soldiers, as Uvani and he himself pointed out. The search for Andreas' brother Hans was almost as negative. Pursuing a hunch that the Slavic exclamation "*Jilitze...Jilitze...*" which the ghost made during the interrogation, might have been "Ulica...Ulica...." I found that a Johannes Ulick (Hans Ulick could be spelled that way) did indeed serve in 1779 in the Second Tryon County Regiment.

The "fifteen stones to the east" to which the ghost referred as the place where he hid the plans may very well have been the walk leading from the house to the log house across the road. Some of these stone steps are still preserved. What happened to the plans, we shall never know. They were probably destroyed by time and weather, or were found and deposited later in obscure hands. No matter which—it is no longer of concern to anyone.

✳ 7

A Revolutionary Corollary: Patrick Henry, Nathan Hale, et al.

NATHAN HALE, AS EVERY schoolboy knows, was the American spy hanged by the British. He was captured at Huntington Beach and taken to Brooklyn for trial. How he was captured is a matter of some concern to the people of Huntington, Long Island. The town was originally settled by colonists from Connecticut who were unhappy with the situation in that colony. There were five principal families who accounted for the early settlement of Huntington, and to this day their descendants are the most prominent families in the area. They were the Sammes, the Downings, the Busches, the Pauldings, and the Cooks. During the Revolutionary War, feelings were about equally divided among the townspeople: some were Revolutionaries and some remained Tories. The consensus of historians is that members of these five prominent families, all of whom were Tories, were responsible for the betrayal of Nathan Hale to the British.

All this was brought to my attention by Mrs. Geraldine P. of Huntington. Mrs. P. grew up in what she considers the oldest house in Huntington, although the Huntington Historical Society claims that theirs is even older. Be that as it may, it was there when the Revolutionary War started. Local legend has it that an act of violence took place on the corner of the street, which was then a crossroads in the middle of a rural area. The house in which Mrs. P. grew up stands on that street. Mrs. P. suspects that the capture—or, at any rate, the betrayal—of the Revolutionary agent took place on that crossroads. When she tried to investigate the history of her house, she found little cooperation on the part of the local historical society. It was a conspiracy of silence, according to her, as if some people wanted to cover up a certain situation from the past.

The house had had a "strange depressing effect on all its past residents," according to Mrs. P. Her own father, who studied astrology and white magic for many years, related an incident that occurred in the house. He awoke in the middle of the night in the master bedroom because he felt unusually cold. He became aware of "something" rushing about the room in wild, frantic circles. Because of his outlook and training, he spoke up, saying, "Can I help you?" But the rushing about became even more frantic. He then asked what was wrong and what could be done. But no communication was possible. When he saw that he could not communicate with the entity, Mrs. P.'s father finally said, "If I can't help you, then go away." There was a snapping sound, and the room suddenly became quiet and warm again, and he went back to sleep. There have been no other recorded incidents at the house in question. But Mrs. P. wonders if some guilty entity wants to manifest, not necessarily Nathan Hale, but perhaps someone connected with his betrayal.

At the corner of 43rd Street and Vanderbilt Avenue, Manhattan, one of the busiest and noisiest spots in all of New York City, there is a small commemorative plaque explaining that Nathan Hale, the Revolutionary spy, was executed on that spot by the British. I doubt that too many New Yorkers are aware of this, or can accurately pinpoint the location of the tragedy. It is even less likely that a foreigner would know about it. When I suggested to my good friend Sybil Leek that she accompany me to a psychically important spot for an experiment, she readily agreed. Despite the noises and the heavy traffic, the spot being across from Grand Central Station, Sybil bravely stood with me on the street corner and tried to get some sort of psychic impression.

"I get the impression of food and drink," Sybil said. I pointed out that there were restaurants all over the area, but Sybil shook her head. "No, I was thinking more of a place for food and drink, and I don't mean in the present. It is more like an inn, a transit place, and it has some connection with the river. A meeting place, perhaps, some sort of inn. Of course, it is very difficult in this noise and with all these new buildings here."

"If we took down these buildings, what would we see?"

"I think we would see a field and water. I have a strong feeling that there is a connection with water and with the inn. There are people coming and going—I sense a woman, but I don't think she's important. I am not sure…unless it would mean foreign. I hear a foreign language. Something like *Verchenen.** I can't quite get it. It is not German."

"Is there anything you feel about this spot?"

"This spot, yes. I think I want to go back two hundred years at least, it is not very clear, 1769 or 1796. That is the period. The connection with the water puzzles me."

"Do you feel an event of significance here at any time?"

"Yes. It is not strong enough to come through to me completely, but sufficiently *drastic* to make me feel a little nervous."

"In what way is it drastic?"

"Hurtful, violent. There are several people involved in this violence. Something connected with water, papers connected with water, that is part of the trouble."

Sybil then suggested that we go to the right to see if the impressions might be stronger at some distance. We went around the corner and I stopped. Was the impression any stronger?

"No, the impression is the same. Papers, violence. For a name, I have the impression of the letters P.T. Peter. It would be helpful to come here in the middle of the night, I think. I wish I could understand the connection with water, here in the middle of the city."

"Did someone die here?"

Sybil closed her eyes and thought it over for a moment. "Yes, but the death of this person was important at that time and indeed necessary. But there is more to it than just the death of the person. The disturbance involves lots of other things, lots of other people. In fact, two distinct races were involved, because I sense a lack of understanding. I think that this was a political thing, and the papers were important."

"Can you get anything further on the nature of this violence you feel here?"

"Just a disturbed feeling, an upheaval, a general disturbance. I am sorry I can't get much else. Perhaps if we came here at night, when things are quieter."

I suggested we get some tea in one of the nearby restaurants. Over tea, we discussed our little experiment and Sybil suddenly remembered an odd experience she had had when visiting the Hotel Biltmore before. (The plaque in question is mounted on the wall of the hotel.) "I receive many invitations to go to this particular area of New York," Sybil explained, "and when I go I always get the feeling of repulsion to the extent where I may be on my way down and get into a telephone booth and call the people involved and say, 'No, I'll meet you somewhere else.' I don't like this particular area we just left; I find it very depressing. *I feel trapped.*"

* * *

I am indebted to R. M. Sandwich of Richmond, Virginia, for an intriguing account of an E.S.P. experience he has connected to Patrick Henry. Mr. Sandwich stated that he has had only one E.S.P. experience and that it took place in one of the early estate-homes of Patrick Henry. He admitted that the experience altered his previously dim view of E.S.P. The present owner of the estate has said that Mr. Sandwich has not been the only one to experience strange things in that house.

The estate-home where the incident took place is called Pine Flash and is presently owned by E. E. Verdon, a personal friend of Mr. Sandwich. It is located in Hanover

*Verplanck's Point, on the Hudson River, was a Revolutionary strongpoint at the time.

A Revolutionary Corollary:

Patrick Henry, Nathan Hale, et al.

County, about fifteen miles outside of Richmond. The house was given to Patrick Henry by his father-in-law. After Henry had lived in it for a number of years, it burned to the ground and was not rebuilt until fifteen years later. During that time Henry resided in the old cottage, which is directly behind the house, and stayed there until the main house had been rebuilt. This cottage is frequently referred to in the area as the honeymoon cottage of young Patrick Henry. The new house was rebuilt exactly as it had been before the fire. As for the cottage, which is still in excellent condition, it is thought to be the oldest wood frame dwelling in Virginia. It may have been there even before Patrick Henry lived in it.

On the Fourth of July, 1968, the Sandwiches had been invited to try their luck at fishing in a pond on Mr. Verdon's land. Since they would be arriving quite early in the morning, they were told that the oars to the rowboat, which they were to use at the pond, would be found inside the old cottage. They arrived at Pine Flash sometime around 6 A.M. Mrs. Sandwich started unpacking their fishing gear and food supplies, while Mr. Sandwich decided to inspect the cottage. Although he had been to the place several times before, he had never actually been inside the cottage itself.

Here then is Mr. Sandwich's report.

"I opened the door, walked in, and shut the door tight behind me. Barely a second had passed after I shut the door when a strange feeling sprang over me. It was the kind of feeling you would experience if you were to walk into an extremely cold, damp room. I remember how still everything was, and then I distinctly heard footsteps overhead in the attic. I called out, thinking perhaps there was someone upstairs. No one answered, nothing. At that time I was standing directly in front of an old fireplace. I admit I was scared half to death. The footsteps were louder now and seemed to be coming down the thin staircase toward me. As they passed me, I felt a cold, crisp, odd feeling. I started looking around for something, anything that could have caused all this. It was during this time that I noticed the closed door open very, very slowly. The door stopped when it was half opened, almost beckoning me to take my leave, which I did at great speed! As I went through that open door, I felt the same cold mass of air I had experienced before. Standing outside, I watched the door slam itself, almost in my face! My wife was still unpacking the car and claims she neither saw nor heard anything."

* * *

Revolutionary figures have a way of hanging on to places they liked in life. Candy Bosselmann of Indiana has had a long history of psychic experiences. She is a budding trance medium and not at all ashamed of her talents. In 1964 she happened to be visiting Ashland, the home of Henry Clay, in Lexington, Kentucky. She had never been to Ashland, so she decided to take a look at it. She and other visitors were shown through the house by an older man, a professional guide, and Candy became somewhat restless listening to his historical ramblings. As the group entered the library and the guide explained the beautiful ash paneling taken from surrounding trees (for which the home is named), she became even more restless. She knew very well that it was the kind of feeling that forewarned her of some sort of psychic event. As she was looking over toward a fireplace, framed by two candelabra, she suddenly saw a very tall, white-haired man in a long black frock coat standing next to it. One elbow rested on the mantel, and his head was in his hand, as if he were pondering something very important.

Miss Bosselmann was not at all emotionally involved with the house. In fact, the guided tour bored her, and she would have preferred to be outside in the stables, since she has a great interest in horses. Her imagination did not conjure up what she saw: she knew in an instant that she was looking at the spirit imprint of Henry Clay.

In 1969 she visited Ashland again, and this time she went into the library deliberately. With her was a friend who wasn't at all psychic. Again, the same restless feeling came over her. But when she was about to go into trance, she decided to get out of the room in a hurry.

* * *

Rock Ford, the home of General Edward Hand, is located four miles south of Lancaster, Pennsylvania, and commands a fine view of the Conestoga River. The house is not a restoration but a well-preserved eighteenth-century mansion, with its original floors, railings, shutters, doors, cupboards, panelings, and window glass. Even the original wall painting can be seen. It is a four-story brick mansion in the Georgian style, with the rooms grouped around a center hall in the design popular during the latter part of the eighteenth century. The rooms are furnished with antiquities of the period, thanks to the discovery of an inventory of General Hand's estate which permitted the local historical society to supply authentic articles of daily usage wherever the originals had disappeared from the house.

Perhaps General Edward Hand is not as well known as a hero of the American Revolution as others are, but to the people of the Pennsylvania Dutch country he is an important figure, even though he was of Irish origin rather than German. Trained as a medical doctor at Trinity College, Dublin, he came to America in 1767 with the Eighteenth Royal Irish Regiment of Foote. However, he resigned British service in 1774 and came to Lancaster to practice medicine and surgery. With the fierce love of liberty so many of the Irish possess, Dr. Hand joined the Revolutionaries in July of 1775, becoming a lieutenant colonel in the Pennsylvania Rifle Battalion. He served in the army until 1800, when he was discharged as a major general. Dr. Hand was present at the Battle of Trenton, the

Battle of Long Island, the Battle of White Plains, the Battle of Princeton, the campaign against the Iroquois, and the surrender of Cornwallis at Yorktown. He also served on the tribunal which convicted Major John André the British spy, and later became the army's adjutant general. He was highly regarded by George Washington, who visited him in his home toward the end of the war. When peace came, Hand became a member of the Continental Congress and served in the Assembly of Pennsylvania as representative of his area. He moved into Rock Ford when it was completed in 1793 and died there in September 1802.

Today, hostesses from a local historical society serve as guides for the tourists who come to Rock Ford in increasing numbers. Visitors are taken about the lower floor and basement and are told of General Hand's agricultural experiments, his medical studies, and his association with George Washington. But unless you ask specifically, you are not likely to hear about what happened to the house after General Hand died. To begin with, the General's son committed suicide in the house. Before long the family died out, and eventually the house became a museum since no one wanted to live in it for very long. At one time, immigrants were contacted at the docks and offered free housing if they would live in the mansion. None stayed. There was something about the house that was not as it should be, something that made people fear it and leave it just as quickly as they could.

Mrs. Ruth S. lives in upstate New York. In 1967 a friend showed her a brochure concerning Rock Ford, and the house intrigued her. Since she was travelling in that direction, she decided to pay Rock Ford a visit. With her family, she drove up to the house and parked her car in the rear. At that moment she had an eerie feeling that something wasn't right. Mind you, Mrs. S. had not been to the house before, had no knowledge about it nor any indication that anything unusual had occurred in it. The group of visitors was quite small. In addition to herself and her family, there were two young college boys and one other couple. Even though it was a sunny day, Mrs. S. felt icy cold.

"I felt a presence before we entered the house and before we heard the story from the guide," she explained. "If I were a hostess there, I wouldn't stay there alone for two consecutive minutes." Mrs. S. had been to many old houses and restorations before but had never felt as she did at Rock Ford.

* * *

It is not surprising that George Washington should be the subject of a number of psychic accounts. Probably the best known (and most frequently misinterpreted) story concerns General Washington's vision which came to him during the encampment at Valley Forge, when the fortunes of war had gone heavily in favor of the British, and the American army, tattered and badly fed, was just about falling to pieces. If there ever was a need for divine guid-

ance, it was at Valley Forge. Washington was in the habit of meditating in the woods at times and saying his prayers when he was quite alone. On one of those occasions he returned to his quarters more worried than usual. As he busied himself with his papers, he had the feeling of a presence in the room. Looking up, he saw opposite him a singularly beautiful woman. Since he had given orders not to be disturbed, he couldn't understand how she had gotten into the room. Although he questioned her several times, the visitor would not reply. As he looked at the apparition, for that is what it was, the General became more and more entranced with her, unable to make any move. For a while he thought he was dying, for he imagined that the apparition of such unworldly creatures as he was seeing at that moment must accompany the moment of transition.

Finally, he heard a voice, saying, "Son of the Republic, look and learn." At the same time, the visitor extended her arm toward the east, and Washington saw what to him appeared like white vapor at some distance. As the vapor dissipated, he saw the various countries of the world and the oceans that separated them. He then noticed a dark, shadowy angel standing between Europe and America, taking water out of the ocean and sprinkling it over America with one hand and over Europe with the other. When he did this, a cloud rose from the countries thus sprinkled, and the cloud then moved westward until it enveloped America. Sharp flashes of lightning became visible at intervals in the cloud. At the same time, Washington thought he heard the anguished cries of the American people underneath the cloud. Next, the strange visitor showed him a vision of what America would look like in the future, and he saw villages and towns springing up from one coast to the other until the entire land was covered by them.

"Son of the Republic, the end of the century cometh, look and learn," the visitor said. Again Washington was shown a dark cloud approaching America, and he saw the American people fighting one another. A bright angel then appeared wearing a crown on which was written the word Union. This angel bore the American Flag, which he placed between the divided nation, saying, "Remember, you are brethren." At that instant, the inhabitants threw away their weapons and became friends again.

Once more the mysterious voice spoke. "Son of the Republic, look and learn." Now the dark angel put a trumpet to his mouth and sounded three distinct blasts. Then he took water from the ocean and sprinkled it on Europe, Asia, and Africa. As he did so, Washington saw black clouds rise from the countries he had sprinkled. Through the black clouds, Washington could see red light and hordes of armed men, marching by land and sailing by sea to America, and he saw these armies devastate the entire country, burn the villages, towns, and cities, and as he lis-

A Revolutionary Corollary:

Patrick Henry, Nathan Hale, et al.

87

tened to the thundering of the cannon, Washington heard the mysterious voice saying again, "Son of the Republic, look and learn."

Once more the dark angel put the trumpet to his mouth and sounded a long and fearful blast. As he did so, a light as of a thousand suns shone down from above him and pierced the dark cloud which had enveloped America. At the same time the angel wearing the word Union on his head descended from the heavens, followed by legions of white spirits. Together with the inhabitants of America, Washington saw them renew the battle and heard the mysterious voice telling him, once again, "Son of the Republic, look and learn."

For the last time, the dark angel dipped water from the ocean and sprinkled it on America; the dark cloud rolled back and left the inhabitants of America victorious. But the vision continued. Once again Washington saw villages, towns, and cities spring up, and he heard the bright angel exclaim, "While the stars remain and the heavens send down dew upon the earth, so long shall the Union last." With that, the scene faded, and Washington beheld once again the mysterious visitor before him. As if she had guessed his question, the apparition then said:

"Son of the Republic, what you have seen is thus interpreted: Three great perils will come upon the Republic. The most fearful is the third, during which the whole world united shall not prevail against her. Let every child of the Republic learn to live for his God, his land, and his Union." With that, the vision disappeared, and Washington was left pondering over his experience.

One can interpret this story in many ways, of course. If it really occurred, and there are a number of accounts of it in existence which lead me believe that there is a basis of fact to this, then we are dealing with a case of prophecy on the part of General Washington. It is a moot question whether the third peril has already come upon us, in the shape of World War II, or whether it is yet to befall us. The light that is stronger than many suns may have ominous meaning in this age of nuclear warfare.

Washington himself is said to have appeared to Senator Calhoun of South Carolina at the beginning of the War between the States. At that time, the question of secession had not been fully decided, and Calhoun, one of the most powerful politicians in the government, was not sure whether he could support the withdrawal of his state from the Union. The question lay heavily on his mind when he went to bed one hot night in Charleston, South Carolina. During the night, he thought he awoke to see the apparition of General George Washington standing by his bedside. The General wore his presidential attire and seemed surrounded by a bright outline, as if some powerful source of light shone behind him. On the senator's desk lay the declaration of secession, which he had not yet signed. With Calhoun's and South Carolina's support, the Confederacy

would be well on its way, having closed ranks. Earnestly, the spirit of George Washington pleaded with Senator Calhoun not to sign the declaration. He warned him against the impending perils coming to America as a divided nation; he asked him to reconsider his decision and to work for the preservation of the Union. But Calhoun insisted that the South had to go its own way. When the spirit of Washington saw that nothing could sway Senator Calhoun, he warned him that the very act of his signature would be a black spot on the Constitution of the United States. With that, the vision is said to have vanished.

One can easily explain the experience as a dream, coming as it did at a time when Senator Calhoun was particularly upset over the implications of his actions. On the other hand, there is this to consider: Shortly after Calhoun had signed the document taking South Carolina into the Confederacy, a dark spot appeared on his hand, a spot that would not vanish and for which medical authorities had no adequate explanation.

* * *

Mrs. Margaret Smith of Orlando, Florida, has had a long history of psychic experiences. She has personally seen the ghostly monks of Beaulieu, England; she has seen the actual lantern of Joe Baldwin, the famous headless ghost of Wilmington, North Carolina; and she takes her "supernatural" experiences in her stride the way other people feel about their musical talents or hobbies. When she was only a young girl, her grandmother took her to visit the von Steuben house in Hackensack, New Jersey. (General F. W. A. von Steuben was a German supporter of the American Revolution who aided General Washington with volunteers who had come over from Europe because of repressions, hoping to find greater freedom in the New World.) The house was old and dusty, the floorboards were creaking, and there was an eerie atmosphere about it. The house had been turned into an historical museum, and there were hostesses to take visitors through.

While her grandmother was chatting with the guide downstairs, the young girl walked up the stairs by herself. In one of the upstairs parlors she saw a man sitting in a chair in the corner. She assumed he was another guide. When she turned around to ask him a question about the room, he was gone. Since she hadn't heard him leave, that seemed rather odd to her, especially as the floorboards would creak with every step. But being young she didn't pay too much attention to this peculiarity. A moment later, however, he reappeared. As soon as she saw him, she asked the question she had on her mind. This time he did not disappear but answered her in a slow, painstaking voice that seemed to come from far away. When he had satisfied her curiosity about the room, he asked her some questions about herself, and finally asked the one which stuck in her mind for many years afterward—"What is General Washington doing now about the British?"

Margaret was taken aback at this question. She was young, but she knew very well that Washington had been dead for many years. Tactfully, she told him this and added that Harry Truman was now president and that the year was 1951. At this information, the man looked stunned and sat down again in the chair. As Margaret watched him in fascinated horror, he faded away.

✳ **8**

The Vindication of Aaron Burr

VERY FEW HISTORICAL figures have suffered as much from their enemies or have been as misunderstood and persistently misrepresented as the onetime Vice-President of the United States, Aaron Burr, whose contributions to American independence are frequently forgotten while his later troubles are made to represent the man.

Burr was a lawyer, a politician who had served in the Revolutionary forces and who later established himself in New York as a candidate of the Democratic-Republican party in the elections of 1796 and 1800. He didn't get elected in 1796, but in 1800 he received exactly as many electoral votes as Thomas Jefferson. When the House of Representatives broke the tie in Jefferson's favor, Burr became Vice-President.

Burr soon realized that Jefferson was his mortal enemy. He found himself isolated from all benefits, such as political patronage, normally accruing to one in his position, and he was left with no political future at the end of his term. Samuel Engle Burr, a descendant of Theodosia Barstow Burr, Aaron's first wife, and the definitive authority on Aaron Burr himself, calls him "the American Phoenix," and truly he was a man who frequently rose from the ashes of a smashed career.

Far from being bitter over the apparent end of his career, Burr resumed his career by becoming an independent candidate for governor of New York. He was defeated, however, by a smear campaign in which both his opponents, the Federalists, and the regular Democratic-Republican party took part.

"Some of the falsehoods and innuendoes contained in this campaign literature," writes Professor Burr in his namesake's biography, "have been repeated as facts down through the years. They have been largely responsible for much of the unwarranted abuse that has been heaped upon him since that time."

Aside from Jefferson, his greatest enemies were the members of the Hamilton-Schuyler family, for in 1791 Burr had replaced Alexander Hamilton's father-in-law, General Philip Schuyler, as the senator from New York. Hamilton himself had been Burr's rival from the days of the Revolutionary War, but the political slurs and statements that had helped to defeat Burr in 1804, and that had been attributed to Hamilton, finally led to the famed duel.

In accepting Burr's challenge, Hamilton shared the illegality of the practice. He had dueled with others before, such as Commodore Nicholson, a New York politician, in 1795. His own son, Philip Hamilton, had died in a duel with New York lawyer George Eacker in 1801. Thus neither party came to Weehawken, New Jersey that chilly July morning in 1804 exactly innocent of the rules of the game.

Many versions have been published as to what happened, but to this day the truth is not clear. Both men fired, and Burr's bullet found its mark. Whether or not the wound was fatal is difficult to assess today. The long voyage back by boat and the primitive status of medicine in 1804 may have been contributing factors to Hamilton's death.

That Alexander Hamilton's spirit was not exactly at rest I proved a few years ago when I investigated the house in New York City where he had spent his last hours after the duel. The house belonged to his physician, but it has been torn down to make room for a modern apartment house. Several tenants have seen the fleeting figure of the late Alexander Hamilton appear in the house and hurry out of sight, as if trying to get someplace fast. I wonder if he is trying to set the record straight, a record that saw his opponent Burr charged with *murder* by the State of New Jersey.

Burr could not overcome the popular condemnation of the duel; Hamilton had suddenly become a martyr, and he, the villain. He decided to leave New York for a while and went to eastern Florida, where he became acquainted with the Spanish colonial system, a subject that interested him very much in his later years. Finally he returned to Washington and resumed his duties as the Vice-President of the United States.

In 1805 he became interested in the possibilities of the newly acquired Louisiana Territory, and tried to interest Jefferson in developing the region around the Ouachita River to establish there still another new state.

Jefferson turned him down, and finally Burr organized his own expedition. Everywhere he went in the West he was cordially received. War with Spain was in the air, and Burr felt the United States should prepare for it and, at the right time, expand its frontiers westward.

Since the government had given him the cold shoulder, Burr decided to recruit a group of adventurous colonists to join him in establishing a new state in Louisiana Territory and await the outbreak of the war he felt was sure to come soon. He purchased four hundred thousand acres of land in the area close to the Spanish-American frontier and planned on establishing there his dream state, to be called Burrsylvania.

In the course of his plans, Burr had worked with one General James Wilkinson, then civil governor of Louisiana Territory and a man he had known since the Revolutionary War. Unfortunately Burr did not know that Wilkinson was actually a double agent, working for both Washington and the Spanish government.

In order to bolster his position with the Jefferson government, Wilkinson suggested to the President that Burr's activities could be considered treasonable. The immediate step taken by Wilkinson was to alter one of Burr's coded letters to him in such a way that Burr's statement could be used against him. He sent the document along with an alarming report of his own to Jefferson in July of 1806.

Meanwhile, unaware of the conspiracy against his expedition, Burr's colonists arrived in the area around Natchez, when a presidential proclamation issued by Jefferson accused him of treason. Despite an acquittal by the territorial government of Mississippi, Washington sent orders to seize him.

Burr, having no intention of becoming an insurrectionist, disbanded the remnants of his colonists and returned east. On the way he was arrested and taken to Richmond for trial. The treason trial itself was larded with paid false witnesses, and even Wilkinson admitted having forged the letter that had served as the basis for the government's case. The verdict was "not guilty," but the public, inflamed against him by the all-powerful Jefferson political machine, kept condemning Aaron Burr.

Under the circumstances, Burr decided to go to Europe. He spent the four years from 1808 to 1812 traveling abroad, eventually returning to New York, where he reopened his law practice with excellent results.

The disappearance at sea the following year of his only daughter Theodosia, to whom he had been extremely close, shattered him; his political ambitions vanished, and he devoted the rest of his life to an increasingly successful legal practice. In 1833 he married for the second time—his first wife, Theodosia's mother, also called Theodosia, having died in 1794. The bride was the widow of a French wine merchant named Stephen Jumel, who had left Betsy Jumel a rich woman indeed. It was a stormy marriage, and ultimately Mrs. Burr sued for divorce. This was granted on the 14th of September 1836, the very day Aaron Burr died. Betsy never considered herself anything but the *widow* of the onetime Vice-President, and she continued to sign all documents as Eliza B. Burr.

Burr had spent his last years in an apartment at Port Richmond, Staten Island, overlooking New York Harbor. His body was laid to rest at Princeton, the president of

which for many years had been Burr's late father, the Reverend Aaron Burr.

I had not been familiar with any of this until after the exciting events of June 1967, when I was able to make contact with the person of Aaron Burr through psychic channels.

My first encounter with the name Aaron Burr came in December of 1961. I was then actively investigating various haunted houses in and around New York City as part of a study grant by the Parapsychology Foundation. My reports later grew into a popular book called *Ghost Hunter*.

One day a publicist named Richard Mardus called my attention to a nightclub on West Third Street doing business as the Cafe Bizarre. Mr. Mardus was and is an expert on Greenwich Village history and lore, and he pointed out to me that the club was actually built into remodeled stables that had once formed part of Richmond Hill, Aaron Burr's estate in New York City. At the time of Burr's occupancy this was farmland and pretty far uptown, as New York City went.

But Mardus did not call to give me historical news only: Psychic occurrences had indeed been observed at the Burr stables, and he asked me to look into the matter. I went down to have a look at the edifice. It is located on a busy side street in the nightclub belt of New York, where after dark the curious and the tourists gather to spend an evening of informal fun. In the daytime, the street looks ugly and ordinary, but after dark it seems to sparkle with an excitement of its own.

The Cafe Bizarre stood out by its garish decor and posters outside the entrance, but the old building housing it, three stories high, was a typical nineteenth-century stone building, well preserved and showing no sign of replacement of the original materials.

Inside, the place had been decorated by a nightmarish array of paraphernalia to suggest the bizarre, ranging from store dummy arms to devil's masks, and colorful lights played on this melee of odd objects suspended from the high ceiling. In the rear of the long room was a stage, to the left of which a staircase led up to the loft; another staircase was in back of the stage, since a hayloft had occupied the rear portion of the building. Sawdust covered the floor, and perhaps three dozen assorted tables filled the room.

It was late afternoon and the atmosphere of the place was cold and empty, but the feeling was nevertheless that of the unusual—uncanny, somehow. I was met by a pretty, dark-haired young woman, who turned out to be the owner's wife, Mrs. Renée Allmen. She welcomed me to the Cafe Bizarre and explained that her husband, Rick, was not exactly a believer in such things as the psychic, but that she herself had indeed had unusual experiences here. On my request, she gave me a written statement testifying about her experiences.

In the early morning of July 27, 1961, at 2:20 A.M., she and her husband were locking up for the night. They walked out to their car when Mrs. Allmen remembered that she had forgotten a package inside. Rushing back to the cafe, she unlocked the doors again and entered the deserted building. She turned on the lights and walked toward the kitchen, which is about a third of the way toward the rear of the place. The cafe was quite empty, and yet she had an eerie sensation of not being alone. She hurriedly picked up her package and walked toward the front door again. Glancing backward into the dark recesses of the cafe, she then saw the apparition of a man, staring at her with piercing black eyes. He wore an antique ruffled shirt and seemed to smile at her when she called out to him, "Who is it?"

But the figure never moved or reacted.

"What are you doing here?" Renée demanded, all the while looking at the apparition.

There was no answer, and suddenly Renée's courage left her. Running back to the front door, she summoned her husband from the car, and together they returned to the cafe. Again unlocking the door, which Renée had shut behind her when she fled from the specter, they discovered the place to be quite empty. In the usual husbandly fashion, Mr. Allmen tried to pass it off as a case of nerves or tired eyes, but his wife would not buy it. She knew what she had seen, and it haunted her for many years to come.

Actually, she was not the first one to see the gentleman in the white ruffled shirt with the piercing black eyes. One of their waiters also had seen the ghost and promptly quit. The Village was lively enough without psychic phenomena, and how much does a ghost tip?

I looked over the stage and the area to the left near the old stairs to see whether any reflecting surface might be blamed for the ghostly apparition. There was nothing of the sort, nothing to reflect light. Besides, the lights had been off in the rear section, and those in the front were far too low to be seen anywhere but in the immediate vicinity of the door.

Under the circumstances I decided to arrange for a visit with psychic Ethel Johnson Meyers to probe further into this case. This expedition took place on January 8, 1962, and several observers from the press were also present.

The first thing Mrs. Meyers said, while in trance, was that she saw three people in the place, psychically speaking. In particular she was impressed with an older man with penetrating dark eyes, who was the owner. The year, she felt, was 1804. In addition, she described a previous owner named Samuel Bottomslee, and spoke of some of the family troubles this man had allegedly had in his lifetime. She also mentioned that the house once stood back from the road, when the road passed farther away than it does today. This I found to be correct.

"I'm an Englishman and I have my rights here," the spirit speaking through Mrs. Meyers thundered, as we sat spellbound. Later I found out that the property had belonged to an Englishman before it passed into Burr's hands.

The drama that developed as the medium spoke haltingly did not concern Aaron Burr, but the earlier settlers. Family squabbles involving Samuel's son Alan, and a girl named Catherine, and a description of the building as a stable, where harness was kept, poured from Ethel's lips. From its looks, she could not have known consciously that this was once a stable.

The period covered extended from 1775 to 1804, when another personality seemed to take over, identifying himself as one John Bottomsley. There was some talk about a deed, and I gathered that all was not as it should have been. It seemed that the place had been sold, but that the descendants of Samuel Bottomslee didn't acknowledge this too readily.

Through all this the initials A.B. were given as prominently connected with the spot.

I checked out the facts afterward; Aaron Burr's Richmond Hill estate had included these stables since 1797. Before that the area belonged to various British colonials.

When I wrote the account of this séance in my book *Ghost Hunter* in 1963, I thought I had done with it. And I had, except for an occasional glance at the place whenever I passed it, wondering whether the man with the dark, piercing eyes was really Aaron Burr.

Burr's name came to my attention again in 1964 when I investigated the strange psychic phenomena at the Morris-Jumel Mansion in Washington Heights, where Burr had lived during the final years of his life as the second husband of Mme. Betsy Jumel. But the spectral manifestations at the Revolutionary house turned out to be the restless shades of Mme. Jumel herself and that of her late first husband, accusing his wife of having murdered him.

* * *

One day in January 1967 I received a note from a young lady named Alice McDermott. It concerned some strange experiences of hers at the Cafe Bizarre—the kind one doesn't expect at even so oddly decorated a place. Miss McDermott requested an interview, and on February 4 of the same year I talked to her in the presence of a friend.

She had been "down to the Village" for several years as part of her social life—she was now twenty—and visited the Bizarre for the first time in 1964. She had felt strange, but could not quite pinpoint her apprehension.

"I had a feeling there was *something* there, but I let it pass, thinking it must be my imagination. But there was something on the balcony over the stage that seemed to stare down at me—I mean something besides the dummy suspended from the ceiling as part of the decor."

At the time, when Alice was sixteen, she had not yet heard of me or my books, but she had had some ESP experiences involving premonitions and flashes of a psychic nature.

* * *

Alice, an only child, works as a secretary in Manhattan. Her father is a barge officer and her mother an accountant. She is a very pretty blonde with a sharp mind and a will of her own. Persuaded to try to become a nun, she spent three months in a Long Island convent, only to discover that the religious life was not for her. She then returned to New York and took a job as a secretary in a large business firm.

After she left the convent she continued her studies also, especially French. She studied with a teacher in Washington Square, and often passed the Cafe Bizarre on her way. Whenever she did, the old feeling of something uncanny inside came back. She did not enter the place, but walked on hurriedly.

But on one occasion she stopped, and something within her made her say, "Whoever you are in there, you must be lonely!" She did not enter the place despite a strong feeling that "someone wanted to say hello to her" inside. But that same night, she had a vivid dream. A man was standing on the stage, and she could see him clearly. He was of medium height, and wore beige pants and black riding boots. His white shirt with a kind of Peter Pan collar fascinated her because it did not look like the shirts men wear today. It had puffy sleeves. The man also had a goatee, that is, a short beard, and a mustache.

"He didn't look dressed in today's fashion, then?"

"Definitely not, unless he was a new rock 'n' roll star." But the most remarkable features of this man were his dark, piercing eyes, she explained. He just stood there with his hands on his hips, looking at Alice. She became frightened when the man kept looking at her, and walked outside.

That was the end of this dream experience, but the night before she spoke to me, he reappeared in a dream. This time she was speaking with him in French, and also to a lady who was with him. The lady wore glasses, had a pointed nose, and had a shawl wrapped around her—"Oh, and a plain gold band on her finger."

The lady also wore a Dutch type white cap, Alice reported. I was fascinated, for she had described Betsy Jumel in her old age—yet how could she connect the ghostly owner of Jumel Mansion with her Cafe Bizarre experience? She could not have known the connection, and yet it fit perfectly. Both Burr and Betsy Jumel spoke French fluently, and often made use of that language.

"Would you be able to identify her if I showed you a picture?" I asked.

"If it were she," Alice replied, hesitatingly.

I took out a photograph of a painting hanging at Jumel Mansion, which shows Mme. Jumel in old age.

I did not identify her by name, merely explaining it was a painting of a group of people I wanted her to look at.

"This is the lady," Alice said firmly, "but she is younger looking in the picture than when I saw her."

What was the conversation all about? I wanted to know.

Apparently the spirit of Mme. Jumel was pleading with her on behalf of Burr, who was standing by and watching the scene, to get in touch with *me!* I asked Alice, who wants to be a commercial artist, to draw a picture of what she saw. Later, I compared the portrait with known pictures of Aaron Burr. The eyes, eyebrows, and forehead did indeed resemble the Burr portraits. But the goatee was not known.

After my initial meeting with Alice McDermott, she wrote to me again. The dreams in which Burr appeared to her were getting more and more lively, and she wanted to go on record with the information thus received. According to her, Aaron poured his heart out to the young girl, incredible though this seemed on the face of it.

The gist of it was a request to go to "the white house in the country" and find certain papers in a metal box. "This will prove my innocence. I am not guilty of treason. There is written proof. Written October 18, 1802 or 1803." The message was specific enough, but the papers of course were long since gone.

The white house in the country would be the Jumel Mansion.

I thanked Alice and decided to hold another investigation at the site of the Cafe Bizarre, since the restless spirit of the late Vice-President of the United States had evidently decided to be heard once more.

At the same time I was approached by Mel Bailey of Metromedia Television to produce a documentary about New York haunted houses, and I decided to combine these efforts and investigate the Burr stables in the full glare of television cameras.

On June 12, 1967 I brought Sybil Leek down to the Bizarre, having flown her in from California two days before. Mrs. Leek had no way of knowing what was expected of her, or where she would be taken. Nevertheless, as early as June 1, when I saw her in Hollywood, she had remarked to me spontaneously that she "knew" the place I would take her to on our next expedition—then only a possibility—and she described it in detail. On June 9, after her arrival in New York, she telephoned and again gave me her impressions.

"I sense music and laughter and drumbeat," she began, and what better is there to describe the atmosphere at the Cafe Bizarre these nights? "It is a three-story place, not a house but selling something; two doors opening, go to the right-hand side of the room and something is raised up from the floor, where the drumbeat is."

Entirely correct; the two doors lead into the elongated room, with the raised stage at the end.

"Three people...one has a shaped beard, aquiline nose, he is on the raised part of the floor; very dark around the eyes, an elegant man, lean, and there are two other people near him, one of whom has a name starting with a Th...."

In retrospect one must marvel at the accuracy of the description, for surely Sybil Leek had no knowledge of either the place, its connection with Burr, nor the description given by the other witnesses of the man they had seen there.

This was a brief description of her first impressions given to me on the telephone. The following day I received a written account of her nocturnal impressions from Mrs. Leek. This was still two days *before* she set foot onto the premises!

In her statement, Mrs. Leek mentioned that she could not go off to sleep late that night, and fell into a state of semiconsciousness, with a small light burning near her bed. Gradually she became aware of the smell of fire, or rather the peculiar smell when a gun has just been fired. At the same time she felt an acute pain, as if she had been wounded in the left side of the back.

Trying to shake off the impression, Mrs. Leek started to do some work at her typewriter, but the presence persisted. It seemed to her as if a voice was trying to reach her, a voice speaking a foreign language and calling out a name, Theo.

I questioned Mrs. Leek about the foreign language she heard spoken clairvoyantly.

"I had a feeling it was French," she said.

Finally she had drifted into deeper sleep. But by Saturday afternoon the feeling of urgency returned. This time she felt as if someone wanted her to go down to the river, not the area where I live (uptown), but "a long way the other way," which is precisely where the Burr stables were situated.

* * *

Finally the big moment had arrived. It was June 12, and the television crews had been at work all morning in and around the Cafe Bizarre to set up cameras and sound equipment so that the investigation could be recorded without either hitch or interruption. We had two cameras taking turns, to eliminate the need for reloading. The central area beneath the "haunted stage" was to be our setting, and the place was reasonably well lit, certainly brighter than it normally is when the customers are there at night.

Everything had been meticulously prepared. My wife Catherine was to drive our white Citroën down to the Bizarre with Sybil at her side. Promptly at 3 P.M. the car arrived, Sybil Leek jumped out and was greeted at the outer door by me, while our director, Art Forrest, gave the signal for the cameras to start. "Welcome to the Cafe Bizarre," I intoned and led my psychic friend into the semidark inside. Only the central section was brightly lit.

I asked her to walk about the place and gather impressions at will.

"I'm going to those drums over there," Sybil said firmly, and walked toward the rear stage as if she knew the way.

"Yes—this is the part. I feel cold. Even though I have not been here physically, *I know this place.*"

"What do we have to do here, do you think?" I asked.

"I think we have to relieve somebody, somebody who's waited a long time."

"Where is this feeling strongest?"

"In the rear, where this extra part seems to be put on."

Sybil could not know this, but an addition to the building was made years after the original had been constructed, and it was precisely in that part that we were now standing.

She explained that there was more than one person involved, but one in particular was dominant; that this was something from the past, going back into another century. I then asked her to take a chair, and Mrs. Renée Allmen and my wife Catherine joined us around a small table.

This was going to be a séance, and Sybil was in deep trance within a matter of perhaps five minutes, since she and I were well in tune with one another, and it required merely a signal on my part to allow her to "slip out."

At first there was a tossing of the head, the way a person moves when sleep is fitful.

Gradually, the face changed its expression to that of a man, a stern face, perhaps even a suspicious face. The hissing sound emanating from her tightly closed lips gradually changed into something almost audible, but I still could not make it out.

Patiently, as the cameras ground away precious color film, I asked "whoever it might be" to speak louder and to communicate through the instrument of Mrs. Leek.

"Theo!" the voice said now. It wasn't at all like Sybil's own voice.

"Theo...I'm lost...where am I?" I explained that this was the body of another person and that we were in a house in New York City.

"Where's Theo?" the voice demanded with greater urgency. "Who are you?"

I explained my role as a friend, hoping to establish contact through the psychic services of Mrs. Leek, then in turn asked who the communicator was. Since he had called out for Theo, he was not Theo, as I had first thought.

"Bertram Delmar. I want Theo," came the reply.

"Why do you want Theo?"

"Lost."

Despite extensive research I was not able to prove that Bertram Delmar ever existed or that this was one of the cover names used by Aaron Burr; but it is possible that

The Cafe Bizarre—once Aaron Burr's stables

he did, for Burr was given to the use of code names during his political career and in sensitive correspondence.

What was far more important was the immediate call for Theo, and the statement that she was "lost." Theodosia Burr was Burr's only daughter and truly the apple of his eye. When she was lost at sea on her way to join him, in 1813, he became a broken man. Nothing in the up-and-down life of the American Phoenix was as hard a blow of fate than the loss of his beloved Theo.

The form "Theo," incidentally, rather than the full name Theodosia, is attested to by the private correspondence between Theodosia and her husband, Joseph Alston, governor of South Carolina. In a rare moment of foreboding, she had hinted that she might soon die. This letter was written six months before her disappearance in a storm at sea and was signed, "Your wife, your fond wife, Theo."

After the séance, I asked Dr. Samuel Engle Burr whether there was any chance that the name Theo might apply to some other woman.

Dr. Burr pointed out that the Christian name Theodosia occurred in modern times only in the Burr family. It was derived from Theodosius Bartow, father of Aaron

Burr's first wife, who was mother of the girl lost at sea. The mother had been Theodosia the elder, after her father, and the Burrs had given their only daughter the same unusual name.

After her mother's passing in 1794, the daughter became her father's official hostess and truly "the woman in the house." More than that, she was his confidante and shared his thoughts a great deal more than many other daughters might have. Even after her marriage to Alston and subsequent move to South Carolina, they kept in touch, and her family was really all the family he had. Thus their relationship was a truly close one, and it is not surprising that the first thought, after his "return from the dead," so to speak, would be to cry out for his Theo!

I wasn't satisfied with his identification as "Bertram Delmar," and insisted on his real name. But the communicator brushed my request aside and instead spoke of another matter.

"Where's the gun?"

"What gun?"

I recalled Sybil's remark about the smell of a gun having just been fired. I had to know more.

"What are you doing here?"

"Hiding."

"What are you hiding from?"

"You."

Was he mistaking me for someone else?

"I'm a friend," I tried to explain, but the voice interrupted me harshly.

"You're a soldier."

In retrospect one cannot help feeling that the emotionally disturbed personality was reliving the agony of being hunted down by U.S. soldiers prior to his arrest, confusing it, perhaps, in his mind with still another unpleasant episode when he was being hunted, namely, after he had shot Hamilton!

I decided to pry farther into his personal life in order to establish identity more firmly.

"Who is Theo? What is she to you?"

"I have to find her, take her away . . . it is dangerous, the French are looking for me."

"Why would the French be looking for you?" I asked in genuine astonishment. Neither I nor Mrs. Leek had any notion of this French connection at that time.

"Soldiers watch. . . ."

Through later research I learned that Burr had indeed been in France for several years, from 1808 to 1812. At first, his desire to have the Spanish American colonies freed met with approval by the then still revolutionary Bonaparte government. But when Napoleon's brother Joseph Napoleon was installed as King of Spain, and thus also ruler of the overseas territories, the matter became a political horse of another color; now Burr was advocating the overthrow of a French-owned government, and that could no longer be permitted.

Under the circumstances, Burr saw no point in staying in France, and made arrangements to go back to New York. But he soon discovered that the French government wouldn't let him go so easily. "All sorts of technical difficulties were put in his way," writes Dr. Samuel Engle Burr, "both the French and the American officials were in agreement to the effect that the best place for the former Vice-President was within the Empire of France." Eventually, a friendly nobleman very close to Napoleon himself managed to get Burr out. But it is clear that Burr was under surveillance all that time and probably well aware of it!

I continued my questioning of the entity speaking through an entranced Sybil Leek, the entity who had glibly claimed to be a certain Bertram Delmar, but who knew so many things only Aaron Burr would have known.

What year was this, I asked.

"Eighteen ten."

In 1810, Burr had just reached France. The date fit in well with the narrative of soldiers watching him.

"Why are you frightened?" I asked.

"The soldiers, the soldiers...."

"Have you done anything wrong?"

"Who are you?"

"I'm a friend, sent to help you!"

"Traitor! You...you betrayed me...."

"Tell me what you are doing, what are you trying to establish here?"

"Traitor!"

Later, as I delved into Burr's history in detail, I thought that this exchange between an angry spirit and a cool interrogator might refer to Burr's anger at General James Wilkinson, who had indeed posed as a friend and then betrayed Burr. Not the "friend" ostensibly helping Burr set up his western colony, but the traitor who later caused soldiers to be sent to arrest him. It certainly fit the situation. One must understand that in the confused mental state a newly contacted spirit personality often finds himself, events in his life take on a jumbled and fragmentary quality, often flashing on the inner mental screen like so many disconnected images from the emotional reel of his life. It is then the job of the psychic researcher to sort it all out.

*   *   *

I asked the communicator to "tell me all about himself" in the hope of finding some other wedge to get him to admit he was Aaron Burr.

"I escaped...from the French."

"Where are the French?"

"Here."

This particular "scene" was apparently being reenacted in his mind, during the period he lived in France.

"Did you escape from any particular French person?" I asked.

"Jacques...de la Beau...."

The spelling is mine. It might have been different, but it sounded like "de la Beau."

"Who is Jacques de la Beau?"

Clenched teeth, hissing voice—"I'm...not...telling you. Even...if you...kill me."

I explained I had come to free him, and what could I do for him?

"Take Theo away...leave me...I shall die...."

Again I questioned him about his identity. Now he switched his account and insisted he was French, born at a place called Dasney near Bordeaux. Even while this information was coming from the medium's lips, I felt sure it was a way to throw me off his real identity. This is not unusual in some cases. When I investigated the ghost of General Samuel Edward McGowan some years ago, it took several weeks of trance sessions until he abandoned an assumed name and admitted an identity that could later be proven. Even the discarnates have their pride and emotional "hangups."

The name Jacques de la Beau puzzled me. After the séance, I looked into the matter and discovered that a certain Jacques Prevost (pronounced pre-voh) had been first husband of Aaron Burr's first wife, Theodosia. Burr, in fact, raised their two sons as his own, and there was a close link between them and Burr in later years. But despite his French name, Prevost was in the British service.

*   *   *

When Burr lived in New York, he had opened his home to the daughter of a French admiral, from whom she had become separated as a consequence of the French Revolution. This girl, Natalie, became the close companion of Burr's daughter Theodosia, and the two girls considered themselves sisters. Natalie's father was Admiral de Lage de Volade. This name, too, has sounds similar to the "de la Beau" I thought I had understood. It might have been "de la voh" or anything in between the two sounds. Could the confused mind of the communicator have drawn from both Prevost and de Lage de Volade? Both names were of importance in Burr's life.

"Tell me about your wife," I demanded now.

"No. I don't like her."

I insisted, and he, equally stubborn, refused.

"Is she with you?" I finally said.

"Got rid of her," he said, almost with joy in the voice.

"Why?"

"No good to me...deceived me...married...."

There was real disdain and anger in the voice now.

Clearly, the communicator was speaking of the second Mrs. Burr. The first wife had passed away a long time before the major events in his life occurred. It is perfectly true that Burr "got rid of her" (through two separations and one divorce action), and that she "deceived him," or rather tricked him into marrying her: He thought she was wealthier than she actually was, and their main difficulties were about money. In those days people did not always marry for love, and it was considered less immoral to have married someone for money than to deceive someone into marrying by the prospects of large holdings when they were in fact small. Perhaps today we think differently and even more romantically about such matters; in the 1830s, a woman's financial standing was as negotiable as a bank account.

*   *   *

The more I probed, the more excited the communicator became; the more I insisted on identification, the more cries of "Theo! Theo!" came from the lips of Sybil Leek.

When I had first broached the subject of Theo's relationship to him, he had quickly said she was his sister. I brought this up again, and in sobbing tones he admitted this was not true. But he was not yet ready to give me the full story.

"Let me go," he sobbed.

"Not until you can go in peace," I insisted. "Tell me about yourself. You are proud of yourself, are you not?"

"Yes," the voice came amid heavy sobbing, "the disgrace...the disgrace...."

"I will tell the world what you want me to say. I'm here as your spokesman. Use this chance to tell the world your side of the facts!"

There was a moment of hesitation, then the voice, gentler started up again.

"I...loved...Theo....I have to...find her...."

The most important thought, evidently, was the loss of his girl. Even his political ambitions took a back seat to his paternal love.

"Is this place we're in part of your property?"

Forlornly, the voice said,

"I had...a lot...from the river...to here."

Later I checked this statement with Mrs. Leroy Campbell, curator of the Morris-Jumel mansion, and a professional historian who knew the period well.

"Yes, this is true," Mrs. Campbell confirmed, "Burr's property extended from the river and Varick Street eastward."

"But the lot from the river to here does not belong to a Bertram Delmar," I said to the communicator. "Why do you wish to fool me with names that do not exist?"

I launched this as a trial balloon. It took off.

"She *calls me* Bertram," the communicator admitted now. "I'm not ashamed of my name."

I nodded. "I'm here to help you right old wrongs, but you must help me do this. I can't do it alone."

"I didn't kill...got rid of her...." he added, apparently willing to talk.

"You mean, your wife?"

"Had to."

"Did you kill *anyone?*" I continued the line of discussion.

"Killed...to protect...not wrong!"

"How did you kill?"

"A rifle...."

Was he perhaps referring to his service in the Revolutionary War? He certainly did some shooting then.

But I decided to return to the "Bertram Delmar" business once more. Constant pressure might yield results.

"Truthfully, will you tell us who you are?"

Deliberately, almost as if he were reading an official communiqué, the voice replied, "I am Bertram Delmar and I shall not say *that* name...."

"You must say 'that name' if you wish to see Theo again." I had put it on the line. Either cooperate with me, or I won't help you. Sometimes this is the only way you can get a recalcitrant spirit to "come across"—when this cooperation is essential both to his welfare and liberation and to the kind of objective proof required in science.

There was a moment of ominous quiet. Then, almost inaudibly, the communicator spoke.

"An awful name...*Arnot.*"

After the investigation I played the sound tapes back to make sure of what I had heard so faintly. It was quite clear. The communicator had said "*Arnot.*"

My first reaction was, perhaps he is trying to say Aaron Burr and pronounce Aaron with a broad ah. But on checking this out with both Mrs. Campbell and Dr. Burr I found that such a pronunciation was quite impossible. The night after the séance I telephoned Dr. Burr at his Washington home and read the salient points of the transcript to him.

When I came to the puzzling name given by the communicator I asked whether Arnot meant anything, inasmuch as I could not find it in the published biographies of Burr. There was a moment of silence on the other end of the line before Dr. Burr spoke.

"Quite so," he began. "It is not really generally known, but Burr did use a French cover name while returning from France to the United States, in order to avoid publicity. *That name was Arnot.*"

But back to the Cafe Bizarre and our investigation.

Having not yet realized the importance of the word Arnot, I continued to insist on proper identification.

"You must cleanse yourself of ancient guilt," I prodded.

"It is awful...awful...."

"Is Theo related to you?"

"She's mine."

"Are you related to her?"

"Lovely...little one...*daughter.*"

Finally, the true relationship had come to light.

"If Theo is your daughter, then you are not 'Bertram.'"

"You tricked me . . . go away . . . or else I'll kill you!"

The voice sounded full of anger again.

"If you're not ashamed of your name, then I want to hear it from your lips."

Again, hesitatingly, the voice said,

"*Arnot.*"

"Many years have gone by. Do you know what year we're in now?"

"Ten. . . ."

"It is not 1810. A hundred fifty years have gone by."

"You're mad."

"You're using the body of a psychic to speak to us. . . ."

The communicator had no use for such outrageous claims.

"I'm not going to listen. . . ."

But I made him listen. I told him to touch the hair, face, ears of the "body" he was using as a channel and to see if it didn't feel strange indeed.

Step by step, the figure of Sybil, very tensed and angry a moment before, relaxed. When the hand found its way to the chin, there was a moment of startled expression:

"No beard. . . ."

I later found that not a single one of the contemporary portraits of Aaron Burr shows him with a chin beard. Nevertheless, Alice McDermott had seen and drawn him with a goatee, and now Sybil Leek, under the control of the alleged Burr, also felt for the beard that was not there any longer.

Was there ever a beard?

"Yes," Dr. Burr confirmed, "there was, although this, too, is almost unknown except of course to specialists like myself. On his return from France, in 1812, Burr sported a goatee in the French manner."

* * *

By now I had finally gotten through to the person speaking through Sybil Leek, that the year was 1967 and not 1810.

His resistance to me crumbled.

"You're a strange person," he said, "I'm tired."

"Why do you hide behind a fictitious name?"

"People . . . ask . . . too many . . . questions."

"Will you help me clear your name, not Bertram, but your real name?"

"I was betrayed."

"Who is the President of the United States in 1810?" I asked and regretted it immediately. Obviously this could not be an evidential answer. But the communicator wouldn't mention the hated name of the rival.

"And who is Vice-President?" I asked.

"Politics . . . are bad . . . they kill you . . . I would not betray anyone. . . . I was wronged . . . politics . . . are bad. . . ."

How true!

"Did you ever kill anyone?" I demanded.

"Not wrong . . . to kill to . . . preserve. . . . I'm alone."

He hesitated to continue.

"What did you preserve? Why did you have to kill another person?"

"*Another* . . . critical . . . I'm not talking!"

"You must talk. It is necessary for posterity."

"I tried . . . to be . . . *the best.* . . . I'm not a traitor . . . soldiers . . . beat the drum . . . then you die . . . politics!!"

As I later listened to this statement again and again, I understood the significance of it, coming, as it did, from a person who had not yet admitted he was Aaron Burr and through a medium who didn't even know *where* she was at the time.

* * *

He killed to *preserve his honor*—the accusations made against him in the campaign of 1804 for the governorship of New York were such that they could not be left unchallenged. Another was indeed *critical* of him, Alexander Hamilton being that person, and the criticisms such that Burr could not let them pass.

He "tried to the best" also—tried to be President of the United States, got the required number of electoral votes in 1800, but deferred to Jefferson, who also had the same number.

No, he was not a traitor, despite continued inference in some history books that he was. The treason trial of 1807 not only exonerated the former Vice-President of any wrongdoing, but heaped scorn and condemnation on those who had tried him. The soldiers beating the drum prior to an execution *could* have become reality if Burr's enemies had won; the treason incident under which he was seized by soldiers on his return from the West included the death penalty if found guilty. That was the intent of his political enemies, to have this ambitious man removed forever from the political scene.

"Will you tell the world that you are not guilty?" I asked.

"I told them . . . trial . . . I am not a traitor, a murderer. . . ."

I felt it important for him to free himself of such thoughts if he were to be released from his earthbound status.

"I . . . want to die . . ." the voice said, breathing heavily.

"Come, I will help you find Theo," I said, as promised.

But there was still the matter of the name. I felt it would help "clear the atmosphere" if I could get him to admit he was Burr.

I had already gotten a great deal of material, and the séance would be over in a matter of moments. I decided to gamble on the last minute or two and try to shock this entity into either admitting he was Burr or reacting to the name in some telling fashion.

I had failed in having him speak those words even though he had given us many incidents from the life of Aaron Burr. There was only one more way and I took it. "Tell the truth," I said, "are you Aaron Burr?"

It was as if I had stuck a red hot poker into his face. The medium reeled back, almost upsetting the chair in which she sat. With a roar like a wounded lion, the voice came back at me,

"Go away...GO AWAY!!...or I'll kill you!"

"You will not kill me," I replied calmly. "You will tell me the truth."

"I will kill you to preserve my honor!!"

"*I'm* here to preserve your honor. I'm your friend."

The voice was like cutting ice.

"You said that once before."

"You are Aaron Burr, and this is part of your place."

"I'M BERTRAM!"

I did not wish to continue the shouting match.

"Very well," I said, "for the world, then, let it be Bertram, if you're not ready to face it that you're Burr."

"I'm Bertram..." the entity whispered now.

"Then go from this place and join your Theo. Be Bertram for her."

"Bertram...you won't tell?" The voice was pleading.

"Very well." He would soon slip across the veil, I felt, and there were a couple of points I wanted to clear up first. I explained that he would soon be together with his daughter, leaving here after all this time, and I told him again how much time had elapsed since his death.

"I tarried...I tarried..." he said, pensively.

"What sort of a place did you have?" I asked.

"It was a big place...with a big desk...famous house...." But he could not recall its name.

Afterward, I checked the statement with Mrs. Campbell, the curator at the Morris-Jumel mansion. "That desk in the big house," she explained," is right here in our Burr room. It was originally in his law office." But the restless one was no longer interested in talking to me.

"I'm talking to Theo..." he said, quietly now, "in the garden....I'm going for a walk with Theo...go away."

Within a moment, the personality who had spoken through Sybil Leek for the past hour was gone. Instead, Mrs. Leek returned to her own self, remembering absolutely nothing that had come through her entranced lips.

"Lights are bright," was the first thing she said, and she quickly closed her eyes again.

But a moment later, she awoke fully and complained only that she felt a bit tired.

I wasn't at all surprised that she did.

*   *   *

Almost immediately after I had returned home, I started my corroboration. After discussing the most important points with Dr. Samuel Engle Burr over the telephone, I arranged to have a full transcript of the séance sent to him for his comments.

So many things matched the Burr personality that there could hardly be any doubt that it *was* Burr we had contacted. "I'm not a traitor and a murderer," the ghostly communicator had shouted. "Traitor and murderer" were the epithets thrown at Burr in his own lifetime by his enemies, according to Professor Burr, as quoted by Larry Chamblin in the Allentown *Call-Chronicle*.

Although he is not a direct descendant of Aaron Burr, the Washington educator is related to Theodosia Barstow Burr, the Vice-President's first wife. A much-decorated officer in both world wars, Professor Burr is a recognized educator and the definitive authority on his famous namesake. In consulting him, I was getting the best possible information.

Aaron Burr's interest in Mexico, Professor Burr explained, was that of a liberator from Spanish rule, but there never was any conspiracy against the United States government. "That charge stemmed from a minor incident on an island in Ohio. A laborer among his colonists pointed a rifle at a government man who had come to investigate the expedition."

Suddenly, the words about the rifle and the concern the communicator had shown about it became clear to me: It had led to more serious trouble for Burr.

Even President Wilson concurred with those who felt Aaron Burr had been given a "raw deal" by historical tradition. Many years ago he stood at Burr's grave in Princeton and remarked, "How misunderstood...how maligned!"

It is now 132 years since Burr's burial, and the falsehoods concerning Aaron Burr are still about the land, despite the two excellent books by Dr. Samuel Engle Burr and the discreet but valiant efforts of the Aaron Burr Association, which the Washington professor heads.

In piecing together the many evidential bits and pieces of the trance session, it was clear to me that Aaron Burr had at last said his piece. Why had he not pronounced a name he had been justly proud of in his lifetime? He had not hesitated to call repeatedly for Theo, identify her as his daughter, speak of his troubles in France and of his political career—why this insistence to remain the fictitious Bertram Delmar in the face of so much proof that he was indeed Aaron Burr?

All the later years of his life, Burr had encountered hostility, and he had learned to be careful whom he chose as friends, whom he could trust. Gradually, this bitterness became so strong that in his declining years he felt himself to be a lonely, abandoned old man, his only daughter gone forever, and no one to help him carry the heavy burden of his life. Passing across into the nonphysical side of life in such a state of mind, and retaining it by that strange quirk of fate that makes some men into ghostly images of their former selves, he would not abandon that one remaining line of defense against his fellow men: his anonymity.

Why should he confide in me, a total stranger, whom he had never met before, a man, moreover, who spoke to him under highly unusual conditions, conditions he himself neither understood nor accepted? It seemed almost natural for Burr's surviving personality to be cautious in admitting his identity.

But this ardent desire to find Theo was stronger than his caution; we therefore were able to converse more or less freely about this part of his life. And so long as he needed not say he was Burr, he felt it safe to speak of his career also, especially when my questions drove him to anger, and thus lessened his critical judgment as to what he could say and what he should withhold from me.

Ghosts are people, too, and they are subject to the same emotional limitations and rules that govern us all.

Mrs. Leek had no way of obtaining the private, specific knowledge and information that had come from her entranced lips in this investigation; I myself had almost

none of it until after the séance had ended, and thus could not have furnished her any of the material from my own unconscious mind. And the others present during the séance—my wife, Mrs. Allmen, and the television people—knew even less about all this.

Neither Dr. Burr nor Mrs. Campbell were present at the Cafe Bizarre, and their minds, if they contained any of the Burr information, could not have been tapped by the medium either, if such were indeed possible.

Coincidence cannot be held to account for such rare pieces of information as Burr's cover name Arnot, the date, the goatee, and the very specific character of the one speaking through Mrs. Leek, and his concern for the clearing of his name from the charges of treason and murder.

That we had indeed contacted the restless and unfree spirit of Aaron Burr at what used to be his stables, now the only physical building still extant that was truly his own, I do not doubt in the least.

The defense rests, and hopefully, so does a happier Aaron Burr, now forever reunited with his beloved daughter Theodosia.

✳ 9

Assassination of a President: Lincoln, Booth, and the Traitors Within

FIVE YEARS AFTER the assassination of President John F. Kennedy we are still not sure of his murderer or murderers, even though the deed was done in the cold glare of a public parade, under the watchful eyes of numerous police and security guards, not to mention admirers in the streets.

While we are still arguing the merits of various theories concerning President Kennedy's assassination, we sometimes forget that an earlier crime of a similar nature is equally unresolved. In fact, there are so many startling parallels between the two events that one cannot help but marvel.

One of the people who marveled at them in a particularly impressive way recently is a New York psychiatrist named Stanley Krippner, attached to Maimonides Medical Center, Brooklyn, who has set down his findings in the learned *Journal of Parapsychology*. Among the facts unearthed by Dr. Krippner is the remarkable "death circle" of presidential deaths: Harrison, elected in 1840, died in 1841; Lincoln, elected twenty years later, in 1860, died in 1865; Garfield, elected in 1880, was assassinated in 1881; McKinley, elected in 1900, died by a murderer's hand in 1901; Harding, elected just twenty years after him, died in office in 1923; Roosevelt, re-elected in 1940, did likewise in 1945; and finally, Kennedy, elected to office in 1960, was

murdered in 1963. Since 1840, every President voted into office in a year ending with a zero has died or been injured in office.

Dr. Krippner speculates that this cycle is so far out of the realm of coincidence that some other reason must be found. Applying the principle of synchronicity or meaningful coincidence established first by the late Professor Carl G. Jung, Dr. Krippner wonders if perhaps this principle might not hold an answer to these astounding facts. But the most obvious and simplest explanation of all should not be expected from a medical doctor: fate. Is there an overriding destiny at work that makes these tragedies occur at certain times, whether or not those involved in them try to avoid them? And if so, who directs this destiny—who, in short, is *in charge of the store?*

Dr. Krippner also calls attention to some amazing parallels between the two most noted deaths among U.S. Presidents, Kennedy's and Lincoln's. Both names have seven letters each, the wives of both lost a son while their husbands were in office, and both Presidents were shot in the head from behind on a Friday and in the presence of their wives. Moreover, Lincoln's killer was John Wilkes Booth, the letters of whose name, all told, add up to fifteen; Lee Harvey Oswald's name, likewise, had fifteen letters. Booth's birth year was 1829; Oswald's, 1939. Both murderers were shot down deliberately in full view of their captors, and both died two hours after being shot. Lincoln was elected to Congress in 1847 and Kennedy in 1947; Lincoln became President in 1860 and Kennedy in 1960. Both were involved in the question of civil rights for African-Americans. Finally, Lincoln's secretary, named Kennedy, advised him not to go to the theater on the fateful day he was shot, and Kennedy's secretary, named Lincoln, urged him not to go to Dallas. Lincoln had a premonitory dream seeing himself killed and Kennedy's assassination was predicted by Jeane Dixon as early as 1952, by Al Morrison in 1957, and several other seers in 1957 and 1960, not to forget President Kennedy's own expressed feelings of imminent doom.

But far be it from me to suggest that the two Presidents might be personally linked, perhaps through reincarnation, if such could be proved. Their similar fates must be the result of a higher order of which we know as yet very little except that it exists and operates as clearly and deliberately as any other law of nature.

But there is ample reason to reject any notion of Lincoln's rebirth in another body, if anyone were to make such a claim. Mr. Lincoln's ghost has been observed in the White House by competent witnesses.

According to Arthur Krock of the *New York Times*, the earliest specter at the White House was not Lincoln but Dolley Madison. During President Wilson's administration, she appeared to a group of workers who were about to move her precious rose garden. Evidently they changed their minds about the removal, for the garden was not touched.

It is natural to assume that in so emotion-laden a building as the White House there might be remnants of people whose lives were very closely tied to the structure. I have defined ghosts as the surviving emotional memories of people who are not aware of the transition called death and continue to function in a thought world as they did at the time of their passing, or before it. In a way, then, they are psychotics unable or unwilling to accept the realities of the nonphysical world into which they properly belong, but which is denied them by their unnatural state of "hanging on" in the denser, physical world of flesh and blood. I am sure we don't know *all* the unhappy or disturbed individuals who are bound up with the White House, and some of them may not necessarily be from the distant past, either. But Abigail Adams was seen and identified during the administration of President Taft. Her shade was seen to pass through the doors of the East Room, which was later to play a prominent role in the White House's most famous ghost story.

That Abraham Lincoln would have excellent cause to hang around his former center of activity, even though he died across town, is obvious: he had so much unfinished business of great importance.

Furthermore, Lincoln himself, during his lifetime, had on the record shown an unusual interest in the psy-

chic. The Lincoln family later vehemently denied that séances took place in the White House during his administration. Robert Lincoln may have burned some important papers of his father's bearing on these sittings, along with those concerning the political plot to assassinate his father. According to the record, he most certainly destroyed many documents before being halted in this foolish enterprise by a Mr. Young. This happened shortly before Robert Lincoln's death and is attested to by Lincoln authority Emanuel Hertz in *The Hidden Lincoln*.

The spiritualists even go so far as to claim the President as one of their own. This may be extending the facts, but Abraham Lincoln was certainly psychic, and even during his term in the White House his interest in the occult was well known. The Cleveland *Plain Dealer*, about to write of Lincoln's interest in this subject, asked the President's permission to do so, or, if he preferred, that he deny the statements made in the article linking him to these activities. Far from denying it, Lincoln replied, "The only falsehood in the statement is that half of it has not been told. The article does not begin to tell the things I have witnessed."

The séances held in the White House may well have started when Lincoln's little boy Willie followed another son, Eddie, into premature death, and Mrs. Lincoln's mind gave way to a state of temporary insanity. Perhaps to soothe her feelings, Lincoln decided to hold séances in the White House. It is not known whether the results were positive or not, but Willie's ghost has also been seen in the White House. During Grant's administration, according to Arthur Krock, a boy whom they recognized as the apparition of little Willie "materialized" before the eyes of some of his household.

The medium Lincoln most frequently used was one Nettie Colburn Maynard, and allegedly the spirit of Daniel Webster communicated with him through her. On that occasion, it is said, he was urged to proclaim the emancipation of the slaves. That proclamation, as everybody knows, became Lincoln's greatest political achievement. What is less known is the fact that it also laid the foundation for later dissension among his Cabinet members and that, as we shall see, it may indirectly have caused his premature death. Before going into this, however, let us make clear that on the whole Lincoln apparently did not need any mediums, for he himself had the gift of clairvoyance, and this talent stayed with him all his life. One of the more remarkable premonitory experiences is reported by Philip van Doren Stern in *The Man Who Killed Lincoln*, and also in most other sources dealing with Lincoln.

It happened in Springfield in 1860, just after Lincoln had been elected. As he was looking at himself in a mirror, he suddenly saw a double image of himself. One, real and lifelike, and an etheric double, pale and shadowy. He was convinced that it meant he would get through his first term safely, but would die before the end of the second. Today, psychic researchers would explain Lincoln's mirror experience in less fanciful terms. What the President saw was a brief "out-of-body experience," or astral projection, which is not an uncommon psychic experience. It merely means that the bonds between conscious mind and the unconscious are temporarily loosened and that the inner or true self has quickly slipped out. Usually, these experiences take place in the dream state, but there are cases on record where the phenomenon occurs while awake.

The President's interpretation of the experience is of course another matter; here we have a second phenomenon come into play, that of divination; in his peculiar interpretation of his experience, he showed a degree of precognition, and future events, unfortunately, proved him to be correct.

This was not, by far, the only recorded dream experienced in Lincoln's life. He put serious stock in dreams and often liked to interpret them. William Herndon, Lincoln's onetime law partner and biographer, said of him that he always contended he was doomed to a sad fate, and quotes the President as saying many times, "I am sure I shall meet with some terrible end."

It is interesting to note also that Lincoln's fatalism made him often refer to Brutus and Caesar, explaining the events of Caesar's assassination as caused by laws over which neither had any control; years later, Lincoln's murderer, John Wilkes Booth, also thought of himself as the new Brutus slaying the American Caesar because destiny had singled him out for the deed!

Certainly the most widely quoted psychic experience of Abraham Lincoln was a strange dream he had a few days before his death. When his strangely thoughtful mien gave Mrs. Lincoln cause to worry, he finally admitted that he had been disturbed by an unusually detailed dream. Urged, over dinner, to confide his dream, he did so in the presence of Ward Hill Lamon, close friend and social secretary as well as a kind of bodyguard. Lamon wrote it down immediately afterward, and it is contained in his biography of Lincoln:

"About ten days ago," the President began, "I retired very late. I had been up waiting for important dispatches from the front. I could not have been long in bed when I fell into a slumber, for I was weary. I soon began to dream. There seemed to be a death-like stillness about me. Then I heard subdued sobs, as if a number of people were weeping. I thought I left my bed and wandered downstairs. There the silence was broken by the same pitiful sobbing, but the mourners were invisible. I went from room to room; no living person was in sight, but the same mournful sounds of distress met me as I passed along. It was light in all the rooms; every object was familiar to me; but where were all the people who were grieving as if their hearts would break? I was puzzled and alarmed. What could be the meaning of all this? Determined to find the cause of a state of things so mysterious and so shocking, I kept on until I arrived at the East Room, which I entered.

"There I met with a sickening surprise. Before me was a catafalque, on which rested a corpse wrapped in funeral vestments. Around it were stationed soldiers who were acting as guards; and there was a throng of people, some gazing mournfully upon the corpse, whose face was covered, others weeping pitifully.

"'Who is dead in the White House?' I demanded of one of the soldiers. 'The President,' was his answer; 'he was killed by an assassin!' Then there came a loud burst of grief from the crowd, which awoke me from my dream. I slept no more that night...."

Lincoln always knew he was a marked man, not only because of his own psychic hunches, but objectively, for he kept a sizable envelope in his desk containing all the threatening letters he had received. That envelope was simply marked "Assassination," and the matter did not frighten him. A man in his position is always in danger, he would argue, although the Civil War and the larger question of what to do with the South after victory had split the country into two factions, made the President's position even more vulnerable. Lincoln therefore did not take his elaborate dream warning seriously, or at any rate, he pretended not to. When his friends remonstrated with him, asking him to take extra precautions, he shrugged off their warnings with the lighthearted remark, "Why, it wasn't me on that catafalque. It was some other fellow!"

But the face of the corpse had been covered in his dream and he really was whistling in the dark.

Had fate wanted to prevent the tragedy and give him warning to avoid it?

Had an even higher order of things decided that he was to ignore that warning?

Lincoln had often had a certain dream in which he saw himself on a strange ship, moving with great speed toward an indefinite shore. The dream had always preceded some unusual event. In effect, he had dreamed it precisely in the same way preceding the events at Fort Sumter, the Battles of Bull Run, Antietam, Gettysburg, Stone River, Vicksburg, and Wilmington. Now he had just dreamed it again on the eve of his death. This was April 13, 1865, and Lincoln spoke of his recurrent dream in unusually optimistic tones. To him it was an indication of impending good news. That news, he felt, would be word from General Sherman that hostilities had ceased. There was a Cabinet meeting scheduled for April 14 and Lincoln hoped the news would come in time for it. It never occurred to him that the important news hinted at by this dream was his own demise that very evening, and that the strange vessel carrying him to a distant shore was Charon's boat ferrying him across the Styx into the nonphysical world.

But had he really crossed over?

Rumors of a ghostly President in the White House kept circulating. They were promptly denied by the government, as would be expected. President Theodore Roosevelt, according to Bess Furman in *White House Profile*, often fancied that he felt Lincoln's spirit, and during the administration of Franklin D. Roosevelt, in the 1930s, a female secretary saw the figure of Abraham Lincoln in his onetime bedroom. The ghost was seated on the bed, pulling on his boots, as if he were in a hurry to go somewhere. This happened in mid-afternoon. Eleanor Roosevelt had often felt Lincoln's presence and freely admitted it.

Now it had been the habit of the administration to put important visitors into what was formerly Lincoln's bedroom. This was not done out of mischief, but merely because the Lincoln room was among the most impressive rooms of the White House. We have no record of all those who slept there and had eerie experiences, for people, especially politically highly placed people, don't talk about such things as ghosts.

Yet, the late Queen Wilhelmina did mention the constant knockings at her door followed by footsteps—only to find the corridor outside deserted. And Margaret Truman, who also slept in that area of the White House, often heard knocking at her bedroom door at 3 A.M. Whenever she checked, there was nobody there. Her father, President Truman, a skeptic, decided that the noises had to be due to "natural" causes, such as the dangerous settling of the floors. He ordered the White House completely rebuilt, and perhaps this was a good thing: It would surely have collapsed soon after, according to the architect, General Edgerton. Thus, if nothing else, the ghostly knockings had led to a survey of the structure and subsequent rebuilding. Or was that the reason for the knocks? Had Lincoln tried to warn the later occupants that the house was about to fall down around their ears?

Not only Lincoln's bedroom, but other old areas of the White House are evidently haunted. There is, first of all, the famous East Room, where the lying-in-state took place. By a strange quirk of fate, President Kennedy also was placed there after his assassination. Lynda Bird Johnson's room happened to be the room in which Willie Lincoln died, and later on, Truman's mother. It was also the room used by the doctors to perform the autopsy on Abraham Lincoln. It is therefore not too surprising that President Johnson's daughter did not sleep too well in the room. She heard footsteps at night, and the phone would ring and no one would be on the other end. An exasperated White House telephone operator would come on again and again, explaining she did not ring her!

But if Abraham Lincoln's ghost roams the White House because of unfinished business, it is apparently a ghost free to do other things as well, something the average specter can't do, since it is tied only to the place of its untimely demise.

Mrs. Lincoln lived on for many more years, but ultimately turned senile and died not in her right mind at the home of her sister. Long before she became unbalanced, however, she journeyed to Boston in a continuing search for some proof of her late husband's survival of bodily death. This was in the 1880s, and word had reached her that a certain photographer named William Mumler had been able to obtain the likenesses of dead people on his photographic plates under strict test conditions. She decided to try this man, fully aware that fraud might be attempted if she were recognized. Heavily veiled in mourning clothes, she sat down along with other visitors in Mumler's experimental study. She gave the name of Mrs. Tyndall; all Mumler could see was a widow in heavy veils. Mumler then proceeded to take pictures of all those present in the room. When they were developed, there was one of "Mrs. Tyndall." In back of her appears a semi-solid figure of Abraham Lincoln, with his hands resting upon the shoulders of his widow, and an expression of great compassion on his face. Next to Lincoln was the figure of their son Willie, who had died so young in the White House. Mumler showed his prints to the assembled group, and before Mrs. Lincoln could claim her print, another woman in the group exclaimed. "Why, that looks like President Lincoln!" Then Mrs. Lincoln identified herself for the first time.

There is, by the way, no photograph in existence showing Lincoln with his son in the manner in which they appeared on the psychic photograph.

Another photographic likeness of Lincoln was obtained in 1937 in an experiment commemorating the President's one-hundredth birthday. This took place at Cassadaga, Florida, with Horace Hambling as the psychic intermediary, whose mere presence would make such a phenomenon possible.

Ralph Pressing, editor of the *Psychic Observer*, was to supply and guard the roll of film to be used, and the exposures were made in dim light inside a séance room. The roll of film was then handed to a local photographer for developing, without telling him anything. Imagine the man's surprise when he found a clearly defined portrait of Abraham Lincoln, along with four other, smaller faces, superimposed on the otherwise black negative.

I myself was present at an experiment in San Francisco, when a reputable physician by the name of Andrew von Salza demonstrated his amazing gift of psychic photography, using a Polaroid camera. This was in the fall of 1966, and several other people witnessed the proceedings, which I reported in my book *Psychic Photography—Threshold of a New Science?*

After I had examined the camera, lens, film, and premises carefully, Dr. von Salza took a number of pictures with the Polaroid camera. On many of them there appeared various "extras," or faces of people superimposed in a manner excluding fraud or double exposure completely. The most interesting of these psychic impressions was a picture showing the face of President Lincoln, with President Kennedy next to him!

Had the two men, who had suffered in so many similar ways, found a bond between them in the nonphysical world? The amazing picture followed one on which President Kennedy's face appeared alone, accompanied by the word "War" written in white ectoplasm. Was this their way to warn us to "mend our ways"?

Whatever the meaning, I am sure of one thing: The phenomenon itself, the experiment, was genuine and in no way the result of deceit, accident, self-delusion, or hallucination. I have published both pictures for all to see.

There are dozens of good books dealing with the tragedy of Abraham Lincoln's reign and untimely death. And yet I had always felt that the story had not been told fully. This conviction was not only due to the reported appearances of Lincoln's ghost, indicating restlessness and unfinished business, but also to my objective historical training that somehow led me to reject the solutions given of the plot in very much the same way many serious people today refuse to accept the findings of the Warren Commission as final in the case of President Kennedy's death. But where to begin?

Surely, if Lincoln had been seen at the White House in recent years, that would be the place to start. True, he was shot at Ford's Theatre and actually died in the Parker House across the street. But the White House was his home. Ghosts often occur where the "emotional center" of the person was, while in the body, even though actual death might have occurred elsewhere. A case in point is Alexander Hamilton, whose shade has been observed in what was once his personal physician's house; it was there that he spent his final day on earth, and his unsuccessful struggle to cling to life made it his "emotional center" rather than the spot in New Jersey where he received the fatal wound.

Nell Gwyn's spirit, as we shall see in a later chapter appeared in the romantic apartment of her younger years rather than in the staid home where she actually died.

Even though there might be imprints of the great tragedy at both Ford's Theatre and the Parker House, Lincoln himself would not, in my estimation, "hang around" there!

My request for a quiet investigation in the White House went back to 1963 when Pierre Salinger was still in charge and John F. Kennedy was President. I never got an answer, and in March 1965 I tried again. This time, Bess Abell, social secretary to Mrs. Johnson, turned me down "for security reasons." Patiently, I wrote back explaining I merely wanted to spend a half hour or so with a psychic, probably Mrs. Leek, in two rarely used areas: Lincoln's bedroom and the East Room. Bess Abell had referred to the White House policy of not allowing visitors into the President's "private living quarters." I pointed out that the President, to my knowledge, did not spend his nights in Lincoln's bedroom, nor was the East Room anything but part of the ceremonial or official government rooms and hardly "private living quarters," especially as tourists are

taken through it every hour or so. As for security, why, I would gladly submit anything I wrote about my studies for their approval.

Back came another pensive missive from Bess Abell. The President and Mrs. Johnson's "restrictive schedules" would not permit my visit.

I offered, in return, to come at any time, day or night, when the Johnsons were out of town.

The answer was still no, and I began to wonder if it was merely a question of not wanting anything to do with ESP?

But a good researcher never gives up hope. I subsequently asked Senator Jacob Javits to help me get into the White House, but even he couldn't get me in. Through a local friend I met James Kerchum, the curator of the State rooms. Would he give me a privately conducted tour exactly like the regular tourist tour, except minus tourists to distract us?

The answer remained negative.

On March 6, 1967, Bess Abell again informed me that the only individuals eligible for admission to the two rooms I wanted to see were people invited for State visits and close personal friends. On either count, that left us out.

I asked Elizabeth Carpenter, whom I knew to be favorably inclined toward ESP, to intervene. As press secretary to Mrs. Johnson, I thought she might be able to give me a less contrived excuse, at the very least. "An impossible precedent," she explained, if I were to be allowed in. I refused to take the tourist tour, of course, as it would be a waste of my time, and dropped the matter for the time being.

But I never lost interest in the case. To me, finding the missing link between what is officially known about Lincoln's murderer and the true extent of the plot would be an important contribution to American history.

The events themselves immediately preceding and following that dark day in American history are known to most readers, but there are, perhaps, some details which only the specialist would be familiar with and which will be found to have significance later in my investigation. I think it therefore useful to mention these events here, although they were not known to me at the time I undertook my psychic investigation. I try to keep my unconscious mind free of all knowledge so that no one may accuse my psychics of "reading my mind," or suggest similar explanations for what transpires. Only at the end of this amazing case did I go through the contemporary record of the assassination.

* * *

The War between the States had been going on for four years, and the South was finally losing. This was obvi-

Assassination of a President:
Lincoln, Booth, and the Traitors Within
103

ous even to diehard Confederates, and everybody wanted only one thing to get it over with as quickly as possible and resume a normal life once again.

While the South was, by and large, displaying apathy, there were still some fanatics who thought they could change the course of events by some miracle. In the North, it was a question of freeing the slaves and restoring the Union. In the South, it was not only a question of maintaining the economic system they had come to consider the only feasible one, but also one of maintaining the feudal, largely rural system their ancestors had known in Europe and which was being endangered by the industrialized North with its intellectuals, labor forces, and new values. To save the South from such a fate seemed a noble cause to a handful of fanatics, among them John Wilkes Booth, the man who was to play so fateful a role. Ironically, he was not even a true Southerner, but a man born on the fringe of the South, in Maryland, and his family, without exception, considered itself to be of the North.

John Wilkes Booth was, of course, the lesser known of the Booth brothers, scions of a family celebrated in the theater of their age, and when Edwin Booth, "the Prince of Players," learned of the terrible crime his younger brother had committed, he was genuinely shocked, and immediately made clear his position as a longtime supporter of Abraham Lincoln.

But John Wilkes Booth did not care whether his people were with him or not. Still in his early twenties, he was not only politically immature but also romantically inspired. He could not understand the economic changes that were sure to take place and which no bullet could stop.

And so, while the War between the States was drawing to a close, Booth decided to become the savior of his adopted Dixie, and surrounded himself with a small and motley band of helpers who had their secret meetings at Mrs. Mary Surratt's boarding house in Washington.

At first, they were discussing a plot to abduct President Lincoln and to deliver him to his foes at the Confederate capitol in Richmond, but the plot never came into being. Richmond fell to the Yankees, and time ran out for the cause of the Confederacy. As the days crept by and Booth's fervor to "do something drastic" for his cause increased, the young actor started thinking in terms of killing the man whom he blamed for his country's defeat. To Booth, Lincoln was the center of all he hated, and he believed that once the man was removed all would be well.

Such reasoning, of course, is the reasoning of a demented mind. Had Booth really been an astute politician, he would have realized that Lincoln was a moderate compared to some members of his Cabinet, that the President was indeed, as some Southern leaders put it when news of the murder reached them, "the best friend the South had ever had."

Had he appraised the situation in Washington correctly, he would have realized that any man taking the place of Abraham Lincoln was bound to be far worse for Southern aspirations than Lincoln, who had deeply regretted the war and its hardships and who was eager to receive the seceded states back into the Union fold with as little punishment as possible.

Not so the war party, principally Stanton, the Secretary of War, and Seward, the Secretary of State. Theirs was a harsher outlook, and history later proved them to be the winners—but also the cause of long years of continuing conflict between North and South, conflict and resentment that could have been avoided had Lincoln's conciliatory policies been allowed to prevail.

The principal fellow conspirators against Lincoln were an ex-Confederate soldier named Lewis Paine; David Herold, a druggist's clerk who could not hold a job; George Atzerodt, a German born carriagemaker; Samuel Arnold, a clerk; Michael O'Laughlin, another clerk; Mrs. Mary Surratt, the Washington boarding house keeper at whose house they met; and finally, and importantly, John Harrison Surratt, her son, by profession a Confederate spy and courier. At the time of the final conspiracy Booth was only twenty-six, Surratt twenty-one, and Herold twenty-three, which perhaps accounts for the utter folly of their actions.

The only one, besides Booth, who had any qualities of leadership was young Surratt. His main job at the time was traveling between Washington and Montreal as a secret courier for the Washington agents of the Confederacy and the Montreal, Canada headquarters of the rebels. Originally a clerk with the Adams Express Company, young Surratt had excellent connections in communications and was well known in Washington government circles, although his undercover activities were not.

When Booth had convinced Surratt that the only way to help the Confederacy was to murder the President, they joined forces. Surratt had reservations about this course, and Mrs. Surratt certainly wanted no part of violence or murder. But they were both swept up in the course of events that followed.

Unfortunately, they had not paid enough attention to the presence in the Surratt boarding house on H Street of a young War Department clerk named Louis Weichmann. Originally intending to become a priest, young Weichmann was a witness to much of the coming and going of the conspirators, and despite his friendship for John Surratt, which had originally brought him to the Surratt boarding house, he eventually turned against the Surratts. It was his testimony at Mrs. Surratt's trial that ultimately led to her hanging.

Originally, Mrs. Surratt had owned a tavern in a small town thirteen miles south of Washington then called Surrattsville and later, for obvious reasons, renamed Clinton, Maryland. When business at the tavern fell off, she leased it to an innkeeper named John Lloyd, and moved to

Washington, where she opened a boarding house on H Street, between Sixth and Seventh Streets, which house still stands.

Certainly she was present when the plans for Lincoln's abduction were made, but she never was part of the conspiracy to kill him. That was chiefly Booth's brain child, and all of his confederates were reluctant, in varying degrees, to go along with him; nevertheless, such was his ability to impress men that they ultimately gave in to his urgings. Then, too, they had already gotten into this conspiracy so deeply that if one were caught they'd all hang. So it seemed just as well that they did it together and increased their chances of getting away alive.

Booth himself was to shoot the President. And when he discovered that the Lincolns would be in the State box at Ford's Theatre, Washington, on the evening of April 14, 1865, it was decided to do it there. Surratt was to try to "fix the wires" so that the telegraph would not work during the time following the assassination. He had the right connections, and he knew he could do it. In addition, he was to follow General Grant on a train that was to take the general and his wife to New Jersey. Lewis Paine was to kill Secretary Seward at the same time.

Booth had carefully surveyed the theater beforehand, making excellent use of the fact that as an actor he was known and respected there. This also made it quite easy to get inside the strategic moment. The play on stage was "Our American Cousin" starring Laura Keene. Booth's plans were furthermore helped by a stroke of luck—or fate, if you prefer, namely, one of the men who was supposed to guard the President's box was momentarily absent from his post.

The hour was shortly after 10 P.M. when Booth quickly entered the box, killed Lincoln with a small Derringer pistol, struggled with a second guard and then, according to plan, jumped over the box rail onto the stage below.

Lincoln lived through the night but never regained consciousness. He expired in the Parker House across from Ford's theatre, where he had been brought. Booth caught his heel on an American flag that adorned the stage box, and fell, breaking his leg in the process. Despite intense pain, he managed to escape in the confusion and jump on the horse he had prepared outside.

When he got to the Navy Yard bridge crossing the Anacostia River, the sentry on this road leading to the South stopped him. What was he doing out on the road that late? In wartime Washington, all important exits from the city were controlled. But Booth merely told the man his name and that he lived in Charles County. He was let through, despite the fact that a nine o'clock curfew was being rigidly enforced at that moment. Many later historians have found this incident odd, and have darkly pointed to a conspiracy: It may well be that Surratt did arrange for the easy passage, as they had all along planned to use the road over the Anacostia River bridge to make good their escape.

A little later, Booth was joined on the road by David Herold. Together they rode out to the Surratt tavern, where they arrived around midnight. The purpose of their visit there at that moment became clear to me only much later. The tavern had of course been a meeting place for Booth and Surratt and the others before Mrs. Surratt moved her establishment to Washington. Shortly after, the two men rode onward and entered the last leg of their journey. After a harrowing escape interrupted by temporary stays at Dr. Mudd's office at Bryantown—where Booth had his leg looked after—and various attempts to cross the Potomac, the two men holed up at Garrett's farm near Port Royal, Virginia. It was there that they were hunted down like mad dogs by the Federal forces. Twelve days after Lincoln's murder, on April 26, 1865, Booth was shot down. Even that latter fact is not certain: Had he committed suicide when he saw no way out of Garrett's burning barn, with soldiers all around it? Or had the avenger's bullet of Sergeant Boston Corbett found its mark, as the soldier had claimed?

It is not my intent here to go into the details of the flight and capture, as these events are amply told elsewhere. The mystery is not so much Booth's crime and punishment, about which there is no doubt, but the question of who *really* plotted Lincoln's death. The State funeral was hardly over when all sorts of rumors and legends concerning the plot started to spring up.

Mrs. Surratt was arrested immediately, and she, along with Paine, Atzerodt, and Herold were hanged after a trial marked by prejudice and the withholding of vital information, such as Booth's own diary, which Secretary of War Stanton had ordered confiscated and which was never entered as an exhibit at the trial. This, along with the fact that Stanton was at odds politically with Lincoln, gave rise to various speculations concerning Stanton's involvement in the plot. Then, too, there was the question of the role John Surratt had played, so much of it covered by secrecy, like an iceburg with only a small portion showing above the surface!

After he had escaped from the United States and gone to Europe and then to Egypt, he was ultimately captured and extradited to stand trial in 1867. But a jury of four Northerners and eight Southerners allowed him to go free, when they could not agree on a verdict of guilty. Surratt moved to Baltimore, where he went into business and died in 1916. Very little is known of his activities beyond these bare facts. The lesser conspirators, those who merely helped the murderer escape, were convicted to heavy prison terms.

There was some to do about Booth's body also. After it had been identified by a number of people who knew

Assassination of a President:
Lincoln, Booth, and the Traitors Within
105

him in life, it was buried under the stone floor of the Arsenal Prison in Washington, the same prison where the four other conspirators had been executed. But in 1867, the prison was torn down and the five bodies exhumed. One of them, presumed to be Booth's, was interred in the family plot in Greenmount Cemetery, Baltimore. Yet a rumor arose, and never ceased, that actually someone else lay in Booth's grave and, though most historians refuse to take this seriously, according to Philip Van Doren Stern, "the question of whether or not the man who died at Garrett's Farm was John Wilkes Booth is one that doubtless will never be settled."

No accounts of any psychic nature concerning Booth have been reported to date, and Booth's ghost does not walk the corridors of Ford's Theatre the way Lincoln's does in the White House. The spot where Garrett's farm used to stand is no longer as it was, and a new building has long replaced the old barn.

If I were to shed new light or uncover fresh evidence concerning the plot to kill Lincoln, I would have to go to a place having emotional ties to the event itself. But the constant refusal of the White House to permit me a short visit made it impossible for me to do so properly.

The questions that, to me, seem in need of clarification concerned, first of all, the strange role John H. Surratt had played in the plot; secondly, was Booth really the one who initiated the murder, and was he really the leader of the plot? One notices the close parallel between this case and the assassination of President Kennedy.

As I began this investigation, my own feelings were that an involvement of War Secretary Stanton could be shown and that there probably was a northern plot to kill Lincoln as well as a southern desire to get rid of him. But that was pure speculation on my part, and I had as yet nothing to back up my contention. Then fate played a letter into my hands, out of left field, so to speak, that gave me new hope for a solution to this exciting case.

A young girl by the name of Phyllis Amos, of Washington, Pennsylvania, had seen me on a television show in the fall of 1967. She contacted me by letter, and as a consequence I organized an expedition to the Surratt tavern, the same tavern that had served as home to Mrs. Mary Surratt and as a focal point of the Lincoln conspiracy prior to the move to H Street in Washington.

Phyllis' connection with the old tavern goes back to 1955. It was then occupied by a Mrs. Ella Curtain and by Phyllis' family, who shared the house with this elderly lady. Mrs. Curtain's brother, B. K. Miler, a prosperous supermarket owner nearby, was the actual owner of the house, but he let his sister live there. Since it was a large house, they subleased to the Amos family, which then consisted of Mr. and Mrs. Amos and their two girls, about two years apart in age.

Phyllis, who is now in her twenties, occupied a room on the upper floor; across the narrow hall from her room was Ella Curtain's room—once the room where John Wilkes Booth had hidden his guns. To the right of Phyllis' bedroom and a few steps down was a large room where the conspirators met regularly. It was shielded from the curious by a small anteroom through which one would have to go to reach the meeting room. Downstairs were the parents' room and a large reception room. The house stood almost directly on the road, surrounded by dark green trees. A forlorn metal sign farther back was the sole indication that this was considered a historical landmark: If you didn't know the sign was there, you wouldn't find it unless you were driving by at very slow speed.

Mrs. Amos never felt comfortable in the house from the moment they moved in, and after eight months of occupancy the Amos family left. But during those eight months they experienced some pretty strange things. One day she was alone in the house when it suddenly struck her that someone was watching her intently. Terrified, she ran to her bedroom and locked the door, not coming out until her husband returned. The smaller of the two girls kept asking her mother who the strange men were she saw sitting on the back stairs. She would hear them talk in whispers up there.

The other occupant of the house, Mrs. Curtain, was certainly not a steadying influence on them. On one occasion she saw the figure of a woman "float" down the front steps. That woman, she felt sure, was Mary Surratt. The house had of course been Mary Surratt's true home, her only safe harbor. The one she later owned in Washington was merely a temporary and unsafe abode. Mightn't she have been drawn back here after her unjust execution to seek justice, or at the very least to be among surroundings she was familiar with?

The floating woman returned several times more, and ultimately young Phyllis was to have an experience herself. It was in April of 1955 and she was in bed in her room, wide awake. Her bed stood parallel to the room where the conspirators used to meet, separated from it only by a thin wall, so that she might have heard them talk had she been present at the time. Suddenly, she received several blows on the side of her face. They were so heavy that they brought tears to her eyes. Were the ghosts of the conspirators trying to discourage her from eavesdropping on their plans?

Both Phyllis and her mother have had ESP experiences all their lives, ranging from premonitions to true dreams and other forms of precognition.

I decided to contact the present owner and ask for permission to visit with a good medium. Thomas Miller, whose parents had owned the Surratt tavern and who now managed it prior to having it restored, at great cost, to the condition it was in a hundred years ago, readily assented. So it was that on a very chilly day in November of 1967, Sybil Leek and I flew down to Washington for a look at the ghosts around John Wilkes Booth: If I couldn't interview the victim, Lincoln, perhaps I could have a go at the murderer?

A friend, Countess Gertrude d'Amecourt, volunteered to drive us to Clinton. The directions the Millers had given us were not too clear, so it took us twice as long as it should have to get there. I think we must have taken the wrong turn off the highway at least six times and in the end got to know them all well, but got no nearer to Clinton. Finally we were stopped by a little old woman who wanted to hitch a ride with us. Since she was going in the same direction, we let her come with us, and thanks to her we eventually found Miller's supermarket, about two hours later than planned. But ghosts are not in a hurry, even though Gertrude had to get back to her real estate office, and within minutes we set out on foot to the old Surratt tavern, located only a few blocks from the supermarket. Phyllis Amos had come down from Pennsylvania to join us, and as the wind blew harder and harder and our teeth began to chatter louder and louder in the unseasonable chill of the late afternoon, we pushed open the dusty, padlocked door of the tavern, and our adventure into the past began.

Before I had a chance to ask Sybil Leek to wait until I could put my tape recording equipment into operating condition, she had dashed past us and was up the stairs as if she knew where she was headed. She didn't, of course, for she had no idea why she had been brought here or indeed where she was. All of us—the Millers, Phyllis, Gertrude d'Amecourt, and myself—ran up the stairs after Sybil. We found her staring at the floor in what used to be the John Wilkes Booth bedroom. Staring at the hole in the floor where the guns had been hidden, she mumbled something about things being hidden there...not budging from the spot. Thomas Miller, who had maintained a smug, skeptical attitude about the whole investigation until now, shook his head and mumbled, "But how would she know?"

It was getting pretty dark now and there was no electric light in the house. The smells were pretty horrible, too, as the house had been empty for years, with neighborhood hoodlums and drunks using it for "parties" or to sleep off drunken sprees. There is always a broken back window in those old houses, and they manage to get in.

We were surrounding Sybil now and shivering in unison. "This place is different from the rest of the house," Sybil explained, "cold, dismal atmosphere...this is where something happened."

"What sort of thing do you think happened here?"

"A chase."

How right she was! The two hunted men were indeed on a chase from Washington, trying to escape to the South. But again, Sybil would not know this consciously.

"This is where someone was a fugitive," she continued now, "for several days, but he left this house and went to the woodland."

Booth hiding out in the woods for several days after passing the tavern!

"Who is the man?" I asked, for I was not at all sure who she was referring to. There were several men connected with "the chase," and for all we knew, it could have been a total stranger somehow tied up with the tavern. Lots of dramatic happenings attach themselves to old taverns, which were far cries from Hilton hotels. People got killed or waylaid in those days, and taverns, on the whole, had sordid reputations. The *good* people stayed at each other's homes when traveling.

"Foreign...can't get the name...hiding for several days here...then there is...a brother...it is very confusing."

*   *   *

The foreigner might well have been Atzerodt, who was indeed hiding at the tavern at various times. And the brother?

*   *   *

"A man died suddenly, violently." Sybil took up the impressions she seemed to be getting now with more depth. We were still standing around in the upstairs room, near the window, with the gaping hole in the floor.

"How did he die?" I inquired.

"Trapped in the woods...hiding from soldiers, I think."

That would only fit Booth. He was trapped in the woods and killed by soldiers.

"Why?"

"They were chasing him...he killed someone."

"Who did he kill?"

"I don't know...birthday...ran away to hide...I see a paper...invitation...there is another place we have to go to, a big place...a big building with a gallery..."

Was she perhaps describing Ford's Theatre now?

"Whose place is it?" I asked.

Sybil was falling more and more under the spell of the place, and her consciousness bordered now on the trance state.

"No one's place...to see people...I'm confused...lot of people go there...watching...a gathering...with music...I'm not going there!!"

*   *   *

"Who is there?" I interjected. She must be referring to the theater, all right. Evidently what Sybil was getting here was the entire story, but jumbled as psychic impressions often are, since they do not obey the ordinary laws of time and space.

"My brother and I," she said now. I had gently led her toward another corner of the large room where a small chair stood, in the hope of having her sit in it. But she was already too deeply entranced to do it, so I let her lean toward the chair, keeping careful watch so she would not topple over.

"My brother is mad...," she said now, and her voice was no longer the same, but had taken on a harder, metallic sound. I later wondered about this remark: Was this Edwin Booth, talking about his renegade brother John who was indeed considered mad by many of his contemporaries? Edwin Booth frequently appeared at Ford's Theatre, and so did John Wilkes Booth.

"Why is he mad?" I said. I decided to continue the questioning as if I were agreeing with all she—or he—was saying, in order to elicit more information.

* * *

"Madman in the family...," Sybil said now, "killed —a—friend...."

"Whom did he kill?"

"No names...he was mad...."

"Would I know the person he killed?"

"Everybody—knows...."

"What is your brother's name?"

"John."

"What is *your* name?"

"Rory."

At first it occurred to me this might be the name of a character Edwin Booth had played on the stage and he was hiding behind it, if indeed it was Edwin Booth who was giving Sybil this information. But I have not found such a character in the biographies of Edwin Booth. I decided to press further by reiterating my original question.

"Whom did John kill?"

An impatient, almost impertinent voice replied, "I won't tell you. You can read!"

"What are you doing in this house?"

"Helping John...escape...."

"Are you alone?"

"No...Trevor...."

"How many of you are there here?"

"Four."

"Who are the others?"

"Traitors...."

"But what are their names?"

"Trevor...Michael...John...."

These names caused me some concern afterward: I could identify Michael readily enough as Michael O'Laughlin, school chum of Booth, who worked as a livery stable worker in Baltimore before he joined forces with his friend. Michael O'Laughlin was one of the conspirators, who was eventually sentenced to life imprisonment. But on Stanton's orders he and the other three "lesser" conspirators were sent to the Dry Tortugas, America's own version

of Devil's Island, off Florida, and it was there that Michael O'Laughlin died of yellow fever in 1868.

* * *

John? Since the communicator had referred to his brother's name as John, I could only surmise this to mean John Wilkes Booth. But Trevor I could not identify. The only conspirator whose middle name we did not know was Samuel Arnold, also an ex-classmate of Booth. Was Trevor perhaps the familiar name by which the conspirators referred to this Maryland farmhand and Confederate deserter?

I pressed the point further with Sybil.

"Who is in the house?"

"Go away...."

I explained my mission: to help them all find peace of mind, freedom, deliverance.

"I'm going to the city...." the communicator said.

"Which city?"

"The big city."

"Why?"

"To stop him...he's mad...take him away...to the country to rest...to help him...give him rest...."

"Has he done anything wrong?"

"He...he's my brother!"

"Did he kill anyone?"

"Killed that man...."

"Why did he kill him?"

Shouting at me, the entranced medium said, "He was unjust!"

"Toward whom?"

"He was unjust toward the Irish people."

Strange words, I thought. Only Michael O'Laughlin could be considered a "professional" Irishman among the conspirators, and one could scarcely accuse Lincoln of having mistreated the Irish.

"What did he do?" I demanded to know.

"He did nothing...."

"Why did he kill him then?"

"He was mad."

"Do you approve of it?"

"Yes!! He did not like him because he was unjust... the law was wrong...his laws were wrong...free people... he was confused...."

Now if this were indeed Edwin Booth's spirit talking, he would most certainly not have approved of the murder. The resentment for the sake of the Irish minority could only have come from Michael O'Laughlin. But the entity kept referring to his brother, and only Edwin Booth had a brother named John, connected with this house and story! The trance session grew more and more confusing.

"Who else was in this?" I started again. Perhaps we could get more information on the people *behind* the plot. After all, we already knew the actual murderer and his accomplices.

"Trevor...four...."

"Did you get an order from someone to do this?"

There was a long pause as the fully entranced psychic kept swaying a little, with eyes closed, in front of the rickety old chair.

I explained again why I had come, but it did not help. "I don't believe you," the entity said in great agitation, "Traitors...."

"You've long been forgiven," I said, "but you must speak freely about it now. What happened to the man he killed?"

"My brother—became—famous...."

This was followed by bitter laughter.

"What sort of work did your brother do?"

"Writing...acting...."

"Where did he act?"

"Go away...don't search for me...."

"I want to help you."

"Traitor...shot like a dog...the madman...."

Sybil's face trembled now as tears streamed freely from her eyes. Evidently she was reliving the final moments of Booth's agony. I tried to calm the communicator.

"Go away..." the answer came, "go away!"

But I continued the questioning. Did anyone put him up to the deed?

"He was mad," the entity explained, a little calmer now.

"But who is guilty?"

"The Army."

"Who in the Army?"

"He was wild...met people...they said they were Army people...Major General...Gee...I ought to go now!!"

Several things struck me when I went over this conversation afterward. To begin with, the communicator felt he had said too much as soon as he had mentioned the person of Major General Gee, or G., and wanted to leave. Why? Was this something he should have kept secret?

Major General G.? Could this refer to Grant? Up to March 1864 Grant was indeed a major general; after that time Lincoln raised him to the rank of lieutenant general. The thought seemed monstrous on the face of it, that Grant could in any way be involved with a plot against Lincoln. Politically, this seemed unlikely, because both Grant and Lincoln favored the moderate treatment of the conquered South as against the radicals, who demanded stern measures. Stanton was a leading radical, and if anyone he would have had a reason to plot against Lincoln. And yet, by all appearances, he served him loyally and well. But Grant had political aspirations of a personal nature, and he succeeded Lincoln after Johnson's unhappy administration.

I decided to pursue my line of questioning further to see where it might lead.

I asked Sybil's controlling entity to repeat the name of this Army general. Faintly but clear enough it came from her entranced lips:

"Gee...G-E-E-...Major General Robert Gee."

Then it wasn't Grant, I thought. But who in blazes was it? If there existed such a person I could find a record, but what "if it was merely a cover name?"

"Did you see this man yourself?"

"No."

"Then did your brother tell you about him?"

"Yes."

"Where did they meet?"

Hesitatingly, the reply came.

"In the city. This city. In a club...."

I decided to change my approach.

"What year is this?" I shot at him.

"Forty-nine."

"What does forty-nine mean to you?"

"Forty-nine means something important...."

"How old are you now?"

"Thirty-four."

He then claimed to have been born in Lowell, Virginia, and I found myself as puzzled as ever: It did not fit Edwin, who was born in 1833 on the Booth homestead at Belair, Maryland. Confusion over confusion!

"Did anyone else but the four of you come here?" I finally asked.

"Yes...Major...Robert Gee...."

"What did he want?"

"Bribery."

"What did he pay?"

"I don't know."

"Did he give him any money?"

"Yes."

"What was he supposed to do?"

"Cause a disturbance. In the gallery. Then plans would be put into operation. To hold up the law."

"Did your brother do what he was supposed to do?"

"He was mad...he killed him."

"Then who was guilty?"

"Gee...."

"Who sent Gee? For whom did he speak?"

We were getting close to the heart of the matter and the others were grouping themselves closely around us, the better to hear. It was quite dark outside and the chill of the November afternoon crept into our bones with the result that we started to tremble with the wet cold. But nobody moved or showed impatience. American history was being relived, and what did a little chill matter in comparison?

"He surveyed..."

"Who worked with him?"

"The government."

"Who specifically?"

"I don't know."

It did not sound convincing. Was he still holding out on us?

"Were there others involved? Other men? Other women?"

A derisive laughter broke the stillness. "Jealous...jealousy...his wife...."

"Whose wife?"

"The one who was killed...shot."

* * *

That I found rather interesting, for it is a historical fact that Mrs. Lincoln was extremely jealous and, according to Carl Sandburg, perhaps the most famous Lincoln biographer, never permitted her husband to see a woman alone—for any reason whatever. The Lincolns had frequent spats for that reason, and jealousy was a key characteristic of the President's wife.

"Why are we in this room?" I demanded.

"Waiting for...what am I waiting for?" the communicator said, in a voice filled with despair.

"I'd like to know that myself," I nodded. "Is there anything of interest for you here?"

"Yes...I have to stay here until John comes back. Where's John?"

"And what will you do when he comes back?"

"Take him to Lowell...my home...."

"Whom do you live with there?"

"Julia...my girl...take him to rest there."

"Where is John now?"

"In the woods...hiding."

"Is anyone with him?"

"Two...they should be back soon."

Again the entity demanded to know why I was asking all those questions and again I reassured him that I was a friend. But I have to know everything in order to help him. Who then was this Major General Gee?

"Wants control," the voice said, "I don't understand the Army...politics...he's altering the government...."

"Altering the government?" I repeated, "On whose side is he?"

"Insurgent side."

"Is he in the U. S. Government?"

"My brother knows them...they have the government."

"But who are they? What are their names?"

"They had numbers. Forty-nine. It means the area. The area they look after."

"Is anyone in the government involved with these insurgents?"

"John knows...John's dead...knew too much...the names...he wasn't all...he's mad!"

"Who killed him?"

"Soldier."

"Why did he kill him?" I was now referring to John Wilkes Booth and the killing of the presidential assassin by Sergeant Boston Corbett, allegedly because "God told him to," as the record states.

"Hunted him."

"But who gave the order to kill him?"

"The government."

"You say, he knew too much. What did he know?"

"I don't know the names, I know only I wait for John. John knows the names. He was clever."

"Was anyone in this government involved?"

"Traitors...in the head of the Army....Sher...must not tell you, John said not to speak...."

"You must speak!" I commanded, almost shouting.

"Sherman...Colonel...he knows Sherman....John says to say nothing...."

"Does Sherman know about it?"

"I don't know...I am not telling you any more..." he said, trembling again with tears, "Everybody asks questions. You are not helping me."

"I will try to help you if you don't hold back," I promised. "Who paid your brother?"

"Nothing...promised to escape...look after him...promised a ticket...."

"How often did your brother see this officer?"

"Not too often. Here. John told me...some things. John said not to talk. He is not always mad."

"Who is the woman with him?" I tried to see if it would trick him into talking about others.

"She's a friend," the communicator said without hesitation.

"What is her name?"

"Harriet."

"Where does she live?"

"In the city."

"How does he know her?"

"He went to play there...he liked her...."

Evidently this was some minor figure of no importance to the plot. I changed directions again. "You are free to leave here now, John wants you to go," I said, slowly. After all, I could not let this poor soul, whoever he was, hang on here for all eternity!

"Where are we?" he asked, sounding as confused as ever.

"A house...."

"My house?...No, Melville's house...."

"Who is Melville?"

"Friend of Gee. Told me to come here, wait for John."

"You are free to go, free!" I intoned.

"Free?" he said slowly. "Free country?"

"A hundred years have gone by. Do you understand me?"

"No."

The voice became weaker as if the entity were drifting away. Gradually Sybil's body seemed to collapse and I was ready to catch her, should she fall. But in time she "came back" to herself. Awakening, as if she had slept a long time, she looked around herself, as completely confused as the entity had been. She remembered absolutely nothing of the conversation between the ghost and myself.

For a moment none of us said anything. The silence was finally broken by Thomas Miller, who seemed visibly impressed with the entire investigation. He knew very well that the hole in the floor was a matter *he* was apt to point out to visitors in the house, and that no visitors had come here in a long time, as the house had been in disrepair for several years. How could this strange woman with the English accent whom he had never met before in his life, or for that matter, how could I, a man he only knew by correspondence, know about it? And how could she head straight for the spot in the semi-darkness of an unlit house? That was the wedge that opened the door to his acceptance of what he had witnessed just now.

* * *

"It's cold," Sybil murmured, and wrapped herself deeper into her black shawl. But she has always been a good sport, and did not complain. Patiently, she waited further instructions from me. I decided it was time to introduce everybody formally now, as I had of course not done so on arrival in order to avoid Sybil's picking up any information or clues.

Phyllis Amos then showed us the spot where she had been hit by unseen hands, and pointed out the area where her younger sister Lynn, seven at the time and now nineteen, had heard the voices of a group of men whom she had also seen huddled together on the back stairs.

"I too thought I heard voices here," Phyllis Amos commented. "It sounded like the din of several voices but I couldn't make it out clearly."

I turned to Thomas Miller, who was bending down now toward the hole in the floor.

"This is where John Wilkes Booth hid his guns," he said, anticlimactically. "The innkeeper, Lloyd, also gave him some brandy, and then he rode on to where Dr. Mudd had his house in Bryantown."

"You heard the conversation that came through my psychic friend, Mr. Miller," I said. "Do you care to comment on some of the names? For instance, did John Wilkes Booth have a brother along those lines?"

"My father bought this property from John Wilkes' brother," Miller said, "the brother who went to live in Baltimore after John Wilkes was killed; later he went to England."

That, of course, would be Edwin Booth, the "Prince of Players," who followed his sister Asia's advice to try his luck in the English theater.

* * *

I found this rather interesting. So Surratt's tavern had once belonged to Edwin Booth—finger of fate!

Mr. Miller pointed out something else of interest to me. While I had been changing tapes, during the interro-

gation of the communicator speaking through Sybil, I had missed a sentence or two. My question had been about the ones behind the killing.

"S-T-..." the communicator had whispered. Did it mean Stanton?

"John Wilkes Booth was very familiar with this place, of course," Miller said in his Maryland drawl. "This is where the conspirators used to meet many times. Mary Surratt ran this place as a tavern. Nothing has changed in this house since then."

* * *

From Thomas Miller I also learned that plans were afoot to restore the house at considerable cost, and to make it into a museum.

* * *

We thanked our host and piled into the car. Suddenly I remembered that I had forgotten my briefcase inside the house, so I raced back and recovered it. The house was now even colder and emptier, and I wondered if I might hear anything unusual—but I didn't. Rather than hang around any longer, I joined the others in the car and we drove back to Washington.

I asked Countess d'Amecourt to stop once more at a house I felt might have some relationship with the case. Sybil, of course, had no idea why we got out to look at an old house on H Street. It is now a Chinese restaurant and offers no visible clues to its past.

"I feel military uniforms, blue colors here," Sybil said as we all shuddered in the cold wind outside. The house was locked and looked empty. My request to visit it had never been answered.

"What period?"

"Perhaps a hundred years...nothing very strong here...the initial S...a man...rather confusing...a meeting place more than a residence...not too respectable...meeting house for soldiers...Army...."

"Is there a link between this house and where we went earlier this afternoon?"

"The Army is the link somehow...."

* * *

After I had thanked the Countess d'Amecourt for her help, Sybil and I flew back to New York.

For days afterward I pondered the questions arising from this expedition. Was the "S" linking the house on H Street—which was Mary Surratt's Washington boarding house—the same man as the "S-T-..." Sybil had whispered to me at Mary Surratt's former country house? Were both initials referring to Secretary Stanton and were the rumors true after all?

* * *

The facts of history, in this respect, are significant. Lincoln's second term was actively opposed by the forces of the radical Republicans. They thought Lincoln too soft on the rebels and feared that he would make an easy peace with the Confederacy. They were quite right in this assumption, of course, and all through Lincoln's second term of office, his intent was clear. That is why, in murdering Abraham Lincoln, Booth actually did the South a great disservice.

In the spring of 1864, when the South seemed to be on its last legs, the situation in Washington also came to a point where decisions would have to be made soon. The "hawks," to use a contemporary term, could count on the services of Stanton, the War Secretary, and of Seward, Secretary of State, plus many lesser officials and officers, of course. The "doves" were those in actual command, however—Lincoln himself, Grant, and Vice President Johnson, himself a Southerner. Logically, the time of crisis would be at hand the moment Grant had won victory in his command and Sherman, the other great commander, on his end of the front. By a strange set of circumstances, the assassination took place precisely at that moment: Both Grant and Sherman had eminently succeeded and peace was at hand.

* * *

Whenever Booth's motive in killing Lincoln has been described by biographers, a point is made that it was both Booth's madness and his attempt to avenge the South that caused him to commit the crime. Quite so, but the assassination made a lot more sense in terms of a *northern* plot by conveniently removing the chief advocate of a soft peace treaty just at the right moment!

This was not a trifling matter. Lincoln had proposed to go beyond freeing the slaves: to franchise the more intelligent ones among them to vote. But he had never envisioned general and immediate equality of newly freed blacks and their former masters. To the radicals, however, this was an absolute must as was the total takeover of southern assets. While Lincoln was only too ready to accept any southern state back into the Union fold that was willing to take the oath of loyalty, the radicals would hear of no such thing. They foresaw a long period of military government and rigid punishment for the secessionist states.

Lincoln often expressed the hope that Jefferson Davis and his chief aides might just leave the country to save him the embarrassment of having to try them. Stanton and his group, on the other hand, were pining for blood, and it was on Stanton's direct orders that the southern conspirators who killed Lincoln were shown no mercy; it was Stanton who refused to give in to popular sentiment against the hanging of a woman and who insisted that Mrs. Surratt share the fate of the other principal conspirators.

Stanton's stance at Lincoln's death—his remark that "now he belongs to the ages" and his vigorous pursuit of the murderers in no way mitigates a possible secret involvement in a plot to kill the President. According to Stefan Lorant, he once referred to his commander-in-chief Lincoln as "the original gorilla." He frequently refused to carry out Lincoln's orders when he thought them "too soft." On April 11, three days prior to the assassination, Lincoln had incurred not only Stanton's anger but that of the entire Cabinet by arranging to allow the rebel Virginia legislature to function as a state government. "Stanton and the others were in a fury," Carl Sandburg reports, and the uproar was so loud Lincoln did not go through with his intent. But it shows the deep cleavage that existed between the liberal President and his radical government on the very eve of his last day!

* * *

Then, too, there was the trial held in a hurry and under circumstances no modern lawyer would call proper or even constitutional. Evidence was presented in part, important documents—such as Booth's own diary—were arbitrarily suppressed and kept out of the trial by order of Secretary Stanton, who also had impounded Booth's personal belongings and any and all documents seized at the Surratt house on H Street, giving defense attorneys for the accused, especially Mrs. Mary Surratt, not the slightest opportunity to build a reasonable defense for their clients.

That was as it should be, from Stanton's point of view: fanning the popular hatred by letting the conspirators appear in as unfavorable a light as possible, a quick conviction and execution of the judgment, so that no sympathy could rise among the public for the accused. There was considerable opposition to the hanging of Mrs. Surratt, and committees demanding her pardon were indeed formed. But by the time these committees were able to function properly, the lady was dead, convicted on purely circumstantial evidence: Her house had been the meeting place for the conspirators, but it was never proven that she was part of the conspiracy. In fact, she disapproved of the murder plot, according to the condemned, but the government would not accept this view. Her own son John H. Surratt, sitting the trial out in Canada, never lifted a hand to save his mother—perhaps he thought Stanton would not dare execute her.

* * *

Setting aside for the moment the identity of the spirit communicator at the Surratt tavern, I examined certain aspects of this new material: Certainly Sherman himself could not have been part of an anti-Lincoln plot, for he was a "dove," strictly a Lincoln man. But a member of his staff—perhaps the mysterious colonel—might well have been involved. Sybil's communicator had stated that Booth knew all about those Army officers who were either using him or were in league with him, making, in fact, the assassination a dual plot of southern avengers and northern hawks. If Booth knew these names, he might have put the information into his personal diary. This diary was written during his fight, while he was hiding from his pursuers in the wooded swamplands of Maryland and Virginia.

At the conspiracy trial, the diary was not even mentioned, but at the subsequent trial of John H. Surratt, two years later, it did come to light. That is, Lafayette Baker, head of the Secret Service at the time of the murder, mentioned its existence, and it was promptly impounded for the trial. But when it was produced as evidence in court, only two pages were left in it—the rest had been torn out by an unknown hand! Eighteen pages were missing. The diary had been in Stanton's possession from the moment of its seizure until now, and it was highly unlikely that Booth himself had so mutilated his own diary the moment he had finished writing it! To the contrary, the diary was his attempt to justify himself before his contemporaries, and before history. The onus of guilt here falls heavily upon Secretary Stanton again.

It is significant that whoever mutilated the diary had somehow spared an entry dated April 21, 1865:

"Tonight I will once more try the river, with the intention to cross; though I have a greater desire and almost a mind to return to Washington, and in a measure clear my name, which I feel I can do."

* * *

Philip Van Doren Stern, author of *The Man Who Killed Lincoln*, quite rightfully asks, how could a self-confessed murderer clear his name unless he knew something that would involve other people than himself and his associates? Stern also refers to David Herold's confession in which the young man quotes Booth as telling him that there was a group of *thirty-five men in Washington* involved in the plot.

Sybil's confused communicator kept saying certain numbers, "forty-nine" and "thirty-four." Could this be the code for Stanton and a committee of thirty-four men?

Whoever they were, not one of the northern conspirators ever confessed their part in the crime, so great was the popular indignation at the deed.

John H. Surratt, after going free as a consequence of the inability of his trial jury to agree on a verdict, tried his hand at lecturing on the subject of the assassination. He only gave a single lecture, which turned out a total failure. Nobody was interested. But a statement Surratt made at that lecture fortunately has come down to us. He admitted that another group of conspirators had been working independently and simultaneously to strike a blow at Lincoln.

That Surratt would make such a statement fits right in with the facts. He was a courier and undercover man for the Confederacy, with excellent contacts in Washington. It was he who managed to have the telegraph go out of order during the murder and to allow Booth to pass the sentry at the Navy Yard bridge without difficulty. But was the communicator speaking through Mrs. Leek not holding back information at first, only to admit finally that John Wilkes *knew* the names of those others, after all?

This differs from Philip Van Doren Stern's account, in which Booth was puzzled about the identities of his "unknown" allies. But then, Stern didn't hold a trance session at the Surratt tavern, either. Until our visit in November of 1967, the question seemed up in the air.

Surratt had assured Booth that "his sources" would make sure that they all got away safely. In other words, Booth and his associates were doing the dirty work for the brain trust in Washington, with John Surratt serving both sides and in a way linking them together in an identical purpose—though for totally opposite reasons.

Interestingly enough, the entranced Sybil spoke of a colonel who knew Sherman, and who would look after him...he would supply a ticket...! That ticket might have been a steamer ticket for some foreign ship going from Mexico to Europe, where Booth could be safe. But who was the mysterious Major General Gee? Since Booth's group was planning to kill Grant as well, would he be likely to be involved in the plot on the northern end?

Lincoln had asked Grant and Mrs. Grant to join him at Ford's Theatre the fateful evening; Grant had declined, explaining that he wished to join his family in New Jersey instead. Perhaps that was a natural enough excuse to turn down the President's invitation, but one might also construe it differently: Did he know about the plot and did he not wish to see his President shot?

Booth's choice of the man to do away with Grant had fallen on John Surratt, as soon as he learned of the change in plans. Surratt was to get on the train that took Grant to New Jersey. But Grant was not attacked; there is no evidence whatever that Surratt ever took the train, and he himself said he didn't. Surratt, then, the go-between of the two groups of conspirators, could easily have warned Grant himself: The Booth group wanted to kill Lincoln *and* his chief aides, to make the North powerless; but the northern conspirators would have only wanted to have Lincoln removed and certainly none of their own men. Even though Grant was likely to carry out the President's "soft" peace plans while Lincoln was his commander-in-chief, he was a soldier accustomed to taking orders and would carry out with equal loyalty the hard-line policies of Lincoln's successor! Everything here points to Surratt as having been, in effect, a double agent.

But was the idea of an involvement of General Grant really so incredible?

Wilson Sullivan, author of a critical review of a recently published volume of *The Papers of Andrew*

Johnson, has this to say of Grant, according to the *Saturday Review of Literature,* March 16, 1968:

"Despite General Grant's professed acceptance of Lincoln's policy of reconciliation with the Southern whites, President Grant strongly supported and implemented the notorious Ku Klux Act in 1871."

This was a law practically disenfranchising Southerners and placing them directly under federal courts rather than local and state authorities.

It was Grant who executed the repressive policies of the radical Republican Congress and who reverted to the hard-line policies of the Stanton clique after he took political office, undoing completely whatever lenient measures President Johnson had instituted following the assassination of his predecessor.

But even before Grant became President, he was the man in power. Since the end of the Civil War, civil administrations had governed the conquered South. In March 1867, these were replaced by military governments in five military districts. The commanders of these districts were directly responsible to General Grant and disregarded any orders from President Johnson. Civil rights and state laws were broadly ignored. The reasons for this perversion of Lincoln's policies were not only vengeance on the Confederacy, but political considerations as well: By delaying the voting rights of Southerners, a Republican Congress could keep itself in office that much longer. Sullivan feels that this attitude was largely responsible for the emergence of the Ku Klux Klan and other racists organizations in the South.

Had Lincoln lived out his term, he would no doubt have implemented a policy of rapid reconciliation, the South would have regained its political privileges quickly, and the radical Republican party might have lost the next election.

That party was led by Secretary Stanton and General Grant!

What a convenient thing it was to have a southern conspiracy at the proper time! All one had to do is get aboard and ride the conspiracy to the successful culmination—then blame it all on the South, thereby doing a double job, heaping more guilt upon the defeated Confederacy and ridding the country of the *one* man who could forestall the continuance in power of the Stanton-Grant group!

That Stanton might have been the real leader in the northern plot is not at all unlikely. The man was given to rebellion when the situation demanded it. President Andrew Johnson had tried to continue the Lincoln line in the face of a hostile Congress and even a Cabinet dominated by radicals. In early 1868, Johnson tried to oust Secretary Stanton from his Cabinet because he realized that Stanton was betraying his policies. But Stanton defied his chief and barricaded himself in the War Department. This

intolerable situation led to Johnson's impeachment proceedings, which failed by a single vote.

There was one more tragic figure connected with the events that seemed to hold unresolved mysteries: Mrs. Mary Surratt, widow of a Confederate spy and mother of another. On April 14, 1865, she invited her son's friend, and one of her boarders, Louis Weichman, to accompany her on an errand to her old country home, now a tavern, at Surrattsville. Weichmann gladly obliged Mrs. Surratt and went down to hire a buggy. At the tavern, Mrs. Surratt went out carrying a package which she described to Weichmann as belonging to Booth. This package she handed to tavernkeeper John Lloyd inside the house to safekeep for Booth. It contained the guns the fugitives took with them later, after the assassination had taken place.

Weichmann's testimony of this errand, and his description of the meetings at the H Street house, were largely responsible for Mrs. Surratt's execution, even though it was never shown that she had anything to do with the murder plot itself. Weichmann's testimony haunted him all his life, for Mrs. Surratt's "ghost," as Lloyd Lewis puts it in *Myths After Lincoln,* "got up and walked" in 1868 when her "avengers" made political capital of her execution, charging Andrew Johnson with having railroaded her to death.

Mrs. Surratt's arrest at 11:15 P.M., April 17, 1865, came as a surprise to her despite the misgivings she had long harbored about her son's involvement with Booth and the other plotters. Lewis Paine's untimely arrival at the house after it had already been raided also helped seal her fate. At the trial that followed, none of the accused was ever allowed to speak, and their judges were doing everything in their power to link the conspiracy with the confederate government, even to the extent of producing false witnesses, who later recanted their testimonies.

If anyone among the condemned had the makings of a ghost, it was Mary Surratt.

Soon after her execution and burial, reports of her haunting the house on H Street started. The four bodies of the executed had been placed inside the prison walls and the families were denied the right to bury them.

When Annie Surratt could not obtain her mother's body, she sold the lodging house and moved away from the home that had seen so much tragedy. The first buyer of the house had little luck with it, however. Six weeks later he sold it again, even though he had bought it very cheaply. Other tenants came and went quickly, and according to the Boston *Post,* which chronicled the fate of the house, it was because they saw the ghost of Mrs. Surratt clad in her execution robe walking the corridors of her home! That was back in the 1860s and 1870s. Had Mary Surratt found peace since then? Her body now lies buried underneath a simple gravestone at Mount Olivet Cemetery.

The house at 604 H Street, N.W. still stands. In the early 1900s, a Washington lady dined at the house. During dinner, she noticed the figure of a young girl appear and walk up the stairs. She recognized the distraught girl as the spirit of Annie Surratt, reports John McKelway in the Washington *Star*. The Chinese establishment now occupying the house does not mind the ghosts, either mother or daughter. And Ford Theatre has just been restored as a legitimate theatre, to break the ancient jinx.

Both Stern and Emanuel Hertz quote an incident in the life of Robert Lincoln, whom a Mr. Young discovered destroying many of his father's private papers. When he remonstrated with Lincoln, the son replied that "the papers he was destroying contained the documentary evidence of the treason of a member of Lincoln's Cabinet, and he thought it best for all that such evidence be destroyed."

Mr. Young enlisted the help of Nicholas Murray Butler, later head of Columbia University, New York, to stop Robert Lincoln from continuing this destruction. The remainder of the papers were then deposited in the Library of Congress, but we don't know how many documents Robert Lincoln had already destroyed when he was halted.

There remains only the curious question as to the identity of our communicator at the Surratt tavern in November 1967.

"Shot down like a dog," the voice had complained through the psychic.

"Hunted like a dog," Booth himself wrote in his diary. Why would Edwin Booth, who had done everything in his power to publicly repudiate his brother's deed, and who claimed that he had little direct contact with John Wilkes in the years before the assassination—why would he want to own this house that was so closely connected with the tragedy and John Wilkes Booth? Who would think that the "Prince of Players," who certainly had no record of any involvement in the plot to kill Lincoln, should be drawn back by feelings of guilt to the house so intimately connected with his brother John Wilkes?

But he did own it, and sell it to B. K. Miller, Thomas Miller's father!

I couldn't find any Lowell, Virginia on my maps, but there is a Laurel, Maryland not far from Surrattsville, or today's Clinton.

Much of the dialogue fits Edwin Booth, owner of the house. Some of it doesn't, and some of it might be deliberate coverup.

Mark you, this is not a "ghost" in the usual sense, for nobody reported Edwin Booth appearing to them at this house. Mrs. Surratt might have done so, both here and at her town house, but the principal character in this fascinating story has evidently lacked the inner torment that is the basis for ghostly manifestations beyond time and space. Quite so, for to John Wilkes Booth the deed was the work of a national hero, not to be ashamed of at all. If anything, the ungrateful Confederacy owed him a debt of thanks.

No, I decided, John Wilkes Booth would not make a convincing ghost. But Edwin? Was there more to his relationship with John Wilkes than the current published record shows? "Ah, there's the rub..." the Prince of Players would say in one of his greatest roles.

Then, too, there is the peculiar mystery of John Surratt's position. He had broken with John Wilkes Booth weeks before the murder, he categorically stated at his trial in 1867. Yes, he had been part of the earlier plot to abduct Lincoln, but murder, no. That was not his game.

* * *

It was my contention, therefore, that John Surratt's role as a dual agent seemed highly likely from the evidence available to me, both through objective research and psychic contacts. We may never find the mysterious colonel on Sherman's staff, nor be able to identify with *certainty* Major General "Gee." But War Secretary Stanton's role looms ominously and in sinister fashion behind the generally accepted story of the plot.

* * *

If Edwin Booth came through Sybil Leek to tell us what he knew of his brother's involvement in Lincoln's death, perhaps he did so because John Wilkes never got around to clear his name himself. Stanton may have seen to that, and the disappearing diary and unseeming haste of the trial all fall into their proper places.

* * *

It is now over a hundred years after the event. Will we have to wait that long before we know the complete truth about another President's murder?

A Visit with Woodrow Wilson

THE WASHINGTON POST may have published an occasional phantom story over the years, but not too many ghost stories. Thus it was with a degree of skepticism that I picked up a copy of that ebullient newspaper dated May 4, 1969. It had been sent to me by a well-meaning friend and fan living in Washington. Mrs. Charles Marwick, herself a writer and married to a medical writer, is of Scottish ancestry and quite prone to pick up a ghost story here and there.

The piece in question had attracted her attention as being a little bit above the usual cut of the journalistic approach to that sort of material. Generally, my newspaper colleagues like to make light of any psychic report, and if the witnesses are respectable, or at least rational on the surface of it, they will report the events but still add a funny tag line or two to make sure that no one takes their own attitude toward the supernatural too seriously.

Thus, when I saw the headline, "Playing Host to Ghosts?" I was worried. This looked like one of those light-hearted, corny approaches to the psychic, I thought, but when I started to read the report by Phil Casey I realized that the reporter was trying to be fair to both his editor and the ghosts.

The Woodrow Wilson House at 2340 S St. NW is a quiet, serene place most of the time, with only about 150 visitors a week, but sometimes at night there's more noise than José Vasquez, the house man, can stand.

Vasquez has been hearing queer, and sometimes loud, noises in the night a couple of times a year for the past four years, but they didn't bother him much until the stroke of midnight, Saturday, April 5.

"It was depressing," he said. "If I were a nervous man, it would be very bad."

Vasquez, who is 32, is from Peru, speaks four languages, plays the piano and is a student at D.C. Teachers College, where he intends to major in psychology. He doesn't believe in ghosts, but he's finding it hard to hold that position, the way things are going around that house.

He was downstairs playing the piano that night, he said, and he was all alone (his wife, a practical nurse, was at work at the National Institute of Health).

"I felt that someone was behind me, watching me," he said. "My neck felt funny. You know? But there was no one there. I looked."

Later, Vasquez was walking up to his fourth-floor apartment when he heard something behind him on the third floor, near the bedrooms of the World War I President and his wife.

"The steps were loud," he said, "and heavy, like a man."

The footsteps went into Mrs. Wilson's bedroom, and Vasquez went in, too. He kept hearing the steps in the room, and was in a state of almost total unhappiness.

"I go to this corner," he said, going to the corner, "and I stand here and wait. I waited a long time and then I hear the steps again, going into the hall and to Mr. Wilson's bedroom. I follow."

At that point, listening to the heavy footsteps at the foot of the President's four-poster bed, Vasquez decided to hurry upstairs.

"And when I do, the steps they came running behind me," he said, "and they follow me, bump, bump, bump, up the stairs. I am very nervous."

The back stairway is iron, and noisy, which didn't help any, Vasquez said, but he went on up to his apartment.

And then, he heard no more footsteps and he was glad about that.

Once, some time back, Vasquez was in his tub when he heard some knocking noises on the tub.

"I knock right back, like this," he said, thumping the tub, "and the noise stops."

His wife has never heard the footsteps or the tub knocking, but she hears an occasional noise and sometimes she wakes up in the night under the impression that someone is standing at the foot of the bed. There never is anyone she can see.

I talked to Mr. Vasquez, and he sounded like a very nice, rational fellow. He had nothing to add to the story that had appeared in the *Post*, but he referred me to the curator of the Wilson House for permission to visit.

I contacted Ruth Dillon and patiently explained the purpose of my investigation. As much as I tried to stress the historic aspects of it, she already knew from my name what I was after, and to my surprise did not object; so long as I did not publish anything untrue, she did not mind my talking about any specters that might be on the premises, famous or otherwise.

I knew very little about the late Woodrow Wilson myself, except what one generally knows of any President of the United States, and I made it a point not to read up on him. Instead I called Ethel Johnson Meyers, my good friend and many times my medium, and arranged for her to accompany me to Washington in the near future. Due to a sudden cancellation in Mrs. Meyers' busy schedule, the date we were able to set was May 6, 1969, three days after the reporter had written his article. A good friend of mine, Mrs. Nicole Jackson, offered to drive us around since I do not drive a car, and the three of us arrived at the Woodrow Wilson House at the appointed hour.

That hour was 11 A.M., on a sunny and very warm May 6. The house was majestic, even from the outside. It looked the very essence of a presidential mansion. It looked that way to me today, although I gather that in the days when this house was built, such houses were not considered ostentatious but rather ordinary elegant town houses for those who could afford them.

Now the property of the National Trust, the house has been turned into a museum, and visitors are admitted at certain hours of the day. Four stories high, it also boasts a magnificent garden in the back and offers the privacy of a country estate along with the convenience of a town house. It is difficult to accurately describe the style of this building. Built for Henry Parker Fairbanks in 1915, the red-brick Georgian house was designed by the architect Waddy B. Wood. Late in 1920, as President Wilson's second term neared its end, Mrs. Wilson searched for an appropriate residence. She happened to be passing the house on S Street, which she is later quoted as describing as "an unpretentious, comfortable, dignified house, fitted to the needs of a gentleman." On December 14 of that year, according to the brochure published by the National Trust about the Woodrow Wilson House, Mr. Wilson insisted that his wife attend a concert, and when she returned, presented her with the deed to the property. The next day they visited the house, where Mr. Wilson gave her a piece of sod, representing the land, and the key to one of the doors, representing the house—telling her this was an old Scottish custom.

The Wilsons made certain changes, such as the installation of an elevator and the addition of a billiard room. They also constructed a brick garage and placed iron gates at the entrance to the drive. Some of the rooms were changed, and a large library was constructed to hold Mr. Wilson's eight thousand books. Today the library contains a large collection of items connected with President Wilson and his contemporaries. These are mainly presentation copies of books and documents.

President Wilson lived in the house with his second wife, Edith Bolling Wilson. She was a devoted companion to him during his last years, went to Europe with him to attend peace conferences, and generally traveled with the President. She liked to read to him and he, conversely, liked to read to her, and in general they were a very close and devoted couple.

At the end of his second term he retired to this house, and died here three years later on February 3, 1924. Mrs. Wilson, who later presented the house to the American people under the guardianship of the National Trust, also lived and died there on December 28, 1961, which happened to be the 105th anniversary of President Wilson's birth.

By and large the rooms have been kept as they were during their tenancy, with the sole addition of certain items such as furniture, antiquities, and documents pertaining to the Wilsons' careers and lifetimes. If the house is a museum, it doesn't look like one. It is more like a shrine—but not an ostentatious one—to what many consider a great American.

As is my custom, I let Ethel Meyers—who did not know she was in the Wilson House—roam the premises under investigation at will, so that she could get her psychic bearings. She walked to and fro, puzzled here, sure of

something or other there, without saying anything. I followed her as close as I could. Finally, she walked up the stairs and came down again in a hurry, pointing up towards the top floors.

"What is it?" I asked Ethel.

"Someone up there," she mumbled, and looked at me.

"Let us go in here," I suggested, as some visitors were coming in through the front door. I did not want to create a sensation with my investigation, as I had promised to do the whole thing quietly and unobtrusively.

We stepped into a parlor to one side of the main entrance. There I asked Ethel to take a seat in one of the old chairs and try to give me her impressions of what she had just experienced upstairs.

At this point, the medium's control personality, Albert, took over.

"So many detached things are coming in. I'm getting the *presence* of an individual here. I haven't had an impression like this before, it seems. Heed kindly the light which we throw on this to you now. *That is a hymn*—'Lead, Kindly Light.'"

"Is there anything in this house that is causing disturbances?"

"There is restlessness, where those who remember certain things. They are like fertile fields, to create over a past that is not understood."

"Who is the communicator, do you think?"

Albert replied: "I would say it is *himself*, in the picture on the mantelpiece."

"What does he want you to do, or say?"

"I heard him distinctly say that the family rows should not be made public. That those are thought levels in the house. Angry voices sometimes rise. There are also others who have things to say for themselves, beyond that."

"What is the row?"

"Let them speak for themselves."

"What is there that he wants to do—is there anything specific he would like us to know?"

"That the world going forward is more pleasant now than going for me backwards, because true statements are coming forth to make wider reach for man *when he shakes his hands across oceans with his neighbors.* So now they are, not before; they were in your back yard so to speak under the shade of other trees."

The "resident spirit" was now talking directly to us.

"I want to say, if you will give me audience while I am here, that this is my pleasurable moment, to lift the curtain to show you that the mortal enemy will become the great friend, soon now. That my puny dream of yesteryear has been gradually realized—the brotherhood of man. And it becomes clearer, closer to the next century. It is here, for us on *our* side. I see it more clearly from here. I am not sure about that designated time. But it is the brotherhood of man, when the religious problem is lifted and the truth is seen, and all men stand equal to other men, neighbors, enemies."

"Who are you referring to?"

"I come back again to tell you, that the hands that will reach over the mighty ocean will soon clasp! Hands lean forward to grasp them. My puny dream, my puny ideal, takes form, and I look upon it and I am proud as a small part but an integral part of that. It will bloom, the period of gestation is about over, when this will come to light. And I give great thanks to the withinness that I have had so small a part in the integral whole. I tell you it is all a part of the period of gestation before the dawn."

"When will the dawn come?"

"Just before the turn of the century. Eighty-eight, –nine."

"And until then?"

"The period of gestation must go through its tortuous ways. But it will dawn, it will dawn and not only on this terra firma. It will dawn even over this city, and it will be more a part of world-state as I saw it in my very close view of the world. I was given this dream, and I have lived by it."

"Do you want us to do anything about your family, or your friends? Tell them anything specifically?"

"That my soul lives on, and that it will return when I see the turn of the century, and that I may look face to face with that which I saw; that which was born within my consciousness."

"Whom should we give this message to?"

"The one living member of my family."

"What is this member's name?"

"Alice."

"Anything else?"

"Just mundane moments of the lives of many fallible mortals are inconsequential. Posterity has no need for it. It has only the need for that which is coming—the bright new dawn. We live to tell you this too. God rest the soul of man; it will win. Science will win. Man's soul will be free to know its own importance. I have forgotten the future; I look upon it all, here, as my integral part of the world."

"We will then go and have a look at that which was your house. Thank you for telling me what you did."

"God bless you—that is, the God that is your own true God."

"Thank you."

"Hello—Albert."

"Albert—is everything alright?"

"She's fine. I will release her."

"Thank you."

"I guess you know with whom you were speaking."

"Yes."

"It was difficult for him to take over."

Now Ethel came out of trance, none the worse for it. I questioned her about the room we were in.

"Deals have been made in this room."

"What kind of deals?"

"Political deals. There is a heavy-set man with sideburns here."

"Is he somebody of importance?"

"I would say so. He has not too much hair up here. Could have a beard."

"What would he be doing here?"

"Well he seems to take over the room. To make a deal, of some kind."

"What kind of deal?"

"I don't think he's an American."

"If you saw him would you recognize him?"

"I think I would, yes."

I walked Ethel into the huge room with the fireplace, pointing at various photographs lined up on top of it. "Would this be the man?"

"Oh, that's George isn't it?"

"No. Could this be the man?"

"That's Richard then."

"No, it's not Richard and it's not George, but is it the man that you saw?"

"He's a little more gray here than he was when I—if that's the man. But it could be, yes." She had just identified a world-famous statesman of World War I vintage.

We had now arrived on the third floor. A guide took us around and pointed out the elevator and the iron stairs. We walked down again and stopped at the grand piano.

"Ethel," I asked, "do you think that this piano has been used recently?"

"I would say it has. Ghostly, too. I think this is a whirlpool right here. I don't know whether Wilson was a good pianist or not, but he has touched it."

"Do you feel he is the one that is in the house?"

"I don't think that he is *haunting* it, but present, yes."

* * *

I carefully checked into the history of the house, to see whether some tragedy or other unusual happenings might have produced a genuine ghost. There was nothing in the background of the house to indicate that such an event had ever taken place. How then was one to explain the footsteps? What about the presence Mr. Vasquez had felt? Since most of the phenomena occurred upstairs, one is led to believe that they might be connected with some of the servants or someone living at that level of the house. At the period when the Wilsons had the house, the top floor was certainly used as servants' quarters. But the Wilsons' own bedroom and living quarters were also upstairs, and the footsteps and the feeling of a presence was not restricted to the topmost floor, it would appear.

Then, too, the expressions used by the entranced medium indicate a person other than an ordinary servant. There are several curious references in the transcript of the tape taken while Ethel Johnson Meyers was in trance, and afterwards when she spoke to me clairvoyantly. First of all, the reference to a hymn, "Lead, Kindly Light," would indeed be in character for President Wilson. He was a son of a Presbyterian minister, and certainly grew up under the influence of his father as far as religion and expressions were concerned. The references to "hands across the sea" would be unimportant if Ethel Johnson Meyers had known that she was in the Wilson House. However, she did not connect the house with President Wilson at the time she made the statement. The "puny dream" referred to of uniting the world was certainly President Wilson's uppermost thought and desire. Perhaps Woodrow Wilson will be known as the "Peace President" in future history books—even though he was in office during a war, he went into that war with a genuine and sincere desire to end all wars. "To make the world safe for democracy" was one of his best-known slogans. Thus, the expressions relayed by the medium seem to me to be entirely in keeping with that spirit.

True, the entity speaking through the medium did not come forward and say, "I am Woodrow Wilson." I would not have expected it. That would have been ostentatious and entirely out of character for the quiet, soft-spoken gentleman Wilson was.

* * *

Is the Woodrow Wilson House haunted? Is the restless spirit of the "Peace President" once more about,

because of what is transpiring in his beloved Washington? Is he aroused by the absence of peace even in his own homeland, let alone abroad? Truly, the conditions to cause a restless entity to remain disturbed are all present.

Why is he trying to make contact with the physical world at this time? The man who reported his experiences to the *Washington Post* evidently is mediumistic. There are very few people staying overnight in the house at the present time. Very likely the restless spirit of President Wilson—if indeed it is his spirit—found it convenient to contact this man, despite his comparatively unimportant position. But because he was psychic he presented a channel through which the President—if it was indeed he—could express himself and reach the outer world, the world that seems to be so much in need of peace today.

In a sense he has succeeded in his efforts. Because of the experiences of Mr. Vasquez I became aware of the hauntings at the Wilson House. My visit and the trance condition into which I placed Ethel Johnson Meyers resulted in a certain contact. There is every reason to believe that this contact was the President himself.

As we left the house, I questioned Mrs. Meyers once again about the man she had clairvoyantly seen walking about the house. Without thinking, she described the tall dignified figure of Woodrow Wilson. It may not constitute absolute proof in terms of parapsychology, of course, but I have the feeling that we did indeed make contact with the restless and truly perturbed spirit of Woodrow Wilson, and that this spirit somehow wants me to tell the world how concerned he is about the state it is in.

Ring Around the White House

I DON'T THINK ANYONE has had more trouble getting into the White House for a specific purpose than I except, perhaps, some presidential aspirants such as Thomas E. Dewey. Mr. Dewey's purpose was a lot easier to explain than mine, to begin with. How do you tell an official at the presidential mansion that you would like to go to the Lincoln Bedroom to see whether Lincoln's ghost is still there? How do you make it plain that you're not looking for sensationalism, that you're not bringing along a whole covey of newspaper people, all of which can only lead to unfavorable publicity for the inhabitants of the White House, whoever they may be at the time?

Naturally, this was the very difficult task to which I had put myself several years ago. Originally, when I was collecting material for *Window to the Past*, I had envisioned myself going to the Lincoln Bedroom and possibly the East

Room in the White House, hoping to verify and authenticate apparitions that had occurred to a number of people in those areas. But all my repeated requests for permission to visit the White House in the company of a reputable psychic were turned down. Even when I promised to submit my findings and the writings based on those findings to White House scrutiny prior to publication, I was told that my request could not be granted.

The first reason given was that it was not convenient because the President and his family were in. Then it was not convenient because they would be away. Once I was turned down because my visit could not be cleared sufficiently with Security, and anyway, that part of the White House I wanted to visit was private.

I never gave up. Deep down I had the feeling that the White House belongs to the people and is not a piece of real estate on which even the presidential family may hang out a sign, "No Trespassers." I still think so. However, I got nowhere as long as the Johnsons were in the White House.

I tried again and again. A colonel stationed in the White House, whom I met through Countess Gertrude d'Amecourt, a mutual friend, tried hard to get permission for me to come and investigate. He too failed.

Next, I received a letter, quite unexpectedly, from the Reverend Thomas W. Dettman of Niagara, Wisconsin. He knew a number of very prominent men in the federal government and offered to get me the permission I needed. These men, he explained, had handled government investigations for him before, and he was sure they would be happy to be of assistance if he asked them. He was even sure they would carry a lot of weight with the President. They knew him well, he asserted. Mr. Dettman had been associated with the Wisconsin Nixon for President Committee, and offered to help in any way he could.

After thanking Mr. Dettman for his offer, I heard nothing further for a time. Then he wrote me again explaining that he had as yet not been able to get me into the Lincoln Bedroom, but that he was still working on it. He had asked the help of Representative John Byrnes of Wisconsin in the matter, and I would hear further about it. Then Mr. Dettman informed me that he had managed to arrange for me to be given "a special tour" of the White House, and, to the best of his knowledge, that included the East Room. He then asked that I contact William E. Timmons, Assistant to the President, for details.

I was, of course, elated. Imagine, a special tour of the White House! What could be better than that?

With his letter, Mr. Dettman had included a letter from Senator William Proxmire of Wisconsin, in which the Senator noted that I would not be able to do research in the Lincoln Bedroom, but that I would be given the special tour of the White House.

I hurriedly wrote a thank-you note to Mr. Dettman, and started to make plans to bring a medium to Washington with me. A few days later Mr. Dettman wrote me again.

He had received a call from the White House concerning the tour. He could, he explained, in no way guarantee what *kind* of tour I would be given, nor what I would see. He had done everything possible to help me and hoped I would not be disappointed.

Whether my own sixth sense was working or not, I suddenly thought I had better look into the nature of that "special tour" myself. I wrote and asked whether I would be permitted to spend half an hour in the East Room, since the Lincoln Bedroom had been denied me. Back came a letter dated May 14, 1970, on White House stationery, and signed by John S. Davies, Special Assistant to the President, Office White House Visitors.

Senator Proxmire's recent letter to Mr. William Timmons concerning your most recent request to visit the White House has been referred to me, as this office is responsible for White House visitors. Unfortunately, as we have pointed out, we are unable to arrange for you to visit the Lincoln Bedroom, as this room is in the President's personal residence area, which is not open to visitors. If you wish to arrange an early-morning special tour, I suggest you contact Senator Proxmire's office. You are also most welcome to come to the White House any time during the regular visiting hours.

I decided to telephone Mr. Davies since the day of my planned visit was close at hand. It was only then that I realized what that famous "special tour" really was. It meant that I, along with who else might be present at the time at the White House gates, would be permitted to walk through the part of the White House open to all visitors. I couldn't bring a tape recorder. I could not sit down or tarry along the way. I had to follow along with the group, glance up at whatever might be interesting, and be on my way again like a good little citizen. What, then, was so special about that tour, I inquired? Nothing really, I was told, but that is what it is known as. It is called a special tour because you have to have the request of either a Senator or a Representative from your home state.

I canceled my visit and dismissed the medium. But my reading public is large, and other offers to help me came my way.

Debbie Fitz is a teenage college student who wanted me to lecture at her school. In return, she offered to get me into the White House, or at least try to. I smiled at her courage, but told her to go right ahead and try. She wrote a letter to Miss Nixon, whom she thought would be favorable to her request, being of the same age group and all that. After explaining her own interest in ESP research and the importance this field has in this day and age for the young, she went on to explain who I was and that I had previously been denied admittance to the White House areas I wished to do research in. She wrote:

All he wants to do is take a psychic medium into the room and scientifically record any phenomena that may exist. This will not involve staying overnight; it can be done during the day at your convenience. All investigations are conducted in a scientific manner and are fully documented. It is well known that Lincoln himself was psychic and held séances in the White House. Wouldn't you, as a student of White House history and a member of the young, open-minded generation, like to find out whether or not this room is really haunted? This will also provide an opportunity for young people who are interested in other things besides riots and demonstrations to benefit intellectually from Mr. Holzer's efforts.

Debbie Fitz never received a reply or an acknowledgment. I, of course, never heard about the matter again.

Try as I would, I was rebuffed. Just the same, interest in the haunted aspects of the nation's Executive Mansion remains at a high level. Several Washington newspapers carried stories featuring some of the psychic occurrences inside the White House, and whenever I appeared on Washington television, I was invariably asked about the ghosts at the White House. Perhaps the best account of the psychic state of affairs at number 1600 Pennsylvania Avenue was written by the *Washington Post* reporter, Jacqueline Lawrence.

"The most troubled spirit of 1600 Pennsylvania Avenue is Abraham Lincoln, who during his own lifetime claimed to receive regular visits from his two dead sons, Pat and Willie." After reporting the well-known premonitory dream in which Lincoln saw himself dead in a casket in the East Room, Miss Lawrence goes on to report that Mrs. Franklin Delano Roosevelt's servant, Mary Evan, had reported seeing Lincoln on the bed in the northwest bedroom, pulling on his boots. "Other servants said they had seen him lying quietly in his bed, and still others vowed that he periodically stood at the oval window over the main entrance of the White House. Mrs. Roosevelt herself never saw Lincoln, but she did admit that when working late she frequently felt a ghostly sort of presence."

Amongst the visitors to the White House who had experienced psychic occurrences was the late Queen Wilhelmina of the Netherlands. Asleep in the Queen's Bedroom, she heard someone knock at her door, got up, opened it, and saw the ghost of President Lincoln standing there looking at her. She fainted, and by the time she had come to he was gone.

"According to the legend, the spirit of Lincoln is especially troubled and restless on the eve of national calamities such as war." Under the circumstances, one should expect the shade of President Lincoln to be in around-the-clock attendance these days and nights.

* * *

But Lincoln is not the only ghost at the White House. Household members of President Taft have observed the ghost of Abigail Adams walking right through the closed doors of the East Room with her arms outstretched. And who knows what other specters reside in these ancient and troubled walls?

That all is not known about the White House may be seen from a dispatch of the New York *Daily News* dated November 25, 1969, concerning two new rooms unearthed at the White House. "Two hitherto unknown rooms,

believed to date back to the time of Thomas Jefferson, have been unearthed in the White House a few yards away from the presidential swimming pool. The discovery was made as excavation continued on the larger work area for the White House press corps. The subterranean rooms, which White House curator James Ketchum described as storage or coal bins, were believed among the earliest built at the White House. Filled with dirt, they contained broken artifacts believed to date back to President Lincoln's administration."

When I discussed my difficulties in receiving permission for a White House investigation with prominent people in Washington, it was suggested to me that I turn my attention to Ford's Theatre, or the Parker House—both places associated with the death of President Lincoln. I have not done so, for the simple reason that in my estimation the ghost of Lincoln is nowhere else to be found but where it mattered to him: in the White House. If there is a transitory impression left behind at Ford's Theatre, where he was shot, or the Parker House, where he eventually died some hours later, it would only be an imprint from the past. I am sure that the surviving personality of President Lincoln is to a degree attached to the White House because of unfinished business. I do not think that this is unfinished only of his own time. So much of it has never been finished to this very day, nor is the present administration in any way finishing it. To the contrary. If there ever was any reason for Lincoln to be disturbed, it is now. The Emancipation Proclamation, for which he stood and which was in a way the rebirth of our country, is still only in part reality. Lincoln's desire for peace is hardly met in these troubled times. I am sure that the disturbances at the White House have never ceased. Only a couple of years ago, Lynda, one of the Johnson daughters, heard someone knock at her door, opened it, and found no one outside. Telephone calls have been put through to members of the presidential family, and there has been no one on the other end of the line. Moreover, on investigating, it was found that the White House operators had not rung the particular extension telephones.

It is very difficult to dismiss such occurrences as products of imagination, coincidence, or "settling of an old house." Everyone except a moron knows the difference between human footsteps caused by feet encased with boots or shoes, and the normal noises of an old house settling slowly and a little at a time on its foundation.

✳ 12

The Ill-fated Kennedys: From Visions to Ghosts

"When are you going to go down to Dallas and find out about President Kennedy?" the pleasant visitor inquired. He was a schoolteacher who had come to me to seek advice on how to start a course in parapsychology in his part of the country.

The question about President Kennedy was hardly new. I had been asked the same question in various forms ever since the assassination of John F. Kennedy, as if I and my psychic helpers had the duty to use our combined talents to find out what really happened at the School Book Depository in Dallas. I suppose similar conditions prevailed after the death of Abraham Lincoln. People's curiosity had been aroused, and with so many unconfirmed rumors making the rounds the matter of a President's sudden death does become a major topic of conversation and inquiry.

I wasn't there when Lincoln was shot; I was around when President Kennedy was murdered. Thus I am in a fairly good position to trace the public interest with the assassination from the very start.

I assured my visitor that so far I had no plans to go down to Dallas with a medium and find out what "really" happened. I have said so on television many times. When I was reminded that the Abraham Lincoln murder also left some unanswered questions and that I had indeed investigated it and come up with startlingly new results in my book *Window to the Past*, I rejoined that there was one basic difference between the Kennedy death and the assassination of President Lincoln: Lincoln's ghost has been seen repeatedly by reliable witnesses in the White House; so far I have not received any reliable reports of ghostly sightings concerning the late President Kennedy. In my opinion, this meant that the restlessness that caused Lincoln to remain in what used to be his working world has not caused John F. Kennedy to do likewise.

But I am not a hundred per cent sure any longer. Having learned how difficult it is to get information about such matters in Washington, or to gain admission to the White House as anything but a casual tourist—or, of course, on official business—I am also convinced that much may be suppressed or simply disregarded by those to whom experiences have happened simply because we live in a time when psychic phenomena can still embarrass those to whom they occur, especially if they have a position of importance.

But even if John Fitzgerald Kennedy is not walking the corridors of the White House at night, bemoaning his untimely demise or trying to right the many wrongs that have happened in this country since he left us, he is apparently doing something far better. He communicates, under special conditions and with special people. He is far from "dead and gone," if I am to believe those to whom these experiences have come. Naturally, one must sift the fantasy from the real thing—even more so when we are dealing with a famous person. I have done so, and I have looked very closely at the record of people who have reported to me psychic experiences dealing with the Kennedy family. I have eliminated a number of such reports simply because I could not find myself wholly convinced that the one who reported it was entirely balanced. I have also eliminated many other reports, not because I had doubts about the emotional stability of those who had made the reports, but because the reports were far too general and vague to be evidential even in the broadest sense. Material that was unsupported by witnesses, or material that was presented after the fact, was of course disregarded.

With all that in mind, I have come to the conclusion that the Kennedy destiny was something that could not have been avoided whether or not one accepts the old Irish Kennedy curse as factual.

Even the ghostly Kennedys are part and parcel of American life at the present. Why they must pay so high a price in suffering, I cannot guess. But it is true that the Irish forebears of the American Kennedys have also suffered an unusually high percentage of violent deaths over the years, mainly on the male side of the family. There is, of course, the tradition that way back in the Middle Ages a Kennedy was cursed for having incurred the wrath of some private local enemy. As a result of the curse, he and all his male descendants were to die violently one by one. To dismiss curses as fantasies, or at the very best workable only because of fear symptoms, would not be accurate. I had great doubts the effectiveness of curses until I came across several cases that allowed of no other explanation. In particular, I refer back to the case of the Wurmbrand curse reported by me in *Ghosts of the Golden West*. In that case the last male descendant of an illustrious family died under mysterious circumstances quite unexpectedly even while under the care of doctors in a hospital. Thus, if the Kennedy curse is operative, nothing much can be done about it.

Perhaps I should briefly explain the distinction between ghosts and spirits here, since so much of the Kennedy material is of the latter kind rather than the former. Ghosts are generally tied to houses or definite places where their physical bodies died tragically, or at least in a state of unhappiness. They are unable to leave the premises, so to speak, and can only repeat the pattern of their final moments, and are for all practical purposes not fully cognizant of their true state. They can be compared with psychotics in the physical state, and must first be freed from their own self-imposed delusions to be able to answer, if possible through a trance medium, or to leave and become free spirits out in what Dr. Joseph Rhine of

Duke University has called "the world of the mind," and which I generally refer to as the non-physical world.

Spirits, on the other hand, are really people, like you and me, who have left the physical body but are very much alive in a thinner, etheric body, with which they are able to function pretty much the same as they did in the physical body, except that they are now no longer weighed down by physical objects, distances, time, and space. The majority of those who die become free spirits, and only a tiny fraction are unable to proceed to the next stage but must remain behind because of emotional difficulties. Those who have gone on are not necessarily gone forever, but to the contrary they are able and frequently anxious to keep a hand in situations they have left unfinished on the earth plane. Death by violence or under tragic conditions does not necessarily create a ghost. Some such conditions may indeed create the ghost syndrome, but many others do not. I should think that President Kennedy is in the latter group—that is to say, a free spirit capable of continuing an interest in the world he left behind. Why this is so, I will show in the next pages.

* * *

The R. Lumber Company is a prosperous firm specializing in the manufacture and wholesale of lumber. It is located in Georgia and the owners, Mr. and Mrs. Bernard R., are respected citizens in their community. It was in April of 1970 that Mrs. R. contacted me. "I have just finished reading your book, *Life After Death*, and could not resist your invitation to share a strange experience with you," she explained, "hoping that you can give me some opinion regarding its authenticity.

"I have not had an opportunity to discuss what happened with anyone who is in any way psychic or clairvoyant. I have never tried to contact anyone close to the Kennedys about this, as of course I know they must have received thousands of letters. Many times I feel a little guilty about not even trying to contact Mrs. Kennedy and the children, if indeed it could have been a genuine last message from the President. It strikes me as odd that we might have received it or imagined we received it. We were never fans of the Kennedys, and although we were certainly sympathetic to the loss of our President, we were not as emotionally upset as many of our friends were who were ardent admirers.

"I am in no way psychic, nor have I ever had any supernatural experience before. I am a young homemaker and businesswoman, and cannot offer any possible explanation for what happened.

"On Sunday night, November 24, 1963, following John F. Kennedy's assassination, my family and I were at home watching on television the procession going through the Capitol paying their last respects. I was feeling very depressed, especially since that afternoon Lee Oswald had also been killed and I felt we would never know the full story of the assassination. For some strange reason, I sud-denly thought of the Ouija board, although I have never taken the answers seriously and certainly have never before consulted it about anything of importance. I asked my teenage daughter to work the board with me, and we went into another room. I had never tried to 'communicate with the dead.' I don't know why I had the courage to ask the questions I did on that night, but somehow, I felt compelled to go on:

Question: Will our country be in danger without Kennedy?

Answer: Strong with, weak without Kennedy, plot—stop.

Question: Will Ruby tell why President was killed?

Answer: Ruby does not know, only Oswald and I know. Sorry.

Question: Will we ever know why Kennedy was killed?

Answer: Underground and Oswald know, Ruby does not know, gangland leader caught in plot.

Question: Who is gangland leader?

Answer: Can't tell now.

Question: Why did Oswald hate President?

Answer: Negroes, civil rights bill.

Question: Have Oswald's and Kennedy's spirits met?

Answer: Yes. No hard feelings in Heaven.

Question: Are you in contact with Kennedy?

Answer: Yes.

Question: Does Kennedy have a message he would send through us?

Answer: Yes, yes, yes, tell J., C., and J.J. about this. Thanks, JFK.

Question: Can Kennedy give us some nickname to authenticate this?

Answer: Only nickname 'John John.'

Question: Do you really want us to contact someone?

Answer: Yes, but wait 'til after my funeral.

Question: How can we be sure Jackie will see our letter?

Answer: Write personal, not sympathy business.

Question: Is there something personal you could tell us to confirm this message?

Answer: Prying public knows all.

Question: Just one nickname you could give us?

Answer: J.J. (John John) likes to swim lots, called 'Daddy's little swimmer boy.' Does that help? JFK.

Question: Anything else?

Answer: J.J. likes to play secret game and bunny.

Question: What was your Navy Serial number?

Answer: 109 P.T. (jg) Skipper—5905. [seemed confused]

Question: Can we contact you again?

Answer: You, JFK, not JFK you.

Question: Give us address of your new home.

Answer: Snake Mountain Road.

Question: Will Mrs. Kennedy believe this, does she believe in the supernatural?

Answer: Some—tired—that's all tonight.

"At this point the planchette slid off the bottom of the board marked 'Good-by' and we attempted no further questions that night.

"The board at all times answered our questions swiftly and deliberately, without hesitation. It moved so rapidly, in fact, that my daughter and I *could not keep up with the message as it came.* We called out the letters to my eleven-year-old daughter who wrote them down, and we had to unscramble the words *after* we had received the entire message. We *had no intention* of trying to communicate *directly* with President Kennedy. I cannot tell you how frightened I was when I asked if there was a message he would send and the message came signed 'JFK.'

"For several days after, I could not believe the message was genuine. I have written Mrs. Kennedy several letters trying to explain what happened, but have never had the courage to mail them.

"None of the answers obtained are sensational, most are things we could have known or guessed. The answers given about 'John John' and 'secret game' and 'bunny' were in a magazine which my children had read and I had not. However, the answer about John John being called 'Daddy's little swimmer boy' is something none of us have ever heard or read. I have researched numerous articles written about the Kennedys during the last two years and have not found any reference to this. I could not persuade my daughter to touch the board again for days. We tried several times in December 1963, but were unsuccessful. One night, just before Christmas, a friend of mine persuaded my daughter to work the board with her. Perhaps the most surprising message came at this time, and it was also the last one we ever received. We are all Protestant and the message was inconsistent with our religious beliefs. When they asked if there was a message from President Kennedy, the planchette spelled out immediately "Thanks for your prayers while I was in Purgatory, JFK.'"

* * *

I have said many times in print and on television that I take a dim view of Ouija boards in general. Most of the material obtained from the use of this instrument merely reflects the unconscious of one or both sitters. Occasionally, however, Ouija boards have been able to tap the psy-chic levels of a person and come up with the same kind of veridical material a clairvoyant person might come up with. Thus, to dismiss the experiences of Mrs. R. merely because the material was obtained through a Ouija board would not be fair. Taking into account the circumstances, the background of the operators, and their seeming reluctance to seek out such channels of communication, I must dismiss ulterior motives such as publicity-seeking reasons or idle curiosity as being the causative factor in the event. On the other hand, having just watched a television program dealing with the demise of President Kennedy, the power of suggestion might have come into play. Had the material obtained through the Ouija board been more specific to a greater extent, perhaps I would not have to hesitate to label this a genuine experience. While there is nothing in the report that indicates fraud—either conscious or unconscious—there is nothing startling in the information given. Surely, if the message had come from Kennedy, or if Kennedy himself had been on the other end of the psychic line, there would have been certain pieces of information that would have been known only to him and that could yet be checked out in a way that was accessible. Surely, Kennedy would have realized how difficult it might have been for an ordinary homemaker to contact his wife. Thus, it seems to me that some other form of proof of identity would have been furnished. This, however, is really only speculation. Despite the sincerity of those reporting the incident, I feel that there is reasonable doubt as to the genuineness of the communication.

* * *

By far the majority of communications regarding President Kennedy relate to his death and are in the nature of premonitions, dreams, visions, and other warnings prior to or simultaneous with the event itself. The number of such experiences indicates that the event itself must have been felt ahead of its realization, indicating that some sort of law was in operation that could not be altered, even if President Kennedy could have been warned. As a matter of fact, I am sure that he was given a number of warnings, and that he chose to disregard them. I don't see how he could have done otherwise—both because he was the President and out of a fine sense of destiny that is part and parcel of the Kennedy make-up. Certainly Jeane Dixon was in a position to warn the President several times prior to the assassination. Others, less well connected in Washington, might have written letters that never got through to the President. Certainly one cannot explain these things away merely by saying that a public figure is always in danger of assassination, or that Kennedy had incurred the wrath of many people in this country and abroad. This simply doesn't conform to the facts. Premonitions have frequently been very precise, indicating in great detail the manner, time, and nature of the assassination. If it were merely a matter of vaguely foretelling the sudden death of the President, then of course one could say that this comes from a study of the situation or from a general feeling about the times in which we live. But this is not so. Many of the startling predictions couldn't have been made by anyone, unless they themselves were in on the planning of the assassination.

Mrs. Rose LaPorta lives in suburban Cleveland, Ohio. Over the years she has developed her ESP faculties—partially in the dream state and partially while awake. Some of her premonitory experiences are so detailed that they cannot be explained on the basis of coincidence, if there is such a thing, or in any other rational terms. For instance, on May 10, 1963, she dreamed she had eaten something with glass in it. She could even feel it in her mouth, so vividly that she began to spit it out and woke up. On October 4 of the same year, after she had forgotten the peculiar dream, she happened to be eating a cookie. There was some glass in it, and her dream became reality in every detail. Fortunately, she had told several witnesses of her original dream, so she was able to prove this to herself on the record.

At her place of work there is a superintendent named Smith, who has offices in another city. There never was any close contact with that man, so it was rather startling to Mrs. LaPorta to hear a voice in her sleep telling her, "Mr. Smith died at home on Monday." Shocked by this message, she discussed it with her coworkers. That was on May 18, 1968. On October 8 of the same year, an announcement was made at the company to the effect that "Mr. Smith died at home on Monday, October 7."

Mrs. LaPorta's ability to tune in on future events reached a national subject on November 17, 1963. She dreamed she was at the White House in Washington on a dark, rainy day. There were beds set up in each of the porticoes. She found herself, in the dream, moving from one bed to another, because she wanted to shelter herself from the rain. There was much confusion going on and many men were running around in all directions. They seemed to have guns in their hands and pockets. Finally, Mrs. LaPorta, in the dream, asked someone what was happening, and they told her they were Secret Service men. She was impressed with the terrible confusion and atmosphere of tragedy when she awoke from her dream. That was five days before the assassination happened on November 22, 1963. The dream is somewhat reminiscent of the famed Abraham Lincoln dream, in which he himself saw his own body on the catafalque in the East Room, and asked who was dead in the White House. I reported on that dream in *Window to the Past*.

* * *

Marie Howe is a Maryland housewife, fifty-two years old, and only slightly psychic. The night before the assassination she had a dream in which she saw two brides with the features of men. Upon awakening she spoke of her dream to her husband and children, and interpreted it that someone was going to die very soon. She thought that two

persons would die close together. The next day, Kennedy and Oswald turned into the "brides of death" she had seen in her dream.

* * *

Bertha Zelkin lives in Los Angeles. The morning of the assassination she suddenly found herself saying, "What would we do if President Kennedy were to die?" That afternoon the event took place.

* * *

Marion Confalonieri, a forty-one-year-old housewife and a native of Chicago, has worked as a secretary, and lives with her husband, a draftsman, and two daughters in a comfortable home in California. Over the years she has had many psychic experiences, ranging from déjà vu feelings to psychic dreams. On Friday, November 22, the assassination took place and Oswald was captured the same day. The following night, Saturday, November 23, Mrs. Confalonieri went to bed exhausted and in tears from all the commotion. Some time during the night she dreamed that she saw a group of men, perhaps a dozen, dressed in suits and some with hats. She seemed to be floating a little above them, looking down on the scene, and she noticed that they were standing very close in a group. Then she heard a voice say, "Ruby did it." The next morning she gave the dream no particular thought. The name Ruby meant absolutely nothing to her nor, for that matter, to anyone else in the country at that point. It wasn't until she turned her radio on and heard the announcement that Oswald had been shot by a man named Ruby that she realized she had had a preview of things to come several hours before the event itself had taken place.

* * *

Another one who tuned in on the future a little ahead of reality was the famed British author, Pendragon, whose real name was L. T. Ackerman. In October 1963, he wrote, "I wouldn't rule out the possibility of attempted assassination or worse if caught off guard." He wrote to President Kennedy urging him that his guard be strengthened, especially when appearing in public.

* * *

Dr. Robert G. is a dentist who makes his home in Rhode Island. He has had psychic experiences all his life, some of which I have described elsewhere. At the time when Oswald was caught by the authorities, the doctor's wife wondered out loud what would happen to the man. Without thinking what he was saying, Dr. G. replied, "He will be shot in the police station." The words just popped out of his mouth. There was nothing to indicate even a remote possibility of such a course of action.

He also had a premonition that Robert Kennedy would be shot, but he thought that the Senator would live on with impaired faculties. We know, of course, that Senator Kennedy died. Nevertheless, as most of us will remember, for a time after the announcement of the shooting there was hope that the Senator would indeed continue to live, although with impaired faculties. Not only did the doctors think that might be possible, but announcements were made to that effect. Thus, it is entirely feasible that Dr. G. tuned in not only on the event itself but also on the thoughts and developments that were part of the event.

As yet we know very little about the mechanics of premonitions, and it is entirely possible that some psychics cannot fine-tune their inner instruments beyond a general pickup of future material. This seems to relate to the inability of most mediums to pinpoint exact time in their predictions.

* * *

Cecilia Fawn Nichols is a writer who lives in Twenty-nine Palms, California. All her life she has had premonitions that have come true and has accepted the psychic in her life as a perfectly natural element. She had been rooting for John F. Kennedy to be elected President because she felt that his Catholic religion had made him a kind of underdog. When he finally did get the nod, Miss Nichols found herself far from jubilant. As if something foreboding were preying heavily on her mind, she received the news of his election glumly and with a feeling of disaster. At the time she could not explain to herself why, but the thought that the young man who had just been elected was condemned to death entered her mind. "When the unexpected passes through my mind, I know I can expect it," she explained. "I generally do not know just how or when or what. In this case I felt some idiot was going to kill him because of his religion. I expected the assassination much sooner. Possibly because of domestic problems, I wasn't expecting it when it did happen."

On Sunday morning, November 24, she was starting breakfast. Her television set was tuned to Channel 2, and she decided to switch to Channel 7 because that station had been broadcasting the scene directly from Dallas. The announcer was saying that any moment now Oswald would be brought out of jail to be taken away from Dallas. The camera showed the grim faces of the crowd. Miss Nichols took one look at the scene and turned to her mother. "Mama, come in the living room. Oswald is going to be killed in a few minutes, and I don't want to miss seeing it."

There was nothing to indicate such a course of action, of course, but the words just came out of her mouth as if motivated by some outside force. A moment later, the feared event materialized. Along with the gunshot, however, she distinctly heard words said that she was never

again to hear on any rerun of the televised action. The words were spoken just as Ruby lifted his arm to shoot. As he began pressing the trigger, the words and the gunshot came close together. Afterwards Miss Nichols listened carefully to many of the reruns but never managed to hear the words again. None of the commentators mentioned them. No account of the killing mentions them. And yet Miss Nichols clearly heard Ruby make a statement even as he was shooting Oswald down.

The fact that she alone heard the words spoken by Ruby bothered Miss Nichols. In 1968 she was with a group of friends discussing the Oswald killing, and again she reported what she had heard that time on television. There was a woman in that group who nodded her head. She too had heard the same words. It came as a great relief to Miss Nichols to know that she was not alone in her perception. The words Ruby spoke as he was shooting Oswald were words of anger: "Take this, you son of a bitch!"

This kind of psychic experience is far closer to truthful tuning in on events as they transpire, or just as they are formulating themselves, than some of the more complicated interpretations of events after they have happened.

* * *

Two Cincinnati amateur mediums by the names of Dorothy Barrett and Virginia Hill, who have given out predictions of things to come to the newspapers from time to time, also made some announcements concerning the Kennedy assassination. I have met the two ladies at the home of the John Straders in Cincinnati, at which time they seemed to be imitating the Edgar Cayce readings in that they pinpointed certain areas of the body subject to illness. Again, I met Virginia Hill recently and was confronted with what she believes is the personality of Edgar Cayce, the famous seer of Virginia Beach. Speaking through her, I questioned the alleged Edgar Cayce entity and took notes, which I then asked Cayce's son, Hugh Lynn Cayce, to examine for validity. Regrettably, most of the answers proved to be incorrect, thus making the identity of Edgar Cayce highly improbable. Nevertheless, Virginia Hill is psychic and some of her predictions have come true.

On December 4, 1967, the Cincinnati *Inquirer* published many of her predictions for the following year. One of the more startling statements is that there were sixteen people involved in the Kennedy assassination, according to Virginia's spirit guide, and that the leader was a woman. Oswald, it is claimed, did not kill the President, but a policeman (now dead) did.

In this connection it is interesting to note that Sherman Skolnick, a researcher, filed suit in April of 1970 against the National Archives and Records Services to release certain documents concerning the Kennedy assassination—in particular, Skolnick claimed that there had been a prior Chicago assassination plot in which Oswald and an accomplice by the name of Thomas Arthur Vallee and three or four other men had been involved. Their plan to kill the President at a ball game had to be abandoned when Vallee was picked up on a minor traffic violation the day before the game. Skolnick, according to *Time* magazine's article, April 20, 1970, firmly believes that Oswald and Vallee and several others were linked together in the assassination plot.

* * *

When it comes to the assassination of Senator Robert Kennedy, the picture is somewhat different. To begin with, very few people thought that Robert Kennedy was in mortal danger, while John F. Kennedy, as President, was always exposed to political anger—as are all Presidents. The Senator did not seem to be in quite so powerful a position. True, he had his enemies, as have all politicians. But the murder by Sirhan Sirhan came as much more of a surprise than the assassination of his brother. It is thus surprising that so much premonitory material exists concerning Robert Kennedy as well. In a way, of course, this material is even more evidential because of the lesser likelihood of such an event transpiring.

Mrs. Elaine Jones lives in San Francisco. Her husband is a retired businessman; her brother-in-law headed the publishing firm of Harper & Row; she is not given to hallucinations. I have reported some of her psychic experiences elsewhere. Shortly before the assassination of Robert Kennedy she had a vision of the White House front. At first she saw it as it was and is, and then suddenly the entire front seemed to crumble before her eyes. To her this meant death of someone connected with the White House. A short time later, the assassination of the Senator took place.

* * *

Months before the event, famed Washington seer Jeane Dixon was speaking at the Hotel Ambassador in Los Angeles. She said that Robert Kennedy would be the victim of a "tragedy right here in this hotel." The Senator was assassinated there eight months later.

* * *

A young Californian by the name of Lorraine Caswell had a dream the night before the assassination of Senator Kennedy. In her dream she saw the actual assassination as it later happened. The next morning, she reported her nightmare to her roommate, who had served as witness on previous occasions of psychic premonition.

* * *

Ellen Roberts works as a secretary and part-time volunteer for political causes she supports. During the campaign of Senator Robert Kennedy she spent some time at headquarters volunteering her services. Miss Roberts is a member of the Reverend Zenor's Hollywood Spiritualist Temple. Reverend Zenor, while in trance, speaks with the voice of Agasha, a higher teacher, who is also able to foretell events in the future. On one such occasion, long before the assassination of John F. Kennedy, Agasha—through Reverend Zenor—had said, "There will be not one assassination, but two. He will also be quite young. Victory will be almost within his grasp, but he will die just before he assumes the office, if it cannot be prevented."

The night of the murder, Ellen Roberts fell asleep early. She awakened with a scene of Robert Kennedy and President Kennedy talking. John F. Kennedy was putting his arm around his brother's shoulders and she heard him say, "Well, Bobby, you made it—the hard way." With a rueful smile they walked away. Miss Roberts took this to mean the discomfort that candidate Robert Kennedy had endured during the campaign—the rock-throwing, the insults, name-callings, and his hands had actually become swollen as he was being pulled. Never once did she accept it as anything more sinister. The following day she realized what her vision had meant.

* * *

A curious thing happened to Mrs. Lewis H. Mac-Kibbel. She and her ten-year-old granddaughter were watching television the evening of June 4, 1968. Suddenly the little girl jumped up, clasped her hands to her chest, and in a shocked state announced, "Robert Kennedy has been shot. Shot down, Mama." Her sisters and mother teased her about it, saying that such an event would have been mentioned on the news if it were true. After a while the subject was dropped. The following morning, June 5, when the family radio was turned on, word of the shooting came. Startled, the family turned to the little girl, who could only nod and say, "Yes I know. I knew it last night."

* * *

Mrs. Dawn Chorley lives in central Ohio. A native of England, she spent many years with her husband in South Africa, and has had psychic experiences at various times in her life. During the 1968 election campaign she and her husband, Colin Chorley, had been working for Eugene McCarthy, but when Robert Kennedy won the primary in New Hampshire she was very pleased with that too. The night of the election, she stayed up late. She was very keyed up and thought she would not be able to sleep because of the excitement, but contrary to her expectations she fell immediately into a very deep sleep around midnight. That night she had a curious dream.

"I was standing in the central downstairs' room of my house. I was aware of a strange atmosphere around me and felt very lonely. Suddenly I felt a pain in the left side of my head, toward the back. The inside of my mouth started to crumble and blood started gushing out of my mouth. I tried to get to the telephone, but my arms and legs would not respond to my will; everything was disoriented. Somehow I managed to get to the telephone and pick up the receiver. With tremendous difficulty I dialed for the operator, and I could hear a voice asking whether I needed help. I tried to say, 'Get a doctor,' but the words came out horribly slurred. Then came the realization I was dying and I said, 'Oh my God, I am dying,' and sank into oblivion. I was shouting so loud I awoke my husband, who is a heavy sleeper. Shaking off the dream, I still felt terribly depressed. My husband, Colin, noticed the time. Allowing for time changes, it was the exact minute Robert Kennedy was shot."

* * *

Jill Taggart of North Hollywood, California, has been working with me as a developing medium for several years now. By profession a writer and model, she has been her own worst critic, and in her report avoids anything that cannot be substantiated. On May 14, 1968, she had meant to go to a rally in honor of Senator Robert Kennedy in Van Nuys, California. Since the parade was only three blocks from her house, it was an easy thing for her to walk over. But early in the evening she had resolved not to go. To begin with, she was not fond of the Senator, and she hated large crowds, but more than anything she had a bad feeling that something would happen to the Senator while he was in his car. On the news that evening she heard that the Senator had been struck in the temple by a flying object and had fallen to his knees in the car. The news also reported that he was all right. Jill, however, felt that the injury was more serious than announced and that the Senator's reasoning faculties would be impaired henceforth. "It's possible that it could threaten his life," she reported. "I know that temples are tricky things." When I spoke to her further, pressing for details, she indicated that she had then felt disaster for Robert Kennedy, but her logical mind refused to enlarge upon the comparatively small injury the candidate had suffered. A short time later, of course, the Senator was dead—not from a stone thrown at him but from a murderer's bullet. Jill Taggart had somehow tuned in on both events simultaneously.

* * *

Seventeen-year-old Debbie Gaurlay, a high school student who also works at training horses, has had ESP experiences for several years. Two days prior to the assassination of Robert Kennedy she remarked to a friend by the name of Debbie Corso that the Senator would be shot very shortly. At that time there was no logical reason to assume an attempt upon the Senator's life.

* * *

John Londren is a machine fitter, twenty-eight years old, who lives with his family in Hartford, Connecticut.

Frequently he has had dreams of events that have later transpired. In March 1968 he had a vivid dream in which he saw Senator Robert Kennedy shot while giving his Inaugural Address. Immediately he told his wife and father about the dream, and even wrote a letter to the Senator in April but decided not to send it until after the election. Even the correct names of the assassin and of two people present occurred in his dream. But Mr. Londren dismissed the dream since he knew that Roosevelt Grier and Rafe Johnson were sports figures. He felt they would be out of place in a drama involving the assassination of a political candidate. Nevertheless, those were the two men who actually subdued the killer.

In a subsequent dream he saw St. Patrick's Cathedral in New York during Senator Kennedy's funeral. People were running about in a state of panic, and he had the feeling that a bombing or shooting had taken place. So upset was Mr. Londren by his second dream that he asked his father, who had a friend in Washington, to make some inquiries. Eventually the information was given to a Secret Service man who respected extrasensory perception. The New York City bomb squad was called in and the security around the Cathedral was doubled. A man with an unloaded gun was caught fifteen minutes before the President arrived for the funeral at the Cathedral. Mr. Londren's second dream thus proved to be not only evidential but of value in preventing what might have been another crime.

* * *

Another amateur prophet is Elaine Morganelli, a Los Angeles housewife. In May 1967 she predicted in writing that President Johnson would be assassinated on June 4, and sent this prediction along with others to her brother, Lewis Olson. What she actually had heard was "President assassination June 4." Well, President Johnson was not assassinated, but on June 5, 1968, Robert Kennedy, a presidential candidate, was shot to death.

A sixteen-year-old teen-ager from Tennessee named John Humphreys experienced a vision late in 1963. This happened while he was in bed but not yet fully asleep. As he looked at the floor of his room he saw several disembodied heads. One of the heads was that of President Kennedy, who had just been assassinated. The others, he did not recognize at the time. Later, he realized who they had been. One was the head of Robert Kennedy; the other of Martin Luther King. He had the feeling at the time of the vision that all three men would be shot in the head. He also remembered two other heads—that of a Frenchman and of a very large Englishman—but no names.

* * *

On April 16, 1968, a Canadian by the name of Mrs. Joan Holt wrote to the *Evening Standard* premonition bureau conducted by Peter Fairley, their science editor,

"Robert Kennedy to follow in his brother's footsteps and face similar danger."

"There is going to be a tragic passing in the Kennedy family very soon," said British medium Minie Bridges at a public sitting the last week of May 1968.

* * *

It seems clear to me that even the death of Senator Kennedy was part of a predestined master plan, whether we like it or not. Frequently, those who are already on the other side of life know what will happen on earth, and if they are not able to prevent it, they are at least ready to help those who are coming across make the transition as painlessly as possible under the circumstances.

To many people of Ireland, the Kennedys are great heroes. Both these thoughts should be kept in mind as I report still another psychic experience concerning the death of Robert Kennedy.

* * *

A fifty-three-year-old secretary by the name of Margaret M. Smith of Chicago, Illinois, was watching the Robert Kennedy funeral on television. As his casket was being carried out of the church to the hearse, she noticed a row of men standing at either side of the casket with their backs to it. They were dressed in gray business suits, very plain, and wore gray hats. These men looked very solemn and kept their eyes cast down. To her they looked like natives of Ireland. In fact, the suits looked homespun. As the casket went past, one of the men in the line turned his head and looked at the casket. Miss Smith thought that a person in a guard of honor should not do that, for she had taken the man in the gray suit as part of an honor guard. Then it occurred to her that the two lines of men were a little hazy, in a lighter gray. But she took this to be due to the television set, although other figures were quite clear. Later she discussed the funeral with a friend of hers in another city who had also seen the same broadcast. She asked her friend if she knew who the men in gray had been. Her friend had not seen the men in gray, nor had any of the others she then asked about them. Soon it became clear to Miss Smith that she alone had seen the spirit forms of what she takes to be the Kennedys' Irish ancestors, who had come to pay their last respects in a fitting manner.

* * *

An Indiana amateur prognosticator with a long record of predictions, some of which have already come true while others are yet in the future, has also contributed to the material about the Kennedys. On August 7, 1968, D. McClintic stated that Jackie Kennedy would be married. At the time no such event was in the offing. On September 21, 1968, Mr. McClintic stated that there would be an attempted kidnapping of one of the Kennedy boys. At the same time he also predicted that the heads of the FBI and

the draft would be replaced within a short time. "J. E. Hoover is near the end of being director. Also the director of the draft, Hershey, is on the way out."

* * *

D. McClintic predicted on January 18, 1969, that Edward Kennedy would not run for President in 1972 because he might still be worried about his nephews. Mr. McClintic didn't spell out why Senator Kennedy should be concerned about his nephews.

* * *

Another amateur psychic, Robert E., however, did. On March 10, 1970, the psychic schoolteacher stated, "I mentioned before that around Easter another Kennedy, one of Senator Robert Kennedy's boys, will drown in a boating accident off the coast of Virginia, and the body will be found between April 1st and April 5th in a muddy shallow near a place with the word 'mile' in it. However, within a month or so it will come out that Senator Ted Kennedy covered for his nephew, who was actually the one who was in the car with the girl at Chappaquiddick Island. The Senator was not involved, and when this evidence becomes known Kennedy's popularity will soar." Naturally, the two psychics do not know of each other, nor did they ever have any contact with each other.

One cannot dismiss Mr. McClintic too lightly when one considers that on January 18, 1969, he predicted that at the next election in England, Labor would be kicked out of office; that Joseph Kennedy would die—which he did shortly afterward; that the war in Vietnam would go on and some American troops would be withdrawn, but not too many; that there would be more attacks on Israeli airplanes carrying passengers; and that Jordan's throne would be shaky again.

* * *

A different kind of prognosticator is Fredric Stoessel. A college graduate and former combat Naval officer, he heads his own business firm in New York, specializing in market analysis and financing. Mr. Stoessel is a student of Christian Science and has had psychic experiences all his life. I have written of his predictions concerning the future of the world in a book entitled *The Prophets Speak*. However, his involvement with the Kennedy family, especially the future of Ted Kennedy, is somewhat more elaborate than his predictions pertaining to other events. In May 1967 he wrote an article entitled, "Why Was President Kennedy Shot?" In Mr. Stoessel's opinion a Communist plot was involved. Mr. Stoessel bases his views on a mixture of logical deduction, evaluations of existing political realities, and a good measure of intuition and personal insight ranging all the way to sixth sense and psychic impressions.

"There is some growing evidence to indicate Senator Ted Kennedy may have been set up for this incident. By whom is not certain, but we suspect the fine hand of organized crime." Thus stated Fredric Stoessel in February of 1970. I discussed this matter with him on April 3 of the same year at my home. Some of the things he told me were off the record and I must honor his request. Other details may be told here. Considering Fredric Stoessel's background and his very cautious approach when making statements of importance at a time the Chappaquiddick incident was still in the news, I felt that perhaps he might come up with angles not covered by anyone else before.

"What then is your intuitive feeling about Kennedy and the girl? Was it an accident?" I asked. I decided to use the term "intuitive" rather than "psychic," although that is what I really meant.

Mr. Stoessel thought this over for a moment. "I don't think it was an accident. I think it was staged, shall we say."

"What was meant to happen?"

"What was meant to happen was political embarrassment for Teddy Kennedy. They were just trying to knock him out as a political figure."

"Do you think that he was aware of what had happened—that the girl had drowned?"

"No, I do not. I think he was telling the truth when he said that he was in a state of shock."

"How did 'they' engineer the accident?"

"I assume that he may have been drinking, but frankly it's an assumption. I think they would just wait until they had the right setup. I'm sure a man like that was watched very carefully."

"Have you any feelings about Kennedy's future?"

"I think Ted Kennedy will make a very strong bid for the presidency in 1972. I do not think he will be elected."

"Do you have any instinctive feelings about any attack upon him?"

"I have had an instinctive feeling that there would be an attack on Ted Kennedy from the civil rights elements. In other words, I think he would be attacked so that there would be a commotion over civil rights. Undoubtedly Ted Kennedy will be the civil rights candidate."

"When you say 'attack,' can you be more specific?"

"I think it will be an assassination attempt; specific, shot."

"Successful or not?"

"No, unsuccessful. This is instinctive."

"How much into the future will this happen?"

"I think it will happen by 1972. I'm not too sure exactly when, but I think when he is being built up for a candidate."

"As far as the other Kennedys were concerned, did you at any time have any visions, impressions, dreams, or other feelings concerning either the President or Bobby Kennedy?"

"Well, I had a very strong sensation—in fact I wrote several people—that he would not be on the ticket in 1964. I had a strong impression that John F. Kennedy would *not be around* for some reason or another."

"When did you write this?"

"That was written to Perkins Bass, who was a Congressman in New Hampshire, in 1962."

"Did you have any impressions concerning the true murderer of John F. Kennedy and the entire plot, if any?"

"As soon as the assassination occurred, in those three days when we were all glued to the television sets, I was inwardly convinced that Oswald did not kill him. My impression of that was immediately reinforced, because Oswald was asking for an attorney named John Abt, who was a lawyer for the Communist Party. My instinctive feeling was that Castro had a lot to do with it."

"Prior to the killing of Robert Kennedy, did you have any inkling that this was going to happen?"

"My wife reminded me that I had always said Bobby would be assassinated. I said that for several months after John died."

"Do you believe there is a Kennedy curse in operation?"

"Yes. I think there are forces surrounding the Kennedy family that will bring tragedy to most every one of them."

"Will we have another Kennedy President?"

"I don't think so. Although I think Teddy will make a strong bid for it this next time."

* * *

Certainly if a direct pipeline could be established to one of the Kennedys—those on the other side of life, that is—even more interesting material could be obtained. But to make such an attempt at communication requires two very definite things: one, a channel of communication— that is to say, a medium of the highest professional and ethical reputation—and two, the kind of questions that could establish, at least to the point of reasonable doubt, that communication really did occur between the investigator and the deceased.

✳ 13

Michie Tavern, Jefferson, and the Boys

"THIS TYPICAL PRE-REVOLUTIONARY tavern was a favorite stopping place for travelers," the official guide to Charlottesville says. "With its colonial furniture and china, its beamed and paneled rooms, it appears much the way it did in the days when Jefferson and Monroe were visitors. Monroe writes of entertaining Lafayette as his guest at dinner here, and General Andrew Jackson, fresh from his victory at New Orleans, stopped over on his way to Washington."

The guide, however, does not mention that the tavern was moved a considerable distance from its original place to a much more accessible location where the tourist trade could benefit from it more. Regardless of this comparatively recent change of position, the tavern is exactly as it was, with everything inside, including its ghosts, intact. At the original site, it was surrounded by trees which framed it and sometimes towered over it. At the new site, facing the road, it looks out into the Virginia countryside almost like a manor house. One walks up to the wooden structure over a number of steps and enters the old tavern to the left or, if one prefers, the pub to the right, which is nowadays a coffee shop. Taverns in the eighteenth and early nineteenth centuries were not simply bars or inns; they were meeting places where people could talk freely, sometimes about political subjects. They were used as headquarters for Revolutionary movements or for invading military forces. Most taverns of any size had ballrooms in which the social functions of the area could be held. Only a few private individuals were wealthy enough to have their own ballrooms built into their manor houses.

What is fortunate about Michie Tavern is the fact that everything is pretty much as it was in the eighteenth century, and whatever restorations have been undertaken are completely authentic. The furniture and cooking utensils, the tools of the innkeeper, the porcelain, the china, the metal objects are all of the period, whether they had been in the house or not. As is customary with historical restorations or preservations, whatever is missing in the house is supplied by painstaking historical research, and objects of the same period and the same area are substituted for those presumably lost during the intervening period.

The tavern has three floors and a large number of rooms, so we would need the two hours we had allowed ourselves for the visit. After looking at the downstairs part of the tavern, with its "common" kitchen and the over-long wooden table where two dozen people could be fed, we mounted the stairs to the second floor.

Ingrid, the medium, kept looking into various rooms, sniffing out the psychic presences, as it were, while I followed close behind. Horace Burr and Virginia Cloud kept a respectable distance, as if trying not to "frighten" the ghosts away. That was all right with me, because I did not want Ingrid to tap the unconscious of either one of these very knowledgeable people.

Finally we arrived in the third-floor ballroom of the old tavern. I asked Ingrid what she had felt in the various rooms below. "In the pink room on the second floor I felt an argument or some sort of strife but nothing special in any of the other rooms."

"What about this big ballroom?"

"I can see a lot of people around here. There is a gay atmosphere, and I think important people came here; it is rather exclusive, this room. I think it was used just on special occasions."

By now I had waved Horace and Virginia to come closer, since it had become obvious to me that they wanted very much to hear what Ingrid was saying. Possibly new material might come to light, unknown to both of these historians, in which case they might verify it later on or comment upon it on the spot.

"I'm impressed with an argument over a woman here," Ingrid continued. "It has to do with one of the dignitaries, and it is about one of their wives."

"How does the argument end?"

"I think they just had a quick argument here, about her infidelity."

"Who are the people involved?"

"I think Hamilton. I don't know the woman's name."

"Who is the other man?"

"I think Jefferson was here."

"Try to get as much of the argument as you can."

Ingrid closed her eyes, sat down in a chair generally off limits to visitors, and tried to tune in on the past. "I get the argument as a real embarrassment," she began. "The woman is frail, she has a long dress on with lace at the top part around the neck, her hair is light brown."

"Does she take part in the argument?"

"Yes, she has to side with her husband."

"Describe her husband."

"I can't see his face, but he is dressed in a brocade jacket pulled back with buttons down the front and breeches. It is a very fancy outfit."

"How does it all end?"

"Well, nothing more is said. It is just a terrible embarrassment."

"Is this some sort of special occasion? Are there other people here?"

"Yes, oh, yes. It is like an anniversary or something of that sort. Perhaps a political anniversary of some kind. There is music and dancing and candlelight."

While Ingrid was speaking, in an almost inaudible voice, Horace and Virginia were straining to hear what she was saying but not being very successful at it. At this point Horace waved to me, and I tiptoed over to him. "Ask her to get the period a little closer," he whispered in my ear.

I went back to Ingrid and put the question to her. "I think it was toward the end of the war," she said, "toward the very end of it. For some time now I've had the figure 1781 impressed on my mind."

Since nothing further seemed to be forthcoming from Ingrid at this point, I asked her to relax and come back to the present, so that we could discuss her impressions freely.

"The name Hamilton is impossible in this connection," Horace Burr began. But I was quick to interject that the name Hamilton was fairly common in the late eighteenth and early nineteenth centuries and that Ingrid need not have referred to *the* Alexander Hamilton. "Jefferson was here many times, and he could have been involved in this," Burr continued. "I think I know who the other man might have been. But could we, just for once, try questioning the medium on specific issues?"

Neither Ingrid nor I objected, and Horace proceeded to ask Ingrid to identify the couple she had felt in the ballroom. Ingrid threw her head back for a moment, closed her eyes, and then replied, "The man is very prominent in politics, one of the big three or four at the time, and one of the reasons this is all so embarrassing, from what I get, is that the other man is of much lower caliber. He is not one of the big leaders; he may be an officer or something like that."

While Ingrid was speaking, slowly, as it were, I again felt the strange sense of transportation, of looking back in time, which had been coming to me more and more often

recently, always unsought and usually only of fleeting duration. "For what it is worth," I said, "while Ingrid is speaking, I also get a very vague impression that all this has something to do with two sisters. It concerns a rivalry between two sisters."

"The man's outfit," Ingrid continued her narrative, "was sort of gold and white brocade and very fancy. He was the husband. I don't see the other man."

Horace seemed unusually agitated at this. "Tell me, did this couple live in this vicinity or did they come from far away on a special anniversary?"

"They lived in the vicinity and came just for the evening."

"Well, Horace?" I said, getting more and more curious, since he was apparently driving in a specific direction. "What was this all about?"

For once, Horace enjoyed being the center of attraction. "Well, it was a hot and heavy situation, all right. The couple were Mr. and Mrs. John Walker—he was the son of Dr. Walker of Castle Hill. And the man, who wasn't here, was Jefferson himself. Ingrid is right in saying that they lived in the vicinity—Castle Hill is not far away from here."

"But what about the special festivity that brought them all together here?"

Horace wasn't sure what it could have been, but Virginia, in great excitement, broke in. "It was in this room that the waltz was danced for the first time in America. A young man had come from France dressed in very fancy clothes. The lady he danced with was a closely chaperoned girl from Charlottesville. She was very young, and she danced the waltz with this young man, and everybody in Charlottesville was shocked. The news went around town that the young lady had danced with a man holding her, and that was just terrible at the time. Perhaps that was the occasion. Michie Tavern was a stopover for stagecoaches, and Jefferson and the local people would meet here to get their news. Downstairs was the meeting room, but up here in the ballroom the more special events took place, such as the introduction of the waltz."

I turned to Horace Burr. "How is it that this tavern no longer stands on the original site? I understand it has been moved here for easier tourist access."

"Yes," Horace replied. "The building originally stood near the airport. In fact, the present airport is on part of the old estate that belonged to Colonel John Henry, the father of Patrick Henry. Young Patrick spent part of his boyhood there. Later, Colonel Henry sold the land to the Michies. This house was then their main house. It was on the old highway. In turn, they built themselves an elaborate mansion which is still standing and turned this house into a tavern. All the events we have been discussing took place while this building was on the old site. In 1926 it was moved here. Originally, I think the ballroom we are standing in now was just the loft of the old Henry house. They raised part of the roof to make it into a ballroom because they had no meeting room in the tavern."

In the attractively furnished coffee shop to the right of the main tavern, Mrs. Juanita Godfrey, the manager, served us steaming hot black coffee and sat down to chat with us. Had anyone ever complained about unusual noises or other inexplicable manifestations in the tavern? I asked.

"Some of the employees who work here at night do hear certain sounds they can't account for," Mrs. Godfrey replied. "They will hear something and go and look, and there will be nothing there."

"In what part of the building?"

"All over, even in this area. This is a section of the slave quarters, and it is very old."

Mrs. Godfrey did not seem too keen on psychic experiences, I felt. To the best of her knowledge, no one had had any unusual experiences in the tavern. "What about the lady who slept here one night?" I inquired.

"You mean Mrs. Milton—yes, she slept here one night." But Mrs. Godfrey knew nothing of Mrs. Milton's experiences.

However, Virginia had met the lady, who was connected with the historical preservation effort of the commu-

Monticello—Thomas Jefferson's home

nity. "One night when Mrs. Milton was out of town," Virginia explained, "I slept in her room. At the time she confessed to me that she had heard footsteps frequently, especially on the stairway down."

"That is the area she slept in, yes," Mrs. Godfrey confirmed. "She slept in the ladies' parlor on the first floor."

"What about yourself, Virginia? Did *you* hear anything?"

"I heard noises, but the wood sometimes behaves very funny. She, however, said they were definitely footsteps. That was in 1961."

What had Ingrid unearthed in the ballroom of Michie Tavern? Was it merely the lingering imprint of America's first waltz, scandalous to the early Americans but innocent in the light of today? Or was it something more—an involvement between Mrs. Walker and the illustrious Thomas Jefferson? My image of the great American had always been that of a man above human frailties. But my eyes were to be opened still further on a most intriguing visit to Monticello, Jefferson's home.

✳ 14

A Visit with the Spirited Jefferson

"YOU'RE WELCOME TO VISIT Monticello to continue the parapsychological research which you are conducting relative to the personalities of 1776," wrote James A. Bear, Jr., of the Thomas Jefferson Memorial Foundation, and he arranged for us to go to the popular tourist attraction after regular hours, to permit Ingrid the peace and tranquility necessary to tune in on the very fragile vibrations that might hang on from the past.

Jefferson, along with Benjamin Franklin, is a widely popular historical figure: a play, a musical, and a musical film have brought him to life, showing him as the shy, dedicated, intellectual architect of the Declaration of Independence. Jefferson, the gentle Virginia farmer, the man who wants to free the slaves but is thwarted in his efforts by other Southerners; Jefferson, the ardent but bashful lover of his wife; Jefferson, the ideal of virtue and American patriotism—these are the images put across by the entertainment media, by countless books, and by the tourist authorities which try to entice visitors to come to Charlottesville and visit Jefferson's home, Monticello.

Even the German tourist service plugged itself into the Jefferson boom. "This is like a second mother country for me," Thomas Jefferson is quoted as saying while traveling down the Rhine. "Everything that isn't English in our country comes from here." Jefferson compared the German Rhineland to certain portions of Maryland and Pennsylvania and pointed out that the second largest ethnic group in America at the time were Germans. In an article in the German language weekly *Aufbau*, Jefferson is described as the first prominent American tourist in the Rhineland. His visit took place in April 1788. At the time Jefferson was ambassador to Paris, and the Rhine journey allowed him to study agriculture, customs, and conditions on both sides of the Rhine. Unquestionably, Jefferson, along with Washington, Franklin, and Lincoln, represents one of the pillars of the American edifice.

Virginia Cloud, ever the avid historian of her area, points out that not only did Jefferson and John Adams have a close relationship as friends and political contemporaries but there were certain uncanny "coincidences" between their lives. For instance, Jefferson and Adams died within hours of each other, Jefferson in Virginia and Adams in Massachusetts, on July 4, 1826—exactly fifty years to the day they had both signed the Declaration of Independence. Adams's last words were, "But Jefferson still lives." At the time that was no longer true, for Jefferson had died earlier in the day.

Jefferson's imprint is all over Charlottesville. Not only did the talented "Renaissance man" design his own home, Monticello, but he also designed the Rotunda, the focal point of the University of Virginia. Jefferson, Madison, and Monroe were members of the first governing board of the University, which is now famous for its school of medicine—and which, incidentally, is the leading university in the study of parapsychology, since Dr. Ian Stevenson teaches there.

On our way to Monticello we decided to visit the old Swan Tavern, which had some important links with Jefferson. The tavern is now used as a private club, but the directors graciously allowed us to come in, even the ladies, who are generally not admitted. Nothing in the appointments reminds one of the old tavern, since the place has been extensively remodeled to suit the requirements of the private club. At first we inspected the downstairs and smiled at several elderly gentlemen who hadn't the slightest idea why we were there. Then we went to the upper story and finally came to rest in a room to the rear of the building. As soon as Ingrid had seated herself in a comfortable chair in a corner, I closed the door and asked her what she felt about this place, of which she had no knowledge.

"I feel that people came here to talk things over in a lighter vein, perhaps over a few drinks."

"Was there anyone in particular who was outstanding among these people?"

"I keep thinking of Jefferson, and I'm seeing big mugs; most of the men have big mugs in front of them."

Considering that Ingrid did not know the past of the building as a tavern, this was pretty evidential. I asked her about Jefferson.

"I think he was the figurehead. This matter concerned him greatly, but I don't think it had anything to do with his own wealth or anything like that."

"At the time when this happened, was there a warlike action in progress?"

"Yes, I think it was on the outskirts of town. I have the feeling that somebody was trying to reach this place and that they were waiting for somebody, and yet they weren't really expecting that person."

Both Horace Burr and Virginia Cloud were visibly excited that Ingrid had put her finger on it, so to speak. Virginia had been championing the cause of the man about whom Ingrid had just spoken. "Virginians are always annoyed to hear about Paul Revere, who was actually an old man with a tired horse that left Revere to walk home," Virginia said, somewhat acidly, "while Jack Jouett did far more—he saved the lives of Thomas Jefferson and his legislators. Yet, outside of Virginia, few have ever heard of him."

"Perhaps Jouett didn't have as good a press agent as Paul Revere had in Longfellow, as you always say, Virginia," Burr commented. I asked Virginia to sum up the incident that Ingrid had touched on psychically.

"Jack Jouett was a native of Albemarle County and was of French Huguenot origin. His father, Captain John Jouett, owned this tavern."

"We think there is a chance that he also owned the Cuckoo Tavern in Louisa, forty miles from here," Burr interjected.

"Jouett had a son named Jack who stood six feet, four inches and weighed over two hundred pounds. He was an expert rider and one of those citizens who signed the oath of allegiance to the Commonwealth of Virginia in 1779.

"It was June 3, 1781, and the government had fled to Charlottesville from the advancing British troops. Most of Virginia was in British hands, and General Cornwallis very much wanted to capture the leaders of the Revolution, especially Thomas Jefferson, who had authored the Declaration of Independence, and Patrick Henry, whose motto, 'Give me liberty or give me death,' had so much contributed to the success of the Revolution. In charge of two hundred fifty cavalrymen was Sir Banastre Tarleton. His mission was to get to Charlottesville as quickly as possible to capture the leaders of the uprising. Tarleton was determined to cover the seventy miles' distance between Cornwallis' headquarters and Charlottesville in a single twenty-four-hour period, in order to surprise the leaders of the American independence movement.

"In the town of Louisa, forty miles distant from Charlottesville, he and his men stopped into the Cuckoo Tavern for a brief respite. Fate would have it that Jack Jouett was at the tavern at that moment, looking after his father's business. It was a very hot day for June, and the men were thirsty. Despite Tarleton's orders, their tongues loosened, and Jack Jouett was able to overhear their destination. Jack decided to outride them and warn Charlottesville. It was about 10 P.M. when he got on his best horse, determined to take shortcuts and side roads, while the British would have to stick to the main road. Fortunately it was a moonlit night; otherwise he might not have made it in the rugged hill country.

"Meanwhile the British were moving ahead too, and around 11 o'clock they came to a halt on a plantation near Louisa. By 2 A.M. they had resumed their forward march. They paused again a few hours later to seize and burn a train of twelve wagons loaded with arms and clothing for the Continental troops in South Carolina. When dawn broke over Charlottesville, Jouett had left the British far behind. Arriving at Monticello, he dashed up to the front entrance to rouse Jefferson; however, Governor Jefferson, who was an early riser, had seen the rider tear up his driveway and met him at the door. Ever the gentleman, Jefferson offered the exhausted messenger a glass of wine before allowing him to proceed to Charlottesville proper, two miles farther on. There he roused the other members of the government, while Jefferson woke his family. Two hours later, when Tarleton came thundering into Charlottesville, the government of Virginia had vanished."

"That's quite a story, Virginia," I said.

"Of course," Burr added, "Tarleton and his men might have been here even earlier if it hadn't been for the fact that they first stopped at Castle Hill. Dr. and Mrs. Walker entertained them lavishly and served them a sumptuous breakfast. It was not only sumptuous but also delaying, and Dr. Walker played the perfect host to the hilt, showing Tarleton about the place despite the British commander's impatience, even to measuring Tarleton's orderly on the living-room door jamb. This trooper was the tallest man in the British army and proved to be 6'9¼" tall. Due to these and other delaying tactics—the Walkers made Jack Jouett's ride a complete success. Several members of the legislature who were visiting Dr. Walker at the time were captured, but Jefferson and the bulk of the legislature, which had just begun to convene that morning, got away.

After Thomas Jefferson had taken refuge at the house of Mr. Cole, where he was not likely to be found, Jouett went to his room at his father's tavern, the very house we were in. He had well deserved his rest. Among those who were hiding from British arrest was Patrick Henry. He arrived at a certain farmhouse and identified himself by saying, "I'm Patrick Henry." But the farmer's wife replied, "Oh, you couldn't be, because my husband is out there fighting, and Patrick Henry would be out there too." Henry managed to convince the farmer's wife that his life depended on his hiding in her house, and finally she understood. But it was toward the end of the Revolutionary War and the British knew very well that they had for all intents and purposes been beaten. Consequently, shortly afterward, Cornwallis suggested to the Virginia legislators that they return to Charlottesville to resume their offices.

It was time to proceed to Monticello; the afternoon sun was setting, and we would be arriving just after the last tourists had left. Monticello, which every child knows from its representation on the American five-cent piece, is probably one of the finest examples of American architecture, designed by Jefferson himself, who lies buried there in the family graveyerd. It stands on a hill looking down in to the valley of Charlottesville. Carefully landscaped grounds surround the house. Inside, the house is laid out in classical proportions. From the entrance hall with its famous clock, also designed by Jefferson, one enters a large, round room, the heart of the house. On both sides of this central area are rectangular rooms. To the left is a corner room, used as a study and library from where Jefferson, frequently in the morning before anyone else was up, used to look out on the rolling hills of Virginia. Adjacent to it is a very small bedroom, almost a bunk. Thus, the entire west wing of the building is a self-contained apartment in which Jefferson could be active without interfering with the rest of his family. In the other side of the round central room is a large dining room leading to a terrace which, in turn, continues into an open walk with a magnificent view of the hillside. The furniture is Jefferson's own, as are the silver and china, some of it returned to Monticello by history-conscious citizens of the area who had previously purchased it.

The first room we visited was Jefferson's bedroom. Almost in awe herself, Ingrid touched the bedspread of what was once Jefferson's bed, then his desk, and the books he had handled. "I feel his presence her," she said, "and I think he did a lot of his work in this room, a lot of planning and working things out, till the wee hours of the night." I don't think Ingrid knew that Jefferson was in the habit of doing just that, in this particular room.

I motioned Ingrid to sit down in one of Jefferson's chairs and try to capture whatever she might receive from the past. "I can see an awful lot of hard work, sleepless nights, and turmoil. Other than that, nothing."

We went into the library next to the study. "I don't think he spent much time here really, just for reference." On we went to the dining room to the right of the central room. "I think this was his favorite room, and he loved to meet people here socially." Then she added, "I get the words 'plum pudding' and 'hot liquor.'"

"Well," Burr commented, "he loved the lighter things of life. He brought ice cream to America, and he squirted milk directly from the cow into a goblet to make it froth. He had a French palate. He liked what we used to call floating island, a very elaborate dessert."

"I see a lot of people. It is a friendly gathering with glittering glasses and candlelight." Ingrid said. "They are elegant but don't have on overcoats. I see their white silken shirts. I see them laughing and passing things around. Jefferson is at the table with white hair pulled back, leaning over and laughing."

The sun was setting, since it was getting toward half past six now, and we started to walk out the French glass doors onto the terrace. From there an open walk led around a sharp corner to a small building, perhaps twenty or twenty-five yards in the distance. Built in the same classical American style as Monticello itself, the building contained two fair-sized roooms, on two stories. The walk led to the entrance to the upper story, barricaded by an iron grillwork to keep tourists out. It allowed us to enter the room only partially, but sufficiently for Ingrid to get her bearings. Outside, the temperature sank rapidly as the evening approached. A wind had risen, and so it was pleasant to be inside the protective walls of the little house.

"Horace, where are we now?" I asked.

"We are in the honeymoon cottage where Thomas Jefferson brought his bride and lived at the time when his men were building Monticello. Jefferson and his family lived here at the very beginning, so you might say that whatever impressions there are here would be of the pre-Revolutionary part of Jefferson's life."

I turned to Ingrid and asked for her impressions. "I feel everything is very personal here and light, and I don't feel the tremendous starin in the planning of things I felt

in the Monticello building. As I close my eyes, I get a funny feeling about a bouquet of flowers, some very strong and peculiar exotic flowers. They are either pink or light red and have a funny name, and I have a feeling that a woman involved in this impression is particularly fond of a specific kind of flower. He goes out of his way to get them for her, and I also get the feeling of a liking for a certain kind of china porcelain. Someone is a collector and wants to buy certain things, being a connoisseur, and wants to have little knick-knacks all over the place. I don't know if any of this makes any sense, but this is how I see it."

"It makes sense indeed," Horace Burr replied. "Jefferson did more to import rare trees and rare flowering shrubs than anyone else around here. In fact, he sent shipments back from France while he stayed there and indicated that they were so rare that if you planted them in one place they might not succeed. So he planted only a third at Monticello, a third at Verdant Lawn, which is an old estate belonging to a friend of his, and a third somewhere else in Virginia. It was his idea to plant them in three places to see if they would thrive in his Virginia."

"The name Rousseau comes to mind. Did he know anyone by that name?" Ingrid asked.

"Of course, he was much influenced by Rousseau."

"I also get the feeling of a flickering flame, a habit of staying up to all hours of the morning. Oh, and is there any historical record of an argument concerning this habit of his, between his wife and himself and some kind of peacemaking gesture on someone else's part?"

"I am sure there was an argument," Horace said, "but I doubt that there ever was a peacemaking gesture. You see, their marriage was not a blissful one; she was very wealthy and he spent her entire estate, just as he spent Dabney Carr's entire estate and George Short's entire estate. He went through estate after estate, including his own. Dabney Carr was his cousin, and he married Jefferson's sister, Martha. He was very wealthy, but Jefferson gathered up his sister and the children and brought them here after Carr's death. He then took over all the plantations and effects of Mr. Carr.

"Jefferson was a collector of things. He wrote three catalogues of his own collection, and when he died it was the largest collection in America. You are right about the porcelain, because it was terribly sophisticated at that time to be up on porcelain. The clipper trade was bringing in these rarities, and he liked to collect them."

Since Ingrid had scored so nicely up to now, I asked her whether she felt any particular emotional event connected with this little house.

"Well, I think the wife was not living on her level, her standard, and she was unhappy. It wasn't what she was used to. It wasn't grand enough. I think she had doubts about him and his plans."

"In what sense?"

"I think she was dubious about what would happen. She was worried that he was getting too involved, and she didn't like his political affiliations too well."

I turned to Horace for comments. To my surprise, Horace asked me to turn off my tape recorder since the information was of a highly confidential nature. However, he pointed out that the material could be found in *American Heritage*, and that I was free to tell the story in my own words.

Apparently, there had always been a problem between Jefferson and his wife concerning other women. His associations were many and varied. Perhaps the most lasting was with a beautiful young black woman, about the same age as his wife. She was the illegitimate natural child of W. Skelton, a local gentleman, and served as a personal maid to Mrs. Jefferson. Eventually, Jefferson had a number of children by this woman. He even took her to Paris. He would send for her. This went on for a number of years and eventually contributed to the disillusionment of this woman. She died in a little room upstairs, and they took the coffin up there some way, but when they put it together and got her into the coffin, it wouldn't come

downstairs. They had to take all the windows out and lower her on a rope. And what was she doing up there in the first place? All this did not contribute to Mrs. Jefferson's happiness. The tragedy is that, after Jefferson's death, two of his mulatto children were sent to New Orleans and *sold* as prostitutes to pay his debts. There are said to be some descendants of that liaison alive today, but you won't find any of this in American textbooks.

Gossip and legend intermingle in small towns and in the countryside. This is especially true when important historical figures are involved. So it is said that Jefferson did not die a natural death. Allegedly, he committed suicide by cutting his own throat. Toward the end of Jefferson's life, there was a bitter feud between himself and the Lewis family. Accusations and counteraccusations are said to have gone back and forth. Jefferson is said to have had Merriweather Lewis murdered and, prior to that, to have accused Mr. Lewis of a number of strange things that were not true. But none of these legends and rumors can be proved in terms of judicial procedure; when it comes to patriotic heroes of the American Revolution, the line between truth and fiction is always rather indistinct.

✳ 15

Major André and the Question of Loyalty

"MAJOR JOHN ANDRÉ'S fateful excursion from General Sir Henry Clinton's headquarters at Number I Broadway to the gallows on the hill at Tappan took less than a week of the eighteenth century, exactly one hundred seventy years ago at this writing. It seems incredible that this journey should make memorable the roads he followed, the houses he entered, the roadside wells where he stopped to quench his thirst, the words he spoke. But it did." This eloquent statement by Harry Hansen goes a long way in describing the relative importance of so temporary a matter as the fate and capture of a British agent during the Revolutionary War.

In the Tarrytowns, up in Westchester County, places associated with André are considered prime tourist attractions. More research effort has been expended on the exploration of even the most minute detail of the ill-fated André's last voyage than on some far worthier (but less romantic) historical projects elsewhere. A number of good books have been written about the incident, every schoolboy knows about it, and John Andé has gone into history as a gentlemanly but losing hero of the American Revolutionary War. But in presenting history to schoolchildren as well as to the average adult, most American texts ignore the basic situation as it then existed.

To begin with, the American Revolutionary War was more of a civil war than a war between two nations. Independence was by no means desired by all Americans; in fact, the Declaration of Independence had difficulty passing the Continental Congress and did so only after much negotiating behind the scenes and the elimination of a number of passages, such as those relating to the issue of slavery, considered unacceptable by Southerners. When the Declaration of Independence did become the law of the land—at least as far as its advocates were concerned—there were still those who had not supported it originally and who felt themselves put in the peculiar position of being disloyal to their new country or becoming disloyal to the country they felt they ought to be loyal to. Those who preferred continued ties with Great Britain were called Tories, and numbered among them generally were the more influential and wealthier elements in the colonies. There were exceptions, of course, but on the whole the conservatives did not support the cause of the Revolution by any means. Any notion that the country arose *as one* to fight the terrible British is pure political make-believe. The issues were deep and manifold, but they might have been resolved eventually through negotiations. There is no telling what might have happened if both England and the United Colonies had continued to negotiate for a better relationship. The recent civil war in Spain was far more a war between two distinct groups than was the American Revolutionary War. In the latter, friends and enemies lived side by side in many areas, the lines were indistinctly drawn, and members of the same family might support one side or the other. The issue was not between Britain, the invading enemy, and America, the attacked; on the contrary, it was between the renunciation of all ties with the motherland and continued adherence to some form of relationship. Thus, it had become a political issue far more than a purely patriotic or national issue. After all, there were people of the same national background on both sides, and nearly everyone had relatives in England.

Under the circumstances, the question of what constituted loyalty was a tricky one. To the British, the colonies were in rebellion and thus disloyal to the king. To the Americans, anyone supporting the British government after the Declaration of Independence was considered disloyal. But the percentage of those who could not support independence was very large all through the war, far more than a few scattered individuals. While some of these Tories continued to support Britain for personal or commercial reasons, others did so out of honest political conviction. To them, helping a British soldier did not constitute high treason but, to the contrary, was their normal duty. Added to this dilemma was the fact that there were numerous cases of individuals crossing the lines on both sides, for local business reasons, to remove women and children caught behind the lines, or to parley about military matters, such as the surrender of small detachments incapable of rejoining their regiments, or the obtaining of help for wounded soldiers. The Revolutionary War was not savagely fought; it was, after all, a war between gentlemen. There were no atrocities, no concentration camps, and no slaughter of the innocent.

In the fall of 1780 the situation had deteriorated to a standstill of sorts, albeit to the detriment of the American forces. The British were in control of the entire South, and they held New York firmly in their grip. The British sloop *Vulture* was anchored in the middle of the Hudson River opposite Croton Point. In this position, it was not too far from that formidable bastion of the American defense system, West Point. Only West Point and its multiple fortifications stood in the way of total defeat for the American forces.

Picture, if you will, the situation in and around New York. The British Army was in full control of the city, that is to say, Manhattan, with the British lines going right through Westchester County. The Americans were entrenched on the New Jersey shore and on both sides of the Hudson River from Westchester County upward. On the American side were first of all, the regular Continental Army, commanded by General Washington, and also various units of local militia. Uniforms for the militia men ran the gamut of paramilitary to civilian, and their training and backgrounds were also extremely spotty. It would have

been difficult at times to distinguish a soldier of the Revolutionary forces from a civilian.

The British didn't call on the citizens of the area they occupied for special services, but it lay in the nature of this peculiar war that many volunteered to help either side. The same situation which existed among the civilian population in the occupied areas also prevailed where the Revolution was successful. Tory families kept on giving support to the British, and when they were found out they were charged with high treason. Nevertheless, they continued right on supplying aid. Moreover, the lines between British and American forces were not always clearly drawn. They shifted from day to day, and if anyone wanted to cross from north of Westchester into New Jersey, for instance, he might very well find himself in the wrong part of the country if he didn't know his way around or if he hadn't checked the latest information. To make matters even more confusing, Sir Henry Clinton was in charge of the British troops in New York City, while Governor Clinton ruled the state of New York, one of the thirteen colonies, from Albany.

In the spring of 1779 Sir Henry Clinton received letters from an unknown correspondent who signed himself only "Gustavus." From the content of these letters, the British commander knew instantly that he was dealing with a high-ranking American officer. Someone on the American side wished to make contact in order to serve the British cause. Clinton turned the matter over to his capable adjutant general, Major John André. André, whose specialty was what we call intelligence today, replied to the letters, using the pseudonym John Anderson.

André had originally been active in the business world but purchased a commission as a second lieutenant in the British Army in 1771. He arrived in America in 1774 and served in the Philadelphia area. Eventually he served in a number of campaigns and by 1777 had been promoted to captain. Among the wealthy Tory families he became friendly with during the British occupation of Philadelphia was the Shippen family. One of the daughters of that family later married General Benedict Arnold.

André's first major intelligence job was to make contact with a secret body of Royalists living near Chesapeake Bay. This group of Royalists had agreed to rise against the Americans if military protection were sent to them. Essentially, André was a staff officer, not too familiar with field work and therefore apt to get into difficulties once faced with the realities of rugged terrain. As the correspondence continued, both Clinton and André suspected that the Loyalist writing the letters was none other than General Benedict Arnold, and eventually Arnold conceded this.

After many false starts, a meeting took place between Major General Benedict Arnold, the commander of West Point, and Major John André on the night of September 21, 1780, at Haverstraw on the Hudson. At the time, Arnold made his headquarters at the house of Colonel Beverley Robinson, which was near West Point.

The trip had been undertaken on André's insistence, very much against the wishes of his immediate superior, Sir Henry Clinton. As André was leaving, Clinton reminded him that under no circumstances was he to change his uniform or to take papers with him. It was quite sufficient to exchange views with General Arnold and then to return to the safety of the British lines.

Unfortunately, André disobeyed these commands. General Arnold had with him six papers which he persuaded André to place between his stockings and his feet. The six papers contained vital information about the fortifications at West Point, sufficient to allow the British to capture the strongpoint with Arnold's help. "The six papers which Arnold persuaded André to place between his stockings and his feet did not contain anything of value that could not have been entrusted to André's memory or at most contained in a few lines in cipher that would not have been intelligible to anyone else," states Otto Hufeland in his book *Westchester County during the American Revolution.* But it is thought that André still distrusted General Arnold and wanted something in the latter's handwriting that would incriminate him if there was any deception.

It was already morning when the two men parted. General Arnold returned to his headquarters by barge, leaving André with Joshua Smith, who was to see to his safe return. André's original plan was to get to the sloop *Vulture* and return to New York by that route. But somehow Joshua Smith convinced him that he should go by land. He also persuaded André to put on a civilian coat, which he supplied. General Arnold had given them passes to get through the lines, so toward sunset André, Smith, and a servant rode down to King's Ferry, crossing the river from Stony Point to Verplanck's Point and on into Westchester County.

Taking various back roads and little-used paths which made the journey much longer, André eventually arrived at a spot not far from Philipse Castle. There he ran into three militia men: John Paulding, Isaac Van Wart, and David Williams. They were uneducated men in their early twenties, and far from experienced in such matters as how to question a suspected spy. The three fellows weren't looking for spies, however, but for cattle thieves which were then plaguing the area. They were on the lookout near the Albany Post Road when Van Wart saw André pass on his horse. They stopped him, and that is where André made his first mistake. Misinterpreting the Hessian coat Paulding wore (he had obtained it four days before when escaping from a New York prison) and thinking that he was among British Loyalists, he immediately identified himself as a British officer and asked them not to detain him. But the three militia men made him dismount and undress, and then the documents were discovered. It has been said that they weren't suspicious of him at all, but that the elegant boots, something very valuable in those days, tempted them, and that they were more interested in André's clothing than in what he might have on him.

Whatever the motivation, André was brought to Colonel Jameson's headquarters at Sand's Mill, which is called Armonk today.

Jameson sent the prisoner to General Arnold, a strange decision which indicates some sort of private motive. The papers, however, he sent directly to General Washington, who was then at Hartford. Only upon the return of his next-in-command, Major Tallmadge, did the real state of affairs come to light. On Tallmadge's insistence, the party escorting André to General Arnold was recalled and brought back to Sand's Mills. But a letter telling General Arnold of André's capture was permitted to continue on its way to West Point!

Benedict Arnold received the letter the next morning at breakfast. The General rose from the table, announced that he had to go across the river to West Point immediately, and went to his room in great agitation. His wife followed him, and he informed her that he must leave at once, perhaps forever. Then he mounted his horse and dashed down to the riverside. Jumping into his barge, he ordered his men to row him to the *Vulture,* some seventeen miles below. He explained to his men that he came on a flag of truce and promised them an extra ration of rum if they made it particularly quickly. When the barge arrived at the British vessel, he jumped aboard and even tried to force the bargemen to enter the King's service on the threat of making them prisoners. The men refused, and the *Vulture* sailed on to New York City. On arrival, General Clinton freed the bargemen, a most unusual act of gallantry in those days.

Meanwhile André was being tried as a spy. Found guilty by a court-martial at Tappan, he was executed by hanging on October 2, 1780. The three militia men who had thus saved the very existence of the new republic were voted special medals by Congress.

* * *

The entire area around Tappan and the Tarrytowns is "André" country. At Philipse Castle there is a special exhibit of André memorabilia in a tiny closet under the stairs. There is a persistent rumor that André was trying to escape from his captors. According to Mrs. Cornelia Beekman, who then lived at the van Cortlandt House in Peekskill, there was in her house a suitcase containing an American army uniform and a lot of cash. That suitcase was to be turned over to anyone bringing a written note from André. Joshua Hett Smith, who had helped André escape after his meeting with Arnold, later asked for the suitcase; however, as Smith had nothing in writing, Beekman refused to give it to him. However, this story came to light only many years after the Revolution, perhaps because Mrs. Beekman feared to be drawn into a treason trial or because she had some feelings of her own in the matter.

Major André and the Question of Loyalty

Our next stop was to be the van Cortlandt mansion, not more than fifteen minutes away by car. Obviously, Pat Smith was in a good mood this morning. In her little foreign car she preceded us at such a pace that we had great difficulty keeping up with her. It was a sight to behold how this lady eased her way in and out of traffic with an almost serpentine agility that made us wonder how long she could keep it up. Bravely following her, we passed Sleepy Hollow Cemetery and gave it some thought. No, we were not too much concerned with all the illustrious Dutch Americans buried there, nor with Washington Irving and nearby Sunnyside; we were frankly concerned with ourselves. Would we also wind up at Sleepy Hollow Cemetery, or would we make it to the van Cortlandt mansion in one piece...?

The mansion itself is a handsome two-story building, meticulously restored and furnished with furniture and artworks of the eighteenth century, some of it from the original house. Turned into a tourist attraction by the same foundation which looked after Philipsburg Manor, the house, situated on a bluff, is a perfect example of how to run an outdoor museum. Prior to climbing the hill to the mansion itself, however, we visited the ferryboat house at the foot of the hill. In the eighteenth century and the early part of the nineteenth century, the river came close to the house, and it was possible for the ships bringing goods to the van Cortlandts to come a considerable distance inland to discharge their merchandise. The Ferryboat Inn seemed a natural outgrowth of having a ferry at that spot: the ferry itself crossed an arm of the Hudson River, not very wide, but wide enough not to be forded on foot or by a small boat. Since so much of these buildings had been restored, I wondered whether Ingrid would pick up anything from the past.

The inn turned out to be a charming little house. Downstairs we found what must have been the public room, a kitchen, and another room, with a winding staircase leading to the upper story. Frankly, I expected very little from this but did not want to offend Pat Smith, who had suggested the visit.

"Funny," Ingrid said, "when I walked into the door, I had the feeling that I had to force my way *through a crowd.*"

The curator seemed surprised at this, for she hadn't expected anything from this particular visit either. "I can't understand this," she said plaintively. "This is one of the friendliest buildings we have."

"Well," I said, "ferryboat inns in the old days weren't exactly like the Hilton."

"I feel a lot of activity here," Ingrid said. "Something happened here, not a hanging, but connected with one."

We went upstairs, where I stopped Ingrid in front of a niche that contained a contemporary print of André's execution. As yet we had not discussed Major André or his connection with the area, and I doubt very much whether

Ingrid realized there was a connection. "As you look at this, do you have any idea who it is?" I asked.

Ingrid, who is very nearsighted, looked at the picture from a distance and said, "I feel that he may have come through this place at one time." And so he might have.

As we walked up the hill to the van Cortlandt mansion, the time being just right for a visit as the tourists would be leaving, I questioned Pat Smith about the mansion.

"My mother used to know the family who owns the house," Pat Smith began. "Among the last descendants of the van Cortlandts were Mrs. Jean Brown and a Mrs. Mason. This was in the late thirties or the forties, when I lived in New Canaan. Apparently, there were such manifestations at the house that the two ladies called the Archbishop of New York for help. They complained that a spirit was 'acting up,' that there were the sound of a coach that no one could see and other inexplicable noises of the usual poltergeist nature."

"What did they do about it?"

"Despite his reluctance to get involved, the Archbishop did go up to the manor, partly because of the prominence of the family. He put on his full regalia and went through a ritual of exorcism. Whether or not it did any good, I don't know, but a little later a psychic sensitive went through the house also and recorded some of these noises. As far as I know, none of it was ever published, and for all I know, it may still be there—the specter, that is."

We now had arrived at the mansion, and we entered the downstairs portion of the house. Two young ladies dressed in colonial costumes received us and offered us some cornmeal tidbits baked in the colonial manner. We went over the house from top to bottom, from bottom to top, but Ingrid felt absolutely nothing out of the ordinary. True, she felt the vibrations of people having lived in the house, having come and gone, but no tragedy, no deep imprint, and, above all, no presence. Pat Smith seemed a little disappointed. She didn't really *believe* in ghosts as such, but, having had some ESP experiences at Sunnyside, she wasn't altogether sure. At that instant she remembered having left her shopping bag at the Ferryboat Inn. The bag contained much literature on the various colonial houses in the area, and she wanted to give it to us. Excusing herself, she dashed madly back down the hill to the Ferryboat Inn. She was back in no time, a little out of breath, which made me wonder whether she had wanted to make her solo visit to the Ferryboat Inn at dusk just as *brief* as humanly possible.

* * *

In a splendid Victorian mansion surmounted by a central tower, the Historical Society of the Tarrytowns functions as an extremely well organized local museum as well as a research center. Too prudent to display items of general interest that might be found elsewhere in greater quantity and better quality, the Historical Society concentrates on items and information pertaining to the immediate area. It is particularly strong on pamphlets, papers, maps, and other literature of the area from 1786 onward. One of the principal rooms in the Society's museum is the so-called Captors' Room. In it are displays of a sizable collection of material dealing with the capture of Major André. These include lithographs, engravings, documentary material, letters, and, among other things, a chair. It is the chair André sat in when he was still a free man at the Underhill home, south of Yorktown Heights. Mrs. Adelaide Smith, the curator, was exceptionally helpful to us when we stated the purpose of our visit. Again, as I always do, I prevented Ingrid from hearing my conversation with Mrs. Smith, or with Miss Smith, who had come along now that she had recovered her shopping bag full of literature. As soon as I could get a moment alone with Ingrid, I asked her to touch the chair in question.

"I get just a slight impression," she said, seating herself in the chair, then getting up again. "There may have been a meeting in here of some kind, or he may have been sentenced while near or sitting in this chair. I think there was a meeting in this room to determine what would happen."

But she could not get anything very strong about the chair. Looking at the memorabilia, she then commented, "I feel he was chased for quite a while before he was captured. I do feel that the chair in this room has something to do with his sentence."

"Is the chair authentic?"

"Yes, I think so."

"Now concerning this room, the Captors' Room, do you feel anything special about it?"

"Yes, I think this is where it was decided, and I feel there were a lot of men here, men from town and from the government."

Had Ingrid wanted to manufacture a likely story to please me, she could not have done worse. Everything about the room and the building would have told her that it was of the nineteenth century, and that the impression she had just described seemed out of place, historically speaking. But those were her feelings, and as a good sensitive she felt obliged to say whatever came into her mind or whatever she was impressed with, not to examine it as to whether it fit in with the situation she found herself in. I turned to the curator and asked, "Mrs. Smith, what was this room used for, and how old is the building itself?"

"The building is about one hundred twenty-five years old; our records show it was built between 1848 and 1850 by Captain Jacob Odell, the first mayor of Tarrytown. It was built as one house, and since its erection two families have lived here. First, there were the Odells, and later Mr. and Mrs. Aussie Case. Mrs. Case is eighty-seven now and retired. This house was purchased for the Society to become their headquarters. It has been used as our headquarters for over twenty years."

"Was there anything on this spot before this house was built?"

"I don't know."

"Has anyone ever been tried or judged in this room?"

"I don't know."

Realizing that a piece of furniture might bring with itself part of the atmosphere in which it stood when some particularly emotional event took place, I questioned Mrs. Smith about the history of the chair.

"This chair, dated 1725, was presented to us from Yorktown. It was the chair in which Major André sat the morning of his capture, when he and Joshua Smith stopped at the home of Isaac Underhill for breakfast."

The thoughts going through André's head that morning, when he was almost sure of a successful mission, must have been fairly happy ones. He had succeeded in obtaining the papers from General Arnold; he had slept reasonably well, been fed a good breakfast, and was now, presumably, on his way to Manhattan and a reunion with his commanding general, Sir Henry Clinton. If Ingrid felt any meetings around that chair, she might be reaching back beyond André's short use of the chair, perhaps into the history of the Underhill home itself. Why, then, did she speak of sentence and capture, facts she would know from the well-known historical account of Major André's mission? I think that the many documents and memorabilia stored in the comparatively small room might have created a common atmosphere in which bits and snatches of past happenings had been reproduced in some fashion. Perhaps Ingrid was able to tune in on this shallow but nevertheless still extant psychic layer.

Major André became a sort of celebrity in his own time. His stature as a British master spy was exaggerated far out of proportion even during the Revolutionary War. This is understandable when one realizes how close the cause of American independence had come to total defeat. If André had delivered the documents entrusted to him by Major General Arnold to the British, West Point could not have been held. With the fall of the complicated fortifications at the point, the entire North would have soon been occupied by the British. Unquestionably, the capture of Major André was a turning point in the war, which had then reached a stalemate, albeit one in favor of the British. They could afford to wait and sit it out while the Continental troops were starving to death, unable to last another winter.

General Arnold's betrayal was by no means a sudden decision; his feelings about the war had changed some time prior to the actual act. The reasons may be seen in his background, his strong Tory leanings, and a certain resentment against the command of the Revolutionary Army. He felt he had not advanced quickly enough; the command at West Point was given him only three months prior to André's capture. Rather than being grateful for the belated recognition of his talents by the Continental command, Arnold saw it as a godsend to fulfill his own nefarious task. For several months he had been in correspondence with Sir Henry Clinton in New York, and his decision to betray the cause of independence was made long before he became commander of West Point.

But André wasn't the master spy later accounts try to make him out: his bumbling response when captured by the three militia men shows that he was far from experienced in such matters. Since he had carried on his person a *laissez-passer* signed by General Arnold, he needed only to produce this document and the men would have let him go. Instead, he volunteered the information that he was a British officer. All this because one of the militia men wore a Hessian coat. It never occurred to André that the coat might have been stolen or picked up on the battlefield! But there was a certain weakness in André's character, a certain conceit, and the opportunity of presenting himself as a British officer on important business was too much to pass up when he met the three nondescript militia men. Perhaps his personal vanity played a part in this fateful decision; perhaps he really believed himself to be among troops on his own side. Whatever the cause of his strange behavior, he paid with his life for it. Within weeks after the hanging of Major André, the entire Continental Army knew of the event, the British command was made aware of it, and in a detailed document Sir Henry Clinton explained what he had had in mind in case Arnold would have been able to deliver West Point and its garrison to the British. Thus, the name André became a household word among the troops of both sides.

* * *

In 1951 I investigated a case of a haunting at the colonial house belonging to the late *New York News* columnist Danton Walker. The case was first published, under the title "The Rockland County Ghost," in *Tomorrow* magazine and, later, in *Ghost Hunter*. Various disturbances had occurred at the house between 1941 and 1951 that had led Mr. Walker to believe that he had a poltergeist in his domicile. The late Eileen Garrett offered to serve as medium in the investigation, and Dr. Robert Laidlaw, the eminent psychiatrist, was to meet us at the house to supervise the proceedings along with me. Even before Mrs. Garrett set foot in the house, however, she revealed to us the result of a "traveling clairvoyance" expedition in which she had seen the entity "hung up" in the house. His name, she informed us, was Andreas, and she felt that he was attached to the then owner of the house.

The visit to the house was one of the most dramatic and perhaps traumatic psychic investigations into haunted houses I have ever conducted. The house, which has since changed ownership owing to Mr. Walker's death, stands on a hill that was once part of a large farm. During the Revolutionary War, the house served as headquarters for a detachment of troops on the Revolutionary side. General Anthony Wayne, known as "Mad" Anthony, had his headquarters very near this site, and the Battle of Stony Point was fought just a few miles away in 1779. The building served as a fortified roadhouse used for the storage of arms, ammunitions, food, and at times for the safekeeping of prisoners.

At the time Danton Walker bought the house, it was in a sad state of disrepair, but with patience and much money he restored it to its former appearance. During the time when the house was being rebuilt, Walker stayed at a nearby inn but would occasionally take afternoon naps on an army cot in the upstairs part of his house. On these occasions he had the distinct impression of the presence of a Revolutionary soldier in the same room with him. Psychic impressions were nothing new for the late *News* columnist; he had lived with them all his life. During the first two years of his tenancy, Walker did not observe anything further, but by 1944 there had developed audible and even visible phenomena.

One afternoon, while resting in the front room downstairs, he heard a violent knocking at the front door caused by someone moving the heavy iron knocker. But he found no one at the front door. Others, including Walker's man Johnny, were aroused many times by knocking at the door, only to find no one there. A worker engaged in the restoration of the house complained about hearing someone with heavy boots on walking up the stairs in mid-afternoon, at a time when he was alone in the place. The sound of heavy footfalls, of someone, probably male, wearing boots, kept recurring. During the summer of 1952, when Walker had guests downstairs, everyone heard the heavy thumping sound of someone falling down the stairs. Other, more tangible phenomena added to the eerie atmosphere of the place: the unmistakable imprint of a heavy man's thumb on a thick pewter jar of the seventeenth century, inexplicable on any grounds; the mysterious appearance on a plate rail eight feet above the kitchen floor of a piece of glass that had been in the front-door window; pictures tumbling down from their places in the hallway; and a pewter pitcher thrown at a woman guest from a bookshelf behind the bed.

One evening, two Broadway friends of Danton Walker's, both of them interested in the occult but not really believers, came to the house for the weekend. One of the men, L., a famous Broadway writer, insisted on spending the night in the haunted bedroom upstairs. An hour later the pajama-clad guest came down to Walker's little studio at the other end of the estate, where Walker was now sleeping because of the disturbances, and demanded an end to the "silly pranks" he thought someone was playing on him. The light beside his bed was blinking on and off, while all the other lights in the house were burning steadily, he explained. Walker sent him back to bed with an explanation about erratic power supply in the country.

A little over an hour later, L. came running back to Walker and asked to spend the rest of the night in Walker's studio.

In the morning he explained the reasons for his strange behavior: he had been awakened from deep sleep by the sensation of someone slapping him violently about the face. Sitting bolt upright in bed, he noticed that the shirt he had placed on the back of a rocking chair was being agitated by the breeze. The chair was rocking ever so gently. It then occurred to L. that there could be no breeze in the room, since all the windows had been closed!

Many times, Walker had the impression that someone was trying desperately to get into the house, as if for refuge. He recalled that the children of a previous tenant had spoken of some disturbance near a lilac bush at the corner of the house. The original crude stone walk from the road to the house passed by this lilac bush and went on to the well, which, according to local tradition, had been used by Revolutionary soldiers.

Our group of investigators reached the house on November 22, 1952, on a particularly dark day, as if it had been staged that way. Toward 3 o'clock in the afternoon, we sat down for a séance in the upstairs bedroom. Within a matter of seconds, Eileen Garrett had disappeared, so to speak, from her body, and in her stead was another person. Sitting upright and speaking in halting tones with a distinct Indian accent, Uvani, one of Mrs. Garrett's spirit guides, addressed us and prepared us for the personality that would follow him.

"I am confronted myself with a rather restless personality, a very strange personality, and one that might appear to be, in his own life, perhaps not quite of the right mind," he explained to us. The control personality then added that he was having difficulty maintaining a calm atmosphere owing to the great disturbance the entity was bringing into the house. As the control spoke, the medium's hands and legs began to shake. He explained that she was experiencing the physical condition of the entity that would soon speak to us, a disease known as classical palsy. Dr. Laidlaw nodded and asked the entity to proceed.

A moment later, the body of Eileen Garrett was occupied by an entirely new personality. Shaking uncontrollably, as if in great pain, the entity tried to sit up in the chair but was unable to maintain balance and eventually crashed to the floor. There, one of the legs continued to vibrate violently, which is one of the symptoms of palsy, a disease in which muscular control is lost. For two minutes or more, only inarticulate sounds came from the entranced medium's lips. Eventually we were able to induce the possessing entity to speak to us. At first there were only halting sounds, as if the entity were in great pain. From time to time the entity touched his leg, and then his head, indicating that those were areas in which he experienced pain. Dr. Laidlaw assured the personality before us that we had come as friends and that he could speak with us freely and

without fear. Realizing what we were attempting to convey, the entity broke into tears, extremely agitated, and at the same time tried to come close to where Dr. Laidlaw sat.

We could at last understand most of the words. The entity spoke English, but with a marked Polish accent. The voice sounded rough, uncouth, not at all like Eileen Garrett's own.

"Friend...friend...mercy. I know...I know...," and he pointed in the direction of Danton Walker. As we pried, gently and patiently, more information came from the entity on the floor before us. "Stones, stones....Don't let them take me. I can't talk." With that he pointed to his head, then to his tongue.

"No stones. You will not be stoned," Dr. Laidlaw assured him.

"No beatin'?"

Laidlaw assured the entity that he *could* talk, and that we were friends. He then asked what the entity's name might be.

"He calls me. I have to get out. I cannot go any further. In God's name, I cannot go any further."

With that, the entity touched Danton Walker's hands. Walker was visibly moved. "I will protect you," he said simply.

The entity kept talking about "stones," and we assumed that he was talking about stones being thrown at him. Actually, he was talking about stones under which he had hidden some documents. But that came later. Meanwhile he pointed at his mouth and said, "Teeth gone," and he graphically demonstrated how they had been kicked in. "Protect me," the entity said, coming closer to Walker again. Dr. Laidlaw asked whether he lived here. A violent gesture was his answer. "No, oh, no. I hide here. Cannot leave here."

It appeared that he was hiding from another man and that he knew the plans, which he had hidden in a faraway spot. "Where did you hide the plans?" Walker demanded.

"Give me map," the entity replied, and when Walker handed him a writing pad and a pen, the entity, using Mrs. Garrett's fingers, of course, picked it up as if he were handling a quill. The drawing, despite its unsteady and vacillating lines due to palsy, was nevertheless a valid representation of where the entity had hidden the papers. "In your measure, Andreas hid...not in the house...timber house, log house...under the stones...fifteen stones...plans for the whole shifting of men and ammunitions I have for the French. Plans I have to deliver to log house, right where the sun strikes window. Where sun strikes the window...fifteen stones under in log house...there I have put away plans."

This was followed by a renewed outburst of fear, during which the entity begged us not to allow him to be taken again. After much questioning, the entity told us that he was in need of protection, that he was Polish and had come to this country as a young man. He threw his arms around Walker, saying that he was like a brother to him. "Gospodin, gospodin," the entity said, showing his joy at finding who he thought was his brother again. "Me André, you Hans," he exclaimed. Walker was somewhat nonplussed at the idea of being Hans. "My brother" the entity said, "he killed too...I die...big field, battle. Like yesterday, like yesterday...I lie here...English all over. They are terrible."

"Were you with the Americans?" Dr. Laidlaw asked.

Apparently the word meant nothing to him. "No, no. Big word. Republic Protection. The stars in the flag, the stars in the flag. Republic.... They sing."

"How long have you been hiding in this house?"

"I go away a little, he stays, he talk, he here part of the time."

Uvani returned at this point, taking Andreas out of Eileen's body, explaining that the Polish youngster had been a prisoner. Apparently, he had been in other parts of the country with the French troops. He had been friendly with various people in the Revolutionary Army, serving as a jackboot for all types of men, a good servant. But he hadn't understood for whom he was working. "He refers to an André," Uvani went on to say, "with whom he is in contact for some time, and he likes this André very much because of the similar name...because he is Andrewski. There is this similarity to André. It is therefore he has been used, as far as I can see, as a cover-up for this man. Here then is the confusion. He is caught two or three times by different people because of his appearance; he is a dead-ringer, or double. His friend André disappears, and he's lost and does what he can with this one and that one and eventually he finds himself in the hands of the British troops. He is known to have letters and plans, and these he wants me to tell you were hidden by him due east of where you now find yourselves, in what he says was a temporary building of sorts in which were housed different caissons. In this there is also a rest house for guards. In this type kitchen he will not reveal the plans and is beaten mercilessly. His limbs are broken and he passes out, no longer in the right mind, but with a curious break on one side of the body, and his leg is damaged. It would appear that he is from time to time like one in a coma—he wakes, dreams, and loses himself again, and I gather from the story that he is not always aware of people."

We sat in stunned silence as Uvani explained the story to us. Then we joined in prayer to release the unfortunate one. To the best of my knowledge, the house has been free from further disturbances ever since. The papers, of course, were no longer in their hiding place. French auxiliary troops under Rochambeau and Lafayette had been all over the land, and papers must have gone back and forth between French detachments and their American allies. Some of these papers may have been of lesser importance

and could have been entrusted even to so simple a man as Andreas.

The years went by, Danton Walker himself passed away, and the house changed hands, but the pewter jar which Danton had entrusted to my care was still in my hands. Johnny, who had served the late columnist so well for all those years, refused to take it. To him, it meant that the ghost might attach himself to *him* now. Under the circumstances, I kept the jar and placed it in a showcase in my home along with many other antiquities and did not give the matter much thought. But roughly on the twentieth anniversary of the original expedition to the house in Rockland County, I decided to test two good mediums I work with, to see whether any of the past secrets clinging to the pewter might yet be unraveled.

On September 25, 1972, I handed Shawn Robbins a brown paper bag in which the pewter jar had been placed. But Shawn could not make contact, so I took out the object and placed it directly into her hands. "I pick up three initials and a crest," she began. "The first thing I see are these initials, someone's name, like B.A.R.; then I see a man with a beard, and he may have been very important. There is another man, whom I like better, however. They look Nordic to me, because of the strange helmets they wear."

"The person you sense here—is he a civilian or a soldier?"

"I'm thinking of the word 'crown.' There is someone here who wears a crown; the period is the 1700s, perhaps the 1600s. The King wore a crown and a white, high neck, like a ruffled collar, and then armor. That is *one* of the layers I get from this object."

I realized, of course, that the object was already old when the American Revolution took place. Danton Walker had acquired it in the course of his collecting activities, and it had no direct connection with the house itself.

It seemed to me that Shawn was psychometrizing the object quite properly, getting down to the original layer when it was first created. The description of a seventeenth-century English king was indeed quite correct. "The armor is a rough color, but all in one piece and worn over something else, some velvet, I think. On his head, there is a crown, and yet I see him also wearing a hat." I couldn't think of a better description of the way King Charles II dressed, and the pewter pitcher originated during his reign.

"What are some of the other layers you get?" I asked.

"There is a man here who looks as if he either broke his neck or was *hanged*. This man is the strongest influence I feel with this object. He is bearded and slightly baldish in front."

"Stick with him then and try to find out who he was."

Shawn gave the object another thorough investigation, touching it all over with her hands, and then reported, "He is important in the sense that the object is haunted by him. He was murdered by a person who had an object in his hand that looks like a scepter to me, but I don't know what it is. The man in back of him killed him: he got it in the back of his neck. The man who killed him is in a position of power."

"What about the victim—what was his position?"

"The only initials I pick up are something like Pont, or perhaps Boef."

While this did not correspond to Andreas, it seemed interesting to me that she picked up two French names. I recalled that the unlucky Polish jackboot had served the French auxiliaries. "Can you get any country of origin?"

"It is hard to say, but the man who was murdered had something to do with England. Perhaps the man who killed him did."

I then instructed Shawn to put her thumb into the dent in the wall of the pitcher where the ghostly hand of Andreas had made a depression. Again, Shawn came up with the name Boef. Since I wasn't sure whether she was picking up the original owner of the pewter pitcher or perhaps one of its several owners, I asked her to concentrate on the *last* owner and the time during which he had had the object in his house.

"The letter V is an important initial here," she said, "and I sense a boat coming up."

I couldn't help thinking of the sloop *Vulture*, which Major André had wanted to use for his getaway but didn't, and which saved the life of General Arnold. "Do you feel any suffering with this object?" I asked.

"Yes," Shawn replied. "A man was murdered, and a woman was involved: a woman, an older person, and the murderer; this was premeditated murder. The victim is a good-looking man, not too old, with a moustache or beard, and it looks as if they are taking something away from him which is part of him, something that belonged to him."

"Was it something he had on his person?"

"When he was murdered, he didn't have it on him, and *it is still buried somewhere*," Shawn replied.

Shawn, of course, had no idea that there was a connection between the object she was psychometrizing and the Rockland County Ghost, which I had written about in the 1960s. "What is buried?" I asked, becoming more intrigued by her testimony as the minutes rolled by.

"There is something he owns that is buried some-where, and I think it goes back to a castle or house. It is not buried inside but *outside*. It is buried near a grave, and whoever buried it was very smart."

"Why was he killed?" I asked.

"I see him, and then another man, besides, who is involved. He was murdered *because he was a friend of this man* and his cause. They are wearing something funny on their heads. One of them is holding up his two hands, with an object with a face on it, a very peculiar thing."

"Can you tell me where the object he buried is located?"

"I can't describe it unless I can draw it. Give me a pencil. There is the initial 'A' here."

"Who is this 'A'?"

"'K' would be another initial of importance. This is the hat they are wearing."

Shawn then drew what looked to me like the rough outlines of a fur-braided hat, the kind soldiers in the late eighteenth century would wear in the winter. The initial "A" of course startled me, since it might belong to Andreas. The "K" I thought might refer to Kosciuszko, the leader of the Polish auxiliary forces in America during the Revolutionary War, who wore fur hats. "The hat is part metal, but there is a red feather on it, actually red and green," she said. The colors were quite correct for the period involved.

"This man is in love with an older woman; he is a very good looking fellow. This is how he looks to me." Shawn drew a rough portrait of a man in the wig and short tie of an eighteenth-century gentleman. She then drew the woman also, and mentioned that she wore a flower or some sort of emblem. It reminded her of a flower or a crest and was important. "It is a crude way of saying something, and the letters V.A.R. come in here also. A crest with V.A.R. across it," Shawn said.*

"Tell me Shawn," I said, steering her in a somewhat different direction, "has there ever been any psychic manifestation associated with this object?"

"Somebody's heavy footsteps are associated with this. Things would move in a house. By themselves."

"Is there any entity attached to this object?"

"I want to say the name Victor." Was she getting Walker?

As I questioned Shawn further about the object, it became increasingly clear that she was speaking of the period when it was first made. She described, in vivid words, the colors and special designs on the uniforms of the men who were involved with the object. All of it fit the middle or late seventeenth century but obviously had nothing to do with the Revolutionary War. I was not surprised, since I had already assumed that some earlier layer would be quite strong. But then she mentioned a boat and remarked that it was going up a river. "I must be way off on this," Shawn said, somewhat disappointed, "because I see a windmill."

The matter became interesting again. I asked her what became of "A." "There are three or four men in the boat," Shawn said. "They are transporting someone, and I think it is 'A' on his way to his execution."

"What did he do?"

"He didn't do anything—that is the sad part of it. He was just a victim of circumstances. He is an innocent victim."

"Who did his captors think he was?"

*Richard Varick, of noble Dutch descent, became Aide-de-Camp to General Arnold in August 1780, six weeks prior to the treason. He was not involved in it, however.

"An important person."

"Did this important person commit a crime or did he have something they wanted?"

"He had nothing on him, but the initials K.A.E.A. are of importance here. That is an important name. But they have the wrong man. But they kill him anyway. There is a design on his cloak, which looks to me like the astrological Cancer symbol, like the crab."

"What happens further on?"

"They are leaving the windmill now. But something is going to happen because they are headed that way. Other people are going to die because of this. Many." Without my telling her to, Shawn touched the object again. "I feel the period when Marie Antoinette lived. I have the feeling they are going off in that direction. They are going to France. There is a general here, and I get the initials L.A.M.* He, too, was killed in the war."

"But why is 'A' brought to this general?"

"Well, 'A' looks to me as if he had changed clothes, and now he wears black with a little piece of white here. They are obviously conferring about something. 'A' is conferring with someone else. It doesn't look like someone in the military, and he is hard to describe, but I never saw a uniform like this before. He has on a beret and a medal."

"What about 'A'? Is he a civilian or an officer?"

"Truthfully, he is really an officer. I think this is what the whole thing is all about. I think they captured someone really important. He probably was an officer in disguise, not wearing the right coloring. It is treason, what else? Could he have sold papers, you know, secrets?"

Shawn felt now that she had gotten as much as she could from the object. I found her testimony intriguing, to say the least. There were elements of the André story in it, and traces of Andreas's life as well. Just as confusing, it seemed to me, as the mistaken-identity problems which had caused Andreas' downfall. All this time, Shawn had no idea that Major André was involved in my investigation, no idea of what the experiment was all about. As far as she was concerned, she had been asked to psychometrize an old pewter jar, and nothing else.

On October 3, 1972, I repeated the experiment with Ethel Johnson Meyers. Again, the pitcher was in the brown paper bag. Again, the medium requested to hold it directly in her hands. "I see three women and a man with heavy features," she began immediately. "Something is going on, but the language doesn't sound English. Now there is a man here who is hurt, blood running from his left eye."

"How did he get hurt?"

"There are some violent vibrations here. I hear loud talking, and I feel as if he had been hit with this pitcher. He has on a waistcoat or brown jacket, either plush or vel-

*General John Lamb was sent by General Washington on September 25, 1780, to secure Kings Ferry on the eve of Arnold's treason.

veteen, and a wide collar. Black stockings and purple shoes. Knickers that go down to here, and of the same material as the coat."

"Can you pinpoint the period?"

"I would guess around the time of Napoleon," Ethel said, not altogether sure. That too was interesting since she obviously wasn't judging the jar (which was far older than the Napoleonic period) by its appearance. As far as the Major André incident was concerned, she was about twenty years off. "I am hearing German spoken," Ethel continued. "I think this object has seen death and horror, and I hear violence and screams. There is the feeling of murder, and a woman is involved. I hear a groan, and now there is more blood. I feel there is also a gash on the neck. Once in a while, I hear an English word spoken with a strange accent. I hear the name Mary, and I think this is at least the seventeenth century."

I realized that she was speaking of the early history of the object, and I directed her to tune in on some later vibrations. "Has this object ever been in the presence of a murder?" I asked directly.

"This man's fate is undeserved. He has been crossing over from a far distance into a territory where he is not wanted by many, and he is not worthy of that protection which he has. He has not deserved this; he has no political leanings; he has not offended anyone purposely. His presence is unwanted. God in heaven knows that."

It sounded more and more the way Andreas spoke when Eileen Garrett was his instrument. *Protection*! That was the word he kept repeating, more than any other word, protection from those who would do him injustice and hurt him.

"What nationality is he?"

"It sounds Italian."

"What name does he give you?"

"Rey…Rey.†…Man betrayed." Ethel was sinking now into a state of semi-trance, and I noticed some peculiar facial changes coming over her; it was almost as if the entity were directing her answers.

"Betrayed by whom?" I asked, bending over to hear every word.

"The ones that make me feel safe."

"Who are they?"

"Bloody Englishmen."

"Who are your friends?"

"I'm getting away from English."

"Is there something this person has that someone else wants?"

"Yes, that is how it is."

"Who is this person to whom all these terrible things are happening."

"Coming over. A scapegoat."

Again, Ethel managed to touch both the earlier layer and the involvement with the Revolutionary period, but in

†AndR Eas?

a confusing and intertwined manner which made it difficult for me to sort out what she was telling me. Still, there were elements that were quite true and which she could not have known, since she, like Shawn, had no idea what the object was or why I was asking her to psychometrize it. It was clear to me that no ghostly entity had attached to the object, however, and that whatever the two mediums had felt was in the past. A little lighter in my heart, I replaced the object in my showcase, hoping that it would in time acquire some less violent vibrations from the surrounding objects.

As for Andreas and André, one had a brief moment in the limelight, thanks chiefly to psychical research, while the other is still a major figure in both American and British history. After his execution on October 2, 1780, at Tappan, André was buried at the foot of the gallows. In 1821 his body was exhumed and taken to England and reburied at Westminster Abbey. By 1880 tempers had sufficiently cooled and British-American friendship was firmly enough established to permit the erection of a monument to the event on the spot where the three militia men had come across Major André. Actually, the monument itself was built in 1853, but on the occasion of the centennial of André's capture, a statue and bronze plaque were added

and the monument surrounded with a protective metal fence. It stands near a major road and can easily be observed when passing by car. It is a beautiful monument, worthy of the occasion. There is only one thing wrong with it, be it ever so slight: *It stands at the wrong spot.* My good friend, Elliott Schryver, the eminent editor and scholar, pointed out the actual spot at some distance to the east.

In studying Harry Hansen's book on the area, I have the impression that he shares this view. In order to make a test of my own, we stopped by the present monument, and I asked Ingrid to tell me what she felt. I had purposely told her that the spot had no direct connection with anything else we were doing that day, so she could not consciously sense what the meaning of our brief stop was. Walking around the monument two or three times, touching it, and "taking in" the atmosphere psychically, she finally came up to me, shook her head, and said, "I am sorry, Hans, there is absolutely nothing here. Nothing at all."

But why not? If the Revolutionary taverns can be moved a considerable distance to make them more accessible to tourists, why shouldn't a monument be erected where everyone can see it instead of in some thicket where a prospective visitor might break a leg trying to find it? Nobody cares, least of all Major André.

✳ 16

Benedict Arnold's Friend

"I WAS COMPLETELY FASCINATED by your recent book," read a letter by Gustav J. Kramer of Claverack, New York. Mr. Kramer, it developed, was one of the leading lights of the Chamber of Commerce in the town of Hudson and wrote a column for the *Hudson Register-Star* on the side. "During the past three years I have specialized in writing so-called ghost stories for my column," he explained. "We have a number of haunted houses in this historic section of the Hudson Valley. President Martin Van Buren's home is nearby and is honestly reputed to be the scene of some highly disturbing influences. Aaron Burr, the killer of Alexander Hamilton, hid out in a secret room of this estate and has reliably been reported to have been seen on numerous occasions wandering through the upper halls."

This was in 1963, and I had not yet investigated the phenomena at Aaron Burr's stables in lower Manhattan at the time. Perhaps what people saw in the house was an imprint of Burr's thought forms.

From this initial letter developed a lively correspondence between us, and for nearly two years I promised to come to the Hudson Valley and do some investigating, provided that Mr. Kramer came up with something more substantial than hearsay.

It wasn't until July 1965 that he came up with what he considered "*the* house." He explained that it had a cold spot in it and that the owner, a Mrs. Dorothea Connacher, a teacher by profession, was a quiet and reserved lady who had actually had a visual experience in the attic of this very old house.

My brother-in-law's untimely and unexpected death postponed our journey once again, so we—meaning Ethel Johnson Meyers, the medium, my wife Catherine, and I— weren't ready to proceed to Columbia County, New York, until early February 1966. GHOST HUNTER VISITS HUDSON, Gus Kramer headlined in his column. He met us at the exit from the Taconic Parkway and took us to lunch before proceeding further.

It was early afternoon when we arrived at Mrs. Connacher's house, which was situated a few minutes away on a dirt road, standing on a fair-sized piece of land and surrounded by tall, old trees. Because of its isolation, one had the feeling of being far out in the country, when in fact the thruway connecting New York with Albany passes a mere ten minutes away. The house is gleaming white, or nearly so, for the ravages of time have taken their toll. Mr. and Mrs. Connacher bought it twenty years prior to our visit, but after divorcing Mr. Connacher, she was unable to keep it up as it should have been, and gradually the interior especially fell into a state of disrepair. The outside still showed its noble past, those typically colonial manor house traits, such as the columned entrance, the Grecian influence in the construction of the roof, and the beautiful colonial shutters.

New York State in the dead of winter is a cold place indeed. As we rounded the curve of the dirt road and saw the manor house looming at the end of a short carriage way, we wondered how the lady of the house was able to heat it. After we were inside, we realized she had difficulties in that respect.

For the moment, however, I halted a few yards away from the house and took some photographs of this visually exciting old house. Ethel Johnson Meyers knew nothing about the house or why we were there. In fact, part of our expedition was for the purpose of finding a country home to live in. Ethel thought we were taking her along to serve as consultant in the purchase of a house, since she herself owns a country home and knows a great deal about houses. Of course, she knew that there were a couple of interesting places en route, but she took that for granted, having worked with me for many years. Even while we were rounding the last bend and the house became visible to us, Ethel started getting her first impressions of the case. I asked her to remain seated in the car and to tell me about it.

"I see two people, possibly a third. The third person is young, a woman with a short, rather upturned nose and large eyes, but she seems to be dimmer than the impression of the men. The men are very strong. One of them has a similar upturned nose and dark skin. He wears a white wig. There is also an older woman. She seems to look at me as if she wants to say, Why are you staring at me that way?" Ethel explained to the spirit in an earnest tone of voice why she had come to the house, that she meant no harm and had come as a friend, and if there were anything she could do for them, they should tell her.

While this one-sided conversation was going on, Catherine and I sat in the car, waiting for it to end. Gus Kramer had gone ahead to announce our arrival to Mrs. Connacher.

"What sort of clothing is the woman wearing—I mean the older woman?" I asked.

"She's got on some kind of a white dusting cap," Ethel replied, "and her hair is sticking out."

"Can you tell what period they are from?"

"He wears a wig, and she has some sort of kerchief, wide at the shoulders and pointed in back. The blouse of her dress fits tight. The dress goes down to the floor, as far as I can see. The bottom of the dress is ruffled. I should say she is a woman in her sixties, perhaps even older."

"What about the man?"

"I think one of the women could be his daughter, because the noses are alike, sort of pug noses."

"Do you get any names or initials?"

"The letter 'B' is important."

"Do you get any other people?"

"There is a woman with dark hair parted in the middle, and there is a man with a strange hat on his head. Then there is someone with an even stranger hat, octagonal in shape and very high. I've never seen a hat like that before. There is something about a B.A. *A Bachelor of Arts?* Now I pick up the name Ben. I am sorry, but I don't think I can do any more outside."

"In that case," I said, "let us continue inside the house." But I asked Ethel to wait in the car while I interviewed the owner of the house. Afterward, she was to come in and try trance.

Mrs. Dorothea Connacher turned out to be a smallish lady in her later years, and the room we entered first gave the impression of a small, romantic jumble shop. Antiquities, old furniture, a small new stove so necessary on this day, pictures on the walls, books on shelves, and all of it in somewhat less than perfect order made it plain that Mrs. Connacher wasn't quite able to keep up with the times, or rather that the house demanded more work than one person could possibly manage. Mrs. Connacher currently lived there with her son, Richmond, age thirty-six. Her husband had left three years after she had moved into the house. I asked her about any psychic experiences she might have had.

"Both my husband and I are freelance artists," she began, "and my husband used to go to New York to work three days a week, and the rest of the time he worked at home. One day shortly after we had moved in, I was alone in the house. That night I had a dream that my husband would leave me. At the time I was so happy I couldn't understand how this could happen."

The dream became reality a short time later. It wasn't the only prophetic dream Mrs. Connacher had. On previous occasions she had had dreams concerning dead relatives and various telepathic experiences.

"What about the house? When did it start here?"

"We were in the house for about five months. We had been told that everything belonging to the former owners had been taken out of the house—there had been an auction, and these things had been sold. There really wasn't anything up in the attic, so we were told. My husband and I had been up a couple of times to explore it. We were fascinated by the old beams, with their wooden pegs dating back to the eighteenth century. There was nothing up there except some old picture frames and a large trunk. It is still up there.

"Well, finally we became curious and opened it, and there were a lot of things in it. It seemed there were little pieces of material all tied up in bundles. But we didn't look too closely; I decided to come up there some day when I had the time to investigate by myself. My husband said he was too busy right then and wanted to go down.

"A few days later, when I was home alone, I decided to go upstairs again and look through the trunk. The attic is rather large, and there are only two very small windows in the far corner. I opened the trunk, put my hands into it, and took out these little pieces of material, but in order to see better I took them to the windows. When I got to the bottom of the trunk, I found a little waistcoat, a hat, and a peculiar bonnet, the kind that was worn before 1800. I thought, what a small person this must have been who could have worn this! At first I thought it might have been for a child; but no, it was cut for an adult, although a very tiny person."

As Mrs. Connacher was standing there, fascinated by the material, she became aware of a pinpoint of light out of the corner of her eye. Her first thought was, I must tell Jim that there is a hole in the roof where this light is coming through. But she kept looking and, being preoccupied with the material in the trunk, paid no attention to the light. Something, however, made her look up, and she noticed that the light had now become substantially larger. Also, it was coming nearer, changing its position all the time. The phenomenon began to fascinate her. She wasn't thinking of ghosts or psychic phenomena at all, merely wondering what this was all about. As the light came nearer and nearer, she suddenly thought, why, that looks like a human figure!

Eventually, it stopped near the trunk, and Mrs. Connacher realize it was a human figure, the figure of an elderly lady. She was unusually small and delicate and wore the very bonnet Mrs. Connacher had discovered at the bottom of the trunk! The woman's clothes seemed gray, and Mrs. Connacher noticed the apron the woman was wearing. As she watched the ghostly apparition in fascinated horror, the little lady used her apron in a movement that is generally used in the country to shoo away chickens. However, the motion was directed against *her*, as if the apparition wanted to shoo her away from "her" trunk!

"I was frightened. I saw the bonnet and the apron and this woman shooing me away, and she seemed completely solid," Mrs. Connacher said.

"What did you do?"

"I walked around in back of the trunk to see whether she was still there. She was. I said, all right, all right. But I didn't want to look at her. I could feel my hair stand up and decided to go down. I was worried I might fall down the stairs, but I made it all right."

"Did you ever see her again?"

"No. But there were all sorts of unusual noises. Once my husband and I were about to go off to sleep when it sounded as if someone had taken a baseball bat and hit the wall with it right over our heads. That was in the upstairs bedroom. The spot isn't too far from the attic, next to the staircase."

"Have other people had experiences here?"

"Well, my sister Clair had a dream about the house before she had been here. When she came here for the first time she said she wanted to see *the attic*. I was surprised, for I had not even told her that there was an attic. She

rushed right upstairs, but when she saw it, she turned around, and her face was white; it was exactly what she had seen in her dream. Then there was this carpenter who had worked for me repairing the attic and doing other chores on the property. After he came down from the attic, he left and hasn't been back since. No matter how often I ask him to come and do some work for me, he never shows up."

"Maybe the little old lady shooed him away too," I said. "What about those cold spots Gus has been telling me about?"

"I only have a fireplace and this small heater here. Sometimes you just can't get the room warm. But there are certain spots in the house that are always cold. Even in the summertime people ask whether we have air conditioning."

"When was the house built?"

"One part has the date 1837 engraved in the stone downstairs. The older part goes back two hundred years."

"Did any of the previous owners say anything about a ghost?"

"No. Before us were the Turners, and before them the Link family owned it for a very long time. But we never talked about such things."

I then questioned Gus Kramer about the house and about his initial discussions with Mrs. Connacher. It is not uncommon for a witness to have a better memory immediately upon telling of an experience than at a later date when the story has been told and told again. Sometimes it becomes embroidered by additional, invented details, but at other times it loses some of its detail because the storyteller no longer cares or has forgotten what was said under the immediate impression of the experience itself.

"Mrs. Connacher was holding an old, musty woman's blouse at the time when the apparition appeared," Gus said. "At the time she felt that there was a connection between her holding this piece of clothing and her sighting."

"Have you yourself ever experienced anything in the Connacher house?"

"Well, the last time I visited here, we were sitting in the dim, cluttered living room, when I noticed the dog follow an imaginary something with his eyes from one bedroom door to the door that leads to the attic, where Mrs. Connacher's experience took place. He then lay down with his head between his paws and his eyes fastened on the attic door. I understand he does this often and very frequently fastens his gaze on 'something' behind Mrs. Connacher's favorite easy chair when she is in it. I assure you, the hairs on the back of my neck stood up like brush bristles while watching that dog."

I decided to get Ethel out of the car, which by now must have become a cold spot of its own. "Ethel," I said, "you are standing in the living room of this house now. There is another story above this one and there is an attic.

I want you to tell me if there is any presence in this house and, if so, what area you feel is most affected.

"The top," Ethel replied, without a moment's hesitation.

"Is there a presence there?"

"Yes," Ethel said firmly. We had stepped into the next room, where there was a large, comfortable easy chair. I tried to get Ethel to sit down in it, but she hesitated. "No, I want to go somewhere." I had the distinct impression that she was gradually falling into trance, and I wanted her in a safe chair when the trance took hold. Memories of an entranced Ethel being manipulated by an unruly ghost were too fresh in my mind to permit such chance-taking. I managed to get her back into the chair all right. A moment later, a friendly voice spoke, saying, "Albert, Albert," and I realized that Ethel's control had taken over. But it was a very brief visit. A moment later, a totally different voice came from the medium's entranced lips. At first, I could not understand the words. There was something about a wall. Then a cheery voice broke through. "Who are you, and what the hell are you doing here?"

When you are a psychic investigator, you sometimes answer a question with another question. In this case, I demanded to know who was speaking. "Loyal, loyal," the stranger replied. I assured "him" that we had come as friends and that he—for it sounded like a man—could safely converse with us. "Will you speak to me then?" he asked.

"Can I help you?" I replied.

"Well, I'll help others; they need help."

"Is this your house? Who are you?" But the stranger wouldn't identify himself just yet. "Why were you brought in? Who brought you here?"

"My house, yes. My house, my house."

"What is your name, please?" I asked routinely. Immediately, I felt resistance.

"What is that to you, sir?"

I explained that I wanted to introduce myself properly.

"I'm loyal, loyal," the voice assured me.

"Loyal to whom, may I ask?"

"His Majesty, sir; do you know that George?"

I asked in which capacity the entity was serving His Majesty. "Who are you? You ask for help. Help for what?"

We weren't getting anywhere, it seemed to me. But these things take time, and I have a lot of patience.

"Can you tell me who you are?"

Instead, the stranger became more urgent. "When is he coming, when is he coming? When is he coming to help me?"

"Whom do you expect?" I replied. I tried to assure him that whomever he was expecting would arrive soon, at

the same time attempting to find out whom he was talking about. This, of course, put him on his guard.

"I don't say anymore."

Again I asked that he identify himself so I could address him by his proper name and rank.

"You are not loyal, you, you, who are in my house?"

"Well, I was told you needed help."

But the entity refused to give his name. "I fear."

"There is no need to fear. I am a friend. You are making it very difficult for me. I am afraid I cannot stay unless you—" I hinted.

"When will he come? When will he come?"

"Who are you waiting for?"

"Horatio. Horatio Gates. Where is he? Tell me, I am a loyal subject. Where is he? Tell me."

"Well, if you are loyal, you will identify yourself. You have to identify yourself before I can be of any service to you."

Instead, the entity broke into bitter laughter. "My name, ha ha ha. Trap! Trap!"

I assured him it was no trap. "You know me, you do," he said. I assured him that I didn't. "You know me if you come here, ha ha ha."

I decided to try a different tack. "What year are we in?"

This didn't go down well with him either. "Madman, madman. Year, year. You're not of this house. Go."

"Look," I said, "we've come a long distance to speak with you. You've got to be cooperative if we are going to help you." But the stranger insisted, and repeated the question: When will he come? I started to explain that "he" wouldn't come at all, that a lot of time had gone by and that the entity had been "asleep."

Now it was the entity's turn to ask who I was. But before I could tell him again, he cried out, "Ben, where are you?" I wanted to know who Ben was, at the same time assuring him that much time had passed and that the house had changed hands. But it didn't seem to make any impression on him. "Where is he? Are you he? Is that you? Speak to me!"

I decided to play along to get some more information. But he realized right away that I was not the one he was expecting. "You are not he, are you he? I can't hang by my throat. I will not hang by my throat. No, no, no."

"Nobody's threatening you. Have you done anything that you fear?"

"My own Lord God knows that I am innocent. If I have a chance. Why, why, why?"

"Who is threatening you? Tell me. I'm on your side."

"But you will get me."

"I've come to help you. This is your house, is it not? What is your name? You have to identify yourself so that I know that I haven't made a mistake," I said, pleading with him. All the time this was going on, Gus Kramer, Mrs. Connacher, and my wife watched in fascinated silence.

Ethel looked like an old man now, not at all like her own self. There was a moment of hesitation, a pause. Then the voice spoke again, this time, it seemed to me, in a softer vein.

"Let me be called Anthony."

"Anthony what?"

"Where is he? I wait. I've got to kill him." I explained how it was possible for him to speak to us *in our time*. But it seemed to make no impression on him. "He was here. He was here. I know it."

"Who was here?" I asked, and repeated that he had to identify himself.

"But I may go?" There was a sense of urgency in his voice.

"Would you like to leave this house?"

"My house, why my house? To hang here. My daughter, she may go with you."

"What is your daughter's name?"

"Where you lead, I go, she says. But she too will hang here if I do not go. She too. God take me, you will take me."

I assured him that he could leave the house safely and need not return again. "You will be safe. You'll see your daughter again. But you must understand, there is no more war. No more killing."

"She died right here, my sweet daughter, she died right here."

"What happened to you after that?"

"I sit here; you see me. I sit here. I will go."

"How old are you?"

"I'm not so old that I can't go from here, where the fields are fertile, and oh! no blood."

"Where would you like to go from here?"

"Far away. Sweet Jennie died. Take me from here. He does not come."

"I promise to take you. Just be calm."

"Oh, Horatio, Horatio, you have promised. Why did he come instead of you, Horatio?"

"Did you serve under Horatio Gates?"

"Arnold, are you he? No."

"If you're looking for Arnold, he's dead."

"You lie."

Again, I explained, tactfully, about the passage of time. But he would hear none of it.

"You lie to me. He will come. You lie."

"No," I replied. "It is true. Arnold is dead."

"Why? Why, why, why? He is gone, is he?"

"Is your name Anthony?"

Eagerly he replied: "Oh, yes, it is. They don't want me to go from here, but I must go, they'll hang me. Don't let them hang me." I assured him that I wouldn't. "My daughter, my sweet child. Oh why, because we swear allegiance to... Now I hang here. They will come to get me; they will come. Where is he? He has forsaken me."

"A lot of time has gone by. You have passed on."

"No. Madness. John, John, help me. Come quick."

I informed the entity that he was speaking through a female instrument, and to touch his instrument's hair. That way, he would be convinced that it wasn't his own body he was in at present.

"John, John, where are you? I'm dreaming."

I assured him that he wasn't dreaming, and that I was speaking the truth.

"I am mad, I am mad."

I assured him that he was sane.

"They hold me. Oh, Jesus Christ!"

I began the usual rescue-circle procedure, explaining that by wanting to be with his daughter, who had gone on before him, he could leave this house where his tragedy had kept him. "Go from this house. You are free to join your daughter. Go in peace; we'll pray for you. There is nothing to fear." A moment later, the entity was gone and Albert had returned to Ethel Meyers's body.

Usually, I question Albert, the control personality, concerning any entity that has been permitted to speak through Ethel Meyers' instrumentality. Sometimes additional information or the previous information in more detailed and clarified form emerges from these discussions. But Albert explained that he could not give me the man's name. "He gives false names. As far as we can judge here, he believes he was hanged. He was a Loyalist, refusing to take refuge with Americans. He didn't pose as a Revolutionary until the very end, when he thought he could be saved." Albert explained that this had taken place in this house during the Revolutionary War.

"Why does he think he was hanged? Was he?"

"I don't see this happening in this house. I believe he was taken from here, yes."

"What about other entities in this house?"

"There have been those locked in secret here, who have had reason to be here. They are all still around. There is a woman who died and who used to occupy this part of the house and up to the next floor. Above, I think I hear those others who have been wounded and secreted here."

I asked Albert if he could tell us anything further about the woman who had been seen in the house. "I remember I showed this to my instrument before. She was wearing a white, French-like kerchief hat with lace and little black ribbons. There are two women, but one is the mother to this individual here. I am talking about the older woman."

"Why is she earthbound?"

"Because she passed here and remained simply because she wanted to watch her husband's struggles to save himself from being dishonored and discredited. Her husband is the one who was speaking to you."

"Can you get anything about the family?"

"They have been in this country for some time, and they are Loyalists."

"Why is the woman up there in the attic and not down here in the rest of the house?"

"She comes down, but she stays above, for she passed there."

"Do you get her name?"

"Elsa, or Elva."

"Is she willing to speak to us?"

"I can try, but she is a belligerent person. You see, she keeps reliving her last days on earth, and then the hauntings in her own house, while her husband and daughter were still living here. Sometimes they clash one with the other."

"What about the other woman? Can you find out anything about her?

"I can describe her, but I can't make her speak. She has dark hair parted in the middle and an oval face, and she wears a high-necked dress of a dark color. Black with long sleeves, I think. However, I feel she is from a later period."

"Why is she earthbound in the house?"

"She had been extremely psychic when she lived here, and she has been bothered by these other ghosts that were here before her. Her name was Drew. Perhaps Andrew, although I rather think Drew was the family name. She died in this house. There was a man who went before her. A curse had been put on her by a woman who was here before her. It was a ghostly kind of quarrel between the two women. One was angry that she should be here, and the other was angry because she owned the house and found it invaded by those unwanted 'guests,' as she called them."

I asked Albert to make sure that the house was now "clean" and to bring Ethel back to her own self. "I will not need to take the woman by the hand," he explained. "She will go away with her husband, now that he has decided to leave for fear they will hang him." With that, I thanked Albert for his help, and Ethel returned to herself a few moments later, remembering nothing of what had transpired, as is usual with her when she is in deep trance.

We had not yet been to the upper part of the house. Even though Ethel would normally be quite tired after a trance session, I decided to have a look at the second story and the attic. Ethel saw a number of people in the upper part of the house, both presences and psychometric impressions from the past. I felt reasonably sure that the disturbed gentleman who had called himself Anthony was gone from the house, as was his daughter. There remained the question of the other woman, the older individual who had frightened Mrs. Connacher. "I see what looks like a small boy," Ethel suddenly exclaimed as we were standing in the attic. "I rather think it is a woman, a short woman."

"Describe her, please."

"She seems to wear a funny sort of white cap. Her outfit is pinkish gray, with a white handkerchief over her shoulders going down into her belt. She looks like a girl and is very small, but she is an older woman, nevertheless."

En route to another house at Hudson, New York, I asked Gus Kramer to comment. "Benedict Arnold was brought to this area after the battle of Saratoga to recuperate for one or two nights," Kramer explained, and I reminded myself that General Arnold, long before he turned traitor to the American cause, had been a very successful field commander and administrative officer on the side of the Revolution. "He spent the night in the Kinderhook area," Gus continued. "The location of the house itself is not definitely known, but it is known that he spent the night here. Horatio Gates, who was the American leader in the battle of Saratoga, also spent several nights in the immediate area. It is not inconceivable that this place, which was a mansion in those days, might have entertained these men at the time."

"What about the hanging?"

"Seven Tories were hanged in this area during the Revolutionary War. Some of the greatest fighting took place here, and it is quite conceivable that something took place at this old mansion. Again, it completely bears out what Mrs. Meyers spoke of while in trance."

I asked Gus to pinpoint the period for me. "This would have been in 1777, toward October and November."

"What about that cold spot in the house?"

"Outside of the owner," Gus replied, "there was an artist named Stanley Bate, who visited the house and complained about an unusually cold spot. There was one particular room that was known as the Sick Room; we have found out from a later investigation that it is one of the bedrooms upstairs. It was used for mortally sick people, when they became so ill that they had to be brought to this bedroom, and eventually several of them died in it. You couldn't notice it today, because the whole house was so cold, but we have noticed a difference of at least twenty-five to thirty degrees in the temperature between that room and the surrounding part of the house. This cannot be attributed to drafts or open windows."

"Did your artist friend who visited the house experience anything else besides the cold spot?"

"Yes, he had a very vivid impression of someone charging at him several times. There was a distinct tugging on his shirt sleeve. This was about two years ago, and though he knew that the house was haunted, he had not heard about the apparition Mrs. Connacher had seen."

It appeared to me that the entity, Anthony, or whatever his name might have been, had pretty good connections on both sides of the Revolutionary War. He was in trouble, that much was clear. In his difficulty, he turned to Benedict Arnold, and he turned to General Horatio Gates, both American leaders. He also cried out to John to save him, and I can't help wondering, common though the name is, whether he might not also have known major John André.

✳ 17

The Haverstraw Ferry Case

HAVERSTRAW IS A SLEEPY little town about an hour's ride from New York City, perched high on the west side of the Hudson River. As its name implies, it was originally settled by the Dutch. On the other side of the river, not far away, was Colonel Beverley Robinson's house, where Benedict Arnold made his headquarters. The house burned down some years ago, and today there are only a few charred remnants to be seen on the grounds. At Haverstraw also was the house of Joshua Smith, the man who helped Major John André escape, having been entrusted with the British spy's care by his friend, Benedict Arnold. At Haverstraw, too, was one of the major ferries to cross the Hudson River, for during the Revolutionary period there were as yet no bridges to go from one side to the other.

I had never given Haverstraw any particular thought, although I had passed through it many times on my way upstate. In August 1966 I received a letter from a gentleman named Jonathan Davis, who had read some of my books and wanted to let me in on an interesting case he thought worthy of investigation. The house in question stands directly on the river, overlooking the Hudson and, as he put it, practically in the shadow of High Tor. Including the basement there are four floors in all. But rather than give me the information secondhand, he suggested to the owner, a friend, that she communicate with me directly. The owner turned out to be Laurette Brown, an editor of a national women's magazine in New York City.

"I believe my house is haunted by one or possibly two ghosts: a beautiful thirty-year-old woman and her two-year-old daughter," she explained. Miss Brown had shared the house with another career woman, Kaye S., since October 1965. Kaye, a lovely blonde woman who came from a prominent family, was extremely intelligent and very creative. She adored the house overlooking the river, which the two women had bought on her instigation. Strangely, though, Kaye frequently said she would never leave it again *alive*. A short a time later, allegedly because of an unhappy love affair, she drove her car to Newburgh, rigged up the exhaust pipe, and committed suicide along with the child she had had by her second husband.

"After she died, and I lived here alone, I was terribly conscious of a spirit trying to communicate with me," Miss Brown explained. "There was a presence, there were unnatural bangings of doors and mysterious noises, but I denied them. At the time, I wanted no part of the so-called supernatural." Since then, Miss Brown has had second thoughts about the matter, especially as the phenomena continued. She began to wonder whether the restless spirit wanted something from her, whether there was something she could do for the spirit. One day, her friend Jonathan Davis was visiting and mentioned that he very much wanted the

red rug on which he was standing at the time and which had belonged to Kaye. Before Miss Brown could answer him, Davis had the chilling sensation of a presence and the impression that a spirit was saying to him, "No, you may not take *my* rug."

"Since that time, I have also heard footsteps, and the crying of a child. Lately, I wake up, out of a deep sleep, around midnight or 2 A.M., under the impression that someone is trying to reach me. This has never happened to me before."

Miss Brown then invited me to come out and investigate the matter. I spoke to Jonathan Davis and asked him to come along on the day when my medium and I would pay the house a visit. Davis contributed additional information. According to him, on the night of August 6, 1966, when Miss Brown had awakened from deep sleep with particularly disturbed thoughts, she had gone out on the balcony overlooking the Hudson River. At the same time, she mixed herself a stiff drink to calm her nerves. As she stood on the balcony with her drink in hand, she suddenly felt another presence with her, and she knew at that instant, had she looked to the right, she would have seen a person. She quickly gulped down her drink and went back to sleep. She remembered, as Mr. Davis pointed out, that her former housemate had strongly disapproved of her drinking.

"It may interest you to know," Miss Brown said, "that the hills around High Tor Mountain, which are so near to our house, are reputed to be inhabited by a race of dwarves that come down from the mountains at night and work such mischief as moving road signs, et cetera. That there is some feeling of specialness, even enchantment, about this entire area, Kaye always felt, and I believe that if spirits can roam the earth, hers is here at the house she so loved."

The story sounded interesting enough, even though I did not take Miss Brown's testimony at face value. As is always the case when a witness has preconceived notions about the origin of a psychic disturbance, I assume nothing until I have investigated the case myself. Miss Brown had said nothing about the background of the house. From my knowledge of the area, I knew that there were many old houses still standing on the river front.

Ethel Johnson Meyers was my medium, and Catherine, my wife, drove the car, as on so many other occasions. My wife, who had by then become extremely interested in the subject, helped me with the tape recording equipment and the photography. Riverside Avenue runs along the river but is a little hard to locate if you don't know your way around Haverstraw. The medium-size house turned out to be quite charming, perched directly on the water's edge. Access to it was now from the street side, although I felt pretty sure that the main entrance had been either from around the corner or from the water itself. From the looks of the house, it was immediately clear to me that we were dealing with a pre-Revolutionary building.

Miss Brown let us into a long verandah running alongside the house, overlooking the water. Adjacent to it was the living room, artistically furnished and filled with antiquities, rugs, and pillows. Mr. Davis could not make it after all, owing to some unexpected business in the city.

Ethel Meyers sat down in a comfortable chair in the corner of the living room, taking in the appointments with the eye of a woman who had furnished her own home not so long before. She knew nothing about the case or the nature of our business here.

"I see three men and a woman," she began. "The woman has a big nose and is on the older side; one of the men has a high forehead; and then there is a man with a smallish kind of nose, a round face, and long hair. This goes back some time, though."

"Do you feel an actual presence in this house?"

"I feel as if someone is looking at me from the back," Ethel replied. "It might be a woman. I have a sense of disturbance. I feel as if I wanted to run away—I'm now speaking as if I were *her*, you understand—I'm looking for the moment to run, to get away."

Ethel took a deep breath and looked toward the verandah, and beyond it to the other side of the Hudson River. "Somebody stays here *who keeps looking out a window* to see if anyone is coming. I can't seem to find the window. There is a feeling of panic. It feels as if I were afraid of somebody's coming. A woman and two men are involved. I feel I want to protect someone."

"Let the individual take over, then, Ethel," I suggested, hoping that trance would give us further clues.

But Ethel wasn't quite ready for it. "I've got to find that window," she said. "She is full of determination to find that window."

"Why is the window so important to her?"

"She wants to know if someone is coming. She's got to look out the window."

I instructed Ethel to tell the spirit that we would look for the window, and to be calm. But to the contrary, Ethel seemed more and more agitated. "Got to go to the window...the window...the window. The window isn't here anymore, but I've got to find it. Who took away the.... No, it is not here. It is not this way. It is that way." By now Ethel was gradually sinking into trance, although by no means a complete one. At certain moments she was still speaking as herself, giving us her clairvoyant impressions, while at other moments some alien entity was already speaking through her directly.

"Very sick here, very sick," she said, her words followed by deep moaning. For several minutes I spoke to the entity directly, explaining that whatever he was now experiencing was only the passing symptoms remembered and had no validity in the present.

The moaning, however, continued for some time. I assured the entity that he could speak to me directly, and that there was nothing to be afraid of, for we had come as friends.

Gradually, the moaning became quieter, and individual words could be understood. "What for? What for? The other house..." This was immediately followed by a series of moans. I asked who the person was and why he was here, as is my custom. Why are you bringing him here?" the entranced medium said. That man, that man, why are you bringing him here? Why? Why?" This was followed by heavy tears.

As soon as I could calm the medium again, the conversation continued. "What troubles you? What is your problem? I would like to help you," I said.

"Talk, talk, talk...too many...too many."

"Be calm, please."

"No! Take him away! I can't tell. They have left. Don't touch me! Take it away! Why hurt me so?"

"It's all right now; much has happened since," I began.

Heavy tears was the response. "They went away. Don't bother me! They have gone. Don't touch! Take him away! Take them off my neck!"

"It's all right," I said again, in as soothing a tone of voice as I could muster. "You are free. You need not worry or fear anything."

Ethel's voice degenerated into a mumble now. "Can't talk...so tired...go away."

"You may talk freely about yourself."

"I'll tell you when they've gone. I didn't help....I didn't help....I didn't know."

"Who are the people you are talking about?"

"I don't know. They took it over."

"Tell me what happened."

"They went away over the water. Please take this off so I can talk better."

Evidently, the entity thought that he was still gagged or otherwise prevented from speaking clearly. In order to accommodate him, I told him I was taking off whatever was bothering him, and he could speak freely and clearly now. Immediately, there was a moaning sound, more of relief than of pain. But the entity would not believe that I had taken "it" off and called me a liar instead. I tried to explain that he was feeling a memory from the past, but he did not understand that. Eventually he relented.

"What is your name?" I asked.

"You know, you know." Evidently he had mistaken me for someone else. I assured him that I did not know his name.

"You are a bloody rich man, that is what you are," he said, not too nicely. Again, he remembered whatever was preventing him from speaking, and, clutching his throat, cried, "I can't speak...the throat..." Then, suddenly, he realized there was no more pain and calmed down considerably. "I didn't have that trouble after all," he commented.

"Exactly. That is why we've come to help you."

"Enough trouble.... I saw them come up, but they went away."

All along I had assumed that we were talking to a male. Since the entity was using Ethel's voice, there were of course some female tinges to it, but somehow it sounded more like a masculine voice than that of a woman. But it occurred to me that I had no proof one way or another.

"What is your name? Are you a gentleman or..."

"Defenseless woman. Defenseless. I didn't take anyone. But you won't believe me."

I assured her that I would.

"You won't believe me.... It was dark. It was dark here.... I told him, take care of me."

"Is this your house?"

"Yes."

"What is your name?"

"My name is Jenny."

"Why are you here?"

"Where is my window? Where is it?"

I ignored the urgency of that remark and continued with my questioning. "What is your family name?"

"Smith... Smith."

"Where and when were you born?"

There was no reply.

"What day is this today?" I continued.

"July."

"What year are we in?"

"'80."

"What went on in this house? Tell me about it."

"They brought him here. They came here." Evidently the woman wasn't too happy about what she was about to tell me.

"Whose house is this?"

"Joshua. Joshua Smith."

"How is he related to you?"

"Husband. They brought him.... I told them, tell them! No... no one was coming. That is all I told them. I don't know why they hurt me."

"You mean, they thought you knew something?"

"Yah... my friends. All that noise. Why don't they stop? Oh, God, I feel pain. They got away. I told you they got away."

"Who are the people you fear?"

"Guns—I must look in the window. They are coming. All is clear... time to go... they get away... they got away.... See, look, they got away. It is dark. They are near the water. I get the money for it."

"What is the money for?"

"For helping."

At the time, I hadn't fully realized the identity of the speaker. I therefore continued the interrogation in the hope of ferreting out still more evidential material from her. "Who is in charge of this country?"

"George... George... nobody... *everybody is fighting.*"

"Where were you born?"

"Here."

"Where was your husband born?"

Instead of answering the question, she seemed to say, faintly, but unmistakably, "André."

"Who is André?"

"He got away. *God Bless His Majesty.* He got away."

"You must go in peace from this house," I began, feeling that the time had come to free the spirit from its compulsion. "Go in peace and never return here, because much time has gone on since, and all is peaceful now. You mustn't come back. You mustn't come back."

"They will come back."

"Nobody will come. It all happened a long time ago. Go away from here."

"Johnny... Johnny."

"You are free, you are free. You can go from this house."

"Suckers... bloody suckers.... They are coming, they are coming now. I can see them. I can see them! God Bless the Majesty. They got away, they got away!"

It was clear that Jenny was reliving the most dramatic moment of her life. Ethel, fully entranced now, sat up in the chair, eyes glazed, peering into the distance, as if she were following the movements of people we could not see!

"There is the horse," the spirit continued. "Quick, get the horse! I am a loyal citizen. Good to the Crown. They got away. Where is my window?" Suddenly, the entity realized that everything wasn't as it should be. An expression of utter confusion crept over Ethel's face. "Where am I, where am I?"

"You are in a house that now belongs to someone else," I explained.

"Where is that window? I don't know where I am."

I continued to direct her away from the house, suggesting that she leave in peace and go with our blessings. But the entity was not quite ready for that yet. She wouldn't go out the window, either. "The soldiers are there."

"Only in your memory," I assured her, but she continued to be very agitated."

"Gone... a rope.... My name is Jenny.... Save me, save me!"

At this point, I asked Albert to help free the entity, who was obviously tremendously embroiled in her emotional memories. My appeal worked. A moment later, Albert's crisp, matter-of-fact voice broke through. "We have taken the entity who was lost in space and time," he commented.

If ever there was proof that a good trance medium does not draw upon the unconscious minds of the sitters—that is to say, those in the room with her—then this was it. Despite the fact that several names had come through Ethel's entranced lips, I must confess they did not ring a bell with me. This is the more amazing as I am historian and should have recognized the name Joshua Smith. But the fact is, in the excitement of the investigation, I did not, and I continued to press for better identification and background. In fact, I did not even connect John with André and continued to ask who John was. Had we come to the house with some knowledge that a Revolutionary escape had taken place here, one might conceivably attribute the medium's tremendous performance to unconscious or even conscious knowledge of what had occurred in the place. As it was, however, we had come because of a suspected ghost created only a few years ago—a ghost that had not the slightest connection with pre-Revolutionary America. No one, including the owner of the house, had said anything about any historical connotations of the house. Yet, instead of coming up with the suspected restless girl who had committed suicide, Mrs. Meyers went back into the eighteenth century and gave us authentic information—information I am sure she did not possess at the time, since she is neither a scholar specializing in pre-Revolutionary Americana nor familiar with the locality or local history.

When Albert took over the body of the instrument, I was still in the dark about the connections between this woman and Smith and André. "Albert," I therefore asked with some curiosity, "who is this entity?"

"There are three people here," Albert began. "One is gone on horseback, and one went across. They came here to escape because they were surrounded. One of them was Major André."

"The historical Major André?" I asked incredulously.

"Yes," Albert replied. "They took asylum here until the coast was clear, but as you may well know, André did not get very far, and Arnold escaped across the water."

"What about the woman? Is her real name Smith?"

"Yes, but she is not related to Joshua Smith. She is a woman in charge of properties, living here."

"Why does she give the name Jenny Smith?"

"She was thinking more of her employer than of herself. She worked for Joshua Smith, and her name was Jennifer."

"I see," I said, trying to sort things out. "Have you been able help her?"

"Yes, she is out of a vacuum now, thanks to you. We will of course have to watch her until she makes up her mind that it is not 1780."

"Are there any others here in the house?" I asked.

"There are others. The Tories were always protected around this neck of the woods, and when there was an escape, it was usually through here."

"Are all the disturbances in this house dating back to the period?"

"No, there are later disturbances here right on top of old disturbances."

"What is the most recent disturbance in this house?"

"A woman and a child."

Immediately this rang a bell. It would have been strange if the medium had not also felt the most recent emotional event in this house, that involving a woman and a child. According to Jonathan Davis, Mrs. Brown had heard the sound of a child in a room that was once used as a nursery. Even her young daughter, then age five, had heard the sounds and been frightened by them. But what about the woman?

"The woman became very disturbed because of the entity you have just released," Albert responded. "In fact, she had been taken over. This was not too long ago."

"What happened to her?"

"She became possessed by the first woman, Jennifer, and as a result felt very miserable."

"Am I correct in assuming that Jennifer, the colonial woman, was hanged?"

"That is right."

"And am I further correct in assuming that the more recent woman took on the symptoms of the unfortunate Jennifer?"

"That is right, too."

"I gather Jennifer died in this house. How?"

"Strangulation."

"What about the more recent case? How did she die?"

"Her inner self was tortured. She lost her breath. She was badly treated by men who did not understand her aberration, the result of her possession by the first spirit in the house. Thus, she committed suicide. It was poison or strangulation or both, I am not sure."

"Do you still sense her in the house now?"

"Yes. She is always following people around. She is here all right, but we did not let her use the instrument, because she could stay on, you know. However, we have her here, under control. She is absolutely demented now. At the time she committed suicide, she was possessed by this woman, but we cannot let her speak because she would possess the instrument. Wait a moment. All right, thank you, they have taken her." Evidently, Albert had been given the latest word by his helpers on the other side. It appeared that Kaye was in safe hands, after all.

"Is there any connection between this woman and the present occupants of the house?" I asked.

"Yes, but there will be no harm. She was not in the right mind when she died, and she is not yet at rest. I'm sure she would want to make it clear that she was possessed and did not act as herself. Her suicide was not of her own choosing. I am repeating words I am being told: *it was not of her own volition.* She suffered terribly from the possession, because the colonial woman had been beaten and strangled by soldiers."

"Before you withdraw, Albert, can we be reasonably sure that the house will be quiet from now on?"

"Yes. We will do our best."

With that, Albert withdrew, and Ethel returned to her own self, seemingly a bit puzzled at first as to where she was, rubbing her eyes, yawning a couple of times, then settling back into the comfortable chair and waiting for me to ask further questions, if any. But for the moment I had questions only for the owner of the house. "How old is this house, and what was on the spot before it was built?"

"It is at least a hundred years old, and I remember someone telling me that something happened down here on this spot, something historical, like an escape. There were soldiers here during the Revolutionary War, but I really don't know exactly what happened."

It is important to point out that even Miss Brown, who had lived in the area for some time, was not aware of the full background of her house. The house, in fact, was far more than a hundred years old. It stood already in September 1780, when Major John André had visited it. At that time, there was a ferry below the house that connected with the opposite shore, and the house itself belonged to Joshua Smith, a good friend of General Benedict Arnold. It was to Joshua Smith that Arnold had entrusted the escape of Major André. Everything Ethel had said was absolutely true. Three people had tried to escape: André, a servant, and, of course, General Arnold, who succeeded. Smith was a Loyalist and considered his help a matter of duty. To the American Army he was a traitor. Even though André was later captured, the Revolutionary forces bore down heavily on Smith and his property. Beating people to death in order to elicit information was a favorite form of treatment used in the eighteenth century by both the British and the American armies. Undoubtedly, Jennifer had been the victim of Revolutionary soldiers, and Kaye, perhaps psychic herself, the victim of Jennifer.

Ethel Meyers had once again shown what a superb medium she is. But there were still some points to be cleared up.

"How long have you had the house now, Miss Brown?" I asked.

"A year and a half. Kaye's suicide took place after we had been here for two months. We had bought the house together. She had been extremely upset because her husband was going to cut off his support. Also, he had announced a visit, and she didn't want to see him. So she took off on a Sunday with her child, and in Newburgh she committed suicide along with the child. They didn't find her until Thursday."

"After her death, what unusual things did you experience in the house?"

"I always felt that someone was trying to communicate with me, and I was fleeing from it in terror. I still feel her presence here, but now I *want* it to be here. She always said that she wanted to stay here, that she loved this river bank. We both agreed that she would always stay here. When I heard all sorts of strange noises after her death, such as doors closing by themselves and footsteps where no one could be seen walking, I went into an alcoholic oblivion and on a sleeping-pill binge, because I was so afraid. At the time, I just didn't want to communicate."

"Prior to these events, did you have any psychic experiences?"

"I had many intuitive things happen to me, such as knowing things before they happened. I would know when someone was dead before I got the message; for instance, prior to your coming, I had heard noises almost every night and felt the presence of people. My little girl says there is a little Susan upstairs, and sometimes I too hear her cry. I hear her call and the way she walks up and down the stairs."

"Did you ever think that some of this might come from an earlier period?"

"No, I never thought of that."

"Was Kaye the kind of person who might commit suicide?"

"Certainly not. It would be completely out of character for her. She used to say, there was always a way, no matter what the problem, no matter what the trouble. She was very optimistic, very reliable, very resourceful. And she considered challenges and problems things one had to surmount. After her death, I looked through the mail, through all her belongings. My first impression was that she had been murdered, because it was so completely out of character for her. I even talked to the police about it. Their investigation was in my opinion not thorough enough. They never looked into the matter of where she had spent the four days and four nights between Sunday and Thursday, before she was found. But I was so broken up about it myself, I wasn't capable of conducting an investigation of my own. For a while I even suspected her husband of having killed her."

"But now we know, don't we," I said.

The ferry at Haverstraw hasn't run in a long, long time. The house on Riverside Avenue still stands, quieter than it used to be, and it is keeping its secrets locked up tight now. The British and the Americans have been fast friends for a long time now, and the passions of 1780 belong to history.

"Ship of Destiny": The U. S. F. Constellation

THE DARK BUICK RACED through the windy night, turning corners rather more sharply than it should: But the expedition was an hour late, and there were important people awaiting our arrival. It was 9 o'clock in the evening, and at that time Baltimore is pretty tame: Traffic had dwindled down to a mere trickle, and the chilly October weather probably kept many pedestrians indoors, so we managed to cross town at a fast clip.

Jim Lyons had come to pick us up at the hotel minutes before, and the three committee members awaiting us at the waterfront had been there since 8 o'clock. But I had arrived late from Washington, and Sybil Leek had only just joined us: She had come down from New York without the slightest idea why I had summoned her. This was all good sport to my psychic associate, and the dark streets which we now left behind for more open territory meant nothing to her. She knew this was Baltimore, and a moment later she realized we were near water: You couldn't very well mistake the hulls of ships silhouetted against the semidark sky, a sky faintly lit by the reflections from the city's downtown lights.

The car came to a screeching halt at the end of a pier. Despite the warmth of the heater, we were eager to get out into the open. The excitement of the adventure was upon us.

As we piled out of Jim Lyons' car, we noticed three shivering men standing in front of a large, dark shape. That shape, on close inspection, turned out to be the hull of a large sailing ship. For the moment, however, we exchanged greetings and explained our tardiness: little comfort to men who had been freezing for a full hour!

The three committee members were Gordon Stick, chairman of the *Constellation* restoration committee, Jean Hofmeister, the tall, gaunt harbormaster of Baltimore, and Donald Stewart, the curator of the ancient ship and a professional historian.

Although Sybil realized she was in front of a large ship, she had no idea of what sort of ship it was; only a single, faint bulb inside the hull cast a little light on the scene, and nobody had mentioned anything about the ship or the purpose of our visit.

There was no superstructure visible, and no masts, and suddenly I remembered that Jim Lyons had casually warned me—the old ship was "in repair" and not its true self as yet. How accurate this was I began to realize a moment later when we started to board her. I was looking for the gangplank or stairway to enter.

The harbormaster shook his head with a knowing smile.

"I'm afraid you'll have to rough it, Mr. Holzer," he said.

He then shone his miner's lamp upon the black hull. There was a rope ladder hanging from a plank protruding from the deck. Beyond the plank, there seemed to be a dark, gaping hole, which, he assured me, led directly into the interior of the ship. The trick was not to miss it, of course. If one did, there was a lot of water below. The ship lay about two yards from the pier, enough room to drown, if one were to be so clumsy as to fall off the ladder or miss the plank. I looked at the rope ladder swaying in the cold October wind, felt the heavy tape recorder tugging at my back and the camera around my neck, and said to myself, "Hans, you're going for a bath. *How do I get out of all this?*"

* * *

Now I'm not a coward normally, but I hate taking chances. Right now I wished I were someplace else. Anyplace except on this chilly pier in Baltimore. While I was still wrestling with words to find the right formula that would get me off the hook, I saw Sybil Leek, who is not a small woman, hurry up that rope ladder with the agility of a mother hen rushing home to the coop for supper. In a second, she had disappeared into the hull of the ship. I swallowed hard and painfully and said to myself, if Sybil can do it, so can I. Bravely, I grabbed the ladder and hauled myself up, all the while sending thought messages to my loved ones, just in case I didn't make it. Step by step, farther and farther away from firm ground I went. I didn't dare look back, for if I had I am sure the others would have looked like dwarfs to me by now. Finally I saw the wooden plank sticking out of the hull, and like a pirate-condemned sailor in reverse I walked the plank, head down, tape recorder banging against my ribs, camera hitting my eyeballs, not daring to stand up lest I hit the beams—until I was at the hole; then, going down on my knees, I half crawled into the hull of the ship where I found Sybil whistling to herself, presumably a sailor's tune. At least I had gotten inside. How I would eventually get back out again was a subject too gruesome to consider at that moment. It might well be that I would have to remain on board until a gangplank had been installed, but for the moment at least I was safe and could begin to feel human again. The others had now followed us up the ladder, and everybody was ready to begin the adventure.

There was just enough light to make out the ancient beams and wooden companionways, bunks, bulkheads, and what have you: A very old wooden ship lay before us, in the state of total disrepair with its innards torn open and its sides exposed, but still afloat and basically sound and strong. Nothing whatever was labeled or gave away the name of our ship, nor were there any dates or other details as the restoration had not yet begun in earnest and only the

outer hull had been secured as a first step. Sybil had no way of knowing anything about the ship, except that which her own common sense told her—a very old wooden ship. For that reason, I had chosen the dark of night for our adventure in Baltimore, and I had pledged the men to keep quiet about everything until we had completed our investigation.

* * *

I first heard about this remarkable ship, the frigate *Constellation*, when Jim Lyons, a TV personality in Baltimore, wrote to me and asked me to have a psychic look at the historic ship. There had been reports of strange happenings aboard, and there were a number of unresolved historical questions involving the ship. Would I come down to see if I could unravel some of those ancient mysteries? The frigate was built in 1797, the first man-of-war of the United States. As late as World War II she was still in commission—something no other ship that old ever accomplished. Whenever Congress passed a bill decommissioning the old relic, *something* happened to stay its hands: Patriotic committees sprang up and raised funds, or individuals in Washington would suddenly come to the rescue, and the scrappy ship stayed out of the scrapyard. It was as if something, or *someone*, was at work, refusing to let the ship die. Perhaps some of this mystic influence rubbed off on President Franklin Roosevelt, a man who was interested in psychic research as was his mother, Sarah Delano Roosevelt. At any rate, when the *Constellation* lay forgotten at Newport, Rhode Island, and the voices demanding her demolition were louder than ever, Roosevelt reacted as if the mysterious power aboard the frigate had somehow reached out to him: In 1940, at the height of World War II, he decreed that the frigate *Constellation* should be the flagship of the U. S. Atlantic Fleet!

* * *

Long after our remarkable visit to Baltimore on a windy October night, I got to know the remarkable ship a lot better. At the time, I did not wish to clutter my unconscious mind with detailed knowledge of her history, so that Sybil Leek could not be accused of having obtained data from it.

The year was 1782. The United States had been victorious in its war for independence, and the new nation could well afford to disband its armed forces. Commerce with foreign countries thrived, and American merchant ships appeared in increasing numbers on the high seas. But a nation then as now is only as strong as her ability to defend herself from enemy attacks. Soon the marauding freebooters of North Africa and the Caribbean made American shipping unsafe, and many sailors fell into pirate hands. Finally, in 1794, Congress decided to do something about this situation, and authorized the construction of six men-of-war or frigates to protect American shipping abroad. The bill was duly signed by George Washington, and work on the ships started immediately. However, only three of these ships, meant to be sister ships, were built in time for immediate action. The first frigate, and thus the very oldest ship in the U. S. Navy, was the U. S. F. *Constellation*, followed by the *Constitution* and the *United States*. The *Constellation* had three main masts, a wooden hull, and thirty-six guns, while the other two ships had forty-four guns each. But the *Constellation's* builder, David Stodder of Baltimore, gave her his own patented sharp bow lines, a feature later famous with the Baltimore Clippers. This design gave the ships greater speed, and earned the *Constellation*, after she had been launched, the nickname of "Yankee Race Horse."

"Ship of Destiny": The U. S. F. Constellation

* * *

On June 26, 1798, the brand-new frigate put out to sea from Baltimore, then an important American seaport, and headed for the Caribbean. She was under the command of a veteran of the Revolutionary War by the name of Thomas Truxtun, who was known for his efficiency and stern views in matters of discipline. A month after the ship had arrived in the area to guard American shipping, she saw action for the first time. Although the North African menace had been subdued for the time being in the wake of a treaty with the Barbary chieftains, the French menace in the Caribbean was as potent as ever.

Consequently, it was with great eagerness that the crew of the *Constellation* came upon the famous French frigate *L'Insurgente* passing near the island of Nevis on a balmy February day in 1799. Within an hour after the first broadside, the French warship was a helpless wreck. This first United States naval victory gave the young nation a sense of dignity and pride which was even more pronounced a year later when the *Constellation* met up with the French frigate *La Vengeance*. Although the American ship had increased its guns by two, to a total of thirty-eight, she was, still outclassed by the French raider sporting fifty-two guns. The West Indian battle between the two naval giants raged for five hours. Then the French ship, badly battered, escaped into the night.

America was feeling its oats now; although only a handful of countries had established close relations with the new republic, and the recently won freedom from Britain was far from secure, Congress felt it would rather fight than submit to blackmail and holdup tactics.

Although Captain Truxtun left the *Constellation* at the end of 1801, his drill manual and tactical methods became the basis for all later U. S. Navy procedures. Next to command the *Constellation* was Alexander Murray, whose first mission was to sail for the Mediterranean in 1802 to help suppress the Barbary pirates, who had once again started to harass American shipping. During the ensuing blockade of Tripoli, the *Constellation* saw much action, sinking two Arab ships and eventually returning to her home port in late 1805 after a peace treaty had finally been concluded with the Arab pirates.

* * *

For seven years there was peace, and the stately ship lay in port at Washington. Then in 1812, when war with Britain erupted again, she was sent to Hampton Roads, Virginia, to help defend the American installations at Fort Craney. But as soon as peace returned between the erstwhile colonies and the former motherland, the Barbary pirates acted up again, and it was deemed necessary to go to war against them once more.

This time the *Constellation* was part of Stephen Decatur's squadron, and remained in North African waters until 1817 to enforce the new peace treaty with Algeria.

America was on the move, expanding not only overland and winning its own West, but opening up new trade routes overseas. Keeping pace with its expanding merchant fleet was a strong, if small, naval arm. Again, the *Constellation* guarded American shipping off South America between 1819 and 1821, then sailed around the Cape to the Pacific side of the continent, and finally put down the last Caribbean pirates in 1826. Later she was involved in the suppression of the Seminole Indian rebellion in Florida, and served as Admiral Dallas's flagship. In 1840 she was sent on a wide-ranging trip, sailing from Boston to Rio de Janeiro under the command of Commodore Lawrence Kearny. From there she crossed the Pacific Ocean to open up China for American trade; returning home via Hawaii, Kearny was able, in the proverbial nick of time, to prevent a British plot to seize the islands.

The British warship H. M. S. *Caryfoot* had been at anchor at Honolulu when the *Constellation* showed up. Hastily, the British disavowed a pledge by King Kamehameha III to turn over the reins of government to the ship's captain, and native rule was restored.

For a few years, the famous old ship rested in its berth at Norfolk, Virginia. She had deserved her temporary retirement, having logged some 58,000 miles on her last trip alone, all of it with sail power only. In 1853 it was decided to give her an overhaul. After all, the Navy's oldest ship was now fifty-five years old and showed some stress and strain. The rebuilding included the addition of twelve feet to her length, and her reclassification as a twenty-two-gun sloop of war. Most of her original timber was kept, repairing and replacing only what was worn out. Once more the veteran ship sailed for the Mediterranean, but the handwriting was already on the wall: In 1858, she was decommissioned.

Here the mysterious force that refused to let the ship die came into play again.

When civil war seemed inevitable between North and South, the *Constellation* was brought back into service in 1859 to become the flagship of the African squadron. Her job was intercepting slave ships bound for the United States, and she managed to return a thousand slaves to their native Africa.

Outbreak of war brought her back home in 1861, and after another stint in the Mediterranean protecting United States shipping from marauding Confederate raiders, she became a receiving and training ship at Hampton Roads, Virginia.

Sailing ships had seen their day, and the inevitable seemed at hand: Like so many wooden sailing ships, she would eventually be destined for the scrapheap. But again she was saved from this fate. The Navy returned her to active service in 1871 as a training ship at the Annapolis Naval Academy. The training period was occasionally interrupted by further sea missions, such as her errand of mercy to Ireland during the 1880 famine. Gradually, the old ship had become a symbol of American naval tradition and was known the world over. In 1894, almost a hundred years old now, the still-seaworthy man-of-war returned to Newport for another training mission. By 1914, her home port Baltimore claimed the veteran for a centennial celebration, and she would have continued her glorious career as an active seagoing ship of the U. S. Navy, forever, had it not been for World War II. More important matters took precedence over the welfare of the *Constellation*, which lay forgotten at the Newport berth. Gradually, her condition worsened, and ultimately she was no longer capable of putting out to sea.

When the plight of this ancient sailor was brought to President Roosevelt's attention, he honored her by making her once again the flagship of the U. S. Atlantic Fleet. But the honor was not followed by funds to restore her to her erstwhile glory. After the war she was berthed in Boston, where attempts were made to raise funds by allowing visitors aboard. By 1953, the ship was in such poor condition that her total loss seemed only a matter of time.

At this moment, a committee of patriotic Baltimore citizens decided to pick up the challenge. As a first step, the group secured title to the relic from the U. S. Navy. Next, the ship was brought home to Baltimore, like a senior citizen finally led back to its native habitat. All the tender care of a sentimental association was lavished on her, and with the help of volunteers, the restoration committee managed to raise the necessary funds to restore the *Constellation* to its original appearance, inside and out. At the time of our nocturnal visit, only the first stage of the restoration had been undertaken: to make her hull seaworthy so she could safely stay afloat at her berth. In the summer of 1968, the rest of the work would be undertaken, but at the time of our visit, the inside was still a raw assortment of wooden beams and badly hinged doors, her superstructure reduced to a mastless flat deck and the original corridors and companionways in their grime-covered state. All this would eventually give way to a spick-and-span ship, as much the pride of America in 1968 as she was back in 1797 when she was launched.

But apart from the strange way in which fate seemed to prevent the destruction of this proud sailing ship time and again, other events had given the *Constellation* the reputation of a haunted ship. This fame was not especially welcomed by the restoration committee, of course, and it was never encouraged, but for the sake of the record, they did admit and document certain strange happenings aboard the ship. In Donald Stewart, the committee had the services of a trained historian, and they hastened to make him the curator of their floating museum.

* * *

Whether or not any psychic occurrences took place aboard the *Constellation* prior to her acquisition by the

The U. S. F. Constellation today

committee is not known, but shortly after the Baltimore group had brought her into Baltimore drydock, a strange incident took place. On July 26, 1959, a Roman Catholic priest boarded the ship, which was then already open to the public, although not in very good condition. The priest had read about the famous ship, and asked curator Donald Stewart if he might come aboard even though it was before the 10 A.M. opening hour for visitors. He had to catch a train for Washington at eleven, and would never be able to face his flock back in Detroit without having seen so famed a vessel. The curator gladly waived the rules, and the good father ascended. However, since Mr. Stewart was in the midst of taking inventory and could not spare the time to show him around, he suggested that the priest just walk around on his own.

At 10:25, the priest returned from below deck, looking very cheerful. Again the curator apologized for not having taken him around.

"That's all right," the man of the cloth replied, "the old gent showed me around."

"What old gent?" the curator demanded. "There is nobody else aboard except you and me."

The priest protested. He had been met by an old man in a naval uniform, he explained, and the fellow had shown him around below. The man knew his ship well, for he was able to point out some of the gear and battle stations.

"Ridiculous," bellowed Mr. Stewart, who is a very practical Scotsman. "Let's have a look below."

Both men descended into the hull and searched the ship from bow to stern. Not a living soul was to be found outside of their own good selves.

When they returned topside, the priest was no longer smiling. Instead, he hurriedly left, pale and shaken, to catch that train to Washington. He *knew* he had met an old sailor, and he *knew* he was cold sober when he did.

Donald Stewart's curiosity, however, was aroused, and he looked into the background of the ship a bit more closely. He discovered then that similar experiences had happened to naval personnel when the ship was at Newport, Rhode Island, and to watchmen aboard the *Constellation*. Nobody liked to talk about them, however. On one occasion during the summer a figure was seen aboard on the gun deck after the ship had closed for the day and no visitors could be aboard. The police were called to rout the burglar or intruder and they brought with them a police dog, a fierce-looking German shepherd, who was immediately sent below deck to rout the intruder. But instead of following orders as he always did, the dog stood frozen to the spot, shivering with fear, hair on his neck bristling, and refused to budge or go below. It is needless to point out that no human intruder was found on that occasion.

Another time a group of Sea Scouts was holding a meeting aboard. The idea was to give the proceedings a real nautical flavor. The fact that the ship was tied up solidly and could not move did not take away from the atmosphere of being aboard a real seagoing vessel. Suddenly, as if moved by unseen hands, the wheel spun from port to starboard rapidly. Everyone in the group saw it, and pandemonium broke loose. There wasn't any wind to account for a movement of the ship. Furthermore, the spool of the wheel was not even linked to the rudder!

The *Constellation* had returned to Baltimore in August 1955. While still under Navy jurisdiction, the first of the unusual incidents took place. The vessel was then tied up beside the U. S. S. *Pike* at the Naval Training Center. There was never anyone aboard at night. The dock was well guarded, and strangers could not approach without being challenged. Nevertheless, a Navy commander and his men reported that they had seen "someone in an early uniform" walking the quarterdeck at night. The matter was investigated by the Baltimore *Sun*, which also published the testimonies of the Navy personnel. When the newspaper sent a photographer aboard the *Constellation*, however, every one of his photographs was immediately seized by naval authorities without further explanation.

Jim Lyons, a longtime Baltimore resident, was able to add another detail to the later uncanny events recorded by the curator. During a Halloween meeting of the Sea Scouts, which was followed by a dance, one of the girls present had an unusual experience. Seated on a wall bench, she turned to speak to what she thought was her escort, and instead looked directly into the face of an old sailor, who smiled at her and then disappeared! Since she had never heard of any alleged hauntings aboard ship, her mind was not impressed with any such suggestion. She described the apparition exactly as the priest had described his ghostly guide below deck. Very likely other visitors to the ship may have had strange encounters of this sort without reporting them, since people tend to disregard or suppress that which does not easily fall into categories they can accept.

It was clear from these reports that some restless force was still active aboard the old vessel, and that it wanted the *Constellation* to go on unharmed and as she was in her heyday. But why did the ghostly sailor make such an effort to manifest and to cling to this ship? What was the secret that this "ship of destiny" harbored below deck?

*   *   *

We were standing in a small group on the main deck of the ship when Sybil said hurriedly, "Must go down below," and before we could even ask her why, she had descended the narrow ladder leading to the next lower level. There she deftly made for the after orlop deck, where she stopped abruptly and remarked, "There is much evil here!"

Before we had all come aboard, she had been wandering about the ship in almost total darkness. "I personally have been with the ship for eleven years," the curator later observed, "and I would not attempt such a feat without light, although I know the ship like the back of my hand." Earlier, while we were still en route to the harbor, Sybil had suddenly mumbled a date out of context and apparently for no particular reason. That date was 1802. When I had questioned her about it she only said it had significance for the place we were going to visit. Later I discovered that the first captain of the *Constellation* had left the frigate at the end of 1801, and that 1802 signified a new and important chapter in the ship's career.

How could Sybil deduce this from the modern streets of nocturnal Baltimore through which we had been driving at the time?

And now we were finally aboard, waiting for developments. These were not long in coming. As Sybil went down into the hold of the ship, we followed her. As if she knew where she was going, she directed her steps toward the ladder area of the after orlop deck.

"I'm frightened," she said, and shuddered. For a person like Sybil to be frightened was most unusual. She showed me her arms, which were covered with gooseflesh. It was not particularly cold inside the hold, and none of us showed any such symptoms.

"This area has a presence, lots of atmosphere...very cruel. And I heard what sounded like a baby crying. Why would a baby cry aboard a ship like this?"

Why indeed?

"A peculiar death...a boy...a gun...big gun...a bad deed...."

"Is this boy connected with the ship?"

Instead of answering, she seemed to take in the atmosphere. More and more dissociating herself from us and the present, she mumbled, "Seventeen sixty-five."

The date had no significance for the ship, but probably for its first captain, then still in British service.

"French guns...."

This would refer to the two great engagements with the French fleet in 1799 and 1800.

I tried to get back to the boy.

"He walked around this boat a lot," Sybil said. "Something happened to him. Have to find the gun. Doesn't like guns. He's frightened. Killed here. Two men...frightening the boy. Powder...powder boy. Eleven."

"Who were those two men?"

"Seventy-two...sixty-six...their boat is not here...."

"Is there an entity present on this boat *now*?"

"Three people. Boy and the two men."

"Who are the two men?"

Belabored, breathing heavily, Sybil answered,

"Thraxton...captain...Thomas...T-h-r...I can't get the middle of it...1802...other man...to the gun...."

When these words came from Sybil's now half-entranced lips, the little group around me froze. I heard a gasp from one of them and realized that Sybil must have hit on something important. Only later did I learn that Captain Thomas Truxtun was the ship's first captain, and that he had been replaced by another at the beginning of 1802. If he was one of the ghostly presences here, he certainly had a reason to stay with the ship that he had made great and whose name was forever linked with his own in naval history.

Sybil came out of her semi-trance momentarily and complained she wasn't getting through too well. "Name ending in son," she said now. "Harson...can't hear it too well. I hear a lot of noise from guns. Attacking. Seventy-two. Sixty-four. French. I can't see what happened to the boy. He didn't come back. But he's here *now*. It's confusing me. Fire!"

"Can you get more about the two men with the boy?" I asked.

"One is important, the other one is...a...armory... the guns...tends to the guns...he's still here...has to be forgiven...for his adventures...he was a coward...he hid away...he was killed by the men on this boat, not the enemy...blew him up...his friends did it because he was a coward...in action...."

"What was his name?"

"Harson...Larson...I don't know....He was an armorer...."

"Where was he from?"

"Sweden."

At this point, when we were leaning over to catch every word of Sybil's testimony, my tape recorder went out of order. No matter how I shook it, it would not work again. Quickly, I tore out a sheet of paper and took notes, later comparing them with those of the curator, Don Stewart.

As I pressed my psychic friend—and her communicators—for more information, she obliged in halting, labored sentences.

This man had been done an injustice, she explained, for he was not a coward. Captain Thomas "Thr-ton," an American, had given the order and he was killed by being blown to bits through a cannon. Finally, the seventy-two sixty-six figures she had mentioned earlier fell into place. That was the spot where the killing happened, she explained, at sea. The position, in other words.

"The guns are a bad influence," she mumbled, "if you take the third gun away it would be better...bad influence here, frightens people...third gun. This ship would be with another...*Const...ation*, and *Con...federation*...something like that...should be at sea...not a sister ship but of the same type with a similar spelling of the name, even though this ship was slightly older, they belong together!"

* * *

This of course was perfectly true, but she could not have known it from standing in an almost dark hull. The *Constellation* preceded the *Constitution* by a very short time.

"1795 important to this boat."

That was the year work on her had begun.

Gradually, I was able to sort out the various tenants of the ship's netherworld.

The eleven-year-old boy was somehow tied to the date of August 16, 1822. He was, Mrs. Leek stated, the victim of murder by two crew members in the cockpit of the orlop deck. Mr. Stewart later confirmed that very young boys were used aboard old ships to serve as lolly boys or servants to naval surgeons. The area where the ghostly boy was most active, according to the psychic, was precisely what had been the surgeon's quarters!

The man who had been executed as a coward during action against the French, as the medium had said, could not materialize because he was in bits and pieces and thus remembered "himself" in this gruesome fashion.

The man who had condemned him was Captain Thomas Truxtun, and the man's name was something like Harsen. But here confusion set in. For she also felt the influence of a person named Larsen—a Swede, she thought —and he gave two figures *similar* to the other figures mentioned before, 73 and 66, and we'd know him by those numerals!

It now became clear to me that Mrs. Leek was getting impressions from several layers at the same time and that I would have to separate them to come to any kind of rational evaluation of the material.

I brought her out of her semi-trance state and we started to discuss what had come through her, when all of a sudden the large doors at the bottom of the ladder approximately ten feet away slowly opened by themselves. The curator, who saw this, reports that a rush of cold air followed. He had often noticed that there was a temperature differential of some five degrees between the after crew's ladder area and the rest of the ship, for which there was no satisfactory explanation.

It was 10 o'clock when we left the ship, and one by one we descended the perilous ladder. It wasn't easy for me until I left my equipment behind for the moment and bravely grabbed the rope ladder in the dark. The fact that I am writing this account is proof I did not plunge into chilly Baltimore Harbor, but I wouldn't want to try it again for all the ghosts in America!

* * *

We repaired to a harbor tavern, and I started to question Mr. Stewart about the information received through Mrs. Leek. It was there that I first learned about Captain Truxtun, and his connection with the ship. It should be noted that only I was in close proximity of Mrs. Leek during most of the séance—the others kept a certain distance. Thus, any "reading of the minds" of the others who knew this name is not likely, and I did not as yet have this knowledge in my own mind.

But there was more, much more. It would appear that a man was indeed executed for cowardice during the action against the French in 1799, just as Mrs. Leek had said. It was during the battle with *L'Insurgente*. A sailor named Neil Harvey deserted his position at gun number 7 on the portside. Found by a Lieutenant Starrett, the traditional account has it, he was instantly run through by the officer.

Had Sybil's "Harsen" anything to do with Harvey?

She had stated the gun was number 3, not 7, but on checking it was found that the gun position numbers had been changed later—after the killing—at the time the ship was rebuilt, so that what is today gun 7 was actually gun 3 in 1799!

It was customary in the British (and early American) navies to execute traitors by strapping them to the mouths of cannon and blowing them to bits. If Lieutenant Starrett, in hot anger, had run the sailor through—and we don't know if he was dead from it—it may well be that the captain, when apprised of the event, had ordered the man, wounded or already dead, subjected to what was considered a highly dishonorable death: no body, no burial at sea. These bits of information were found by the curator, Mr.

Stewart, in the original ship's log preserved at the Navy Department in Washington.

Apparently, Neil Harvey's job was that of a night watchman as well as gunner. This may have given rise to another version of the tradition, researched for me by Jim Lyons. In this version, Harvey was found fast asleep when he should have stood watch, and, discovered by Captain Truxtun himself, was cursed by his master forever to walk the decks of his ship, after which the captain himself ran him through with his sword.

The records, however, report the killing by Lieutenant Starrett and even speak of the court-martial proceedings against the sailor. He was condemned, according to the log, for deserting his position and was executed aboard by being shot. This would bear out my suggestion that the sword of Lieutenant Starrett did not finish the unfortunate man off altogether.

I had now accounted for the boy, the captain, and the unhappy sailor named Neil Harvey, blown to bits by the gun. But there was still an unresolved portion to the puzzle: the "Swede" Sybil felt present. By no stretch of the imagination could Neil Harvey be called a Scandinavian. Also, the man, she felt, had "spent the happiest days of his life aboard ship as an employee."

One can hardly call an eighteenth-century sailor an employee, and Harvey did not spend any happy days aboard; certainly, at least, this would not be his memory at the time of sudden death.

But the curator informed me that another watchman, curiously enough, had seen Harvey's ghost, or what looked like an old sailor, while playing cards aboard ship. He looked up from his game, casually, and saw the transparent figure going through the wall in front of him. He quit his position in 1963, when an electric burglary alarm system was installed aboard. Originally a Royal Navy cook, the man had come from Denmark—not Sweden—and his name was Carl Hansen. It occurred to me then that Sybil had been confused by two different entities—a Harvey and a Hansen, both of them watchmen, albeit of different periods.

After Hansen retired from his job aboard the *Constellation*, he evidently was very lonely for his old home—he had lived aboard from 1958 to 1963. He had written hundreds of letters to the *Constellation* restoration committee begging them to let him have his old position back, even though he had planned to retire to a farm. It was not possible to give him back his job, but the old man visited the ship on many occasions, keeping up a strong emotional tie with it. He died in 1966 at age seventy-three.

Here again one of those strange similarities had confused Sybil. On one occasion she had mentioned the figures seventy-two and sixty-six as applying to a position at sea, while later saying that the man from Sweden could be recognized by the numerals 73 and 66. It struck the curator that he was giving his age and death year in order to be identified properly!

Who then, among these influences aboard, was responsible for the continued resurgence of the old ship? Who wanted her to stay afloat forever, if possible?

Not the eleven-year-old boy, to whom the ship had meant only horror and death.

But perhaps the other three had found at last, something in common: their love for the U. S. F. *Constellation*.

Captain Truxtun certainly would feel himself bound to his old ship, the ship that shared his glories.

Neil Harvey might have wished to find justice and to clear his name. So long as the ship existed, there was a chance that the records would bear him out.

And lastly, the twentieth-century watchman Hansen, inexorably mixed up with the ship's destiny by his love for her and his lack of any other real focal point, might just have "gotten stuck" there upon death.

The only thing I can say with reasonable certainty is that the *Constellation* is not likely to disappear from the sea, whether out in the open ocean or safely nestled at her Baltimore dock. She's got three good men to look after her now.

✳ 19

The Truth About Camelot

WAS THERE A CAMELOT?

Did King Arthur preside in its splendid halls over the Round Table and its famous knights amid medieval splash and chivalry?

Musical comedy writers Lerner and Loewe thought so when they created the Broadway musical *Camelot*. Basically, this version presents Arthur as the champion of justice in a world of corruption and violence. He and his chosen knights of the Round Table challenge the sinister elements around them—and usually win. The religious elements are subdued, and Arthur emerges as a good man eventually hurt by his closest friend, when Lancelot runs off with Queen Guinevere. This treachery makes Arthur's world collapse. The major point made here is that breach of faith can only lead to disaster.

* * *

I have been fascinated by the King Arthur tradition for many years, wondering if there ever was a Camelot—if, indeed, there ever was a *real* King Arthur. Historians have had a go at all this material over the years, of course, and the last word isn't in yet, for the digs are still fresh and new evidence does turn up in forgotten or lost manuscripts. Also, reinterpretations of obscure passages shed new light on ancient mysteries.

In 1965 I stood in the inner portions of the ruined abbey of Glastonbury in the west of England. Near me was a bronze tablet neatly stuck into the wet soil. "King Arthur's tomb," it read, and a little farther on I found Queen Guinevere's tomb. I had not come to search for these tombs, however, but to see for myself the remnants of this "holiest spot in all Britain," which had been discovered through a combination of archaeological prowess and psychic gifts. A professional archeologist named Bligh Bond had discovered that he was also psychic. Far from being incredulous, he did not reject this gift, but put it to a

prolonged and severe test. As a result of this test, he received alleged communications from a monk who claimed to have lived at Glastonbury in the early Middle Ages. These communications came to Bond through automatic writing, his hands being guided by the unseen person of the monk. This, of course, sounds fantastic, and Bond was attacked for his lapse into what his fellow professionals thought was pure fantasy.

The location of Glastonbury Abbey was unknown then, yet Bond's communicator claimed that it was there, beneath the grassy knoll near the present town of Glastonbury. He even supplied Bond with exact details of its walls, layout, and walks. Eventually, Bond managed to have excavations started, and the abbey emerged from its grave very much as predicted by the ghostly monk.

As I said, though, I had not come to study King Arthur's grave, but to look at Glastonbury Abbey. Yet the trail seemed to lead to Camelot just the same. Glastonbury is 12½ miles due northwest of the area I later learned was the site of Camelot. Originally a Celtic (or British) settlement, it is the Avalon of the Arthurian legends.

My interest in the subject of King Arthur and Camelot was temporarily put aside when more urgent projects took up my time, but I was suddenly brought back to it in 1967 when I was contacted by a man named Paul Johnstone, who had read one of my previous books.

Johnstone is a scholar who specializes in historical research and is also a free-lance writer. His articles on British history have appeared in *Antiquity* and *Notes and Queries*, his fiction in *Blue Book* and other magazines. His writing leans toward medieval historical subjects, and after twenty-five years of research, in 1963 he completed a book called *The Real King Arthur*. That year his mother passed on, and he felt that her spirit might want to communicate with him. Although Paul Johnstone is a rationally inclined individual, he had never discounted the possibility of such communications, particularly in view of the fact that as a youngster he had had some ESP experiences. By means of a "fortune-telling board" he had purchased for his own amusement, he was able to come into communication with his late mother, and although at first he asked her only the most obvious questions, she eventually made it known to him that Artorius wanted to talk to him.

Now, the legendary King Arthur and his Camelot were merely fictional re-creations of old ballads, mainly French, which Sir Thomas Malory condensed into *La Morte d'Artur* in the fifteenth century. These ballads, however, in turn were only re-creations of older Welsh tales that, while not accurate, were nevertheless closer to the truth. According to Godfrey Turton in *The Emperor Arthur*, the medieval trappings "are completely inappropriate to the historical Arthur, who lived nearly a thousand years before Malory was born."

The only contemporary source extant from the late fifth century when Arthur lived is a book called *De Excidio Britanniae*, written by Gildas, a monk who later became an abbot. Arthur himself is not mentioned in this work, but according to *The Life of Gildas*, Gildas and Arthur had been enemies since Arthur had put the monk's brother to death for piracy.

In the ninth century a man named Nenius described Arthur's reign and victories in great detail. This Arthur was a late-Roman chieftain, a provincial commander whose military leadership and good judgment led him to be chosen to succeed the British chief Ambrosius as head and defender of post-Roman Britain. At this period in history, the Saxons had not completely taken over Britain and the Western part in particular was still free of their savage rule. Although the Romans no longer occupied Britain, centuries of occupation had left their mark, and Artorius was as much a Roman general as any of his Italian colleagues.

Because of Johnstone's twenty-five years devoted to research into King Arthur's life and times, he had evidently attracted the attention of the King's spirit, who now wished to reward him by conversing with him directly and setting the record straight wherever he, Johnstone, might have erred in his research. According to Johnstone's mother, Arthur had for years tried to tell Johnstone his side of the story directly, though Johnstone had not been aware of it. But now, with her arrival on the other side, a missing link had been supplied between Arthur and Johnstone, and they could establish direct communication.

I have examined the transcripts of these conversations, and since Johnstone himself is writing a book about his experiences with communicators like Arthur and others, it will suffice to say that they are amazing and detailed. The question of course immediately presents itself: Is this really King Arthur of the Britons speaking, or is it a figment of Johnstone's imagination, caused by his preoccupation with the subject and fed by the accumulated knowledge in his conscious and unconscious minds? That

this also occurred to Johnstone is clear and he started the talks by asking the alleged Artorius a number of questions that had not been satisfactorily answered before, such as exact sites of battles and places mentioned in the records but not yet discovered. The answers came via the board in a mixture of Welsh, Latin, and modern English. Many of the names given were unknown to Johnstone, but he looked them up and found that they fit.

Paul Johnstone questioned the communicator calling himself Artorius extensively about the main events of his life, and thus was able to adjust or confirm some of his own earlier ideas about the period—ideas obtained purely archeologically and through research, not psychically. Thus we have a date for Arthur's birth, 459 A.D., and another for the battle at Badon Hill, 503, where Arthur decisively defeated a coalition of Saxons and their allies, and established his kingdom firmly for twenty peaceful years.

To me it did not even matter whether Arthur spoke through Johnstone or whether Johnstone, the psychic, obtained factual information not previously known or confirmed. The knowledge was gained, one way or the other, through paranormal means. When I brought up this delicate point, Johnstone referred to a number of instances where his own knowledge and opinion had been totally different from what he received psychically from Arthur. For example, when he asked what Castle Guinnion was, he was told it was a refuge of the Picts. His own views had been that it was a British stronghold, assailed by the Picts.

* * *

All this correspondence came to a sudden climax when Johnstone informed me that new digs were going on at what might or might not be the true site of Camelot.

* * *

Now the question as to where Arthur's famed stronghold was situated—if there was indeed a Camelot—has occupied researchers for centuries. The Tourist Board insists it is Tintagel Castle in Cornwall. Arthur spent his boyhood there, according to Mr. Johnstone, and there was a monastery on the spot, but the castle itself is many centuries later than Arthur. Cadbury Hill, west of Ilchester, was a more logical choice for the honor. This hill fort in Somerset overlooks the plains all the way to Glastonbury, which one can clearly see from its ramparts. Johnstone suggested it as the site of the true Camelot when he wrote his book in 1963. His opinion was based on archeological evidence, but the "establishment" of professionals rejected this possibility then. The Cadbury Hill ruins were considered pre-Roman, and any connection with Arthur's fifth-century Britain denied. It was the opinion of Leslie Alcock of the University of Wales, one of the men digging at Cadbury, that in Arthur's time warfare did not use fortified positions of this size. But after digging at the site in the summer of 1966, he expressed a different view in the March 1967 issue of *Antiquity*: Cadbury was a vital strongpoint in Arthur's time.

What Johnstone suggested to me was simply this: Why not take a good medium to Cadbury and see what she can get? Let us find out, he asked, if Cadbury Hill is Camelot. He himself would not come along with us, so that no one might accuse my medium of being influenced by knowledge in his mind or subconscious. But he was willing to give me exact instructions on how to get to the site, and to a few other sites also connected with the Arthur-Camelot lore, and afterward help me evaluate the material I might obtain on the spot.

I enthusiastically agreed to this, and made arrangements to visit Britain in the early fall of 1967, with Sybil Leek serving as my psychic bloodhound.

Our plans would be made in such a manner that Sybil could not guess our purpose or where we were headed, and I would take great pains in avoiding all sensory clues that might give away our destination. Thus I made my arrangements with the driver whenever Sybil was not within sight, and confined our conversations to such innocent topics as the weather, always a good one in uncertain Britain.

Paul Johnstone had given me two sites to explore: Cadbury Hill, allegedly the true Camelot, and a point in Hampshire where he thought England was founded. If his calculations were correct, then the latter place would be the actual site of Cardic's barrow, or grave, a spot where the first king of Wessex, precursor of modern England, was buried.

"It's at Hurstbourne Priors in Hampshire," he wrote, "halfway between Winchester and Salisbury, but closer to Andover. But there is a drawback to this one. Nobody seems to know the exact site."

Since Cardic was one of the local rulers Arthur fought at Badon Hill, I felt we should include the visit, especially as it was not out of our way to Camelot.

Johnstone was able, however, to give me one more clue, this one not archeological, but psychic:

In 1950 he had had a strange dream about Cardic's grave. He saw that a nineteenth-century church had been erected over the site, on the hill where the barrow was. Cardic's grave, called Ceardicesboerg in the original tongue, had escaped even so renowned an archeologist as Professor O. G. S. Crawford, the founder of *Antiquity*, and a man whose home territory this was, as he lived in nearby Southampton.

Thus armed with a meager clue and the story of a strange dream, we set out from London on September 22, 1967. Sybil Leek was to meet us at the Andover railroad station.

I had with me an ordnance map of the area so that even the smallest piece of territory could be quickly explored. Our driver had long realized we were no ordinary tourists (by "we" I mean Catherine and myself, and now, Mrs. Leek).

We left Andover and drove three miles northeast to the little village of Hurstbourne Priors. In fact, we drove right through it, several times, actually, before we realized that we were going too fast. As we turned the car around once more, I spotted a narrow country lane, covered by the shadows of huge old trees, opening to our left. And at the bottom of the lane, a church—our church. We had found it, exactly as Paul Johnstone had dreamed it in 1950!

Johnstone had never visited Europe, nor did he have access to the fact that an early nineteenth-century-type church would stand there at the end of this country lane. But there it was, and we piled out.

Built in the traditional Church of England neo-Gothic style, this church had earlier beginnings, but its essence was indeed early nineteenth century. It stood in the middle of a romantic churchyard filled with ancient gravestones, some still upright, but the majority leaning in various directions due to age. Farther back were a number of huge trees. Suddenly the busy country road we had just left did not intrude any longer, and we were caught up in a time warp where everything was just as it must have always been. It was close to noon now, and not a living soul around.

We entered the little church and found it the very model of a country chapel.

The driver stayed outside near the car while we started to walk around the soft green grounds.

"The church is not important here," Sybil said right away, "it's the ground that is."

We stood near the biggest of the trees now.

"We should be on a hill," she said, "a small hill, a rise in the ground that has been utilized for a practical purpose."

I became interested and moved in closer. The funerary bowers of old were just that.

"There is some connection with a disease . . . people congregating here because of a disease. . . . I expected to find the hill here."

Considering the changes possible in the course of fifteen centuries, I was not at all surprised that the hill no longer existed, or at least that it was no longer prominent, for there was a rise in back of the cemetery.

"Why is this hill important?" I asked.

"A long time ago . . . comes in in flickering movements, but I can see the hill distinctly. There is a male dominance here. This is not a local thing. I can't quite see his legs. He dominates, though there are other people. He has a tall rod, which he is holding. There is a bird on the rod. It's not a flag, but it's like a flag. The hill is important to him . . . J . . . initial J. This is in connection with the flag thing. I can see his face and his head."

"Is there anything on his head?"

"Yes, there is, a headgear—it is related to the thing he is holding. I can't see it very clearly. The bird is also on

Camelot today—only the earth works are left

his headgear, swept up from it. An outdoor man of great strength. *He is a soldier.* A very long time ago."

"What period are we in with him, would you say?" I asked softly. Nothing in the appearance of the place related to a soldier. Sybil was of course getting the right "vibrations," and I was fascinated by it.

"So far back I can't be sure."

"Is he an important man?"

"Yes. I'm looking at letters. C-Caius...C-a-i-s... Caius. He is very important. The hill is connected with him, yet he is foreign. But he needs the hill. He faces west. West is the road he has to go...from east to west is the journey...."

"What has he done?"

"The thing in his hand is related to his position. Coins...trading...a lot of people in one spot but he dominates...."

Sybil felt at this point that we should move back farther for better "reception" of the faint waves from the past. She pointed to the two oldest trees at the extreme end of the churchyard and remarked that the strongest impression would be there.

"Kill...someone was killed between those two trees," she now asserted, "he was chased, there is an old road beneath this cemetery. He had to go this way, make the way as he went. Not just walk over. Almost on this spot, I have the feeling of someone meeting sudden death. Violent death. And yet it was not war. More like an attack, an ambush. There is a big connection with the west. That's what he wants to do, go west. This man was very dominant."

We were now in the corner of the old cemetery. The silence was unbroken by anything except an occasional jet plane soaring overhead. There is an airbase situated not far away.

"There ought to be a clearing where you look out to a hill," Sybil insisted. "This man was here before those trees. The trees are at least a thousand years old."

I did some fast arithmetic. That would get us back to about the ninth century. It was before then, Sybil asserted.

With that, she turned around and slowly walked back to the car. We had lots more mileage to cover today, so I thought it best not to extend our visit here, especially as we had found interesting material already.

When I saw Paul Johnstone in St. Louis in February of the following year, I played the tape of our investigation for him. He listened with his eyes half-closed, then nodded. "You've found it, all right. Just as I saw it in my dream."

"What exactly did you dream?"

"I was there...I was looking at the hill...there was a church on the hill, not a particularly ancient church, and there was a bronze memorial of a British soldier in it...then I was looking at a book, a book that does not exist, but it was telling of Cardic of Wessex, and that he was buried on this hill where stood this nineteenth-century church. The church had obliterated the traces of his grave, that is why it had not been found. I simply wrote this dream down, but never did anything about it until you came along."

The reference to Cardic's grave goes back to the tenth century, Johnstone pointed out. I questioned him about the name CAIUS which Sybil tried to spell for us.

"In his own time, Cardic would have spelled his name C-a-r-a-t-i-c-u-s....Mrs. Leek got the principal letters of the name, all right. The long rod with the bird on it is also very interesting. For in the Sutton Hoo find of ancient British relics there was a long bronze spear with a stag atop it. This was a standard, and Cardic might well have had one with a bird on it. This founder of Wessex undoubtedly was a "dominant personality," as Sybil put it —and again some interesting things fall into place. Cardic's father was a Jute, as were most of his people—remember the letter, J, that Sybil used to describe him and his kind?"

Johnstone then went on to explain the role Cardic played in history. I had not wanted to have this knowledge before, so that Sybil could not get it from my mind or unconscious.

Both Cardic and Artorius served as officers of British King Ambrose, and when Ambrose died in 485 A.D. Cardic went over to the Saxon enemy. In 495 he invaded Hampshire with his Jutes, and ruled the country as a local chieftain. In 503, when Arthur fought the Battle of Badon Hill against the Saxons and their allies, Cardic's people were among those allies. According to Johnstone, he arrived a little late and made his escape, living on to 516, at which time he might have been ambushed at the barrow site and buried there with the honors due him. This site was very close to his western frontier, and the ambushers would have been Britons from Ambrose's old kingdom, based at Salisbury, rather than men from the distant Camelot. Johnstone does not think Arthur could have ordered Cardic murdered: They had been friends for years, and though their kingdoms were close to one another, there was no war between them between 503 and 516, a pretty long time of peace in those days. Arthur could have crushed Cardic's kingdom, which was based at what is now Winchester, yet be chose for some reason not to do so. But Ambrose's heirs might not have felt as charitable about their neighbor, and it is there that we must look for the killers of Cardic.

Johnstone also suggested that the long rod with the eagle on top and the helmet might very well have been Roman, inasmuch as Roman culture was still very dominant in the area and Cardic certainly trained as an officer in that tradition.

The name Cardic itself is Welsh, and Johnstone suggested that Cardic's father, Elesa, was of Anglo-Jute origin, his mother Welsh, and he himself a native of Britain, perhaps the reason for his divided loyalties in those turbulent times.

I questioned my expert concerning the remark, made by Mrs. Leek, that the man wanted to go west and had come from the east.

"As a Saxon commander, he naturally came from the east and wanted to extend his power westward, but he was fought to a standstill," Johnstone replied.

It seemed fitting to me to visit the last resting place of the man who had been Arthur's counterplayer, and yet a friend once too, before proceeding to Arthur's lair, Camelot, some two hours' driving time farther to the southwest.

Finding Cadbury Hill proved no easier than discovering Cardic's bower. We passed through South Cadbury twice, and no one knew where the excavations were to be found. Evidently the fame of Cadbury Hill did not extend beyond its immediate vicinity. It was already the latter part of the afternoon when we finally came upon the steep, imposing hill that once held a succession of fortified encampments from the dawn of history onward—including, perhaps, the fabled Camelot?

A twisting road led up the hill, and we decided it best to leave the car behind. After crossing a wooded section and passing what appeared to be remnants of old stone fortifications, we finally arrived on the plateau. The sight that greeted our eyes was indeed spectacular. Windswept and chilly, a slanting plateau presented itself to our eyes: earth ramparts surrounding it on all four sides, with the remnants of stone walls here and there still in evidence. The center of the area was somewhat higher than the rest, and it was there that a team of volunteer archeologists had been digging. The sole evidence of their efforts was a crisscross network of shallow trenches and some interesting

artifacts stored in a local museum, most of it of Roman or pre-Roman origin, however, which had led to the assumption that this was nothing more than a native Celtic fortress the Romans had taken over. Was this the great palace of Camelot with its splendid halls and the famed Round Table?

* * *

At the moment, a herd of cows was grazing on the land and we were the only bipeds around. The cows found us most fascinating and started to come close to look us over. Until we were sure that they were cows and that there were no bulls among them, this was somewhat of a nerve-wracking game. Then, too, my tape recording of what Sybil had to say was frequently interrupted by the ominous and obvious sound of cow droppings, some of which came awfully close for comfort. But the brave explorer that I am stood me in good stead: I survived the ordeal with at least as much courage as did Arthur's knights of old survive the ordeal of combat. There we were, Catherine in a wine red pants suit, the driver somewhere by himself looking down into the village, and Sybil and I trying to tune in the past.

If this was indeed the true Camelot, I felt that Mrs. Leek should pick up something relating to it. She had no conscious notion as to where we were or why I had caused her to walk up a steep hill in the late afternoon, a hill evidently given over to cows. But she saw the trenches and diggings and may have assumed we were looking at some ancient Roman site. Beyond that I honestly don't think she knew or cared why we were here: She has always trusted me and assumed that there is a jolly good reason.

After walking around for few moments, I cornered her near the diggings and begin my questioning.

"What do you think this place is?" I began.

"I think it's a sanctuary," came the odd reply, "a retreat. A spiritual retreat."

"Can you visualize what stood here?"

"As I was coming up the hill I had the feeling of a monastery, but I am not thinking in terms of pure religion —more like a place where people come to contemplate, a spiritual feeling. I see more the end of the period than the buildings."

"How did it end?"

"The breaking up of a clan . . . a number of people, not in a family, but tied by friendship. . . ."

"How far back?"

"I'll try to get some letters. . . ." She closed her eyes and swayed a little in the strong wind, while I waited. "G-w-a-i-n-e-l-o-d. . . ."

My God, I thought, is she trying to say "Camelot"?

"A meeting place," Sybil continued, gradually falling more and more into trance, "not a war place, a good place, friendship...this place has had for many years a religious association. A very special one."

"Is there some leader?" I asked.

"Abbot *Erlaile*...not of necessity in the same period."

"When were these people here?"

"A long, long time ago. Not much power behind it, very diffuse. I can only catch it from time to time. There are many Gwaine letters, a lot of those."

"You mean people whose names sound like that or start with Gwaine?"

"Yes."

"Are they male?"

"Not all male. But the friendship is male. Coming up from the sea. This was their sanctuary."

"Who were these men?"

"Gwaine is one."

"Who ruled over them?"

"It's a very mixed thing...not easy to catch...thirteen people...tied together by friendship...."

"Do they have any name as a group?"

"Templars."

Later, when I examined the evidence, it became clear to me that Sybil was getting more than one layer of history when she made contact with the imprint left upon these storied rocks.

Paul Johnstone, my Arthurian expert friend, assured me later that Camelot was derived from the Welsh *Camallt,* meaning crooked slope, which is a pretty good description of the place at that.

In his psychic contact with the historical Arthur, Johnstone, using his dowsing board, established the name as *Cambalta,* which is pretty close to the modern Welsh form. But on earlier occasion, again using the board, Johnstone questioned his communicator (as he described it in an article, "News from Camelot," in *Search* magazine, March 1968) about the ancient name of the hill at South Cadbury. This time the answer differs.

"Dinas Catui," Johnstone quotes his informant, and explains that it means Fort of Cado. But he also gives an alternate name: Cantimailoc. Thus, even the "horse's mouth" wasn't always sure what the name was, it would seem. Unless, of course, there was more than one name. This is precisely what I think. As its owners changed, so the name might have changed: When Cado was king, perhaps it was Dinas Catui, which would be the post-Latin form, or Cantimailoc, the local Welsh form. Then when Arthur succeeded his erstwhile colleague, the name might have left out the reference to King Cado and become Cambalta, referring to the geographical peculiarity of the place, rather than incorporating Arthur's name, a modesty quite consistent with the character of the historical Artorius. But when Gwaine became prominent in the area, he might not have held such modest views as Arthur, and thus the forti-

fied hill might have become known as Gwaine's slope or Gwainelot.

Mrs. Leek, getting her impressions at the same time and with varying degrees of intensity, could not possibly distinguish between the various layers that cling to the place. Certainly, from what I heard, there were at least two sixth-century layers, that of Artorius himself and that of Gwaine, and a third layer not directly connected either in time or relationship with the two earlier ones, but somehow also concerned with the overall aspects of the site. This strange discrepancy would require some sorting out, I thought immediately, but surely there must be a connection. I knew enough of Mrs. Leek's work to take nothing lightly or dismiss any bit of information obtained through her as unimportant.

After our return, I went over the tapes very carefully to try to make sense out of what had come through. To begin with, the sanctuary and Abbot Erlaile and the Templars would certainly have to be much later than the thirteen men tied together in friendship, and the man she called Gwaine, and yet there might have been a strong link.

Gwainelod—was that a contemporary name for Camelot? Gwaine himself was the son of a northern chieftain whom Arthur had taken under his wing. Sometimes styled Gawain, this historical knight with the Welsh name actually lived in the early sixth century, and shows up also as a fictional hero in the medieval Arthur legend, where he is called Sir Gawain. The many people with names beginning with Gwaine to which the medium referred might very well have included Queen Gwainewere, better known as Guinevere, Arthur's first wife. According to Johnstone, the one who did most of the things the medieval Guinevere was supposed to have done was not this queen, who died after a short time, but her successor, Arthur's second queen named Creirwy.

Now the Knights Templars belong to a much later period, that of the Crusades. Strangely, the legend of the Holy Grail is set during that latter time, incorporating much of the Arthurian traditions. Was there a connection somewhere between a post-Roman local ruler and a Christian mystical upholder of the faith? Was Camelot reoccupied long after its fall and destruction by Arthur's nephew Mordred, in the Saxon period by a group of monks who established a sanctuary there, linking the Arthurian traditions with their early medieval Christianity? In other words, did a group of monks during the early Crusades occupy the hill at Cadbury, and found upon the ruins of Arthur's sanctuary and palace a new sanctuary dedicated to the revived belief in the Holy Grail of nearby Glastonbury?

All these thoughts came to me much later, when I sifted the material back in New York.

At the moment we were standing atop Cadbury Hill, and the air was getting chilly as the sun started to disappear behind the horizon.

"There was some link with the sea, but they were finished, they had to move...very suddenly...came here for sanctuary and tried to build up...the same meeting place...feeling...."

"What was the place called then?" I asked with bated breath. "B-r-y-n-w-T-o-r-," Sybil answered.

"Brynw Tor?" I repeated. Nearly Glastonbury came to mind. A tor is high, craggy hill that in England usually has a temple on it.

"What was here actually?" I pointed to the ground.

"The home of....I see a face lying down...with gray things hanging...*chains*. It's a good man, in chains. Loss of freedom must cause suffering...tied here."

Later I wondered who the prisoner she felt might have been. I found that Arthur himself was thrown into prison by one of the sons of King Ambrose, after the king had died. Arthur had become embroiled in the quarrel among Ambrose's sons and successors. Eventually Arthur was freed by his men. Could Sybil be picking up this mental image of that event in the far past?

Again I asked, who was the leader here, and Sybil replied, she did not know. When I saw Paul Johnstone in St. Louis many months later, he informed me that he had had contact with Arthur, through his psychic board. Arthur had informed him that he had not been present when I came to look for Camelot, even though I had come to the right place.

"Do you sense any leader at all?" I insisted, and looked at Sybil.

"Two leaders. Two men."

This, I discovered later, was also interesting. Arthur ruled jointly with King Cado at Camelot when Arthur first came there. Later, Arthur became sole ruler. Cado is remembered today in the place name for Cadbury, site of Camelot.

"What does the place look like?" I continued my questioning.

"There is a circle...the circle is important...building, too, but there must be a circle...the knights...brave men...Welsh names...*Monserrey*...."

I was overcome with the importance of what we were doing and spoke in a subdued voice, even though I could have shouted and nobody but the cows would have heard me.

"Are we here..." I asked. *"Is this Monserrey?"*

"The place is here, but the cavity is not here."

"Where is the cavity?"

"West...toward the sun...."

"What is in the cavity?"

"The chains."

"What is kept here?"

"No one must know. Not ready. Not ready for knowledge."

"Before the circle...."

"Who is at the head of the circle?"

"He's dead. You should not look yet."

"What is the secret kept here?"

"I will not say the name."

The conversation was getting more and more into the realms of mysticism, I felt. What Sybil had brought through made sense although I would not be able to sort it out until afterward, on my return to New York. The circle could refer to the Round Table, the knights with Welsh names were certainly Arthur's men, but Monserrey (or Montserrat) belonged to the legend of the Holy Grail. Again, Sybil was fusing into one story two periods separated by many centuries.

The cavity containing the chains also interested me. Was she referring to a relic kept, perhaps, at Glastonbury? Was there something besides the cup and the sprig Joseph of Arimathaea had brought with him from Palestine? Were these chains of later origin? I was hardly going to get any objective proof for these statements, and yet the picture, although confused, was intriguing, especially so as Sybil had no way of connecting the windswept hill we were standing on with either King Arthur or the Holy Grail!

"Who is the communicator?" I demanded. I had the feeling it was not Artorius, and it wasn't Sybil any longer, and my curiosity was aroused: Who was it?

"Don't say communicator...communicant!"

"Very well, what is the communicant's name, then?"

"The King."

I was surprised, taken aback.

"I have to have proof."

"The name is not ready....It is wrong to discover more than you can hope to learn....I want to protect the secret with magic."

"What is your name?"

"She knows me...." he said, referring to the medium, and all at once I, too, knew who my informant was, incredible though it seemed at that instant!

"I know you, too," I heard myself say, "and I'm a friend, you need not fear me."

"I'm a bird," the voice coming from Sybil's entranced lips said, a little mockingly.

Merlin! Of course...Merlin means "small hawk." How apt the name fit the wise counselor of Arthur.

Was there a Merlin?

Not one, but two, Paul Johnstone assured me, and one of them did serve as an adviser to Artorius. Whether or not he was also a magician is a moot question. But a historical figure Merlin (or Medwin) certainly was.

"Link between the sea and here...stranger...must come....When will that be? When the hawk...when the birds fly in the sky like me.... *Man flies in the sky.... The link is a bad one...."*

"And who will the stranger be?" I asked.

"Erfino...a bird...."

"Where will he come from?"

"From out of the earth?"

"Inside the earth?" I asked incredulously.

"Out of the earth...will rise again."

"You speak in riddles."

"I know the answers!"

"Why not give them to me now?"

"You are a man.... There have to be *twelve others* ... the *bird* is the secret...."

I began to understand the implications of this prophecy and, forgetting for the moment my mission here, said only, "Is there nothing I can do?"

But Merlin was gone.

Sybil was back.

The change in expression and personality was incredible: One moment ago, her face had been the wizened, serene face of a timeless wise man, and now it was Sybil Leek, voluble author and voluntary medium, merely standing on a hill she didn't know, and it was getting dark and chilly.

We quickly descended the steep hill and got into the car, the driver turned on the heat, and off we went, back to London.

But the experience we had just been through was not easily assimilated. If it was indeed Arthur's counselor Merlin, speaking for the King—and how could I disprove it even if I had wanted to?—then Sybil had indeed touched on the right layer in history. The implications of Merlin's prophecy also hit home: Was he speaking of a future war that was yet to come and that would drive the human race underground, to emerge only when it was safe to do so, and build once again the sanctuary?

* * *

The idea of a council of twelve is inherent in most secret doctrines, from Rosicrucian to White Brotherhood, and even in the twelve apostles and the esoteric astrologers' twelve planets (of which we know only nine presently) this number is considered important.

The prophecy of birds (airplanes) he calls hawks (warlike) that represent a bad link needs, I think, no explanation, and the subsequent destruction forcing man to live in caves was reminiscent of H. G. Wells' strangely prophetic *The Shape of Things to Come.*

But what was the meaning of the bird named Erfine, or perhaps Irfine, or some such spelling, since I only heard the word and did not see it spelled out?

When I confronted Paul Johnstone in his friend Dr. Saussele's offices in St. Louis in February of 1968, I questioned him about the Camelot material.

"I think Sybil got several periods there," he began. "The Templars were prominent in England in the 1200s, but that is of course seven hundred years after Arthur."

"Did Arthur build a sanctuary on the hilltop?"

"Not to my knowledge. He built a fortress and occupied a dwelling on the hilltop. Some invading Celtic tribes built a hilltop fort there around 200 B.C. Then the Romans came and chased these people away. The hill was semi-

deserted for quite a while. Then Cado reestablished himself there. Cado was a kinsman to Arthur, and around 510 A.D., after the victorious Battle of Badon Hill, he invited Arthur to share his kingdom with him, which Arthur did."

"Any other comments?"

"No, except to say that Sybil Leek was getting something real."

"Thus the real Camelot can no longer be sought at Tintagel, or in Wales, or on the Scottish border: nowhere but atop the breezy hill at Cadbury near Ilchester. There are several other Cadburys in Somerset and Devon, but the one that once belonged to King Arthur lies at a spot marked Cadbury Castle on most maps. You can't miss it if you have an ordnance map, and even if you don't, have Sybil Leek with you!

But to my mind Sybil had done more than merely establish via psychometry the reality of Camelot and the Arthurian presence at Cadbury. The puzzling dual impression of sixth-century Arthur and a twelfth-century Grail tradition at this spot seemed to me to point in a direction no other author has ever traveled. Could it be that the romantic, almost fictional Arthur of the Christian chivalry period was not merely the result of the continuous rewriting and distortion of ancient legends? Was there a kernel of truth in linking Artorius with the story of the Grail?

According to my psychic friend, Sybil Leek, the hallowed ground where Arthur tried to save Briton from the barbarians overrunning it at the time was later turned into another sanctuary by the Knights Templars. We know that the legend of the Grail became known about that period, when the monks of Glastonbury started to spread it.

So much of this part of the world is as yet underground, awaiting the spade of the archeologist. Perhaps some day in the not-too-distant future, additional digging will reveal tangible proof for what is now mainly information and deduction, but certainly not fantasy or make-believe.

The early Christian leadership of Arthur may very well have been the example the Templars wished to follow in their endeavor to found a sanctuary of their own in a period no less turbulent than Arthur's. In time, the two struggles might have become intertwined until one could no longer tell them apart. The thirteenth- and fourteenth-century authors merely picked up what they heard and uncritically embroidered it even further.

Unraveling the confused yarn is not an easy task, but through the talents of a psychic like Sybil Leek we could at least assure ourselves of a totally fresh and independent approach. There can be no doubt that Mrs. Leek picked up impressions out of the past at Cadbury, and not thoughts in my mind, for most of the material she obtained was unknown to me at the time of our expedition.

It probably matters little to the producers of the magnificent film that the *real Camelot* looks a lot less glamorous than their version of it; no matter, Arthur would have liked it, I'm almost sure.

✳ 20

Her Name Was Trouble: The Secret Adventure of Nell Gwyn

PICTURE THIS, IF YOU WILL: All England is rejoicing, the long and bloody Civil War is finally over. Thousands of dead cavaliers and matching thousands of roundheads will never see the light of day again, smoking ruins of burned-down houses and churches and estates have finally cooled off, and England is back in the family of nations. The Puritan folly has had its final run: King Charles II has been installed on his father's throne, and Whitehall Palace rings once again with pleasant talk and music.

The year is 1660. One would never suspect that a scant eleven years before, the King's father had been executed by the parliamentary government of Oliver Cromwell. The son does not wish to continue his revenge. Enough is enough. But the Restoration does not mean a return to the old ways, either. The evils of a corrupt court must not be repeated lest another Cromwell arise. Charles II is a young man with great determination and skill in the art of diplomacy. He likes his kingship, and he thinks that with moderation and patience the House of Stuart would be secure on the English throne for centuries to come. Although the Puritans are no longer running the country, they are far from gone. The King does not wish to offend their moral sense. He will have his fun, of course, but why flaunt it in their faces?

With the Restoration came not only a sigh of relief from the upper classes, that all was well once again and one could *play*, but the pendulum soon started to swing the other way: Moral decay, excesses, and cynicism became the earmarks of the Restoration spirit. Charles II wanted no part of this, however. Let the aristocracy expose themselves; he would always play the part of the monarch of the people, doing what he wanted quietly, out of sight.

One of the nicest sights in the young King's life was an actress of sorts by the name of Nell Gwyn. She and her mother had come to London from the country, managed to meet the King, and found favor in his eyes. She was a pale-skinned redhead with flash and lots of personality, and evidently she had the kind of attractions the King fancied. Kings always have mistresses, and even the Puritans would not have expected otherwise. But Charles II was also worried about his own friends and courtiers: He wanted the girl for himself, he knew he was far from attractive, and though he was the King, to a woman of Nell's spirit, that might be enough.

The thing to do was simply not to sneak her in and out of the Whitehall rear doors for a day or two, and possibly run into the Queen and a barrage of icy stares. A little privacy would go a long way, and that was precisely what Charles had in mind. Nell was not his only mistress by any means—but she was the only one he *loved*. When he gazed into the girl's sky-blue eyes or ran his hands

through her very British red hair, it electrified him and he felt at peace. Peace was something precious to him as the years of his reign rolled by. The religious problem had not really been settled; even the Stuarts were split down the middle among Protestants and Catholics. The Spaniards were troublesome, and Louis XIV in league with the "godless" Turks was not exactly a good neighbor. Yes, Charlie needed a place in the country where the pressures of Whitehall would not intrude.

*   *   *

His eyes fell upon a partially dilapidated old manor house near St. Albans, about an hour and a half from London by today's fast road, in the vicinity of an old Roman fortress dominating the rolling lands of Herfordshire. Nearby was the site of the Roman strong city of Verulamium, and the place had been a fortified manor house without interruption from Saxon times onward. It had once belonged to the Earl of Warwick, the famed "King maker," and in 1471, during an earlier civil war period, the War of the Roses, the house had been in the very center of the Battle of Barnet. To this day the owners find rusty fifteenth-century swords and soldiers' remains in the moat or on the grounds.

By the middle of the sixteenth century, however, the manor house, known as Salisbury Hall, had gradually fallen into a state of disrepair, partially due to old age and partially as a consequence of the civil war, which was fought no less savagely than the one two centuries later which brought Charles II to the throne.

A certain country squire named John Cutte had then acquired the property, and he liked it so much he decided to restore the manor house. He concentrated his rebuilding efforts on the center hall, lavishing on the building all that sixteenth-century money could buy. The wings later fell into ruins, and have now completely disappeared. Only an old battlement, the moat surrounding the property, or an occasional corridor abruptly ending at a wall where there had once been another wing to the house remind one of its early period.

One day Charles and Nell were driving by the place, and both fell in love with it instantly. Discreetly Charles inquired whether it might be for sale, and it so happened it was, not merely because he was the King, but because of financial considerations: The recent political affairs had caused the owners great losses, and they were glad to sell the house. Once again it was almost in ruins, but Charles restored it in the style of his own period. This was a costly operation, of course, and it presented a problem, even for a king. He could not very well ask Parliament for the money to build his mistress a country house. His personal coffers were still depleted from the recent war. There was only one way to do it, and Charles II did not hesitate: He borrowed

Nell Gwyn's old home; later became the Royal Saddlery; a night club today

The nightclub known as the Gargoyle occupied part of the four-story building, the balance being what is now called the Nell Gwyn Theatre, and various offices and dressing rooms. In the 1920s, Noel Coward was one of the founding members of this club, and Henri Matisse designed one of the rooms. It was highly respectable and private then, and many of the leading artists of the 1920s and 1930s made it their hangout for late-night parties. As Soho became more and more a nightclub area, the Gargoyle could not remain aloof: It became London's best-known strip-tease club. The acts at the Gargoyle are never vulgar. It isn't the place to take your maiden aunt, but you *can* take your wife. The last time I visited Jimmy Jacobs and his club, I was somewhat startled by the completely nude bartenders, female, popping up behind the bar of the upstairs club; it seemed a bit incongruous to think that these girls dress to go to work, then take their clothes off for their work, and get dressed to go home. But I think Nell Gwyn would have been quite understanding. A girl's got to make a living, after all. The decor inside is flashy and very much in the style of the 1920s, for Jimmy Jacobs has not touched any of it.

In this "town house" Nell Gwyn lived for many years. But she actually died of a stroke in another house in the Mall which the King had given her in the days when they were close. According to *Burnet's Own Time*, Vol. I, p. 369, she continued in favor with the King for many years, even after she was no longer his mistress, and it is true that the King had words of concern for her on his deathbed: "Let not poor Nelly starve," he asked of his brother and successor on the English throne, James II.

That of course might have been an expression of remorse as much as a sign of caring. When her royal protector was gone, Nell was most certainly in great debt, and among other things was forced to sell her personal silver. The *Dictionary of National Biographies* is our source of reference for these events that filled her last remaining years. She survived Charles II by only two years, leaving this vale of tears on November 13, 1687, at the age of thirty-seven, considered middle age in those day, especially for a woman!

But there were periods during which Nell was at odds with her King, periods in which he refused to look after her. Nell, of course, was not a shy wallflower: On one occasion she stuck her head out of her window, when some sightseers were staring at her house, and intoned, "I'm a Protestant whore!" Although her profession had been listed as actress, she herself never made any bones about what she thought she was.

During those lean years she badgered the Court for money, and the sentimental King sent it to her now and then. Their relationship had its ups and downs, and there were periods when Nell was in financial trouble and the King would not help her. Whatever help he gave her was perhaps because of their offspring. The first-born child later became the Duke of St. Albans, taking the title from

the money from discreet sources, and soon after installed his lady love at Salisbury Hall.

As time went on, the King's position grew stronger, and England's financial power returned. Also, there was no longer any need for the extreme caution that had characterized the first few years after the Restoration. The King did not wish to bury Nell Gwyn at a distance in the country, especially as he did not fancy riding out there in the cold months of the year. He therefore arranged for her to have a private apartment in a house built above the Royal Saddlery near the Deanery, in the London suburb called Soho.

In the second half of the seventeenth century, Soho was pretty far uptown from Whitehall, and the young things flitting to and fro through its woods were still four-legged. Today, of course, Soho is the sin-studded nightclub section of London's West End. The old house, built in 1632, still stands, but it has changed over many times since. Next door to it was the Royalty Theatre, where Nell Gwyn had once been among the hopeful young actresses—but not for long. It seems odd to find a theater next door to the stables, but Soho was a hunting suburb and it seemed then logical to have all the different sporting events and facilities close together. Besides, Nell did not mind; she liked peeking in at the Royalty Theatre when she was not otherwise engaged. Unfortunately, the theater is no more; an unfriendly Nazi bomb hit it during World War II. But the Saddlery did not get a scratch and that is all to the good, for today it houses a most interesting emporium.

Charles's romantic memory still attaching to his and Nell's early days (and nights) at Salisbury Hall near St. Albans. The descendants of this child still thrive, and the present duke is the thirteenth to hold the title. Gradually the King's interest started to wander, but not his possessiveness of her. While he allowed himself the luxury of casting an appreciative eye in other directions, he took a dim view of anyone else doing likewise toward his Nell.

There are popular stories that Nell died broke and lonely, but the fact seems to be that while she had years when she was indeed poor and unhappy, at the very end she had a measure of comfort due perhaps to the personal belongings she had managed to save and which she was later able to sell off. The house in the Mall was still hers, and it was there that she passed on. In a final gesture, Nell left the house to the Church and was buried properly in the crypt at St. Martin's in the Fields.

We know very little about her later years except the bare facts of her existence and continued relationship with the King. But this knowledge is only a skeleton without the flesh and blood of human emotions. The story fascinated me always from the purely historical point of view, but it was not until 1964 that I became interested in it as a case of psychic phenomena.

The English actress Sabrina, with whom I shared an interest in such matters, called my attention to an incident that had occurred a short time before my arrival in London.

One of the girls in the show got locked in by mistake. It was late at night, and she was the only one left in the building. Or so she thought. While she was still trying to find a way to get out, she became aware of the sounds of footsteps and noises. Human voices, speaking in excited tones, added to her terror, for she could not see anyone. Not being a trained psychic researcher, she reacted as many ordinary people would have reacted: She became terrified with fear, and yelled for help. Nobody could hear her, for the walls of the building are sturdy. Moreover, she was locked in on the top floor, and the noises of the Soho streets below drowned out her cries for help. Those who did hear her took her for a drunk, since Soho is full of such people at that time of the night. At any rate, she became more and more panicky, and attempted to jump out the window. At that point the fire department finally arrived and got her out.

Jimmy Jacobs was so impressed with her story that he asked the editor of the *Psychic News* to arrange for an investigation, which yielded two clues: that the Royal Stables were once located in the building, and that Jimmy Jacobs himself was very psychic. The first fact he was able to confirm objectively, and the second came as no surprise to him either. Ever since he had taken over the club, he had been aware of a psychic presence.

"When I bought this place in 1956, I hadn't bargained for a ghost as well, you know," Jimmy Jacobs explained to me, especially as the subject of ESP had always fascinated him and running a burlesque show with psychic overtones wasn't what he had in mind. But he could not discount the strange experiences his employees kept having in the old building, even though he had given explicit instructions to his staff never to tell any new dancer anything about the psychic connotations of the building. If they were to learn of them, they would do so by their own experiences, not from gossip or hearsay, he decided.

One night in 1962, Jimmy was standing in the reception room on the top floor. It was 3 o'clock in the morning, after the club had shut down and he was, in fact, the only person in the building. He was about to call it a night when he heard the elevator come up to his floor. His first thought was that someone, either an employee or perhaps a customer, had forgotten something and was coming back to get it. The hum of the elevator stopped, the elevator came to a halt, and Jimmy looked up toward it, curious to see who it was. But the doors did not open. Nobody came out of the elevator. His curiosity even more aroused, Jimmy stepped forward and opened the outer iron gates, then the inner wooden gates of the small elevator, which could accommodate only three people at one time. It was empty.

Jimmy swallowed hard. He was well aware of the operating mechanism of this elevator. To make it come up, someone had to be *inside* it to press the button, or someone had to be where *he* was, to call it up. He had not called it up. Nobody was inside it. How did the elevator manage to come up?

For days after the event he experimented with it to try and find another way. But there just wasn't any other way, and the mechanism was in perfect working order.

Jimmy stared at the elevator in disbelief. Then, all of a sudden, he became aware of a shadowy, gray figure, about five yards away from him across the room. The figure was dressed in a period costume with a high waist; it wore a large hat and had its face turned away from him— as if it did not wish to be recognized. Jimmy later took this to be a sign that the girl was "an imposter" posing as Nell Gwyn, and did not wish to be recognized as such. That he was wrong in his conclusion I was to learn later.

For the moment Jimmy stared at the shadowy girl, who did not seem to walk the way ordinary humans do, but instead was gliding toward him slightly above floor level. As she came nearer to where he was rooted, he was able to distinguish the details of her hat, which was made of a flowered material. At the same time, his nostrils filled with the strong aroma of gardenias. For days afterward he could not shake the strong smell of this perfume from his memory.

The figure glided past him and then disappeared into the elevator shaft! Since Jimmy was only a yard away from the figure at this point, it was clear that she was not a human being simply taking the elevator down. The elevator did not budge, but the figure was gone nevertheless.

The next morning, when Jimmy returned to his club, he began to put all reports of a psychic nature into a semblance of order, so that perhaps someone—if not he—could make head or tail of it. Clearly, *someone* not of flesh and blood was there because of some unfinished business. But who, and why?

The interesting part seemed to be that most of the disturbances of a psychic nature occurred between 1962 and 1964, or exactly two hundred years after the heyday of Nell Gwyn. It almost looked as if an anniversary of some sort were being marked!

An exotic dancer named Cherry Phoenix, a simple country woman, had come to London to make her fame and fortune, but had wound up at the Gargoyle making a decent enough salary for not-so-indecent exposure, twice nightly. The men (and a few women, too) who came to see her do it were from the same country towns and villages she had originally come from, so she should have felt right at home. That she didn't was partially due to the presence of something other than flesh-and-blood customers.

For the first months of her stay she was too busy learning the routines of her numbers and familiarizing herself with the intricate cues and electrical equipment that added depth to her otherwise very simple performance to allow anything unusual to intrude on her mind. But as she became more relaxed and learned her job better, she was increasingly aware that she was often not alone in her dressing room upstairs. One night she had come in fifteen minutes early, and the stairwell leading up to the roof was still totally dark. But she knew her way around, so she walked up the winding old stairs, using her hands to make sure she would not stumble. Her dressing room was a smallish room located at the top of the stairs and close to a heavy, bolted door leading out to the flat rooftop of the building. There were other dressing rooms below hers, in back of the stage, of course, but she had drawn this particular location and had never minded it before. It was a bit lonesome up there on the top floor, and if anything should happen to her, no one was likely to hear her cries, but she was a self-sufficient young woman and not given to hysterics.

That evening, as she reached the top of the stairs, she heard a peculiar flicking sound. Entering her dressing room in the darkness, she made her way to the familiar dressing table on the right side of the room. Now the noise was even more pronounced. It sounded to her as if someone were turning the pages of a book, a sound for which there was no rational source. Moreover, she suddenly became aware of a clammy, cold feeling around her. Since it was a warm evening, this too surprised her. "I went goosey all over," the girl commented to me in her provincial accent.

In the dark, she could not be sure if there wasn't someone else in the dressing room. So she called out the names of the other two girls, Barbara and Isabelle, who shared the room with her. There was no answer. Cherry Phoenix must have stood on that spot for about fifteen minutes without daring to move. Finally, she heard the noise of someone else coming up the stairs. The steps came nearer, but it was one of her dressing roommates. With that, the spell was broken and the noise stopped. Casually, the other girl turned the lights on. Only then did Cherry talk about her experience. She got very little sympathy from the other girl, for she had heard the strange noise herself on many occasions. For the first time Cherry found out that the ghost of "Nell" was responsible for all these shenanigans, and was told not to worry about it.

This was of little comfort to the frightened girl. The more so as other uncanny happenings added to her worries. The door to the roof was always secured by a heavy iron bolt. It would be impossible to open it from the outside, and the girls were safe in this respect even in Soho. But it could be pulled back by someone on the inside of the door, provided the person attempting this had great physical strength. The bolt was rarely pulled as this was an emergency exit only, and it was stiff and difficult to move. Nevertheless, on a number of occasions, when the girls knew there was no one else upstairs, they had found the bolt drawn back and the door to the roof wide open. In fact, it soon became apparent that the rooftop and that door were focal points of the mysterious haunting.

The last time Cherry found the rooftop door wide open was in 1964, and even after she left the show in 1965, it continued to "open itself" frequently to the consternation of newcomers to the dressing room.

One night, when Cherry was getting ready to leave—about the same time as Jimmy Jacobs' encounter with the gray lady—she heard a rattling sound, as if someone wanted to get out of a cage! There was such an air of oppression and violence about the area then that she could not get out of the dressing room and down the stairs fast enough.

When I visited the haunted stairwell in September of 1966, I clearly heard those terrifying sounds myself. They sounded far away, as if they were coming to my ears through a hollow tunnel, but I could make out the sound of metal on metal...such as a sword hitting another sword in combat. Was that perhaps the rattling sound Cherry Phoenix had heard earlier? At the time I heard these metallic sounds I was quite alone on the stairs, having left two friends in the theater with Jimmy Jacobs. When they joined me outside on the stairs a few moments later, the sounds had stopped, but the whole area was indeed icy.

Cherry Phoenix never saw the gray lady the way her boss had seen her. But another girl named Tracy York had been in the Gargoyle kitchen on the floor below the top floor, when she saw to her horror the outline of a woman's figure in a pale lilac dress. She ran out of the kitchen screaming, into the arms of choreographer Terry Brent, who calmed her down. In halting words, Tracy York reported her experience, and added that she had wanted to talk about the strange voice she kept hearing—a voice calling her name! The voice belonged to a woman, and Miss York thought that one of her colleagues had called her. At the time she was usually in the top-floor dressing room, and she assumed the voice was calling her from the next lower floor. When she rushed down, she found there was no one there, either. Terry Brent remembered the incident with the gray lady very well. "Tracy said there was a kind of mistiness about the figure, and that she wore a period costume. She just appeared and stood there."

Brent was not a believer in the supernatural when he first came to work at the Gargoyle. Even the mounting testimony of many girls—noises, apparitions, metallic rattlings, cold spots—could not sway him. He preferred to ascribe all this to the traditional rumors being told and embroidered more and more by each successive tenant of the top-floor dressing room. But one night he came in to work entering through the theater. It was still early, but he had some preliminary work to do that evening. Suddenly he heard the laughter of a woman above his head, coming from the direction of that top-floor dressing room. He naturally assumed that one of the girls had come in early, too. He went upstairs and found Isabelle Appleton all by herself in the dressing room. The laughter had not been hers, nor had the voice sounded like hers at all. The girl was pale with fear. She, too, had heard the violent laughter of an unseen woman!

When I had investigated the Gargoyle and also Salisbury Hall for the first time, I had wondered whether the restless shade of Nell Gwyn might be present in either of the houses. According to my theory she could not very well be in both of them, unless she were a "free spirit" and not a troubled, earthbound ghost. Had there been evidence of Nell Gwyn's presence at Salisbury Hall, once her country retreat?

Some years ago, Sir Winston Churchill's stepfather, Cornwallis-West, had an experience at Salisbury Hall. A guards officer not the least bit interested in psychic phenomena, Mr. Cornwallis-West was sitting in the main hall downstairs when he became aware of a figure of a beautiful girl with blue eyes and red hair coming down the stairs toward him. Fascinated by her unusual beauty, he noticed that she wore a pale cream dress with blue chiffon, and he heard clearly the rustling of silk. At the same time he became conscious of the heavy scent of perfume, a most unusual scent for which there was no logical explanation, such as flowers or the presence of a lady. The figure reached the heavy oaken door near the fireplace and just disappeared *through* it. Cornwallis-West was aware of her ethereal nature by now, and realized it was a ghost. His first thought, however, was that perhaps something dreadful had happened to his old nanny, for the girl reminded him of her. Immediately he telephoned his sister and

A chorine showing the door that kept opening mysteriously

inquired if the woman was all right. He was assured that she was. Only then did it strike him that he had seen an apparition of Nell Gwyn, for the nanny had always been considered a veritable double of the celebrated courtesan. He quickly reinforced his suspicions by inspecting several contemporary portraits of Nell Gwyn, and found that he had indeed seen the onetime owner of Salisbury Hall!

Others living at the Hall in prior years had also met the beautiful Nell. There was the lady with several daughters who occupied Salisbury Hall around 1890. On one of several occasions she was met by a beautiful young girl, perhaps in her late teens, with a blue shawl over her shoulders and dressed in a quaint, old-fashioned costume of an earlier age. The lady assumed it was one of her daughters masquerading to amuse herself, and she followed the elusive girl up the stairs. It was nighttime, and the house was quiet. When the girl with the blue shawl reached the top landing of the stairs, she vanished into thin air!

On checking out all her family, she found them safely asleep in their respective rooms. Nobody owned an outfit similar to the one she had seen the vanished girl wear.

But the phenomena did not restrict themselves to the wraith of beautiful Nell. Christopher, the young son of Mr. and Mrs. Walter Goldsmith, the present owners of the

Her Name Was Trouble: The Secret Adventure of Nell Gwyn

Nell Gwyn in her prime

Charles II and Nell? History is vague about her later years. She had not been murdered nor had she committed suicide, so we cannot ascribe her "continuous presence" in what were once her homes to a tragic death through violence. *What other secret was Nell Gwyn hiding from the world?*

* * *

In September of 1966, I finally managed to take up the leads again and visit the house at 69 Deane Street. This time I had brought with me a psychic by the name of Ronald Hearn, who had been recommended to me by the officers of the College of Psychic Science, of which I am a member. I had never met Mr. Hearn, nor he me, nor did he seem to recognize my name when I telephoned him. At any rate, I told him only that we would need his services for about an hour or so in London, and to come to my hotel, the Royal Garden, where we would start.

Promptly at 9 P.M. Mr. Hearn presented himself. He is a dark-haired, soft-spoken young man in his early thirties, and he did not ask any questions whatever. With me were two New Yorkers, who had come along because of an interest in producing a documentary motion picture with me. Both men were and are, I believe, skeptics, and knew almost nothing about the case or the reasons for our visit to 69 Deane Street, Soho.

It was just a few minutes before ten when we jumped out of a taxi at a corner a block away from the Gargoyle Club. We wanted to avoid Mr. Hearn seeing the entrance sign, and he was so dazzled by the multitude of other signs and the heavy nightclub traffic in the street that he paid no attention to the dark alleyway into which I quickly guided him. Before he had a chance to look around, I had dragged him inside the Gargoyle entrance. All he could see were photographs of naked girls, but then the whole area is rich in this commodity. Nothing in these particular photographs was capable of providing clues to the historical background of the building we had just entered.

I immediately took Hearn up the back stairs toward the dressing rooms to see if it meant anything to him. It did.

"I've got a ghastly feeling," he said suddenly. "I don't want to come up the stairs...almost as if I am afraid to come up and come out here...."

We were standing on the roof now. Jimmy Jacobs had joined us and was watching the medium with fascination. He, too, was eager to find out who was haunting his place.

"My legs are feeling leaden as if something wants to stop me coming out onto this rooftop," Hearn explained. "I feel terribly dizzy. I didn't want to come but something kept pushing me; I've *got* to come up!"

I inquired if he felt a "living" presence in the area. Hearn shook his head in deep thought.

"More than one person," he finally said. "There's a fight going on...someone's trying to get hold of a man,

Hall, reports an experience he will never forget. One night when he occupied his brother Robin's room upstairs, just for that one night, he had a terrifying dream, or perhaps a kind of vision: Two men were fighting with swords—two men locked in mortal combat, and somehow connected with this house.

Christopher was not the only one who had experienced such a fight in that room. Some years before a girl also reported disturbed sleep whenever she used that particular room, which was then a guest room. Two men would "burst out" of the wall and engage in close combat.

There is an earlier specter authenticated for the Hall, dating back to the Cromwellian period. It is the unhappy ghost of a cavalier who was trapped in the Hall by roundheads outside, and, having important documents and knowledge, decided to commit suicide rather than brave capture and torture. The two fighting men might well have reference to that story, but then again they might be part of Nell's—as I was to find out much later.

* * *

The mystery of Nell Gwyn remained: I knew she had died almost forgotten, yet for many years she had been the King's favorite. Even if she had become less attractive with her advancing years, the King would not have withdrawn his favors unless there was another reason. Had something happened to break up that deep-seated love between but someone else doesn't want him to...two people battling...I feel so dizzy...more on the staircase...."

We left the chilly roof and repaired to the staircase, carefully bolting the "haunted door" behind us. We were now standing just inside the door, at the entrance to the dressing room where Cherry Phoenix had encountered the various phenomena described earlier. Unfortunately, music from the show going on below kept intruding, and Hearn found it difficult to let go. I decided to wait until the show was over. We went down one flight and sat down in Jimmy Jacobs' office.

Hearn took this opportunity to report a strange occurrence that had happened to him that afternoon.

"I had no idea where I was going tonight," he explained, "but I was with some friends earlier this evening and out of the blue I heard myself say, 'I don't know where I'm going tonight, but wherever it is, it is associated with Nell Gwyn.' My friend's name is Carpenter and he lives at 13, Linton Road, Kilburn, N.W. 6. His telephone is Maida Vale 1871. This took place at 7:30 P.M."

My skeptic friend from New York thereupon grabbed the telephone and dialed. The person answering the call confirmed everything Hearn had reported. Was it a putup job? I don't think so. Not after what followed.

We went down into the third-floor theater, which was now completely dark and empty. Clouds of stale smoke hanging on in the atmosphere gave the place a feeling of constant human presences. Two shows a night, six days a week, and nothing really changes, although the women do now and then. It is all done with a certain amount of artistic finesse, this undressing and prancing around under the hot lights, but when you add it up it spells the same thing: voyeurism. Still, compared to smaller establishments down the street, Jimmy Jacobs' emporium was high-class indeed.

We sat down at a table to the right hand of the stage, with the glaring night light onstage providing the only illumination. Against this background Ronald's sharp profile stood out with eerie flair. The rest of us were watching him in the dim light, waiting for what might transpire.

"Strange," the psychic said, and pointed at the rotund form of proprietor Jimmy Jacobs looming in the semidarkness, "but I feel some sort of psychic force floating round him, something peculiar, something I haven't met up with before. There's something about you, sir."

Jimmy chuckled.

"You might say there is," he agreed, "you see, I'm psychic myself."

The two psychics then started to compare feelings.

"I feel very, very cold at the spine," Jimmy said, and his usual joviality seemed gone.

He felt apprehensive, he added, rather unhappy, and his eyes felt hot.

"I want to laugh," Hearn said slowly, "but it's not a happy laugh. It's a forced laugh. Covering up something. I feel I want to get out of here, actually. I feel as though in

coming here *I'm trapped.* It's in this room. Someone used to sit here with these feelings, I've been brought here, but I'm trapped, I want to get out! It's a woman. Voluptuous. Hair's red. Long and curled red hair."

We sat there in silent fascination. Hearn was describing the spitting image of Nell Gwyn. But how could he know consciously? It was just another nightclub.

"Fantastic woman...something in her one could almost love, or hate...there's a beauty spot on her cheek ...very full lips, and what a temper...."

Hearn was breathing with difficulty now, as if he were falling into trance. Jimmy sat there motionless, and his voice seemed to trail off.

"Do you know where the Saddlery is?" Jimmy mumbled now, before I could stop him. I wanted one medium at a time.

"Below here," Hearn answered immediately, "two floors below."

"Who'd be in the Saddlery?" Jimmy asked. I motioned him to stay out of it, but he could not see me.

"John," Hearn murmured.

"What's his rank?" Jimmy wanted to know. It was hard to tell whether Jimmy Jacobs, medium, or Jimmy Jacobs, curious proprietor of the Gargoyle Club, was asking.

"Captain," Hearn answered. He was now totally entranced.

"Who was this Captain John?"

"A friend of the King's."

"What did he serve in?"

"Cavalry," the voice coming from Hearn's lips replied.

Jimmy nodded assent. Evidently he was getting the same message.

"What duty?" he asked now.

"In charge of the guard."

Hearn's own personality was completely gone now, and I decided to move in closer.

"Brought here," I heard him mumble.

"Who was brought here?" I asked.

"They made me...to hide...from the King...jealous...."

"For what reason?" The breathing was labored and heavy.

"Tell us who you are!"

"Oh God it's Car...Charles...." The voice was now so excited it could scarcely be understood.

"Whose house is this?" I demanded to know.

"I...." The communicator choked.

"What is your name?"

But the entity speaking through Hearn would not divulge it.

A moment later, the medium awoke, grimacing with pain. He was holding his left arm as if it had been hurt.

"Almost can't move it," he said, with his usual voice.

I often get additional information from a psychic just after the trance ends.

"Was the entity female or male?"

"Female."

"Connected with this house?"

"Yes, yes. She must have lived here, for some time at least."

"Is she still here?"

"Yes."

"What does she want?"

"*She can't leave.* Because she is ashamed of having caused something to happen. She felt responsible for somebody's death."

"Whose death?"

"It was her lover. Somebody was murdered. It has to do with the stairs."

"Is she here alone?"

"No, I think there is somebody else here. There was a fight on the stairs. Two men."

"Who was the other man?"

"He was sent...terrible, I feel like banging my head very hard...."

Evidently Hearn was in a semi-trance state now, not fully out, and not really in, but somewhere in between.

"What period are we in now?" I continued the questioning.

"Long curls and white hats...big hats...Charles the First...."

"Who was the other man who was killed?"

"I can't be sure...."

A sudden outburst of bitter laughter broke through the clammy, cold silence of the room. Hearn was being seized by a spell of laughter, but it wasn't funny at all. I realized he was again being taken over. I asked why he was laughing so hard.

"Why shouldn't I?" came the retort, and I pressed again for a name.

"Are you ashamed of your name?"

"Yes," came the reply, "trouble...*my name was trouble* ...always trouble...I loved too much...."

"Why are you here?"

"Why shouldn't I be here? It is my house."

"Who gave it to you?"

"Charles."

"What do you seek?"

Mad laughter was my answer. But I pressed on, gently and quietly.

"Oh, no...you could pay, love...but the King wouldn't like it...." The voice was full of bitterness and mock hilarity.

"Are you here alone?" I asked.

"No...."

"Who is with you?"

"He is...my lover...John."

"What is his name?"

"He has many names...many...."

Evidently the communicator was having her little fun with me. "What happened to him?"

"He was killed."

"By whom?"

"The King's men."

"Which ones of the King's men?"

"Fortescue."

"What is his rank?"

"Lieutenant."

"Regiment?"

"Guards."

"Who sent him?"

"The King."

"How did he find out?"

"Sometimes...beyond talking...."

"Did you cheat on the King?"

"Yes, many times." Great satisfaction in the voice now.

"Did he give you this house?"

"He did."

"Then why did you cheat?"

"Because he wasn't satisfactory...." It was said with such disdain I almost shuddered. Here was a voice, presumably from the 1660s or 1670s, and still filled with the old passions and emotional outbursts.

"How many years since then?" I said. Perhaps it was time to jolt this entity into understanding the true situation.

"Oh, God...what's time? What's time?! Too much time...."

"Are you happy?"

"No!!" the voice shouted, "No! He killed my lover!"

"But your lover is dead and should be with you now. Would that not give you happiness?" I asked.

"No," the entity replied, "because my lover was the same cheat. Cheat! Oh, my God...that's all these men ever cared about...hasn't changed much, has it? Hahaha...."

Evidently the ghostly communicator was referring to the current use to which her old house was being put. It seemed logical to me that someone of Nell Gwyn's class (or lack of it) would naturally enjoy hanging around a burlesque theater and enjoy the sight of men hungering for women.

"Not much difference from what it used to be."

"How did it used to be?"

"The same. They wanted entertainment, they got it."

If this was really Nell Gwyn and she was able to observe goings-on in the present, then she was a "free spirit," only partially bound to these surroundings. Then, too, she would have been able to appear both here and at her country house whenever the emotional memories pulled her hither or yon.

"Is this your only house?" I asked now.

"No... Cheapside... don't live there much... Smithfield... God, why all these questions?" The voice flared up.

"How do we know you are the person you claim to be?" I countered. "Prove it."

"Oh, my God," the voice replied, as if it were below her dignity to comply.

I recalled Jimmy Jacobs' view that the ghost was an imposter posing as Nell Gwyn.

"Are you an imposter?"

"No..." the voice shot back firmly and a bit surprised.

"Where were you born?"

"Why do you want to know?...What does it matter?..."

"To do you honor."

"Honor? Hahaha.... Sir, you speak of honor?"

"What is your name?"

"I used to have a name.... What does it matter now?"

She refused and I insisted, threatened, cajoled.

Finally, the bitterness became less virulent.

"It is written," she said, "all over... Nell... Nell... God!!!"

There was a moment of silence, and I continued in a quieter vein. Was she happy in this house? Sometimes. Did she know that many years had passed? Yes. Was she aware of the fact that she was not what she used to be?

"What I used to be?" she repeated, "Do you know what I used to be? A slut. A slut!!"

"And what are you now," I said, quietly, "now you're a ghost."

"A ghost," she repeated, pensively, playing with the dreaded word, as I continued to explain her status to her. "Why did they have to fight?" she asked.

"Did you know he was coming?"

"Yes."

"Why didn't you warn him?"

"What could I do? My life or his!"

"I don't understand—do you mean he would have killed *you*?"

"The King was a jealous man," she replied, "always quarrels... he was bald... bald... hahaha... with his wig...."

"Why are you in this part of the building? What is there here for you?"

"Don't I have a right?"

I explained that the house belonged to someone else.

"Do I—disturb—?"

"What are you looking for here?"

"I'm not looking for anything...."

Again, the name Fortescue came from the entranced lips of the medium. "Where did this Fortescue do the

Nell Gwyn, the Royal actress

killing?" I asked. Almost as if every word were wrought with pain, the voice replied.

"On the stairs... near the top...."

"What time was that?"

"Oh, God, time! It was the autumn...."

"Was there anyone with him?"

"Outside."

"Where did you yourself pass over?" I said as gently as I could. There was moment of silence as if she did not understand the question. "You do know you've passed over?" I said.

"No."

"You don't remember?"

"What is there to remember, nobody cares. Why do they use this house, these people?" she demanded to know now. I explained it was a theater.

"Is there any other place you go to, or are you here all the time?"

"I think so...."

"What are the noises for? What do you want?"

"Do you want me to stop the fighting, you hear them fighting on the stairs?..."

"What was John's full name?"

"Molyneaux."

"He was a lieutenant?"

"Captain... in the Guards."

"And Fortescue, what was he?"

"Lieutenant...King's Guards. He was sent by the King."

"What was the order?"

"Kill him...I was terrified...fight with swords...I was below...the salon...."

"What can I do to help you find peace?"

"What is peace?"

"Do you know Salisbury Hall?" I decided to see what the reaction would be.

"You want to know I was his mistress....I was there...sometimes...."

I demanded to have further proof of her identity, but the visitor from beyond demurred.

"Let me go...Why have you come here?"

Again, following Jimmy Jacobs' suggestion, I accused her of being an actress impersonating Nell Gwyn. But the entity did not budge. She was Nell Gwyn, she said, and would not discuss anything about her family.

In retrospect I feel sure she was speaking the truth.

Shortly after, Ronald Hearn woke up. He seemed tired and worn out, but could not recollect anything that had come through him the past hour or so. At any rate he stated he didn't, and while I can never objectively *prove* these absences of a medium's true self, I have no reason to doubt their statements either. We left, and Hearn was driven back to his home in the suburbs.

On September 24, I came back to the Gargoyle Club with Trixie Allingham. It was the end of a very long day which we had spent at Longleat, the ancestral seat of the Marquess of Bath, and I didn't expect too much of Trixie, as even mediums get tired.

But time was short and we had to make the best of our opportunities, so I took her quickly upstairs to the same spot where we had brought Ronald Hearn, a table in the rear of the clubroom.

Trixie looked at the somewhat seedy surroundings of the old place in astonishment. It was clear she had never been in or near anything like it. After all, she was originally a nurse who had turned professional psychic later in life when she discovered her great gift. This wasn't her kind of place, but she was willing to have a go at whatever I wanted of her. It was late afternoon, before the club was open for business, and quite dark already. She did not realize where she was, except that it was some Soho nightclub, and she wanted to get out of it as soon as possible!

* * *

There was a curiously depressing atmosphere all around us, as we sat down in the empty club, breathing stale air mixed with the smoke of the previous night.

"There's a man and a woman concerned," she said immediately, "there's a tragedy...the one she loves is killed." She then continued, "She's tall, rather lovely, dark eyes, pale face."

I wanted to know how she died, but Trixie does not like direct questions as it throws her off her thought track. So I decided to just let her get into the atmosphere of the place by herself, as we watched her intently.

"I'm conscious of a stab...a knife goes through me...there's some triviality here to do *with a garter*." The King of England, of course, was the head of the Order of the Garter, which is considered a royal symbol. Trixie's psychometry was working fine.

"There's something to do with a triangle here," she continued, "also something to do with money...*initial R*...some people looking at a body on the ground... stabbed...she is most unhappy now, tears pouring down her face. I think she said 'marry'....Why on earth am I seeing a bear?!"

While Trixie wondered about the bearskin she was seeing, one of my companions, the American writer Victor Wolfson, commented that the Royal Guards wear a bearskin. I don't like to have any information disclosed during an investigation, but I thanked him and requested that he hold back comments until later.

Meanwhile I asked Trixie to press the female ghost for some proof of her identity, and further personal data.

"Some extraordinary link with the Palace.... Does that sound crazy?" Trixie said, hesitatingly, for her logical mind could not conceive of any connection between a Soho striptease club and Whitehall. I reassured her, and let her continue. "That's what I'm getting...something in French...my French is so poor, what did you say, dear? Someone is to guard her...I'm going back in time for this picture...two men to guard her...darkish men, they've got European dress on, band of silk here...." She indicated the waistline. "Can't quite see them...turbans...M...link with royalty...acting and royalty...and heartache...someone linked with her at the time was ill...Harry...*clandestine meetings* ...real love...betrayal...two men fighting...castle is linked with all this...I hear the words, 'Save for the world...passion...save and deliver me!'"

We were all listening very quietly as the drama unfolded once again.

"It was nighttime," Trixie continued in a halting voice as if the memory were painful. "There was a fog outside...C...Charles...now I'm seeing a prior coming into the room from that door and he is saying, 'Time this was remedied! I've called you here.'...Now I'm seeing a cherub child leading her away and I hear the prior saying, 'Go in peace, you have done what was necessary.'" Trixie put her head into her arms and sighed. "That's all I can give you. I feel so sick."

Since so much of her testimony had matched Ronald Hearn's, and as it was obvious that she was at the end of her psychic day, I felt it would do no harm to try to stimulate some form of reaction with material obtained by Hearn in the hope that it would be further enlarged upon by the second medium. "Does the name Fortescue mean anything to you?" I asked casually. Her facial expression remained the same. It didn't mean anything to her. But she then added, "If it's got to do with an *ancient house*, then it's right. All ancient lineage."

On later checking I found that the Fortescue family was indeed one of England's oldest, although the name is by no means common or even well-known today.

Trixie explained the girl was now gone, but the prior was still around and could be questioned by her psychically.

I asked about Salisbury. Just that one word, not indicating whether I was referring to a man or a place.

"A tall and rather grim-looking place," Trixie commented, "isolated, cold, and gray...dreary...."

The description did indeed fit Salisbury Hall at the time Charles II bought it.

I asked the prior to tell us who the girl was.

"Some link here with royalty." Trixie answered after a moment, presumably of consultation with the invisible priest, "She came and she went...some obscure...linked up with this royal...setup...she rose...then something happened...she was cast off...that caused this tragedy...beautiful person, dark, I don't mean jet-black, but dark by comparison with a blonde, and curls...down to her shoulder...N...*Nell...this is Nell* Gwyn!"

We all rose and cheered. Everything Trixie had said made sense.

Having shot her bow, Trixie now almost collapsed, mumbling, "I'm sorry, that's all I can do. I'm tired."

The spirit had left her in more ways than one, but it was no longer important. Gently we led her downstairs, and one of us took her home to the suburbs where she lives a respectable, quiet life.

On examination of the tapes, it struck me at once how both mediums hit on many similar details of the story. Since neither medium had had any foreknowledge of the place we were going to visit, nor, on arrival, any inkling as to why we were there, nor any way of knowing of each other, one cannot help but assume that both psychics were tuning in on the same past.

There were a number of extraordinary details not otherwise stressed in conventional history.

Both mediums described a triangle, with two men fighting on the roof—where all the hauntings had been observed—and one man going down in death. King Charles, also mentioned by name, had sent one of them, because someone had told him his mistress Nell was deceiving him.

Hearn had described the two men as Captain John Molyneaux of the Cavalry or Royal Guards (who were horseguards), and a Lieutenant Fortescue, also of the Guards. Captain John was the lover, who lived below in the Saddlery, and whose job it had been to guard her for the King. Instead, he had fallen in love with her. Lieutenant Fortescue (sometimes the name is also spelled Fortesque) was dispatched by the King to avenge him and kill the unfaithful officer at the house of his mistress. No first name is given for Fortescue by medium Hearn, but medium Allingham refers to the initial R. Trixie had added that money was involved, and I assumed that the murderer had been promised a bounty, which would seem natural in view of the fact that the killing was not the sort of thing a court of law would condone even if it were the King who had been cuckolded. Thus the need for an inducement to the young officer who did Charles' dirty work!

Evidently, Nell and John had planned to elope and marry, but were betrayed by someone to the King, who

Her Name Was Trouble: The Secret

Adventure of Nell Gwyn

took revenge in the time-honored fashion of having the rival killed and the ex-mistress disgraced. We do know from the records that Nell fell into disfavor with the King during her heyday and died in modest circumstances. The plot became very clear to me now. Nell had seen a chance at a respectable life with a man she loved after years as the King's mistress. That chance was brutally squashed and the crime hushed up—so well, in fact, that none of the official or respected books on the period mention it specifically.

But then, who would know? In the dark of night, a troop of horsemen arrives at the house in the suburbs; quickly and quietly, Fortescue gains entrance, perhaps with the help of the servant who had tipped off the Palace. He races up the narrow stairs to Nell's apartments, find John Molyneaux there and a duel to the finish ensues, up the stairs to the roof. The captain dies at his woman's feet, sending her into a shock that lasts three centuries. The murderer quickly identifies his foe, perhaps takes an object with him to prove that he had killed him, and departs to collect his bounty money.

Behind him a woman hysterical with grief awaits her fate. That fate is not long in coming. Stripped of all her wealth, the result of royal patronage, she is forced to leave the house near the Deanery and retire to more modest quarters. Her health and royal support gone, she slips into obscurity and we know little about her later years.

* * *

But I needed objective proof that Nell Gwyn really lived at that house and, more importantly, that these two men existed. If they were officers, there would have to be some sort of records.

Inquiry at the British Museum revealed that Nell lived in a house at the junction of Meard Street and the Deanery. This is the exact spot of the Gargoyle Club. As far as Fortescue and Molyneaux are concerned, I discovered that both names belonged to distinguished Royalist families. From Edward Peacock's *The Army Lists of the Roundheads and Cavaliers* I learned also that these families were both associated with the Royal Cavalry, then called Dragoons. During the Royalist expedition against Ireland in 1642, under the King's father, Charles I, the third "troop of horse," or cavalry regiment, was commanded by Sir Faithful Fortescue. With him served a younger member of the family by the name of Thomas Fortescue, a cornet at the time, but later most likely advanced to a lieutenancy. I didn't find any "R" Fortescue in the regimental records. But I reread the remark Trixie Allingham had made about his person, and discovered that she mentioned R is being present to identify the body of a slain person! Very likely, the murderer, Fortescue, had wanted to make sure there was no doubt about Molyneaux's identity so he could collect his bounty. Also, Molyneaux came from a family as prominent as his own, and he would not have wanted to leave the body of the slain officer unattended. No, the thing to have done would have been to call in a member of Molyneaux's own family, both to provide identification— and burial!

Was there an R Molyneaux?

I searched the records again, and in C. T. Atkinson's *History of the Royal Dragoons* I discovered that a Richard Molyneaux, being head of the family at that time, had raised two regiments for Charles II. I also found that the name John was frequently used in the Molyneaux family, even though I haven't located a John Molyneaux serving in the Royal Guards at the exact period under discussion. Was his name stricken from the records after the murder? The King could order such drastic removal from official records, of course.

* * *

I should emphasize at this point that linking the family names of Molyneaux and Fortescue with Charles II and his time is highly specialized knowledge of history, and not the sort of thing that is taught in schools or found in well-known books about the period.

Thus we knew who the ghostly woman at the Gargoyle Club was and why she could not find rest. We knew the cause of the tragedy, and had discovered an obscure chapter in the life of not-so-Good King Charles.

In the process of this investigation, a royal trollop had turned into a woman who found love too late and death too soon.

Judging from similar investigations and the techniques employed in them, I can safely say, however, that Nell and her John are at last united in a world where the Royal Guards have no power and even King Charles can walk around without a wig, if he so desires.

Ghosts Around Vienna

WHAT GHOSTS ARE, you know by now, and those of my readers who are unfamiliar with the term *gemütlichkeit* ought to be told that it is a German word meaning "pleasant, go-easy way of life." When we flew into Hamburg, we did not expect *gemütlichkeit*, which is mostly found in southern countries like Switzerland and Austria anyway. But we found a genuine interest in psychic matters among radio and television people, although the vast masses of Germans are quite unaware of the seriousness with which sixth-sense experiences are studied in the Anglo-Saxon world. A small, keenly intelligent minority is, of course, trying to establish research on a respectable basis. Hans Bender and his parapsychological laboratory at Freiburg are unique, though. In Hamburg, we met with Erich Maria Koerner, author and translator of books on extrasensory perception, and Milo Renelt, a medium, called "the seer of Hamburg." But, simply because people are reluctant to talk, we could not find any leads to haunted houses, of which there must be many.

Upon arriving in Vienna, Austria, we went to see Countess Zoe Wassilko-Serecki, the president of the Austrian society for psychical research. She brought us up to date on the situation in Austria, where the press was openly hostile and derisive of any serious efforts to report parapsychological studies. An American of Austrian descent myself, I found the use of the local tongue most helpful when I called on the television and radio people the next day. I quickly found out that radio would have nothing to do with me, since a local magician had convinced the responsible producers that all psychic experiences were hokum and could be reproduced by him at will. Somewhat more of an open mind awaited me at the newly created television headquarters of Austrian TV, which is about ten years behind ours, but full of good will and operating under great handicaps of low budgets and pressures. Finally, a reporter named Kaiser agreed to accompany Catherine and me on a ghost hunt and to do a straight reporting job, without bias or distortion. I must say he kept his word.

We drove to the Imperial Castle, which is a sprawling array of buildings in the very heart of Vienna. There we went on foot into the portion known as Amalienburg, the oldest part of the castle. All I had to go on was a slim report that a ghost had been observed in that area.

Right off the bat, Kaiser turned to the police officer at the gate and asked him if he knew of any ghosts.

"Ghosts?" the officer asked, somewhat perplexed, and scratched his head. "None that I know of." He suggested we pay the *Burghauptmann*, or governor, a visit.

The governor was a fortyish gentleman with the unusual name of Neunteufel, which means Nine Devils. Far from being hellish, however, he invited us into his office and listened respectfully, as Kaiser explained me to him. Considering that we were in arch-Catholic Vienna, in the inner offices of a high government official, I admired his courage. But then Kaiser had admitted to me, privately, that he had experienced an incident of telepathy he could not dismiss. His open-mindedness was not a drafty head but sincere.

"Well," the governor finally said, "I am so sorry, but I've only been in this post for five years. I know nothing whatever about ghosts. But there is an old employee here who might be able to help you."

My heart had begun to falter and I saw myself being ridiculed on television. "Please, boys," I said inaudibly, addressing my friends upstairs, "help us a little."

Mr. Neunteufel dialed and asked to speak to a Mr. Sunday. There was a pause. "Oh, I see," he then said. "You mean Mr. Sunday isn't in on Friday?" Black Friday, I thought! But then the governor's face brightened. Mr. Sunday would be over in a moment.

The man turned out to be a quiet, soft-spoken clerk in his later years. He had worked here practically all his adult life. "Yes," he nodded. "There is indeed a ghost here; but not in the Amalienburg. Come, I'll show you where."

You could have heard a pin drop, or, for that matter, a ghost walk, when he had spoken. Kaiser gave me a look of mixed admiration and puzzlement. He and his cameraman were already on their feet.

With the governor at our side, we followed Sunday up and down a number of stairs, along corridors, through musty halls, and again up a staircase into a back portion of the castle.

"I've never been here myself," the governor apologized to me, as we walked. "In fact, I didn't even know this part existed," he added.

What the hell! I thought. It's a big house.

Now we stood in front of a *Marterl*, a peculiarly Austrian type of Blessed Virgin altar built into the wall and protected by a metal screen. To the left were the stairs we had come up on, and to our right was another, smaller stairway, closed off by a wooden door.

"Where are we?" Kaiser asked.

"This is the private apartment of Baroness Vecera," Sunday said.

Baroness Vecera was the sweetheart of Crown Prince Rudolph. They were central characters of the famed Meyerling tragedy, resulting in a major national scandal that rocked the Austria of the 1880s.

"The Crown Prince arranged for this flat," Sunday explained, "so he could see his lady friend quietly and privately. These stairs are not marked on the plans of the building."

"No wonder!" The governor sighed with relief.

Part of the castle had evidently been rented out to private citizens in recent years, since the Republic had toppled the monarchy, and the officials of the castle had paid scant attention to that wing since then.

"Has anyone seen a ghost here?" I inquired.

Sunday nodded. "A *Jaeger* reported seeing a white woman here some years ago, under the Empire." A *Jaeger* is a soldier belonging to a Tyrolean or other Alpine regiment. "Then there is the guard Beran," Sunday continued, "who saw this white woman right here, by the altar of the Virgin Mary. As a matter of fact, many servants have seen her, too."

"When did all this start—I mean, how far back has she been seen?" I asked.

"Not too far back," Sunday answered, "about eighty years or so."

Since the death of Rudolph and Vecera, then, I thought. Of course! This was their home, the only refuge where they could meet in secrecy. There are among historians growing voices that say the suicide of Meyerling wasn't a suicide at all, but an execution.

Would the restless ghost of Baroness Vecera demand satisfaction or was the specter of her remorseful form praying by the shrine, seeking forgiveness for the tragedy she had caused?

Sunday now took us farther down the narrowing corridor into what must have been the oldest part of the castle. The thick walls and tiny slit windows suggested a fortress rather than a showplace of the Habsburgs.

"Not long ago," he said, "a patient of Dr. Schaefer, who had his offices here, saw a Capuchin monk walk down the corridor."

"What would a monk be doing here?" I demanded.

"In the early days, the Emperors kept a small number of monks here for their personal needs. There was a Capuchin monastery built into the castle at this very spot."

We waited for a while, but no Capuchin showed up. They were probably all too busy down in the Imperial Crypt, where the Capuchin Fathers do a thriving tourist business letting visitors look at the gaudy Imperial coffins for fifty cents a head.

I looked at Kaiser, and there was a thoughtful expression on his face.

We returned to the TV studio and filmed some footage, showing me with photographs of haunted houses. Then a reporter took down my dialogue, and the following day, as is their custom, the daily newsreel commentator read the story of our ghost hunt to some seven million Austrians who had never before been told of psychic research.

The chain of events is sometimes composed of many links. A friend of a friend in New York introduced me to Herta Fisher, a medium and student of the occult, who, in turn, suggested that I contact Edith Riedl when in Vienna.

Mrs. Riedl offered to take us to the two haunted castles I wanted to visit in southern Austria. In fact, even before I arrived in Vienna, she was able to help me. The *Volksblatt*, a local newspaper, had published a highly distorted report of my activities two weeks before our arrival. Mrs. Riedl sent me the clipping for such action as I might see fit to take.

I picked up the phone and dialed the *Volksblatt*.

"The 'responsible editor,' please," I said, in German. Austrian newspapers employ "responsible editors," usually minor clerks, who must take the blame whenever the newspaper publishes anything libelous.

"Hello," said a pleasantly soft voice on the other end of the line.

"Hello, yourself," I replied. "Did you not publish a piece about Hans Holzer, the Ghost Hunter, recently?"

"*Ja, ja,*" the voice said. "We did."

"Well," I said in dulcet tones, "I am he, and I'm suing you for five million schillings."

There was a gasp at the other end. "Wait!" the voice pleaded. "Let us talk this over."

The following afternoon, Turhan Bey drove us to the editorial offices of the newspaper, awaiting our return in a nearby café. I had a 3 o'clock appointment with the publisher. At 3:15 I reminded the receptionist that time was of the essence. When nothing further had happened five minutes later, I sent in my card with a note: "Sorry can't wait —am on my way to my lawyer, from whom you will hear further."

Faster than you can say "S. O. B.," the publisher came running. I repaired to his offices, where I was joined by his editor and a man named Hannes Walter, a reporter.

It was agreed that I could indeed sue for libel.

But they were willing to print another piece, far more thorough and bereft of any libelous matter. Would I agree?

I always believe in giving felons a second chance. When I read the piece a few weeks later, I realized I should have sued instead. Mainly the brain child of Herr Walter, it was still full of innuendoes, although it did report my activities with some degree of accuracy. Austrian TV is only ten years old and its press goes back several hundred years—yet the only fair treatment I received in public was on the home screens. As is the case in many countries, newspapermen frequently underestimate the intelligence of their readers. That is why so many TV sets are sold.

Mrs. Riedl turned out to be a cultured lady in her late fifties or early sixties, capable of speaking several languages, and full of intellectual curiosity. Of noble Hungarian ancestry, she is married to one of the owners of the Manners chocolate factory, and lives in a sprawling villa in the suburb of Dornbach.

At first, she was to drive us to the Burgenland Province in her car, but, when Turhan Bey offered to come along, we switched to his larger car. The four of us made a marvelous team as we discovered mutual bonds in many areas. I wanted to know more about Edith Riedl's mediumship, and asked her to tell me all about herself.

We were rolling towards the south, that part of Austria annexed in 1919 which had been a Hungarian province for many centuries, although the people of the area always spoke both German and Hungarian. Soon we left the sprawling metropolis of Vienna behind us and streaked down the southern highway towards the mountains around Wiener Neustadt, an industrial city of some importance. Here we veered off onto a less-traveled road and began our descent into the Burgenland, or Land of Castles.

"Tell me, Mrs. Riedl," I asked, "when did you first notice anything unusual about yourself—I mean, being psychic?"

Speaking in good English interlarded with an occasional German or French word, the lively little lady talked freely about herself. "I was only three years old when I had my first experience," she replied. "I was in my room when I saw, outside my window smoke billowing, as if from a fire. This, of course, was only an impression—there was no smoke."

"'We'll get a war!' I cried, and ran to my mother. Imagine a small child talking about war. I certainly did not know the meaning of the word I was using!"

"Amazing," Turhan Bey said, and I agreed. I had never before heard of psychic experiences at such an early age.

"Thirty years later, the house was hit by a bomb, and smoke rose indeed at the spot where I had seen it as a child, and the house burned down."

"When was the next time you experienced anything unusual along psychic lines?" I asked. The countryside was getting more and more rustic and we encountered fewer cars now.

"I was seventeen years old. A cousin of mine served with the Hungarian Hussar Regiments, and we were engaged to be married. The First World War was already on, but he did not serve at the front. He was stationed deep inside the country, near Heidenschaft."

"'I don't mind fighting at the front,' he often told me. 'I'm not afraid of the enemy. The only thing I'm afraid of, somehow, is fog.'"

"Fog?" I said. "Strange for a Hussar officer in Hungary to worry about fog. You don't have much fog down here, do you?"

"No, I couldn't understand why fog could be something for him to fear. Well, Christmas came, and I sent him a card, showing an angel. Without thinking much about it, I wrote the word 'Peace' into the halo of the angel, and sent the card off to my fiancé."

"Later, I regretted this—after all, one should wish a soldier victory, not peace—I wanted the card back, because the whole idea bothered me. I got the card back all right—with a notation by a strange hand across it, reading, 'Died in service, December 22nd.'"

"I couldn't understand how he could have died in the war at Heidenschaft, where there was no enemy within many hundred miles. I felt terrible. I wanted to die, too. I went to my room and put out the lights; I wanted to go to bed early. I was not yet asleep—in fact, still wide awake—when I saw a kind of light near me, and within this luminous disc I recognized a rock, a tree, and at the bottom of the tree, a crumbled mass of something I did not have the courage to look at closely. I knew at this moment that I could either join him in death, or live on. Being very young, my life force triumphed. As I decided to stick to the world of the living, the vision slowly lost color and faded away. But I still wondered how he could have died where he was stationed. The vision immediately returned, but my power of observation was weakening; perhaps the excitement was too much for me. At any rate, I could not make it out clearly.

"The next morning, I reported the incident to my parents. Mother and father looked at each other. 'It is better to tell her,' mother said, but my father shook, his head. A year passed by, but I had never forgotten my fiancé.

"One day I helped my father sort some papers in his study. As I helped him go through his desk, my eyes fell on a letter with a black border. I had the feeling it had to do with Francis, my fiancé. I asked my father if I could take it, and my father, preoccupied with his own affairs, nodded in affirmation.

"I immediately went to my own room and opened the black-bordered letter. It was from one of Francis' friends, and he told the family how my fiancé had died. He was flying a small plane on a reconnaissance mission towards the Italian front, but he was stopped short by sudden fog. In the dense fog, he underestimated his altitude and hit a rock. The plane broke into pieces and his body was later found at the foot of a tree. Just as I had seen in my vision!"

"I believe you mentioned to me some startling experiences with premonitions—your ability to warn of impending disaster," I said.

"It happens quite often," Mrs. Riedl replied. "During the last war, for instance, on one occasion when my children were away at Laa on Theyer, in school, I went to visit them by school bus along with many children and a few mothers. I was seated behind the driver, when there was one of those sudden thunderstorms we have in the area. Suddenly, I heard myself shout to the driver, 'Stop, stop at once!'

"He stopped and turned around. 'Are you out of your mind? What is it?' he demanded. Before he had finished talking, a huge tree fell onto the road hitting the spot where the bus would have been if I hadn't stopped it.

"On another occasion, after the last war, my daughter and I were invited to go to Mistelbach, out in the country, to a wedding. At that time it was not possible to use your own car, trains weren't running yet, and transportation was quite primitive.

"There were two groups of people: one was our wedding party, the other was a funeral party also going in that direction. Transportation was by bus. Our numbers were called, and we were about to board the bus, when I cried out to my daughter, 'Come back, this isn't our bus.'

"Our entire group turned back and I was asked why I had recalled them, when our numbers had obviously been called.

"I could not tell them. I never know why I do these things. All I know is I must do it.

"Meanwhile the other party, those going to that funeral, boarded the bus, taking our place. I said, 'The bus is supposed to return to take us next.'"

"Did it?" I asked.

"The bus was supposed to come back in half an hour. Three hours went by and no bus. Then the news came—there had been an accident. We were saved by my warning, but the funeral party were badly hurt."

"How often have you had these warning flashes?"

"Maybe twenty times during the last five years."

"You also have the ability to sense where objects might be safe, as well as people, isn't that right?"

"Yes," Mrs. Riedl nodded. "As you know my husband has a valuable collection of rare books. When war broke out, he decided to send the most valuable ones to a safe place in the country. But as soon as the books had been unloaded there, I had to order the driver to take them back again. I felt the place was far from safe. We went to a parish house and tried to hide them there, but again something warned me against the location. Finally, we did unload the books at another parish house. The priest had already received some books belonging to a Vienna book seller and invited me to add ours to this pile. But I politely refused. Instead, I went around until I found what my inner voice told me was the only safe place in the house: the washroom!"

"How did the priest take that?"

"Well, he didn't like it. He remonstrated with me, but to no avail. As it turned out, the house was consumed by fire, except the washroom, and our books were safe at the end of the war!"

"Have you accepted this gift of yours as something that is part of you?"

"Certainly. Just think how much good it has brought me already."

By now we had reached the border country where Hungary met Austria, and we had to be careful not to pierce the Iron Curtain accidentally by taking the wrong road. The land was green and fertile and the road ran between pleasant-looking hills sometimes crowned by ancient castles or fortresses, a striking demonstration of how the country got its name—Land of Castles.

Our destination was Forchtenstein, a yellow-colored compound of imposing buildings sitting atop a massive hill that rises straight out of the surrounding landscape. As we wound our way up the hill we could see its towers beckoning to us.

Shortly after, we drove up at the imposing castle and Turhan parked the car. This is one of the biggest of Esterhazy castles, of which there are many, since that family was wealthy and powerful in Hungary and southeastern Austria for many centuries, and though the Communists have taken the Esterhazy lands in Hungary, the family still controls huge estates in Austria, and is likely to continue to do so. Today, Forchtenstein is run as a museum. Its fortifications, long, vaulted galleries and rooms, its magnificent collection of paintings, and enough medieval and seventeenth-century arms to equip a small army make it a major tourist attraction in this part of Central Europe. Although it was started in the fourteenth century, it really reached importance only in the time of the Turkish wars, when the Crescent and Star were very near indeed.

During that time also the Court of Justice for the entire land was held here and executions took place in the courtyard.

We passed over the front ditch, over a wooden bridge, into the outer courtyard.

"There are noises and all sorts of goings on in this castle," Mrs. Riedl explained.

"There is a well, four hundred and twenty feet deep, dug out by Turkish prisoners of war. When the well was completed, the prisoners were thrown into it. I am sure some of them are still around."

"How do you know?"

"Many people have heard sighing in the vicinity of the well."

Turhan Bey, who is half Turkish, half Austrian, smiled. "I am here as an ambassador of peace," he said.

"Also chain rattling," Mrs. Riedl continued.

"Did you ever feel anything unusual here?"

"I was here once before," Mrs. Riedl replied, "and whenever I could be by myself, away from the others in the group being shown around, I felt a presence. Someone wanted to tell me something, perhaps to plead with me for help. But the guide drove us on, and I could not find out who it was."

If there is one thing I dislike intensely, it is guided tours of anything. I went to the local guide and asked him for a private tour. He insisted I buy a dozen tickets, which is the smallest number of people he could take around. We started out at once, four humans, and eight ghosts. At least I paid for eight ghosts.

We walked into the inner courtyard now, where a stuffed crocodile hung high under the entrance arch, which reminded us of the days when the Esterhazys were huntsmen all over the world.

"This is supposed to scare away evil spirits," Mrs. Riedl remarked.

"They must have had a bad conscience, I guess," I said grimly. The Hungarians certainly equaled the Turks in brutality in those days.

We walked past the monument to Paul Esterhazy, ornamented with bas-reliefs showing Turkish prisoners of war in chains, and into the castle itself. Our guide led us up the stairs onto the roof which is now overgrown with shrubbery and grass.

Suddenly, Mrs. Riedl grabbed my arm. "Over there, I feel I am drawn to that spot. Somebody suffered terribly here."

We retraced our steps and followed to where she pointed. The ground was broken here, and showed a small opening, leading down into the castle.

"What is underneath?" I asked our guide.

"The dungeon," he replied. He didn't believe in ghosts. Only in tourists.

Quickly we went down into the tower. At the gate leading into the deep dungeon itself, we halted our steps. Mrs. Riedl was trembling with deep emotion now.

"Somebody grabbed my skirts up there," she said, and pointed to the roof we had just left, "as if trying to call attention to itself."

I looked down into the dimly lit dungeon. A clammy feeling befell all of us. It was here that the lord of the castle threw his enemies to die of starvation. One time he was absent from the castle, leaving its administration to his wife, Rosalie. She mistreated some of his guests and on his return he had her thrown into this dungeon to die herself.

Her ghost is said to haunt the castle, although her husband, taken with either remorse or fear of the ghost, built a chapel dedicated to Rosalie, on a nearby hill.

"What do you feel here?" I asked Mrs. Riedl.

"A woman plunged down here from a very high place. I feel her very strongly."

"What does she want?"

Mrs. Riedl kept still for a moment, then answered in a trembling voice, "I think she wants us to pray for her."

With the guide pointing the way, we walked up another flight of stairs into the private chapel of the Esterhazys. To a man with twelve tickets there were no closed doors.

Mrs. Riedl quickly grabbed the railing of the gallery and started to pray fervently. Underneath, in the chapel itself, the lights of many candles flickered.

After a moment or two, Edith Riedl straightened up. "I think she feels relieved now," she said.

We continued our inspection of the building. "This is the execution chamber," the guide said casually, and pointed out the execution chair and sword. Then the guide, whose name is Leitner, took us to the prisoners' well, showing us its enormous depth by dropping a lighted flare into it. It took the flare several seconds to hit bottom. "Five thousand Turks built it in thirteen years' time," he said.

Mrs. Riedl stepped closer to the opening of the well, then shrank back. "Terrible," she mumbled. "I can't go near it."

I wondered how many of the murdered Turks were still earthbound in this deep shaft.

*　*　*

Outside, there was sunshine and one of those very pleasant late-summer afternoons for which southern Austria is famous.

We passed the chapel dedicated to Rosalie, but in our hearts we knew that it had not done much good. Quite possibly our visit had done more for the tormented spirit of the ancient *Burgfrau* than the self-glorifying building atop the hill.

We consulted the maps, for our next destination, Bernstein, lay some thirty miles or more to the west. We drove through the backwoods of the land, quiet little villages with nary a TV aerial in sight, and railroad tracks that hadn't seen a train in years. It was getting cooler and darker and still no sign of Bernstein!

I began to wonder if we had not taken a wrong turn somewhere when all of a sudden we saw the castle emerge from behind a turn in the road.

Not as imposing as Forchtenstein, Bernstein impresses one nevertheless by its elegance and Renaissance-like appearance within a small but cultured park. There is a mine of semiprecious stones called *smaragd* nearby, and the downstairs houses a shop where these stones are on display. This is a kind of wild emerald, not as valuable as a real one, of course, but very pretty with its dark green color and tones.

Bernstein castle goes back to the thirteenth century and has changed hands continuously between Austrian and Hungarian nobles. Since 1892 it has belonged to the Counts Almassy, Hungarian "magnates" or aristocrats.

We arrived at a most inappropriate time. The Count had a number of paying guests which helped defray the expenses of maintaining the large house, and it was close to dinner time. Nevertheless, we were able to charm him into taking us to the haunted corridor.

On November 11, 1937, Count Almassy, a tall, erect man now in his late sixties, was sitting in his library when one of his guests asked for a certain book. The library can be reached only by walking down a rather narrow, long corridor connecting it with the front portion of the building.

"I left the library, walked down the passage with a torch—I don't like to turn on the main lights at night— well, when I came to this passage, I saw by the light of my torch [flashlight] a female figure kneeling in front of a wooden Madonna that stands at that spot. It was placed there in 1914 by my mother when both my brothers and I were away in the war. Of course I had often heard talk of a

'White Lady of Bernstein,' so I realized at once that I was seeing a ghost. My first impression was that she looked like a figure cast in plaster of Paris with hard lines. She wore a Hungarian noblewoman's dress of the fifteenth century, with a woman's headgear and a big emerald-green stone on her forehead which threw a dim, green light around her. She had her hands folded under her left cheek."

"What did you do when you saw her?" I asked.

"I had time to switch on the light in the passage," the Count replied, "so that I had her between two lights, that of my torch and the electric light overhead. There was no possible mistake, I saw her clearly. Then just as suddenly, she vanished."

"What is the tradition about this ghost, Count Almassy?" I asked.

"Well, she is supposed to be an Italian woman, Catherine Freschobaldi—of a Florentine family which still exists, in fact—mentioned in Dante's *Inferno*. She married a Hungarian nobleman, Count Ujlocky, of a very old Hungarian family. Her husband was the last King of Bosnia. The family died out. He was very jealous, without any reason, and so he killed her, according to one version, by stabbing her; according to another, by walling her in. That is the story."

"Has anyone else seen the White Lady of Bernstein?"

"Many people. When I was a boy, I remember every year someone or other saw her. When I was in the army,

between 1910 and 1913, she was seen many, many times. In 1921 she was seen again when there were Hungarian occupation troops garrisoned at Bernstein during the short-lived Austro-Hungarian campaign of that year—and the ghostly lady chased them away! Then, of course, in 1937, as I told you, and that was the last time I saw her."

"I believe also that a friend of yours saw her in Africa in the Cameroons? How does this fit in?"

Count Almassy laughed. "Well, that's another story, that one. An Army friend of mine—I really did not know him too well, I met him in 1916, and he left Austria in 1937 and bought a farm in the Cameroons. He became a wealthy man. In 1946 he experienced a strange incident.

"An apparition very much like the White Lady of Bernstein (although he knew nothing whatever about our ghost) appeared to him and spoke to him in Italian.

"In 1954 he came to see me to check on the story this ghost had told him. The ghost claimed to be the famous White Lady and he decided to come to Austria to see if there was such a ghost."

"Remarkable," I said. "I can only assume that the apparition in the Cameroons was a thought projection, unless, of course, your ghost is no longer bound to this castle."

The Count thought for a moment. "I do hope so," he finally said. "This is a drafty old castle and Africa is so much warmer."

✳ 22

The Secret of Mayerling

IN A WORLD RIFE with dramatic narratives and passionate love stories, with centuries of history to pick and choose from, motion picture producers of many lands have time and again come back to Mayerling and the tragic death of Crown Prince Rudolph of Austria as a subject matter that apparently never grows stale.

This is probably so because the romantic Mayerling story satisfies all the requirements of the traditional tear-jerker: a handsome, misunderstood prince who cannot get along too well with his stern father, the Emperor; a loving but not too demonstrative wife whom the prince neglects; a brazen young girl whose only crime is that she loves the prince—these are the characters in the story as seen through Hollywood eyes.

To make sure nobody objects to anything as being immoral, the two lovers are shown as being truly in love with each other—but as the prince is already married, this love cannot be and he must therefore die. The Crown Princess gets her husband back, albeit dead. In the motion

picture version the political differences between father and son are completely neglected, and the less-than-sterling qualities of the young Baroness Vetsera are never allowed to intrude on the perfect, idyllic romance.

The prince goes to the Prater Park in Vienna, sees and falls in love with the young woman, secret meetings are arranged, and love is in bloom. But then the piper must be paid. Papa Franz Josef is upset, reasons of state must be considered, and commoners (to a crown prince a mere baroness is like a commoner!) do not marry the heir to the imperial throne. They could run away and chuck it all—but they don't. In this perhaps, the movie versions come closer to the truth than they realized: Rudolph would never have run off, and Vetsera was too much in love with him to do anything against his wishes.

Nothing is made of the Emperor's political jealousy or the total lack of love between the crown prince and the wife that was forced upon him by his father. In the pictures, she is the wronged woman, a pillar of moral concern to the millions of married moviegoers who have paid to see this opus.

There is apparently a never-ending attraction in the yarn about an unhappy, melancholy prince in love with a young woman who wants to die for and with him. Perhaps the thrill of so close a juxtaposition of life-creating love and life-taking death holds the secret to this powerful message, or perhaps it is the age-old glamor of princely intrigue and dashing romance that keeps moviegoers enthralled from generation to generation.

But does this tell the *true* story of the tragedy that came to a head at the imperial hunting lodge at Mayerling, or were the real secrets of Mayerling quite different?

To seek an understanding of the unfortunately rather grim facts from which the screenwriters have spun their romantic versions, we must, first of all, look at the secret undercurrents of political life in the Austrian Empire of the 1880s.

For decades, the military powers of the great empire had been declining, while Germany's star had kept rising. A reactionary political system holding sway over Austria seemed out of step with the rest of Europe. A reluctance on the part of a starchy court and its government to grant any degree of self-determination to the many foreign elements in the empire's population was clearly leading toward trouble.

Especially there was trouble brewing with the proud Hungarians. Never reconciled to the incorporation of their kingdom into the Austrian Empire, the Magyars had openly rebelled in 1848 and done it with such force that the Austrians had to call for Russian troops to help them.

In 1849 the revolt was quashed, and Hungary became more enslaved than ever. But the struggle that had been lost on the battlefield continued in Parliament and the corridors of the Imperial Palace. Hungary pressed for its national identity until, in 1867, the government gave in: the so-called *Ausgleich*, or reconciliation, acknowledged the existence of a Hungarian nation, and the Empire was changed into a dual monarchy, with separate Austrian and Hungarian parliaments, ministers, and of course languages, all under the rule of the Habsburg Emperor.

Austro-Hungary was now a weaker, but less turbulent giant, united only around the person of its ruler, the aging Emperor Franz Josef. Still, the Hungarian magnates pursued a separatist policy, gradually driving wedges between the two halves of the Danube monarchy, while the Germanic Austrian ruling class tried everything within its power to contain the Hungarians and to keep a firm upper hand.

By the 1880s there was no question of another armed insurrection. The Hungarians knew it would be unsuccessful, and they weren't going to take a chance unless they were sure of positive results. But they thought they could get greater attention for Hungarian affairs, greater influence by Hungarians in the councils of state and in trade matters. The Magyars were on the march again, but without a leader.

Then they found a sympathetic ear in the most unlikely quarter, however: Rudolph, the crown prince, who had grown up in the shadow of his illustrious father, but who was also very critical of his father's political accomplishments, because he did not share his father's conservative views.

Rudolph was born in 1858, and in 1888 he was exactly thirty years old. Although he was the heir apparent and would some day take over the reins of the government, he was permitted little more than ceremonial duties. He had himself partly to blame for this situation, for he was outspoken, and had made his sympathies with the underdogs of the Empire well known. He did not hold his tongue even among friends, and soon word of his political views reached the Court. Even if his father had wanted to overlook these views, the Prime Minister, Count Eduard von Taaffe, could not. To him, an archconservative, Rudolph was clearly not "on the team," and therefore had to be watched.

Hoping to keep Rudolph from the center of political activity, Count von Taaffe managed to get the crown prince and the crown princess sent to Hungary, but it turned out to be a mistake after all. While residing in Budapest, Rudolph endeared himself to the Hungarian partisans, and if he had nurtured any doubts as to the justice of their cause, he had none when he returned to Vienna.

Also, during his sojourn in Hungary, Rudolph had learned to be cautious, and it was a sober, determined man who re-entered the princely apartments of the Imperial Castle. Located on the second floor in the central portion of the palace and not very close to the Emperor's rooms, these apartments could easily be watched from both inside the walls and from the outside, if one so desired, and Count von Taaffe desired just that.

Perhaps the most fascinating of recent Mayerling books is a bitter denunciation of the Habsburg world and its tyranny underneath a façade of Viennese smiles. This book was written in English by Hungarian Count Carl Lonyay, whose uncle married the widowed ex-Crown Princess Stephanie. Lonyay inherited the private papers of that lady after her death, and with it a lot of hitherto secret information. He did a painstaking job of using only documented material in this book, quoting sources that still exist and can be checked, and omitting anything doubtful or no longer available, because of Franz Josef's orders immediately after the tragedy that some very important documents pertaining to Rudolph's last days be destroyed.

"Rudolph was a virtual prisoner. He was kept under strict surveillance. No one could visit him unobserved. His correspondence was censored." Thus Lonyay describes the situation after Rudolph and Stephanie returned to the old Imperial Castle.

Under the circumstances, the Crown Prince turned more and more to the pursuit of women as a way to while away his ample free time. He even kept a diary in which each new conquest was given a rating as to standing and desirability. Although Rudolph's passing conquests were many, his one true friend in those days was Mizzi Kaspar,

The Secret of Mayerling: The hunting lodge, now a Carmelite monastery today

an actress, whom he saw even after he had met the Baroness Vetsera.

Mizzi was more of a confidante and mother confessor to the emotionally disturbed prince, however, than she was a mistress. Moodiness runs in the Habsburg family, and mental disease had caused the death of his mother's cousin, Louis II of Bavaria. Thus, Rudolph's inheritance was not healthy in any sense, and his knowledge of these facts may have contributed to his fears and brooding nature, for it is true that fear of unpleasant matters only hastens their arrival and makes them worse when they do occur, while rejection of such thoughts and a positive attitude tend to smooth their impact.

There is a persistent hint that Rudolph's illness was not only mental, but that he had somehow also contracted venereal disease along the highways and byways of love. In the latter years of his life he often liked the company of common people in the taverns of the suburbs, and found solace among cab drivers and folksingers.

As Rudolph's frustrations grew and he found himself more and more shunted away from the mainstream of political activity, he often hinted that he wished to commit suicide. Strangely, he did not expect death to end all his problems: He was not a materialist, but he had mystical beliefs in a hereafter and a deep curiosity about what he would find once he crossed the threshold.

Perhaps this direction of his thoughts got its start after an incident during his residence in Prague some years before. At that time, the daughter of a Jewish cantor saw him pass by and immediately fell in love with the prince. Her parents sent her away from Prague, but she managed

to get back and spent the night sitting underneath his windows. The next morning she had contracted pneumonia, and in short order she died. Word got to the Crown Prince and he was so touched by this that he ordered flowers put on her grave every day. Although he had conquered many women and immediately forgotten them, the attachment of the one girl he had never even met somehow turned into a romantic love for her on his part. Until he crossed paths with Mary Vetsera, this was the only true love of his life, unfulfilled, just as his ambitions were, and very much in character with his nihilistic attitudes.

Now, in the last year of life, he kept asking people to commit suicide with him so that he need not enter the new world alone. "Are you afraid of death?" he would ask anyone who might listen, even his coachmen. A classical Austrian answer, given him a day before his own death, came from the lips of his hired cab driver, Bratfisch:

"When I was in the Army, no, I wasn't afraid of death. *I wasn't permitted to.* But now? Yes."

It didn't help to put Rudolph's mind at rest. But people who announce beforehand their intentions to do away with themselves, seldom carry out their threat.

"Rudolph announced his decision to commit suicide, verbally and in writing, to a number of persons. Of these, not even his father, his wife, his cousin, or the two officers on his staff ever made a serious attempt to prevent him from carrying out his plan, although it was clear for all to see that Rudolph's state of mind gave rise to grave concern," Lonyay reports.

But despite this longing for death, Rudolph continued a pretty lively existence. It was on November 5, 1888 that he saw Mary Vetsera for the first time in the Freudenau, a part of the large Prater Park that was famed for its racing. She was not yet eighteen, but had led anything but a sheltered life. The daughter of the widowed Baroness Helen Vetsera had already had a love affair with a British officer in Cairo at age sixteen, and was developed beyond her years. Her mother's family, the Baltazzis, were of "Levantine" origin, which in those days meant anything beyond the Hungarian frontiers to the east. Lonyay calls them Greeks, but Lernet-Holenia describes them as Jewish or part-Jewish. Their main claim to fame was interest in, and a knowledge of, horse breeding, and since Vienna was a horsey city, this talent opened many doors to them that would otherwise have remained closed. Helen's husband, Victor von Vetsera, had been an interpreter at the Austrian Embassy in Constantinople, and this later enabled her to move to Vienna with her daughter Mary.

What struck Rudolph immediately when he saw the girl was her similarity to the cantor's daughter who had died for him in Prague. Although they had never spoken, he had once glimpsed her and did remember her face. Mary had lots to offer on her own: She was not beautiful in the strictest sense, but she appeared to be what today we call "very sexy."

After the initial casual meeting in the Freudenau, Mary herself wrote the prince a letter expressing a desire to meet again. Rudolph was, of course, interested, and asked his cousin, Countess von Larisch, to arrange matters for him discreetly. Marie Larisch gladly obliged her cousin, and the two met subsequently either in Prater Park or at various social functions. So far there had been no intimate relations between them. The relationship was a purely romantic one as Rudolph found himself drawn to the young woman in a way none of his other conquests had ever attracted him. It wasn't until January 13, 1889, that the two became lovers in Countess Larisch's apartment at the Grand Hotel.

Eventually, Mary's mother found out about the meetings, and she did not approve of them. Her daughter was not about to become the crown prince's mistress if *she* could help it, and Rudolph became aware of the need to be very circumspect in their rendezvous. Shortly after, he requested Countess Larisch to bring Mary to him at the Imperial Castle. This was a daring idea and Marie Larisch didn't like it at all. Nevertheless, she obeyed her cousin. Consequently, she and Mary arranged for the visit at the lion's den.

Dressed in "a tight-fitting olive green dress," according to Countess Larisch's own memoirs, Mary was led to a small iron gate which already stood open, in the castle wall. They were received by Rudolph's valet, Loschek, who led the two women up a dark, steep stairway, then opened a door and stopped. They found themselves on the flat roof of the castle! Now he motioned them on, and through a window they descended into the corridor below. At the end of this passage, they came to an arsenal room filled with trophies and hunting equipment. From there, they contin-

The altar—site where the bedroom stood and the murder took place in 1889

ued their journey through the back corridors of the castle into Rudolph's apartments.

Rudolph came to greet them, and abruptly took Mary Vetsera with him into the next room, leaving his cousin to contemplate the vestibule. Shortly after, Rudolph returned and, according to Countess Larisch's memoir, told her that he would keep Mary with him for a couple of days. That way Mary's mother might realize he was not to be trifled with. Countess Larisch was to report that Mary had disappeared from her cab during a shopping expedition, while she had been inside a store.

Marie Larisch balked at the plan, but Rudolph insisted, even threatening her with a gun. Then he pressed five hundred florins into her hand to bribe the coachman, and ushered her out of his suite.

* * *

Evidently Mary Vetsera was in seventh heaven, for the next two weeks were spent mainly at Rudolph's side. She had returned home, of course, but managed to convince her mother that she was serious in her love for the Crown Prince. Baroness Helen had no illusion about the

Madonna statue near the foot of the bed site

outcome. At best, she knew, Rudolph would marry her daughter off to some wealthy man after he tired of her. Nevertheless, she acquiesced, and so Mary kept coming to the castle via the secret stairs and passages.

The Imperial Castle is a huge complex of buildings, spanning several centuries of construction. It is not difficult to find a way into it without being seen by either guards or others living at the castle, and the back door was reasonably safe. Although rumors had Rudolph meet his lady love within the confines of the castle, nobody ever caught them, and chances are that their relationship might have continued for some time in this manner had not the tragedy of Mayerling cut their lives short.

As we approach the momentous days of this great historical puzzle, we should keep firmly in mind that much of the known stories about it are conjecture, and that some of the most significant details are unknown because of the immediate destruction of Rudolph's documents—those he left behind without proper safeguard, that is.

The accounts given by Lonyay and the historian and poet Alexander Lernet-Holenia are not identical, but on the whole, Lonyay has more historical detail and should be

believed. According to his account, on January 27, 1889, at a reception celebrating the birthday of German Emperor William II, Franz Josef took his estranged son's hand and shook it—a gesture for public consumption, of course, to please his German hosts, with whom he had just concluded a far-reaching military alliance. This gesture was necessary, perhaps, to assure the German allies of Austria's unity. Rudolph took the proffered hand and bowed. This was the last time the Emperor and his only son met.

* * *

At noon, the following day, Rudolph ordered a light carriage, called a gig, to take him to his hunting lodge at Mayerling, about an hour's drive from Vienna. He had arranged with his trusted driver Bratfisch to pick up Mary Vetsera at her home in the third district and to bring her to Mayerling by an alternate, longer route. Mary, wearing only a cloak over her negligee, slipped out from under her mother's nose and was driven by Bratfisch to the village of Breitensee, halfway between Vienna and Mayerling. There she joined her lover, who dismissed his gig and continued the journey with Mary in Bratfisch's cab.

At this point, reports Lernet-Holenia, the carriage was halted by a group consisting of Mary's uncle Henry Baltazzi, a doctor, and two seconds, who had come to challenge the crown prince to a duel. In the ensuing scuffle, Henry was wounded by his own gun. This encounter is not of great importance except that it furnishes a motive for the Baltazzis to take revenge on Rudolph—Henry had wanted Mary for himself, even though she was his niece.

As soon as the pair reached the safety of the Mayerling castle walls, Lernet-Holenia reports, the Countess Larisch arrived in great haste and demanded he send the girl back to Vienna to avoid scandal. The mother had been to the chief of police and reported her daughter as missing. Lonyay evidently did not believe this visit occurred, for he does not mention it in *his* account of the events at Mayerling on that fateful day. Neither does he mention the fact that Rudolph gave the countess, his favorite cousin, a strongbox to safekeep for him.

"The Emperor may order my rooms searched at any moment," the countess quotes him in her memoirs. The strongbox was only to be handed over to a person offering the secret code letters R.I.U.O.

After the tragedy, this strongbox was picked up by Archduke John Salvator, close friend to Rudolph, and it is interesting to note that Henry W. Lanier, in a 1937 book titled *He Did Not Die at Mayerling*, claims that Rudolph and John Salvator escaped together to America after another body bad been substituted for Rudolph's. Both archdukes, he says, had been involved in an abortive plot to overthrow Franz Josef, but the plot came to the Emperor's attention.

However interesting this theory, the author offers no tangible evidence which makes us go back to Lernet-

Holenia's account of Countess Larisch's last words with Rudolph.

She left Mayerling, even though very upset by the prince's insistence that he and Mary were going to commit suicide. Yet, there was no privacy for that, if we believe Lernet-Holenia's version, which states that immediately after the countess's carriage had disappeared around the bend of the road, Rudolph received a deputation of Hungarians led by none other than Count Stephan Karolyi, the Prime Minister. Karolyi's presence at Mayerling is highly unlikely, for it surely would have come to the attention of the secret police almost immediately, thereby compromising Rudolph still further. Lonyay, on the other hand, speaks of several telegrams Rudolph received from the Hungarian leader, and this is more logical.

What made a contact between the Hungarians and Rudolph on this climactic day so imperative really started during a hunting party at Rudolph's Hungarian lodge, Görgény. Under the influence of liquor or drugs or both, Rudolph had promised his Hungarian friends to support actively the separation of the two halves of the monarchy and to see to it that an independent Hungarian army was established in lieu of the militia, at that time the only acknowledgment that Hungary was a separate state.

Austria at this juncture of events needed the support of the Hungarian parliament to increase its armed forces to the strength required by its commitments to the German allies. But Karolyi opposed the government defense bill for increased recruiting, and instead announced on January 25 that he had been assured by Rudolph that a separate Hungarian army would be created. This of course turned the crown prince into a traitor in the eyes of Count von Taaffe, the Austrian Prime Minister and father of the defense bill, and Rudolph must have been aware of it. At any rate, whether the Hungarian deputation came in person or whether Karolyi sent the telegrams, the intent was the same. Rudolph was now being asked to either put up or shut up. In the face of this dilemma, he backed down. The telegrams no longer exist, but this is not surprising, for a file known as "No. 25—Journey of Count Pista Karolyi to the Crown Prince Archduke Rudolph re defense bill in the Hungarian parliament" was removed from the state archives in May 1889, and has since disappeared. Thus we cannot be sure if Karolyi did go to Mayerling on this day in January or not.

But all existing sources seem to agree that two men saw Rudolph on January 29: his brother-in-law, Philip von Coburg, and his hunting companion, Count Joseph Hoyos. Rudolph begged off from the shoot, and the two others went alone; later Philip went back to Vienna to attend an imperial family dinner, while Rudolph sent his regrets, claiming to have a severe cold.

The next morning, January 30, Philip von Coburg was to return to Mayerling and together with Hoyos, who had stayed the night in the servants' wing of the lodge, continue their hunting. Much of what follows is the

The Imperial Castle—Vienna. Through this entrance the Crown prince and Mary went to their rooms.

account of Count Hoyos, supported by Rudolph's valet, Loschek.

Hoyos and Coburg were to have breakfast with Rudolph at the lodge at 8 A.M. But a few minutes before eight, Hoyos was summoned by Loschek, the valet, to Rudolph's quarters. Now the lodge was not a big house, as castles go. From the entrance vestibule, one entered a reception room and a billiards room. Above the reception area were Rudolph's private quarters. A narrow, winding staircase led from the ground floor directly into his rooms.

On the way across the yard, Loschek hastily informed Hoyos why he had called him over. At 6:30, the crown prince had entered the anteroom where Loschek slept, and ordered him to awaken him again at 7:30. At that time he also wanted breakfast and have Bratfisch, the cab driver, ready for him. The prince was fully dressed, Loschek explained, and, whistling to himself, had then returned to his rooms.

When Loschek knocked to awaken the prince an hour later, there was no response. After he saw that he was unable to rouse the prince—or the Baroness Vetsera, who,

An altar near the spot where Mary's ghost had been seen

the news of Mary Vetsera's presence at the lodge was completely suppressed.

Rudolph had been found with his hand still holding a revolver, but since fingerprints had not yet become part of a criminal investigation procedure, we don't know whose revolver it was and whether he had actually used it. But there wasn't going to be any kind of inquest in this case, anyway. Mary's body was immediately removed from the room and hidden in a woodshed, where it lay unattended for two days. Finally, on the thirty-first the Emperor ordered Rudolph's personal physician, Dr. Auchenthaler, to go to Mayerling and certify that Mary Vetsera had committed suicide. At the same time, Mary's two uncles, Alexander Baltazzi and Count Stockau, were instructed to attend to the body. Without any argument, the two men identified the body and then cosigned the phony suicide document which had been hastily drawn up. Then they wrapped Mary's coat around the naked body, and sat her upright in a carriage with her hat over her face to hide the bullet wound. In the cold of the night, at midnight to be exact, the carriage with the grotesque passenger raced over icy roads toward the monastery of Heiligenkreuz, where the Emperor had decided Mary should be buried. When the body threatened to topple over, the men put a cane down her back to keep it upright. Not a word was spoken during the grim journey. At the Cistercian monastery, there was some difficulty at first with the abbot, who refused to bury an apparent suicide, but the Emperor's power was so great that he finally agreed.

And so it was that Mary Vetsera was buried in the dead of night in a soil so frozen that the coffin could be properly lowered into it only with difficulty.

Today, the grave is a respectable one, with her name and full dates given, but for years after the tragedy it was an unmarked grave, to keep the curious from finding it.

Rudolph, on the other hand, was given a state funeral, despite objections from the Holy See. His head bandaged to cover the extensive damage done by the bullet, he was then placed into the Capuchins' crypt alongside all the other Habsburgs.

However, even before the two bodies had been removed from Mayerling, Franz Josef had already seized all of Rudolph's letters that could be found, including farewell letters addressed by the couple to various people. Although most of them were never seen again, one to Rudolph's chamberlain, Count Bombelles, included a firm request by the crown prince to be buried with Mary Vetsera. Strangely enough, the count was never able to carry out Rudolph's instructions even had he dared to, for he himself died only a few months later. At the very moment his death became known, the Emperor ordered all his papers seized and his desk sealed.

In a letter to a former lover, the Duke of Braganza, Mary is said to have stated, "We are extremely anxious to find out what the next world looks like," and in another one, this time to her mother, she confirms her desire to die

he explained, was *with* the prince—he became convinced that something was wrong, and wanted Count Hoyos present in case the door had to be broken down. Hardly had Hoyos arrived at the prince's door, which was locked, as were all other doors to the apartment, when Philip von Coburg drove up. Together they forced the door open by breaking the lock with a hatchet. Loschek was then sent ahead to look for any signs of life. Both occupants were dead, however. On the beds lay the bodies of the two lovers, Rudolph with part of his head shot off seemingly by a close blast, and Mary Vetsera also dead from a bullet wound.

Hoyos wired the imperial physician, Dr. Widerhofer, to come at once, but without telling him why, and then drove back to Vienna in Bratfisch's cab.

At the Imperial Castle it took some doing to get around the protocol of priority to inform the imperial couple of the tragedy. Franz Josef buried his grief, such as it was, under the necessity of protecting the Habsburg *image*, and the first announcements spoke of the prince having died of a heart attack. After a few days, however, this version had to be abandoned and the suicide admitted. Still, and asks her mother's forgiveness. Since the letter to the Duke of Braganza also bore Rudolph's signature, it would appear that Rudolph and Mary had *planned* suicide together. But, according to Lonyay, a fragment of Rudolph's letter to his mother somehow became known, and in this farewell note, Rudolph confessed that he had murdered Mary Vetsera and therefore had no right to live. Thus, apparently, Rudolph shot the girl first but then had lacked the courage to kill himself until the next morning. Many years later, when the Emperor could no longer stop the truth from coming out, reports were made by two physicians, Kerzl and Auchenthaler, in further support of the view that Mary had died some ten hours before Rudolph.

In the letter to her mother, Mary had requested that she be buried with Rudolph, but to this day, *that desire has not been honored:* Her remains are still at the Heiligenkreuz cemetery, and his are in the crypt in Vienna.

After the deaths, Mary Vetsera's mother was brusquely told to leave Austria; the daughter's belongings were seized by police and, on higher orders, were burned.

Ever since, speculation as to the reasons for the double "suicide" had raced around the world. In Austria, such guessing was officially discouraged, but it could hardly be stopped. Lonyay dismisses various reasons often advanced for the suicide: that Franz Josef had refused his son a divorce so he could marry Mary Vetsera; that a lovers' pact between Rudolph and Vetsera had taken place; or that his political *faux pas* had left Rudolph no alternative but a bullet. Quite rightly Lonyay points out that suicide plans had been on Rudolph's mind long before things had come to a head. He also discounts Rudolph's great love for the girl, hinting that the crown prince simply did not wish to die *alone,* and had made use of her devotion to him to take her with him. Thus it would appear that Mary Vetsera, far from being the guilty party, was actually the victim—both of Rudolph's bullets, and of his motives. No one doubts Mary's intention to commit suicide if Rudolph did and if he asked her to join him.

But—is the *intention* to commit suicide the same as actually doing it?

Too many unresolved puzzles and loose ends remained to satisfy even the subdued historians of those days, to say nothing of the unemotional, independent researcher of today, who is bent only on discovering what really happened.

The official report concerning the two deaths was finally signed on February 4, 1889, and handed to the Prime Minister for depositing in the Court archives. Instead, Count von Taaffe took it with him to his private home in Bohemia for "safekeeping." It has since disappeared.

Of course, there was still Loschek, the valet. He could not help wondering why the Prime Minister was in such good spirits after the crown prince's death, and especially when the report was filed, thus officially ending the

Dr. Hans Holzer interviewing castle employee who witnessed the apparition of Mary Vetsera

whole affair. While the ordinary Viennese mourned for their prince, von Taaffe seemed overjoyed at the elimination of what to him and his party had been a serious threat. And in the meantime Franz Josef now maintained that he and Rudolph had always been on the best of terms and that the suicide was a mystery to one and all.

Helen Vetsera wrote a pamphlet telling the family's side of the story: but it was seized by the police, and so the years passed and gradually the Mayerling events became legendary.

The Austro-Hungarian monarchy fell apart in 1918, just as Rudolph had foreseen, and the Habsburgs ceased to be sacrosanct, but still the secret of Mayerling was never really resolved nor had the restless spirit of the woman, who suffered most in the events, been quieted.

True, the Emperor had changed the hunting lodge into a severe monastery immediately after the tragedy: Where the bedroom once stood there is now an altar, and nuns sworn to silence walk the halls where once conviviality and laughter prevailed. In Vienna, too, in the corridor of the Imperial Castle where the stairs once led to Rudolph's apartment, a *marterl,* a typically Austrian niche containing a picture of the Virgin Mary, has been placed.

But did these formal expressions of piety do anything to calm the spirit of Mary Vetsera? Hardly. Nor was everything as quiet as the official Court powers would have liked it to be.

The English Prime Minister, Lord Salisbury, had some misgivings about the official version of the tragedy.

In a letter that Edward, the Prince of Wales, wrote to his mother, Queen Victoria, we find:

"Salisbury is sure that poor Rudolph and that unfortunate young lady were murdered."

But perhaps the most interesting details were supplied by the autopsy report, available many years later:

"The gun wound of the crown prince did not go from right to left as has been officially declared and would have been natural for *suicide*, but from left, behind the ear toward the top of the head, where the bullet came out again. Also, other wounds were found on the body. The revolver which was found next to the bed had *not* belonged to the crown prince; all six shots had been fired.

"The shotgun wound of the young lady was not found in the temple as has been claimed, but on top of the head. She, too, is said to have shown other wounds."

Had Count von Taaffe seized upon the right moment to make a planned suicide appear just that, while actually murdering the hesitant principals?

We have no record of secret agents coming to Mayerling that day, but then we can't be sure that they didn't come, either. So confusing is this comparatively recent story that we can't be too sure of *anything*, really. Certainly there was a motive to have Rudolph eliminated. Von Taaffe knew all about his dealings with Karolyi, and could not be sure that Rudolph might not accept a proffered Hungarian crown. To demand that Rudolph be restrained or jailed would not have sat well with the image-conscious Emperor. Yet the elimination of Rudolph, either as an actual traitor or as a potential future threat to von Taaffe's concepts, was certainly an urgent matter, at that moment.

Just as von Taaffe was aware of the Hungarian moves and had read the telegrams from Karolyi, so he knew of Rudolph's suicide talk. Had the Karolyi move prompted him to act immediately, and, seeing that the crown prince had gone to Mayerling with Mary Vetsera, given him an idea to capitalize on what *might* happen at Mayerling...but to make sure it did? Rudolph's lack of courage was well known. Von Taaffe could not be sure the crown prince would really kill himself. If Rudolph returned from Mayerling alive, it would be too late. The Hungarian defense bill had to be acted upon at once. Rebellion was in the air.

Perhaps von Taaffe did not have to send any agents to Mayerling. Perhaps he already *had* an agent there. Was someone around the crown prince in von Taaffe's employ?

These and other tantalizing questions went through my mind in August of 1964 when I visited the old part of the Imperial Castle with my wife Catherine. I was following a slender thread: a ghostly white lady had been observed in the Amalienburg wing. Our arrival was almost comical: Nobody knew anything about ghosts and cared less. Finally, more to satisfy the curiosity of this American writer, the *burghauptmann* or governor of the castle summoned one of the oldest employees, who had a reputation

for historical knowledge. The governor's name was Neunteufel, or "nine devils," and he really did have a devil of a time finding this man whose Christian name was Sonntag, or "Sunday."

"Is Herr Sonntag in?" he demanded on the intercom. Evidently the answer was disappointing, for he said, "Oh, Herr Sunday is not in on Friday?"

Fortunately, however, the man was in and showed us to the area where the phenomenon had been observed.

Immediately after the Mayerling tragedy, it seemed, a guard named Beran was on duty near the staircase leading up toward the late crown prince's suite. It was this passage that had been so dear to Mary Vetsera, for she had had to come up this way to join her lover in his rooms. Suddenly, the guard saw a white figure advancing toward him from the stairs. It was plainly a woman, but he could not make out her features. As she got to the *marterl*, she vanished. Beran was not the only one who had such an unnerving experience. A Jaeger, a member of an Alpine regiment serving in the castle, also saw the figure one afternoon. And soon the servants started talking about it. Several of them had encountered the "white woman," as they called her, in the corridor used by Mary Vetsera.

I looked at the *marterl*, which is protected by an iron grillwork. Next to it is a large wooden chest pushed flush against the wall. And behind the chest I discovered a wooden door.

"Where does this door lead to?" I asked.

"No place," Sonntag shrugged, "but it used to be a secret passage between the outside and Rudolph's suite."

Aha! I thought. So that's why there is a ghost here. But I could not do anything further at that moment to find out *who* the ghost was.

On September 20, 1961 I returned to Vienna. This time I brought with me a Viennese lady who was a medium. Of course she knew where we were—after all, everybody in Vienna knows the Imperial Castle. But she had no idea why I took her into the oldest, least attractive part of the sprawling building, and up the stairs, finally coming to an abrupt halt at the mouth of the corridor leading toward the haunted passage.

It was time to find out what, if anything, my friend Mrs. Edith Riedl could pick up in the atmosphere. We were quite alone, as the rooms here have long been made into small flats and let out to various people, mainly those who have had some government service and deserve a nice, low-rent apartment.

With us were two American gentlemen who had come as observers, for there had been some discussion of a motion picture dealing with my work. This was their chance to see it in its raw state!

"Vetsera stairs...." Mrs. Riedl suddenly mumbled. She speaks pretty good English, although here and there she mixes a German or French word in with it. Of noble Hungarian birth, she is married to a leading Austrian manufacturer and lives in a mansion, or part of one, in the suburb of Doebling.

"She stopped very often at this place," she continued now, "waiting, till she got the call...."

"Where did the call come from?" I asked.

"From below."

Mrs. Riedl had no knowledge of the fact that Mary Vetsera came this way and *descended* into Rudolph's rooms by this staircase.

"The Madonna wasn't here then...but she prayed here."

She walked on, slowly, as if trying to follow an invisible trail. Now she stopped and pointed at the closed-off passage.

"Stairway...that's how she went down to Rudolph...over the roof...they met up here where the Madonna now is...and sometimes he met her part of the way up the stairs."

No stairs were visible to any of us at this point, but Mrs. Riedl insisted that they were in back of the door.

"She had a private room here, somewhere in the castle," she insisted. Officially, I discovered, no such room belonging to Mary Vetsera is recorded.

"There were two rooms she used, one downstairs and another one farther up," Mrs. Riedl added, getting more and more agitated. "She changed places with her maid, you see. That was in case they would be observed. In the end, they were no longer safe here, that's when they decided to go to Mayerling. That was the end."

I tried to pinpoint the hub of the secret meetings within the castle.

"Rudolph's Jaeger...." Mrs. Riedl replied, "Bratfisch...he brought the messages and handed them to the maid...and the maid was standing here and let her know...they could not go into his rooms because his wife was there, so they must have had some place of their own...."

We left the spot, and I followed Mrs. Riedl as she walked farther into the maze of passages that honeycomb this oldest part of castle. Finally, she came to a halt in a passage roughly opposite where we had been before, but on the other side of the flat roof.

"Do you feel anything here?" I asked.

"Yes, I do," she replied "this door...number 77...79...poor child...."

The corridor consisted of a number of flats, each with a number on the door, and each rented to someone whose permission we would have had to secure, should we have wished to enter. Mrs. Riedl's excitement became steadily greater. It was as if the departed girl's spirit was slowly but surely taking over her personality and making her relive her ancient agony all over again.

"First she was at 77, later she changed...to 79... these two apartments *must* be connected...."

Now Mrs. Riedl turned to the left and touched a window giving onto the inner courtyard. Outside the win-

The oldest wing of the Imperial Castle, Vienna, where the apartment of the Crown prince was located

dow was the flat roof Countess Larisch had mentioned in her memoirs!

"She same up the corridor and out this window," the medium now explained, "something of her always comes back here, because in those days she was happiest here."

"How did she die?" I shot at her.

"She wouldn't die. She was killed."

"By whom?"

"Not Rudolph."

"Who killed him?"

"The political plot. He wanted to be Hungarian King. Against his father. His father knew it quite well. He took her with him to Mayerling because he was afraid to go alone; he thought with her along he might not be killed."

"Who actually killed them?"

"Two officers."

"Did he know them?"

"She knew them, but he didn't. She was a witness. That's why she had to die."

"Did Franz Josef have anything to do with it?"

"He knew, but he did not send them.... *Das kann ich nicht sagen!*" she suddenly said in German, "I can't say this!"

What couldn't she say?

"I cannot hold the Emperor responsible...please don't ask me...."

Mrs. Riedl seemed very agitated, so I changed the subject. Was the spirit of Mary Vetsera present, and if so, could we speak to her through the medium?

The stair leading up to the apartment of the Crown prince

"She wants us to pray downstairs at that spot..." she replied, in tears now. "Someone should go to her grave...."

I assured her that we had just come from there.

"She hoped Rudolph would divorce his wife and make her Queen, poor child," Mrs. Riedl said. "She comes up those stairs again and again, trying to live her life over but making it a better life...."

We stopped in front of number 79 now. The name on the door read "Marschitz."

"She used to go in here," Mrs. Riedl mumbled. "It was a hidden door. Her maid was at 75, opposite. This was her apartment."

At the window, we stopped once more.

"So much has changed here," the medium said.

She had never been here before, and yet she *knew*.

Later I discovered that the area had indeed been changed, passage across the flat roof made impossible.

"There is something *in between*," she insisted.

A wall perhaps? No, not a wall. She almost *ran* back to the Madonna. There the influence, she said, was still strongest.

"Her only sin was vanity, not being in love," Mrs. Riedl continued. "She wishes she could undo something...she wanted to take advantage of her love, and that was wrong."

Suddenly, she noticed the door, as if she had not seen it before.

"Ah, the door," she said with renewed excitement. "That is the door I felt from the other side of the floor. There should be some connection...a secret passage so she could not be seen...waiting here for the go-ahead

signal...no need to use the big door...she is drawn back here now because of the Virgin Mary.... Mary was her name also...she can pray here...."

I asked Mrs. Riedl to try to contact the errant spirit.

"She is aware of us," my medium replied after a pause in which she had closed her eyes and breathed deeply. "She smiles at us and I can see her eyes and face. I see this door *open* now and she stands in the door. Let us pray for her release."

On Mrs. Riedl's urging, we formed a circle and clasped hands around the spot. At this moment I thought I saw a slim white figure directly in front of us. The power of suggestion? "She is crying," Mrs. Riedl said.

We then broke circle and left. My American friends were visibly shaken by what they had witnessed, although to me it was almost routine.

The following day, we returned to the castle. This time we had permission from the governor to open the secret door and look for the passage Mrs. Riedl had said was there. At first, the door would not yield, although two of the castle's burly workmen went at it with heavy tools. Finally, it opened. It was evident that it had not been moved for many years, for heavy dust covered every inch of it. Quickly, we grouped ourselves around the dark, gaping hole that now confronted us. Musty, moist air greeted our nostrils. One of the workmen held up a flashlight, and in its light we could see the inside of the passage. It was about a yard wide, wide enough for one person to pass through, and paralleled the outer wall. A stairway had once led from our door down to the next lower floor—directly into Crown Prince Rudolph's apartment. But it had been removed, leaving only traces behind. Likewise, a similar stairway had led over from the opposite side where it must have once linked up with the corridor we had earlier been in—the window Mrs. Riedl had insisted was significant in all this.

* * *

The castle's governor shook his head. The secret passage was a novelty to him. But then the castle had all sorts of secrets, not the least of which were corridors and rooms that did not show on his "official" maps. Some parts of the Imperial Castle date back to the thirteenth century; others, like this one, certainly as far back as Emperor Frederick III, around 1470. The walls are enormously thick and can easily hide hollow areas.

* * *

I had taken a number of photographs of the area, in Mrs. Riedl's presence. One of them showed the significant "reflections" in psychically active areas. The day of our first visit here, we had also driven out to Mayerling with the help of Dr. Beatrix Kempf of the Austrian Government Press Service, who did everything to facilitate our journey. Ghosts or no ghosts, tourists and movie producers are good business for Austria.

At Mayerling, we had stood on the spot where the two bodies had been found on that cold January morning in 1889. I took several pictures of the exact area, now taken up by the altar and a cross hanging above it. To my surprise, one of the color pictures shows instead a whitish mass covering most of the altar rail, and an indistinct but obviously male figure standing in the right corner. When I took this exposure, nobody was standing in that spot. Could it be? My camera is double exposure proof and I have occasionally succeeded in taking psychic pictures.

If there is a presence at Mayerling, it must be Rudolph, for Mary Vetsera surely has no emotional ties to the cold hunting lodge, where only misery was her lot. If anywhere, she would be in the secret passageway in the Vienna castle, waiting for the signal to come down to join her Rudolph, the only place where her young heart ever really was.

I should point out that the sources used by me in my Mayerling research were only read long *after* our investigation, and that these are all rare books which have long been out of print.

Like all Viennese, Mrs. Riedl certainly knew about the Mayerling tragedy in a general way. But there had been no book dealing with it in circulation at the time of our visit to the castle, nor immediately before it; the personal memoirs of Countess Maria Larisch, published back in 1913, which contained the reference to the walk across the flat roof and entry by the window, is available only in research libraries. Mrs. Riedl had not been told what our destination or desire would be that hot September afternoon in 1966. Consequently, she would have had no time to study any research material even if she had wanted to— but the very suggestion of any fraud is totally out of character with this busy and well-to-do lady of society.

Until I put the pieces together, no one else had ever thought of connecting the meager reports of a ghost in the old Amalienburg wing of the castle with Mary Vetsera's unhappy death. Amtsrat Josef Korzer, of the governor's staff, who had helped us so much to clear up the mystery of the secret passage, could only shake his head: So the castle had some ghosts, too. At least it gave the Viennese some competition with all those English haunts!

The question remains unanswered: Who killed the pair, if murder it was? The medium had named two officers. Were they perhaps able to bring off their deed because they were well known to the crown prince? Had Count von Taaffe managed to pervert to his cause two of Rudolph's good friends?

If that is so, we must assume that the Hoyos report is nothing more than a carefully constructed alibi.

On the last day of his life, Rudolph had gotten into an argument with his brother-in-law, Philip von Coburg. The subject was the Habsburg family dinner that night. By failing to make an appearance, Rudolph was, in fact, withdrawing from the carefully laid plans of his cousins. The young archdukes and their in-laws had intended to pres-

Mayerling today: turned into a Carmelite Monastery soon after the tragedy

sure the aging Emperor into reforming the government, which the majority of them felt could alone save the monarchy from disaster. The most important link in this palace revolution was Rudolph. In refusing to join up, was he not in fact siding with the Emperor?

If Rudolph had been murdered, was he killed because of his pro-Hungarian leanings, or because he failed to support the family palace revolution? And if it was indeed death by his own hands, can one call such a death, caused by unbearable pressure from conditions beyond his control, a voluntary one? Is it not also murder, albeit with the prince himself as the executioner?

There may be some speculation as to which of the three alternate events took place. But there is no longer any doubt about Mary Vetsera's death. *She did not commit suicide.* She was brutally murdered, sacrificed in a cause not her own. Moreover, there is plenty of "unfinished business" to plague her and make her the restless ghost we found her to be: her last wish not granted—not buried with Rudolph, as both had desired; her personal belongings burned; her family mistreated; and her enemies triumphant.

According to the autopsy report, Rudolph could have killed Mary Vetsera, but he could not have killed *himself.* Whose gun was it that was found in his hand? At the funeral, Rudolph's right hand had to be covered because the fingers were still bent around the trigger of a gun. Had someone forced the fingers *after* Rudolph's death to make it appear he pulled the trigger? The conditions of the hand seem to suggest this. No investigation, of course, in the usual criminal sense had been permitted; thus we cannot now answer such vital questions. It is now a century later and still the mystery remains. No trace of any unknown person or persons having had access to the hunting lodge at Mayerling has turned up, nor has the strongbox Archduke John Salvator claimed appeared. But then, John Salvator himself got lost, not much later, "in a storm at sea," or if Henry Lanier's tale is true, living a new life as a farmer in South America.

We may never know the full truth about Rudolph's death. But we do know, at last, that Mary Vetsera was not a suicide. A planned suicide never leads to the ghostly phenomena observed in this case. Only a panic death, or murder, leaving unresolved questions, can account for her presence in the castle. To the unfortunate victim, a century is as nothing, of course. All others who were once part of this tragedy are dead, too, so we may never know if Count von Taaffe ordered Rudolph killed, or the royal family, or if he himself committed the act.

The strange disappearance of the most vital documents and the way things were hushed up leads me personally to believe that the medium had the right solution: The Hungarian plot was the cause of Rudolph's downfall. There was neither suicide nor a suicide pact at the time the pair was in Mayerling. There was an earlier *intention*, yes, but those letters were used as a smoke screen to cover the real facts. And without accusing some presently honorable names, how can I point the finger at Rudolph's murderers?

Let the matter rest there.

*　*　*

But the matter did not rest there, after all. In the late 1970's, documents bearing on the case were discovered by accident—apparently contained in the long-lost box of the late Archduke John Salvator who had so mysteriously "disappeared."

From these documents, it was clear that Mayerling was not suicide, but cold-blooded murder.

✳ 23

Royalty and Ghosts

ACCORDING TO THE German newspaper, *Neues Zeitalter* of April 18, 1964, Queen Elizabeth II has had a number of psychic experiences. She accepts the reality of spirit survival and maintains a lively interest in the occult. In this respect she follows in the tradition of the House of Windsor, which has always been interested in psychic phenomena. King George V, for instance, took part in séances and, after his death, communicated with noted researchers through a number of mediums, including the late Geraldine Cummins. It was the same Miss Cummins, parenthetically, who brought through some extremely evidential messages from the late President Franklin D. Roosevelt. This is not surprising, since Miss Cummins was a disciplined medium, well trained to receive intricate and detailed messages.

Whenever word of Spiritualist séances at Buckingham Palace gets out, the press has a field day, especially the British press, which displays, with rare exceptions, a singularly disrespectful attitude towards the reality of psychic phenomena. Under the circumstances one cannot blame the palace for the usual blanket denial of such rumors, even if they happen to be based on fact.

But a Frenchman by the name of François Veran claimed to have had reliable information that Spiritualist séances were taking place in Buckingham Palace and that Queen Elizabeth II had confided in friends that her late father, King George VI, had appeared to her no fewer than six times after his death. There had been a particularly close relationship between father and daughter, and prior to his death King George VI had assured his daughter he would always be with her in times of need, even from the beyond. The queen's sister, Princess Margaret, is known to be interested in psychic research, and Prince Philip, the royal consort, has lent his name as patron to a research effort by the great medical pioneer Dr. Douglas Baker, a parapsychologist and member of the College of Surgeons. This cautious involvement by members of the British royal family is not a recent inclination, however, for Queen Victoria maintained a close and continuing relationship with seers of her time, notably John Brown, who served ostensibly as the queen's gilly or orderly, but whose real attraction lay in his pronounced psychic gift, which he put at the disposal of his queen.

Nearly all the royal residences of Britain are haunted. There is a corridor in the servants' quarters of Sandringham, the castle where Queen Elizabeth II was born, where servants have frequently observed the ghost of a footman of an earlier age. There is Windsor Castle near London, where the face of George III has appeared to witnesses, and there is the Bloody Tower of London with all its grisly memories and the ghost of at least two queens. There may be others at the Tower, for nobody has yet had a chance to go in with a competent trance medium and ferret out all the psychic remains. British authorities, despite reputations to the contrary, take a dim view of such endeavors, and I for one have found it difficult to get much cooperation from them. Cooperation or not, the ghosts are there.

Probably the most celebrated of British royal ghosts is the shade of unlucky Queen Anne Boleyn, the second wife of Henry VIII, who ended her days on the scaffold. Accused of infidelity, which was a form of treason in the sixteenth century, she had her head cut off despite protestations of her innocence. In retrospect, historians have well established that she was speaking the truth. But at the time of her trial, it was a political matter to have her removed from the scene, and even her uncle, who sat in judgment of her as the trial judge, had no inclination to save her neck.

Anne Boleyn's ghost has been reported in a number of places connected with her in her lifetime. There is, first of all, her apparition at Hampton Court, attested to by a number of witnesses over the years, and even at Windsor Castle, where she is reported to have walked along the eastern parapet. At the so-called Salt Tower within the confines of the Tower of London, a guard observed her ghost walking along headless, and he promptly fainted. The case is on record, and the man insisted over and over again that he had not been drinking.

Perhaps he would have received a good deal of sympathy from a certain Lieutenant Glynn, a member of the Royal Guard, who has stated, also for the record, "I have seen the great Queen Elizabeth and recognized her, with her olive skin color, her fire-red hair, and her ugly dark teeth. There is no doubt about it in my mind." Although Elizabeth died a natural death at a ripe old age, it is in the nature of ghosts that both the victims and the perpetrators of crimes sometimes become restless once they have left the physical body. In the case of good Queen Bess, there was plenty to be remorseful over. Although most observers assume Queen Elizabeth "walks" because of what she did to Mary Queen of Scots, I disagree. Mary had plotted against Elizabeth, and her execution was legal in terms of the times and conditions under which the events took place. If Queen Elizabeth I has anything to keep her restless, it would have to be found among the many lesser figures who owed their demise to her anger or cold cunning, including several ex-lovers.

Exactly as described in the popular English ballad, Anne Boleyn had been observed with "her 'ead tucked under," not only at the Tower of London, but also at Hever Castle, in Kent, where she was courted by King Henry VIII. To make things even more complicated, on the anniversary of her execution she allegedly drives up to the front door of Blickling Hall, Norfolk, in a coach driven by a headless coachman and drawn by four headless horses, with herself sitting inside holding her head in her lap. That, however, I will have to see before I believe it.

A number of people have come forward to claim, at the very least, acquaintanceship with the unlucky Anne Boleyn in a previous life, if not identity with her. Naturally, one has to be careful to differentiate between the real thing and a romantically inclined person's fantasizing herself or himself back into another age, possibly after reading some books dealing with the period or after seeing a film.

The circumstances surrounding Anne are well known; her history has been published here and abroad, and unless the claimant comes up with some hitherto unknown facet of the queen's life, or at the very least some detail that is not generally known or easily accessible in the existing literature, a prima facie case cannot really be established.

As I am firmly convinced of the reality of reincarnation and have published two books dealing with this subject, I am perhaps in a position to judge what is a real reincarnation memory and what is not. Thus, when Mrs. Charlotte Tuton of Boston contacted me in early 1972 with a request to regress her hypnotically, I was impressed with her attitude and previous record. To begin with, Mrs. Tuton is the wife of a prominent professional man in her community, and her attitude has been one of cautious observation rather than firm belief from the beginning. "I feel such a strong attachment to the person of Anne Boleyn," she explained to me, "and have from the time I was about eleven or twelve years old. Many features of my own life and circumstances lead me to believe that I either *was* she or was very closely associated with her."

It didn't occur to Mrs. Tuton until recently to put all these so-called clues together, although she has lived with them all her life. Her interest in the subject of reincarnation was aroused by the literature in the field, notably Ruth Montgomery's work. Eventually she read my book *Born Again* and approached me. "At the age of eleven I read a book called *Brief Gaudy Hour* by Margaret Campbell. It concerned the life of Anne Boleyn and her short time as Queen of England. The odd fact is that though I read scores of historical novels and literally hundreds of other books all through childhood and adolescence, majoring eventually in French literature at Wellesley, I never had a feeling—visceral knowledge—to compare with that which I had experienced as a child reading the short life of Anne Boleyn."

From early childhood, Mrs. Tuton had an almost pathological terror of knives and sharp metallic objects, while other weapons did not affect her in the least. The very mention of a blade produced an attack of goose bumps and shivers in her. "I also have frequently experienced a severe sensation of the cutting of a major nerve at the back of my neck, a physical feeling intense enough for me to have consulted a neurosurgeon at the Lahey Clinic about it. No known physiological cause for the sensation could be found, yet it continues to appear from time to time."

Mrs. Tuton also pointed out to me that her given names were Charlotte and Anne, yet from her earliest recollections she had told her mother that Charlotte was the wrong name for her and that she should have been known only as Anne. Her mother had named her Charlotte after her own name but had selected Anne as the second name from an obscure relative, having given the choice of a second name for her child a great deal of thought and finally settling upon one that she considered perfect.

"Another theme has run through my life which is rather twofold," Mrs. Tuton continued her account. "It is a sense of having lost a way of life in high places, among people whose decisions affected the course of history at every turn, and an accompanying sense of having been wrongly accused of some act that I did not commit, or some attitude that I did not hold. None of these feelings can be explained in any way by my present lifetime."

* * *

Mrs. Betty Thigpen of South Carolina spent her childhood and adolescence in what she describes as "uneventful middle-class surroundings" and worked for some time as private secretary to a local textile executive. Later she became the personal secretary of a well-known United States senator and eventually managed his South Carolina office. After her marriage to a banking executive, she retired and devoted herself to her children. Mrs. Thigpen's interest in reincarnation is of comparatively recent origin and was prompted by certain events in her own life.

"Since early childhood, I have had certain strong identification feelings with the personality of Anne Boleyn. From the time I was old enough to read, I have also been captivated by sixteenth-century English history," Mrs. Thigpen explained. "I have never been to England but feel strong ties with that country, as well as with France. When I saw the movie, *Anne of the Thousand Days*, sitting almost hypnotized, I felt somehow as if all of it had happened before, but to me. I am almost embarrassed to admit feelings of spiritual kinship with a queen, so I keep telling myself that if there is some connection, perhaps it is just that I knew her, maybe as scullery maid or lady in waiting, but in any event I do feel a definite identification with Anne Boleyn and that period of history that I have never felt with anyone or anything else."

I would like to note that I tried to hypnotize both Mrs. Tuton of Boston and Mrs. Thigpen of South Carolina, but without much success. Both ladies seemed too tense to be able to relax sufficiently to go under to the third stage of hypnosis where regression into a possible previous life might be attempted. Under the circumstances, it is difficult to assess the evidential value of the ladies' statements, but there were far more glamorous and luckier queens to identify with, if this were merely a question of associating oneself with someone desirable. Possibly, as time goes on, these individuals will remember some historical detail that they would not otherwise know, and in this way the question of who they were, if indeed they were, in Queen Anne Boleyn's days may be resolved.

* * *

If Anne Boleyn had just cause to be dissatisfied with her sudden death, a relative of hers who also made it to the throne was not so innocent of the charges leveled against her. I am speaking, of course, of Catherine Howard, whom Henry VIII married when he was of advanced years and she was much younger. Catherine took a lover or two and unfortunately was discovered in the process and accused of high treason. She too lost her head. According to the magazine *Country Life*, Hampton Court is the place where she does her meandering, causing all sorts of disturbances as a result. "Such was the fear of an apparition," states Edward Perry, "that for many years the haunted gallery was shut off. Servants slipped past its doors hastily; the passage outside it is rarely used at night. And still inexplicable screams continue."

* * *

No other historical figure has attracted so much identification attention as Mary Queen of Scots, with the possible exception of Cleopatra. This is not surprising, as Mary was a highly controversial figure in her own time. She has been the subject of several plays and numerous books, the best of which is, I believe, Elizabeth Byrd's *Immortal Queen*. Her controversial status is due not so much to an untimely demise at the hands of the executioner, acting on orders from her cousin, Queen Elizabeth I, as to the reasons why Mary was dispatched into eternity in the first place. Nearly all dramatizations and books make a great deal of Queen Elizabeth's hatred and envy of her cousin, and a lot less of the fact that Mary was next in line to the English throne and conspired to get it. While the justice of Mary's imprisonment by Elizabeth may be open to question and could be construed as an act of envy and hatred, Mary's execution, after so many years of imprisonment "in style" in a country castle, is directly traceable to overt actions by Mary to remove Elizabeth from the throne. Under the circumstances, and following the rather stern dictates of her time, Elizabeth was at least legally justified in ordering Mary's execution.

Much has also been made in literature of Queen Mary's four ladies in waiting, all first-named Mary as well. They shared her triumphant days at Holyrood Castle in Edinburgh, and they shared her exile in England. "The Four Marys" are reasonably well known to students of history, although these details are not taught on the high school or even average college level in the United States. I think it is important to know the background of what I am about to relate in order to evaluate the relative likelihood of its being true.

In July of 1972 I was approached by Marilyn Smith, a young housewife from St. Louis, Missouri, who had strong reincarnation memories she wished to explore further. At least two of the reincarnation memories, or previous lives, had nothing to do with Scotland, but seemed rather evidential from the details Mrs. Smith was able to communicate to me when we met the following spring in

St. Louis. Despite the reincarnation material, Mrs. Smith does not have a strong history of ESP, which is in line with my thinking that true reincarnation memories preclude mediumship. Her involvement with Scottish history began eighteen years before she met me, in 1954.

"When I was seventeen years old, I was curled up in a chair reading and halfway watching television, where a live performance of *Mary Queen of Scots* was being presented. One particular scene caught my attention. In it, Mary, the Queen, is ready to board a boat for an ill-fated journey to England. A woman is clinging to Mary, pleading with her not to go to England. Suddenly I said to myself, 'That woman there, the one who is pleading, is me,' but immediately I dismissed this notion. When the queen did get into the boat, I felt a terrible, cowardly guilt."

Mrs. Smith has no Scottish blood in her, has never been to Scotland or England, and has not even read much about it. A few months later she had a vision. "I lived in the country at the time, and because it was a hot summer night, I took my pillow and a blanket and crawled upon a huge wagonload of hay to sleep. I lay there looking up at the beautiful starlit sky, wondering why I hadn't appreciated its beauty before. Then I felt a magnetic force engulf me, and I began predicting the future for myself. 'The stars will play a very important role in my life someday and I'm going to be very rich and famous because of them.' Then I saw the face of a very beautiful blond woman, and somehow I knew she would play an important role in my future. 'We *were* almost like sisters,' I said to myself. But then I caught myself. How could we have been like sisters when I hadn't even met her yet? At this moment I suddenly recalled the television program I had watched with such strange feelings, and the word Mary seemed to be connected with this face. Also, something about a Mary Beaton or Mary Seaton came through, but I didn't understand it."

During the ensuing years, bits and pieces from a previous lifetime seemed to want to come through to the surface, but Mrs. Smith repressed them. Years passed, and Mrs. Smith became interested in the occult, reincarnation, and especially astrology. She began to study astrology and is now erecting horoscopes professionally.

"At my very first astrology lesson," Mrs. Smith explained, "I met another student whose name was Pat Webbe, a very attractive blonde woman. There was an almost instant rapport between us. Hers was the face I had seen in my vision many years before, and I decided to tell her of it. However, I didn't inform her of the fact that the name Mary had also been attached to her face, assuming that it had referred to the Blessed Virgin Mary, to whom I was very devoted at all times."

About a year before she met Marilyn Smith, Pat Webbe had a strange dream. In the dream she was dressed in a period gown of several centuries ago. She was in what seemed to be a castle and was waiting to escape.

"It was a large castle and cold, and I remember going into one room, and there were men in it with long halberds who were jabbing at each other. I saw two headgears crushed, and then I was back in the other room and there seemed to be fire everywhere in front of the castle. I hear myself tell a servant to hurry and get the children and make sure they have their coats on, because we have to go out into the snow. I can see the light coming down from where the servant is getting the children, and we go out through a little trap door and there is a large dog out there, but I am not afraid of the dog for some reason, although in my present life I am very much afraid of dogs. The dream ends, but I know at the very end that I am concerned about my oldest daughter not being there."

"Did you see yourself in this dream?" I asked.

"Yes, but it was really just a form; I couldn't distinguish a face or anything."

"What other details do you recall?"

"I recall the period costume and the hooped dresses, but everything was sort of gray, except for the snow and the fire, which was red, and the swords, which were black. I heard thunder, but I can't explain it. But ever since I was a child I have had a recurrent dream. My mother and I were in a boat, and it looked as though we were glad we were in that boat, escaping."

Mrs. Webbe has no strong feeling of having lived before. She has never been to Europe, and she does not have a strong desire to visit Scotland or England, though she does feel she would like to go to France.

"When you met Marilyn Smith for the first time, did you have any peculiar feelings about her, as if you had known her before?" I asked.

"No, but we took up with each other immediately. We were like sisters within six months, almost as if we had been friends all our lives."

Some time after meeting Marilyn Smith, Pat had another unusual dream. In it, she saw herself in bed, and a woman who was supposed to take care of her. Somehow Mrs. Webbe got the name Merrick.

"I remember she had to leave, but I didn't want her to. I begged her to stay, but she had to go anyway. I remember I was sitting at a child-sized piano and playing it beautifully. I could see a great massive door, and a man came in wearing a period costume. It was gray and had some kind of chain belt around it; he had blond hair, and I remember throwing myself at his feet and saying. 'Help her, help her,' and adding, 'She's leaving in a boat, help her,' but he swore and said something about 'Goddamn insurrectionists,' and that was the end of the dream."

"Pat and I often discussed our dreams with each other," Marilyn Smith said. "One day she called me very excitedly about a dream she had just had."

"Well, I thought it was rather silly," Mrs. Webbe explained, "but in the dream my husband and I were at some sort of banquet and we were walking through a long corridor which was very ornately decorated in the French style. There was a couch in one corner with two swords on it. One was very large and ornate, the other small and made of silver, and I handed the latter to my husband. As I handed him the sword, I pricked my finger, and I went to a little room to clean the blood from my hand, and the blood disappeared. When I looked into a mirror in this room, I saw myself dressed as a French boy. Then I said to myself, 'I am Mary Queen of Scots,' and I ran back into the other room and told my husband, 'I am Mary Queen of Scots.' Shortly afterwards I awoke from my dream, singing a song with the words, 'I am Mary Queen of Scots!'"

The two ladies came to the conviction that they had been together in a previous life in Scotland; to be exact, as Mary Queen of Scots and Mary Beaton or Seaton, one of the four ladies in waiting. At first, the idea of having been a Scottish queen was difficult for Pat to accept, and she maintained a healthy attitude of skepticism, leaving the more enthusiastic support of this theory to her friend Marilyn. Nevertheless, the two ladies discussed the matter intelligently and even went so far as to compare horoscopes, since both of them were now immensely interested in astrology. There were a number of incidents into which they read some significance, incidents which taken individually seem to me to have no meaning whatever, but which, taken together in relation to this particular situation, are, at the very least, curious. These include such incidents as Marilyn Smith visiting a folk theater in Arkansas while on vacation and hearing a folk singer render "The Ballad of Mary Queen of Scots" the minute she arrived. Similarly, there was the time when Pat Webbe attended a floor show in Las Vegas, with one of the principal performers impersonating Mary Queen of Scots.

"I also thought it kind of strange that I never liked the name Mary," Pat Webbe added. "I have five daughters, and my husband had wanted to call our first daughter Mary, but I just wouldn't have it. I wanted something different, but somehow I was compelled to add the name Mary to each one of my daughters somewhere, not because my husband suggested it, but for some unknown reason. So it happened that every one of my daughters has Mary as part of her name."

Since the two ladies, professional astrologers by now, tried to tie in their own rebirth with the horoscope of Mary Queen of Scots and her lady in waiting, they asked that I ascertain the birth data of Mary Beaton and Mary Seaton, if I could. With the help of my friend Elizabeth Byrd, I was able to establish that Mary Queen of Scots was born December 8, 1542, but the inquiry at the Royal Register House supplied only the rather vague information that Mary Seaton seems to have been born around 1541, and there was no reference to the birth of Mary Beaton. Mari-

lyn Smith found it significant that the queen's rising sign had been 29° Taurus, and Pat Webbe, supposed reincarnation of the queen, had a moon in 29° Taurus in her natal chart. She believes that astrology can supply valid information concerning reincarnation identities.

Elizabeth Page Kidder, who lives with her parents near Washington, D.C., happened to be in Scotland at age seven.

"We were on the bus from the airport, going to Edinburgh. Suddenly my father said, 'Look up at the hill; that's where Mary Queen of Scots used to live.' At that, I went into trance, sort of a deep sleep." Somehow her father's reference to Mary Queen of Scots had touched off a buried memory in her. Two days after their arrival in the Scottish capital the Kidders went shopping. While they were looking at kilts, Elizabeth insisted upon getting a Stuart plaid, to the exclusion of all others. In the end, she settled for a MacDonald plaid, which fit in with her family background. A while later, the family went to visit Madame Tussaud's Wax Museum in London. When Elizabeth got a good look at the representation of Mary Queen of Scots being beheaded, she was shattered. Although the seven-year-old girl had never heard of the queen before, she insisted that the execution had been unjust and became extremely vehement about it. None of the other exhibits in the museum affected her in the least. When the family visited Westminster Abbey, Elizabeth went straight to Mary's grave and began to pray for her. Now eighteen years old, Elizabeth Kidder has read a number of books dealing with Mary Queen of Scots, and in particular the references to Mary Seaton have interested her.

Her daughter's strange behavior in Edinburgh and London made Mrs. Kidder wonder about reincarnation and the validity of such incidents. Many years later, when she heard of an organization called The Fellowship of Universal Guidance in Los Angeles, specializing in life studies along the lines of Edgar Cayce's work, she submitted the necessary data to them for a reading concerning her daughter. Did her daughter have any connection with Mary Queen of Scots, she wanted to know. Back came the answer that she had been her lady-in-waiting. Mrs. Kidder went further, accepting the so-called life reading at face value, and began to put her daughter into hypnosis, finding her a good subject. Under hypnosis Elizabeth disclosed further details of her life as lady-in-waiting to Mary Queen of Scots and claimed that her school friend Carol was, in fact, Mary Queen of Scots reincarnated. Carol Bryan William, who had come along to visit me in New York, had often dreamed that she was a richly dressed person standing in an ornately carved room with royal-blue hangings. Bent on proving the truth of these amazing claims, Mrs. Kidder contacted Ruth Montgomery and, in her own words, "was able to verify through her that her daughter Elizabeth was Mary Seaton and her friend Carol was Mary Queen of Scots."

Carol, who is a little older than Elizabeth, said that when she was little she always thought that she was from England. Her father is of English descent, but since she is an adopted child, that would have little meaning in this instance. She does have recurrent dreams involving a castle and a certain room in it, as well as a countryside she likes to identify as English.

I had previously put Elizabeth under hypnosis, but without significant results. I next tried my hand with Carol. She turned out to be a better subject, sliding down to the third level easily. I asked her to identify the place she was now in.

"I think it is the sixteenth century. I see lots of townspeople. They are dressed in burlap, loose-fitting cloth gathered in by a rope around the waist. I see myself standing there, but it is not me. I am a boy. He is small, has fair hair, and is kind of dirty."

On further prodding, it turned out that the boy's name was John, that his mother was a seamstress and his father a carpenter, working for the king. The king's name was James. He had dark hair and a beard and was on the tall side.

"Do you know anyone else in the city?" I asked.

"I know a woman. People don't like her very much because she is not Catholic. She is Episcopal."

"What are you?"

"Catholic."

"Is everybody Catholic in your town?"

"Some people aren't, but if you are not, you are in trouble. It is the law."

"Who is the man who leads the ones who are not Catholic?"

"Henry VIII."

"Does he like King James?"

"I don't think so."

"What happened to King James?"

"He is killed. He died a violent death."

"Did Henry VIII have anything to do with it?"

"There was a discrepancy over the religions. Henry VIII did not want to be Catholic, and the only way he could abolish Catholic rule was to get rid of James."

"Who wins?"

"I think Henry VIII does, but he does and he doesn't. Everybody does not follow Henry VIII. There are still people who are faithful to the Catholic religion."

After I returned Carol to the conscious state, I questioned her about her studies. It turned out she was taking an English course at college and had had one year of English history thus far. She had no particular interest in Scottish history, but she seemed unusually attached to the subject of the Catholic religion. She can't understand why, because she is an Episcopalian.

Mrs. Kidder wasn't too pleased that her protégé, Carol, remembered only having been a boy in sixteenth-century England, and not the eminent Mary Queen of Scots. But then where would that leave Pat Webbe of St. Louis? It was all just as well.

* * *

Linda Wise is a young lady living in the Midwest whose ancestors came over on the *Mayflower*. She is part Scottish, part English and part German, and just about her only link with Scotland is a family legend from her grandmother's side that several members of the family were forced to leave Scotland in the 1700s on very short notice. These cousins, if they were that, were named Ewing, but Miss Wise hasn't researched it further. She has never had any particular interest in Scotland or Great Britain, hasn't studied the history of the British Isles, and, living in the Midwest, has very little contact with English or Scottish people. Nevertheless, she has had periodic feelings of wanting to *go back to* Scotland, as if she had been there before. In 1971 she became acquainted with a Scottish couple and they became pen pals. As a result, she went to visit them in August, 1972. As soon as she arrived in Scotland, she had a strange experience.

"When I first got there, we took a bus from Aberdeen to Elgin, where my friends live. I could see the mountains in a certain area and suddenly I had goose bumps. I just felt as if I had come home, as if I had known the area from before."

Later she went to visit England, but all the time she was in England she felt extremely uneasy, wanting to return to Scotland as soon as possible. "For some reason, I felt much safer once the train crossed the border at Berwick-on-Tweed."

But the most haunting experience of her journey took place at the battleground of Culloden, where Bonnie Prince Charlie led the Scottish clans against King George in the Uprising of 1745. This battlefield, situated several miles east of Inverness, is now a historical site. Miss Wise had a vague knowledge that an important battle had taken place at Culloden, and that it had been extremely bloody. The forest at Culloden contains many grave markers, and people go there to observe and sometimes pray.

"Suddenly I felt as if I were being pulled in two directions—to continue and yet to get back to the main road as fast as I could," Linda Wise explained to me. "At a certain point I could not take it any longer, so I left to rejoin the friends I had come with. They too commented on the eerie sensations they were having."

"What exactly did you feel at Culloden?"

"I felt that something or someone was after me, that I wasn't alone," Miss Wise explained. "I really didn't feel as if I were by myself." When Miss Wise rejoined her friends, she took with her some small stones from the area. On returning to the Midwest, she handed a small stone from Culloden to her mother to use in an attempt at psychometry. Immediately Mrs. Wise picked up the impression of a group of men, wearing predominantly red and yellow uniforms, coming over a hill. This experiment was part of a regular session undertaken by a home development circle among people interested in psychic research.

"We asked my mother to describe the uniform she was impressed with," Miss Wise continued. "She said Scottish; she did not see any kilts or straight-legged pants, however. She physically felt her own eyes becoming very heavy as if they were being pushed in. Since my mother knew that there was nothing wrong with her own eyes, she mentally asked what was the cause of it and in her mind's eye saw a form, or rather the etheric image of a large man who said he wanted his eyeballs back! He explained that he had been hanging around for a long time for that reason and did not know what to do."

"You mean, he had lost his eyes?"

"Yes," Linda confirmed. "My mother realized that this was an emotional situation, so she calmed his fears and told him his eyes were well again and to go on, sending him love, energy, and assurance at the same time."

Some time after her return to the United States, Miss Wise bought a record on which the famous Black Watch Regiment was playing. It upset her greatly, but her emotional involvement became even stronger when she went to a midwestern festival where various ethnic groups participated. "It was the first pipe band I had seen since I had been to Scotland, and I got tears in my eyes and felt like being back in Scotland."

The battle of Culloden, and the fate of Bonnie Prince Charlie, at one time King Charles III of Scotland and England, has also affected my own life for many years, because of some as yet indistinct memories of having lived during that time. People have given me objects from Culloden, or concerning Prince Charles; books, sometimes of very obscure origin, have found their way into my hands. Moreover, I own a silver touch piece with the name of Charles III, a great rarity as medals go, acquired under strange circumstances. At the time I saw it listed in the catalogue of a well-known London art dealer, the catalogue had been on its way to me for some time, having been sent by sea mail. Nevertheless, undaunted, I sent away for the piece but had very little hope that the modestly priced touch piece would still be there. Picture my surprise when I was nevertheless able to acquire it. How the many Scottish collectors of such items passed over this most desirable medal, so that it could await my letter, seems to me beyond pure chance or logic. It was almost as if the medal were *meant* to be mine.

✳ 24

A Visit with Robert Louis Stevenson

HELEN LILLIE MARWICK is a newspaperwoman and writer who lives with her science-writer husband Charles in a delightful old house in Georgetown, Washington, D.C. It was on her insistence that I decided to pay a visit to the house once owned by Robert Louis Stevenson in Heriot Row, Edinburgh.

"A delightful Irish girl, Mrs. John Macfie, has bought the old Robert Louis Stevenson house and reports that the friendly ghost of R. L. S. himself has been around, and she hopes to keep him," Helen wrote.

I arranged for a visit during my stay in Edinburgh, and on May 4, 1973, I arrived at the Stevenson House barely in time for tea. We had been asked for 5 o'clock, but our adventures in the countryside had caused us to be an hour late. It wasn't so much the countryside as the enormous downpour which had accompanied this particular ghost hunt, and though it gave it a certain aura, it created havoc with our schedule. But Kathleen Macfie shook hands with us as if we were old friends and led us into the high-ceilinged drawing room, one flight up. The large French windows allowed us to look out on what is probably one of the finest streets in Edinburgh, and I could see at a glance that Mrs. Macfie had refurbished the Stevenson House in a manner that would have made Stevenson feel right at home: a gentle blend of Victorian and earlier furniture pieces and casual displays of artwork in the manner of a home rather than a museum. Her own strong vibrations, as the owner, filled the place with an electrifying atmosphere of the kind that is so very conducive to psychic occurrences. Our hostess had blue eyes, red hair, and a direct practical approach to everything, including ghosts. After we had had a glass of sherry, she gave us the grand tour of the house. It had been the home of Robert Louis Stevenson from 1857 to 1880.

"This was Mrs. Stevenson's domain," our hostess explained. The magnificently furnished drawing room was pretty much the way it must have been in Stevenson's day, except for the addition of electric light and some of the personal belongings of the Macfies. In particular, there was a chair by the window which Stevenson is said to have sat in when resting from his work. As we walked in, I felt a distinct chill down my back, and I knew it wasn't due to the weather. It was a definite touch of some sort. I asked Alanna whether she had felt anything. She confirmed that she too had been touched by unseen hands, *a very gentle kind of touch.* "I feel a presence. There is definitely someone here other than ourselves." I turned to Mrs. Macfie. "What exactly have you felt since you came to this house?"

"I am most sensitive to a feeling when I am alone in the house, but maybe that isn't right, because I never feel alone here. There is always somebody or something here, a friendly feeling. Actually, there are two people here. At first I thought, perhaps because of what I had read about Robert Louis Stevenson, I was imagining things. But then the Irish writer James Pope Hennessey came to stay with us. Mr. Hennessey had been to Vailina, on Samoa, where Robert Louis Stevenson lived and ended his days. There, in the South Seas, he had seen an apparition of Stevenson, and in this house he had seen it also. It happened in his own room because he slept back there in what we called the master bedroom."

"Have *you* seen anything?"

"No, but I feel it all the time. It is as though I would look around and there was somebody behind me. Sometimes, when I wake up early in the morning, especially in the winter, I feel as if there is somebody moving about. It is very difficult to talk about it. You see, my husband is an utter skeptic. He thinks it is the central heating. Even my small son would say 'Oh, don't listen to Mother. She sees ghosts everywhere.' You see, the family doesn't support me at all."

Kathleen Macfie admits to having had similar "feelings" in other houses where she has lived. When she arrived at the Stevenson House eighteen months prior to our conversation, she soon realized that it was happening again.

"While the movers were still bringing the stuff in, I didn't pay any attention to what I felt or heard. I thought it was just the noise the movers were making. But then the feeling came: you know, when you are looking in a certain way you have peripheral vision and feelings; you don't have to look straight at anything to see it. You know that it is there. But it is a comforting, marvelous feeling."

Some of the poet's personal belongings were still in the house, intermingled with period pieces carefully chosen by the Macfies when they bought the house. "There is an invitation which he sent to his father's funeral, with his own signature on it," Mrs. Macfie commented. "But when his father died, his mother took nearly all the furniture out of here and went to live in Samoa with her son. When Stevenson himself died, the mother came back to Edinburgh to live with her sister, but Robert Louis Stevenson's widow brought all the furniture back to St. Helena, California, where she ended her days. By the way, this is his parents' room. His own room is up one flight. Originally the top story was only half a story, and it was for the servants, but Stevenson's parents wanted him to have proper accommodations up there, so that he could study and work. The house was built between 1790 and 1810. The Stevensons bought it from the original builders, because they wanted a house on drier ground."

Mrs. Macfie explained that she was in the process of turning part of the house into a private museum, so that people could pay homage to the place where Robert Louis Stevenson lived and did so much of his work.

We walked up to the second floor, Stevenson's own study. The room was filled with bookcases, and next to it was a bedroom, which Mr. Macfie uses as a dressing room. Nowadays there is a bed in the study, but in Stevenson's time there was no bed; just a large desk, a coal scuttle, and of course lots of books. I turned to Alanna and asked if she received any impressions from the room. She nodded.

"Near the fireplace I get an impression of *him*. When I just came in through the door it was as if somebody were there, standing beside the door."

While she was speaking, it seemed to me as if I, too, were being shown some sort of vague scene, something that sprang to my mind unexpectedly and most certainly not from my own unconscious. Rather than suppress it or attribute it to our discussion of Robert Louis Stevenson, of whom I knew very little at that point, I decided to "let it rip," saying whatever I felt and seeing if it could be sorted out to make some sense.

"Is there a person connected with this house wearing a rather dark coat and a light-colored or white shirtwaist type of thing with a small tie? He has rather dark eyes and his hair is brushed down. He has bushy eyebrows and he seems rather pale and agitated, and at this moment he is tearing up a letter."

Miss Macfie seemed amazed. "Yes, that is him exactly. His desk used to be where you're standing, and this was where his mother used to leave food for him on a little stool outside. She would come back hours later and it would still be there."

"I get something about age thirty-four," I said.

"Well, he was married then. On May 9, 1880, in fact." This was May 4, almost an anniversary.

We stepped into the adjacent room, which was once Stevenson's bedroom. I asked Alanna whether she felt anything special. "The presence is much stronger here than in the other room," she said. Even while she was talking, I again had the strange urge to speak about something I knew nothing about.

"I have the impression of someone being desperately ill from a high fever and very lonely and near death. He's writing a letter to someone. He expects to die but survives nevertheless."

Both ladies nodded simultaneously. "During his teenage period, he was always desperately ill and never expected to survive," Alanna commented. "It was consumption, which today is called emphysema, an inflammation of the lungs."

Alanna Knight was eminently familiar with Robert Louis Stevenson, as she was working on a play about him. My knowledge of the great writer was confined to being aware of his name and what he had written, but I had not known anything about Stevenson's private life when I entered the house. Thus I allowed my own impressions to take the foreground, even though Alanna was far more qualified to delve into the psychic layer of the house.

"Was there any kind of religious conflict, a feeling of wanting to make up one's mind one way or the other? Is there any explanation of the feeling I had for his holding a crucifix and putting it down again, of being desperate, of going to consult with someone, of coming back and not knowing which way to turn?" I asked.

"This is absolutely accurate," Mrs. Macfie confirmed, "because he had a tremendous revulsion from the faith he had been brought up in, and this caused trouble with his father. He was Presbyterian, but he toyed with atheism and the theories of the early German philosophers. All of this created a terrible furor with his father."

"Another thing just went through my mind: was he at any time interested in becoming a doctor, or was there a doctor in the family?"

"He was trained as a lawyer, very reluctantly," Mrs. Macfie replied; "his father wanted him to become an engineer. But because of his uncertain health he never practiced law. His uncle, Dr. Louis Balfour, insisted that he leave Edinburgh for his health. His wife, Fannie Osborne, was very interested in medicine; she helped keep him alive."

Alanna seemed puzzled by something she "received" at this moment. "Was there a dog of a very special breed, a very elegant dog? When he died, was there great upheaval because of it? I feel that there was a very strong attachment to this dog." Mrs. Macfie beamed at this. "There was a West Highland terrier that he took all over. The dog's name was Rogue and he was very attached to it."

We thanked our hostess and prepared to leave the house. It was almost dinner time and the rain outside had stopped. As we opened the heavy door to walk out into Heriot Row, I looked back at Kathleen Macfie, standing on the first-floor landing smiling at us. Her husband had just returned and after a polite introduction excused himself to go upstairs to his room—formerly Robert Louis Stevenson's study and bedroom. Except for him and for Mrs. Macfie on the first-floor landing, the house was empty at this moment. Or was it? I looked back into the hallway and had the distinct impression of a dark-eyed man standing there, looking at us with curiosity, not sure whether he should come forward or stay in the shadows. But it probably was only my imagination.

✳ 25

Bloody Mary's Ghost

SAWSTON HALL LIES a few miles south of the great English university town of Cambridge, and can be reached from London in about two and a half hours. When I heard that reliable witnesses had seen a ghost in this old manor house, I contacted the owner, Captain Huddleston, about a visit. The Captain's nephew, Major A. C. Eyre, wrote back saying how delighted they would be to receive us. Like so many British manor houses, Sawston Hall is open to the public at certain times and, of course, I wanted to avoid a day when the tourists were sure to interfere with our quest. Although I usually avoid getting secondhand information on hauntings, and prefer to talk to the witnesses directly when I see them, I like to know the general background of a haunted house before I approach it. This gives me a better idea as to what I might encounter in the way of atmosphere, mementos, and such. As a trained historian, I have no trouble finding my way around English history. I picked up one of the little booklets the Major had prepared for the visitors, to familiarize myself with the history of Sawston Hall while the car, driven by the imperturbable Mr. Brown, rolled quietly through the picturesque countryside. The booklet read:

Sawston Hall has been the home of the Huddleston family for over 400 years and is noteworthy for being one of the few old manor houses in Cambridgeshire built out of stone. In 1553 Edward VI was ailing and entirely dominated by the ambitious Duke of Northumberland. The King was already dead when his half sister, Princess Mary, afterwards Queen Mary Tudor, who was living in Norfolk, received a message purporting to be from him, begging her to come to him. Mary immediately set out for London and at Hoddesdon she received word that the message was a trap. On her way back, she accepted the hospitality of John Huddleston, the then Squire of Sawston, and spent the night at the Hall. During the night, however, the Duke's supporters from Cambridge who learnt she was there, set out to capture her. John Huddleston just got her to safety in time by disguising her as a dairy maid.

When we arrived at Sawston Hall, it was already 4 o'clock, a little late for tea, but our gracious hosts, the Huddlestons, had waited to serve until we got there. By now the light was not quite so strong as I would have liked it for the sake of my motion-picture camera. But I never use artificial lighting, only the available light.

We started up the stairs, and Mrs. Huddleston explained the treasures of the house to us. We admired, but quickly passed through the imposing Great Hall with its magnificent portrait of Queen Mary Tudor, the drawing room with its harpsichord in perfect playing condition, as if Queen Mary were about to use it, and proceeded past the Little Gallery and a paneled bedroom into the Tapestry

Bedroom, so called because its walls are hung with a set of Flemish tapestries showing the life of King Solomon. Dominating this room is a four-poster bed in which Queen Mary is said to have slept, back during the dark days of 1553 when she was running for her life. To the right of the bed, there is a small marble fireplace and farther down the wall an oaken door opening onto a passage which ultimately leads to the priest's hiding hole. I think these connections are of some importance if the ghost is that of Queen Mary, who was Catholic.

We stood in front of the four-poster when I started my examination.

"Tell me, Mrs. Huddleston, what are the facts about the hauntings here?"

Mrs. Huddleston, a soft-spoken, well-organized lady in her middle years, smiled a friendly smile. "Something always seems to take place in this room we're standing in. The original story is that in the middle of the night you suddenly hear three slow knocks at the door, and the door slowly swings open and a lady in gray slowly floats across the room and disappears into that tapestry. A great many people have slept in this room and there are a great many different stories of various things that have happened to them."

"What sort of things?"

"One girl woke up in the night very frightened, because she heard someone next to her in the bed breathe very heavily."

"What did she do, scream?"

"No, she just crawled to the bottom of the bed and tried to forget all about it."

"I can't say that I blame her under the circumstances. Did anyone else have trouble in this bed?"

"Well, there was a young man who was sleeping in this room, and he wasn't very well when he went to bed. When he came down to breakfast the next morning, he said, 'You know I was quite all right last night, you needn't have bothered to come to see me.' So I said, 'But I didn't.' He insisted, 'Oh, yes, you did; you knocked on the door three times, and rattled on the latch, and I got awfully frightened, and kept saying, "Come in, come in," and nothing happened, and I suddenly felt really, really frightened, so I crept down to the bottom of the bed and tried to forget all about it.'"

"Seems habit-forming," I said, "that bottom-of-the-bed business. Of course, it *is* a huge bed."

"Well, he insisted, 'it must have been you; you must have come to see me,' but I told him, 'No, I'm sorry. I never came near you; you weren't nearly sick enough.' That was that."

"How long ago did this take place?"

"Four years ago."

"Did you yourself ever hear or see anything unusual?"

"When I was first married and came here as a bride, I heard distinctly some very tinkly music rather like a spinet or virginal, and I asked my husband who it was, and he said, oh, he had heard nothing and that it was all nonsense. However, I heard it again the next night and again a little later. He kept telling me this was all rubbish, so I felt very triumphant when about a month later a visitor came down to breakfast, and said, 'Do tell me, what is this music I keep hearing.'"

"Who do you think is playing the instrument?"

"The general opinion is that it is Queen Mary Tudor herself."

"You mean her ghost?"

"Yes. Of course, you know she slept in this bed and was very fond of this house. But the reason I think that it is really she is that she was a very good performer on the virginal, in fact she was so good that her father, Henry VIII, had her brought down from the nursery as a child to play for the Flemish ambassadors when they came over."

"And you are sure you heard the music?"

"Absolutely. It was quite clear."

"Has anyone else had psychic experiences in this room?"

"Oh, yes; quite a few, really," Mrs. Huddleston said with typical English understatement. To her, a ghost was no worse than a famous actor or politician in the family. In England, one need not be looked at askance just because one believes in ghosts. It is rather respectable and all that.

"One day I was taking a rather large group around the house, and when we were in this room an old lady suddenly stepped forward, and said, 'You know, I knew this house long before you did! You see I was employed here as a young girl, as a house maid. Once I was kneeling down, attending to the fire, and suddenly I felt very cold, looked up, and I saw the door slowly opening and a gray figure swept across the room and disappeared into the tapestry there. I was so frightened I flung myself out of the room and fell headlong from the top to the bottom of the stairs and hurt myself so badly that I've never dared come back to this house until this very day.'"

"That's quite a story," I said. "Did you check on it?"

"Yes. You see, you can't see the bottom of the stairs when you're upstairs, and so she must have been absolutely right in the way she remembered things, because when we'd finished the round, and were at the bottom of the stairs, she suddenly called out, 'Oh, that's the place, I remember it, that's where I fell!'"

"And there was such a place?"

"Yes, there was."

"Have there been any manifestations here lately?"

"Not long ago, Tom Corbett, the well-known psychic, slept in this bed. He reported a presence bending over him every hour of the night. His alarm clock, which he had set for 7 o'clock, went off at one, two, three, four, five, six. When it did so this presence kept bending over him. Mr. Corbett had the impression the ghost was that of a night

watchman with one eye, and a name that sounded to him like Cutlass or Cutress."

"Did this make sense to you?"

"Well, I thought it simply meant he was carrying a cutlass with him, but Tom Corbett insisted it was a name. I made inquiries after Mr. Corbett had left, and I found to my amazement there was a man named Cutress living in the village. I had never heard of him. But the people who did the research for me said, 'That can't possibly have any connection with the night watchman, since he's only just arrived from London.'

"About a month later, the butler here was standing next to a stranger in the local pub, and he said, 'What is your name?' The stranger replied, 'Oh, my name is Cutress, and I've just come here a short time ago.' The butler wondered why he had come to this rather out-of-the-way place. 'Oh,' the man replied, 'my family's lived in Sawston for generations. I wanted to come back to the old family place.'"

"Tom Corbett certainly hit the nail on the head on that one," I acknowledged. "Any other interesting witnesses to uncanny phenomena?"

"I was taking an old lady round, and it was broad daylight, and I was showing her the tapestries, and was so busy with that, I didn't notice the change that had come over her face. When I looked around at her, she looked simply terrible, as if she were going to pass out. I asked her if I should get a doctor, but she assured me she would be all right.

"'It's really this room,' she explained. 'It's the ghosts in this room.'"

We left the haunted bedroom and went along the Long Gallery to the priest's hiding hole, which was ingeniously hidden in the thickness of the wall, barely large enough for a man to sit in, and accessible to the outer world only through a small trapdoor which could easily be covered during a raid.

I wondered if any hauntings had been observed in connection with the hiding hole, since so much tragedy and emotional turmoil adhered to the atmosphere around it.

"Not by the hole itself, but there is a nearby bedroom where there have been some ghostly experiences during the last few years. That room just above the staircase. A friend of ours, a well-known Jesuit priest, was sleeping in it, and he had so much disturbance during the night, knocking at the door, and noises outside, that he got up several times to see what was happening."

CHAPTER FIVE: **Famous Ghosts**

"Did he find anything or anyone?"

"No, of course not. They never do."

"Was there anyone else who experienced anything out of the ordinary around that staircase?"

"A lady from South Africa came here for a first visit. She arrived rather unexpectedly, so we put her into the haunted room, but the next morning she reported that she had had a good night and not been disturbed at all. Maybe the ghost had moved away? 'Anyway,' she bragged, 'I always know when there is a ghost around, because I get very cold and get goose pimples all up my arms.' So we forgot all about the ghost and started to show her around the house. But when she got to this same big staircase, which leads to this room I have just talked about, she suddenly gave a little scream and said, 'Oh, there's no doubt about it, *this* is where the ghost is!' I hurriedly looked at her arms, and she was, in fact, covered with goose pimples.

"Tom Corbett also went up these stairs and he distinctly felt someone walking after him, so much so, he turned around to speak to him, but there was nobody there."

There we had it.

The Gray Lady floating across the haunted bedroom, and the haunted staircase.

During the years of religious persecution, Sawston Hall was the principal refuge for those of the Catholic faith, including a number of priests and lay brothers. Many atrocities were perpetrated in those days in the name of the Reformed Religion, and the atmosphere at Sawston Hall is soaked with the tragedy and suffering of those martyrs.

Then, too, one must realize that Mary Tudor, later known as Bloody Mary, had found the old manor house her salvation when the Huddlestons saved her life by hiding her. Her ghost might, indeed, be drawn back there even though she did not die there. I don't think the Gray Lady is merely an etheric impression without personality; the behavior is that of a bona fide ghost.

✳ 26

Spectral Mary, Queen of Scots

BACK OF HOLYROOD PALACE, Edinburgh, residence of Mary Queen of Scots and other Scottish monarchs, stands a little house of modest appearance going by the quaint name of Croft-en-Reigh. This house was once owned by James, Earl of Moray, half brother of Mary, and Regent of Scotland in her absence. Today, the house is subdivided into three apartments, one of which belongs to a Mrs. Clyne. But several years ago this was the official residence of the warden of Holyrood Palace. The warden is the chief guide who has charge of all tourist traffic. David Graham, the onetime warden, has now retired to his house in nearby Portobello, but fourteen years ago he had a most unusual experience in this little house.

"There were twelve of us assembled for a séance, I recall," he said, "and we had Helen Duncan, who is now dead, as our medium. There we were, seated quietly in the top floor of Croft-en-Reigh, waiting for developments."

They did not have to wait long. A figure materialized before their astonished eyes and was recognized instantly: Mary Queen of Scots herself, who had been to this house many times in moments of great emotional turmoil. Within a moment, she was gone.

On several occasions, Mr. Graham recalls, he saw the ghost of a short man in sixteenth-century clothes. "I am French," the man insisted. Graham thought nothing of it until he accidentally discovered that the house was built by an architect named French!

✳ 27

Renvyle

ALL ALONG THE Irish countryside, whenever I got to talk about ghosts, someone mentioned the ghost at Renvyle. Finally, I began to wonder about it myself. In Dublin, I made inquiries about Renvyle and discovered that it was a place in the West of Ireland. Now a luxury hotel, the old mansion of Renvyle in Connemara was definitely a place worth visiting sometime, I thought. As luck would have it, the present manager of the Shelbourne in Dublin had worked there at one time.

I immediately requested an interview with Eoin Dillon, and that same afternoon I was ushered into the manager's office tucked away behind the second floor suites of the hotel.

Mr. Dillon proved to be an extremely friendly, matter-of-fact man, in his early middle years, impeccably dressed as is the wont of hotel executives.

"I went to Renvyle in 1952," he explained, "as manager of the hotel there. The hotel was owned originally by the Gogarty family, and St. John Gogarty, of course, was a famous literary figure. He had written a number of books; he was also the original Buck Mulligan in Joyce's *Ulysses*, and he was a personal friend of every great literary figure of his period.

"The house itself was built by Sir Edward Lutchins about 1932, but it stood on the site of the original Gogarty house, which was burnt down in the Troubled Times, some say without any reference to critical facts."

What Mr. Dillon meant was that the I.R.A. really had no business burning down this particular mansion. More great houses were destroyed by the Irish rebels for reasons hardly worthy of arson than in ten centuries of warfare. Ownership by a Britisher, or alleged ownership by an absentee landlord, was enough for the partisans to destroy the property. It reminded me of the Thirty Years' War in Europe when mere adherence to the Catholic or Protestant faith by the owner was enough to have the house destroyed by the opposition.

"What happened after the fire?" I asked.

"The site being one of the most beautiful in Ireland, between the lake and the sea, the hotel was then built. This was in 1922. Following the rebuilding of the house, Gogarty, who ran it as a rather literary type of hotel, collected there a number of interesting people, among them the poet and Nobel-prize winner W. B. Yeats, whose centenary we are celebrating this year. And Yeats, of course, was very interested in psychic phenomena of one kind or another and has written a number of plays and stories on the subject. He also went in for séances. We were told that some of the séances held at Renvyle were very successful.

"Now the background to the piece of information which I have is that during the years preceding my arrival it had been noted that one particular room in this hotel was causing quite a bit of bother. On one or two occasions people came down saying there was *somebody* in the room, and on one very particular occasion, a lady whom I knew as a sane and sensible person complained that a man was looking over her shoulder while she was making her face up at the mirror. This certainly caused some furor."

"I can imagine—watching a lady put on her 'face' is certainly an invasion of privacy—even for a ghost," I observed.

"Well," Mr. Dillon continued, "when I went there the hotel had been empty for about a year and a half. It had been taken over by a new company and I opened it for that new company. My wife and I found some very unpleasant sensations while we were there."

"What did you do?"

"Finally, we got the local parish priest to come up and do something about it."

"Did it help?"

"The entire house had this atmosphere about it. We had Mass said in the place, during which there was a violent thunderstorm. We somehow felt that the situation was under control. About August of that particular year, my wife was ill and my father was staying in the hotel at the time. I moved to that particular room where the trouble had been. It is located in the center of the building facing into a courtyard. The house is actually built on three sides of a courtyard. It is one flight up. This was thirteen years ago now, in August of 1952."

"What happened to you in the haunted room, Mr. Dillon?" I asked.

"I went to sleep in this room," he replied, "and my father decided he would sleep in the room also. He is a particularly heavy sleeper, so nothing bothers him. But I was rather tired and I had worked terribly hard that day, and as I lay in bed I suddenly heard this loud, clicking noise going on right beside my ears as if someone wanted to get me up! I refused to go—I was too tired—so I said, 'Will you please go away, whoever you are?'—and I put my blanket over my head and went to sleep."

"What do you make of it?" I said.

"There is a strong tradition that this room is the very room in which Yeats carried out these séances, and for that reason there was left there as a legacy actually some being of some kind which is certainly not explainable by ordinary standards."

"Has anyone else had experiences there?"

"Not the finger clicking. I assume that was to get my attention. But the wife of a musician here in town, whom I know well, Molly Flynn—her husband is Eamon O'Gallcobhair, a well-known Irish musician—had the experience with the man looking over her shoulder. He was tall and dressed in dark clothes."

"Have more people slept in this room and had experiences?"

"Over the years, according to the staff, about ten different people have had this experience. None of them knew the reputation the house had as being haunted, incidentally."

The reports of an intruder dated back only to Yeats' presence in the house, but of course something might have been latently present, perhaps "held over" from the earlier structure, and merely awakened by the séances.

It was not until the following summer that our hopes to go to Renvyle House were realized. Originally we had asked our friend Dillon to get us rooms at this renowned resort hotel so we could combine research with a little loafing in the sun—but as fate would have it, by the time we were ready to name a date for our descent upon the Emerald Isle, every nook and cranny at Renvyle House had been taken. Moreover, we could not even blame our ever-present countrymen, for the American tourist, I am told, waits far too long to make his reservations. The Britisher, on the other hand, having been taught caution and prevision by a succession of unreliable governments, likes to "book rooms," as they say, early in the season, and consequently we found that Connemara was once again British—for the summer, anyway.

We were given the choice of bedding down at nearby Leenane where Lord French is the manager of a rather modern hotel built directly upon the rocky Connemara soil on the shore of a lough several miles deep. These loughs, or fjords, as they are called in Norway, are remnants of the ice ages, and not recommended for swimming, but excellent for fishing, since the Connemara fish apparently don't mind the cold.

I should explain at this point that Connemara is the name of an ancient kingdom in the westernmost part of Ireland, which was last—and least—in accepting English custom and language, and so it is here in the cottages along the loughs and the magnificent Connemara seacoast that you can hear the softly melodic tongue of old Erin still spoken as a natural means of expression. The lilting brogue and the strange construction of sentences is as different from what you can hear across the Straits as day and night. There is, of course, a small percentage of literary and upper-class Irish, especially in Dublin, whose English is so fine it out-shines that spoken in Albion, and that, too, is a kind of moral victory over the English.

But we have left Lord French waiting for our arrival at the Hotel Leenane, and await us he did, a charming, middle-thirtyish man wild about fishing and genially aware of the lure the area has for tourists. Leenane was pleasant and the air was fresh and clear, around 65 degrees at a time when New York was having a comfortable 98 in the shade. My only complaint about the hotel concerned the walls, which had the thickness of wallpaper.

The weather this month of July, 1966, was exceptionally fine and had been so for weeks, with a strong sun shining down on our heads as we set out for Renvyle after lunch. The manager, Paul Hughes, had offered to come and fetch us in his car, and he—the manager, not the car —turned out to be far younger than I had thought. At 27, he was running a major hotel and running it well. It took us about three-quarters of an hour, over winding roads cut through the ever-present Connemara rock, to reach the coastal area where Renvyle House stands on a spot just about as close to America—except for the Atlantic—as any land could be in the area. The sea was fondling the very shores of the land on which the white two-story house stood, and cows and donkeys were everywhere around it, giving the entire scene a bucolic touch. Mr. Hughes left us alone for a while to take the sun in the almost tropical garden. After lunch I managed to corner him in the bar. The conversation, in Sybil Leek's presence, had avoided all references to ghosts, of course. But now Sybil was outside, looking over the souvenir shop, and Hughes and I could get down to the heart of the matter.

Mr. Hughes explained that the hotel had been rebuilt in 1930 over an older house originally owned by the Blakes, one of the Galway tribes, who eventually sold it to Oliver St. John Gogarty. I nodded politely, as Mr. Dillon had already traced the history of the house for me last summer.

"He was a doctor in Dublin," Hughes explained, "and he came here weekends and entertained people such as Joyce and Yeats and Augustus John."

Thank goodness, I thought, they did not have autograph hounds in Connemara!

Mr. Hughes had been the manager for three years, he explained.

"Ever notice anything unusual about any of the rooms?" I prodded.

"No, I haven't, although many of the staff have reported strange happenings. It seems that one of the maids, Rose Coine, saw a man in one of the corridors upstairs—a man who disappeared into thin air."

Miss Coine, it developed, was middle-aged, and rather shy. This was her week off, and though we tried to coax her later, at her own cottage, to talk about her experiences, she refused.

"She has experienced it a few times," Mr. Hughes continued. "I don't know how many, though."

"Has anyone else had unusual impressions anywhere in the hotel?"

"They say since the hotel was rebuilt it isn't as strong anymore."

"But didn't Miss Coine have her experience *after* the fire?"

"Yes," the manager admitted, "last year."

I decided to pay the haunted room, number 27, a visit. This was the room mentioned by Eoin Dillon in which he had encountered the ghostly manifestations. We ascended the wooden staircase, with Sybil joining us—my wife and I, and Mr. Hughes, who had to make sure the guests of number 27 were outside for the moment. The room we entered on the second floor was a typical vacation-time hotel room, fairly modern and impersonal in decor, except for a red fireplace in the center of the left wall. I later learned that the two rooms now numbered 27 and 18 were originally one larger room. I took some photographs and let Sybil gather impressions. Hughes quickly closed the outside door to make sure nobody would disturb us. Sybil sat down in the chair before the fireplace. The windows gave onto the courtyard.

"I have the feeling of something overlapping in time," Sybil Leek began. Of course, she had no idea of the "two Renvyles" and the rebuilding of the earlier house.

"I have a peculiar feeling around my neck," she continued, "painful feeling, which has some connection with this particular room, for I did not feel it a moment ago downstairs."

"Do you feel a presence here?" I asked directly.

"Yes," Sybil replied at once, "something...connected with pain. I feel as if my neck's broken."

I took some more pictures; then I heard Sybil murmur "1928." I immediately questioned her about the significance of this date. She felt someone suffered in the room we were in at that time. Also, the size of the room has been changed since.

"There is a presence in this area," she finally said with resolution. "A noisy presence. This person is rough."

After Sybil remarked that it might be difficult to get the fireplace going, we went to the adjoining room to see if the impressions there might be stronger.

"What do you sense here?" I asked.

"Fear."

"Can it communicate?"

"It is not the usual thing we have . . . just pain, strong pain."

"Someone who expired here?"

"Yes, but did not finish completely."

"Is the person here now?"

"Not the person, but an impression."

"How far back?"

"I only get as far back as 1928."

I questioned Paul Hughes. That was indeed the time of the Yeats séances.

"What sort of people do you feel connected with this room?"

"There is this overlapping period . . . 1928 I feel very vital, but beyond that we go down in layers . . . traveling people, come here, do not live here . . . does the word 'off-lander' mean anything?"

It did not to me.

"We're in 1928 now. Men in long dresses . . . religious, perhaps . . . men in long clothes? A group of men, no women. Perhaps ten men. Long coats. Sitting in front of a big fire."

"The one you feel hung up in the atmosphere here—is he of the same period?"

"No," Sybil replied, "this is of a later period."

"How did he get here?"

"This is someone who was living here . . . died in this room . . . fire . . . the people in the long clothes are earlier, can't tell if they're men or women, could be monks, too . . . but the one whom I feel in the atmosphere of this room, he is from 1928."

We left the room and walked out into the corridor, the same corridor connecting the area in which we had just been with number 2, farther back in the hotel. It was here that the ghost had been observed by the maid, I later learned. Sybil mentioned that there were ten people with long clothes, but she could not get more.

"Only like a photograph," she insisted.

We proceeded to the lovely library, which is adorned with wooden paneling and two rather large paintings of Saints Brigid and Patrick—and I noticed that St. Brigid wore the long, robe-like dress of the ancient Gaelic women, a dress, incidentally, that some of Ireland's nineteenth-century poets imitated for romantic reasons. It reminded Sybil of what she had felt in the room upstairs.

From her own knowledge, she recalled that William Butler Yeats had a lady friend fond of wearing such ancient attire! Far-fetched though this sounded, on recollection I am not so sure. We left the house, and Paul Hughes drove us up a mountain road to the cottage in which the maid who had seen the ghost lived.

Hughes would go in first and try and persuade her to talk to me. Should he fail, he would then get the story once more from her and retell it to us afresh. We waited about fifteen minutes in his car while the manager tried his native charm on the frightened servant woman. He emerged and shook his head. But he had at least succeeded in having her tell of her experiences to him once more.

"About a year ago," Hughes began, "in the ground floor corridor leading to room number 2, Mrs. Coine saw a man come through the glass door and go into room 2."

"What did she do?" I interrupted.

"It suddenly struck Miss Coine that there was nobody staying in room 2 at the time. So she went down into room 2 and could not see anybody! She suddenly felt weak, and the housekeeper was coming along wondering what had happened to her. But she would not talk about it at first for she thought it would be bad for business at the hotel."

"Ridiculous," I said. "American tourists adore ghosts."

"Well," Hughes continued, "earlier this year—1966—there was a lady staying in room 2. Her daughter was in room 38. After two nights, she insisted on leaving room 2 and was happy to take a far inferior room instead. There were no complaints after she had made this change."

I discovered that rooms 2 and 27 were in distant parts of the hotel, just about as far apart as they could be.

There was a moment of silence as we sat in the car and I thought it all over.

"Did she say what the man looked like that she saw?" I finally asked, referring to Miss Coine's ghost.

"Yes," Hughes replied and nodded serenely. "*A tall man*, a very tall man."

"And a flesh and blood man could not have left the room by other means?"

"Impossible. At that stage the new windows had not yet been put in and the windows were inoperable with the exception of a small fan window. This happened about lunchtime, after Mass, on Sunday. In 1965."

"And the strange behavior of the lady?"

"Between Easter and Whitsun, this year, 1966."

We walked back into the main lobby of the hotel. There, among other memorabilia, were the framed pictures of great Irish minds connected with Renvyle House.

Among them, of course, one of William Butler Yeats.

I looked at it, long and carefully. Yeats was *a tall man*, a very tall man. . . .

* * *

In the winter of 1952–1953, Oliver St. John Gogarty wrote a brief article for *Tomorrow* magazine, entitled "Yeats and the Ghost of Renvyle Castle."

To begin with, the term castle was applied by *Tomorrow*'s editors, since Gogarty knew better than to call Renvyle House a castle. There *is* a Renvyle castle all right and it still stands, about two miles south of the hotel, a charred ruin of medieval masonry, once the property of the celebrated Irish pirate queen Grania O'Malley.

Gogarty's report goes back to the house that stood there prior to the fire. Our visit was to the new house, built upon its ruins. The popular tale of séances held at the Renvyle House must refer to the earlier structure, as none were held in the present one, as far is I know.

Gogarty's report tells of Yeats and his own interest in the occult; of one particular time when Mrs. Yeats, who was a medium, told of seeing a ghostly face at her window; of a séance held in an upstairs room in which the restless spirit of a young boy manifested who had died by his own hands there. Morgan Even, a Welshman who apparently was also a trance medium, was among the guests at the time, and he experienced an encounter with the ghost which left him frightened and weak.

"I felt a strange sensation. A feeling that I was all keyed up just like the tension in a nightmare, and with that terror that nightmares have. Presently, I saw a boy, stiffly upright, in brown velvet with some sort of shirt showing at his waist. He was about twelve. Behind the chair he stood, all white-faced, hardly touching the floor. It seemed that if he came nearer some awful calamity would happen to me. I was just as tensed up as he was—nightmare terrors, tingling air; but what made it awful was my being wide awake. The figure in the brown velvet only looked at me, but the atmosphere in the room vibrated. I don't know what else happened. I saw his large eyes, I saw the ruffles on his wrists. He stood vibrating. His luminous eyes reproved. He looked deeply into mine.

"The apparition lifted his hands to his neck and then, all of a sudden, his body was violently seized as if by invisible fiends and twisted into horrible contortions in mid-air. He was mad! I sympathized for a moment with his madness and felt myself at once in the electric tension of Hell."

Suicide! Suicide! Oh, my God, he committed suicide in this very house."

As it transpired, the ghost had communicated with Yeats through automatic writing. He objected to the presence of strangers in his house. But Yeats responded to his objection with a list of demands of his own such as the ghost could hardly have expected. First, he must desist from frightening the children in their early sleep. He must cease to moan about the chimneys. He must walk the house no more. He must not move furniture or terrify those who sleep nearby. And, finally, he was ordered to name himself to Yeats. And this he did.

How could Yeats, a visitor, have known that the children used at times to rush down crying from their bedroom? Nor could he have guessed that it was the custom of the Blake family to call their sons after the Heptarchy. And yet he found out the ghost's particular name. A name Gogarty had never gleaned from the local people though he lived for years among them.

The troubled spirit had promised to appear in the ghost room to Mrs. Yeats, as he was before he went mad sixty years before.

Presently, Mrs. Yeats appeared carrying a lighted candle. She extinguished it and nodded to her husband. "Yes, it is just as you said."

"My wife saw a pale-faced, red-haired boy of about fourteen years of age standing in the middle of the north room. She was by the fireplace when he first took shape. He had the solemn pallor of a tragedy beyond the endurance of a child. He resents the presence of strangers in the home of his ancestors. He is Harold Blake."

And now it became clear to me *what* Sybil Leek had felt! Upstairs, in the room nearly on the same spot where the ghostly boy had appeared in the *old* house, she had suddenly felt a terrible discomfort in her neck—just as the psychic Welshman had, all those years ago! Was she reliving the tragedy or was the pale boy still about?

But the maid had seen a tall stranger, not a young boy, and not in the haunted room, but far from it. Yeats had been terribly attached to this house, and, being a man of great inquisitiveness, was just the type to stay on even after death. If only to talk to the melancholy boy from his own side of the veil!

✳ 28

Is This You, Jean Harlow?

IF ANY MOVIE actress deserved the name of "the vamp," it certainly was Jean Harlow. The blonde actress personified the ideal of the 1930s—slim and sultry, moving her body in a provocative manner, yet dressing in the rather elegant, seemingly casual style of that period. Slinky dresses,

sweaters, and colorful accessories made Jean Harlow one of the outstanding glamor girls of the American screen. The public was never let in on any of her personal secrets or, for that matter, her personal tragedies. Her life story was carefully edited to present only those aspects of her personality that fit in with the preconceived notion of what a glamorous movie star should be like. In a way, Jean Har-

low was the prototype of all later blonde glamor girls of the screen, culminating with Marilyn Monroe. There is a striking parallel, too, in the tragic lives and sometimes ends of these blonde movie queens. Quite possibly the image they projected on the screen, or were forced to project, was at variance with their own private achievements and helped pave the way to their tragic downfalls.

To me, Jean Harlow will always stand out as the glamorous goddess of such motion pictures as *Red Dust*, which I saw as a little boy. The idea that she could have had an earthbound life after death seems to be very far from the image the actress portrayed during her lifetime. Thus it was with some doubt that I followed up a lead supplied by an English newspaper, which said the former home of the screen star was haunted.

The house in question is a handsome white stucco one-family house set back somewhat from a quiet residential street in Westwood, a section of Los Angeles near the University generally considered quiet and upper middle class. The house itself belonged to a professional man and his wife who shared it with their two daughters and two poodles. It is a two-story building with an elegant staircase winding from the rear of the ground floor to the upper story. The downstairs portion contains a rather large oblong living room which leads into a dining room. There are a kitchen and bathroom adjacent to that area and a stairway leading to the upper floor. Upstairs are two bedrooms and a bathroom.

When I first spoke on the telephone to Mrs. H., the present occupant of the house, asking permission to visit, she responded rather cordially. A little later I called back to make a definite appointment and found that her husband was far from pleased with my impending visit. Although he himself had experienced some of the unusual phenomena in the house, as a professional, and I suppose as a man, he was worried that publicity might hurt his career. I assured him that I was not interested in disclosing his name or address, and with that assurance I was again welcomed. It was a sunny afternoon when I picked up my tape recorder and camera, left my taxicab in front of the white house in Westwood, and rang the bell.

Mrs. H. was already expecting me. She turned out to be a petite, dark-blonde lady of around thirty, very much given to conversation and more than somewhat interested in the occult. As a matter of fact, she had read one of my earlier books. With her was a woman friend; whether the friend had been asked out of curiosity or security I do not know. At any rate the three of us sat down in the living room and I started to ask Mrs. H. the kind of questions I always ask when I come to an allegedly haunted house.

"Mrs. H., how long have you lived in this house?"

"Approximately four years."

"When you bought it, did you make any inquiries as to the previous owner?"

"I did not. I didn't really care. I walked into the house and I liked it and that was that."

"Did you just tell your husband to buy it?"

"Yes. I told him, 'This is our house.' I had the realtor go ahead and draw up the papers before he saw it because I knew he would feel as I did."

"Where did you live before?"

"All over—Brentwood, West Los Angeles, Beverly Hills. I was born in Canada."

"How many years have you been married?"

"Seventeen."

"You have children?"

"I have two daughters, nine and twelve."

"Did the real-estate man tell you anything about the house?"

"He did not."

"After you moved in and got settled, did you make some changes in it?"

"Yes; it was in kind of sad shape. It needed somebody to love it."

"Did you make any structural changes?"

"No. When we found out the history of the house we decided we would leave it as it was."

"So at the time you moved in, you just fixed it?"

"Yes."

"When was the first time that you had any *unusual* feelings about the house?"

"The day before we moved in I came over to direct the men who were laying the carpet. I walked upstairs and I had an experience at that time."

"What happened?"

"My two dogs ran barking and growling into the upstairs bedrooms; I went up, and I thought I heard something whisper in my ear. It scared me."

"That was in one of the upstairs bedrooms?"

"No, in the hallway just before the master bedroom. The dogs ran in barking and growling as if they were going to get somebody, and then when they got in there they looked around and there was nobody there."

"What did you hear?"

"I could swear I heard somebody say, *'Please help me!'* It was a soft whisper, sort of hushed."

"What did you do?"

"I talked to myself for a few minutes to get my bearings. I had never experienced anything like that, and I figured, 'Well, if it's there, fine.' I've had other ESP experiences before, so I just went about my business."

"Those other experiences you've had—were they before you came to this house?"

"Yes. I have heard my name being called."

"In this house or in another?"

"In other homes."

"Anyone you could recognize?"

"No, just female voices."

"Did you *see* anything unusual at any time?"

"I saw what I assume to be ectoplasm. . . . It was like cigarette smoke. It moved, and my dogs whined, tucked their tails between their legs, and fled from the room."

"Did you tell your husband about the whisper?"

Jean Harlow's old bed upstairs

"I did not. My husband is skeptical. I saw no reason to tell him."

"When was the next time you had any feeling of a presence here?"

"The night we moved in, my husband and I were lying in bed. Suddenly, it was as if the bed were hit by a very strong object three times. My husband said 'My God, I'm getting out of here. This place is haunted.' I replied, 'Oh, shush. It's all right if someone is trying to communicate. It's not going to hurt.' And to the ghost I said, 'You're welcome—how do you do; but we've got to get some sleep—we're very, very tired—so please let us be.'"

"And did it help?"

"Yes."

"How long did the peace last?"

"Well, the jerking of the bed never happened again. But other things happened. There is a light switch on my oven in the kitchen. For a long time after we moved in, the switch would go on every so often—by itself."

"Would it take anyone to turn it physically, to turn on the light?"

"Yes, you'd have to flip it up."

"Was there anybody else in the house who could have done it?"

"No, because I would be sitting here and I'd hear the click and I would go there and it would be *on.* It's happened ten or fifteen times, but recently it has stopped."

"Any other phenomena?"

"Something new one time, at dusk. I was walking from one room to the other. I was coming through the dining room, and for some reason I looked up at the ceiling. There it was, this light—"

"Did it have any particular shape?"

"No. It moved at the edges, but it really didn't have a form. It wasn't a solid mass, more like an outline. It was floating above me."

"Did you hear anything?"

"Not at that time. I have on one occasion. I was sitting right in the chair I am in now. My Aunt Mary was in that chair, and we both heard sobs. Terrible, sad, wrenching sobs coming from the corner over there by the mailbox. It was very upsetting, to say the least."

"Were these a woman's sobs?"

"Definitely."

"Did you see anything at the time?"

"No. I just felt terribly sad, and the hair stood up on my arms. Also, in this house there are winds at times, when there is no window open."

"Are there any cold spots that cannot be explained rationally?"

"Very frequently. Downstairs, usually here or in the upstairs bedroom, sometimes also in the kitchen."

"At the time your Aunt Mary was sitting here and you heard the sobs, did she also hear them?"

"Oh, she did, and I had to give her a drink."

"Have you heard any other sounds?"

"Footsteps. Up and down the stairs when nobody was walking up or down."

"Male or female?"

"I would say female, because they are light. I have also felt things brush by my face, touching my cheek."

"Since you came to this home, have you had any unusual dreams?"

"Definitely. One very important one. I was in bed and just dozing off, when I had a vision. I saw very vividly a picture of the upstairs bathroom. I saw a hand reaching out of a bathtub full of water, going up to the light switch, the socket where you turn power on and off. It then turned into a vision of wires, and brisk voltage struck the hand; the hand withered and died. It upset me terribly. The next morning my husband said, 'You know, I had the strangest dream last night.' He had had the *identical dream!*"

"Identical?"

"Practically. In his version, the hand didn't wither, but he saw the sparks coming out of it. I went into the bathroom and decided to call in an electrician. He took out the outdated switch. He said, 'Did you know this is outlawed? If anybody had been in the tub and reached up and touched the switch, he would have been electrocuted!' We moved the switch so the only way you can turn the switch on is *before* you go into the bathroom. You can no longer reach it from the tub. Whoever helped me with this—I'm terribly grateful to her."

"Is there anything else of this kind you would care to tell me?"

"I have smelled perfume in the upstairs children's bedroom, a very strong perfume. I walked into the room. My little daughter who sleeps there doesn't have perfume. That's the only place I smell it, my little girl's bedroom."

"Has any visitor ever come to this house without knowledge of the phenomena and complained about anything unusual?"

"A friend named Betty sat in the kitchen and said, 'My gosh, I wish you'd close the windows. There's such a draft in here.' But everything was shut tight."

"Has your husband observed anything unusual except for the dream?"

"One evening in the bedroom he said, 'Boy, there's a draft in here!' I said there couldn't be. All the windows were closed."

"What about the children?"

"My youngest daughter, Jenny, has complained she hears a party in her upstairs closet. She says that people are having a party in it. She can hear them."

"When was the house built?"

"I believe in 1929."

"Was it built to order for anyone?"

"No. It was just built like many houses in this area, and then put up for sale."

"Who was the first tenant here?"

"It was during the Depression. There were several successive tenants."

"How did Jean Harlow get involved with the house?"

"She was living in a small home, but the studio told her she should live in a better area. She rented this house in the early '30s and moved into it with her parents."

"How long did she live here?"

"About four years. She paid the rent on it longer, however, because after she married, her folks stayed in this house. I believe she married her agent."

"How did she die?"

"She died, I understand, as the result of a beating given to her by her husband which damaged her kidneys. The story goes that on the second night, after their honeymoon, he beat her. She came back to this house, took her mother into the bathroom and showed her what he had done to her. She was covered with bruises. She tried to make up with him, but to no avail. The night he killed himself, she was in this house. There was a rumor that he was impotent or a latent homosexual. He shot himself. When she heard the news, she was in her upstairs bedroom. She tried to commit suicide, because she thought she was the reason. She took an overdose of sleeping pills."

"Did she succeed?"

"She did not. Her parents put pressure on her to move out of this house. She built another one and subsequently died of a kidney disease."

"Not immediately after the beating?"

"No—a few years later. Her parents were Christian Scientists, and she didn't have ordinary medical help at the time."

"Then what took place in this house, emotionally speaking? The marriage to Paul Bern, the news of his suicide, and her own attempt to commit suicide upstairs. Which rooms were particularly connected with these events?"

"The living room. She was married there. And the bathroom upstairs. I left it as it was."

"Do you have any feelings about it?"

"I have a feeling about the bathroom. I know she's been in that bathroom many times. I don't know if she tried to commit suicide in the bathroom or if she took the pills in the bedroom."

"Where did the actual beating take place?"

"They say it was in the bathroom downstairs."

"Which is the bathroom you have such a weird feeling in, the downstairs or the upstairs?"

"Downstairs."

"Anything pertaining to the front or the outside of the house?"

"There are knocks at our front door when there is nobody there; visitors would say, 'There's someone at your door,' and there wasn't. . . . It happens all the time."

"Are you sure other people hear the knocks too?"

"Yes."

"Somebody couldn't have done it and run away in a hurry?"

"No: It's a funny knock. Kind of gentle. It isn't like a 'let-me-in' type knock. Flesh-and-blood people wouldn't knock on a door that way."

"When was the last time you had any feeling of a presence in this house?"

"Maybe two or three months ago."

"Do you feel she's still around?"

"Yes. Also, I feel she was very upset at the way she was portrayed as a kind of loose woman without morals. Her biography presents her as something she was not."

"Do you think she's trying to express herself through you?"

"No, but I think it's terrible what they've done to her reputation. They had no right to do that."

"Do you feel that she's trying to set the record straight?"

"I would imagine. I can only put myself in her place. If I were to cross over under those circumstances, I would be very unhappy. I hope some day somebody will write another book about Harlow and go into it with a sensitive, loving attitude instead of sensationalism as a way to make a fast buck."

I thanked Mrs. H. and prepared to leave the house that had once been Jean Harlow's. Perhaps the lady of the house was merely reliving the more emotional aspects of the late screen star's life, the way an old film is rerun from time to time on television. Was she picking up these vibrations from the past through psychometry? Or was there perhaps something of the *substance* of Jean Harlow still present in the atmosphere of this house? As I walked out the front door into the still-warm late afternoon, I looked back at Mrs. H., who stood in the doorway waving me good-bye. Her blonde hair was framed by the shadow cast by the door itself. For a fleeting moment, some of the blonde glamor of the late Jean Harlow seemed to have impressed itself upon her face. Perhaps it was only my imagination, but all of a sudden I felt that Jean Harlow hadn't really left the house where so much of her emotional life had taken place.

✳ 29

Do The Barrymores Still Live Here?

PAULA DAVIDSON IS A charming, introspective woman from Cleveland, Ohio, who decided that a career in the entertainment field could be best achieved by moving to Los Angeles. In 1969 she arrived in Beverly Hills and took a job with a major advertising agency. The job was fine, but there was something peculiar about the house into which she had moved. In the first place, it was far too large to be a one-family home, and yet she had been told that it once belonged to one family—the family of Lionel Barrymore. Perched high in the Hollywood hills, the house gives a deceptive impression if one approaches it from the street. From that side it presents only two stories, but the rear of the house looks down into a deep ravine, perhaps as much as five or six stories deep. There is even a private cable car, no longer in use. The once-beautiful gardens have long since fallen into disrepair and now present a picture of sad neglect.

On the whole, the house was and is the kind of palatial mansion a Barrymore would have felt at home in. Although the gardens have been neglected for years, the house itself is still bright, having been painted recently, and its Spanish decor adds to the mystique of its background. When Paula Davidson took up residence there, the owner had been forced to sublet part of the house in order to hold on to the house itself. One of the rooms in what used to be the former servants' quarters was rented to Heidi, a composer who wrote musical scores for films. She was in the habit of practicing her music in the music room on the first level. Since the house was quiet during the daytime, everyone having gone off to work, Heidi liked to practice during that part of the day. In the stillness of the empty house she would frequently hear footsteps approaching as if someone unseen were listening to her playing. On one occasion she clearly heard a baby cry when there was no baby in the house.

I promised Paula to look into the matter, and on May 31, 1969, she picked me up at the Continental Hotel to take me to the Barrymore mansion. With us was another friend named Jill Taggart. Jill had worked with me before. A writer and parttime model, Jill had displayed ESP talents at an early age and shown amazing abilities with clairvoyance and psychometry. It occurred to me that taking her to a place she knew nothing about, without of course telling her where we were going and why, might yield some interesting results. Consequently I avoided discussing anything connected with the purpose of our visit.

When we arrived at the mansion, the owner of the house greeted us cordially. Paula, Heidi, the owner and I started out following Jill around the house as my psychic friend tried to get her bearings. Unfortunately, however, we had picked an evening when some of the other tenants in the house were having a party. What greeted us on our arrival was not the serene stillness of a night in the Hollywood hills but the overly loud blaring of a jukebox and the stamping of many feet in one of the basement rooms.

I have never worked under worse conditions. Under the circumstances, however, we had no choice but to try to get whatever we could. Even before we entered the house Jill remarked that she felt two people, a man and a woman, hanging on in the atmosphere, and she had the feeling that someone was watching us. Then she added, "She died a long time after he did." I questioned her further about the entities she felt present. "She's old; he's young. He must have been in his thirties; she is considerably older. I get the feeling of him as a memory. Perhaps only her memory of him, but whichever one of the entities is here, it is madder than hell at the moment." With the noise of the music going on downstairs I couldn't rightly blame the ghost for being mad. Jill then pointed at a corner of the house and said, "I keep seeing the corner of the house up there."

I later discovered that the top room was a kind of ballroom with a balcony. In it Heidi frequently heard a telephone ring, but that was not the only part of the house where an invisible telephone kept ringing. "I used to be down in the bottom room, the one right next to where the noise is now," Heidi explained, "practicing my music, but I'd constantly have to stop, thinking I heard the telephone ring. Of course there was no telephone." I took Heidi aside so that Jill could not hear her remarks. Jill would not have been interested anyway, for she was engrossed in her study of the house now, walking up and down the stairs, peering into rooms with a quizzical expression on her face.

"Tell me," I asked Heidi, "what else did you experience in this house?"

"Frequently when I was down in that room playing the piano I would hear people walking on the stairs; this happened at all times of the day, and there was never anyone up there."

Jill was passing by us now. "I picked up a name," she said. "Grace—and then there is something that sounds like Hugen." I looked at the owner of the house. Jill was out of earshot again. "The party who had the house before us was Arty Erin," the owner said, shrugging.

"Did anyone ever die of violence in this house?" I asked.

"I've heard rumors, something having to do with the cable car, but I don't know for sure."

We all walked over to the cable car, covered with rust and dirt and long out of commission. Jill placed her hands on it to see if she could get any psychometric impression from it. "This cable car has been much loved, I should say, and much enjoyed." Then her facial expression changed to one of absolute horror. Quickly she took her hands off the cable car.

"What is it, Jill?" I asked.

"Someone came down violently, down the hill in the cable car. Later he wound up here near the pulley."

We walked down to the bottom of the ravine, where there was a magnificent swimming pool. The pool itself was still in operating condition, and there was a pool house on the other side of it. Down here the sound of the music was largely muted, and one could hear one's voice again. Jill obviously had strong impressions now, and I asked her what she felt about the place.

"I feel that a very vicious man lived here once, but I don't think he is connected with the name Grace I got before. This may have been at a different time. Oh, he had some dogs, kind of like mastiffs. I think there were two and possibly three. They were vicious dogs, trained to be vicious."

"What did this man do?"

"I see him as a sportsman, quick with words. There were also two young people connected with this man, a boy and a girl. I see them laughing and romping about and having a wonderful time here as teenagers. He seems not to like it at all but is tolerating it. But the dogs seemed to have played a very big part in his life. Nobody would dare enter his property without his permission because of those dogs. Permission, I feel, was rarely given except with a purpose in mind. He has exerted the strongest influence on this house, but I don't think he was the first owner."

"Do you feel that anyone well-known was connected with this house?"

"Yes. More than one well-known person, in fact." I asked Jill to describe the personality that she felt was strongest in the atmosphere of the house.

"I see this man with a small moustache, dark thinning hair, exceedingly vain, with a hawklike nose. He has brownish eyes; they have dark circles under them. He doesn't look dissipated by an excess of drink or food, but he does look dissipated through his own excesses. That is, his own mind's excesses. He prides himself on having the eye of the eagle and so affects an eagle-eyed look. I also suspect that he is nearsighted. I see him wearing a lot of smoking jackets. One in particular of maroon color."

The description sounded more and more fascinating. What profession did she think the man followed?

"I see him with a microphone in his hand, also a cigarette and a glass. He might be an actor or he might be a director."

I asked Jill whether this man owned the house or was merely a visitor.

The question seemed to puzzle her. "He might be a visitor, but I see him down here so much he might be staying here. The young people I described before might belong to the owner of the house."

I wondered if the man in the maroon jacket was one of the disturbing entities in the house.

Jill nodded. "I think this man is as well aware now of what he does as when he was alive. *I think he is still here.*"

"Can you get an indication of his name?"

"I get the letter *S*, but that's because he reminds me so much of Salvador Dali."

"Anything else?"

"Yes, there is an *L* connected with him. The *L* stands for a name like Lay or Lee or Leigh, something like that. Oh, and there is something else. A Royal typewriter is important. I don't know if it's important to him because he writes letters or what, but *Royal* is important."

I was about to turn to the owner of the house when Jill's arm shot up, pointing to the balcony. "That woman up there—she acts very much the owner of the house. I imagine it's Grace." Since none of us could see the woman, I asked Jill for description of what she saw.

"She's a woman in her sixties, with gray or white hair. And it's very neat. She is very statuesque—slender and tall—and she wears a long flowing dress that has pleats all over. She seems to be raising her hand always, very dramatically, like an actress."

I thanked Jill for her work and turned to Marie, the owner of the house. How did all this information stack up with the knowledge she had of the background of her house—for instance, the business of telephones ringing incessantly when there were no telephones about?

"At one time this house was owned by a group of gamblers. They had a whole bunch of telephones all over the house. This goes back several years."

"What about this Grace?"

"The name rings a bell with me, but I can't place it."

"And the baby Heidi keeps hearing?"

"Well, of course, the house used to belong to actor Lionel Barrymore. He and his wife had two babies who died in a fire, although it was not in this house."

Apparently Lionel Barrymore had owned this house, while his brother John lived not far away on Tower Road. Thus John was in a very good position to visit the house

frequently. Jill had spoken of a man she saw clairvoyantly as reminding her of Salvador Dali. That, we all agreed, was a pretty good description of the late John Barrymore. Jill had also mentioned the name Lee or Leigh or something like it. Perhaps she was reaching for Lionel.

The mention of the word *Royal* I found particularly fascinating. On the one hand, the Barrymores were often referred to as the royal family of the theater. On the other hand, if a typewriter was meant, one must keep in mind that John Barrymore had been hard at work on his autobiography in his later years, though he had never completed it. Yet the matter of finishing it had been very much on his mind. As for the teenagers Jill felt around the premises, the two children, Diana and John, Jr., had been at the house a great deal when they were teenagers. John Barrymore, however, didn't like children at all; he merely tolerated them.

I asked Marie (who had been here for more than a year prior to our visit) if she had ever seen or heard anything uncanny.

"No, but I can feel a presence."

The house has twelve rooms altogether, but according to local tradition, the three bottom rooms were added on somewhat later. "Has anything tragic ever occurred in this house, to your knowledge?"

"A man fell down those stairs head first and was killed. But it was an accident."

Obviously the house had been lived in for many years both before and after the Barrymore tenancy. It seems only natural that other emotional events would leave their mark in the atmosphere of the old house. Despite all this, Jill was able to pick up the personalities of both John and Lionel Barrymore and perhaps even of sister Ethel, if she was the lady in the gray robe. We left the house with a firm promise to dig into the Hall of Records for further verification.

Two weeks later I received a letter from Paula Davidson. She was having lunch with a friend of hers, director William Beaudine, Sr., who had been well acquainted with both John and Lionel Barrymore. Paula mentioned her experience at the house with Jill and me and the description given by Jill of the entity she had felt present in the house. When she mentioned the vicious dogs, Mr. Beaudine remarked that he remembered only too well that John had kept some Great Danes. They might very well have been the vicious dogs described by Jill.

Since that time Paula Davidson has moved away from the house on Summit Ridge. Others have moved in, but no further reports have come to me about the goings-on at the house. If the noisy party we witnessed during our visit was any indication of the present mood of the house, it is most unlikely that the Barrymores will put in an appearance. For if there was one thing the royal family of the theater disliked, it was noisy competition.

The Latest Adventures of The Late Clifton Webb

WHEN I WAS in my twenties Clifton Webb was one of the funniest men on the screen. To me, at least, he represented the epitome of Anglo-Saxon coolness and wit. Only later did I learn that Mr. Webb came from the Midwest and that his English accent and manner were strictly stage-induced. There is hardly anyone in this country who doesn't remember his capers as Mr. Belvedere, the deadpan babysitter, or his many other roles in which he portrayed the reserved yet at times explosive character that contained so much of Clifton Webb himself. I saw him on the New York stage in one of Noel Coward's plays, and in the flesh he acted exactly as he had on the screen: cool, deadpan, with a biting, satirical sense of humor.

With the success of his Mr. Belvedere and several motion pictures based on it, Webb moved into a new-found financial security and consequently went casting about for a home corresponding to his status in the movie industry. His eyes fell upon a white stucco building in one of the quieter parts of Beverly Hills. The house, set back somewhat from a side street not far from busy Sunset Boulevard, had a vaguely Spanish-style wing paralleling the street, to which a shorter wing toward the rear of the house was attached, creating an enclosed courtyard—again in the Spanish tradition. The house was and still is surrounded by similar buildings, all of them belonging to the well-to-do of Beverly Hills. It has had a number of distinguished owners. Grace Moore, the singer, spent some of her happiest years in it. Later, actor Gene Lockhart lived there, and his daughter June, who is quite psychic, had a number of uncanny experiences in it at that time. Clifton Webb himself was on friendly footing with the world of the unseen. He befriended Kenny Kingsley, the professional psychic, and on more than one occasion confided that he had seen Grace Moore's spirit in his house. Evidently the restless spirit of the late singer stayed on in the house throughout its occupation by Clifton Webb and his mother, Maybelle. For it appears to me that the "dancing figure of a woman," which the current lady of the house has reportedly seen, goes back to the Grace Moore period rather than to the time of Clifton Webb.

Clifton Webb was inordinately happy in this house. At the height of his motion picture career, surrounded by friends, he made up for the arid years of his youth when he had had to struggle for survival. In 1959 his mother passed away, bringing an end to a close and sometimes overpowering relationship. Webb had never married, nor would he have wanted to. His leanings had never been hidden from the world, and he was quite content to let matters be as they were. When his mother died, Webb became more and more of a recluse. In semi-retirement, he kept to his house most of the time, seeing fewer friends as the years went on. In mid-October of 1966 he himself died, almost eight years after his mother. During those eight years, he probably continued his relationship with Maybelle, for Clifton Webb was psychic and believed in life after death. Her clothes and belongings remained in a locked room in the house right up to the time of Clifton's death.

During his twenty years of residence in this house, Webb had remodeled it somewhat and added a room that he dubbed the Greek room, which he had furnished and decorated to his particular taste, taking great care that everything should be exactly as he wanted it to be. By mid-January of 1967 the house was on the market. Word of the availability of this house came to the attention of a producer at one of the major motion picture studios in Hollywood. He and his writer-wife had been looking for precisely such a house. Within a matter of days they purchased it and prepared to move in. With the need for redecorating and making certain alterations on the house, the C.s were not able to move in until sometime in May. Two days before their actual move, they were showing the house to a friend. While they were busy in another part of the house, the gentleman found himself alone in the Greek room. He was wearing contact lenses and felt the need to clean his lenses at that point. There is a bathroom, decorated in gray, off the Greek room. He entered the bathroom, put the contact lenses on the shelf and turned on the water faucet. When he raised his head from the sink the lenses were no longer there. He searched everywhere but couldn't locate them, and they were never found.

The new owners of the house thought nothing of the matter, but shortly afterwards another event took place that shook their confidence. On the first night of their stay in the house Mr. C.'s mother happened to be staying in the Greek room. Unfamiliar with the bathroom, she found herself unable to locate either a toothbrush receptacle or a glass. She therefore left her toothbrush on the sink. The next morning when she entered the bathroom she found the wall receptacle open and exposed and her toothbrush firmly placed into it. Since there had been no one in the room during the night but herself, she became frightened and tried to run from the room. To her amazement the door was locked and resisted opening. In panic, she fled through the window. Later, calmed down, she returned to the room.

The following morning she awoke in bed and found her cigarettes broken in half, tobacco scattered all over the bed and the package crushed. It then occurred to Mr. and Mrs. C. that the late Clifton Webb had been vehemently against smoking in his final years.

Earlier that night Mr. and Mrs. C and Mr. C.'s mother had been standing near the pool in the courtyard. All three were looking toward the house through the master bedroom into what was then Mrs. C.'s bathroom. Suddenly they saw a ghostly swaying figure looking somewhat like the legendary ectoplasmic ghost. They rubbed their eyes and looked again, but the figure had disappeared.

Over the next few weeks several more apparitions were observed by the C.s. In the courtyard in front of the house they always saw the same tall gray forms, shadowy, yet with some substance. There was no doubt in their minds that they were seeing human figures.

Late in July Mrs. C. was coming home one night around midnight. Stepping into the courtyard, she saw a form like an hourglass (this time completely stationary) in the living room to the left of the couch. Finally she got up enough courage to move closer; when she did so, the form remained still until it gradually dissolved.

All during those first few weeks the animals in the house behaved strangely. The C.s had several cats and dogs, and whenever they would go to certain spots in the house they would scream in terror and bolt from the area. One of the dogs would not go into the Greek room no matter how much he was coaxed. Instead he would howl at it, and his hackles would rise.

Even the master bedroom was not free from phenomena. Frequently the C.s would awaken in the middle of the night to the sound of curtains rustling and perceive a form of sorts standing in the corner of the room, observing them.

At first the producer and his wife wondered whether their own imagination and their knowledge of the background of the house were creating fantasies in them. Their doubts were dispelled, however, when they gave a dinner party and were showing a number of guests through the house. One friend, a producer who was staying with the C.s, suddenly stopped dead while walking from the master bedroom into the hallway, which was then being used as Mr. C.'s study. He claimed he felt something cold enveloping him. Since he is a man not given to hallucinations and has no interest in the occult, his statement carried weight with the C.s. At the time, the producer employed two servants, a Mexican maid and a butler who slept in a cottage to the rear of the house. On several occasions the maid claimed that a cold presence had attacked her and that lights had gone on and off without explanation. It terrified her and she wanted to know what was going on. The producer could only shake his head, saying he wished he knew himself.

The Greek room seemed to be the center of the activities. Women, especially, staying in the Greek room often had personal articles moved. Mr. C.'s sister, a great skeptic, visited them and was put up in that room. On the third night of her stay she awoke toward dawn feeling a warm, enveloping embrace from behind her. She screamed, jumped out of bed, and turned on the lights. There was no one in the room. The bathroom adjoining that room was also the scene of many experiences. The toilet paper in it unrolled itself on numerous occasions. Even more fantastic, the toilet had several times been used by parties unknown during the night and left unflushed, even though no human being had been in the bathroom.

In September Mrs. C. took on additional duties as a writer and hired a secretary and assistant who worked in the house with her. But it appeared as if "someone" wasn't too pleased with the arrangements. All during the winter, things kept disappearing from her office or getting moved about. Her engagement calendar would turn up in the Greek room, and certain files that were kept in cabinets in her office would disappear and turn up in other parts of the house, although no one had placed them there. It appeared that someone was creating havoc in her professional life, perhaps to discourage her or perhaps only to play a prank and put the new owners of the house on notice that a previous resident hadn't quite left.

The worst was yet to come. In October there was an occurrence the C.s will never forget. All that evening the dog had been howling and running about the house wildly as if anticipating something dreadful. Sounds were heard for which there seemed to be no natural explanation. Then, in the middle of the night, Mr. and Mrs. C. woke up because of noises both of them heard. Someone was moaning in their bedroom, and as they looked up they saw a gray figure forming in the corner of the room.

The next morning they realized they had been through the night on which Clifton Webb had died, exactly one year to the day. What they had heard was a reenactment of that terrible moment. From then on the moaning seemed to abate.

Although neither Mr. nor Mrs. C. were exactly believers in the occult, they were open-minded enough to realize that something was terribly wrong in their house. By now they knew that the previous owner, most likely Clifton Webb, was dissatisfied with their presence in the house. They did not understand why, however. True, they had made certain changes in the house; they had rearranged the furniture, and they had used the Greek room as a guest room. They had also made some changes in the garden and courtyard, especially around the rose bushes, which had been Mr. Webb's favorites. But was that enough of a reason for Mr. Webb to want them out of the house?

In January of 1968 they were approached by a real estate agent, out of the blue, on behalf of a couple who had passed the house once and immediately become interested in acquiring it. The C.s had no intention of selling, so they named a fantastically high price, thinking this would end the matter. They discovered to their surprise that the couple wanted to buy the house anyway. The C.s then reconsidered and decided to look for another house. But they discovered that prices for similar houses had risen so much that they might as well stay where they were, and after some discussion they decided to turn down the offer.

That very night Mrs. C. was awakened at 3:30 A.M. by a rustling sound among the curtains in the master bedroom. She looked toward the disturbance and noticed an ectoplasmic form moving across the room and back. As she stared at it in disbelief, she heard a voice saying, "Well, well," over and over. It had the sound of a fading echo and gradually disappeared along with the apparition. Several days in a row Mrs. C. saw the same figure and heard the voice exclaim, as if in amusement, "Well, well, well, well." At the same time, she received the telepathic impression that the ghost was not feeling unfriendly toward her anymore and that he wanted her and her husband to know that he didn't mind their staying on in the house.

By now Mrs. C. was convinced that the ghost was none other than Clifton Webb, and she approached F. M., another producer, who had been a close personal friend of the actors, with a view toward asking some personal questions about him. When she reported the voice's saying, "Well, well, well, well" over and over, Mr. M. remarked that Webb had been in the habit of saying "Well, well" frequently, sometimes for no apparent reason. With that Mrs. C. felt that the identity of the ghostly visitor was firmly established.

That night she was awakened again by a feeling that she was not alone. She looked up and saw the silhouette of a man. This time it was clearly Clifton Webb. He was standing just outside the bedroom window in the courtyard. As she looked at the apparition, it occurred to her that he seemed taller than he had been in his movie roles. For what seemed to her several minutes, but may have been only a few seconds, she was able to observe the shadowy apparition of the actor looking into the house directly at her. Shortly afterward it dissolved into thin air. The tall appearance of the figure puzzled her somewhat, so she checked into it. To her amazement she discovered that Webb had actually been six feet tall in life.

A few days later she encountered Mr. Webb again. Her attention was drawn by the strange behavior of her cats, which ran into her office from the courtyard. She was in the habit of taking a shortcut from her office to the kitchen by walking diagonally across the courtyard. As she did so this time, she noticed the tall, erect figure of Mr. Webb in the living room. He seemed to be walking slowly across the living room as if in search of something.

It had become clear to Mr. and Mrs. C. that Webb was not altogether satisfied with the way things were, even though he seemed to be somewhat more friendly toward them. So they invited me to the house to investigate the situation with the help of a reputable psychic. I in turn asked Sybil Leek to come along with me.

On a Thursday night in October 1968 a group of us met at the house. Besides Sybil and me there were my wife Catherine, Sybil's son Julian, and several people who had known Clifton Webb intimately. They had been asked not out of curiosity but to help identify any material of an evidential nature that might come through Sybil in trance. There was the distinguished playwright Garson Kanin, his actress wife, the late Ruth Gordon, Rupert Allen, a public relations man who had worked for Webb for many years, and two or three others who had known him.

Sybil, of course, knew nothing about the circumstances of the case, nor why she had been brought to this house. During dinner I was careful to steer the conversation away from the occult, and Sybil and I stayed out of the Greek room. But on her way to the house Sybil had already had her first clairvoyant impression. She described a tall, slender and "sexless" individual who had not been born in California. She also mentioned that she felt the initial V or something sounding like it connected with a personality in the house.

After we had grouped ourselves around Sybil in the Greek room, I began the proceedings, as is my custom, by asking the medium for clairvoyant impressions. My hope was that Mr. Webb might pay us a visit, or at any rate tell Sybil what it was that he wanted or what had kept him tied to his former home in so forceful and physical a manner.

"Sybil," I said, "do you get any impressions about the room?"

"I don't like this room," Sybil said sternly. "I wouldn't choose to be in it. I have a strange feeling on my right-hand side toward the window. I feel somebody died here very suddenly. Also I've had for some time now the initial V and the word *Meadows* on my mind. I would say this is the least likable room in the house. The strange thing is, I don't feel a male or a female presence; I feel something sexless."

"What sort of person is this?"

"I feel an atmosphere of frustration, an inability to do anything."

"Why is this personality frustrated?"

"Bad relationships."

I decided it was time to begin trance. After brief suggestions Sybil went under quickly and completely. I addressed myself now to the unseen presences in the atmosphere. "Whoever might be present in this room, come forward, please, peacefully and as a friend, so that we may speak to you. We have assembled here as friends. We have come to help you find peace and happiness in this house. Use this instrument, the medium; come peacefully and speak to us so that we may be of help to you in whatever may trouble you."

After a moment Sybil started to toss, eyes closed, breathing heavily. "Can't do it, won't do it. No, I won't do it," she mumbled.

I asked that whoever was speaking through her speak somewhat louder since I had difficulty making out the words. A sardonic smile stole across Sybil's face now, very unlike her own expression. "I'm thirsty, I want a drink, get me a drink."

I promised the entity a drink a little later, but first I wanted to know who it was who had come to speak to us. Instead, Sybil sighed, "It's so cold here, chill, chill. I want to sing and sing. Sing, sing, sing, la, la, la, jolly good time."

"What kind of a song do you want to sing?" I asked, going along with the gag.

"Dead men tell no tales."

"Wouldn't you like to talk to us and tell us about yourself?"

"I want to sing."

"What are you doing here?"

"Writing, writing a song."

"Are you a writer?"

"I do a lot of things."

"What else can you do?"

"Anything, anything."

"Come on, tell me about it."

"No."

"How do I know you can do those things?" I said, using the teasing method now. "You haven't even told me your name."

A snort came from Sybil's lips. "Webb of intrigue."

"What did you say? Would you mind repeating it?"

"Webb, Webb, W-E-B-B."

"Is that your name?"

"Webb, Webb, Webb."

"Why are you here?"

"I need friends."

"Well, you've got them."

"Need friends. I'm lonely. I need to sing."

"Are you a singer?"

"I sing music; music is good."

"Why are you in this particular house?"

"I have a right to be here."

"Tell us why. What does it mean to you?"

"Money, friendship."

"Whose friendship?"

"Where is Wade? Wade, to drink with. People drive me mad."

"What is it that troubles you?" I asked, as softly as I could.

"I won't tell anyone. No help from anyone. There is no help."

"Trust me."

"I'll drink another glass."

"I've come all the way from New York to help you."

"New York—I'll go to New York and watch the people, shows, singing."

"Are you alone?"

"Yes. Nobody wants people like me."

"That isn't true, for I wouldn't be here if we didn't have the feeling of friendship toward you. Why do you think we've come here?"

"Curiosity. There is a reason behind everything. Who are you?"

I explained who I was and that I'd come to try and understand him and if possible set him free from his earthly ties. He had difficulty understanding what I was talking about.

"I want to help you."

"Late."

"Please let me help you."

"Webb."

"Yes, I heard the name," I acknowledged.

"It means nothing."

"I believe there was an actor by that name."

Sybil started to sob now. "Acting, acting all my life."

"What about this house: why are you here?"

"I like it."

"What does it mean to you?"

"What does it mean to me? Lots of money here. Friends. Friends who look after me."

"Do I know them?"

"A newspaperman; I hate newspapermen. Nosey bastards. Let's have a drink. Why don't we have some music?"

"What do you do here all day long?"

"I'm here to drink, look around for a friend or two. I'd like to know a few people. Get some work."

"What kind of work?"

"Contracts. Contracts must be somehow fulfilled."

"Contracts with whom?"

"There's a man called Meadows. Harry Meadows."

"Do you have a contract with him?"

"No good."

"What were you supposed to do?"

"Sign away the house."

"What sort of business is he in?"

"Don't know what to tell you."

"Where did you meet him?"

"He came here. Sixty-four."

"I'd like to help you find peace, Mr. Webb," I said seriously.

The entity laughed somewhat bitterly. "Mr. Webb."

"How else would you want me to call you?"

"Mr. Webb—it's finished."

"Perhaps I can help you."

"Who cares, Cathy."

"Who's Cathy?"

"Where am I, I am lost."

I assured the entity that he was not lost but merely speaking through the medium of another person. Webb obviously had no idea that such things as trance mediumship were possible. He was, of course, quite shocked to find himself in the body of Sybil Leek, even temporarily. I calmed him down and again offered to help. What was it that troubled him most?

"I can't do anything now. I am drunk, I want to sing."

Patiently I explained what his true status was. What he was experiencing were memories from his past; the future was quite different.

"I want to say a lot, but nobody listens."

"I am listening."

"I'm in trouble. Money, drink, Helen,"

"What about Helen?"

"I'm peculiar."

"That's your own private affair, and nobody's criticizing you for being peculiar. Also you are very talented."

"Yes." One could tell that he liked the idea of being acclaimed even after his death.

"Now tell me about Helen. Is she in one of your wills?"

"She's dead, you idiot. I wouldn't leave anything to a dead woman. She was after my money."

"What was Helen's full name?"

"Helen T. Meadows."

"How old were you on your last birthday?"

"We don't have birthdays here."

"Ahah," I said, "but then you know where you are and what you are."

"I do," the entity said, stretching the *oo* sound with an inimitable comic effect. Anyone who has ever heard Clifton Webb speak on screen or stage would have recognized the sound.

"You know then that you're over there. Good. Then at least we don't have to pretend with each other that I don't know and you don't know."

"I'm tired."

"Was there any other person who knew you and Helen?"

"Cathy, Cathy was a little thing that came around."

"Was there a male friend you might remember by name?"

There was distrust in Sybil's voice when the entity answered. "You're a newspaperman."

"I'm not here as a journalist but primarily to help you. Does the name Conrad mean anything to you?" I'd been told by friends of the late Clifton Webb to ask this. I myself had no idea who this Conrad was or is.

"Hmmm," the entity replied, acknowledging the question. "Initial V, V for Victory." At the same time, Sybil took hold of a chain she used as a belt and made an unmistakable gesture as if she were about to strangle someone with it.

"Who was Conrad? Are you trying to show me something?"

Unexpectedly Sybil broke into sobbing again. "Damn you, leave me alone."

The sobbing got heavier and heavier. I decided it was time to release the entity. "Go in peace then; go in peace and never be drawn back to this house where you've had such unhappy experiences. Go and join the loved ones awaiting you on the other side of life. Good-bye, Mr. Webb. Go in peace. Leave this instrument now and let her return to her own body without any memory of what has come through her entranced lips."

A few moments later Sybil awoke, startled, rubbing her eyes and trying to figure out where she was for a moment. "I do feel a bit peculiar," Sybil said, slightly shaken. "Maybe I will have a glass of wine."

After everyone had recovered from the tense attention given to Sybil's trance performance, I invited discussion of what had just transpired. Those who had known Clifton Webb in life volunteered the information that at times Sybil's face had looked somewhat like Webb's, at least to the extent that a woman's face can look like a man's. Her voice, too, had reminded them of the actor's voice—especially in the middle of the session when the trance seemed to have been deepest. As for the names mentioned, Rupert Allen explained that the "Cathy" Sybil had named was a secretary whom Webb had employed for only a week. Also, the Helen Meadows mentioned was probably Helen Mathews, a long-time secretary and assistant of the late actor. There had been a great deal of discussion about a will in which the assistant figured. Quite possibly, Webb and Miss Mathews had been at odds toward the end of his life. As for his wanting to sing, Rupert Allen reminded us that long before Clifton Webb had become a famous actor he had been one of the top song-and-dance men on Broadway, had appeared in many musicals and musical revues and had always loved the musical theater. The mannerisms and some of the phrases, Mr. Allen confirmed, were very much in the style of Clifton Webb, as was his negative reaction to the idea of having a newspaperman present.

There had been no near relatives living at the time of Webb's death. Under the circumstances the estate, including the house, would go to whomever he had chosen in his will. Was there a second will that had never been found? Was it this need to show the world that a second will existed that kept Clifton Webb tied to his former home?

After the memorable séance with Sybil Leek, I inquired of the owners from time to time whether all was quiet. For a while it was. But then reports of Mr. Webb's reappearance reached me. I realized, if course, that the producer's wife herself, being phychic to a great extent, was supplying some of the energies necessary for Webb to manifest himself in this manner. But I was equally sure that she did not do so consciously. If anything, she wanted a quiet house. But the apparition of Webb and perhaps of Grace Moore, if indeed it was she in the garden, managed to convince Mrs. C. of the reality of psychic phenomena. She no longer feared to discuss her experiences in public. At first her friends looked at her askance, but gradually they came to accept the sincerity and objectivity of her testimony. Others who had never previously mentioned any unusual experiences admitted they had felt chills and uncanny feelings in various parts of the house while visiting the place.

Clifton Webb continues to maintain a foothold in the house, for better or for worse. Perhaps he likes the attention, or perhaps he's merely looking for that other will. At any rate, he no longer seems to delight in surprising the current owners of the house. After all, they know who he is and what he's up to. Mr. Webb always knew the value of a good entrance. In time, I am sure, he will also know how to make his exit.

✳ 31

The Haunted Rocking Chair at Ash Lawn

NOT ONLY HOUSES are haunted, even furniture can be the recipient of ghostly attention. Not very far from Castle Hill, Virginia is one of America's most important historical buildings, the country home once owned by James Monroe, where he and Thomas Jefferson often exchanged conversation and also may have made some very big political decisions in their time. Today this is a modest appearing cottage, rather than a big manor house, and it is well kept. It may be visited by tourists at certain hours, since it is considered an historical shrine. If any of my readers are in the area and feel like visiting Ash Lawn, I would suggest they do not mention ghosts too openly with the guides or caretakers.

Actually the ghostly goings-on center around a certain wooden rocking chair in the main room. This has been seen to rock without benefit of human hands. I don't know how many people have actually seen the chair rock, but Mrs. J. Massey, who lived in the area for many years, has said to me when I visited the place, "I will tell anyone and I have no objection to its being known, that I've seen not once but time and time again the rocking chair rocking exactly as though someone were in it. My brother John has seen it too. Whenever we touched it it would stop rocking."

This house, though small and cozy, nevertheless was James Monroe's favorite house even after he moved to the bigger place which became his stately home later on in his career. At Ash Lawn he could get away from his affairs of state, away from public attention, to discuss matters of great concern with his friend Thomas Jefferson who lived only two miles away at Monticello.

Who is the ghost in the rocking chair? Perhaps it is only a spirit, not an earthbound ghost, a spirit who has become so attached to his former home and refuge from the affairs of state, that he still likes to sit now and then in his own rocking chair thinking things over.

Ash Lawn—Monroe's cottage in Virginia

The haunted chair at Ash Lawn

✳ 32

A Visit with Carole Lombard's Ghost

IN 1967 I FIRST HEARD of a haunted house where the late Carole Lombard had lived. Adriana S. was by vocation a poet and writer, but she made her living in various ways, usually as a housekeeper. In the late forties she had been engaged as such by a motion picture producer of some renown. She supervised the staff, a job she performed very well indeed, being an excellent organizer. Carefully inspecting the house before agreeing to take the position, she had found it one of those quiet elegant houses in the best part of Hollywood that could harbor nothing but good. Confidently, Adriana took the job.

A day or two after her arrival, when she was fast asleep in her room, she found herself aroused in the middle of the night by someone shaking her. Fully awake, she realized that she was being shaken by the shoulder. She sat up in bed, but there was no one to be seen. Even though she could not with her ordinary sight distinguish any human being in the room, her psychic sense told her immediately that there was someone standing next to her bed. Relaxing for a moment and closing her eyes, Adriana tried to tune in on the unseen entity. Immediately she saw, standing next to her bed, a tall, slim woman with blonde hair down to her shoulders. What made the apparition or psychic impression the more upsetting to Adriana was the fact that the woman was bathed in blood and quite obviously suffering.

Adriana realized that she had been contacted by a ghostly entity but could not get herself to accept the reality of the phenomenon, and hopefully ascribed it to an upset stomach, or to the new surroundings and the strains of having just moved in. At the same time, she prayed for the restless one. But six or seven days later the same thing happened again. This time Adriana was able to see the ghost more clearly. She was impressed with the great beauty of the woman she saw and decided to talk about her experience with her employers in the morning. The producer's wife listened very quietly to the description of the ghostly visitor, then nodded. When Adriana mentioned that the apparition had been wearing a light suit covered with blood, the lady of the house drew back in surprise. It was only then that Adriana learned that the house had once been Carole Lombard's and that the late movie star had lived in it very happily with Clark Gable. Carole Lombard had died tragically in an airplane accident during World War II, when her plane, en route to the East where she was going to do some USO shows, hit a mountain during a storm. At the time, she was wearing a light-colored suit.

Several years afterward I investigated the house in the company of an actress who is very psychic. It so happened that the house now belonged to her doctor, a lady by the name of Doris A. In trance, my actress friend was able to make contact with the spirit of Carole Lombard. What kept her coming back to the house where she once lived was a feeling of regret for having left Clark Gable, and also the fact that she and Gable had had a quarrel just before her death. Luckily, we were able to pacify the restless spirit, and presumably the house is now peaceful.

✳ 33

Mrs. Surratt's Ghost at Fort McNair

FORT McNAIR IS one of the oldest military posts in the United States and has had many other names. First it was known as the Arsenal, then called the Washington Arsenal, and in 1826 a penitentiary was built on its grounds, which was a grim place indeed. Because of disease, President Lincoln ordered the penitentiary closed in 1862, but as soon as Lincoln had been murdered, the penitentiary was back in business again.

Among the conspirators accused of having murdered President Lincoln, the one innocent person was Mrs. Mary Surratt, whose sole crime consisted of having run a boarding house where her son had met with some of the conspirators. But as I have shown in a separate investigation of the boarding house in Clifton, Maryland, her son John Surratt was actually a double-agent, so the irony is even greater. She was the first woman hanged in the United States, and today historians are fully convinced that she was totally innocent. The trial itself was conducted in a most undemocratic manner, and it is clear in retrospect that the conspirators never had a chance. But the real power behind the Lincoln assassination, who might have been one of his own political associates, wanted to make sure no one was left who knew anything about the plot, and so Mary Surratt had to be sacrificed.

There is a small, ordinary looking building called Building 21 at Fort McNair, not far from what is now a pleasant tennis court. It was in this building that Mary Surratt was imprisoned and to this day sobs are being heard in the early hours of the morning by a number of people being quartered in the building. The penitentiary stands no more and the land itself is now part of the tennis court. Next to Building 21 is an even smaller house, which serves as quarters for a number of officers. When I visited the post a few years ago, the Deputy Post Commander was quartered there. Building 20 contains five apartments, which have been remodeled a few years ago. The ceilings have been lowered, the original wooden floors have been replaced with asbestos tile. Unexplained fires occurred there in the 1960s. The execution of the conspirators, including Mrs. Mary Surratt, took place just a few yards from where Building 21 now stands. The graves of the hanged conspirators were in what is now the tennis court, but the coffins were removed a few years after the trial and there are no longer any bodies in the ground.

Captain X.—and his name must remain secret for obvious reasons—had lived in apartment number 5 for several years prior to my interviewing him. He has not heard the sobbing of Mary Surratt but he has heard a strange sound, like high wind.

However, Captain and Mrs. C. occupied quarters on the third floor of Building 20 for several years until 1972. This building, incidentally, is the only part of the former penitentiary still standing. The C.s' apartment consisted of the entire third floor and it was on this floor that the conspirators, including John Wilkes Booth, who was already dead, were tried and sentenced to die by hanging. Mary Surratt's cell was also located on the third floor of the building. Mrs. C. has had ESP experiences before, but she was not quite prepared for what occurred to her when she moved onto the post at Fort McNair.

"My experiences in our apartment at Fort McNair were quite unlike any other I have ever known.

"On several occasions, very late at night, someone could be heard walking above, yet we were on the top floor." One night the walking became quite heavy, and a window in the room which had been Mrs. Surratt's cell was continually being rattled, as if someone were trying to get in or out, and there seemed to be a definite presence in

The haunted prison at Fort McNair where Mrs. Surrat was held

the house. This happened in April, as did the trial of the conspirators.

I doubt that it would be easy to visit Fort McNair for any except official reasons, such as perhaps an historical investigation. But for better or for worse the building in question is located on the northeast corner of the tennis courts and Fort McNair itself is in Washington, D.C., at the corner of Fourth and P Streets and easy to reach from the center of the city.

CHAPTER SIX

This House is Haunted

PROBABLY NO OTHER word picture has had a more profound influence on people's imagination than the idea of a truly haunted house. After all, a haunted house is not a home the way people like to think of a home. Sharing it with someone who happens to be dead can be very upsetting, both to the flesh-and-blood inhabitants of the house and the ghost who happens to be stuck in it.

Most people think of a haunted house as something sinister, threatening, and altogether undesirable. In Ireland, calling someone's house haunted can bring a very substantial lawsuit for defamation of character—of the house's character, that is. In America, on the other hand, such a reputation, deserved or not, generally enhances the value of the property.

WHAT EXACTLY *IS* A HAUNTED HOUSE?

It can be a house, apartment, or an abode of any kind where people live, eat, and sleep. What distinguishes a haunted home from all others is the fact that one (or more) of the previous tenants or owners has not quite left the premises, and considers herself or himself fully in residence.

These are neither aliens from afar nor are they monsters but simply folks like you who used to live there, died, and somehow got trapped into not being able to leave for better places—the other side of life, or what religion likes to call Heaven, though there really is no such place in the sense that religion describes it. Even the devil gets short shrift in parapsychology. But the next dimension, a world as real as this one, does exist, and people live in it. These are the people who passed over without problems. Those who experienced some sort of trouble and did not pass over are the ones we call earthbound spirits or ghosts.

With haunted houses, the emphasis, and thus the emotional bond, is the house, not the people living in it. The house can contain either pleasant memories or, more often, traumatic ones, which prevented the transition from occurring at the time of physical death in the first place.

Ghosts may appear or make themselves heard in any spot that had meaning for them when they were living, and particularly during the time of their death. Thus, a ghost does not necessarily need a house in which to manifest. But a truly haunted house does need a ghost or ghosts to qualify for the expression, unless of course we are talking about psychic impressions from the past only. Of this, more later.

* * *

Thanks to movies and television, haunted houses are inevitably portrayed as sinister-looking, dilapidated places, manor houses, castles—anything but a clean, up-to-date apartment on Park Avenue. The truth is that for a haunting to occur, the appearance, age, or nature of the house is totally *immaterial*, if you will pardon the pun. Thus, there are bona fide haunted houses all over the world, of any age, from ancient castles to recently built skyscrapers, from rural hideaways to modern night clubs.

What they all have in common is the *presence* of an earthbound spirit, a ghost, unable to break free of the emotional turmoil of his or her physical passing.

Usually there are certain phenomena associated with a haunting, such as cold spots or the "feel" of a human presence, though the presence remains unseen. These phenomena are not manufactured by the resident ghost but are the natural by-products of its presence and owe their impact purely to electromagnetic reactions to the presence of a human being in the etheric body or aura, which is, after all, a strong electromagnetic field itself.

FINALLY, SHOULD YOU BE AFRAID OF GHOSTS?

No, not even if you're a kid. Be afraid of television programs espousing violence and drugs instead.

Ghosts are so caught up in their own confusion and misery, they are not about to harm you. They are not in the business of frightening people either. But, in certain cases on record, the resident ghost has put in appearances or caused phenomena, with the intent of ridding the house of the new tenants.

Just as some folks call in a "Ghost Hunter" to rid the house of these unwanted pests, the ghosts fight back by making the new tenants feel uncomfortable. After all, they were there first.

Unfortunately, for both house owner or tenant and ghost, there is a terrible lack of knowledge regarding the qualifications a true investigator of the paranormal must have. Charlatans abound, claiming expertise masquerading as curiosity; they "look around" the haunted premises with Geiger counters and electronic instruments such as oscilloscopes and proclaim the presence of ghosts just because their instruments show fluctuations. Real, academically trained parapsychologists don't do this; they work with trained, reputable sensitive psychics with good track records. Television programs introduce such pseudo-investigators as "renowned parapsychologists," which they are not. In fact, they have day jobs as waiters and clerks. One particularly obnoxious "investigator" goes around accompanied by his psychic-reader wife, a former priest, and a former police officer—looking for demons and the devil's hoof prints in haunted houses that would require only the visit of a trained psychical researcher, perhaps with a good trance medium, to resolve the problem.

One needs neither the likes of "demonologists" or "vampyrists" to come to grips with an unwanted haunting. Common sense will prevail when you realize you are faced only with a past event and someone—a human being—in trouble at the time of passing.

People have come to me for counsel and help when they could not understand the nature of their haunting. Frequently, I have visited them, often in the company of a good psychic, and managed to answer many questions.

FEAR IS THE ABSENCE OF INFORMATION

Haunted houses know neither barriers in time nor space, nor distance. Some of these can be visited, at least on the outside, since a road is never (or hardly ever) private. Many, however, are private houses, and it would take a great deal of ingenuity to persuade the owner to let you in. Some sites, like the Queen Mary, or a haunted garden, such as Versailles and Trianon, may charge nominal admission because of their status as tourist attractions, not because they have ghosts "on the payroll." In some cases, the ghost is gone but an imprint remains, and you might still feel something of it. In other cases, the ghost has never left.

✳ 34

The Bank Street Ghost

ON JUNE 26, 1957, I picked up a copy of the *New York Times*, that most unghostly of all newspapers, and soon was reading Meyer Berger's column, "About New York." That column wasn't about houses or people this particular day. It was about ghosts.

Specifically, Mr. Berger gave a vivid description of a house at 11 Bank Street, in Greenwich Village, where a "rather friendly" ghost had apparently settled to share the appointments with the flesh-and-blood occupants. The latter were Dr. Harvey Slatin, an engineer, and his wife, Yeffe Kimball, who is of Osage Indian descent and well known as a painter.

The house in which they lived was then 125 years old, made of red brick, and still in excellent condition.

Digging into the past of their home, the Slatins established that a Mrs. Maccario had run the house as a nineteen-room boarding establishment for years before selling it to them. However, Mrs. Maccario wasn't of much help when questioned. She knew nothing of her predecessors.

After the Slatins had acquired the house and the other tenants had finally left, they did the house over. The downstairs became one long living room, extending from front to back, and adorned by a fireplace and a number of good paintings and ceramics. In the back part of this room, the Slatins placed a heavy wooden table. The rear door led to a small garden, and a narrow staircase led to the second floor.

The Slatins were essentially "uptown" people, far removed from any Bohemian notions or connotations. What attracted them about Greenwich Village was essentially its quiet charm and artistic environment. They gathered around them friends of similar inclinations, and many an evening was spent "just sitting around," enjoying the tranquil mood of the house.

During these quiet moments, they often thought they heard a woman's footsteps on the staircase, sometimes crossing the upper floors, sometimes a sound like a light hammering. Strangely enough, the sounds were heard more often in the daytime than at night, a habit most unbecoming a traditional haunt. The Slatins were never frightened by this. They simply went to investigate what might have caused the noises, but never found any visible evidence. There was no "rational" explanation for them, either. One Sunday in January of 1957, they decided to clock the noises, and found that the ghostly goings-on lasted all day; during these hours, they would run upstairs to trap the trespasser—only to find empty rooms and corridors. Calling out to the unseen brought no reply, either. An English carpenter by the name of Arthur Brodie was as well adjusted to reality as are the Slatins, but he also heard the footsteps. His explanation that "one hears all sorts of noises in old houses" did not help matters any. Sadie, the maid,

heard the noises too, and after an initial period of panic, got accustomed to them as if they were part of the house's routine—which indeed they were!

One morning in February, Arthur Brodie was working in a room on the top floor, hammering away at the ceiling. He was standing on a stepladder that allowed him to just about touch the ceiling. Suddenly, plaster and dust showered down on his head, and something heavy fell and hit the floor below. Mrs. Slatin in her first-floor bedroom heard the thump. Before she could investigate the source of the loud noise, there was Brodie at her door, saying: "It's me, Ma'am, Brodie. I'm leaving the job! I've found the body!" But he was being facetious. What he actually found was a black-painted metal container about twice the size of a coffee can. On it there was a partially faded label, reading: *"The last remains of Elizabeth Bullock, deceased. Cremated January 21, 1931."* The label also bore the imprint of the United States Crematory Company, Ltd., Middle Village, Borough of Queens, New York, and stamped on the top of the can was the number—37251. This can is in the Slatins' house to this very day.

Mrs. Slatin, whose Indian forebears made her accept the supernatural without undue alarm or even amazement, quietly took the find and called her husband at his office. Together with Brodie, Dr. Slatin searched the hole in the ceiling, but found only dusty rafters.

Curiously, the ceiling that had hidden the container dated back at least to 1880, which was long before Elizabeth Bullock had died. One day, the frail woman crossed Hudson Street, a few blocks from the Slatin residence. A motorist going at full speed saw her too late, and she was run over. Helpful hands carried her to a nearby drugstore, while other by-standers called for an ambulance. But help arrived too late for Mrs. Bullock. She died at the drugstore before any medical help arrived. But strangely enough, when Dr. Slatin looked through the records, he found that Mrs. Bullock had never lived at 11 Bank Street at all!

Still, Mrs. Bullock's ashes were found in that house. How to explain that? In the crematory's books, her home address was listed at 113 Perry Street. Dr. Slatin called on Charles Dominick, the undertaker in the case. His place of business had been on West 11th Street, not far from Bank Street. Unfortunately, Mr. Dominick had since died.

The Slatins then tried to locate the woman's relatives, if any. The trail led nowhere. It was as if the ghost of the deceased wanted to protect her secret. When the search seemed hopeless, the Slatins put the container with Mrs. Bullock's ashes on the piano in the large living room, feeling somehow that Mrs. Bullock's ghost might prefer that place of honor to being cooped up in the attic. They got so used to it that even Sadie, the maid, saw nothing extraordinary in dusting it right along with the rest of the furniture and bric-a-brac.

The house of the "Little Old Lady" Ghost on Twelfth Street

Her ashes after their discovery in the attic

Still, the Slatins hoped that someone would claim the ashes sooner or later. Meanwhile, they considered themselves the custodians of Mrs. Bullock's last remains. And apparently they had done right by Elizabeth, for the footsteps and disturbing noises stopped abruptly when the can was found and placed on the piano in the living room.

One more strange touch was told by Yeffe Kimball to the late Meyer Berger. It seems that several weeks before the ashes of Mrs. Bullock were discovered, someone rang the doorbell and inquired about rooms. Mrs. Slatin recalls that it was a well-dressed young man, and that she told him they would not be ready for some time, but that she would take his name in order to notify him when they were. The young man left a card, and Mrs. Slatin still recalls vividly the name on it. It was E. C. Bullock. Incidentally, the young man never did return.

It seems odd that Mrs. Slatin was not more nonplussed by the strange coincidence of the Bullock name on the container and card, but, as I have already stated, Mrs. Slatin is quite familiar with the incursions from the nether world that are far more common than most of us would like to think. To her, it seemed something odd, yes, but also something that no doubt would "work itself out." She was neither disturbed nor elated over the continued presence in her living room of Mrs. Bullock's ashes. Mrs. Slatin

is gifted with psychic talents, and therefore not afraid of the invisible. She takes the unseen visitors as casually as the flesh-and-blood ones, and that is perhaps the natural way to look at it, after all.

Greenwich Village has so many haunted or allegedly haunted houses that a case like the Slatins' does not necessarily attract too much attention from the local people. Until Meyer Berger's interview appeared in the *Times*, not many people outside of the Slatins' immediate circle of friends knew about the situation.

Mr. Berger, who was an expert on Manhattan folklore, knew the Slatins, and also knew about ghosts. He approached the subject sympathetically, and the Slatins were pleased. They had settled down to living comfortably in their ghost house, and since the noises had stopped, they gave the matter no further thought.

I came across the story in the *Times* in June of 1957, and immediately decided to follow up on it. I don't know whether my friend and medium, Mrs. Ethel Meyers, also read the article; it is possible that she did. At any rate, I told her nothing more than that a haunted house existed in the Village and she agreed to come with me to investigate it. I then called the Slatins and, after some delay, managed to arrange for a séance to take place on July 17, 1957, at 9:30 P.M. Present were two friends of the Slatins, Mr. and Mrs. Anderson, Meyer Berger, the Slatins, Mrs. Meyers, and myself.

Immediately upon entering the house and sitting down at the table, around which we had grouped ourselves, Mrs. Meyers went into trance. Just as she "went under" and was still in that borderline condition where clairvoyance touches true trance, she described the presence of a little woman who walked slowly, being paralysed on one side, and had a heart condition. "She's Betty," Mrs. Meyers murmured, as she went under. Now the personality of Betty started to use the vocal apparatus of the medium.

Our medium continued in her trance state: "He didn't want me in the family plot—my brother—I wasn't even married in their eyes.... But I was married before God... Edward Bullock.... I want a Christian burial in the shades of the Cross—any place where the cross is—*but not with them!*" This was said with so much hatred and emotion that I tried to persuade the departed Betty to desist, or at least to explain her reasons for not wishing to join her family in the cemetery.

"I didn't marry in the faith," she said, and mentioned that her brother was Eddie, that they came from Pleasantville, New York, and that her mother's maiden name was Elizabeth McCuller. "I'm at rest now," she added in a quieter mood.

How did her ashes come to be found in the attic of a house that she never even lived in?

"I went with Eddie," Betty replied. "There was a family fight... my husband went with Eddie... steal the ashes... pay for no burial... he came back and took them from Eddie... hide ashes... Charles knew it... made a roof over the house... ashes came through the roof... so Eddie can't find them..."

I asked were there any children?

"Eddie and Gracie. Gracie died as a baby, and Eddie now lives in California. Charlie protects me!" she added, referring to her husband.

At this point I asked the departed what was the point of staying on in this house now? Why not go on into the great world beyond, where she belonged? But evidently the ghost didn't feel that way at all! "I want a cross over my head... have two lives to live now... and I like being with you!" she said, bowing toward Mrs. Slatin. Mrs. Slatin smiled. She didn't mind in the least having a ghost as a boarder. "What about burial in your family plot?" That would seem the best, I suggested. The ghost became vehement.

"Ma never forgave me. I can never go with her and rest. I don't care much. When she's forgiven me, maybe it'll be all right... only where there's a green tree cross—and where there's no more fighting over the bones... I want only to be set free, and there should be peace.... I never had anything to do with them.... Just because I loved a man out of the faith, and so they took my bones and fought over them, and then they put them up in this place, and let them smoulder up there, so nobody could touch them... foolish me! When they're mixed up with the Papal State...."

Did her husband hide the ashes all by himself?

"There was a Peabody, too. He helped him."

Who cremated her?

"It was Charles' wish, and it wasn't Eddie's and therefore, they quarreled. Charlie was a Presbyterian... and he would have put me in his Church, but I could not offend them all. They put it beyond my reach through the roof; still hot... they stole it from the crematory."

Where was your home before, I asked.

"Lived close by," she answered, and as if to impress upon us again her identity, added—"Bullock!"

Throughout the séance, the ghost had spoken with a strong Irish brogue. The medium's background is not Irish, and I have a fine ear for authenticity of language, perhaps because I speak seven of them, and can recognize many more. This was not the kind of brogue a clever actor puts on. This was a real one.

As the entranced medium served the cause of Mrs. Bullock, I was reminded of the time I first heard the tape recordings of what became later known as Bridie Murphy. I remember the evening when the author of *The Search for Bridie Murphy*, Morey Bernstein, let me and a small group of fellow researchers in on an exciting case he had recently been working on. The voice on the tape, too, had an authentic Irish brogue, and a flavor no actor, no matter how brilliant, could fully imitate!

Now the medium seemed limp—as the ghost of Elizabeth Bullock withdrew. A moment later, Mrs. Meyers awoke, none the worse for having been the link between two worlds.

After the séance, I suggested to Mrs. Slatin that the can containing the ashes be buried in her garden, beneath the tree I saw through the back window. But Mrs. Slatin wasn't sure. She felt that her ghost was just as happy to stay on the piano.

I then turned my attention to Mrs. Slatin herself, since she admitted to being psychic. A gifted painter, Yeffe Kimball *knew* that Mrs. Meyers had made the right contact when she heard her describe the little lady with the limp at the beginning of the séance; she herself had often "seen" the ghost with her "psychic eye," and had developed a friendship for her. It was not an unhappy ghost, she contended, and particularly now that her secret was out—why deprive Elizabeth Bullock of "her family"? Why indeed?

The house is still there on Bank Street, and the can of ashes still graces the piano. Whether the E. C. Bullock who called on the Slatins in 1957 was the Eddie whom the ghost claimed as her son, I can't tell. My efforts to locate him in California proved as fruitless as the earlier attempts to locate any other kin.

So the Slatins continue to live happily in their lovely, quiet house in the Village, with Elizabeth Bullock as their star boarder. Though I doubt the census taker will want to register her.

The Bank Street Ghost

The Whistling Ghost

ONE OF MY DEAR FRIENDS is the celebrated clairvoyant Florence Sternfels of Edgewater, New Jersey, a lady who has assisted many a police department in the apprehension of criminals or lost persons. Her real ambition, however, was to assist serious scientists to find out what makes her "different," where that power she has—"the forces," as she calls them—comes from. Many times in the past she had *volunteered* her time to sit with investigators, something few professional mediums will do.

I had not seen Florence in over a year when one day the telephone rang, and her slightly creaky voice wished me a cheery hello. It seemed that a highly respected psychiatrist in nearby Croton, New York, had decided to experiment with Florence's psychic powers. Would I come along? She wanted me there to make sure "everything was on the up-and-up." I agreed to come, and the following day Dr. Kahn himself called me, and arrangements were made for a young couple, the Hendersons, to pick me up in their car and drive me out to Croton.

When we arrived at the sumptuous Kahn house near the Hudson River, some thirty persons, mostly neighbors and friends of the doctor's, had already assembled. None of them was known to Florence, of course, and few knew anything about the purpose of her visit. But the doctor was such a well-known community leader and teacher that they had come in great expectation.

The house was a remodeled older house, with an upstairs and a large garden going all the way down to the river.

Florence did not disappoint the good doctor. Seated at the head of an oval, next to me, she rapidly called out facts and names about people in the room, their relatives and friends, deceased or otherwise, and found quick response and acknowledgment. Startling information, like "a five-year-old child has died, and the mother, who is paralyzed in the legs, is present." She certainly was. "Anyone here lost a collie dog?" Yes, someone had, three weeks before. Florence was a big success.

When it was all over, the crowd broke up and I had a chance to talk to our hostess, the doctor's young wife. She seemed deeply interested in psychic matters, just as was her husband; but while it was strictly a scientific curiosity with Dr. Kahn, his wife seemed to be intuitive and was given to "impressions" herself.
"You know, I think we've got a ghost," she said, looking at me as if she had just said the most ordinary thing in the world.

We walked over to a quiet corner, and I asked her what were her reasons for this extraordinary statement—

unusual for the wife of a prominent psychiatrist. She assured me it was no hallucination.

"He's a whistling ghost," she confided, "always whistling the same song, about four bars of it—a happy tune. I guess he must be a happy ghost!"

"When did all this start?" I asked.

"During the past five years I've heard him about twenty times," Mrs. Kahn replied. "Always the same tune."

"And your husband, does he hear it, too?"
She shook her head.

"But he hears raps. Usually in our bedroom, and late at night. They always come in threes. My husband hears it, gets up, and asks who is it, but of course there is nobody there, so he gets no answer.

"Last winter, around three in the morning, we were awakened by a heavy knocking sound on the front door. When we got to the door and opened it, there was no one in sight. The path leading up to the road was empty, too, and believe me, no one could have come down that path and not be still visible by the time we got to the door!"

"And the whistling—where do you hear it usually?"

"Always in the living room—here," Mrs. Kahn replied, pointing at the high-ceilinged, wood-paneled room, with its glass wall facing the garden.

"You see, this living room used to be a stage...the house was once a summer theater, and we reconverted the stage area into this room. Come to think of it, I also heard that whistling in the bedroom that was used by the former owner of the house, the man who built both the theater and the house."

"What about this man? Who was he?"

"Clifford Harmon. He was murdered by the Nazis during World War II, when he got trapped in France. The house is quite old, has many secret passageways—as a matter of fact, only three weeks ago, I dreamed I should enter one of the passages!"

"You dreamed this?" I said. "Did anything ever come of it, though?"

Mrs. Kahn nodded. "The next morning, I decided to do just what I had done in my dream during the night. I entered the passage I had seen myself enter in the dream, and then I came across some musty old photographs."

I looked at the pictures. They showed various actors of both sexes, in the costumes of an earlier period. Who knows what personal tragedy or joy the people in these photographs had experienced in this very room? I returned the stack of pictures to Mrs. Kahn.

"Are you mediumistic?" I asked Mrs. Kahn. It seemed to me that she was the catalyst in this house.

"Well, perhaps a little. I am certainly clairvoyant. Some time ago, I wrote to my parents in Miami, and for some unknown reason, addressed the letter to 3251 South 23rd Lane. There was no such address as far as I knew, and the letter was returned to me in a few days. Later, my parents wrote to me telling me they had just bought a house at 3251 South 23rd Lane."

At this point, the doctor joined the conversation, and we talked about Harmon.

"He's left much unfinished business over here, I'm sure," the doctor said. "He had big plans for building and improvements of his property, and, of course, there were a number of girls he was interested in."

I had heard enough. The classic pattern of the haunted house was all there. The ghost, the unfinished business, the willing owners. I offered to hold a "rescue circle" type of séance, to make contact with the "whistling ghost."

We decided to hold the séance on August 3, 1960, and that I would bring along Mrs. Meyers, since this called for a trance medium, while Florence, who had originally brought me to this house, was a clairvoyant and psychometrist. A psychometrist gets "impressions" by holding objects that belong to a certain person.

Again, the transportation was provided by Mrs. Henderson, whose husband could not come along this time. On this occasion there was no curious crowd in the large living room when we arrived. Only the house guests of the Kahns, consisting of a Mr. and Mrs. Bower and their daughter, augmented the circle we formed as soon as the doctor had arrived from a late call. As always, before sliding into trance, Mrs. Meyers gave us her psychic impressions; before going into the full trance it is necessary to make the desired contact.

"Some names, said Mrs. Meyers, "a Robert, a Delia, a Harold, and the name Banks...Oh...and then a Hart." She seemed unsure of the proper spelling.

At this very moment, both Mrs. Kahn and I distinctly heard the sound of heavy breathing. It seemed to emanate from somewhere above and behind the sitters. "Melish and Goldfarb!" Mrs. Meyers mumbled, getting more and more into a somnambulant state. "That's strange!" Dr. Kahn interjected. "There was a man named Elish here, some fifteen years ago...and a Mr. Goldwag, recently!"

"Mary...something—Ann," the medium now said. Later, after the séance, Dr. Kahn told me that Harmon's private secretary, who had had full charge of the big estate, was a woman named—Mary Brasnahan....

Now Mrs. Meyers described a broad-shouldered man with iron-gray hair, who, she said, became gray at a very early age. "He wears a double-breasted, dark blue coat, and has a tiny mustache. His initials are R. H." Then she added, "I see handwriting...papers...signatures...and there is another, younger man, smaller, with light brown hair—and he is concerned with some papers that belong in files. His initials are J. B. I think the first man is the boss, this one is the clerk." Then she added suddenly, "Deborah!"

At this point Mrs. Meyers herself pulled back, and said: "I feel a twitch in my arm; apparently this isn't for

publication!" But she continued and described other people whom she "felt" around the house; a Gertrude, for instance, and a bald-headed man with a reddish complexion, rather stout, whom she called B. B. "He has to do with the settlements on Deborah and the other girls."

Mrs. Meyers knew of course nothing about Harmon's alleged reputation as a bit of a ladies' man.

"That's funny," she suddenly commented, "I see two women dressed in very old-fashioned clothes, much earlier than their own period."

I had not mentioned a word to Mrs. Meyers about the theatrical usage which the house had once been put to. Evidently she received the impressions of two actresses.

"Bob...he's being called by a woman."

At this point, full trance set in, and the medium's own personality vanished to allow the ghost to speak to us directly, if he so chose. After a moment Albert, the medium's control, came and announced that the ghost would speak to us. Then he withdrew, and within seconds a strange face replaced the usual benign expression of Mrs. Meyer's face. This was a shrewd, yet dignified man. His voice, at first faint, grew in strength as the seconds ticked off.

"So...so it goes...Sing a Song of Sixpence...all over now...."

Excitedly Mrs. Kahn grabbed my arm and whispered into my ear: "That's the name of the song *he* always whistled...I couldn't think of it before." Through my mind went the words of the old nursery rhyme—

Sing a Song of Sixpence,
A pocket full of rye,
Four and Twenty Blackbirds,
Baked in a pie.
When the pie was opened,
The birds began to sing
Isn't that a dainty dish
To set before the King?

Like a wartime password, our ghost had identified himself through the medium.

Why did Harmon pick this song as his tune? Perhaps the gay lilt, the carefree air that goes with it, perhaps a sentimental reason. Mrs. Kahn was aglow with excitement.

The communicator then continued to speak: "All right, he won't come anymore. She isn't here...when you're dead, you're alive."

I thought it was time to ask a few questions of my own. "Why are you here?"

"Pleasant and unpleasant memories. My own thoughts keep me...happy, loved her. One happiness—*he* stands in the way. She didn't get what was hers. Jimmy may get it for her. *He* stands in the way!"

"Why do you come to this house?"

"To meet with her. It was our meeting place in the flesh. We still commune in spirit though she's still with you, and I return. We can meet. It is my house. My thought-child."

What he was trying to say, I thought, is that in her dream state, she has contact with him. Most unusual, even for a ghost! I began to wonder who "she" was. It was worth a try.

"Is her name Deborah?" I ventured. But the reaction was so violent our ghost slipped away. Albert took over the medium and requested that no more painfully personal questions be asked of the ghost. He also explained that our friend was indeed the owner of the house, the other man seen by the medium, his secretary, but the raps the doctor had heard had been caused by another person, the man who is after the owner's lady love.

Presently the ghost returned, and confirmed this.

"I whistle to call her. He does the rappings, to rob...."

"Is there any unfinished business you want to tell us about?" That should not be too personal, I figured.

"None worth returning for, only love."

"Is there anything under the house?" I wondered....

"There is a small tunnel, but it is depleted now." At this, I looked searchingly toward the doctor, who nodded, and later told me that such a tunnel did indeed exist.

"What is your name?"

"Bob. I only whistle and sing for happiness."

Before I could question him further, the gentleman slipped out again, and once more Albert, the control, took over:

"This man died violently at the hands of a firing squad," he commented, "near a place he thinks is Austerlitz...but is not sure. As for the estate, the other woman had the larger share."

There was nothing more after that, so I requested that the séance be concluded.

After the medium had returned to her own body, we discussed the experience, and Dr. Kahn remarked that he was not sure about the name Harmon had used among his friends. It seemed absurd to think that Clifford, his official first name, would not be followed by something more familiar—like, for instance, Bob. But there was no certainty.

"Did the Nazis really kill him?" I asked. There was total silence in the big room now. You could have heard a pin drop, and the Bowers, who had never been to any séances before, just sat there with their hands at their chins, wide-eyed and full of excitement. Albert, through his "instrument," as he called his medium, took his time to answer me.

"I'm afraid so. But I don't think it was a firing squad that killed him. He was beaten to death!" I looked with

horror at Dr. Kahn, trying to get confirmation, but he only shrugged his shoulders.

Actually, nobody knows exactly how Harmon died, he revealed later. The fact is that the Nazis murdered him during the war. Could he have meant *Auschwitz* instead of Austerlitz?

I didn't feel like pursuing the subject any further. With Albert's assistance, we ended the séance, bringing the medium out of her trance state as quickly as possible.

The lights, which had been subdued during the sitting, were now allowed to be turned back on again. Mrs. Meyers recalled very little of what had transpired, mostly events and phrases at the onset and very end of her trance condition, but nothing that happened in the middle portion, when her trance state was at its deepest.

It was now midnight, and time to return to New York. As I said good night to my mediumistic friend, I expressed my hope that all would now be quiet at Croton.

This was wishful thinking.

The following morning, Mrs. Kahn telephoned me long distance. Far from being quiet—the manifestations had increased around the house.

"What exactly happened?" I inquired. Mrs. Kahn bubbled over with excitement.

"We went to bed shortly after you left," she replied, "and all seemed so peaceful. Then, at 3 A.M., suddenly the bedroom lights went on by themselves. There is only one switch. Neither my husband nor I had gotten out of bed to turn on that switch. Nevertheless, when I took a look at the switch, it was *turned down*, as if by human hands!"

"Amazing," I conceded.

"Oh, but that isn't all," she continued. "Exactly one hour later, at 4 o'clock, the same thing happened again. By the way, do you remember the drapery covering the bedroom wall? There isn't a door or window nearby. Besides, they were all shut. No possible air current could have moved those draperies. All the same, I saw the draperies move by their own accord, plainly and visibly."

"I suppose he wants to let you know he's still there!" I said, rather meekly. Ghosts can be persistent at times. But Mrs. Kahn had more to tell me.

"Our house guest, Mrs. Bower, has the room that used to be Harmon's bedroom. Well, this morning she was dressing in front of the big closet. Suddenly she saw the door to the room open slowly, and then, with enormous force, pin her into the closet! There was nobody outside the room, of course."

"Anything else?" I asked quietly.

"Not really. Only, I had a dream last night. It was about a man in a blue suit. You remember Mrs. Meyers saw a man in a blue suit, too. Only with me, he said, 'Miller.' Said it several times, to make sure I got it. I also dreamed of a woman in a blue dress, with two small children, who was in danger somehow. But Miller stood out the strongest."

I thanked Mrs. Kahn for her report, and made her promise me to call me the instant there were any further disturbances.

I woke up the following morning, sure the phone would ring and Mrs. Kahn would have more to tell me. But I was wrong. All remained quiet. All remained peaceful the next morning, too. It was not until four days later that Mrs. Kahn called again.

I prepared myself for some more of the ghost's shenanigans. But, to my relief, Mrs. Kahn called to tell me no further manifestations had occurred. However, she had done a bit of investigating. Since the name "Miller" was totally unknown to her and the doctor, she inquired around the neighborhood. Finally, one of the neighbors did recall a Miller. He was Harmon's personal physician.

"One thing I forgot to mention while you were here," she added. "Harmon's bed was stored away for many years. I decided one day to use it again. One night my husband discovered nails similar to carpet tacks under the pillow. We were greatly puzzled—but for lack of an explanation, we just forgot the incident. Another time I found something similar to crushed glass in the bed, and again, although greatly puzzled—forgot the incident. I don't know whether or not these seemingly unexplainable incidents mean anything."

Could it be that Harmon objected to anyone else using his bed? Ghosts are known to be quite possessive of their earthly goods, and resentful of "intruders."

All seemed quiet at the Kahns, until I received another call from Mrs. Kahn the last days of October.

The whistling ghost was back.

This was quite a blow to my prestige as a ghost hunter, but on the other hand, Harmon's wraith apparently was a happy spirit and liked being earthbound. To paraphrase a well-known expression, you can lead a ghost to the spirit world, but you can't make him stay—if he doesn't want to. Next morning a note came from Mrs. Kahn.

"As I told you via phone earlier this evening, we again heard our whistler last night about 1 A.M., and it was the loudest I have ever heard. I didn't have to strain for it. My husband heard it too, but he thought it was the wind in the chimney. Then, as it continued, he agreed that it was some sort of phenomena. I got out of bed and went toward the sound of the whistle. I reached the den, from where I could see into the living room. Light was coming through a window behind me and was reflected upon the ceiling of the living room...I saw a small white mist, floating, but motionless, in front of the table in the living room. I called to my husband. He looked, but saw nothing. He said he would put the light on and I watched him walk *right through the mist*—he turned the lamp on and everything returned to normal."

I haven't spoken with the Kahns in several months now.

Is the whistling ghost still around? If he is, nobody seems to mind. That's how it is sometimes with happy ghosts. They get to be one of the family.

✳ 36

The Metuchen Ghost

ONE DAY LAST SPRING, while the snow was still on the ground and the chill in the air, my good friend Bernard Axelrod, with whom I have shared many a ghostly experience, called to say that he knew of a haunted house in New Jersey, and was I still interested.

I was, and Bernard disclosed that in the little town of Metuchen, there were a number of structures dating back to colonial days. A few streets down from where he and his family live in a modern, up-to-date brick building, there stands one wooden house in particular which has the reputation of being haunted, Bernard explained. No particulars were known to him beyond that. Ever since the Rockland County Ghost in the late Danton Walker's colonial house had acquainted me with the specters from George Washington's days, I had been eager to enlarge this knowledge. So it was with great anticipation that I gathered a group of helpers to pay a visit to whoever might be haunting the house in Metuchen. Bernard, who is a very persuasive fel-

low, managed to get permission from the owner of the house, Mr. Kane, an advertising executive. My group included Mrs. Meyers, as medium, and two associates of hers who would operate the tape recorder and take notes, Rosemarie de Simone and Pearl Winder. Miss de Simone is a teacher and Mrs. Winder is the wife of a dentist.

It was midafternoon of March 6, 1960, when we rolled into the sleepy town of Metuchen. Bernard Axelrod was expecting us, and took us across town to the colonial house we were to inspect.

Any mention of the history or background of the house was studiously avoided en route. The owners, Mr. and Mrs. Kane, had a guest, a Mr. David, and the eight of us sat down in a circle in the downstairs living room of the beautifully preserved old house. It is a jewel of a colonial country house, with an upper story, a staircase and very few structural changes. No doubt about it, the Kanes had good taste, and their house reflected it. The furniture was all in the style of the period, which I took to be about the turn of the eighteenth century, perhaps earlier. There were several cats smoothly moving about, which helped me greatly to relax, for I have always felt that no house is wholly bad where there are cats, and conversely, where there are several cats, a house is bound to be wonderfully charming. For the occasion, however, the entire feline menagerie was put out of reach into the kitchen, and the tape recorder turned on as we took our seats in a semicircle around the fireplace. The light was the subdued light of a late winter afternoon, and the quiet was that of a country house far away from the bustling city. It was a perfect setting for a ghost to have his say.

As Mrs. Meyers eased herself into her comfortable chair, she remarked that certain clairvoyant impressions had come to her almost the instant she set foot into the house.

"I met a woman upstairs—in spirit, that is—with a long face, thick cheeks, perhaps forty years old or more, with ash-brown hair that may once have been blonde. Somehow I get the name Mathilda. She wears a dress of striped material down to her knees, then wide plain material to her ankles. She puts out a hand, and I see a heavy wedding band on her finger, *but it has a cut in it,* and she insists on calling my attention to the cut. Then there is a man, with a prominent nose, tan coat, and black trousers, standing in the back of the room looking as if he were sorry about something...he has very piercing eyes...I think she'd like to find something she has lost, and he blames her for it."

We were listening attentively. No one spoke, for that would perhaps give Mrs. Meyers an unconscious lead, something a good researcher will avoid.

"That sounds very interesting," I heard Bernard say, in his usual noncommittal way. "Do you see anything else?"

"Oh, yes," Mrs. Meyers nodded, "quite a bit—for one thing, there are *other* people here who don't belong to *them* at all...they come with the place, but in a different period...funny, halfway between upstairs and downstairs, I see one or two people *hanging.*"

At this remark, the Kanes exchanged quick glances. Evidently my medium had hit pay dirt. Later, Mr. Kane told us a man committed suicide in the house around 1850 or 1860. He confirmed also that there was once a floor in between the two floors, but that this later addition had since been removed, when the house was restored to its original colonial condition.

Built in 1740, the house had replaced an earlier structure, for objects inscribed "1738" have been unearthed here.

"Legend has always had it that a revolutionary soldier haunts the house," Mr. Kane explained after the séance. "The previous owners told us they did hear peculiar noises from time to time, and that they had been told of such goings-on also by the owner who preceded them.

Perhaps this story has been handed down from owner to owner, but we have never spoken to anyone in our generation who has heard or seen anything unusual about the place."

"What about you and your wife?" I inquired.

"Oh, we were a bit luckier—or unluckier—depending on how you look at it. One day back in 1956, the front door knocker banged away very loudly. My wife, who was all alone in the house at the time, went to see who it was. There was nobody there. It was winter, and deep snow surrounded the house. *There were no tracks in the snow.*"

"How interesting," Bernard said. All this was new to him, too, despite his friendship with the family.

Mr. Kane slowly lit a pipe, blew the smoke toward the low ceiling of the room, and continued.

"The previous owners had a dog. Big, strapping fellow. Just the same, now and again he would hear some strange noises and absolutely panic. In the middle of the night he would jump into bed with them, crazed with fear. But it wasn't just the dog who heard things. They, too, heard the walking—steps of someone walking around the second floor, and in their bedroom, on the south side of the house—at times of the day when they knew for sure there was nobody there."

"And after you moved in, did you actually see anything?" I asked. Did they have any idea what the ghost looked like?

"Well, yes," Mr. Kane said. "About a year ago, Mrs. Kane was sleeping in the Green Room upstairs. *Three nights in a row, she was awakened in the middle of the night, at the same time, by the feeling of a presence.* Looking up, she noticed a white form standing beside her bed. Thinking it was me, at first, she was not frightened. But when she spoke to it, it just disappeared into air. She is sure it was a man."

Although nothing unusual had occurred since, the uncanny feeling persisted, and when Bernard Axelrod mentioned his interest in ghosts, and offered to have me come to the house with a qualified medium, the offer was gladly accepted. So there we were, with Mrs. Meyers slowly gliding into trance. Gradually, her description of what she saw or heard blended into the personalities themselves, as her own personality vanished temporarily. It was a very gradual transition, and well controlled.

"She is being blamed by him," Mrs. Meyers mumbled. "Now I see a table, she took four mugs, four large mugs, and one small one. Does she mean to say, four older people and a small one? I get a name, Jake, John, no, *Jonathan!* Then there are four Indians, and they want to make peace. *They've done something they should not have,* and they want to make peace." Her visions continued.

"Now instead of the four mugs on the table, there's a whole line of them, fifteen altogether, but I don't see the small mug now. There are many individuals standing around the table, with their backs toward me—then someone is calling and screaming, and someone says 'Off above the knees.'"

I later established through research that during the Revolutionary War the house was right in the middle of many small skirmishes; the injured may well have been brought here for treatment.

Mrs. Meyers continued her narrative with increasing excitement in her voice.

"Now there are other men, all standing there with long-tailed coats, white stockings, and talking. Someone says 'Dan Dayridge' or 'Bainbridge,' I can't make it out clearly; he's someone with one of these three-cornered hats, a white wig, tied black hair, a very thin man with a high, small nose, not particularly young, with a fluffy collar and large eyes. Something took place here in which he was a participant. He is one of the men standing there with those fifteen mugs. It is night, and there are two candles on either side of the table, food on the table—*smells like chicken*—and then there is a paper with red seals and gold ribbon. But something goes wrong with this, and now there are only four mugs on the table…I think it means, only four men return. *Not the small one.* This man is one of the four, and somehow the little mug is pushed aside, I see it put away on the shelf. I see now a small boy, he has disappeared, he is gone…but always trying to *come back*. The name *Allen*…he followed the man, but the Indians got him and he never came back. They're looking for him, trying to find him…."

Mrs. Meyers now seemed totally entranced. Her features assumed the face of a woman in great mental anguish, and her voice quivered; the words came haltingly and with much prodding from me. For all practical purposes, the medium had now been taken over by a troubled spirit. We listened quietly, as the story unfolded.

"Allen's coming back one day…call him back…my son, do you hear him? They put those Indians in the tree, do you hear them as they moan?"

"Who took your boy?" I asked gently.

"They did…he went with them, with the men. With his father, *Jon*."

"What Indians took him?"

"Look there in the tree. They didn't do it. I know they didn't do it."

"Where did they go?"

"To the *river*. My boy, did you hear him?"

Mrs. Meyers could not have possibly known that there was a river not far from the house. I wanted to fix the period of our story, as I always do in such cases, so I interrupted the narrative and asked what day this was. There was a brief pause, as if she were collecting her thoughts. Then the faltering voice was heard again.

"December one…."

December one! The old-fashioned way of saying December first.

"What year is this?" I continued.

This time the voice seemed puzzled as to why I would ask such an obvious thing, but she obliged.

"Seventeen…seventy…six."

"What does your husband do?"

"Jonathan…?"

"Does he own property?"

"The field…."

But then the memory of her son returned. "Allen, my son Allen. He is calling me…."

"Where was he born?"

"Here."

"What is the name of this town?"

"Bayridge."

Subsequently, I found that the section of Metuchen we were in had been known in colonial times as *Woodbridge*, although it is not inconceivable that there also was a Bayridge.

The woman wanted to pour her heart out now. "Oh, look," she continued, "they didn't do it, they're in the tree…those Indians, dead ones. They didn't do it, I can see their souls and they were innocent of this…in the cherry tree."

Suddenly she interrupted herself and said—"Where am I? Why am I so sad?"

It isn't uncommon for a newly liberated or newly contacted ghost to be confused about his or her own status. Only an emotionally disturbed personality becomes an earthbound ghost.

I continued the questioning.

Between sobs and cries for her son, Allen, she let the name "Mary Dugan" slip from her lips, or rather the lips of the entranced medium, who now was fully under the unhappy one's control.

"Who is Mary Dugan?" I immediately interrupted.

"He married her, Jonathan."

"Second wife?"

"Yes…I am under the tree."

"Where were you born? What was your maiden name?"

"Bayridge…Swift…my heart is so hurt, so cold, so cold."

"Do you have any other children?"

"Allen…Mary Anne…Gorgia. They're calling me, do you hear them? Allen, he knows I am alone waiting here. He thought he was a *man!*"

"How old was your boy at the time?" I said. The disappearance of her son was the one thing foremost in her mind.

"My boy…eleven…December one, 1776, is his birthday. That was his birthday all right."

I asked her if Allen had another name, and she said, Peter. Her own maiden name? She could not remember.

"Why don't I know? They threw me out…it was Mary took the house."

"What did your husband do?"

"He was a *potter*. He also was paid for harness. His shop...the road to the south. Bayridge. In the tree orchard we took from two neighbors."

The neighborhood is known for its clay deposits and potters, but this was as unknown to the medium as it was to me until *after* the séance, when Bernard told us about it.

In *Boyhood Days in Old Metuchen*, a rare work, Dr. David Marshall says: "Just south of Metuchen there are extensive clay banks."

But our visitor had enough of the questioning. Her sorrow returned and suddenly she burst into tears, the medium's tears, to be sure, crying—"I want Allen! Why is it I look for him? I hear him calling me, I hear his step...I know he is here...why am I searching for him?"

I then explained that Allen was on "her side of the veil" too, that she would be reunited with her boy by merely "standing still" and letting him find her; it was her frantic activity that made it impossible for them to be reunited, but if she were to calm herself, all would be well.

After a quiet moment of reflection, her sobs became weaker and her voice firmer.

"Can you see your son now?"

"Yes, I see him." And with that, she slipped away quietly.

A moment later, the medium returned to her own body, as it were, and rubbed her sleepy eyes. Fully awakened a moment later, she remembered nothing of the trance. Now for the first time did we talk about the house and its ghostly visitors.

"How much of this can be proved?" I asked impatiently.

Mr. Kane lit another pipe, and then answered me slowly.

"Well, there is quite a lot," he finally said. "For one thing, this house used to be a tavern during revolutionary days, known as the Allen House!"

Bernard Axelrod, a few weeks later, discovered an 1870 history of the town of Metuchen. In it, there was a remark anent the house, which an early map showed at its present site in 1799:

"In the house...lived a Mrs. Allen, and on it was a sign 'Allentown Cake and Beer Sold Here.' Between the long Prayer Meetings which according to New England custom were held mornings and afternoons, with half hour or an hour intermission, it was not unusual for the young men to get ginger cake and a glass of beer at this famous restaurant...."

"What about all those Indians she mentioned?" I asked Mr. Kane.

"There were Indians in this region all right," he confirmed.

"Indian arrowheads have been found right here, near the pond in back of the house. Many Indian battles were fought around here, and incidentally, during the War for Independence, both sides came to this house and had their ale in the evening. This was a kind of no-man's land between the Americans and the British. During the day, they would kill each other, but at night, *they ignored each other over a beer at Mrs. Allen's tavern!*"

"How did you get this information?" I asked Mr. Kane.

"There was a local historian, a Mr. Welsh, who owned this house for some thirty years. He also talked of a revolutionary soldier whose ghost was seen plainly 'walking' through the house about a foot off the ground."

Many times have I heard a ghostly apparition described in just such terms. The motion of walking is really unnecessary, it seems, for the spirit form *glides* about a place.

There are interesting accounts in the rare old books about the town of Metuchen in the local library. These stories spoke of battles between the British and Americans, and of "carts loaded with dead bodies, after a battle between British soldiers and Continentals, up around Oak Tree on June 26th, 1777."

No doubt, the Allen House saw many of them brought in along with the wounded and dying.

I was particularly interested in finding proof of Jonathan Allen's existence, and details of his life.

So far I had only ascertained that Mrs. Allen existed. Her husband was my next goal.

After much work, going through old wills and land documents, I discovered a number of Allens in the area. I found the will of his father, Henry, leaving his "son, Jonathan, the land where he lives," on April 4, 1783.

A 1799 map shows a substantial amount of land marked "Land of Allen," and Jonathan Allen's name occurs in many a document of the period as a witness or seller of land.

The Jonathan Allen I wanted had to be from Middlesex County, in which Metuchen was located. I recalled that he was an able-bodied man, and consequently must have seen some service. Sure enough, in the *Official Register of the Officers and Men of New Jersey in the Revolutionary War*, I found my man—"Allen, Jonathan—Middlesex."

It is good to know that the troubled spirit of Mrs. Allen can now rest close to her son's; and perhaps the other restless one, her husband, will be accused of negligence in the boy's death no more.

✳ 37

A Greenwich Village Ghost

BACK IN 1953, when I spent much of my time writing and editing material of a most mundane nature, always, of course, with a weather eye cocked for a good case of hunting, I picked up a copy of *Park East* and found to my amazement some very palatable grist for my psychic mills. "The Ghost of Tenth Street," by Elizabeth Archer, was a well-documented report of the hauntings on that celebrated Greenwich Village street where artists make their headquarters, and many buildings date back to the eighteenth century. Miss Archer's story was later reprinted by *Tomorrow* magazine, upon my suggestion. In *Park East*, some very good illustrations accompany the text, for which there was no room in *Tomorrow*.

Up to 1956, the ancient studio building at 51 West Tenth Street was a landmark known to many connoisseurs of old New York, but it was demolished to make way for one of those nondescript, modern apartment buildings.

Until the very last, reports of an apparition, allegedly the ghost of artist John La Farge, who died in 1910, continued to come in. A few houses down the street is the Church of the Ascension; the altar painting, "The Ascension," is the work of John La Farge. Actually, the artist did the work on the huge painting at his studio, No. 22, in 51 West Tenth Street. He finished it, however, in the church itself, "in place." Having just returned from the Far East, La Farge used a new technique involving the use of several coats of paint, thus making the painting heavier than expected. The painting was hung, but the chassis collapsed; La Farge built a stronger chassis and the painting stayed in place this time. Years went by. Oliver La Farge, the great novelist and grandson of the painter, had spent much of his youth with his celebrated grandfather. One day, while working across the street, he was told the painting had fallen again. Dashing across the street, he found that the painting had indeed fallen, and that his grandfather had died *that very instant!*

The fall of the heavy painting was no trifling matter to La Farge, who was equally as well known as an architect as he was a painter. Many buildings in New York for which he drew the plans seventy-five years ago are still standing. But the construction of the chassis of the altar painting may have been faulty. And therein lies the cause for La Farge's ghostly visitations, it would seem. The artists at No. 51 insisted always that La Farge could not find rest until he had corrected his calculations, searching for the original plans of the chassis to find out what was wrong. An obsession to redeem himself as an artist and craftsman, then, would be the underlying cause for the persistence with which La Farge's ghost returned to his old haunts.

The first such return was reported in 1944, when a painter by the name of Feodor Rimsky and his wife lived in No. 22. Late one evening, they returned from the opera. On approaching their studio, they noticed that a light was on and the door open, although they distinctly remembered having left it shut. Rimsky walked into the studio, pushed aside the heavy draperies at the entrance to the studio itself, and stopped in amazement. In the middle of the room, a single lamp plainly revealed a stranger behind the large chair in what Rimsky called his library corner; the man wore a tall black hat and a dark, billowing velvet coat. Rimsky quickly told his wife to wait, and rushed across the room to get a closer look at the intruder. But the man *just vanished* as the painter reached the chair.

Later, Rimsky told of his experience to a former owner of the building, who happened to be an amateur historian. He showed Rimsky some pictures of former tenants of his building. In two of them, Rimsky easily recognized his visitor, wearing exactly the same clothes Rimsky had seen him in. Having come from Europe but recently, Rimsky knew nothing of La Farge and had never seen a picture of him. The ball dress worn by the ghost had not been common at the turn of the century, but La Farge was known to affect such strange attire.

Three years later, the Rimskys were entertaining some guests at their studio, including an advertising man named William Weber, who was known to have had psychic experiences in the past. But Weber never wanted to discuss this "special talent" of his, for fear of being ridiculed. As the conversation flowed among Weber, Mrs. Weber, and two other guests, the advertising man's wife noticed her husband's sudden stare at a cabinet on the other side of the room, where paintings were stored. She saw nothing, but Weber asked her in an excited tone of voice—"Do you see that man in the cloak and top hat over there?"

Weber knew nothing of the ghostly tradition of the studio or of John La Farge; no stranger could have gotten by the door without being noticed, and none had been expected it this hour. The studio was locked from the *inside.*

After that, the ghost of John La Farge was heard many times by a variety of tenants at No. 51, opening windows or pushing draperies aside, but not until 1948 was he *seen* again.

Up a flight of stairs from Studio 22, but connected to it—artists like to visit each other—was the studio of illustrator John Alan Maxwell. Connecting stairs and a "secret rest room" used by La Farge had long been walled up in the many structural changes in the old building. Only the window of the walled-up room was still visible from the outside. It was in this area that Rimsky felt that the restless spirit of John La Farge was trapped. As Miss Archer puts it in her narrative, "walled in like the Golem, sleeping through the day and close to the premises for roaming through the night."

After many an unsuccessful search of Rimsky's studio, apparently the ghost started to look in Maxwell's studio. In the spring of 1948, the ghost of La Farge made his initial appearance in the illustrator's studio.

It was a warm night, and Maxwell had gone to bed naked, pulling the covers over himself. Suddenly he awakened. From the amount of light coming in through the skylight, he judged the time to be about one or two in the morning. *He had the uncanny feeling of not being alone in the room.* As his eyes got used to the darkness, he clearly distinguished the figure of a tall woman, bending over his bed, lifting and straightening his sheets several times over. Behind her, there was a man staring at a wooden filing cabinet at the foot of the couch. Then he opened a drawer, looked in it, and closed it again. Getting hold of himself, Maxwell noticed that the woman wore a light red dress of the kind worn in the last century, and the man a white shirt and dark cravat of the same period. It never occurred to the illustrator that they were anything but people; probably, he thought, models in costume working for one of the artists in the building.

The woman then turned to her companion as if to say something, but did not, and walked off toward the dark room at the other end of the studio. The man then went back to the cabinet and leaned on it, head in hand. By now Maxwell had regained his wits and thought the intruders must be burglars, although he could not figure out how they had entered his place, since he had locked it from the *inside* before going to bed! Making a fist, he struck at the stranger, yelling, "Put your hands up!"

His voice could be heard clearly along the empty corridors. *But his fist went through the man and into the filing cabinet.* Nursing his injured wrist, he realized that his visitors had dissolved into thin air. There was no one in the dark room. The door was still securely locked. The skylight, 150 feet above ground, could not very well have served as an escape route *to anyone human.* By now Maxwell knew that La Farge and his wife had paid him a social call.

Other visitors to No. 51 complained about strange winds and sudden chills when passing La Farge's walled-up room. One night, one of Maxwell's lady visitors returned, shortly after leaving his studio, in great agitation, yelling, "That man! That man!" The inner court of the building was glass-enclosed, so that one could see clearly across to the corridors on the other side of the building. Maxwell and his remaining guests saw nothing there.

But the woman insisted that she saw a strange man under one of the old gaslights in the building; he seemed to lean against the wall of the corridor, dressed in old-fashioned clothes and possessed of a face so cadaverous and death-mask-like, that it set her ascreaming!

This was the first time the face of the ghost had been observed clearly by anyone. The sight was enough to make her run back to Maxwell's studio. Nobody could have left without being seen through the glass-enclosed corridors and no one had seen a stranger in the building that evening. As usual, he had vanished into thin air.

So much for Miss Archer's account of the La Farge ghost. My own investigation was sparked by her narrative, and I telephoned her at her Long Island home, inviting her to come along if and when we held a séance at No. 51.

I was then working with a group of parapsychology students meeting at the rooms of the Association for Research and Enlightenment (Cayce Foundation) on West Sixteenth Street. The director of this group was a phototechnician of the *Daily News*, Bernard Axelrod, who was the only one of the group who knew the purpose of the meeting; the others, notably the medium, Mrs. Meyers, knew nothing whatever of our plans.

We met in front of Bigelow's drugstore that cold evening, February 23, 1954, and proceeded to 51 West Tenth Street, where the current occupant of the La Farge studio, an artist named Leon Smith, welcomed us. In addition, there were also present the late *News* columnist, Danton Walker, Henry Belk, the noted playwright Bernays, Marguerite Haymes, and two or three others considered students of psychic phenomena. Unfortunately, Mrs. Belk also brought along her pet chihuahua, which proved to be somewhat of a problem.

All in all, there were fifteen people present in the high-ceilinged, chilly studio. Dim light crept through the tall windows that looked onto the courtyard, and one wished that the fireplace occupying the center of the back wall had been working.

We formed a circle around it, with the medium occupying a comfortable chair directly opposite it, and the sitters filling out the circle on both sides; my own chair was next to the medium's.

The artificial light was dimmed. Mrs. Meyers started to enter the trance state almost immediately and only the loud ticking of the clock in the rear of the room was heard for a while, as her breathing became heavier. At the threshold of passing into trance, the medium suddenly said—

"Someone says very distinctly, *Take another step and I go out this window!* The body of a woman...close-fitting hat and a plume...close-fitting bodice and a thick skirt...lands right on face...I see a man, dark curly hair, *hooked nose, an odd, mean face*...cleft in chin...light tan coat, lighter britches, boots, whip in hand, cruel, mean...."

There was silence as she described what I recognized as the face of La Farge.

A moment later she continued: "I know the face is not to be looked at anymore. It is horrible. It should have hurt but I didn't remember. Not long. I just want to scream and scream."

The power of the woman who went through the window was strong. "I have a strange feeling," Mrs. Meyers said, "I *have to go out that window* if I go into trance." With a worried look, she turned to me and asked, "If I stand up and start to move, *hold me.*" I nodded assurance and the séance continued. A humming sound came from her lips, gradually assuming human-voice characteristics.

The next personality to manifest itself was apparently a woman in great fear. "They're in the courtyard.... He is coming...they'll find me and whip me again. I'll die first. Let me go. I shouldn't talk so loud. Margaret! Please don't let him come. See the child. My child. Barbara. Oh, the steps, I can't take it. Take Bobby, raise her, I can't take it. He is coming...*let me go!* I am free!"

With this, the medium broke out of trance and complained of facial stiffness, as well as pain in the shoulder.

Was the frantic woman someone who had been mistreated by an early inhabitant of No. 22? Was she a runaway slave, many of whom had found refuge in the old houses and alleys of the Village?

I requested of the medium's "control" that the most prominent person connected with the studio be allowed to speak to us. But Albert, the control, assured me that the woman, whom he called Elizabeth, was connected with that man. "He will come only if he is of a mind to. He entered the room a while ago."

I asked Albert to describe this man.

"Sharp features, from what I can see. You are closest to him. Clothes...nineties, early 1900s."

After a while, the medium's lips started to move, and a gruff man's voice was heard: "Get out...get out of my house."

Somewhat taken aback by this greeting, I started to explain to our visitor that we were his friends and here to help him. But he didn't mellow.

"I don't know who you are...who is everybody here. Don't have friends."

"I am here to help you," I said, and tried to calm the ghost's suspicions. But our visitor was not impressed.

"I want help, but not from you...*I'll find it!*"

He wouldn't tell us what he was looking for. There were additional requests for us to get out of his house. Finally, the ghost pointed the medium's arm toward the stove and intoned—"I put it there!" A sudden thought inspired me, and I said, lightly—"We found it already."

Rage took hold of the ghost in an instant. "You took it...you betrayed me...it is mine...I was a good man."

I tried in vain to pry his full name from him.

He moaned. "I am sick all over now. Worry, worry, worry. Give it to me."

I promised to return "it," if he would cooperate with us.

In a milder tone he said, "I wanted to make it so pretty. *It won't move.*"

I remembered how concerned La Farge had been with his beautiful altar painting, and that it should not fall *again.* I wondered if he knew how much time had passed.

"Who is President of the United States now?" I asked.

Our friend was petulant. "I don't know. I am sick. William McKinley." But then he volunteered—"I knew him. Met him. In Boston. Last year. Many years ago. Who are you? I don't know any friends. *I am in my house.*"

"What is your full name?"

"Why is that so hard? I know William and I don't know my *own* name."

I have seen this happen before. A disturbed spirit sometimes cannot recall his own name or address.

"Do you know you have passed over?"

"I live here," he said, quietly now. "Times changed. I know I am not what I used to be. *It is there!*"

When I asked what he was looking for, he changed the subject to Bertha, without explaining who Bertha was.

But as he insisted on finding "it," I finally said, "You are welcome to get up and look for it."

"I am bound in this chair and can't move."

"Then tell us where to look for it."

After a moment's hesitation, he spoke. "On the chimney, in back...it was over there. I will find it, but I can't move now...*I made a mistake...I can't talk like this.*"

And suddenly he was gone.

As it was getting on to half past ten, the medium was awakened. The conversation among the guests then turned to any feelings they might have had during the séance. Miss Archer was asked about the building.

"It was put up in 1856," she replied, "and is a copy of a similar studio building in Paris."

"Has there ever been any record of a murder committed in this studio?" I asked.

"Yes...between 1870 and 1900, *a young girl went through one of these windows.* But I did not mention this in my article, as it *apparently* was unconnected with the La Farge story."

"What about Elizabeth? And Margaret?"

"That was remarkable of the medium," Miss Archer nodded. "You see, Elizabeth was La Farge's wife...and Margaret, well, she also fits in with his story."

For the first time, the name La Farge had been mentioned in the presence of the medium. But it meant nothing to her in her conscious state.

Unfortunately, the ghost could not be convinced that his search for the plans was unnecessary, for La Farge's genius as an architect and painter has long since belonged to time.

A few weeks after this séance, I talked to an advertising man named Douglas Baker. To my amazement, he, too, had at one time occupied Studio 22. Although aware of the stories surrounding the building, he had scoffed at the idea of a ghost. But one night he was roused from deep sleep by the noise of someone opening and closing drawers. Sitting up in bed, he saw a man in Victorian opera clothes in his room, which was dimly lit by the skylight and windows. Getting out of bed to fence off the intruder, he found himself alone, just as others had before him.

No longer a scoffer, he talked to others in the building, and was able to add one more episode to the La Farge case. It seems a lady was passing No. 51 one bleak afternoon when she noticed an odd-looking gentleman in opera clothes standing in front of the building. For no reason at all, the woman exclaimed, "My, you're a funny-looking man!"

The gentleman in the opera cloak looked at her in rage. "Madam—how dare you!"

And with that, *he went directly thought the building—the wall of the building, that is!*

Passers-by revived the lady.

* * *

Now there is a modern apartment building at 51 West Tenth Street. Is John La Farge still roaming its ugly modern corridors? Last night, I went into the Church of the Ascension, gazed at the marvelous altar painting, and prayed a little that he shouldn't have to.

✳ 38

The Hauntings at Seven Oaks

ELEANOR SMALL IS A charming woman in her late forties who dabbles in real estate and business. She comes from a very good family which once had considerable wealth, and is what is loosely termed "social" today. She wasn't the kind of person one would suspect of having any interest in the supernatural.

One evening, as we were discussing other matters, the conversation got around to ghosts. To my amazement, Eleanor was fascinated by the topic; so much so, that I could not help asking her if by chance she knew of a haunted house somewhere for me to investigate!

"Indeed I do," was the reply, and this is how I first heard about Seven Oaks. In Mamaroneck, New York, up in posh Westchester County, there stood until very recently a magnificent colonial mansion known as Seven Oaks. Situated near the edge of Long Island Sound, it was one of the show places of the East. Just as did so many fine old mansions, this one gave way to a "development," and now there are a number of small, insignificant, ugly modern houses dotting the grounds of the large estate.

During the Battle of Orient Point, one of the bloodier engagements of the Revolutionary War, the mansion was British-held, and American soldiers, especially the wounded, were often smuggled out to Long Island Sound via an "underground railway," passing through the mansion.

"When I was a young girl," Eleanor said, "I spent many years with my mother and my stepfather at Seven Oaks, which we then owned. I was always fascinated by the many secret passageways which honeycombed the house."

The entrance was from the library; some books would slide back, and a slender wooden staircase appeared. Gaslight jets had been installed in the nineteenth century to light these old passages. A butler working for Eleanor's parents stumbled onto them by chance.

"When did you first hear about ghosts?" I asked.

"We moved into the house about June 1932. Right away, a neighbor by the name of Mabel Merker told us that the place was *haunted*. Of course, we paid no attention to her."

"Of course." I nodded wryly.

"But it wasn't too long before Mother changed her mind about that."

"You mean she saw the ghost?"

Eleanor nodded. "Regularly, *practically every night.*" Eleanor's mother had described her as a woman of about forty-five, with long blond hair and sweet expression on her face. One of these apparitions had its comic aspects, too.

"Mother had her private bathroom, which connected directly with her bedroom. One night, after all doors had been locked and Mother knew there was no one about any more, she retired for the night. Entering the bathroom from her bedroom, she left the connecting door open in the knowledge that her privacy could not possibly be disturbed! Suddenly, looking up, *she saw, back in her room, the ghost standing and beckoning to her in the bathroom,* as if she wanted to tell her something of utmost urgency. There was such an expression of sadness and frustration on the wraith's face, Mother could never forget it."

"But what did she *do?*" I asked.

"She approached the apparition, but when she got halfway across the room, the ghost just evaporated into thin air."

"And this was in good light, and the apparition was not shadowy or vaporous?"

"Oh no, it looked just like someone of flesh and blood—until that last moment when she *dissolved before Mother's eyes.*"

"Was your mother very upset?"

"Only at first. Later she got used to the idea of having a ghost around. Once she saw her up on the second floor, in the master bedroom. There she was standing in front of the two beds. Mother wondered what she could do to help her, but the ghost again vanished."

"Did she ever hear her talk or make any kind of noise?" I asked.

"Not talk, but noise—well, at the time Mother moved into the house, the previous owner, Mrs. Warren, still maintained a few things of her own in a closet in the house, and she was in the habit of returning there occasionally to pick some of them up, a few at a time. One evening Mother heard some footsteps, but thought them to be Mrs. Warren's.

"The next day, however, she found out that no one had been to the house. Our family dog frequently barked loudly and strongly before the fireplace, at *something* or *someone* we could not see, but evidently he could."

"Did anyone else see the ghost?"

"The servants constantly complained of *being pulled from their beds*, in the servants' quarters, by unseen hands. It was as if someone wanted their attention, but there never was anyone there when the lights were turned on."

"She probably wanted to talk to someone, as ghosts often do!" I said. Communication and inability to be heard or seen by the people of flesh and blood is the main agony of a wraith.

"That must be so," Eleanor nodded, "because there was another incident some years later that seems to confirm it. My stepfather's son and his seventeen-year-old bride came to live at Seven Oaks. The girl was part Indian, and extremely sensitive. They were given a room on the top floor of the old mansion, with a double bed in the center.

"One night they retired early, and the son was already in bed, while his wife stood nearby in the room. Suddenly, as she looked on with horror, she saw her *husband bodily pulled out of bed by unseen hands.* His struggle was in vain.

"The next morning, the young couple left Seven Oaks, never to return."

✳ 39

The Central Park West Ghost

MRS. M. DALY HOPKINS was a lady of impeccable taste, and gracious surroundings meant a great deal to her and her husband. Consequently, when they decided to look for a new apartment, they directed their steps toward Central Park West, which in the thirties had become one of New York's more desirable residential areas.

As they were walking up the tree-lined street, they noticed a man in working overalls hanging up a sign on a building, reading "Apartment for Rent." The man turned out to be the superintendent of one of three identical gray five-story buildings on the corner of 107th Street and Central Park West.

Mrs. Hopkins, who reported her uncanny experiences in a story entitled "Ten Years with a Ghost,"* was overjoyed. The location was perfect; now if only the apartment suited them! With hearts beating a trifle faster, the Hopkinses approached the building.

The apartment for rent was on the top floor, that is, it occupied the southeast corner of the fifth floor of the building, and it contained a total of eight rooms. This seemed ideal to the Hopkinses, who needed plenty of space for themselves, their small son, and his nurse.

It seemed the former tenants had just moved out, after living in the apartment for many years. Most of the

people in the building, the superintendent added, had been there a long time. By November of the same year, the Hopkins family was settled in the new apartment.

Nothing unusual happened during the first few weeks of their stay, except that on a number of occasions Mrs. Hopkins heard her housekeeper cry out, as if surprised by someone or something!

Finally, the middle-aged woman came to Mrs. Hopkins, and said: "Something's strange about this place. I often feel someone standing behind me, and yet, when I turn around, there is nobody there!"

Mrs. Hopkins, naturally, tried to talk her out of her apprehensions, but to no avail. For two years Annie, the housekeeper, tolerated the "unseen visitor." Then she quit. She just could not go on like this, she explained. "*Somebody keeps turning my doorknob.* I am not a superstitious person, but I do believe you have a *ghost* here."

Mrs. Hopkins wondered why no one else in the apartment noticed anything unusual. After Annie left, Josephine was hired, and slept in the apartment. Before long, Josephine, too, kept exclaiming in surprise, just as Annie had done for so long.

Finally, Josephine came to see Mrs. Hopkins and asked if she could talk to her. Mrs. Hopkins sat back to listen.

"This apartment is haunted," Josephine said.

Mrs. Hopkins was not surprised. She admitted openly now that there was an "unseen guest" at the apartment,

*Fate, July, 1954.

but she loved the apartment too much to give it up. "We'll just have to live with that ghost!" she replied. Josephine laughed, and said it was all right with her, too.

She felt the ghost was female, and from that day on, for seven-and-a-half years, Josephine would speak aloud to the ghost on many occasions, addressing her always as "Miss Flossie" and asking the unquiet spirit to tell her what was troubling her so much. Finally, one morning, Josephine came into Mrs. Hopkins' room and told her that she knew why "Miss Flossie" could not find rest.

"Miss Flossie killed herself, Ma'am," she said quietly.

Josephine never actually *saw* the ghost, for "no matter how quick I turn, the ghost is even quicker" to disappear. But as is the case so often with children, the Hopkinses' small son *did* see her. The boy was then just four years old.

He had been asleep for several hours that particular night, when Mrs. Hopkins heard him call out for her. Since the "nanna" was out for the evening, Mrs. Hopkins rushed to his side. The boy said a "lady visitor waked me up when she kissed me." Mrs. Hopkins insisted that she and her husband were the only ones at home. The boy insisted that he had seen this woman, and that she looked like "one of those dolls little girls play with."

Mrs. Hopkins calmed her boy, and after he had returned to sleep, she went to her husband and brought him up to date on this entire ghost business. He didn't like it at all. But somehow the household settled down to routine again, and it was several years before another manifestation occurred, or was noticed, at least.

One night, while her son was in boarding school and her husband out of town on business, Mrs. Hopkins found herself all alone in the apartment. The "nanna" had returned to England. It was a quiet, rainy night, and Mrs. Hopkins did not feel unduly nervous, especially as "Miss Flossie" had not been active for so long.

Sometime after going to bed, Mrs. Hopkins was awakened by someone calling her name. "Mrs. Hop-kins! Mrs. Hop-kins!" There was a sense of urgency about the voice, which seemed to be no different from that of someone close by. Mrs. Hopkins responded immediately. "Yes, what is it?" Fully awake now, she noticed by her clock that the time was 1 A.M. Suddenly she became aware of an entirely different sound. Overhead, on the roof, there were footsteps, and somehow she knew it was a burglar. Jumping from bed, Mrs. Hopkins examined the hall door. The three locks were all off. She tried to telephone the superintendent, but found the line had been cut! Without a moment's hesitation, she retraced her steps to the bedroom, and *locked herself in the room.*

The next morning, the superintendent informed Mrs. Hopkins that the two other houses in the block had their top floor apartments burglarized during the night, but her apartment had somehow been spared! Mrs. Hopkins smiled wanly. How could she explain that a ghost had saved her that night?

One evening Mrs. Hopkins and her husband returned from the theater and found a small black kitten crying on the front doorstep of the house. She felt pity for the kitten, and took it into the apartment, locking it into the maid's room for the night. At first they thought it was a neighbor's cat, but nobody came to claim it, and in the end they kept it.

The cat behaved strangely right from the start. Dashing through the apartment with fur disarranged, she seemed terrified of something. Josephine assured Mrs. Hopkins that the ghost hated the kitten, and would kill it before long.

A week later, Mrs. Hopkins sat alone in a comfortable chair, reading. It was evening, and the kitten was curled up, sleeping peacefully nearby. Suddenly the cat looked toward the doorway leading into the hall. Getting up, she seemed to see someone enter the room, pass in front of Mrs. Hopkins, and finally stand directly behind her. The cat seemed terrified. Finally, Mrs. Hopkins said, "Kitty, don't be afraid of Miss Flossie." The cat relaxed, but not Mrs. Hopkins, who felt a terrible chill.

When her husband returned, she insisted they give up the apartment. The ghost had become too much for her. No sooner said than done, and two weeks later, they were living at the other end of town.

One night at dinner Mr. Hopkins mentioned that he had just learned more about their former apartment from one of the old tenants he had accidentally met. At the time when they rented the place, the superintendent told them the previous tenants had moved out "ten minutes before." What he had neglected to tell them, however, was *how.* The Hopkinses had come there *ten minutes after the funeral.* The wife of the former tenant had committed suicide in the living room. Mrs. Hopkins' curiosity was aroused. She went to see a Mrs. Foran, who lived at the old place directly below where their apartment had been.

"What sort of woman was this lady who died here?" she asked her.

Well, it seemed that the couple had been living elsewhere before their marriage without benefit of clergy. After they got married, they moved to this place, to make a fresh start.

But the wife was still unhappy. During the three years of their tenancy, she *imagined* the neighbors were gossiping about her. Actually, the neighbors knew nothing of their past, and cared less. "But," Mrs. Foran added as an afterthought, "she didn't *belong* here."

"Why not?" wondered Mrs. Hopkins.

"Because she had bleached hair, that's why!" replied Mrs. Foran.

Mrs. Hopkins couldn't help smiling, because she realized how right Josephine had been in calling the spook "Miss Flossie."

In July 1960, I decided to pay "Miss Flossie" a visit. I first located Mrs. Hopkins in Newmarket, Canada. My request for information was answered by Mrs. Hopkins' sister, Helena Daly.

"Since my sister is very handicapped following a stroke," she wrote, "I shall be pleased to give you the information you wish, as I lived there with them for a short time, but did not meet the ghost.

"The location is at 471 Central Park West, northwest corner of 106th Street, a top-floor apartment with windows facing south and also east, overlooking Central Park.

"Wishing you every success, yours truly, Helena M. Daly."

I located the house all right, even though it was at 107th Street. The apartment on the top floor was locked. I located a ground-floor tenant who knew the name of the family now living in it. The name was Hernandez, but that didn't get me into the apartment by a long shot. Three letters remained unanswered. The rent collector gave me the name of the superintendent. He didn't have a key either. The entire neighborhood had changed greatly in character since the Hopkinses lived there. The whole area, and of course the building at 471 Central Park West, was now populated by Spanish-speaking Puerto Ricans.

Weeks went by. All my efforts to contact the Hernandez family proved fruitless. There was no telephone, and they never seemed to be home when I called. Finally, I decided to send a letter announcing my forthcoming visit three days hence at 1:30 in the afternoon, and would they please be in, as I had the permission of their landlord to see them.

I was determined to hold a séance *outside* their very doorstep, if necessary, hoping that my sensitive, Mrs. Meyers, would somehow catch at least part of the vibratory element and atmosphere of the place. I also invited a Mr. Lawrence, a newspaper writer, to come along as a witness.

To my surprise, the séance on the doorstep was unnecessary. When the three of us arrived at the apartment, somewhat out of breath after climbing four flights of stairs on a hot summer day, the door was immediately opened by a nicely-dressed young man who introduced himself as Mr. Hernandez, owner of the flat. He led us through the large apartment into the living room at the corner of the building, the very room I was most interested in.

Mr. Hernandez spoke excellent English. He explained that he was a furniture repairman employed by one of the large hotels, and that he and his family—we saw a young wife and child—lived in the apartment. They had never seen nor heard anything unusual. He did not believe in "vibrations" or the supernatural, but had no objection to our sitting down and gathering what impressions we could. I had maintained in my letters all along that "a famous literary figure" had once occupied his apartment and we wanted to visit the rooms for that reason, as I was doing an article on this person. It doesn't pay to tell the person whose apartment you want to visit that it's his ghost you're after.

Mrs. Meyers sat down on the comfortable couch near the window, and the rest of us took seats around her. Her first impressions of the room came through immediately.

"I hear a woman's voice calling Jamie or Janie.... There is an older woman, kind of emaciated looking, with gray hair, long nose, wide eyes, bushy eyebrows. Then there is a black cat. Something is upsetting Jamie. There's a squeaking rocking chair, a man with a booming voice, reciting lines, heavy-set, he wears a cutaway coat...man is heavy in the middle, has a mustache, standup collar with wings, dark tie...there's something wrong with his finger...a wedding band? A remark about a *wedding band?*"

Mrs. Meyers looked around the carefully furnished, spotlessly clean room, and continued. "A small boy, about twelve. Someone here used to live *with the dead* for a very long time, treated as if they were alive. Just stay here, never go out, if I go out, *he* is not going to come back again, so I'll remain here! I look from the window and see him coming out of the carriage. We have dinner every night." Suddenly, Mrs. Meyers started to inhale rapidly, and an expression of fear crept upon her face.

"Gas—always have one burner—gas! Somebody is still disturbed about Jamie. I get the letters M. B. or B. M. I feel lots of people around. There is a to-do in court. Now someone walks around the outside that can't be seen. Wants to come in by the window.

"It's like a nightmare, very dark, can't look out the window. I am a mess, and I'm going to fall if I let go. There's a body laid in a casket in this room, but very few flowers; the name on the silver plaque reads Stevens or Stevenson; the curtains are drawn, it's very dark, there are candles and a body in the casket."

I asked Mrs. Meyers if she felt any restless spirits about the place still. "The restlessness is dimming," she replied. "It was there in the past, but is much dimmer now, because a religious person lives here."

Did she get any other impressions? "The police had something to do here, they wear long coats, the coffin contains a person in black."

After we had left the apartment, I compared Mrs. Meyers' impressions to the material in the 1954 story, which I had never shown or mentioned to her. There was a small son, and the description of the "older woman" fitted Mrs. Hopkins, as did the black cat. Mrs. Meyers' statement, that "something was wrong with his finger...a wedding band!" recalled the fact that the couple had been living together as man and wife for years without being married, and had this fact not disturbed the ghost so much?

The gas explosion and the funeral following "Miss Flossie's" suicide were factual. M. is Mrs. Hopkins' initial and "M. B." may have been "M. D.," which is M. Daly, Mrs. Hopkins' maiden name. "Someone walking on the outside" refers to the burglar episode. Police and the coffin make sense where suicide is involved.

Shortly after our séance, I received word that Mrs. Hopkins had passed on. Now perhaps she and "Miss Flossie" can become better acquainted.

✳ 40

The Ghosts at St. Mark's

DESPITE THE FACT that most religious faiths, and their clergy, take a dim view of ghosts and hauntings, there are many recorded cases of supernormal goings-on in churches and cemeteries. One such place of worship is New York's famed old St. Mark's-In-the-Bowerie church, located at the corner of Second Avenue and Tenth Street.

Originally the site of a chapel erected in 1660 by Peter Stuyvesant for the Dutch settlers of New Amsterdam, it became the governor's burial ground in 1672. The Stuyvesant vault was permanently sealed in 1953, when the last member of the family died. A century after the death of the governor, the family had adopted the Episcopalian faith, and a grandson, also named Peter Stuyvesant, gave the land and some cash to build on the same spot the present church of St. Mark's. It was completed in 1799 and has been in service continuously since. No major repairs, additions, or changes were made in the building.

The surrounding neighborhood became one of the worst in New York, although it was once a highly respected one. But even in the confines of the Bowery, there is a legend that St. Mark's is a haunted church.

I talked to the Reverend Richard E. McEvoy, Archdeacon of St. John's, but for many years rector of St. Mark's, about any apparitions he or others might have seen in the church. Legend, of course, has old Peter Stuyvesant rambling about now and then. The Reverend proved to be a keen observer, and quite neutral in the matter of ghosts. He himself had not seen anything unusual. But there was a man, a churchgoer, whom he had known for many years. This man always sat in a certain pew on the right side of the church.

Queried by the rector about his peculiar insistence on that seat, the man freely admitted it was because from there he could see "her"—the "her" being a female wraith who appeared in the church to listen to the sermon, and then disappeared again. At the spot he had chosen, he could always be next to her! I pressed the rector about any *personal* experiences. Finally he thought that he had seen something like a figure in white out of the corner of one

St. Mark's-in-the-Bowerie, New York

eye, a figure that passed, and quickly disappeared. That was ten years ago.

On the rector's recommendation, I talked to Foreman Cole, the man who comes to wind the clock at regular intervals, and who has been in and around St. Mark's for the past twenty-six years.

Mr. Cole proved to be a ready talker. Some years ago, Cole asked his friend Ray Bore, organist at a Roman Catholic church nearby, to have a look at the church organ. The church was quite empty at the time, which was 1 A.M. Nevertheless, Cole saw "someone" in the balcony.

About fifteen years ago, Cole had another unusual experience. It was winter, and the church was closed to the public, for it was after 5 P.M. That evening it got dark early, but there was still some light left when Cole let himself into the building. Nobody was supposed to be in the church at that time, as Cole well knew, being familiar with the rector's hours.

Nevertheless, to his amazement, *he clearly saw a woman standing in the back of the church*, near the entrance door, in the center aisle. Thinking that she was a late churchgoer who had been locked in by mistake, and worried that she might stumble in the semidarkness, he called

The haunted nave

Governor Peter Stuyvesant is buried in the vault

A psychic photograph of the haunted nave

out to her, "Wait, lady, don't move till I turn the lights on."

He took his eyes off her for a moment and quickly switched the lights on. But he found himself alone; she had vanished into thin air from her spot well within the nave of the church.

Unnerved, Cole ran to the entrance door and found it firmly locked. He then examined all the windows and found them equally well secured.

I asked Cole if there was anything peculiar about the woman's appearance. He thought for a moment, then said, "Yes, there was. She seemed to ignore me, looked right through me, and did not respond to my words."

Six weeks later, he had another supernormal experience. Again alone in the church, with all doors locked, he saw a man who looked to him like one of the Bowery derelicts outside. He wore shabby clothes, and did not seem to "belong" here. Quickly, Cole switched on the lights to examine his visitor. But he had vanished, exactly as the woman had before.

Cole has not seen any apparitions since, but some pretty strange noises have reached his ears. For one thing, there is frequent "banging" about the church, and "uncanny" feelings and chills in certain areas of the old church. On one occasion, Cole clearly heard someone coming up the stairs leading to the choir loft. Thinking it was the sexton, he decided to give him a scare, and hid to await the man at the end of the staircase. Only, nobody came. The steps were those of an *unseen man!*

Cole has no idea who the ghosts could be. He still takes care of the clock, and is reluctant to discuss his experiences with ordinary people, lest they think him mad. A

The Ghosts at St. Mark's

man of forty-one, and quite healthy and realistic, Cole is sure of his memories.

Several days later, I asked Mary R. M., a singer and gifted psychic, to accompany me to the church and see if she could get any "impressions." It turned out that my friend had been to the church once before, last November, when she was rehearsing nearby. At that time, she was sure the place was haunted. We sat in one of the right-hand pews, and waited. We were quite alone in the church; the time was three in the afternoon, and it was quite still.

Within a minute or so, Mary told me she felt "a man with a cane walking down the middle aisle behind us." Peter Stuyvesant, buried here, walked with a cane.

Then my friend pointed to the rear, and advised me that she "saw" a woman in wide skirts standing near the rear door of the church. She added: "I see a white shape floating away from that marble slab in the rear!"

So if you ever see someone dissolve into thin air at St. Mark's—don't be alarmed. It's only a ghost!

✳ 41

The Clinton Court Ghosts

WHILE CASUALLY LEAFING through the pages of *Tomorrow* magazine, a periodical devoted to psychical research in which my byline appears on occasion, I noticed a short piece by Wainwright Evans, called "Ghost in Crinoline." The article, written in the spring of 1959, told of a spectral inhabitant at number 422½ West Forty-Sixth Street, in New York City. It seemed that Ruth Shaw, an artist who had for years lived in the rear section of the old building, which she had turned into a studio for herself, had spoken to Mr. Evans about her experiences. He had come to see her at Clinton Court, as the building was called. There was a charming iron gate through which you pass by the main house into a court. Beyond the court rose an arcaded rear section, three stories high and possessed of an outdoor staircase leading to the top. This portion dates back to 1809, or perhaps even before, and was at one time used as the coach house of Governor DeWitt Clinton.

Miss Shaw informed Evans about the legends around the place, and in her painstaking manner told him of her conversations with ninety-year-old Mr. Oates, a neighborhood druggist. An English coachman with a Danish wife once lived in the rooms above the stables. The first ghost ever to be seen at Clinton Court was that of "Old Moor," a sailor hanged for mutiny at the Battery, and buried in Potter's Field, which was only a short block away from the house. Today, this cemetery has disappeared beneath the teeming tenement houses of the middle Westside, Hell's Kitchen's outer approaches. But "Old Moor," as it were, did not have far to go to haunt anyone. Clinton Court was the first big house in his path. The coachman's wife saw the apparition, and while running away from "Old Moor," fell down the stairs. This was the more unfortunate as she was expecting a child at the time. She died of the fall, but the child survived.

The irony of it was that soon the mother's ghost was seen around the Court, too, usually hanging around the

baby. Thus, Ghost Number 2 joined the cast at the Governor's old house.

One of the grandchildren of the Clinton family, who had been told these stories, used to play "ghost" the way children nowadays play cops and robbers. This girl, named Margaret, used to put on old-fashioned clothes and run up and down the big stairs. One fine day, she tripped and fell down the stairs making the game grim reality. Many have seen the pale little girl; Miss Shaw was among them. She described her as wearing a white blouse, full sleeves, and a crinoline. On one occasion, she saw the girl ghost skipping down the stairs *in plain daylight*—skipping is the right word, for a ghost need not actually "walk," but often floats just a little bit above ground, not quite touching it.

I thought it would be a good idea to give Miss Shaw a ring, but discovered there was no telephone at the address. Miss Shaw had moved away and even the local police sergeant could not tell me where the house was. The police assured me *there was no such number* as 422½ West Forty-Sixth Street. Fortunately, I have a low opinion of police intelligence, so my search continued. Perhaps a dozen times I walked by numbers 424 and 420 West Forty-Sixth Street before I discovered the strange archway at Number 420. I walked through it, somehow driven on by an inner feeling that I was on the right track. I was, for before me opened Clinton Court. It simply was tucked away in back of 420 and the new owners had neglected to put the 422½ number anywhere within sight. Now an expensive, remodeled apartment house, the original walls and arrangements were still intact.

On the wall facing the court, Number 420 proudly displayed a bronze plaque inscribed "Clinton Court—ca. 1840—Restored by the American Society for Preservation of Future Antiquities"! The rear building, where Miss Shaw's studio used to be, was now empty. Apparently the carpenters had just finished fixing the floors and the apartment was up for rent. I thought that fortunate, for it meant we could get into the place without worrying about a tenant. But there was still the matter of finding out who the landlord was, and getting permission. It took me several weeks and much conversation, until I finally got permission to enter the place one warm evening in August 1960.

Clinton Court—the outside gate to the old carriage house

Clinton Court—the haunted courtyard

Meanwhile I had been told by the superintendent that an old crony by the name of Mrs. Butram lived next door, at Number 424, and that she might know something of interest. I found Mrs. Butram without difficulty. Having been warned that she kept a large number of pets, my nose led me to her door. For twenty-five years, she assured me, she had lived here, and had heard many a story about the ghost next door. She had never seen anything herself, but when I pressed her for details, she finally said—

"Well, they say it's a young girl of about sixteen.... One of the horses they used to keep back there broke loose and frightened her. Ran down the stairs, and fell to her death. That's what they say!"

I thanked Mrs. Butram, and went home. I called my good friend Mrs. Meyers, and asked her to accompany me to a haunted house, without telling her any more than that.

To my surprise, Mrs. Meyers told me on the phone that she thought she could see the place clairvoyantly that very instant.

"There is a pair of stairs outside of a house, and a woman in white, in a kind of backyard."

This conversation took place on August 9, a week before Mrs. Meyers knew anything about the location or nature of our "case."

About a week later, we arrived together at Clinton Court, and proceeded immediately into the ground-floor studio apartment of the former coach house. In subdued light, we sat quietly on the shabby, used-up furniture.

"Let me look around and see what I get," Mrs. Meyers said, and rose. Slowly I followed her around the apartment, which lay in ghostly silence. Across the yard, the windows of the front section were ablaze with light and the yard itself was lit up by floodlights. But it was a quiet night. The sounds of Hell's Kitchen did not intrude into our atmosphere, as if someone bent on granting us privacy for a little while were muffling them.

"I feel funny in the head, bloated...you understand I am *her* now...there are wooden steps from the right on the outside of the place—"

Mrs. Meyers pointed at the wall. "There, where the wall now is; they took them down, I'm sure." On close inspection, I noticed traces of something that may have been a staircase.

"A woman in white, young, teenager, she's a bride, she's fallen down those steps on her wedding night, her head is battered in—"

Horror came over Mrs. Meyers' face. Then she continued. "It is cold, the dress is so flimsy, flowing; she is disappointed, for someone has disappointed *her*."

Deep in thought, Mrs. Meyers sat down in one of the chairs in a little room off the big, sunken living room that formed the main section of the studio apartment now, as the new owners had linked two apartments to make one bigger one.

"She has dark hair, blue eyes, light complexion, I'd say she's in her middle teens and wears a pretty dress, almost like a nightgown, the kind they used to have seventy-five or a hundred years ago. But now I see her in a gingham or checkered dress with high neck, long sleeves, a white hat, she's ready for a trip, only someone doesn't come. There is crying, disappointment. Then there is a seafaring man also, with a blue hat with shiny visor, a blue coat. He's a heavy-set man."

I thought of "Old Moor." Mrs. Meyers was getting her impressions all at the same time. Of course, she knew nothing of either the young girl ghost nor the sailor.

Now the medium told a lively tale of a young girl ready to marry a young man, but pursued by another, older man. "I can hear her scream!" She grabbed her own throat, and violently suppressed a scream, the kind of sound that might have invited an unwelcome audience to our séance!

"Avoiding the man, she rushes up the stairs, it is a slippery and cold day around Christmas. She's carrying something heavy, maybe wood and coal, and it's the eve of her marriage, but she's pushed off the roof. There are two women, the oldest one had been berating the girl, and pushed her out against the fence, and over she went. It was cold and slippery and nobody's fault. But instead of a wedding, there is a funeral."

The medium was now in full trance. Again, a scream is suppressed, then the voice changes and another personality speaks through Mrs. Meyers. "Who are you?" I said, as I always do on such occasions. Identification is a must when you communicate with ghosts.

Instead, the stranger said anxiously—"Mathew!"
"Who is Mathew?" I said.
"Why won't he come, where is he? Why?"
"Who are you?"
"Bernice."
"How old are you?"
"Seventeen."
"What year is this?"
"Eighty."
But then the anguish came to the fore again.
"Where is he, he has the ring...my head...Mathew, Mathew...she pushed me, she is in hell. I'm ready to go, I'm dressed, we're going to father. I'm dressed...."

As she repeated her pleas, the voice gradually faded out. Then, just as suddenly as she had given way to the stranger, Mrs. Meyers' own personality returned.

As we walked out of the gloomy studio apartment, I mused about the story that had come from Mrs. Meyers' lips. Probably servant girls, I thought, and impossible to trace. Still, she got the young girl, her falling off the stairs, the stairs themselves, and the ghostly sailor. Clinton Court is still haunted all right!

I looked up at the reassuringly lighted modern apartments around the yard, and wondered if the ghosts knew the difference. If you ever happen to be in Hell's Kitchen, step through the archway at 420 West Forty-Sixth Street into the yard, and if you're real, real quiet, and a bit lucky, of course, perhaps you will meet the teen-age ghost in her white dress or crinoline—but beware of "Old Moor" and his language—you know what sailors are like!

✳ 42

Hungry Lucy

"June Havoc's got a ghost in her townhouse," Gail Benedict said gaily on the telephone. Gail was in public relations, and a devoted ghost-finder ever since I had been able to rid her sister's apartment of a poltergeist the year before.

The house in question was 104 years old, stashed away in what New Yorkers call "Hell's Kitchen," the old area in the 40s between Ninth and Tenth Avenues, close to the theater district. Built on the corner of Forty-fourth Street and Ninth Avenue, it had been in the possession of the Rodenberg family until a Mr. Payne bought it. He remodeled it carefully, with a great deal of respect for the old plans. He did nothing to change its quaint Victorian appearance, inside or out.

About three years later, glamorous stage and television star June Havoc bought the house, and rented the upper floors to various tenants. She herself moved into the downstairs apartment, simply because no one else wanted it. It didn't strike her as strange at the time that no tenant had ever renewed the lease on that floor-through downstairs apartment, but now she knows why. It was all because of *Hungry Lucy*.

The morning after Gail's call, June Havoc telephoned me, and a séance was arranged for Friday of that week. I immediately reached British medium Sybil Leek, but I gave no details. I merely invited her to help me get rid of a noisy ghost. Noise was what June Havoc complained about.

"It seems to be a series of *insistent* sounds," she said. "First, they were rather soft. I didn't really notice them three years ago. Then I had the architect who built that balcony in the back come in and asked him to investigate these sounds. He said there was nothing whatever the matter with the house. Then I had the plumber up, because I thought it was the steam pipes. He said it was not that either. Then I had the carpenter in, for it is a very old house, but he couldn't find any structural defects whatever."

"When do you hear these tapping noises?"

"At all times. Lately, they seem to be more insistent. More demanding. We refer to it as 'tap dancing,' for that is exactly what it sounds like."

The wooden floors were in such excellent state that Miss Havoc didn't cover them with carpets. The yellow pine used for the floorboards cannot be replaced today.

June Havoc's maid had heard loud tapping in Miss Havoc's absence, and many of her actor friends had remarked on it.

"It is always in this area," June Havoc pointed out, "and seems to come from underneath the kitchen floor. It has become impossible to sleep a full night's sleep in this room."

The kitchen leads directly into the rear section of the floor-through apartment, to a room used as a bedroom. Consequently, any noise disturbed her sleep.

Underneath Miss Havoc's apartment, there was another floor-through, but the tenants had never reported anything unusual there, nor had the ones on the upper floors. Only Miss Havoc's place was noisy.

We now walked from the front of the apartment into the back half. Suddenly there was a loud tapping sound from underneath the floor as if someone had shot off a machine gun. Catherine and I had arrived earlier than the rest, and there were just the three of us.

"There, you see," June Havoc said. The ghost had greeted us in style.

I stepped forward at once.

"What do you want?" I demanded.

Immediately, the noise stopped.

While we waited for the other participants in the investigation to arrive, June Havoc pointed to the rear wall.

"It has been furred out," she explained. "That is to say, there was another wall against the wall, which made the room smaller. Why, no one knows."

Soon *New York Post* columnist Earl Wilson and Mrs. Wilson, Gail Benedict, and Robert Winter-Berger, also a publicist, arrived, along with a woman from *Life* magazine, notebook in hand. A little later Sybil Leek swept into the room. There was a bit of casual conversation, in which nothing whatever was said about the ghost, and then we seated ourselves in the rear portion of the apartment. Sybil took the chair next to the spot where the noises always originated. June Havoc sat on her right, and I on her left. The lights were very bright since we were filming the entire scene for Miss Havoc's television show.

Soon enough, Sybil began to "go under."

"Hungry," Sybil mumbled faintly.

"Why are you hungry?" I asked.

"No food," the voice said.

The usually calm voice of Sybil Leek was panting in desperation now.

"I want some food, some food!" she cried.

June Havoc's former townhouse—haunted by a colonial soldier's lady friend

I promised to help her and asked for her name.

"Don't cry. I will help you," I promised.

"Food...I want some food...," the voice continued to sob.

"Who are you?"

"Lucy Ryan."

"Do you live in this house?"

"No house here."

"How long have you been here?"

"A long time."

"What year is this?"

"Seventeen ninety-two."

"What do you do in this house?"

"No house...people...fields...."

"Why then are you here? What is there here for you?"

The ghost snorted.

"Hm...men."

"Who brought you here?"

"Came...people sent us away...soldiers...follow them...sent me away...."

"What army? Which regiment?"

"Napier."

Hungry Lucy

The haunted area of Miss Havoc's living room

"How old are you?"

"Twenty."

"Where were you born?"

"Hawthorne...not very far away from here."

I was not sure whether she said "Hawthorne" or "Hawgton," or some similar name.

"What is you father's name?"

Silence.

"Your mother's name?"

Silence.

"Were you baptized?"

"Baptized?"

She didn't remember that either.

I explained that she had passed on. It did not matter.

"Stay here...until I get some food...meat...meat and corn..."

"Have you tried to communicate with anyone in this house?"

"Nobody listens."

"How are you trying to make them listen?"

"I make noise because I want food."

"Why do you stay in one area? Why don't you move around freely?"

"Can't. Can't go away. Too many people. Soldiers."

"Where are your parents?"

"Dead."

"What is your mother's name?"

"Mae."

"Her maiden name?"

"Don't know."

"Your father's first name?"

"Terry."

"Were any of your family in the army?"

Ironical laughter punctuated her next words.

"Only...me."

"Tell me the names of some of the officers in the army you knew."

"Alfred...Wait."

"Any rank?"

"No rank."

"What regiment did you follow?"

"Just this...Alfred."

"And he left you?"

"Yes. I went with some other man, then I was hungry and I came here."

"Why here?"

"I was sent here."

"By whom?"

"They made me come. Picked me up. Man brought me here. Put me down on the ground."

"Did you die in this spot?"

"Die, die? I'm not dead. *I'm hungry.*"

I then asked her to join her parents, those who loved her, and to leave this spot. She refused. She wanted to walk by the river, she said. I suggested that she was not receiving food and could leave freely. After a while, the ghost seemed to slip away peacefully and Sybil Leek returned to her own body, temporarily vacated so that Lucy could speak through it. As usual, Sybil remembered absolutely nothing of what went on when she was in deep trance. She was crying, but thought her mascara was the cause of it.

Suddenly, the ghost was back. The floorboards were reverberating with the staccato sound of an angry tap, loud, strong, and demanding.

"What do you want?" I asked again, although I knew now what she wanted.

Sybil also extended a helping hand. But the sound stopped as abruptly as it had begun.

A while later, we sat down again. Sybil reported feeling two presences.

"One is a girl, the other is a man. A man with a stick. Or a gun. The girl is stronger. She wants something."

Suddenly, Sybil pointed to the kitchen area.

"What happened in the corner?"

Nobody had told Sybil of the area in which the disturbances had always taken place.

"I feel her behind me now. A youngish girl, not very well dressed, Georgian period. I don't get the man too well."

At this point, we brought into the room a small Victorian wooden table, a gift from Gail Benedict.

Within seconds after Sybil, June Havoc, and I had lightly placed our hands upon it, it started to move, seemingly of its own volition!

Rapidly, it began to tap out a word, using a kind of Morse code. While Earl Wilson was taking notes, we

Heavy knocking in the floorboards were heard here every night at 3 A.M.

The late medium Sybil Leek making contact. Notice the psychic energy covering the floor and making it mirror-like.

allowed the table to jump hither and yon, tapping out a message.

None of us touched the table top except lightly. There was no question of manipulating the table. The light was very bright, and our hands almost touched, so that any pressure by one of us would have been instantly noticed by the other two. This type of communication is slow, since the table runs through the entire alphabet until it reaches the desired letter, then the next letter, until an entire word has been spelled out.

"L-e-a-v-e," the communicator said, not exactly in a friendly mood.

Evidently she wanted the place to herself and thought *we* were the intruders.

I tried to get some more information about her. But instead of tapping out another word in an orderly fashion, the table became very excited—if that is the word for emotional tables—and practically leapt from beneath our hands. We were required to follow it to keep up the contact, as it careened wildly through the room. When I was speaking, it moved toward me and practically crept onto my lap. When I wasn't speaking, it ran to someone else in the room. Eventually, it became so wild, at times entirely off the floor, that it slipped from our light touch and, as the power was broken, instantly rolled into a corner—just another table with no life of its own.

We repaired to the garden, a few steps down an iron staircase, in the rear of the house.

"Sybil, what do you feel down here?" I asked.

"I had a tremendous urge to come out here. I didn't know there was a garden. Underneath my feet almost is the cause of the disturbance."

We were standing at a spot adjacent to the basement wall and close to the center of the tapping disturbance we had heard.

"Someone may be buried here," Sybil remarked, pointing to a mound of earth underneath our feet. "It's a girl."

"Do you see the wire covering the area behind you?" June Havoc said. "I tried to plant seeds there, and the wire was to protect them—but somehow nothing, nothing will grow there."

"Plant something on this mound," Sybil suggested. "It may well pacify *her*."

We returned to the upstairs apartment, and soon after broke up the "ghost hunting party," as columnist Sheila Graham called it later.

The next morning, I called June Havoc to see how things were. I knew from experience that the ghost would either be totally gone, or totally mad, but not the same as before.

Lucy, I was told, was rather mad. Twice as noisy, she still demanded her pound of flesh. I promised June Havoc that we'd return until the ghost was completely gone.

A few days passed. Things became a little quieter, as if Lucy were hesitating. Then something odd happened the

The dark shape on the right was not visible to the eye

The living room in normal condition

next night. Instead of tapping from her accustomed corner area, Lucy moved away from it and tapped away from above June's bed. She had never been heard from that spot before.

I decided it was time to have a chat with Lucy again. Meanwhile, corroboration of the information we had obtained had come to us quickly. The morning after our first séance, Bob Winter-Berger called. He had been to the New York Public Library and checked on Napier, the officer named by the medium as the man in charge of the soldier's regiment.

The *Dictionary of National Biography* contained the answer. Colonel George Napier, a British officer, had served on the staff of Governor Sir Henry Clinton. How exciting, I thought. The Clinton mansion once occupied the very ground we were having the séance on. In fact, I had reported on a ghost in Clinton Court, two short blocks to the north, in *Ghost Hunter* and again in *Ghosts I've Met*. As far as I knew, the place was still not entirely free of the uncanny, for reports continued to reach me of strange steps and doors opening by themselves.

Although the mansion itself no longer stands, the carriage house in the rear was now part of Clinton Court, a reconstructed apartment house on West Forty-sixth Street. How could Sybil Leek, only recently arrived from England, have known of these things?

Napier was indeed the man who had charge of a regiment on this very spot, and the years 1781–82 are given as the time when Napier's family contracted the dreaded yel-

low fever and died. Sir Henry Clinton forbade his aide to be in touch with them, and the Colonel was shipped off to England, half-dead himself, while his wife and family passed away on the spot that later became Potter's Field.

Many Irish immigrants came to the New World in those years. Perhaps the Ryan girl was one of them, or her parents were. Unfortunately, history does not keep much of a record of camp followers.

On January 15, 1965, precisely at midnight, I placed Sybil Leek into deep trance in my apartment on Riverside Drive. In the past we had succeeded in contacting *former* ghosts once they had been pried loose in an initial séance in the haunted house itself. I had high hopes that Lucy would communicate I wasn't disappointed.

"Tick, tock, tickety-tock, June's clock stops, June's clock stops," the entranced medium murmured, barely audibly.

"Tickety-tock, June's clock stops, tickety-tock..."

"Who are you?" I asked.

"Lucy."

"Lucy, what does this mean?"

"June's clock stops, June's clock stops, frightened June, frightened June," she repeated like a child reciting a poem.

"Why do you want to frighten June?"

"Go away."

"Why do you want her to go away?"

"People there...too much house...too much June... too many clocks...she sings, dances, she makes a lot of noise...I'm hungry, I'm always hungry. You don't do a thing about it...."

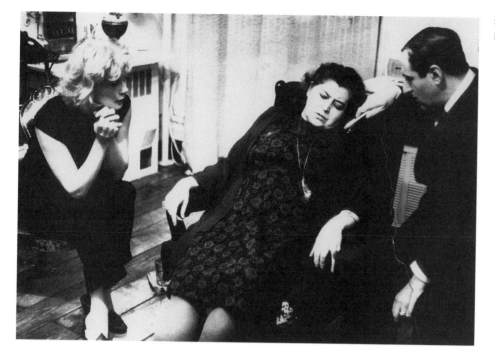

"Will you go away if I get you some food? Can we come to an agreement?"

"Why?"

"Because I want to help you, help June."

"Ah, same old story."

"You're not happy. Would you like to see Alfred again?"

"Yes... he's gone."

"Not very far. I'll get you together with Alfred if you will leave the house."

"Where would I go?"

"Alfred has a house of his own for you."

"Where?"

"Not very far."

"Frightened to go... don't know where to go... nobody likes me. She makes noises, I make noises. I don't like that clock."

"Where were you born, Lucy?"

"Larches by the Sea... Larchmont... by the Sea... people disturb me."

Again I asked her to go to join her Alfred, to find happiness again. I suggested she call for him by name, which she did, hesitatingly at first, more desperately later.

"No... I can't go from here. He said he would come. He said *wait*. Wait... here. Wait. Alfred, why don't you come? Too many clocks. Time, time, time... noisy creature. Time, time... 3 o'clock."

"What happened at 3 o'clock?" I demanded.

"He said he'd come," the ghost replied. "I waited for him."

"Why at 3 o'clock in the middle of the night?"

"Why do you think? Couldn't get out. Locked in. Not allowed out at night. I'll wait. He'll come."

"Did you meet any of his friends?"

"Not many... what would *I* say?"

"What was Alfred's name?"

"Bailey... Alfred said, 'Wait, wait... I'll go away,' he said. 'They'll never find me.'"

"Go to him with my love," I said, calmly repeating over and over the formula used in rescue circle operations to send the earthbound ghost across the threshold.

As I spoke, Lucy slipped away from us, not violently as she had come, but more or less resignedly.

I telephoned June Havoc to see what had happened that night between midnight and 12:30. She had heard Lucy's tapping precisely then, but nothing more as the night passed—a quiet night for a change.

Was Lucy on her way to her Alfred?

We would know soon enough.

In the weeks that followed, I made periodic inquiries of June Havoc. Was the ghost still in evidence? Miss Havoc did not stay at her townhouse all the time, preferring the quiet charm of her Connecticut estate. But on the nights when she did sleep in the house on Forty-fourth Street, she was able to observe that Lucy Ryan had changed considerably in personality—the ghost had been freed, yes, but had not yet been driven from the house. In fate, the terrible noise was now all over the house, although less frequent and less vehement—*as if she were thinking things over.*

I decided we had to finish the job as well as we could and another séance was arranged for late March, 1965. Present were—in addition to our hostess and chief sufferer—my wife Catherine and myself; Emory Lewis, editor of *Cue* magazine; Barry Farber, WOR commentator; and two friends of June Havoc. We grouped ourselves around a table in the *front room* this time. This soon proved to be a mistake. No Lucy Ryan. No ghost. We repaired to the other room where the original manifestations had taken place, with more luck this time.

Sybil, in trance, told us that the girl had gone, but that Alfred had no intention of leaving. He was waiting for *her* now. I asked for the name of his commanding officer and was told it was Napier. This we knew already. But who was the next in rank?

"Lieutenant William Watkins."

"What about the commanding general?"

He did not know.

He had been born in Hawthorne, just like Lucy, he told Sybil. I had been able to trace this Hawthorne to a place not far away in Westchester County.

There were people all over, Sybil said in trance, and they were falling down. They were ill.

"Send Alfred to join his Lucy," I commanded, and Sybil in a low voice told the stubborn ghost to go.

After an interlude of table tipping, in which several characters from the nether world made their auditory appearance, she returned to trance. Sybil in trance was near the river again, among the sick.

But no Lucy Ryan. Lucy's gone, she said.

"The smell makes me sick," Sybil said, and you could see stark horror in her sensitive face.

"Dirty people, rags, people in uniform too, with dirty trousers. There is a big house across the river."

"Whose house is it?"

"Mr. Dawson's. Doctor Dawson. Dr. James Dawson...Lee Point. Must go there. Feel sick. Rocks and trees, just the house across the river."

"What year is this?"

"Ninety-two."

She then described Dr. Dawson's house as having three windows on the left, two on the right, and five above, and said that it was called Lee Point—Hawthorne. It sounded a little like Hawgton to me, but I can't be sure.

Over the river, she said. She described a "round thing on post" in front of the house, like a shell. For messages, she thought.

"What is the name of the country we're in?" I asked.

"Vinelands. Vinelands."

I decided to change the subject back to Hungry Lucy. How did she get sick?

"She didn't get any food, and then she got cold, by the river.

"...Nobody helped them there. Let them die. Buried them in a pit."

"What is the name of the river?"

"Mo...Mo-something."

"Do you see anyone else still around?"

"Lots of people with black faces, black shapes."

The plague, I thought, and how little the doctors could do in those days to stem it.

I asked about the man in charge and she said "Napier" and I wondered who would be left in command after Napier left, and the answer this time was, "Clinton ...old fool. Georgie."

There were a Henry Clinton and a George Clinton, fairly contemporary with each other.

"What happened after that?"

"Napier died."

"Any other officers around?"

"Little Boy Richardson...Lieutenant."

"What regiment?"

"Burgoyne."

Sybil, entranced, started to hiss and whistle. "Signals," she murmured. "As the men go away, they whistle."

I decided the time had come to bring Sybil out of trance. She felt none the worse for it, and asked for something to drink. *Hungry*, like Lucy, she wasn't.

We began to evaluate the information just obtained. Dr. James Dawson may very well have lived. The A.M.A. membership directories aren't that old. I found the mention of Lee Point and Hawthorne interesting, inasmuch as the two locations are quite close. Lee, of course, would be Fort Lee, and there is a "point" or promontory in the river at that spot.

The town of Vinelands does exist in New Jersey, but the river beginning with "Mo-" may be the Mohawk. That Burgoyne was a general in the British army during the Revolution is well known.

So there you have it. Sybil Leek knows very little, if anything, about the New Jersey and Westchester countryside, having only recently come to America. Even I, then a New York resident for 27 years, had never heard of Hawthorne before. Yet there it is on the way to Pleasantville, New York.

The proof of the ghostly pudding, however, was not the regimental roster, but the state of affairs at June Havoc's house.

A later report had it that Lucy, Alfred, or whoever was responsible had quieted down considerably.

They were down, but not out.

I tactfully explained to June Havoc that feeling sorry for a hungry ghost makes things tough for a parapsychologist. The emotional pull of a genuine attachment, no matter how unconscious it may be, can provide the energies necessary to prolong the stay of the ghost.

Gradually, as June Havoc—wanting a peaceful house especially at 3 A.M.—allowed practical sense to outweigh sentimentality, the shades of Hungry Lucy and her soldierboy faded into the distant past, whence they came.

The House Ghost of Bergenville

ABOUT A YEAR ago, Mrs. Ethel Meyers, who has frequently accompanied me on ghost-hunting expeditions, heard from friends living in Bergen County, New Jersey, about some unusual happenings at their very old house. They are busy people of considerable prominence in the theater, but eventually the "safari for ghost" was organized, and Mr. B., the master of the house, picked us up in his car and drove us to Bergen County. The house turned out to be a beautifully preserved pre-Revolutionary house set within an enclosure of tall trees and lawns.

The building had been started in 1704, I later learned, and the oldest portion was the right wing; the central portion was added in the latter part of the eighteenth century, and the final, frontal portion was built from old materials about fifty years ago, carefully preserving the original style of the house. The present owners had acquired it about a year ago from a family who had been in possession for several generations. The house was then empty, and the B.s refurbished it completely in excellent taste with antiques of the period.

After they moved into the house, they slept for a few days on a mattress on the enclosed porch, which skirted the west wing of the house. Their furniture had not yet arrived, and they didn't mind roughing it for a short while. It was summer, and not too cool.

In the middle of the night, Mrs. B. suddenly awoke with the uncanny feeling that there was *someone else* in the house, besides her husband and herself. She got up and walked toward the corridor-like extension of the enclosed porch running along the back of the house. There she clearly distinguished the figure of a man, seemingly white, with a beard, wearing what she described as "something ruffly white." She had the odd sensation that this man belonged to a much earlier period than the present. The light was good enough to see the man clearly for about five minutes, in which she was torn between fear of the intruder and curiosity. Finally, she approached him, and saw him *literally dissolve before her very eyes!* At the same time, she had the odd sensation that the stranger came to look *them* over, wondering what they were doing in *his* house! Mrs. B., a celebrated actress and choreographer, is not a scoffer, nor is she easily susceptible. Ghosts to her are something one can discuss intelligently. Since her husband shared this view, they inquired of the former owner about any possible hauntings.

"I've never heard of any or seen any," Mr. S. told them, "but my daughter-in-law has never been able to sleep in the oldest part of the house. Said there was too much going on there. Also, one of the neighbors claims he saw *something*."

Mr. S. wasn't going to endanger his recent real-estate transaction with too many ghostly tales. The B.s thanked him and settled down to life in their colonial house.

But they soon learned that theirs was a busy place indeed. Both are artistic and very intuitive, and they soon became aware of the presence of unseen forces.

One night Mrs. B. was alone at home, spending the evening in the upper story of the house. There was nobody downstairs. Suddenly she heard the downstairs front door open and shut. There was no mistaking the very characteristic and complex sound of the opening of this ancient lock! Next, she heard footsteps, and sighed with relief. Apparently her husband had returned much earlier than expected. Quickly, she rushed down the stairs to welcome him. There was nobody there. There was no one in front of the door. All she found was the cat in a strangely excited state!

Sometime after, Mr. B. came home. For his wife these were anxious hours of waiting. He calmed her as best he could, having reservations about the whole incident. Soon these doubts were to be dispelled completely.

This time Mrs. B. was away and Mr. B. was alone in the downstairs part of the house. The maid was asleep in her room, the B.s' child fast asleep upstairs. It was a peaceful evening, and Mr. B. decided to have a snack. He found himself in the kitchen, which is located at the western end of the downstairs part of the house, *when he suddenly heard a car drive up.* Next, there were the distinct sounds of the front door opening and closing again. As he rushed to the front door, he heard the dog bark furiously. But again, there was no one either inside or outside the house!

Mr. B., a star and director, and as rational a man as could be, wondered if he had imagined these things. But he knew he had not. What he had heard were clearly the noises of an arrival. While he was still trying to sort out the meaning of all this, another strange thing happened.

A few evenings later, he found himself alone in the downstairs living room, when he heard carriage wheels outside grind to a halt. He turned his head toward the door, wondering who it might be at this hour. The light was subdued, but good enough to read by. He didn't have to wait long. A short, husky man walked into the room *through* the closed door; then, without paying attention to Mr. B., turned and walked out into the oldest part of the house, again *through a closed door!*

"What did he look like to you?" I asked.

"He seemed dotted, as if he were made of thick, solid dots, and he wore a long coat, the kind they used to wear around 1800. He probably was the same man my wife encountered."

"You think he is connected with the oldest part of the house?"

"Yes, I think so. About a year ago I played some very old lute music, the kind popular in the eighteenth century, in there—and something happened to the atmosphere in the room. As if someone were listening quietly and peacefully."

But it wasn't always as peaceful in there. A day before our arrival, Mrs. B. had lain down, trying to relax. But she could not stay in the old room. "There was someone there," she said simply.

The B.s weren't the only ones to hear and see ghosts. Last summer, two friends of the B.s were visiting them, and everybody was seated in the living room, when in plain view of all, the screen door to the porch opened and closed again by its own volition! Needless to add, the friends didn't stay long.

Only a day before our visit, another friend had tried to use the small washroom in the oldest part of the house. Suddenly, he felt chills coming on and rushed out of the room, telling Mrs. B. that "someone was looking at him."

At this point, dinner was ready, and a most delicious repast it was. Afterwards we accompanied the B.s into the oldest part of their house, a low-ceilinged room dating back to the year 1704. Two candles provided the only light. Mrs. Meyers got into a comfortable chair, and gradually drifted into trance.

"Marie . . . Catherine . . . who calls?" she mumbled.

"Who is it?" I inquired.

"Pop . . . live peacefully . . . love. . . ."

"What is your name?" I wanted to know.

"Achabrunn. . . ."

I didn't realize it at the time, but a German family named Achenbach had built the house and owned it for several generations. Much later still, I found out that one of the children of the builder had been called Marian.

I continued my interrogation.

"Who rules this country?"

"The Anglish. George."

"What year is this?"

"Fifty-six. Seventeen fifty-six."

"When did you stay here?"

"Always. Pop. My house. *You* stay with *me*."

Then the ghost spoke haltingly of his family, his children, of which he had nine, three of whom had gone away.

"What can we do for you?" I said, hoping to find the reason for the many disturbances.

"Yonder over side hill, hillock, three buried . . . flowers there."

"Do you mean," I said, "that we should put flowers on these graves?"

The medium seemed excited.

"*Ach Gott, ja, machs gut.*" With this the medium crossed herself.

"What is your name?" I asked again.

"Oterich . . . Oblich. . . ." The medium seemed hesitant as if the ghost were searching his memory for his own name. Later, I found that the name given was pretty close to that of another family having a homestead next door.

The ghost continued.

"She lady . . . I not good. I very stout heart, I look up to good-blood lady, I make her good . . . Kathrish, holy lady, I worship lady . . . they rest on hill too, with three. . . ."

After the séance, I found a book entitled *Pre-Revolutionary Dutch Houses in Northern New Jersey and New York*. It was here that I discovered the tradition that a poor shepherd from Saxony married a woman above his station, and built this very house. The year 1756 was correct.

But back to my interrogation. "Why don't you rest on the hillock?"

"I take care of . . . four . . . hillock . . . Petrish, Ladian, Annia, Kathrish. . . ."

Then, as if taking cognizance of us, he added—"To care for you, that's all I want."

Mrs. B. nodded and said softly, "You're always welcome here."

Afterward, I found that there were indeed some graves on the hill beyond the house. The medium now pointed toward the rear of the house, and said, "Gate . . . we put intruders there, he won't get up any more. Gray Fox made trouble, Indian man, I keep him right there."

"Are there any passages?"

"Yeah. Go dig through. When Indian come, they no find."

"Where?"

"North hillock, still stone floor there, ends here."

From Mr. B. I learned that underground passages are known to exist between this house and the so-called "Slave House," across the road.

The ghost then revealed that his wife's father, an Englishman, had built the passage, and that stores were kept in it along with Indian bones.

"Where were you born?" I inquired.

"Here. Bergenville."

Bergenville proved to be the old name of the township.

I then delicately told him that this was 1960. He seemed puzzled, to say the least.

"In 1756 I was sixty-five years old. I am not 204 years older?"

At this point, the ghost recognized the women's clothing the medium was wearing, and tore at them. I explained how we were able to "talk" to him. He seemed pacified.

"You'll accept my maize, my wine, my whiskey. . . ."

I discovered that maize and wine staples were the mainstays of the area at that period. I also found that Indian wars on a small scale were still common in this area in the middle 1700s. Moreover, the ghost referred to the "gate" as being in the *rear* of the house. This proved to be correct, for what is now the back of the house was then its front, facing the road.

Suddenly the ghost withdrew and after a moment another person, a woman, took over the medium. She complained bitterly that the Indians had taken one of her children, whose names she kept rattling off. Then she too withdrew, and Mrs. Meyers returned to her own body, none the worse for her experiences, none of which, incidentally, she remembered.

Shortly afterward, we returned to New York. It was as if we had just come from another world. Leaving the poplar-lined road behind us, we gradually re-entered the world of gasoline and dirt that is the modern city.

Nothing further has been reported from the house in Bergen County, but I am sure the ghost, whom Mrs. B. had asked to stay as long as he wished, is still there. There is of course now no further need to bang doors, to call attention to his lonely self. *They know he is there with them.*

✳ 44

The Riverside Ghost

PLEASE HELP ME find out what this is all about," pleaded the stranger on the telephone. "I'm being attacked by a ghost!" The caller turned out to be a young jeweler, Edward Karalanian of Paris, now living in an old apartment building on Riverside Drive.

For the past two years, he had lived there with his mother; occasionally he had heard footsteps where no one could have walked. Five or six times he would wake up in the middle of the night to find several strangers in his room. They seemed to him people in conversation, and disappeared as he challenged them on fully awakening.

In one case, he saw a man coming toward him, and threw a pillow at the invader. To his horror, the pillow did not go through the ghostly form, but slid off it and fell to the floor, as the spook vanished!

The man obviously wanted to attack him; there was murder in his eyes—and Mr. Karalanian was frightened by it all. Although his mother could see nothing, he was able to describe the intruder as a man wearing a white "uniform" like a cook, with a hat like a cook, and that his face was mean and cruel.

On March 9, I organized a séance at the apartment, at which a teacher at Adelphi College, Mr. Dersarkissian,

and three young ladies were also present; Mrs. Ethel Meyers was the medium.

Although she knew nothing of the case, Mrs. Meyers immediately described a man and woman arguing in the apartment and said there were structural changes, which Mr. Karalanian confirmed.

"Someone is being strangled...the man goes away... now a woman falls and her head is crushed...they want to hide something from the family." Mrs. Meyers then stated that someone had gone out through the twelfth floor window, after being strangled, and that the year was about 1910.

In trance, the discarnate victim, Lizzy, took over her voice and cried pitifully for help. Albert, Mrs. Meyers' control, added that this was a maid who had been killed by a hired man on the wife's orders. Apparently, the girl had an affair with the husband, named Henry. The murderer was a laborer working in a butcher's shop, by the name of Maggio. The family's name was Brady, or O'Brady; the wife was Anne.

After the séance, I investigated these data, and found to my amazement that the 1912 *City Directory* listed an "A. Maggio, poultry," and both an Anne Brady and Anne O'Grady. The first name was listed as living only one block away from the house! Oh, yes—Mr. Karalanian found out that a young girl, accused of stealing, had killed herself by jumping from that very room!

✳ 45

"Ocean-Born" Mary

AMONG THE GHOSTLY legends of the United States, that of "Ocean-Born" Mary and her fascinating house at Henniker, New Hampshire, is probably one of the best known. To the average literate person who has heard about the colorful tale of Mary Wallace, or the New Englander who knows of it because he lives "Down East," it is, of course, a legend—not to be taken too seriously.

I had a vague idea of its substance when I received a note from a lady named Corinne Russell, who together

with her husband, David, had bought the Henniker house and wanted me to know that it was still haunted.

That was in October of 1963. It so happens that Halloween is the traditional date on which the ghost of six-foot Mary Wallace is supposed to "return" to her house in a coach drawn by six horses. On many a Halloween, youngsters from all around Henniker have come and sat around the grounds waiting for Mary to ride in. The local press had done its share of Halloween ghost hunting, so much so

that the Russells had come to fear that date as one of the major nuisance days of their year.

After all, Halloween visitors do not pay the usual fee to be shown about the house, but they do leave behind destruction and litter at times. Needless to say, nobody has ever seen Mary ride in her coach on Halloween. Why should she when she lives there *all year round?*

To explain this last statement, I shall have to take you back to the year 1720, when a group of Scottish and Irish immigrants was approaching the New World aboard a ship called the *Wolf,* from Londonderry, Ireland. The ship's captain, Wilson, had just become the father of a daughter, who was actually born at sea. Within sight of land, the ship was boarded by pirates under the command of a buccaneer named Don Pedro. As the pirates removed all valuables from their prize, Don Pedro went below to the captain's cabin. Instead of gold, he found Mrs. Wilson and her newborn baby girl.

"What's her name?" he demanded.

Unafraid, the mother replied that the child had not yet been baptized, having been recently born.

"If you will name her after my mother, Mary," the pirate said, overcome with an emotion few pirates ever allow into their lives, "I will spare everybody aboard this ship."

Joyously, the mother made the bargain, and "Ocean-Born" Mary received her name. Don Pedro ordered his men to hand back what they had already taken from their prisoners, to set them free, and to leave the captured ship.

The vicious-looking crew grumbled and withdrew to their own ship.

Minutes later, however, Don Pedro returned alone. He handed Mrs. Wilson a bundle of silk.

"For Mary's wedding gown," he said simply, and left, again.

As soon as the pirate ship was out of sight, the *Wolf* continued her voyage for Boston. Thence Captain and Mrs. Wilson went on to their new home in Londonderry, New Hampshire, where they settled down, and where Mary grew up.

When she was eighteen she married a man named Wallace, and over the years they had four sons. However, shortly after the birth of the fourth son, her husband died and Mary found herself a widow.

Meanwhile, Don Pedro—allegedly an Englishman using the Spanish *nom de pirate* to disguise his noble ancestry—had kept in touch with the Wilsons. Despite the hazards of pirate life, he survived to an old age when thoughts of retirement filled his mind. Somehow he managed to acquire a land grant of 6,000 acres in what is now Henniker, New Hampshire, far away from the sea. On this land, Pedro built himself a stately house. He employed his ship's carpenters, as can be seen in the way the beams are joined. Ship's carpenters have a special way of building, and "Ocean-Born" Mary's house, as it later became known, is an example of this.

The house was barely finished when the aging pirate heard of Mary Wallace's loss of her husband, and he asked Mary and her children to come live with him. She accepted his invitation, and soon became his housekeeper.

The house was then in a rather isolated part of New England, and few callers, if any, came to interrupt the long stillness of the many cold winter nights. Mary took up painting and with her own hands created the eagle that can still be seen gracing the house.

The years went by peacefully, until one night some-one attacked Don Pedro and killed him. Whether one of his men had come to challenge the pirate captain for part of the booty, or whether the reputation of a retired pirate had put ideas of treasure in the mind of some local thief, we may never know. All we know is that by the time Mary Wallace got out into the grove at the rear of the house, Don Pedro was dying with a pirate cutlass in his chest. He asked her to bury him under the hearthstone in the kitchen, which is in the rear of the house.

Mary herself inherited the house and what went with it, treasure, buried pirate, and all. She herself passed on in 1814, and ever since then the house had been changing hands.

Unfortunately, we cannot interview the earlier owners of the house, but during the 1930s, it belonged to one Louis Roy, retired and disabled and a permanent guest in what used to be his home. He sold the house to the Russells in the early sixties.

During the great hurricane of 1938, Roy claims that Mary Wallace's ghost saved his life 19 times. Trapped out-side the house by falling trees, he somehow was able to get back into the house. His very psychic mother, Mrs. Roy, informed him that she had actually seen the tall, stately fig-ure of "Ocean-Born" Mary moving behind him, as if to help him get through. In the 1950s, *Life* told this story in an illustrated article on famous ghost-haunted houses in America. Mrs. Roy claimed she had seen the ghost of Mary time and time again, but since she herself passed on in 1948, I could not get any details from *her*.

Then there were two state troopers who saw the ghost, but again I could not interview them, as they, too, were on the other side of the veil.

A number of visitors claimed to have felt "special vibrations" when touching the hearthstone, where Don Pedro allegedly was buried. There was, for instance, Mrs. James Nisula of Londonderry, who visited the house sev-eral times. She said that she and her "group" of ghost buffs had "felt the vibrations" around the kitchen. Mrs. David Russell, the owner who contacted me, felt nothing.

I promised to look into the "Ocean-Born" Mary haunting the first chance I got. Halloween or about that time would be all right with me, and I wouldn't wait around for any coach!

"There is a lady medium I think you should know," Mrs. Russell said when I spoke of bringing a psychic with me. "She saw Mary the very first time she came here."

My curiosity aroused, I communicated with the lady. She asked that I not use her married name, although she was not so shy several months after our visit to the house, when she gave a two-part interview to a Boston newspaper columnist. (Needless to say, the interview was not autho-rized by me, since I never allow mediums I work with to talk about their cases for publication. Thus Lorrie shall remain without a family name and anyone wishing to reach this medium will have to do so without my help.)

Lorrie wrote me she would be happy to serve the cause of truth, and I could count on her. There was noth-ing she wanted in return.

We did not get up to New Hampshire that Hal-loween. Mr. Russell had to have an operation, the house was unheated in the winter except for Mr. Roy's room, and New England winters are cold enough to freeze any ghost.

Although there was a caretaker at the time to look after the house and Mr. Roy upstairs, the Russells did not stay at the house in the winter, but made their home in nearby Chelmsford, Massachusetts.

I wrote Mrs. Russell postponing the investigation until spring. Mrs. Russell accepted my decision with sonic disappointment, but she was willing to wait. After all, the ghost at "Ocean-Born" Mary's house is not a malicious type. Mary Wallace just lived there, ever since she died in 1814, and you can't call a lady who likes to hold on to what is hers an intruder.

"We don't want to drive her out," Mrs. Russell repeatedly said to me. "After all, it *is* her house!"

Not many haunted-house owners make statements like that.

But something had happened at the house since our last conversation.

"Our caretaker dropped a space heater all the way down the stairs at the 'Ocean-Born' Mary house, and when it reached the bottom, the kerosene and the flames started to burn the stairs and climb the wall. There was no water in the house, so my husband went out after snow. While I stood there looking at the fire and powerless to do anything about it, the fire went right out all by itself right in front of my eyes; when my husband got back with the snow it was out. It was just as if someone *had smothered it with a blan-ket*."

This was in December of 1963. I tried to set a new date, as soon as possible, and February 22 seemed possible. This time I would bring Bob Kennedy of WBZ, Boston and the "Contact" producer Squire Rushnell with me to record my investigation.

Lorrie was willing, asking only that her name not be mentioned.

"I don't want anyone to know about my being differ-ent from them," she explained. "When I was young my family used to accuse me of spying because I knew things from the pictures I saw when I touched objects."

Psychometry, I explained, is very common among psychics, and nothing to be ashamed of.

I thought it was time to find out more about Lorrie's experiences at the haunted house.

"I first saw the house in September of 1961," she began. "It was on a misty, humid day, and there was a haze over the fields."

Strange, I thought, I always get my best psychic results when the atmosphere is moist.

Lorrie, who was in her early forties, was Vermont born and raised; she was married and had one daughter, Pauline. She was a tall redhead with sparkling eyes, and, come to think of it, not unlike the accepted picture of the ghostly Mary Wallace. Coincidence?

A friend of Lorrie's had seen the eerie house and suggested she go and see it also. That was all Lorrie knew about it, and she did not really expect anything uncanny to occur. Mr. Roy showed Lorrie and her daughter through the house and nothing startling happened. They left and started to walk down the entrance steps, crossing the garden in front of the house, and had reached the gate when Pauline clutched at her mother's arm and said:

"Mamma, what is that?"

Lorrie turned to look back at the house. In the upstairs window, a woman stood and looked out at them. Lorrie's husband was busy with the family car. Eventually, she called out to him, but as he turned to look, the apparition was gone.

She did not think of it again, and the weeks went by. But the house kept intruding itself into her thoughts more and more. Finally she could not restrain herself any longer, and returned to the house—even though it was 120 miles from her home in Weymouth, Massachusetts.

She confessed her extraordinary experience to the owner, and together they examined the house from top to bottom. She finally returned home.

She promised Roy she would return on All Hallow's Eve to see if the legend of Mary Wallace had any basis of fact. Unfortunately, word of her intentions got out, and when she finally arrived at the house, she had to sneak in the back to avoid the sensation-hungry press outside. During the days between her second visit and Halloween, the urge to go to Henniker kept getting stronger, as if someone were possessing her.

By that time the Russells were negotiating to buy the house, and Lorrie came up with them. Nothing happened to her that Halloween night. Perhaps she was torn between fear and a desire to fight the influence that had brought her out to Henniker to begin with.

Mediums, to be successful, must learn to relax and not allow their own notions to rule them. All through the following winter and summer, Lorrie fought the desire to return to "Ocean-Born" Mary's house. To no avail. She returned time and time again, sometimes alone and sometimes with a friend.

Things got out of hand one summer night when she was home alone.

Exhausted from her last visit—the visits always left her an emotional wreck—she went to bed around 9:30 P.M.

"What happened that night?" I interjected. She seemed shaken even now.

"At 11 P.M., Mr. Holzer," Lorrie replied, "I found myself driving on the expressway, wearing my pajamas and robe, with no shoes or slippers, or money, or even a handkerchief. I was ten miles from my home and heading for Henniker. Terrified, I turned around and returned home, only to find my house ablaze with light, the doors open as I had left them, and the garage lights on. I must have left in an awful hurry."

"Have you found out why you are being pulled back to that house?"

She shook her head.

"No idea. But I've been back twice, even after that. I just can't seem to stay away from that house."

I persuaded her that perhaps there was a job to be done in that house, and the ghost wanted her to do it.

We did not go to Henniker in February, because of bad weather. We tried to set a date in May 1964. The people from WBZ decided Henniker was too far away from Boston and dropped out of the planning.

Summer came around, and I went to Europe instead of Henniker. However, the prospect of a visit in the fall was very much in my mind.

It seemed as if someone were keeping me away from the house very much in the same way someone was pulling Lorrie toward it!

Come October, and we were really on our way, at last.

Owen Lake, a public relations man who dabbles in psychic matters, introduced himself as "a friend" of mine and told Lorrie he'd come along, too. I had never met the gentleman, but in the end he could not make it anyway. So just four of us—my wife Catherine and I, Lorrie, and her nice, even-tempered husband, who had volunteered to drive us up to New Hampshire—started out from Boston. It was close to Halloween, all right, only two days before. If Mary Wallace were out haunting the countryside in her coach, we might very well run into her. The coach is out of old Irish folktales; it appears in numerous ghost stories of the Ould Sod. I'm sure that in the telling and retelling of the tale of Mary and her pirate, the coach got added.

The countryside is beautiful in a New England fall. As we rolled toward the New Hampshire state line, I asked Lorrie some more questions.

"When you first saw the ghost of "Ocean-Born" Mary at the window of the house, Lorrie," I said, "what did she look like?"

"A lovely lady in her thirties, with auburn-colored hair, smiling rather intensely and thoughtfully. She stayed there for maybe three minutes, and then suddenly, *she just wasn't there.*"

"What about her dress?"

"It was a white dress."

Lorrie never saw an apparition of Mary again, but whenever she touched anything in the Henniker house, she received an impression of what the house was like when Mary had it, and she had felt her near the big fireplace several times.

Did she ever get an impression of what it was Mary wanted?

"She was a quick-tempered woman; I sensed that very strongly," Lorrie replied. "I have been to the house maybe twenty times altogether, and still don't know why. She just keeps pulling me there."

Lorrie had always felt the ghost's presence on these visits.

"One day I was walking among the bushes in the back of the house. I was wearing shorts, but I never got a scratch on my legs, because I kept feeling heavy skirts covering my legs. I could feel the brambles pulling at this invisible skirt I had on. I felt enveloped by something, or someone."

Mrs. Roy, the former owner's mother, had told of seeing the apparition many times, Lorrie stated.

"As a matter of fact, I have sensed her ghost in the house, too, but it is not a friendly wraith like Mary is."

Had she ever encountered this other ghost?

"Yes, my arm was grabbed one time by a malevolent entity," Lorrie said emphatically. "It was two years ago, and I was standing in what is now the living room, and my arm was taken by the elbow and pulled.

"I snatched my arm back, because I felt she was not friendly."

"What were you doing at the time that she might have objected to?"

"I really don't know."

Did she know of anyone else who had had an uncanny experience at the house?

"A strange thing happened to Mrs. Roy," Lorrie said. "A woman came to the house and said to her, 'What do you mean, the *rest* of the house?' The woman replied, 'Well, I was here yesterday, and a tall woman let me in and showed me half of the house.' But, of course, there was nobody at the house that day."

What about the two state troopers? Could she elaborate on their experience?

"They met her walking down the road that leads to the house. She was wearing a colonial-type costume, and they found that odd. Later they realized they had seen a ghost, especially as no one of her description lived in the house at the time."

Rudi D., Lorrie's husband, was a hospital technician. He was with her on two or three occasions when she visited the house. Did he ever feel anything special?

"The only thing unusual I ever felt at the house was that I wanted to get out of there fast," he said.

"The very first time we went up," Lorrie added, "something kept pulling me toward it, but my husband insisted we go back. There was an argument about our

The house the pirate Don Pedro built: "Ocean-Born" Mary's

continuing the trip, when suddenly the door of the car flew open of its own volition. Somehow we decided to continue on to the house."

An hour later, we drove up a thickly overgrown hill and along a winding road at the end of which the "Ocean-Born" Mary house stood in solitary stateliness, a rectangular building of gray stone and brown trim, very well preserved.

We parked the car and walked across the garden that sets the house well back from the road. There was peace and autumn in the air. We were made welcome by Corinne Russell, her husband David, and two relatives who happened to be with them that day. Entering the main door beneath a magnificent early American eagle, we admired the fine wooden staircase leading to the upstairs—the staircase on which the mysterious fire had taken place—and then entered the room to the left of it, where the family had assembled around an old New England stove.

During the three years the Russells had lived at the house, nothing uncanny had happened to Mrs. Russell, except for the incident with the fire. David Russell, a man almost typical of the shrewd New England Yankee who weighs his every word, was willing to tell me about *his* experiences, however.

"The first night I ever slept in what we call the Lafayette room, upstairs, there was quite a thundershower on, and my dog and I were upstairs. I always keep my dog with me, on account of the boys coming around to do damage to the property.

"Just as I lay down in bed, I heard very heavy footsteps. They sounded to me to be in the two rooms which we had just restored, on the same floor. I was quite annoyed, almost frightened, and I went into the rooms, but there nobody there or anywhere else in the house."

"Interesting," I said. "Was there more?"

"Now this happened only last summer. A few weeks later, when I was in that same room, I was getting undressed when I suddenly heard somebody pound on my door. I said to myself, "Oh, it's only the house settling," and I got into bed. A few minutes later, the door knob turned back and forth. I jumped out of bed, opened the door, and there was absolutely nobody there. The only other people in the house at the time were the invalid Mr. Roy, locked in his room, and my wife downstairs."

What about visual experiences?

"No, but I went to the cellar not long ago with my dog, about four in the afternoon, or rather tried to—this dog never leaves me, but on this particular occasion, something kept her from going with me into the cellar. Her hair stood up and she would not budge."

The Lafayette room, by the way, is the very room in which the pirate, Don Pedro, is supposed to have lived. The Russells did nothing to change the house structurally, only restored it as it had been and generally cleaned it up.

I now turned to Florence Harmon, an elderly neighbor of the Russells, who had some recollections about the house. Mrs. Harmon recalls the house when she herself was very young, long before the Russells came to live in it.

"Years later, I returned to the house and Mrs. Roy asked me whether I could help her locate 'the treasure' since I was reputed to be psychic."

Was there really a treasure?

"If there was, I think it was found," Mrs. Harmon said. "At the time Mrs. Roy talked to me, she also pointed out that there were two elm trees on the grounds—the only two elm trees around. They looked like some sort of markers to her. But before the Roys had the house, a Mrs. Morrow lived here. I know this from my uncle, who was a stone mason, and who built a vault for her."

I didn't think Mrs. Harmon had added anything material to my knowledge of the treasure, so I thanked her and turned my attention to the other large room, on the right hand side of the staircase. Nicely furnished with period pieces, it boasted a fireplace flanked by sofas, and had a rectangular piano in the corner. The high windows were curtained on the sides, and one could see the New England landscape through them.

We seated ourselves around the fireplace and hoped that Mary would honor us with a visit. Earlier I had inspected the entire house, the hearthstone under which Don Pedro allegedly lay buried, and the small bedrooms upstairs where David Russell had heard the footsteps. Each of us had stood at the window in the corridor upstairs and

stared out of it, very much the way the ghost must have done when she was observed by Lorrie and her daughter.

And now it was Mary's turn.

"This was her room," Lorrie explained, "and I do feel her presence." But she refused to go into trance, afraid to "let go." Communication would have to be via clairvoyance, with Lorrie as the interpreter. This was not what I had hoped for. Nevertheless we would try to evaluate whatever material we could obtain.

"Sheet and quill," Lorrie said now, and a piece of paper was handed her along with a pencil. Holding it on her lap, Lorrie was poised to write, if Mary wanted to use her hand, so to speak. The pencil suddenly jumped from Lorrie's hand with considerable force.

"Proper quill," the ghost demanded.

I explained about the shape of quills these days, and handed Lorrie my own pencil.

"Look lady," Lorrie explained to the ghost. "I'll show you it writes. I'll write my name."

And she wrote in her own, smallish, rounded hand, "Lorrie."

There was a moment of silence. Evidently, the ghost was thinking it over. Then Lorrie's hand, seemingly not under her own control, wrote with a great deal of flourish "Mary Wallace." The "M" and "W" had curves and ornamentation typical of eighteenth-century calligraphy. It was not at all like Lorrie's own handwriting.

"Tell her to write some more. The quill is working," I commanded.

Lorrie seemed to be upset by something the ghost told her.

"No," she said. "I can't do that. No."

"What does she want?" I asked.

"She wants me to sleep, but I won't do it."

Trance, I thought—even the ghost demands it. It would have been so interesting to have Mary speak directly to us through Lorrie's entranced lips. You can lead a medium to the ghost, but you can't make her go under if she's scared.

Lorrie instead told the ghost to tell *her*, or to write through her. But no trance, thank you. Evidently, the ghost did not like to be told how to communicate. We waited. Then I suggested that Lorrie be very relaxed and it would be "like sleep" so the ghost could talk to us directly.

"She's very much like me, but not so well trimmed," the ghost said of Lorrie. Had she picked her to carry her message because of the physical resemblance, I wondered.

"She's waiting for Young John," Lorrie now said. Not young John. The stress was on young. Perhaps it was one name—Young-john.

"It happened in the north pasture," Mary said through Lorrie now. "He killed Warren Langerford. The Frazier boys found the last bone."

I asked why it concerned her. Was she involved? But there was no reply.

Then the ghost of Mary introduced someone else standing next to her.

"Mrs. Roy is with her, because she killed her daughter," Lorrie said, hesitatingly, and added, on her own, "but I don't believe she did." Later we found out that the ghost was perhaps not lying, but of course nobody had any proof of such a crime—if it were indeed a crime.

"Why do you stay on in this house?" I asked.

"This house is my house, h-o-u-s-e!" "Ocean-Born" Mary reminded me.

"Do you realize you are what is commonly called dead?" I demanded. As so often with ghosts, the question brought on resistance to face reality. Mary seemed insulted and withdrew.

I addressed the ghost openly, offering to help her, and at the same time explaining her present position to her. This was her chance to speak up.

"She's very capricious," Lorrie said. "When you said you'd bring her peace, she started to laugh."

But Mary was gone, for the present anyway.

We waited, and tried again a little later. This time Lorrie said she heard a voice telling her to come back tonight.

"We can't," I decided. "If she wants to be helped, it will have to be now."

Philip Babb, the pirate's real name (as I discovered later), allegedly had built a secret passage under the house. The Russells were still looking for it. There were indeed discrepancies in the thickness of some of the walls, and there were a number of secret holes that didn't lead anywhere. But no passage. Had the pirate taken his secrets to his grave?

I found our experience at Henniker singularly unsatisfactory since no real evidence had been forthcoming from the ghost herself. No doubt another visit would have to be made, but I didn't mind that at all. "Ocean-Born" Mary's place was a place one can easily visit time and again. The rural charm of the place and the timeless atmosphere of the old house made it a first-rate tourist attraction. Thousands of people came to the house every year.

We returned to New York and I thought no more about it until I received a letter from James Caron, who had heard me discuss the house on the "Contact" program in Boston. He had been to the house in quest of pirate lore and found it very much haunted.

James Caron was in the garage business at Bridgewater, Massachusetts. He had a high school and trade school education, and was married, with two children. Searching for stories of buried treasure and pirates was a hobby of his, and he sometimes lectured on it. He had met Gus Roy about six years before. Roy complained that his deceased mother was trying to contact him for some reason. Her picture kept falling off the wall where it was hung, and he constantly felt "a presence." Would Mr. Caron know of a good medium?

In August of 1959, James Caron brought a spiritualist named Paul Amsdent to the "Ocean-Born" Mary house. Present at the ensuing séance were Harold Peters, a furniture salesman; Hugh Blanchard, a lawyer; Ernest Walbourne, a fireman and brother-in-law of Caron; Gus Roy; and Mr. Caron himself. Tape recording the séance, Caron had trouble with his equipment. Strange sounds kept intruding. Unfortunately, there was among those present someone with hostility toward psychic work, and Gus Roy's mother did not manifest. However, something else did happen.

"There appear to be people buried somewhere around or in the house," the medium Amsdent said, "enclosed by a stone wall of some sort."

I thought of the hearthstone and of Mrs. Harmon's vault. Coincidence?

Mr. Caron used metal detectors all over the place to satisfy Gus Roy that there was no "pirate treasure" buried in or near the house.

A little later, James Caron visited the house again. This time he was accompanied by Mrs. Caron and Mr. and Mrs. Walbourne. Both ladies were frightened by the sound of a heavy door opening and closing with no one around and no air current in the house.

Mrs. Caron had a strong urge to go to the attic, but Mr. Caron stopped her. Ernest Walbourne, a skeptic, was alone in the so-called "death" room upstairs, looking at some pictures stacked in a corner. Suddenly, he clearly heard a female voice telling him to get out of the house. He looked around, but there was nobody upstairs. Frightened, he left the house at once and later required medication for a nervous condition!

Again, things quieted down as far as "Ocean-Born" Mary was concerned, until I saw a lengthy story—two parts, in fact—in the *Boston Record-American*, in which my erstwhile medium Lorrie had let her hair down to columnist Harold Banks.

It seemed that Lorrie could not forget Henniker, after all. With publicist Owen Lake, she returned to the house in November, 1964, bringing with her some oil of wintergreen, which she claimed Mary Wallace asked her to bring along.

Two weeks later, the report went on, Lorrie felt Mary Wallace in her home in Weymouth near Boston. Lorrie was afraid that Mary Wallace might "get into my body and use it for whatever purpose she wants to. I might wake up some day and *be* Mary Wallace."

That's the danger of being a medium without proper safeguards. They tend to identify with a personality that has come through them. Especially when they read all there is in print about them.

I decided to take someone to the house who knew nothing about it, someone who was not likely to succumb to the wiles of amateur "ESP experts," inquisitive columnists and such, someone who would do exactly what I required of her: Sybil Leek, famed British psychic.

It was a glorious day late in spring when we arrived at "Ocean-Born" Mary's house in a Volkswagen station wagon driven by two alert young students from Goddard College in Vermont: Jerry Weener and Jay Lawrence. They had come to Boston to fetch us and take us all the way up to their campus, where I was to address the students and faculty. I proposed that they drive us by way of Henniker, and the two young students of parapsychology agreed enthusiastically. It was their first experience with an actual séance and they brought with them a lively dose of curiosity.

Sybil Leek brought with her something else: "Mr. Sasha," a healthy four-foot boa constrictor someone had given her for a pet. At first I thought she was kidding when she spoke with tender care of her snake, coiled peacefully in his little basket. But practical Sybil, author of some nine books, saw still another possibility in "Life with Sasha" and for that reason kept the snake on with her. On the way to Henniker, the car had a flat tire and we took this opportunity to get acquainted with Sasha, as Sybil gave him a run around the New Hampshire countryside.

Although I have always had a deep-seated dislike for anything reptilian, snakes, serpents, and other slitherers, terrestrial or maritime, I must confess that I found this critter less repulsive than I had thought he would be. At any rate, "Mr. Sasha" was collected once more and carefully replaced in his basket and the journey continued to Henniker, where the Russells were expecting us with great anticipation.

After a delightful buffet luncheon—"Mr. Sasha" had his the week before, as snakes are slow digesters—we proceeded to the large room upstairs to the right of the entrance door, commonly called the Lafayette room, and Sybil took the chair near the fireplace. The rest of us—the Russells, a minister friend of theirs, two neighbors, my wife Catherine and I, and our two student friends—gathered around her in a circle.

It was early afternoon. The sun was bright and clear. It didn't seem like it would be a good day for ghosts. Still, we had come to have a talk with the elusive Mary Wallace in her own domain, and if I knew Sybil, she would not disappoint us. Sybil is a very powerful medium, and something *always* happens.

Sybil knew nothing about the house since I had told our hosts not to discuss it with her before the trance session. I asked her if she had any clairvoyant impressions about the house.

"My main impressions were outside," Sybil replied, "near where the irises are. I was drawn to that spot and felt very strange. There is something outside this house which means more than things inside!"

"What about inside the house? What do you feel here?"

"The most impressive room I think is the loom room," Sybil said, and I thought, that's where Ernest Walbourne heard the voice telling him to get out, in the area that's also called the "death" room.

"They don't want us here...there is a conflict between two people...somebody wants something he can't have..."

Presently, Sybil was in trance. There was a moment of silence as I waited anxiously for the ghost of Mary Wallace to manifest itself through Sybil. The first words coming from the lips of the entranced medium were almost unintelligible.

Gradually, the voice became clearer and I had her repeat the words until I could be sure of them.

"Say-mon go to the lion's head," she said now. "To the lion's head. Be careful"

"Why should I be careful?"

"In case he catches you."

"Who are you?"

"Mary Degan."

"What are you doing here?"

"Waiting. Someone fetch me."

She said "*Witing*" with a strong cockney accent, and suddenly I realized that the "*say-mon*" was probably a seaman.

"Whose house is this?" I inquired.

"Daniel Burn's." (Perhaps it was "Birch.")

"What year is this?"

"1798."

"Who built this house?"

"Burn..."

"How did you get here?"

"All the time, come and go...to hide...I have to wait. He wants the money. Burn. Daniel Burn."

I began to wonder what had happened to Mary Wallace. Who was this new member of the ghostly cast? Sybil knew nothing whatever of a pirate or a pirate treasure connected by legend to this house. Yet her very first trance words concerned a *seaman* and *money*.

Did Mary Degan have someone else with her, I hinted. Maybe this was only the first act and the lady of the house was being coy in time for a second act appearance.

But the ghost insisted that she was Mary Degan and that she lived here, "with the old idiot."

"Who was the old idiot?" I demanded.

"Mary," the Degan girl replied.

"What is Mary's family name?"

"Birch," she replied without hesitation.

I looked at Mrs. Russell, who shook her head. Nobody knew of Mary Wallace by any other name. Had she had another husband we did not know about?

Was there anyone else with her, I asked.

"Mary Birch, Daniel, and Jonathan," she replied.

"Who is Jonathan?"

"Jonathan Harrison Flood," the ghostly woman said.

A week or so later, I checked with my good friend Robert Nesmith, expert in pirate lore. Was there a pirate by that name? There had been, but his date is given as 1610, far too early for our man. But then Flood was a very common name. Also, this Flood might have used another name as his *nom de pirate* and Flood might have been his real, civilian name.

"What are they doing in this house?" I demanded.

"They come to look for their money," Sybil in trance replied. "The old idiot took it."

"What sort of money was it?"

"Dutch money," came the reply. "Very long ago."

"Who brought the money to this house?"

"Mary. Not me."

"Whose money was it?"

"Johnny's."

"How did he get it?"

"Very funny...he helped himself...so we did."

"What profession did he have?"

"Went down to the sea. Had a lot of funny business. Then he got caught, you know. So they did him in."

"Who did him in?"

"The runners. In the bay."

"What year was that?"

"Ninety-nine."

"What happened to the money after that?"

"She hid it. Outside. Near the lion's head."

"Where is the lion's head?"

"You go down past the little rocks, in the middle of the rocks, a little bit like a lion's head."

"If I left the house by the front entrance, which way would I turn?"

"The right, down past the little rock on the right. Through the trees, down the little..."

"How far from the house?"

"Three minutes."

"Is it under the rock?"

"Lion's head."

"How far below?"

"As big as a boy."

"What will I find there?"

"The gold. Dutch gold."

"Anything else?"

"No, unless she put it there."

"Why did she put it there?"

"Because he came back for it."

"What did she do?"

"She said it was hers. Then he went away. Then they caught him, and good thing, too. He never came back and she went off, too."

"When did she leave here?"

"Eighteen three."

"What was she like? Describe her."

"Round, not as big as me, dumpy thing, she thought she owned everything."

"How was Jonathan related to Daniel?"

"Daniel stayed here when Johnny went away and then they would divide the money, but they didn't because of Mary. She took it."

"Did you see the money?"

"I got some money. Gold. It says 1747."

"Is anyone buried in this ground?"

"Sometimes they brought them back here when they got killed down by the river."

"Who is buried in the house?"

"I think Johnny."

I now told Mary Degan to fetch me the other Mary, the lady of the house. But the girl demurred. The other Mary did not like to talk to strangers.

"What do *you* look like?" I asked. I still was not sure if Mary Wallace was not masquerading as her own servant girl to fool us.

"Skinny and tall."

"What do you wear?"

"A gray dress."

"What is your favorite spot in this house?"

"The little loom room. Peaceful."

"Do you always stay there?"

"No." The voice was proud now. "I go where I want."

"Whose house is this?" Perhaps I could trap her if she was indeed Mary Wallace.

"Mary Birch."

"Has she got a husband?"

"They come and go. There's always company here—that's why I go to the loom room."

I tried to send her away, but she wouldn't go.

"Nobody speaks to me," she complained. "Johnny... she won't let him speak to me. Nobody is going to send me away."

"Is there a sea captain in this house?" I asked.

She almost shouted the reply. *"Johnny!"*

"Where is he from?"

"Johnny is from the island."

She then explained that the trouble with Johnny and Mary was about the sea. Especially about the money the captain had.

"Will the money be found?" I asked.

"Not until I let it."

I asked Mary Degan to find me Mary Wallace. No dice. The lady wanted to be coaxed. Did she want some presents, I asked. That hit a happier note.

"Brandy...some clothes," she said. "She needs some hair...hasn't got much hair."

"Ask her if she could do with some oil of wintergreen," I said, sending up a trial balloon.

"She's got a bad back," the ghost said, and I could tell from the surprised expression on Mrs. Russell's face that Mary Wallace had indeed had a bad back.

"She makes it... people bring her things... rub her back... back's bad she won't let you get the money... not yet... may want to build another house, in the garden... in case she needs it... sell it... she knows she is not what she used to be because her back's bad... she'll never go. Not now."

I assured her that the Russells wanted her to stay as long as she liked. After all, it was her house, too.

"Where is Johnny's body buried?" I now asked.

"Johnny's body," she murmured, "is under the fireplace."

Nobody had told Sybil about the persistent rumors that the old pirate lay under the hearthstone.

"Don't tell anyone," she whispered.

"How deep?"

"Had to be deep."

"Who put him there?"

"I shan't tell you."

"Did you bury anything with him?"

"I shan't tell. He is no trouble now. Poor Johnny."

"How did Johnny meet Mary?"

"I think they met on a ship."

"Ocean-Born" Mary, I thought. Sybil did not even know the name of the house, much less the story of how it got that name.

"All right," I said. "Did Mary have any children?"

"Four... in the garden. You can never tell with her."

"Did anyone kill anyone in this house at any time?"

"Johnny was killed, you know. Near the money. The runners chased him and he was very sick, we thought he was dead, and then he came here. I think she pushed him when he hurt his leg. We both brought him back and put him under the fireplace. I didn't think he was dead."

"But you buried him anyway?" I said.

"She did," the ghost servant replied. "Better gone, she said. He's only come back for the money."

"Then Mary and Johnny weren't exactly friendly?"

"They were once."

"What changed things?"

"The money. She took his money. The money he fought for. Fighting money."

Suddenly, the tone of voice of the servant girl changed.

"I want to go outside, " she begged. "She watches me. I can go out because her back is bad today. Can't get up, you see. So I can go out."

I promised to help her.

Suspiciously, she asked, "What do you want?"

"Go outside. You are free to go," I intoned.

"Sit on the rocks," the voice said. "If she calls out? She can get very angry."

"I will protect you," I promised.

"She says there are other places under the floor...," the girl ghost added, suddenly.

"Any secret passages?" I asked.

"Yes. Near the old nursery. First floor. Up the stairs, the loom room, the right hand wall. You can get out in the smoke room!"

Mr. Russell had told me of his suspicions that on structural evidence alone there was a hidden passage behind the smoke room. How would Sybil know this? Nobody had discussed it with her or showed her the spot.

I waited for more. But she did not know of any other passages, except one leading to the rear of the house.

"What about the well?"

"She did not like that either, because she thought *he* put his money there."

"Did he?"

"Perhaps he did. She used to put money in one place, he into another, and I think he put some money into the smoke room. He was always around there. Always watching each other. Watch me, too. Back of the house used to be where he could hide. People always looking for Johnny. Runners."

"Who was Mr. Birch?"

"Johnny had a lot to do with his house, but he was away a lot and so there was always some man here while he was away."

"Who paid for the house originally?"

"I think Johnny."

"Why did he want this house?"

"When he got enough money, he would come here and stay forever. He could not stay long ever, went back to the sea, and she came."

I tried another tack.

"Who was Don Pedro?" That was the name given the pirate in the popular tale.

She had heard the name, but could not place it.

"What about Mary Wallace?"

"Mary Wallace was Mary *Birch*," the ghost said, as if correcting me. "She had several names."

"Why?"

"Because she had several husbands."

Logical enough, if true.

"Wallace lived here a little while, I think," she added.

"Who was first, Wallace or Birch?"

"Birch. Mary Wallace, Mary Birch, is good enough."

Did the name Philip Babb mean anything to her? That allegedly was the pirate's real name.

"She had a little boy named Philip," the ghost said, and I thought, why not? After all, they had named Mary for the pirate's mother, why not reciprocate and name *her* son for the old man? Especially with all that loot around.

"If I don't go now, she'll wake up," the girl said. "Philip Babb, Philip Babb, he was somewhere in the back room. That was his room. I remember him."

How did Philip get on with Johnny? I wanted to know if they were one and the same person or not.

"Not so good," the ghost said. "Johnny did not like men here, you know."

I promised to watch out for Mary, and sent the girl on her way.

I then brought Sybil out of her trance.

A few moments later, we decided to start our treasure hunt in the garden, following the instructions given us by Mary Degan.

Sybil was told nothing more than to go outside and let her intuition lead her toward any spot she thought important. The rest of us followed her like spectators at the National Open Golf Tournament.

We did not have to walk far. About twenty yards from the house, near some beautiful iris in bloom, we located the three stones. The one in the middle looked indeed somewhat like a lion's head, when viewed at a distance. I asked the others in the group to look at it. There

was no doubt about it. If there was a lion's head on the grounds, this was it. What lay underneath? What indeed was underneath the hearthstone in the house itself?

The Russells promised to get a mine detector to examine the areas involved. If there was metal in the ground, the instrument would show it. Meanwhile, the lore about "Ocean-Born" Mary had been enriched by the presence in the nether world of Mary Degan, servant girl, and the intriguing picture of two pirates—Johnny and Philip Babb. Much of this is very difficult to trace. But the fact is that Sybil Leek, who came to Henniker a total stranger, was able, in trance, to tell about a man at sea, a Mary, a pirate treasure, hidden passages, a child named Philip, four children of Mary, and the presence of a ghost in the loom room upstairs. All of this had been checked.

Why should not the rest be true also? Including, perhaps, the elusive treasure?

Only time will tell.

✳ 46

The Ghosts of Stamford Hill

"Mr. Holzer," the voice on the phone said pleasantly, "I've read your book and that's why I'm calling. We've got a ghost in our house."

Far from astonished, I took paper and pencil and, not unlike a grocery-store clerk taking down a telephone order, started to put down the details of the report.

Robert Cowan is a gentleman with a very balanced approach to life. He is an artist who works for one of the leading advertising agencies in New York City and his interests range widely from art to music, theater, history and what have you. But not to ghosts, at least not until he and his actress-wife, Dorothy, moved into the 1780 House in Stamford Hill. The house is thus named for the simplest of all reasons: it was built in that year.

Mr. Cowan explained that he thought I'd be glad to have a look at his house, although the Cowans were not unduly worried about the presence of a non-rent-paying guest at their house. It was a bit disconcerting at times, but more than that, curiosity as to what the ghost wanted, and who the specter was, had prompted Bob Cowan to seek the help of The Ghost Hunter.

I said, "Mr. Cowan, would you mind putting your experiences in writing, so I can have them for my files?"

I like to have written reports (in the first person, if possible) so that later I can refer back to them if similar cases should pop up, as they often do.

"Not at all," Bob Cowan said, "I'll be glad to write it down for you."

The next morning I received his report, along with a brief history of the 1780 House.

Here is a brief account of the experiences my wife and I have had while living in this house during the past nine-and-a-half years. I'll start with myself because my experiences are quite simple.

From time to time (once a week or so) during most of the time we've lived here I have noticed unidentifiable movements out of the corner of my eye...day or night. Most often, I've noticed this while sitting in our parlor and what I see moving seems to be in the living room. At other times, and only late at night when I am the only one awake, I hear beautiful but unidentified music seemingly played by a full orchestra, as though a radio were on in another part of the house.

The only place I recall hearing this is in an upstairs bedroom and just after I'd gone to bed. Once I actually got up, opened the bedroom door to ascertain if it was perhaps music from a radio accidently left on, but it wasn't.

Finally, quite often I've heard a variety of knocks and crashes that do not have any logical source within the structural setup of the house. A very loud smash occurred two weeks ago. You'd have thought a door had fallen off its hinges upstairs but, as usual, there was nothing out of order.

My wife, Dorothy, had two very vivid experiences about five years ago. One was in the kitchen, or rather outside of a kitchen window. She was standing at the sink in the evening and happened to glance out the window when she saw a face glaring in at her. It was a dark face but not a Negro, perhaps Indian; it was very hateful and fierce.

The Stamford Hill house—the restless stairs

At first she thought it was a distorted reflection in the glass but in looking closer, it was a face glaring directly at her. All she could make out was a face only and as she recalls it, *it seemed translucent*. It didn't disappear, *she did!*

On a summer afternoon my wife was taking a nap in a back bedroom and was between being awake and being asleep when she heard the sounds of men's voices and the sound of working on the grounds—rakes, and garden tools—right outside the window. She tried to arouse herself to see who they could be, but she couldn't get up.

At that time, and up to that time we had only hired a single man to come in and work on the lawn and flower beds. It wasn't until at least a year later that we hired a crew that came in and worked once a week and we've often wondered if this was an experience of precognition. My wife has always had an uneasy feeling about the outside of the back of the house and still sometimes hears men's voices outside and will look out all the windows without seeing anyone.

She also has shared my experiences of seeing "things" out of the corner of her eye and also hearing quite lovely music at night. She hasn't paid attention to household noises because a long time ago I told her "all old houses have odd structural noises"...which is true enough.

Prior to our living here the house was lived in for about 25 years by the Clayton Rich family, a family of five. Mr. Rich died towards the end of their stay here. By the time we bought it, the three children were all married and had moved away.

For perhaps one year prior to that a Mrs. David Cowles lived here. She's responsible for most of the restoration along with a Mr. Frederick Kinble.

Up until 1927 or 1928, the house was in the Weed family ever since 1780. The last of the line were two sisters who hated each other and only communicated with each other through the husband of one of the sisters. They had divided the house and used two different doors, one used the regular front door into the stair hall and the other used the "coffin door" into the parlor.

Mr. Cowan added that they were selling the house—not because of ghosts, but because they wanted to move to the city again. I assured him that we'd be coming up as soon as possible.

Before we could make arrangements to do so, I had another note from the Cowans. On February 9, 1964, Bob Cowan wrote that they heard a singing voice quite clearly downstairs, and music again.

It wasn't until the following week, however, that my wife and I went to Stamford Hill. The Cowans offered to have supper ready for us that Sunday evening, and to pick us up at the station, since nobody could find the house at night who did not know the way.

It was around six in the evening when our New Haven train pulled in. Bob Cowan wore the Scottish beret he had said he would wear in order to be recognized by us at once. The house stood at the end of a winding road which ran for about ten minutes through woodland and past shady lanes. An American eagle over the door, and the date 1780 stood out quite clearly despite the dusk which had started to settle on the land. The house has three levels, and the Cowans used for their dining room the large room next to the kitchen in what might be called the cellar or ground level.

They had adorned it with eighteenth-century American antiques in a most winning manner, and the fireplace added a warmth to the room that seemed miles removed from bustling New York.

On the next level were the living room and next to that a kind of sitting room. The fireplace in each of these rooms was connected one to the other. Beyond the corridor there was the master bedroom and Bob's rather colorful den. Upstairs were two guest rooms, and there was a small attic accessible only through a hole in the ceiling and by ladder. Built during the American Revolution, the house stands on a wooded slope, which is responsible for its original name of Woodpecker Ridge Farm.

Many years ago, after the restoration of the house was completed, Harold Donaldson Eberlin, an English furniture and garden expert, wrote about it:

With its rock-ribbed ridges, its boulder-strewn pastures and its sharply broken contours like the choppy surface of a wind-blown sea, the topographical conditions have inevitably affected the domestic architecture. To mention only two particulars, the dwellings of the region have had to accommodate themselves to many an abrupt hillside site and the employment of some of the omnipresent granite boulders. Part of the individuality of the house at Woodpecker Ridge Farm lies in the way it satisfies these conditions without being a type house.

Before communal existence, the country all thereabouts bore the pleasantly descriptive name of Woodpecker Ridge, and Woodpecker Ridge Farm was so called in order to keep alive the memory of this early name. Tradition says that the acres now comprised within the boundaries of Woodpecker Ridge Farm once formed part of the private hunting ground of the *old Indian chief Ponus*.

Old Ponus may, perhaps, appear a trifle mythical and shadowy, as such long-gone chieftains are wont to be. Very substantial and real, however, was Augustus Weed, who built the house in 1780. And the said Augustus was something of a personage.

War clouds were still hanging thick over the face of the land when he had the foundation laid and the structure framed. Nevertheless, confident and forward-looking, he not only reared a staunch and tidy abode, indicative of the spirit of the countryside, but he seems to have put into it some of his own robust and independent personality as well.

It is said that Augustus was such a notable farmer and took such justifiable pride in the condition of his fields that he was not afraid to make a standing offer of one dollar reward for every daisy that anyone could find in his hay.

About 1825 the house experienced a measure of remodeling in accordance with the notions prevalent at the time. Nothing very extensive or ostentatious was attempted, but visible traces of the work then undertaken remain in the neo-Greek details that occur both outside and indoors.

It is not unlikely that the "lie-on-your-stomach" windows of the attic story date from this time and point to either a raising of the original roof or else some alteration of its pitch. These "lie-on-your-stomach" windows —so called because they were low down in the wall and had their sills very near the level of the floor so that you had almost to lie on your stomach to look out of them— were a favorite device of the *néo-Grec* era for lighting attic rooms. And it is remarkable how much light they actually do give, and what a pleasant light it is.

The recent remodeling that brought Woodpecker Farmhouse to its present state of comeliness and comfort impaired none of the individual character the place had acquired through the generations that had passed since hardy Augustus Weed first took up his abode there. It needs no searching scrutiny to discern the eighteenth-century features impressed on the structure at the beginning—the stout timbers of the framing, the sturdy beams and joists, the wide floor boards, and the generous fireplaces. Neither is close examination required to discover the marks of the 1825 rejuvenation.

The fashions of columns, pilasters, mantelpieces and other features speak plainly and proclaim their origin.

The aspect of the garden, too, discloses the same sympathetic understanding of the environment peculiarly suitable to the sort of house for which it affords the natural setting. The ancient well cover, the lilac bushes, the sweetbriers, the August lilies and the other denizens of an old farmhouse dooryard have been allowed to keep their long-accustomed places.

In return for this recognition of their prescriptive rights, they lend no small part to the air of self-possessed assurance and mellow contentment that pervades the whole place.

After a most pleasant dinner downstairs, Catherine and I joined the Cowans in the large living room upstairs. We sat down quietly and hoped we would hear something along musical lines.

As the quietness of the countryside slowly settled over us, I could indeed distinguish faraway, indistinct musical sounds, as if someone were playing a radio underwater or at great distance. A check revealed no nearby house or parked car whose radio could be responsible for this.

After a while we got up and looked about the room itself. We were standing about quietly admiring the furniture, when both my wife and I, and of course the Cowans, clearly heard footsteps overhead.

They were firm and strong and could not be mistaken for anything else, such as a squirrel in the attic or other innocuous noise. Nor was it an old house settling.

"Did you hear that?" I said, almost superfluously.

"We all heard it," my wife said and looked at me.

"What am I waiting for?" I replied, and faster than you can say Ghost Hunter, I was up the stairs and into the room above our heads, where the steps had been heard. The room lay in total darkness. I turned the switch. There was no one about. Nobody else was in the house at the time, and all windows were closed. We decided to assemble upstairs in the smaller room next to the one in which I had heard the steps. The reason was that Mrs. Cowan had experienced a most unusual phenomenon in that particular room.

"It was like lightning," she said, "a bright light suddenly come and gone."

I looked the room over carefully. The windows were arranged in such a manner that a reflection from passing cars was out of the question. Both windows, far apart and on different walls, opened into the dark countryside away from the only road.

Catherine and I sat down on the couch, and the Cowans took chairs. We sat quietly for perhaps twenty minutes, without lights except a small amount of light filtering in from the stairwell. It was very dark, certainly dark enough for sleep and there was not light enough to write by.

As I was gazing towards the back wall of the little room and wondered about the footsteps I had just heard so clearly, I saw a blinding flash of light, white light, in the corner facing me. It came on and disappeared very quickly, so quickly in fact that my wife, whose head had been turned in another direction at the moment, missed it. But

Dorothy Cowan saw it and exclaimed, "There it is again. Exactly as I saw it."

Despite the brevity I was able to observe that the light cast a shadow on the opposite wall, so it could not very well have been a hallucination.

I decided it would be best to bring Mrs. Meyers to the house, and we went back to New York soon after. While we were preparing our return visit with Mrs. Meyers as our medium, I received an urgent call from Bob Cowan.

"Since seeing you and Cathy at our house, we've had some additional activity that you'll be interested in. Dottie and I have both heard knocking about the house but none of it in direct answer to questions that we've tried to ask. On Saturday, the 29th of February, I was taking a nap back in my studio when I was awakened by the sound of footsteps in the room above me...the same room we all sat in on the previous Sunday.

"The most interesting event was on the evening of Thursday, February 27. I was driving home from the railroad station alone. Dottie was still in New York. As I approached the house, I noticed that there was a light on in the main floor bedroom and also a light on up in the sewing room on the top floor, a room Dottie also uses for rehearsal. I thought Dottie had left the lights on. I drove past the house and down to the garage, put the car away and then walked back to the house and noticed that the light in the top floor was now off.

"I entered the house and noticed that the dogs were calm (wild enough at seeing me, but in no way indicating that there was anyone else in the house). I went upstairs and found that the light in the bedroom was also off. I checked the entire house and there was absolutely no sign that anyone had just been there...and there hadn't been, I'm sure."

* * *

On Sunday, March 15, we arrived at the 1780 House, again at dusk. A delicious meal awaited us in the downstairs room, then we repaired to the upstairs part of the house.

We seated ourselves in the large living room where the music had been heard, and where we had been standing at the time we heard the uncanny footsteps overhead.

"I sense a woman in a white dress," Ethel said suddenly. "She's got dark hair and a high forehead. Rather a small woman."

"I was looking through the attic earlier," Bob Cowan said thoughtfully, "and look what I found—a waistcoat that would fit a rather smallish woman or girl."

The piece of clothing he showed us seemed rather musty. There were a number of articles up there in the attic that must have belonged to an earlier owner of the house—much earlier.

A moment later, Ethel Meyers showed the characteristic signs of onsetting trance. We doused the lights until only one back light was on.

At first, only inarticulate sounds came from the medium's lips. "You can speak," I said, to encourage her, "you're among friends." The sounds now turned into crying.

"What is your name?" I asked, as I always do on such occasions. There was laughter—whether girlish or mad was hard to tell.

Suddenly, she started to sing in a high-pitched voice.

"You can speak, you can speak," I kept assuring the entity. Finally she seemed to have settled down somewhat in control of the medium.

"Happy to speak with you," she mumbled faintly.

"What is your name?"

I had to ask it several times before I could catch the answer clearly.

"Lucy.

"Tell me, Lucy, do you live here?"

"God be with you."

"Do you life in this house?"

"My house."

"What year is this?"

The entity hesitated a moment, then turned towards Dorothy and said, "I like you."

I continued to question her.

"How old are you?"

"Old lady."

"How old?"

"God be with you."

The conversation had been friendly, but when I asked her, "What is your husband's name?" the ghost drew back as if I had spoken a horrible word.

"What did you say?" she almost shouted, her voice trembling with emotion. "I have no husband—God bless you—what were you saying?" she repeated, then started to cry again. "Husband, husband," she kept saying it as if it was a thought she could not bear.

"You did not have a husband, then?"

"Yes, I did."

"Your name again?"

"Lucy...fair day...where is he? The fair day...the pretty one, he said to me look in the pool and you will see my face."

"Who is he?" I repeated.

But the ghost paid no heed to me. She was evidently caught up in her own memories.

"I heard a voice, Lucy, Lucy—fair one—alack—they took him out—they laid him cold in the ground...."

"What year was that?" I wanted to know.

"Year, year?" she repeated. "Now, now!"

"Who rules this country now?"

"Why, he who seized it."

"Who rules?"

"They carried him out.... The Savior of our country. General Washington."

"When did he die?"

"Just now."

I tried to question her further, but she returned to her thoughts of her husband.

"I want to stay here—I wait at the pool—look, he is there!" She was growing excited again.

"I want to stay here now, always, forever—rest in peace—he is there always with me."

"How long ago did you die?" I asked, almost casually. The reaction was somewhat hostile.

"I have not died—never—All Saints!"

I asked her to join her loved one by calling for him and thus be set free of this house. But the ghost would have none of it.

"Gainsay what I have spoke—"

"How did you come to this house?" I now asked.

"Father—I am born here."

"Was it your father's house?"

"Yes."

"What was his name?" I asked, but the restless spirit of Lucy was slipping away now, and Albert, the medium's control, took over. His crisp, clear voice told us that the time had come to release Ethel.

"What about this woman, Lucy?" I inquired. Sometimes the control will give additional details.

"He was not her husband...he was killed before she married him," Albert said.

No wonder my question about a husband threw Lucy into an uproar of emotions.

In a little while, Ethel Meyers was back to her old self, and as usual, did not remember anything of what had come through her entranced lips.

* * *

Shortly after this my wife and I went to Europe.

As soon as we returned, I called Bob Cowan. How were things up in Stamford Hill? Quiet? Not very.

"Last June," Bob recalled, "Dottie and I were at home with a friend, a lady hair dresser, who happens to be psychic. We were playing around with the Ouija board, more in amusement than seriously. Suddenly, the Sunday afternoon quiet was disrupted by heavy footsteps coming up the steps outside the house. Quickly, we hid the Ouija board, for we did not want a potential buyer of the house to see us in this unusual pursuit. We were sure someone was coming up to see the house. But the steps stopped abruptly when they reached the front door. I opened, and there was no one outside."

"Hard to sell a house that way," I commented. "Anything else?"

"Yes, in July we had a house guest, a very balanced person, not given to imagining things. There was a sudden crash upstairs, and when I rushed up the stairs to the sewing room, there was this bolt of material that had been standing in a corner, lying in the middle of the room as if thrown there by unseen hands! Margaret, our house guest, also heard someone humming a tune in the bathroom, although there was no one in there at the time. Then in November, when just the two of us were in the house, someone knocked at the door downstairs. Again we looked, but there was nobody outside. One evening when I was in the ship room and Dottie in the bedroom, we heard footfalls coming down the staircase.

"Since neither of us was causing them and the door was closed, only a ghost could have been walking down those stairs."

"But the most frightening experience of all," Dorothy Cowan broke in, "was when I was sleeping downstairs and, waking up, wanted to go to the bathroom without turning on the lights, so as not to wake Bob. Groping my way back to bed, I suddenly found myself up on the next floor in the blue room, which is pretty tricky walking in the dark. I had the feeling someone was forcing me to follow them into that particular room."

I had heard enough, and on December 15, we took Ethel Johnson Meyers to the house for another go at the restless ones within its confines. Soon we were all seated in the ship room on the first floor, and Ethel started to drift into trance.

"There is a baby's coffin here," she murmured. "Like a newborn infant's."

The old grandfather clock in back of us kept ticking away loudly.

"I hear someone call Maggie," Ethel said, "Margaret."

"Do you see anyone?"

"A woman, about five foot two, in a long dress, with a big bustle in the back. Hair down, parted in the middle, and braided on both sides. There is another young woman ...Laurie...very pretty face, but so sad...she's looking at you, Hans...."

"What is it she wants?" I asked quietly.

"A youngish man with brown hair, curly, wearing a white blouse, taken in at the wrists, and over it a tan waistcoat, but no coat over it..."

I asked what he wanted and why he was here. This seemed to agitate the medium somewhat.

"Bottom of the well," she mumbled, "stones at bottom of the well."

Bob Cowan changed seats, moving away from the coffin door to the opposite side of the room. He complained of feeling cold at the former spot, although neither door nor window was open to cause such a sensation.

"Somebody had a stick over his shoulder," the medium said now, "older man wearing dark trousers, heavy stockings. His hair is gray and kind of longish; he's got that stick."

I asked her to find out why.

"Take him away," Ethel replied. "He says, 'Take him away!'"

"But he was innocent, he went to the well. Who is down the well? Him who I drove into the well, him...I mistook..."

Ethel was now fully entranced and the old man seemed to be speaking through her.

What is your name?" I asked.

"She was agrievin'," the voice replied, "she were grievin' I did that."

"What is your name?"

"Ain't no business to you."

"How can I help you?"

"They're all here...accusin' me...I see her always by the well."

"Did someone die in this well?" Outside, barely twenty yards away, was the well, now cold and silent in the night air.

"Him who I mistook. I find peace, I find him, I put him together again."

"What year was that?"

"No matter to you now...I do not forgive myself...I wronged, I wronged...I see always her face look on me."

"Are you in this house now?" I asked.

"Where else can I be and talk with thee?" the ghost shot back.

"This isn't your house any more," I said quietly.

"Oh, yes it is," the ghost replied firmly. "The young man stays here only to look upon me and mock me. It will not be other than mine. I care only for that flesh that I could put again on the bone and I will restore him to the bloom of life and the rich love of her who suffered through my own misdemeanor."

"Is your daughter buried here?" I asked, to change the subject. Quietly, the ghostly voice said "Yes."

But he refused to say where he himself was laid to final—or not so final—rest.

At this point the ghost realized that he was not in his own body, and as I explained the procedure to him, he gradually became calmer. At first, he thought he was in his own body and could use it to restore to life the one he had slain. I kept asking who he was. Finally, in a soft whisper, came the reply, "Samuel."

"And Laurie?"

"My daughter....oh, he is here, the man I wronged...Margaret, Margaret!" He seemed greatly agitated with fear now.

The big clock started to strike. The ghost somehow felt it meant him.

"The judgment, the judgment...Laurie....they smile at me. I have killed. He has taken my hand! He whom I have hurt."

But the excitement proved too much for Samuel. Suddenly, he was gone, and after a brief interval, an entirely different personality inhabited Ethel's body. It was Laurie.

"Please forgive him," she pleaded, "I have forgiven him."

The voice was sweet and girlish.

"Who is Samuel?"

"My grandfather."

"What is your family name?"

"Laurie Ho-Ho-...if I could only get that name."

But she couldn't.

Neither could she give me the name of her beloved, killed by her grandfather. It was a name she was not allowed to mention around the house, so she had difficulty remembering now, she explained,

"What is your mother's name?" I asked.

"Margaret."

"What year were you born?"

Hesitatingly, the voice said, "Seven-teen-fifty-six."

"What year is this now?"

"Seventeen seventy-four. We laid him to rest in seventeen seventy-four."

"In the church?"

"No, Grandfather could not bear it. We laid him to rest on the hill to the north. We dug with our fingers all night.

"Don't tell Grandpa where we put it."

"How far from here is it?"

"No more than a straight fly of the lark.

"Is the grave marked?"

"Oh, no."

"What happened to your father?"

"No longer home, gone."

I explained to Laurie that the house would soon change hands, and that she must not interfere with this. The Cowans had the feeling that their ghosts were somehow keeping all buyers away, fantastic though this may be at first thought. But then all of psychic research is pretty unusual and who is to say what cannot be?

Laurie promised not to interfere and to accept a new owner of "their" house. She left, asking again that her grandfather be forgiven his sins.

I then asked Albert, Ethel's control, to take over the medium. That done, I queried him regarding the whole matter.

"The father is buried far from here, but most of the others are buried around here," he said, "during the year 1777...grandfather was not brought here until later when there was forgiveness. The body was removed and put in Christian burial."

"Where is the tombstone?" I asked.

"Lying to the west of a white structure," Albert replied in his precise, slightly accented speech, "on these grounds. The tombstone is broken off, close to the earth. The top has been mishandled by vandals. The old man is gone, the young man has taken him by the hand."

"What was the young man's name?"

"She called him Benjamin."

"He was killed in the well?"

"That is right. He has no grave except on the hill."

"Is the old man the one who disturbs this house?"

"He is the main one who brings in his rabble, looking for the young man."

"Who is Lucy?" I asked, referring back to the girl who had spoken to us at the last séance in the late spring.

"That is the girl you were talking about, Laurie. Her name is really Lucy. One and the same person."

"She was not actually married to the young man?"

"In her own way, she was. But they would not recognize it. There were differences in religious ideas....But we had better release the medium for now."

I nodded, and within a moment or two, Ethel was back to herself, very much bewildered as to what went on while she was in trance.

"How do you reconcile these dates with the tradition that this house was built in 1780?" I asked Bob Cowan.

He shook his head.

"It is only a tradition. We have no proof of the actual date."

We went to the upstairs sewing room where the latest manifestations had taken place, and grouped ourselves around the heavy wooden table. Ethel almost immediately fell into trance again. She rarely does twice in one sitting.

The voice reverberating in the near-darkness now was clearly that of a man, and a very dominating voice it was.

"Who are you?" I demanded.

"Sergeant-major...." No name followed. I asked why was he here in this house.

"One has pleasant memories."

"Your name?"

"Sergeant-major Harm."

"First name?"

Instead of giving it, he explained that he once owned the house and was "friend, not foe." I looked at Bob Cowan, who knows all the owners of the property in the old records, and Bob shook his head. No Harm.

"When I please, I come. I do not disturb willingly. But I will go," the new visitor offered, "I will take him with me; you will see him no more. I am at peace with him now. He is at peace with me."

"How did you pass over?" I inquired.

"On the field of battle. On the banks of the Potomac...1776."

"What regiment were you in?" I continued.

"York....Eight....I was a foot soldier...18th regiment..."

"What Army?"

"Wayne...Wayne..."

"Who was your commanding general?"

"Broderick."

"Who was the Colonel of your regiment?"

"Wayne, Wayne."

"You were a Sergeant-major?"

"Sergeant-major, 18th regiment, foot infantry."

"Where were you stationed?"

"New York."

"Where in New York?"

"Champlain."

"Your regimental commander again?"

"Broderick." Then he added, not without emotion, "I died under fire, first battle of Potomac."

"Where are you buried?"

"Fort Ticonderoga, New York."

I wondered how a soldier fighting on the banks of the Potomac could be buried in upstate New York. But I must confess that the word "Potomac" had come so softly that I could have been mistaken.

"The date of your death?"

"1776."

Then he added, as the voice became more and more indistinct, "I will leave now, but I will protect you from those who... who are hungry to..." The voice trailed off into silence.

A few moments later, Ethel emerged from the trance with a slight headache, but otherwise her old self.

* * *

We returned to New York soon after, hoping that all would remain quiet in the Cowan house, and, more importantly, that there would soon be a new laird of the manor at the 1780 House.

I, too, heard the ghostly music, although I am sure it does not connect with the colonial ghosts we were able to evoke. The music I heard sounded like a far-off radio, which it wasn't, since there are no houses near enough to be heard from. What I heard for a few moments in the living room sounded like a full symphony orchestra playing the music popular around the turn of this century.

Old houses impregnated with layers upon layers of people's emotions frequently also absorb music and other sounds as part of the atmosphere.

What about the Sergeant-major?

I checked the regimental records. No soldier named Harm, but a number of officers (and men) named Harmon. I rechecked my tapes. The name "Harm" had been given by the ghost very quietly. He could have said Harmon. Or perhaps he was disguising his identity as they sometimes will.

But then I discovered something very interesting. In the Connecticut state papers there is mention of a certain Benjamin Harmon, Jr. Lt., who was with a local regiment in 1776. The murdered young man had been identified as "Benjamin." Suddenly we have another ghost named Harm or Harmon, evidently an older personality. Was he the father of the murdered young man?

The 1780 House is, of course, recorded as dating back to 1780 only. But could not another building have occupied the area? Was the 1780 house an adaptation of a smaller dwelling of which there is no written record?

We can neither prove nor disprove this.

It is true, however, that General "Mad" Anthony Wayne was in charge of the Revolutionary troops in the New York area at the time under discussion.

At any rate, all this is knowledge not usually possessed by a lady voice teacher, which is what Ethel Meyers is when not being a medium.

✳ 47

The "Spy House" Ghosts of New Jersey

IN JUNE, 1696, ONE Daniel Seabrook, aged 26 and a planter by profession, took his inheritance of 80 pounds sterling and bought 202 acres of property from his stepfather, Thomas Whitlock. For 250 years this plantation was in the hands of the Seabrook family who worked the land and sailed their ships from the harbor. The "Spy House" is probably one of the finest pieces of colonial architecture available for inspection in the eastern United States, having been restored meticulously over the years.

The house is built in the old manner, held together with wooden pegs. There are handmade bricks, filled with clay mortar. The house has two stories and is painted white. Every room has its own fireplace as that was the only way in which colonial houses could be heated.

The house, which is located near Middletown, New Jersey, can easily be reached from New York City. It was kept by a group headed by curator Gertrude Neidlinger, helped by her historian-brother, Travis Neidlinger, and as a museum it displays not only the furniture of the Colonial period but some of the implements of the whalers who were active in the area well into the nineteenth century. As an historical attraction, it is something that should not be missed by anyone, apart from any ghostly connections.

One of the rooms in the house is dedicated to the period of the Battle of Monmouth. This room, called the spy room by the British for good reasons, as we shall see, has copies of the documents kept among General Washington's private papers in the Library of Congress in Washington, D.C.

In 1778, the English were marching through Middletown, pillaging and burning the village. Along the shoreline the Monmouth militia and the men who were working the whale boats, got together to try to cut down the English shipping. General Washington asked for a patriot from Shoal Harbor, which was the name of the estate where the

spy house is located, to help the American side fight the British. The volunteer was a certain Corporal John Stillwell, who was given a telescope and instructions to spy on the British from a hill called Garrett's Hill, not far away, the highest point in the immediate area.

The lines between British and Americans were intertwined and frequently intercut each other, and it was difficult for individuals to avoid crossing them at times. The assignment given Corporal Stillwell was not an easy one, especially as some of his own relatives favored the other side of the war. Still, he was able to send specific messages to the militia who were able to turn these messages into attacks on the British fleet.

At that point, Stillwell observed there were 1,037 vessels in the fleet lying off the New Jersey coastline, at a time when the American forces had no navy at all. But the fishermen and their helpers on shore did well in this phase of the Revolutionary War. John Stillwell's son, Obadiah Stillwell, 17 years old, served as message carrier from his father's observation point to the patriots.

Twenty-three naval battles were fought in the harbor after the battle of Monmouth. The success of the whaleboat operation was a stunning blow to the British fleet and a great embarrassment. Even daylight raids became so bold and successful that in one day two pilot boats were captured upsetting the harbor shipping.

Finally, the British gave the order to find the spy and end the rebel operation. The searching party declared the Seabrook homestead as a spy house, since they knew its owner, Major Seabrook, was a patriot. They did not realize that the real spy was John Stillwell, operating from Garrett's Hill. Nevertheless, they burned the spy house. It was,

of course, later restored. Today, descendants of John Stillwell are among the society of friends of the museum, supporting it.

Gertrude Neidlinger turned to me for help with the several ghosts she felt in the house. Considering the history of the house, it is not surprising that there should be ghosts there. Miss Neidlinger, herself, has felt someone in the entrance room whenever she has been alone in the house, especially at night. There is also a lady in white who comes down from the attic, walks along the hall and goes into what is called the blue and white room, and there tucks in the covers of a crib or bed. Then she turns and goes out of sight. Miss Neidlinger was not sure who she was, but thought she might have been the spirit of Mrs. Seabrook, who lived through the Revolutionary War in a particularly dangerous position, having relatives on both sides of the political fence.

In 1976, I brought Ingrid Beckman, my psychic friend, to the spy house, which is technically located in Keansburg, New Jersey, near Middletown. The number on the house is 119, but of course everyone in the area calls it the Spy House. As Ingrid walked about the place, she immediately pointed out its ancient usage as an outpost. While we were investigating the house, we both clearly heard footsteps overhead where there was no one walking. Evidently, the ghosts knew of our arrival.

Without knowing anything about the history of the house, Ingrid commented, "Down here around the fireplace I feel there are people planning strategy, worried about

British ships." Then she continued, "This was to mobilize something like the minutemen, farming men who were to fight. This was a strategic point because it was the entry into New York."

I then asked Ingrid to tell me whether she felt any ghosts, any residues of the past still in the house.

When we went upstairs, Ingrid tuned into the past with a bang. "There's a woman here. She ties in with this house and something about spying, some kind of spying went on here." Then she added, "Somebody spied behind the American lines and brought back information."

Upstairs near the window on the first floor landing, Ingrid felt a man watching, waiting for someone to come his way. Ingrid felt there was a man present who had committed an act of treason, a man who gave information back to the British. His name was Samuels. She felt that this man was hanged publicly. The people call him an ex-patriot. This is the entity, Ingrid said, who cannot leave this house out of remorse.

Ingrid also asserted that the house was formerly used as a public house, an inn, when meetings took place here. The curator, Miss Neidlinger, later confirmed this. Also, Ingrid felt that among the families living in the area, most of the members served in the patriot militia, but that there were occasional traitors, such as George Taylor. Colonel George Taylor might have been the man to whom Ingrid was referring. As for the man who was hanged, it would have been Captain Huddy, and he was hanged for having caused the death of a certain Philip White. Captain Joshua Huddy had been unjustly accused of having caused the death of the patriot Philip White and despite his inno-

cence, was lynched by the patriots. Again, Ingrid had touched on something very real from history.

But the ghostly lady and the man who was hanged and the man who stared out the window onto the bay are not the only ghosts at the spy house. On the Fourth of July, 1975, a group of local boys were in the house in the blue and white room upstairs. Suddenly, the sewing machine door opened by itself and the pedals worked themselves without benefit of human feet. One of the boys looked up, and in the mirror in the bureau across the room, he could see a face with a long beard.

Another boy looked down the hall and there he saw a figure with a tall black hat and a long beard and sort of very full trousers as they were worn in an earlier age. That was enough for them and they ran from the house and never went back again.

One of the ladies who assists the curator, Agnes Lyons, refuses to do any typing in the upstairs room because the papers simply will not stand still. A draft seems to go by all the time and blow the papers to the floor even though the windows are closed. A Mrs. Lillian Boyer also saw the man with the beard standing at the top of the stairs, wearing a black hat and dressed in the period of the later 1700s. He had very large eyes, and seemed to be a man in his forties. He just stood there looking at her and she of course wouldn't pass him. Then he seemed to flash some sort of light back and forth, a brilliant light like a flashlight. And there were footsteps all over the house at the same time. She could even hear the man breathe, yet he was a ghost!

✳ 48

The Strange Case of the Colonial Soldier

Somerton, Pennsylvania, is now a suburb of Philadelphia, albeit a pretty outlaying one. It takes you all of an hour by car from downtown Philadelphia, but when you get there, it's worth it, especially Byberry Road. How the builders of modern chunks of concrete managed to overlook this delightful country lane in the backyard of the big city is beyond my knowledge, but the fact is that we have here a winding, bumpy road, good enough for one car at a time, that goes for several miles without a single high-rise building. Instead, old homes line it in respectable intervals, allowing even a bit of green and open spaces between the dwellings.

One of the most unusual sights along this winding road is a pretty, wooden colonial house built in 1732, and

untouched except for minor alterations, mainly inside the house. That in itself is a rarity, of course, but the owners who lived here since the Revolutionary period evidently were house-proud people who *cared*.

The current tenants are David and Dolores Robinson, whose greatest pleasure is being in that house. They don't advertise the fact they've got an authentic pre-Revolutionary home, but they're not exactly shy about it either; to them, it is a thrill to live as our ancestors did, without the constant urge to "improve" things with shiny new gadgets that frequently don't work, or to tear down some portion of their home just because it looks old or has been used for a long time.

The Robinsons are house-proud, and they have a keen sense of the antiquarian without any formal education in that area. Mr. Robinson works for the telephone company and his wife works for her brother, a photographer, as a retouch artist. Both are in early middle age and they have three children in the preteenage group.

Theirs is a happy family without problems or frustrations: They'd like to make a little more money, advance a little faster, get a better car—but that is the normal average American's dream. With the Robinsons lives Mr. Robinson Senior, an elderly gentleman whose main occupation seemed to be watching TV.

I first heard of the Robinsons and their homestead when I appeared on a local radio show in the area, and I was fascinated by the prospect of an apparently untouched house with many layers of history clinging to it that a psychic might be able to sense. I put the house on my mental list of places to visit for possible psychometry experiments.

Finally, in April of 1967, that opportunity arose and a friend, Tom Davis, drove us out to Byberry Road. There is something strange about Philadelphia distances; they grow on you somehow, especially at night. So it was with considerable delay that we finally showed up at the house, but we were made welcome just the same by the owners.

The house could not be missed even in the dark of night. It is the only one of its kind in the area, and sits back a bit from the road. With its graceful white pillars that support the roof of the porch, it is totally different from anything built nowadays or even in Victorian times. From the outside it looks smaller than it really is. There are three stories, and a storage room beneath the rear part of the house, the oldest portion. We entered through the front door and found ourselves in a delightfully appointed living room leading off to the left into the older portion of the house. The house had a mixture of Colonial and Victorian furniture in it, somehow not out of context with the over-all mood of the place, which was one of remoteness from the modern world. Across the narrow hall from the downstairs living room, a staircase led to the next floor, which contained bedrooms and one of the largest bathrooms I ever saw. Considering the Colonial reluctance to bathe to excess, it struck me as incongruous, until I realized later that the house had had some quasi-public usage at one period.

A few steps led from the living room to the rear section, which was the original portion of the house. A large fireplace dominates it. Next to it is a rear staircase also leading to the upper stories, and the low ceiling shows the original wooden beams just as they were in pre-Revolutionary days.

The Robinsons weren't particularly addicted to the psychic even though they're both Irish, but Mrs. Robinson admits to having had ESP experiences all her life. Whether this is her Irishness (with a well-developed sense of imagination, as she puts it) or just a natural ability, it's there for better or worse. When she was fourteen, she was reading in bed one night, and it was very, very late. This was against the rules, so she had made sure the door to her bedroom was shut. Suddenly, the door opened and her brother Paul stood there looking at her reproachfully. He had been dead for eight years. Dolores screamed and went under the covers. Her mother rushed upstairs to see what was the matter. When she arrived, the door was still wide

open! Since that time, Mrs. Robinson has often known things before they really happened—such as who would be at the door before she answered it, or just before the telephone rang, who would be calling. Today, this is just a game to her, and neither her husband nor she takes it too seriously. Both of them are high school graduates, Dolores has had some college training, and her husband has electro-engineering skills which he uses professionally; nevertheless they don't scoff at the possibility that an old house might contain some elements from its violent past.

When they first moved into the house in 1960, Mrs. Robinson felt right at home in it, as if she had always lived there. From the very first, she found it easy to move up and down the stairs even in the dark without she slightest accident or need to orient herself. It was almost as if the house, or someone it, were guiding her steps.

* * *

But soon the Robinsons became acutely aware that the house was *alive*: There were strange noises and creaking boards, which they promptly ascribed to the settling of an old building. But there were also human footsteps that both husband and wife heard, and there were those doors. The doors, in particular, puzzled them. The first time Mrs. Robinson noticed anything unusual about the doors in their house was when she was working late over some photography assignments she had brought home with her. Her husband was out for the evening and the three children were fast asleep upstairs. The children have their bedrooms on the third floor, while the Robinsons sleep on the second floor. Suddenly Mrs. Robinson heard footsteps on the ceiling above her bedroom. Then the door of the stairwell opened, steps reverberated on the stairs, then the door to the second floor opened, and a blast of cold air hit her. Without taking her eyes from her work, Mrs. Robinson said, "Go back to bed!" assuming it was one of her children who had gotten up for some reason. There was no answer.

She looked up, and there was no one there. Annoyed, she rose and walked up the stairs to check her children's rooms. They were indeed fast asleep. Not satisfied and thinking that one of them must be playing tricks on her, she woke them one by one and questioned them. But they had trouble waking up, and it was evident to Mrs. Robinson that she was on a fool's errand; her children had not been down those stairs.

That was the beginning of a long succession of incidents involving the doors in the house. Occasionally, she would watch with fascination when a door opened quite by itself, without any logical cause, such as wind or draft; or to see a door open for her just as she was about to reach for the doorknob. At least, whatever presence there was in the old house, was polite: It opened the door to a lady! But reassuring it was not, for to live with the unseen can be

A haunted colonial house in Pennsylvania

infuriating, too. Many times she would close a door, only to see it stand wide open again a moment later when she knew very well it could not do that by itself.

She began to wonder whether there wasn't perhaps a hidden tunnel beneath their back living room. Frequently they would hear a booming sound below the floor, coming from the direction of the cold storage room below. The doors would continually open for her now, even when she was alone in the house and the children could not very well be blamed for playing pranks on her. During the summer of 1966, there were nights when the activities in the house rose to frenzy comparable only with the coming and going of large crowds. On one occasion her daughter Leigh came down the stairs at night wondering who was in the living room. She could hear the noises up to the top floor! That night Mrs. Robinson was awakened six times by footsteps and closing doors.

Around that time also, her father-in-law reported a strange experience in his room on the second floor. He was watching television when his door opened late one night, and a woman came in. He was so startled by this unexpected visitor, and she disappeared again so quickly, he did not observe her too closely, but he thought she had either long black hair or a black veil. There was of course no one of that description in the house at the time.

Then there were those moments when an invisible rocking chair in the living room would rock by itself as if someone were in it.

Just prior to our visit, Mrs. Robinson's patience was being sorely tried. It was the week of April 4, and we had

already announced our coming about a week or so afterward. Mrs. Robinson was on the cellar stairs when she heard a clicking sound and looked up. A rotisserie rack was sailing down toward her! Because she had looked up, she was able to duck, and the missile landed on the stairs instead of on her head. But she thought this just too much. Opening doors, well, all right, but rotisserie racks? It was high time we came down to see her.

I carefully went all over the house, examining the walls, floors, and especially the doors. They were for the most part heavy hinged doors, the kind that do not slide easily but require a healthy push before they will move. We looked into the back room and admired the beams, and I must confess I felt very uneasy in that part of the house. Both Catherine and I had an oppressive feeling, as if we were in the presence of something tragic, though unseen, and we could not get out of there fast enough.

I promised the Robinsons to return with a good psychometrist and perhaps have a go at trance, too, if I could get Mrs. Leek to come down with me on her next visit east. The prospect of finding out what it was that made their house so lively, and perhaps even learn more about its colorful past, made the mysterious noises more bearable for the Robinsons, and they promised to be patient and bear with me until I could make the required arrangements.

It was not until June 1967 that the opportunity arose, but finally Mrs. Leek and I were planning to appear on Murray Burnett's radio program together, and when I mentioned what else we intended doing in the area, Murray's eyes lit up and he offered to include himself in the expedition and drive us to and fro.

The offer was gladly accepted, and after a dinner at one of Murray's favorite places—during which not a word was exchanged about the Robinson house—we were off in search of adventure in his car. "If there's one thing I do well," he intoned, as we shot out onto the expressway, "it's driving an automobile." He did indeed. He drove with verve and so fast we missed the proper exit, and before long we found ourselves at a place called King of Prussia, where even a Prussian would have been lost.

We shrugged our combined shoulders and turned around, trying to retrace our steps. Murray assured me he knew the way and would have us at the Robinson house in no time at all. There was a time problem, for we all had to be back in the studio by eleven so that we could do the radio program that night. But the evening was still young and the Pennsylvania countryside lovely.

It was just as well that it was, for we got to see a good deal of it that evening. There was some confusion between Roosevelt Boulevard and Roosevelt Avenue, and the directions I had faithfully written down were being interpreted by us now the way two of Rommel's Afrika Korps officers must have studied the caravan routes.

"We should have turned off where we didn't," I finally remarked, and Murray nodded grimly. The time was about an hour after our appointed hour. No doubt the Robinsons must be thinking we're lost, I thought. At least I hoped that that's what they would think, not that we had abandoned the project.

The neighborhood seemed vaguely familiar now; no doubt it was. We had been through it several times already that same evening. Were the "forces" that kept opening and closing doors at the Robinson homestead preventing our coming so that they could continue to enjoy their anonymity?

When you're lost in Pennsylvania, you're really lost. But now Murray came to a decision. He turned north and we entered an entirely different part of town. It bore no similarity to the direction in which we wanted to go, but at least it was a well-lit section of town. I began to understand Murray's strategy: He was hoping we would run across someone—no, that's an unhappy word—*find* someone who just might know which way Somerton was. We met several motorists who didn't and several others who thought they did but really didn't, as we found out when we tried to follow their directions.

Ultimately, Murray did the smart thing: He hailed the first cop he saw and identified himself, not without pride. Everybody in Philadelphia knew his radio show.

"We're lost, officer," he announced, and explained our predicament.

"It's Mercury retrograding," Sybil mumbled from the back seat. All during our wild ghost chase she had insisted that astrologically speaking it was not at all surprising that we had gotten lost.

"Beg your pardon?" the officer said, and looked inside.

"Never mind Mercury," Murray said impatiently, "will you please show us the way?"

"I'll do better than that, sir," the policeman beamed back, "I'll personally escort you."

The Strange Case of the Colonial Soldier

The dining room, never quite still

And so it came to pass that we followed a siren-tooting patrol car through the thick and thin of suburban Philadelphia.

Suddenly, the car in front of us halted. Murray proved how skillful a driver he really was. He did not hit anyone when he pulled up short. He merely jumbled *us*.

"Anything wrong, officer?" Murray asked, a bit nervously. It was half past nine now.

"My boundary," the officer explained. "I've already telephoned for my colleague to take you on further."

We sat and waited another ten minutes, then another police car came up and whisked us in practically no time to our destination. When the Robinsons saw the police car escort us to their house, they began to wonder what on earth we had been up to. But they were glad to see us, and quickly we entered the house. Sybil was hysterical with laughter by now, and if we had had something to drink en route, the whole odyssey might have been a jolly good party. But now her face froze as she entered the downstairs portion of the house. I watched her change expression, but before I had a chance to question her, she went to the lady's room. On emerging from it she reported that the first word that had impressed itself upon her was a name—"Ross."

She explained that she felt the strongest influence of this person to the right of the fireplace in the oldest part of the house, so I decided we should go to that area and see what else she might pick up.

Although the house itself was started in 1732, the particular section we were in had definitely been dated to 1755 by local historians, all of whom admired the Robin-

son house as a showcase and example of early American houses.

"1746 is what I get," Sybil commented.

"Sybil's underbidding you," I remarked to Mrs. Robinson.

"This is some kind of a meeting place," Sybil continued her appraisal of the room, "many people come here... 1744...and the name Ross. The whole house has an atmosphere which is not unpleasant, but rather *alive*." Just as Mrs. Robinson had felt on first contact with the house, I thought. As for the meeting place, I later found out that the house was used as a Quaker meeting house in the 1740s and later, and even today the "Byberry Friends" meet down the road! John Worthington, the first owner of the house, was an overseer for the meeting house in 1752.

"There are many impressions here," Sybil explained as she psychometrized the room more closely, "many people meeting here, but this is superimposed on one dominant male person, this Ross."

After a moment of further walking about, she added, "The date 1774 seems to be very important."

She pointed at a "closet" to the right of the ancient fireplace, and explained that this personality seemed to be strongest there.

"It's a staircase," Mrs. Robinson volunteered, and opened the door of the "closet." Behind it a narrow, winding wooden staircase led to the upper floors.

I motioned to Sybil to sit down in a comfortable chair near the fireplace, and we grouped ourselves around her. We had perhaps thirty minutes left before we were to return to Philadelphia, but for the moment I did not worry about that. My main concern was the house: What would it tell us about its history? What tragedies took place here and what human emotions were spent in its old walls?

Soon we might know. Sybil was in deep trance within a matter of minutes.

"Ross," the voice speaking through Sybil said faintly now, "I'm Ross. John Ross.... Virtue in peace...."

"Is this your house?"

"No."

"Then what are you doing here?"

"Praying. Hope for peace. Too much blood. People must pray for peace."

"Is there a war going on?"

"I say there's war...the enemies are gone...."

"Are you a soldier?"

"Captain—John—Ross," the voice said, stressing each word as if it were painful to pronounce it.

"What regiment?" I shot back, knowing full well that regimental lists exist and can be checked out for names.

"Twenty-first."

"Calvary or Infantry?"

"I—am—for—peace."

"But what branch of the Army were you in?"

"Twenty-first of Horse."

This is an old English expression for cavalry.

"Who is your superior officer?" I asked.

"Colonel Moss is bad...he must pray...."

"Who commands?"

"Albright."

"Where did you serve?"

"Battle...here...."

He claimed to be thirty-eight years old, having been born in 1726. This would make him thirty-eight in the year 1764. His place of birth was a little place named Verruck, in Holstein, and when he said this I detected a very faint trace of a foreign accent in the entranced voice of the medium.

"Are you German then?" I asked.

"German?" he asked, not comprehending.

"Are you American?"

"American—is good," he said, with appreciation in his voice. Evidently we had before us a mercenary of the British Army.

"Are you British?" I tried.

"Never!" he hissed back.

"Whom do you serve?"

"The thirteen...pray...."

Was he referring to the thirteen colonies, the name by which the young republic was indeed known during the revolutionary war?

"This Albrecht....What is his first name?"

"Dee-an-no...I don't like him....Peace for this country!!! It was meant for peace."

I could not make out what he meant by Dee-an-no, or what sounded like it. I then questioned the personality whether he was hurt.

"I wait for them to fetch me," he explained, haltingly, "sickness, make way for me!"

"Why are you in this house—what is there here?"

"Meeting place to pray."

"What religion are you?"

"Religion of peace and silence."

Suddenly, the medium broke into almost uncontrollable sighs and cries of pain. Tears flowed freely from Sybil's closed eyes. The memory of something dreadful must have returned to the communicator.

"I'm dying...hands hurt....Where is my hand?"

You could almost see the severed hand, and the broken tone of voice realizing the loss made it the more immediate and dramatic.

"I—am—for peace...."

"What sort of people come here?"

"Silent people. To meditate."

What better way to describe a Quaker meeting house?

"Don't stop praying," he beseeched us.

We promised to pray for him. But would he describe his activities in this house?

"Send for the Friend...dying."

He wanted spiritual guidance, now that he was at death's door. The term Friend is the official name for what we now call a Quaker.

Was there someone he wanted us to send for?

"William Proser...my brother...in England."

"Were you born in England?"

"No. William."

"He is your brother?"

"All—men—are brothers."

He seemed to have trouble speaking. I started to explain what our mission was and that we wanted to help him find the elusive peace he so longed for.

"Name some of your fellow officers in the regiment," I then requested.

"Erich Gerhardt," the voice said. "Lieutenant Gerhardt."

"Was he in the cavalry? What regiment?"

"My—cavalry—Twenty-first—"

"What year did you serve together? What year are we in now?"

"Seventy-four."

"Where are you stationed?"

Sybil was completely immersed in the past now, with her face no longer hers; instead, we were watching a man in deep agony, struggling to speak again. Murray Burnett had his fingers at his lips, his eyes focused on the medium. It was clear he had never witnessed anything like it, and the extraordinary scene before him was bound to leave a deep and lasting impression, as indeed it did.

But the question went unanswered. Instead, Sybil was suddenly back again, or part of her, anyway. She seemed strangely distraught, however.

"Hands are asleep," she murmured, and I quickly placed her back into the hypnotic state so that the personality of Captain Ross might continue his testimony.

"Get me out, get me out," Sybil screamed now, "my hands...my hands are asleep...."

I realized that the severed hand or hands of the Colonial soldier had left a strong imprint. Quickly I suggested that she go back into trance. I then recalled her to her own self, suggesting at the same time that no memory of the trance remain in her conscious mind.

Pearls of sweat stood on Sybil's forehead as she opened her eyes. But she was in the clear. Nothing of the preceding hour had remained in her memory. After a moment of heavy silence, we rose. It was time to return to the city, but Murray did not care. He knew that his producer, Ted Reinhart, would stall for time by playing a tape, if need be. The Robinsons offered us a quick cup of coffee, which tasted even more delicious than it must have been, under the circumstances. Everybody was very tense and I thought how wise it had been of Mrs. Robinson to keep the children away from the séance.

Hurriedly, we picked up our gear and drove back to the station. It took us about one-fifth of the time it had taken us to come out. Murray Burnett showed his skill behind the wheel as he literally flew along the expressway. Traffic was light at this hour and we managed to get back just as the announcer said, "And now, ladies and gentlemen, Murray Burnett and his guests...."

As if nothing had happened, we strode onto the platform and did a full hour of light banter. By the time we left Philadelphia to return to New York, though, Sybil was exhausted. When we staggered out of our coaches in New York, it was well past one in the morning. The silence of the night was a welcome relief from the turbulent atmosphere of the early evening.

The following day I started to research the material obtained in the Robinson homestead.

To begin with, the Robinsons were able to trace previous ownership back only to 1841, although the local historical society assured her that it was built in 1732. The early records are often sketchy or no longer in existence because so many wars—both of foreign origin and Indian—have been fought around the area, not counting fire and just plain carelessness.

The Robinsons were the ninth family to own the place since the Civil War period. Prior to that the only thing known for certain was that it was a Quaker meeting house and this fit in with the references Sybil had made in trance.

But what about Ross?

The gentleman had claimed that he was Captain John Ross, and the year, at the beginning of our conversation, was 1764.

In W. C. Ford's *British Officers Serving in America 1754–1774*, I found, on page 88, that there was a certain Captain John Ross, commissioned November 8, 1764. This man of course was a Tory, that is, he would have fought on the side of the British. Now the Revolutionary War started only in April 1775, and the man had expressed a dislike for the British and admiration for the "thirteen," the American colonies. Had he somehow switched sides during the intervening year? If he was a German mercenary, this would not have been at all surprising. Many of these men, often brought here against their desire, either left the British armies or even switched sides. Later on he referred to the date 1774, and Sybil had said it was important. At that time the war was already brewing even though no overt acts had happened. But the atmosphere in this area was tense. It was the seat of the Continental Congress, and skirmishes between Tories and Revolutionaries were not uncommon, although they were on a smaller or even individual level. What traumatic experience had happened to Captain Ross at that time? Did he lose his hands then?

* * *

I needed additional proof for his identity, of course. The name John Ross is fairly common. A John Ross was Betsy Ross's husband. He was guarding munitions on the Philadelphia waterfront one night in 1776 when the munitions and Ross blew up. Another John Ross was a purchasing agent for the Continental Army, and he used much of his own money in the process. Although Robert Morris later tried to help him get his money back, he never really did, and only a year ago his descendants petitioned Congress for payment of this ancient debt of honor. Neither of these was our man, I felt, especially so as I recalled his German accent and the claim that he was born in a little place called Verruck in Holstein. That place name really had me stumped, but with the help of a librarian at the New York Public Library I got hold of some German source books. There is a tiny hamlet near Oldesloe, Holstein, called Viertbruch. An English-speaking person would pronounce this more like "Vertbrook." Although it is not on any ordinary map, it is listed in Mueller's *Grosses Deutsches Wortbuch*, published in Wuppertal in 1958, on page 1008.

Proser, his brother's name, is a German name. Why had he adopted an English name? Perhaps he had spent many years in England and felt it more expedient. He also mentioned belonging to the 21st Cavalry Regiment. The Captain John Ross I found in the records served in the 31st, not the 21st. On the other hand, there is, curiously enough, another Ross, first name David, listed for the 21st Regiment for the period in question, 1774.

I could not trace the superior named Albright or Albrecht, not knowing whether this was someone German or English. Since the first name given us by the communicator was unclear, I can't even be sure if the Philip Albright, a captain in the Pennsylvania Rifles 1776–77,

according to F. B. Heitman, *Historical Register of the Continental Army during the War of the Revolution*, is this man. This Philip Albright was a rebel, and if he was only a captain in 1776 he could not have been John Ross commanding officer in 1774, unless he had changed sides, of course.

I was more successful with the fellow officer Lieutenant "Gerhardt," who also served in "his" 21st Regiment, Ross had claimed. Spellings of names at that period are pretty free, of course, and as I only heard the names without any indication as to proper spelling, we must make allowances for differences in the letters of these names. I did trace a Brevet Lieutenant Gerard (first name not given) of the Dragoons, a cavalry regiment, who served in the Pulaski Legion from September 3, 1778 to 1782.

Is this our man? Did he change sides after the Revolutionary War started in earnest? He could have been a regimental comrade of John Ross in 1774 and prior. The source for this man's data is F. B. Heitman's *Historical Register of the Continental Army*, Volume 1775–83, page 189. The Pulaski Legion was not restricted to Polish volunteers who fought for the new republic, but it accepted voluntary help from any quarters, even former Britishers or mercenaries so long as they wanted to fight for a free America. Many Germans also served in that legion.

* * *

The Colonel Moss who was "bad" might have been Colonel Mosses Allen, a Tory, who was from this area and who died February 8, 1779. He is listed in Saffell's *Records of the Revolutionary War.*

It was a confusing period in our history, and men changed their minds and sides as the need of the times demanded. Had the unfortunate soldier whom we had found trapped here in this erstwhile Quaker meeting house been one of those who wanted to get out from under, first to join what he considered "the good boys," and then, repelled by the continuing bloodshed, could he not even accept *their* war? Had he become religiously aware through his Quaker contacts and had he been made a pacifist by them? Very likely, if one is to judge the words of the colonial soldier from the year 1774 as an indication. His plea for peace sounds almost as if it could be spoken today.

* * *

Captain John Ross was not an important historical figure, nor was he embroiled in an event of great significance in the overall development of the United States of America. But this very anonymity made him a good subject for our psychometric experiment. Sybil Leek surely could not have known of Captain Ross, his comrades, and the Quaker connections of the old house on Byberry Road. It was her psychic sense that probed into the impressions left behind by history as it passed through and onward relentlessly, coating the house on Byberry Road with an indelible layer of human emotions and conflict.

* * *

I sincerely hope we managed to "decommission" Captain Ross in the process of our contact, to give him that much-desired "peace and silence" at last.

✳ 49

The House on Plant Avenue

PLANT AVENUE IS a charming suburban boulevard running through one of the better sectors of Webster Groves, Missouri, in itself a better-than-average small town, near St. Louis. Plant Avenue is not known for anything in particular except perhaps that it does have some plants, mainly very old trees that give it a coolness other streets lack, even in the heat of summer when this part of the country can be mighty unpleasant.

Webster Groves wasn't much of a landmark either until *Life* magazine published an article on its high school activities, and then it had a short-lived flurry of excitement as the "typical" American upper-middle-class town with all its vices and virtues. But now the town has settled back to being just one of many such towns and the people along Plant Avenue sigh with relief that the notoriety has ebbed. They are not the kind that enjoy being in the headlines and the less one pays attention to them, the happier they are.

In the three hundred block of Plant Avenue there are mainly large bungalow type houses standing in wide plots and surrounded by shrubbery and trees. One of these houses is a two-story wood and brick structure of uncertain style, but definitely distinguished looking in its own peculiar way. The roof suggests old English influences and the wide windows downstairs are perhaps southern, but the overall impression is that of a home built by an individualist who wanted it his way and only his way. It does not look like any other house on the block, yet fits in perfectly and harmoniously. The house is somewhat set back and there is a garden around it, giving it privacy. From the street one walks up a front lawn, then up a few stairs and into the house. The downstairs contains a large living room, a day room and a kitchen with a rear exit directly into the garden. From the living room, there is a winding staircase to the upper floor where the bedrooms are located.

The house was built in the final years of the last century by a man of strange character. The neighborhood knew little enough about this Mr. Gehm. His business was the circus and he seems to have dealt with various circus performers and represented them in some way. He was not a good mixer and kept mainly to himself and ultimately died in the house he had built for himself.

This much was known around the neighborhood, but to tell the truth, people don't much care what you do so long as you don't bother them, and the real estate agent who took on the house after Mr. Gehm passed away was more concerned with its wiring and condition than Mr. Gehm's unusual occupation. As the house had a certain nobility about it, perhaps due to the German background of its builder, it seemed a good bet for resale and so it turned out to be.

In 1956 the house passed into the hands of Mr. and Mrs. S. L. Furry, who had been married twenty years at the time, and had two young daughters, now long married also.

Mrs. Furry's ancestry was mainly English and she worked for the Washington University Medical school in St. Louis, having been a major in psychology in college.

Thus she found herself more than shaken when she discovered some peculiarities about the house they had moved into—such as being awakened, night after night at precisely 2 A.M. with a feeling of having been shaken awake. On one occasion, she clearly heard a heavy hammer hit the headboard of her bed, turned on the lights only to discover everything intact where she was sure she would find splinters and a heavy indentation. Soon this was amplified by the sound of something beating against the windows at night. "It sounds just like a heavy bird," Mrs. Furry thought, and shuddered. There was nothing visible that could have caused the sounds.

One morning she discovered one of the heavy wall sconces, downstairs, on the floor. Yet it had been securely fastened to the wall the night before. On examination she discovered no logical reason for how the piece could have fallen.

By now she realized that the footsteps she kept hearing weren't simply caused by overwrought nerves due to fatigue or simply her imagination. The footsteps went up and down the stairs, day and night, as if someone were scurrying about looking for something and not finding it. They always ended on the upstairs landing.

At first, she did not wish to discuss these matters with her husband because she knew him to be a practical man who would simply not believe her. And a woman is always vulnerable when it comes to reporting the psychic. But eventually he noticed her concern and the problem was brought out into the open. He readily remarked he had heard nothing to disturb his sleep and advised his wife to forget it.

But shortly after, he sheepishly admitted at the breakfast table that he, too, had heard some odd noises. "Of course, there must be a logical explanation," he added quickly. "It is very likely only the contraction and expansion of the old house. Lots of old houses do that." He seemed satisfied with this explanation, but Mrs. Furry was not. She still heard those scurrying footfalls and they did not sound to her like a house contracting.

Eventually, Mr. Furry did not insist on his explanation, but had no better one to offer and decided to shrug the whole thing off. One night he was awakened in the bedroom adjoining his wife's boudoir because of something strange: he then noticed a filmy, white shape go *through the door* into the hall and proceed into their little girl's room. He jumped out of bed and looked into the room, but could see nothing. "Must have been the reflection of car lights from the street," he concluded. But it never happened again, and cars kept passing the house at all hours.

The years went on and the Furry's got somewhat used to their strange house. They had put so much money and work into it, not to say love, that they were reluctant to let a ghost dislodge them. But they did become alarmed when their three-year-old child kept asking at breakfast, "Who is the lady dressed in black who comes into my room at night?" As no lady in black had been to the house at any time, this of course upset the parents.

"What lady?" Mrs. Furry demanded to know.

"The lady," the three-year-old insisted. "She's got a little boy by the hand."

Some time later, the child complained about the lady in black again. "She spanks me with a broom, but it doesn't hurt," she said. Mrs. Furry did not know what to do. Clearly there was something in the house the real estate people had failed to tell her about. After nine years, they found a better house—one more suitable to their needs—and moved. Again, the house on Plant Avenue was for sale. It wasn't long until a new tenant for the handsome house appeared.

In the middle of November 1965, the Walshes rented the house and moved in with two of their three children, ten-year-old Wendy and twenty-year-old Sandy. They had of course not been told anything about the experiences of the previous owners and they found the house pleasant and quiet, at least at first.

A short time after moving in, Mrs. Walsh was preparing dinner in the kitchen. She was alone except for her dog. The time was 6:30. Suddenly, she noticed the dog cringe with abject fear. This puzzled her and she wondered what the cause was. Looking up, she noticed a white cloud, roughly the shape and height of a human being, float in through the open door leading into the living room. The whole thing only lasted a moment but she had never seen anything like it.

"A ghost!" she thought immediately, for that was exactly what is looked like. Clare Walsh is not a simple-minded believer in the supernatural. She has a master's degree in biochemistry and did research professionally for five years. But what she saw was, indeed a ghost! She wasn't frightened. In fact, she felt rather good, for her sneaking suspicion had been confirmed. On the day she first set foot into the house, when they had not yet taken it, she had had a deep feeling that there was a presence there. She dismissed it as being a romantic notion at the time, but evidently her intuition had been correct. With a sigh Mrs. Walsh accepted her psychic talents. This wasn't the first time that they had shown themselves.

At the time her husband's ship was torpedoed, she dreamed the whole incident in detail. When she was a child, her aunt died, and she saw her aunt's apparition before anyone in the family knew she had passed on. Since then she had developed a good deal of telepathy, especially with her daughters.

She dismissed the apparition she had seen in the kitchen, especially since nothing similar followed. But the nights seemed strangely active. At night, the house came to life. Noises of human activity seemed to fill the halls and rooms and in the darkness Mrs. Wash felt unseen presences roaming about her house at will. It wasn't a pleasant feeling but she decided to brave it our and wait for some kind of opening wedge, whereby she could find out more about the background of her house. In February 1966, her neighbors next door invited them to dinner.

Over dinner, the question of the house came up and casually Mrs. Walsh was asked how quiet the house was. With that, she confessed her concern and reported what she had seen and heard. The neighbors—a couple named Kurus—nodded to each other with silent understanding.

"There seems to be a pattern to these noises," Mrs. Walsh said, "it's always at 4 A.M. and upstairs."

The Kurus had almost bought the house themselves but were dissuaded from it by the experiences of another neighbor who lived across the street. The man had been a frequent house guest at the house and while there, had encountered ghostly phenomena sufficient to convince him that the house was indeed haunted. The Kurus then bought the house next door instead. When Mrs. Walsh obtained the name of the man across the street, she called him and asked what he knew about their house.

"The original owner has hidden some valuables in a number of places, niches, all over the houses," the gentleman explained, "and now he's looking for his treasures."

One of those secret hiding places apparently was the fireplace downstairs. Upon putting down the receiver, Mrs. Walsh started to examine the fireplace. There was a strange hollow sound in one spot, but unless she took tools to pry it open, there was no way of telling what, if anything, was hidden there.

The vague promise of hidden treasure was not sufficient to outweigh the pride of ownership in a handsome fireplace, so she did not proceed to cut open the fireplace, but instead went to bed.

About midnight she was awakened by a peculiar, musty odor in the room. She got up and walked about the room, but the musty door lingered on. It reminded her of the smell of death.

The next morning she told her husband about it.

"Ridiculous," he laughed, but the following morning the same odor invaded his bedroom and he, too, smelled it. Since Mr. Walsh works for a large chemical concern odors are his business, in a manner of speaking. But he could not classify the peculiar odor he was confronted with in his own house.

After that, not much happened beyond the 4 A.M. noises that kept recurring with punctuality—almost of Germanic character.

But Mrs. Walsh noticed that the door to the attic was always open. The stairs leading up to the attic from the second story have a stair whose tread lifts. Underneath the stairs she discovered a hollow space! So the tales of hidden treasure might have some basis of fact after all, she mused. The secret space was once completely closed, but the catch had long disappeared.

On one occasion, when Mr. Walsh was down with the flu, he used an adjoining bedroom. While Mrs. Walsh was resting she heard the attic door open and close again four times, and thought it was her husband going to the bathroom. But he had only been up once that night. The other three times, it was another person, one they could not see.

As time went on, Mrs. Walsh kept notes of all occurrences, more as a sport than from fear. Both she and her husband, and soon the children, kept hearing the footsteps going up to the attic, pausing at the now empty hiding place. Each following morning the attic door, securely closed the night before, was found wide open. It got to be such a routine they stopped looking for *real* people as the possible culprits. They knew by now they wouldn't find anyone.

One morning she went up to the attic and closed the door again, then continued with her breakfast work in the kitchen. Suddenly she had the strange urge to return to the attic once more. Almost as if led by a force outside of herself, she dropped the bread knife and went up the stairs. The door was open again, and she stepped through it into a small room they had never used for anything but storage. It was chock-full of furniture, all of it securely fastened and closed.

To her amazement, when she entered the little room, things were in disorder. The heavy chest of drawers at one side had a drawer opened wide. She stepped up to it and saw it was filled with blueprints. She picked one of them up, again as if led by someone, and at the bottom of the blueprint saw the name "Henry Gehm."

She had been looking in the attic for a supposedly hidden doorway and had never been able to locate it. Was it after all just gossip and was there no hidden door?

At this moment, she had held the blueprints of the house in her hands, she received the distinct impression she should look in a certain spot in the attic. As she did, she noticed that the furniture against that wall had recently been moved. No one of flesh and blood had been up there for years, of course, and this discovery did not contribute to her sense of comfort. But as she looked closer she saw there was now a door where before a large piece of furniture had blocked the view!

Who had moved the furniture?

She felt a chill run down her back as she stood there. It wasn't the only time she had felt cold. Many times a cold blast of air, seemingly out of nowhere, had enveloped

her in the bedroom or in the kitchen. As she thought of it now, she wondered why she had not investigated the source of that air but taken it for granted. Perhaps she did not want to know the results.

The events in the attic occurred on March 1, 1966. The following day, she was awakened quite early by incessant footsteps in the hallway. Someone was walking up and down, someone she could not see.

She got up. At that moment, she was distinctly impressed with the *command* to take out an old music box that had belonged to her mother. The box had not played for years and was in fact out of order. She opened the box and it started to play. It has remained in working order ever since. Who had fixed it and was this a reward for having looked at the blueprints for "someone?"

On March 5, she was roused from deep sleep once more at the "witching hour" of 4 A.M., but the house was quiet, strangely so, and she wondered why she had been awakened. But she decided to have a look downstairs. In the dining room, the breakfront which she had left closed the night before, stood wide open. The teaspoons in one of the drawers had been rearranged by unseen hands! A plant had a shoot broken off and the twig lay on the table nearby. Since the dog had not been in the room, there was no one who could have done this.

The next day, her sleep was interrupted again at 4 o'clock. This time the drawer containing her underclothes was all shaken up. Suddenly it dawned on her that her ten-year-old daughter might have spoken the truth when she reported "someone" in her mother's bedroom opening and closing the dresser when Mrs. Walsh knew for sure she had not been in the room.

She realized now what it was. The bedroom she occupied had been Henry Gehm's room. If he had hidden anything in it, he might be mistaking her dresser for his own furniture and still keep looking.

On March 8 Mrs. Walsh was in the basement, and her ten-year-old girl, Wendy, was in the garden playing. The house was quite empty.

Suddenly, she heard the sound of a child running at a mad pace through the dining room and kitchen. It must be Sandy, she thought, and called out to her. She received no reply. She went upstairs to investigate and found the house empty and quiet. Yet the footsteps had been those of a child, not the same footfalls she had so often heard on the stairs and in the attic. So there were two of them now, she thought, with a shudder.

It was then also that she recalled the baby hair she had found under the couch shortly after they had first moved in. At the time she had dismissed it as unimportant, even though no one with *blond* hair lived in the house. The hair was very fine, clearly blond and seemed like the hair of a very young child.

"Like angel's hair," she thought and wondered.

Five days later all but Mr. Walsh were out of the house, in church. He was still in bed, but after the family had left for church he came downstairs, and fixed himself breakfast in the kitchen. At that moment, he thought he heard Wendy running upstairs.

He assumed the child was not well and had been left behind, after all. Worried, he went upstairs to see what was the matter. No child. He shook his head and returned to his breakfast, less sure that the house didn't have "something strange" in it.

Upon the return of the others, they discussed it and came to the conclusion that the house was haunted by at least two, possibly three, people. It was a large enough house, but to share one's home with people one could not see was not the most practical way to live.

A few days later Mrs. Walsh was again in the basement, doing the laundry. A sweater hanging from the rafters on the opposite side of the basement suddenly jumped down from the rafters, hanger and all, and landed in front of her. The windows were firmly closed and there was no breeze. What amazed Mrs. Walsh even more was the way the sweater came down. Not straight as if pulled by gravity, but in an ark, as if held by unseen hands.

"Mrs. Gehm," she heard herself exclaiming. "What did you do that for?"

There she was talking to a ghost.

What is your first name, anyway? she heard herself think.

Instantly, a counterthought flashed into her mind. My name is Mary.

On March 16 she woke again early in the morning with the sure sensation of not being alone. Although she could not see anyone, she knew there was someone upstairs again. However she decided to stay in bed this time. First thing in the morning, as soon as its was *light*, she ventured up the stairs to the attic. In the little room the furniture had been completely reshuffled! She then recalled having heard a dull thud during the night.

A trunk had been moved to the center of the room and opened; a doll house had been placed from one shelf to a much lower shelf, and a tool box she had never seen before had suddenly appeared in the room. There were fresh markings in the old dust of the room. They looked like a child's scrawl....

Mrs. Walsh looked at the scrawl. It looked as if someone had made a crude attempt to write a name in the dust. She tried to decipher it, but could not. The next day she returned to the room. No one had been there. The children were by now much too scared to go up there.

The scribbled signature was still there, and not far from it, someone had made handprint in the dust. *A small child's hand!*

As Mrs. Walsh stared at the print of the child's hand, it came back to her how she had the month before heard a child's voice crying somewhere in the house. None of her children had been the cause of the crying, she knew, and yet the crying persisted. Then on another occasion, a humming sound such as children like to make, had come to her attention, but she could determine no visible source for it.

Two days later, still bewildered by all this, she found herself again alone in the house. It was afternoon, and she clearly heard the muffled sound of several voices talking. She ran up the stairs to the attic—for it seemed to her that most of the phenomena originated here—and sure enough the door to the attic, which she had shut earlier, was wide open again.

Early the next morning Mrs. Walsh heard someone calling a child up in the attic. Who was up there? Not any of the Walshes, she made sure. Slowly it dawned upon her that a family from the past was evidently unaware of the passage of time and that the house was no longer theirs. But how to tell them?

A busy family it was, too. At 5 A.M. one morning a typewriter was being worked. The only typewriter in the house stood in Wendy's room. Had she used it? She hadn't, but that morning she found her typewriter *had* been used by someone. The cover had been put back differently from the way she always did it. A doll she had left next to the machine the night before was now on top of it.

That night, while the family was having dinner in the kitchen, the lights in the living were turned on by unseen forces. Pieces of brightly wrapped candy disappeared from a tray and were never seen again.

The dog, too, began to change under the relentless turn of events. She would refuse to sleep in the basement or go near certain spots where most of the psychic phenomena had occurred. The seven-year-old dog, once the very model of a quiet suburban canine, soon turned into a neurotic, fear-ridden shadow of her former self.

It got to be a little too much for the Walshes.

The treasure Mr. Gehm was haunting had no doubt long ago been found and taken away by some earlier tenant or stranger. As for the house itself, the ghosts could have it, if they wanted it that much. The Walshes decided to build a new home of their own, from scratch. No more old homes for them. That way, they would not inherit the ghosts of previous owners.

They notified the owner of their intent to move and as soon as the new home was ready, they moved out.

Even on the last day, the sounds of footsteps scurrying up the stairs could be heard.

Plant Avenue gossips can add another chapter to the lore of the Gehm house, but the sad little girl up in the attic won't have any playmates now. Even if they couldn't see her, the children knew she was *there*.

And that's all a ghost can hope for, really.

The Whaley House Ghosts

I FIRST HEARD about the ghosts at San Diego's Whaley House through an article in *Cosmic Star*, Merle Gould's psychic newspaper, back in 1963. The account was not too specific about the people who had experienced something unusual at the house, but it did mention mysterious footsteps, cold drafts, unseen presences staring over one's shoulder and the scent of perfume where no such odor could logically be—the gamut of uncanny phenomena, in short. My appetite was whetted. Evidently the curators, Mr. and Mrs. James Redding, were making some alterations in the building when the haunting began.

I marked the case as a possibility when in the area, and turned to other matters. Then fate took a hand in bringing me closer to San Diego.

I had appeared on Regis Philbin's network television show and a close friendship had developed between us. When Regis moved to San Diego and started his own program there, he asked me to be his guest.

We had already talked of a house he knew in San Diego that he wanted me to investigate with him; it turned out to be the same Whaley House. Finally we agreed on June 25th as the night we would go to the haunted house and film a trance session with Sybil Leek, then talk about it the following day on Regis' show.

Sybil Leek came over from England a few years ago, after a successful career as a producer and writer of television documentaries and author of a number of books on animal life and antiques. At one time she ran an antique shop in her beloved New Forest area of southern England, but her name came to the attention of Americans primarily because of her religious convictions: she happened to be a witch. Not a Halloween type witch, to be sure, but a follower of "the Old Religion," the pre-Christian Druidic cult which is still being practiced in many parts of the world. Her personal involvement with witchcraft was of less interest to me than her great abilities as a trance medium. I tested her and found her capable of total "dissociation of personality," which is the necessary requirement for good trance work. She can get "out of her own body" under my prodding, and lend it to whatever personality might be present in the atmosphere of our quest. Afterwards, she will remember nothing and merely continue pleasantly where we left off in conversation prior to trance—even if it is two hours later! Sybil Leek lends her ESP powers exclusively to my research and confines her "normal" activities to a career in writing and business.

We arrived in sunny San Diego ahead of Regis Philbin, and spent the day loafing at the Half Moon Inn, a romantic luxury motel on a peninsula stretching out into San Diego harbor. Regis could not have picked a better

place for us—it was almost like being in Hawaii. We dined with Kay Sterner, president and chief sensitive of the local California Parapsychology Foundation, a charming and knowledgeable woman who had been to the haunted Whaley House, but of course she did not talk about it Sybil's presence. In deference to my policy she waited until Sybil left us. Then she told me of her forays into Whaley House, where she had felt several presences. I thanked her and decided to do my own investigating from scratch.

My first step was to contact June Reading, who was not only the director of the house but also its historian. She asked me to treat confidentially whatever I might find in the house through psychic means. This I could not promise, but I offered to treat the material with respect and without undue sensationalism, and I trust I have not disappointed Mrs. Reading too much. My readers are entitled to all the facts as I find them.

Mrs. Reading herself is the author of a booklet about the historic house, and a brief summary of its development also appears in a brochure given to visitors, who keep coming all week long from every part of the country. I quote from the brochure.

The Whaley House, in the heart of Old Town, San Diego—restored, refurnished and opened for public viewing—represents one of the finest examples extant of early California buildings.

Original construction of the two-story mansion was begun on May 6, 1856, by Thomas Whaley, San Diego pioneer. The building was completed on May 10, 1857. Bricks used in the structure came from a clay-bed and kiln—the first brick-yard in San Diego—which Thomas Whaley established 300 yards to the southwest of his projected home.

Much of "old San Diego's" social life centered around this impressive home. Later the house was used as a theater for a traveling company, "The Tanner Troupe," and at one time served as the San Diego County Court House.

The Whaley House was erected on what is now the corner of San Diego Avenue and Harney Street, on a 150-by-217-foot lot, which was part of an 8½-acre parcel purchased by Whaley on September 25, 1855. The North room originally was a granary without flooring, but was remodeled when it became the County Court House on August 12, 1869.

Downstairs rooms include a tastefully furnished parlor, a music room, a library and the annex, which served as the County Court House. There are four bedrooms upstairs, two of which were leased to "The Tanner Troupe" for theatricals.

Perhaps the most significant historical event involving the Whaley House was the surreptitious transfer of the county court records from it to "New Town," present site of downtown San Diego, on the night of March 31, 1871.

Despite threats to forcibly prevent even legal transfer of the court house to "New Town," Col. Chalmers Scott, then county clerk and recorder, and his henchmen removed the county records under cover of darkness and transported them to a "New Town" building at 6th and G Streets.

The Whaley House would be gone today but for a group of San Diegans who prevented its demolition in 1956 by forming the Historical Shrine Foundation of San Diego County and buying the land and the building.

Later, the group convinced the County of San Diego that the house should be preserved as an historical museum, and restored to its early-day spendor. This was done under the supervision and guidance of an advisory committee including members of the Foundation, which today maintains the Whaley House as an historical museum.

Most of the furnishings, authenticated as in use in Whaley's time, are from other early-day San Diego County homes and were donated by interested citizens.

The last Whaley to live in the house was Corinne Lillian Whaley, youngest of Whaley's six children. She died at the age of 89 in 1953. Whaley himself died December 14, 1890, at the age of 67. He is buried in San Diego in Mount Hope Cemetery, as is his wife, Anna, who lived until February 24, 1913.

When it became apparent that a thorough investigation of the haunting would be made, and that all of San Diego would be able to learn of it through television and newspapers, excitement mounted to a high pitch.

Mrs. Reading kept in close touch with Regis Philbin and me, because ghosts have a way of "sensing" an impending attempt to oust them—and this was not long in coming. On May 24th the "activities" inside the house had already increased to a marked degree; they were of the same general nature as previously noticed sounds.

Was the ghost getting restless?

I had asked Mrs. Reading to prepare an exact account of all occurrences within the house, from the very first moment on, and to assemble as many of the witnesses as possible for further interrogation.

Most of these people had worked part-time as guides in the house during the five years since its restoration. The phenomena thus far had occurred, or at any rate been observed, mainly between 10 A.M. and 5:30 P.M., when the house closes to visitors. There is no one there at night, but an effective burglar alarm system is in operation to prevent flesh-and-blood intruders from breaking in unnoticed. Ineffective with the ghostly kind, as we were soon to learn!

I shall now quote the director's own report. It vouches for the accuracy and caliber of witnesses.

PHENOMENA OBSERVED AT WHALEY HOUSE

By Visitors

Oct 9, 1960—Dr. & Mrs. Kirbey, of New Westminster, B.C., Canada, 1:30—2:30 P.M. (He was then Director of the Medical Association of New Westminster.)

The Whaley House—San Diego, California

While Dr. Kirbey and his wife were in the house, she became interested in an exhibit in one of the display cases and she asked if she might go through by herself, because she was familiar with the Victorian era, and felt very much at home in these surroundings. Accordingly, I remained downstairs with the Doctor, discussing early physicians and medical practices.

When Mrs. Kirbey returned to the display room, she asked me in a hesitating fashion if I had ever noticed anything unusual about the upstairs. I asked her what she had noticed. She reported that when she started upstairs, she felt a breeze over her head, and though she saw nothing, felt a pressure against her, that seemed to make it hard for her to go up. When she looked into the rooms, she had the feeling that someone was standing behind her, in fact so close to her that she turned around several times to look. She said she expected someone would tap her on the shoulder. When she joined us downstairs, we all walked toward the courtroom. As we entered, again Mrs. Kirbey turned to me and asked if I knew that someone inhabited the courtroom. She pointed to the bailiff's table, saying as she did, "Right over there." I asked her if the person was clear enough for her to describe, and she said:

"I see a small figure of a woman who has a swarthy complexion. She is wearing a long full skirt, reaching to the floor. The skirt appears to be of calico or gingham, small print. She has a kind of cap on her head, dark hair and eyes and she is wearing gold hoops in her pierced ears. She seems to stay in this room, lives here, I gather, and I get the impression we are sort of invading her privacy."

Mrs. Kirbey finished her description by asking me if any of the Whaley family were swarthy, to which I replied, "No."

This was, to my knowledge, the only description given to an apparition by a visitor, and Mrs. Kirbey the only person who brought up the fact in connection with the courtroom. Many of the visitors have commented

Today, a haunted museum, the Whaley House attracts many tourists

upon the atmosphere in this room, however, and some people attempting to work in the room mentioned upon the difficulty they have in trying to concentrate here.

By Persons Employed at Whaley House

April, 1960, 10:00 A.M. By myself, June A. Reading, 3447 Kite St. Sound of Footsteps—in the Upstairs.

This sound of someone walking across the floor, I first heard in the morning, a week before the museum opened to the public. County workmen were still painting some shelving in the hall, and during this week often arrived before I did, so it was not unusual to find them already at work when I arrived.

This morning, however, I was planning to furnish the downstairs rooms, and so hurried in and down the hall to open the back door awaiting the arrival of the trucks with the furnishings. Two men followed me down the hall; they were going to help with the furniture arrangement. As I reached up to unbolt the back door, I heard the sound of what seemed to be someone walking across the bedroom floor. I paid no attention, thinking it was one of the workmen. But the men, who heard the sounds at the time I did, insisted I go upstairs and find out who was in the house. So, calling out, I started to mount the stairs. Halfway up, I could see no lights, and that the outside shutters to the windows were still closed. I made some comment to the men who had followed me, and turned around to descend the stairs. One of the men joked with me about the spirits coming in to look things over, and we promptly forgot the matter.

However, the sound of walking continued. And for the next six months I found myself going upstairs to see if someone was actually upstairs. This would happen during the day, sometimes when visitors were in other parts of the house, other times when I was busy at my desk trying to catch up on correspondence or bookwork.

At times it would sound as though someone were descending the stairs, but would fade away before reaching the first floor. In September, 1962, the house was the subject of a news article in the *San Diego Evening Tribune*, and this same story was reprinted in the September 1962 issue of *Fate* magazine.

* * *

Oct. & Nov. 1962 We began to have windows in the upper part of the house open unaccountably. We installed horizontal bolts on three windows in the front bedroom, thinking this would end the matter. However, the really disturbing part of this came when it set off our burglar alarm in the night, and we were called by the police and San Diego Burglar Alarm Co. to come down and see if the house had been broken into. Usually, we would find nothing disturbed. (One exception to this was when the house was broken into by vandals, about 1963, and items from the kitchen display stolen.)

In the fall of 1962, early October, while engaged in giving a talk to some school children, a class of 25 pupils, I heard a sound of someone walking, which seemed to come from the roof. One of the children interrupted me, asking what that noise was, and excusing myself from them, I went outside the building, down on the street to see if workmen from the County were repairing the roof. Satisfied that there was no one on the roof of the building, I went in and resumed the tour.

Residents of Old Town are familiar with this sound, and tell me that it has been evident for years. Miss Whaley, who lived in the house for 85 years, was aware of it. She passed away in 1953.

Mrs. Grace Bourquin, 2938 Beech St. Sat. Dec. 14, 1963, noon—Was seated in the hall downstairs having lunch, when she heard walking sound in upstairs.

Sat. Jan. 10, 1964, 1:30 P.M.—Walked down the hall and looked up the staircase. On the upper landing she saw an apparition—the figure of a man, clad in frock

coat and pantaloons, the face turned away from her, so she could not make it out. Suddenly it faded away.

Lawrence Riveroll, resides on Jefferson St., Old Town. Jan. 5, 1963, 12:30 noon—Was alone in the house. No visitors present at the time. While seated at the desk in the front hall, heard sounds of music and singing, described as a woman's voice. Song "Home Again." Lasted about 30 seconds.

Jan. 7, 1963, 1:30 P.M.—Visitors in upstairs. Downstairs, he heard organ music, which seemed to come from the courtroom, where there is an organ. Walked into the room to see if someone was attempting to play it. Cover on organ was closed. He saw no one in the room.

Jan. 19, 1963, 5:15 P.M.—Museum was closed for the day. Engaged in closing shutters downstairs. Heard footsteps in upper part of house in the same area as described. Went up to check, saw nothing.

Sept. 10–12, 1964—at dusk, about 5:15 P.M.— Engaged in closing house, together with another worker. Finally went into the music room, began playing the piano. Suddenly felt a distinct pressure on his hands, as though someone had their hands on his. He turned to look toward the front hall, in the direction of the desk, hoping to get the attention of the person seated there, when he saw the apparition of a slight woman dressed in a hoop skirt. In the dim light was unable to see clearly the face. Suddenly the figure vanished.

J. Milton Keller, 4114 Middlesex Dr. Sept. 22, 1964, 2:00 P.M.—Engaged in tour with visitors at the parlor, when suddenly he, together with people assembled at balustrade, noticed crystal drops hanging from lamp on parlor table begin to swing back and forth. This occurred only on one side of the lamp. The other drops did not move. This continued about two minutes.

Dec. 15, 1964, 5:15 P.M.—Engaged in closing house along with others. Returned from securing restrooms, walked down hall, turned to me with the key, while I stepped into the hall closer to reach for the master switch which turns off all lights. I pulled the switch, started to turn around to step out, when he said, "Stop, don't move, you'll step on the dog!" He put his hands out, in a gesture for me to stay still. Meantime, I turned just in time to see what resembled a flash of light between us, and what appeared to be the back of a dog, scurry down the hall and turn into the dining room. I decided to resume a normal attitude, so I kidded him a little about trying to scare me. Other people were present in the front hall at the time, waiting for us at the door, so he turned to them and said in a rather hurt voice that I did not believe him. I realized then that he had witnessed an apparition, so I asked him to see if he could describe it. *He said he saw a spotted dog, like a fox terrier, that ran with his ears flapping, down the hall and into the dining room.*

May 29, 1965, 2:30 P.M.—Escorting visitors through house, upstairs. Called to me, asking me to come up. Upon going up, he, I and visitors all witnessed a black rocking chair, moving back and forth as if occupied by a person. It had started moving unaccountably, went on about three minutes. Caused quite a stir among visitors.

Dec. 27, 1964, 5:00 P.M.—Late afternoon, prior to closing, *saw the apparition of a woman dressed in a green plaid gingham dress.* She had long dark hair, coiled up in a bun at neck, was seated on a settee in bedroom.

Feb. 1965, 2:00 P.M.—Engaged in giving a tour with visitors, when two elderly ladies called and asked him to come upstairs, and step over to the door of the nursery. These ladies, visitors, called his attention to a sound that was like the cry of a baby, about 16 months old. All three reported the sound.

More psychic photographs taken by the Whaley House staff

March 24, 1965, 1:00 P.M.—He, together with Mrs. Bourquin and his parents, Mr. and Mrs. Keller, engaged in touring the visitors, when for some reason his attention was directed to the foot of the staircase. He walked back to it, and heard the sound of someone in the upper part of the house whistling. No one was in the upstairs at the time.

Mrs. Suzanne Pere, 106 Albatross, El Cajon. April 8, 1963, 4:30 P.M.—Was engaged in typing in courtroom, working on manuscript. Suddenly she called to me, calling my attention to a noise in the upstairs. We both stopped work, walked up the stairs together, to see if anyone could possibly be there. As it was near closing time, we decided to secure the windows. Mrs. Pere kept noticing a chilly breeze at the back of her head, had the distinct feeling that someone, though invisible, was pre-

sent and kept following her from one window to another.

Oct. 14, 21; Nov. 18, 1964—During the morning and afternoon on these days, called my attention to the smell of cigar smoke, and the fragrance of perfume or cologne. This occurred in the parlor, the upstairs hall and bedroom. In another bedroom she called my attention to something resembling dusting powder.

Nov. 28, 1964, 2:30 P.M.—Reported seeing an apparition in the study. A group of men there, dressed in frock coats, some with plain vests, others figured material. One of this group had a large gold watch chain across vest. Seemed to be a kind of meeting; all figures were animated, some pacing the floor, others conversing; all serious and agitated, but oblivious to everything else. One figure in this group seemed to be an official, and stood off by himself. This person was of medium stocky build, light brown hair, and mustache which was quite full and long. He had very piercing light blue eyes, penetrating gaze. Mrs. Pere sensed that he was some kind of official, a person of importance. He seemed about to speak. Mrs. Pere seemed quite exhausted by her experience witnessing this scene, yet was quite curious about the man with the penetrating gaze. I remember her asking me if I knew of anyone answering this description, because it remained with her for some time.

Oct. 7, 1963, 10:30 A.M.—Reported unaccountable sounds issuing from kitchen, as though someone were at work there. Same day, she reported smelling the odor of something baking.

Nov. 27, 1964, 10:15 A.M.—Heard a distinct noise from kitchen area, as though something had dropped to the floor. I was present when this occurred. She called to me and asked what I was doing there, thinking I had been rearranging exhibit. At this time I was at work in courtroom, laying out work. Both of us reached the kitchen, to find one of the utensils on the shelf rack had disengaged itself, fallen to the floor, and had struck a copper boiler directly below. No one else was in the house at the time, and we were at a loss to explain this.

Mrs. T.R. Allen, 3447 Kite Street—Was present *Jan. 7, 1963, 1:30 P.M.* Heard organ music issue from courtroom, when Lawrence Riveroll heard the same (see his statement).

Was present *Sept. 10–12, 1964,* at dusk, with Lawrence Riveroll, when she witnessed apparition. Mrs. Allen went upstairs to close shutters, and as she ascended them, described a chill breeze that seemed to come over her head. Upstairs, she walked into the bedroom and toward the windows. Suddenly she heard a sound behind her, as though something had dropped to the floor. She turned to look, saw nothing, but again experienced the feeling of having someone, invisible, hovering near her. She had a feeling of fear. Completed her task as quickly as possible, and left the upstairs hastily. Upon my return, both persons seemed anxious to leave the house.

May, 1965 (the last Friday), 1:30 P.M.—Was seated in the downstairs front hall, when she heard the sound of footsteps.

Regis Philbin himself had been to the house before. With him on that occasion was Mrs. Philbin, who is highly sensitive to psychic emanations, and a teacher-friend of theirs considered an amateur medium.

They observed, during their vigil, what appeared to be a white figure of a person, but when Regis challenged it, unfortunately with his flashlight, it disappeared immediately. Mrs. Philbin felt extremely uncomfortable on that occasion and had no desire to return to the house.

By now I knew that the house had three ghosts, a man, a woman and a baby—and a spotted dog. The scene observed in one of the rooms sounded more like a psychic impression of a past event to me than a bona fide ghost.

I later discovered that still another part-time guide at the house, William H. Richardson, of 470 Silvery Lane, El Cajon, had not only experienced something out of the ordinary at the house, but had taken part in a kind of séance with interesting results. Here is his statement, given to me in September of 1965, several months *after* our own trance session had taken place.

In the summer of 1963 I worked in Whaley House as a guide.

One morning before the house was open to the public, several of us employees were seated in the music room downstairs, and the sound of someone in heavy boots walking across the upstairs was heard by us all. When we went to investigate the noise, we found all the windows locked and shuttered, and the only door to the outside from upstairs was locked. This experience first sparked my interest in ghosts.

I asked June Reading, the director, to allow several of my friends from Starlight Opera, a local summer musical theatre, to spend the night in the house.

At midnight, on Friday, August 13, we met at the house. Carolyn Whyte, a member of the parapsychology group in San Diego and a member of the Starlight Chorus, gave an introductory talk on what to expect, and we all went into the parlor to wait for something to happen.

The experience was that of a cool breeze blowing through the room, which was felt by several of us despite the fact that all doors and windows were locked and shuttered.

The next thing that happened was that a light appeared over a boy's head. This traveled from his head across the wall, where it disappeared. Upon later investigation it was found to have disappeared at the portrait of Thomas Whaley, the original owner of the house. Footsteps were also heard several times in the room upstairs.

At this point we broke into groups and dispersed to different parts of the house. One group went into the study which is adjacent to the parlor, and there witnessed a shadow on the wall surrounded by a pale light which moved up and down the wall and changed shape as it did so. There was no source of light into the room and one could pass in front of the shadow without disturbing it.

Another group was upstairs when their attention was directed simultaneously to the chandelier which began to swing around as if someone were holding the bottom and twisting the sides. One boy was tapped on the leg several times by some unseen force while seated there.

Meanwhile, downstairs in the parlor, an old-fashioned lamp with prisms hanging on the edges began to act strangely. As we watched, several prisms began to swing by themselves. These would stop and others would start, but they never swung simultaneously. There was no breeze in the room.

At this time we all met in the courtroom. Carolyn then suggested that we try to lift the large table in the room.

We sat around the table and placed our fingertips on it. A short while later it began to creak and then slid across the floor approximately eight inches, and finally lifted completely off the floor on the corner where I was seated.

Later on we brought a small table from the music room into the courtroom and tried to get it to tip, which it did. With just our fingertips on it, it tilted until it was approximately one inch from the floor, then fell. We righted the table and put our fingertips back on it, and almost immediately it began to rock. Since we knew the code for yes, no and doubtful, we began to converse with the table. Incidentally, while this was going on, a chain across the doorway in the courtroom was almost continually swinging back and forth and then up and down.

Through the system of knocking, we discovered that the ghost was that of a little girl, seven years old. She did not tell us her name, but she did tell us that she had red hair, freckles, and hazel eyes. She also related that there were four other ghosts in the house besides herself, including that of a baby boy. We conversed with her spirit for nearly an hour.

At one time the table stopped rocking and started moving across the floor of the courtroom, into the dining room, through the pantry, and into the kitchen. This led us to believe that the kitchen was her usual abode. The table then stopped and several antique kitchen utensils on the wall began to swing violently. Incidentally, the kitchen utensils swung for the rest of the evening at different intervals.

The table then retraced its path back to the courtroom and answered more questions.

At 5:00 a.m. we decided to call it a night—a most interesting night. When we arrived our group of 15 had had in it a couple of real believers, several who half believed, and quite a few who didn't believe at all. After the phenomena we had experienced, there was not one among us who was even very doubtful in the belief of some form of existence after life.

It was Friday evening, and time to meet the ghosts. Sybil Leek knew nothing whatever about the house, and when Regis Philbin picked us up the conversation remained polite and non-ghostly.

When we arrived at the house, word of mouth had preceded us despite the fact that our plans had not been announced publicly; certainly it had not been advertised that we would attempt a séance that evening. Nevertheless, a sizable crowd had assembled at the house and only Regis' polite insistence that their presence might harm whatever results we could obtain made them move on.

It was quite dark now, and I followed Sybil into the house, allowing her to get her clairvoyant bearings first, prior to the trance session we were to do with the cameras rolling. My wife Catherine trailed right behind me carrying the tape equipment. Mrs. Reading received us cordially. The witnesses had assembled but were temporarily out of reach, so that Sybil could not gather any sensory impres-

sions from them. They patiently waited through our clairvoyant tour. All in all, about a dozen people awaited us. The house was lit throughout and the excitement in the atmosphere was bound to stir up any ghost present!

And so it was that on June 25, 1965, the Ghost Hunter came to close quarters with the specters at Whaley House, San Diego. While Sybil meandered about the house by herself, I quickly went over to the court house part of the house and went over their experiences with the witnesses. Although I already had their statements, I wanted to make sure no detail had escaped me.

From June Reading I learned, for instance, that the court house section of the building, erected around 1855, had originally served as a granary, later becoming a town hall and court house in turn. It was the only two-story brick house in the entire area at the time.

Not only did Mrs. Reading hear what sounded to her like human voices, but on one occasion, when she was tape recording some music in this room, the tape also contained some human voices—sounds she had not herself heard while playing the music!

"When was the last time you yourself heard anything unusual?" I asked Mrs. Reading.

"As recently as a week ago," the pert curator replied, "during the day I heard the definite sound of someone opening the front door. Because we have had many visitors here recently, we are very much alerted to this. I happened to be in the court room with one of the people from the Historical Society engaged in research in the Whaley papers, and we both heard it. I went to check to see who had come in, and there was no one there, nor was there any sound of footsteps on the porch outside. The woman who works here also heard it and was just as puzzled about it as I was."

I discovered that the Mrs. Allen in the curator's report to me of uncanny experiences at the house was Lillian Allen, her own mother, a lively lady who remembered her brush with the uncanny only too vividly.

"I've heard the noises overhead," she recalled. "Someone in heavy boots seemed to be walking across, turning to come down the stairway—and when I first came out here they would tell me these things and I would not believe them—but I was sitting at the desk one night, downstairs, waiting for my daughter to lock up in the back. I heard this noise overhead and I was rushing to see if we were locking someone in the house, and as I got to almost the top, a big rush of wind blew over my head and made my hair stand up. I thought the windows had blown open but I looked all around and everything was secured."

"Just how did this wind feel?" I asked. Tales of cold winds are standard with traditional hauntings, but here we had a precise witness to testify.

"It was cold and I was chilly all over. And another thing, when I lock the shutters upstairs at night, I feel like someone is breathing down the back of my neck, like they're going to touch me—at the shoulder—that happened often. Why, only a month ago."

A Mrs. Frederick Bear now stepped forward. I could not find her name in Mrs. Reading's brief report. Evidently she was an additional witness to the uncanny goings-on at this house.

"One evening I came here—it was after 5 o'clock; another lady was here also—and June Reading was coming down the stairs, and we were talking. I distinctly heard something move upstairs, as if someone were moving a table. There was no one there—we checked. That only happened a month ago."

Grace Bourquin, another volunteer worker at the house, had been touched upon in Mrs. Reading's report. She emphasized that the sounds were those of a heavy man wearing boots—no mistake about it. When I questioned her about the apparition of a man she had seen, about six weeks ago, wearing a frock coat, she insisted that he had looked like a real person to her, standing at the top of the stairs one moment, and completely gone the next.

"He did not move. I saw him clearly, then turned my head for a second to call out to Mrs. Reading, and when I looked again, he had disappeared."

I had been fascinated by Mrs. Suzanne Pere's account of her experiences, which seemed to indicate a large degree of mediumship in her makeup. I questioned her about anything she had not yet told us. "On one occasion June Reading and I were in the back study and working with the table. We had our hands on the table to see if we could get any reaction."

"You mean you were trying to do some table-tipping."

"Yes. At this point I had only had some feelings in the house, and smelled some cologne. This was about a year ago, and we were working with some papers concerning the Indian uprising in San Diego, and all of a sudden the table started to rock violently! All of the pulses in my body became throbbing, and in my mind's eye the room was filled with men, all of them extremely excited, and though I could not hear any sound, I knew they were talking, and one gentleman was striding up and down the center of the room, puffing on his cigar, and from my description of him June Reading later identified him as Sheriff McCoy, who was here in the 1850s. When it was finished I could not talk for a few minutes. I was completely disturbed for a moment."

McCoy, I found, was the leader of one of the factions during the "battle" between Old Town and New Town San Diego for the county seat.

Evidently, Mrs. Bourquin had psychically relived that emotion-laden event which did indeed transpire in the very room she saw it in!

"Was the court house ever used to execute anyone?" I interjected.

Mrs. Reading was not sure; the records were all there but the Historical Society had not gone over them as yet

for lack of staff. The court functioned in this house for two years, however, and sentences certainly were meted out in it. The prison itself was a bit farther up the street.

A lady in a red coat caught my attention. She identified herself as Bernice Kennedy.

"I'm a guide here Sundays," the lady began, "and one Sunday recently, I was alone in the house and sitting in the dining room reading, and I heard the front door open and close. There was no one there. I went back to continue my reading. Then I heard it the second time. Again I checked, and there was absolutely no one there. I heard it a third time and this time I took my book and sat outside at the desk. From then onward, people started to come in and I had no further unusual experience. But one other Sunday, there was a young woman upstairs who came down suddenly very pale, and she said the little rocking chair upstairs was rocking. I followed the visitor up and I could not see the chair move, but there was a clicking sound, very rhythmic, and I haven't heard it before or since."

The chair, it came out, once belonged to a family related to the Whaleys.

"I'm Charles Keller, father of Milton Keller," a booming voice said behind me, and an imposing gentleman in his middle years stepped forward.

"I once conducted a tour through the Whaley House. I noticed a lady who had never been here act as if she were being pushed out of one of the bedrooms!"

"Did you see it?" I said, somewhat taken aback.

"Yes," Mr. Keller nodded, "I saw her move, as if someone were pushing her out of the room."

"Did you interrogate her about it?"

"Yes, I did. It was only in the first bedroom, where we started the tour, that it happened. Not in any of the other rooms. We went back to that room and again I saw her being pushed out of it!"

Mrs. Keller then spoke to me about the ice-cold draft she felt, and just before that, three knocks at the back door! Her son, whose testimony Mrs. Reading had already obtained for me, then went to the back door and found no one there who could have knocked. This had happened only six months before our visit.

I then turned to James Reading, the head of the Association, responsible for the upkeep of the museum and house, and asked for his own encounters with the ghosts. Mr. Reading, in a cautious tone, explained that he did not really cotton to ghosts, but —

"The house was opened to the public in April 1960. In the fall of that year, October or November, the police called me at 2 o'clock in the morning, and asked me to please go down and shut off the burglar alarm, because they were being flooded with complaints, it was waking up everybody in the neighborhood. I came down and found two officers waiting for me. I shut off the alarm. They had meantime checked the house and every door and shutter was tight."

"How could the alarm have gone off by itself then?"

"I don't know. I unlocked the door, and we searched the entire house. When we finally got upstairs, we found one of the upstairs front bedroom windows open. We closed and bolted the window, and came down and tested the alarm. It was in order again. No one could have gotten in or out. The shutters outside that window were closed and hooked on the inside. The opening of the window had set off the alarm, but it would have been impossible for anyone to open that window and get either into or out of the house. Impossible. This happened *four times*. The second time, about four months later, again at two in the morning, again that same window was standing open. The other two times it was always that same window."

"What did you finally do about it?"

"After the fourth incident we added a second bolt at right angles to the first one, and that seemed to help. There were no further calls."

Was the ghost getting tired of pushing *two* bolts out of the way?

I had been so fascinated with all this additional testimony that I had let my attention wander away from my favorite medium, Sybil Leek. But now I started to look for her and found to my amazement that she had seated herself in one of the old chairs in what used to be the kitchen, downstairs in back of the living room. When I entered the room she seemed deep in thought, although not in trance by any means, and yet it took me a while to make her realize where we were.

Had anything unusual transpired while I was in the court room interviewing?

"I was standing in the entrance hall, looking at the postcards," Sybil recollected, "when I felt I just had to go to the kitchen, but I didn't go there at first, but went halfway up the stairs, and a child came down the stairs and into the kitchen and I followed her."

"A child?" I asked. I was quite sure there were no children among our party.

"I thought it was Regis' little girl and the next thing I recall I was in the rocking chair and you were saying something to me."

Needless to say, Regis Philbins' daughter had *not* been on the stairs. I asked for a detailed description of the child.

"It was a long-haired girl," Sybil said. "She was very quick, you know, in a longish dress. She went to the table in this room and I went to the chair. That's all I remember."

I decided to continue to question Sybil about any psychic impressions she might now gather in the house.

"There is a great deal of confusion in this house," she began. "Some of it is associated with another room upstairs, which has been structurally altered. There are two centers of activity."

Sybil, of course, could not have known that the house consisted of two separate units.

"Any ghosts in the house?"

"Several," Sybil assured me. "At least four!"

Had not William Richardson's group made contact with a little girl ghost who had claimed that she knew of four other ghosts in the house? The report of that séance did not reach me until September, several months after our visit, so Sybil could not possibly have "read our minds" about it, since our minds had no such knowledge at that time.

"This room where you found me sitting," Sybil continued, "I found myself drawn to it; the impressions are very strong here. Especially that child—she died young."

We went about the house now, seeking further contacts.

"I have a date now," Sybil suddenly said, "1872."

The Readings exchanged significant glances. It was just after the greatest bitterness of the struggle between Old Town and New Town, when the removal of the court records from Whaley House by force occurred.

"There are two sides to the house," Sybil continued. "One side I like, but not the other."

Rather than have Sybil use up her energies in clairvoyance, I felt it best to try for a trance in the court room itself. This was arranged for quickly, with candles taking the place of electric lights except for what light was necessary for the motion picture cameras in the rear of the large room.

Regis Philbin and I sat at Sybil's sides as she slumped forward in a chair that may well have held a merciless judge in bygone years.

But the first communicator was neither the little girl nor the man in the frock coat. A feeble, plaintive voice was suddenly heard from Sybil's lips, quite unlike her own, a voice evidently parched with thirst.

"Bad...fever everybody had the fever..."

"What year is this?"

"Forty-six."

I suggested that the fever had passed, and generally calmed the personality who did not respond to my request for identification.

"Send me...some water...." Sybil was still in trance, but herself now. Immediately she complained about there being a lot of confusion.

"This isn't the room where we're needed...the child...she is the one...."

What is her name?"

"Anna...Bell...she died very suddenly with something, when she was thirteen...chest...."

"Are her parents here too?"

"They come...the lady comes."

"What is this house used for?"

"Trade...selling things, buying and selling."

"Is there anyone other than the child in this house?"

"Child is the main one, because she doesn't understand anything at all. But there is something more vicious. Child would not hurt anyone. There's someone else. A man. He knows something about this house...about thirty-two, unusual name, C...Calstrop...five feet ten, wearing a green coat, darkish, mustache and side whiskers, he goes up to the bedroom on the left. He has business here. His business is with things that come from the sea. But it is the papers that worry him."

"What papers?" I demanded.

"The papers...1872. About the house. Dividing the house was wrong. Two owners, he says."

"What is the house being used for, now, in 1872?"

"To live in. Two places...I get confused for I go one place and then I have to go to another."

"Did this man you see die here?"

"He died here. Unhappy because of the place...about the other place. Two buildings. Some people quarrelled about the spot. He is laughing. He wants all this house for himself."

"Does he know he is dead?" I asked the question that often brings forth much resistance to my quest for facts from those who cannot conceive of their status as "ghosts."

Sybil listened for a moment.

"He does as he wants in this house because he is going to live here," she finally said. "It's his house."

"Why is he laughing?"

A laughing ghost, indeed!

"He laughs because of people coming here thinking it's their house! When he knows the truth."

"What is his name?" I asked again.

"Cal...Calstrop...very difficult as he does not speak very clearly...he writes and writes...he makes a noise...he says he will make even more noise unless you go away."

"Let him," I said, cheerfully hoping I could tape-record the ghost's outbursts.

"Tell him he has passed over and the matter is no longer important," I told Sybil.

"He is upstairs."

I asked that he walk upstairs so we could all hear him. There was nobody upstairs at this moment—everybody was watching the proceedings in the court room downstairs.

We kept our breath, waiting for the manifestations, but our ghost wouldn't play the game. I continued with my questions.

"What does he want?"

"He is just walking around, he can do as he likes," Sybil said. "He does not like new things...he does not like any noise...except when he makes it...."

"Who plays the organ in this house?"

"He says his mother plays."

"What is her name?"

"Ann Lassay...that's wrong, it's Lann—he speaks so badly...Lannay...his throat is bad or something...."

I later was able to check on this unusual name. Anna Lannay was Thomas Whaley's wife!

At the moment, however, I was not aware of this fact and pressed on with my interrogation. How did the ghost die? How long ago?

"'89...he does not want to speak; he only wants to roam around...."

Actually, Whaley died in 1890. Had the long interval confused his sense of time? So many ghosts cannot recall exact dates but will remember circumstances and emotional experiences well.

"He worries about the house...he wants the whole house...for himself...he says he will leave them... papers...hide the papers...he wants the other papers about the house...they're four miles from here...several people have these papers and you'll have to get them back or he'll never settle...never...and if he doesn't get the whole house back, he will be much worse...and then, the police will come...he will make the lights come and the noise...and the bell...make the police come and see him, the master...of the house, he hears bells upstairs...he doesn't know what it is...he goes upstairs and opens the windows, wooden windows...and looks out...and then he pulls the...no, it's not a bell...he'll do it again...when he wants someone to know that he really is the master of the house...people today come and say he is not, but he is!"

I was surprised. Sybil had no knowledge of the disturbances, the alarm bell, the footsteps, the open window...and yet it was all perfectly true. Surely, her communicator was our man!

"When did he do this the last time?" I inquired.

"This year...not long...."

"Has he done anything else in this house?"

"He said he moved the lights. In the parlor."

Later I thought of the Richardson séance and the lights they had observed, but of course I had no idea of this when we were at the house ourselves.

"What about the front door?"

"If people come, he goes into the garden...walks around because...he meets mother there."

"What is in the kitchen?"

"Child goes to the kitchen. I have to leave him, and he doesn't want to be left...it was an injustice, anyway, don't like it...the child is twelve...chest trouble...something from the kitchen...bad affair...."

"Anyone's fault?"

"Yes. Not chest...from the cupboard, took something...it was an acid like salt, and she ate it...she did not know...there is something strange about this child, someone had control of her, you see, she was in the way...family...one girl...those boys were not too good...the other boys who came down...she is like two people...someone controlled her...made her do strange things and then...could she do that."

"Was she the daughter of the man?"

"Strange man, he doesn't care so much about the girl as he does about the house. He is disturbed."

"Is there a woman in this house?"

"Of course. There is a woman in the garden."

"Who is she?"

"Mother. Grandmother of the girl."

"Is he aware of the fact he has no physical body?"

"No."

"Doesn't he see all the people who come here?"

"They have to be fought off, sent away."

"Tell him it is now seventy years later."

"He says seventy years when the house was built."

"Another seventy years have gone by," I insisted. "Only part of you is in the house."

"No, part of the house...you're making the mistake," he replied.

I tried hard to convince him of the real circumstances. Finally, I assured him that the entire house was, in effect, his.

Would this help?

"He is vicious," Sybil explains. "He will have his revenge on the house."

I explained that his enemies were all dead.

"He says it was an injustice, and the court was wrong and you have to tell everyone this is his house and land and home."

I promised to do so and intoned the usual formula for the release of earthbound people who have passed over and don't realize it. Then I recalled Sybil to her own self, and within a few moments she was indeed in full control.

I then turned to the director of the museum, Mrs. Reading, and asked for her comments on the truth of the material just heard.

"There was a litigation," she said. "The injustice could perhaps refer to the County's occupancy of this portion of the house from 1869 to 1871. Whaley's contract, which we have, shows that this portion of the house was leased to the County, and he was to supply the furniture and set it up as a court room. He also put in the two windows to provide light. It was a valid agreement. They adhered to the contract as long as the court continued to function here, but when Alonzo Horton came and developed New Town, a hot contest began between the two communities for the possession of the county seat. When the records were forcefully removed from here, Whaley felt it was quite an injustice, and we have letters he addressed to the Board of Supervisors, referring to the fact that his lease had been broken. The Clerk notified him that they were no longer responsible for the use of this house—after all the work he had put in to remodel it for their use. He would bring the matter up periodically with the Board of Supervisors, but it was tabled by them each time it came up."

"In other words, this is the injustice referred to by the ghost?"

"In 1872 he was bitterly engaged in asking redress from the County over this matter, which troubled him some since he did not believe a government official would act in this manner. It was never settled, however, and Whaley was left holding the bag."

"Was there a child in the room upstairs?"

"In the nursery? There were several children there. One child died here. But this was a boy."

Again, later, I saw that the Richardson séance spoke of a boy ghost in the house.

At the very beginning of trance, before I began tapping the utterances from Sybil's lips, I took some handwritten notes. The personality, I now saw, who had died of a bad fever had given the faintly pronounced name of Fedor and spoke of a mill where he worked. Was there any sense to this?

"Yes," Mrs. Reading confirmed, "this room we are in now served as a granary at one time. About 1855 to 1867."

"Were there ever any Russians in this area?"

"There was a considerable otter trade here prior to the American occupation of the area. We have found evidence that the Russians established wells in this area. They came into these waters then to trade otters."

"Amazing," I conceded. How could Sybil, even if she wanted to, have known of such an obscure fact?

"This would have been in the 1800s," Mrs. Reading continued. "Before then there were Spaniards here, of course."

"Anything else you wish to comment upon in the trance session you have just witnessed?" I asked.

Mrs. Reading expressed what we all felt.

"The references to the windows opening upstairs, and the ringing of these bells...."

How could Sybil have known all that? Nobody told her and she had not had a chance to acquaint herself with the details of the disturbances.

What remained were the puzzling statements about "the other house." They, too were soon to be explained. We were walking through the garden now and inspected the rear portion of the Whaley House. In back of it, we discovered to our surprise still another wooden house standing in the garden. I questioned Mrs. Reading about this second house.

"The Pendington House, in order to save it, had to be moved out of the path of the freeway...it never belonged to the Whaleys although Thomas Whaley once tried to rent it. But it was always rented to someone else."

No wonder the ghost was angry about "the other house." It had been moved and put on his land...without his consent!

The name *Cal...trop* still did not fall into place. It was too far removed from Whaley and yet everything else that had come through Sybil clearly fitted Thomas Whaley. Then the light began to dawn, thanks to Mrs. Reading's detailed knowledge of the house.

"It was interesting to hear Mrs. Leek say there was a store here once..." she explained. "This is correct, there was a store here at one time, but it was not Mr. Whaley's."

"Whose was it?"

"It belonged to a man named Wallack...Hal Wallack...that was in the seventies."

Close enough to Sybil's tentative pronunciation of a name she caught connected with the house.

"He rented it to Wallack for six months, then Wallack sold out," Mrs. Reading explained.

I also discovered, in discussing the case with Mrs. Reading, that the disturbances really began after the second house had been placed on the grounds. Was that the straw that broke the ghost's patience?

Later, we followed Sybil to a wall adjoining the garden, a wall, I should add, where there was no visible door. But Sybil insisted there had been a French window there, and indeed there was at one time. In a straight line from this spot, we wound up at a huge tree. It was here, Sybil explained, that Whaley and his mother often met—or are meeting, as the case may be.

I was not sure that Mr. Whaley had taken my advice to heart and moved out of what was, after all, his house. Why should he? The County had not seen fit to undo an old wrong.

We left the next morning, hoping that at the very least we had let the restless one know someone cared.

A week later Regis Philbin checked with the folks at Whaley House. Everything was lively—chandelier swinging, rocker rocking; and June Reading herself brought me up to date on July 27th, 1965, with a brief report on activities—other than flesh-and-blood—at the house.

Evidently the child ghost was also still around, for utensils in the kitchen had moved that week, especially a cleaver which swings back and forth on its own. Surely that must be the playful little girl, for what would so important a man as Thomas Whaley have to do in the kitchen? Surely he was much to preoccupied with the larger aspects of his realm, the ancient wrong done him, and the many intrusions from the world of reality. For the Whaley House is a busy place, ghosts or not.

On replaying my tapes, I noticed a curious confusion between the initial appearance of a ghost who called himself Fedor in my notes, and a man who said he had a bad fever. It was just that the man with the fever did not have a foreign accent, but I distinctly recalled "fedor" as sounding odd.

Were they perhaps two separate entities?

My suspicions were confirmed when a letter written May 23, 1966—almost a year later—reached me. A Mrs. Carol DeJuhasz wanted me to know about a ghost at Whaley House...no, not Thomas Whaley or a twelve-year-old girl with long hair. Mrs. DeJuhasz was concerned with an historical play written by a friend of hers, dealing with the unjust execution of a man who tried to steal a harbor boat in the 1800s and was caught. Make no mistake about it, nobody had observed this ghost at Whaley House. Mrs. DeJuhasz merely thought he ought to be there, having been hanged in the backyard of the house.

Many people tell me of tragic spots where men have died unhappily but rarely do I discover ghosts on such spots just because of it. I was therefore not too interested in Mrs. DeJuhasz' account of a possible ghost. But she thought that there ought to be present at Whaley House the ghost of this man, called Yankee Jim Robinson. When captured, he fought a sabre duel and received a critical wound in the head. Although alive, he became delirious and was tried without representation, *sick of the fever*. Sentenced to death, he was subsequently hanged in the yard behind the Court House.

Was his the ghostly voice that spoke through Sybil, complaining of the fever and then quickly fading away? Again it was William Richardson who was able to provide a further clue or set of clues to this puzzle. In December of 1966 he contacted me again to report some further experiences at the Whaley House.

"This series of events began in March of this year. Our group was helping to restore an historic old house which had been moved onto the Whaley property to save it from destruction. During our lunch break one Saturday, several of us were in Whaley House. I was downstairs when Jim Stein, one of the group, rushed down the stairs to tell me that the cradle in the nursery was rocking by itself. I hurried upstairs but it wasn't rocking. I was just about to chide Jim for having an overactive imagination when it began again and rocked a little longer before it stopped. The cradle is at least ten feet from the doorway, and a metal barricade is across it to prevent tourists from entering the room. No amount of walking or jumping had any effect on the cradle. While it rocked, I remembered that it had made no sound. Going into the room, I rocked the cradle. I was surprised that it made quite a bit of noise. The old floorboards were somewhat uneven and this in combination with the wooden rockers on the cradle made a very audible sound.

"As a matter of fact, when the Whaleys were furnishing carpeting for the house, the entire upstairs portion was carpeted. This might explain the absence of the noise.

"In June, Whaley House became the setting for an historical play. The play concerned the trial and hanging of a local bad man named Yankee Jim Robinson. It was presented in the court room and on the grounds of the mansion. The actual trial and execution had taken place in August of 1852. This was five years before Whaley House was built, but the execution took place on the grounds.

"Yankee Jim was hanged from a scaffold which stood approximately between the present music room and front parlor.

"Soon after the play went into rehearsal, things began to happen. I was involved with the production as an actor and therefore had the opportunity to spend many hours in the house between June and August. The usual footsteps kept up and they were heard by most of the members of the cast at one time or another. There was a group of us within the cast who were especially interested in the phenomenon: myself, Barry Bunker, George Carroll, and his fiancée, Toni Manista. As we were all dressed in period costumes most of the time, the ghosts should have felt right at home. Toni was playing the part of Anna, Thomas Whaley's wife. She said she often felt as if she were being followed around the house (as did we all).

"I was sitting in the kitchen with my back to the wall one night, When I felt a hand run through my hair. I quickly turned around but there was nothing to be seen. I have always felt that it was Anna Whaley who touched me. It was my first such experience and I felt honored that she had chosen me to touch. There is a chair in the kitchen which is made of rawhide and wood. The seat is made of thin strips of rawhide crisscrossed on the wooden frame. When someone sits on it, it sounds like the leather in a saddle. On the same night I was touched, the chair made sounds as if someone were sitting in it, not once but several times. There always seems to be a change in the temperature of a room when a presence enters. The kitchen is no exception. It really got cold in there!

"Later in the run of the show, the apparitions began to appear. The cast had purchased a chair which had belonged to Thomas Whaley and placed it in the front parlor. Soon after, a mist was occasionally seen in the chair or near it. In other parts of the house, especially upstairs, inexplicable shadows and mists began to appear. George Carroll swears that he saw a man standing at the top of the stairs. He walked up the stairs and through the man. The man was still there when George turned around but faded and disappeared almost immediately.

"During the summer, we often smelled cigar smoke when we opened the house in the morning or at times when no one was around. Whaley was very fond of cigars and was seldom without them.

"The footsteps became varied. The heavy steps of the man continued as usual, but the click-click of high heels was heard on occasion. Once, the sound of a small child running in the upstairs hall was heard. Another time, I was alone with the woman who took ticket reservations for *Yankee Jim*. We had locked the doors and decided to check the upstairs before we left. We had no sooner gotten up the stairs than we both heard footfalls in the hall below. We listened for a moment and then went back down the stairs and looked. No one. We searched the entire house, not really expecting to find anyone. We didn't. Not a living soul.

"Well, this just about brings you up to date. I've been back a number of times since September but there's nothing to report except the usual footfalls, creaks, etc.

"I think that the play had much to do with the summer's phenomena. Costumes, characters, and situations which were known to the Whaleys were reenacted nightly. Yankee Jim Robinson certainly has reason enough to haunt. Many people, myself included, think that he got a bad deal. He was wounded during his capture and was unconscious during most of the trial. To top it off, the judge was a drunk and the jury and townspeople wanted blood. Jim was just unlucky enough to bear their combined wrath.

"His crime? He had borrowed (?) a boat. Hardly a hanging offense. He was found guilty and condemned. He was unprepared to die and thought it was a joke up to the minute they pulled the wagon out from under him. The scaffold wasn't high enough and the fall didn't break his neck. Instead, he slowly strangled for more than fifteen minutes before he died. I think I'd haunt under the same circumstances myself.

"Two other points: another of the guides heard a voice directly in front of her as she walked down the hall. It said, 'Hello, hello.' There was no one else in the house at the time. A dog fitting the description of one of the Whaley dogs has been seen to run into the house, but it can never be found."

Usually, ghosts of different periods do not "run into" one another, unless they are tied together by a mutual problem or common tragedy. The executed man, the proud owner, the little girl, the lady of the house—they form a lively ghost population even for so roomy a house as the Whaley House is.

Mrs. Reading doesn't mind. Except that it does get confusing now and again when you see someone walking about the house and aren't sure if he has bought an admission ticket.

Surely, Thomas Whaley wouldn't dream of buying one. And he is not likely to leave unless and until some action is taken publicly to rectify the ancient wrong. If the County were to reopen the matter and acknowledge the mistake made way back, I am sure the ghostly Mr. Whaley would be pleased and let matters rest. The little girl ghost has been told by Sybil Leek what has happened to her, and the lady goes where Mr. Whaley goes. Which brings us down to Jim, who would have to be tried again and found innocent of stealing the boat.

There is that splendid courtroom there at the house to do it in. Maybe some ghost-conscious county administration will see fit to do just that.

I'll be glad to serve as counsel for the accused, at no charge.

✳ 51

The Ghost at the Altar

I HAD HEARD RUMORS for some time of a ghost parson in a church near Pittsburgh, and when I appeared on the John Reed King show on station KDKA-TV in the spring of 1963, one of the crew came up to me after the telecast and told me how much he enjoyed hearing about ghosts.

"Have you ever visited that haunted church in M——?" he asked, and my natural curiosity was aroused. A ghost here in Pittsburgh, and I haven't met him? Can't allow that. But my stay was over and I had to return to New York.

Still, the ghostly person of M—— was very much on my mind. When I returned to Pittsburgh in September of 1963, I was determined to have a go at that case.

With the help of Jim Sieger and his roving reporter, John Stewart, at station KDKA, we got together a car, a first-class portable tape recorder, and photographer Jim Stark. Immediately following my telecast, we set out for Milvale.

Fate must have wanted us to get results, for the attendant of the first gasoline station we stopped at directed us to the Haunted Church. Both the name of the church and its current pastor must remain hidden at their own request, but the story is nevertheless true.

The Haunted Church is an imposing Romanesque building of stone, erected at the turn of the century on a bluff overlooking the Pittsburgh River. It is attached to a school and rectory and gives a clean and efficient impression, nothing haunted or mysterious about it.

When I rang the doorbell of the rectory, a portly, imposing man in sweater and slacks opened the door. I asked to talk to him about the history of the church. Evidently he had more than a share of the sixth sense, for he knew immediately what I was after.

"I am priest," he said firmly, with a strong Slavic accent. I was somewhat taken aback because of his casual clothes, but he explained that even priests are allowed to relax now and then. Father X., as we shall call him, was a well-educated, soft-spoken man of about forty-five or fifty, and he readily admitted he had heard the rumors about "spirits," but there was, of course, nothing to it. Actually, he said, the man to talk to was his superior, Father H.

A few moments later, Father H. was summoned and introduced to me as "the authority" on the subject. When the good Father heard I was a parapsychologist and interested in his ghost, he became agitated. "I have nothing to say," he emphasized, and politely showed us the door. I chose to ignore his move.

Instead, I persisted in requesting either confirmation or denial of the rumors of hauntings in his church. Evidently, Father H. was afraid of the unusual. Many priests are not and discuss freely that which they know exists. But Father H. had once met with another writer, Louis

Adamic, and apparently this had soured him on all other writers, like myself.

It seems that Adamic, a fellow Croatian, had mentioned in one of his books the story about the ghost at the altar—and seriously at that—quite a feat for a nonbeliever as Adamic was said to have been. Father H. had nothing to say for publication.

"No, no, no—nothing. I bless you. Good-bye." He bowed ceremoniously and waited for us to depart. Instead, I turned and smiled at Father X., the assistant pastor.

"May we see the church?" I said and waited. They couldn't very well refuse. Father H. realized we weren't going to leave at once and resigned himself to the fact that his assistant pastor would talk to us.

"Very well. But without me!" he finally said, and withdrew. That was all Father X. had needed. The field was clear now. Slowly he lit a cigarette and said, "You know, I've studied parapsychology myself for two years in my native Croatia."

After his initial appearance, nothing about Father X. surprised me. As we walked across the yard to the church, we entered into an animated discussion about the merits of psychic research. Father X. took us in through the altar door, and we saw the gleaming white and gold altar emerging from the semidarkness like a vision in one of Raphael's Renaissance paintings.

There was definitely something very unusual about this church. For one thing, it was a typically European, Slavonically tinged edifice and one had the immediate feel of being among an ethnic group of different origin from one's own. The large nave culminated in a balcony on which an old-fashioned—that is, nonelectric, nonautomatic—organ was placed in prominent position. No doubt services at this church were imposing and emotionally satisfying experiences.

We stepped closer to the altar, which was flanked on either side by a large, heavy vigil light, the kind Europeans call Eternal Light. "See this painting," Father X. said and pointed at the curving fresco covering the entire inner cupola behind the altar, both behind it and above it. The painting showed natives of Croatia in their costumes, and a group of Croatians presenting a model of their church.

These traditional scenes were depicted with vivid colors and a charming, primitive style not found elsewhere. I inquired about the painter. "Maxim Hvatka," the priest said, and at once I recognized the name as that of a celebrated Yugoslav artist who had passed on a few years ago. The frescos were done in the early part of the century.

As we admired the altar, standing on its steps and getting impressions, Father X. must again have read my mind, for he said without further ado, "Yes, it is this spot where the 'spirits were seen.'"

There was no doubt in my mind that our assistant pastor was quite convinced of the truth of the phenomena.

The haunted church at M——, Pennsylvania

"What exactly happened?" I asked.

"Well, not so long ago, Father H. and this painter Hvatka, they were here near the altar. Hvatka was painting the altar picture and Father H. was here to watch him. Suddenly, Hvatka grabbed Father's arm and said with great excitement, 'Look, Father—this person—there is someone here in the church, in front of the altar!'

"Father H. knew that the church was locked up tight and that only he and the painter were in the building. There *couldn't* be another person. 'Where? Who?' he said and looked hard. He didn't see anything. Hvatka insisted he had just seen a man walk by the altar and disappear into nothing. They stepped up to the vigil light on the left and experienced a sudden chill. Moreover, *the light was out.*

"Now to extinguish this light with anything less than a powerful blower or fan directly above it is impossible. Glass-enclosed and metal-covered, these powerful wax candles are meant to withstand the wind and certainly ordinary drafts or human breath. Only a supernormal agency could have put out that vigil light, gentlemen."

Father X. paused. I was impressed by his well-told story, and I knew at once why Father H. wanted no part of us. How could he ever admit having been in the presence of a spirit without having seen it? Impossible. We took some photographs and walked slowly towards the exit.

Father X. warmed up to me now and volunteered an experience from his own youth. It seems that when he was studying theology in his native Croatia, he lived among a group or perhaps a dozen young students who did not share his enthusiasm for psychic studies—who, in fact, ridiculed them.

One young man, however, who was his roommate, took the subject seriously, so seriously in fact that they made a pact—whoever died first would let the other know. A short time later, Father X., asleep on a warm afternoon, suddenly woke up. He *knew* his friend had died that instant, for he saw him sitting on a chair near his bed, laughing and waving at him. It was more than a mere dream, a vividly powerful impression. Father X. was no longer asleep at that moment; the impression had actually awakened him.

He looked at his watch; it was just three in the afternoon. Quickly, he made inquiries about is friend. Within a few hours he knew what he had already suspected—his friend had died in an accident at precisely the moment he had seen him in his room, back at the seminary!

"You're psychic then," I said.

Father X. shrugged. "I know many psychic cases," he said obliquely. "There was that nun in Italy, who left her hand prints on the church door to let her superiors know she was now in purgatory."

Father X. spoke softly and with the assurance of a man who knows his subject well. "There are these things, but what can we do? We cannot very well admit them."

A sudden thought came to my mind. Did he have any idea who the ghost at the altar was? Father X. shook his head.

"Tell me," I continued, "did anyone die violently in the church?"

Again, a negative answer.

"That's strange," I said. "Was there another building on this spot before the present church?"

"No," Father X. said nonchalantly.

"That's even stranger," I countered, "for my research indicates there was a priest here in the nineteenth century, and it is his ghost that has been seen."

Father X. swallowed hard.

"As a matter of fact," he said now, "you're right. There was an earlier wooden church here on this very spot. The present stone building only dates back to about 1901. Father Ranzinger built the wooden church."

"Was that around 1885," I inquired. That is how I had it in my notes.

"Probably correct," the priest said, and no longer marveled at my information.

"What happened to the wooden church, Father?" I asked, and here I had a blank, for my research told me nothing further.

"Oh, it burned down. Completely. No, nobody got hurt, but the church, it was a total loss."

Father Ranzinger's beloved wooden church went up in flames, it appeared, and the fifteen years he had spent with his flock must have accumulated an emotional backlog of great strength and attachment. Was it not conceivable that Father Ranzinger's attachment to the building was transferred to the stone edifice as soon as it was finished?

Was it his ghost the two men had seen in front of the altar? Until he puts in another appearance, we won't know, but Pittsburgh's Haunted Church is a lovely place in which to rest and pray—ghost or no ghost.

✳ 52

A Ghost's Last Refuge

NEAR CHARLOTTESVILLE, VIRGINIA, stands a farmhouse built during Revolutionary days, now owned by Mary W., a lady in her early fifties, who, some years ago, had a fleeting interest in the work of Professor Rhine at Duke University.

Her own psychic talents are acknowledged, but she insists she has not done any automatic writing lately and isn't really very much interested anymore. Later I realized that her waning interest must have some connection with the events at the house which we shall call Wickham, since the real name must at present remain veiled in deference to the owner's request.

Virginia Cloud had come along to serve as a combination guide and clairvoyant, and writer Booton Herndon also came along to observe what he had always found a fascinating subject. Thus a caravan of two cars made its way to Wickham one bright May morning when nature's brilliance belied the sober subject of our goal.

On arrival, my wife, Catherine, and I sat down with Mary W. to hear her tell of her own experiences in the haunted house. Only after she had done so did Virginia Cloud enter the house.

The oldest part of the house, rather skilfully connected to the rest, consists of a hall or main room and a small bedroom reached by a narrow winding staircase.

This portion, dating back to 1781, has been the location of some uncanny happenings beginning at the time when Mrs. W. acquired the house and acreage in 1951. Whether previous owners had had any experiences couldn't be ascertained.

Emotionally keyed at the time, Mrs. W. recalls, she was in a small adjoining room downstairs, which has been turned into a small home bar, when she clearly heard footsteps in the main room, and a noise like that made by riding clothes, swishing sounds; she called out, but she knew it was not her husband; the steps continued; someone was walking up and down in the room. Mrs. W. took a look through the window and saw her entire family outside near the barn, some twenty yards away.

This alarmed her even more and she stepped into the main room. There was no one there. But the eerie thing was that even in her presence the steps continued, reached

The door that kept coming open by itself

the doorway and then went back across the room to the stairway where they stopped abruptly at the landing leading to old room above.

The previous owner, by the name of Deauwell, had told Mary W. that when his predecessor at the house, Mrs. Early, had died, there had been a strange noise *as if someone were falling down stairs.*

Two years later, in 1953, Mrs. W.'s two girls, aged twelve and nine at the time, were playing in the upstairs room while the parents were entertaining some guests in the nearby cottage apart from the main house. It was 10 P.M. when the girls distinctly heard someone walk around downstairs in the empty house. They called out, but got no answer. They thought it was a friend of their parents, but

The fireplace—center of psychic phenomena

later checking revealed nobody had left the party to return to the main house even for a moment.

Around 1960–61, Mrs. W. again heard the by-now-familiar footsteps in the same spot. They started, then stopped, then started up again. Although Mrs. W. admitted some psychic talent, her automatic writing had yielded no one claiming to be connected with the house except perhaps a slave girl named Rebecca, who claimed to have been captured by Indians who cut out her tongue; she was found by the Early sons, and became their servant since; Mrs. W. also claimed a guide or control named Robert.

The place had been in litigation for many years, and there are no less than three family cemeteries on the grounds. The house itself was built by one Richard Durrette in 1781. When the fireplace was rebuilt prior to 1938, before Mrs. W. owned the place, an inscription turned up explaining that Hessian-soldier prisoners from a nearby barracks had helped build the chimney in 1781. Three thousand prisoners were kept in barracks nearby. Some stayed afterwards and married local girls.

This was *not* discussed in the presence of Virginia Cloud, who soon went into semi-trance in the presence of Mary W. and myself. She "saw" an Albert or Alfred, in white shirt, boots, trousers, but not a uniform, dragging

himself into the house; perhaps he was an injured Hessian entering an empty house, chased here by Redcoats. "The British are farther away.... Something was burned near here." At this point, both Mary W. and I smelled smoke.

Independent of Virginia Cloud's testimony, both of us also heard a faint knock at the entrance door, two short raps.

Virginia, in her chair near the stairway, started to shiver. "The ghost remembers his mother and calls her, but she is not here any more...only a memory; he may have died here, since I don't see him leave again. His arm is hurt by metal, perhaps a shell."

Mary W. had lived through tragedy in her own life. Her husband, Kenneth, had committed suicide in the very house we were visiting. I had the feeling that Mary's interest in the occult coincided with this event, and that perhaps she thought the ghostly footsteps were actually her late husband's restless movements in the room he had called his own.

But the noises and disturbances go back farther than Mary's tenancy of the house. Premeditated suicide seldom yields ghosts. I am convinced that the ghost at Wickham is not Mary's husband, but the Hessian deserter who wanted to find refuge from the pursuing British.

The Octagon Ghosts

COLONEL JOHN TAYLOE, in 1800, built his mansion, the magnificent building now known as the Octagon because of its shape. It stood in a fashionable part of Washington, but now houses the offices and exhibit of the American Institute of Architects.

In the early 1800s the Colonel's daughter ran away with a stranger and later returned home, asking forgiveness. This she did not get from her stern father and in despair she threw herself from the third-floor landing of the winding staircase that still graces the mansion. She landed on a spot near the base of the stairs, and this started a series of eerie events recorded in the mansion over the years.

Life magazine reported in an article in 1962 on haunted mansions that some visitors claim to have seen a shadow on the spot where the girl fell, while others refuse to cross the spot for reasons unknown; still others have heard the shriek of the falling girl.

The July, 1959, issue of the *American Institute of Architects Journal* contains a brief account of the long service record of employee James Cypress. Although he himself never saw any ghosts, he reports that at one time when his wife was ill, the doctor saw a man dressed in the clothes of one hundred fifty years ago coming down the spiral staircase. As the doctor looked at the strange man in puzzlement, the man just disappeared *into thin air.*

After some correspondence with J. W. Rankin, Director of the Institute, my wife and I finally started out for Washington on May 17, 1963. It was a warm day and the beautiful Georgian mansion set back from one of the capital's busier streets promised an adventure into a more relaxed past.

Mr. Rankin received us with interest and showed us around the house which was at that time fortunately empty of tourists and other visitors. It was he who supplied some of the background information on the Octagon, from which I quote:

The White House and the Octagon are relations, in a way. Both date from the beginning of government in the national capital; the White House was started first but the Octagon was first completed. Both have served as the official residence of the President.

It was early in 1797 that Colonel John Tayloe of Mount Airy, Virginia, felt the need for a town house. Mount Airy was a magnificent plantation of some three thousand acres, on which the Colonel, among many activities, bred and raced horses, but the call of the city was beginning to be felt, even in that early day; Philadelphia was the Colonel's choice, but his friend General Washington painted a glowing picture of what the new national capital might become and persuaded

The Octagon ghosts—Washington, D.C.

him to build the Octagon in surroundings that were then far removed from urbanity.

Dr. William Thornton, winner of the competition for the Capitol, was Colonel Tayloe's natural selection of architect.

On April 19, 1797, Colonel Tayloe purchased for $1,000 from Gustavus W. Scott—one of the original purchasers from the Government on November 21, 1796 —Lot 8 in Square 170 in the new plot of Washington. Although, as the sketch of 1813 shows, the site was apparently out in a lonely countryside, the city streets had been definitely plotted, and the corner of New York Avenue and Eighteenth Street was then where it is today.

Obviously, from a glance at the plot plan, Colonel Tayloe's house derived its unique shape from the angle formed at the junction of these two streets. In spite of the name by which the mansion has always been known, Dr. Thornton could have had no intention of making the plan octagonal; the house planned itself from the street frontages.

Work on the building started in 1798 and progressed under the occasional inspection of General Washington, who did not live to see its completion in 1800. The mansion immediately took its place as a center of official and nonofficial social activities. Through its hospitable front door passed Madison, Jefferson, Monroe, Adams, Jackson, Decatur, Porter, Webster, Clay, Lafayette, Von Steuben, Calhoun, Randolph, Van Renssalaer and their ladies.

Social activities were forgotten, however, when the War of 1812 threatened and finally engulfed the new

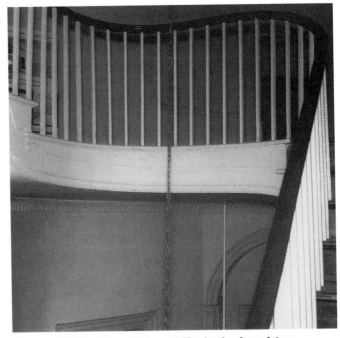

The winding staircase at the Octagon and the chandelier that moves at times

From this landing Colonel Taylor's daughter jumped to her death

nation's capital. On August 24, 1814, the British left the White House a fire-gutted ruin. Mrs. Tayloe's foresight in establishing the French Minister—with his country's flag—as a house guest may have saved the Octagon from a like fate.

Colonel Tayloe is said to have dispatched a courier from Mount Airy, offering President Madison the use of the mansion, and the Madisons moved in on September 8, 1814.

For more than a year Dolly Madison reigned as hostess of the Octagon. In the tower room just over the entrance President Madison established his study, and here signed the Treaty of Ghent on February 17, 1815, establishing a peace with Great Britain which endures to this day.

After the death of Mrs. John Tayloe in 1855, the Octagon no longer served as the family's town house. That part of Washington lost for a time its residential character and the grand old mansion began to deteriorate.

In 1865 it was used as a school for girls. From 1866 to 1879 the Government rented it for the use of the Hydrographic Office. As an office and later as a studio dwelling, the Octagon served until about 1885, when it was entrusted by the Tayloe heirs to a caretaker.

Glenn Brown, longtime secretary of the American Institute of Architects, suggested in 1889 that the house would make an appropriate headquarters for the Institute.

When the architects started to rehabilitate the building, it was occupied by ten Negro families. The fine old drawing room was found to be piled four feet deep with rubbish. The whole interior was covered with grime, the fireplaces closed up, windows broken, but the structure,

built a century before, had been denied no effort or expense to make it worthy of the Tayloes, and it still stood staunch and sound against time and neglect.

Miraculously the slender balusters of the famous stairway continued to serve, undoubtedly helped by the fact that every fifth baluster is of iron, firmly jointed to the handrail and carriage. Even the Coade Stone mantels in drawing room and dining room, with their deeply undercut sculpture, show not a chip nor scar. They had been brought from London in 1799 and bear that date with the maker's name.

On January 1, 1899, the Institute took formal possession of the rehabilitated mansion, its stable, smokehouse and garden.

So much for the house itself. I was given free rein to interview the staff, and proceeded to do so. I carefully tabulated the testimony given me by the employees individually, and checked the records of each of them for reliability and possible dark spots. There were none.

In view of the fact that nobody was exactly eager to be put down as having heard or seen ghosts, far from seeking publicity or public attention, I can only regard these accounts as respectable experiences of well-balanced individuals.

The building itself was then and still is in the care of Alric H. Clay, a man in his thirties, who is an executive with the title of superintendent. The museum part of the Octagon, as different from the large complex of offices of the American Institute of Architects, is under the supervision of Mrs. Belma May, who is its curator. She is assisted by a staff of porters and maids, since on occasion formal

The haunted stairs

The carpet where the girl landed and died continues to fling itself back and forth by unseen hands

dinners or parties take place in the oldest part of the Octagon.

Mrs. May is not given to hallucinations or ghost stories, and in a matter-of-fact voice reported to me what she had experienced in the building. Most of her accounts are of very recent date.

Mrs. May saw the big chandelier swing of its own volition while all windows in the foyer were tightly shut; she mentioned the strange occurrence to a fellow worker. She also hears strange noises, not accounted for, and mostly on Saturdays. On one occasion, Mrs. May, accompanied by porters Allen and Bradley, found tracks of human feet in the otherwise undisturbed dust on the top floor, which had long been closed to the public. The tracks looked to her as "if someone were standing on toes, tiptoeing across the floor." It was from there that the daughter of Colonel Tayloe had jumped.

Mrs. May often smells cooking in the building when there is no party. She also feels "chills" on the first-floor landing.

Caretaker Mathew reports that when he walks up the stairs, he often feels as if someone is walking behind him, especially on the second floor. This is still happening to him now.

Ethel Wilson, who helps with parties, reports "chills" in the cloakroom.

Porter Allen was setting up for a meeting on the ground floor in the spring of 1962, when he heard noises "like someone dragging heavy furniture across the floor upstairs." In March, 1963, he and his colleague saw the steps "move as if someone was walking on them, but there was no one there." This happened at 9:30 A.M.

Porter Bradley has heard groaning, but the sound is hard to pin down as to direction. Several times he has also heard footsteps.

Alric H. Clay was driving by with his wife and two children one evening in the spring of 1962, when he noticed that the lights in the building were on. Leaving his family in the car, he entered the closed building by the back door and found everything locked as it should be. However, in addition to the lights being on, he also noticed that the *carpet edge was flipped* up at the spot where the girl had fallen to her death in the 1800s.

Clay, not believing in ghosts, went upstairs; there was nobody around, so he turned the lights off, put the carpet back as it should be, and went downstairs into the basement where the light controls are.

At that moment, *on the main floor above* (which he had just left) *he clearly heard someone* walk from the drawing room to the door and back. Since he had just checked all doors and knew them to be bolted firmly, he was so upset he almost electrocuted himself at the switches. The steps were heavy and definitely those of a man.

In February of 1963 there was a late party in the building. After everybody had left, Clay went home secure in the knowledge that he alone possessed the key to the back door. The layout of the Octagon is such that nobody can hide from an inspection, so a guest playing a prank by staying on is out of the question.

At 3 A.M. the police called Clay to advise him that all lights at the Octagon were blazing and that the building was wide open. Mr. Woverton, the controller, checked and together with the police went through the building, turning off all lights once more. Everything was locked up again, in the presence of police officers.

At 7 A.M., however, they returned to the Octagon once more, only to find the door unlocked, the lights again burning. Yet, Clay was the only one with the key!

"Mr. Clay," I said, "after all these weird experiences, do you believe in ghosts?"

"No, I don't," Clay said, and laughed somewhat uneasily. He is a man of excellent educational background and the idea of accepting the uncanny was not at all welcome to him. But there it was.

"Then how do you explain the events of the past couple of years?"

"I don't," he said and shrugged. "I just don't have a rational explanation for them. But they certainly happened."

From the testimony heard, I am convinced that there are two ghosts in the Octagon, restlessly pacing the creaking old floors, vying with each other for the attention of the flesh-and-blood world outside.

There are the dainty footsteps of Colonel Tayloe's suicide daughter, retracing the walks she enjoyed but too briefly; and the heavy, guilt-laden steps of the father, who cannot cut himself loose from the ties that bind him to his house and the tragedy that darkened both the house and his life.

✳ 54
The Octagon Revisited

BACK IN 1965 I published a comprehensive account of the hauntings and strange goings-on at one of Washington's most famous houses. Frequently referred to as "the second White House" because it served in that capacity to President Madison during the War of 1812, the Octagon still stands as a superb monument to American architecture of the early nineteenth century. Most people hear more about the Pentagon than about the Octagon when referring to Washington these days, but the fact is that the Octagon is still a major tourist attraction, although not for the same reasons that brought me there originally. As a matter of fact, The American Institute of Architects, who own the building, were and are quite reluctant to discuss their unseen tenants. It took a great deal of persuasion and persistence to get various officials to admit that there was something amiss in the old building.

After my first account appeared in *Ghosts I've Met*, which Bobbs-Merrill published in 1965, I received a number of calls from people in Washington who had also been to the Octagon and experienced anything ranging from chills to uncanny feelings. I also found that the executives of The American Institute of Architects were no longer quite so unfriendly towards the idea of a parapsychologist investigating their famous old headquarters. They had read my account and found in it nothing but truthful statements relating to the history and psychic happenings in the house, and there really was nothing they could complain about. Thus, over the years I remained on good terms with the management of The American Institute of Architects. I had several occasions to test the relationship because once in a while there seemed to be a chance to make a documentary film in Washington, including, of course, the

Octagon. It didn't come to pass because of the difficulties involved not with The American Institute of Architects but the more worldly difficulties of raising the needed capital for such a serious-minded film.

* * *

Originally I became aware of the potential hauntings at the Octagon because of a *Life* magazine article in 1962. In a survey of allegedly haunted houses, *Life* claimed that some visitors to the Octagon had seen a shadow on the spot where a daughter of Colonel Tayloe, who had built the house, had fallen to her death. As far as I could ascertain at the time, there was a tradition in Washington that Colonel John Tayloe, who had been the original owner of the Octagon, had also been the grieving father of a daughter who had done the wrong thing marriage-wise. After she had run away from home, she had later returned with her new husband asking forgiveness from her stern father and getting short shrift. In desperation, so the tradition goes, she then flung herself from the third-floor landing of the winding staircase, landing on a spot near the base of the stairs. She died instantly. That spot, by the way, is one of those considered to be the most haunted parts of the Octagon.

A somewhat different version is given by Jacqueline Lawrence in a recent survey of Washington hauntings published by the *Washington Post* in October of 1969. According to Miss Lawrence, Colonel Tayloe had more than one daughter. Another daughter, the eldest one, had fallen in love with a certain Englishman. After a quarrel with her father, who did not like the suitor, the girl raced up the stairs and when she reached the second landing, went over the bannister and fell two flights to her death. This, then, would have been not a suicide but an accident. As for the other daughter, the one who had brought home the wrong suitor according to tradition, Miss Lawrence reports that she did not marry the man after all. Her father thought of this young Washington attorney as a man merely after his daughter's money and refused to accept him. This was especially necessary as he himself had already chosen a wealthy suitor for his younger daughter. Again an argument ensued, during which he pushed the girl away from him. She fell over that same ill-fated bannister, breaking her neck in the fall. This also according to Miss Lawrence was an accident and not suicide or murder.

In addition to these two unfortunate girls, she also reports that a slave died on that same staircase. Pursued by a British naval officer, she threw herself off the landing rather than marry him. According to Miss Lawrence, the young man immediately leaped after her and joined her in death.

It is a moot question how easily anyone could fall over the bannister, and I doubt that anyone would like to try it as an experiment. But I wondered whether perhaps the story of the two girls had not in the course of time become confused into one tradition. All three deaths would have had to take place prior to 1814. In that year Washington was taken by the British, and after the burning of the White House President Madison and his family moved temporarily into the Octagon. They stayed there for one full year, during which the Octagon was indeed the official White House.

Only after President Madison and his family had left the Octagon did accounts of strange happenings there become known. People in Washington started to whisper that the house was haunted. Allegedly, bells could be heard when there was no one there to ring them. The shade of a girl in white had been observed slipping up the stairway. The usual screams and groans associated with phantoms were also reported by those in the know. According to Miss Lawrence, seven years after the Civil War five men decided to stay in the house after dark to prove to themselves that there was nothing to the stories about the haunting. They too were disturbed by footsteps, the sound of a sword rattling, and finally, human shrieks. Their names, unfortunately, are not recorded, but they did not stay the night.

After some correspondence with J. W. Rankin, Director of the Institute, my wife, Catherine, and I finally started out for Washington on May 17, 1963. The beautiful Georgian mansion greeted us almost as if it had expected us. At the time we did not come with a medium. This was our first visit and I wanted to gain first impressions and interview those who actually had come in contact with the uncanny, be it visual or auditory. First I asked Mr. Rankin to supply me with a brief but concise rundown on the history of the house itself. It is perhaps best to quote here my 1965 report in *Ghosts I've Met*. (See quote on page 313.)

Only one prior account of any unusual goings-on at the Octagon had come to my attention before my visit in 1963. The July 1959 issue of *The American Institute of Architects' Journal* contains a brief account of the long service record of a certain employee named James Cypress.

Although Mr. Cypress himself had never seen any ghosts, he did report that there was an unusual occurrence at one time when his wife was ill and in need of a doctor. The doctor had reported that he had seen a man dressed in the clothes of about one hundred fifty years ago coming down the spiral staircase. The doctor looked at the stranger somewhat puzzled. At that instant the apparition dissolved into thin air, leaving the medical man even more bewildered. A short time before publication of *Ghosts I've Met*, Joy Miller of the Associated Press wrote to me about the Octagon ghosts, adding a few more details to the story.

Legend has it that on certain days, particularly the anniversary of the tragic affair, no one may cross the hall at the foot of the stairway where the body landed without unconsciously going around an unseen object lying there.

The story of the bells that ring without due cause also is embroidered in this account.

Once, so a story goes, a skeptic leaped up and caught hold of the wires as they started to ring. He was lifted off the floor but the ringing kept on. To keep superstitious servants, the house was entirely rewired, and this apparently did the trick.

Of course, accounts of this kind are usually anonymous, but as a parapsychologist I do not accept reports no matter how sincere or authentic they sound unless I can speak personally to the one to whom the event has occurred.

When I started to assemble material for this book, I wondered what had happened at the Octagon since 1963. From time to time I keep reading accounts of the hauntings that used to be, but nothing startling or particularly new had been added. It became clear to me that most of these newspaper articles were in fact based on earlier pieces and that the writers spent their time in the research libraries rather than in the Octagon. In April of 1969 I contacted The American Institute of Architects again, requesting permission to revisit the Octagon, quietly and discreetly but with a medium. The new executive director, William H. Scheick, replied courteously in the negative: "The Octagon is now undergoing a complete renovation and will be closed to visitors until this work is completed. We hope the Octagon will be ready for visitors in early 1970. I am sorry that you and your guest will not be able to see the building when you are in Washington."

But Mr. Scheick had not reckoned with the persistence and flexibility of an erstwhile ghost hunter. I telephoned him and after we had become somewhat better acquainted, he turned me over to a research staff member who requested that I let him remain anonymous. For the purpose of this account, then, I will refer to him simply as a research assistant. He was kind enough to accompany us on a tour of the Octagon, when we managed to come to Washington, despite the fact that the house was in repair or, rather, disrepair.

The date was May 6, 1969; the day was hot and humid, as so many days in May are in Washington. With me was my good friend Ethel Johnson Meyers, whom I had brought to Washington for the purpose of investigating several houses, and Mrs. Nicole Jackson, a friend who had kindly offered to drive us around. I can't swear that Mrs. Meyers had not read the account of my earlier investigation of the Octagon. We never discussed it particularly, and I doubt very much that she had any great interest in matters of this kind, since she lives in New York City and rarely goes to Washington. But the possibility exists that she had read the chapter, brief as it is, in my earlier book. As we will see in the following pages, it really didn't matter whether she had or had not. To her, primary impressions were always the thing, and I know of no instance where she referred back to anything she had done before or read before.

* * *

When we arrived at the Octagon, we first met with the research assistant. He received us courteously and first showed us the museum he had installed in the library. We then proceeded through the garden to the Octagon building itself, which is connected with the library building by a short path. Entering the building from the rear rather than the imposing front entrance as I had in 1963, we became immediately aware of the extensive work that was going on inside the old building. Needless to say, I regretted it, but I also realized the necessity of safeguarding the old structure. Hammering of undetermined origin and workmen scurrying back and forth were not particularly conducive to any psychic work, but we had not choice. From noon to 1 o'clock was the agreed-upon time for us, and I hoped that we could at least learn something during this brief period. I urged Ethel to find her own bearings the way she always does, and the three of us followed her, hoping to catch what might come from her lips clairvoyantly or perhaps even in trance.

Immediately inside the building, Ethel touched me, and I tried to edge closer to catch what came from her. She was quite herself and the impressions were nothing more than clairvoyant descriptions of what raced through her mind. We were standing in the room to the left of the staircase when I caught the name "Alice."

"What about Alice?" I asked. "Who is she?"

"I don't know. It just hit me."

"I won't tell you any more than that you should try to find your way around this general area we are in now, and upstairs as far as you feel like."

"Oh yes, my goodness, there's so many, they won't stay still long enough. There's one that has *quite a jaw*—I don't see the top of the face yet; just a *long jaw*."

"Man or woman?"

"Man."

"Is this an imprint from the past or is this a person?"

"From the past."

"Go over to this bannister here, and touch the bannister and see whether this helps you establish contact."

"I see a *horse face*."

"Is this part of his character or a physical impairment?"

"Physical impairment."

"What is his connection with this house?"

"I just see him here, as if he's going to walk out that door. Might have a high hat on, also. I keep hearing, 'Alice. Alice.' As if somebody's calling."

"Are there several layers in this house, then?"

"I would say there are several layers."

"Is there anything about this area we're standing in that is in any way interesting to you?" We were now in front of the fatal banister.

"Well, this is much more vivid. This is fear."

She seemed visibly agitated now, gripping the banister with both hands. Gently, I pried her loose and led her up a few steps, then down again, carefully watching her every move lest she join the hapless Tayloe girls. She stopped abruptly at the foot of the stairs and began to describe a man she sensed near the staircase—a phantom man, that is. Connected with this male ghost, however, was another person, Ethel indicated.

"Someone has been carried down these steps after an illness, and out of here. That's not the man, however. It seems to be a woman."

"What sort of illness?"

"I don't know. I just see the people carrying her down—like on a stretcher, a body, a sick person."

"Was this person alive at the time when she was carried down?"

"Alive, but very far gone."

"From where did she come?"

"I think from down here." Ethel pointed toward the spot beneath the bannister. "There is also a Will, but during this time I don't think Will is alive, when this happens. I also find the long-faced man walking around. *I can see through him.*"

"Is he connected with the person on the stretcher?"

"I would say so, because he follows it." Then she added, "Someone comes here who is still alive from *that*. Moved around."

"A presence, you mean?" She nodded. "This man with the horse face—what sort of clothes did he wear?"

"A formal suit with a long coat. Turn of the century or the twenties?"

"The *nineteen*-twenties?"

"Somewhere in here, yes."

"And the person on the stretcher—do you see her?"

"No, she's covered up. It is the woman I still see in here."

"Why don't you go up those stairs, to about the first landing."

"I am afraid of that, *for some reason or other.*"

"Why do you suppose that is?"

"I don't like it."

"Did something happen in that area?"

"I don't know. I'm just getting a feeling as if I don't want to go. But I'll go *anyway.*"

"See whether you get any more impressions in doing that!"

"I'm getting a cerebral heaviness, in the back of the head."

"Was somebody hurt there?"

"I would say. Or—stricken."

"What is the connection? Take one or two steps only, and see whether you feel anything further in doing this. You're now walking up the stairs to the first landing."

"Oh, my head. Whew!"

"You feel—?"

"Numb."

"We're not going further than the first landing. If it is too difficult, don't do it."

"No. I'll take it for what it is." Suddenly, she turned. "Don't push me!"

"Somebody's trying to push you?"

"Yes."

I didn't feel like testing the matter. "All right, come back here. Let us stand back of the first landing."

"I get a George, too. And Wood, and something else. I'm holding onto my head, that hurts, very badly."

"Do you know who is this connected with, the injury to the head?"

"It sounds like Jacques."

"Is he connected with this house in any official capacity?"

"Well, this is a definite ghost. He's laughing at me. I don't like it!"

"Can you get any name for this person?"

"Again I get Jacques."

"Did anything tragic ever happen here?"

"I would say so. I get two individuals here—the long-faced man, and a shorter-faced man who is much younger."

"Are they of the same period?"

"No."

"Where does the woman on the stretcher fit in?"

"In between, or earlier."

"What is this tragic event? What happened here?"

"I can hardly get anything. It feels like my brains are gone."

"Where do you think it happened? In what part of the building?"

"Here, of course, *here.*"

"Did somebody die here? Did somebody get hurt?"

"According to my head, I don't know how anybody got through this. It is like *blown off.* I can't feel it at all. I have to put my hand up to find it."

"Are the presences still here?"

Instead of replying, Ethel put up her hands, as if warding off an unseen attack. "Oh, no!"

"Why did you just move like this? Did you feel anyone present?"

"Yes—as if somebody was trying to get hold of me, and I don't want that. I don't know how long I can take the head business, right here..."

"All right, we'll go down. Tell them, whoever might be present, that if they have to say something, they should say it. Whatever information they have to pass on, we are willing to listen. Whatever problem they might have."

Ethel seemed to struggle again, as if she were being possessed.

"There's something foreign here, and I can't make out what is being said."

"A foreign language?"

"Yes."

"What language is it?"

"I'm not sure; it's hard to hear. It sounds more Latin than anything else."

"A Latin language? Is there anything about this house that makes it different from any other house?"

"There's a lot of foreign influence around it."

"Was it used in any way other than as a dwelling?"

"There were séances in this place."

"Who do you think held them?"

"Mary."

"Who is this Mary?"

"She parted her hair in the middle. Heavy girl. I've got to put my hand up, always to my head, *it hurts so.*"

"Do you get the names of the people involved in this horrible accident, or whatever it is that you describe, this painful thing?"

"That has to be Mary who's taken down the steps. I think it's this one."

"The tragedy you talk about, the pain..."

"It seems like it should be *here,* but it could have been somewhere else. I don't understand. There are two layers here."

"There may be many layers."

"There are so many people around here, it's so hard to keep them separate."

"Do you get the impression of people coming and going? Is there anything special about the house in any way?"

"I would say there is. *The highest people in the land have lived here.* I'm positively torn by the many things. Someone married here with the name of Alice. *That* has nothing to do with the head."

"Alice is another layer?"

"That's right."

"Mary has the injury to her head. Is the marriage of Alice later or earlier?"

"Much later." Then she added. "This house is terribly psychic, as it were—it is as if I have been able to find the easiest possible connections with a lot of people through what has been done here, psychically. There's a psychic circle around this place. From the past."

"Do you feel that these manifestations are still continuing?"

"I would say there are, yes. I don't know what all this rebuilding is doing to it, particularly when the painting starts. Has Lincoln had anything to do with this house? I feel that I see him here."

"What would be his connection with the house?"

"Nothing at all, but *he's been here.*"

"Why would he be here?"

"I see an imprint of him."

"As a visitor?"

"I would say, yes. Some other high people have been here, too."

"As high as he?"

"That's right."

"Before him or after him?"

"After."

"What about before? Has anybody been as high as he here?"

"I would say so." Ethel, somewhat sheepishly, continued. "The man with the long face, he looks like Wilson!"

At that I raised my eyebrows. The mention of President Lincoln, and now Wilson, was perhaps a little too much name-dropping. On the other hand, it immediately occurred to me that both of these dignitaries must have been present at the Octagon at one time or other in their careers. Even though the Octagon was not used as a second White House after the disastrous War of 1812, it had frequently been used as a major reception hall for official or semiofficial functions. We do not have any record as to President Lincoln's presence or, for that matter, Wilson's but it is highly likely that both of these men visited and spent time at the Octagon. If these occasions included some festivities, an emotional imprint might very well have remained behind in the atmosphere and Ethel would, of course, pick that up. Thus her mention of Lincoln and Wilson wasn't quite as outlandish as I had at first thought.

* * *

For several minutes now I had noticed a somewhat disdainful smile on the research assistant's face. I decided to discontinue questioning Ethel, especially as it was close to 1 o'clock now and I knew that the assistant wanted to go to lunch.

I wondered whether any of the foregoing material made any sense to him. Frankly, I didn't have much hope that it did, since he had been honest enough to communicate his lack of faith in the kind of work I was doing. But he had been kind enough to come along, so the very least I could do was use his services such as they might turn out to be.

The name Alice meant nothing to him, but then he was tuned in on the history of the Octagon rather than Washington history in general. Later, at the Wilson House I realized that Ethel was in some peculiar way catapulting her psychic readings. It appeared that Alice meant a good deal in the history of President Wilson.

What about Lincoln? The assistant shook his head.

"The family left the house about 1854, and I guess Lincoln was a Congressman then. He could have been here, but..."

"You're not sure?"

"I mean, he's not on the list that we have of people who have been here. I have no knowledge of it."

Colonel Tayloe died in 1854, and the house was owned by the family until after 1900 when the Institute bought it. But it was not occupied by the Tayloe family after the Colonel's death. I wondered why.

As to the names of the Tayloes' daughters, the research assistant wasn't very helpful either. He did have the names of some of the daughters, but he couldn't put his hands on them right now. He did not remember Mary. But, on reflection, there might have been.

I turned to Ethel. It was clear to me that the noise of the returning workmen, who had just finished their lunch hour, and the general tone of the conversation did not help to relax her. I thanked the assistant for his presence, and we left the building. But before we had walked more than a few steps, Ethel stopped suddenly and turned to me and said, "Somebody was murdered here, or badly wounded at least." She felt it was the woman on the stretcher. She was not completely sure that death had been due to murder, but it was certainly of a violent kind. I pointed at a portrait on the wall; the picture was that of Colonel Tayloe. Did Ethel recognize the man in the picture, I asked, without of course indicating who he was. Perhaps she knew anyway. She nodded immediately.

"That's the man. I saw him."

He was one of the men she had seen walking about with a peculiar tall hat. She was quite sure. The face somehow had stuck in her mind. Ethel then pointed at another portrait. It was a photograph of Mrs. Wilson. She too had been at the Octagon. Ethel felt the presence.

"Would this be 1958?" she asked somewhat unsure. The date seemed possible.

In evaluating Ethel's performance, I kept in mind that she had rarely if ever been wrong in pinpointing presences in haunted houses. Under the circumstances, of course, there was no possibility of Ethel going into full trance. Her contact with the entities was at the very best on the surface. Nevertheless, if three lady ghosts mentioned by Jacqueline Lawrence in her article had been present, then Ethel would surely have felt, seen, or otherwise indicated them. I am quite sure that Ethel never saw the article in the *Washington Post*. I am also equally sure that had she seen it, it would have made no difference to her, for she is a dedicated and honest medium. In the building itself she found her way to the psychic "hot spot" without my help, or in any way relying on my guidance. Had she been there before it would have made no difference, since the renovation had completely altered the impression and layout of the downstairs. I myself was hard put to find my way around, even though I had been to the Octagon on two previous occasions.

Thus, Ethel Johnson Meyers tended to confirm the original contention published by me in 1965. One girl ghost and one male ghost, daughter and father, would be the logical inhabitants of the Octagon at this time. Whether or not the entities themselves are aware of their plight is a moot question.

It appears to be equally difficult to ascertain the true nature of the girl's problem. Had she merely brought home a suitor whom her father did not like, or had she actually gotten married? Strange as it seems, the records are not clear in this case. What appears to be certain, at least to me, is her death by falling from the upper story. Ethel Johnson Meyers would not have picked up the "passing condition" had she not genuinely felt it. Furthermore, these impressions were felt by the medium on the very spot where traditionally the girl landed. Thus, Ethel was able to confirm the continuous presence of an unfortunate young woman in what used to be her father's house. Since the two

Presidents whom the medium felt in some way attached to the house are hardly of the ghostly kind, it remains for Colonel Tayloe himself to be the man whose footsteps have been identified by a number of witnesses.

* * *

The American Institute of Architects no longer considers the Octagon the kind of museum it was before the renovation. It prefers that it be known primarily as their headquarters. Also, it is doubtful that the frequent parties and social functions that used to take place inside its walls will be as frequent as in the past, if indeed the Institute will permit them altogether.

If you are a visitor to the nation's capital and are bent on unusual sights, by all means include the Octagon in your itinerary. Surely once the renovation is completed there can be no reason—I almost said no earthly reason—for a visitor to be denied the privilege of visiting the American Institute of Architects. And as you walk about the Octagon itself and look up at the staircase perhaps wondering whether you will be as fortunate, or unfortunate as the case may be, as to see one of the two phantoms, remember that they are only dimly aware of you if at all. You can't command a ghost to appear. If you manage to wangle an invitation to spend the night, perhaps something uncanny might happen—but then again, it might not. What you can be sure of, however, is that I haven't "deghosted" the Octagon by any means even though a medium, Ethel Johnson Meyers, was briefly almost on speaking terms with its two prominent ghosts.

It remains to be seen, or heard, whether further psychic phenomena take place at the Octagon in the future.

☀ 55

The Integration Ghost

DURING THE HOT, HUMID July days of 1964, while blacks rioted in Harlem and Brooklyn and the black-and-white struggle was being brought to fever pitch by agitators on both sides, I was fortunate enough to help free a black gentleman from his unhappy state between the two worlds.

It all started with my appearance on a program called "To Tell the Truth," which, to tell the truth, frequently doesn't—in the interest of good showmanship, of course.

The program, as most Americans know, consists of a panel of three so-called celebrities, who shoot questions at three guests, and try to determine, by their answers, which one is the real McCoy, and which two are imposters.

I appeared as one of three alleged ghost hunters, two of whom were frauds. One of my imposters, incidentally, was later involved in a real fraud, but my ESP wasn't work-

ing well at the time of my meeting with him, or I would have objected to his presence.

I played it cool, appearing neither too knowing nor exactly stupid. Nevertheless, the majority of the panel knew which of us was the Ghost Hunter and I was unmasked. Panelist Phyllis Newman thought I was pale enough to be one of my own ghosts, and comedian Milton Kamen wondered about the love life of my ghosts, to which I deadpanned, "I never invade the private lives of my clients."

Artie Shaw wanted to know if I had read a certain book, but of course I had to inform him that I usually read only *Ghost Hunter*, especially on network television shows.

Actually, I almost became a ghost myself on this program, for the lights so blinded me I nearly fell off the high stage used to highlight the three guests at the start of the show.

On October 10, 1963, I received a note from the receptionist of the program, who had apparently read *Ghost Hunter* and had something of special interest to tell me.

Alice Hille is a young lady of considerable charm, as I later found, whose family was originally from Louisiana, and who had always had an interest in ghost stories and the like.

The experience she was about to report to me concerned a staffer at Goodson-Todman, Frank R., a television producer, and about as levelheaded a man as you'd want to find.

It was he who had had the uncanny experience, but Alice thought I ought to know about it and, if possible, meet him. Since she herself, being African-American, had an interest in an intelligent approach to integration, the particularities of the case intrigued her even more. She wrote me:

It seems that there was a colored man named John Gray. He was a personal friend of Frank's. Mr. Gray had renounced his race and had proceeded to live in the "white world," dressing with only the finest of taste. He died of cancer after a long illness, and his family provided him with a real old-fashioned Southern funeral. Mr. Gray would have been appalled at the way he was being laid to rest, as he had once said, should he die, he wanted to be cremated, and his ashes spread over the

areas of Manhattan where he would not have been allowed to live, had he been known as a Negro.

Alice then proceeded to tell me of Frank's uncanny experience, and gave me the address of the apartment where it happened.

It took me three or four months to get hold of Frank R. and get the story firsthand. Finally, over a drink at Manhattan's fashionable Sheraton-East Hotel, I was able to pin him down on details.

Frank had met John Gray through his roommate, Bob Blackburn. At the time Bob and Frank lived not far from what was now the haunted apartment, and when they heard that John Gray was ill, they went to see him in the hospital. This was the year 1961. Gray, only thirty-three, knew he was dying. To the last he complained that his friends did not come to visit him often enough. He had been an employee of the Department of Welfare, with odd working hours which usually had brought him home to his apartment in the middle of the afternoon.

Three months after John Gray's death, the two friends took over his vacated apartment. Not long after, Frank R. found himself alone in the apartment, resting in bed, with a book. It was the middle of the afternoon.

Suddenly, he clearly heard the front door open and close. This was followed by a man's footsteps which could be heard clearly on the bare floor.

"Who is it?" Frank called out, wondering. Only his roommate Bob had a key, and he certainly was not due at that time. There was no reply. The footsteps continued slowly to the bedroom door, which lies to the right of the large living-room area of the small apartment.

He heard the characteristic noise of the bedroom door opening, then closing, and footsteps continuing on through the room towards the bed. There they abruptly stopped.

Frank was terrified, for he could not see anything in the way of a human being. It was 3 P.M., and quite light in the apartment. Sweat started to form on his forehead as he lay still, waiting.

After a moment, he could hear the unseen visitor's footsteps turn around, slowly walk out again, and the noise of the door opening and closing was repeated in the same way as a few moments before. Yet despite the noise, the door did not actually open!

At first Frank thought he was ill, but a quick check showed that he did not suffer from a fever or other unusual state. He decided to put the whole incident out of his mind and within a day or so he had ascribed it to an overactive imagination. What, however, had brought on just this particular imaginary incident, he was never able to say.

He also thought better of telling Bob about it, lest he be branded superstitious or worse. There the matter stood until about six weeks later, when Bob Blackburn had the same experience. Alone in bed, he heard the steps, the doors open and close, but he did not panic. Somehow an incipient psychic sense within him guided him, and he *knew* it was his departed friend, John Gray, paying his former abode a visit.

The atmosphere had taken on a tense, unreal tinge, electrically loaded and somehow different from what it had been only a moment before.

Without thinking twice, Bob Blackburn leaned forward in bed and said in a low, but clear voice, "May your soul rest in peace, John."

With that, the unseen feet moved on, and the footsteps went out the way they had come in. Somehow, after this the two roommates got to discussing their psychic experiences. They compared them and found they had met John Gray's ghost under exactly the same conditions.

They left the apartment for a number of reasons, and it was not until about three years later that the matter became of interest again to Frank R.

At a party in the same neighborhood—Thirty-fourth Street and Third Avenue, New York—one of the guests, a Chilean named Minor, talked of his friend Vern who had just moved out of a haunted apartment because he could not stand it any longer.

Frank R., listening politely, suddenly realized, by the description, that Minor was talking about John Gray's old apartment.

"People are walking all over the place," Vern was quoted as saying, and he had moved out, a complete nervous wreck.

The apartment remained empty for a while, even though the rent was unusually low. The building passed into the hands of the owners of a fish restaurant downstairs. Most of the tenants in the five-story walkup are quiet artists or business people. The building is well kept and the narrow staircase reveals a number of smallish, but cozy flatlets, of which Manhattan never has enough to satisfy the needs of the younger white-collar workers and artists.

John Gray must have been quite comfortable in these surroundings and the apartment on Third Avenue probably was a haven and refuge to him from the not-so-friendly world in which he had lived.

"Very interesting," I said, thanking Frank R. for his story. I asked if he himself had had other psychic experiences.

"Well, I'm Irish," he said, and smiled knowingly, "and I'm sort of intuitive a lot of times. When I was very young, I once warned my mother not to go to the beach on a certain day, or she would drown. I was only fourteen years old at the time. Mother went, and did have an accident. Almost drowned, but was pulled out just in time."

"That explains it," I said. "You must be psychic in order to experience the footsteps. Those who have uncanny experiences are mediumistic to begin with, otherwise they would not have heard or seen the uncanny."

Frank R. nodded. He quite understood and, moreover, was willing to attend a séance I was going to try to arrange if I could talk to the present occupants of the haunted apartment. On this note we parted company, and Frank promised to make inquiries of the landlord as to whether the apartment was still vacant.

Apartment 5A was far from empty. A young and attractive couple by the name of Noren had occupied it for the past six months.

When I called and identified myself, they were puzzled about the nature of my business.

"Do you by any chance hear footsteps where no one is walking, or do you experience anything unusual in your apartment?" I asked innocently.

It was like a bombshell. There was a moment of stunned silence, then Mrs. Noren answered, "Why, yes, as a matter of fact, we do. Can you help us?"

The following day I went to visit them at the haunted apartment. Mr. Noren, a film editor for one of the networks, had not had any unusual experiences up to that time. But his wife had. Two or three months before my visit, when she was in the shower one evening, she suddenly and distinctly heard footsteps in the living room. Thinking it was her husband and that something was wrong, she rushed out only to find him still fast asleep in the bedroom. They decided it must have been he, walking in his sleep!

But a few weeks later, she heard the footsteps again. This time there was no doubt in her mind—they had a ghost.

I arranged for a séance on July 22, 1964, to make contact with the ghost.

My medium was Ethel Johnson Meyers, who was, of course, totally unaware of the story or purpose of our visit.

Among those present were three or four friends of the Norens, Frank R., Bob Blackburn, Alice Hille, an editor from Time-Life, a Mrs. Harrington, student of psychic science, the Norens, my wife, Catherine, myself—and two tiny black kittens who—in complete defiance of all tradition laid down for familiars and black cats in general—paid absolutely no attention to the ghost. Possibly they had not yet been told how to behave.

In a brief moment of clairvoyance, Ethel Meyers described two men attached to the place: one a white-haired gentleman whom Bob Blackburn later acknowledged as his late father, and a "dark-complexioned man," not old, not terribly young.

"He is looking at you and you," she said, not knowing the names of the two men. Frank and Bob tensed up in expectation. "He looks at you with one eye, sort of," she added. She then complained of breathing difficulties and I remembered that John Gray had spent his last hours in an oxygen tent.

Suddenly, the ghost took over. With a shriek, Mrs. Meyers fell to the floor and, on her knees, struggled over to where Bob Blackburn and Frank sat. Picking out these two contacts from among the many present was a sure sign of accuracy, I thought. Naturally, Mrs. Meyers knew nothing of their connection with the case of the ghost.

She grabbed Bob Blackburn's hand amid heavy sobs, and the voice emanating now from her throat was a deep masculine voice, not without a trace of a Southern accent. "It's a dream," he mumbled, then began to complain that Bob had not come to visit him!

Soothing words from Bob Blackburn and myself calmed the excited spirit.

When I tried to tell him that he was "dead," however, I was given a violent argument.

"He's mad," the ghost said, and sought solace from his erstwhile friend.

"No, John, he's right," Bob said.

"You too?" the ghost replied and hesitated.

This moment was what I had hoped for. I proceeded to explain what had happened to him. Gradually, he understood, but refused to go.

"Where can I go?" he said. "This is my house."

I told him to think of his parents, and join them in this manner.

"They're dead," he replied.

"So are you," I said.

Finally I requested the assistance of Ethel's control, Albert, who came and gently led the struggling soul of John Gray over to the "other side" of life.

"He isn't all there in the head," he commented, as he placed the medium back into her chair quickly. "Narcotics before passing have made him less than rational."

Was there any unsettled personal business? I wanted to know.

"Personal wishes, yes. Not all they should have been."

Albert explained that he had brought John's parents to take his arm and help him across, away from the apartment which had, in earth life, been the only refuge where he could really be "off guard."

An hour after trance had set on Mrs. Meyers, she was back in full command of her own body, remembering absolutely nothing of either the trance experience with John Gray, or her fall to the floor.

It was a steaming hot July night as we descended the four flights of stairs to Third Avenue, but I felt elated at the thought of having John Gray roam no more where he was certainly not wanted.

✳ 56

The Ardmore Boulevard Ghosts

ARDMORE BOULEVARD LIES in a highly respected and rather beautiful section of Los Angeles. It is a broad street, richly adorned by flowers, and substantial homes line it on both sides for a distance of several miles north and south.

The people who live here are not prone to ghost stories, and if something uncanny happens to them, they prefer that their names be kept secret.

Since that was the only condition under which I could have access to the house in question, I reluctantly agreed, although the names and addresses of all concerned in this case are known to me and to the American Society for Psychic Research, represented, in the investigation I made, in the person of its California head, Mrs. George Kern.

It all started unbeknown to me when I was a panelist on a television program emanating from the Linden Theatre in Los Angeles in December of 1963.

Shortly after, I received a letter from a lady whom we shall identify as Helen L. She wrote:

I consider myself lucky that I tuned in on the show you appeared on. You see, I live in a haunted house, and I do need help desperately.

I have heard a terrible struggle and fight in the middle of the night when I have gotten up to go to the bathroom! The other night I was reading in bed and smoking a cigarette. It was about 9:30, and I was completely engrossed in my book. Suddenly, I would say about a couple of feet to my right, a champagne cork popped loud and clear and then I heard it [champagne] being poured into a glass! I saw nothing, yet heard it all, and the horror of it is that it all took place right beside me.

I telephoned Helen L. as soon as I received a second letter from her.

There was no immediate possibility of going to Los Angeles to help her, but I wanted to establish personal contact and perhaps get a better idea of her personality in the process.

Miss L. struck me as a person of good educational background; her voice was well modulated and not at all hysterical. She sounded rather embarrassed by the whole thing and begged me to keep her name and exact address confidential. I explained that unfortunately there was no foundation to pay for an expedition to Los Angeles post-haste, nor was there as yet a television series to finance such a trip as part of its legitimate research.

Consequently, I had to provide the funds myself, and an author's funds are never enough.

I would go as soon as there was an opportunity to do so—an engagement to speak or to appear on the home screen which would take me to the coast. Meanwhile, would she write me whenever anything new was happening in the house. Also, could she give me a chronological account of the strange goings on in her house, blow by blow. On January 23, the lady obliged. Her letter seemed a bit more composed this time; evidently the promise of my coming out to see her had helped calm her nerves.

Just as I had asked her, she started at the beginning:

My mother bought our home around thirty-eight years ago. It had just been completed when we moved in. My mother had been widowed a few years previously and she brought my two sisters and myself from the Middle West to California because we were always sickly due to the fierce winters that we left behind.

About a couple of years after we moved in, we unfortunately lost almost everything. My mother then rented our house furnished and we lived elsewhere. She rented the house on a lease basis to five different tenants over an eight or nine year period.

There was an oil man who had a young wife and baby. My mother can only describe him as a great brute of a man with a surly disposition.

Our next-door neighbors called my mother while these people were living here and said that there had been a terrible fight at our house the night before and four other men were involved. They said that they could hear furniture being broken, and that they had almost called the police.

As to furniture being broken—it was all too true—as my mother discovered when they moved out.

In the back of the house are two bedrooms and a small room that we use as a den. These three rooms all have French doors and then screened doors that open onto a good-sized patio.

Things didn't start to happen right away after we moved back. It was quiet for a while, but then it started.

The first thing I remember was when I was about nineteen or twenty years old. Everyone had gone to bed, my sister had gone out, and I was writing a letter in my bedroom. Suddenly my locked French doors started to rattle and shake as if someone were desperately trying to get in. It just so happened that we had had our outside patio floor painted that very afternoon. I couldn't wait until I got out there the next morning to look for footprints in the paint. There weren't any. There wasn't even a dent.

I touched my finger to the freshly painted patio floor and a little of it adhered to my fingers.

We would also keep hearing a light switch being pushed every now and then, and no one in the room!

Sometimes my mother would ask me in the morning why I had been rapping on her bedroom door at night. I have never rapped on her door and she knows it now because that's another thing that goes on every now and then. Three raps on your bedroom door, usually late at night. I was married during World War II, and after the war my husband and I lived here for three years. I had a most unhappy married life and eventually we separated and I secured a divorce.

One night, while I was still married, my mother and sister were visiting relatives in the Middle West.

I was all alone, as my husband had gone out for a while. I had locked all the doors that lead to the back of the house as I always did when I was alone. It was only around 9 P.M. Suddenly I heard someone slowly turning the knob of the door that leads from the laundry to the den. Then it would stop and a few minutes later "it" would try again, turning and turning that knob!

My husband came home less than an hour later and we both went through the house together. Every window was bolted, every door was locked.

Then later, there was the man I kept steady company with for a long time. We met about eleven years ago and I remember so well after we had been out and he'd walk me up to my front door at night we would both hear these footsteps inside the house making a great deal of noise running to the front door as if to meet us!

Then, sometimes for weeks at a time, every night tapping on my furniture would start while I'd be in bed reading. "It" would go around and tap on all of my furniture, usually two or three taps at a time. I used to get so fed up with it all I'd yell out "Get out and leave me alone!" That didn't do any good because "it" would always come back.

When I used to sleep with my lights out up to five years ago, three times I was nearly smothered to death.

I always sleep on my left side—but for some strange reason I would slowly wake up lying flat on my stomach trying desperately to breathe.

Something seemed to have me in a vise wherein I absolutely could not move any part of my body, and would keep pressing my face into the pillow! I would try desperately to scream and fight it off, but I was absolutely powerless. Just when I knew I couldn't stand it any longer and was suffocating to death—I would be released, slowly!

But each time this happened—"it" would suffocate me a little longer. I felt that I would never live through it again, and hence have slept with my lights on ever since.

The same thing happened to my mother once when she had that room prior to my having it. She never told me about her own experience, however, until I told her of mine.

The champagne cork popping and the liquid being poured (it even bubbled) right beside me, without being seen, happened three times last year at approximately six-week intervals.

That too was in my bedroom; it happened once in my mother's bedroom also.

The loud shrill whistling in my right ear occurred last March or April when I came home one evening around 10 P.M. It was so loud it was more like a blast. It started as a whistle into my right ear just as soon as I opened the front door and stepped into the darkness of the house. I screamed and ran to the kitchen and when I turned the light on it stopped. The whistling sounded like the beginning of a military march, but there were just a few notes.

Occasionally we hear a whistling outside our house at night—but it is a *different* tune and sounds more as if it is calling to us.

My mother has heard articles on her dressing table being moved around while she was in bed at night. This happened twice last year.

Noises in our kitchen wake me up at night. They sound as if something were moving around, kettles being handled, and cupboards being opened.

One night about three years ago, I got up around midnight to go to the bathroom. While I was in the bathroom, I heard loudly and clearly a terrible fight going on in the living room. It was a wordless and desperate struggle!

How I got the courage to open the door to the living room I'll never know, but I did. It was completely dark—I saw nothing and the fighting stopped the instant I opened the door!

Some months later, my mother, sister, and I were awakened at night by a terrible fight going on right outside of our bedroom's French doors. It sounded as if every stick of our patio furniture were being broken by people who were fighting desperately but wordlessly. It lasted all of several minutes.

We didn't go outside, but the next morning we did. None of our furniture on the patio had been touched, everything was in its place and looked as pretty as it always had. Yet we had all been awakened by the terrible noise—and what sounded like the complete destruction of everything on our patio.

This blasted ghost even walks around outside in the back yard and on our driveway and sidewalks.

Several times when we have had relatives staying with us for a few days, my mother and my sister slept in our double garage on some of our patio chaise longues. They have always been awakened at night by heavy footsteps walking up to the garage door and then they hear nothing else. There are never any footsteps heard that indicate "it" is walking away! Let me also mention it would be almost impossible for a human intruder to get into our back yard. Everything is enclosed by high fences and a steel gate across the driveway.

Several years ago when I had fallen asleep on the couch in the den while looking at television, I awakened around 11 P.M. and turned the television off. Then I stretched and was just walking to my bedroom when I heard a voice enunciating most distinctly, and saying loudly and clearly, but slowly—"Oh woe—woe—woe—you've got to go—go—go!"

Last month I heard footsteps every night in the den, even after I had left that room only five minutes before.

I decided to seek verification of the experience with the footsteps from inside an empty house. The young man Helen had mentioned, William H., is a chemist and rather on the practical side.

"On quite a few instances upon returning to Helen's home and entering the house I heard what sounded to me noises of footsteps approaching to greet us as we entered the living room. I investigated to assure myself as well as Helen that there was no one there. I cannot explain it, but I definitely heard the noises."

I had encouraged Helen L. to report to me any further happenings of an uncanny nature, and I did not have to wait long. On February 3, 1964, she wrote me an urgent note:

On January 28th I woke up about 11:30 P.M. to go to the bathroom for a glass of water. As I turned on the light I pushed the bathroom door open, and I heard a loud, screeching, rusty sound. It sounded like some heavy oaken door that one might hear in a horror movie! I examined the bolts at the top and the bottom of the door and there was nothing wrong; the door was as light to the touch and easy to open as it always had been.

Incidentally, while the door was making those terrible noises, it woke my mother up. She had heard it, too.

On Friday night, January 31, I was in the small room that we call the den, in the back of the house.

I suddenly heard footsteps outside, walking very distinctly on the sidewalks right by the den windows and then suddenly they just ceased as they always do—outside!

They are definitely a man's footsteps, and I would say the footsteps of a man that knows exactly where he's going! It's always the same measured pace, and then they suddenly stop!

I asked Miss L. whether anyone had ever died in the house, whether by violence, or through ordinary ways. "As far as we know, nobody ever died," she replied.

I promised to make arrangements soon to visit the house with a medium. Miss L. meanwhile wanted me to know all about her mother and sister:

My sister here at home is retarded due to an injury at birth. Also, my mother is 80 years of age, an arthritic with crippled hands and feet and suffers from the added complication of heart disease.

Last night, February 2, I was reading in bed. It was around 10:30 P.M. Suddenly it sounded as if a body were thrown against my bedroom door.

Since this was the first I had heard of the sister's retarded condition, I naturally questioned her role in creating the strange phenomena. Knowing full well that a retarded person is often exactly like a youngster prior to puberty as far as the poltergeist phenomena are concerned, it occurred to me that the woman might be supplying the force required to perform some of the uncanny actions in the haunted house.

I tactfully suggested this possibility to Helen L., but she rejected any such possibility:

Her power of concentration is impaired and her nervous system more or less disorganized. You must also bear in mind that every door in this house that leads to another room is locked. There is only one door that we don't lock and that is the door that leads from the kitchen to the laundry.

She couldn't possibly produce the phenomena that even other friends of mine have witnessed when my sister has been over 3,000 miles away visiting relatives in Minnesota.

One thing I haven't told you is that I seem to have inherited a tendency of my mother's. We both dream dreams that come true—and have all of our lives. Many of them don't concern me at all or even people that are close to me, but they always come true.

One night I dreamt I saw this ghost who has been haunting our house. I was in bed and he was sitting on my cedar chest just looking at me. He seemed to be dressed in some early Grecian style—had rather curly hair—a frightfully mischievous expression and the most peculiar eyes. They were slanted up at the corners but he was not Oriental. His eyes were rather dark and very bright but his face looked bloated—an unhealthy looking pasty white skin—and it was too fat. He was a pretty big young man. He looked anything but intelligent, in fact the expression on his face was quite idiotic! Now—can you make anything out of this?

The picture began to get clearer. For one thing, Helen L. had not understood my references to her retarded sister. I never suggested conscious fraud, of course. The possibility that her energies were used by the ghost began to fade, however, when Helen told me that the manifestations continued unabated in her absence from Los Angeles. Poltergeists don't work long distance.

Then, too, the incidents of earlier clairvoyance and premonitory dreams in Helen's life made it clear to me at this point that she herself must be the medium, or at least one of the mediums, supplying the force needed for the manifestations.

The psychic photo of the girl who died at a wild party in the house on Ardmore Boulevard, Los Angeles

Her strange dream, in which she saw the alleged ghost, had me puzzled. Could he be an actor?

As I began to make preparations for my impending visit to California, I was wondering about other witnesses who might have heard the uncanny footsteps and other noises. Helen L. had told me that a number of her friends had experienced these things, but were reluctant to talk:

There was only *one* time in my life that I was glad that this wretched ghost around here made himself known. I had a close lady friend for a number of years with whom I used to work. After I had known her a few years I took her into my confidence and told her that our house was haunted. She laughed and said of course there was no such thing as a ghost, and that I must be the victim of my own imagination. I didn't argue the point because I knew it was useless.

About one month later she called me on the phone on a Sunday afternoon and asked me if she could stop by and visit. She came by around 4 P.M., and I fixed a cup of coffee which I brought to my bedroom. She was sitting in my bedroom chair jabbering away—and I was sitting on my bed drinking my coffee. It was still daylight. Suddenly, this ghost started walking and thumping from the living room right up to my bedroom door and stopped. Margaret looked up at me brightly and said, "Why, Helen, I thought you said you were all alone—who on earth could that be?" I said, "Margaret, I am all alone here—no living person is in this house except you and me, and what you hear is what you call my imagination!"

She couldn't get out of this house fast enough, wouldn't even go out through the living room, but rushed out of my French doors that lead to the patio and that's the last I saw of her.

On February 23, Helen L. wrote again. There had been additional disturbances in the house, and she was able to observe them a little more calmly, perhaps because I had assured her that soon I would try to get rid of the nuisance once and for all.

Since I last wrote to you two or three weeks ago—for almost one solid week I would hear someone moving around in the den which adjoins my bedroom; sometimes within only 5 or 10 minutes after I would leave the den, lock the door, climb into bed and read—I would keep hearing these *furtive movements*. This time the walking would be soft—and "it" would keep bumping into the furniture; of late I am awakened quite frequently by someone that has thrown himself forcibly against the den door leading to my bedroom. This has happened several times at exactly 11:30 P.M., but has also happened as early as 8:30 P.M. The only way I can describe it is that someone is pretty damned mad at me for closing and locking that door and is registering a violent reaction in protest.

It actually sounds as if the door is about to be broken down. Then "it" has begun to rap loudly on the bedroom walls, two loud raps.

A week before I was due to arrive in Los Angeles, I had another note from Helen. On April 9, she wrote:

Last Saturday night I got home around midnight and went to bed with my book as usual. I was just about ready to doze off when a "bull-whip" cracked right over my head! The next night someone hit the bedboard of my bed real hard while I was sitting there in bed trying to read.

I've told you about the heavy man's footsteps outside, what I neglected to tell you is that my mother and sister are both awakened every once in a while between 3 and 4 A.M. by a woman's fast clicking shoes hurrying up our driveway and stopping at the gate that crosses the driveway towards the rear of the house! The last time was less than two weeks ago.

I wonder what the neighbors think when they hear her!

I arrived in Los Angeles on April 16 and immediately called Helen L. on the phone. We arranged for a quick initial visit the following day. Meanwhile I would make inquiries for a good medium. Once I had found the right person, I would return with her and the exorcism could begin.

The quick visit after my lecture, delivered to the Los Angeles branch of the American Society for Psychic Research, was of value inasmuch as I got to know Helen L.

a little better and could check on some of her reports once again. The house on Ardmore Boulevard was as comfortable and pleasant-looking as its owner had described it, and I would never have guessed that it had a sinister history.

That's the way it is sometimes with haunted houses; they just don't look the part!

Dick Simonton, an executive deeply interested in extra-sensory perception studies, accompanied me to the house. He, too, was impressed by Miss L.'s apparent levelheadedness under trying conditions.

Fortunately, I did not have to look far for a suitable medium or, at least, clairvoyant. Several months before my California trip, I had received a letter from a Mrs. Maxine Bell, who had seen me on a local television show:

I am a sincere medium willing to offer my talents for your research and experiments. For the past 20 years I have been doing much work for individuals with definite problems. Not once have I run into a poltergeist type, for my work is more spiritually oriented. Deep trance is not even necessary for me to work as I am extremely sensitive.

I am a woman in her late 40's who has had the gift of perception since 1938 and I have worked on the most serious cases of possession and some haunted-house cases as well. I would be most happy to serve you in any way.

I called Mrs. Bell and asked her to meet us the following day in front of the house. The time was 3 P.M. and it was one of those lovely California afternoons that are hard to reconcile with a ghost.

Obviously, Mrs. Bell had no chance to dig into the past of the house or even get to know the present owner. I told her to meet us at the corner but volunteered neither name nor details.

Soon she had seated herself in the living room across from Helen L., myself, Mrs. George Kern of the American Society for Psychic Research, and an associate of hers, Mr. G., who was psychic to a certain extent.

The house impressed him strongly. "I felt chilly on entering this house," he said. "There are two people here— I mean ghosts—one is a man in his middle years, and a young female who died by suffocation."

I immediately thought of Helen L.'s report of how she was almost suffocated a number of times by unseen hands!

"These two seek each other," Mr. G., an engineer by profession, continued. "The young person is about ten or twelve years old, feminine or a male with feminine characteristics. This child is lost and asking for help. There is wildness, she wants to do 'things,' she says, 'I want....'" Mr. G. was now breathing heavily, as if he were assuming the personality of the young ghost.

"This child may be a little older," he finally said, "maybe as much as fifteen years. She is very nervous... crying because of unexpressed emotions... this child lived in this house but had sad times here, too much discipline. I think both people died about the same time. I'd say at least fifteen to twenty years ago."

I thanked the engineer and turned to Mrs. Bell, who had quietly watched the "reading" of the house.

"I never interfere with another medium's impressions," she finally said, "but if he's finished, I'd like to add mine."

I nodded for her to go ahead.

"A Philip Stengel died here in 1934," she began. I looked at Helen L. The name did not register. But then her mother did not recall all of their tenants. There were quite a few.

"Ten years ago a person was murdered here," Mrs. Bell continued. "No—in 1948. There were violent arguments. Two men, one of them named Howard. Arguments in the driveway outside. The neighbors heard it, too. Two parties came here, there was that violent argument, and one was killed. Wounded in the abdomen. The body was lifted into a vehicle. One of them is staying here in this house, but there is also another person in the house. I feel sudden violence and money involved. A lady fled. Lots of money was at stake. Two people were here, the woman, however, had the house. The quarrel was due to a misunderstanding about money."

I was amazed. Unless Mrs. Bell had read Helen L.'s letters to me or spoken to her before coming here, she could not have known many of these details. The description of the quarrel and the attitude of the neighbors were exactly as described to me by Helen L.

I looked at the owner of the house who sat somewhat stunned by what she had heard.

"Well," she finally said to me, "there are two different kinds of footsteps—the ones in the back of the house sound like those of a man, while the ones in front are certainly more like a child's steps, very fast. The steps we hear around three or four in the morning are also woman's, I think. I'm sure the whistler we've heard is a man."

What were the facts around that quarrel?

Helen L. had looked into the matter further since my arrival.

"There was a fight," she said quietly. "An oilman lived here, he was married to a much younger woman, and they had a baby. He went away and a friend came to the house. There was a wild fight here."

"What about those rather quaint words you heard?" I questioned Miss L.

"You mean, 'Woe, woe, woe, you've got to go, go, go!'—why, they were spoken with a definite British accent."

"Or a theatrical phony British accent?"

"Perhaps."

We moved on to the bedroom where so much commotion had been observed. Mrs. Bell stood opposite the bed and the rest of us formed a circle around her. I asked the entity to leave, in a ritual known as a rescue circle, a verbal exorcism, which usually works. There are exceptions, of course.

I then took some photographs with my Super Ikonta B camera, a camera which is double-exposure proof because of a special arrangement of the transport and shutter systems. I used Agfa Record film and no artificial light. There was enough light coming in from the French windows. To my amazement, two of the pictures showed figures that were not visible to the naked eye, at least not to mine. One of the two clearly shows a female figure, rather young and slender, standing near the window in what looks like a diaphanous gown. Evidently the ghost wanted us to know she was watching us. I have since enlarged this picture and shown it on television.

There is no doubt about the figure, and I didn't put it there, either.

We returned to the living room and took our leave. I felt sure the evil entity had been dislodged or at least shaken up. Sometimes an additional visit is necessary to conclude the deed, but I could not stay any longer.

I had hardly touched New York soil, when a letter from Helen L. arrived:

I haven't written you sooner because I wanted to be sure that "it" has left, and I feel that "it" hasn't left entirely. I am suffering from a dreadful fatigue of mind and body and soul—and I'd like to cry and cry and never stop! On the Saturday night you were here, I woke up about 11:30 P.M. and walked into the kitchen, when I heard heavy footsteps walking in the dining room to the swinging kitchen door. Needless to say, I got out of there fast.

On May 17, Helen L. finally wrote to me some of the corroboration I asked her for. I wanted to know if any more of the material obtained by Maxine Bell could be checked out, and if so, with what results:

When Miss Bell was here, she said there was kindly gray-haired man standing before her who had died suddenly in my bedroom, years ago, of a heart attack. He hadn't expected to die, and had so much unfinished business. In talking to my mother later she feels that it was a man she had as a tenant here who was married for the second time, to a much younger woman. She said he had been ill with a heart condition and he was an extremely busy man with more than one business, including a railroad he owned. He had a baby daughter by his second wife and was quite cheerful and happy—and confident that he was over the heart attack he had previously suffered.

Nevertheless he did die suddenly and my mother always felt that he did die in this house, although his wife denied it. Even so, my mother released her from the lease. He was a gray-haired, very distinguished-looking man.

Now about the murder that Miss Bell mentioned and the terrible fight that took place that our neighbors reported to my mother.

Miss Bell was right when she said that the fight started toward the back of the house on the driveway. In fact, our neighbor came out and asked what was going on and the man he asked, whom he didn't know (probably a guest of our tenant's at that time) said, "Oh, nothing," and gave him his card which had an address on this street. Nevertheless the fight started again, and it was terrible—furniture being broken, etc. The neighbors didn't call the police because they didn't wish to become involved. My mother said that this particular tenant was a big brutish-looking man, married also to a young woman, and they too had a baby daughter.

The wife and baby were not here, according to our neighbors. They were away visiting relatives over the weekend.

My mother also told me that after they moved she did find blood spots on our floors.

For a while, I heard nothing further from the haunted address on Ardmore. Then a letter arrived, dated July 4. It was no fireworks message, but it contained the melancholy news that Helen L. was being plagued again by footsteps, thuds, movements, and other poltergeist manifestations.

I explained that I thought her own mediumistic powers made the manifestations possible and her fear of them might very well bring back what had been driven out. Such is the nature of anxiety that it can open the door to the uncanny where the strong in heart can keep it closed forever.

I also hinted that her own emotional state was extremely conducive to paranormal occurrences. Frustrations, even if unconscious, can create the conditions under which such manifestations flourish.

But Helen L. could not accept this.

"They'll always come back, no matter who lives here," she said, and looked forward to the day when she would sell the house.

What was needed was such a little thing—the firm conviction that "they" *could* be driven out, never to return. Instead, through apprehension as to whether the uncanny had *really* left, Helen L. had turned the closed door into a revolving door for herself.

✳ 57

The Ghost Who Refused to Leave

ONE OF THE MOST spectacular cases I reported in *Ghosts I've Met* concerned the hauntings at a house on Ardmore Boulevard, Los Angeles.

The house itself, barely thirty years old, was being plagued by the noises of a wild party going on at night, during which apparently someone was killed, by footsteps where nobody was seen walking and by other uncanny noises, including voices resounding in the dark, telling the current owners to get out of *their* house!

I had been to this house several times and brought Maxine Bell, a local psychic, on one occasion. That visit proved memorable not only because of material obtained by Miss Bell, in semi-trance, which proved accurate to a large degree, but because of my own photographic work.

Left alone in the most haunted part of the house, I took at random a number of black and white pictures of a particular bedroom which of course was empty, at least to my eyes.

On one of the pictures, taken under existing daylight conditions and from a firm surface, the figure of a young girl dressed in a kind of negligee appears standing near the window. As my camera is double exposure proof and both film and developing beyond reproach, there is no other rational explanation for this picture. Since that time, I have succeeded in taking other psychic photographs, but the "girl at the window" will always rank as one of my most astounding ones.

The whistling noises, the popping of a champagne bottle in the dark of night followed by laughter, the doors opening by themselves, and all the other psychic phenomena that had been endured by the owner of the house, Helen L., for a long time would not yield to my usual approach: trance session and order to the ghost to go away. There were complications in that Miss L. herself had mediumistic talents, although unsought and undeveloped, and there was present in the household a retarded sister, often the source of energies with which poltergeist phenomena are made possible.

Nevertheless, when we left the house on Ardmore Boulevard I had high hopes for a more peaceful atmosphere in the future. For one thing, I explained matters to Miss L., and for another, I suggested that the garden be searched for the body of that murder victim. We had already established that a fight had actually occurred some years ago in the house, observed by neighbors. It was entirely possible that the body of one of the victims was still on the grounds.

In July 1964 the noises resumed, and thuds of falling bodies, footfalls and other noises started up again in the unfortunate house. Quite rightly Helen L. asked me to continue the case. But it was not until the spring of 1965 that I could devote my energies toward this matter again.

All I had accomplished in the interim was a certain lessening of the phenomena, but not their elimination.

On March 14, 1965, Helen L. communicated with me in a matter of great urgency. For the first time, the ghost had been seen! At 3 A.M. on March 13, her mother had been awakened by strange noises, and looking up from the bed, she saw the figure of a man beside the bed. The noise sounded to her as if someone were tearing up bed-sheets. Frightened, the old lady pulled the covers over her head and went back to sleep. Helen L. also heard heavy footsteps all over the house that same night. Needless to say, they had no visitors from the flesh-and-blood world.

"Are you going to be here in April? Help!!" Helen L. wrote. I answered I would indeed come and bring Sybil Leek with me to have another and, hopefully, final go at this ghost. But it would have to be in June, not April. During the first week of May, Helen awoke on Sunday morning to hear a man's voice shushing her inches away from her pillow. She could hardly wait for our arrival after that. Finally, on June 28, I arrived at the little house with Sybil to see what she might pick up.

"I know there is a presence here," Sybil said immediately as we seated ourselves in the little office that is situated in back of the bedroom where most of the disturbances had occurred. I turned the light out to give Sybil a better chance to concentrate, or rather, to relax, and immediately she felt the intruder.

"It is mostly in the bedroom," she continued. "There are two people; the man dominates in the bedroom area, and there is also a woman, a young girl."

I decided Sybil should attempt trance at this point, and invited the ghost to make himself known. After a few moments, Sybil slipped into a state bordering on trance, but continued to be fully conscious.

"Morton," she mumbled now, "there is something terribly intense... have a desire to *break* something... Morton is the last name."

I repeated my invitation for him to come forward and tell his story.

"The girl goes away," Sybil intoned, "and he says he comes back to find her. And she isn't here. He was going to celebrate. He must find her. Wedding party, celebration... for the girl. She wasn't happy here; she had to go away. This man is a foreigner."

"You're right." The booming voice of Helen L. spoke up in the dark across the room. Evidently Sybil had described someone she recognized.

"Jane Morton," Sybil said now, flatly, "something to do with building, perhaps he had something to do with building this house... he's an older man. Jane... is young... I'm trying to find out where Jane is... that's what *he* wants to know... I will tell him it didn't matter about the party... she would have gone anyway... she hated the old man... this man fell... head's bad... fell against the stable..."

"Did he die here?" I pressed.

"1837," Sybil said, somewhat incongruously, "1837. Came back... went out again, came back with people, was drunk, hurt his head, left hand side...."

Despite my urging, the entity refused to speak through Sybil in trance. I continued to question her nevertheless.

The ghost's name was Howell Morton, Sybil reported, although I was not sure of the spelling of the first name, which might have been Hawall rather than Howell.

"He came here to do some building, someone was accidentally killed and buried in the garden..."

"Who buried this person?"

"Boyd Johnson... Raymond McClure... Dell... Persilla..." The voice was faltering now and the names not too clear.

"Is the girl dead too?"

"Girl's alive...."

"Is there anyone dead in this house outside of Morton?"

"Morton died here."

"Who was the figure I photographed here?"

"Jane... he wants to draw her back here... but I think she's alive... yet there are things of hers buried..."

Sybil seemed confused at this point.

"Meri... Meredith...." she said, or she could have said. "Married her." It just was not clear enough to be sure. Morton and some of his friends were doing the disturbing in the house, Sybil explained. He died at the party.

"There was violence outside," Sybil added and Helen L. nodded emphatically. There was indeed.

"Drunk... 4 o'clock... he died accidentally..."

Where is he buried in the garden, Helen L. wanted to know, anxiously.

"Straight down by the next building," Sybil replied. "It wasn't built completely when he died."

Later we all went into the garden and identified the building as the garage in back of the house.

But Helen was not yet ready to start digging. What would the neighbors think if we found a body? Or, for that matter, what would they think if we didn't? There we left it, for her to think over whether to dig or not to dig—that was the question.

I returned to New York in the hope that I would not hear anything further from Helen L. But I was mistaken. On July 5 I heard again from the lady on Ardmore Boulevard.

Her other sister, Alma, who lives in Hollywood but has stayed at the house on Ardmore on occasion, called the morning after our visit. It was then that she volunteered information she had been holding back from Helen L. for two years for fear of further upsetting her, in view of events at the house. But she had had a dream-like impression at the house in which she "saw" a man in his middle years, who had lived in a lean-to shack attached to the garage.

She knew this man was dead and got the impression that he was a most stubborn person, difficult to dislodge or reason with. What made this dream impression of interest to us, Miss L. thought, was the fact that her sister could not have known of Sybil Leek's insistence that a man lay buried at that very spot next to the garage! No shack ever stood there to the best of Helen L.'s knowledge, but of course it may have stood there before the present house was built.

Also, Helen reminded me that on those occasions when her mother and sister slept in the garage, when they had company in the main house, both had heard heavy footsteps coming up to the garage and stopping dead upon reaching the wall. Helen L.'s mother had for years insisted that there was "a body buried there in the garden" but nobody had ever tried to find it.

Nothing more happened until May 8, 1966, when Sybil Leek and I again went to the house because Helen L. had implored us to finish the case for her. The disturbances had been continuing on and off.

With us this time was Eugene Lundholm, librarian and psychic researcher. Trance came quickly. Perhaps Sybil was in a more relaxed state than during our last visit, but whatever the reason, things seemed to be more congenial this time around.

"I'm falling," her voice whispered, barely audible, "I'm hungry..."

Was someone reliving moments of anguish?

"Who are you?" I demanded.

"Can't breathe...."

"What is your name?"

"Ha...Harold..."

He had great difficulties with his breathing and I suggested he relax.

"Kill her..." he now panted, "kill her, kill the woman..."

"Did you kill her?"

"NO!"

"I've come to help you. I'm your friend."

"Kill her before she goes away...."

"Why?"

"No good here...where's he taken her? Where is she?"

The voice became more intelligible now.

"What is her name?"

"Where is she...I'll kill her."

"Who's with her?"

"Porter."

"Is he a friend of yours?"

"NO!"

"Who are you?"

"Harold Howard."

"Is this your house?"

"My house."

"Did you build it?"

"No."

"Did you buy it?"

Evidently my questioning got on his nerves, for he shouted, "Who are you?" I explained, but it didn't help.

"Too many people here...I throw them out...take those people out of here!"

Strangely enough, the voice did not sound like Sybil's at all; it had lost all trace of a British flavor and was full of anger. Evidently the ghost was speaking of the revellers he had found at his house and wanted them out.

"His friends...take them away...she brought them..."

"While you were away?" He was somewhat calmer now.

"Yes," he confirmed.

"Where were you?"

"Working."

"What do you do?"

"Miner."

"Where do you work?"

"Purdy Town." He may have said Purgory Town, or something like it.

"What happened when you came home?"

Again he became upset about the people in his house and I asked that he name some of them.

"Margaret..." he said, more excited now. "Mine... twenty-five...I came home...they were here...too many people...party here...."

"Did you hurt anyone?"

"I'm going to kill her," he insisted. Evidently he had not done so.

"Why?"

"Because of him." Jealousy, the great ghost-maker.

"Who is he?"

"Porter."

"Who is he?"

"He took my place. Eric Porter."

"What year is this?"

It was high time we got a "fix" on the period we were in.

"Forty-eight."

"What happened to you...afterwards?"

"People went away...Porter...outside...I want to go away now..."

It became clear to me that the girl must have been killed but that a shock condition at the time of the crime had prevented this man from realizing what he had done, thus forcing him to continue his quest for the girl. I told him as much and found him amazed at the idea of his deed.

"Why did he follow me...he followed me...then I hit him in the guts..."

"What did you do with him then?"

"Put him away."

He became cagey after that, evidently thinking I was some sort of policeman interrogating him.

"I watch him," he finally said. "I look after him...in the garden. I won't let him in the house."

I asked him further about himself, but he seemed confused.

"Where am I?"

He asked me to leave the other man in the garden, in the ground. He would never go away because he had to watch this other man.

"Margaret comes back," he said now. Was there a foursome or were we dealing with more than one level of consciousness?

"Keep him away from her," the ghost admonished me.

"I will," I promised and meant it.

I then told him about his death and that of the others, hoping I could finally rid the house of them all.

"She'll come back," his one-track mind made him say. "I'll wait till she is in bed and then I'll kill her."

I explained again that killing the other man wouldn't do any good since he was already dead.

"My head's bad," the ghost complained.

"You cannot stay at this house," I insisted firmly now.

"Not leaving," he shot back just as firmly. "My house!"

I continued my efforts, explaining also about the passage of time.

"Forty-eight..." he insisted, "I fight...I fight..."

"You've been forgiven," I said and began the words that amount to a kind of exorcism. "You are no longer guilty. You may go."

"Carry him," he mumbled and his voice weakened somewhat. "Where is she? Who'll clean up?"

Then he slipped away.

I awakened Sybil. She felt fine and recalled nothing. But I recalled plenty.

For one thing, it occurred to me that the ghost had spoken of the year '48, but not indicated whether it was 1948 or 1848, and there was something in the general tone of the voice that made me wonder if perhaps we were not in the wrong century. Certainly no miner worked in Los Angeles in 1948, but plenty did in 1848. Eugene Lundholm checked the records for me.

In the forties mines sprang up all over the territory. In 1842 Francisco Lopez had discovered gold near the San Fernando Mission, and in 1848 a much larger gold deposit was found near Sacramento.

In 1848 also was the famous gold strike at Sutter's Mill. But already in the 1840s mining existed in Southern California, although not much came of it.

After we went back to New York, Helen L. reached me again the last week of July 1966.

Her mother refused to leave the house, regardless of the disturbances. Thus a sale at this time as out of the question, Miss L. explained.

Something or someone was throwing rocks against the outside of the house and on the roof of their patio—but no living person was seen doing it. This, of course, is par for the poltergeist course. Just another attention-getter. Loud crashes on the patio roof and nobody there to cause them. Even the neighbors now heard the noises. Things were getting worse. I wrote back, offering to have another look at the haunted house provided she was willing to dig. No sense leaving the corpus delicti there.

But on September 18 Miss L. had some more to tell me. Rocks falling on the driveway behind the house brought out the neighbors in force, with flashlights, looking for the "culprits." Who could not be found. Nor could the rocks, for that matter. They were invisible rocks, it would seem.

This took place on numerous occasions between 6:15 and 7:30 P.M. and only at that time. To top it off, a half ripe lemon flew off their lemon tree at Miss L. with such force that it cracked wide open when it landed on the grass beside her. It could not have fallen by itself and there was no one in the tree to throw it.

I promised to get rid of the lemon-throwing ghost if I could, when we came to Los Angeles again in October. But when I did, Miss L.'s mother was ill and the visit had to be called off.

I have not heard anything further about this stubborn ghost. But the area was populated in 1848 and it could be that another house or camp stood on this site before the present house was erected. There is a brook not far away. So far, neither Mr. Morton nor Mr. Howard has been located and Jane and Margaret are only ghostly facts. A lot of people passed through the house when Miss L.'s family did not own it, and of course we know nothing whatever about the house that preceded it.

One more note came to me which helped dispel any notion that Helen L. was the only one bothered by the unseen in the house on Ardmore.

It was signed by Margaret H. Jones and addressed *To Whom It May Concern*. It *concerned* the ghost.

"Some years ago, when I was a guest in Miss L.'s home at ____ Ardmore Boulevard, in Los Angeles, I heard what seemed to be very heavy footsteps in a room which I *knew* to be empty. Miss L. was with me at the time and I told her that I heard this sound. The footsteps seemed to advance and to recede, and this kept up for several minutes, and though we investigated we saw no one. They ceased with the same abruptness with which they began."

I fondly hoped the manifestations would behave in a similar manner. Go away quietly.

But on October 6, 1967, Helen L. telephoned me in New York. She had spent a sleepless night—part of a night, that is.

Up to 4 A.M. she had been sleeping peacefully. At that hour she was awakened by her cat. Putting the animal down, she noticed a strange light on her patio, which is located outside her bedroom windows. She hurriedly threw on a robe and went outside.

In the flower bed on her left, toward the rear of the garden, she noticed something white. Despite her dislike of the phenomena which had for so long disturbed her home, Helen L. advanced toward the flower bed.

Now she could clearly make out the figure of a woman, all in white. The figure was not very tall and could have been that of a young girl. It seemed to watch her intently, and looked somewhat like the conventional white bedsheet type of fictional ghost.

At this point Miss L.'s courage left her and she ran back to her room.

The next morning, her eyes red with exhaustion, she discussed her experience with her aged mother. Until now she had been reluctant to draw her mother into these matters, but the impression had been so overpowering that she just had to tell *someone.*

To her surprise, her mother was not very upset. Instead, she added her own account of the "White Lady" to the record. The night before, the same figure had apparently appeared to the mother in a dream, telling her to pack, for she would soon be taking her away!

When Helen L. had concluded her report, I calmed her as best I could and reminded her that *some* dreams are merely expressions of unconscious fears. I promised to pay the house still another visit, although I am frankly weary of the prospect: I know full well that you can't persuade a ghost to go away when there may be a body, once the property of said ghost, buried in a flower bed in the garden.

After all, a ghost's got rights, too!

✳ 58

The Haunted Motorcycle Workshop

LEIGHTON BUZZARD SOUNDED like a species of objectionable bird to us, when we first heard it pronounced. But it turned out to be a rather pleasant-looking English country town of no particular significance or size, except that it was the site of a poltergeist that had been reported in the local press only a short time before our arrival in England.

The *Leighton Buzzard Observer* carried a report on the strange goings on at Sid Mularney's workshop.

When Leighton motorcycle dealer, Mr. Sid Mularney, decided to extend his workshop by removing a partition, he was taking on more than he anticipated. For he is now certain that he has offended a poltergeist.

Neighbors are blaming "Mularney's Ghost" for weird noises that keep them awake at night, and Mr. Mularney, who claims actually to have witnessed the poltergeist's pranks, is certain that the building in Lake-street, Leighton, is haunted.

It was about a fortnight ago when he decided to take down the partition in the workshop which houses racing motorcycles used by the world-champion rider, Mike Hailwood.

The following morning, said Mr. Mularney, he went to the door, opened it, and found three bikes on the floor. The machines, which are used by local rider Dave Williams, had their fairings smashed.

A few days later Mr. Mularney was working on a racing gear box, and when he realized he couldn't finish it unless he worked late, he decided to stay on. And it wasn't until three o'clock that he finished.

As he was wiping his hands, weird things started to happen.

"I felt something rush by me. I looked round and spanners flew off hooks on the wall and a tarpaulin, covering a bike, soared into the air," he declared.

"You would have to see it to believe it. I was scared stiff. I grabbed a hammer, got out of the room as fast as I could and made straight for home. My wife was asleep and I woke her up to tell her about it."

Since then other peculiar things have been taking place, and neighbors have been complaining of weird noises in the night.

Mrs. Cynthia Ellis, proprietress of the Coach and Horses Restaurant, next door in Lake-street, said she had been woken during the night several times "by strange bangings and clatterings."

"I looked out of the window, but there was never anything there."

She said her young son, Stephen, was the first to wake up and hear noises.

"We thought it was just a child's imagination, but we soon changed our minds," she said.

"The atmosphere round here has become very tense during the past fortnight. It's all very odd," said Mrs. Ellis.

Since his strange experience Mr. Mularney has discovered odd happenings in the workshop. One morning he found a huge box of nuts and bolts "too heavy for me to lift," scattered all over the floor. Since then he has discovered petrol tanks which have been moved about and even large bolts missing, which, he claims, he could never mislay.

I contacted the editor of the *Observer*, Mr. McReath, who confirmed all this information and gave me his private estimation of Mr. Mularney's character and truthfulness, which were A-1. I then arranged with Mr. Mularney to be at his place at noon the next day to look into the matter personally.

Located on a busy main street, the motorcycle workshop occupies the front half of a large yard. Much of it is rebuilt, using some very old timbers and bricks. Mr. Mularney, a large, jovial man with a bit of an Irish brogue, greeted us warmly and showed us around the rather crowded workshop. There were three rooms, leading from one into the other like a railroad flat, and all of this space was chockfull of motorcycles and tools.

"What exactly happened, Mr. Mularney?" I opened the conversation.

"When we finish off in the evening, my partner and I clean our hands and put all the tools back onto the bench. Just then, for some unknown reasons, the spanners (wrenches) jumped off the hooks on the bench and landed on the bench in front of me."

"You mean, the wrenches flew off the hooks by themselves?"

"Yes."

"You saw this with your own eyes?"

"Oh, yes, definitely."

"There was enough light in the shop?"

"Yes, the shop was lit."

"What did you think it was?"

"Well, at the moment I didn't take much notice of it but, later, there was a noise in the rear of the workshop, something came across the floor, and caught my foot, and my toe, and my eyes, and so I began to look around; on the other side of the shop we had some metal sprockets which were standing there. They started to spin around on a pivot bolt. Later, a huge piece of rubber foam came off the wall and flew into the middle of the room."

"By its own volition?"

"Yes."

"Did you think it was something unusual?"

"I did then, yes. Then we had a racing motorcycle covered by a waterproof sheet, and this rose completely up—"

"You mean, in the air?"

"Yes, it stayed up. By that time I was ready to leave the shop."

"Did you think something supernatural was taking place then?"

"I did. I sat in the van for a moment to think about it, then went home and woke my wife up. I explained to her what I had seen, and she thought I'd been drinking."

"Did anything else happen after that?"

"Yes, we had the Swedish motorcycle champion leave his motorcycle here for repairs. He left some pieces on the bench and went to have tea. When he went back, they had completely disappeared and could never be found again. There was no one in the shop at the time who could have taken them, and we had locked up tight.

"I had the same experience myself," Sid Mularney added. "We were taking a cycle apart, two of us working

The haunted motorcycle workshop

here. One compartment, big enough to see, just disappeared."

"You have, of course, looked into the possibility of pranksters?"

"Oh, yes, we have. But there's only two of us who use the shop. About five weeks ago, the two of us took another motorcycle to pieces. We put some of the nuts and bolts into a waterproof pan to wash them. We locked up for the night, but when we returned in the morning, the whole lot was scattered all over the room."

A number of amateur "ghost chasers" had offered Mr. Mularney their services, but he turned them all down since the shop housed some pretty valuable motorcycles and they did not want to have things disappear by natural means on top of their supernatural troubles.

I realized by now that a mischievous spirit, a poltergeist, was at work, to disrupt the goings on and call attention to his presence, which is the classical pattern for such disturbances.

"Tell me, what was on this spot before the repair shop was built?"

"Years ago it used to be an old-fashioned basket works, and there used to be about fourteen men working here. After that, the shed stood empty completely for five or six years. When we came here to open the shop, it was full of old baskets and things. We rebuilt it and made it into this workshop."

"I understand the phenomena started only after you knocked down a wall?"

"Yes, we knocked down that wall on a Saturday evening. We came back Sunday morning and three motorcycles were in the corner, as if somebody had thrown them there. As if in anger."

"Did something dramatic ever take place here before you took it over, Mr. Mularney?" I asked.

"Somebody hanged himself here years ago when it was the basket works. That's all we know."

I went back into the third of the three rooms and examined the spot where the wall had been removed. The wooden beams still left showed signs of great age, certainly far beyond the current century.

Quite possibly, in removing the partition wall, Sid Mularney had interfered with the memory picture of a ghost who did not wish to leave the spot. The three of us stood quiet for a moment, then I addressed myself to the poltergeist, asking that he discontinue annoying the present owners of the place. I left my card with Mr. Mularney and instructed him to telephone me the moment there was any further disturbance.

All was quiet in the weeks that have followed, so I can only assume that the poltergeist has accepted the redesigning of the place. Then, too, he might have become offended by the kind of clientele that rides motorcycles nowadays. Basket weaving is a gentle art, and "mods" and "rockers" are best avoided by gentle folk. Even ghosts.

✳ 59

Encountering the Ghostly Monks

WHEN KING HENRY VIII broke with Rome as the aftermath of not getting a divorce, but also for a number of more weighty reasons, English monastic life came to an abrupt halt. Abbeys and monasteries were "secularized," that is, turned into worldly houses, and the monks thrown out. Now and again an abbot with a bad reputation for greed was publicly executed. The first half of the sixteenth century was full of tragedies and many an innocent monk, caught up in the new turmoil of religious matters, was swept to his doom.

The conflict of the abolished monk or nun and the new owners of their former abode runs through all of England, and there are a number of ghosts that have their origin in this situation.

The "act of dissolution" which created a whole new set of homeless Catholic clerics also created an entirely new type of haunting. Our intent was to follow up on a few of the more notorious ghosts resulting from the religious schism.

I should be happy to report that it was a typically glorious English fall day when we set out for Southampton very early in the morning. It was not. It rained cats and dogs, also typically English. I was to make an appearance on Southern TV at noon, and we wanted a chance to visit the famed old Cathedral at Winchester, halfway down to Southampton. My reason for this visit was the many persistent reports of people having witnessed ghostly processions of monks in the church, where no monks have trod since the sixteenth century. If one stood at a certain spot in the nave of the huge cathedral, one might see the transparent monks pass by. They would never take notice of you; they weren't that kind of ghost. Rather, they seemed like etheric impressions of a bygone age, and those who saw them re-enact their ceremonial processions, especially burial services for their own, were psychic people able to pierce the veil. In addition, a rather remarkable report had come to me of some photographs taken at Winchester. The *Newark Evening News* of September 9, 1958, relates the incident:

Amateur photographer T. L. Taylor thought he was photographing empty choir stalls inside Winchester Cathedral, but the pictures came out with people sitting in the stalls.

Taylor took two pictures inside the cathedral nearly a year ago. The first shows the choir stalls empty. The second, taken an instant later, shows 13 figures in the stalls, most of them dressed in medieval costume. Taylor swears he saw no one there.

Taylor's wife, their 16-year-old daughter Valerie, and a girl friend of Valerie's said they were with him when he took the pictures. They saw nothing in the stalls. "It gives me the creeps," Valerie said.

Taylor, a 42-year-old electrical engineer whose hobby is photography, is convinced that the films were not double exposed. He said his camera has a device to prevent double exposures and the company which made the film confirmed the ghosts were not caused through faulty film.

As I already reported in *Ghost Hunter*, I take psychic photography very seriously. Not only John Myers, but others have demonstrated its authenticity under strictest test conditions, excluding all kinds of possible forgery or deception. The camera, after all, has no human foibles and emotions. What it sees, it sees. If ghostly impressions on the ether are emotionally triggered electric impulses in nature, it seems conceivable that a sensitive film inside the camera may record it.

My own camera is a Zeiss-Ikon Super Ikonta B model, a fifteen-year-old camera which has a device making double exposures impossible. I use Agfa Record film, size 120, and no artificial light whatever except what I find in the places I photograph. I don't use flash or floodlights, and have my films developed by commercial houses. I wouldn't know how to develop them myself, if I had to.

When we arrived at Winchester, it was really pouring. My wife and I quickly jumped from the car and raced into the church. It was 11 o'clock in the morning and the church was practically empty, except for two or three visitors in the far end of the nave. Light came in through the high windows around the altar, but there was no artificial light whatever, no electricity, only the dim light from the windows and the faraway entrance gate. The high wooden chairs of the choir face each other on both sides of the nave, and there are three rows on each side. Prayer books rest on the desks in front of each seat. The entire area is surrounded by finely carved Gothic woodwork, with open arches, through which one can see the remainder of the nave. There wasn't a living soul in those chairs.

The solitude of the place, the rain outside, and the atmosphere of a distant past combined to make us feel really remote and far from worldly matters. Neither of us was the least bit scared, for Ghost Hunters don't scare.

I set up my camera on one of the chair railings, pointed it in the direction of the opposite row of choir chairs, and exposed for about two seconds, all the while keeping the camera steady on its wooden support. I repeated this process half a dozen times from various angles. We then left the cathedral and returned to the waiting car. The entire experiment took not more than fifteen minutes.

When the films came back from the laboratory the following day, I checked them over carefully. Four of the six taken showed nothing unusual, but two did. One of them quite clearly showed a transparent group or rather procession of hooded monks, seen from the rear, evidently walking somewhat below the present level of the church floor. I checked and found out that the floor used to be below its present level, so the ghostly monks would be walking on the floor level *they* knew, not ours.

I don't claim to be a medium, nor is my camera supernatural. Nevertheless, the ghostly monks of Winchester allowed themselves to be photographed by me!

* * *

We left Southampton after my television show, and motored towards Salisbury. South of that old city, at Downton, Benson Herbert maintains his "paraphysical laboratory" where he tests psychic abilities of various subjects with the help of ingenious apparatus. One of his "operators," a comely young lady by the name of Anne Slowgrove, also dabbles in witchcraft and is a sort of younger-set witch in the area. Her abilities include precognition and apparently she is able to influence the flickering of a light or the sound of a clock by will power, slowing them down or speeding them up at will. A devoted man, Benson Herbert was introduced to me by Sybil Leek, medium and "White Witch" of the New Forest. We wit-

nessed one of his experiments, after which we followed his car out of the almost inaccessible countryside towards our next objective, Moyles Court, Ringwood.

The ghostly goings-on at Moyles Court had come to my attention both through Sybil Leek, and through an article in the September issue of *Fate* magazine.

The original house goes back to the eleventh century and there is a wing certainly dating back to the Tudor period; the main house is mostly sixteenth century, and is a fine example of a large country manor of the kind not infrequently seen in the New Forest in the south of England.

Lilian Chapman, the author of the *Fate* article, visited the place in 1962, before it was sold to the school which now occupies it. The Chapmans found the house in a sad state of disrepair and were wondering if it could be restored, and at what cost.

Mrs. Chapman, wandering about the place, eventually found herself seated on the window sill near the landing leading to the second floor, while the rest of the party continued upstairs. As she sat there alone, relaxing, she felt herself overcome with a sense of fear and sadness:

As I looked toward the doors which led to the Minstrels Gallery, I was amazed to see, coming through them, a shadowy figure in a drab yellow cloak. There seemed more cloak than figure. The small cape piece nearly covered a pair of hands which were clasped in anguish or prayer. The hands clasped and unclasped as the apparition came towards me. I felt no fear, only an intense sorrow. And I swear I heard a gentle sigh as the figure passed me and drifted to the end of the landing. From there it returned to go down the stairs, seeming to disappear through a window facing the chapel.

I, too, have sat on that spot, quietly, relaxed. And I have felt a chill and known a heaviness of heart for which there was no logical reason.

The Chapmans did not buy the house, but the Manor House School did at the subsequent auction sale. Unknown to Mrs. Chapman at the time, Dame Lisle, one-time owner of the manor house, was tried and executed at nearby Winchester by the notorious "hanging judge" Jeffreys in 1685. The sole crime committed by the aged lady was that she had given shelter overnight to two fugitives from the battle of Sedgemoor. The real reason, of course, was her Puritan faith. As described by Mrs. Chapman in detail, it was indeed the apparition of the unfortunate lady she had witnessed.

I contacted the headmistress of the school, Miss V. D. Hunter, for permission to visit, which she granted with the understanding that no "publicity" should come to the school in England. I agreed not to tell any English news of our visit.

Where the monks of Beaulieu are still being heard

When we arrived at Moyles Court, it was already five o'clock, but Miss Hunter had left on an urgent errand. Instead, a Mrs. Finch, one of the teachers, received us.

"What is the background of the haunting here?" I inquired.

"Dame Lisle hid her two friends in the cellar here," she said, "where there was an escape tunnel to the road. There were spies out watching for these people, they discovered where they were, and she was caught and tried before Judge Jeffreys. She was beheaded, and ever since then her ghost was said to be wandering about in this house."

"Has anyone ever seen the ghost?"

"We have met several people who had lived here years ago, and had reared their families here, and we know of one person who definitely has seen the ghost at the gates of the house—and I have no reason to disbelieve her. This was about twenty-five years ago, but more recently there has been somebody who came into the house just before we took it over when it was covered in cobwebs and in a very bad state. She sat in the passage here and said that she had seen the ghost walking along it."

"How was the ghost described?"

"She has always been described as wearing a saffron robe."

"Does the ghost ever disturb anyone at the house?"

"No, none. On the contrary, we have always heard that she was a sweet person and that there is nothing whatever to be afraid of. We've had television people here, but we don't want the children to feel apprehensive and as a matter of fact, the older children rather look forward to meeting the ghostly lady."

I thanked Mrs. Finch, and we were on our way once more, as the sun started to settle. We were hoping to make it to Beaulieu before it was entirely dark. As we drove through the nearly empty New Forest—empty of people, but full of wild horses and other animals—we could readily understand why the present-day witches of England choose this natural preserve as their focal point. It is an eerie, beautifully quiet area far removed from the gasoline-soiled world of the big cities.

We rolled into Beaulieu around 6 o'clock, and our hosts, the Gore-Brownes, were already a bit worried about us.

My contact with Beaulieu began a long time before we actually arrived there. Elizabeth Byrd, author of *Immortal Queen* and *Flowers of the Forest*, introduced us to the Gore-Brownes, who had been her hosts when she spent some time in England. Miss Byrd is keenly aware of the psychic elements around us, and when she heard we were going to visit Beaulieu—it consists of the manor house itself owned by Lord Montague and known as the Palace House; "The Vineyards," a smaller house owned by the Gore-Brownes and, of course, the ruins of the once magnificent Abbey and gardens—she implored me to have a look from a certain room at "The Vineyards."

"When you go to Beaulieu please ask Margaret to take you up to 'The Red Room'—my room—and leave you alone there a while. It is not the room but the view from the window that is strange. If even *I* feel it, so should you have a very strong impression of static time. I have looked from that window at various seasons of the year at various times of day and always have sensed a total

hush...as though life had somehow stopped. The trees are as fixed as a stage-set, the bushes painted. Nothing seems quite real. As you know, I am a late riser, but I was always up at dawn at Beaulieu when that view was nearly incredible to me—not just fog, something more, which I can only call permanent and timeless and marvelously peaceful. I would not have been surprised (or afraid) to see monks tending the vineyards. It would have seemed perfectly natural. If one could ever enter a slit in time it would be at Beaulieu."

The vivid description of the view given us by Elizabeth Byrd was only too accurate. Although it was already dusk when we arrived, I could still make out the scenery and the ruins of the Abbey silhouetted against the landscape. My wife was rather tired from the long journey, so I left her to warm herself at the comfortable fireplace, while Colonel Gore-Browne took me down to the Abbey, to meet a friend, Captain B., who had been a longtime resident of Beaulieu. The Palace House, comparatively new, was not the major center of hauntings.

A modern Motor Museum had been built next to it by Lord Montague, and has become a major tourist attraction. I have no objections to that, but I do find it a bit peculiar to have a washroom built into an ancient chapel, with a large sign on the roof indicating its usage!

The Abbey itself had not been commercialized, but lay tranquil on the spot of land between "The Vineyards" and an inlet of water leading down to the channel called "the Splent," which separates the Hampshire coast from the Isle of Wight. Here we stood, while the Captain looked for his keys so we could enter the Abbey grounds.

"What exactly happened here in the way of a haunting, Captain?"I asked, as we entered the churchyard surrounding the ruined Abbey walls.

"A young lady who lived in Beaulieu was walking across this little path toward what we call 'the parson's wicked gate,' when she saw a brown-robed figure which she thought was a visitor. She had been walking along with her eyes on the ground and she raised them when she got near to where she thought the man would be so as not to run into him—but he just wasn't there!"

We were now standing in the ruined "garth" or garden of the Abbey. Around us were the arched walls with their niches; back of us was the main wall of what is now the Beaulieu church, but which was once the monks' dining hall or refectory.

"Has anyone seen anything here?"I inquired.

"Well, there were two ladies who lived in the little flat in the *domus conversorum*. One of them, a retired trained nurse of very high standing, told me that one Sunday morning she came out onto the little platform outside her flat and she looked, and in the fifth recess there she saw a monk sitting reading a scroll."

"What did she do?"

"She watched him for a minute or two, then unfortunately she heard her kettle boiling over and she had to go in. When she came out again, of course, he was gone."

"Did it ever occur to her that he was anything but flesh and blood?"

"Oh, yes, she knew that he couldn't have been flesh and blood."

"Because there are no monks at Beaulieu."

"Yes."

"Was she frightened?"

"Not in the least."

"Are there any other instances of ghosts in this area?"

The Captain cleared his throat. "Well, old Mr. Poles, who was Vicar here from 1886 to 1939, used to talk of meeting and seeing the monks in the church, which was the lay brothers' refectory and which is now behind us. He also used to hear them as a daily occurrence."

We walked back to the church and entered its dark recesses. The interior is of modern design hardly consistent with its ancient precursor, but it is in good taste and the mystic feeling of presences persists.

This was the place where the Vicar had met the ghostly monks.

"He not only heard them singing," the Captain said, "but he also saw them. They were present."

"Has anyone else seen the ghostly apparitions in this church?"

"A few years ago," the Captain replied in his calm, deliberate voice, as if he were explaining the workings of a new gun to a recruit, "I was waiting for the funeral procession of a man who used to work here, and two ladies came into the church. We got to talking a little, and one of them said, 'When I came to this church about thirty years ago, with my friend, she saw it as it was.'

"I didn't quite understand what she meant and I said, 'Oh, I know, the church was completely altered in 1840.'

"'Oh, no,' she said, 'I mean—we both saw it—as it was, *when the monks had it.*'

"I questioned her about this.

"'We came in,' she said, 'and we saw the church laid out apparently as a dining room. We were rather surprised, but we really did not think anything very much of it, and then we went out. But when we got home, we talked it over, and we came to the conclusion that there was something rather extraordinary, because we hadn't seen it as a parish church at all. Then we made inquiries and, of course, we realized that we had seen into the past.'"

The ladies had evidently been catapulted back in time to watch the monks of Beaulieu at supper, four hundred years ago!

I walked out into the middle of the nave and in a hushed voice invited the monks to show themselves. There was only utter silence in the darkened church, for it was now past the hour when even a speck of light remains in the sky.

As I slowly walked back up the aisle and into the present, I thought I heard an organ play softly somewhere overhead. But it may have been my imagination. Who is to tell? In that kind of atmosphere and having just talked about it, one must not discount suggestion.

Others have heard the ghostly monks in the garden, burying their own. Burial services are very important to a monk, and King Henry had deprived them of the privilege of being laid to rest in the proper manner. Where could the dead monks go? The Abbey was the only place they knew on earth, and so they clung to it, in sheer fear of what lay beyond the veil.

Quite possibly, too, the ghostly brothers cannot accept the strange fact that their sacred burial ground, their cemetery, has never been found! There is a churchyard around the Abbey, but it belonged and still belongs to the people of Beaulieu. The monks had their own plot and no one knows where it is. I have a feeling that there will be ghostly monks walking at Beaulieu until someone stumbles onto that ancient burial ground, and reconsecrates it properly.

The massive manor house, or Palace House, also incorporates much of the abbot's palace within its structure. Monks have been seen there time and again. When I appeared on the Art Linkletter program in January of 1964, I was contacted by a Mrs. Nancy Sullivan, of the Bronx, New York, who was once employed as a cook at Palace House.

"Palace House used to have a moat all around," she explained, "and a spiral staircase running down from the top to the bottom. It was claimed Mary Queen of Scots escaped down that staircase, and a man was waiting in the moat in a boat, making good her escape. Some say her ghost still runs down those stairs!

"The help had their rooms on the top floor; there were five girls then, and every night we heard someone walking down those stairs, although we knew that the doors were safely locked, top and bottom. We were scared stiff, so much so, we all moved into one room."

Whether it was Mary Stuart getting away from Beaulieu, or perhaps an older ghost, is hard to tell. What is interesting is that the steps were heard where no one was seen to walk.

Television cameras have overrun Beaulieu in quest of the supernatural. When all has quieted down, I intend to go back and bring a good trance medium with me. Perhaps then we can find out directly what it is the monks want.

✳ 60

The Somerset Scent (Pennsylvania)

SOMERSET IS ONE OF THOSE nondescript small towns that abound in rural Pennsylvania and that boast nothing more exciting than a few thousand homes, a few churches, a club or two and a lot of hardworking people whose lives pass under pretty ordinary and often drab circumstances. Those who leave may go on to better things in the big cities of the East, and those who stay have the comparative security of being among their own and living out their lives peacefully. But then there are those who leave not because they want to but because they are driven, driven by forces greater than themselves that they cannot resist.

The Manners are middle-aged people with two children, a fourteen-year-old son and a six-year-old daughter. The husband ran a television and radio shop which gave them an average income, neither below middle-class standards for a small town, nor much above it. Although Catholic, they did not consider themselves particularly religious. Mrs. Manner's people originally came from Austria, so there was enough European background in the family to give their lives a slight continental tinge, but other than that, they were and are typical Pennsylvania people without the slightest interest in, or knowledge of, such sophisticated matters as psychic research.

Of course, the occult was never unknown to Mrs. Manner. She was born with a veil over her eyes, which to many means the second sight. Her ability to see things before they happened was not "precognition" to her, but merely a special talent she took in her stride. One night she had a vivid dream about her son, then miles away in the army. She vividly saw him walking down a hall in a bathrobe, with blood running down his leg. Shortly after she awakened the next day, she was notified that her son had been attacked by a rattlesnake and, when found, was near death. One night she awoke to see an image of her sister standing beside her bed. There was nothing fearful about the apparition, but she was dressed all in black.

The next day that sister died.

But these instances did not frighten Mrs. Manner; they were glimpses into eternity and nothing more.

As the years went by, the Manners accumulated enough funds to look for a more comfortable home than the one they were occupying, and as luck—or fate—would have it, one day in 1966 they were offered a fine, old house in one of the better parts of town. The house seemed in excellent condition; it had the appearance of a Victorian home with all the lovely touches of that bygone era about it. It had stood empty for two years, and since it belonged to an estate, the executors seemed anxious to finally sell the house. The Manners made no special inquiries about their projected new home simply because everything seemed so right and pleasant. The former owners had been wealthy people, they were informed, and had lavished much money and love on the house.

When the price was quoted to them, the Manners looked at each other in disbelief. It was far below what they had expected for such a splendid house. "We'll take it," they said, almost in unison, and soon the house was theirs.

"Why do you suppose we got it for such a ridiculously low price?" Mr. Manner mused, but his wife could only shrug. To her, that was not at all important. She never believed one should look a gift horse in the mouth.

It was late summer when they finally moved into their newly acquired home. Hardly had they been installed when Mrs. Manner knew there was something not right with the place.

From the very first, she had felt uncomfortable in it, but being a sensible person, she had put it down to being in a new and unaccustomed place. But as this feeling persisted she realized that she was being *watched* by some unseen force all the time, day and night, and her nerves began to tense under the strain.

The very first night she spent in the house, she was aroused at exactly 2 o'clock in the morning, seemingly for no reason. Her hair stood up on her arms and chills shook her body. Again, she put this down to having worked so hard getting the new home into shape.

But the "witching hour" of 2 A.M. kept awakening her with the same uncanny feeling that something was wrong, and instinctively she knew it was not her, or someone in her family, who was in trouble, but the new house.

With doubled vigor, she put all her energies into polishing furniture and getting the rooms into proper condition. That way, she was very tired and hoped to sleep through the night. But no matter how physically exhausted she was, at 2 o'clock the uncanny feeling woke her.

The first week somehow passed despite this eerie feeling, and Monday rolled around again. In the bright light of the late summer day, the house somehow seemed friendlier and her fears of the night had vanished.

She was preparing breakfast in the kitchen for her children that Monday morning. As she was buttering a piece of toast for her little girl, she happened to glance up toward the doorway. There, immaculately dressed, *stood a man.* The stranger, she noticed, wore shiny black shoes, navy blue pants, and a white shirt. She even made out his tie, saw it was striped, and then went on to observe the man's face. The picture was so clear she could make out the way the man's snowy white hair was parted.

Her immediate reaction was that he had somehow entered the house and she was about to say hello, when it occurred to her that she had not heard the opening of a door or any other sound—no footfalls, no steps.

"Look," she said to her son, whose back was turned to the apparition, but by the time her children turned around, the man was gone like a puff of smoke.

Mrs. Manner was not too frightened by what she had witnessed, although she realized her visitor had not been of the flesh and blood variety. When she told her husband about it that evening, he laughed.

Ghost, indeed!

The matter would have rested there had it not been for the fact that the very next day something else happened. Mrs. Manner was on her way into the kitchen from the backyard of the house, when she suddenly saw a woman go past her refrigerator. This time the materialization was not as perfect. Only half of the body was visible, but she noticed her shoes, dress up to the knees, and that the figure seemed in a hurry.

This still did not frighten her, but she began to wonder. All those eerie feelings seemed to add up now. What had they gotten themselves into by buying this house? No wonder it was so cheap. It was haunted!

Mrs. Manner was a practical person, the uncanny experiences notwithstanding, or perhaps because of them. They had paid good money for the house and no specters were going to dislodge them!

But the fight had just begun. A strange kind of web began to envelop her frequently, as if some unseen force were trying to wrap her into a wet, cold blanket. When she touched the "web," there was nothing to be seen or felt, and yet, the clammy, cold force was still with her. *A strange scent of flowers* manifested itself out of nowhere and followed her from room to room. Soon her husband smelled it too, and his laughing stopped. He, too, became concerned: their children must not be frightened by whatever it was that was present in the house.

It soon was impossible to keep doors locked. No matter how often they would lock a door in the house, it was found wide open soon afterwards, the locks turned by unseen hands. One center of particular activities was the old china closet, and the scent of flowers was especially strong in its vicinity.

"What are we going to do about this?" Mrs. Manner asked her husband one night. They decided to find out more about the house, as a starter. They had hesitated to mention anything about their plight out of fear of being ridiculed or thought unbalanced. In a small town, people don't like to talk about ghosts.

The first person Mrs. Manner turned to was a neighbor who had lived down the street for many years. When she noticed that the neighbor did not pull back at the mention of weird goings-on in the house, but, to the contrary, seemed genuinely interested, Mrs. Manner poured out her heart and described what she had seen.

In particular, she took great pains to describe the two apparitions. The neighbor nodded gravely.

"It's them, all right," she said, and started to fill Mrs. Manner in on the history of their house. This was the first time Mrs. Manner had heard of it and the description of the man she had seen tallied completely with the appearance of the man who had owned the house before.

"He died here," the neighbor explained. "They really loved their home, he and his wife. The old lady never wanted to leave or sell it."

"But what do you make of the strange scent of flowers?" Mrs. Manner asked.

"The old lady loved flowers, had fresh ones in the house every day."

Relieved to know what it was all about, but hardly happy at the prospect of sharing her house with ghosts, Mrs. Manner then went to see the chief of police in the hope of finding some way of getting rid of her unwanted "guests."

The chief scratched his head.

"Ghosts?" he said, not at all jokingly. "You've got me there. That's not my territory."

But he promised to send an extra patrol around in case it was just old-fashioned burglars.

Mrs. Manner thanked him and left. She knew otherwise and realized the police would not be able to help her.

She decided they had to learn to live with their ghosts, especially as the latter had been in the house before them. Perhaps it wouldn't be so bad after all, she mused, now that they knew who it was that would not leave.

Perhaps one could even become friendly, sort of one big, happy family, half people, half ghosts? But she immediately rejected the notion. What about the children? So far, they had not *seen* them, but they knew of the doors that wouldn't stay shut and the other uncanny phenomena.

Fortunately, Mrs. Manner did not understand the nature of poltergeists. Had she realized that the very presence of her teen-age son was in part responsible for the physical nature of the happenings, she would no doubt have sent him away. But the phenomena continued unabated, day and night.

One night at dinner, with everyone accounted for, an enormous crash shook the house. It felt as if a ton of glass had fallen onto the kitchen floor. When they rushed into the kitchen, they found everything in order, nothing misplaced.

At this point, Mrs. Manner fell back on her early religious world.

"Maybe we should call the minister?" she suggested, and no sooner said than done. The following day, the minister came to their house. When he had heard their story, he nodded quietly and said a silent prayer for the souls of the disturbed ones.

He had a special reason to do so, it developed. They had been among his parishioners when alive. In fact, he had been to their home for dinner many times, and the house was familiar to him despite the changes the present owners had made.

If anyone could, surely their own minister should be able to send those ghosts away.

Not by a long shot.

Either the couple did not put much stock into their minister's powers, or the pull of the house was stronger, but the phenomena continued. In fact, after the minister had tried to exorcise the ghosts, things got worse.

Many a night, the Manners ran out into the street when lights kept going on and off by themselves. Fortunately, the children slept through all this, but how long would they remain unaffected?

At times, the atmosphere was so thick Mrs. Manner could not get near the breakfast nook in the kitchen to clear the table. Enveloped by the strong vibrations, she felt herself tremble and on two occasions fainted and was thus found by her family.

They were seriously considering moving now, and let the original "owners" have the house again. They realized now that the house had never been truly "empty" for those two years the real estate man had said it was not in use.

It was 2 A.M. when they finally went up to bed.

Things felt worse than ever before. Mrs. Manner clearly sensed three presences with her now and started to cry.

"I'm leaving this house," she exclaimed. "You can have it back!" Her husband had gone ahead of her up the stairs to get the bedding from the linen closet. She began to follow him and slowly went up the stairs. After she had climbed about halfway up, something forced her to turn around and look back.

What she saw has remained with her ever since, deeply impressed into her mind with the acid of stark fear.

Down below her on the stairway, was a big, burly man, trying to pull himself up the stairs.

His eyes were red with torture as he tried to talk to her.

Evidently he had been hurt, for his trousers and shirt were covered with mud. Or was it dried blood?

He was trying to hang on to the banister and held his hands out towards her.

"Oh, God, it can't be true," she thought and went up a few more steps. Then she dared look down again.

The man was still holding out his hand in a desperate move to get her attention. When she failed to respond, he threw it down in a gesture of impatience and frustration.

With a piercing scream she ran up the stairs to her husband, weeping out of control.

The house had been firmly locked and no one could have gained entrance. Not that they thought the apparitions were flesh and blood people. The next morning, no trace of the nocturnal phenomenon could be found on the stairs. It was as if it had never happened.

But that morning, the Manners decided to pack and get out fast. "I want no more houses," Mrs. Manner said

firmly, and so they bought a trailer. Meanwhile, they lived in an apartment.

But their furniture and all their belongings were still in the house, and it was necessary to go back a few more times to get them. They thought that since they had signed over the deed, it would be all right for them to go back. After all, it was no longer *their* house.

As Mrs. Manner cautiously ascended the stairs, she was still trembling with fear. Any moment now, the specter might confront her again. But all seemed calm. Suddenly, the scent of flowers was with her again and she knew the ghosts were still in residence.

As if to answer her doubts, the doors to the china closet flew open at that moment.

Although she wanted nothing further to do with the old house, Mrs. Manner made some more inquiries. The terrible picture of the tortured man on the stairs did not leave her mind. Who was he, and what could she have done for him?

Then she heard that the estate wasn't really settled, the children were still fighting over it. Was that the reason the parents could not leave the house in peace? Was the man on the stairs someone who needed help, someone who had been hurt in the house?

"Forget it," the husband said, and they stored most of their furniture. The new house trailer would have no bad vibrations and they could travel wherever they wanted, if necessary.

After they had moved into the trailer, they heard rumors that the new owners of their house had encountered problems also. But they did not care to hear about them and studiously stayed away from the house. That way, they felt, the ghosts would avoid them also, now that they were back in what used to be their beloved home!

But a few days later, Mrs. Manner noticed a strange scent of flowers wafting through her brand-new trailer. Since she had not bought any flowers, nor opened a perfume bottle, it puzzled her. Then, with a sudden impact that was almost crushing, she knew where and when she had smelled this scent before. It was the personal scent of the ghostly woman in the old house! Had she followed her here into the trailer?

When she discussed this new development with her husband that night, they decided to fumigate the trailer, air it and get rid of the scent, if they could. Somehow they thought they might be mistaken and it was just coincidence. But the scent remained, clear and strong, and the feeling of a presence that came with it soon convinced them that they had not yet seen the last of the Somerset ghosts.

They sold the new trailer and bought another house, a fifty-seven-year-old, nice, rambling home in a nearby Pennsylvania town called Stoystown, far enough from Somerset to give them the hope that the unseen ones would not be able to follow them there.

Everything was fine after they had moved their furniture in and for the first time in many a month, the Manners could relax. About two months after they had moved to Stoystown, the scent of flowers returned. Now it was accompanied by another smell, that resembling burned matches.

The Manners were terrified. Was there no escape from the uncanny? A few days later, Mrs. Manner observed a smoky form rise up in the house. Nobody had been smoking. The form roughly resembled the vague outlines of a human being.

Her husband, fortunately, experienced the smells also, so she was not alone in her plight. But the children, who had barely shaken off their terror, were now faced with renewed fears. They could not keep running, running away from what?

They tried every means at their command. Holy water, incense, a minister's prayer, their own prayers, curses and commands to the unseen: but the scent remained.

Gradually, they learned to live with their psychic problems. For a mother possessed of definite mediumistic powers from youth and a young adult in the household are easy prey to those among the restless dead who desire a continued life of earthly activities. With the physical powers drawn from these living people, they play and continue to exist in a world of which they are no longer a part.

As the young man grew older, the available power dwindled and the scent was noticed less frequently. But the tortured man on the stairs of the house in Somerset will have to wait for a more willing medium to be set free.

✳ 61

The House of Evil (New York)

PARKER KEEGAN IS A practical man not much given to daydreaming or speculation. That is as it should be. For Parker makes his living, if you can call it that, driving a truck with high explosives, tanks containing acetylene, oxygen, nitrogen, and other flammable substances for a welding company in upstate New York.

So you see, he has to have his mind on his work all the time, if he wants to get old.

His wife Rebecca is a more emotional type. That, too, is as it should be. She is an artist, free-lancing and now and again making sales. There is some Indian blood in her and she has had an occasional bout with the supernatural. But these were mainly small things, telepathy or dream experiences and nothing that really worried her. Neither she nor her husband had any notions that such things as haunted houses really existed, except, of course, in Victorian novels.

Now the Keegans already had one child and Rebecca was expecting her second, so they decided to look for a larger place. As if by the finger of fate, an opportunity came their way just about then. Her teen-age cousin Jane telephoned Rebecca at her parents' home to tell them of a house they might possibly rent. It developed she did this not entirely out of the goodness of her heart, but also because she didn't like being alone nights in the big place she and her husband lived in. He worked most of the night in another city.

"There are two halves to this house," Jane explained, and she made it so enticing that Parker and Rebecca decided then and there to drive over and have a look at it.

Even though they arrived there after dark, they saw immediately that the house was attractive, at least from the outside. Built in pre-Civil War days, it had stood the test of time well. As is often the case with old houses, the servant quarters are in a separate unit and parallel, but do not intrude upon, the main section of the house. So it was here, and it was the former servant quarters that Jane and Harry occupied. As the visitors had not spoken to the landlord about their interest, they entered the unused portion of the building from their cousin's apartment. This was once the main house and contained eight rooms, just what they needed.

The ground floor consisted of a large front room with two windows facing the road and two facing the other way. Next to it was an old-fashioned dining room, and branching off from it, a narrow kitchen and a small laundry room. In the dim light they could make out a marvelous staircase with a lovely, oiled banister. It was at this point that the two apartments which made up the house connected, and one could be entered into from the other. Underneath the front stairway was a closet and the door leading to the other side of the house, but they found another, enclosed, stairway leading from the bedroom at the top of the front stairs into the dining room. Exactly below this enclosed staircase were the cellar stairs leading into the basement. There were three cellars, one under the servant quarters, one underneath the front room, and one below the dining room.

As Rebecca set foot into the cellar under the dining room, which had apparently served as a fruit cellar, she grew panicky for a moment. She immediately dismissed her anxiety with a proper explanation: they had seen the thriller "Psycho" the night before and this cellar reminded her of one of the gruesome incidents in that movie. But later she was to learn that the feeling of panic persisted whenever she came down into this particular part of the basement, even long after she had forgotten the plot of that movie.

For the present, they inspected the rest of the house. The upstairs portion contained two large bedrooms and two smaller ones. Only the larger rooms were heated. There was an attic but nobody ever investigated it during their entire stay in the house.

They decided the house was just what they wanted and the next morning they contacted the owner.

George Jones turned out to be a very proper, somewhat tight-lipped man. He inquired what they did for a living and then added, "Are you religious people?"

Rebecca thought this an odd question, but since she had told him she was an artist, she assumed he considered artists somewhat unreliable and wanted to make sure he had responsible and "God-fearing" tenants. Only much later did it occur to her that Jones might have had other reasons.

It was a cold, miserable day in December 1964 when the Keegans moved into their new home. They were happy to get into a home full of atmosphere, for Rebecca was an avid amateur archaeologist who read everything on antiques she could get her hands on. At the same time they were doing a good deed for her cousin, keeping her company on those long nights when her husband was away at work. It all seemed just right and Rebecca did not even mind the difficulties the moving brought them. For one thing, they could not afford professional moving men, but had turned to friends for help. The friends in turn had borrowed a truck that had to be back in the garage by nightfall, so there was a lot of shoving and pushing and bad tempers all around. On top of that, the stinging cold and snow made things even more uncomfortable, and Rebecca could do little to help matters, being pregnant with their second child at the time.

Late that first night, they finally climbed the stairs to the large bedroom. They were both exhausted from the day's work and as soon as they fell into bed, they drifted off into deep sleep.

But even though they were very tired, Rebecca could not help noticing some strange noises, crackling sounds emanating seemingly from her cousin's side of the house. She put them down to steam pipes and turned to the wall.

When the noises returned night after night, Rebecca began to wonder about them. Parker also worked nights now and she and Jane sat up together until after the late show on television was over, around 1:30 A.M. All that time, night after night, they could hear the steam pipes banging away. Nobody slept well in the house and Jane became jumpier and jumpier as time went on. Her mood would change to a certain sullenness Rebecca had not

noticed before, but she dismissed it as being due to the winter weather, and of no particular significance.

Then one night, as she was thinking about some of the events of the recent past while lying awake in bed, Rebecca heard heavy footsteps coming up the stairs. They were the steps of a heavy man, and since she had not heard the characteristic clicking of the front door lock, she knew it could not be her husband.

Alarmed, and thinking of burglars, she got out of bed and called out to her cousin. She then went to the top of the stairs and was joined by Jane coming through the connecting door, and standing at the foot of the stairs. What the two women saw from opposite ends of the staircase was far from ordinary. Someone was walking up the stairs and the stairs were bending with each step as if a heavy person were actually stepping upon them!

Only there was no one to be seen. They did not wait until the footsteps of the invisible man reached the top of the stairs. Rebecca dove back into her bedroom banging the door shut after her. Just before she did, she could still hear her young cousin downstairs screaming, before she, too, ran back into the assumed safety of her bedroom.

The experience on the stairs made Jane even moodier than before and it was not long afterward that she took her little girl and left her husband. There had been no quarrel, no apparent reason for her sudden action. He was a handsome young man who had treated her well, and Jane loved him. Yet, there it was—she could not stand the house any longer and did what her panicky mind told her to do.

Rebecca was now left alone nights with the noisy wraith on the stairs and she scarcely welcomed it. Soon after the incident, Jane's abandoned husband sold his belongings and moved away, leaving the former servant quarters empty once again.

It was then that Rebecca kept hearing, in addition to the heavy footsteps, what seemed to be someone crying in the empty side of the house. She convinced herself that it wasn't just a case of nerves when the noises continued at frequent intervals while she was fully awake. Her time was almost at hand, and as often happens with approaching motherhood, she grew more and more apprehensive. It did not help her condition any when she heard a loud banging of the cupboards in the dining room at a time when she was all alone in the house. Someone was opening and closing the doors to the cupboard in rapid succession soon after she had retired for the night. Of course she did not run downstairs to investigate. Who would?

Fortunately, Parker came home a little earlier that night, because when he arrived he found Rebecca in a state of near hysteria. To calm her fears as much as to find out for himself, he immediately went downstairs to investigate. There was no one there and no noise. Getting into bed with the assurance of a man who does not believe in the supernatural, he was about to tell his wife that she must have dreamed it all, when he, too, clearly heard the cupboard doors open and close downstairs.

He jumped out of bed and raced down the stairs. As he took the steps two at a time, he could clearly hear the doors banging away louder and louder in the dining room. It must be stated to Parker's eternal credit, that not once did he show fear or worry about any possible dangers to himself: he merely wanted to know what this was all about.

The noise reached a crescendo of fury, it seemed to him, when he stood before the dining room door. Quickly he opened the door and stepped into the dark expanse of the chilly dining room.

Instantly, the noise stopped as if cut off with a knife.

Shaking his head and beginning to doubt his own sanity, or at least, power of observation, Parker got into bed once more and prepared to go to sleep. Rebecca looked at him anxiously, but he did not say anything. Before she could question him, the ominous noise started up again downstairs.

Once more, as if driven by the furies, Parker jumped out of bed and raced down the stairs. Again the noise stopped the moment he opened the dining room door.

He slowly went up the stairs again and crawled into bed. Pulling the cover over his ears, he cursed the ghosts downstairs, but decided that his badly needed sleep was more important than the answer to the puzzle.

Shortly after, their son was born. When they returned from the hospital, they were greeted by a new couple, the Winters, who had meanwhile moved into the other half of the house. Although friendly on the surface, they were actually stern and unbending and as they were also much older than the Keegans, the two families did not mingle much. Mrs. Winters was a tough and somewhat sassy old woman and did not look as if anything could frighten her. Her husband worked as a night watchman, and there were no children. It was not long before Mrs. Winters knocked at Rebecca's door in fear.

"Someone is trying to break in," she whispered, and asked to be let in. Rebecca knew better but did not say anything to frighten the old woman even further.

It seemed as if winter would never yield to spring, and if you have ever lived in the cold valleys of upstate New York, you know how depressing life can be under such circumstances.

To brighten things a little, the Keegans acquired a female German shepherd dog for the children, and also for use as a watchdog.

All this time Rebecca was sure she was never alone in the house. There was someone watching her, night and day. Her husband no longer scoffed at her fears, but could do little about them. The strange noises in the walls continued on and off and it got so that Rebecca no longer felt fear even when she saw the doorknob of a perfectly empty room turn slowly by its own volition. By now she knew the house was haunted, but as yet she did not realize the nature of the uncanny inhabitants.

One day she left the baby securely strapped in his seat while she ran to catch her little girl who was climbing the front stairs and was in immediate danger of falling off. Just at that precise moment, the strap broke and the baby fell to the floor, fracturing his skull.

All during their stay at the house, someone was always having accidents or becoming unaccountably ill. Their debts increased as their medical expenses grew higher, so it was decided that Rebecca should go to work and earn some money. In addition, Parker started working extra shifts. But far from helping things, this only served to incite the landlord to raise their rent, on the theory that they were earning more. To make things even more difficult for them, Rebecca could not find a proper baby-sitter to stay with the children while she was at work. Nobody would stay very long in the house, once they got to know it.

She turned to her mother for help, and her mother, after a short stay, refused to spend any more time in the house, but offered to take the children to her own home. There was no explanation, but to Rebecca it seemed ominous and obvious. Finally, her teenage sister consented to become a baby-sitter for them. She could use the money for school, but soon her enthusiasm waned. She began to complain of a closed-in feeling she experienced in the old house and of course she, too, heard all the strange noises. Each day, Mary became more and more depressed and ill, whereas she had been a happy-go-lucky girl before.

"There are prowlers about," she kept saying, and one day she came running to Rebecca in abject fear. On a moonless night she happened to be glancing out a living room window when she saw what appeared to be a face. Rebecca managed to calm her by suggesting she had seen some sort of shadow, but the incessant barking of the dog, for no apparent reason, made matters worse. Added to this were incidents in which objects would simply fly out of their hands in broad daylight. The end of the rope was reached one day when they were all in the front room. It was afternoon and Mary was holding a cup in her hand, about to fill it with tea. That instant it flew out of her hands and smashed itself at Parker's feet. Without saying another word, the young girl went up the stairs to her room. Shortly after, her things all packed, she came down again to say goodbye.

Once again they were without help, when Rebecca's sister-in-law Susan saved the day for them. A simple and quite unimaginative person, she had put no stock into all the tales of goings-on she had heard and was quite willing to prove her point.

Within a day after her arrival, she changed her tune.

"Someone is watching me," she complained, and refused to stay alone in the house. She, too, complained of things flying off the shelves seemingly by their own volition and of cupboard doors opening and closing as if some-one were looking into the drawers for something or other.

The footsteps up the stairs continued and Susan heard them many times. She took the dog into the house with her but that was of little use: the dog was more afraid than all of the people together.

Incredible though it seemed to the Keegans, two years had passed since they had come to the House of Evil. That they still had their sanity was amazing, and that they had not moved out, even more of a miracle. But they simply could not afford to, and things were difficult enough in the physical world to allow the unseen forces to add to their problems. So they stuck it out.

It was the night before Christmas of 1966, and all through the house a feeling of ominous evil poisoned the atmosphere. They were watching television in order to relax a little. Rebecca suddenly saw a presence out of the corner of her eye, a person of some kind standing near the window in back of the sofa where her sister-in-law was sitting. Without raising her voice unduly or taking her eyes off the spot, she said, "Susan, get the rifle!" They had a rifle standing ready in the corner of the room.

Only then did Susan take a sharp look at the face peering into the window. It was a man's face, either Indian or Negro, and so unspeakably evil it took her breath away. Scowling at them with hatred, the face remained there for a moment, while Susan grabbed the gun. But when she pointed it towards the window, the face had disappeared.

Immediately, they rushed outside. The ground was frozen hard, so footprints would not have shown, had there been any. But they could not see anyone nor hear anyone running away.

The dog, chained at a spot where an intruder would be visible to her, evidently did not feel anything. She did not bark. Was she in some strange way hypnotized?

Soon after Christmas, Susan had to leave and the Keegans no longer could afford a baby-sitter. Rebecca had quit her job, and things were rough financially again.

To help matters, they invited a young couple with a small child to move in with them and help share expenses. The husband did not believe in the supernatural and the wife, on being told of their "problems," showed herself open-minded, even interested, although skeptical.

What had appeared to be a sensible arrangement soon turned out a disaster and additional burden to an already overburdened family. The Farmers weren't going to contribute to the household, but spend what money they earned on liquor and racing. The tension between the Keegans and the Farmers mounted steadily. But the monetary problems were not the sole cause. The Farmers, too, noticed the noises and the unbearable, heavy atmosphere of the house and instinctively blamed the Keegans for these things. Then there was a quilt with an early American eagle and ship motif printed on it. Soon the wife noticed that *someone* had turned the quilt around after she had put it away safely for the night. In the morning, the motif would face the opposite way. They could not blame the Keegans for that, since the quilt had been stored out of anyone's reach, and they dimly realized that the house was indeed haunted.

As the tension grew, the two couples would scarcely speak to each other even though they naturally shared the same quarters. Rebecca began to realize that no matter how gay a person might have been on the outside, once such a person moved into the House of Evil, there would be changes of personality and character. Although far from superstitious, she began to believe that the house itself was dangerous and that prolonged life in it could only destroy her and her loved ones.

Early in April Rebecca and Parker were in the bedroom upstairs one night, when they saw a form cross from where their telephone was, over their bed, and then down the stairs. As it crossed past the telephone, the phone rang. An instant later, as the form reached the bottom of the stairs, the downstairs telephone also rang.

This brought the Farmers out screaming and demanding to know what was going on?

For once, there was unison in the house as the four adults gathered together soberly downstairs to discuss what they just witnessed and compare impressions.

They agreed there was a blue-white light around the form, a light so intense it hurt the eyes. They all had felt an icy chill as the form passed them. Only Parker bravely insisted it might have been lightning. But nobody had heard any thunder.

For the Farmers, this was the ghost that broke their patience's back. They moved out immediately.

Left once again to themselves, Rebecca and her husband decided it was time for them to look elsewhere, too.

Tired from the long struggle with the uncanny, they moved soon afterwards.

As soon as they had settled in a new house, life took on a different aspect: where ominous presences had dampened their spirits, there was now gaiety and a zest for life they had not known for four years. Nobody has been sick in the family since and they have no problems getting and keeping baby-sitters.

The House of Evil still stands on lonely Route 14, and there are people living in it now. But whenever Parker has occasion to pass Route 14 in his car, he steps on the gas and drives just a little bit faster. No sense taking chances!

✳ 62

The Specter in the Hallway
(Long Island)

PORT WASHINGTON IS A busy little town on Long Island, about forty-five minutes from New York City. A lot of people who live there commute daily to their jobs downtown or midtown, and the flavor of the town is perhaps less rustic than other places further out on Long Island. Still, there are a few back roads and quiet lanes that are as quiet and removed from the pace of Main Street as any small town might boast. Such a street is Carlton, and a house in about the middle of the block not far from the waterfront fits the description of a country home to a tee. It is a two-story wooden structure about fifty years old, well-preserved and obviously redecorated from time to time. The house sits back from the street on a plot of land, and all in all, one could easily overlook it if one were not directly searching for it. There is nothing spectacular about this house on Carlton, and to this day the neighbors think of it only as a nice, old house usually owned by nice, respectable people whose lives are no different from theirs and whose problems are never of the kind that make headlines.

But the house behind the nice, old trees has not always been so pleasant looking. When Mr. and Mrs. F. first saw it, it was nothing more than a dilapidated shell of its former splendor, yet it was imbued with a certain nobility that translated itself, in their minds, into the hope of being capable of restoration, provided someone lavished enough care and money on the place. Mr. F. was not wealthy, but he had a going business and could afford a good-sized house.

Mrs. F.'s own father had been involved in the building of the house on Carlton though she did not realize it at the time she first saw it. He had been in the building trade in this town, and Mrs. F. had grown up here. It seemed the natural thing to her to settle in a town she was familiar with, now that their two girls were of school age, and she had to think of the future. The house was for sale and as they walked through it they realized that it had been neglected for some time. The real estate man was properly vague about previous owners, and would say only that it had been built by respectable people fifty-three years ago, and they could have it very reasonably. Real estate agents are not historians, they are not even concerned with the present, but only the future: tomorrow's sale and commission. If the F.s did not want to buy the old house, sooner or later someone else would, or perhaps the house could be torn down and another one built here. The land was almost more valuable than the house itself. Suburbia was stretching further and further and Port Washington was a most convenient location.

But the F.s did buy the house in 1961 and even though the place was a shambles, they managed to move in right away and live in it while they were restoring and redecorating it. There were twelve rooms in all, on two floors. A broad staircase with two landings led up to the second story. The second landing led directly into a hallway. To the left was the master bedroom, to the right a second bedroom they turned over to their two girls, aged thirteen and eight. The first few days were busy ones indeed, as the family tried to settle down in unfamiliar surroundings. Mr. F. worked in the city, and the girls were in school mornings, so Mrs. F. was alone in the house a good part of the day. The master bedroom in particular was an eyesore, dark and forbidding as it was, and wholly depressing to her.

She decided to start work immediately on the bedroom, and had it painted white. That caused some problems in the mornings when one wanted to sleep late, for they had morning sun, and the white walls made the room even brighter. But this occasional inconvenience was more than offset by the general cheerfulness the change in color gave the room. Mrs. F. felt optimistic about the house and was sure it would make a splendid home for them.

One day soon after their arrival, she was hanging curtains in the bedroom. Suddenly she felt a hostile glare in back of her and turned to see who had entered the room. There was no one to be seen. And yet, she was sure another person was next to her in the room, a person whose hatred she could literally feel!

Immediately, Mrs. F. put down the curtains and left the house. For a few hours, she went shopping in town. As it became time to return home, she dismissed the whole incident as imagination. She had no interest in the occult even though over the years she had shown a marked degree of ESP powers. Whenever someone close to her, or even a mere acquaintance, was involved in a tragedy, she knew it beforehand. Often she would anticipate what someone was about to say to her, but she had learned to play down this peculiar talent lest people in the community might think her an oddball. If anything, she hated being "different," or causing her husband dismay for leanings that did not sit well with his employers or the people they socialized with.

Shortly after this incident, she was in bed asleep when she awoke the incessant ringing of the telephone. The telephone was downstairs, so she got up and started on her way down the stairs to answer it. Who would call them at that hour? Theirs was an unlisted number.

She was fully awake as she reached the stairs. The phone was still demanding her attention. As she put one foot onto the top step, she felt herself pushed by unseen hands and fell down to the first landing. As soon as she fell, the telephone stopped ringing. As a consequence of this "accident," she was crippled for several months. Her husband ascribed the fall to her drowsiness, but she knew better. She had felt a hard push in the back: she had not slipped on the stairs. They patiently went over the entire list of those who had their unlisted phone number. None of them had called.

* * *

From this moment on, her optimistic outlook about the house changed. She longed for the time she could be outside the house, have the choice of running away from it when she felt like it. But her legs were still bruised and the time passed slowly.

Then one evening, while her husband was away, she sat quietly in the living room downstairs, reading a book. For some unexplainable reason, she suddenly felt that someone was watching her. She lifted her eyes from the book, turned, and glanced up at the stairway. There, at the very spot where she had fallen, stood a man. His face was in the shadows, but he was tall and wearing dark clothes. She stared at the figure with amazement for several moments. When she was fully aware of it, the apparition vanished, as if it had only wanted to let her know of its presence.

Too horrified to move from the chair, Mrs. F. just sat there until her husband returned. She knew the man on the stairs wanted her to come up to him, and she could not bring herself to do it. Neither could she tell her husband what had happened.

Much later, when she confided in him, she found out that he did not think her mad, and his compassion only increased their deep affection for each other.

The larger incidents were accompanied by a continuing plethora of odd sounds, creaking noises on the stairs or in the master bedroom. Most of the latter noises she had heard downstairs in the living room, which is located directly underneath the master bedroom. Old houses make odd noises, she rationalized to herself, and probably the house was just settling. But to make sure, she decided to call in some termite specialists. They came and removed paneling from some of the basement walls in that part of the house and gave the place a thorough examination. As she watched, they inspected the beams and the foundation of the house. They found nothing. The house was neither settling nor shifting, the experts explained, thus removing the pat explanation Mrs. F. had given to herself for the odd noises. She wished she had never called in the termite experts, for now that she knew there were no natural causes for the disturbances, what was she to do?

So far neither her husband nor her children had noticed anything odd, or if they had, they had not said anything to her. Mrs. F. dreaded the thought of discussing such matters with her children. One night she busied herself in the living room after dinner. Her husband was out and the two girls were presumably in their own room upstairs. Suddenly there was a loud thumping and knocking overhead in the master bedroom.

"The girls are out of their beds," she thought, and called up to them to go back to bed immediately. There was no reply. When she went upstairs to check, she found both girls fast asleep in their room. She went back to continue her chores in the living room. Immediately, the noises started up again overhead. Despite her fears that *he* was up there waiting for her, Mrs. F. went up again. There are seven doors opening onto that hallway and yet she knew immediately which door *he* was lurking behind: her bedroom's. She turned around and grabbed the banister of the stairs firmly. This time he wasn't going to push her down again. Slowly, she descended the stairs. She knew in her heart the specter would not follow her down. His domain was the upstairs part of the house. She soon realized that the uncanny house guest had his limitations as far as movements were concerned and it gave her unsuspected strength: she knew he could not follow her outside, or even into the living room; there she was safe from him. Often, when she was outside in the yard, she could *feel* him peering out at her, watching, always watching with slow-burning eyes. When she went out to market and closed the door behind her, a wave of hatred hit her from inside the empty house. He resented being left alone. Had the ghostly presence developed an attachment toward her?

Psychic feelings had been a subject studiously avoided by Mrs. F. in her conversations, but when she mentioned her problem accidentally to her mother, she was surprised to find not a questioning gaze but an understanding acknowledgment.

"I too have always felt there is *someone* in the house," her mother admitted, "but I think it's friendly."

Ms. F. shook her head. She knew better. Her mother then suggested that a portrait of Jesus be placed in the entrance foyer to ward off "evil influences." Mrs. F. was not religious, but under the circumstances, she was willing to try *anything*. So a portrait of Christ was duly placed in the foyer at the landing. It apparently made a difference, for the presence of the man in black faded away from the spot from that day. However, he was as strongly present as ever in the bedroom.

One night, the F.'s intimate relationship was literally interrupted by the ghostly presence, and it took them years to get over the shock. They could never be sure that they were truly "alone," and even if they moved to another room, Mrs. F. feared the jealous specter would follow them there.

During the day, she continuously felt a call to go up to the bedroom, but she never went when she was alone in the house. That was "his" domain and she had hers in the downstairs area of the house.

One evening, while her husband was taking a shower, she felt encouraged enough to venture alone into the bedroom. A thought ran through her mind, "Why, he isn't here after all!" Scarcely had she finished thinking this, when she clearly heard a voice shout into her ear: "I am here!" And as if to underscore his presence, a necktie rose off its clasp and placed itself on her shoulder!

Mrs. F. tried to behave as if that happened every day of her life. As if speaking to herself she said, aloud, "Oh, stupid tie, falling like *that!*" But she knew she was not fooling him, that he knew he had terribly frightened her with this performance.

The same evening, she and her husband had a quiet discussion about the house. They both loved it and they had spent considerably money and much time in fixing it up. It was most inconvenient to move after four years. But what were they to do? Share it forever with a ghost?

She found that her husband had felt odd in the house for a long time also, and had thought of selling it. While he failed to see how a ghost could possibly harm them—having had plenty of chances to do so and not having done so, apart from the "accident" on the stairs—he did not wish to subject his family to any form of terror.

They placed an ad in the *New York Times* and listed their telephone for the first time. At least, Mrs. F. thought, if the phone rang now, it would be someone calling about the house, not a ghost trying to rouse her from deep sleep.

But houses do not always sell overnight, especially old ones. They wanted to sell, but they didn't want to lose money. Still, having made the decision to move eventually made things easier for Mrs. F. She was even able to muster some curiosity about their unbidden guest and made inquiries among neighbors, especially some old-timers who knew the area well. Nobody, however, could shed any light on the situation. Of course, Mrs. F. did not come right out and speak of her experiences in the house, but she did ask if any unusual events had ever occurred in it or what the history of the house had been. Still, the result was not encouraging and they realized they would leave the house without ever knowing who it was that had caused them to do so!

Then Mrs. F. discovered that she was, after all, a natural medium. She would simply sit back in her chair and rest and gradually her senses would become clouded and another person would speak to her directly. It felt as if that person was very close to her and she could take the message the way a telegraph operator takes down a telegram, word for word, and the more relaxed she was and the less fear she showed, the more clear the words were to her.

She fought this at first, but when she realized that it meant only more discomfort, she relaxed. Then, too, she knew the specter would not harm her—their relationship had somehow changed since the time he had pushed her down those stairs. She felt no fear of him, only compassion, and sensed he needed help badly and that she was willing to extend it to him.

While they were waiting for a buyer for the house, she would often lapse into semiconsciousness and commune with her tormentor, who had now become a kind of friend. Gradually she pieced together his story and began to understand his reasons for doing what he was doing to get her attention. As she listened to the ghost, his anger gave way to an eagerness to be heard and understood.

A young man of about seventeen and of small build, he had light hair, high cheekbones, and deep-set eyes. At that tender age he was lost at sea as a member of the Canadian Navy. A French Canadian, he desperately wanted her to deliver a message to someone, but she was unable to clearly get either the message or the name of the individual. Perhaps the very emotionalism of such an attempt caused its failure. But she did get the name of his ship, something that sounded to her like Tacoma. Whenever Mrs. F. awoke from her trance state, that word stood strongly in her mind. Finally she wrote to the United States Navy Department. Unfortunately, there had been four ships by that name! But her intuition told her to contact the Canadian Navy also. The boy had been lost during World War II, while on duty, and while she did not have his name, perhaps the name of the ship could be traced. No, the Canadians did not have a Tacoma, but they did have a mine sweeper named Transcona, and instantly she felt that was the right ship. It had been in war service from 1942 to 1945.

As her inquiries went on, she felt the atmosphere in the house change. It was no longer heavy with frustration, but the presence was still there. Twice during that month he was seen by the children. The thirteen-year-old girl wanted to know who was "the big boy walking back and forth in the hallway all night" and Mrs. F. told her she had dreamed it all, for there was no one in the hall that night.

Either unable or unwilling to question this explanation, the girl thought no further about it. The younger girl, however, reported another incident a few days later. She knew nothing of her older sister's experience. As she was bathing, a young man had opened the door and then turned and walked into her sister's room! Mrs. F. was hard put to explain *that* away, but eventually she managed to calm the little girl.

* * *

But despite Mrs. F.'s willingness to let him communicate with her in trance, the young man was unable to give either his name or that of the person whom he tried to reach. His own emotions were still pitched high from the sudden death he had suffered and he did not know how to cope with the situation.

In October of that year, after a wait of half a year, they sold the house. The new owner was a police officer in retirement with little sympathy for ghosts. Both he and his wife are devout Catholics and any suggestion at investigating the disturbances to free the unfortunate soul was simply not answered. The F.s had moved out but stayed in town, so they could not help hearing some of the local gossip concerning the house.

If the police officer was bothered by the ghostly sailor, he certainly did not speak of it to anyone. But word of mouth was that the new owners were disappointed with their new home: it wasn't as happy a place to them as they had anticipated when they bought it. Lots of little things were going wrong seemingly for no apparent reasons. For example, no matter how often the bedroom door was opened, it would "close itself."

Mrs. F. smiled wryly, for she remembered that the ghostly sailor always liked that door *open*. She too, had closed it to have privacy, only to find it opened by unseen hands. Finally, she understood that it wasn't curiosity or evil thoughts on his part, but simple loneliness, the desire not to be shut out from the world, and she left it open, the way he wanted it.

How long would it take the lieutenant to understand the lad? She mused and wondered if perhaps he could leave the house of his own free will, now that he had told her at least part of his story. Shortly after, the F.s moved to Florida. They wondered if the power for the manifestations had come from their young daughters, who were at the time of "poltergeist" age. If so, the police lieutenant will have the same problem: he has six children of his own.

✳ 63

The Bayberry Perfume Ghost (Philadelphia)

IF THERE IS ANYTHING more staid than a North Philadelphia banker I wouldn't know it. But even bankers are human and sometimes psychic. In William Davy's case there had been little or no occasion to consider such a matter except for one long-forgotten incident when he was eight years of age. At that time he lived with his parents in Manchester, England. On one particular morning, little William insisted that he saw a white shadow in the shape of a man passing in front of the clock. The clock, it so happened, was just striking the hour of 8:30 A.M. His mother, reminded by the sound of the clock, hurriedly sent the boy off to school, telling him to stop his foolishness about white shadows.

By the time the boy returned home, word had reached the house that his favorite grandfather, who lived halfway across England in Devon, had passed away. The time of his death was 8:30 A.M. Eventually, Mr. Davy moved to Philadelphia where he is an officer in a local bank, much respected in the community and not the least bit interested in psychic matters. His aged father, William Sr., came to live with him and his family in the home they bought in 1955. The house is a splendid example of Victorian architecture, built on three levels on a plot surrounded by tall trees in what is now part of North Philadelphia, but what was at the time the house was built a separate community, and originally just farmland.

The ground floor has a large kitchen to one side, a large living room, with fireplace, separated from a dining room by a sliding double door. Upstairs are bedrooms on two floors, with the third floor the one-time servant quarters, as was customary in Victorian houses. The Davy family did some remodelling downstairs, but essentially the house is as it was when it was first built, sometime in the late 1880s, according to a local lawyer named Huston, who is an expert on such things. At any rate, in 1890 it already stood on the spot where it is today.

William Sr. was a true English gentleman given to historical research, and a lover of ghost stories, with which he liked to regale his family on many occasions. But what started as a purely literary exercise soon turned into grim reality. Shortly after his arrival, William Sr. complained of hearing unusual noises in the house. He had a room on the third floor and was constantly hearing strange noises and floor boards creaking as if someone were walking on them.

His son laughed at this and ascribed it to his father's vivid imagination, especially after his many fictional ghost stories had set the mood for the sort of thing. But the older Davy insisted to his last day that he was being troubled by an unseen entity. After he passed away in February 1963, Mr. and Mrs. Davy thought no more of the matter. The house was a peaceful home to them and they enjoyed life.

* * *

Several months later, Mr. Davy was sitting by himself in the living room, reading. He was tired, and the time was 10 P.M. He decided to call it a day, and got up to go to bed. As he walked toward the hallway between the living room and the staircase, he literally stepped into a cloud of very pungent perfume which he instantly identified as a very strong bayberry smell. For a moment he stood in utter amazement, then slowly continued into the hall and up the stairs. The perfume still surrounded him, as if someone invisible, wearing this heavy perfume, were walking alongside him!

Upon reaching the first landing he went into the bedroom. At that point, the perfume suddenly left him, just as suddenly as it had come.

"Mary," he asked his wife, "did you by any chance spill some perfume?" She shook her head emphatically. She did not even own any such scent, and there had been no one else in the house that day or evening.

Puzzled but not particularly upset, Mr. Davy let the matter drop and he would have forgotten it entirely had not another event taken him by surprise.

Several months later he was again sitting in the living room, the time being around 10 P.M. He put down his book, and went toward the hallway. Again, he walked into a heavy cloud of the same perfume! Again it followed him up the stairs. As he climbed he felt something—or someone—brush against his right leg. It made a swishing sound but he could not see anything that could have caused it. When he got to the landing, he stopped and asked Mary to come out to him.

His wife had suffered a fractured skull when she was young and as a consequence had lost about 70% of her sense of smell.

When Mary joined him at the landing, he asked her if she smelled anything peculiar. "Oh my word," she said, immediately, "what a heavy perfume!" They were standing there looking at each other in a puzzled state. "What on earth is it?" Mary finally asked. He could only shrug his shoulders.

At that precise moment, they clearly heard footsteps going up the stairs from where they were standing, to the third floor!

Since neither of them saw any person causing the footsteps, they were completely unnerved, and refused to investigate. They did not follow the footsteps up to the third floor. They knew only too well that there wasn't any living soul up there at the moment.

One evening Mary was reading in bed, on the second floor, when she found herself surrounded by the same bayberry perfume. It stayed for several seconds, then died away. Since she was quite alone in the house and had been all evening, this was not very reassuring. But the Davys are not the kind of people that panic easily, if at all, so she shrugged it off as something she simply could not explain. On another occasion, Mr. Davy saw a patch of dull, white light move through the living room. From the size of the small cloud it resembled in height either a large child or a small adult, more likely a woman than a man. This was at 3 A.M. when he had come downstairs because he could not sleep that night.

In April 1966 the Davys had gone to Williamsburg, Virginia for a visit. On their return, Mr. Davy decided to take the luggage directly upstairs to their bedroom. That instant he ran smack into the cloud of bayberry perfume. It was if some unseen presence wanted to welcome them back!

One of Mary's favorite rings, which she had left in her room, disappeared only to be discovered later in the garden. How it got there was as much of a mystery then as it is now, but no one of flesh and blood moved that ring. Naturally, the Davys did not discuss their unseen visitor

with anyone. When you're a Philadelphia banker you don't talk about ghosts.

In September of the same year, they had a visit from their niece and her husband, Mr. and Mrs. Clarence Nowak. Mr. Nowak is a U.S. government employee, by profession a chemical engineer. Their own house was being readied and while they were waiting to move in, they spent two weeks with their uncle and aunt. The niece was staying on the second floor, while Mr. Nowak had been assigned the room on the third floor that had been the center of the ghostly activities in the past. After they had retired, Mr. Nowak started to read a book. When he got tired of this, he put the book down, put the lights out and got ready to doze off.

At that precise moment, he clearly heard footsteps coming up and he was so sure it was Mary coming up to say goodnight that he sat up and waited. But nobody came into his room and the footsteps continued!

Since he is a man of practical outlook, this puzzled him and he got out of bed and looked around. The corridor was quite empty, yet the footsteps continued right in front of him. Moreover, they seemed to enter the room itself and the sound of steps filled the atmosphere of the room as if someone were indeed walking in it. Unable to resolve the problem, he went to sleep.

The next night, the same thing happened. For two weeks, Mr. Nowak went to sleep with the footsteps resounding promptly at 10 P.M. But he had decided to ignore the whole thing and went to sleep, steps or no steps.

"It seemed, when I was in bed," he explained to his aunt, somewhat sheepishly, "the footsteps were coming up the stairs, and when I was lying there it seemed as if they were actually in the room, but I could not distinguish the actual location. When I first heard them I thought they were Mary's, so I guess they must have been the footsteps of a woman."

Mr. Nowak is not given to any interest in psychic phenomena, but on several occasions his wife, also named Mary, as is her aunt, did have a rapport bordering on telepathic communication with him. These were minor things, true, but they were far beyond the possibilities of mere chance. Thus it is very likely that the chemist's natural tendency towards ESP played a role in his ability to hear the steps, as it certainly did in the case of the banker, Mr. Davy, whose own childhood had shown at least one marked incident of this sort.

But if the ghostly presence favored anyone with her manifestations, it would seem that she preferred men. Mary Nowak slept soundly through the two weeks, with nary a disturbance or incident.

Clifford Richardson, another nephew of the Davys, came from Oklahoma to visit the Nowaks one time, and in the course of the visit he decided to stay a night at the Davys. Mr. Richardson is the owner of an insurance agency and not the least bit interested in the occult. On his return to the Nowaks the following day, he seemed unusually pensive and withdrawn. Finally, over coffee, he opened up.

"Look, Mary," he said, "your husband Bucky has stayed over at Uncle Ned's house for a while. Did he sleep well?"

"What do you mean?" Mary asked, pretending not to know.

"Did he ever hear any sounds?"

Mary knew what he meant and admitted that her husband had indeed "heard sounds."

"Thank God," the insurance man sighed. "I thought I was going out of my mind when I heard those footsteps."

He, too, had slept in the third floor bedroom.

What was the terrible secret the little bedroom held for all these years?

The room itself is now plainly but adequately furnished as a guest room. It is small and narrow and undoubtedly was originally a maid's room. There is a small window leading to the tree-studded street below. It must have been a somewhat remote room originally where a person might not be heard, should he/she cry for help for any reason.

The Davys began to look into the background of their house. The surrounding area had been known as Wright's Farm, and a certain Mrs. Wright had built houses on the property towards the late 1880s. The house was owned by four sets of occupants prior to their buying it and despite attempts to contact some of those who were still alive, they failed to do so. They did not discuss their "problem" with anyone, not even Mary's aged mother who was now staying with them. No sense frightening the frail old lady. Then again the Davys weren't really frightened, just curious. Mary, in addition to being a housewife, was also a student of group dynamics and education at nearby

Temple University, and the phenomena interested her mildly from a researcher's point of view. As for William Davy, it was all more of a lark than something to be taken seriously, and certainly not the sort of thing one worries about.

* * *

When their inquiries about the history of the house failed to turn up startling or sensational details, they accepted the presence as something left over from the Victorian age and the mystique of it all added an extra dimension, as it were, to their fine old home.

Then one day, in carefully looking over the little room on the third floor, Mr. Davy made an interesting discovery. At waist height, the door to the room showed heavy dents, as if someone had tried to batter it down! No doubt about it, the damage showed clear evidence of attempted forcing of the door.

Had someone violated a servant up there against her wishes? Was the door to the bedroom battered down by one of the people in the house, the son, perhaps, who in that age was sacrosanct from ordinary prosecution for such a "minor" misdeed as having an affair with the maid?

The strong smell of bayberry seemed to indicate a member of the servant class, for even then, as now, an overabundance of strong perfume is not a sign of good breeding.

* * *

There have been no incidents lately but this does not mean the ghost is gone. For a Victorian servant girl to be able to roam the *downstairs* at will is indeed a pleasure not easily abandoned—not even for the promised freedom of the other side!

✳ 64

The Headless Grandfather (Georgia)

GROVER C. WAS ONE OF those colorful old-timers you hardly see anymore these days, not even in the deep South. It wasn't that Grover had any particular background in anything special, far from it; he was an untutored man who owed his success solely to his own willpower and an insatiable curiosity that led him places his education—or lack of it—would have prevented him from ever reaching.

* * *

He saw the light of day just before the turn of the century in rural North Carolina. At the age of nineteen he married for the first time, but his wife Fannie and the child she bore him both died from what was then called "childbed fever," or lack of proper medical treatment. He

had not yet chosen any particular career for himself, but was just "looking around" and did odd jobs here and there. A year later he was married again, to a lady from Georgia who is still living. After their first girl was born, they moved to Columbus, Georgia, and Mr. C. worked in a local mill for a while. This didn't satisfy his drive, however, and shortly afterward he and his brother Robert opened a grocery store. The store did right well until "the Hoover panic," as they called it, and then they managed to sell out and buy a farm in Harris County.

Life was pretty placid, but after an accident in which he lost his daughter, Mr. C. moved back to Columbus and tried his hand at the grocery business once more. About this time, the restless gentleman met a lady from Alabama, as a result of which he became the father of an "extracurricular" little girl, in addition to his own family, which eventually consisted of a wife and nine children, two of whom are dead, the others still living.

When his second-born child died of an infectious disease, Mr. C. had his long-delayed breakdown, and for several years, he was unable to cope with his life. During those rough years of slow, gradual recuperation, his daughter Agnes ran the store for him and supported the family.

As his health improved and he began to return to a happier and more constructive outlook on life, he developed an interest in real estate. With what money he could spare, he bought and sold property, and before long, he did so well he could dispense with the grocery store.

Soon he added a construction business to his real estate dealings and was considered a fairly well-to-do citizen in his hometown. This status of course attracted a variety of unattached women and even some who were attached, or semi-detached, as the case may have been, and Mr. C. had himself a good time. Knowledge of his interest in other ladies could not fail to get to his wife and eventually he was given a choice by his wife: it was either her or *them*.

He picked them, or, more specifically, a lady next door, and for thirteen years he was reasonably faithful to her. Eventually she disliked living with a man she was no married to, especially when he happened to be married to someone else, even though he had bought her a cute little house of her own in Columbus. Mr. C. was not particularly happy about this state of affairs either, for he developed a penchant for drinking during those years. After they separated, the lady next door left town and got married.

Far from returning to the bosom of his family, now that the "other woman" had given him the gate, Grover looked elsewhere and what he found apparently pleased him. By now he was in his late sixties, but his vigorous personality wasn't about to be slowed down by so silly a reason as advancing age!

* * *

About 1962 he met a practical nurse by the name of Madeline, who turned out to be the opposite of what the doctor had ordered. After a particularly heavy argument, she kicked him in the nose. When it did not stop bleeding, she became alarmed and took him to the hospital. The family went to see him there even though his wife had not exactly forgiven him. But at this point it mattered little. Mr. C. also complained of pain in his side and the children firmly believed that the practical nurse had also kicked him in that area. Since he died shortly afterward, it was a moot question whether or not she had done so because Mrs. C's abilities no longer corresponded to her amorous expectations. The old gent certainly did not discuss it with his family. He was seventy when he died and Madeline was a mere sixty. Death was somewhat unexpected despite the

fact Mr. C. had suffered from various ailments. During the days he had been alone in his room at the hospital. At first, he shared the room with another older man, but several days later a young man was sent in to be with him. The young man's complaint was that he had a lollipop stick stuck in his throat. There probably aren't too many young men with such a predicament in medical annals, and even fewer in Columbus, Georgia. The family found this mighty peculiar, even more so since the young man was a close relative of Madeline, the very practical nurse.

They complained to the hospital authorities and the young man was moved. It is not known whether the lollipop stick was ever removed from his throat, but chances are it was or we would have heard more of it. Young men with lollipop sticks in their throats either die from them or become sideshow attractions in the circus; the records show neither so it must be assumed that the lollipop stick got unstuck somehow somewhere along the line. At any rate, Mr. C. was now guarded by one of his children each night, the children taking turns.

They are firmly convinced that the practical nurse slipped her erstwhile benefactor some poison and that perhaps the boy with the lollipop stick stuck in his throat might have done her bidding and administered it to the old gent. This is a pretty sticky argument, of course, and hard to prove, especially as no autopsy was ever performed on Mr. C. But it is conceivable that Madeline made a discovery about her friend that could have induced her to speed his failure to recover and do so by any means at her command. She knew her way around the hospital and had ready access to his room. She also had equally ready access to his office and thereby hangs a strange tale.

* * *

On one of the infrequent occasions when Mr. C. slept at home, his estranged wife was making up the bed. This was five months before his demise. As she lifted the mattress, she discovered underneath it a heavy envelope, about six by ten inches in size, crammed full with papers. She looked at it and found written on it in Mr. C.'s large lettering, the words:

"This is not to be opened until I am dead. I mean good and dead, Daddy."

She showed the envelope to her daughter, Agnes, but put it back since she did not wish to enter into any kind of controversy with her husband. Evidently the envelope must have been taken by him to his office sometime later, for when she again made his bed two weeks before his passing, when he was still walking around, she found it gone. But there was a second, smaller envelope there, this one not particularly marked or inscribed. She left it there. A short time later Mr. C. was taken to the hospital. When Mrs. C. made the bed she found that the small envelope had also disappeared.

While the C.'s house in Columbus was not exactly a public place, neither was it an impregnable fortress, and anyone wishing to do so could have walked in at various times and quickly removed the envelope. As far as the office was concerned, that was even easier to enter and the family had no doubt whatever that Madeline took both envelopes for reasons best known to herself, although they could not actually prove any of it. At no time did the old gent say an unkind word about his Madeline, at least not to his children, preferring perhaps to take his troubles with him into the great beyond.

*　*　*

After his death, which came rather suddenly, the family found a proper will, but as Mr. C. had generously built homes for most of his children during his lifetime, in the 1950s, there was only a modest amount of cash in the bank accounts, and no great inheritance for anyone.

The will named Mrs. C. as executor, and as there was nothing to contest, it was duly probated. But the family did search the office and the late Mr. C.'s effects at the house for these two envelopes that were still missing. Only the wife and daughter Agnes knew of them, even though "nobody and everybody" had access to the house. The servants would not have taken them, and the safe was empty. As the old gent had occasionally slept in his office on a couch, the family looked high and low in his office but with negative results. The only thing that turned up in addition to the will itself was the neatly typed manuscript of a book of Biblical quotations. Mr. C. had been a serious Bible scholar, despite his uneducated status, and the quotes arranged by subject matter and source represented many thousands of hours of work. When his daughter Marie had seen him working on this project in 1962, she had suggested he have the scribbled notes typed up and she had prevailed upon her Aunt Catherine to undertake the job, which the latter did. Somewhat forlornly, Marie picked up the manuscript and wondered whether someone might not buy it and put a little cash into the estate *that* way.

The mystery of the disappearing envelopes was never solved. Even greater than the puzzle of their disappearance was the question about their content: what was in them that was so important that the old gent had to hide them under the mattress? So important that someone took them secretly and kept them from being turned over to the family, as they should have been?

Although there is no evidence whatever for this contention, Marie thinks there might have been some valuables left to Grover C.'s love child, the one he had with the lady from Alabama early in his romantic life.

At any rate, after several months of fruitless searches, the family let the matter rest and turned to other things. Grover C. would have gone on to his just reward, especially in the minds of his family, if it weren't for the matter of some peculiar, unfinished business.

About a year after Grover's death, Lewis C., one of the sons of the *deceased*, as they say in the police records, was busy building a brick flower planter in his home in Columbus. This was one of the houses his father had erected for his children, and Mr. C., the son, had been living in it happily without the slightest disturbance. Lewis was thirty years old and the mystery of his father's disappearing envelopes did not concern him very much at this point. Here he was, at 4 o'clock in the afternoon, on a brisk March day in 1967, working on his planter. Giving him a hand with it, and handing him one brick after another, was a professional bricklayer by the name of Fred, with whom he had worked before. They were in the living room and Lewis was facing the back door, Fred the front door.

"A brick, please" said Lewis, without turning around.

No brick came. He asked again. Still no brick. He then looked up at his helper and saw him frozen to the spot, gazing at the front door.

"What's the matter, Fred?" he inquired. He had never seen Fred so frightened.

Finally, as if awakening from a bad dream, Fred spoke.

"I've just seen Mr. C.," he said, "big as life."

"But Mr. C. has been dead for a year," the son replied.

Fred had worked for Grover for many years and he knew him well.

"What did he look like?" the son inquired.

"White…light," Fred replied and then went on to describe the figure in white pants he had seen at the door. Although it was only the bottom half of a man, he had instantly recognized his late employer. Grover was bow-legged and the white pants facing him surely were as bow-legged as old Grover had been. There was no doubt about whose lower half it was that had appeared and then gone up in a puff again.

Lewis shook his head and went on with his work. But a short time later he began to appreciate what Fred had experienced. In the middle of the night he found himself suddenly awake by reason of something in the atmosphere —undefinable, but still very real.

The lights in his bedroom were off, but he could see down the hallway. And what he saw was a man wearing a white shirt, dark pants…and…with no head. The headless gentleman was tiptoeing down the hallway toward him.

Lewis could only stare at the apparition which he instantly recognized as his late father, head or no head. When the ghost saw that Lewis recognized him, he took three leaps *backward* and disappeared into thin air.

Unfortunately, Catherine, Lewis' wife did not believe a word of it. For several months the subject of father's headless ghost could not be mentioned in conversation. Then in December 1968 Lewis and Catherine were asleep one night, when at about 2:30 A.M. they were both roused by the sound of heavy footsteps walking down the hall from the bedrooms toward the living room. As they sat up and listened with nary a heartbeat, they could clearly hear how the steps first hit the bare floor and then the carpet, sounding more muffled as they did. Finally, they resounded louder again as they reached the kitchen floor. Lewis jumped out of bed, ready to fight what he was sure must be an intruder. Although he looked the house over from top to bottom he found no trace of a burglar, and all the doors were locked.

* * *

In retrospect they decided it was probably Grover paying them a visit. But why? True, he had built them the house. True, they had some of his effects, especially his old pajamas. But what would he want with his old pajamas where he *now* was? Surely he could not be upset by the fact that his son was wearing them. They decided then that Grover was most likely trying to get their attention because of those envelopes that were still missing or some other unfinished business, but they didn't like it, for who would like one's headless father popping in the middle of the night?

* * *

But apparently Grover did not restrict his nocturnal visits to his son Lewis' place. His granddaughter Marie, who lives in Atlanta, had come to visit at her grandfather's house in the spring of 1968. The house had no city water but used water from its own well system. It was therefore necessary to carry water into the house from outside. On one such occasion, when she had just done this and was returning with an *empty* basin, Marie stepped into what looked like a puddle of water. She started to mop up the puddle only to find that the spot was actually totally dry. Moreover, the puddle was ice cold, while the water basin she had just carried was still hot. She found this most unusual but did not tell anyone about it. Within a matter of hours eight-year-old Randy reported seeing a man in a dark suit in the bathroom, when the bathroom was obviously empty.

Apparently the old gent liked children, for little Joel was playing the piano in his Atlanta home in February of 1969, when he heard the sound of shuffling feel approach. Then there was the tinkling of glasses and all this time no one was visible. Grover had always liked a shot and a little music.

Soon Marie began to smell carnations in her house when no one was wearing them or using any perfume. This lingered for a moment and then disappeared, as if someone wearing this scent was just passing through the house.

In 1967, her Aunt Mary came to visit her in Atlanta and the conversation turned to the mysterious scent. "I'm glad you mentioned this," the aunt exclaimed, and reported a similar problem: both she and her husband would smell the same scent repeatedly in their own house, sometimes so

strongly they had to leave the house and go out for some fresh air. But the scent followed them, and on one occasion "sat" with them in their car on the way to church on Sunday morning!

They weren't too sure whether it was more like carnations or just a funeral smell, but it surely was a smell that had no rational explanation. Then in 1968, Mary informed her niece that a new perfume had suddenly been added to their list of phenomena: this one was a spicy scent, like a man's after-shave lotion.

Not long after this report, Marie smelled the same sharp, men's perfume in her own house in Atlanta, in her den. This was particularly upsetting, because they had shut off that room for the winter and no perfume or anyone wearing it had been in it for months.

In 1969, she had occasion to visit her grandfather's house in Columbus once again. She found herself wandering into her late grandfather's old bedroom. She stopped at his dresser and opened the drawer. There she found her spicy scent: a bottle of Avon hair lotion he had used. None of her husband's eau de cologne bottles had a similar smell. This was it. But how had it traveled all the way to Atlanta? Unless, of course, Grover was wearing it.

Marie is a thirty-year-old housewife, has worked for years as a secretary to various business firms, and is married to a postal clerk.

She was upset by her grandfather's insistence on continuing to visit his kinfolk and not staying in the cemetery as respectable folk are supposed to do, at least according to the traditional view of the dead.

Evidently Grover was far from finished with this life, and judging from the lively existence he had led prior to his unexpected departure from this vale of tears, he had a lot of energy left over.

That, combined with a genuine grievance over unfinished business—especially the missing two envelopes—must have been the cause for his peripatetic visits. Marie decided not to wait for the next one, and went to see a card reader in Columbus. The card reader could tell her only that she had a restless grandfather who wished her well.

Unfortunately, even if the cause for Grover's continued presence could be ascertained, there was no way in which the missing envelopes could be legally recovered.

Marie tried, in vain, to get a local psychic to make contact with her grandfather. Finally, she turned her attention to the manuscript of Bible quotes. Perhaps it was the book he wanted to see published.

Whatever it was, she must have done the right thing, or perhaps all that talk about the headless grandfather had pleased the old gent's ego enough to pry him loose from the earth plane. At any rate, no further appearances have been reported and it may well be that he has forgotten about those envelopes by now, what with the attractions of his new world absorbing his interest.

Unless, of course, he is merely resting and gathering strength!

The Old Merchant's House Ghost (New York City)

WHEN NEW YORK was still young and growing, that which is now a neighborhood given over to derelicts and slums was an elegant, quiet area of homes and gardens, and the world was right and peaceful in the young republic circa 1820.

Gradually, however, the "in" people, as we call them nowadays, moved further uptown, for such is the nature of the city confined to a small island that it can only move up, never down or out. Greenwich Village was still pretty far uptown, although the city had already spread beyond its limits and the center of New York was somewhere around the city hall district, nowadays considered way downtown.

Real state developers envisioned the east side of Fifth Avenue as the place to put up elegant homes for the well-to-do. One of the more fashionable architects of that time was John McComb, who had plans for a kind of terrace of houses extending from Lafayette Street to the Bowery, with the back windows of the houses opening upon John Jacob Astor's property nearby. Now Mr. Astor was considered somewhat uncouth socially by some of his contemporaries —on one occasion he mistook a lady's voluminous sleeve for a dinner napkin—but nobody had any second thoughts about his prosperity or position in the commercial world. Thus, any house looking out upon such a desirable neighborhood would naturally attract a buyer, the builders reasoned, and they proved to be right.

Called brownstones because of the dark brick material of their facades, the houses were well-appointed and solid. Only one of them is still left in that area, while garages, factories and ugly modern structures have replaced all the others from the distant past.

The house in question was completed in 1830 and attracted the eagle eye of a merchant named Seabury Tredwell, who was looking for a proper home commensurate with his increasing financial status in the city. He bought it and moved in with his family.

Mr. Tredwell's business was hardware, and he was one of the proud partners in Kissam & Tredwell, with offices on nearby Dey Street. A portly man of fifty, Mr. Tredwell was what we would today call a conservative. One of his direct ancestors had been the first Protestant Episcopal bishop of New York, and though a merchant, Tredwell evinced all the outward signs of an emerging mercantile aristocracy. The house he had just acquired certainly looked the part: seven levels, consisting of three stories, an attic and two cellars, large, Federal-style windows facing Fourth Street, a lovely garden around the house, and an imposing columned entrance door that one reached after ascending a flight of six marble stairs flanked by wrought-iron gate lanterns—altogether the nearest a merchant

prince could come to a real nobleman in his choice of domicile.

Inside, too, the appointments were lavish and in keeping with the traditions of the times: a Duncan Phyfe banister ensconcing a fine staircase leading to the three upper stories, and originating in an elegant hall worthy of any caller.

As one stepped into this hall, one would first notice a huge, high-ceilinged parlor to the left. At the end of this parlor were mahogany double doors separating the room from the dining room, equally as large and impressive as the front room. The Duncan Phyfe table was set with Haviland china and Waterford crystal, underlining the Tredwell family's European heritage. Each room had a large fireplace and long mirrors adding to the cavernous appearance of the two rooms. Large, floor-to-ceiling windows on each end shed light into the rooms and when the mahogany doors were opened, the entire area looked like a ballroom in one of those manor houses Mr. Tredwell's forebears lived in in Europe.

The furniture—all of which is still in the house—was carefully chosen. Prominent in a corner of the parlor was a large, rectangular piano. Without a piano, no Victorian drawing room was worth its salt. A music box was placed upon it for the delight of those unable to tinkle the ivories yet desirous of musical charms. The box would play "Home Sweet Home," and a sweet home it was indeed.

Further back along the corridor one came upon a small "family room," and a dark, ugly kitchen, almost L-shaped and utterly without charm or practical arrangements, as these things are nowadays understood. But in Victorian New York, this was a proper place to cook. Maidservants and cooks were not to be made cheerful, after all, theirs was to cook and serve, and not to enjoy.

On the first floor—or second floor, if you prefer, in today's usage—two large bedrooms are separated from each other by a kind of storage area, or perhaps a dressing room, full of drawers and cabinets. Off the front bedroom there is a small bedroom in which a four-poster bed took up almost all the available space. The bed came over from England with one of Mrs. Tredwell's ancestors.

Leading to the third floor, the stairs narrow and one is well-advised to hold on to the banister lest he fall and break his neck. The third floor nowadays serves as the curator's apartment, for the Old Merchant's House is kept up as a private museum and is no longer at the mercy of the greedy wrecker.

But when Seabury Tredwell lived in the house, the servants' rooms were on the third floor. Beyond that, a low-ceilinged attic provided additional space, and still another apartment fills part of the basement, also suitable for servants' usage.

Three views of the Old Merchant's House—Lower Manhattan

All in all, it was the kind of house that inspired confidence in its owner and Mr. Tredwell proceeded to establish himself in New York society as a force to be reckoned with, for that, too, was good for his expanding business.

He was eminently aided in this quest by the fact that his wife Eliza, whom he had married while still on his way up, had given him six daughters. Three of the girls made good marriages and left the parental homestead and apparently made out very well, for not much was heard about

them one way or another. Of the remaining three girls, however, plenty is recorded, and lots more is not, though it's undoubtedly true.

The three "bachelor girls" were named Phoebe, Sarah, and Gertrude. Phoebe's main interest was the Carl Fischer piano in the parlor and she and her sister Sarah would often play together. Gertrude, the last of the Tredwell children, born in 1840, was different from the rest of them and kept herself apart. There were also two boys, but somehow they did not amount to very much, it is said, for it became necessary at a later date, when of all the children only they and Gertrude were left, to appoint a cousin, Judge Seabury, to supervise the management of the estate. Brother Horace, in particular, was much more interested in tending the four magnolia trees that dominated the view from the tearoom.

To this day, nobody knows the real reason for a secret passage from a trap door near the bedrooms to the East River, a considerable distance. It has lately been walled up to prevent rats from coming up through it, but it is still there, holding onto its strange mystery—that is, to those who do not *know*.

Some of the things that transpired behind the thick walls of the Old Merchant's House would never have been brought to light were it not for the sensitive who walked its corridors a century later and piece-by-piece helped reconstruct what went on when the house was young. Only then did the various pieces of the jigsaw puzzle slowly sink into place, pieces that otherwise might never have found a common denominator.

When the house finally gave up its murky secrets a strange calm settled over it, as if the story had wanted to be told after all those years and free it from the need of further hiding from the light.

Seabury Tredwell's stern Victorian ways did not sit well with all members of his family. The spinster girls in particular were both afraid of and respectful toward their father, and found it difficult to live up to his rigid standards. They wanted to marry but since no suitable person came along they were just as happy to wait. Underneath this resignation, however, a rebellious spirit boiled up in Sarah. Five years older than Gertrude, she could not or would not wait to find happiness in an age where the word scarcely had any personal meaning.

Tredwell ruled the family with an iron hand, demanding and getting blind submission to his orders. Thus it was with considerable misgivings that Sarah encouraged a budding friendship with a young man her father did not know, or know of, whom she had met accidentally at a tearoom. That in itself would have been sufficient reason for her father to disallow such as friendship. He was a man who considered anyone who referred to chicken *limbs* as legs, indecent, a man who ordered the legs of his chairs and tables covered so they might not incite male visitors to unsavory ideas!

It took a great deal of ingenuity for Sarah to have a liaison with a strange man and not get caught. But her mother, perhaps out of rebellion against Tredwell, perhaps out of compassion for her neglected daughter, looked the other way, if not encouraged it. And ingenious Sarah also found another ally in her quest for love. There was a black servant who had known and cared for her since her birth and he acted as a go-between for her and the young man. For a few weeks, Sarah managed to sneak down to meet her paramour. Accidentally, she had discovered the secret passageway to the river, and used it well. At the other end it led to what was then pretty rough ground and an even rougher neighborhood, but the young man was always there waiting with a carriage and she felt far safer with him than in the cold embrace of her father's fanatical stare. Although Tredwell boasted to his friends that his house had "seven hundred locks and seven hundred keys," there was one door he had forgotten about.

Why an architect in 1830 would want to include a secret passage is a mystery on the surface of it, but there were still riots in New York in those years and the British invasion of 1812 was perhaps still fresh in some people's memories. A secret escape route was no more a luxury in a patrician American home than a priest hole was in a Catholic house in England. One never knew how things might turn. There had been many instances of slave rebellions, and the "underground railroad," bringing the unfortunate escapees up from the South was in full swing then in New York.

One meeting with the young man, who shall remain nameless here, led to another, and before long, nature took its course. Sarah was definitely pregnant. Could she tell her father? Certainly not. Should they run off and marry? That seemed the logical thing to do, but Sarah feared the long arm of her family. Judge Seabury, her father's distinguished cousin, might very well stop them. Then too, there was the question of scandal. To bring scandal upon her family was no way to start a happy marriage.

Distraught, Sarah stopped seeing the young man. Nights she would walk the hallways of the house, sleepless from worry, fearful of discovery. Finally, she had to tell someone, and that someone was her sister Gertrude. Surprisingly, Gertrude did understand and comforted her as best she could. Now that they shared her secret, things were a little easier to bear. But unfortunately, things did not improve. It was not long before her father discovered her condition and all hell broke loose.

With the terror of the heavy he was, Tredwell got the story out of his daughter, except for the young man's name. This was especially hard to keep back, but Sarah felt that betraying her lover would not lead to a union with him. Quite rightfully, she felt her father would have him killed or jailed. When the old merchant discovered that there had been a go-between, and what was more, a man in his employ, the old man was hauled over the coals. Only the fact that he had been with them for so many years and

The fireplace supposedly incapable of being photographed . . .

that his work was useful to the family, prevented Tredwell from firing him immediately. But he abused the poor man and threatened him until the sheer shock of his master's anger changed his character: where he had been a pleasant and helpful servant, there was now only a shiftless, nervous individual, eager to avoid the light and all questions.

This went on for some weeks or months. Then the time came for the baby to be born and the master of the house had another stroke of genius. He summoned the black servant and talked with him at length. Nobody could hear what was said behind the heavy doors, but when the servant emerged his face was grim and his eyes glassy. Nevertheless, the old relationship between master and servant seemed to have been restored, for Tredwell no longer abused the man after this meeting.

What happened then we know only from the pieces of memory resurrected by the keen insight of a psychic: no court of law would ever uphold the facts as true in the sense the law requires, unfortunately, even if they are, in fact, facts. One day there was a whimpering heard from the trapdoor between the two bedrooms upstairs, where there is now a chest of drawers and the walled-off passageway

The Old Merchant's House Ghost

(New York City)

The actual dress worn by Gitty, whose ghost has never left the house

down to the river. Before the other servants in the house could investigate the strange noises in the night, it was all over and the house was silent again. Tredwell himself came from his room and calmed them.

"It is nothing," he said in stentorian tones, "just the wind in the chimney."

Nobody questioned the words of the master, so the house soon fell silent again.

But below stairs, in the dank, dark corridor leading to the river, a dark man carried the limp body of a newborn baby that had just taken its first, and last, breath.

Several days later, there was another confrontation. The evil doer wanted his pay. He had been promised a certain sum for the unspeakable deed. The master shrugged. The man threatened. The master turned his back. Who would believe a former slave, a run-away slave wanted down South? Truly, he didn't have to pay *such* a person. Evil has its own reward, too, and the man went back to his little room. But the imprint of the crime stuck to the small passage near the trapdoor and was picked up a century later by a psychic. Nobody saw the crime. Nobody may rightfully claim the arrangement between master and servant ever took place. But the house knows and in its silence, speaks louder than mere facts that will stand up in court.

When Sarah awoke from a stupor, days later, and found her infant gone, she went stark raving mad. For a time, she had to be restrained. Somehow, word leaked out into the streets of the city below, but no one ever dared say anything publicly. Sarah was simply "indisposed" to her friends. Weeks went by and her pain subsided. Gradually a certain relief filled the void in her insides. She had lost everything, but at least her lover was safe from her father's clutches. Although she never knew for sure, whenever she glanced at the manservant, she shrank back: his eyes avoided hers and her heart froze. Somehow, with the illogical knowledge of a mother, she *knew*. Then, too, she avoided the passage near the trap door. Nothing could get her to walk through it. But as her health returned, her determination to leave also received new impetus. She could not go on living in this house where so much had happened. One day, she managed to get out of the door. It was a windy fall night and she was badly dressed for it. Half-mad with fear of being followed, she roamed the streets for hours. Darkness and mental condition took their toll. Eventually she found herself by the water. When she was found, she was still alive, but expired before she could be brought back to the house.

Her death—by her own hands—was a blow to the family. Word was given out that Sarah had died in a carriage accident. It sounded much more elegant, and though no one ever found out what carriage, as she had been in bed for so long, and just learned to walk about the house again, it was accepted because of the unspoken code among the Victorians: one man's tragedy is never another's gossip. Then, too, the question of suicide was a thorny one to resolve in an age that had not yet freed the human personality even in the flesh: it had to be an accident.

Thus Sarah was laid to rest along with the others of her family in the Christ Churchyard in Manhasset, Long Island, properly sanctified as behooves the daughter of an important citizen whose ancestor was a bishop.

What had happened to Sarah did not pass without making a deep and lasting impression on the youngest girl, Gertrude, whom they liked to call Gitty in her younger years. She tried not to talk about it, of course, but it made her more serious and less frivolous in her daily contacts.

She was now of the age where love can so easily come, yet no one had held her hand with the slightest effect on her blood pressure. True, her father had introduced a number of carefully screened young men, and some not so young ones, in the hope that she might choose one from among them. But Gertrude would not marry just to please her father, yet she would not marry against his wishes. There had to be someone she could love and whom her father could also accept, she reasoned, and she was willing to wait for him.

While she was playing a game with time, spring came around again and the air beckoned her to come out into the garden for a walk. While there, she managed to catch the eye of a young man on his way past the house. Words were exchanged despite Victorian propriety and she felt gay and giddy.

She decided she would not make the mistake her sister had made in secretly seeing a young man. Instead, she encouraged the shy young man, whose name was Louis, to seek entry into her house openly and with her father's knowledge, if not yet blessings. This he did, not without difficulties, and Seabury Tredwell had him investigated immediately. He learned that the young man was a penniless student of medicine.

"But he'll make a fine doctor someday," Gertrude pleaded with her father.

"Someday," the old man snorted, "and what is he going to live on until then? I tell you what. My money."

Tredwell assumed, and perhaps not without reason, that everybody in New York knew that his daughters were heiresses and would have considerable dowries as well. This idea so established itself in his mind, he suspected every gentleman caller as being a fortune hunter.

The young man was, of course, he argued, not after his daughter's love, but merely her money and that would never do.

Gertrude was no raving beauty, although possessed of a certain charm and independence. She was petite, with a tiny waistline, blue eyes and dark hair, and she greatly resembled Britain's Princess Margaret when the latter was in her twenties.

Tredwell refused to accept the young medical student as a serious suitor. Not only was the young man financially unacceptable, but worse, he was a Catholic. Tredwell did not believe in encouraging marriages out of the faith and even if Louis had offered to change religion, it is doubtful the father would have changed his mind. In all this he paid absolutely no heed to his daughter's feelings or desires, and with true Victorian rigidity, forbade her to see the young man further.

There was finally a showdown between father and daughter. Tredwell, no longer so young, and afflicted with the pains and aches of advancing age, pleaded with her not to disappoint him in his last remaining years. He wanted a good provider for her, and Louis was not the right man. Despite her feelings, Gertrude finally succumbed to her father's pleading, and sent the young man away. When the doors closed on him for the last time, it was as if the gates of Gertrude's heart had also permanently closed on the outside world: hence she lived only for her father and his well-being and no young man ever got to see her again.

Seabury Tredwell proved a difficult and thankless patient as progressive illness forced him to bed permanently. When he finally passed away in 1865, the two remaining sisters, Gertrude and Phoebe, continued to live in the house. But it was Gertrude who ran it. They only went out after dark and only when absolutely necessary to buy food. The windows were always shuttered and even small leaks covered with felt or other material to keep out the light and cold.

As the two sisters cut themselves off from the outside world, all kinds of legends sprang up about them. But after

A secret trap door leading to a passage connecting the house to the East river

Phoebe died and left Gertrude all alone in the big house, even the legends stopped and gradually the house and its owner sank into the oblivion afforded yesterday's sensation by a relentless, ever-changing humanity.

Finally, at age ninety-three, Gertrude passed on. The year was 1933, and America had bigger headaches than what to do about New York's last authentic brownstone. The two servants who had shared the house with Gertrude to her death, and who had found her peacefully asleep, soon left, leaving the house to either wreckers or new owners, or just neglect. There was neither electricity nor telephone in it, but the original furniture and all the fine works of art Seabury Tredwell had put into the house were still there. The only heat came from fireplaces with which the house was filled. The garden had long gone, and only the house remained, wedged in between a garage and a nondescript modern building. Whatever elegance there had been was now present only inside the house or perhaps in the aura of its former glories.

The neighborhood was no longer safe, and the house itself was in urgent need of repairs. Eventually, responsible city officials realized the place should be made into a museum, for it presented one of the few houses in America with everything—from furniture to personal belongings and clothes—still intact as it was when people lived in it in the middle of the nineteenth century. There were legal

The Old Merchant's House Ghost
(New York City)

problems of clearing title, but eventually this was done and the Old Merchant's House became a museum.

When the first caretaker arrived to live in the house, it was discovered that thieves had already broken in and made off with a pair of Sheffield candelabra, a first edition of Charlotte Brönte, and the Tredwell family Bible. But the remainder was still intact and a lot of cleaning up had to be done immediately.

One of the women helping in this work found herself alone in the house one afternoon. She had been busy carrying some of Miss Gertrude's clothing downstairs so that it could be properly displayed in special glass cases. When she rested from her work for a moment, she looked up and saw herself being watched intently by a woman on the stairs. At first glance, she looked just like Princess Margaret of England, but then she noticed the strange old-fashioned clothes the woman wore and realized she belonged to another age. The tight fitting bodice had a row of small buttons and the long, straight skirt reached to the floor. As the volunteer stared in amazement at the stranger, wondering who it could be, the girl on the stairs vanished.

At first the lady did not want to talk about her experience, but when it happened several times, and always when she was alone in the house, she began to wonder whether she wasn't taking leave of her senses. But soon another volunteer moved into the picture, a lady writer who had passed the house on her way to the library to do some research. Intrigued by the stately appearance of the house, she looked further and before long was in love with the house.

There was a certain restlessness that permeated the house after dark, but she blamed it on her imagination and the strange neighborhood. She did not believe in ghosts nor was she given to fancies, and the noises didn't really disturb her.

She decided that there was a lot of work to be done if the museum were to take its proper place among other showplaces, and she decided to give the tourists and other visitors a good run for their money—all fifty cents' worth of it.

The next few weeks were spent in trying to make sense out of the masses of personal effects, dresses, gowns, shoes, hats, for the Tredwells had left everything behind them intact—as if they had intended to return to their earthly possessions one of these days and to resume life as it was.

Nothing had been given away or destroyed and Mrs. R., writer that she was, immediately realized how important this intact state of the residence was for future research of that period. She went to work at once and as she applied herself to the job at hand, she began to get the *feel* of the house as if she had herself lived in it for many years.

She started her job by taking inventory of the late Gertrude Tredwell's wardrobe once again. This time the job had to be done properly, for the visitors to the museum were entitled to see a good display of period costumes. As she picked up Gertrude's vast wardrobe one article at a time, she had the uncanny feeling of being followed step-for-step. The house was surrounded by slums and the danger of real break-ins very great, but this was different: no flesh and blood intruders followed her around on her rounds from the third floor down to the basement and back again for more clothes.

Often a chilly feeling touched her as she walked through the halls, but she attributed that to the moist atmosphere in the old house.

One day when she entered the front bedroom that used to be Gertrude's from the hall bedroom, she had the distinct impression of another presence close to her. Something was brushing by her to reach the other door that opened into the front bedroom before she did!

When this happened again sometime later, she began to wonder if the stories about the house being haunted, that circulated freely in the neighborhood, did not have some basis of fact. Certainly there was a presence, and the sound of another person brushing past her was quite unmistakable.

While she was still deliberating whether or not to discuss this with any of her friends, an event took place that brought home even more the suspicion that she was never quite alone in the house.

It was on a morning several months after her arrival, that she walked into the kitchen carrying some things to be put into the display cases ranged along the wall opposite the fireplace. Out of the side of her eye she caught sight of what looked like the figure of a small, elegant woman standing in front of this huge fireplace. While Mrs. R. was able to observe the brown taffeta gown she was wearing, her head was turned away, so she could not see her features. But there were masses of brown hair. The whole thing was in very soft focus, rather misty without being insubstantial. Her hands, however, holding a cup and saucer, were very beautiful and quite sharply defined against her dark gown.

Mrs. R. was paralyzed, afraid to turn her head to look directly at her. Suddenly, however, without any conscious volition, she spun around and quickly walked out of the room into the hall. By the time she got to the stairs she was covered with cold perspiration and her hands were shaking so violently she had to put down the things she was carrying.

Now she knew that Gertrude Tredwell was still around, but not the way she looked when she died. Rather, she had turned back her memory clock to that period of her life when she was gayest and her young man had not yet been sent away by a cruel and unyielding father.

When the realization came to Mrs. R. as to who her ghostly friend was, her fears went away. After all, who would have a better right to be in this house than the one who had sacrificed her love and youth to it and what it stood for in her father's view. This change of her attitude must have somehow gotten through to the ghostly lady as well, by some as yet undefinable telegraph connecting all things, living and dead.

Sometime thereafter, Mrs. R. was arranging flowers for the table in the front parlor. The door was open to the hallway and she was quite alone in the house. Mrs. R. was so preoccupied with the flower arrangement, she failed to notice that she was no longer alone.

Finally, a strange sound caught her attention and she looked up from the table. The sound was that of a taffeta gown swishing by in rapid movement. As her eyes followed the sound, she saw a woman going up the stairs. It was the same, petite figure she had originally seen at the fireplace sometime before. Again she wore the brown taffeta gown. As she rounded the stairs and disappeared from view, the sound of the gown persisted for a moment or two after the figure herself had gotten out of sight.

This time Mrs. R. did not experience any paralysis or fear. Instead, a warm feeling of friendship between her and the ghost sprang up within her, and contentedly, as if nothing had happened, she continued with her flower arrangement.

All this time the actual curator of the Old Merchant's House was a professional antiquarian named Janet Hutchinson who shared the appointments with her friend Emeline Paige, editor of *The Villager,* a neighborhood newspaper, and Mrs. Hutchinson's son, Jefferson, aged fourteen. In addition, there was a cat named Eloise who turned out to be a real "fraiddicat" for probably good and valid reasons.

Although Mrs. Hutchinson did not encounter anything ghostly during her tenure, the lady editor did feel very uneasy in the back bedroom, where much of the tragedy had taken place.

Another person who felt the oppressive atmosphere of the place, without being able to rationalize it away for any good reasons, was Elizabeth Byrd, the novelist and her friend, whom I must call Mrs. B., for she shies away from the uncanny in public. Mrs. B. visited the house one evening in 1964. As she stood in what was once Gertrude's bedroom, she noticed that the bedspread of Gertrude's bed was indented *as if someone had just gotten up from it.* Clearly, the rough outline of a body could be made out.

As she stared in disbelief at the bed, she noticed a strange perfume in the air. Those with her remarked on the scent, but before anyone could look for its source, it had evaporated. None of the ladies with Mrs. B. had on any such perfume and the house had been sterile and quiet for days.

Since that time, no further reports of any unusual experiences have come to light. On one occasion in 1965, photographs of the fireplace near which Mrs. R. had seen the ghost of Gertrude Tredwell were taken simultaneously by two noted photographers with equipment previously tested for proper performance. This was done to look into the popular legend that this fireplace could not be photographed and that whenever anyone so attempted, that person would have a blank film as a result. Perhaps the legend was started by a bad photographer, or it was just that, a legend, for both gentlemen produced almost identical images of the renowned fireplace with their cameras. However, Gertrude Tredwell was not standing in front of it.

This is as it should be. Mrs. R., the untiring spirit behind the Historical Landmarks Society that keeps the building going and out of the wreckers' hands, feels certain that Gertrude need not make another appearance now that everything is secure. And to a Victorian lady, that matters a great deal.

✳ 66

The House on Fifth Street (New Jersey)

NORTH FIFTH STREET in Camden, New Jersey, was in a part of town that is best avoided, especially at night. But even in the daytime it had the unmistakable imprint of a depressed—and depressing—area, downtrodden because of economic blight. The people leaning against shabby doors, idle and grim-looking, are people out of step with progress, people who don't work or can't work and who hate those who do. This is what it looks like today, with the busy factories and the smelly buildings of industrial Camden all around it, the super-modern expressway cutting a swath

through it all as if those on it wouldn't want to stop even long enough to have a good look at what is on both sides of the road.

This grimy part of town wasn't always a slum area, however. Back in the 1920s, when Prohibition was king, some pretty substantial people lived here and the houses looked spic-and-span then.

Number 522, which has since given up its struggle against progress by becoming part of a city-wide improvement program, was then a respectable private residence. Situated in the middle of a short block, it was a gray, conservative-looking stone building with three stories and a backyard. The rooms are railroad flats, that is, they run from one to the other and if one were to go to the rear of the house one would have to enter from the front and walk through several rooms to get there. It wasn't the most inspiring way of building homes, but to the lower, or even the higher, middle classes of that time, it seemed practical and perfectly all right.

From the ground floor—with its front parlor followed by other living rooms and eventually a kitchen leading to the backyard—rose a turning staircase leading up to two more flights. This staircase was perhaps the most impressive part of the house and somehow overshadowed the simplicity of the rest of the layout. A nicely carved wooden banister framed it all the way up and though the house, in keeping with the custom of the times, was kept quite dark, the many years of handling the banister had given it a shine that sparkled even in so subdued an illumination. Heavy dust lay on stairs and floors and what there was of furniture was covered with tarpaulins that had grown black in time. Clearly, the house had seen better days but those times were over, the people were gone, and only a short time stood between the moment of rest and the sledge hammer of tomorrow.

Edna Martin is a bright young woman working for a local radio station in Camden, and spooks are as far removed from her way of thinking as anything could possibly be. When her parents moved into what was then a vacant house, she laughed a little at its forbidding appearance, but being quite young at the time, she was not at all frightened or impressed. Neither was her mother, who is a woman given to practical realities. There is a sister, Janet, and the two girls decided they were going to enjoy the big old house, and enjoy it they did.

Eventually, Edna began to notice some peculiar things about their home: the noise of rustling silk, the swish of a dress nearby when no one who could be causing these sounds was to be seen. On one occasion, she was having a quiet evening at home when she heard someone come up the stairs and enter the middle bedroom.

At that moment, she heard someone sigh as if in great sadness. Since she was quite sure that no one but herself was upstairs, she was puzzled by these things and entered the middle bedroom immediately. It was more out of curiosity than any sense of fear that she did so, not knowing for sure what she might find, if anything.

Before she entered the room, she heard the bedsprings squeak as if someone had lain down on the bed. She examined the bedspread—there was no indication of a visitor. Again, the rustling of clothes made her keenly aware of another presence in the room with her. Thoughtfully, she went back to her own room.

The parents and their married daughters, with their husbands and children, eventually shared the big house, and with so many people about, extraneous noises could very easily be overlooked or explained away.

And yet, there were ominous signs that the house was home to others besides themselves.

Janet woke up one night soon after the incident in the middle bedroom, and listened with a sharpened sense of hearing, the kind of super-hearing one sometimes gets in the still of night. Something very light was walking up the stairs, and it sounded like the steps of a very light person, such as a child. The steps came gradually nearer. Now they were at the top of the stairs and then down the hall, until they entered the girl's room. She could hear every single floor board creak with the weight of an unseen person. Frozen with fright, she dared not to move or speak. Even if she had wanted them to, her lips would not have moved. Then, as she thought she could stand it no longer, the steps came to a sudden halt beside her bed. She clearly felt the presence of a person near her staring at her!

Somehow, she managed to fall asleep, and nothing happened after that for a few weeks. She had almost forgotten the incident when she came home late one night from a date in town.

It was her custom to undress in the middle bedroom, and put her clothes on the bed, which was not occupied. She did not wish to wake the others, so she undressed hurriedly in the dark. As she threw her clothes upon the bed, *someone in the bed* let out a sigh, and turned over, as if half-awakened from deep sleep. Janet assumed her niece had come to visit and that she had been given the room. So she gathered her clothes from the bed and placed them on the chair instead, thinking nothing further about the matter.

Next morning, she went downstairs to have breakfast and at the same time have a chat with her niece, Miki. But the girl wasn't around. "Where is Miki, Mother?" she inquired. Her mother looked at her puzzled.

"I haven't the faintest idea," she shrugged. "She hasn't been here for weeks."

Janet froze in her tracks. Who had turned with a sigh in the empty bed?

The two girls had a close friend, Joanne, with whom they shared many things, including the eerie experiences in the house that somehow increased as the years went on. One evening Joanne was typing in the front bedroom on the second floor while Janet lay on the bed on her stomach.

Joanne's back was turned towards Janet at the time and the two girls were both spending the evening in their own way. Suddenly, Janet felt a strange sensation on the sole of her shoe. It felt as if someone had hit her in that spot, and hit her hard. The noise was so strong Joanne turned around and asked what had happened. Janet, who had jumped up and moved to the window, could only shrug. Was someone trying to communicate with her in this strange way?

Then there was the time the three girls were sitting on the bed and their attention was drawn to the foot of the bed, somehow. There, wriggling about five inches into the night air, was a greenish "thing" that had materialized out of nowhere. Letting out a shriek, Janet stared at it. Evidently she was the only one who could see it. As she looked through horror-stricken eyes, she could vaguely make out a small head nearby. Memories of the ghostly footsteps she had taken for a child some time ago came back to haunt her. Was there not a connection? Then the "thing" vanished.

The girls did not talk about these things if they could help it, for by now they knew there was something very peculiar about the house. But as yet they were not willing to believe in such things as ghosts of the departed. It all seemed terribly unreal to them.

When Edna was not yet married, the man she later married was an airman stationed at a base near Trenton, New Jersey. After one visit to her in Camden, he happened to miss the midnight bus back to camp, and there was nothing to be done but wait up for the next one, which was at 2:20 A.M. Since Edna had to get up early the next day, she went upstairs to get ready for bed. She left her fiancée downstairs where there was a couch he could use, to rest up before going out to catch his bus. The young airman settled back with a smoke and relaxed.

Suddenly he heard the front door open. The door is a very heavy, old-fashioned one, with a lock that is hard to open unless you have the key. The airman was puzzled because he himself had seen Edna set the lock a few moments ago. Before he could try to figure this out, he heard the vestibule door open and suddenly there was an icy atmosphere in the room. True, it was winter, but until then he had not been cold. He immediately assumed a burglar had entered the house and rolled up his sleeves to receive him properly.

But then he experienced an eerie feeling quite different from anything he had ever felt before. His hair stood up as if electric current were going through it, and yet he was not the least bit frightened. Then a bell started to ring. The bell was inside a closed case, standing quietly in the corner. He suddenly realized that a bell could not clang unless someone first lifted it. When he came to that conclusion and saw no flesh-and-blood invader, he decided he'd rather wait for his bus *outside*. He spent the next hour or so at a drafty corner, waiting for his bus. Somehow it seemed to him a lot cozier.

That same night, Edna was awakened from light sleep by the sound of a disturbance downstairs. As her senses returned she heard someone clanging against the pipes downstairs. She immediately assumed it was her fiance playing a trick on her, for he had a talent for practical jokes. She hurriedly put on her robe and went downstairs. Immediately the noise stopped. When she reached the vestibule, her fiancée was not there.

When she told him about this later and he reported the incident of the bell, she thought that he was now sufficiently impressed to accept the reality of ghosts in the house. But the young airman did not take the psychic

occurrences too seriously despite his own encounter. He thought the whole thing extremely funny and one night he decided to make the ghosts work overtime. By then he and Edna were married. That night, he tied a string to the door of their bedroom, a door leading out into the hall. The other end of the string he concealed so that he could pull it and open the door, once they were in bed.

As soon as the lights were out, but sufficient light coming in through the windows remained, he started to stare at the door so as to attract his wife's attention to that spot. While she looked, he pointed at the door and said in a frightened voice, "Look, it's opening by itself!"

And so it was. He pulled off the trick so well, Edna did not notice it and in near-panic sprinkled the door with holy water all over. This made him laugh and he confessed his joke.

"Don't ever do such a thing," she warned him, when she realized she had been made a fool of. But he shrugged. She returned to bed and admonished him never to tempt the unseen forces lest they "pay him back" in their own kind.

She had hardly finished, when the door to the middle room began to open slowly, ever so slowly, by its own volition. As her husband stared in amazement, and eventually with mounting terror, the door kept swinging open until it had reached the back wall, then stopped. For a moment, neither of them moved. There was nothing else, at least not for the moment, so they jumped out of bed and the airman tried the door to see if he could explain "by natural means" what had just taken place before their eyes. But they both knew that this particular door had been taken off its hinges sometime before and had been propped into a closed position. In addition, in order to open it at all, it would have had to be lifted over two rugs on the floor. For several hours they tried to make this door swing open, one way or another. It would not move. Edna held the door by the hinges to keep it from falling forward while her husband tried to open it. It was impossible. Then they managed to get it to stay on the hinges, finally, and started to open it. It swung out about an inch before the rugs on the floor stopped it. What superior force had lifted the door over the rugs and pushed it against the back wall?

Still, he argued, there *had* to be some logical explanation. They let the matter rest and for a while nothing unusual happened in the house. Then, Edna and her husband had moved to the Middle West and were no longer aware of day-to-day goings-on in Camden. When they came to visit the family in Camden, after some time, they naturally wondered about the house but preferred not to bring up the subject of ghosts. Actually, Edna prayed that nothing should mar their homecoming.

Then it was time to leave again, and Edna's husband, good-naturedly, reminded her that he had neither seen nor heard any ghosts all that time. On that very day, their little son took sick, and they had to stay longer because of his condition.

They set up a cot for him in the living room, where they were then sleeping. If the boy were in need of help, they would be close by. During the night, they suddenly heard the cot collapse. They rushed over and quickly fixed it. The boy had not even awakened, luckily. As they were bent over the cot, working on it, they heard someone coming down the stairs.

Edna paid no particular attention to it, but her husband seemed strangely affected.

"Did you hear someone just come down the stairs?" he finally asked.

"Of course I did," Edna replied, "that was probably Miss Robinson."

Miss Robinson was a boarder living up on the third floor.

"No, it wasn't," her husband said, and shook his head, "I watched those stairs closely. I saw those steps bend when someone walked over them—but there was no Miss Robinson, or for that matter, anyone else."

"You mean...?" Edna said and for the first time her husband looked less confident. They made a complete search of the house from top to bottom. No one else was home at the time but the two of them and the sick child.

Edna, who is now a divorcee, realized that her family home held a secret, perhaps a dark secret, that somehow defied a rational explanation. Her logical mind could not accept any other and yet she could not find any answers to the eerie phenomena that had evidently never ceased.

If there was a ghostly presence, could she help it get free? What was she to do? But she knew nothing about those things. Perhaps her thoughts permeated to the ether areas where ghostly presences have a shadowy existence, or perhaps the unhappy wraith simply drew more and more power from the living in the house to manifest.

Sometime later, Joanne, Edna's close friend, came to her for help in the matter of a costume for a barn dance she had been asked to attend. Perhaps Edna had some suitable things for her? Edna had indeed.

"Go down to the basement," she directed her friend. "There are some trunks down there filled with materials. Take what you can use." Joanne, a teacher, nodded and went down into the cellar.

Without difficulty, she located the musty trunks. It was not quite so easy to open them, for they had evidently not been used for many years. Were those remnants left behind by earlier tenants of the house? After all, the present tenants had taken over a partially furnished house and so little was known about the people before them. The house was at least sixty years old, if not older.

As Joanne was pulling torn dresses, some of them clearly from an earlier era, she was completely taken up with the task at hand, that of locating a suitable costume for the dance. But she could not help noticing that something very strange was happening to her hair. It was a strange sensation, as if her hair suddenly stood on end! She passed her hand lightly over her forehead and felt that her hair was indeed stiff and raised up! At the same time she had a tingling sensation all over her body.

She dropped the dress she had been holding and waited, for she was sure someone was standing and staring at her. Any moment now, that person would speak. But as the seconds ticked away and no one spoke, she began to wonder. Finally, she could no longer contain herself and turned slowly around.

Back a few yards was a whirlpool of smoke, whirling and moving at rapid pace. It had roughly the shape of a human figure, and as she looked at this "thing" with mounting terror, she clearly saw that where the face should be there was a gray mass of smoke, punctuated only by two large holes—where the eyes would normally be!

As she stared in utter disbelief, the figure came toward her. She felt the air being drawn from her lungs at its approach and knew that if she did not move immediately she would never get out of the cellar.

Somehow she managed to inch her way toward the stairs and literally crawled on all fours up to the ground floor. When she reached the fresh air, she managed to gather her wits sufficiently to tell Edna what she had seen.

But so terrible was the thought of what she had witnessed she preferred not to accept it, as time went by. To her, to this day, it was merely the shadow of someone passing by outside the cellar windows....

Meanwhile the footsteps on the stairs continued but somehow the fury was spent. Gradually, the disturbances receded or perhaps the people in the house became used to them and paid them no further heed.

After Edna finally left the house and moved into a modern, clean flat, the house was left to its own world of ghosts until the wreckers would come to give it the *coup de grace*.

But Edna had not forgotten her years of terror, so when she heard of a famed psychic able to communicate with such creatures as she imagined her house was filled with, she tried to make contact and invite the lady to the house. She herself would not come, but the door was open.

It was a muggy day in July 1967 that the psychic lady and a friend and co-worker paid the house a fleeting visit. Perhaps an hour at the most, then they would have to go on to other, more urgent things and places. In that hour, though, they were willing to help the unseen ones out of their plight, if they cared to be helped.

The psychic had not been inside the musty living room for more than ten seconds when she saw the woman on the stairs.

"There is a little boy, also, and the woman has fallen to her death on the stairs," she said, quietly, and slowly walked back and forth, her footsteps echoing strangely in the empty, yet tense old house.

"Go home," she pleaded with the woman. "You've passed over and you mustn't stay on here where you've suffered so much."

"Do you get any names?" asked her companion, ever the researcher. The psychic nodded and gave a name, which the gentleman quickly wrote down.

"All she wants is a little sympathy, to be one of the *living*," the psychic explained, then turned again to the staircase which still gleamed in the semi-darkness of the vestibule. "Go home, woman," she intoned once more and there seemed a quiet rustling of skirts as she said it.

Time was up and the last visitors to the house on Fifth Street finally left.

The next day, the gentleman matched the name his psychic friend had given him with the name of a former owner of the house.

But as their taxi drew away in a cloud of gasoline fumes, they were glad they did not have to look back at the grimy old house.

For had they done so, they would have noticed that one of the downstairs curtains, which had been down for a long time, was now drawn back a little—just enough to let someone peek out from behind it.

✳ 67

Morgan Hall (Long Island)

ALICE IS A TWENTY-TWO-YEAR-OLD blonde, way above average in looks and intelligence. She lives in Manhattan, has a decent, law-abiding seaman for a father and an Irish heritage going back, way back, but mixed in with some French and various other strains that have blended well in Alice's face, which is one of continual curiosity and alertness. Alice's work is routine, as are most of her friends. She takes this in her stride now, for she has another world waiting for her where nothing is ever ordinary.

* * *

When she was born, her parents moved into an old house in Brooklyn that had the reputation of being queer. Alice was only a few months old when they left again, but during those months she would not go into her mother's bedroom without a fierce struggle, without breaking into tears immediately—a behavior so markedly different from her otherwise "good" behavior as a baby that it could not help but be noticed by her parents. While her father had no interest in such matters, her mother soon connected the child's strange behavior with the other strange things in the house: the doors that would open by themselves, the footsteps, the strange drafts, especially in the bedroom little Alice hated so much.

When Alice was about twelve years old, and the family had moved from the old neighborhood into another house, she found herself thinking of her grandmother all of a sudden one day. Her grandparents lived a distance away upstate and there had been no recent contact with them.

"Grandmother is dead," Alice said to her mother, matter-of-factly. Her mother stared at her in disbelief. Hours later the telephone rang. Grandmother, who had been in excellent health, had suddenly passed away.

Her mother gave the girl a queer look but she had known of such gifts and realized her daughter, an only child, was something special. Within six months, the telephone rang twice more. Each time, Alice looked up and said:

"Grandfather's dead."

"Uncle's dead."

And they were.

While her father shook his head over all this "foolishness," her mother did not scoff at her daughter's powers. Especially after Alice had received a dream warning from her dead grandmother, advising her of an impending car accident. She was shown the exact location where it would happen, and told that if her mother were to sit in front, she would be badly hurt but it Alice were to change places with her, Alice would not be as badly hurt.

After the dream, without telling her mother her reasons, she insisted on changing places with her on the trip. Sure enough, the car was hit by another automobile. Had her mother been where Alice sat, she might not have reacted quickly enough and been badly hurt. But Alice was prepared and ducked—and received only a whiplash.

Afterward, she discussed all this with her mother. Her mother did not scoff, but asked her what grandmother, who had given them the warning, had looked like in the vision.

"She had on a house dress and bedroom slippers," Alice replied. Her mother nodded. Although the grandmother had lost both legs due to diabetes, she had been buried with her favorite bedroom slippers in the coffin. Alice had never seen nor known this.

When she was seventeen years of age, Alice had a strong urge to become a nun. She felt the world outside had little to offer her and began to consider entering a convent. Perhaps this inclination was planted in her mind when she was a camp counselor for a Catholic school on Long Island. She liked the serenity of the place and the apparently quiet, contemplative life of the sisters.

* * *

On her very first visit to the convent, however, she felt uneasy. Morgan Hall is a magnificently appointed mansion in Glen Cove, Long Island, that had only been converted to religious purposes some years ago. Prior to that it was the Morgan estate with all that the name of that wealthy family implies. Nothing about it was either ugly or frightening in the least, and yet Alice felt immediately terrified when entering its high-ceilinged corridors.

As a prospective postulant, it was necessary for her to visit the place several times prior to being accepted, and on each occasion her uneasiness mounted.

But she ascribed these feelings to her lack of familiarity with the new place. One night, her uncle and grandfather appeared to her in a dream and told her not to worry, that everything would be all right with her. She took this as an encouragement to pursue her religious plans and shortly after formally entered the convent.

She moved in just a few days before her eighteenth birthday, looking forward to a life totally different from that of her friends and schoolmates. The room she was assigned to adjoined one of the cloisters, but at first she was alone in it as her future roommate was to arrive a week late. Thus she spent her very first days at Morgan Hall alone in the room. The very first night, after she had retired, she heard someone walking up and down outside the door. She thought this strange at that hour of the night, knowing full well that convents like their people to retire early. Finally her curiosity overcame her natural shyness of being in a new place, and she peaked out of her door into the corridor. The footsteps were still audible. But there was no one walking about outside. Quickly, she closed the door and went to bed.

The next morning, she discussed the matter with six other postulants in rooms nearby. They, too, had heard the footsteps that night. In fact, they had heard them on many other nights as well when there was positively no one walking about outside.

As she got used to convent routine, Alice realized how impossible it would be for one of them—or even one of the novices, who had been there a little longer than they —to walk around the place at the hour of the night when she heard the steps. Rigid convent rules included a bell, which rang at 10 P.M. Everybody had to be in their rooms and in bed at that time, except for dire emergencies. One just didn't walk about the corridors at midnight or later for the sheer fun of it at Morgan Hall, if she did not wish to be expelled. All lights go out at ten also and nothing moves.

At first, Alice thought the novices were playing tricks on the new arrivals by walking around downstairs to create the footsteps, perhaps to frighten the postulants in the way college freshmen are often hazed by their elder colleagues.

But she soon realized that this was not so, that the novices were no more allowed out after ten than they were.

Her psychic past did not allow Alice to let matters rest there and her curiosity forced her to make further inquiries as best she could under the circumstances. After all, you don't run to the Mother Superior and ask, Who walks the corridors at night, Ma'am?

It was then she learned that the house had been J. P. Morgan's mansion originally and later had been used by the Russian Embassy for their staff people. She recalled the battles the Russians had fought with the Glen Cove township over taxes and how they finally vacated the premises in less than perfect condition. As a sort of anticlimax, the Catholic nuns had moved in and turned the Hall into a convent and school.

A conversation with the convent librarian wasn't particularly fruitful, either. Yes, Mr. Morgan built the house in 1910. No, he didn't die here, he died in Spain. Why did she want to know?

Alice wondered about Mr. Morgan's daughter.

Alice Morgan had lived in this house and died here of typhoid fever in the early years of her life.

But try as she might, she never got the librarian to tell her anything helpful. Naturally, Alice did not wish to bring up the real reason for her curiosity. But it seemed as if the librarian sensed something about it, for she curtly turned her head sideways when speaking of the Morgans as if she did not wish to answer.

Frustrated in her inquiry, Alice left and went back to her chores. One night in October 1965, Alice was walking in the hall of the postulancy, that part of the building reserved for the new girls who were serving their apprenticeship prior to being admitted to the convent and to taking their final vows.

It was a cool night, and Alice had walked fairly briskly to the extreme end of the hall and then stopped for a moment to rest. As she turned around and faced toward the opposite end of the hall, whence she had just come, she noticed a girl standing there who had not been there before. She wore a long, black dress similar to the dresses the postulants wore and Alice took her to be her girl friend.

She noticed the figure enter the room at the end of the hall. This room was not a bedroom but used by the postulants for study purposes.

"It's Vera," Alice thought, and decided to join her and see what she was up to in that room.

Quickly, she walked towards the room and entered it. The lights were off and Alice thought this peculiar. Was her friend perhaps playing games with her? The room at this hour was quite dark.

So she turned on the lights, and looked around. There was no one in the room now, and there was no way anyone could have left the room without her noticing it, Alice reasoned. She examined the windows and found them tightly closed. Not that she expected her friend to exit the room by that way, but she wanted to be sure the person—whoever she might have been—could not have left that way. This was on the third floor and anyone trying to leave by the windows would have had to jump, or have a ladder outside.

Suddenly it hit Alice that she had not heard anything at all. All the time she had seen the figure walk into the room, there had been no footsteps, no noise of a door opening, nothing at all. Morgan Hall's doors open with a considerable amount of squeaking and none of that was audible when she had seen the figure before.

Alice quickly left and hurried to her own room to figure this out quietly.

On recollection, she visualized the figure again and it occurred to her at once that there was something very odd about the girl. For one thing, the long gown the postulants wear moves when they walk. But the figure she had seen was stiff and seemed to glide along the floor rather than actually walk on it. The corridor was properly lit and she had seen the figure quite clearly. What she had not seen were her ankles and socks, something she would have observed had it been one of her friends.

Although the door was not closed, the room was actually a corner room that could be entered in only one way, from the front door. Alice was sure she had not seen the figure emerge from it again. There was no place to hide in the room, had this been her girlfriend playing a joke on her. Alice had quickly examined the closet, desk, and beds—and no one was hiding anywhere in that room.

Eventually, she gathered up enough courage to seek out her friend Vera and discuss the matter with her. She found that there was a "joke" going around the convent that Alice Morgan's ghost was roaming the corridors, but that the whole matter was to be treated strictly as a gag. Yet she also discovered that there was one part of the hall that was off limits to anyone *alone*. In what the girls called the catacombs, at ground level, was the laundry room. The third section, way back, was never to be entered by any of them at night, and in the daytime only if in pairs. Yet, the area was well lit. Alice could not get any information for the reasons for this strange and forbidding order. In a convent, speaking to anyone but one's own group is extremely difficult without "proper permission" and this was not a fitting subject to discuss.

The novices, whom she approached next, suddenly became serious and told her to forget it: there were things going on in the building that could not be explained. She was not to pay attention, and pray hard instead.

Alice wondered about this attitude, and perhaps it was then that her first doubts concerning her ecclesiastical future began to enter her mind.

Shortly after, it was still October 1965, she lay awake in bed at night, thinking of her future at the convent. The clock had just chimed eleven and she was still wide awake. Night after night, she had heard the walking in the hall. After weeks of these manifestations, her nerves began to get edgy and she could not sleep as easily as she used to when she still lived in Brooklyn. Sure enough, there they were again, those incessant footsteps. They seemed to her the steps of a medium-heavy person, more like a woman's than a man's, and they seemed to be bent on some definite business, scurrying along the hall as if in a hurry.

Suddenly the night was pierced by a shriek: it seemed directly outside her door, but below. Since she was on the top floor, the person would have to be on the second floor. There was no mistaking it, this was the outcry of a woman in great pain, in the agony of being hurt by someone!

This time she was almost too scared to look, but she did open the door only to find the corridor abandoned and quiet now.

She ran in to speak to the other postulants, regulations or no regulations. She found them huddled in their beds in abject fear. All eight of them had heard the blood-curdling scream!

By now Alice was convinced that something strange had taken place here and that a restless personality was stalking the corridors. A short time later, she and Vera were in their room, getting ready to retire.

It was a cold night, but no wind was about. The windows were the French window type that locked with a heavy iron rod from top to bottom. No one could open the window from the outside, the only way it could be opened would be from the inside, by pushing the rod up.

"We don't have to lock the window tonight, do we?" Vera said. "It isn't windy."

But they decided to do it anyway as they did every night. They put their shoes on the window sill, something they were in the habit of doing so that the small draft coming in below the windows would "air them out."

After the window was locked, they retired.

It was well into the night, when the girls awoke to a loud noise. The French window had broken open by itself and the shoes had been tossed inside the room as if by a strong storm!

They checked and found the air outside totally still. Whatever had burst their window open had not been the wind. But what was it?

The room was ice cold now. They shuddered and went back to bed.

There is only a small ledge for pigeons to sit on outside the window, so no one could have opened the window from that vantage point. One could hardly expect pigeons to burst a window open, either.

The girls then realized that the novices who had been complaining about the windows in their room being constantly open had not been fibbing. Alice and Vera always kept their windows closed, yet some unseen force had apparently opened them from inside on a number of occasions. Now they had seen for themselves how it happened.

Alice realized that the window had been broken open as if by force from *inside*, not outside.

"Someone's trying to get out, not in," she said, and her roommate could only shudder.

There were other peculiar things she soon noticed. Strange cold drafts upstairs and in the attic. Crosses nailed to the wall next to the entrance to the upstairs rooms. Only to those rooms, and to no others, and not inside the rooms, as one might expect in a convent, but just outside as if they had been placed there to keep something, or someone evil out!

In the main dining room, a door, when closed, could not be distinguished from the surrounding wall. A trick window near the head of the table was actually a mirror which allowed the man at the head of the table to see who was coming towards him from all sides.

Banker Morgan lived in considerable fear of his life, whether imagined or real, but certainly the house was built to his specifications. In fact, trick mirrors were so placed in various parts of the main house so that no one could approach from downstairs and surprise anyone upstairs, yet no one could see the one watching them through the mirrors.

Shortly after Alice had moved into the convent, she began to have strange dreams in which a blonde young girl named Alice played a prominent role.

In the dream, the girl's blonde hair changed to curls, and she heard a voice say, "This is Alice Morgan, I want to introduce you to her."

But when she woke up Alice thought this was only due to her having discussed the matter with the novices. Alice Morgan was not the disturbed person there, her psychic sense told her.

To her, all ghostly activities centered around that attic. There were two steps that always squeaked peculiarly when someone stepped on them. Many times she would hear them squeak and look to see who was walking on them, only to find herself staring into nothingness. This was in the daytime. On other occasions, when she was at work cleaning garbage cans downstairs—postulants do a lot of ordinary kitchen work—she would feel herself observed closely by a pair of eyes staring down at her from the attic. Yet, no one was up there then.

The torture of the nightly footsteps together with her doubts about her own calling prompted her finally to seek release from the convent and return to the outside world, after three months as a postulant. After she had made this difficult decision, she felt almost as if all the burdens had lifted from the room that had been the center of the psychic manifestations.

She decided to make some final inquiries prior to leaving and since her superiors would not tell her, she looked the place over by herself, talked to those who were willing to talk and otherwise used her powers of observation. Surely, if the haunted area was upstairs, and she knew by now that it was, it could not be Alice Morgan who was the restless one.

But then who was?

The rooms on the third floor had originally been servant quarters as is customary in the mansions of the pre-World War I period. They were built to house the usually large staffs of the owners. In the case of the Morgans, that staff was even larger than most wealthy families.

Was "the restless one" one of the maids who had jumped out the window in a final burst for freedom, freedom from some horrible fate?

Then her thoughts turned to the Communist Russian occupancy of the building. Had they perhaps tortured someone up there in her room? The thought was melodramatically tempting, but she dismissed it immediately. The figure she had seen in the hall was dressed in the long dress of an earlier period. She belonged to the time when the Morgan Hall was a mansion.

No, she reasoned, it must have been a young girl who died there while the Morgans had the place and perhaps her death was hushed up and she wanted it known. Was it suicide, and did she feel in a kind of personal hell because of it, especially now that the place was a convent?

Somehow Alice felt that she had stumbled upon the right answers. That night, the last night she was to spend at the convent prior to going home, she slept soundly.

For the first time in three months, there were no footsteps outside her door.

For a while she waited, once the 10 o'clock bell had sounded, but nothing happened. Whoever it was had stopped walking.

The Guardian of the Adobe (California)

CASA ALVARADO IS California's best preserved adobe house, one of the few Spanish houses still standing and inhabited by people descended from the original settlers who had come to this land with Don Gaspar de Portola and Padre Junipero Serra in 1769.

The *casa* stands on an ever-shrinking piece of land which was once the proud property of two Spanish gentlemen named Ygnacio Palomares and Ricardo Vejar. They received it jointly in a Mexican land grant in April 1837, the Mexican Republic having by then replaced the Spanish crown as the dispenser of such favors. It was fertile, but empty, territory before then and the government liked to encourage potential ranchers in settling here. To get an idea of the immenseness of such sweeping grants, one must only remember that the ranch, even as late as 1875 when the original grant was reconfirmed by the American authorities, encompassed 22,340 acres.

The two gentlemen divided the land between them, with Señor Palomares taking the lower half, which became known as Lower San Jose, while his friend and partner Vejar took the Upper San Jose for his estate. The choice of the name of San Jose for the land was not entirely accidental.

It was on March 19, 1837, that the above named two gentlemen, in the company of a certain Padre Salvidea of San Gabriel Mission, were taking a break from the day's activities underneath a giant oak tree on the property. They had been surveying the land that was soon to become theirs officially and the good Padre decided to bless it right then and there. Since it was the feast day of St. Joseph, they dedicated it to that saint, and St. Joseph has been venerated in the area ever since as a special "local" protector.

Señor Palomares realized he had a huge piece of land on his hands, and, being a gregarious fellow, invited some of his neighbors and relatives to come with him and settle in this fertile valley. Among them was a certain Ygnacio Alvarado and his wife Luisa Avila, who were deeded a piece of land south of the Palomares home itself. The only stipulation was that a room be set aside in the new house to accommodate St. Joseph and to serve as a sanctuary for religious services.

The Alvarado home was duly built of adobe and wood as was the custom in 1840, in this part of the world. Adobe is a natural plaster mixture of soil and is made into bricks that can withstand the ravages of time, if not of human desecration.

The house consists of a spacious *sala* or parlor, forty-two feet long, and originally there were ten adobe rooms making up the square building, a shingled roof, and portico running alongside the house on all sides, graduated to the surrounding ground by three wooden steps. One of the adobe bedroom wings was destroyed by a later owner, the Nichols family, who replaced it with three new redwood rooms containing Victorian fireplaces. They don't exactly fit in with the rest of the house but some day, perhaps, the house may be restored completely to its original splendor.

The main portion contained, in addition to aforementioned *sala*, a large, square dining room, a den, two kitchens and a winery and blacksmith shop. The Nichols family had no use for the latter two items and replaced them with a water tower.

That large *sala* was the sanctuary the original owner had promised to maintain, and the altar stood at the north end during services to St. Joseph. However, the Mexicans are also a practical and joyous people, so after each Mass, the altar was turned to the wall and a fiesta held in the same room, which was obviously suitable for both church and ballroom!

That homey practice came to an end when the Pomona Land and Water Company acquired the estate. At the same time, the parish priest of St. Joseph's in Pomona took over the Mass which was no longer followed by a fiesta, churches being what they are.

As the years went on, Señor Alvarado was stricken with paralysis, and confined to his bed. But he ordered his house to be kept open to all his friends, and despite the owner's illness, it continued to be filled with many people, coming and going, and the sounds of hospitality. Doña Luisa, the owner's wife, ministered to the throngs, dressed in black, as was the Spanish custom, and wearing a white neck scarf over the shoulder, pinned at the throat with a brooch of Spanish gold. The Alvarado dances continued to be gay affairs.

The community that had sprung up around the estate produced many children and before long it became necessary to build a school, because the Casa Alvarado, where the sessions had first been held, proved much too small.

In the early 1870s, therefore, a plain frame building, the new school, was erected southeast of the adobe.

The two adobe houses—the Palomares site and the Casa Alvarado—became the property of the Nichols family, owners of the Pomona Land and Water Company, in 1887, but eventually the heirs sold the Palomares house. They kept the Casa Alvarado and one day a couple from Sherman Oaks, by the name of Fages, visited the house and immediately fell in love with it. They were and are antiquarians, and the *casa* was just what they wanted. Devout people, they asked St. Joseph to intercede on their behalf, and sure enough, six years later the house was for sale. What made their possession even more appropriate was the fact that Mrs. Isabella Fages is a direct descendant of the original Alvarado family and thus it was in a way a homecoming for both family and house.

After moving in, they had a priest, Father Mathew Poetzel, bless and rededicate the house and grounds to St.

Joseph, and they placed a plaque telling its remarkable history upon the outside wall. The land had dwindled over the years and was now not much more than the ground required to have a homestead.

A little to the south there was once a wooden barn, part of the estate. That barn, dating back to the 1840s, had long since been turned into a house. Despite its proximity to the Casa Alvarado, it belongs to different owners, and has been separated from the rest of the estate for many years. But to those who see the Rancho San Jose as one entity, it is of course still part and parcel of the original land grant.

Of course, the city of Pomona has now grown up all around this spot and the air isn't as clear as it used to be when Don Alvarado rode about his ranch. The freeway comes close to the *casa* now and gasoline fumes do too, but no one can touch the grounds themselves. The *casa* is secure from greedy speculators and the shrine to St. Joseph will probably outlast them all.

All of the energies of the Alvarado family have been directed toward the preservation of the landmark in its original state and no sacrifice is too large to safeguard it.

It goes without saying that nothing has been changed in the *casa* since the house passed back into the family again. But the partial destruction by the Nichols family, whose New England practicality did not understand the sentimental attachment of the Spanish settlers for their own ways, had left the house scarred, if not damaged. This must not happen again, and Mrs. Fages watches the construction work around her with a wary eye. In a way she holds the fort against incursions from hostile strangers exactly as the first settlers did.

What happened to the barn between the time the Nichols family sold the Casa Alvarado and the moving in of the present owners is not certain, but just prior to their occupation of the place it was a home already, and not a barn. A Mr. and Mrs. Bolt lived in it. Mrs. Bolt died in it, of cancer, often rending the night air with screams of pain.

In the meantime the house suffered somewhat from the weather and when the Leimbach family moved in a few years ago, it was clear to them that they would have to do some repairing and remodeling to make the old barn into a fine home. Meanwhile they are, of course, living in the house. It is only about thirty miles from Los Angeles on the freeway, and most convenient in terms of Los Angeles suburban living conditions. The entrance to the house is from the side, and downstairs there is a kitchen, a bedroom, and the living room, from which a staircase leads to the upper story. Two bedrooms make up that part of the house.

After they moved in the Leimbachs knew their house had once been used as a barn and hayloft: they even found a hay hook in the downstairs bedroom and knew that horses had once lived in it! But this did not bother them in the least, of course, nor did it bother their two daughters, Denise and Dana. The two girls were aged twelve and ten respectively at the time of their arrival at the house.

Jo Ann Leimbach, a woman in her thirties, her husband, somewhat older, the two girls, and an occasional cleaning woman, Mrs. Irene Nuñez, were the only people occupying the house.

Or so it seemed at first, anyway.

*　*　*

Mrs. Leimbach wasn't particularly interested in psychic phenomena, but as a child she had had a little precognition, such as the time she had known her grandfather had died, although he was far away from the family, and how her mother would tell her about his death.

But this had been a long time ago and none of these things were in her mind when she and her family moved into the converted barn on the Alvarado estate.

On September 12, 1967, she was in her sewing room, which is located in a separate building away from the main house. The main house was empty except for Mrs. Nuñez, who was cleaning the guest bedroom upstairs. Normally a courageous woman, Mrs. Nuñez felt uneasy this morning, as if she were being watched by someone she could not see.

This was the first time she had been alone in the house. Was it getting on her nerves? She is a woman of Mexican descent and the area is closely tied up with her people, so it could not be that she was out of her element, and yet she felt very much estranged at this moment. She turned around to see if there was perhaps someone in the room, after all.

As she turned, she clearly heard footsteps coming toward her. Immediately she froze in her tracks and the footsteps went right past her. There was no one to be seen, yet the floorboards reverberated with the weight of a person, quite heavy apparently, rushing past her! She caught herself running down the stairs, but then thought better of it and returned upstairs. The uneasy feeling was still present, but seemed quiet now.

Had she told her employer about her experience she would have encountered understanding, not scorn. For Mrs. Leimbach had already found out by then that there was someone other than flesh-and-blood people in this house. In February of the same year, she found herself in the house with her two girls, while her husband had gone out to attend to his income tax report. The girls, then aged ten and twelve, were in the kitchen with her that evening, when she clearly heard heavy footsteps upstairs.

This was immediately followed by the sound of someone opening and closing various drawer and of doors being violently opened and slammed shut. It sounded as if someone were very angry at not finding what he was looking for, and frantically going from room to room searching for *something*.

Thinking of how it would affect her children, since she could not possibly explain these sounds to them ratio-

nally, she jumped for the radio and turned it on loud so the noise would cover the sounds upstairs. Then she went out and brought the dog into the house and tried to get her to accompany her up the stairs. Tried is right, for the animal absolutely refused to budge and sat at the foot of the stairs and howled in utter terror.

Somehow Mrs. Leimbach did not feel up to going it alone, so she just sat there and waited. For a full ten minutes, the racket went on upstairs. Then it stopped as abruptly as it had begun. About half an hour later, her sister-in-law Doris and her son's fiancée, Marion, arrived at the house. Reinforced by her relatives, Mrs. Leimbach finally dared go upstairs. From the sound of the commotion she was sure to find various drawers open and doors jammed. But when she entered the rooms upstairs, she found everything completely untouched by human hands.

All windows were closed tightly so one could not blame drafts of air for the disturbances. All doors stood wide open, yet she had distinctly heard the sound of doors being violently slammed shut.

There is no house within earshot of theirs, and no noises in the area that could possibly mimic such sounds.

"I wonder what he is looking for," she mumbled, more to herself than for anyone's benefit. To her, the heavy footfalls were those of a man.

She did not discuss any of this with her girls, of course, and somehow managed to keep it from them although she felt disturbed herself by all this. Surely there was something wrong with the house, but what? She need not have worried about her girls since they already had a pretty good idea what it was that caused the trouble.

The previous July, Mrs. Leimbach and her husband were having coffee in the kitchen downstairs. It was a clear, sunny afternoon and all seemed peaceful and quiet. Denise, the elder daughter, was upstairs, sitting at her window seat and reading a book. For a moment, she took her eyes off the book, for it had seemed to her that a slight breeze had disturbed the atmosphere of the room. She was right, for she saw a large man walk across the room and enter the large walk-in closet at the other end of it. She assumed it was her father, of course, and asked what he was looking for. When she received no reply, she got up and went to the closet herself. It struck her funny that the closet door was closed. She opened it, wondering if her father was perhaps playing games with her. The closet was empty. Terrified, she rushed downstairs.

"What are you doing? What are you doing?" she demanded to know, sobbing, as her father tried to calm her.

Only after he had assured her that he wasn't playing tricks on her, did she relent. But if not her father, who had been upstairs in her room? The Leimbachs tried to explain the matter lightly, trying everything from "tired eyes" due to too much reading, to "shadows from the trees" outside. But the girl never believed any of it.

There was now an uneasy truce around the house and the subject of the phenomena was not discussed for the moment. The truce did not last very long, however.

Soon afterward, the two girls woke up in the middle of the morning even though they were usually very sound sleepers. The time was 2 A.M. and there was sufficient light in the room for them to distinguish the figure of a large man in black standing by their beds! He seemed to stare down at them without moving. They let out a scream almost in unison, bringing their parents up the stairs. By that time, the apparition had dissolved.

The war of nerves continued, however. A few nights later, the girls' screams attracted the parents and when they raced upstairs they found the girls barricaded inside the room, holding the door as if someone were trying to force it open.

For a moment, the parents could clearly see that some unseen force was balancing the door against the weight of the two young girls on the other side of it—then it slacked and fell shut. Almost hysterical with panic now, the girls explained, between sobs, that someone had tried to enter their room, that they had wakened and sensed it and pushed against the door—only to find the force outside getting stronger momentarily. Had the parents not arrived on the scene at this moment, the door would have been pushed open and whatever it was that did this, would have entered the bedroom.

But the door did not stop the black, shadowy intruder from entering that room. On several occasions, the girls saw him standing by their bedside and when they fully woke and jumped out of bed, he disappeared.

The Leimbachs and their girls were, however, not the only ones who had encountered the stranger. Even more sensitive to the invisible vibrations of a haunted house, Mrs. Nuñez had already had her initial experience with the man upstairs. But as yet she had not laid eyes on him and surely did not want to. But it so happened that in the summer of that year the family decided to go on vacation, and asked Mrs. Nuñez to look after their mail, water the plants and clean up the house, even though it would be empty. In addition, the local police were told of the possibility of prowlers and asked to keep an eye on the house while the family was away on vacation. The police gladly obliged and the house was put under surveillance.

Mrs. Nuñez accepted the assignment with mixed emotions. She wasn't a superstitious woman, but she always felt watched in that house, never alone, and somehow she had the impression that the force in the house was far from friendly. But she had decided to brave it out and try to get her job done as quickly as possible, and definitely only in the daylight.

As she approached the house this morning, it seemed strangely quiet and peaceful. The air was warm, as the California air usually is, and the humming of bees indicated that summer at its fullest was upon them.

She parked her car in front of the house and went toward the entrance door. Lumber for the structural changes the Leimbachs were making was still lying about all over the front yard. She put the key into the lock and opened the front door.

Carefully closing it behind her, she then turned and to her horror saw a figure turn into the hallway and head for the stairs! At the same time, she heard the heavy footsteps of a man scurrying out of earshot, then going up the stairs, and she clearly heard the floor boards squeaking overhead as the weight of a person was placed upon them —or so it seemed.

Despite her abject fear and the pearls of sweat that now stood on her forehead, she rallied and went after the intruder up the stairs. The footfalls had stopped by now and there was no one upstairs. She searched in every nook and cranny, opened every closet door and even looked down the stairs and in the cellar. Nothing. The house was as empty as it should be.

Only then did she remember how strangely icy the hallway had been when she had entered the house. In the excitement of seeing the human figure disappear around the corner she had completely overlooked this fact. But now, as she sat quietly on the upstairs bed, she recalled it and shuddered even though it was no longer cold.

Her chores done, she left the house and went home.

When her next day to visit came, she tried hard not to go, but her sense of propriety forced her to do what was expected of her.

This time she took her son Richard along for the ride. She quickly parked the car, opened the door, and looked inside. Again, the icy, clammy atmosphere began to envelop her. Quickly she threw the mail she had collected from the box onto the table in the entrance hall and slammed the door shut. She could not go further today.

When the Leimbachs returned, she resumed her visits, but whenever she approached the house after that, she almost "saw" the figure of a man standing by the entrance door staring out at her with hostile, cold eyes.

The Leimbachs finally received an answer to their problem.

A famous psychic lady walked through their house and immediately felt its hostile atmosphere.

"Something threatens this house," she mumbled, "and it has to do with both houses and the land, not just this house."

Suddenly it occurred to the Leimbachs that their troubles had started only when they had decided to make major structural changes in the house.

"Aha," the psychic said, "there is your problem."

While the main house, the Casa Alvarado, had remained untouched by any change, except for that unfortunate addition inflicted upon it in the last century, the barn, once part of the estate, had been remodeled. But until the arrival of the Leimbachs, no wall had yet been removed nor had the basic construction undergone changes. This was their intent, however, to correspond with their needs for a modern home.

Had this activity awakened the ire of the guardian wraith?

Then, too, there was the presence in the house of two sub-teenage girls, natural sources for poltergeist activities.

The man in black staring out at a hostile world, which had done so much to his erstwhile domain, was he the restless spirit of Señor Alvarado himself?

There seemed no need for his watchfulness in the main house, where the statue of St. Joseph looked out for dangers. But here, in the barn, there seemed need for a watchful eye.

After this, the Leimbachs proceeded with greater caution in their plans to change the house. Perhaps the question of their justified improvements having been openly discussed somehow reassured the unseen ears of the guardian.

It has been quiet at the house of late, but of course one can never tell. The early Spanish settlers knew how to take care of themselves, and of their own. And the old barn is still part of the Alvarado ranch, television aerial and garage notwithstanding.

☀ 69

The Mynah Bird (Canada)

"COME ON, BOY! Come on, boy!" the shrill voice of a mynah bird called out from its perch on the wall. The corridor of the old house was deliberately kept dimly lit to go with the atmosphere of the place. After all, this was and is Toronto's first and only topless nightclub. Since it is also nonalcoholic, due to the absence of a beverage license, it has to rely heavily on other attractions. The other attractions are such that nobody very much misses the lack of spirits in the bottle, especially as there are other spirits—the real kind—lingering about the place. Of that, anon. As for the black, yellow-beaked mynah bird, he was brought back from Bombay by the current owner of the club, Colin Kerr, from one of his many journeys to India.

Mr. Kerr is not only the owner of a bird, but also a professional golfer whose activities have taken him all over the world. He got into the nightclub business when his eye was caught by an attractive, almost romantic looking old house in Toronto's Yorkville district, an area roughly equivalent to New York's Greenwich Village or London's Soho. He installed his father-in-law on the third floor of the dark, brick and wood townhouse, with the task of keeping the building clean and in good shape. That was in 1963 and for two years he ran the place as any other club in the area was run; dancing, an occasional singer, and lots of romance. Still no liquor, but the Victorian atmosphere of the place more than made up for it and for a while it was an off-beat club for young couples to hold hands in. To make the feeling of remoteness from the outside world even stronger, Mr. Kerr dimmed his overhead lights, added heavy red drapes and Victorian furniture to the place and put in as many antiques of the period as he could garner in the local antique shops and flea markets.

Mr. Kerr is a slightly built man in his thirties and soft spoken. He is scarcely the image of the typical nightclub manager and being in this strange house provided him in a way with self-expression.

The place itself had been an antique shop prior to his arrival and before that an artist had had his studio upstairs where Mr. Kerr built a little stage. All kinds of people congregated in the area and there was an atmosphere of adventure and a certain wildness all around the house that somehow blended well with its insides.

Two years after his arrival on the scene, he decided to buy the house which he had at first only rented. This was not without good reason. Mr. Kerr had become aware of a new, exciting trend in the nightclub business and felt Toronto was about ready for the innovations first brought about in the pioneering domain of San Francisco's North Beach.

The topless dancers would be a far better attraction than his dance bands had been. But Mr. Kerr's artistic ambitions reached even further into the possibilities of creative expression: why not let the customers get in on the show? It was all well and good to sit there and watch a naked young woman shake and wriggle under the fluorescent lights. That had its good points and Mr. Kerr knew the attractions he offered brought in the crowds. But a more intimate touch was needed and he provided it.

"Paint our bare-breasted girl!" the Mynah Bird club advertised in all the Toronto papers. For a two-dollar fee, any customer could dip his brush in paint thoughtfully provided by management, and paint a design upon the naked torso of a young woman. It wasn't as good as finger painting, but it was the next best thing to it and the customers were given free rein to express their various artistic viewpoints. The club can hold about seventy people downstairs, in what must have been a parlor once, and another forty in the "theater" on the second floor. The third floor was used for living quarters.

The innovation caught on like wildfire. The Mynah Bird remained Canada's only place of this kind, and soon people from other cities came to do the painting bit. Strangely, there was nothing particularly shocking about all this. The women, to be sure, were young and pretty and wore only tiny panties which provided the anchor for what-

The haunted Mynah Bird Cafe—Toronto

ever artistic motifs the amateur painters wished to paint upon the girls' skin. The paint used was fluorescent and with the lights low, this made a pretty picture indeed. When there was no more empty space left on a woman's bare skin, the painting session ended, the customers returned to their seats, and the painted girl began to dance.

All this happened two or three times a night, six days a week. Mr. Kerr, despite his sexy attractions, found it unnecessary to hire a body guard or bouncer for his emporium. Perhaps Canadians do not mash so readily as Americans, or more likely the absence of intoxicating beverages kept the men at a distance. At any rate, the predominantly male audience kept their distance when not painting women's breasts. But the proceedings did do something to the men's eyes. They became hard and narrow as if they were watching an arena fight somewhere in ancient Rome. And the young women, mostly from the outlying provinces, became hard and cold looking, too, whenever they caught those glances.

Still, it was a successful operation and still is. Who is to say that painting designs on bare-breasted women is not some sort of artistic expression? The women themselves love it and it isn't just the touch of the wet brush that fascinates them, but the thought behind it all. They are in the center of the ring and love the male attention. But, like the stripper on stage, they also hate being stared at *in that way* at the same time. Colin Kerr watches over his seven girls and makes sure they are not molested, and the women consider their club a kind of home where they are appreciated for their contribution. The latter are not merely being painted in the nude. There is the girl in the fish tank, for instance, a trick done with mirrors, since the tank is only

the two gallon kind. (It is similar to another tank in which Mr. Kerr keeps a live piranha, though he is not part of the show. So far, anyway.) The woman in the fish tank is completely nude but she is only inches high to the viewer. Sometimes the viewers do not believe they are looking at a live girl, but the girl waves at them and convinces them pretty fast.

In a club serving soft drinks and even sandwiches there is bound to be some dishwashing and other nonglamorous jobs. Everybody takes turns here at doing everything, from the painting bit, the fish tank, the topless dancing, to checking of customers' coats, seeing them to their tables and serving them. The girls like being one thing today and another tomorrow for it gives them a sense of variety and Mr. Kerr has no complaints from disgruntled waitresses or tired dishwashers that way.

The girls range from eighteen to twenty-one years in age and come mostly from lower-middle-class homes, usually outside the cities. Whenever Kerr needs a replacement, there is a long line of applicants, which proves—if nothing else—that some women do like their breasts painted with fluorescent paint.

But something strange happened when Kerr changed the club's policy from straight dancing to the topless business. Whether it was his daring approach to night life or the sudden influx of a group of very young females that caused the disturbances is a moot question. Perhaps it was both. Shortly after the club had changed its policy, Mr. Kerr found that he could not keep the lights turned off at times.

It was almost as if someone were trying to annoy him, or perhaps only signal him for some reason, but the light switches kept turning themselves on regularly. Since they had not done anything of the kind during the first two years of his occupancy, this naturally caused some concern. But there seemed to be no natural explanation for this behavior. Then some musical instruments—leftovers from the band days—moved by themselves, very much to the consternation of Mr. Kerr who discovered that none of the girls had even been near them. He began to wonder whether perhaps some psychic force was at work here, although he had never been particularly interested in such things.

About that time, his father-in-law reported being addressed by some unseen person on several occasions. Since Kerr had also added movies to his attractions—the latter being stag films from Europe shown in the second floor "theater" after the downstairs show closed—he thought that perhaps one of the customers had sneaked up to the third floor and talked to his in-law. But Mr. Alfred Lawrence, the custodian, assured his son-in-law that he could tell a flesh-and-blood stag movie patron from an invisible ghost.

Things were going well with the Mynah Bird: the club was having sellouts six nights a week, and Raj, the bird himself, was being sought for TV appearances left and right. This led to a record album and Mr. Kerr found that his bird was making more money than he was. This did not trouble him, however, since he was, after all, paying the bird in seeds and the bird was happy and learned a lot of new words from the customers ogling the bare-breasted women.

Under the circumstances Mr. Kerr felt it wise to insure his twelve-year-old mynah with Lloyds of London. Raj was the first and only feathered insurance policy holder in the history of that austere company. Ever watchful to inform his doting public, Mr. Kerr let the newspapers know about this and the crowds that came to see the mynah bird in the cage became even larger. Of course, they all stayed for the show.

The rumbling of psychic disturbances did not escape the women's attention even though Kerr and his wife, Mrs. Jessamyn Kerr, took great pains not to alarm them by drawing their attention to these phenomena.

Although they once had a woman work for them who claimed to be a full-fledged witch, this woman did not have any uncanny experiences at the place, or perhaps to her they were not noteworthy. She was eighteen, from Hamilton, and named Lizerina, and she fit right in with the decor of the club.

After her departure for greener, or at least, better lit pastures, it was Joy Nicholls who became one of the hardest workers at the Mynah Bird. She arrived in 1967 fresh from the far northern portion of Canada, the daughter of a construction foreman. Perhaps she expressed more openly what every woman dreams of and perhaps she went about it in a rather unorthodox way, but Joy honestly believed in her work and liked her surroundings and to her the Mynah Bird was the most wonderful place in the world.

One month after her arrival, she found herself resting up at the end of one night. It was about 2:30 in the morning and time to quit. Upstairs, all was quiet, since the last customer had gone home. Just then she clearly heard chairs move overhead as if someone were rearranging them. She knew for a fact that there was no one else about but forgetting all fear for the moment, she ran up the stairs to see who the intruder was.

As she opened the door of the "theater," she found that the chairs which she had left a little earlier neatly arranged in rows for next evening's show, were now in disarray and strewn all over the place. She put them in order once more and left.

Many times after this initial exposure to unseen forces, the same phenomenon happened. Always after the stag films had been shown, it seemed as if someone threw the chairs about in great anger.

Then Joy realized that the place used as a theater now was originally the artist's studio. Perhaps his sensitive artistic taste recoiled at the kind of movies shown here, so delicately advertised by Kerr as "Only for those who will not be offended."

A short time after the initial incident with the moving chairs, Joy was downstairs when she heard someone walk overhead and then continue down the stairs. But nobody appeared. Yet, within a fraction of a moment, she strongly felt that someone was standing close to her, staring at her, coldly and with piercing eyes. Now she did not see this but felt it with an inner awareness that had always been acute in her. She knew at once it was a man and she knew he was angry. Or perhaps sad. Being a generous person she wondered how she could help the stranger. Perhaps her thoughts somehow pierced the veil of silence.

Shortly after, she found herself alone again in the hall when she heard her name being called.

"Joy," a soft, almost hoarse voice seemed to say, and more urgently repeated, "Joy!"

She turned around to see who was calling out to her, but of course she was quite alone.

About the same time, Nancy Murray, another one of the women, complained about someone whom she could not see staring at her. Joy was a gay, life-loving blonde with a spectacular figure, while Nancy was more the slim, sultry type, quiet and introverted—despite her occupation —but both had a psychic awareness in common, it would appear.

Despite her bad eyes, Nancy saw someone when she was alone in the downstairs room. The continual stares of someone she could not see made Nancy far more apprehensive than the very visual stares of the men in the audience when she was being painted. After all, she knew what went through men's minds, but what do ghosts think?

With the women adding to the number of psychic incidents almost daily, Kerr finally concluded there was something the matter with his place. He decided to hold a séance and, if possible, find out.

It so happened that one of his featured girls, a folksinger named Tony Stone, had often served as a clairvoyant medium at séances and she readily agreed to try. The first of what became later an almost daily séance, was held entirely privately, after the customers had left. Only the Kerrs and the women attended. Upon instruction from Tony Stone, one candle was placed on the table, which was covered by an ordinary tablecloth.

After holding hands and generally relaxing their thoughts for a while, the group looked about. The room was quite dark in its further recesses and the flicker of the candle gave the entire procedure an even eerier glow.

Suddenly and without warning, the tablecloth was yanked off the table, almost toppling the candle. With a scream, Nancy rose. Some unknown force had managed to get the tablecloth off the table and threw it with great violence some distance from them on the floor.

Horror in her eyes, Nancy left the room and has refused to attend any séances ever since. But Mr. Kerr was so impressed with the performance he decided to add the séance to his regular program: each night, after the show, and after the stag films, the customers were invited to stay on for an impromptu séance. Sometimes, when the spirit moved them, they put the séance on even *before* the stag movies.

Soon the Mynah Bird "family" discovered that these séances—the only public séances of their kind in Canada—brought on additional disturbances in the house. Dishes in the kitchen in the rear downstairs would suddenly start to rattle. Once when Kerr and his wife ran back to see what was happening, they found the kitchen empty. But as they looked with amazement into the well-lit kitchen, they saw a big kitchen knife balance itself as if held by unseen hands. Kerr grabbed it and examined it. While he was trying to see if he could balance it by natural means—ever the skeptic—another stack of dishes came tumbling down on them. There was no earthly reason for this. Since that first time, dish rattling follows almost all séances. It is as if their sittings release some power within the women that creates the phenomena. Or perhaps someone up there on the second floor is not entirely happy with the whole thing.

The first time an audience stayed behind for a séance, Nancy almost went into deep trance. She had sworn she would not attend another séance, but her presence was required in the room as part of her job and she kept a distance from the medium. Nevertheless, she felt herself sink into trance and fought it. After that, she spoke to Kerr and was given permission to stay away from all further séances.

To Nancy, the world of ghosts was scarcely unknown. It was precisely because of prior experiences that she had to beg off. Not long ago, while on a visit to a friend in downtown Toronto, she came upon an old house on nearby Gloucester Street. That was on the last day of February 1968 and she will never forget the date.

The old house had been closed down, but she was curious, and opened the front door to peek in. As she did so, she perceived coming down the broad staircase, a strange looking man. He was a soldier in a very unusual uniform, not one she was familiar with, and he looked quite as real as any man walking down a staircase. She even heard his canteen rattle and the steps of his boots as he came closer toward where she was standing. But as he came close she could see his face, such a sad face, and it looked straight at her. But where his neck should have been, there was a gaping hole. The wallpaper could be seen right through it and as she realized this she fled in terror. The uniform was of World War I vintage, she later learned.

The first public séance had other results, though, than to frighten Nancy. With her head bowed, medium Tony Stone spoke of a resident ghost she felt close by.

Superimposed on the face of a lady customer sitting across the table from her, she described the figure of an old man with gray hair and a beard, but she could not get his name that time.

Then, somewhat later, at another séance, she excitedly described the man again.

"He's behind me now," she exclaimed and her lips started to tremble as if the ghost was trying to take her over.

"Lawrence…Oliver…Kendall…" she finally managed to say, slowly, while fighting off the unseen force.

"He's a very sad person," she added, but she could not find out why he was here in the club. As more and more of the public attended the séances, less and less happened at them which is not at all surprising. They degenerated into just another number on the bill and no one took them seriously anymore. Especially not the resident specters. They resolutely refused to put on appearances, unpaid, by command, to amuse the out-of-town visitors.

Even the introduction of an ouija board did not help. It did establish that Tony Stone was a good clairvoyant but little else.

She managed to predict accurately the names of several people who would be in the audience the next night. But the Mynah Bird scarcely needs to know who its customers are. There are so many of them.

As to Mr. Kendall, he has not yet been identified from among the many tenants of the old house.

On separate occasions, Nancy and Joy smelled strong perfume in the downstairs area when neither of them was wearing any. It was a sudden wafting in of a woman's perfume, somehow reminiscent of a bygone era.

When Joy also heard the swishing sound of taffeta skirts whisking by her one night, she knew that the sad old man upstairs was not the only spectral boarder at the club. Somehow it did not frighten the women as much as the fury of the man moving those chairs. Was the woman responsible for the throwing about of the dishes in the kitchen perhaps?

Late at night, when the customers have gone, nothing in the world could induce the girls to go up the narrow corridors and stairwells to find out if one of the denizens of the nether world is still lurking about in anger. So far Mr. Kerr does not consider their presence dangerous or even undesirable. After all, who else offers his clientele bare-breasted women and ectoplastic presences for the same ticket?

✳ 70

The Terror on the Farm
(Connecticut)

NORTH WOODSTOCK, CONNECTICUT, is New England at its best and quietest: rolling farmland seldom interrupted by the incursions of factories and modern city life.

The village itself seems to have weathered the passage of time rather well and with a minimum of change. Except for the inevitable store signs and other expressions of contemporary American bad taste, the village is as quiet today as it must have been, say, two hundred years ago, when America was young.

On Brickyard Road, going toward the outer edges of the village, and standing somewhat apart from the inhabited areas, was an old farm house. It had obviously seen better days, but now it was totally dilapidated and practically beyond repair. Still, it was a house of some size and quite obviously different from the ordinary small farmhouse of the surrounding countryside.

There were sixteen rooms in the house, and for the past fifty years it had been the property of the Duprey family. The house itself was built in pre-Revolutionary times by the Lyons family, who used it as a tavern. The place was a busy spot on the Boston-Hartford road and a tavern here did well indeed in the days when railroads had not yet come into existence.

After the Lyons Tavern changed hands, it belonged successfully to the Potters, Redheads, Ides, and then the Dupreys, but it was now a private dwelling, the center of the surrounding farm, and no longer a public house.

Very little is known about its early history beyond that, at least that is what Mrs. Florence Viner discovered when she considered buying the house. She did discover, however, that Mrs. Emery Duprey, the previous owner, had suffered great tragedy in the house. One morning she had taken a group of neighbors' children to school. The school was in a one-room house, less than a mile distant. Her fourteen-year-old daughter Laura was left behind at the house because she had not been feeling well that day.

When Mrs. Duprey returned home a short time later, she found the girl gone. Despite every effort made, the girl was never found again nor was any trace found of her disappearance.

Mr. and Mrs. Charles Viner decided to buy the house in 1951 despite its deplorable condition. They wanted a large country house and did not mind putting it in good condition; in fact, they rather looked forward to the challenge and task.

It was on Good Friday of that year that they moved in. Immediately they started the restoration, but they stayed at the house and made do, like the pioneers they felt they had now become.

The farm itself was still a working farm and they retained a number of farm workers from the surrounding area to work it for them. The only people staying at the house at all times were the Viners, their daughter Sandra, and the help.

Two months had gone by after their arrival when one evening Mrs. Viner and her daughter, then eleven years old, were alone in the house, sitting in the kitchen downstairs, reading.

"Who is upstairs?" the girl suddenly inquired.

Mrs. Viner had heard furtive footsteps also, but had decided to ignore them. Surely, the old house was settling or the weather was causing all sorts of strange noises.

But the footsteps became clearer. This was no house settling. This was someone walking around upstairs. For several minutes, they sat in the kitchen, listening as the steps walked all over the upper floor. Then Mrs. Viner rose resolutely, went to her bedroom on the same floor and returned with a 22-revolver she had in the drawer of her night table just in case prowlers would show up. The moment she re-entered the kitchen, she clearly heard two heavy thumps upstairs. It sounded as if a couple of heavy objects had fallen suddenly and hit the floor. Abruptly, the walking ceased as if the thumps were the end of a scene being re-enacted upstairs.

Too frightened to go up and look into what she knew to be an empty room, Mrs. Viner went to bed. When her husband returned a little later, however, they investigated upstairs together. There was nothing out of place nor indeed any sign that anyone had been up there.

But a few days later, the same phenomenon recurred. First, there were the footsteps of someone walking up and down upstairs, as if in great agitation. Then two heavy thumps and the sound of a falling object and abrupt silence. The whole thing was so exactly the same each time it almost became part of the house routine and the Viners heard it so many times they no longer became panicky because of it. When the house regained its former splendor, they began to have overnight guests. But whenever anyone stayed at the house, inevitably, the next morning they would complain about the constant walking about in the corridor upstairs.

Mrs. Ida Benoit, Mrs. Viner's mother, came downstairs the morning after her first night in the house.

"I'll never sleep in *this* house again," she assured her daughter. "Why, it's haunted. Someone kept walking through my bedroom."

Her daughter could only shrug and smile wanly. She knew very well what her mother meant. Naturally, the number of unhappy guests grew, but she never discussed the phenomena with anyone beforehand. After all, it was just possible that *nothing* would happen. But in ten years of occupancy, there wasn't a single instance where a person using a bedroom upstairs was not disturbed.

A year after they had moved in, Mrs. Viner decided to begin to renovate a large upstairs bedroom. It was one of those often used as a guest room. This was on a very warm day in September, and despite the great heat, Mrs. Viner liked her work and felt in good spirits. She was painting the window sash and singing to herself with nothing particular on her mind. She was quite alone upstairs at the time and for the moment the ghostly phenomena of the past were far from her thoughts.

Suddenly, she felt the room grow ice cold. The chill became so intense she began to shudder and pulled her arms around herself as if she were in mid-winter on an icy road. She stopped singing abruptly and at the same time she felt the strong presence of another person in the room with her.

"Someone's resenting very much what I'm doing," she heard herself think.

Such a strong wave of hatred came over her she could not continue. Terrified, she nevertheless knew she had to turn around and see who was in the room with her. It seemed to take her an eternity to muster sufficient strength to move a single muscle.

Suddenly, she felt a cold hand at her shoulder. Someone was standing behind her and evidently trying to get her attention. She literally froze with fear. When she finally moved to see who it was the hand just melted away.

With a final effort, she jerked herself around and stared back into the room. There was no one there. She ran to the door, screaming, "I don't know who you are or what you are, but you won't drive me out of this house."

Still screaming, she ran down the stairs and onto the porch. There she caught her breath and quieted down. When her daughter came home from school, she felt relieved. The evil in that room had been overpowering, and she avoided going up there as much as possible after that experience.

"I'll never forget that hand, as long as I live," she explained to her husband.

In the years that followed, they came to terms with the unseen forces in the house. Perhaps her determined effort not to be driven out of their home had somehow gotten through to the specter, but at any rate, they were staying and making the house as livable as they could. Mrs. Viner gave birth to two more children, both sons, and as Sandra grew up, the phenomena seemed to subside. In 1958 a second daughter was born and Sandra left for college. But three weeks later the trouble started anew.

One night in September she was sitting in the downstairs living room watching television with James Latham, their farm worker. The two boys and the baby had been in bed for hours. Suddenly, there was a terrific explosion in the general direction of the baby's room. She ran into the room and found it ice cold—as if it had been an icebox. From the baby's room, another door leads out into the hall,

and it is usually closed for obvious reasons. But now it stood wide open, and evidently it had been thrust open with considerable force. The lock was badly bent from the impact and the radiator, which the door had hit in opening, was still reverberating from it. The baby was not harmed in any way, but Mrs. Viner wondered if perhaps the oil burner had blown up.

She went down into the basement to check but found everything normal. As she returned to the baby's room she suddenly had the distinct impression that the phenomenon somehow connected with the presence of a young girl.

She tried to reason this away, since no young girl was present in the household, nor was there any indication that tied in in any way with the tragic disappearance of Mrs. Duprey's girl, of which she, of course, knew. Try as she might, she could not shake this feeling that a young girl was the focal point of the disturbances at the house.

One night her sister had joined her in the living room downstairs. Suddenly there was a loud crash overhead in what they knew was an empty bedroom. Mrs. Viner left her worried sister downstairs and went up alone. A table in the bedroom had been knocked over. No natural force short of a heavy quake could have caused this. The windows were closed and there was no other way in which the table could topple over by itself. She was so sure that this could not have been caused by anything but human intruders, she called the state police.

The police came and searched the house from top to bottom but found no trace of any intruder.

Mrs. Viner then began to wonder about the goings-on. If these unseen forces had the power to overturn heavy tables, surely they might also harm people. The thought frightened her, and where she had until then considered living with a ghost or ghosts rather on the chic side, it now took on distinctly threatening overtones. She discussed it with her husband but they had put so much work and money into the house that the thought of leaving again just did not appeal to them.

It was inevitable that she should be alone in the house, except for the children, at various times. Her husband was away on business and the farm help out where they belonged. Often Mrs. Viner found herself walking through the rooms hoping against rational reasoning that she would come face-to-face with the intruder. Then she could address her or him—she was not sure how many there were—and say, "look, this is my house now, we've bought it and rebuilt it, and we don't intend to leave it. Go away and don't hang around, it's no use." She often rehearsed her little speech for just such a confrontation. But the ghost never appeared when she was ready.

Meanwhile the footsteps followed by the heavy thumps kept recurring regularly, often as many as four times in a single week. It was usually around the same time of the evening, which led her to believe that it represented some sort of tragedy that was being re-enacted upstairs by the ghostly visitors. Or was she merely tuning in on a past tragedy and what she and the others were hearing was in fact only an echo of the distant past? She could not believe this, especially as she still remembered vividly the ice cold hand that grabbed her shoulder in the bedroom upstairs on that hot September day. And a memory would not cause a heavy door to swing open by itself with such violence that it burst the lock.

No, these were not memory impressions they were hearing. These were actual entities with minds of their own, somehow trapped between two states of being and condemned by their own violence to live forever in the place where their tragedy had first occurred. What a horrible fate, Mrs. Viner thought, and for a moment she felt great compassion for the unfortunate ones.

But then her own involvement reminded her that it was, after all, her house and her life that was being disrupted. She had a better right to be here than they had, even if they had been here before.

Defiantly, she continued to polish and refine the appointments in the house until it looked almost as if it had never been a dilapidated, almost hopelessly derelict house. She decided to repaper one of the bedrooms upstairs, so that her guests would sleep in somewhat more cheerful surroundings. The paper in this particular room was faded and very old and deserved to be replaced. As she removed the dirty wallpaper, the boards underneath became visible again. They were wide and smooth and obviously part of the original boards of the house.

After she had pulled down all the paper from the wall facing away from the window, she glanced up at it. The wall, exposed to light after goodness knows how many years, was spattered with some sort of paint.

"This won't do at all," she decided, and went downstairs to fetch some rags and water. Returning to the room, she started to remove what she took for some very old paint. When she put water on the stains, the spots turned a bright red!

Try as she might, she could not remove the red stains. Finally she applied some bleach, but it only turned the spots a dark brown. It finally dawned on her that this wasn't paint but blood. On closer investigation, her suspicion was confirmed. She had stumbled upon a blood-spattered wall—but what had taken place up here that had caused this horrible reminder?

Somehow she felt that she had gotten a lead in her quest for the solution to the phenomena plaguing the house. Surely, someone had been killed up there, but who and why?

She went into the village and started to talk to the local people. At first, she did not get much help, for New Englanders are notoriously shy about family matters. But eventually Mrs. Viner managed to get some information from some of the older local people who had known about the house on Brickyard Road for a long time.

When the house was still a public tavern, that is somewhere around the turn of the nineteenth century or the very end of the eighteenth, there had been two men at the tavern who stayed overnight as guests. Their names are shrouded in mystery and perhaps they were very unimportant, as history goes.

But there was also a young girl at the tavern, the kind innkeepers used to hire as servant girls in those days. If the girl wanted to be just that, well and good; if she wanted to get involved with some of the men that passed through on their way to the cities, that was her own business. Tavern keepers in those days were not moral keepers and the hotel detective had not yet been conceived by a puritan age. So the servant girls often went in and out of the guests' rooms, and nobody cared much.

It appears that one such young girl was particularly attractive to two men at the same time. There were arguments and jealousy. Finally the two men retired to a room upstairs and a fight to the finish followed. As it was upstairs, most likely it was in the girl's own room, with one suitor discovering the other obtaining favors he had sought in vain, perhaps. At any rate, as the horrified girl looked on, the two men killed each other with their rapiers, and their blood, intermingled in death, spattered upon the wall of the room.

As she walked back from the village with this newly-gained knowledge, Mrs. Viner understood clearly for the first time, why her house was indeed haunted. The restless footsteps in the room upstairs were the hurried steps of the unhappy suitor. The scuffling noises that followed and the sudden heavy thumps would be the fight and the two falling bodies—perhaps locked in death. The total silence that always ensued after the two heavy falls, clearly indicated to her that the stillness of death following the struggle was being re-enacted along with the tragedy itself.

And how right she had been about a girl being the central force in all this!

But why the hostility towards her? Why the icy hand at the shoulder? Did the girl resent her, another woman, in this house? Was she still hoping her suitor would come for her, and did she perhaps take Mrs. Viner for "competition?" A demented mind, especially when it has been out of the body for one hundred fifty years, can conjure up some strange ideas.

But her fighting energies were somehow spent, and when an opportunity arose to sell the house, Mrs. Viner agreed readily to do so. Those house then passed into the hands of Samuel Beno, after the Viners had lived in it from 1951 to 1961. For five years, Mr. Beno owned the house but never lived in it. It remained unoccupied, standing quietly on the road.

Only once was there a flurry of excitement. In 1966, someone made off with $5,000 worth of plumbing and copper piping. The owner naturally entrusted the matter to the state police hoping the thieves would eventually return for more. The authorities even placed tape recorders on the ready into the house in case some thieves did return.

Since then not much has been heard about the house and one can only presume that the tragic story of the servant girl and her two suitors has had its final run. But one can't be entirely sure until the next tenant moves into the old Lyons Tavern. After all, blood does not come off easily, either from walls or from men's memories.

✳ 71

A California Ghost Story

LITTLE DID I KNOW when I had successfully investigated the haunted apartment of Mrs. Verna Kunze in San Bernardino, that Mrs. Kunze would lead me to another case equally as interesting as her own, which I reported on in my book, *Ghosts of the Golden West*.

Mrs. Kunze is a very well-organized person, and a former employee in the passport division of the State Department. She is used to sifting facts from fancy. Her interest in psycho-cybernetics had led to her to a group of like-minded individuals meeting regularly in Orange County. There she met a gentleman formerly with the FBI by the name of Walter Tipton.

One day, Mr. Tipton asked her help in contacting me concerning a most unusual case that had been brought to his attention. Having checked out some of the more obvious details, he had found the people involved truthful and worthy of my time.

So it was that I first heard of Mrs. Carole Trausch of Santa Ana.

What happened to the Trausch family and their neighbors is not just a ghost story. Far more than that, they found themselves in the middle of an old tragedy that had not yet been played out fully when they moved into their spanking new home.

Carole Trausch was born in Los Angeles of Scottish parentage and went to school in Los Angeles. Her father is a retired policeman and her mother was born in Scotland. Carole married quite young and moved with her husband, a businessman, to live first in Huntington Beach and later in Westminster, near Santa Ana.

Now in her early twenties, she is a glamorous-looking blonde who belies the fact that she has three children aged eight, six, and two, all girls.

Early the previous year, they moved into one of two hundred two-story bungalows in a new development in Westminster. They were just an ordinary family, without any particular interest in the occult. About their only link the world of the psychic were some peculiar dreams Carole had had.

The first time was when she was still a little girl. She dreamed there were some pennies hidden in the rose bed in the garden. On awakening, she laughed at herself, but out of curiosity she did go to the rose bed and looked. Sure enough, there were some pennies in the soil below the roses. Many times since then she has dreamed of future events that later came true.

One night she dreamed that her husband's father was being rolled on a stretcher, down a hospital corridor by a nurse, on his way to an operation. The next morning there was a phone call informing them that such an emergency had indeed taken place about the time she dreamed it. On several occasions she sensed impending accidents or other unpleasant things, but she is not always sure what kind. One day she felt sure she or her husband would be in a car accident. Instead it was one of her little girls, who was hit by passing car.

When they moved into their present house, Mrs. Trausch took an immediate disliking to it. This upset her practical-minded husband. They had hardly been installed when she begged him to move again. He refused.

The house is a white-painted two-story bungalow, which was built about five years before their arrival. Downstairs is a large, oblong living room, a kitchen, and a dining area. On the right, the staircase leads to the upper story. The landing is covered with linoleum, and there are two square bedrooms on each side of the landing, with wall-to-wall carpeting and windows looking onto the yard in the rear bedroom and onto the street in the front room.

There is a large closet along the south wall of the rear bedroom. Nothing about the house is unusual, and there was neither legend nor story nor rumor attached to the house when they rented it from the local bank that owned it.

And yet there was something queer about the house. Mrs. Trausch's nerves were on edge right from the very first when they moved in. But she accepted her husband's decision to stay put and swept her own fears under the carpet of everyday reason as the first weeks in their new home rolled by.

At first the children would come to her with strange tales. The six-year-old girl complained of being touched by someone she could not see whenever she dropped off for her afternoon nap in the bedroom upstairs. Sometimes this presence would shake the bed, and then there was a shrill noise, somewhat like a beep, coming from the clothes closet. The oldest girl, eight years old, confirmed the story and reported similar experiences in the room.

Carole dismissed these reports as typical imaginary tales of the kind children will tell.

But one day she was resting on the same bed upstairs and found herself being tapped on the leg by some unseen person.

This was not her imagination; she was fully awake, and it made her wonder if perhaps her intuition about this house had not been right all along.

She kept experiencing the sensation of touch in the upstairs bedrooms only, and it got to be a habit with her to make the beds as quickly as possible and then rush downstairs where she felt nothing unusual. Then she also began to hear the shrill, beep like sounds from the closet. She took out all the children's clothes and found nothing that could have caused the noise. Finally she told her husband about it, and he promptly checked the pipes and other structural details of the house, only to shake his head. Nothing could have made such noises.

For several months she had kept her secret, but now that her husband also knew, she had Diane, the oldest, tell her father about it as well.

It was about this time that she became increasingly aware of a continuing presence upstairs. Several times she would hear footsteps walking upstairs, and on investigation found the children fast asleep. Soon the shuffling steps became regular features of the house. It would always start near the closet in the rear bedroom, then go toward the stair landing.

Carole began to wonder if her nerves weren't getting the better of her. She was much relieved one day when her sister, Kathleen Bachelor, who had come to visit her, remarked about the strange footsteps upstairs. Both women knew the children were out. Only the baby was upstairs, and on rushing up the stairs, they found her safely asleep in her crib. It had sounded to them like a small person wearing slippers.

Soon she discovered, however, that there were two kinds of footsteps: the furtive pitter-patter of a child, and the heavy, deliberate footfalls of a grownup.

Had they fallen heir to two ghosts? The thought seemed farfetched even to ESP-prone Carole, but it could not be dismissed entirely. What was going on, she wondered. Evidently she was not losing her mind, for others had also heard these things.

Once she had gone out for the evening and when she returned around 10 P.M., she dismissed the babysitter. After the girl had left, she was alone with the baby. Suddenly she heard the water running in the bathroom upstairs. She raced up the stairs and found the bathroom door shut tight. Opening it, she noticed that the water was on and there was some water in the sink.

On January 27 of the next year, Carole had guests over for lunch, two neighbors name Pauline J. and Joyce S., both young women about the same age as Carole. The children were all sleeping in the same upstairs front bedroom, the two older girls sharing the bed while the baby

girl occupied the crib. The baby had her nap between 11 and 2 P.M. At noon, however, the baby woke up crying, and, being barely able to talk at age two, kept saying "Baby scared, Mommy!"

The three ladies had earlier been upstairs together, preparing the baby for her crib. At that time, they had also put the entire room carefully in order, paying particular attention to making the covers and spread on the large bed very smooth, and setting up the dolls and toys on the chest in the corner.

When the baby cried at noon, all there women went upstairs and found the bed had wrinkles and an imprint as though someone had been sitting on it. The baby, of course, was still in her crib.

They picked up the child and went downstairs with her. Just as they got to the stairway, all three heard an invisible child falling down the stairs about three steps ahead of where they were standing.

It was after this experience that Mrs. Trausch wondered why the ghost child never touched any of the dolls. You see, the footsteps they kept hearing upstairs always went from the closet to the toy chest where the dolls are kept. But none of the dolls was ever disturbed. It occurred to her that the invisible child was a boy, and there were no boys' toys around.

The sounds of a child running around in the room upstairs became more and more frequent; she knew it was not one of her children, having accounted for her own in other ways. The whole situation began to press on her nerves, and even her husband—who had until now tended to shrug off what he could not understand—became concerned. Feelers were put out to have me come to the house as soon as possible, but I could not make it right away and they would have to cope with their unseen visitors for the time being, or until I arrived on the scene.

All during February the phenomena continued, so much so that Mrs. Trausch began to take them as part of her routine. But she kept as much to the downstairs portion of the house as she could. For some unknown reason, the phenomena never intruded on that part of the house.

She called in the lady who managed the development for the owners and cautiously told her of their problem. But the manager knew nothing whatever about the place, except that it was new and to her knowledge no great tragedies had occurred there in her time.

When the pitter-patter of the little feet continued, Carole Trausch decided she just had to know. On March 16, she decided to place some white flour on the linoleum-covered portion of the upstairs floor to trap the unseen child. This was the spot where the footsteps were most often heard, and for that past two days the ghost child had indeed "come out" there to run and play.

In addition, she took a glass or water with some measuring spoons of graduated sizes in it, and set it all down in a small pan and put it into her baby's crib with a cracker in the pan beside the glass. This was the sort of thing a little child might want—that is, a living child.

She then retired to the downstairs portion of the house and called in a neighbor. Together the two women kept watch, waiting for the early afternoon hours when the ghost child usually became active upstairs.

As the minutes ticked off, Carole began to wonder how she would look if nothing happened. The neighbor probably would consider her neurotic, and accuse her of making up the whole story as an attention-getter in this rather quiet community.

But she did not have to worry long. Sure enough, there were the footsteps again upstairs. The two women waited a few moments to give the ghost a chance to leave an impression, then they rushed upstairs.

They saw no child, but the white flour had indeed been touched. There were footmarks in the flour, little feet that seemed unusually small and slender. Next to the prints there was the picture of a flower, as if the child had bent down and finger-painted the flower as a sign of continuing presence. From the footprints, they took the child to be between three and four years of age. The water and pan in the crib had not been touched, and as they stood next to the footprints, there was utter silence around them.

Mrs. Trausch now addressed the unseen child gently and softly, promising the child they would not hurt it. Then she placed some boys' toys, which she had obtained for this occasion, around the children's room and withdrew.

There was no immediate reaction to all this, but two days later the eight-year-old daughter came running down the stairs to report that she had seen the shadow of a little boy in front of the linen closet in the hall. He wore striped shirt and pants, and was shorter than she.

When I heard of the footprints by telephone, I set the week of June 2 aside for a visit to the house. Meanwhile I instructed the Trausches to continue observing whatever they could.

But the Trausches had already resolved to leave the house, even if I should be able to resolve their "problem." No matter what, they could never be quite sure. And living with a ghost—or perhaps two ghosts—was not what they wanted to do, what with three living children to keep them on their toes.

Across from the Trausch apartment, and separated from it by a narrow lane, is another house just like it and built about the same time, on what was before only open farmland—as far as everyone there knows. A few years before, the area was flooded and was condemned, but it dried out later. There is and always has been plenty of water in the area, a lowland studded with ponds and fishing holes.

The neighbor's name was Bonnie Swanson and she too was plagued by footsteps that had no human causing them. The curious thing is that these phenomena were heard only in the upstairs portion of her house, where the bedrooms are, just as in the Trausch house.

Twice the Swansons called in police, only to be told that there was no one about causing the footsteps. In April, the Swansons had gone away for a weekend, taking their child with them. When they returned, the husband opened the door and was first to step into the house. At this moment he distinctly heard footsteps running very fast from front to rear of the rooms, as if someone had been surprised by their return. Mrs. Swanson, who had also heard this, joined her husband in looking the house over, but there was no stranger about and no one could have it left.

Suddenly they became aware of the fact that a light upstairs was burning. They knew they had turned it off when they left. Moreover, in the kitchen they almost fell over a child's tricycle. Last time they saw this tricycle, it had stood in the corner of their living room. It could not have gotten to the kitchen by itself, and there was no sign of anyone breaking and entering in their absence. Nothing was missing.

It seemed as if my approaching visit was somehow getting through to the ghost or ghosts, for as the month of June came closer, the phenomena seemed to mount in intensity and frequency.

On the morning of May 10, 9:30, Mrs. Trausch was at her front bedroom window, opening it to let in the air. From her window she could see directly into the Swanson house, since both houses were on the same level with the windows parallel to each other. As she reached her window and casually looked out across to the Swanson's rooms, which she knew to be empty at this time of day (Mr. Swanson was work, and Mrs. Swanson and a houseguest were out for the morning) she saw to her horror the arm of a woman pushing back the curtain of Mrs. Swanson's window.

There was a curiously stiff quality about this arm and the way it moved the curtain back. Then she saw clearly a woman with a deathlike white mask of a face staring at her. The woman's eyes were particularly odd. Despite her excitement, Mrs. Trausch noticed that the woman had wet hair and was dressed in something filmy, like a white nylon negligee with pink flowers on it.

For the moment, Mrs. Trausch assumed that the houseguest must somehow have stayed behind, and so she smiled at the woman across from her. Then the curtain dropped and the woman disappeared. Carole Trausch could barely wait to question her neighbor about the incident, and found that there hadn't been anyone at the house when she saw the woman with the wet hair.

Now Mrs. Trausch was sure that there were two unseen visitors, a child and a woman, which would account for the different quality of the footsteps they had been hearing.

She decided to try and find out more about the land on which the house stood.

A neighbor living a few blocks away on Chestnut Street, who had been in her house for over twenty years, managed to supply some additional information. Long before the development had been built, there had been a farm there.

In the exact place where the Trausches now lived there had been a barn. When the house was built, a large trench was dug and the barn was pushed into it and burned. The people who lived there at the time were a Mexican family named Felix. They had a house nearby but sold the area of the farm to the builders.

But because of the flooded condition of the area, the houses stood vacant for a few years. Only after extensive drainage had taken place did the houses become inhabitable. At this time the Trausches were able to move into theirs.

The area was predominantly Mexican and the development was a kind of Anglo-Saxon island in their midst.

All this information was brought out only after our visit, incidentally, and neither Sybil Leek, who acted as my medium, nor I had any knowledge of it at the time.

Mrs. Trausch was not the only adult member of the family to witness the phenomena. Her husband finally confessed that on several occasions he had been puzzled by footsteps upstairs when he came home late at night. That was around 1 A.M., and when he checked to see if any of the children had gotten out of bed, he found them fast asleep. Mr. Trausch is a very realistic man. His business is manufacturing industrial tools, and he does not believe in ghosts. But he heard the footsteps too.

The Trausches also realized that the shuffling footsteps of what appeared to be a small child always started up as soon as the two older girls had left for school. It was as if the invisible boy wanted to play with their toys when they weren't watching.

Also, the ghost evidently liked the bathroom and water, for the steps resounded most often in that area. On one occasion Mrs. Trausch was actually using the bathroom when the steps resounded next to her. Needless to say, she left the bathroom in a hurry.

Finally the big day had arrived. Mr. Trausch drove his Volkswagen all the way to Hollywood to pick up Mrs. Leek and myself, and while he did not believe in ghosts, he didn't scoff at them either.

After a pleasant ride of about two hours, we arrived at Westminster. It was a hot day in June, and the Santa Ana area is known for its warm climate. Mr. Trausch parked the car, and we went into the house where the rest of the family was already awaiting our visit.

I asked Sybil to scout around for any clairvoyant impressions she might get of the situation, and as she did

so, I followed her around the house with my faithful tape recorder so that not a word might be lost.

As soon as Sybil had set foot in the house, she pointed to the staircase and intoned ominously, "It's upstairs."

Then, with me trailing, she walked up the stairs as gingerly as trapeze artist while I puffed after her.

"Gooseflesh," she announced and held out her arm. Now whenever were are in haunted area Sybil does get gooseflesh—not because she is scared but because it is a natural, instant reaction to whatever presence might be there.

We were in the parents' room now, and Sybil looked around with the expectant smile of a well-trained bird dog casing the moors.

"Two conflicting types," she then announced. "There's anger and resentfulness toward someone. There's something here. Has to do with the land. Two people."

She felt it centered in the children's room, and that there was a vicious element surrounding it, an element of destruction. We walked into the children's room and immediately she made for the big closet in the rear. Behind that wall there was another apartment, but the Trausches did not know anything about it except that the people in it had just recently moved in.

"It's that side," Sybil announced and waved toward the backyard of the house where numerous children of various ages were playing with the customary racket.

"Vincent," Sybil added, out of the blue. "Maybe I don't have the accent right, but it is Vincent. But it is connected with all this. Incidentally, it is the land that's causing the trouble, not the house itself."

The area Sybil had pointed out just a moment before as being the center of the activities was the exact spot where the old barn had once stood.

"It's nothing against this house," Sybil said to Mrs. Trausch, "but something out the past. I'd say 1925. The name Vincent is important. There's fire involved. I don't feel a person here but an influence...a thing. This is different from our usual work. It's the upper part of the building where the evil was."

I then eased Sybil into a chair in the children's room and we grouped ourselves silently around her, waiting for some form of manifestation to take place.

Mrs. Trausch was nervously biting her lips, but otherwise bearing up under what must have been the culmination of a long and great strain for her. Sybil was relaxing now, but she was still awake.

"There's some connection with a child," she said now, "a lost child...1925...the child was found here, dead."

"Whose child is it?" I pressed.

"Connected with Vincent...dark child...nine years old...a boy...the children here have to be careful..."

"Does this child have any connection with the house?"

"He is lost."

"Can you seem him; can he see you?"

"I see him. Corner...the barn. He broke his neck. Two men...hit the child, they didn't like children, you see...they left him...until he was found...woman... Fairley...name...Pete Fairley..."

By now Sybil had glided into a semi-trance and I kept up the barrage of questions to reconstruct the drama in the barn.

"Do they live here?" I inquired.

"Nobody lives here. Woman walked from the water to find the boy. He's dead. She has connection with the two men who killed him. Maniacs, against children."

"What is her connection with the boy?"

"She had him, then she lost him. She looked after him."

"Who were the boy's parents then?"

"Fairley. Peter Fairley. 1925."

Sybil sounded almost like a robot now, giving the requested information.

"What happened to the woman?" I wanted to know.

"Mad...she found the boy dead, went to the men... there was a fight...she fell in the water...men are here... there's a fire..."

"Who were these men?"

"Vincent...brothers...nobody is very healthy in this farm...don't like women..."

"Where did the child come from?"

"Lost...from the riverside..."

"Can you see the woman?"

"A little...the boy I can see clearly."

It occurred to me how remarkable it was for Sybil to speak of a woman who had fallen into the water when the apparition Mrs. Trausch had seen had had wet hair. No one had discussed anything about the house in front of Sybil, of course. So she had no way of knowing that the area had once been a farm, or that a barn had stood there where she felt the disturbances centered. No one had told her that it was a child the people in the house kept hearing upstairs.

"The woman is out of tempo," Sybil explained. "That makes it difficult to see her. The boy is frightened."

Sybil turned her attention to the little one now and, with my prodding, started to send him away from there.

"Peter go out and play with the children...outside," she pleaded.

"And his parents...they are looking for him," I added.

"He wants the children here to go with him," Sybil came back. Mrs. Trausch started to swallow nervously.

"Tell him he is to go first," I instructed.

"He wants to have the fair woman come with him," Sybil explained and I suggest that the two of them go.

"She understands," Sybil explained, "and is willing, but he is difficult. He wants the children."

I kept pleading with the ghost boy. Nothing is harder than dealing with a lost one so young.

"Join the other children. They are already outside," I said.

There was a moment of silence, interrupted only by the muffled sounds of living children playing outside.

"Are they still here?" I cautiously inquired a little later.

"Can't see them now, but I can see the building. Two floors. Nobody there now."

I decided it was the time to break the trance which had gradually deepened and at this point was full trance. A moment later Sybil Leek "was back."

Now we discussed the matter freely and I researched the information just obtained.

As I understood it, there had been this boy, age nine, Peter Fairley by name, who had somehow gotten away from his nanny, a fair woman. He had run into a farm and gone up to the upper story of a barn where two brothers named Vincent had killed him. When the woman found him, she went mad. Then she looked for the men whom she knew, and there was a fight during which she was drowned. The two of them are ghosts because they are lost; the boy lost in a strange place and the woman lost in guilt for having lost the boy.

Mrs. Kunze and Mrs. Trausch volunteered to go through the local register to check out he names and to see if anything bearing on this tragedy could be found in print.

Unfortunately the death records for the year 1925 were incomplete, as Mrs. Trausch discovered at the Santa Ana *Register*; and this was true even at the local Hall of Records in the court house. The County Sheriff's Office was of no help either. But they found an interesting item in the *Register* of January 1, 1925:

Deputies probe tale of "burial" in orange grove. Several Deputy Sheriffs, in a hurried call to Stanton late last night, failed to find any trace of several men who were reported to be "burying something" in a isolated orange grove near that town, as reported to them at the Sheriff's office here.

Officers rushing to the scene were working under the impression that a murder had been committed and that the body was being interred, but a thorough search in that vicinity failed to reveal anything unusual, according to a report made by Chief Criminal Deputy Ed McClellan, on their return. Deputy Sheriffs Joe Scott and Joe Ryan accompanied McClellan.

Mrs. Kunze, a long-time resident of the area and quite familiar with its peculiarities, commented that such a burial in an isolated orange grove could easily have been covered up by men familiar with the irrigating system, who could have flooded that section, thus erasing all evidence of a newly made grave.

I wondered about the name Peter Fairley. Of course I did not expect to find the boy listed somewhere, but was there a Fairley family in these parts in 1925?

There was.

In the Santa Ana County Directories, S.W. Section, for the year 1925, there is a listing for a Frank Fairley, carpenter, at 930 W. Bishop, Santa Ana. The listing continues at the same address the following year also. It was not in the 1924 edition of the directory, however, so perhaps the Fairleys were new to the area then.

At the outset of the visit Mrs. Leek had mentioned a Felix connected with the area. Again consulting the County Directories for 1925, we found several members of the Felix family listed. Andres Felix, rancher, at Golden West Avenue and Bolsa Chica Road, post office Westminster, Adolph and Miguel Felix, laborers, at the same address—perhaps brothers—and Florentino Felix, also a rancher, at a short distance from the farm of Andres Felix. The listing also appears in 1926.

No Vincent or Vincente, however. But of course not all members of the family need to have been listed. The directories generally list only principals, i.e., those gainfully employed or owners of business or property. Then again, there may have been two hired hands by that name, if Vincente was a given name rather than a Christian name.

The 1911 *History of Orange County*, by Samuel Armor, described the areas as consisting of a store, church, school, and a few residences only. It was then called Bolsa, and the main area was used as ranch and stock land. The area abounds in fish hatcheries also, which started around 1921 by a Japanese named Akiyama. Thus was explained the existence of water holes in the area along with fish tanks, as well as natural lakes.

With the help of Mrs. Kunze, I came across still another interesting record.

According to the *Los Angeles Times* of January 22, 1956, "an ancient residence at 14611 Golden West Street, Westminster, built 85 years ago, was razed for subdivision."

This was undoubtedly the farm residence and land on which the development we had been investigating was later built.

And there we have the evidence. Three names were given by our psychic friend: Felix, Vincent, and Peter Fairley. Two of them are found in the printed record, with some difficulty, and with the help of local researchers familiar with the source material, which neither Mrs. Leek nor I was prior to the visit to the haunted house. The body of the woman could easily have been disposed of without leaving a trace by dumping it into one of the fish tanks or other water holes in the area, or perhaps in the nearby Santa Ana River.

About a month after our investigation, the Trausch family moved back to Huntington Beach, leaving the Westminster house to someone else who might some day appear on the scene.

But Carole Trausch informed me that from the moment of our investigation onward, not a single incident had marred the peace of their house.

So I can only assume that Sybil and I were able to help the two unfortunate ghosts out into the open, the boy to find his parents, no doubt also on his side of the veil, and the woman to find peace and forgiveness for her negligence in allowing the boy to be killed.

It is not always possible for the psychic investigator to leave a haunted house free of its unseen inhabitants, and when it does happen, then the success is its own reward.

✳ 72

The Ghostly Usher of Minneapolis

FOR THIS ACCOUNT, I am indebted to a twenty-two-year-old creative production assistant in a Minneapolis advertising agency, by the name of Deborah Turner. Miss Turner got hooked on some of my books, and started to look around in the Twin Cities for cases that might whet my appetite for ghost hunting. Being also musically inclined with an interest in theater, it was natural that she should gravitate toward the famed Guthrie Theater, named after the famous director, which is justly known as the pride of Minneapolis. At the theater she met some other young people, also in their early twenties, and shared her interest in psychic phenomena with them. Imagine her surprise

when she discovered that she had stumbled upon a most interesting case.

Richard Miller was born in Manhattan, Kansas in 1951. Until age ten, he lived there with his father, a chemist in government service. Then his father was transferred to England, and Richard spent several years going to school in that country. After that, he and his family returned to the United States and moved to Edina. This left Richard not only with a vivid recollection of England, but also somewhat of an accent which, together with his childhood in Kansas, gave him somewhat unusual personality.

His strange accent became the subject of ridicule by other students at Edina Morningside High School where he went to school, and it did not go down well with the shy, introspective young man. In the tenth grade at this school, he made friends with another young man, Fred Koivumaki, and a good and close relationship sprang up between the two boys. It gave Fred a chance to get to know Richard better than most of the other fellows in school.

As if the strange accent were not enough to make him stand out from the other boys in the area. Richard was given to sudden, jerky movements, which made him a good target for sly remarks and jokes of his fellows students. The Millers did not have much of a social life, since they also did not quite fit into the pattern of life in the small town of Edina.

During the years spent in an English school, Richard had known corporal punishment, since it is still part of the system in some English schools. This terrified him, and perhaps contributed towards his inability to express himself fully and freely. Somehow he never acquired a girlfriend as the other students did, and this, too, bothered him a lot. He couldn't for the world understand why people didn't like him more, and often talked about it to his friend Fred.

When both young men reached the age of sixteen, they went to the Guthrie Theater where they got jobs as ushers. They worked at it for two years. Richard Miller got along well with the other ushers, but developed a close friendship only with Fred Koivumaki and another fellow, Barry Peterson. It is perhaps a strange quirk of fate that both Richard Miller and Barry Peterson never reached manhood, but died violently long before their time.

However, Richard's parents decided he should go to the university, and quit his job. In order to oblige his parents, Richard Miller gave up the job as usher and moved into Territorial Hall for his first year at the university.

However, the change did not increase his ability to express himself or to have a good social life. Also, he seemed to have felt that he was catering to his parent's wishes, and became more antagonistic toward them. Then, too, it appears that these students also made him the butt of their jokes. Coincidentally, he developed a vision problem, with cells breaking off his retinas and floating in the inner humor of the eye. This caused him to see spots before his eyes, a condition for which there is no cure. However, he enjoyed skiing because he knew how to do it well, and joined the university ski club.

But Richard's bad luck somehow was still with him. On a trip to Colorado, he ran into a tree, luckily breaking only his skis. When summer came to the area, Richard rode his bike down a large dirt hill into rough ground and tall weeds at the bottom injuring himself in the process. Fortunately, a motorcyclist came by just then, and got Richard to the emergency ward of a nearby hospital. All this may have contributed towards an ultimate breakdown; or, as the students would call it, Richard just "flipped out."

He was hospitalized at the university hospital and was allowed home only on weekends. During that time he was on strong medication, but when the medication did not improve his condition, the doctor took him off it and sent him home.

The following February 4, he decided to try skiing again, and asked his father to take him out to Buck Hill, one of the skiing areas not far from town. But to his dismay Richard discovered that he couldn't ski anymore, and this really depressed him. When he got home, there was a form letter waiting for him from the university, advising him that because he had skipped all the final exams due to his emotional problems at the time, he had received Fs in all his classes and was on probation.

All this seemed too much for him. He asked his mother for $40, ostensibly to buy himself new ski boots. Then he drove down to Sears on Lake Street, where he bought a high-powered pistol and shells. That was on Saturday, and he killed himself in the car. He wasn't found until Monday morning, when the lot clearing crew found him with most of his head shot off.

Richard Miller was given a quiet burial in Fort Snelling National Cemetery. His parents, Dr. and Mrs. Byron S. Miller, requested that memorials to the Minnesota Association for Mental Health be sent instead of flowers. Richard's mother had always felt that her son's best years had been spent as an usher at the Guthrie Theater; consequently he was cremated wearing his Guthrie Theater blazer. The date was February 7, and soon enough the shock of the young man's untimely death wore off, and only his immediate family and the few friends he had made remembered Richard Miller.

A few weeks after the death of the young usher, a woman seated in the theater in an aisle seat came up to the usher in charge of this aisle and asked him to stop the other usher from walking up and down during the play. The usher in charge was shocked, since he had been at the top of the aisle and had seen no one walk up and down. All the other ushers were busy in their respective aisles. However, the lady insisted that she had seen this young man walk up and down the aisle during the play. The usher in charge asked her to describe what she had seen. She described Richard Miller, even to the mole on his cheek. The incident is on record with the Guthrie Theater. *Minneapolis Tribune* columnist Robert T. Smith interviewed Craig Scherfenberg, director of audience development at the theater, concerning the incident. "There was no one in our employ at the time who fit the description," the director said, "but it fit the dead young man perfectly."

In the summer several years later, two ushers were asked to spend the night in the theater to make sure some troublesome air conditioning equipment was fully repaired. The Guthrie Theater has a thrust stage with openings onto the stage on all three sides; these openings lead to an actors' waiting area, which in turn has a door opening onto an area used as a lounge during intermissions.

The two young men were sitting in this waiting area with both doors open, and they were the only people in the building. At 1 o'clock in the morning, they suddenly heard the piano on stage begin to play. Stunned by this, they watched in silence when they saw a cloud-like form floating through the lounge door and hovering in the center of the room. One of the ushers thought the form was staring at him. As quickly as they could gather their wits they left the room.

One of Deborah Turner's friends had worked late one evening shortly after this incident, repairing costumes needed for the next day's performance. She and a friend were relaxing in the stage area while waiting for a ride home. As she glanced into the house, she noticed that the lights on the aisle that had been the dead usher's were going on and off, as if someone were walking slowly up and down. She went to the ladies' room a little later, and suddenly she heard pounding on one wall, eventually circling the room and causing her great anxiety, since she knew that she and her friend were the only people in the house.

When the Guthrie Theater put on a performance of *Julius Caesar*, one of the extras was an older woman by the name of Mary Parez. She freely admitted that she was psychic and had been able to communicate with her dead sister. She told her fellow actors that she could sense Richard Miller's presence in the auditorium. Somehow she thought that the ghost would make himself known during Mark Antony's famous speech to the Romans after Caesar's death.

The scene was lit primarily by torches when the body of Julius Caesar was brought upon the stage. Jason Harlen, a young usher, and one of his colleagues, were watching the performance from different vantage points in the theater. One man was in one of the tunnels leading to the stage, the other in the audience. Both had been told of Mary Parez's prediction, but were disappointed when nothing happened at that time. In boredom, they began to look around the theater. Independently of each other, they saw smoke rising to the ceiling, and shaping itself into a human form. Both young men said that the form had human eyes.

The aisle that the late Richard Miller worked was number eighteen. Two women in the acting company of *Julius Caesar*, named Terry and Gigi, complained that they had much trouble with the door at the top of aisle eighteen for no apparent reason. Bruce Benson, who now worked aisle eighteen, told that people complained of an usher walking up and down the aisle during performances. Bruce Margolis, who works the stage door, leaves the building after everyone else. When he was there one night all alone, the elevator began running on its own.

All this talk about a ghost induced some of the young ushers to try and make contact with him via the Ouija board. Dan Burg, head usher, took a board with him to the stage, and along with colleagues Bruce Benson and Scott Hurner, tried to communicate with the ghost. For a while nothing happened. Then, all of a sudden the board spelled, "Tiptoe to the tech room." When they asked why, the board spelled the word ghost. They wanted to know which tech room the ghost was referring to: downstairs? "No," the communicator informed them, "upstairs." Then the board signed off with the initials MIL. At that, one of the men tipped over the board and wanted nothing further to do with it.

In November of the next year, an usher working at the theater told columnist Robert Smith, "It was after a night performance. Everyone had left the theater but me. I had forgotten my gloves and returned to retrieve them. I glanced into the theater and saw an usher standing in one of the aisles. It was him. He saw me and left. I went around to that aisle and couldn't find anything."

There is also an opera company connected with the Guthrie Theater. One night, one of the ladies working for the opera company was driving home from the Guthrie Theater. Suddenly she felt a presence beside her in the car. Terrified, she looked around, and became aware of a young man with dark curly hair, glasses, and a mole on his face. He wore a blue coat with something red on the pocket— the Guthrie Theater blazer. With a sinking feeling, she realized that she was looking at the ghost of Richard Miller.

For two years after, however, no new reports have come in concerning the unfortunate young man. Could it be that he has finally realized that there await him greater opportunities in the next dimension, and though his life on earth was not very successful, his passing into the spiritual life might give him most of the opportunities his life on earth had denied him? At any rate things have now quieted down in aisle eighteen at the Guthrie Theater, in Minneapolis, Minnesota.

✳ 73

The Ghostly Adventures of a North Carolina Family

TONI S. IS YOUNG WOMAN of good educational background, a psychologist by profession, who works for a large business concern. She is not given to daydreaming or fantasizing. She is the daughter of Mrs. Elizabeth K., or rather the daughter of Mrs. K.'s second marriage. The thrice-married Mrs. K. is a North Carolina lady of upper middle-class background, a socially prominent woman who has traveled extensively.

Neither was the kind of person who pulls out a Ouija board to while away the time, or to imagine that every shadow cast upon the wall is necessarily a ghost. Far from it; but both ladies were taken aback by what transpired in their old house at the town of East La Porte, built on very old ground.

Originally built about fifty years ago, it was to be a home for Mrs. K.'s father who then owned a large lumber company, and the tract of timber surrounding the house extended all the way across the Blue Ridge Parkway. Undoubtedly an older dwelling had stood on the same spot, for Mrs. K. has unearthed what appears to be the remains of a much older structure. The house was renovated and a second story was built on about thirty-five years ago. At that time, her father had lost one leg as the result of an automobile accident, and retired from his lumber mill activities to East La Porte, where he intended to spend his remaining years in peace and quiet. He had liked the climate to begin with, and there was a sawmill nearby, which he could oversee. The house is a doubleboxed frame house, perhaps fifty-by-fifty square, containing around fifteen rooms.

Mrs. K.'s family refer to it as the summer cottage, even though it was full-sized house; but they had other houses that they visited from time to time, and the house in East La Porte was merely one of their lesser properties. Downstairs there is a thirty-by-fifteen-foot reception room, richly carpeted with chestnut from Furnace Creek, one of the sawmills owned by the family. It was in this room that Mrs. K.'s father eventually passed on.

The house itself is built entirely from lumber originating in one of the family's sawmills. There was a center hall downstairs and two thirty-foot rooms, then there were three smaller rooms, a bath, a card room, and what the family referred to as a sleeping porch. On the other side of the center hall was a lounge, a kitchen, and a laundry porch. Running alongside the south and east walls of the house is a veranda. Upstairs is reached by a very gentle climb up the stairs in the middle of the floor, and as one climbs the steps, there is a bedroom at the head of the stairs. In back of the stairs, there are two more bedrooms,

then a bathroom, and finally a storage room; to the left of the stairs are three bedrooms.

The attic is merely a structure to hold up the roof, and does not contain any rooms. There is a cellar, but it contains only a furnace. Although the acreage surrounding the house runs to about sixty acres, only three acres belong to the house proper. All around the house, even today, there is nothing but wilderness, and to get to the nearest town, East La Porte, one needs a car.

Mrs. K. enjoyed traveling, and didn't mind living in so many residences; in fact, she considered the house at East La Porte merely a way-station in her life. She was born in Alaska, where the family also had a sawmill. Her early years were spent traveling from one sawmill to another, accompanying her parents on business trips.

Under the circumstances, they were never very long in residence at the house in East La Porte. Any attempt to find out about the background of the land on which the house stood proved frutiless. This was Cherokee territory, but there is little written history concerning the time before the Cherokees. Anything remotely connected with physic phenomena was simply not discussed in the circles in which Mrs. K. grew up.

The first time Mrs. K. noticed anything peculiar about the house was after her father had passed away. She and her father had been particularly close, since her mother had died when she was still a small child. That particular day, she was sitting at her father's desk in the part of the house where her father had died. The furniture had been rearranged in the room, and the desk stood where her father's bed had previously been. Her father was on her mind, and so she thought it was all her imagination when she became aware of a distinctive sound like someone walking on crutches down the hall.

Since Mrs. K. knew for a fact that she was the only person in the house at the time, she realized that something out of the ordinary was happening. As the footsteps came closer, she recognized her father's tread. Then she heard her father's familiar voice say, "Baby." It came from the direction of the door. This gave her a feeling of great peace, for she had been troubled by emotional turmoil in her life. She felt that her late father was trying to console her, and give her spiritual strength.

Nothing happened until about a year later. It was August, and she had been in New York for awhile. As she was coming down the stairs of the house, she found herself completely enveloped with the fragrance of lilacs. She had not put any perfume on, and there were no lilacs blooming in August. No one was seen, and yet Mrs. K. felt a presence although she was sure it was benign and loving.

A short time later, she was sitting at a desk in what used to be her father's study upstairs, thinking about nothing in particular. Again she was startled by the sound of footsteps, but this time they were light steps, and certainly not her father's. Without thinking, she called out to her daughter, "Oh, Toni, is that you?" telling her daughter that she was upstairs.

But then the steps stopped, and no one came. Puzzled, Mrs. K. went to the head of the stairs, called out again, but when she saw no one, she realized that it was not a person of flesh and blood who had walked upon the stairs.

During the same month, Mrs. K.'s daughter Toni was also at the house. Her first experience with the unseen happened that month, in an upstairs bedroom.

She was asleep one night when someone shook her hard and said, "Hey, you!" Frightened, she did not open her eyes, yet with her inner eyes, she "saw" a man of about fifty years of age. She was much too frightened to actually look, so instead she dove underneath the covers and lay there with her eyes shut. There was nothing further that night.

In the fall of the same year, Toni decided to have a pajama party and spent the night with a group of friends. Her mother had gone to bed because of a cold. Toni and her friends returned to the house from bowling at around 11:30. They were downstairs, talking about various things, when all of a sudden one of Toni's girlfriends said, "Your mother is calling you."

Toni went out into the hallway, turning on the lights as she approached the stairs. Footsteps were coming down the stairs, audible not only to her but to her two girlfriends who had followed her into the house. And then they heard a voice out of nowhere calling out, "Toni, it is time to go to bed." It was a voice Toni had never heard before.

She went up the stairs and into her mother's room, but her mother was fast asleep, and had not been out of bed. The voice had been a woman's, but it had sounded strangely empty, as if someone were speaking to her from far away.

The following years, Toni was married and left the house. Under the circumstances, Mrs. K. decided to sublease part of the house to a tenant. This turned out to be a pleasant woman by the name of Alice H. and her husband. The lady had been injured and was unable to go far up the mountain where she and her husband were building a summer home at the time. Although Mrs. K. and her new tenants were not associated in any way except that they were sharing the same house, she and Alice H. became friendly after a while. One afternoon, Alice H. came to Mrs. K.'s apartment in order to invite her to have supper with her and her husband that night. She knew that Mrs. K. was in her apartment at the time because she heard her light footsteps inside the apartment. When there was no reply from inside the apartment Alice was puzzled, so she descended to the ground floor, thinking that perhaps Mrs. K. was downstairs.

Sure enough, as she arrived downstairs, she saw a shadow of what she assumed to be Mrs. K.'s figure walking along the hallway. She followed this shadowy woman all the way from the ground floor guest room, through the bath into Mrs. K.'s bedroom, and then through another hallway and back to the bedroom. All the time she saw the shadowy figure, she also heard light footsteps. But when she came to the bedroom again, it suddenly got very cold and she felt all the blood rush to her head. She ran back to her husband in their own apartment, and informed him that there was a stranger in Mrs. K.'s rooms.

But there was no one in the house at the time except themselves, for Mrs. K. had gone off to Asheville for the day. The experience shook Alice H. to the point where she could no longer stand the house, and shortly afterward she and her husband left for another cottage.

In August of the same year, Toni S. returned to her mother's house. But now she was a married lady, and she was coming for a visit only. Her husband was a car dealer, in business with his father. At the time of the incident, he was not in the house. It was raining outside, and Toni was cleaning the woodwork in the house.

Suddenly her Pekinese dog came running down the stairs, nearly out of her mind with terror, and barking at the top of her lungs. Toni thought the dog had been frightened by a mouse, so she picked her up and proceeded up the stairs. But the dog broke away from her and ran behind the door. All of a sudden, Toni felt very cold. She kept walking down the hall and into the room, where there was a desk standing near the window. Someone was going through papers on her desk as if looking for a certain piece of paper, putting papers aside and continuing to move them! But there was no one there. No one, that is, who could be seen. Yet the papers were moving as if someone were actually shuffling them. It was 2 o'clock in the afternoon, and the light was fairly good.

Suddenly, one letter was pulled out of the piles of papers on the desk, as if to catch her attention. Toni picked it up and read it. It was a letter her father had sent her in February, at the time she got married, warning her that the marriage would not work out after all, and to make sure to call him if anything went wrong. Things *had* gone wrong since, and Toni understood the significance of what she had just witnessed.

At that very moment, the room got warm again, and everything returned to normal. But who was it standing at her desk, pulling out her father's letter? The one person who had been close to her while he was in the flesh was her grandfather.

During Toni's visit at the house, her husband, now her ex-husband, also had some uncanny experiences. Somebody would wake him in the middle of the night by calling out, "Wake up!" or "Hey you!" This went on night after night, until both Toni and her husband awoke around two in the morning because of the sound of loud laughing, as if a big party were going on downstairs.

Toni thought that the neighbors were having a party, and decided to go down and tell them to shut up. She looked out the window and realized that the neighbors were also fast asleep. So she picked up her dog and went downstairs, and as she arrived at the bottom of the stairs, she saw a strange light, and the laughing kept going on and on. There were voices, as if many people were talking all at once, having a social. In anger, Toni called out to them to shut up, she wanted to sleep, and all of a sudden the house was quiet, quiet as the grave. Evidently, Southern ghosts have good manners!

After her daughter left, Mrs. K. decided to sublease part of the house to a group of young men from a national fraternity who were students at a nearby university. One of the students, Mitchell, was sleeping in a double bed, and he was all alone in the house. Because the heat wasn't turned up, it being rather costly, he decided to sleep in a sleeping bag, keeping warm in this manner. He went to sleep with his pillow at the head of the bed, which meant due east, and his feet going due west. When he awoke, he found himself facing in the opposite direction, with his head where his feet should have been, and vice versa. It didn't surprise the young man though, because from the very first day his fraternity brothers had moved into the house, they had heard the sounds of an unseen person walking up and down the stairs.

One of their teachers, a pilot who had been a colonel in the Korean War, also had an experience at the house. One day while he was staying there, he was walking up the stairs, and when he reached about the halfway mark, someone picked him up by the scruff of his neck and pushed him up the rest of the way to the landing.

But the night to remember was Halloween Eve. Mrs. K. was in the house, and the night was living up to its reputation: it sounded as if someone wearing manacles were moving about. Mrs. K. was downstairs, sleeping in one of the bunk beds, and a noise came from an upstairs hall. This went on for about two hours straight. It sounded as if someone with a limp were pulling himself along, dragging a heavy chain. Mrs. K. was puzzled about this, since the noise did not sound anything like her father. She looked into the background of the area, and discovered that in the pre-colonial period, there had been some Spanish settlers in the area, most of whom kept slaves.

Toni S. takes her involvement with hauntings in stride. She has had psychic experiences ever since she can remember; nothing frightening, you understand, only such things as events before they actually happen—if someone is going to be sick in the family, for instance, or who might be calling. Entering old houses is always a risky business for her: she picks up vibrations from the past, and sometimes she simply can't stand what she feels and must leave at once.

But she thought she had left the more uncanny aspects of the hauntings behind when she came to New York to work. Somehow the wound up residing in a house that is one hundred ten years old.

After a while, she became aware of an old man who liked sitting down on her bed. She couldn't actually see him, but he appeared to her more like a shadow. So she asked some questions, but nobody ever died in the apartment and it was difficult for Toni to accept the reality of the phenomena under the circumstances. As a trained psychologist, she had to approach all this on a skeptical level, and yet there did not seem to be any logical answers.

Soon afterward, she became aware of footsteps where no one was walking, and of doors closing by themselves, which were accompanied by the definite feeling of another personality present in the rooms.

On checking with former neighbors upstairs, who had lived in the house for seventeen years, Toni discovered that they too had heard the steps and doors closing by themselves. However, they had put no faith in ghosts, and dismissed the matter as simply an old structure settling. Toni tried her innate psychic powers, and hoped that the resident ghost would communicate with her. She began to sense that it was a woman with a very strong personality. By a process of elimination, Toni came to the conclusion that the last of the original owners of the house, a Mrs. A., who had been a student of the occult, was the only person who could be the presence she was feeling in the rooms.

Toni doesn't mind sharing her rooms with a ghost, except for the fact that appliances in the house have a way of breaking down without reason. Then, too, she has a problem with some of her friends; they complain of feelings extremely uncomfortable and cold, and of being watched by someone they cannot see. What was she to do? But then Toni recalled how she had lived through the frightening experiences at East La Porte, North Carolina, and somehow come to terms with the haunts there. No ordinary Long Island ghost was going to dispossess her!

With that resolve, Toni decided to ignore the presence as much as she could, and go about her business—the business of the living.

✳ 74

Reba's Ghosts

REBA B. IS A SENSITIVE, fragile-looking lady with two grown children. She was born in Kentucky, and hails from an old family in which the name Reba has occurred several times before. She works as a medical secretary and doctor's assistant, and nowadays shares her home with three cats, her children having moved away. Mrs. B., who is divorced, wondered whether perhaps she had a particular affinity for ghosts, seeing that she has encountered denizens of the other world so many times, in so many houses. It wasn't that it bothered her to any extent, but she had gotten used to living by herself except for her cats, and the idea of having to share her home with individuals who could pop in and out at will, and who might hang around her at times when she could not see them, did not contribute to her comfort.

Her psychic ability goes back to age three, when she was living with her grandparents in Kentucky. Even then she had a vivid feeling of presences all around her, not that she actually say them with her eyes. It was more a sensitivity to unseen forces surrounding her—an awareness that she was never quite alone. As soon as she would go to bed as a child, she would see the figure of a man bending over her, a man she did not know. After a long period of this she wondered if she was dreaming, but in her heart she knew she was not. However, she was much too young to worry about such things, and as she grew up, her ability became part of her character, and she began to accept it as "normal."

This incident begins when she happened to be living in Cincinnati, already divorced. Her mother shared an old house with her, a house that was built around 1900; it had all the earmarks of the post-Victorian era: brass door knobs, little doorbells that were to be turned by hand, and the various trimmings of that age. The house consisted of three floors; the ground floor contained an apartment, and the two ladies took the second and third floor of the house. Reba had her bedroom on the third floor; it was the only bedroom up there situated in the middle of the floor.

One day she was coming up those stairs, and was approaching the window when she saw a man standing by it. He vanished as she came closer, and she gave this no more thought until a few days later. At that time she happened to be lying in bed, propped up and reading a book.

She happened to look up and saw a man who had apparently come up the stairs. She noticed his features fully: his eyes were brown, and he also had brown hair. Immediately she could sense that he was very unhappy, even angry. It wasn't that she heard his voice, but somehow his thoughts communicated themselves to her, mind to mind.

From her bed she could see him approach, walking out to a small landing and standing in front of her door. Next to her room was a storage room. He looked straight at Reba, and at that moment she received the impression that he was very angry because she and her mother were in the house, because they had moved into *his* house.

Although Reba B. was fully conscious and aware of what was going on, she rejected the notion that she was hearing the thoughts of a ghost. But it did her no good; over and over she heard him say or think, "Out, out, I want you out, I don't want you here." At that moment he raised his arm and pointed outward, as if to emphasize his point. The next moment he was gone. Reba thought for a moment whether she should tell her mother whose bedroom was downstairs. She decided against it, since her mother had a heart condition and because she herself wasn't too sure the incident had been quite real. Also, she was a little frightened and did not want to recall the incident any more than she had to. After a while, she went off to sleep.

Not too long after that her daughter, who was then fourteen, and eleven-year-old son were home with her from school. It was a weekend, and she wanted the children to enjoy it. Consequently, she did not tell them anything about her ghostly experience. She had gone into the front storage room, when she thought she saw someone sitting on the boxes stacked in the storage area.

At first she refused to acknowledge it, and tried to look away, but when her gaze returned to the area, the man was still sitting there, quietly staring at her. Again she turned her head, and when she looked back, he was gone. The following weekend, her children were with her again. They had hardly arrived when her daughter returned from the same storage room asked, "Mother, is there someone sitting in there?" and all Reba could do was nod, and acknowledge that there was. Her daughter then described the stranger and the description matched what her mother had seen. Under the circumstances, Reba B. freely discussed the matter with her children. But nothing further was done concerning the matter, and no inquiries were made as to the background of the house.

Summer came, and another spring and another summer, and they got into the habit of using the entrance at the side of the house. There were some shrubs in that area, and in order to enter the apartment in which they lived, they had to come up the stairs where they would have a choice of either walking into the living room on the second floor, or continuing on to the third floor where Reba's bedroom was. The tenant who had the ground floor apartment also had his own entrance.

One warm summer evening, she suddenly felt the stranger come into the downstairs door and walk up the stairs. When she went to check, she saw nothing. Still, she *knew* he was in the house. A few days passed, and again she sensed the ghost nearby. She looked, and as her eyes peered down into the hall, she saw him walking down the hall towards her. While she was thinking, "I am imagining this, there is no such thing as a ghost," she slowly walked toward him. As he kept approaching her, she walked right through him! It was an eerie sensation: for a moment she could not see, and then he was gone. The encounter did not help Reba to keep her composure, but there was little she could do about it.

Many times she sensed his presence in the house without seeing him, but early one evening, on a Sunday, just as it got dark, she found herself in the living room on the second floor of the house. She had turned on the television set, which was facing her, and she kept the volume down so as not to disturb her mother, whose room was on the same floor. She had altered the furniture in the room somewhat, in order to be closer to the television set, and there were two lounge chairs, one of which she used, and the other one close by, near the television set, so that another person could sit in it and also view the screen. She was just watching television, when she sensed the stranger come up the stairs again and walk into the living room. Next he sat down in the empty chair close to Reba, but this time the atmosphere was different from that first encounter near the door of her room. He seemed more relaxed and comfortable, and Reba was almost glad that he was there keeping her company. Somehow she felt that he was glad to be in the room with her, and that he was less lonely because of her. He was no longer angry; he just wanted to visit.

Reba looked at the stranger's face and noticed his rather high-bridged nose. She also had a chance to study his clothes; he was wearing a brown suit, rather modern in style. Even though the house was quite old, this man was not from the early years, but his clothes seemed to indicate a comparatively recent period. As she sat there, quietly studying the ghost, she got the feeling that he had owned the house at one time, and that their living room had been the sitting room where the ghost and his wife had received people.

Reba somehow knew that his wife had been very pretty—a fair-complexioned blonde, and she was shown a fireplace in the living room with a small love seat of the French Provincial type next to it, drawn up quite close to the fireplace. She saw this in her mind's eye, as if the man were showing her something from his past. At the same time, Reba knew that some tragedy had occurred between the ghost and his wife.

Suddenly, panic rose in Reba, as she realized she was sharing the evening with a ghost. Somehow her fears communicated themselves to her phantom visitor, for as she looked close, he had vanished.

As much as she had tried to keep these things from her mother, she could not. Her mother owned an antique

covered casserole made of silver, which she kept at the head of her bed. The bed was a bookcase bed, and she used to lift the cover and put in receipts, tickets, and papers whenever she wanted.

One day, Reba and her mother found themselves at the far end of her bedroom on the second floor. Her bed was up against the wall, without any space between it and the wall. As the two ladies were looking in the direction of the bed, they suddenly saw the silver casserole being picked up, put down on the bed, turned upside down and everything spilled out of it. It didn't fly through the air, but moved rather slowly, as if some unseen force were holding it. Although her mother had seen it, she did not say anything because she felt it would be unwise to alarm her daughter; but later on she admitted having seen the whole thing. It was ironic how the two women were trying to spare each other's feelings—yet both knew that what they had witnessed was real.

The ghost did not put in any further appearances after the dramatic encounter in the living room. About a year later, the two ladies moved away into another old house far from this one. But shortly before they did, Reba's mother was accosted on the street by a strange middle-aged lady, who asked her whether she was living in the house just up the street. When Reba's mother acknowledged it, the lady informed her the house had once belonged to her parents. Were they happy in it, Reba's mother wanted to know. "Very happy," the stranger assured her, "Especially my father." It occurred to Reba that it might have been he who she had encountered in the house; someone so attached to his home that he did not want to share it with anyone else, especially flesh-and-blood people like her mother and herself.

The new home the ladies moved into proved "alive" with unseen vibrations also, but by now they didn't care. Reba realized that she had a special gift. If ghosts wanted her company, there was little she could do about it.

She had a friend who worked as a motorcycle patrolman, by the name of John H. He was a young man and well-liked on the force. One day he chased a speeder—and was killed in the process. At the time, Reba was still married, but she had known John for quite a few years before. They were friends, although not really close ones, and she had been out of touch with him for some time. One morning, she suddenly sensed his presence in the room with her; it made no sense, yet she was positive it was John H. After a while, the presence left her. She remarked on this to her mother and got a blank stare in return. The young man had been killed on the previous night, but Reba could not have known this. The news had come on the radio just that morning, but apparently Reba had had advance news of a more direct kind.

Reba B. shared her interest in the occult with an acquaintance, newscaster Bill G. In his position as a journalist, he had to be particularly careful in expressing an opinion on so touchy a subject as ESP. They had met a local restaurant one evening, and somehow the conversation had gotten around to ghosts.

When Mr. G. noticed her apprehension at being one of the "selected" ones who could see ghosts, he told her about another friend, a young medium who had an apartment not far away. One evening she walked out onto her patio, and saw a man in old-fashioned clothes approach her. The man tried to talk to her, but she could not hear anything. Suddenly he disappeared before her eyes. The young lady thought she was having a nervous breakdown, and consulted a psychiatrist; she even went into a hospital to have herself examined, but there was nothing wrong with her. When she returned to her home and went out onto the patio again, she saw the same ghostly apparition once more. This time she did not panic, but instead studied him closely. When he disappeared she went back into her apartment, and decided to make some inquiries about the place. It was then that she discovered that a long time ago, a man of that description had been hanged from a tree in her garden.

"These things *do* happen," Bill G. assured Reba, and asked her not to be ashamed or afraid of them. After all, ghosts are people too. Since then, Reba had come to terms with her ghostly encounters. She has even had an experience with a ghost cat—but that is another story.

✳ 75

Henny from Brooklyn

Clinton Street, Brooklyn is one of the oldest sections of that borough, pleasantly middle-class at one time, still amongst Brooklyn's best neighborhoods, as neighborhoods go. The house in question is in the 300 block, and consists of four stories. There was a basement floor, then a parlor floor a few steps up, as is the usual custom with brownstone houses, with a third and fourth floor above it. If one preferred, one could call the third floor the fourth floor, in which case the basement becomes the first floor; but no matter how one called it, there were four levels in this brownstone, all capable of serving as apartments for those who wished to live there. The house was more than one hundred years old at the time of the events herein described, and the records are somewhat dim beyond a certain point.

In the 1960s, the house was owned by some off-beat people, about whom little was known. Even the Hall of Records isn't of much help, as the owners didn't always live in the house, and the people who lived in it were not necessarily the owners, not to mention tenants, although sharing a part of the house with people legitimately entitled to live there. However, for the purpose of my story, we need only concern ourselves with the two top floors; the third floor contained two bedrooms and a bath, while the fourth or top floor consisted of a living room, dining room, kitchen, and second bath.

At the time my account begins, the first two floors were rented to an architect and his wife, and only the two top floors were available for new tenants.

It was in the summer when two young ladies in their early 20s, who had been living at the Brooklyn YWCA, decided to find a place of their own. Somehow they heard of the two vacant floors in the house on Clinton Street and immediately fell in love with it, renting the two top floors without much hesitation. Both Barbara and Sharon were 23 years old at the time, still going to college, and trying to make ends meet on what money they could manage between them. Two years later, Barbara was living in San Francisco with a business of her own, independently merchandising clothing. Brooklyn was only a hazy memory by then, but on August 1 of the year she and Sharon moved in, it was very much her world.

Immediately after moving in, they decided to clean up the house, which needed it, indeed. The stairway to the top floor was carpeted all the way up, and it was quite a job to vacuum it clean because there were a lot of outlets along the way, and one had to look out for extension cords. Sharon got to the top floor and was cleaning it when she removed the extension cord to plug it in further up. Instead, she just used the regular cord of the vacuum cleaner, which was about 12 feet long, using perhaps three feet of it, which left nine feet of cord lying on the floor.

All of a sudden, the plug just pulled out of the wall. Sharon couldn't believe her eyes; the plug actually pulled itself out of the socket, and flew out onto the floor. She shook her head and put it back in, and turned the vacuum cleaner on again. Only then did she realize that she had turned the switch on the cleaner back on, when she had never actually turned it off in the first place! She couldn't figure out how that was possible. But she had a lot more work to do, so she continued with it. Later she came downstairs and described the incident to her roommate who thought she was out of her mind. "Wait till something happens to you," Sharon said, "there is something strange about this house."

During the next five months, the girls heard strange noises all over the house, but they attributed it to an old houses settling, or the people living downstairs in the building. Five months of "peace" were rudely shattered when Sharon's younger brother came to visit from New Jersey.

He was still in high school, and liked to listen to music at night, especially when it was played as loud as possible. The young people were sitting in the living room, listening to music and talking. It was a nice, relaxed evening. All of a sudden the stereo went off. The music had been rather loud rock and roll, and at first they thought the volume had perhaps damaged the set. Then the hallway light went out, followed by the kitchen light. So they thought a fuse had blown. Barbara ran down four flights of stairs into the basement to check. No fuse had blown. To be on the safe side, she checked them anyway, and switched them around to make sure everything was fine. Then she went back upstairs and asked the others how the electricity was behaving.

But everything was still off. At this point, Sharon's brother decided to go into the kitchen and try the lights there. Possibly there was something wrong with the switches. He went into the hallway where there was an old Tiffany-type lamp hanging at the top of the stairway. It had gone off, too, and he tried to turn it on and nothing happened. He pulled again, and suddenly it went on. In other words, he turned it off first, then turned it on, so it has been on in the first place.

This rather bothered the young man, and he announced he was going into the kitchen to get something to eat. He proceeded into the kitchen, and when he came back to join in the others he was as white as the wall. He reported that the kitchen was as cold as an icebox, but as soon as one left the kitchen, the temperature was normal in the rest of the house. The others then got up to see for themselves, and sure enough, it was icy cold in the kitchen. This was despite the fact that there were four or five radiators going, and all the windows were closed.

That night they knew that they had a ghost, and for want of a better name they called her Hendrix—it happened to have been the anniversary of Jimi Hendrix's death, and they had been playing some of his records.

Shortly afterward, Toby joined the other two girls in the house. Toby moved in on April 1. It had been relatively quiet between the incident in the kitchen and that day, but somehow Toby's arrival was also the beginning of a new aspect of the haunting.

About a week after Toby moved in, the girls were in living room talking. It was about 11 o'clock at night, and they had dimmers on in the living room. Toby was sitting on the couch, and Barbara and some friends were sitting on the other side of the room, when all of a sudden she felt a chilly breeze pass by her. It didn't touch her, but she felt it nonetheless, and just then the lights started to dim back and forth, back and forth, and when she looked up, she actually saw the dial on the dimmer moving by itself. As yet, Toby knew nothing about the haunting, so she decided to say nothing to the others, having just moved in, and not wishing to have her new roommates think her weird.

But things kept happening night after night, usually after 11 o'clock when two girls and their friends sat around talking. After a couple of weeks, she could not stand it any longer, and finally asked the others whether they could feel anything strange in the room. Barbara looked at Sharon, and a strange look passed between them; finally they decided to tell Toby about the haunting, and brought her up to date from the beginning of their tenancy in the house.

Almost every day there was something new to report: cooking equipment would be missing, clothing would disappear, windows were opened by themselves, garbage cans would be turned over by unseen hands. Throughout that period, there was the continued walking of an unseen person in the living room located directly over the third-floor bedroom. And the girls heard it at any hour of the night, and once in a while even during the day. Someone was walking back and forth, back and forth. They were loud, stomping footsteps, more like a woman's but they sounded as if someone were very angry. Each time one of them went upstairs to check they found absolutely nothing.

The girls held a conference, and decided that they had a ghost, make no mistake about it. Toby offered to look into the matter, and perhaps find out what might have occurred at the house at an earlier age. Barbara kept hearing an obscure whistling, not a real tune or song that could be recognized, but a human whistle nevertheless. Meanwhile, Toby heard of a course on witchcraft and the occult being given at New York University, and started to take an interest in books on the subject. But whenever there were people over to visit them and they stayed in the living room upstairs past 11 o'clock at night, the ghost would simply run them out of the room with all the tricks in her ghostly trade.

"She" would turn the stereo on and off, or make the lights go on and off. By now they were convinced it was a woman. There were heavy shutters from the floor to the ceiling, and frequently it appeared as if a wind were coming through them and they would clap together, as if the breeze were agitating them. Immediately after that, they heard footsteps walking away from them, and there was an uncomfortable feeling in the room, making it imperative to leave and go somewhere else, usually downstairs into one of the bedrooms.

As yet, no one had actually seen her. That June, Bruce, Toby's boyfriend, moved into the house with her. They had the master bedroom, and off the bedroom was a bathroom. Since Barbara would frequently walk through in the middle of the night, they left the light on in the bathroom all night so that she would not trip over anything. That particular night in June, Toby and her boyfriend were in bed and she was looking up, not at the ceiling, but at the wall, when suddenly she saw a girl looking at her.

It was just like an outline, like a shadow on the wall, but Toby could tell that she had long hair arranged in braids. Somehow she had the impression that she was an

Indian, perhaps because of the braids. Toby looked up at her and called the apparition to her boyfriend's attention, but by the time he had focused on it she had disappeared.

He simply did not believe her. Instead, he asked Toby to go upstairs to the kitchen and make him a sandwich. She wasn't up there for more than five or ten minutes when she returned to the bedroom and found her boyfriend hidden under the covers of the bed. When she asked him what was wrong, he would shake his head, and so she looked around the room, but could find nothing unusual. The only thing she noticed was that the bathroom was now wide open. She assumed that her boyfriend had gone to the bathroom, but he shook his head and told her that he had not.

He had just been lying there smoking a cigarette, when all of a sudden he saw the handle on the door turn by itself, and the door open.

When he saw that, he simply dove under the covers until Toby returned. From that moment on, he no longer laughed at her stories about a house ghost. The following night, her boyfriend was asleep when Toby woke up at 2 o'clock in the morning. The television set had been left on and she went to shut it off, and when she got back into bed, she happened to glance at the same place on the wall where she had seen the apparition the night before. For a moment or two she saw the same outline of a girl, only this time she had the impression that the girl was smiling at her.

Two weeks after that, Toby and her boyfriend broke up, and this rather shook her. She had come back home one day and didn't know that he had left, then she found a note in which he explained his reasons for leaving, and that he would get in touch with her later. This very much upset her, so much so that her two roommates had to calm her down. Finally, the two girls went upstairs and Toby was lying on the bed trying to compose herself.

In the quiet of the room, she suddenly heard someone sob a little and then a voice said, "Toby." Toby got up from bed and went to the bottom of the stairs and called up, demanding to know what Barbara wanted. But no one had called her. She went back to the room and lay down on the bed again. Just then she heard a voice saying "Toby" again and again. On checking, she found that no one had called out to her—no one of flesh and blood, that is.

Toby then realized who had been calling her, and she decided to talk to "Henny," her nickname for Hendrix, which was the name given by the others to the ghost since that night when they were playing Jimi Hendrix records. In a quiet voice, Toby said, "Henny, did you call me?" and then she heard the voice answer, "Calm down, don't take it so hard, it will be all right." It was a girl's voice, and yet there was no one to be seen. The time was about 5 o'clock in the afternoon, and since it was in June, the room was still fairly light.

Toby had hardly recovered from this experience when still another event took place. Sharon had moved out and another girl by the name of Madeline had moved in. One day her brother came to visit them from Chicago, and he bought a friend along who had had some experience of a spiritual nature. His name was Joey, and both boys were about twenty to twenty-one years old.

Madeline and her brother were much interested in the occult, and they brought a Ouija board to the house. On Saturday, December 19, while it was snowing outside and the atmosphere was just right for a séance, they decided to make contact with the unhappy ghost in the house. They went upstairs into the living room, and sat down with the board. At first it was going to be a game, and they were asking silly questions of it such as who was going to marry whom, and other romantic fluff. But halfway through the session, they decided to try to contact the ghost in earnest. The three girls and Madeline's brother sat down on the floor with their knees touching, and put the board on top. Then they invited Henny to appear and talk to them if she was so inclined. They were prepared to pick up the indicator and place their hands on it so it could move to various letters on the board.

But before their hands ever touched it, the indicator took off by itself! It shot over to the word yes on the board, as if to reassure them that communication was indeed desired. The four of them looked at each other dumbfounded, for they had seen only too clearly what had just transpired. By now they were all somewhat scared. However, Toby decided that since she was going to be interested in psychic research, she might as well ask the questions. She began asking why the ghostly girl was still attached to the house. Haltingly, word for word, Henny replied and told her sad story.

It was a slow process, since every word had to be spelled out letter by letter, but the young people didn't mind the passage of time—they wanted to know why Henny was with them. It appears that the house once belonged to her father, a medical doctor. Her name was Cesa Rist and she had lived in the house with her family. Unfortunately she had fallen in love with a young man and had become pregnant by him. She wanted to marry him and have the baby, but her father would not allow it and forced her to have an abortion. He did it in the house himself, and she died during the abortion.

Her body was taken to Denver, Colorado and buried in the family plot. She realized that her boyfriend was dead also, because this all happened a long time ago. Her reasons for staying on in the house were to find help; she wanted her remains to be buried near her lover's in New York.

"Do you like the people who live in the house?"
"Yes," the ghost replied.
"Is anyone who lives here ever in any danger?"

"Yes, people who kill babies."

This struck the young people as particularly appropriate: a close friend, not present at the time, had just had an abortion. "Will you appear to us?"

"Cesa has," the ghost replied, and as if to emphasize this statement, there suddenly appeared the shadow of a cross on the kitchen wall, for which there was no possible source, except, of course, from the parapsychological point of view.

The girls realized they did not have the means to go to Denver and exhume Cesa's remains and bring it to New York, and they told the ghost as much. "Is there anything else we can do to help you?" "Contact Holzer," she said. By that time, of course, Toby had become familiar with my works, and decided to sit down and write me a letter, telling me of their problem. They could not continue with the Ouija board or anything else that night, they were all much too shaken up.

On Monday, Toby typed up the letter they had composed, and sent it to me. Since they were not sure the letter would reach me, they decided to do some independent checking concerning the background of the house, and if possible, try to locate some record of Cesa Rist. But they were unsuccessful, even at the Hall of Records, the events having apparently transpired at a time when records were not yet kept, or at least not properly kept.

When I received the letter, I was just about to leave for Europe and would be gone two-and-a-half months. I asked the girls to stay in touch with me and after my return I would look into the matter. After Toby had spoken to me on the telephone, she went back into the living room and sat down quietly. She then addressed Henny and told her she had contacted me, and that it would be a couple of months before I could come to the house because I had to go to Europe.

Barbara decided not to wait, however; one night she went upstairs to talk to Henny. She explained the situation to her, and asked why she was still hanging around the house; she explained that her agony was keeping her in the house, and that she must let go of it in order to go on and join her boyfriend in the great beyond. Above all, she should not be angry with them because it was their home now. Somehow Barbara felt that the ghost understood, and nothing happened, nothing frightening at all. Relieved, Barbara sat down in a chair facing the couch. She was just sitting there smoking a cigarette, wondering whether Henny really existed, or whether perhaps she was talking to thin air.

At the moment, an ethereal form entered the room and stood near the couch. It looked as if she were leaning on the arm of the couch or holding onto the side of it. She saw the outline of the head, and what looked like braids around the front of her chest. For half a minute she was there, and then she suddenly disappeared.

It looked to Barbara as if the girl had been five foot four inches, weighing perhaps one hundred twenty pounds. Stunned, Barbara sat there for another ten or fifteen minutes, trying to believe what she had seen. She smoked another five cigarettes, and then walked downstairs to try to go to asleep. But sleep would not come; she kept thinking about her experience.

At the time Sharon left, they were interviewing potential roommates to replace her. One particularly unpleasant girl had come over and fallen in love with the house. Both Barbara and Toby didn't want her to move in, but she seemed all set to join them, so Toby decided to tell her about the ghost. She hoped it would stop the girl from moving in. As Toby delineated their experiences with Henny, the would-be roommate became more and more nervous.

All of a sudden there was a loud crash in the kitchen, and they went to check on it. The garbage can had turned itself over and all the garbage was spilled all over the kitchen, even though no one had been near it. The new girl took one look at this and ran out as fast as she could. She never came back.

But shortly afterward, Toby went on vacation to California. There she made arrangements to move and found employment in the market research department of a large department store. Under the circumstances, the girls decided not to renew the lease, which was up in July, but to move to another apartment for a short period. That September, they moved to California. Under the circumstances, they did not contact me any further, and I assumed that matters had somehow been straightened out, or that there had been a change in their plans. It was not until a year later that we somehow met in California, and I could fill in the missing details of Henny's story.

On the last day of the women's stay at the house on Clinton Street, with the movers going in and out of the house, Toby went back into the house for one more look and to say goodbye to Henny. She went up to the living room and said a simple goodbye, and hoped that Henny would be all right. But there was no answer, no feeling of a presence.

For a while the house stood empty, then it was purchased by the father of an acquaintance of the girls. Through Alan, they heard of the new people who had moved in after the house was sold. One day when they had just been in the house for a few days, they returned to what they assumed to be an empty house.

They found their kitchen flooded with water: there were two inches of water throughout the kitchen, yet they knew they had not left the water taps on. Why had Henny turned the water on and let it run? Perhaps Henny didn't like the new tenants after all. But she had little choice, really. Being a ghost, she was tied to the house.

Following her friends to San Francisco was simply impossible, the way ghosts operate. And unless or until the new tenants on Clinton Street call for my services, there is really nothing I can do to help Henny.

76

Longleat's Ghosts

LONGLEAT IN SOMERSET must be the most publicized haunted house in all of England. If it isn't, at the very least its owner, Lord Bath, is the most publicity-conscious man among British nobility I have ever met: a genial, clever, very businesslike Aquarian who happens to share my birthdate, although a few years my senior. Longleat and its ghosts were first extensively publicized by Tom Corbett, the British society seer, who went there in the company of a British journalist, Diana Norman, who then wrote a book on Corbett's experiences in various British houses called *The Stately Ghosts of England*. Mr. Corbett goes to great pains to explain that he is not a medium but a clairvoyant. He most certainly is not a trance medium, and it takes a good deep-trance medium to really get to the bottom of any haunting. All a clairvoyant can do is pick up vibrations from the past and possibly come into communication with a resident ghost or spirit entity, while it remains for a trance medium to allow the spirit or ghost to speak directly to the investigator.

I began to correspond with Lord Bath in the spring of 1964, but before I could fix a date for my first visit to Longleat, NBC television decided to include the magnificent palace in its itinerary of allegedly haunted houses which its documentary unit wanted to film.

The *Psychic News* of May 23, 1964, headlined, FAMOUS ACTRESS AND MEDIUM TO STAR IN PSYCHIC FILM—WILL CAMERA RECORD SPIRIT FORMS? The newspaper was, of course, referring to Margaret Rutherford, the grand old lady of the British theater, who happened to be interested in ESP phenomena, although by no means a medium herself.

The idea of filming at Longleat and elsewhere was the brainchild of producer-director Frank De Fellitta, who had read the Tom Corbett-Diana Norman tome on Britain's haunted mansions. The NBC team went to Longleat, and immediately after they had set up for the filming all sorts of difficulties arose. Cameras would be out of place, tools would disappear; it seemed as if the resident ghosts were not altogether happy at the invasion taking place. But it is hard to tell how much of the reported difficulty was factual and how much of it a product of the NBC publicity department. One fact, however, was blissfully ignored in its implications by both NBC and the producer. They had set up a time-lapse exposure camera in the haunted corridor at Longleat, a camera which records one frame of film at a time over a long period of time. Such a recording was made during the night when no one was around. On developing the film, a whitish flash of light was discovered for which there was no easy explanation. The flash of light could not be explained as faulty film, faulty laboratory work, or any other logical source. What the camera had recorded was nothing less than the forma-tion of a spirit form. Had Mr. De Fellitta any basic knowledge of parapsychology or had he been in the company of an expert in the field, he might have made better use of this unexpected bonus.

The choice of Margaret Rutherford as hostess of the program was not dictated by psychic ability or her integrity as an investigator, but simply because she looked the part, and in television that is the most important consideration. And she had played the magnificently written comedy role of the medium in Noel Coward's *Blithe Spirit*. Even the austere *New York Times*, which has generally ignored any serious treatment of parapsychology, managed to give the project and Margaret Rutherford quite a bit of space. "Miss Rutherford and company will visit allegedly spirit-ridden mansions. She will give her personal impressions of the hauntings—how they occur, when they occur and, maybe, why they don't occur," wrote Paul Gardner. Nothing of the sort was either intended or delivered, of course, but it read well in the publicity releases.

* * *

My first visit to Longleat took place in September, 1964, long after the hullabaloo and the departure of Margaret Rutherford and the film crew. However, the usual large number of tourists was still milling around, so we had arranged with Lord Bath to come at a time when the grounds were closed to them.

Longleat is in the west of England, about three hours from London by car, and truly a palace, rivaling some of the royal residences in both size and appointments. Lord Bath himself had long ago moved into more modest quarters at nearby Warminster, where he and his wife lived in a charming old mill. Longleat itself is named after a river which runs through the grounds. It has been the home of the Thynne family for four hundred years. Sometime before 1580 Sir John Thynne, direct ancestor of the current Marquess of Bath, began to build Longleat. His successors enlarged the mansion until it assumed the proportions of a palace. To describe the art treasures that fill the palace from top to bottom would take volumes. Suffice it to say that some very important paintings hang at Longleat and among them, perhaps a peculiarity of the present Lord Bath, art work by both Sir Winston Churchill and Adolf Hitler. The latter are in the private portion of the house, however, on one of the upper floors.

The first person Lord Bath wanted us to meet was the old nurse, a certain Miss Marks, who was then in her seventies. At the time when she took care of little Caroline, she had several encounters with a ghost.

"I saw a tall, scholarly looking man," the nurse explained. "He was walking along and looked as if he might be reading something; I only saw his back, but he had a high collar, the wings of it distinctly standing out. I would say, 'I think perhaps that is Grandpa. Shall we

Longleat's Ghosts are strictly family—with one exception

hurry up and speak to him?' We would follow him across the room, but when we got to the door at the end, which was shut, he just wasn't there. I didn't think anything of it, because I saw him lots and lots of times, and in the end I thought, It isn't a person at all. I didn't discuss it with anyone, but I knew it was friendly to me. I loved seeing this person, even after I discovered it was *only a ghost.*"

From the nurse's description and that given by Tom Corbett it was clear to historians that the ghost was none other than the builder of Longleat, Sir John Thynne. Thynne had been a banker in the time of Henry VIII and was known for his sharp business sense. The grounds upon which Longleat stands were a result of his business acumen, and he was very much attached to it in his day. His haunting ground, so to speak, is the Red Library on the ground floor, where he usually appears between 7 and 8 o'clock at night.

Lord Bath then took us up to the haunted corridor, which is now completely bare and gives a rather depressing feeling, ghost or no ghost. This long, narrow passage runs parallel to the sleeping quarters of some of the Thynne family, and it was here that Tom Corbett felt a ghostly presence.

"This is the corridor," Lord Bath explained in a voice that betrayed the fact that he had said it many times before, "where a duel was fought by one of my ancestors, the second Viscount Weymouth, because he found that his wife, Louisa Carteret, had been unfaithful to him. He discovered her in a state, unfortunately, in which he thought a duel ought to be fought with the man she was with. He

fought this duel with the intruder and killed the man, after which he buried him in the cellar. His skeleton was accidentally found when the boiler was put in downstairs six years ago."

One would assume the unfortunate lover to be roaming the corridors at Longleat, seeking revenge, or at least, to frighten the survivors. But apparently he took his fate like a man and remained a spirit rather than a ghost. Not so with Lady Louisa: "People have seen what is assumed to be the ghost of Louisa Carteret," Lord Bath explained. "I haven't seen her myself, because I don't have that power. My mother has seen the ghost in the Red Library downstairs, but not this one." I asked about visitors. Lord Bath explained that visitors were never taken to the part of the house where we were, so there was no way of telling whether they had experienced anything. I took a good look at the portrait of Lady Louisa. She was indeed worth fighting over: lovely face, beautiful eyes, slim figure in a green dress.

Shortly afterwards we left Longleat with the firm promise to return someday with a trance medium so that we could have a go at contacting the resident ghosts. But it wasn't until two years later that the opportunity came along.

* * *

It was in September, 1966, when I brought the London medium and former nurse, Trixie Allingham, to Longleat, introduced her to Lord Bath, and proceeded to enter the palace in the hope of really coming to grips with the phantoms that had never been dislodged, nor indeed fully contacted before. For the next two hours, Lord Bath, my friends and I went through one of the most fascinating and gripping sessions we'd ever experienced.

All along, Trixie, a frail lady, had been unhappy in the car, partly because it was a rough ride and partly because she sensed some great tragedy ahead which would shortly involve her personally. As we were rounding the last long curve of the driveway leading to the palace, Trixie turned to me and said, "I saw the painting of a fair young woman. I thought she had something to do with my visit here, and she showed me an opened window as if she were telling me that there had been a tragedy connected with that window. Either she was pushed out, or somebody she loved had flung himself out, and then the vision faded. Then another woman came to me, rather charming and of the same period. She was older and looked rather haughty for a moment. Then she faded."

I had not replied, for I did not wish to give her any clues. A few minutes later we arrived it the main gate to Longleat and got out of the car. I gave Trixie time to "get to herself" and to get the shaky ride out of her system. Then we entered the Red Library, and I asked Trixie to sit down in one of the large antique chairs at the head of the room.

Immediately she said in a quivering, excited voice, "A long time ago something very evil happened here, or someone had a devilish temptation in this room, looking out of that window." She pointed at one of the several large windows on the far side of the room. "I have a feeling that there is a French link here, that either the wife or the daughter was of French ancestry," Trixie continued. "There is some connection with the French Revolution, for I see a guillotine...good heavens!"

"Do you sense a ghost here, Trixie?" I asked.

"As a matter of fact, yes, I get a woman. She has a dress with long sleeves, and she walks as if her hip were bent. There is a crucifix around her neck and she's saying, 'Help me, help me, help me!' This is going back more than a hundred years; her gown is sort of whitish with a mulberry shade. From way back." Trixie paused for a moment as if getting her bearings. Lord Bath, not exactly a believer, was watching her seriously now.

"Now I see a horse and a man galloping away, and I see the woman in tears and I wonder what it means. She sees the man galloping away, and she thinks life is over, and now I see her dead. I feel there is a church nearby, where her effigy is in stone on top of some sort of a sarcophagus. She showed it to me."

I asked Trixie if the woman was the same one she had seen in the car driving tip, but she couldn't be sure, for she hadn't yet seen the woman's face. Were there any other presences in the room?

"Yes," Trixie replied. "Very dimly over there by the door and holding the handle, there is a man with a big hat on, and he wears a collar around the neck. He goes back a long time, I think."

I glanced at Lord Bath: nobody had told Trixie about the apparition seen by the nurse—Sir John Thynne, a man wearing a strange old-fashioned collar! While Trixie was resting for a moment, I walked around the library. I noticed that the shelves were filled with French books and that some of the furniture was obviously of eighteenth-century French origin. Had Trixie simply picked up the atmosphere of the room?

Trixie suddenly said in a rather challenging tone of voice: "Henry—is there a Henry here?" Almost like an obedient schoolboy, Lord Bath stepped forward. Trixie eyed him suspiciously. "You're Henry?"

"I'm the only one."

"Well, they said, 'Go talk to Henry.'"

"Who told you to talk to Henry?" Lord Bath inquired.

"I don't know. It is a man, a very unhappy man. He passed over a long time ago. He killed three people, and I don't mean in battle."

The story was getting more interesting. "How did he kill them?" I demanded to know.

"I look at his hands, and there are brown stains on them which he can't seem to wipe off. The letter H seems to be connected with him, and I have the feeling he did it

Hans Holzer's wife, Catherine, examining the haunted corridor

in vengeance. I see a friar come up to him, and him trying to get absolved and being unable to. The friar is haughty, arrogant, and then the prior comes in and I see this unhappy man on his knees, and yet he does not get absolution, and that is why he comes back here."

"Can you possibly speak to him, Trixie?" I asked.

"I am speaking to him *now*," Trixie replied impatiently, "but he says, 'There is no hope for me.' I tell him we will pray for him. I hear him speak in Latin. I know a fair amount of Latin, and I'm saying it in English: 'Out of the depths I have called unto thee, O God, hear my voice.' Then the monk reappears, and there is also a tall lady here, by his side. I believe this is his wife; she's very slender and beautiful, and she's holding up one of his hands, saying, 'Pray, pray as you've never prayed before.'"

We left the Red Library and slowly walked up the staircase, one of the world's greatest, to the upper stories. When we arrived at the haunted corridor where the famous duel had taken place, Trixie sensed that something had happened around December or January of one particular year—not an ordinary passing. Immediately she explained that it had nothing to do with the haunting downstairs.

"The passing of this person was kept quiet. He was carried out in the dead of night in a gray shroud. I can see this happening. Five people are carrying out this ominous task. The whole situation was tragic and hushed up. He

The haunted "Red Library"

wasn't murdered and it wasn't suicide, but it was a person who came to an untimely end. Above all, they wanted no attention, no attention. He didn't live here, but he stayed here for a while. He came from Spain. I think he died from a wound in his side, yet it wasn't murder or suicide. He was about thirty-five years old. He says 'O my God, my God, to come to such an end.' He was a Catholic, he tells me. He was not shriven here after he passed. I see lanterns; he's not buried in sacred ground. Wait a moment, sir," Trixie suddenly said, turning to Lord Bath. "Is there a name like Winnie or something like that connected with your family?" Lord Bath's interest perked up. Winnie sounded a little like Weymouth.

"Francis, Francis," Trixie said excitedly now. "And I hear the name Fanny. She's just laughing. Did you know her?"

"Yes," Lord Bath replied, "a long, long time ago."

"Was she a very bright person?"

"Well, she was as a child. Her nickname was Fanny."

Evidently Trixie had gotten some more recent spirits mixed in with the old characters. "I see her as a younger woman, lovely, laughing, running along, and she tells me you have in your pocket a coin that is bent, out of order, not a normal coin. Is that true?"

"Yes," Lord Bath said, surprised.

"She just told me; isn't she sweet? Oh, and there is a lord chief justice here. Do you know him?"

"Peculiar," Lord Bath replied. "There was a lord chief justice upstairs."

For a moment Trixie seemed particularly sad, as she reported: "There is a child here named Tim, Timothy, but he died at the age of one-and-a-half. Is this true?"

Lord Bath seemed to struggle with his emotions now. "Yes," he finally said in a low voice.

"He wants me to say, 'I am Tim,' and you should know he is still your son."

Lord Bath confirmed that his oldest son, Tim, had died in infancy, but that the fact was known only to members of the family and had never been publicized.

Trixie then reported a servant woman, continuing to serve in her ghostly condition, and when I didn't show any particular interest, she went on to say that there was also a rather funny-looking man, "someone holding his head under his arm, walking, and I really shouldn't laugh at this sort of thing, but I saw this man with his head under his arm."

Since none of us were laughing, she assumed that it was all right to address the man with his head under his arm. "Can you tell me, sir, how you lost your head, and why?" She listened for a while, apparently getting an answer from the unseen headless specter. Nodding, she turned to us. "There is something about some rebels here; they are linked with France, and these rebels have come in strength. Somebody was being hounded, a person of high birth. He was hidden here, and I don't like it at all."

Lord Bath was visibly impressed. "During the rebellion of the Duke of Monmouth," he explained, "some rebels took refuge here. It is not at all unlikely that one of them was put to death on these grounds."

Trixie now exhibited unmistakable signs of weariness. Under the circumstances, we decided to call it a day and return in the morning. The following morning we started again in the Red Library. On entering, Trixie described a woman walking up and down wringing her hands and saying that her child had died. Trixie identified her as Christina and explained that this had happened no more than a hundred years ago. However, my main interest was in an earlier period, and I asked Trixie to try for full trance if she could. Again she seated herself in the comfortable chair at the far end of the Red Library.

"There is a link here with the tragedy I saw in part yesterday," she began. "I still see the horseman and the woman at the window, and I smell the tragedy. There is something about a rapier wound. Ron is murdered and a Helen is mixed up in this. The man I saw yesterday is still here, by the way, and he looks happier now."

"Ask him to identify himself."

"I get the initial R. He wears a cape and a lace collar."

"Why did he murder the three people?"

"I get the initial P. Someone was in a dungeon here." All of a sudden we weren't hearing Trixie's voice anymore, but a rough male voice coming from her entranced lips. I realized that the ghost had at last taken over the medium and was about to address us directly.

"Who put you into the dungeon?"

"S. Mine enemy, mine enemy."

"Is this your house?"

"Yes, of course."

"Did you build this house?"

"With bad money."

"What is your name, sir?" I insisted.

Suddenly the entity was gone again and Trixie was back. "He was a Catholic by birth," she said, "and he is showing me a very large ruby ring on his finger. His ankles hurt him. He must have been chained for a time, and I see a short dagger in his hand. Now he is fading again."

"Is he the victim or the murderer?" I almost shouted.

"He did it; he says, 'I did it, I have no peace.' He was the owner of the house. He says, 'You will pray for me, you will pray for me.'"

I assured the entity through the medium that we would all pray for him.

"He says someone owes him something."

"But he can be forgiven; tell him that."

"There is a little chapel here somewhere in this mansion. I can see the altar, and he wants Lord Bath to go there, to the chapel. 'If he will do it, he will give me peace; he will give me rest.'"

I promised that we would do it, without even asking Lord Bath, for I knew he would go along with it, although he was not a religious person.

"I can't do any more, I can't do any more," the medium said now, and she looked exhausted. I questioned her about what she remembered.

"I saw two men killed over a woman," Trixie recollected. "There is a lead coffin amongst all the others, one different from the others. It is away from the others. This man is in it, the one who murdered. I hear the name Grace, and someone was hung, hanged from the rafters." Impressions seemed to hit her now from various directions, possibly getting different layers of history confused in the process. It was up to us to sort it out.

"Tom," Trixie now said firmly, and looked at me. I asked her to describe the man. "I see him very dimly; he is old and belongs to an earlier age." Lord Bath then informed me that we were in what used to be the chapel, although the floor had been changed and we were actually above it. Just as I had promised, we grouped ourselves around the spot where the altar once stood below, bowed our heads in prayer, and I said, "May Thomas rest free from worry, happy in his home. May he be free from any guilt or fear. Let us now have a moment of silent prayer."

In the silence I glanced at Lord Bath, a man who had told me before that he thought himself an agnostic. He seemed genuinely affected and moved.

"I don't know whether it was a bishop," Trixie said, "but I saw a man with a gold miter on his head make the sign of the cross and I heard the word 'progression,' and then something very odd happened. A feather was put on his shoulder, but I don't know what it means."

Medium Trixie Allingham in a trance in the Red Library

"Perhaps his soul is now light as a feather?" I suggested. Trixie then asked Lord Bath whether he knew any jeweled crucifix in the mansion. Lord Bath could not remember such an item offhand. Trixie insisted, "It is a jeweled cross with dark stones, and it has to do with your people. I also see three monks who were here when you were praying. Three in a row. But now I feel peace; I feel a man who had a leaden weight on his shoulder is now without it. It was important that he be helped."

I have already mentioned that the name which the medium got in connection with the death of the thirty-five-year-old Spaniard in the haunted passage upstairs sounded very close to Weymouth, the man who killed him in a duel. The medium's description of this death as being neither death nor suicide is of course entirely correct: he was killed in an honest duel, which in those days was not considered murder. Trixie described the man's death as an affair that had to be hushed up, and so it was indeed, not only because a man had been killed, but also because the wife of the Viscount had been unfaithful. A scandal *was* avoided: the body was interred underneath the kitchen floor, and, as Lord Bath confirmed, it had been found several years earlier and been given burial *outside* the house.

More fascinating is Trixie's account of the haunting in the Red Library. The man she described is obviously the same man described by the old nanny whom I interviewed in 1964, and the same man whom Dorothy Coates, former librarian of Longleat, had encountered, as well as a certain Mrs. Grant, former housekeeper in the greathouse.

In a somewhat confused and jumbled way, however, Trixie hit on many of the facts surrounding the ancient palace. I doubt that Trixie would have known of these family secrets, which are never found in tourist guides of Longleat or in popular books dealing with the Thynne family. They are, however, available in research libraries, if one tries hard enough to find the information. There exists, for instance, a contemporary source known as the "John Evelyn Diary," a seventeenth-century chronicle of the London scene. From this source we learned that Thomas Thynne, then already one of the wealthiest men in England and somewhat advanced in years, had fallen in love with a sixteen-year-old heiress by the name of Elizabeth Ogle. He married her despite the great difference in their ages, and after the wedding ceremony preceded her to Longleat, where Lady Elizabeth was to follow him in a few days' time. But Elizabeth never arrived in Longleat. Unwilling to consummate the marriage into which she felt herself forced by her family, she ran away to the Netherlands, where she continued living as if she weren't married. In the Netherlands, Elizabeth Ogle met a certain Count Koenigsmark and fell in love with this somewhat adventurous gentleman. Since divorce was out of the question, and Lady Elizabeth was legally married to Thomas Thynne, the young lovers decided to murder Elizabeth's husband so that she might be free to marry her count.

In view of Thynne's affluence and importance, such a plot was not an easy one to bring off. Koenigsmark therefore engaged the services of three paid murderers, a certain Lieutenant Stern, a Colonel Vratz and a man named Boroski. The murderous foursome arrived in London and immediately set about keeping a close watch on their intended victim. One Sunday night Thynne left a party in London and entered his coach to be driven home. That was the signal they had been waiting for. They followed their victim, and when the coach with Thomas Thynne reached Pall Mall, which was at that time still a country road, the murderers stopped it. Lieutenant Stern, galloping ahead of the coach, put his hands onto the reins of the lead horse. As Thomas Thynne opened the door of the coach and stepped out, a volley of shots hit him in the face.

The restless ghost had called "mine enemy." Could this have been Stern?

The murder created a great deal of attention even in those unruly times. Count Koenigsmark and his henchmen were apprehended just as the count was about to leave England to join Elizabeth. According to John Evelyn, the trial, which took place in 1682, saw the count acquitted by a corrupt jury, but the actual murderers were condemned to death on the gallows. The hired assassins paid with their lives, but the man who had hatched the plot got off scot-free. No wonder the restless spirit of the victim could not find peace! But if one of the ghosts who contacted us through Trixie was indeed Thomas Thynne, the victim of the murder plot, why should he then grieve for the three people who had been put to death for his murder? Undoubtedly, Trixie, in reaching several levels of hauntings, had brought up bits and pieces of John, Thomas, and perhaps even his murderers—all presented in a slightly confusing but essentially evidential package.

Trixie also spoke of "one lead coffin, different from all others." According to the diaries, two weeks after Colonel Vratz had been put to death his body was still not decayed, owing to a new process of preservation which was being used for the first time. "He lay exposed in a very rich coffin lined with *lead*, too magnificent for so daring and horrid a murderer."

So it seems that at least four ghosts occupied the halls of Longleat: the Lady Louisa, who mourned her lover's death at the hands of her husband; the rebel from the Duke of Monmouth's army, who was caught and slaughtered; the builder of Longleat, Sir John Thynne, whose personal attachment and possibly feelings of guilt keep him from leaving his rich estate for greener pastures; and, of course, Thomas Thynne. I should think the latter has departed the premises now, but I am equally sure that Sir John is still around enjoying the spectacles his descendant, the present Lord Bath, is putting on for the tourists. Surely Sir John would have understood the need to install turnstiles in the cafeteria and toilet downstairs, or to bring in lions for a zoo, and to do whatever was possible to raise revenue to keep the magnificent palace in prime condition; for Sir John, not unlike his descendant, was foremost a man of business and common sense.

77

The Ghosts at Blanchland

"THE MOST OBVIOUS THING about Blanchland is its remoteness," writes G. W. O. Addleshaw in his short history of Blanchland. It wasn't as remote for us, because we arrived on a well-planned schedule, by private car, followed about two hours later by a busload of special tourists: participants in a Hunted Britain Tour arranged by Vision Travel, under the guidance of Andre Michalski, Polish nobleman and former orchestra conductor. Over the hills, into the dales, and over still another chain of hills we rode, shaken up all the while, but hopeful of eventually reaching our destination intact. By *we* I mean my wife Catherine and myself and London medium Trixie Allingham, whom I had invited to participate in a rare and unusual experiment. She hadn't the slightest idea why I was bringing her up north. All she knew was that I was on a ghost-hunting expedition, that she would have a quiet room that night and be brought back to London the following day.

When we left the airport at Newcastle, I had no idea that I would soon be in the heart of the Middle Ages, in a small market town so perfectly preserved that it gave one the impression of being in the middle of a motion-picture set in Hollywood. The square commons was reached through a city gate, turreted and fortified, and to the left was a solid-looking gray stone building with a colorful sign dangling from the second story. The sign read "Lord Crewe Arms." This was the unusual hotel which was once a sixteenth-century manor house, which in turn had been converted from a twelfth-century monastery.

The Abbey of Blanchland had been founded by Premonstratensian monks, a strict offshoot of the Benedictines. The land which gave the abbey its income was originally part of the old earldom of Northumbria, expropriated by Henry I for the Norman de Bolbec family. The family itself added some of their own lands in 1214, and it was then that the name Blanchland, which means white land, was mentioned for the first time. Most probably the name is derived from the white habits of the Premonstratensian monks. Up until the middle nineteenth century, the area around Blanchland was wild and desolate, very thinly populated and cut off from the outside world. This was, in a way, most fortunate, because it prevented Blanchland from being embroiled in the political struggles of the intervening centuries and allowed the monks to lead a more contemplative life here than in any other part of England. The monastery was dissolved under Henry VIII, as were all others, and in 1539 the remaining monks were pensioned off, leaving Blanchland Abbey after four hundred years of residence. At first a family named Radcliffe owned the estates and buildings of the dissolved abbey, but in 1623 the Forsters, an old Northumberland family, came into possession of Blanchland. By now the church was in ruins, but a chapel still existed within the main building. Part of the abbey buildings were converted into houses for the village, and the abbot's residence became the manor house. When the last male of the line died, the property passed into the hands of Dorothy Forster, who had married Lord Crewe, Bishop of Durham.

When the owners of Blanchland got into financial difficulties in 1704, Lord Crewe bought the estates, and thus the name Crewe was linked with Blanchland from that moment on. Unfortunately for the family, they became embroiled in the Scottish rebellion of 1715, taking the Jacobite side. The estates eventually passed to a board of trustees, which rebuilt the damaged portion of the village.

A group of buildings, chiefly the kitchen and the prior's house, eventually became an unusual hotel, the Lord Crewe Arms, owned and operated by the Vaux Breweries of Sunderland. The stone-vaulted chamber of the house now serves as a bar. There is an outer stone staircase leading to the gateway and another one leading to what is called the Dorothy Forster Sitting Room, a room I was to know intimately.

We were welcomed by the manager, a Mr. Blenkinsopp, and shown to our quarters. Everything was furnished in eighteenth-century style. Our room, facing the rear, led onto a magnificent garden behind the house: obviously this was the monastery garden, or what remained of it. I understood from previous correspondence with the owner that the area is frequently plunged into sudden mists, but the day of our arrival was a particularly nice day in early August, and the sun was warm as late as 7 o'clock at night. "Mrs. Holzer and yourself are in the Bambrugh Room," the manager said, with a significant raising of the eyebrows, when I came downstairs after unpacking. Then, making sure that no one was listening to our conversation, he added, "This is the room in which most of the activities are reputed to have taken place, you know." I nodded. I had specifically asked to be put up in the "haunted room."

Our arrival had gone unannounced, by my request; however, I offered to give a press interview after we had done our work. While my wife and Trixie rested after the journey from the airport, I took a walk around the premises. The peaceful atmosphere of the place was incredible. It almost belied the rumors of a haunting. A little later we had dinner in the candlelit bar downstairs. My psychic tour had meanwhile arrived and been placed in various rooms of the inn, and they were eager to participate in what for them was a unique and exciting adventure: to witness an actual séance or make contact with an authentic ghost!

It was already dark when we repaired to the room in which we were to sleep that night. Things were a bit on the tight side, with fourteen people trying to squeeze into a double bedroom. But we managed to find everyone a spot, and then Trixie took to a chair in one corner, closed her eyes and leaned back, waiting for the spirits to manifest.

Immediately Trixie looked up at me with a significant nod. "There was a murder in this room, you know," as if it were the most natural thing to expect from a room that was to serve as our sleeping quarters for the night.

"Anything else?" I said, preparing myself for the worst.

"I saw three monks come along, and the odd thing is one dropped his girdle—you know, the cord. It is all very odd."

I agreed that it was, but before I could ask her anything further, she pointed at the bed we were sitting on. "I see a woman lying on this bed, and she is dead. She has been murdered. This happened centuries ago. Now I see a little child running into the room, also wearing a dress of centuries ago. There is an unusual coffin leaving this room. I hear chanting. The coffin is black and shaped like a boat. I have the feeling this happened between the eleventh and thirteenth centuries. Also, I have a feeling of sword play and of a stone, a very special stone standing up somewhere outside."

At this point Trixie called for us to join hands to give her more power for what was to come.

Immediately her face became agitated, as if she were listening to something, something coming to her from far away. "I can hear somebody calling, 'Jesus, Jesus have mercy, Jesus have mercy,' and I see a monk wearing a dark habit, while the others are wearing a grayish white. But this man has on a dark robe which is extraordinary. He is a monk, yet he is really Satanic.

"I think his name is Peter. I don't know whether he committed this murder or got caught up in it. He has a hawk-like face, and there is a very beautiful woman who was tied to this monk. I hear her crying, 'Help me, help me, help me!'"

"How can we help her?" I asked.

"Get on your knees and pray," Trixie replied. "She wants absolution."

"What has she done?"

"*Credo, credo*—what does it mean?"

Trixie seemed puzzled, then she handed me a key. "Go to my room and you'll find a crucifix there. Bring it to me." I asked one of the tour members to get the crucifix from the room down the hall.

"This very beautiful girl died in childbirth, but it was not her husband's child," Trixie explained. "And now she wants absolution for what she had done. I hear 'Ave Maria.' She was buried stealthily outside this area, but she comes back here to visit this guilty love. Her progression is retarded because of her inability to clear her conscience, and yet one part of her wants to cling to the scene here. Wait a minute, I get 'Lord' something. Also, I wonder who was imprisoned for a time, because I see a jailer and rusty keys. It is all very much like looking at a movie screen—I'm getting bits and pieces of a picture. There is a

great sense of remorse; this woman was married, yet she had this love for a monk. The child is lying on a bier. It is all tinged with murder. It seems she killed the child. Now I'm getting something about Spain and the Inquisition, but I don't understand why."

"Tell her she must divulge her name, so that she may be completely cleared," I suggested.

Trixie strained visibly to read the woman's name. "I get the initial F.," she finally said.

"Can you get something about the period when this happened?"

"She said 1260. She's beautiful; her hair is chestnut colored."

"What happened to the monk?"

"He was banished and died in misery, and she says, 'My fault, my fault!'"

I instructed Trixie to relieve the unhappy one of her guilt. Trixie took up the crucifix and intoned in a trembling voice, "You are forgiven and helped in Christ, the Savior!" I asked what was the name of the unlucky monk so that we could pray for him too. "F. F. F." Trixie replied. "He was a monsignor."

At this point, trance set in and Trixie turned more and more into the unhappy woman ghost. "I thought it would be some reparation for the misery I caused if I came back here. I am trying to impress my survival by coming from time to time. I do not see him now. Oh, we are separated from each other. I kneel in the church."

Trixie "returned," and the entity again spoke to her, with the medium relaying her messages to me. "When she was young, this house belonged to the earl." I offered to have some prayers said on her behalf in the church, but in whose name should they be said?

"Just pray for me. I shall know much happiness and I shall be free."

"Then go in peace with our blessings," I replied, and I could see that the entity was fast slipping away. Trixie came out of her psychic state now, visibly tired.

While she was recuperating, I asked the others whether they had felt anything peculiar during the séance. One lady spoke up and said that there was a sort of electric feeling in the room; another admitted to having a strong feeling that she received the impression of a monk who wasn't a real monk at all. Trixie said, "Now I understand about the three monks and one of them putting down his cord. He was being defrocked!"

Mr. Hewitt, one of the managers, had been present throughout the séance, watching with quiet interest. I asked him for verification of the material that had come through Trixie. "It all makes sense," he said, "but the peculiar thing is that the times are all mixed up—everything is correct, but there are two different layers of time involved."

The part of the building where the séance had taken place was the only part of the abbey remaining from the very early period, the Abbey of the White Monks—the white monks seen clairvoyantly by Trixie at the beginning of our session. Mr. Hewitt could not enlighten us concerning the defrocked monk, and when I mentioned it, Trixie filled me in on some of the details of her vision. "It was a terrible thing to see this monk. There he stood in his dark robe, then the cord dropped off and his habit came off, and then I saw him naked being flayed and flayed—it was a terrible thing."

According to the manager, several of the villagers have seen the apparition of a woman in the churchyard and also in the church next door to the hotel. People sleeping in the room we were in had at various times complained of a "presence," but nobody had actually seen her. "She was absolutely beautiful with her rust-colored hair," Trixie said. "I could just see her vaguely, but she had on a light dress, very low, nothing on her head, and her hair was loose." The manager turned to me and asked whether he might bring in a picture of the lady whom they suspected of being the ghost. When Trixie looked at it, she said firmly, "This is the girl I saw." The picture was a portrait of Dorothy Forster—Trixie had named the woman F.— and it was this Dorothy Forster who had played an important role in the history of Blanchland. In 1715, Dorothy's brother Thomas was a general in the Jacobite army, although he was not really qualified for the post. He was captured and imprisoned at Newgate Prison. Three days before his trial for high treason, his sister Dorothy managed to enter the prison, disguised as a servant, get her brother out, and help him escape to France, where he eventually died. Also of interest is the reference to the initials F. F. F. by Trixie. In 1701 a certain John Fenwick killed Ferdinando Forster in a duel at Newcastle. As a result of this, the estate fell into debt and was later sold to Lord Crewe, the Bishop of Durham. He in turn married Dorothy Forster's aunt, also named Dorothy. "There still seems to be some confusion as to which of the two Dorothys haunts the village and the hotel," says S. P. B. Mais in a pamphlet entitled "The Lord Crewe Arms, Blanchland": "She is to be seen walking along the Hexham Road and opens and shuts doors in the haunted wing of the hotel. A portrait of the niece hangs in the sitting room which is named after her, and a portrait of the aunt hangs in the dining room alongside that of her husband, the Bishop of Durham."

I realized by now that Trixie had tuned in on two separate times layers: the grim twelfth and thirteenth centuries, together with the story of a monk who had done wrong and had been punished for it. This particular haunting or impression came as a surprise to the manager, because it had not been reported before. On the other hand, the ghostly presence of Dorothy Forster was generally known around the area. The question was, which Dorothy was the ghost? During the state bordering on trance, Trixie spoke of the house owned by the earl. This was in reply to the question of whose house it was when Dorothy was young. So the ghost could only be the niece, the second Dorothy, because Lord Crewe, the Bishop of Durham, had married her aunt, also named Dorothy. The younger Dorothy would have grown up in her aunt's house. But why was Dorothy Forster, the younger, seeking forgiveness of her sins? Here the mystery remains. On the one hand, Trixie identified the ghost from the portrait shown her by Mr. Hewitt; on the other hand, Dorothy Forster definitely had nothing to do with any monks, since in the eighteenth century there weren't any monks around Blanchland.

The following morning we left for Newcastle and a television interview. A reporter from one of the local papers, *The Northern Echo*, headlined the August 9, 1969, issue with "HAUNTED, YES—BUT WHOSE GHOST IS IT?"

Two psychic sisters from Dallas, Ceil Whitley and Jean Loupot, who had been on the haunted tour with us, decided to jot down their impressions in the haunted room immediately afterwards.

"Both of us feel that Trixie was mistaken in at least one of her impressions. Trixie felt the young woman was inconsolable because she had killed her newborn child, but both of us had the definite impression that she said, 'did away with,' meaning, not killed. We thought it was spirited away by the monks who delivered it. We are so sure of this impression that we do want to go back to Blanchland and see if we can pick up anything further."

On September 15, 1970, the two ladies got in touch with me again. "When we were at Blanchland, Jean 'saw' a woman standing beside a wall at an open gateway. She was quite plump, approximately forty to forty-five years old, and dressed in a black, stiff, full-skirted, long-sleeved dress, nipped in at the waist. There was a laced scarf over her head, crossed in front and back over her shoulders. She stood with her arms crossed in front of her, and her face had a look of sad resignation, as though she were remembering some long-past sadness. We thought it was the girl we 'picked up' last summer, only she was showing us herself in middle age, though still suffering the loss of her child."

78

The Ghosts of Edinburgh

I WOULD NOT BE so familiar with some of the ghosts in and around Edinburgh were it not for the friendship and enormous help given me by Elizabeth Byrd, the author of *Immortal Queen*, and Alanna Knight, author of *October Witch* and many other books, and her husband Alistair. These wonderful friends not only helped plan my recent visit to Scotland but spent much time with me as well. There is something very peculiar about the intellectual atmosphere of the Scottish capital: when you walk along the impressive eighteenth- and early nineteenth-century streets, you feel in the heart of things, yet also removed from the turbulence of the world.

"Guess what? I'm coming to Scotland," I wrote to Elizabeth in March 1973. It was May 3 when I checked in at the George Hotel in the heart of Edinburgh. Shortly after my arrival, Elizabeth paid me a visit with detailed plans for the rest of my stay, pretty much in the manner of one of Napoleon's field marshals when the emperor was about to embark on a campaign. As my first official act on Scottish soil I presented Elizabeth with a large bottle of Scotch, imported from New York. Elizabeth had wanted to take me to one of the famous old hotels where she had had an uncanny experience in the ladies' room. There was some question on how to get me into the ladies' room and what to tell the manager. "Suppose I watched outside and barred any lady from coming in?" Elizabeth suggested. "Five minutes in there should suffice, should you feel any impression." I declined, explaining that I wouldn't mind going to a haunted men's room but then since there wasn't any at that particular hotel, I would pass. But my curiosity had been aroused, so I asked Elizabeth what exactly happened at the ladies' room at the —— Hotel.

"Well," Elizabeth replied in her well-modulated voice, "last year on December 8, which happens to be my birthday, I was in a very happy mood. I was in Edinburgh for business appointments and to celebrate. At noon, I happened to run into a book dealer who invited me for a drink. So we went to the —— Hotel. He ordered the drinks and I went upstairs to primp. The ladies' room is immaculate, new, and neon-lit. Absolutely nothing to frighten anyone, one would think. No one else was in there. I was there for about two minutes when a feeling of absolute terror came over me. Without so much as combing my hair, much less putting on lipstick, I just had to run."

"Did you hear or see anything?"

"No, just this feeling of terror. I went down two flights of stairs and was extremely glad to get that drink from the book dealer, who said, 'You look peculiar.' I kept wondering what had frightened me so. All I knew about

the hotel was that it had been built around 1850. When I told a friend, Kenneth Macrae, what had happened to me in the ladies' room, he said, 'I know something about the history of the hotel.' He suggested I also check with *The Scotsman*."

Elizabeth's greatest terror is fire, so she inquired whether there had been any disastrous fires at the hotel at any time. There had indeed been a fire in May of 1971 in which a woman was killed, and a chef had been found guilty of starting the fire and causing the woman's death. Earlier, in 1967, a fire had broken out in a club nearby and the hotel staff had been evacuated, but the fire had been quickly brought under control. The newspaper librarian regretted that there was no fire of any proportion at the hotel at any time. A little later Elizabeth went to London and while there she received a note from her friend Kenneth Macrae: "Dear Elizabeth, is it possible that your discomfort in the ladies' room was prophetic? A Welsh Rugby supporter was killed in a fire on February 3, 1973, in the hotel."

Miss Byrd thought that was the end of that, but then on April 29, 1973, a really disastrous fire broke out in the hotel, the result of which left two hundred people dead. "It must have been this really big fire I felt, long before it actually happened. I'm glad I wasn't in the hotel at that time."

But Alanna Knight had a different impression of the haunted ladies' room. "Elizabeth insisted on taking me there one day. I must admit I was very skeptical, but as soon as I opened the door I got my unfailing signal—that old, familiar scalp-crawl—and I knew that despite the modern decor, and bright lights, there was something terribly wrong. Luckily we had the place to ourselves for the moment, although I must admit if Elizabeth had not been there, I would have taken to my heels at once!

"I felt immediately that she was mistaken about thinking it had anything to do with a fire. I got an impression of a woman, thirty-five to forty, sometime about 1910, who had suffered such a tragedy that she took her own life in that room. It was a particularly gruesome end, and the room absorbed it. My impression of her was that she was neat but rather shabbily dressed, a 'superior' servant, perhaps a housekeeper or a teacher or someone of that nature."

Because Elizabeth frequently visits the hotel where all this happened, she has asked I not give the hotel's name. She likes the bar, the dining room, and the lounge—everything, in fact, except the ladies' room. Therefore, when the call comes, there is but one thing for Elizabeth to do— leave.

* * *

The telephone rang. It was Ian Groat, who with his friend James Grandison, who would serve as the driver, was to take us to the outskirts of Edinburgh for a look at a haunted country house. During the ride from the center of town up into the hills surrounding it, I had an opportunity to interview Mr. Grandison.

"This happened in 1965, in a modern bungalow built in 1935, on the outskirts of Edinburgh," he began in a soft voice colored by a pleasant Scottish burr. "The place was called Pendleton Gardens, and there had not been anything on the spot before. I lived there for about two years without experiencing anything out of the ordinary, but then strange things started to happen. At first we heard the sound of wood crackling in the fireplace, and when we checked, we found the fire hadn't been lit. Sometimes this noise would also occur in other parts of the place. Then there was the noise of dogs barking inside the house. My wife used to hear it on her own, and I of course discounted the whole thing, saying that there must have been a dog outside. But eventually I began to hear it as well. There were no dogs outside, and I was able to pinpoint the direction whence the bark came. Added to this was the noise of a kettle boiling over on a stove, as if one had to run to the kitchen and turn off the kettle. Whenever we approached the entrance to the kitchen, the noise stopped instantly. While we were still wondering about this, other things began to happen. A door would suddenly slam in our faces, just before we got to it. Or I would go to the bathroom, and the bathroom door would be halfway open, and just as I reached the handle, it would slam violently open, wide open."

"In other words, whoever was causing it was aware of you?"

"Oh, absolutely, yes. Then we started getting knocks on the walls. We tried to communicate by knocking back, and sure enough this thing kept knocking back at us, but we weren't able to establish a code, and apparently this thing didn't have enough energy to carry on indefinitely. We tried to ignore the whole thing, but then something or someone started to knock on the back door. Whenever we answered the door, there was no one there. One day I was lying on the bed while my wife Sadie was in another room with my mother. Suddenly I heard the sound of heavy footsteps walking down the path to the back door and someone knocking on the door. It sounded like a woman's footsteps, but I can't be sure. Then my wife and my mother also heard the footsteps going down the path. We did nothing about answering the door, and after a moment the noise came again, but this time it was a thunderous knock, *bang-bang-bang*. It sounded like someone was very annoyed at not getting in, and this time both my wife and my mother ran to open the door, and again there was no one there and no sound of footsteps receding up the path.

"We were in the habit of going away weekends then and coming back Sunday night. During our absence the house was well locked up, with safety locks on the windows and on the front door. The back door was barred entirely with bolts and quite impregnable; there was no way of getting in. The first time we did this, when we came back we found all sorts of things amiss: the hearth rug in the bedroom had been picked up neatly from the floor and placed in the center of the bed. An ashtray had been taken from the mantelpiece and put in the middle of the hearth rug. We had a loose carpet in the corridor running the length of the house. It was loose and not nailed down. After we got back from our weekend, we found this carpet neatly folded up end-to-end, and we had to unwind the thing again and put it back along the corridor. There was a large piece of wood in the living room, part of the back of a radio-phonograph. When we came back after the weekend, instead of lying against the wall, it was flat on the floor. So the following weekend, we put the piece of wood back against the wall and two chairs up against it so it couldn't possibly fall down. But when we came back, the wood was again right on the floor, yet the chairs had not been disturbed! Whoever it was who did it must have lifted it straight up over the chairs and slipped it out from behind them and placed it in the middle of the floor, as if they were saying, 'Look, I've done it again, even though you tried to stop me.' By now we were pretty sure we had a poltergeist in our house."

"What did you do about it?"

"While we were still trying to figure it out, there was an incident involving a cat. One day we clearly heard a cat purring in the middle of the kitchen floor. But our cat was sitting on a chair, looking down at this imaginary cat as if she could see it. We also heard a terrible crash in the living room, only to find nothing at all disturbed. Once in a while one would hear an odd note on the piano, an odd key being struck, but there was no one near it. This went on and on, gradually building up. At first it was perhaps one incident a week. Eventually it was happening every day. After two years it was getting really ridiculous, and we were beginning to worry in case the neighbors would hear dogs barking *inside* the house and things like that. Finally I asked a medium by the name of James Flanagan to come to the house."

"A professional medium?" I asked.

"It is a hobby with him, but he tells me that his work is his hobby, and the mediumship is his actual profession."

"What happened?"

"He brought another man with him, James Wright, and they had tape recorders with them. He informed us that he felt spirits all over the room, and that he could see them even though we couldn't. He told us it was the original owner of the house, an old lady; she had become strange and was put in a hospital, where she died. She didn't know that she was dead and insisted on coming back to her home. He described her as having reddish hair. Her husband had been a freemason."

"Did you check this out?"

"The person who had shown us round the house when we bought it," Mr. Grandison replied, "was a ginger-haired woman who turned out to have been the daughter of a lady who had died. Also we found a number of things in the attic having to do with freemasonry.

"What advice did the medium give you to get rid of the spook?"

"He asked us to get a basin of clean water and put it in the kitchen and to try to imagine his face in the basin of water after he had left. Also, in two weeks' time the entire phenomenon would disappear—and much to our surprise, it did. Incidents were less frequent and eventually they ceased altogether."

* * *

I had mentioned to Elizabeth Byrd that a certain David Reeves had been in touch with me concerning a poltergeist at his Edinburgh residence and expressed the desire to visit with Mr. Reeves.

"It all started at the beginning of 1970, when my cousin Gladys, her husband Richard, myself, and my wife Aileen were discussing the unknown and life after death," Mr. Reeves had stated to me. "We had heard of other people using a Ouija board, so I drew one on a large piece of paper and placed it on the floor, then placed a tumbler in the center of the paper, and we all put our right forefingers on the glass. After a few minutes I experienced a cold shiver down my back and Richard said he felt the same. Then the glass started to move!"

They received no message, and Mr. Reeves was very skeptical about the whole thing. But the little circle continued using the Ouija board, and eventually they did get evidential messages, from a spirit claiming to be Richard's grandfather. The message was succinct: Richard was to have a crash on his motorbike. A few weeks later he crashed his three-wheeler, which had a motorbike engine. Messages came to them now from different people. One night they received a message stating that the two men were to drink salt water(!) and to make their minds blank at precisely 11 o'clock.

"At 11 I 'fell asleep,' and what happened afterwards is an account told to me by the others," Mr. Reeves explained. In trance, through Mr. Reeves, an entity calling himself St. Francis of Assisi manifested. Since none of the group were Roman Catholics, this was rather surprising to them. The entranced David Reeves then got up, demanded that the light—which he called 'the false light'—be put out, and that the curtains be opened. This done, he demanded that everyone fall to his knees and pray. He himself then proceeded to pray in Latin, a language which neither Mr. Reeves nor any of those present knew.

Unfortunately, Mr. Reeves's cousin Gladys mistook his deep state of trance for illness and put the light on. Immediately he came out of his trance and complained of great pains in his hands.

"When I looked at them, they were covered by blood, and each hand had a hole in the center," Mr. Reeves said. "This was witnessed by everyone present. I quickly ran to the tap and washed the blood away. The holes then vanished."

But the holy tenor of their séances soon changed to something more earthy: Mr. Reeves was impressed with advance information concerning local horse racing and won quite a lot of money because of it. This was followed by what he described as a "distinct evil presence" in the circle, to the point where his wife refused to participate any longer. The other couple, Richard and Gladys, evidently took part of the presence to their own home: poltergeistic activities started and objects moved of their own volition. It was at this point that Mr. Reeves contacted me and wondered what they ought to do next. Unfortunately, I was unable to find him at the address he had given me. Had he been forced to move? I wrote him a note advising him to stay clear of Ouija boards and to consider his experience in trance as a form of psychic hysteria: it could just be that a spirit who *wanted* to be St. Francis had taken over Mr. Reeves's body and expressed this unfulfilled desire for martyrdom.

The discussion of various ghostly events had made the time fly, and suddenly we halted at our destination, Woodhouse Lea. Ian Groat, a gunsmith by profession, had had an uncanny experience here and wanted me to see the place where it all happened. We were on a hill overlooking Edinburgh, and there were a stable and a modern house to our left. Farther up the hill, following the narrow road, one could make out the main house itself. According to my information, Woodhouse Lea had originally stood on another site, farther east, but had been transferred to the present spot. There was a local tradition of a "White Lady of Woodhouse Lea," and it was her appearance that I was after. It was a bitingly cold day for April, so we decided to stay in the car at first, while we sorted out Mr. Groat's experiences.

"In January 1964 I went to Woodhouse Lea in the company of Mr. and Mrs. Peter London," Ian told us. "We waited for several hours in the basement of the house, which had been used to store fodder for horses."

"I gather you went there because of the tradition that a 'White Lady' appeared there?" I asked.

Ian nodded. "After about two hours, a fluorescent light appeared behind one of the doors, which was slightly ajar. It seemed to move backwards and forwards for about five minutes and then disappeared. All three of us saw it. The light was coming from behind that door. We were waiting to see whether anything would actually enter the room, but nothing did, and so we left."

"What was the house like at that point?"

"It was still standing, though several large pieces of masonry had fallen and were lying in front of it. The woodwork was in very poor condition and floorboards were missing, but part of the original grand staircase was still there. It was dangerous to walk in it at night, and even in daylight one had to walk very carefully."

The house could have been restored, if someone had wanted to foot the expense. For a while the monument commission thought of doing it, but nothing came of it, and eventually the owners pulled it down. The decision was made in a hurry, almost as if to avoid publicity about the destruction of this historical landmark. It was all done in one weekend. The masonry and what was still standing was pulled to the ground by heavy machinery, then stamped into the ground to serve as a kind of base for the modern chalet which the owners of the land built on top of it. It reminded me of some of the barbarous practices going on in the United States in pulling down old landmarks in order to build something new and, preferably, profitable.

Peter London was shocked at the sudden disappearance of the old mansion house, and he got to talking to some of the women working in the stables at the bottom of the hill, also part of the estate. Several of them had seen the apparition of a woman in white.

The strange thing is that the British army had invested seven thousand pounds in central heating equipment when they occupied the building. This was during World War II and the building was then still in pretty good shape.

"During the war there was a prisoner-of-war camp that bordered on the actual Woodhouse Lea Estate," Ian continued. "The sentries kept a log of events, and there are fourteen entries of interest, stretching over a three-year period. These concerned sightings of a 'woman in white' who was challenged by the sentries. Incidentally, the stable girls saw her walking about the grounds, *outside* the house, not in the house itself or in the stables."

I decided it was time to pay a visit to the area where the mansion last stood. Since there had been no time to make arrangements for my investigation, Mr. Groat went ahead, and to our pleasant surprise he returned quickly, asking us to come inside the stable office, at the bottom of the hill. There we were received by a jolly gentleman who introduced himself as Cedric Burton, manager of the estate. I explained the purpose of my visit. In Scotland, mentioning ghosts does not create any great stir: they consider it part of the natural phenomena of the area.

"As I know the story," Mr. Burton said, "her name was Lady Anne Bothwell, and originally she lived at the *old* Woodhouse Lea Castle, which is about four miles from here. Once when her husband was away, one of his enemies took over the castle and pushed her out, and she died in the snow. I gather she appears with nothing on at all when she does appear. That's the way she was pushed out —naked. Apparently her ghost makes such a nuisance of itself that the owners decided to move the castle and brought most of the stones over here and built the mansion house called Woodhouse Lea up on the hill. The last person I know of who heard a manifestation was a coachman

named Sutherland, and that was just before electric light was installed. There has been no sign of her since."

"I gather there were a number of reports. What exactly did these people see?"

"Well, it was always the same door on the north side of the building, and on snowy nights there was a fairly vigorous knock on the door; and when someone would go outside to investigate, there was never anyone there—nor were there any footprints in the deep snow. That, I think, was the extent of the manifestations, which are of course tremendously exaggerated by the local people. Some say it is a White Lady, and one has even heard people coming up the drive. I've heard it said, when the old house was standing there empty, lights were seen in the rooms."

"Has the house ever been seriously investigated?"

"Some Edinburgh people asked permission and sat in the old house at midnight on midsummer's eve. However, I pointed out to them that she was only known to appear around seven in the evening and in deep snow. Midnight on midsummer's eve wasn't the most auspicious occasion to expect a manifestation. There was another chap who used to bring his dog up and stand there with his torch from time to time, to see if the dog was bristling."

"When did the actual event occur—the pushing out of the woman?"

"The house was moved to this spot in the early fifteenth century. It was originally built around the old Fulford Tower. It is a bit confusing, because up there also by the house there is an archway built from stones from an entirely different place with the date 1415 on it. This comes from the old Galaspas Hospital in Edinburgh."

"If Woodhouse Lea was moved from the original site to this hill in the early fifteenth century, when was the original house built?"

"Sometime during the Crusades, in the thirteenth century."

While the early history of Woodhouse Lea is shrouded in mystery, there was a Lord Woodhouse Lea in the eighteenth century, a well-known literary figure in Edinburgh. Many other literary figures stayed at the house, including Sir Walter Scott, Alan Ramsey, and James Hogg. Evidently Sir Walter Scott knew that *old* Woodhouse Lea was haunted, because he mentions it in one of his books, and Scottish travel books of the eighteenth century commonly refer to it as 'haunted Woodhouse Lea.' In 1932 control of the house passed into the hands of the army, and much damage was done to the structure. The army held onto it for thirty years.

"Have there been any manifestations reported in recent years?"

"Not really," Mr. Burton replied. "When the bulldozer pulled down the old house, we told people as a joke that the ghost would be trying to burrow her way out of the rubble. Some of the stones from the old house have been incorporated into the new chalet, built on top of the crushed masonry, to give it a sort of continuity."

The chalet is the property of George Buchanan Smith, whose family uses it as a holiday house. He is the son of Lord Balonough, and his younger brother is the Undersecretary of State for foreign affairs in Scotland.

"The house has been talked about tremendously," Mr. Burton said. "It has even been described as the second most haunted house in Scotland. Also, Woseley is not too far from here, and it too has a nude white lady. She has been observed running on the battlements."

"Why did they move the house from the old site to this spot?"

"Because of her. She disturbed them too much."

"And did the manifestations continue on the new site?"

"Yes," Mr. Burton acknowledged. "She came with the stones."

He turned the office over to an assistant and took us up to the chalet. The owner was away, so there was no difficulty in walking about the house. It is a charmingly furnished modern weekend house, with a bit of ancient masonry incorporated into the walls here and there. I gazed at a particularly attractive stone frieze over the fireplace. Inscribed upon it, in Latin, were the words, OCCULTUS NON EXTINCTUS: the occult is not dead (just hidden).

✸ 79

The Ghostly Monk of Monkton

WHEN ELIZABETH BYRD moved into a monastic tower at Old Craig Hall at Musselburgh nine miles outside of Edinburgh, she probably didn't figure on sharing the quarters with a ghost, much less a monk. If there is one thing Elizabeth Byrd doesn't want to share quarters with, it is a monk. As for ghosts, she has an open mind: to begin with, she has had ghostly experiences all through the years.

The monastic tower has two stories and is part of a larger complex of buildings which was once a monastery. Her landlord, who is also a good friend, lives in the main house, while Elizabeth is lady of the manor, so to speak, in her tower—an ideal situation for a romantically inclined writer, and she has been able to turn out several novels since moving into Monkton, as the place is called.

We had left my visit to Monkton for the evening of my second day in Edinburgh, and it turned out to be a foggy, chilly day. Alistair and Alanna Knight brought me in their car, and Ian Groat, the gunsmith whom I had met earlier, was also there.

One walks up a winding stair from the ground floor to the main floor, in which Elizabeth has made her home. The apartment consists of a living room with fireplace, a small kitchen and pantry to one side, and a bedroom to the other. I am sure that when the monks had the place, they did not do nearly so well as Elizabeth does now, so I can readily understand why a monk, especially a ghostly monk, would be attracted to the situation. We grouped ourselves around the fireplace with only a candle illuminating the room.

"I rented this cottage in February, 1972," Elizabeth Byrd began the account of her experiences. "I found it beautifully peaceful and benign. I discovered that the cottage was built in 1459, across a courtyard from a fortified house, which goes back to the twelfth century. Not much is known about my cottage except that it was built by monks. They worked this as an agricultural area, and it was an extension of Newbattle Abbey near Dalkeith. It came to be called 'The Town of the Monks.' From this, the name Monkton developed."

"During the year and a quarter that you have lived here," I said, "have you had any unusual experiences?"

"Yes," Elizabeth replied. "Six months after I got here I was reading in bed one night with the light on when I smelled a marvelous juicy kind of baking of meat, or the roasting of meat, which seemed to emanate from the old stone fireplace. It actually made me hungry. Of course I wasn't doing any cooking. This happened three or four times in the subsequent weeks, but I took it in stride, just looked up from my book and said to myself, 'Oh, there it is again, that smell.' It wasn't the kind of meat that you get in the supermarket: it was more like standing rib roast—expensive, gorgeous meat."

Alanna took up the narrative it this point. "I stayed at this cottage about a year ago for the first time. Of course, I was rather apprehensive of what I might find, but I found nothing but this wonderful feeling of great happiness and content. The first time I stayed here with Alistair, we went off to bed and slept in Elizabeth's room, and she slept in her study; it was a Saturday night. I woke up early Sunday morning and there was the sound of bells ringing. It must have been about 6 o'clock in the morning and I thought, 'Ah, there must be a Catholic church somewhere nearby. This is obviously a call to early Mass.' So I didn't wake my husband, but soon I heard the sound of trotting horses, and again I thought, 'Oh, well, that is somebody out with their horses. After all it is in the country.' When we had breakfast, I asked my husband whether the sound of the bells didn't wake him around 6 o'clock. He said, 'What bells?' I didn't say anything, but when Elizabeth came in I asked her, 'Doesn't the bell wake you up on a Sunday morning? Where is your church near here?' She said, 'We don't have a church here.' Actually, the bell I heard was on the side of the house."

"The bell has never been heard by anyone except by Alanna. There is no church within miles," Elizabeth said.

"Last March I stayed here again," Alanna continued. "I slept in Elizabeth's room, and around eight in the morning I woke up to a wonderful smell of food and thought, 'Oh, good, Elizabeth is making something absolutely delicious for breakfast,' and it was the most gorgeous, juicy smell, a gamey smell. There was also the smell of lovely, fresh bread. I jumped out of bed and rushed into the kitchen. There was no sign of Elizabeth and nothing was cooking. It was all emanating from the bedroom."

Now it was Ian Groat's turn.

"In January, 1973, I was asked to spend a few days' holiday here. On the first night I retired about 4:30. Before falling asleep, I realized that I might see things, not because Elizabeth had told me of anything in particular, but because I suspected there was a good reason why she wanted me to sleep in this particular room."

"Did you, in fact, see anything unusual?"

"Yes," the gunsmith replied. "The first thing I saw was a trap door slightly to the left, in the floor, and a pair of steps leading to the basement. I saw the top of the trap door and a small monk appeared and looked at me. He had climbed the steps into the bedroom and was looking around, but he didn't seem to see me. Since he didn't see me at all, I allowed myself to relax completely. Then I saw a procession come in. One appeared to be a high dignitary of the Roman Catholic Church. He may have been a bishop. He was flanked by monks and they seemed to be chanting. I had a very good look at the bishop. He was clean-shaven, with a very serene face, and he looked very intelligent. The procession walked past me and more or less disappeared.

"Now another apparition appeared which caused me a great deal of confusion. I had decided I could see through the floor if I cared to exercise my faculty to do so. So I looked through the floor, and what I saw were bales of hay, and then I saw what appeared to be an opening in the wall, and through it came what I took to be either Vikings or Saxons. They were dressed in rough clothing. There were three of them—an old man, bearded, with gray hair, and two others, younger and fair-haired, also bearded, and none of them had weapons. I thought them to be farmers. They came through this cavity in the wall and they raised their hands in a greeting sign, but not at me. I was more or less an observer. Then I decided, since I could see through the floor, that I could perhaps see outside the building as well, and I then viewed the building from a height. Now I appeared to be on a parallel which was outside this dwelling, looking down. I saw soldiers coming up the drive and around the corner, and they seemed to be of the middle seventeen hundreds, dressed in gray coats of a very superior material. The accoutrements seemed to be made of white webbing. They were playing their drums and keep-

The Monkton cottage, complete with ghost

ing step with them as they marched. I gained the impression that I was seeing this standing in a tower, but there is no tower there. I tried to see more, but I didn't, so I decided to go to sleep."

"My landlord, John Calderwood Miller," Elizabeth Byrd added, "bought this property in 1956 and restored it. There is a reference to it in Nigel Trentor's book, *The Fortified House in Scotland*. I told Mr. Miller about Ian's experience of having seen the hole in the floor and the monk going down and the hay, and he said, 'That is extraordinary, because in 1956 there *was* a hole in the floor between where your beds are now, and we had to cover it over and make a floor.' There was an exit down to what had been the stables where there were indeed horses. Now it is a garage and sheds."

There was still another witness to the haunting at Monkton: Ian Adam, whom I had interviewed in London, the mediumistic gentleman who had been so helpful to me during my ghost-hunting expedition in April. Originally of Scottish background, Ian liked coming up to Edinburgh. The morning of December 27, 1972, he arrived at 3:45. Elizabeth Byrd remembers it clearly; not too many of her friends drop in at that hour. But he was driving up from Newcastle with a friend, and Elizabeth had gotten worried.

"It was a very cold night, and Elizabeth greeted us as only Elizabeth can," Ian told me. "Immediately we sat down in her sitting room, she asked, 'Do you feel anything here?' but even before she had said it, I had felt that it had a very peaceful atmosphere about it."

"Within ten minutes, out of the blue, Ian, who had never been here, said, 'What a strong scent of rosemary! This place is redolent of rosemary!'" Elizabeth reported Ian as exclaiming, but none of the others could smell it.

"The place was very lovely, really," Ian said, "and I told Elizabeth I was sure there was a woman there, a very industrious lady, perhaps of the fifteenth century. She appeared to me to be wearing a sort of off-white dress and was very busy cooking, as if she had an enormous amount of work to do. She seemed young, and yet old for her years, probably owing to hard work. There was a definite sense of tremendous activity about her, as if she had an awful lot of people to look after. I had a strong feeling that the place was one of healing. I saw a man sitting in a corner on a chair; his leg was being dressed and strapped, and he was being given an old-fashioned jug, or bottle, to drink from by another man. I think it had an anesthetic in it. I remember distinctly there was a great deal of good being done in this place, as if it were a place where people came for shelter and healing, if there were accidents or fighting. It was certainly a place of great spiritual power."

When I checked Ian's testimony with Elizabeth, who had written down his impressions immediately after he had given them to her, she changed the description of the woman ghost somewhat. According to Elizabeth's notes, the woman seemed between thirty and forty years of age, wearing pale gray, sort of looped up on one side.

"Was the impression of the man being helped and of the woman doing the cooking simply an imprint of the past, or do you think these were ghosts that you saw?"

"Oh," Ian said firmly, "they were ghosts all right." He couldn't hear anything, but he did smell the cooking.

"Did anything else happen during that night?"

"No. I had a very peaceful night, although I was absolutely freezing. It must have been the coldest night I've ever lived through. In fact, I got out of bed in the middle of the night and put a jersey over my head to protect myself from the intense cold."

There is one more witness to the haunting at Monkton. James Boyd, by profession a sales representative, but gifted with psychic and healing powers, once stayed overnight in the same bedroom Ian Groat slept in when he had his remarkable experience. This was in early April of 1972.

"In the morning he came to me," Elizabeth said, and reported that there was a woman in a long, dirty-white dress who seemed to be very busy about the fireplace in the bedroom. The two fireplaces in the sitting room, where we are now, and the bedroom next door, were once connected. James Boyd also told me, 'She's very busy and tired because she works so hard.' He had, of course, no knowledge of Ian Adam's experience in the house."

Ian Groat spoke up now. "Two weeks after his visit here, James Boyd telephoned me and said, 'Ian, I have the feeling that there is a well in that courtyard. It is all covered up, but I think if you go down that well, about halfway down, you will find a cavity in the wall and in this cavity lots of silver, household silver that was hidden in times of danger.' I promised I would tell Elizabeth about it and I did."

"There is indeed such a well in the courtyard," Elizabeth confirmed, "but the tower that Ian Groat mentioned no longer exists. It was part of a peel tower, used for defense. When I told Mr. Miller about the well, he said, 'Now that is very extraordinary. About a year ago I went down into the well, about fifteen feet, and when I looked up, the light seemed far away.' Mr. Miller decided to go back up, as he didn't know what he might hit down in the depths. But he did have the feeling that there was a treasure somewhere and encouraged me and my friends to look for it."

Now that everyone had had his say, it was time to tell them of my own impressions. While the others were talking about the bedroom, I had the very distinct impression of a large, rather heavy monk witching from the doorway. He had on a grayish kind of robe, and there was a rather quizzical expression on his face, as if he were studying us. The name Nicholas rushed at me. I also had the feeling that there was some agricultural activity going on around here, with chickens and geese and supplies, and that in some way the military were involved with these supplies. These impressions came to me *before* the others had given their respective testimonies.

"The monk I saw had a gray robe on," Ian Groat confirmed, "and my impression was that I was seeing events that had occurred and not people who were present at that particular moment. It was like seeing a film from the past."

Well, if the monks and the lady at Elizabeth's Monkton Tower are film actors, they are one step ahead of Hollywood: you can actually *smell* the food!

✳ 80

Scottish Country Ghosts

FOR A DAY IN EARLY MAY, the morning certainly looked peculiar: heavy, moist fog was covering most of Edinburgh; fires were burning in all the fireplaces of the hotel; and the electric light had to be turned on at nine in the morning. It didn't seem to bother the natives much, not even when the fog gave way to heavy rain of the kind I know so well from the Austrian mountains. Just the same, a schedule is a schedule. Promptly at 10 Alistair and Alanna Knight called for me at the Hotel George, and we embarked on the trip we had planned well in advance. Alistair was well armed with maps of the area to the south and east of Edinburgh, to make sure that we did not lose time in going off on the wrong road. Since the Knights came from Aberdeen they were not so familiar with the countryside farther south as native Edinburghers might be, and the whole trip took on even more the mood of an adventure. At first we followed one of the main roads leading out of town, but when we got on top of a steep hill in the southeastern suburbs of Edinburgh, the fog returned and enveloped us so thoroughly that Alistair had to halt the car. We decided to trust our intuition, and between Alanna and myself, we put our ESP to work, such as it was, telling Alistair to go straight until he came to a certain side road, which he was to take. To our immense relief, the fog lifted just then and we discovered that we had been on the right road all along.

It all started with a note from Mrs. Agnes Cheyne, who wanted to tell me about an unusual spot eight miles from Edinburgh called Auchindinny, Midlothian. "I was born there in 1898," Mrs. Cheyne had written. "I am no chicken." The ghost who haunts the "Firth Woods" is that of a woman who was jilted by her lover and in great distress jumped from a great height into the river Esh. That, at least, is the tradition. Mrs. Cheyne's aunt, who wasn't convinced of the reality of ghosts, happened to be walking through an abandoned railroad tunnel running through to Dalmor Mill. At the mill, there are two old railroad tunnels left over from a branch of the Edinburgh railroad which has long been abandoned for lack of business. The tracks of course were taken up many years ago, but the tunnels have remained as a silent testimony to the colorful era of railroading. Today, the mill uses the road and trucks to do business with the outside world. It is a quiet, wooded part of the country, very much off the beaten track both to tourists and to business people, and it has retained much of the original charm it must have had throughout the nineteenth century.

The lady walked into the tunnel, and when she came to the middle of it, she suddenly froze in terror. There was a woman coming toward her, seemingly out of nowhere. Her clothes showed her to be from an earlier period, and there were no sounds to her footsteps. Mrs. Cheyne's aunt looked closer, and suddenly the apparition disappeared before her eyes. Although she had never believed in ghosts, that day she returned home to Edinburgh in a very shaken condition.

After about forty-five minutes, we reached a narrow country road, and despite the heavy rain, we managed to see a sign reading "Dalmor Mill." A few moments later, a branch road descended toward the river bank, and there was the mill. We ignored a sign warning trespassers not to park their cars and looked around. There was a tunnel to the right and one to the left. First we investigated the one on the right. Inside, everything was dry, and I remarked what wonderful mushrooms one could grow in it. We had scarcely walked ten yards when Alanna turned back, saying, "This is not the right tunnel. Let's try the other one." As soon as we had walked into the second tunnel, all of us felt an icy atmosphere which was far in excess of what the rainy day would bring about. Besides, the first tunnel was not equally cold. When we reached the middle of the tunnel Alanna stopped. "I wouldn't want to walk through this at night," she said, "and even in the daytime I wouldn't walk through it *alone*."

"What do you feel here?" I asked. I had not told the Knights about Mrs. Cheyne's letter or why we were here.

"There is something about the middle of this tunnel that is very frightening. I have a feeling of absolute panic, and this started when I was halfway through this tunnel." Without further ado, Alanna turned back and sat in the car. I am sure that no amount of persuasion could have gotten her back into that tunnel again.

* * *

Twenty-three miles from Edinburgh, in a fertile valley that was once the center of the mill industry but is now largely agricultural, there stands the town of Peebles. The surrounding countryside is known as Peeblesshire and there are a number of lovely vacation spots in the area, quiet conservative villas and small hotels much favored by the English and the Scottish. One such hotel is the Venlaw Castle Hotel, standing on a bluff on the outskirts of town, seven hundred feet above sea level. It is open for summer guests only and does indeed give the appearance of a castle from the outside. Standing four stories high, with a round tower in one corner, Venlaw Castle represents the fortified house of Scotland rather than the heavy, medieval fortress. Access to the castle, now the hotel, is from the rear; behind it, Venlaw, the hill which gave it its name, rises still further. The present building was erected in 1782 on the site of an old Scottish keep called Smithfield Castle, one of the strong points of the borderland in olden days. One half of the present house was added in 1854, in what is locally known as the mock baronial style.

Venlaw belonged to the Erskine family and in 1914 Lady Erskine offered her mansion to the admiralty as a convalescent hospital for twelve naval officers. According to

James Walter Buchanan's *A History of Peebleshire*, it remained an auxiliary Red Cross hospital to the end of World War I. The same author describes the present dwelling house as being "built on a commanding position with one of the finest views in the County. It is presumed that it occupies the site of the ancient castle of Smithfield, which was in existence until about the middle of the eighteenth century."

In 1949 the house passed into the hands of Alexander Cumming, the father of the present owner, who turned it into a small hotel.

In the summer of 1968 an American couple, Mr. and Mrs. Joseph Senitt, decided to spend a few days at Venlaw Castle. "The room we occupied was at the end of the middle floor with a little turret room which my daughter used," Mrs. Senitt had explained to me. "The very first night we were there, the room was ice cold even though it was July, and we couldn't wait to close the lights and go to sleep. Immediately upon getting into bed, I suddenly heard a long-drawn-out and quite human sigh! It seemed to be near the foot of my bed. For the moment I froze—I was afraid to move or even breathe. If it hadn't been for the fact that my husband was with me, I might have gone into shock. I said nothing to him, as he usually kids me about my ghostly beliefs, and I felt he was probably asleep, as he made no move and said nothing. However, after a moment I got the strongest feeling that if it was a ghost it was friendly, because I felt welcome."

When the Senitts left the castle a few days later, Mrs. Senitt finally mentioned the incident to her husband. To her surprise he confirmed that he too had heard the sound. He had attributed it to their daughter, sleeping in the small room next door. But Mrs. Senitt was sure that the sound came from in front of her, and the turret bedroom where the girl slept was off to a corner in back of the room and the door was closed. Also, the Senitts were the only people staying in that part of the hotel at the time.

It was still raining when we crossed the river Tweed and headed into Peebles. The castle-hotel was easy to find, and a few minutes later we arrived in front of it, wondering whether it would be open, since we had not been able to announce our coming. To our pleasant surprise a soft-spoken young man bade us welcome, and it turned out that he was the owner, the son of the man who had opened the hotel originally, and also that he was the only person in the hotel at the present time, since it was not yet open for the season. I asked him to show us the room on the middle floor with the turret bedroom without, however, indicating my reasons for this request. I merely mentioned that some American friends of mine had enjoyed their stay at Venlaw, and I wanted to see the room they'd occupied. As soon as we had entered the room, Alanna turned to me and said, "There is something here. I'm getting a cold, crawly scalp." While Alanna was getting her psychic bearings, I

took Mr. Cumming aside, out of her earshot, and questioned him about the hotel. Was there, to his recollection, any incident connected with the house, either since it had been turned into a hotel or before, involving death or tragedy or anything unusual?

Mr. Cumming seemed a bit uneasy at this question. "There are things we don't like to speak about," he finally said. "We've only had one traumatic accident. About twenty years ago one of our guests fell from a bedroom window."

Alanna came over at this point and stopped short of the window. "There's something at this window," she said. "Somebody either threw himself out of this window or fell out." But Alanna insisted that the tragedy went back a long time, which puzzled me. Was she confusing her time periods, or did a second death follow an earlier death, perhaps caused by a possessing entity? Those are the kinds of thoughts that race through a psychic investigator's mind at a time like this. Actually, it turned out that the guest fell out of a window one flight higher than the room we were in. He was a miner who had become ill and somehow fallen out the window. His friends carried him back in, but he had a broken neck; they actually killed him by moving him.

Alanna shook her head. "No. What I feel has to do with this window in this room. It may have something to do with the original place that stood here before. I get the feeling of a fire."

"Well," Mr. Cumming said, "Venlaw Hill, where we are standing, was the place where, during the persecutions, witches were burned, or people accused of such."

"I have feelings of intense suffering," Alanna said, "and I sense some noise, the feeling of noise and of a great deal of confusion and excitement. I get the feeling of a crowd of people, and of anger. Someone either fell out of this window or was thrown out, and also there is a feeling of fire. But this is definitely a woman. I feel it not only in this room but down on this terrace below, which seems to have something to do with it."

I questioned Mr. Cumming whether any of his guests had ever complained about unusual phenomena.

"Not really," he replied. "We did have a guest who complained of noises, but she was mentally disturbed. She was a resident here for some time in the 1950s. I didn't know her well; I was very young at the time."

"And where did this lady stay?" I asked.

"Why, come to think of it, in the room next to this one.

I thanked Mr. Cumming and wondered whether the lady guest had really been unhinged, or whether perhaps she had only felt what Mr. and Mrs. Senitt felt some fifteen years later in the same area.

The afternoon was still young, and we had two hours left to explore the countryside. We decided to cross the river Tweed once again and make for Traquair House, making sure, however, to telephone ahead, since this was

not one of the days on which this private manor house could be visited.

Known as the "oldest inhabited house in Scotland," Traquair House at Innerleithen rises to five stories amid a majestic park, in a tranquil setting that gives the illusion of another century, another world. It is now owned by Lord Maxwell Stuart, of a distinguished noble family, related to the royal Stuarts. There is a tradition that the magnificent gates of Traquair, surmounted by fabled animals, shall remain closed until a Stuart king is crowned again in London. This Jacobite sentiment goes back to the times when the earls of Traquair gave support to the Stuart cause, but the present laird, Peter Maxwell Stuart, is more concerned with the quality of the beer he brews. He's also the author of a magnificently illustrated booklet detailing the treasures at Traquair House. These include, in the king's room, the bed in which Mary Queen of Scots slept, with a coverlet made by her ladies-in-waiting. That she slept there is not surprising, since Lady Mary Seaton, the wife of the second earl, was one of Mary's favorite ladies-in-waiting. Also, the very cradle used by Mary Stuart for her son James VI of Scotland now stands at Traquair, and in the many rooms of the house there are displayed treasures, documents, arms, and fine furniture, all of them dating back to the sixteenth and seventeenth centuries, when this great house was at its zenith. Much as we loved the sight of this beautiful house, so romantic on a rainy day, with the fog just lifting, we had come not to admire the antiques but to find out about its ghosts.

The caretaker, Andrew Aiken Burns, who had been at the house since 1934, took us around, painstakingly explaining room after room.

"Have you ever had any psychic experiences here?"

"Yes," he nodded, as if it were the most natural thing in the world to be asked. "It happened in 1936 in the after-noon of a beautiful summer day. I was out with my horse, clearing the brush from the front of the house, near the old ruined cottage in the field. My horse was a chestnut named Ginger, and suddenly he flicked his ears and I looked up. I saw a lady coming down the grass, dressed in a Victorian dress. She walked slowly down through the gate and into the cottage and their through the wicket gate into the garden."

"What was so special about that? Could she not have been a visitor?" I asked.

"Well, I left my horse and went right up to see where this person had gone, and the wicket gate was shut. She had been through the gate, and still the gate was shut."

"Did you ever see her again?"

"No. But later someone showed me some old photographs, and I recognized one is the lady I had seen walking on the grass. It was Lady Louisa Stuart."

Lady Louisa Stuart died in 1875 at age one hundred. She is buried in a vault in the Traquair church-yard, right in back of the castle. Why would she walk the grounds? I wondered.

According to the twentieth laird, Traquair House goes back to the tenth century when a heather hut stood on the place. In 1107 King Alexander I granted a charter to the Traquairs, and he was the first of a long line of Scottish kings who stayed here. Incidentally, Traquair means dwelling on a winding river. In the thirteenth century the building was incorporated into a border peel, a defensive palisade, and it served as such during the long period of border strife. In 1491 James Stuart, the son of the Earl of Buchan, became the first Laird of Traquair, and from him the present family is descended. Over the centuries the building was largely altered and added to, to fit the changing times. What was once an austere border fortress became a Renaissance castle and eventually one of the finer residences in Scotland. During the Civil War in the seventeenth century, Traquair became what the present laird describes as "one of the great bastions of the Catholic faith in Scotland," because of marriages with Catholic ladies. Since Catholicism was not favored in this part of the country, Mass had to be celebrated in secret. To this day, there is a Roman Catholic chapel on the grounds, unfortunately decorated in the most gaudy modern style and totally at variance with the rest of the house. In 1688 the house was raided by a mob from Peebles, and all the religious articles found were destroyed. It wasn't until well into the nineteenth century that Catholicism was freely admitted into Scotland. During the rebellion of 1715, Traquair sided with Bonnie Prince Charles, which brought much misfortune upon the family.

When Charles Stuart, the fourteenth laird, died unmarried in 1861, the property passed into the hands of his sister, Lady Louisa, born in 1775. She also didn't marry and died in 1875 after spending nearly all her time on her estate. All her life she had carried on a love affair with Traquair House. She looked after the gardens, took great pride in keeping the house itself in perfect order, and, though she was the first female head of the family in many centuries, she had the full respect of the villagers and of her servants. When she died, the question of the inheritance had to be settled by the courts. Eventually, Traquair House passed into the hands of Lady Louisa's cousin, the Honorable Henry Constable Maxwell Stuart, who thus became the sixteenth laird. Perhaps Lady Louisa was not altogether happy with the turn of events, for she had been the last in the direct line to hold Traquair. Possibly, her spirit does not wish to relinquish her realms, or perhaps her long residence here has so accustomed her to Traquair that she is unaware of the fact that there might be another, better place for her to go.

"Has anyone else seen the ghost of Lady Louisa?" I asked the caretaker.

"Well, some other people have seen her, but they have only seen a figure and did not recognize her. Some have seen her farther up the road."

"Why is she called The Green Lady?" I asked. I understood from my friends that the legendary Lady of Traquair was referred to by that name.

"Well, the dress I saw her wearing," the caretaker said, "was kind of green, the color of a wood pigeon."

"Is there such a dress in existence?" I asked. Since so much of the old furniture and personal belongings of the family were preserved at the house, perhaps the original dress still existed.

"Well, it is a strange thing: one of the old foresters here—his wife's mother was Lady Louisa's dressmaker. They kept some of the clippings from which the dresses were made, and when I asked her, the granddaughter showed me the materials. I recognized the color and the material of the dress the lady had on when I saw her." Mr. Burns, the caretaker, admitted that he had some psychic abilities. Sometimes he knew things before they actually occurred, but paid it no great heed.

I asked Mr. Burns to take us to Lady Louisa's room. There, beautifully framed on the south wall, was the great lady's portrait. "She was friendly with Sir Walter Scott," the caretaker commented. The room was oblong, with a fireplace on one end. Wine-red chairs, two sofas, and a strange mixture of eighteenth-century and Victorian furniture gave the room a warm, intimate feeling. On one side, one could gaze into the garden, while the other overlooked the driveway, so that Lady Louisa would always know who was coming up to see her. Alanna hadn't said anything for quite a while. I found her standing by the garden windows. The rain had stopped, and the sun began to pierce through the clouds.

"Do you feel her presence?" I asked.

Alanna gave me a curious look. "Don't you?"

I nodded. I had known for several minutes that Lady Louisa Stuart was at home this afternoon, receiving *unexpected* visitors.

* * *

Shortly afterwards, we drove back towards Edinburgh. We crossed the river Tweed again, and the rain started up once more. It was as if fate had held it back for an hour or so to give us a chance to visit Traquair House at its best.

I wondered what it was that bound all British ghosts together. Then it struck me: whether Medieval or Victorian, Renaissance, or Edwardian, they all had *style*.

✳ 81

The Ghost on the Kerry Coast

IF YOU'VE NEVER heard of Ballyheigue—pronounced just like Rodgers and Hammerstein's "Bali-ha'i"—you've really missed one of the most poetic stretches of coastland still unspoiled by human greed. It isn't completely untouched by habitation by any means, but there isn't—as yet—that glass-and-concrete luxury hotel, the nearby airport, the chic clientele. Ballyheigue just sits there, a small fishing village and a majestic castle, looking out onto the Atlantic. This stretch of land used to swarm with smugglers not so long ago, as it was rather difficult for the revenue people to catch up with the wily Irish in the many bays and loughs of Western Ireland.

Now I wasn't looking for smugglers' coves or new sources of poteen, but the spirit that moved me to travel down the Kerry coast had been brought to my attention in a respectable magazine piece, published a couple of years ago in Dublin. The article, entitled "On the Trail of a Ghost," is the factual report of Captain P. D. O'Donnell, about his strange experiences at Ballyheigue in 1962. The magazine, *Ireland of the Welcomes*, is published by the Irish Tourist Board, but this piece is the only instance of a psychic adventure appearing in its pages. Here then is Captain O'Donnell's report:

"It all started during a normal vacation in Ballyheigue in the first, sunny half of June, 1962. Even on holidays, a part-time writer like myself is always on the lookout for new ideas, but on that vacation I was determined to get the most out of a heat wave, and to heck with writing. I relaxed in the quiet atmosphere of the almost deserted village, lazed on the lonely four-mile-long beach with the family, or joined in the beach games with the handful of visitors from the hotel.

"Then, one day—it was the 4th or 5th day of June, be it noted—I took a walk with my eight-year-old son, Frank, up the winding avenue above the cliffs to the burnt-out shell of Ballyheigue Castle. It was purely in deference to my interest in old castles, and to show my son the castle. I had only a vague idea of its history, but knew that from here the strong Crosbie family had once lorded it over most of the north of County Kerry. They left the country when the republicans burnt the castle to the ground during the 'troubles' of 1921.

"For a while we talked to an old man working nearby, and he told us the castle was never explored fully. Then with camera in hand we started. I am one for always trying different angles and unusual shots with a camera, so when our short tour among the ruins satisfied Frank, we started to take a few snaps for the record. The snap that mattered was taken inside the castle. Frank was placed standing against a wall at right angles to the front of the castle, and I stood back. It was shadowy inside the castle, but the sun was slanting strongly through a window on his right. In the viewfinder I was able to get Frank on the left and hoped also to get the view of the beach through the window on the right. The light of the sun coming through the window would be enough, I hoped—no light meters for my amateur photography.

"The story of the rest of the vacation does not matter, except to record that the days were filled with sunshine, battling the breakers, looking for Kerry diamonds on Kerry Head, enjoying the relaxation and joining in the hotel sing-song at night. What did matter, however, was when the color film came back from the developers. The snap which I have described appeared to have another figure in it, partly obscured by the square of light that was the window. This figure held a sword, and its legs were not trousered, but appeared as if clothed in hose or thigh boots! At first I thought this rather frightening, but my wife passed it off as a double exposure.

"However, when she and I examined the other snapshots, we both agreed that there was neither a double exposure nor any other negative which if it was superimposed on the 'ghost' picture could have produced the same effect. What then was the answer, we wondered. Was it really a ghost I had photographed?

"The events that followed, indeed, made the affair more extraordinary. I brought the snap into the office, and passed it around my friends. Two were more interested than the others, and asked to see the negative. When I went home for lunch I slipped the negative into the same envelope with the snapshot—much to my later regret—and they were suitably impressed. That night, however, I gave the envelope to a friend, forgetting that the negative was also inside—and would you believe it—the envelope disappeared most mysteriously. If it was only the snapshot, it would have been all right, but as the negative was with it, all was lost. At least I had twelve witnesses who saw both negative and print, so anyone who says I am a liar can call them liars too.

"Of course, I advertised in the newspapers, and even got leaflets printed offering a very good reward, but my 'ghost' picture never turned up. I was interviewed by a newspaper and on radio, and determined to look into the whole matter of recent Irish ghostly appearances and write a book on the subject. The news travelled, and shortly after, I had queries from Stockholm and from Copenhagen seeking to buy the Swedish and Danish rights of the photographs. They were offering sums from £25 to £30, and if I had the photo, I would probably have been the richer by much more, when other newspapers got interested.

"Why were the Danes so interested in a photograph of a 'ghost' from the wilds of Kerry? That story is extremely interesting. According to old Kerry records a Danish ship, the *Golden Lyon*, of the Danish Asiatic Company, en route from Copenhagen to Tranquebar, was wrecked on the strand at Ballyheigue on October 20, 1730.

At Ballyheigue in Ireland, a ghostly sailor stays on

It had been blown off its course by a fierce storm, but the local story was that the Crosbies of Ballyheigue Castle set up false lights on horses' heads to lure the ship ashore. The ship's captain, thinking the bobbing lights ahead from other shipping, kept on course, only to become a wreck on the Atlantic breakers.

"The crew were rescued by Sir Thomas Crosbie and his tenants. Also salvaged were many bottles of Danish wine, clothing, equipment, *and* twelve chests of silver bars and coin. The last was for the purpose of paying for goods and labor in Tranquebar, and was the cause of six people meeting their deaths. Soon afterwards, Sir Thomas Crosbie died suddenly, by poison it was rumored, and his wife, Lady Margaret, claimed a sum of £4,500 for salvage and the loss of her husband. She said it was because of his labors and exertions on the night of the wreck that he died. The ship's master, Captain J. Heitman, opposed the claim indignantly, and moved the twelve chests of silver down into the cellar under the strong tower of the castle. However, delay followed delay, and by June 1731, he still found he could not get the silver safely to Dublin, and home to Denmark, or on another ship.

"Then one night he was aroused by the sound of many voices outside the castle gates. Jumping up, he was left under no illusions that a raid was in progress. About fifty or sixty men with blackened faces stormed the gates, and attacked the tower. Lady Margaret then arrived and flung herself in front of the captain, saying he would be killed if he ventured outside. Meanwhile, the sentry on the

door to the cellar rushed, bleeding from stab wounds, up to his comrades on the first floor of the tower. He told them that his two fellow sentries lay dead outside, and that the mob had disarmed him. As the other Danes had only one musket between them and little ammunition—another bone of contention between Heitman and Lady Margaret—they retreated to the top room of the tower and were spectators to the scene of the twelve chests of silver being loaded on farm carts. Then the shouting stopped and the carts vanished into the night.

"However, within three days, Sir Edward Denny, the governor of Tralee, had nine men in Tralee gaol. One of the Danes had spotted a nephew of Lady Margaret's in the mob, and it soon became apparent that the whole robbery was planned by friends of the Crosbies. In the dispositions taken before the several trials, a number of the accused stated that four chests of the silver had been laid aside for Lady Margaret. These were never recovered. Lady Margaret denied knowing anything about the affair and the Danes recovered only £5,000 out of a total of £20,000 in silver. Some of the raiders fled across the Shannon to Clare, others left for France in a fishing boat loaded with silver, while the majority simply went to earth and said nothing.

"Two Crosbies, relatives of Lady Margaret, were tried in Dublin and acquitted, but a third man, named Cantillon, a tenant of the castle Crosbies, was found guilty. One man hanged himself in Tralee gaol and another, who turned state's evidence, was found dead in his lodgings in Dublin. It was said he was poisoned, although the castle put it out that he died of typhoid and drinking too much. And the local tradition handed down the story that most of

the gentry of north Kerry were involved. The castle at Ballyheigue was owned by the Cantillons, ancestors of the man found guilty, before the Crosbies arrived in Kerry. They were originally de Cantillons, who came to Ireland with the Norman invaders.

"Pieces of Danish china still exist locally, and in the cellars of Ballyheigue Castle lie some bottles with Danish crests, but of the missing silver there is still no trace. Some of the accused said it was buried in the orchard there, others that it was buried in an orchard three miles away near Banna Strand, and still others that it was buried behind Ballysheen House. If you enquire today in Ballyheigue, you will surely find someone who will tell you that he knows where it is buried, that he and his forefathers were afraid to dig it up, and maybe he might let you into the secret!

"The Danes are naturally still interested. It would make great copy if the 'ghost' photo was of one of the Danish sailors, and besides there is the lost treasure in silver. Long ago in the time of King Brian Boru, Viking ships of Norsemen and Danes raided Ireland, established the cities of Dublin, Wexford and Waterford, and brought loot back to Scandinavia. It was probably a simple matter for those envious of the Danish silver to persuade the local farmers that the presence of Danish silver in Ballyheigue Castle was a chance to reverse the flow of loot, and besides there was the landlord's wife, who lost her husband saving the shipwrecked Danes. However, the affair of the ghost picture has a more interesting history.

"All these historical details were new to me, and I found it highly interesting to read that swordsmen did indeed flash their swords in the castle. What was almost fantastic, however, was a little detail that almost escaped my notice. Remember, I said I had come on vacation to Ballyheigue in June. I arrived on June 1st. The second week was wild and rainy and it was not possible to take any color pictures in that week. The first week, however, was heat wave weather, with sunshine for 15 hours every day. It was after the weekend of 1st/2nd of June that I began to take the second roll of color film, and I am reasonably certain that the 'ghost' picture was taken on the 4th or 5th of June. Now, the record states that the Danish Silver Raid took place at midnight on June 4, 1731! Coincidence? Or do swords flash in Ballyheigue Castle on every June 4th when three Danish sailors died?

"You may bet I will be there next June 4th, with camera at the ready. Do I believe in this ghost? Well, it's a good excuse for visiting that charming spot again. Will I be afraid, while waiting there till midnight? Not on your life. I won't be alone, but somehow I don't believe we will see anything at night. The 'ghost' photo was taken in mid-afternoon with the sun slanting through the window from the west. Possibly, what I photographed was an imprint on the wall. But then again, the Danes were there, they were probably wearing seaboots, and there was swordplay there on the 4th of June."

*   *   *

So much for Captain O'Donnell's experience. The irony of losing his negative can be appreciated—for I too guard my psychic photographs, such as those of the ghostly monks at Winchester Cathedral, England, as if they were treasures, which in a way they are.

I made inquiries about the author of the article and was assured his integrity was the highest. As an officer he was not given to imagining things.

We had been visiting Listowel and decided to continue on to Ballyheigue. On the map it seemed an easy hour's ride, but it was almost sundown by the time we rounded the last hill and saw the sparkling sea before us.

Quickly passing through the village, we drove up to the gate of the castle. There was an old gatekeeper in a tiny house nearby and we had no trouble convincing her that we meant the castle no harm. We opened the old gate ourselves and then the car drove up the winding driveway towards the gray castle, the ruins of which loomed large over the landscape. The gentle slopes reaching from its ramparts to the sandy shore were covered by meadowland, which was moist, as so much of Ireland is. On the land were perhaps two dozen cows and many more mementos of their presence.

We avoided the cows and parked the car close to the castle walls. Then I started to film the scene, while our driver ate a belated luncheon. The cows did not seem to bother him.

The castle looked eerie even in the daytime, with its windows staring out into the country like the eyes of a blind man. Inside, the walking was hazardous, for wet soil had long filled in the rooms. The fire that had devoured the castle in 1921 had left nothing of the interior standing, and the totally gutted heart of the once proud house now looked like an ancient Roman ruin. We walked about the many rooms, and Sybil tried to pick up impressions. Naturally, she knew nothing whatever about the place.

Ultimately, we followed her into one of the first-floor rooms looking out to the sea—a room whence one could have easily observed the ships and all that came and went. Here she stopped and listened, as if from within. Her psychic voice was giving her directions and we waited quietly for her words.

"Sybil, what do you think happened here?" I decided to break the silence.

"Whatever happened here," she replied hesitatingly, "certainly happened at a much lower level than the one we're on. I have a feeling that there is an underground passage connected with the sea."

She did not, of course, know about the Danish sailors and how the silver was hidden.

"I don't think I'm going back more than 150 years," she added, "although I know there are influences here going back three hundred years."

I urged her on, as she hesitated.

"This passage leading to the sea, Sybil—who came through it?" I asked.

"The name I have in mind is Donald," she replied. "I have a feeling of three young men, possibly sons, connected with the house, but Donald was not. The house was a large family house, but the people who came through the passage were travellers ... *seafaring folk*."

Again I thought, how would Sybil know, consciously, of the Danish sailors coming here for refuge? She could not know this.

"Were they of local origin?" I asked.

"Foreign," she shot back, "probably coming from France. Lots of coming and going here."

"Why had these men come to the house?"

"Some connection with food," Sybil replied, not at all sure of her impression now, "food or something for the table."

"Any tragedy here?"

"Not those coming from France but the people living in the house."

"What happened?"

"There is the influence of a woman, the name is, I think, Emily, but the woman is connected with the house. The tragedy is through the woman. At first I had only the feeling of a man here, but now the woman is very strong."

"A man?"

"Men," Sybil corrected herself, and added: "The name Glen comes to me. The man's fate in the house ... something to do with the food. Could it be poison? He was eating, when something happened."

One should realize at this point that Sybil had said several things that were pretty close to the true facts. Sir Thomas Crosbie, owner of the castle, was poisoned shortly after the Danish wreck had been salvaged. Was Lady Margaret as guilty of this sudden death as of the "raid" on the Danish silver staged later on?

Also, the raiders eventually fled to France by boat. Had Sybil felt this event somehow? But I wanted to hear more of what my psychic friend had to say here in the ruined drawing roofs of Ballyheigue Castle.

"I have a feeling of a man going down the passage. I think he was drowned because he disappears in the sea."

"Any fighting here?" I asked.

"I don't feel it now," Sybil said. "The woman is not constant to this house; she comes or goes away. The conflict is between the sea and the house. I think it could be a family feud. There is something else but I am not getting it as clearly as I am getting a foreign influence here."

"Other than French?"

"Also, there is a Northern influence. Many foreign visitors. Beyond Scotland, Sweden. Fair men, Nordic influence. Two periods."

Sybil, of course, knew nothing about the Danish sailors.

Who was Emily? Who was Donald?

Did Captain O'Donnell indeed photograph the Danish silver raid, when the Danish sailors died defending their property in Ballyheigue castle?

Not having examined the photograph, I cannot attest to its genuineness, but I have taken similar pictures elsewhere and know it can be done. Thus I have no reason to doubt the story so movingly told by the Captain.

The silver may still lie somewhere underneath the crumbled walls of the castle. The Danes, as we know, only managed to get a fourth of their treasure out of there in the long run. And there may well be an eighteenth-century swordsman defending it now as of yore.

It really does not matter. When you stand at the empty windows of Ballyheigue Castle and look out into the bay towards Kerry Head as the sun slowly settles behind the water line, you can well believe that the place is haunted.

As we rode back towards County Clare, it became chilly and the moisture in the air came down as light rain.

Nobody spoke much.

At one point, we almost took a wrong turn in the road, perhaps due to the darkness now settling around us, or perhaps we were all a bit tired.

Ballyheigue Castle had disappeared into the night by now and the Danish silver was safe once more.

✳ 82

Haunted Kilkea Castle, Kildare

FROM A DISTANCE, Kilkea Castle looks the very image of an Irish castle. Turreted, gray, proud, sticking up from the landscape with narrow and tall windows which give it a massive and fortified appearance, Kilkea Castle is neverthe-less one of the most comfortable tourist hotels in present-day Ireland. Anyone may go there simply by making a reservation with the genial host, Dr. William Cade.

The castle is about an hour and a half by car from Dublin, in the middle of fertile farmlands. There are beautiful walks all around it, and the grounds are filled with brooks, old trees, and meadows—the latter populated by a fairly large number of cows.

Kilkea was built in 1180 by an Anglo-Norman knight named Sir Walter de Riddleford, and it is said to be the oldest inhabited castle in Ireland, although I have seen this claim put forward in regard to several places. Let there be no mistake: the inside has been modified and very little of the original castle remains. But the haunting is still there.

The castle has four floors, not counting cellars and roof. The rooms are of varying sizes and kinds. The haunted area is actually what must have been the servants' quarters at one time, and it is reached through a narrow passage in the northern section of the castle. The room itself is just large enough for one person, and if you should want to sleep in it, you had better make a reservation way ahead of time. All you need to do is ask Dr. Cade for the haunted room. He will understand.

The story of the haunting goes back to the early Middle Ages. Apparently one of the beautiful daughters of an early owner fell in love with a stableboy. Her proud father disapproved and threatened to kill them both if they continued their association. One night, the father found the young man in his daughter's room. In the struggle that followed the man was killed, but we are not told whether the woman was killed or not. But it is the man's ghost who apparently still roams the corridors, trying to get his sweetheart back.

In the course of rebuilding, this room became part of the servants' quarters. A number of people have reported uncanny feelings in the area. The owner of Kilkea himself, though skeptical, has admitted to witnessing doors opening by themselves for no apparent reason.

Locally, the so-called Wizard Earl is blamed for the happenings at Kilkea Castle, and there is even a legend about him. Apparently to please his lady fair, the earl

Kilkea Castle has its own resident ghost

transformed himself into a bird and sat on her shoulder. But he had not counted on the presence of the castle cat, who jumped up and ate the bird. The legend continues that the earl and his companions still ride at night and will eventually return from the beyond to "put things right in Ireland"—if that is necessary. The legend does not say what happened to the cat. •

✳ 83

The Ghosts at Skryne Castle

ONE FINE DAY we started out from Dublin aboard one of the Murray cars one rents in Ireland if one doesn't have a car of one's own, and as luck would have it, we had a most pleasant and intelligent driver by the name of Guy Crodder, who understood immediately what we were after.

Passing the airport, we started to look for Mara Castle, a ruin James Reynolds had briefly mentioned in his Irish ghost books as being suspect from the ghost-hunting point of view. The suburban town of Newton-Swords was interesting and charming, but nobody there knew of Mara Castle. Since our schedule for the day was heavy, I decided to go farther north. We took some of the quiet back roads, but our driver had a good sense of direction, and by high noon we had arrived at our first destination.

County Meath is much less forbidding than the West of Ireland we had recently left, and the nearness of the river Boyne gave the land an almost Southern charm.

Before us rose majestically the high tower of a ruined church, built in the fourteenth century and dedicated to St. Colmcille, one of Ireland's three most sacred saints. The tower, sixty feet high on a hill of about five hundred feet elevation, dominates the landscape. But it was not this once-magnificent church we were seeking out. The much smaller castle of Skryne or Screen, at the foot of the hill, was our goal.

What had brought me here was a brief story in James Reynolds' *More Ghosts in Irish Houses*, published in 1956. He tells of this castle, smallish as castles go, set back of the river Boyne woodlands, not far from Tara, which he visited when it was owned by a relative of the Palmerston family which had long owned the house.

According to Reynolds, the tragedy that led to the haunting at Skryne happened in 1740. At that time the occupants of the house were one Sir Bromley Casway, and his ward, a beautiful young girl by the name of Lilith Palmerston. Lilith had led a sheltered life here and in

Dublin, and had had little contact with the world of society or men. During her long stay at Skryne, she met a country squire named Phelim Sellers whose house stood not far from Skryne and whose wife had died mysteriously, possibly as the result of a beating administered by the brutish man.

Lilith Palmerston instantly disliked the neighbor. He in turn became a frequent visitor at Skryne Castle, playing cards with her elderly guardian, but always having an eye for her. On one occasion, Reynolds tells us, Sellers attacked her but was thwarted in his design by the gardener. Now Lilith asked that they return to Dublin to escape the unwanted attentions of this man. Her guardian agreed and all was in readiness for their journey down to the city. The last night before their planned departure, Sellers got wind of Lilith's plans, broke into her room and murdered her. Later caught, he was hanged at Galway City.

A number of persons living at the castle have heard shrieks in the night, and seen a woman in white clutching at her throat run out of the house.

Sellers had killed Lilith by forcing foxglove fronds down her throat, thus strangling her.

So much for Reynolds' vivid account of the tragedy at Skryne Castle.

I had not announced our coming, but we were fortunate in that the castle was open. It so happened that the owners were tossing a wedding breakfast for someone in the area; thus the house was bustling with servants. It was even more fortunate that only the downstairs part of the old house was being used for the festivities, leaving us free to roam the upper stories at will.

The house stood across from a cluster of very old trees, and on the meadow between them a lonely goat tended to her luncheon.

Built in 1172, the castle had fallen into disrepair and was rebuilt in the early nineteenth century. I walked around the castle, which looked more like an early Victorian country house than a castle, despite its small tower rising above the second story. The house was covered with ivy from one end to the other. The windows were neat and clean and the garden in back of the house seemed orderly.

I managed to talk to one of the caterers in the house, a lady who had come here on many occasions and slept upstairs now and then. She was Kay Collier, and quite willing to talk to me even about so elusive a subject as ghosts.

"I've never noticed anything unusual myself," she began, "but there is a tradition about a ghost here. It's a tall man walking around with a stick, wearing a hard hat, and a dog with him. He's been seen outside the castle. Mrs. Reilly, of Skryne, she's seen him."

Since she could not tell us anything more, I made a mental note to look up Mrs. Reilly. Then I asked Sybil, who had been sitting quietly outside under the age-old tree, to join Catherine and me in the upstairs rooms of the castle. The salon to the left of the stairs was elaborately and tastefully furnished in early Victorian style, with mirrors on some of the walls, delicate furniture, couches, sofas, and small antiques dressing up the room.

Sybil sat down in one of the comfortable chairs, placed her hand over her eyes and gathered impressions. For a moment, no one spoke. The silence, however peaceful on the surface, was forbidding, and there was, to me at least, an atmosphere of doom hanging rather heavily around us in this room.

"This room immediately attracted me," Sybil said now.

"You know I first turned right, then turned around and came straight to this room instead."

I nodded. She had indeed changed course as if led by some invisible force.

"I feel that this is where a woman has walked," Sybil said slowly, deliberately. "The mirrors have some significance; perhaps there was a door behind the mirror on the right hand side, because she comes from the right. Whether she comes from the garden...."

Was Sybil making contact with the unlucky wraith of Lilith whose favorite spot the garden had been, the same garden where her battered body had been found?

Naturally I had never told her of the tradition surrounding the castle, nor of James Reynolds' account.

"Do you feel her now?" I asked.

"Very slightly," Sybil replied, and looked up. "I don't think that she has been seen for some time. Fifty-eight, fifty-nine. I don't think she has made her presence known for some time, *but she is here.*"

"Can you communicate with her?"

"I'm only conscious of her, but not directly in contact with her. Also, there seem to be two periods, and yet the woman should not be a 'period piece' ghost—and yet she has this link with the past."

"What period do you think she belongs to?"

"I have an early period, of 1624, but the feeling in this room is of a very feminine influence, two periods."

"What did you feel outside the castle?"

"The tree is very important to this house somehow."

"What did you feel by the tree?"

"There I felt conflict. There I felt death. A man. This is the early period. We should go back to the tree, I think."

"Anything else you feel here?"

"I think something happened here in 1959. Perhaps the lady walked. I think you will find a link, something running, not from the house but to the house. That's where the tree comes in. Running from the old place, the church tower to this house—not this house but the one that stood here then."

"Can you describe any figure you see or sense?"

"Here the woman I see has fair hair, arranged in curls; she belongs to the early 1900s—22 comes up—I keep seeing the number 22. Could be her age. Perhaps she is a descendant of the people in the yard."

"Any names?"

"I have the girl's name...there are two names... Mathilda, Mary...Madeleine...*Mathild*....something like that...."

Was Sybil referring to Lilith? How close are the sounds of Lilith and Mathild? Was she repeating a whispered name from the faint lips of a long-ago murder victim?

We left the room now and walked to the tree opposite the castle. Here Sybil sat down again and listened to what her psychic sense would tell her. The tree must have been here centuries ago and its twisted, scarred branches must have witnessed a great deal of history.

"What do you get, Sybil?" I finally asked.

"This is connected with the early part of the house. As I see it, the original drive to the house would be just in front of this tree. Coming down the rough driveway I have the distinct feeling of a horseman. Sixteenth century. He is running away from soldiers, running to this house. The soldiers are not Irish. There is a foreign element here."

"Is the one who is running Irish?"

"He is not Irish, either. But he belongs to this area. The soldiers following him have nothing to do with the area. They're alien. This is the remnant of a battle. He is taking refuge, but he does not reach the house."

"What happens to him?" I asked.

"His stomach is injured. The soldiers come down to the house. His body is near this tree. The injury is because of a horse going over him, I think, and he is left here. He dies here—he does not reach the house."

"Is he a soldier or a civilian?"

"I think he is a civilian, but who is to know in these times...."

"Anything about a name, or rank?"

"I only get a foreign name. It's a French-Italian name. Alien to this country although he lives here."

"Is he still here under this chestnut tree?"

"Yes, he is," Sybil replied. "He still has to reach the house; he is not aware that he is dead. He has the feeling he has to get to the house. But he can't do it."

"Does he wish to talk to us?"

"He has someone close to him, not a blood relation, perhaps a brother-in-law, in the house. This is the person he had to go to. Fian...F-I-A-N-M-E...Fianna...."

"Anything we can do for him?"

"I think that he would have to have some relation here, he has to feel a link. To know that he can go to the house. He is bewildered."

"Tell him the house has changed hands, now belongs to a Mr. Nichols," I said, but Sybil shook her head, indicating the futility of communication at this point.

"It was a much bigger house, much rougher house," Sybil said, and of course the original Skryne castle was all that.

Sybil Leek at Skyrne Castle

"A much straighter house," Sybil continued to describe what she saw in the past, "with the door more to the right than it is now. The door he is heading for. The little garden was part of the house."

I asked Sybil to reassure the ghost that we would help him.

Sybil told the ghost that he was safe from his pursuers, and not to worry about reaching the house.

"Now he is to my right," Sybil said, and a moment later, "I can't find him now. I can only hear this one word —FIANMA—"

I promised to deliver the message, whatever it meant, for him, and suddenly the ghost was gone.

"He's gone now," Sybil said quietly, "and now the house is gone."

We packed up and started back to the village of Skryne, to look for Mrs. Reilly.

Much later I consulted the material about Skryne and I found some interesting information.

A local historian, the Reverend Gerald Cooney, wrote:

"The ancient name of Skryne was Ochil or Cnoc Ghuile, meaning the Hill of Weeping. Following the death

Skyrne Castle—Where a woman was murdered long ago

of Cormac mac Airt, who established the *Fianna*, his son Cairbre became Highking. The Fianna rebelled against their king and the battle of Gabhra (Gowra) was fought at the foot of the hill now called Skryne. The Fianna were utterly defeated but Cairbre was killed in the battle."

The Fianna were the partisans of parliamentary government in medieval Ireland. Had Sybil somehow mixed up her centuries and seen a ghost going back to this battle?

We did not have to drive far. Someone pointed Mrs. Reilly's house out to me and I walked down a little country road to her gate. The house was set back behind a well-kept wall, a neat, reasonably modern country house covered by flowers. I rang the bell at the gate and soon enough Mrs. Reilly came out to greet me. She was a spunky lady in her sunny years, and quite willing to tell me all about her ghostly experiences.

"I can't exactly tell you when it happened," she said with a heavy brogue, "but it was a long time ago. I know about it through an uncle of mine, also named Reilly. I'm Kathleen Reilly."

"What is the story then?" I asked. The Irish have a way of telling someone else's story and sometimes a lot gets lost in the transition—or added. I wanted to be sure the account was believable.

"The ghost, well he was a coachman, and he had a dog. He was seen several times about the castle. And then there was a ghost of a nun seen, too."

"A nun?" I asked.

"A long time ago, the castle was a monastery and there was a nun's room."

"Was there ever any battle around here?"

"The battle of Tara," she replied and pointed toward another hill. "That's Tara over there."

"Has anyone ever come from there and taken refuge in the castle?"

"Not that I ever heard of."

She took me up to the house where I could see across the wooded glen to Skryne Castle.

"You see the spire?" she asked. "Well, right underneath is the nun's room."

The room Sybil had felt the woman's presence in, I realized at once.

"Twenty years ago," Mrs. Reilly volunteered, "a man I know by the name of Spiro slept in that room. He saw the nun, and he would never go back into that room."

"Did anyone ever die violently in the castle?" She was not sure. The house had been in the same family until twenty-five years ago when the present owner, Nichols, bought it.

"The girls often heard noises...the rustling of clothes....I thought I heard footsteps there one night when I was sittin' for the woman who has it now. I did hear footsteps, and there was no one in to my knowledge but myself."

"Where in the house was that?" I asked.

"The part where the nuns are supposed to be there," Mrs. Reilly replied. In other words, the upstairs salon where we had been, which was Lilith's room.

"Have you been there often?"

"Many times. I worked there three years."

"Are you ever afraid?"

"No, I'm not. When I heard the footsteps I was a bit afraid, but it went away."

I thanked Mrs. Reilly and pondered the business about the nuns. Had the witnesses merely drawn on their knowledge of a monastic background of the house to ascribe the rustling of clothes to nuns? Had the figure in a white bed robe seemed like a nun to them? And was it really Lilith's ghost they had encountered?

Puzzle upon puzzle.

Our driver suggested that we drive into the nearby town of Navan, also known in Gaelic as An Uaimh. Here we found a nice restaurant and had a warm meal. The hills of Tara were our next goal, and though I had no reason to suspect a haunting in Ireland's ancient capital, or what was left of it, I nevertheless felt it was a worthwhile excursion. One could always try to see if Sybil got any impressions. Enough mayhem had taken place here over the centuries to create disturbances.

We arrived on the hill where Tara once stood in little more than half an hour. The place is absolutely breathtaking. Except for a hut where a small entrance fee is paid to this national shrine, and a church on a tree-studded hill in the distance, the hill, or rather the hilly plateau, is com-pletely empty. Ancient Tara was built mainly of wood, and not a single building is now above ground.

Here and there a bronze plaque on the ground level indicates where the buildings of the old Irish capital stood. Brian Boru held court here in the eleventh century, and after him, the office of Highking fell into disrepute until foreign invaders made Ireland part of their domain.

As we looked around, the wind howled around us with unabating fury. The view was imposing, for one could look into the distance towards Dublin to the south, or towards Drogheda to the north, and see the rolling hills of Eastern Ireland.

"I don't think I have ever been so moved by a place since I was in Pompeii," Sybil said. "The tremendous Druidic influences are still around and I wish this place were kept in a better state so that people could come here and see it as it was."

As an archaeologist, I could only concur with Sybil. The ominous shapes under the soil surely should be exca-vated. But I learned that only part of the land on which Tara once stood was owned by the nation; a small portion of it was privately owned and therein lies so much of Ireland's trouble: they could not get together to allow for proper excavations, so none took place.

✳ 84

Ghost Hunting in County Mayo

ROSS HOUSE STANDS ON a bluff looking directly out into Clew Bay, halfway between Westport and Newport, and in about as nice a position as anyone would wish. From its windows you can see the many islands dotting the bay, one of which is part of the demesne of the house, and the lush green park in back of the house gives a nice contrast to the salty clime of the frontal portion. All in all, it is a house worthy of its owner, Major M. J. Blackwell, retired officer formerly in the British Army and nowadays in business in Chicago, U.S.A., as the second, but by no means minor, half of the celebrated firm of Crosse & Blackwell.

I shan't tell you how to get to Ross House, for it is not easy, what with Western Irish roads, but then there is no need to go there unless you're invited, is there?—and that might well be, for the Major is hospitality personified and his house always rings with the laughter of young relatives and their friends come over for a holiday.

The house itself is exquisitely furnished in both its stories, the rooms being large and modern, for the house is not too ancient; the broad Georgian staircase is a master-piece unto itself, and, as I found out later, it also attracted one of the resident ghosts frequently. But about this in good time.

I first heard about Ross House from the Major's young nephew, Edwin Stanley, an American living in New Jersey. Mr. Stanley had read my books and thought it might be worth my while to visit the house. Subsequently Major Blackwell himself invited us to come. We finally made it, driving up from Leenane, where we were staying.

As soon as we had met the brood of youngsters assembled in the house, and the two baby cats, I repaired with the Major to his study upstairs, where we could get down to *ghost* business.

"Let's talk about the house first," I began. "When was it built?"

"It is a Georgian house as you can see, but prior to that, there had been another house here of which we are not quite certain, to the back of the present house. It is on the oldest maps. I inherited it from my mother, and it goes back in her family for quite a long time. My mother's side of the family has proven its descent from 779 A.D., but they even have good claims all the way back to 365 A.D."

"That's about the oldest family tree I've heard of," I said, "even counting my wife's, which goes back to the 800s. You yourself, were you born here?"

"No, I was born in England, but I spent most of my childhood here, always loved the place, the boats, the people. Five years ago I inherited the place from my mother. When I'm not here, I live outside of Chicago."

I asked the Major what his mother's family name was and it turned out to be O'Malley—the famous O'Malley clan of which Grania O'Malley, the pirate queen of the sixteenth century, was not its greatest but certainly its best-known member. Then a sudden impulse struck me. During lunch, which we had had in the big downstairs room to the right of the entrance door, Sybil had slipped me a piece of paper, murmuring that it was something that had "come" to her. The name rang a bell and I pulled it out of my pocket now.

Scribbled on it were the words "Timothy . . . Mother . . . O'Malley." There was, of course, a mother O'Malley—the Major's own!

"During the times you've been here, Major," I continued now, "have you ever noticed anything unusual?"

The Major nodded. "About six years ago, the following happened. I was asleep in my room upstairs, when suddenly I woke up; at the end of my bed I saw standing an old maidservant; Annie O'Flynn was her name—she had been a maid of my grandmother's.

"I was completely lucid now, having gone to bed at a normal time the night before. My talking to this ghost woke my wife up, and I pointed her out to my wife, saying —'Look, Annie O'Flynn is here, and she's got a friend with her,' for there was another woman with the maid. When I said this, the ghostly maid smiled at me, apparently happy at being recognized. My wife did not see them, but she can attest to the fact that I was fully awake at the time."

"Amazing," I conceded. "What did you do about it?"

"Well, the next morning I went down to talk to Tommy Moran, an old man who works for us and knows a great deal about the people here, and after I described the other ghost to him he was able to identify her as a local friend of Annie's who had passed on also."

"Was that the first time in your life that you've had a psychic experience?"

"Oh no; for instance when I was in the south of France, where I was brought up, I was going up to see some friends who lived just above Nice, and I was with a friend. We had sat down for a moment on a bridge leading into this chateau when we heard the sound of horses and a coach going at full speed. I said to my friend, let's get out of the way because someone's coach has run away! But the noise just went past us and continued on, no coach, no horses! So we continued to our friend Col. Zane's house. When we told him of our experience he laughed. 'That's nothing, really,' he explained. 'That goes on all the time there. It's a ghost coach.'"

"Any other incidents?" I asked with expectation. Obviously, Major Blackwell was gifted with the sixth sense.

"The only other one was here when I dug up the tomb of Dermot MacGrania." Grania is Irish for grace, incidentally, and it is pronounced more like "gronia."

"I've seen the monolith outside the house, down towards the back end of the estate," I said. "What's the story of that tomb?"

"I started to dig, because I am terribly interested in archaeology. One night I dreamt that I was working on it, as usual, when the stone moved and out from under the stone came this extraordinary figure who was dressed in a kilt and leggings around his feet, and he advanced towards me and I was never so frightened in my life. I couldn't get to sleep at all, and the next morning I went down to the pier, because the two men who had been working on the diggings with me lived across the water and came over by boat.

"Before they landed, they told me immediately, 'We're very, very sorry, but we will not do any more work on the tomb of Dermot MacGrania!'

"Evidently, they too had been frightened off. I have not touched it since then, and that was thirty years ago. I won't permit any digging at the tomb, unless it is for the *good* of it—for I feel that at the time I was not looking into it for that reason, but rather in the hope of finding treasure, and that is why I was stopped."

"This tomb is a pre-Christian relic, is it not?" I asked after a moment of pensive contemplation. Suddenly the twentieth century was gone and the very dawn of history was upon us.

"Similar graves exist up in County Sligo. According to the legend told about this particular grave, when Dermot escaped with Grania, they were caught here and killed and buried here by his enemies. That was about 1500 B.C. This is, of course, the very beginning of Irish history."

"Has anyone else had any unusual experience at this tomb?"

"None that I know of. But there have been psychic experiences in the house itself."

I settled back in the comfortable leather chair in the Major's study and listened as Major Blackwell calmly unfolded the record of ghosts at beautiful Ross House.

"Miss Linda Carvel, a cousin of mine, has seen the old maid walking up and down and my wife and I have heard someone walking up and down where the original stairs used to be."

The Major showed me the spot where the wall now covered the stair landing. Only the main staircase exists today.

The former staircase was at the front of the house but structural changes had made it unnecessary.

"My wife has heard it at least four or five times a week. She has also heard the door knocked on."

"Almost like a maidservant," I observed. "Did anyone see the maid?"

"Yes, Linda Carvel actually saw her walking into that front room. This was only two years ago. Everybody had gone to church, and there was nobody in the house at the time except my wife, myself, my daughter, and Linda. Linda suddenly came into the room to us, white as a sheet. 'I just saw a woman walk into Granny's room,' she said. 'She was dressed in a white and blue uniform—a starched uniform.' I discussed this with Tommy Moran and he confirmed that that was the uniform the maids wore in my grandmother's time!"

"What do you make of it, Major?"

"I think it is the same one, Annie, who came to see me. She died a normal death, but she was fantastically attached to the family and the house. She spent her whole life here. She married a man named John O'Flynn, a tailor, but she adored it here and even after she left she came back all the time bringing us gifts."

"Have any other phenomena been observed here?"

"In the drawing room, downstairs, Tommy Moran and all his sons have seen two people sitting in front of the fireplace. I know nothing about them firsthand, however. My cousin, Peter O'Malley, also has seen them. He is the one also who had a shocking experience. He saw the most terrible face appear in the window of the drawing room."

"What exactly did he see?" I was all ears now. The whole atmosphere seemed loaded with electricity.

"I wasn't here at the time, but he just says it was a most terrible face. That was ten years ago."

"What about Inishdaff Island, Major?" I asked.

"There is an old monastery there I hope to restore. We've got the records back to 1400 and there it says 'church in ruins.' The peninsula we are on now, where the house stands, also turns into an island at high tide, incidentally, and the path of the pilgrims going over to that ruined church can still be traced. The road would not have been built for any other reason."

"You didn't see anything unusual on the island, though?"

"No, I didn't, but Tommy Moran, and some other relatives of mine—actually four people altogether—did. The island has always been considered . . . that there is *something wrong with it*."

We got to talking about the other members of the family now; Mrs. Blackwell had been unable to join us at lunch since she was staying at Castlebar with their fourteen-year-old daughter, who was in the hospital there because of a broken leg. It appeared, however, that there was more to that accident than a casual mishap.

"The extraordinary thing about it is this. The night before it happened, she dreamt that an ambulance drove up to the *front* of the house. Now the front of the house is blocked off to cars, as you saw. So every car must come through the *back*. She saw the ambulance come to the front entrance, however, pick *someone* up and drive off. Also, the ambulance did not have a red cross or other familiar sign on it, but a circular thing in Irish writing! That was exactly the ambulance that came up the next evening and picked *her* up; it was a Volkswagen ambulance with an Irish

Ross House—County Mayo

inscription on the side in a circle just as she had described it to us! Edie is definitely psychic also."

"So it seems," I said. "Anything else about her I might want to know?"

"One time she dreamt she saw Grandmother—my mother—and described her perfectly in every detail. Being terrified of ghosts, Edie, in her dream, pleaded with my mother's apparition not ever to have to see a ghost again. Granny promised her she wouldn't, but she would always *know*."

There were two more points of psychic interest, I discovered. The unexplained putting on of lights and opening of doors in the nursery, and something else that I only learned towards the end of our most enjoyable stay. But in a way it made a perfect finale.

Right now everybody was handed heavy clothing and overshoes, for we would be sailing—well, motorboating—to the island across the bay and it was wet and chilly, the Major assured us. Cathy looked like a real outdoor girl in the Major's fur jacket, and Sybil was so heavily bundled up she scarcely made the entrance to the cabin of the little boat. The assorted cousins of both sexes also came along in a second boat, and within minutes we were out in the open bay crossing over to the island of Inishdaff, all of which belonged to the Major's estate.

We landed on the island ten minutes later. The sandy beach was most inviting to a swim and Major Blackwell admitted he was working on just such a project. What with the absence of sharks, I felt this to be about the most ideal place to swim in any ocean.

We next scaled the heights of the hill, taking the center of the island, upon which stood the ruined abbey. It was at once clear to me that we were standing close to the roof of that church and that the lower part had simply filled in with soil over the centuries. In one corner of the "elevated floor" was the simple grave of one of Tommy Moran's sons, a Celtic cross watching over him. Otherwise the island was empty.

While the others stood around the ruined abbey, Major Blackwell, Tommy, and I mounted the other side of the wall and then descended onto the wet ground. We then proceeded to the top of the island whence we had a magnificent view of all the other islands around us, all the way out to the farthest, which indeed was Ireland's outpost to the sea, beyond which lay America. It was among these many islands and inlets that the pirates of old hid, safe from prosecution by the law.

We fetched some heavy stones from the enclosure of the church and sat down so that Tommy Moran could talk to me about his experiences.

I first questioned him about the frightening face seen here and in the house.

"Mike Sheils told it to me, sir," Tommy Moran began with a heavy brogue. "He worked the glass house with me for years. He was a man not easily frightened. At the time there were blackthorn trees in the burial ground. He was passing through when he heard some noise. He looked over his shoulder and what he saw was a sheep's head with a human body."

"No," I said.

"Yes, sir," Tommy nodded, "it was a head covered with wool the same as sheep. There were three boys in front of Mike. He knocked them down and ran."

"Did you yourself ever have any such experiences here, Tommy?" I reflected that a disheveled human face might very well look like a sheep's head to a simple, imaginative islander used to lots of sheep.

"During me own time, sir," he began, "they were bringing torf to Ross House by boat, that was Mrs. O'Malley's husband, who was gettin' the torf, and they were rowing, two of them, but they had no sail. They wanted to keep as close to the shore as they could. They were brother and sister, Pat Stanton and his sister Bridget. Suddenly a man came down from the burial ground trying to grasp his oar and take it out of the water. Pat rowed like mad to get away; he recalls the man was stark naked, had no clothes on at all. Finally, they got away."

"There was no one living here at the time?"

"No one, no," Tommy assured me, and the Major nodded assent.

I was fascinated by the old man's tales. Surely, Tommy could not have made them up, for what he had said did make some sense when matched with the horrible face looking into the dining room window. Somewhere along the line a human being living like an animal must have found shelter on the desolate island, and, perhaps

brought up by animals, this man was taken for a monster. I did not feel that this was a ghost in the sense I use the term.

Tommy told us other tales, some bordering just barely on the supernormal, and then we rejoined the others and went back to the house. It was time for me to question Sybil Leek about her impressions of the church and burial ground.

"There were impressions, but not a presence as we understand it, Hans," Sybil explained, "but I strongly urge that the place be excavated, for there might be some works of art underneath. There is also a passage, which we discovered this afternoon, on the right hand side. The high altar connecting with the first monastic cell."

We had returned now to the house, and took off the heavy clothing the Major had lent us for the journey. While tea was being prepared, we grouped ourselves around the fireplace, waiting.

It was then that I recalled a chance remark Sybil had made to me earlier about a man she had met when we first came to the house, prior to lunch. Perhaps we could sort this out now, before Tommy Moran left for his chores.

"I left the main party in the house for a while, because I wanted to be on my own," Sybil explained, "so I walked through the path leading to the wrought-iron gate which led into a garden. I walked right down as far as I could go, until I came to an open space which was on the other side of the garden to where I had started. I reached the tomb. I stayed by the tomb for a little while, then I went toward the gate, ready to climb over the gate, and I was in deep thought. So I wasn't surprised to see a man there. To me he looked rather small, but of course I was on higher ground than he was. He wore no hat, but he had peculiar hair, gray hair."

"What did he do when he saw you?"

"He smiled at me, and appeared to come towards me. I was continuing to walk towards him. He said, 'So you have come back again?' and I replied, 'But I haven't been here. I don't know this place.' He turned and walked towards the sea and I turned away and went back."

"Did he look like a ghost to you?"

"You know I never know what a ghost looks like. To me, everything seems the same. I have this difficulty of distinguishing between flesh-and-blood and ghosts."

When I informed Major Blackwell of Sybil's encounter, he was taken aback and said: "My God, she's seen the other one—she's seen the Sea Captain!"

It turned out that there was another ghost he had not told us about when we talked about the house. Sybil, he felt, had not made contact with the ghostly maidservant—perhaps she had found a more permanent niche by now—but somehow had picked up the scent of the ghostly seaman.

I questioned Tommy Moran, who at seventy-five knew the place better than any other person, what this sea captain business was all about.

"I don't know his name, sir," Tommy said, "but he was in the house about a hundred years ago. He bought this place and he thought so much about it, he went out to England to bring back his wife and family. He said when he was gone that he would come back, dead or alive!

"He died at sea, and he has since been seen by many, always in daylight, always smoking a cigar; Mike Sheils saw him sittin' in the drawing room once. Several people saw him on the stairway and he always just disappeared. One of my sons saw him and it frightened him. He had no hat, but always this cigar. Very black hair, as tall as you are, sir, according to Mike Sheils."

There you have it, a sea captain *without his cap* but with a cigar! On recollection, Sybil was not sure whether she heard him say, "So you've come back again" or "See, I've come back again."

✳ 85

The Ghost at La Tour Malakoff, Paris

MAISON-LAFITTE IS A RUSTIC, elegant suburb of metropolitan Paris, reached easily by car within half an hour. Near the race course there is a cluster of townhouses within a park setting, aristocratic reminders of a disappearing elegance. More and more high-rise, high-price apartment houses have replaced the old residences.

On the corner of rue Racine and avenue Montaigne there stands a three-story residence within about an acre of landscaped grounds. When I visited the house it was exactly as it had been since it was built during the Second Empire, in the 1860s. A glass-enclosed conservatory faced toward the garden and a tower reached up beyond the roof in the romantic Victorian manner of the period. The only new addition was a low-ceilinged projection room on the other end of the garden: the last tenant had been motion picture personality Robert Lamoureux.

Inside the house, the appearance of an elegant townhouse in the country was further maintained by the presence of high ceilings, white walls, gold appliances, and wrought-iron staircases in the front and rear.

No. 3 avenue Montaigne was built by Emperor Napoleon III for his own account. Ostensibly a hunting lodge (Maison-Lafitte was then still rural), in reality it housed a favorite mistress, whose portrait the Emperor had had painted and placed on the outside wall.

With the advent of the Republic, the house became state property and was maintained as a "Residence of State" until World War II. Important visitors—but not those important enough to be housed in the Elysée Palace —were lodged there. During World War II German soldiers occupied the house and, in the process, looted it of anything that was not nailed down. When Allied troops took over the property, they completed the job. Subsequently it was purchased by M. DuPrès, a gentleman interested in real estate. When Mme. DuPrès saw the house, she had him take it off the market and moved in with their family.

＊　＊　＊

In the fall of 1949, Mr. and Mrs. D. rented it for their own use. Mr. D. was a high-ranking diplomat at the American Embassy in Paris. Mrs. D., Pennsylvania-born, was of English, Welsh, and Irish descent and was born with a caul, a fact some people regard as a sign of psychic talents. She and Mr. D. have four children and now live near Washington, D.C., where Mr. D. practices law.

When the D.s rented the house, they also took over the services of Paulette, the "bonne-à-tout-faire" who had been with the DuPrès family for many years. The house had meanwhile been tastefully refurnished and the appointments included a fine grand piano in the "salon," the large downstairs reception room where the lady in Napoleon's life presumably met her illustrious lover whenever he visited her.

Mrs. D. liked the house from the start; but she could not help wondering about the oval portrait of the lovely lady attached to the wall of the tower.

Shortly after moving to the house, Mr. D. had to travel for three weeks on government business. Mrs. D. was left with her children, Paulette the maid, and a nursemaid—neither of whom spoke a word of English. Mrs. D.'s French was then almost nonexistent, so she looked forward to a somewhat unusual relationship with her servants.

Several nights after her husband's departure, Mrs. D. was awakened at 3 A.M. by the sound of music. It was a rambling but lovely piano piece being played somewhere nearby. Her first reaction was how inconsiderate the neighbors were to make music at such an hour, until she realized that she had no neighbors near enough to hear anything. It then struck her that the music came from *inside* her house, or, to be specific, from the salon downstairs. She rushed to the bathroom and sat down on an ice-cold bathtub to make sure she was awake. An hour later the playing stopped. During that hour she was much too scared to go down and see who was playing her piano. The music had not been particularly macabre, but rather more on the pleasant side and somewhat rambling.

Who was she to discuss her experience with? The Embassy staff would hardly react favorably to such matters and her French did not permit her to question the servants.

The haunted villa at La Tour Malakoff, Paris

The views from La Tour Malakoff

The next night, the ghostly piano music came on again, promptly at 3 A.M., and stopped just as promptly at 4 A.M. Night after night, she was being treated to a concert by unseen hands. Mrs. D. still would not venture downstairs at the time of the spooky goings-on, but prior to retiring she tried to set traps for her unknown visitor, such as closing the piano lid or leaving sheet music open at certain pages. But the ghost did not respond: everything was exactly as she had left it, and the music was as clear as ever.

She greeted her husband with a sigh of relief on his return. When she told him of her ordeal, he was amazingly understanding. Had the ghost been playing that night, Mr. D. would have sat up to listen, but unfortunately, his return abruptly ended the nocturnal concerts.

Gradually the matter of the ghostly pianist faded into memory, especially as the D.s did a lot of entertaining in the house. Among their guests were Neill O., her husband's assistant, and his wife. One Sunday morning they descended the stairs to breakfast in a somewhat shaken condition. When questioned by Mrs. D., the couple complained about the inconsiderate "neighbor" who had kept them awake playing the piano at 3 A.M. Their room had been exactly above the salon. Mrs. O. added that she had clearly heard a hunting horn outside the house and that it had awakened her.

Other overnight guests of the D.'s complained similarly about nocturnal concerts downstairs. What could the hosts do but say they hoped their guests would sleep better the next night?

Eventually Mrs. D., with the help of Neill O., interrogated the maid about the house in which she had served for so long.

"What about that portrait of a lady outside?" Mrs. D. wanted to know. Apparently Napoleon had wearied of his mistress after a while and left her to live by herself in the house. During those lonely years as a former Imperial mistress she had little company to comfort her: only a grand piano for her amusement, and soon it became her one and only passion. When Mrs. D. asked the maid about a ghost in the house, the girl blanched. Living on the third floor, Paulette had often heard the ghostly piano concert downstairs but had been too scared to investigate. During the DuPrès residency, Paulette had been alone with the children on one occasion when the nurse had gone to sleep.

One of the children started to cry and Paulette rushed to the room. She found the little girl standing in her bed wide awake, pointing to a corner of the room and saying, "Look at the pretty lady!" Paulette, however, could not see anyone or anything.

After the D.s left Paris, the house passed into the hands of Robert Lamoureux, who added the projection room on the grounds but left everything else as it was.

He, too, gave up the house and eventually moved elsewhere. The house then became part of a real estate parcel acquired by speculators for the purpose of tearing down the old houses and erecting a new apartment house on the spot. In August 1968, I was granted permission by the La Tour Malakoff Society to visit the house, with the tense suggestion that I do so as soon as possible if I wanted to find the house still standing.

Finally, in 1969, I did so, and fortunately the wreckers had not yet come. The house already showed its state of abandonment. The once carefully kept garden was over-

grown with weeds, the windows were dirty and the absence of all furniture gave it an eerie, unreal feeling.

I walked up and down the staircase, taking pictures and "listening with an inner ear" for whatever vibrations might come my way. I did not hear any music, but then the grand piano was no longer there. An Italian watchman, who had spent hundreds of nights on the property guarding it from intruders, looked at me and wondered what I wanted there. I asked if he had had any unusual experiences in the house. He shook his head and explained he wouldn't have—he never slept there and wouldn't dream of doing so. Why not? He just smiled somewhat foolishly and changed the subject.

When my photographs were developed by the professional service I use, one of them showed a strange light streak I could not account for. It was a picture of the iron staircase in the house. The shapeless light streak appears between the second and first floors. Was it perhaps Napoleon's lady friend rushing downstairs to welcome her lover?

One can't be sure about those things.

✳ 86

Haunted Wolfsegg Fortress, Bavaria

THE FORTIFIED CASTLE at Wolfsegg, Bavaria, is not State property and can be visited only through the kindness and permission of its owner. It is one of the few privately owned fortresses in the world, I believe, and thereby hangs a tale.

The late Georg Rauchenberger, by profession a painter and the official guardian of monuments for the province of The Upper Palatinate, which is part of the state of Bavaria, purchased this ancient fortress with his own savings. Since he was the man who passed on monies to be spent by the state for the restoration of ancient monuments in the province, he had of course a particularly touchy situation on his hands, for he could not possibly allow any funds to be diverted to his own castle. Consequently, every penny spent upon the restoration of this medieval fortress came from his own pocket. Over the years he gradually restored this relic of the past into a livable, if primitive, medieval fortress. He put in some of the missing wooden floors, and turned the clock back to the eleventh century in every respect.

Two persons, so far, can sleep comfortably in the large fortress, but as it is still in the process of being restored, it will be a long time before it can compare with some of the "tourist attractions" under State control. Nevertheless, small groups of interested visitors have been admitted most days of the week for a guided tour through the Hall of Knights and other parts of the fortress. Ordinarily visitors are not told of the hauntings at Wolfsegg, but I am sure that anyone referring to these lines will find at least a friendly reception.

Because of the nearness of the River Danube, the fortress at Wolfsegg was always of some importance. It rises majestically out of the valley to the equivalent of four or five modern stories. Quite obviously constructed for defense, its thick bulky walls are forbidding, the small windows—high up to discourage aggressors—and the hill upon which the fortress perches making attack very difficult.

Never conquered, Wolfsegg's Twelfth Century bulwarks are formidable

As a matter of fact, Wolfsegg never fell to an enemy, and even the formidable Swedes, who besieged it for a long time during the Thirty Years' War, had to give up. Built in 1028, Wolfsegg belonged to several noble Bavarian families and was always directly or indirectly involved in the intricate dynastic struggles between the various lines of the Wittelsbachs, who ruled Bavaria until 1918. Many of the masters of Wolfsegg made a living by being "Raubritter" —that is to say, robber barons. All in all, the area had an unsavory reputation even as early as the twelfth and thirteenth centuries. The walls are thick and the living quarters located well above ground.

The Knights Hall on the third floor is reached by a broad staircase, and one flight down there is also a lookout tower which has been restored as it was in the sixteenth century. In the inner court there is a wooden gallery running along part of the wall (at one time this gallery covered

The village is remote and depends largely on tourism

Entrance to the fortress Wolfsegg

One of the two rooms "fixed up" by the owner Georg Rauchenberger

the entire length of the wall). The lower stories have not yet been fully restored or even explored.

Georg Rauchenberger himself heard uncanny noises, footsteps, and experienced cold drafts at various times in various parts of the fortress. The late Mrs. Therese Pielmeier, wife of the custodian, actually saw a whitish form in the yard, full of luminescence, and she also heard various unexplained noises. On one occasion, Mr. Rauchenberger saw a young lady coming in with a small group of visitors, and when he turned to speak to her she disappeared.

In the yard, where the ghost of the Countess was seen

The Medieval gallery

I held a séance at Wolfsegg with a Viennese lady who served as my medium at the time. Through the trance mediumship of Mrs. Edith Riedl, I was able to trace the terrible story of a triple murder involving a beautiful woman, once the wife of a Wolfsegg baron, who had become the innocent victim of a political plot. The legend of the beautiful ghost at Wolfsegg had, of course, existed prior to our arrival on the scene. Apparently, greedy relatives of a fourteenth-century owner of Wolfsegg had decided to take over the property, then of considerable value, by trapping the young wife of the owner with another man. The husband, told of the rendezvous, arrived in time to see the two lovers together, killed both of them, and was in turn murdered in "just revenge" by his cunning relatives.

The portrait of the unlucky lady of Wolfsegg hangs in one of the corridors, the work of the father of the current owner, who painted her from impressions received while visiting the castle.

Although I was able to make contact with the atmosphere surrounding the "white woman" of Wolfsegg, and to shed light upon a hitherto unknown Renaissance tragedy, it is entirely possible that the restless baroness still roams the corridors to find recognition and to prove her innocence to the world.

One reaches Wolfsegg on secondary roads in about a half hour's drive from Regensburg, and it is situated near a small and rather primitive village, northwest of the city on the north side of the Danube River. There is only one inn

Strong walls and small windows characterize the early medieval fortress

in this village, and staying overnight, as I once did, is not recommended.

This is a remote and strange area of Germany, despite the comparative nearness of the city of Regensburg. By the way, Regensburg is sometimes also called Ratisbon, and is the center of one of the few remaining strongly Celtic areas in Germany.

✳ 87

A Haunted Former Hospital in Zurich

THE HOUSE IN QUESTION is now a private residence, owned by Colonel and Mrs. Nager. The Colonel is a professional officer and takes a cautious attitude towards psychic phenomena. Mrs. Catherine Nager is not only a talented medium herself, but also serves as secretary to the Swiss Society for Parapsychology headed by the Zurich psychiatrist Dr. Hans Negele-Osjord.

Rather aristocratic in design and appearance, the house stands on upper Hoenger Street at a spot where it overlooks much of downtown Zurich. It is a square, heavy-set stone house with three stories, and an attic above the top story. In this attic there is a window that does not want to stay closed—no matter how often one tries to close it. When this happened all the time, the Nagers kept accusing each other of leaving the window open, only to discover that neither of them had done it.

The house is set back from the road in a heavily protected garden; it is painted a dark gray and there is a wrought-iron lantern over the entrance.

When I first visited the house in the company of the owner, the attic immediately depressed me. The famous window was open again and I had no difficulty closing it. But it could not have opened by its volition.

Down one flight there is a small room which for many years has served as a maid's room. It was here that the most notable phenomena have been observed. A maid named Liesl saw a man wearing a kind of chauffeur's cap standing between the bed and the wall with a candle in his hand. She panicked and ran from the room screaming in terror. Mrs. Nager checked the room immediately and found it empty. No one could have escaped down the stairs in the brief interval. Another servant girl took Liesl's place. A year and a half after the initial incident, the new girl saw the same apparition.

Next to the maid's room is another room famous for uncanny atmospheric feelings. Guests who have stayed there have frequently complained about a restlessness in the room, and nobody ever slept well.

On the third floor there is still another maid's room where a girl named Elsbeth saw the ghostly apparition of a man wearing a peculiar beret. When Mrs. Nager's son was only eight, he saw a man emerge from between the window curtains of his room. He, too, emphasized the peculiar cap the man wore—something not seen today.

Other servants have described the ghost as being a man of about thirty-five, wearing the same peculiarly Swiss cap; they have seen him all over the house.

The explanation is this: during the seventeenth century the house had been a military hospital. Many wounded soldiers who came there died. The cap worn by the apparition was the soldier's cap worn in the period. Most likely the man is lost between two states of being and would like to get out—if only someone would show him the way.

✳ 88

The Lady from Long Island

MAURICE O. IS AN elderly man of Polish extraction, healthy, vigorous, and strong, despite his years. He is firmly rooted in the Roman Catholic faith but is also aware of the psychic world around him. Mr. O. operates a workshop located in a loft occupying the second story of a house on lower Broadway. The section is one of the oldest parts of New York City. This case was brought to my attention by the man's nephew, a teacher on Long Island who had developed an interest in historical research, especially research pertaining to the American Revolutionary period.

When I met Mr. O., he was at first very suspicious of me and my psychic friend, Ingrid Beckman. He didn't understand what parapsychology was or what we were going to do in his place. Patiently, I explained that I wanted Ingrid to get her bearings and to see whether she could pick up something from "the atmosphere." While Ingrid was puttering around in the rear of the place, I convinced Mr. O. that I had to know what had happened to him, so that I could judge the case fairly. He explained that he had been in the neighborhood for fifty-five years. He remembered that, when he was a small boy, another building had stood on the same spot. "I came here from Poland in 1913, when I was ten years old," Mr. O. explained in a halting, heavily accented voice. "In this spot there was an old building, a red brick building with few windows. On the corner there was a United cigar store. Down the block was a saloon. They had girls there; customers could come into the saloon, have the girls, and go upstairs with them. In those days it cost them fifty cents or a dollar. There also used to be a barber shop in the building. In 1920 they tore down the old building and built the present factory loft, but they used the same foundations."

When Mr. O. moved his business into a building he had known all his life, it was a little like a homecoming for him. He was in the business of servicing high-speed sewing machines, which were sent to him from all over the country. Most of the time he did the work alone; for a while, his brother Frank had assisted him. In those days he never gave psychic phenomena any thought, and the many strange noises he kept hearing in the loft didn't really bother him. He thought there must be some natural explanation for them, although there were times when he was sure he heard heavy footsteps going up and down the stairs when he was alone in the building. One Saturday afternoon around 4 o'clock, as he was ready to wash up and go home, he walked back into the shop to wipe his hands. All of a sudden he saw a heavy iron saw fly up into the air on its own volition. It fell down to the floor, broken in two. Mr. O. picked up the pieces and said to nobody in particular, "Ghost, come here. I am not afraid of you; I want to talk to you." However, there was no answer.

"See that latch on the door," Maurice O. said to us, and showed us how he locked the place so that nobody could come in. "Many times I've seen that latch move up and down, as if someone wanted to get in, and when I went outside there was no one there."

Oftentimes he would hear footsteps overhead in the loft above his. When he would go upstairs to check what the noise was all about, he would find the third-floor loft solidly locked up and no one about. Once, when he went to the toilet between 1:30 and 2 P.M., at a time when he knew he was alone in the building, he found himself locked out of his place, yet he knew he had left the door open. Someone, nevertheless, had locked the latch from the *inside*. Finally, with the help of a friend, he broke the door open and of course found the place empty. The incident shook Mr. O. up considerably, as he couldn't explain it, no matter how he tried. During this time, too, he kept seeing shadows, roughly in the shape of human beings. They would move up and down in the back of his workshop and were of a grayish color. "It was the shape of a banana," Mr. O. commented. Curiously, during the first eight years of his occupancy—he had been across the street for forty years before—Mr. O. had had no such problems. It was only in the last two years that he began to notice things out of the ordinary.

However, Mr. O. had heard rumors of strange goings-on in the building. A previous owner of the loft building had a music store and was in the habit of spending Saturday nights in his shop with some invited friends, listening to music. One night, so the story goes, around midnight, everything started to pop out of the shelves, merchandise flying through the air, and the entire building began to shake as if there had been an earthquake. While all this was going on, the people in the music store heard a tremendous noise overhead. They became frightened and called the police. Several radio cars responded immediately but could not find out what was wrong. Everything seemed normal upstairs. Shortly after, the owner sold the building and moved to California.

Mr. O.'s workshop is L-shaped, with a small office immediately behind the heavy steel door that gives access to the corridor, and thence to a steep staircase that leads out into the street. The machine shop itself is to the left and in back of the office. Thus, it is possible to work in the back of the shop and not see anyone coming in through the entrance door. But it is not possible to escape hearing any noises on the floor, since the entire building is not very large.

The day after Thanksgiving 1971 Maurice was alone in the shop, working quietly on some orders he wanted to get out of the way. Since it was the day after Thanksgiving and just before the weekend, the building was very quiet. There was no one upstairs, and Maurice was sure he was the only one in the building at the time. Suddenly, he saw a lady walk into his office. Since he had not heard the heavy door slam, which it always does when someone walks in, he wondered how she had gotten into the building and into his office. She wore what to Maurice seemed a very old-fashioned, very chic dress, white gloves, and a bonnet, and she smelled of a sweet fragrance that immediately captured him. What was so nice a lady doing in his sewing machine shop?

Maurice did not pursue his line of thought, how she had gotten in in the first place, but asked her what she wanted. Somehow, he felt a little frightened. He had noticed that her face was more like a skeleton covered with skin than the face of a flesh-and-blood person. The lady seemed unusually white. There was no reply; she simply stood there, looking around the place. Maurice repeated his question.

"Well," she said finally, in a faraway tone of voice, "I just came here to look at the place. I used to live in this building." Then she went to the window and pointed to the street. "I used to play over there—these houses are all new brick houses. My father and mother had a corn farm where the Federal Building is now, downtown."

"Was there anything peculiar about her tone of voice?" I asked.

"No, it sounded pretty clear to me, real American," O. replied. "She said, 'You know, all these new buildings weren't here during Revolutionary times.' Then she added, rather apologetically, 'I just came around to look.'"

Maurice was standing in back of the counter that separates his office from the short stretch of corridor leading from the entrance door. The lady was standing on the other side of the counter, so Maurice could get a good look at her; but he was too frightened to look her in the face. When he backed up, she started to talk rapidly. "I just wanted to visit the neighborhood. I used to live here." Then, pointing her hand toward the window, she said, "The headquarters of the British Army used to be across the street."

The statement made no impression on Mr. O. Besides, he was much too upset by all this to wonder how a woman standing before him in the year 1971 could remember the location of the headquarters of the British Army, which had left New York almost two hundred years before.

"What did she look like?" I asked.

"She was dressed very nicely, and she looked just like any other person except for her face. I didn't see her hands, but she had on brand new gloves, her dress looked new, and the hat was real nice."

"Did you see her walking?"

"Yes, she was walking."

"What happened next?"

"Well," Maurice explained, swallowing hard at the memory of his experience. "I finally got up enough courage to ask her, 'Where are you going now?'"

The question had seemed to make the lady sad, even upset. "I'm leaving to visit relatives on Long Island," she said finally. "In the cemetery. My relatives, my friends, my father and mother."

Maurice became more and more uneasy at all this. He pretended that he had some business in the rear of the shop and started to back up from the counter.

"I'm going to visit you again," the lady said and smiled.

For about a minute, Mr. O. busied himself in the back of his workshop, then returned to the office. The woman was gone.

"Was the door still closed?"

"The door was closed. No one could have left without slamming this door, and I would have heard it. I quickly opened the door to convince myself that I had really spoken to a person. I looked around; there was nobody outside. Nobody."

Maurice checked both his door and the door downstairs. Neither door had been opened, so he went back up to continue working. He was still very much upset but decided to stay till about 5 o'clock. When he was ready to go home and had put the keys into the door, he suddenly began to smell the same perfume again—the perfume the lady had brought with her. She's back again, he thought, and he looked everywhere. But there was no one about. Quickly he locked the door and ran downstairs.

A year to the day after the apparition, Maurice decided to work late—more out of curiosity than out of any conviction that she would return. But the lady never did.

Mr. O.'s nephew, who is a teacher and a researcher, commented, "With reference to the British headquarters'

being across the street, I have checked this fact out and have found that during the Revolution the British headquarters were across the street from this same building my uncle now occupies. This is a fact I know my uncle couldn't possibly have known."

"Ingrid," I said, after I had asked her to join me and Mr. O. in the front of the workshop, "what do you feel about this place?"

"There is a lot of excitement here," she replied. "I think there is a man here who is kind of dangerous, very treacherous, and I think someone might have been injured here. This happened about twenty-five years ago."

"Do you think there is an earlier presence in this house?"

"I feel that this was a prosperous place, an active, busy spot. A lot of people were coming here. It was part home, part business. Before that I think this building was something else. I think a family lived here. They may have been foreigners, and I think the man was killed. I feel that this man came to this country and invested his savings here. He wanted to build up a family business. I also think there is a woman connected with it. She wears a longish dress, going below the knees."

"What is her connection with this place?"

"She may have spent her childhood here—what happened here might have happened to her father. Perhaps she came here as a young child and spent many years in this building. She has some connection with this man, I feel."

"Does she have any reason to hang onto this place?"

"Maybe she doesn't understand why all this has happened, and she can't accept it yet. Perhaps she has lost a loved one."

Every year, around Thanksgiving, Maurice O. will wait for the lady to come back and talk to him again. Now that he knows that she is "just a ghost," he isn't even afraid of her any longer. As far as the lady is concerned, she need not worry either: when the British Army headquarters stood across the street, the area was a lot safer than it is now, especially at night; but she really needn't worry about muggings either, things being as they are.

✳ 89

The Ghost of the Olympia Theatre

THERE ARE THREE THEATERS of renown in Dublin: the Gate, the Abbey, and the Olympia. The Gate was closed for repairs, and the Olympia was running a musical revue when we visited Dublin for the first time, in the late summer of 1965.

Lona Moran, the stage designer, had first told me of the hauntings at the Olympia, and my appetite was further whetted by Michael MacLiammoir, although he thought the Gate's ghosts were more impressive!

We booked seats for the night of August 19. The revue starred popular Irish comedian Jack Cruise in something called "Holiday Hayride." To tell the truth, it was pleasant without being great, and we laughed frequently at what to sophisticated Americans must have appeared old-hat comedy. Overtones of Palace vaudeville made the show even more relaxing and the absence of boisterous rock-and-roll groups—inevitable in England these days—made it even nicer for us. In a comedy sketch taking off on Dublin police—called here the Garda—one of the cops played by Chris Curran made reference to our TV appearance that morning, proving again how small a town Dublin really is. Or how topical the revue was. At any rate, Lona Moran, who had often worked here before becoming the designer for Telefis Eireann, had arranged to meet us after the show and discuss the haunting with us.

Dick Condon, the house manager, joined us in the bar around eleven, and Miss Moran was not long in coming either. Sybil's purple evening sari drew a lot of attention, but then Sybil is used to that by now.

We decided to repair to the stage itself, since the house had meanwhile gone dark. The stagehands agreed to stay a little late for us that night, and I started my inquiry.

"I've beard some very curious tappings and bangings," Lona Moran began, "and doors being shaken when they were very heavily chained. I have heard windows rattle, outside the room where I was sitting, and when I came out I realized there was no window!"

"How long ago was that?"

"That was about this time last year," Lona Moran replied. "It was in the backstage area, in the dressing room upstairs, number 9. Outside there is a completely blank wall. Actually, Mr. O'Reilly was with me and he heard it too. It was early morning when I went into that room, about half past five. We had been working all night. We went up to the dressing room to make notes and also to make tea, and this awful banging started. It sounded like a window being rattled very, very persistently. I went stiff with fright. I was very tired at the time. At intervals, the noise covered a period of about an hour, I'd say, because we left the room around 6:30 and only then we realized there was no window."

"Did you hear this noise at any other time?"

"Yes, when I worked on stage during the night. I heard a window rattle, and once got as far as the first floor to see if I could see it and then I lost my nerve and came down again."

"There was no possibility of a window making the noise?"

"Well, I suppose a window could have done it—but *what window?*"

"Do you know if any structural changes have taken place here?"

"No, I don't; but the theater is over two hundred years old."

"Do you know if any tragedy or other unusual event took place in this area?"

"I don't know of any, but the theater is supposed to be haunted. By what, I really don't know."

"Did you experience anything unusual before last year?"

"Yes, before then there were lots of bangings. The door of the bar would shake and rattle very badly, on very calm evenings, as if someone were rattling it. The sound of things dropping also. I thought Jeremy, my assistant, was dropping things and accused him rather sharply, but he wasn't."

"Ever hear footsteps?"

"I think I've imagined I heard footsteps—I don't know really whether they were or weren't—always during the night when we were working—two of us would be working on the stage together, and no one else in the theater."

"And what happened on those occasions?"

"Rattling noises and creaking…and something that might be footsteps."

"Have you ever felt another presence?"

"I had the feeling last September that there was something there, when I walked through that door and saw no window."

I asked if she had ever had psychic experiences before she set foot into the theater.

"I simply did not believe, but I do now," Lona Moran replied. She had never experienced anything unusual before coming to the Olympia. She had worked as stage designer for the Olympia Theatre for fourteen months prior to going into television.

I turned to Lona Moran's associate, who had come along to tell of his own experiences here.

"My name is Alfo O'Reilly," the tall young man said, "and I'm theater designer and television designer here in Dublin. I myself have designed only two or three productions here, and last year, for the theater festival, I designed an American production. On the particular evening in question Lona and I worked very late into the night, and I had not heard any stories at all about this theater being haunted. We went up to the dressing room, and we were sitting there quietly exhausted when we heard these incredible noises."

"Those are the noises Miss Moran spoke of," I commented, and Alfo O'Reilly nodded and added:

"I have found that when I'm terribly exhausted, I seem to have a more heightened awareness. We knew there was only one other person in the theater, the night watchman who was roaming elsewhere, and we were alone upstairs. There was certainly nothing in the corridor that could create this kind of noise. I've heard many things, footsteps, at the Gate Theatre, which is certainly haunted, but not here."

I thanked Mr. O'Reilly and turned to a slim young man who had meanwhile arrived onstage.

"My name is Jeremy Swan and I work with Telefís Eireann," he said by way of introduction, "and I used to work here as resident stage manager. About this dressing room upstairs—I remember one season here, during a pantomime, the dressing room was wrecked, allegedly by a poltergeist."

"Would you explain just how?"

"All the clothes were strewn about," Swan explained, "makeup was thrown all around the place—we questioned all the chorus girls who were in the room at the time—that was number 9 dressing room."

The haunted dressing room, I thought.

"Apparently there had been knocking at the door every night and nobody there," the stage manager continued, "at half past nine. One night when I was working here as assistant to Miss Moran I went upstairs to the washroom there, and when I came out I felt and I was almost sure saw a light—just a glow—yellow; it seemed to be in the corner of the corridor. I followed the light round the corner—it moved, you see—and it went into the corridor where number 9 was, where there was another door. The door was open, and now it closed in my face!"

"Incredible," I was forced to say. "What happened then?"

"There was nobody in the theater at all. It was after midnight. Now all the doors in the corridor started to rattle. That was four years ago."

"Have you had any experiences since then?"

"I haven't worked here very much since."

"Did you feel any unusual chill at the time?"

"Yes, I did before I went upstairs to the corridor. It was very cold onstage. Suddenly, I heard whispering from back in the theater."

"What sort of whispering?"

"Sh-sh-sh-sh," Jeremy Swan went on. "It sounded like a voice that didn't quite make it."

"Anything else?"

"Then I heard this banging again. Beside me almost. On stage. I did not want to say anything to Miss Moran,

and then I went up to the washroom where this funny light business started."

"At what height did the light appear?"

"Sort of knee level."

I thanked the young man and looked around. The stagehands had come forward the better to hear the questioning. Somehow they did not mind the overtime; the subject was fascinating to them.

All this time, of course, Sybil Leek was absent, safely out of earshot of anything that might be said about the haunting onstage. I was about to ask that she be brought in to join us, when a middle-aged stagehand stepped forward, scratched his head and allowed as to some psychic experiences that might perhaps interest me.

"What is your name, sir?" I asked the man.

"Tom Connor. I'm an electrician. I've been here fifteen years."

"Anything unusual happen to you here at the Olympia?"

"About eight years ago when I was on night duty here, I heard footsteps coming down the stairs. So I thought it was one of the bosses coming and I went to check and there was nobody, so I went to the top of the house and still didn't see anybody. I came back again and I heard footsteps coming down the gallery, so I went to the switchboard, put on the houselights and searched—but there was nobody there."

"Did you hear this just once?"

"During the same fortnight when that show was on," Tom Connor replied quietly, "I had the same experience again. Footsteps coming down from the dressing rooms. I went and checked. Still, nobody. Couple of nights afterwards, I was having a cup of tea, and I was reading a book, sitting on the rostrum, and the rostrum lifted itself a few inches off the ground! I felt myself coming up and I thought it was one of the bosses, and I said, well, I'm awake! It's all right, I'm awake. But to my surprise, there was nobody there."

"You felt the rostrum physically lifted up?"

"Yes, as if someone of heavy weight had stood on the end of it."

"So what did you do then?"

"When I realized that there was no one there, I got a shock and felt a cold shiver, and put on more lights and had a look around. There was nobody in the theater."

"Did you ever experience anything unusual in the area of the dressing rooms upstairs?" I asked.

"No, except that I heard the footsteps coming down, very clearly."

"Man or woman?"

"Heavy footsteps, like a man's."

"Anything else?"

"Well, at night, half-past twelve, 1 o'clock, I get this cold, clammy feeling—my hair standing on end—I am always very glad to get out of the place."

Meanwhile, Dick Conlon, the house manager, had come onstage, having finished counting his money for the night.

I interrupted my interesting talk with Tom Connor, stagehand, to question Conlon about his experiences, if any, at the Olympia.

"I've been here thirteen months," he said, "but so far I haven't noticed anything unusual."

By now Sybil Leek had joined us.

"Sybil," I said, "when we got to this theater earlier this evening, you did not really know where we were going. But when we got to our seats in stage box 1, you said to me, 'Something is here, I feel very cold.' What was your impression on getting here?"

"There is undoubtedly a presence here and I think it moves around quite a lot. The box has some association with it. I am mainly concerned though with the dressing room that had the number changed. I have not been up to this room, but it is upstairs. Second door, almost faces the stage. The corridor continues and there is a left hand turn. Then there are two doors. Not a particularly healthy presence, I feel. *I don't feel it is connected with the theater.*"

"Then how would it be here?"

"I have an impression that this is something in the year 1916, and something very unruly, something destructive. It is a man. He doesn't belong here. He wishes to get away."

"What is he doing here?" I asked. The story was taking a most unusual turn.

Sybil thought for a moment as if tuning in on her psychic world.

"He stayed here and could not get out, and the name is Dunnevan. That is the nearest I can get it. I can't see him too well; the clearest place where I see him is upstairs, along the corridor that faces the stage on both landings. Near the dressing room that had the number changed."

"This man—is he a soldier or a civilian?" I asked.

"There is so much violence about his nature that he could have been of military character. But again I get a little confusion on this."

"Did he die here?"

"I have a feeling that he did, and that he came to a very unsavory end. Perhaps not within the walls of this place, but having been here, having stayed here for some time. I think he wanted to stay in here. After the theater was closed."

"Is there any fighting involved?"

"Yes, I have the feeling of some violence. More people than this man."

"Is he alone?"

"He is the victim of it."

"What does he want?"

"I think he just is continuing in the same violent way in which he lived."

"Why is he causing these disturbances?"

"He needs to escape. A connection with . . . I think this man has sometime been imprisoned. The noises are really his protestation against the periods of being restricted. He does not know this is a theater. But something vital happened in that top dressing room and the impressions there would be clearer."

Unfortunately, the hour was so late we could not go up there that night.

"This man moves around the theater a lot," Sybil commented. "He was moving around here under pressure."

I thanked Sybil, and not knowing if any of the material obtained from her in this clairvoyant state had validity, I looked around for someone who could either confirm or deny it.

Again a stagehand, Albert Barden, was helpful.

"There was some fighting here," he said in his deliberate voice. "It was during the Easter rebellion, in 1916."

"Any soldiers here?" I asked, and a hush fell over the audience as they listened to the stagehand.

"As a matter of fact," he continued, "there was a civilian shot—he was suspected of I.R.A. activities, but it was discovered afterwards that he had something to do with the Quartermaster stores down in Ironbridge Barracks. *He was shot by mistake.*"

"Where was he shot?"

"In the theater."

"Downstairs?"

The man nodded.

"Though I was only six years old in 1916, I remember it as if it were yesterday. It was sometime between the rebellion and the Black and Tan fighting of 1921, but he surely was shot here."

In Ireland, it is sometimes difficult to distinguish between the two civil wars; as a matter of fact, they run one into the other, for it is true that for five long years all of Eire was a battleground for freedom.

It was very late by now and we had to leave the theater. Outside, Dublin was asleep except for a few pubs still plying their trade.

I thanked Lona Moran and her friends for having come down to help us pin down the specter of the Olympia.

Now at least they know it isn't a fellow thespian unhappy over bad notices—but a man who gave his life in the far grimmer theater of reality.

90

The Haunted Rectory

THE FIRST TIME I heard of the haunted rectory of Carlingford was in August 1965, when its owner, Ernest McDowell, approached me on the advice of an American friend who knew of my work.

"I own an old rectory which is haunted. If you are interested I will show you over the house with pleasure."

Subsequently, I ascertained that Mr. McDowell was a man of standing and intelligence, and his report was to be taken seriously. I arranged for us to go up to the Dundalk area in late July 1966. By this time, two editors from the German fashion magazine *Constanze*, Mr. and Mrs. Peter Rober, had decided to join us for a firsthand report on my methods, and also to act as neutral observers and arbiters should my camera yield some supernormal photographs. For this purpose, an elaborate system of safeguards was devised by Mr. Rober. It consisted of his bringing from Hamburg the very sensitive film I normally use for the purpose and personally inserting it in my Zeiss camera, which he kept in his own possession until we were ready to visit the house in question.

After he had filled the camera with film, he sealed it with string and red scaling wax, so that I could not possibly manipulate the camera or the film inside without breaking the seal. By this method he was in a firm position to attest to the fact that nobody had tampered with my camera and to further attest that if supernormal results were obtained, they had been obtained genuinely and not by fraud. I was happy to oblige the German editors, since an article in that materialistic country, dealing in a positive way with psychic phenomena, would be an important step forward.

The Robers arrived on a hot Saturday evening at Jury's Hotel, and the following morning we set out for Dundalk in one of those huge Princess cars that can seat six comfortably. We arrived at Ballymascanlon Hotel north of Dundalk by lunch time; I had chosen this comfortable inn as our headquarters.

The former Plunkett residence, now fully modernized and really an up-to-date hostelry in every sense of the word, has beginnings going back to the ninth century, although the house itself is only a hundred years old. This area abounds in "giants' tombs" and other pre-Christian relics, and was the center of the Scanlan family for many centuries. Later it belonged to the Cistercian monks of Mellifont, a ruin we had visited the year before when we crossed the river Boyne.

As soon as Mrs. Irene Quinn, the hotel's spunky owner, had settled us into our rooms, we made plans. I put in a telephone call to Ernest McDowell and a pleasant, well-modulated voice answered me on the other end of the

line. He was indeed ready for the expedition; within an hour he had driven over from his own home, a farm south of Dundalk called Heynestown, and we sat down in the comfortable lounge of Ballymascanlon Hotel to go over his experiences in detail.

"Let us start with the history of the house, as far as you know it at this moment," I asked McDowell, a pleasant-looking, well-dressed young man in his fortieth year whose profession was that of a painter, although he helped his brother run their farm as required. By and large Ernest McDowell was a gentleman farmer, but more gentleman than farmer, and rather on the shy side.

"The house was built in the seventeenth century," he began. "It was then a private house, a mansion that belonged to the Stannus family, before it was bought by the Church of Ireland for a rectory. The builder of the newer portion was the grandfather of the celebrated Sadler's Wells ballerina Ninette de Valois. I bought it in 1960."

"Have you moved in yet?"

"I haven't really...the house is empty, except of course for the ghosts."

"Ah yes," I said, "How large a house is it?"

"Twenty-two rooms in all. Nobody has lived there since I bought it, through."

"When was your first visit to the house, after you had acquired it?"

"I went up there every week to see if it was all right."

"Was it?"

"Well, yes, but one summer afternoon, in 1963—it was early September, I recall—my brother and I were at the rectory. My brother was out cutting corn, and I was mowing the lawn. It was rather a hot evening and I thought I was getting a cold. I was very busy, though, and I just happened to look up, towards the door, when I noticed moving towards the door *a figure of a girl in a red dress.*

"The motor of the lawnmower was not in good repair and it had bothered me, and I was taken aback by what I saw. It was a red velvet dress she wore, and before I could see her face, she just vanished!"

"Did she look solid?"

"Solid."

"Did she cast a shadow?"

"Yes."

"Did you see her shoes?"

"There wasn't time. I started from the ground up, and the red dress was the first thing I noticed."

"About that face?"

"I couldn't make it out."

"What period would you say the dress belonged to?"

"It was Edwardian, long."

"What did you do after she vanished?"

"I looked towards the gate—the gate that lets you into the grounds from the road—and coming in the gate was a clergyman with a very high collar, and he vanished, too!"

"Do you recall anything else about him?"

"He wore a rather out-of-date outfit, and a hat."

"What time of day was it?"

"About 5 P.M."

I thought about this ghostly encounter of two restless spirits for a moment, before continuing my questioning of the chief witness.

"Did they react to each other in any way?"

"I should say there was some bond between the two; there was a connection."

"Did you see anything else?"

"No, just the two figures."

"Did your brother see anything?"

"No. But Canon Meissner, who lived at the house for some time, saw the same girl in one of the rooms. She appeared to him on a separate occasion."

"How long ago?"

"About twenty years ago. He described her as a young girl who appeared near his bed and then just disappeared."

"Disconcerting for a Canon, I'd say. What else can you tell me about the haunted rectory?"

"Helen Meissner, his daughter, was in the dining room one night, with the door open, alone, when the other door, on the other end of the room, suddenly started to vibrate as if someone were trying hard to push it open. It opened by itself and the dog with her stood and stared at whatever came through the door, its hackles rising, and then it ran for its life.

"Then, too, Mrs. Meissner, the Canon's wife, and Helen heard footsteps on the backstairs one night. The steps started on the bottom of the stairs and went right up, past them, as they were standing on both sides of the stairs; but they did not see anything. This was about fifteen years ago when Meissner was Rector and lived at the house with his family.

"My sister-in-law, who is very sensitive, went through the house only two weeks ago, and she claimed that the back part of the house gave her a very uncomfortable feeling. She owned a house in Kent, England, that was haunted and we both felt it. I suppose we are both psychic to a degree, since I've on occasion felt things."

"What sort of things?" I asked. I always like to get a full picture of my witnesses to evaluate their testimony. If they have had ghostly experiences prior to the one under investigation, it would indicate mediumistic faculties in them.

"My brother and sister-in-law had bought a house in Kildare and I stayed there one night, and for no reason at all, I sat up in bed from a deep sleep, and I clearly heard both locks on the doors in the room click. But I was quite alone."

The haunted rectory at Carlingford

"To your knowledge, is there any record of any unhappy incident in this house?" I asked, getting back to the haunted rectory.

"No, it has a very happy atmosphere. Only when I go into it sometime, I feel as if there were people in it, yet it is obviously empty. It seems alive to me. Of course, I have heard footsteps in the corridors when I was quite alone in the house. That was mainly upstairs. It's a passage that runs up one stairway and around the house and down the other staircase. The only thing smacking of tragedy I know of was the coachman losing a child in the gatehouse that burned down, but that was not in the house itself."

"Is there any tradition or popular rumor that might refer to the apparitions of the clergyman and the girl in the red dress?"

"None whatever."

Thus it was that all members of our party had no foreknowledge of any event connected with the haunted house, no names, or anything more than what Ernest McDowell had just told us. Sybil, of course, was nowhere near us at this point, since she was to join us only after the preliminaries had been done with.

The Germans took it all down with their tape recorders, and it was for their benefit that I made the point of our total "innocence" as far as facts and names were concerned.

"What is the house called now?" I asked.

"Mount Trevor," Mr. McDowell replied. "It was originally built by the Trevors, a very well-known country family. They also built the town of Rostrevor, across Carlingford Lough."

Empty now, the rectory was once witness to great emotional events

"Are there any chairs in the house now?" I finally asked, since Sybil had to sit down *somewhere* for her trance. McDowell assured me he had thought of it and brought one chair—just one—to the otherwise empty house.

When we arrived at the house after a pleasant drive of about fifteen minutes, Peter Rober gave me back my camera, fully sealed now, and I took pictures at random downstairs and upstairs, and Catherine joined me in taking some shots also, with the same camera.

We entered the grounds, where the grass stood high, and McDowell led us into the house by a side entrance, the only door now in use, although I was immediately impressed that a larger door facing the other way must at one time have existed.

The house is pleasantly situated atop a knoll gently sloping down towards the water of Carlingford Lough, with trees dotting the landscape and sheep grazing under them, giving the place a very peaceful feeling. In back of the house lay a kitchen garden, beyond which the ruined towers of ancient Carlingford Abbey could be seen in the distance. Across the road from the garden gate was the Catholic church house of Carlingford.

The hall was rather small; to the left, the staircase mentioned in the ghostly accounts immediately led to the upper story, while to the right of the door a short passage took us into the large downstairs corner room, where we decided to remain. Large windows all around gave the room sufficient illumination, and there was a fireplace in the rear wall. Next to it stood the lone chair McDowell had mentioned.

CHAPTER SIX: **This House is Haunted**

444

Sybil joined us now inside the house and I hurried to get her first clairvoyant impressions as they occurred.

"Something connected with the period of 1836," she said immediately, poking about the rooms. "I have two names...as we came in the name *Woodward* came to me, and the other is *Devine or Divine*. Something like that. Peculiar name, I think."

"Please don't analyze it," I warned, "just let it come. I'll do the analyzing."

"Woodward and Devine," Sybil repeated. "These names have some meaning in this house. Also, a hall of imprisonment. Someone was imprisoned, I feel."

We followed Sybil, who slowly walked from room to room, Catherine helped me carry the tape recorder and camera, Ernest McDowell following behind looking excited, and three friends of his whose presence he felt might be useful. They were two ladies sharing a house at Ardee, both of them very psychic. Mrs. Bay John and Pat MacAllister had brought a young ward named Julian with them. I secretly hoped there weren't any poltergeists lurking about under the circumstances!

Later, Mrs. MacAllister mentioned seeing a face as if etched onto the wall in the very room upstairs where I took some psychic pictures, though of course I did not know they would turn out to be unusual at the time I took them. I never know these things beforehand.

We were still on the ground floor and Sybil was investigating the rear section, the oldest part of the house. There were some iron bars outside the window of the rather dank room, giving it a very heavy prison-like feeling. It was the original kitchen area.

"Someone was *made* to stay upstairs," Sybil said now, "and I have gooseflesh on my forearms now." We walked up the stairs and I confirmed the latter observation.

Finally we found ourselves in a room about the middle of the upper story, and Sybil came to a halt.

"I feel I want to run away from this room," she observed. "It's a panic-stricken feeling. Someone wants to get away from here; the name Devine comes again here. Someone is hiding here, and then there is imprisonment. Is there a prison somewhere here? Several people are held. This is away from the house, however."

"Is there a presence here?" I asked as I always do when we are at the center of uncanny activities.

"Yes, several. The period is 1836. The strongest presence is someone in brown. A man. There is a connection with business. There are three people here, but of the same period. There is no overlapping of periods here. The main person hiding in this room or forcibly kept here went from here and was hanged, with other people. This was a man. Perhaps we should go downstairs now."

We followed Sybil's advice and repaired to the downstairs parlor.

"Father Devine...should not have left the church for business," Sybil suddenly mumbled. "Someone says that about him. I feel him around, though."

Now I placed Sybil in the one chair we had and the rest of us formed a circle around her as best we could. It was about the same time, 5 o'clock, as the time of the haunting and I was prepared for *anything*.

Presently, Sybil showed all signs of deep trance. My German friends were riveted to the floor, Mrs. Rober clutching the microphone and Mr. Rober taking dozens of pictures with his Rolleiflex camera. The tension mounted as Sybil's lips started to move, though no word came at first through them. Gradually, I coaxed the spirit to take firmer possession of my medium's body and to confide in us, who had come as friends.

"Who are you?" I said softly. The voice now emanating from Sybil was hesitant and weak, not at all like Sybil's normal voice.

"Aileen," the voice murmered.

I could hardly hear her, but my tape recorder picked up every breath.

"Aileen Woodward," the ghost said.

"Is this your house?"

"We live here...where is he? Where is he? Robert!

"Whom are you seeking?"

"Devaine...Robert Devaine...speak slightly...my husband...be quiet...where is he?"

I wondered if she wanted me to keep my voice down so that I would not give her away to some pursuers.

"Where is Robert?" I asked, trying to reverse the line of questioning.

"Where is he, where is he?" she cried instead, becoming more and more upset and the tears, real tears, streaming down Sybil's usually tranquil face.

I calmed her as best I could, promising to help her find Robert, if I could.

"When did you first come to this house?" I asked quietly, while the sobbing continued.

The faces around me showed the great emotions that seemed to have been transferred from the ghostly girl to the witnesses. Not a word was spoken.

At this point, the tape had to be turned over. Unfortunately, it slipped out of our hands and it was several seconds before I started to record again. During those moments I tried to explore her family connections more fully.

Who was Robert and who were his people? Who was Robert's father?

"In the Church," she replied, quieter now.

"Does he like you?" I wanted to know.

There was a moment of quiet reflection before she answered.

"No."

"Why not?"

"The Church must not marry!"

"Is Robert a priest?"

"Shhh!" she said quickly. "Don't speak!"

"I don't quite understand...how does religion enter the picture?"

"Changer," she mumbled, indicating that someone had changed his faith.

"Are you and Robert of the same religion?" I now asked.

"Don't ask it."

"Are you Catholic?"

Utter silence was my answer.

I pleaded with her for more information so I could help her locate Robert. In vain; she would not budge on this question. Finally, she confused me with her enemies.

"You took him...I'm going for a walk now...follow...down the hill...just a walk...to see if he comes...."

"If I get you to see Robert again, will you promise to do as I tell you?" I asked.

"I promise nothing," the frightened ghost replied. "You betray him...how do I know you're a friend?"

"You have to trust me if I am to help, you."

"I don't trust."

Now I gently told her the truth about herself, the time that had come and gone since 1836 and why she could not stay on in this house.

"Don't speak so loud...you drive me mad...I'm going for a walk in the garden..." she said, trying to ignore the light of truth piercing her self-inflicted prison. But it did not work. The door of reality had been opened to her. In a moment she was gone.

Sybil reopened her eyes, confused at first as to where she was. I then asked her to take some fresh air outside the house, since the rain that had come down during part of our séance had now stopped and the countryside was back to its glorious Irish freshness.

With Sybil outside, I turned once more to the owner of the house and asked whether he had ever heard the names Woodward, Aileen, and Devine or Devaine before in connection with the house or area.

"The only thing I know is that Canon Meissner told me that this house was once occupied by a French family named Devine. Since Canon Meissner had the house from 1935 onward, this must have been before his time."

"The girl speaks of a clergyman, and you saw a clergyman ghost, is that correct?"

"Yes," McDowell nodded, "but he wore black, not brown."

In the time we had lost through the tape change, the ghost had described herself as 16 years of age, wearing a red dress, and the dates 1836 and 1846 both were given. Sybil, of course, had no knowledge of McDowell's experience with the girl in the red velvet dress.

I asked Mr. McDowell to look in the local records for confirmation of some of the names and information that had come through the medium. Offhand, none of it was known to those present, so that confirmation would have to await further research.

We returned to Ballymascanlon Hotel, where the eager German journalist had made an appointment with a local photographer so that he could get my films developed while we were still on location, and if there was anything on the negatives that had not been visible to the naked eye, one could make immediate use of the information. I never anticipated anything of this sort, but one can't know these things in advance either. As it turned out, there *were* two pictures in the batch, taken by Catherine and me with my sealed camera, that showed the same mirror-like effects I had observed on the photographs taken in June Havoc's haunted townhouse in New York and in the haunted trailer of Rita Atlanta, near Boston. Wherever there is present in a room a haunted area, represented by a magnetic field or a cold spot sometimes, such an area occasionally shows up on film with mirror-like effects; that is, reflections of objects in the room occur that could not have occurred under ordinary conditions, there being no mirror or other reflecting surface near.

Peter Rober was clearly elated, showing his pleasure about as much as his North German nature permitted him to. There was still another picture that represented a puzzle to us: in the haunted room upstairs where Helen Meissner had seen the door open by its own volition, Catherine took a picture in what seemed to both of us an empty room. We clearly recall that the doors were both shut. Yet, to our amazement, on the picture the door to the left is quite plainly ajar!

Ernest McDowell suggested we talk to the Meissners firsthand, and the following morning, Mr. and Mrs. Rober and I drove across the border to Northern Ireland, where the Meissners now live in a little town called Warrenpoint.

Mrs. Meissner turned out to be a friendly, talkative lady who readily agreed to tell us what had happened to them during their tenancy at the rectory.

"We lived there twenty-five years, and we left the house in 1960," she began her recollections. "We did not notice anything unusual about the house at first, perhaps because we were so glad to get the house.

"Part of the house was almost Queen Anne period, the rest Georgian. We had two indoor maids and we took our gardener with us, too. Everybody was happy. We did lots of entertaining and life was very pleasant. Then I noticed that local people never came to the rectory *in the evening*. They always made an excuse. Finally, I was informed that there was a ghost in the house. It was supposed to have been the ghost of a sea captain who lived here originally and was lost at sea. The older portion of the house was where he had lived, they said. I never was able to find out anything more than that about this sea captain, however. I was a skeptic myself and went gaily about my business. Then summer came, and I used to be outdoors as late as one could. Several evenings, *something white* passed me, something big, and yet I never heard a sound. I

thought this very strange, of course, and wondered if it was a white owl, But there was no sound of wings. Gradually I got to rather expect this phenomenon."

"Any particular time of day?" I interjected.

"At dusk. Outside. And then I saw it from the window. But it had no form, yet I knew it was white. I saw it often, and never a sound."

"After that, did you have any further adventures in the house?" I asked.

"We had a visit from the sister of Ninette de Valois, and she was very interested in the house because it was an ancestor of hers who had owned it. He was a Colonel Stannus. At the same time we had another visitor, a young man from Dublin. The lady and her husband had come rather late in the evening; they were staying at Rostrevor Hotel, and they wanted to see over Carlingford Rectory, and we thought it was rather late in the evening for that, so we asked them to come the next day. At that time the young man from Dublin was here also, but he and the lady had never met.

"When he looked at the lady, he became suddenly white as a sheet. I wondered if he was ill, but he said no, so we moved on to a room that we always regarded as a guest room. The young man from Dublin had often stayed in that room before. But when we entered the room, the lady exclaimed that she had been in that room before! Of course she hadn't.

"The young fellow from Dublin still looked very shaken, so I took him downstairs to one side and said, What is wrong with you?

"Finally he told me.

"'It's the most extraordinary thing,' he said to me. 'That lady is the ghost.'

"'What ghost?' I asked.

"'Often when I slept in that room,' he explained, 'I have been awakened by the feeling of a presence in the room. When I looked up, I saw the face of that lady!'

"What struck me as odd was that he felt something strange immediately upon meeting her and she felt something equally strange about having been to that room before when in fact she hadn't.

"Later, at tea, she asked me if I believed in the transmigration of souls."

The young man, whose name is Ronny Musgrave, evidently was reminded by the lady's appearance of the ghost's, I felt, but that would still not explain *her* reaction to the room, unless she had clairvoyantly foreseen her trip to Carlingford and was now realizing it!

"I've spent so much time in that house," Mrs. Meissner continued, "but I never felt I was alone. My husband's experience was different from mine. He had fallen asleep. He awoke, feeling that there was someone in the room. He thought it was an evil presence and he made the sign of the cross. Then it disappeared. I always thought the presence was female. I've heard footsteps, too. But I never feared this ghost. To me, it was pleasant."

I tried to piece together the past history of the house. Prior to 1932 when the Meissners moved in, there was a rector named Aughmuty there; before that the Reverend Bluett, before him his father-in-law, a Mr. Mailer, and that brings us back to the nineteenth century, when the Stannus family owned the place. It was just a private house then.

Mrs. Meissner did not recognize any of the names obtained during the trance, incidentally.

While she went to fetch her octogenarian husband to supplement some of the data for us, I had a talk with the daughter, now the widowed Mrs. Thompson, who had come over to the house to see us.

"We had a cocker spaniel," she began, "and the dog was with me in that upstairs room. There was a big mirror there then, and as I looked into it, I saw the door at the far end of the room open by itself, and then close again slowly. The dog got up and snarled and growled, but I saw nothing. That was the only experience that I had, but it was enough for me."

Canon Meissner is a lively and kind man who readily answered my questions as best he knew. None of the names rang a bell with him, as far as churchmen were concerned, and as for private origins, he did not really have the sources in his library. He recommended we take it up with Trinity College in Dublin where there are extensive records. The house had become a rectory about 1870 or 1871, he explained, and was directly purchased from the Stannus family at that time. They had built the newer part onto the already existing old portion.

I started to examine the two heavy books the Canon had brought with him from his study.

No Devine or Devaine showed up in the lists of rectors of Carlingford.

In *The Alumni of Trinity College*, London, Williams and Norgate, 1924, on page 217, column I, I found the following entry: "Devine, Charles, admitted to Trinity, November 4, 1822, age 20 [thus born 1802]; son of John Devine, born County Louth."

That, of course, was the right area, for Carlingford was at that time the principal town in the county.

I further found a listing of "Robert Woodward, graduated Trinity, November 5, 1821, aged 16, son of Henry Woodward, M.A. 1832," on page 94 of the same work.

It seemed extraordinary that we had located two names given in trance by Sybil Leek, and that both names were of the right period claimed and in the right location. But the search was far from finished.

While I was trying to get some corroboration from the local librarian at Dundalk—without success—the German editors packed up and left for Hamburg. I left instructions with Ernest McDowell as to what I needed, and then the three of us, my wife and I and Sybil, went on to the western part of Ireland. There we parted company and Sybil went to her home in the south of England while we returned to New York.

The owner Edward McDowell, a painter, examining the grounds

On August 2, 1966, Sybil had a trance-like dream at her house at Ringwood, Hants. In this dream state she saw herself walking back and forth between the rectory and the ruined abbey. There was a young woman who had come from some other place and had been waiting a long time for a man to join her. He had been in India. The woman was terribly upset and said that she had married the man but it was not legal and she had to find a Catholic priest to marry them because the whole thing was making her ill. He did not want to be married by a priest because he was a Protestant and his family would cut him off without any money.

He had left her because of her insistence on being married again, but she loved him and wanted to persuade him to agree to being married by a priest. She had been in England, and he told her to come to Ireland to Carlingford, where he could meet her, but he had not turned up. She had to find a priest who would keep the marriage secret, and this was not easy, as everyone said the marriage had to be written down in a book.

The woman claimed that "everything" could be found in the *Yelverton papers* in Dublin. Sybil was sure there was a court case called the Yelverton case about the 1840–50 period. But then things in the dream-like state got a bit confused as she found herself drifting in and out of the house, sometimes walking to the abbey, talking to a priest, then back to the house, which at that time seemed furnished; and the gateway Sybil saw at the back of the house, not where it is now. The woman seemed to be staying with friends; she did not live at Carlingford permanently and indeed went on from there.

That was on August 2; on the third, Sybil again "dreamt" exactly the same sequence, which again culminated in the search for the Yelverton case papers. But the dream was more vivid this time; in the morning Sybil found that she had gotten up in the middle of the night, taken off her nightgown and put on a long evening dress, and then gone back to bed in it. She had the distinct feeling of wearing the same kind of clothes this girl wore in the 1840s. The girl said in all her moving around she could not get the right clothes to be married in and would have to buy more. The girl seemed to have an accent and spoke Italian and French in between a lot of crying and sniffling, and she seemed familiar to Sybil.

The latter was only too logical, since Sybil had been her instrument of communication, but we had not until now discussed the details of the case or her trance with Sybil; consequently she could not have known about the religious problem, for instance.

That was a monumental week for this case, for on the following day, and quite independently of Sybil's impressions, Ernest McDowell had come across the needed corroboration in a rare local chronicle. In a work entitled *County Families of the United Kingdom, 1800*, the family named Woodhouse, of Omeath Park, near Carlingford, was listed.

Omeath is the next village after Carlingford and quite close to it.

John Woodhouse, born October 6, 1804, married to Mary Burleigh, June 10, 1834; nine children, the fourth of which was Adeline Elizabeth. Now the Irish would pronounce Adeline rather like Ad'lin, and what I had heard from Sybil's entranced lips sounded indeed like A'lin, or Ad'lin!

The Woodhouse family claimed descent from the Woodhouses of Norfolk, England; thus Sybil's reference to the girl having been to England might fit. Perhaps she had gone to visit relatives.

Further in the same source, there is a listing also for the family Woodward of Drumbarrow. A Robert Wood-ward, born June 20, 1805, is given, whose father was Henry Woodward. Robert Woodward, according to the source, married one Esther Woodward and had two sons and three daughters. This marriage took place in 1835. This is the same man also listed in the register of Trinity College.

The similarity of the names Woodward and Woodhouse may have been confusing to the ghostly girl. One was presumably her maiden name and the other that of her husband's family.

Unfortunately, we don't have the birth dates for Adeline. But if her father was married only in 1834, she could not very well have married Robert in 1836 or even 1846. If she was sixteen at the time as she claimed in trance, and if she had been born somewhere between 1835 and 1845, we get to the period of around 1850–60 as the time in which her tragic liaison with Robert might have taken place. But this is speculation.

What we do know concretely is this: nobody, including Sybil Leek, ever heard of a man named Devine, a girl named Adeline Woodhouse, a man named Robert Woodward, before this investigation took place. These names were not in anyone's unconscious mind at the time of our visit to Carlingford Rectory. Yet these people existed in the very area in which we had been and at the approximate time when the ghost had been active there in her lifetime. How can that be explained by any other reasoning than true communication with a restless departed soul?

What were the relationships between the girl in the red velvet dress and her Robert, and how did the father fit into this and which one was the clergyman? Was Devine the clergyman who destroyed their marriage or did he help them? It seems to me that it is his ghost Ernest McDowell observed. Is there a feeling of guilt present that kept him in these surroundings perhaps?

At any rate, the rectory has been quiet ever since our visit and Ernest McDowell is thinking of moving in soon. That is, if we don't buy the place from him. For the peaceful setting is tempting and the chance of ever encountering the girl in the red velvet dress, slim. Not that any of us would have minded.

91

The Haunted Seminary

I FIRST HEARD OF THE haunted room at Maynooth College from Patrick Byrne, who also assured me it would be difficult, if not impossible, to get permission to investigate it. But a Ghost Hunter never says die, so, without further attempting to set up a visit, I decided to read what there was about the seminary itself, and then set out for it.

"Founded through the exertions of the Irish Hierarchy by an Act of the Irish Parliament in 1795, Maynooth College became within a century one of the largest ecclesiastical seminaries in the world. From its small beginnings with forty students and ten professors accommodated in a converted dwelling-house, it has grown into a fair academic city of nearly six hundred students and a teaching staff of forty, with noble buildings, spacious recreation grounds and one of the finest churches in Ireland. Between 9,000 and 10,000 priests have been trained here.

"Eamon De Valera, President of Ireland, was formerly attached to the teaching staff.

"Passing between the *Geraldine Castle* (begun by Maurice Fitzgerald in 1176) and the *Protestant church* with its pre-Reformation tower, the avenue skirts *Silken Thomas's Tree* (sixteenth century) and affords a fine view of the original college. In the center is the two-hundred-year-old *mansion of John Stoyte*, where the first students and professors labored, and behind it the buildings erected for them in 1797–99.

"Spacious cloisters are a feature of the Pugin part of Maynooth, and the cloister beginning at the College Chapel leads through a long array of episcopal portraits and groups of past students to the Library and St. Mary's Oratory.

"The *Junior House* buildings (1832–34) contain the 'Ghost Room' which has been enshrined in a maze of gory legends since its conversion into an oratory (1860). They are flanked by a very pleasant rock garden. Beyond, one glimpses the towering trees of the College Park, stretching to the farm buildings in the distance. Nearby a simple yew glade leads to the *Cemetery*, where so many of the great Maynooth figures of the past now rest, undisturbed by the throbbing life around them as a new generation of Maynooth students prepares to carry on their work."

My appetite was aroused. The following day we started out by car towards Maynooth, which is a little west of Dublin and easily reached within an hour's driving time. Our driver immediately knew what we were looking for, having been with us before, so when we reached the broad gates of the College, he pulled up at the gatekeeper's lodge and suggested I have a chat with him. Unfortunately, it started to rain and the chat was brief, but the man really did not know any more than second- or third-hand information. We decided to see for ourselves and drove past the ruined tower of the old Fitzgerald castle into the College grounds. Walking around just like ordinary tourists, we eventually made our way past the imposing main buildings into the courtyard where, according to the gatekeeper, the haunted dormitory was situated.

It was about four in the afternoon, and very few students were in evidence, perhaps because it was vacation time. The building called Rhetoric House was easy to spot, and we entered without asking permission from anyone—mainly because there was nobody around to ask. We realized, of course, that women were somewhat of an oddity here, but then this was a College and not a Trappist Monastery, and mothers must have visited here now and then, so I felt we were doing nothing sacrilegious by proceeding up the iron stairs of the rather drab-looking dormitory. When we reached the second story—always I first and Catherine and Sybil trailing me, in case they had to beat a hasty retreat—we finally found a human being at Maynooth. A young priest stood in one of the corridors in conversation with another priest, and when he saw me, he abruptly terminated it and came towards me, his curiosity aroused as to what I was doing here. As he later explained to me, some not-so-honest people had on occasion walked in and walked out with various items, so naturally he had learned to be careful about strangers. I dispelled his fears, however, by introducing myself properly, but I must have been slipshod in introducing my wife Catherine and Sybil Leek, for the good father thought Sybil was Cathy's mother—not that Cathy was not honored!

When I asked for his own name, he smiled and said with the humor so often found in Irish priests: "My name is that of a character in one of James Joyce's novels."

"Bloom," I said, smilingly.

"Of course not."

"Well then," I said thoughtfully, "it must be Finnegan."

"You get 'A' for that. Finnegan it is."

And it was thus that I became friendly with a charming gentleman of the cloth, Father Thomas A. Finnegan, a teacher at Maynooth.

I cautiously explained about our interest in the occult, but he did not seem to mind. To the contrary. Leading the way up the stairs, he brought us into the so-called haunted room.

The wall where the mysterious window had been was now boarded up and a statue of St. Joseph stood before the window. The rest of the room was quite empty, the floor shining; there was nothing sinister about it, at least not on first acquaintance.

I took some pictures and filmed the area as Sybil "poked around" in the room and adjacent corridor. Father Finnegan smiled. It was obvious he did not exactly believe in ghosts, nor was he afraid of them if they existed. He was genuinely fond of Maynooth and respected my historical interest along with the psychic.

"'You've heard of the tradition about this room, of course," he said, "but I'm sorry I can't supply you with any firsthand experiences here."

"Do you know of anyone who has had any uncanny feelings in this room?" I asked.

"Well, now, the room was closed in 1860, as you know," the priest replied, "and the people who slept in it prior to that date would not be around now. Otherwise no one has reported anything recently—the room is rarely used, to begin with."

Sybil seemed to sense something unpleasant at this point and hurried out of the room, down the corridor.

"There are two good sources on this room," Father Finnegan said, as if he had read my thoughts. "There is Denis Meehan's book, *Window on Maynooth*, published in 1949, and a somewhat longer account of the same story also can be found in *Hostage to Fortune* by Joseph O'Connor. I'll send you one or both books, as soon as I can get hold of them."

With that, Father Finnegan led us down the stairs and gave us the grand tour of Maynooth College, along the library corridors, the beautiful and truly impressive church of St. Patrick, the garden, and finally the museum, opened only about twenty years ago.

We thanked him and went back to our car. I then told the driver to stop just outside the College gates on a quiet spot in the road. Sybil was still under the sway of what we had just seen and heard and I wanted to get her psychic impressions while they were fresh.

"Where exactly were we?" Sybil asked. Despite the priest's tour she was somewhat vague about the place.

"We're at Maynooth, in County Kildare," I replied, and added, "You've been in a haunted room on the third floor of a certain dormitory."

"It's a strange place, Hans," Sybil said. "The downstairs is typical of any religious place, peaceful—but when we went upstairs I had a great desire to run. It was not fear, and yet—I felt I had to run. I had a strange feeling of an animal."

"An animal?" I repeated.

"A four-legged animal. I had the feeling an animal had followed us down to what is now an oratory."

"What did you feel in the room itself?"

"Fear."

"Any part of the room in particular?"

"Yes, I went straight to the statue."

"Where the window used to be?"

"I felt I wanted to run. I had the feeling of an animal presence. No human."

"Anything else?"

"I developed a tremendous headache—which I generally do when I am where there has been a tragedy. It is gone now. But I had it all the time when I was on that floor."

"Did you feel anyone went out that window?"

"Yes, for at that moment I was integrated into whatever had happened there and *I could have gone out the window!* I was surprised that there was a wall there."

"Did you feel that something unresolved was still present?"

"Yes, I did. But to me it was a case of going back in time. It was a fear of something following you, chasing you."

I thought of the account of the haunting, given by one of the students—the only one who got away with his life—who had seen "a black shape" in the room. Shades of the Hounds of the Baskervilles!

Had someone brought a large dog to the room and had the dog died there? We will never know for sure. Animal ghosts exist and to the novice such an image could indeed be so frightening as to induce him to jump out a window. Then, too, the College was built on old ground where in the Middle Ages a castle had stood, replete with keep, hunters—and dogs. Had something from that period been incorporated into the later edifice?

When we returned to Dublin, I had the pictures taken developed but nothing unusual showed on them.

The following week, Father Finnegan sent me a copy of *Window on Maynooth* by Denis Meehan, a sometime professor at the College who is now a Benedictine monk in the United States, according to Patrick Byrne.

Here then, under the subtitle of "The Buildings of Junior House," is Father Meehan's account of the ghost room at Maynooth.

For the curious, however, the most interesting feature of Rhetoric House will certainly be the ghost room. The two upper floors are altogether residential, and the ghost room is, or rather was, Room No. 2 on the top corridor. It is now an oratory of St. Joseph. Legend, of course, is rife concerning the history of this room; but unfortunately everything happened so long ago that one cannot now guarantee anything like accuracy. The incident, whatever it may have been, is at least dated to some extent by a Trustee's resolution of October 23rd, 1860. "That the President be authorised to convert room No. 2 on the top corridor of Rhetoric House into an Oratory of St. Joseph, and to fit up an oratory of St. Aloysius in the prayer hall of the Junior Students."

The story, as it is commonly now detailed, for the edification of susceptible Freshmen, begins with a suicide. The student resident in this room killed himself one night. According to some he used a razor; but tellers are not too careful about such details. The next inhabitant, it is alleged, felt irresistibly impelled to follow suit, and again, according to some, he did. A third, or it may have been the second, to avoid a similar impulse, and when actually about to use his razor, jumped through the window into Rhetoric yard. He broke some bones, but saved his life. Subsequently no student could be induced to use the room; but a priest volunteered to sleep or keep vigil there for one night. In the morning his hair was white, though no one dares to relate what his harrowing experiences can have been.

Afterwards the front wall of the room was removed and a small altar of St. Joseph was erected.

The basic details of the story have doubtless some foundation in fact, and it is safe to assume that something very unpleasant did occur. The suicide (or suicides), in so far as one can deduce from the oral traditions that remain, seems to have taken place in the period 1842–48. A few colorful adjuncts that used to form part of the stock in trade of the story teller are passing out of memory now. Modern students for instance do not point out the footprint burned in the wood, or the bloodmarks on the walls.

✳ 92

The Ghostly Sailor of Alameda

ONE NIGHT IN THE early spring of 1965, the telephone rang and a pleasant voice said, "I think I've got a case for you, Mr. Holzer. I'm calling from Alameda, California."

Before the young lady could run up an impressive telephone bill, I stopped her and asked her to jot down the main points of her story for my records. She promised this, but it took several months to comply. Evidently the ghost was not so unpleasant as she thought it was the night she had to call me long-distance, or perhaps she had learned to live with the unseen visitor.

It had all started four years before when Gertrude Frost's grandmother bought a house in Alameda, an island in San Francisco Bay connected with the mainland by a causeway and mainly covered by small homes—many of which belong to people connected with the nearby naval installations. The house itself was built around 1917.

After the old lady died, Miss Frost's mother had the house. Noises in the night when no one was about kept Miss Frost and her mother and aunt, who shared the house with her, from ever getting a good night's sleep. It did not sound like a very exciting case and I was frankly skeptical since there are many instances where people *think* they hear unnatural noises when in fact they merely ascribe supernormal character to what is actually natural in origin. But I was going to be in the area, and decided to drop in.

I asked Claude Mann, a news reporter from Oakland's Channel 2, to accompany us—my wife Catherine and my good friend Sybil Leek, who did not have the faintest idea where Alameda was or that we were going there. Not that Sybil cared—it was merely another assignment and she was willing. The date was July 1, 1965, and it was pleasantly warm—in fact, a most unghostly type of day.

As soon as we approached the little house, we quickly unloaded the camera equipment and went inside where two of the ladies were already expecting us. I promptly put Sybil into one of the easy chairs and began my work—or rather Sybil began hers.

Although the house was in the middle of the island and no indication of the ocean could be seen anywhere near it, Sybil at once remarked that she felt the sea was connected with the house in some way; she felt a presence in the house but not associated with it directly.

As soon as Sybil was in deep trance, someone took over her vocal cords.

"What is your name?" I asked.

"Dominic...."

"Do you live in this house?"

"No house... water... fort... tower...."

"What are you doing here?"

"Have to wait... Tiana...."

"What does Tiana mean?"

"*Tiana* ...boat...."

"Where does the boat go?"

"Hokeite... Hokeite...."

"What year is this?"

"1902."

"What is your rank?"

"Mid–ship–man." He had difficulty in enunciating. The voice had a strangely unreal quality, not at all like Sybil's normal speaking voice but more like the thin voice of a young man.

I continued to question the ghostly visitor.

"Are you serving on this boat?"

"Left here," he replied. "I'm going to break... everything up."

"Why do you want to do that?"

"Those things... got to go... because they are untidy ... I shall break them up... they say I'm mad... I'm not mad..."

"How old are you?"

"Thirty-one...."

"Where were you born?"

"I was born... Hakeipe...."

I was not sure whether he said "Hakeipe" or "Hakeite," but it sounded something like that.

"What state?" I had never heard of such a place.

"No state," the ghost said, somewhat indignant because I did not know better.

"Then where is it?" I demanded.

"In Japan," the ghost informed me. I began to wonder if he didn't mean Hakodate, a harbor of some importance. It had a fair number of foreign people at all times, being one of the principal seaports for the trade with America and Europe. It would be pronounced "Hak-o-deit," not too different from what I had heard through Sybil's mediumship.

"Break them up, break them up," the ghost continued to mumble menacingly, "throw those little things ... into ... faces ... I don't like faces ... people...."

"Do you realize time has gone on?"

"Time goes on," the voice said sadly.

"What are you doing here?" I asked.

"What are *they* doing here?" the ghost shot back angrily.

It was his land, he asserted. I asked if he had built anything on it.

"The tower is here," he said cryptically, "to watch the ships. I stay here."

"Are you American?"

"No, I'm Italian."

"Are you a merchant sailor or Navy?"

"Navy ... why don't you go away?"

"What do you want here?"

"Nothing...."

I explained about his death and this evoked cold anger.

"Smash everything...."

I decided to change the subject before the snarling became completely unintelligible.

Claude Mann's cameras were busily humming meanwhile.

"Did you serve in the American Navy?"

"Yes."

"Give me your serial number!"

"Serial ... one ... eight ... eight ... four ... three."

"Where did you enlist?"

"Hakkaite."

It did not make sense to me, so I repeated the question. This time the answer was different. Perhaps he had not understood the first time.

"In 'meda," he said.

Sailors call Alameda by this abbreviation. How could Sybil, newly arrived here, have known this? She could not, and I did not.

"Who's your commanding officer?"

"Oswald Gregory."

"What rank?"

"Captain."

"The name of your ship."

"*Triana*."

"How large a ship?"

"I don't know...."

I asked about his family. Did he have a wife, was he well? He became more and more reluctant. Finally he said:

"I'm not answering questions...."

"Your father's name?" I continued.

"Guiseppe."

"Mother?"

"Matilone...."

"Sister or brothers?"

"Four...."

"They live in Hokkaipe," he added.

"Where did you go to school?"

"Hokkaipe Mission...."

He came to this place in 1902, he asserted, and was left behind because he was sick.

"I wait for next trip ... but they never came back. I had bad headache. I was lying here. Not a house. Water."

I then asked what he was doing to let people know about his presence.

"I can walk—as well as anyone," he boasted. "I play with water, I drop things...."

I reasoned with him. His father and mother were waiting for him to join them. Didn't he want to be with them? I received a flat "No." He wasn't interested in a family reunion. I tried to explain about real estate. I explained that the house was fully paid for and he was trespassing. He could not have cared less.

I questioned his honesty and he did not like that. It made him waver in his determination to break everything up.

I spoke to him of the "other side" of life. He asked that I take him there.

He now recalled his sisters' names, Matild' and Alissi, or something that sounded like it.

"We've come to fetch you, Dominic." I said, suggesting he "go across."

"You're late," he snarled.

"Better late than never," I intoned. Who said I didn't have as much of a sense of humor as a ghost?

"I was never late," he complained. "I can walk ... without you!"

Gratitude was not his forte.

I requested that Sybil return to her own body now, but to remain in trance so as to answer my questions on what she could observe in that state.

Soon Sybil's own voice, feeble at first, was heard again from her lips.

I asked her to describe the scene she saw.

"I see a short, dark man," she replied, "who can't walk very well; he was insane. I think he had fits. Fell down. Violent man."

"Do you see a house?"

"No, I see water, and a gray ship. Big ship, not for people. Not for travelling. Low ship."

"Do you see a name on the ship?"

"...*ana* ... can't see it properly."

"What is this man doing here?"

"He had a fit here, and fell down and died, and somebody left him here. Somebody picked the body up ... into the water...."

Sybil showed signs of strain and I decided to take her out of trance to avoid later fatigue. As soon as she was "back" to her own self, not remembering anything, of course, that had come through her the past hour, turned to Miss Frost to find out what it was exactly that had occurred here of an unusual nature.

"Always this uneasy feeling...causing nervousness ...more at night..." she explained, "and noises like small firecrackers."

Miss Frost is a woman in her thirties, pleasant and soft spoken, and she holds a responsible position in San Francisco business life.

"If you pay no attention to it," she added, "then it becomes more intense, louder."

"Doesn't want to be ignored, eh?" I said.

"Occasionally at night you hear footsteps in the living room."

"When it is empty?"

"Of course.'"

"What does it sound like?"

"As if there were no carpets...like walking on boards...a man's footsteps."

"How often?"

"Maybe three times...last time was about three months ago. We've been here four years, but we only heard it about half a year after we moved in. On one occasion there was a noise inside the buffet as if there were a motor in it, which of course there isn't."

"Has anyone else had any experiences of an unusual nature in this house?"

"A painter who was painting a small room in the rear of the house suddenly asked me for a glass of water because he didn't feel well. Because of the noises."

I turned to Miss Frost's aunt, who had sat by quietly, listening to our conversation.

"Have you heard these footsteps?"

"Yes," she said. "I checked up and there was nobody there who could have caused them. That was around two in the morning. Sometimes around five or six also. They went around the bed. We had the light on, but it continued."

With the help of Miss Frost, I was able to trace the history of the area. Before the house was built here, the ground was part of the Cohen estate. The water is not far from the house although one cannot actually see it from the house.

Originally Alameda was inhabited by Indians and much of it was used as burial ground. Even today bones are dug up now and again.

Prior to Miss Frost, a Mr. Bequette owned the house, but what interested me far more than Mr. Bequette was the fact that many years ago a hospital occupied the land at this spot. Nothing is left of the old hospital.

In 1941, allegedly, a family lived at this house whose son was killed in action during the war. A mysterious letter reached Miss Frost in February of 1961 addressed to a B. Biehm at her address, but she could not locate this man.

None of this takes us back to 1902 when Dominic said he lived. A Japanese-born Italian sailor serving in the U.S. Navy is a pretty unusual combination. Was Dominic his family name?

I decided to query the Navy Department in the hope that they might have some records about such a man, although I had learned on previous occasions that Naval records that far back are not always complete.

On December 29, 1966, I received this reply from the office of the Chief of Naval Operations:

Dear Mr. Holzer:
In reply to your letter of 8 December, we have been unable to find either DOMINIC or Oswald GREGORY in the lists of U.S. Navy officers during this century. The Navy Registers for the period around 1902 list no U.S. Naval ship named TRIANA.
We have very little information on Alameda Island during the early 1900's. The attached extract from the Naval Air Station history, however, may be of some use.
Sincerely yours,
F. KENT LOOMIS
Captain, USN (Ret.)
Asst. Director of Naval History

Captain Loomis enclosed a history of the Alameda installations which seems to confirm the picture painted of the area (prior to that installation) by the ghostly sailor.

The real story of the U.S. Naval Air Station, Alameda, is how it has "arisen from the waters." How it was thrown up from the bottom of San Francisco Bay; how it was anchored to the earth with grass roots; how it was, by accident, the scene of some of the earliest flights in America. This is the romance of Alameda.

The Navy Department first began to consider the site now occupied by the air station toward the end of the First World War. The intention was to utilize the site as a destroyer base, but the war was over before the plans could be perfected. The land then lapsed into oblivion. *It was a rather barren land.* When the tide was out it was odious and disagreeable looking. Since people who boil soap are not fastidious concerning olfactory matters, the Twenty Mule Team Borax Company located the site of their first efforts near the "Mole" which went to San Francisco's ferries.

The main part of Alameda was very pretty, covered with good rich "bottom land" and shade trees, from which it had derived its name during the Spanish occupation days. "Alameda" means "shade" or "shady lane."

In 1776 the land had been granted to Don Luis Peralta, a grizzled old man who immigrated from Tabac in Sonora. His life as a soldier had been crowded with 40 years of service to His Majesty, the King of Spain, and ten children. It was only a small part of the 43,000 acres granted him by a grateful Spain.

He distributed his lands among his children when he felt his time had come. Although the peninsula of Alameda was in the most part fertile, the western tip of it was nothing but barren sands and tidal flats.

In 1876, engineers cut a channel through the peninsula's tip which linked San Leandro Bay with the main bay, and Alameda became an island. Deep water was on the way and dredging was begun to effect this end.

The inability of the U.S. Navy librarian to identify a ship named the *Triana* did not stop me from looking further, of course. Was there ever such a ship? A Captain Treeana commanded one of the three ships of Christopher Columbus and consequently there are towns named for him in the land he and his shipmates helped discover. Spelled nowadays Triana, one of them is in Alabama, and in the city of Huntsville there is a Triana Boulevard. It seems highly likely that so famous a captain's name should at one time or other have been chosen as the name of a ship.

Meanwhile, back at the house, things remained quiet and peaceful for 48 hours. Miss Frost was happy for the first time in years.

And then the footsteps and other noises resumed. Dominic wasn't going to ship out, after all.

That was in July 1965. I made certain suggestions. Close the door mentally; gently tell the ghost he must go, over and over again. He was free now to do so—proof of which was the fact that his footsteps, once confined to the living room area, were now heard all over the house.

A year has gone by and I have had no news from Alameda. Perhaps no news is good news and the ghostly sailor roams no more.

✳ 93

The Ghost Clock

NEW ENGLAND IS FULL of ghosts. A young woman with the improbable first name of Dixie-Lee, and the acquired-by-marriage second name of Danforth, lived in the small town of Milford, just over the border in New Hampshire. She chanced to hear me on a Boston radio program, and presto, there was a note in the mail about something pretty eerie that had happened to her.

In 1954, when Dixie-Lee was seventeen, she took on a two-week job as companion to an elderly lady by the name of Mrs. William Collar. Mrs. Collar, then eighty-two years old, had been a fine artist, and had lived a happy life all over the world. Dixie-Lee found being a companion an easy way to make some extra money. Mrs. Collar's housekeeper went home nights, and the elderly lady wanted someone with her in the large, rambling house, at least until she could find a full-time housekeeper who would sleep in.

The Collars had met in France, both studying there, and though they married against the wishes of their parents, they had a wonderful and happy life together. When Mr. William Collar died, things were never the same. They had occupied a large double room on the second floor, with a bed on either side, and a wash basin for each. They truly lived close together.

After her husband's death, Mrs. Collar moved out of the room, and never slept in it again. She left everything as it was, including a big grandfather clock, which was never wound again after Mr. Collar's passing. Finally, in 1958, she joined her Bill. She may have been able to prepare herself for it, for she was often heard talking to "her Bill" when no one else could be seen in the room.

There was a fight over the will. The Collars had had no children, and a niece inherited the house.

But let me get back to Dixie-Lee and 1954. The young girl had moved into Mrs. Collar's imposing white house at New Ipswich, as the section was called, and given a room on the second floor next to the large bedroom once occupied by Mr. and Mrs. Collar. She had barely enough time to admire the expensive antique furniture around the house, when it was time to retire for the night.

Mrs. Dixie-Lee Danforth had come to Boston to meet me, and I questioned her about what happened then.

"I went to bed," she said, "and in the wee hours of the morning I awoke to the faint sound of footsteps and ticking of a clock. The sound of both kept getting louder—louder—till it seemed to beat against my brain."

At first she thought she was dreaming, but, biting her own hand, she realized she was fully awake. Cold sweat stood on her forehead when she realized that Mrs. Collar was an invalid *who could not walk*. What was more, the big clock had not worked for years. Suddenly, just as suddenly as it had come, it ceased. Dixie-Lee lay still for a while in sheer terror, then she turned on the light. Her bedroom door was firmly closed, just as she had left it before going to bed. She checked the door leading to what was once the Collars' big bedroom. It was shut tight, too. She ventured out onto the narrow landing of the staircase leading to the lower floor. It was shut off from the downstairs part of the house by a hall door. That, too, was shut. She retraced her steps and suddenly noticed a rope and pulley. She pulled it and another door appeared.

"I opened it, heart in my mouth," Dixie-Lee said, "and was relieved to find a pretty, light bedroom behind it. It was furnished with modern furniture, and seemed to me much gayer and more peaceful than the rest of the house. The room was empty."

"What did you do then?" I wondered.

"First, I checked the big clock in my room. It was not going. Just as dead as it had been all those years. I looked around the house for other clocks. The only one in going condition was downstairs in the room occupied by Mrs. Collar, and I'd have to have had superhearing to hear that one tick all the way up to the second floor through three sets of closed doors and a heavy wooden floor!"

I readily agreed that was not very likely, and wondered if she had told anyone of her frightening experience that night.

"I told the daytime housekeeper, with whom I was friendly, and she laughed. But I refused to stay another moment unless someone else stayed with me. She and her young daughter moved in with me upstairs, and stayed the full two weeks. I never heard the footsteps or the ticking of the clock again while they were with me. But after I left, housekeepers came and went. Nobody seemed to stay very long at the big white house in New Ipswich. Possibly they, too, heard the uncanny noises."

I nodded and asked about Mrs. Collar. Could she have gotten out of bed somehow?

"Not a chance," Dixie-Lee replied. "She was a total invalid. I checked on her in the morning. She had never left her bed. She couldn't have. Besides, the footsteps I heard weren't those of a frail old woman. *They were a man's heavy footfalls.* I never told Mrs. Collar about my experience though. Why frighten her to death?"

"Quite so," I agreed, and we talked about Dixie-Lee now. Was she psychic to any degree?

Dixie-Lee came from a most unusual family. Her great-grandmother knew how to work the table. Her grandfather saw the ghost of his sister, and Dixie-Lee herself had felt her late grandfather in his house whenever she visited, and she had numerous premonitions of impending danger.

On at least one such occasion she had a feeling she should not go on a certain trip, and insisted on stopping the car. On investigation, she found the wheels damaged. She might have been killed had she not heeded the warning!

We parted. Mrs. Danforth returned to her somewhat-more-than skeptical husband in Milford, and I took the next plane back to New York.

But the haunted house in New Ipswich never left my mind. I was due back in New England around Halloween, 1963, and decided to join Mrs. Danforth in a little trip up to the New Hampshire border country. A friend of hers, their children, a Boston-teacher friend of ours named Carol Bowman, and my wife and I completed the party that drove up to New Ipswich on that warm fall day. We weren't exactly expected, since I did not know the name of the present owner of the house, But Mrs. Danforth had sent word of our coming ahead. It turned out the word was never received, and we actually were lucky to find anyone

in, luckier yet to be as cordially welcomed as we were by the lady of the house, whom we shall call Mrs. F.

Mrs. Jeanette F. was a sophisticated, well-educated lady whose husband was a psychiatrist, who was once also interested in parapsychology. She asked that I not use her full name here. A strange "feeling" of expecting us made her bid us a cordial welcome. I wasn't surprised to hear this—in this business, nothing surprises me anymore.

The F.s had only had the house for a year when we visited them. They had not intended to buy the house, although they were on the lookout for a home in New England. But they passed it in their car, and fell in love with it . . . or rather were somehow made to buy the place. They discovered it was built in 1789. That wasn't all they discovered after they moved in.

"I always had the feeling," Mrs. F said, "that we were only *allowed* to live here . . . but never really alone. Mrs. Collar's bedroom, for instance. I had the distinct feeling something was buried there under the floorboards. My sister-in-law slept upstairs. The next morning she told me she had 'heard things.' Right after we moved in, I heard footsteps upstairs."

"You too?" marveled Dixie-Lee, shooting a triumphant side glance at me, as if I had doubted her story.

"Last winter at dusk one day, I heard a woman scream. Both of us heard it, but we thought—or rather, *liked* to think—that it was a bobcat. Soon thereafter, we heard it again, only now it sounded more like a *child crying.* We heard it on several occasions and it gave us the willies."

On another occasion, there had been five people in the house when they heard the scream, followed by a growl. They went out to look for a bobcat . . . but there were absolutely no traces in the fresh snow, of either animal or human. There had also been all sorts of noises in the basement.

"Something strange about this child crying," Mrs. F. continued. "When we moved in, a neighbor came to see us and said when they saw we had a child, 'You've brought life back to the Collar house.'"

Dixie-Lee broke in.

"I seem to recall there was something about a child. I mean that they had a child."

"And it died?" I asked.

"I don't know," Mrs. F. said. "But there were diaries —they were almost lost, but one of Bill Collar's best friends, Archie Eaton, saved them. Here they are."

Mrs. F. showed us the remarkable books, all written in longhand. On cursory examination I did not uncover the secret of the child.

There is a hollow area in the basement. We went down to get impressions, and Dixie-Lee felt very uneasy all of a sudden, and didn't feel like joining us downstairs, even though moments before she had been the spirit of adventure personified.

We returned to the ground floor and had some coffee.

I decided to return with a medium, and hold a séance next to the chimney down in the basement, underneath the room where Mrs. F. felt the floorboards held a secret.

But somehow we were thwarted in this effort.

In December 1963, we were told that our visit would have to be postponed, and Mrs. F. asked us to come later in the winter. Too many living relatives in the house were making it difficult to listen for the dead.

"Something happened yesterday," she added, "that will interest you. My housekeeper is a very bright and trusted woman. She has never mentioned anything strange about the house. Yesterday I was telling her about our plans to sell the house. As I spoke, she was looking in the room next to me—I was standing in the kitchen. She was looking into the dining room, when she turned pale and interrupted me. She had seen a short, old woman in a long gray dress walk through the dining room. Now I questioned her about anything she might have seen in the past. She admitted she had seen figures on several occasions, but was afraid to be ridiculed. Strangely enough, she wants to buy the house despite these experiences. She calls it 'the house that watches,' because she always feels she is being observed while she cares for the children, even when she has them in the garden."

In February 1964, we tried to fix a new date to visit the house. My letters remained unanswered. Had the house changed hands again?

But no matter who actually *lived* there. It seemed the *real* owner was still Mrs. Collar.

✳ 94

The Ghost of Gay Street

FRANK PARIS AND T. E. Lewis were puppeteers. Children came to admire the little theater the two puppeteers had set up in the high-ceilinged basement of their old house in Greenwich Village, that old section of New York going back to the 1700s. The house at Number 12 Gay Street was a typical old townhouse, smallish, the kind New Yorkers built around 1800 when "the village" meant *far uptown*.

In 1924, a second section was added to the house, covering the garden that used to grace the back of the house. This architectural graft created a kind of duplex, one apartment on top of another, with small rooms at the sides in the rear.

The ownership of the house in the early days is hazy. At one time a sculptor owned Number 12, possibly before the 1930s. Evidently he was fond of bootleg liquor, for he built a trapdoor in the ground floor of the newer section of the house, probably over his hidden liquor cabinet. Before that, Mayor Jimmy Walker owned the house, and used it *well*, although not *wisely*. One of his many loves is said to have been the tenant there. By a strange set of circumstances, the records of the house vanished like a ghost from the files of the Hall of Records around that time.

Later, real-estate broker Mary Ellen Strunsky lived in the house. In 1956, she sold it to the puppeteer team of Paris and Lewis, who had been there ever since, living in the upstairs apartment and using the lower portion as a workroom and studio for their little theater.

None of this, incidentally, was known to me until after the visit I paid the house in the company of my medium for the evening, Berry Ritter.

It all started when a reporter from the *New York World-Telegram*, Cindy Hughes, came to interview me, and casually dropped a hint that she knew of a haunted house. Faster than you can say *Journal-American*, I had her promise to lead me to this house. On a particularly warm night in May 1963, I followed Miss Hughes down to Gay Street. Berry Ritter knew nothing at all about the case; she didn't even know the address where we were going.

We were greeted warmly by Frank Paris, who led us up the stairs into the upper apartment. The sight of the elaborately furnished, huge living room was surprising. Oriental figurines, heavy drapes, paintings, statuary, and antiques filled the room.

In two comfortable chairs we found awaiting us two friends of the owners: an intense looking man in his thirties, Richard X., who, I later discovered, was an editor by profession, and Alice May Hall, a charming lady of undetermined age.

I managed to get Berry out of earshot, so I could question these people without her getting impressions from our conversation.

"What is this about the house being haunted?" I asked Frank Paris.

He nodded gravely.

"I was working downstairs with some lacquer. It was late, around 3 A.M. Suddenly, I began to smell a strong odor of violets. My black spaniel here also smelled it, for he started to sniff rather strangely. And yet, Ted, my partner, in the same room with me, did not get the strange scent at all. But there is more. People waltz up and down the stairs at night, time and again."

"What do you mean, *waltz*?"

"I mean they go up and down, up and down, as if they had business here," Frank explained, and I thought, perhaps they had, perhaps they had.

"A weekend visitor also had a most peculiar experience here," Frank Paris continued. "He knew nothing about our haunted reputation, of course. We were away on a short trip, and when we got back, he greeted us with—'Say, who are all these people going up and down the stairs?' He had thought that the house next door was somehow connected to ours, and that what he heard were people from next door. But of course, there is no connection whatever."

"And did you ever investigate these mysterious footsteps?" I asked.

"Many times," Frank and Ted nodded simultaneously, "but there was never anyone there—anyone of flesh-and-blood, that is."

I thanked them, and wondered aloud if they weren't psychic, since they had experienced what can only be called psychic phenomena.

Frank Paris hesitated, then admitted that he thought both of them were to some extent.

"We had a little dog which we had to have put away one day. We loved the dog very much, but it was one of those things that had to be done. For over a year after the dog's death, both of us felt him poking us in the leg—a habit he had in life. This happened on many occasions to both of us."

I walked over to where Miss Hall, the gray-haired little lady, sat.

"Oh, there is a ghost here all right," she volunteered. "It was in February 1963, and I happened to be in the house, since the boys and I are good friends. I was sitting here in this very spot, relaxing and casually looking toward the entrance door through which you just came—the one that leads to the hallway and the stairs. There was a man there, wearing evening clothes, and an Inverness Cape—I saw him quite plainly. He had dark hair. It was dusk, and there was still some light outside."

"What did you do?"

"I turned my head to tell Frank Paris about the stranger, and that instant he was gone like a puff of smoke."

Paris broke in.

"I questioned her about this, since I didn't really believe it. But a week later, at dawn this time, I saw the ghost myself, exactly as Alice had described him—wearing evening clothes, a cape, hat, and his face somewhat obscured by the shadows of the hallway. Both Alice and I are sure he was a youngish man, and had sparkling eyes. What's more, our dog also saw the intruder. He went up to the ghost, friendly-like, as if to greet him."

Those were the facts of the case. A ghost in evening clothes, an old house where heaven knows what might have happened at one time or another, and a handful of psychic people.

The ghost on Gay Street making an appearance before the owner and late puppeteer, Frank Paris

I returned to Betty Ritter, and asked her to gather psychic impressions while walking about the house.

"A crime was committed here," the medium said, and described a terrible argument upstairs between two people. She described a gambling den, opium smokers, and a language she could not understand. The man's name was Ming, she said. Ming is a very common Chinese word meaning, I believe, Sun.

Betty also told Frank Paris that someone close to him by the name of John had passed on and that he had something wrong with his right eye, which Paris acknowledged was correct. She told Ted Lewis that a Bernard L. was around him, not knowing, of course, that Lewis' father was named Bernham Lewis. She told Richard X. that he worked with books, and it was not until after the séance that I learned he was an editor by profession. I don't know about the Chinese and the opium den, but they are possibilities in an area so far removed from the bright lights of the city as the Village once was.

We went downstairs and, in the almost total darkness, formed a circle. Betty fell into trance, her neck suddenly falling back as if she were being possessed by a woman whose neck had been hurt.

"Emil," she mumbled, and added the woman had been decapitated, and her bones were still about. She then came out of trance and we walked back up the stairs to the

The Ghost of Gay Street

The late medium Betty Ritter trying to contact the restless one

The Gay Street house

oldest part of the house. Still "seeing" clairvoyantly, Betty Ritter again mumbled "Emil," and said she saw documents with government seals on them. She also felt someone named Mary Ellen had lived here and earlier some "well-known government official named Wilkins or Wilkinson."

Betty, of course, knew nothing about real-estate broker Mary Ellen Strunsky or Jimmy Walker, the former New York Mayor, who had been in this house for so long.

It now remained for us to find those bones Betty had talked about. We returned to the downstairs portion of the house, but Betty refused to go farther. Her impression of tragedy was so strong she urged us to desist.

Thus it was that the Ghost of Gay Street, whoever he may be, would have to wait just a little longer until the bones could be properly sorted out. It wasn't half bad, considering that Frank Paris and Ted Lewis put on a pretty nice puppet show every so often, down there in the murky basement theater at Number 12 Gay Street.

✳ 95

The Ship Chandler's Ghost

IT IS A WELL-KNOWN FACT among ghost hunting experts that structural changes in a house can have dire effects. Take out a wall, and you've got a poltergeist mad as a wet hen. I proved that in the case of the Leighton Buzzard ghost in *Ghosts I've Met*. Take down the building, like the studio building at New York's 51 West Tenth Street, and put up a modern apartment house, and you've got no ghost at all. Just a lot of curious tenants. If the ghost is inside the house before the changes are realized, he may bump into walls and doors that weren't there before—not the way he remembered things at all.

But move a whole house several yards away from the shore where it belongs, and you're asking for trouble. Big trouble. And big trouble is what the historical society in Cohasset, Massachusetts, got when they moved the old Ship's Chandlery in Cohasset. With my good friend Bob Kennedy of WBZ, Boston, I set out for the quaint old town south of Boston on a chilly evening in the fall of 1964.

When we arrived at the wooden structure on a corner of the Post Road—it had a nautical look, its two stories squarely set down as if to withstand any gale—we found several people already assembled. Among them were Mrs. E. Stoddard Marsh, the lively curator of the museum, which was what the Ship's Chandlery became, and her associate lean, quiet Robert Fraser. The others were friends and neighbors who had heard of the coming of a parapsychologist, and didn't want to miss anything. We entered the building and walked around the downstairs portion of it, admiring its displays of nautical supplies, ranging from fishing tackle and scrimshaw made from walrus teeth to heavy anchors, hoists, and rudders—all the instruments and wares of a ship chandler's business.

Built in the late eighteenth century by Samuel Bates, the building was owned by the Bates family; notably by one John Bates, second of the family to have the place, who had died seventy-eight years before our visit. Something of a local character, John Bates had cut a swath around the area as a dashing gentleman. He could well afford the role, for he owned a fishing fleet of twenty-four vessels, and business was good in those far-off days when the New England coast was dotted with major ports for fishing and shipping. A handwritten record of his daily catch can be seen next to a mysterious closet full of ladies' clothes. Mr. Bates led a full life.

After the arrival of Dorothy Damon, a reporter from the *Boston Traveler*, we started to question the curator about uncanny happenings in the building.

"The building used to be right on the waterfront, at Cohasset Cove, and it had its own pier," Mrs. Marsh began, "and in 1957 we moved it to its present site."

"Was there any report of uncanny happenings before that date?"

"Nothing I know of, but the building was in a bad state of disrepair."

"After the building was brought to its present site, then," I said, "what was the first unusual thing you heard?"

"Two years ago we were having a lecture here. There were about forty people listening to Francis Hagerty talk about old sailing boats. I was sitting over here to the left—on this ground floor—with Robert Fraser, when all of a sudden we heard heavy footsteps upstairs and things being moved and dragged—so I said to Mr. Fraser, 'Someone is up there; will you please tell him to be quiet?' I thought it was kids."

"Did you know whether there was in fact anyone upstairs at the time?"

"We did not know. Mr. Fraser went upstairs and after a moment he came down looking most peculiar and said, 'There is no one there.'"

"Now, there is no other way to get down from upstairs, only this one stairway. Nobody had come down it. We were interrupted three times on that evening."

I asked Robert Fraser what he had seen upstairs.

"There was enough light from the little office that is upstairs, and I could see pretty well upstairs, and I looked all over, but there was nobody upstairs."

"And the other times?"

"Same thing. Windows all closed, too. Nobody could have come down or gotten out. But I'm sure those were footsteps."

I returned to Mrs. Marsh and questioned her further about anything that might have occurred after that eventful evening of footsteps.

"We were kept so busy fixing up the museum that we paid scant attention to anything like that, but this summer something happened that brought it all back to us."

"What happened" I asked, and the lady reporter perked up her ears.

"It was on one of the few rainy Sundays we had last July," Mrs. Marsh began, "You see, this place is not open on Sundays. I was bringing over some things from the other two buildings, and had my arms full. I opened the front door, when I heard those heavy footsteps upstairs."

"What did you do—drop everything?"

"I thought it was one of our committee or one of the other curators, so I called out, 'Hello—who's up there?' But I got no answer, and I thought, well, someone sure is pretty stuffy, not answering me back, so I was a little peeved and I called again."

"Did you get a reply?"

"No, but *the steps hesitated* when I called. But then they continued again, and I yelled, 'For Heaven's sake, why don't you answer?' and I went up the stairs, but just as I got to the top of the stairs, they stopped."

There was a man who had helped them with the work at the museum who had lately stayed away for reasons unknown. Could he have heard the footsteps too and decided that caution was the better part of valor?

"The other day, just recently, four of us went into the room this gentleman occupies when he is here, and *the door closed on us*, by itself. It has never done that before."

I soon established that Fraser did not hear the steps when he was *alone* in the building, but that Mrs. Marsh did. I asked her about anything psychic in her background.

"My family has been interested in psychic matters since I was ten years old," she said in a matter-of-fact tone. "I could have become a medium, but I didn't care to. I saw an apparition of my mother immediately after she passed away. My brother also appeared to me six months after his death, to let me know he was all right, I guess."

"Since last July has there been any other manifestation?"

"I haven't been here much," Mrs. Marsh replied. "I had a lot of work with our costume collection in the main building. So I really don't know."

We decided to go upstairs now and see if Mr. Bates —or whoever the ghost might be—felt like walking for us. We quietly waited in the semi-darkness upstairs, near the area where the footsteps had been heard, but nothing happened.

"The steps went back and forth," Mrs. Marsh reiterated. "Heavy, masculine steps, the kind a big man would make."

She showed us how it sounded, allowing of course for the fact she was wearing high heels. It sounded hollow enough for ten ghosts.

I pointed at a small office in the middle of the upstairs floor.

"This was John Bates' office," Mrs. Marsh explained, "and here is an Indian doll that falls down from a secure shelf now and then as if someone were throwing it."

I examined the doll. It was one of those early nineteenth-century dolls that Indians in New England used to make and sell.

"The people at the lecture also heard the noises," Mrs. Marsh said, "but they just laughed and nobody bothered thinking about it."

I turned to one of the local ladies, a Mrs. Hudley, who had come up with us. Did she feel anything peculiar up here, since she had the reputation of being psychic?

"I feel disturbed. Sort of a strange sensation," she began, haltingly, "as though there was a 'presence' who was in a disturbed frame of mind. It's a man."

Another lady, by the name of McCarthy, also had a strange feeling as we stood around waiting for the ghost to make himself known. Of course, suggestion and atmosphere made me discount most of what those who were around us that night might say, but I still wanted to hear it.

"I felt I had to get to a window and get some air," Mrs. McCarthy said. "The atmosphere seemed disturbed somehow."

I asked them all to be quiet for a moment and addressed myself to the unseen ghost.

"John Bates," I began, "if this is you, may I, as a stranger come to this house in order to help you find peace, ask that you manifest in some form so I know you can hear me?"

Only the sound of a distant car horn answered me.

I repeated my invitation to the ghost to come forward and be counted. Either I addressed myself to the wrong ghost or perhaps John Bates disliked the intrusion of so many people—only silence greeted us.

"Mr. Bates," I said in my most dulcet tones, "please forgive these people for moving your beautiful house inland. They did not do so out of irreverence for your person or work. They did this so that many more people could come and admire your house and come away with a sense of respect and admiration for the great man that you were.

It was so quiet when I spoke, you could have heard a mouse breathe.

Quietly, we tiptoed down the haunted stairs, and out into the cool evening air. Cowboy star Rex Trailer and his wife, who had come with us from Boston, wondered about the future—would the footsteps ever come back? Or was John Bates reconciled with the fact that the sea breezes no longer caressed his ghostly brow as they did when his house was down by the shore?

Then, too, what was the reason he was still around to begin with? Had someone given him his quietus in that little office upstairs? There are rumors of violence in the famous bachelor's life, and the number of women whose affections he had trifled with was legion. Someone might very well have met him one night and ended the highly successful career of the ship chandlery's owner.

A year went by, and I heard nothing further from the curator. Evidently, all was quiet at John Bates' old house. Maybe old John finally joined up with one of the crews that sail the ghost ships on the other side of the curtain of life.

✳ 96

The Ghost-Servant Problem at Ringwood Manor

RINGWOOD, IN THE SOUTH of England, has an American counterpart in New Jersey. I had never heard of Ringwood Manor in New Jersey until Mrs. Edward Tholl, a resident of nearby Saddle River, brought it to my attention. An avid history buff and a talented geographer and map maker, Mrs. Tholl had been to the Manor House and on several occasions felt "a presence." The mountain people who still inhabited the Ramapo Mountains of the region wouldn't go near the Manor House at night.

"Robert Erskine, geographer to Washington's army, is buried on the grounds," Mrs. Tholl told me.

The Manor House land was purchased by the Ogden family of Newark in 1740, and an iron-smelting furnace was built on it two years later. The area abounds in mine deposits and was at one time a center of iron mining and smelting. In 1762, when a second furnace was built, a small house was also built. This house still stands and now forms part of the haphazard arrangement that constitutes the Manor House today. One Peter Hasenclever bought the house and iron works in 1764. He ran the enterprise with such ostentation that he was known as "The Baron." But Hasenclever did not produce enough iron to suit his backers, and was soon replaced by Robert Erskine. When the War of Independence broke out, the iron works were forced to close. Erskine himself died "of exposure" in 1780.

By 1807, the iron business was going full blast again, this time under the aegis of Martin Ryerson, who tore down the ramshackle old house and rebuilt it completely. After the iron business failed in the 1830s, the property passed into the hands of famed Peter Cooper in 1853. His son-in-law Abram S. Hewitt, one-time Mayor of New York, lived in the Manor House.

Mrs. Hewitt, Cooper's daughter, turned the drab house into an impressive mansion of fifty-one rooms, very much as it appears today. Various older buildings already on the grounds were uprooted and added to the house, giving it a checkered character without a real center. The Hewitt family continued to live at Ringwood until Erskine Hewitt deeded the estate to the State of New Jersey in 1936, and the mansion became a museum through which visitors were shown daily for a small fee.

During troubled times, tragedies may well have occurred in and around the house. There was a holdup in 1778, and in the graveyard nearby many French soldiers were buried who died there during an epidemic. There is also on record an incident, in later years, when a cook was threatened by a butler with a knife, and there were disasters that took many lives in the nearby iron mines.

One of the Hewitt girls, Sally, had been particularly given to mischief. If anyone were to haunt the place, she'd be a prime candidate for the job. I thanked Claire Tholl for her help, and called on Ethel Johnson Meyers to accompany me to New Jersey. Of course, I didn't give her any details. We arranged to get to the house around dusk, after all the tourists had gone.

My wife Catherine and I, with Ethel Meyers as passenger, drove out to the house on a humid afternoon in May 1965. Jim Byrne joined us at the house with *Saturday Review* writer Haskell Frankel in tow.

We were about an hour late, but it was still light, and the peaceful setting of the park with the Manor House in its center reminded one indeed of similar houses gracing the English countryside.

We stood around battling New Jersey mosquitoes for a while, then I asked Catherine to take Ethel away from the house for a moment, so I could talk to Mrs. Tholl and others who had witnessed ghostly goings-on in the house.

"I've had a feeling in certain parts of the house that I was not alone," Mrs. Tholl said, "but other than that I cannot honestly say I have had uncanny experiences here."

Alexander Waldron had been the superintendent of Ringwood Manor for many years, until a year before, in fact. He consented to join us for the occasion. A jovial, gray-haired man, he seemed rather deliberate in his report, giving me only what to him were actual facts.

"I was superintendent here for eighteen years," Mr. Waldron began. "I was sitting at my desk one day, in the late afternoon, like today, and the door to the next room was closed. My office is on the ground floor. I heard two people come walking toward me at a fast pace. That did not seem unusual, for we do have workmen here frequently. When the steps reached my door, nothing happened. Without thinking too much, I opened the door for them. But there was no one there. I called out, but there was no answer. Shortly after, two workmen did come in

from outside, and together we searched the whole building, but found no one who could have made the sound."

"Could anyone have walked away without being seen by you?"

"Impossible. There was good light."

"Did anything else happen after that?"

"Over the years we've had a few things we could not explain. For instance, doors we had shut at night, we found open the next morning. Some years ago, when I had my boys living here with me, they decided to build a so-called monster down in the basement. One boy was of high-school age, the other in grammar school—sixteen and thirteen. One of them came in by himself one night, when he heard footsteps overhead, on the ground floor. He thought it was his brother who had come over from the house.

"He thought his brother was just trying to scare him, so he continued to work downstairs. But the footsteps continued and finally he got fed up with it and came upstairs. All was dark, and nobody was around. He ran back to the house, where he found his brother, who had never been to the manor at all."

Bradley Waldron probably never worked on his "monster" again after that.

There are stories among the local hill folk of Robert Erskine's ghost walking with a lantern, or sitting on his grave half a mile down the road from the Manor House, or racing up the staircase in the house itself.

Wayne Daniels, who had accompanied Mrs. Tholl to the House, spoke up now. Mr. Daniels had lived in the region all his life, and was a professional restorer of early American structures.

"I have felt strange in one corner of the old dining room, and in two rooms upstairs," he volunteered. "I feel hostility in those areas, somehow."

It was time to begin our search in the house itself.

I asked Ethel Meyers to join us, and we entered the Manor House, making our way slowly along the now-deserted corridors and passages of the ground floor, following Ethel as she began to get her psychic bearings.

Suddenly, Ethel remarked that she felt a man outside the windows, but could not pin down her impression.

"Someone died under a curse around here," she mumbled, then added as if it were an afterthought, "Jackson White...what does that mean?"

I had never heard the name before, but Claire Tholl explained that "Jackson White" was a peculiar local name for people of mixed blood, who live in the Ramapo hills. Ethel added that someone had been in slavery at one time.

Ethel was taken aback by the explanation of "Jackson White." She had taken it for granted that it was an individual name. Jackson Whites, I gathered, are partly American Indian and partly black, but not white.

We now entered a large bedroom elegantly furnished in the manner of the early nineteenth century, with a large bed against one wall and a table against the other. Ethel looked around the room uncertainly, as if looking for something she did not yet see.

"Someone with a bad conscience died in this room," she said. "A man and a woman lived here, who were miles apart somehow."

It was Mrs. Erskine's bedroom we were in. We went through a small door into another room that lay directly behind the rather large bedroom; it must have been a servant's room at one time. Nevertheless, it was elegant, with a marble fireplace and a heavy oak table, around which a number of chairs had been placed. We sat down but before I had time to adjust my tape recorder and camera, Ethel Meyers fell into deep trance. From her lips came the well-modulated voice of Albert, her control. He explained that several layers of consciousness covered the room, that there were blacks brought here by one Jackson, who came in the eighteenth century. One of them seemed present in the room, he felt.

"One met death at the entrance...a woman named Lucy Bell, she says. She was a servant here."

Suddenly, Albert was gone. In his stead, there was a shrill, desperate female voice, crying out to all who would listen.

"No...I didn't...before my God I didn't...I show you where...I didn't touch it...never..."

She seemed to be speaking to an unseen tormentor now, for Ethel, possessed by the ghost, pulled back from the table and cried:

"No...don't...don't!" Was she being beaten or tortured?

"He didn't either!" the ghost added.

I tried to calm her.

"I didn't touch...I didn't touch..." she kept repeating. I asked for her name.

"Lucy," she said in a tormented, high-pitched voice completely different from Ethel Meyers' normal tones.

"I believe you," I said, and told the ghost who we were and why we had come. The uncontrollable crying subsided for the moment.

"He's innocent too," she finally said. "I can't walk," she added. Ethel pointed to her side. Had she been hurt?

"I didn't take it," she reiterated. "It's right there."

What didn't she take? I coaxed her gently to tell me all about it.

"I've come as a *friend*," I said, and the word finally hit home. She got very excited and wanted to know where I was s since she could not see me.

"A friend, Jeremiah, do you hear?" she intoned.

"Who is Jeremiah?"

"He didn't do it either," she replied. Jeremiah, I gathered, lived here, too, but she did not know any family

name—just Jeremiah. Then Ethel Meyers grabbed my hand, mumbling "friend," and almost crushed my fingers. I managed to pull it away. Ethel ordinarily has a very feminine, soft grip—a great contrast to the desperately fierce clasp of the ghost possessing the medium!

"Don't go!"

I promised to stay if she would talk.

"I have never stolen," she said. "It's dark...I can't see now...where do I go to see always?"

"I will show you the way," I promised.

"Marie...Marie...where are you?" she intoned pleadingly.

"What is Jeremiah doing?"

"He is begging for his honor."

"Where is he now?"

"Here with me."

"Who is the person you worked for?" I asked.

"Old lady...I don't want her...."

"If she did you wrong, should we punish her? What is her name?"

"I never wished evil on anyone...I would forgive her...if she forgives me. She is here...I saw her, and she hates me...."

The voice became shrill and emotional again. I started to send her away, and in a few moments, she slipped out. Suddenly, there was an entirely different person occupying Ethel's body. Proudly sitting up, she seemed to eye us, with closed eyes, of course, as if we were riff-raff invading her precincts.

"What is your name?" I demanded.

"I am in no court of justice," was the stiff reply in a proper upper-middle-class accent. "I cannot speak to you. I have no desire. It is futile for you to give me any advice."

"What about this servant girl?" I asked.

"You may take yourself away," the lady replied, haughtily. "Depart!"

"What did the girl take?" I asked, ignoring her outburst of cold fury.

"I am not divulging anything to you."

"Is she innocent then?"

This gave her some thought, and the next words were a little more communicative.

"How come you are in my house?" she demanded.

"Is it your house?"

"I will call the servants and have you taken our by the scruff of your neck," she threatened.

"Will the servants know who you are?" I countered.

"I am lady in my own."

"What is your name?"

"I refuse to reveal myself or talk to you!"

I explained about the passage of time. It made no impression.

"I will call her...Old Jeremiah is under his own disgrace. You are friend to him?"

I explained about Ethel Meyers and how she, the ghost, was able to communicate with us.

She hit the table hard with Ethel's fist.

"The man is mad," the ghost said. "Take him away!"

I didn't intend to be taken away by ghostly men-in-white. I continued to plead with "the lady" to come to her senses and listen. She kept calling for her servants, but evidently nobody answered her calls.

"Jeremiah, if you want to preserve yourself in my estimation and not stand by this girl, take this..."

Somehow the medium's eyes opened for a moment, and the ghost could "see." Then they closed again. It came as a shock, for "the lady" suddenly stopped her angry denunciation and instead "looked" at me in panic.

"What is this? Doctor...where is he...Laura! Laura! I am ill. Very ill. I can't see. I can't see. I hear something talking to me, but I can't see it. Laura, call a doctor. I'm going to die!"

"As a matter of fact," I said calmly, "you have died already."

"It was my mother's." The ghost sobbed hysterically. "Don't let her keep it. Don't let it go to the scum! I must have it. Don't let me die like this. Oh, oh..."

I called on Albert, the control, to take the unhappy ghost away and lead her to the other side of the veil, if possible. The sobbing slowly subsided as the ghost's essence drifted away out of our reach in that chilly Georgian room at Ringwood.

It wasn't Albert's crisp, precise voice that answered me. Another stranger, obviously male, now made his coughing entry and spoke in a lower-class accent.

"What's the matter?"

"Who is this?" I asked.

The voice sounded strangely muffled, as if coming from far away.

"Jeremiah...What's the matter with everybody?" The voice had distinct black overtones.

"I'm so sleepy," the voice said.

"Who owns this house?"

"Ho, ho, I do," the ghost said. "I have a funny dream, what's the matter with everybody?" Then the voice cleared up a little, as he became more aware of the strange surroundings into which he had entered.

"Are you one of these white trashes?" he demanded.

"What is the old lady's name?" I asked.

"She's a Bob," he replied, enigmatically, and added, "real bumby, with many knots in it, many knots in the brain."

"Who else is here?"

"I don't like you. I don't know you and I don't like who I don't know," the servant's ghost said.

"You're white trash," he continued. "I seed you!" The stress was on *white*.

"How long have you been living here?"

"My father...Luke."

Again, I explained about death and consequences, but the reception was even less friendly than I had received from "the lady."

Jeremiah wanted no truck with death.

"What will the old squaw say? What will she say?" he wondered, "She needs me."

The Ghost-Servant Problem

at Ringwood Manor

"Not really," I replied. "After all, she's dead, too." He could hardly believe the news. Evidently, the formidable "squaw" was immune to such events as death in his mind.

"What do you have against my mother?" he demanded now. Things were getting confusing. Was the "old lady" his mother?

"Lucy white trash too," he commented.

"Was she your wife?"

"Call it that."

"Can you see her?"

"She's here."

"Then you know you have died and must go from this house?" I asked.

"'dominable treek, man, 'dominable treek," he said, furiously.

"This house is no longer yours."

"It never was," he shot back. "The squaw is here. We're not dead, Great White Spirit—laugh at you."

"What do you want in this house?"

"Squaw very good," he said. "I tell you, my mother, squaw very good. Lucy Bell, white trash, but good. Like Great White Spirit. Work my fingers down to the bone. I am told! I am thief, too. Just yesterday. Look at my back! Look at my squaw! Red Fox, look at her. Look at my back, look at it!"

He seemed to have spent his anger. The voice became softer now.

"I am so sleepy," he said. "So sleepy...my Lucy will never walk again...angel spirit...my people suffer...her skin should be like mine...help me, help my Lucy...."

I promised to help and to send him to his father, Luke, who was awaiting him.

"I should have listened to my father," the ghost mumbled.

Then he recognized his father, evidently come to guide him out of the house, and wondered what he was doing here.

I explained what I thought was the reason for his father's presence. There was some crying, and then they all went away.

"Albert," I said. " Please take over the instrument."

In a moment, the control's cool voice was heard, and Ethel was brought out of trance rather quickly.

"My hip," she complained. "I don't think I can move."

"Passing conditions" or symptoms the ghost brings are sometimes present for a few moments after a medium comes out of trance. It is nothing to be alarmed about.

I closed Ethel's eyes again, and sent her back into trance, then brought her out again, and this time all was "clear." However, she still recalled a scream in a passage between the two rooms.

I wondered about the Indian nature of the ghost. Were there any Indians in this area?

"Certainly," Mr. Waldron replied. "They are of mixed blood, often Negro blood, and are called Jackson Whites. Many of them worked here as servants."

The footsteps the superintendent had heard on the floor below were of two persons, and they could very well have come from this area, since the room we were in was almost directly above his offices.

There was, of course, no record of any servants named Jeremiah or Lucy. Servants' names rarely get recorded unless they do something that is most unusual.

I asked Mrs. Tholl about ladies who might have fitted the description of the haughty lady who had spoken to us through Ethel Meyers in trance.

"I associate this with the Hewitt occupancy of the house," she explained, "because of the reference to a passage connecting two parts of the house, something that could not apply to an early structure on the spot. Amelia Hewitt, whose bedroom we had come through, was described in literature of the period as 'all placidity and kindliness.' Sarah Hewitt, however, was quite a cut-up in her day, and fitted the character of 'the lady' more accurately."

But we cannot be sure of the identity of the ghost-lady. She elected to keep her name a secret and we can only bow to her decision and let it remain so.

What lends the accounts an air of reality and evidence is, of course, the amazing fact that Ethel Meyers spoke of "Jackson Whites" in this house, an appellation completely new to her and me. I am also sure that the medium had no knowledge of Indians living in the area. Then, too, her selecting a room above the spot where the ghostly steps had been heard was interesting, for the house was sprawling and had many rooms and passages.

✳ 97

The Phantom Admiral

I HAD NEVER HEARD OF Goddard College until I received a letter from Jay Lawrence, a second-semester student at Goddard College in Plainfield, Vermont. Mr. Lawrence was serious about his interest in psychic phenomena and he had some evidence to offer. He did more than ask me to speak at the college on extrasensory perception; he invited me to come and have a look at a ghost he had discovered in Whitefield, New Hampshire, about two hours' drive from Goddard.

The haunted house in Whitefield belonged to the Jacobsen family who used it as a summer home only. The younger Jacobsen, whose first name was Erlend—they're of Norwegian descent—invited us to come stay at the house, or at least have a look at it. The Goddard College boys offered to pick us up in Boston and drive us up through the scenic White Mountains to Whitefield.

We arrived at dusk, when the country tends to be peaceful and the air is almost still. The house was at the end of a narrow, winding driveway lined by tall trees, hidden away from the road. There was a wooden porch around three sides of the wooden structure, which rose up three stories.

We were welcomed by Erlend Jacobsen, his wife, Martha, and their little boy Erlend Eric, a bright youngster who had met the ghost, too, as we were to find out.

Inside the house with its spacious downstairs dining room and kitchen, decorated in a flamboyant style by the Jacobsens, we found Mr. and Mrs. Nelson, two friends of the owners, and Jeff Broadbent, a young fellow student of Jay Lawrence.

Sybil puttered around the house, indulging her interest in antiques. I mounted my tape recorder to hear the testimony of those who had experienced anything unusual in the house. We went upstairs, where Sybil Leek could not very well hear us, and entered a small bedroom on the second floor, which, I was told, was the main center of ghostly activities, although not the only one.

The house was called "Mis 'n Top" by its original owner and builder. I lost no time in questioning Erlend Jacobsen, a tall young man of thirty on the Goddard College faculty as an instructor, about his experiences in the old house.

"When my parents decided to turn the attic into a club room where I could play with my friends," Erlend Jacobsen began, "they cut windows into the wall and threw out all the possessions of the former owner of the house they had found there. I was about seven at the time.

"Soon after, footsteps and other noises began to be heard in the attic and along the corridors and stairs leading toward it. But it was not until the summer of 1956, when I was a senior in college and had just married, that I experienced the first really important disturbance.

"1955, Erlend," the wife interrupted. Wives have a way of remembering such dates. Mr. Jacobsen blushed and corrected himself.

"1955, you're right," he said. "That summer we slept here for the first time in this room, one flight up, and almost nightly we were either awakened by noises or could not sleep, waiting for them to begin. At first we thought they were animal noises, but they were too much like footsteps and heavy objects being moved across the floor overhead, and down the hall. We were so scared we refused to move in our beds or turn on the lights."

But you did know of the tradition that the house was haunted, did you not?" I asked.

"Yes, I grew up with it. All I knew is what I had heard from my parents. The original owner and builder of the house, an admiral named Hawley, and his wife, were both most difficult people. The admiral died in 1933. In 1935, the house was sold by his daughter, who was then living in Washington, to my parents. Anyone who happened to be trespassing on his territory would be chased off it, and I imagine he would not have liked our throwing out his sea chest and other personal possessions."

"Any other experience outside the footsteps?"

"About four years ago," Erlend Jacobsen replied, "my wife and I, and a neighbor, Shepard Vogelgesang, were sitting in the living room downstairs discussing interpretations of the Bible. I needed a dictionary at one point in the discussion and got up to fetch it from upstairs.

"I ran up to the bend here, in front of this room, and there were no lights on at the time. I opened the door to the club room and started to go up the stairs, when suddenly I walked into what I can only describe as a *warm, wet blanket*, something that touched me physically as if it had been hung from wires in the corridor. I was very upset, backed out, and went downstairs. My wife took one look at me and said, 'You're white.' 'I know,' I said. '*I think I just walked into the admiral.*'"

"I suppose he didn't enjoy your bumping into him in this fashion either," I commented. "Anything else?"

"I was alone in the house, in the club room, which is designed like a four-leaf clover—you can see into the section opposite you, but you can't see into the other two. I was lying there, looking out the window at sunset, when I heard someone breathing—rhythmically breathing in, out, in, out."

"What did you do?"

"I held my own breath, because at first I thought I might be doing it. But I was not. The breathing continued right next to me! I became terrified, being then only fifteen years of age, and ran out of the house until my parents returned."

I asked him again about the time *he touched the ghost.*

How did it feel? Did it have the touch of a human body?

The home of the ghostly Admiral in New Hampshire

"Nothing like it. It was totally dark, but it was definitely warm, and it resisted my passage."

"Has anything happened to you here recently?"

"About two-and-a-half weeks ago, I walked into the house at dusk and I heard very faint crying for about fifteen or twenty seconds. I thought it might be a cat, but there was no cat in the house, and just as suddenly as it had started, the crying stopped. It sounded almost as if it were outside this window, here on the second floor."

"Is there any record of a tragedy attached to this house?"

"None that I know of."

"Who else has seen or heard anything uncanny here?"

"My parents used to have a Negro maid who was psychic. She had her share of experiences here all right. Her name is Sarah Wheeler and she is about seventy-five now. The admiral had a reputation for disliking colored people, and she claimed that when she was in bed here, frequently the bedposts would move as if someone were trying to throw her out of bed. The posts would move off the floor and rock the bed violently, held by unseen hands, until she got out of bed, and then they would stop. She was a Catholic and went to the church the next day to fetch some Holy Water. That quieted things down. But the first night of each season she would come without her Holy Water and that was when things were worst for her."

"Poor Sarah," I said.

"She was psychic, and she had an Indian guide," Erlend Jacobsen continued. "I did not put much stock in some of the things she told us, such as there being treasure underneath the house, put there by the old admiral. But eight or nine years ago, I had occasion to recall this. The house has no cellar but rests on stone pillars. We used to throw junk under the house, where wooden steps led down below. I was cleaning up there with a flashlight, when I saw something shiny. It was a cement block with a silver handle sticking out of it. I chipped the cement off, and found a silver bowl, with 'A.H.' engraved on it."

I turned my attention to Mrs. Jacobsen. She had three children, but still gave the impression of being a college sophomore. As a matter of fact, she was taking courses at Goddard.

It was ten years to the day—our visit was on June 11—that the Jacobsens had come to this house as newlyweds.

"We spent one night here, then went on our honeymoon, and then came back and spent the rest of the summer here," Martha Jacobsen said. "The first night I was very, very frightened—hearing this walking up and down the halls, and we the only ones in the house! There was a general feeling of eeriness and a feeling that there was someone else in the house. There were footsteps in the hall outside our bedroom door. At one point before dawn, the steps went up the stairs and walked around overhead. But Erlend and I were the only ones in the house. We checked."

Imagine one's wedding night interrupted by unseen visitors—this could give a person a trauma!

"Two weeks later we returned and stayed here alone," Mrs. Jacobsen continued," and I heard these footsteps several times. Up and down. We've been coming here for the last ten years and I heard it again a couple of weeks ago."

"Must be unnerving," I observed.

"It is. I heard the steps overhead in the club room, and also, while I was downstairs two weeks ago, the door to the kitchen opened itself and closed itself, without anyone being visible. Then the front door did the same thing—opened and shut itself.

"Along with the footsteps I heard things being dragged upstairs, heavy objects, it seemed. But nothing was disarranged afterwards. We checked."

"Any other events of an uncanny nature?" I asked as a matter of record. Nothing would surprise me in *this* house.

"About ten years ago, when we first moved in, I also heard the heavy breathing when only my husband and I were in the house. Then there was a house guest we had, a Mrs. Anne Merriam. She had this room and her husband was sleeping down the hall in one of the single rooms. Suddenly, she saw a figure standing at the foot of her bed."

"What did she do?"

"She called out, 'Carol, is that you?' twice, but got no answer. Then, just as suddenly as it had come, the figure dissolved into thin air.

"She queried her husband about coming into her room, but he told her that he had never left his bed that night. When this happened on another night, she attempted to follow the figure, and found her husband entering through another door!"

"Has anyone else had an encounter with a ghost here?" I asked.

"Well, another house guest went up into the attic and came running down reporting that the door knob had turned in front of his very eyes before he could reach for it to open the door. The dog was with him, and steadfastly refused to cross the threshold. That was Frank Kingston and it all happened before our marriage. Then another house guest arrived very late at night, about five years ago. We had already gone to bed, and he knew he had to sleep in the attic since every other room was already taken. Instead, I found him sleeping in the living room, on the floor, in the morning. He knew nothing about the ghost. 'I'm not going back up there any more,' he vowed, and would not say anything further. I guess he must have run into the admiral."

What a surprise that must have been, I thought, especially if the admiral was all wet.

"Three years ago, my brother came here," Mrs. Jacobsen continued her report. "His name is Robert Gillman. In the morning he complained of having been awake all night. A former skeptic, he knew now that the tales of ghostly footsteps were true, for he, too, had heard them—all night long in fact."

Jeffrey Broadbent was a serious young man who accompanied Jay Lawrence to the house one fine night, to see if what they were saying about the admiral's ghost was true.

They had sleeping bags and stayed up in the attic. It was a chilly November night in 1964, and everything seemed just right for ghosts. Would they be lucky in their quest? They did not have to wait long to find out.

"As soon as we entered the room, we heard strange noises on the roof. They were indistinct and could have been animals, I thought at first. We went off to sleep until Jay woke me up hurriedly around six in the morning. I distinctly heard human footsteps on the roof. They slid down the side to a lower level and then to the ground where they could be heard walking in leaves and into the night. Nothing could be seen from the window and there was nobody up on the roof. We were the only ones in the house that night, so it surely must have been the ghost."

Jay Lawrence added one more thing to this narrative.

"When we first turned out the flashlight up in the attic, I distinctly heard a high-pitched voice—a kind of scream or whine—followed by footsteps. They were of a human foot wearing shoes, but much lighter than the normal weight of a human body would require.

Jerry Weener also had spent time at the haunted house.

"In early March 1965, Jay and I came over and had dinner at the fireplace downstairs. We decided to sleep downstairs and both of us, almost simultaneously, had a dream that night in which we met the admiral's ghost, but unfortunately on awakening, we did not recall anything specific or what he might have said to us in our dreams. A second time when I slept in the house, nothing happened. The third time I came over with friends, I slept in the attic, and I heard footsteps. We searched the house from top to bottom, but there was no one else who could have accounted for those steps."

Erlend Eric, age eight going on nine, was perhaps the youngest witness to psychic phenomena scientifically recorded, but his testimony should not be dismissed because of his age. He had heard footsteps going up and down and back up the stairs. One night he was sleeping in the room across the hall when he heard someone trying to talk to him.

"What sort of voice was it?" I asked. Children are frequently more psychic than adults.

"It was a man's," the serious youngster replied. "He called my name, but I forgot what else he said. That was three years ago."

Miriam Nelson was a petite young woman, the wife of one of Erlend Jacobsen's friends, who had come to witness our investigation that evening. She seemed nervous and frightened and asked me to take her to another room so I could hear her story in private. We went across the hall into the room where the figure had stood at the head of the bed and I began my questioning.

"My first experience was when Erlend and I brought a Welsh Corgi up here; Erlend's parents were here, too. I was downstairs in the library; the dog was in my lap. Suddenly I felt another presence in the room, and I could not breathe anymore. The dog started to bark and insist that I follow him out of the room. I distinctly felt someone there.

"Then on a cold fall day about four years ago, I was sitting by the stove, trying to get warm, when one of the burners lifted itself up about an inch and fell down again. I looked and it moved again. It could not have moved by itself. I was terrified. I was alone in the house."

I had heard all those who had had an encounter with the ghost and it was time to get back downstairs where the Jacobsens had laid out a fine dinner—just the right thing after a hard day's drive. A little later we all went up the stairs to the top floor, where Sybil stretched out on a couch near the window. We grouped ourselves around her in the haunted attic and waited.

"I had a feeling of a *middle* room upstairs," Sybil said, "but I don't feel anything too strongly yet."

Soon Sybil was in deep trance as we awaited the coming of the admiral—or whoever the ghost would be—with bated breath. The only light in the attic room was a garish fluorescent lamp, which we shut off, and replaced with a smaller conventional lamp. It was quiet, as quiet as only a country house can be. But instead of the ghost speaking to us directly and presumably giving us hell for trespassing, it was Sybil herself, in deep trance "on the other side," reporting what she saw—things and people the ordinary eye could not perceive.

"I'm walking around," Sybil said. "There is a man lying dead in the middle room. Big nose, not too much hair in front, little beard cut short now. There is a plant near him."

"Try to get his name, Sybil," I ordered.

"I'll have to go into the room," she said.

We waited.

"He is not in here *all* the time," she reported back. "He came here to die."

"Is this his house?"

"Yes, but there is another house also. A long way off. This man had another house. Hawsley...Hawsley."

Almost the exact name of the admiral, I thought. Sybil could not have known that name.

"He went from one house to another, in a different country. Something Indian."

"Is he still here and what does he want?"

"To find a place to rest because...he does not know in which house it's in!"

"What is he looking for?"

"Little basket. Not from this country. Like a handle...it's shiny...silver...a present. It went to the wrong house. He gave it to the wrong house. He is very particular not to get things confused. It belongs to Mrs. Gerard at the other house. He usually stays in the little room, one flight up. With the fern. By the bed."

"But what about Mrs. Gerard? How can we send the package to her unless we get her address?" I said.

"It's very important. It's in the wrong perspective, he says," Sybil explained.

"What did he have for a profession?" I tried again.

"He says he brought things...seeds."

"What are his initials or first name?"

"A. J. H."

Sybil seemed to listen to someone we could not see.

"He's not troublesome," she said. "He goes when I get near to him. Wants to go to the other house."

"Where is the other house?"

"Liang...Street...Bombay."

"Does he know he is dead?"

"No."

I instructed her to tell him.

"Any family?"

"Two families...Bombay."

"Children?"

"Jacob...Martin."

It was not clear whether the ghost said Jacob or Jacobsen.

"He is shaking himself," Sybil now reported. "What upset him? He worries about names. A. J. A. name on something he is worried about. The names are wrong on a paper. He said Jacobsen is wrong. It should be Jacob Hawsley son."

Evidently the ghost did not approve the sale of his house by his executors, but wanted it to go to his son.

"Because of two houses, two families, he did not know what to do with the other."

"What does 'A.' stand for in his name?"

"Aaron...Aaron Jacob."

"Does he have any kind of title or professional standing?"

"A-something...A-D-M...can't read...Administrator A-D-M...it's on the paper, but I can't read the paper."

Still, she did get the admiral's rank!

I promised to have the gift delivered to Mrs. Gerard, if we could find her, but he must not stay in this house any further.

"Who waters the plants, he asks," Sybil said.

I assured him the plants would be taken care of.

"But what about the other house, who waters the plants there?" the ghost wanted to know.

"How does he go there?" I asked in return.

"He sails," Sybil replied. "Takes a long time."

Again I promised to find the house in India, if I could.

"What about a date?" I asked. "How long ago did all this happen?"

"About 1867," Sybil replied.

"How old was he then?"

"Fifty-nine."

I implored the admiral not to cause any untidiness in the house by upsetting its inhabitants. The reply via Sybil was stiff.

"As a man with an administrative background, he is always tidy," Sybil reported. "But he is going now."

"He is going now," Sybil repeated, "and he's taking the ferns."

I called Sybil back to her own body, so as not to give some unwanted intruder a chance to stop in before she was back in the driver's seat, so to speak.

None the worse for her travels in limbo, Sybil sat up and smiled at us, wondering why we all stared at her so intently. She remembered absolutely nothing.

Erlend Jacobsen spoke up.

"That basket she mentioned," he said. "When my parents first bought the house, there was hanging over the dining room, on a chain, a stuffed armadillo, which had been shellacked from the outside. It had straw handles and had been turned into a *basket*. It was around the house until about five years ago, but I have no idea where it is now. For all we know, it may still be around the house somewhere."

"Better find it," I said. "That is, if you want those footsteps to cease!"

Just as we were leaving the house, the senior Jacobsens returned. Mr. Eric Jacobsen does not care for ghosts and I was told not to try to get him to talk about the subject. But his wife, Josephine, Erlend's mother, had been pushed down the stairs by the ghost—or so she claims. This is quite possible, judging by the way the admiral was behaving in his post-funeral days and nights.

Our job in Whitefield seemed finished and we continued on to Stowe, Vermont, where we had decided to stay at the famous Trapp Family Lodge. Catherine had become interested in Mrs. Trapp's books, and from *The Sound of Music*, we both thought that the lodge would provide a welcome interlude of peace during a hectic weekend of ghost hunting.

The next morning we rested up from the rigors of our investigation and found the world around us indeed peaceful and promising. The following morning we would go down to Goddard College and address students and teachers on the subject of ghosts, which would leave us with a pleasant afternoon back at Stowe, before flying back to Manhattan. But we had reckoned without the commercial spirit at the lodge. Like most overnight lodgings, they wanted us out of our rooms by 11 o'clock Sunday morning, but finally offered to let us stay until two. I declined.

After my talk at the college, we were taken to one of the women's dormitories where uncanny happenings had taken place. The college was situated on the old Martin farm, and the manor had been turned into a most elegant female students' residence, without losing its former Victorian grandeur. Reports of a dead butler still walking the old corridors upstairs had reached my ears. Two students, Madeleine Ehrman and Dorothy Frazier, knew of the ghost. The phenomena were mainly footsteps when no one was about. A teacher who did not believe in ghosts set foot in the manor and later revealed that the name Dawson had constantly impressed itself on her mind. Later research revealed that a butler by that name did in fact live at the manor house long ago.

Sue Zuckerman was a New Yorker studying at Goddard.

"One night last semester," she said, "I was up late studying when I heard footsteps approaching my room. After a few seconds I opened my door—there was nobody there. I closed the door and resumed studying. I then heard footsteps walking away from my door. I looked again, but saw nothing.

"During this time for a period of about three weeks, my alarm clock had been shut off every night. I would set it for about 7:30, but when I woke up much later than that, the alarm button was always off. I began hiding my clock, locking my door—but it still happened.

"Back in 1962, I was toying with a Ouija board I had bought more in fun than as a serious instrument of communication. I had never gotten anything through it that could not have come from my own mind, but that Friday afternoon in 1962, I worked it in the presence of three other friends, and as soon as we put our hands on it, it literally started to leap around. It went very fast, giving a message one of us took down: 'I am dead...of drink.' 'Are you here now in the Manor?' 'One could speak of my presence here.' There was more, but I can't remember it now.

"Afterward, a strange wind arose and as we walked past a tree outside, it came crashing down."

I don't know about strange "wind," and Ouija boards are doubtful things at times, but the footfalls of the restless butler named Dawson must have been a most unusual extracurricular activity for the co-eds at Goddard College.

✳ 98

The Ghosts in The Basement

MARY LIVES IN Atlanta, Georgia, a quiet woman who speaks with a charming southern accent and is rather conservative in her way of life. Even her special talent of being able to read the tarot cards for her friends used to be an embarrassment to her because of her religion and because of what the neighbors might say if they found out, not to mention the fact that everyone would want a reading from her.

At the time I met her she had two lovely daughters, Katie, a 15-year-old, and Boots, who went to college. On the day of Halloween, 1962, she and her girls had moved into an attractive 18-year-old house in Atlanta. It stood in a quiet suburban neighborhood amid other small homes of no particular distinction. Not far from the house are the tracks of a railroad which is nowadays used only for freight. Famous old Fort McPherson is not far away; during the Civil War one of the bloodiest engagements was fought on this spot.

The house has two levels; at street level, there is a large living room which one enters from the front side of the house, then there are three bedrooms, and on the right side of the house, a den leading into a kitchen. From one of the bedrooms a stair secured by an iron railing leads into the basement. There is a closet underneath the stairs. In back of the house there is a large patio and there are also outside stairs leading again into the basement. Only the right-hand third of the basement area is actually used by the family, a laundry room occupies most of the space and a wall seals it off from the undeveloped "dirt" area of the basement.

The house itself feel cozy and warm, the furniture is pleasant and functional, and if it weren't for some unusual events that had occurred in the house, one might never suspect it of being anything but just another ordinary suburban home.

Soon after they had moved in, Mary and her daughters knew there was something very odd about the house. She would wake up in the middle of the night because she heard someone digging down in the basement. She thought this entirely out of the question, but when the noise persisted night after night, she was wondering whether the neighbors might be putting in a water pipe. After a while, she decided to find out who was doing the digging. She left her bed and went downstairs, but there was nothing to be seen. There were no rats or mice which could have caused the strange noise. There was no freshly turned up dirt either. Their neighbors weren't doing any digging. Even more mysterious, Mary and her two daughters kept hearing the noise of someone trying to break into the house, always at two in the morning. And when they checked there was never anyone there. They called the police but the police failed to turn up any clues. Mary installed heavy bolts inside the front and rear doors, but the day she returned from an errand to an empty house she found the heavy bolts ripped away by unseen hands.

At the time Mary was estranged from her doctor husband, and she was afraid to discuss the strange phenomena with him, since he put no stock into psychic phenomena and might have taken advantage of the information to have Mary declared in need of psychiatric treatment. Mary was in the habit of taking afternoon naps but now her naps kept being disturbed by an unseen person entering the house, walking through it as if he or she knew it well, and sometimes even running the water or flushing the toilet! Often, when she was doing her laundry in the basement she would clearly hear footsteps overhead then the sound of drawers being opened and shut and water being run. But when she checked, there was no one about and nothing had changed.

At first she kept the disturbing news from her daughters but soon the discovered that the children had also heard the strange noises. In addition, Katie had felt a pair of hands on her during the night when she knew she was alone in her room. Even in plain daylight such heavy objects as books began to disappear and reappear in other places as if someone were trying to play a game with them. At that time Boots, the older girl, was at college and when she came back from school she had no idea what her sister and mother had been through recently in the house. So it was a shock for her to hear someone using a typewriter in the basement when they all knew that there was no one there and no typewriter in the house. The family held a conference and it was decided that what they had in the house was a ghost, or perhaps several. By now they had gotten used to the idea, however, and it did not frighten them as much as before.

One night Katie was asleep when she awoke with the feeling she was not alone. As she opened her eyes she saw standing by her bedside a shadowy figure. Since her mother was in the other bedroom, she knew that it could not have been her.

Soon, Mary and her girl realized that they weren't dealing with just one ghost. On several occasions the quick footsteps of a child were also heard along with the heavier footsteps of an adult. Then someone seemed to be calling out to them by name. One day in January 1968 when they had gotten accustomed to their unseen visitors Mary awoke to the sound of music coming from the kitchen area. She investigated this at once but found neither a radio nor any other reason for the music that could be accepted on a rational basis. She returned to bed and tried to ignore it. Just then two sets of footfalls reached her ears right through the covers. One set of feet seemed to turn to toward her daughter Katie's room, while the other pair of feet came right toward her bed, where they stopped. Something ice cold then seemed to touch her. She screamed in fear and jumped from her bed and this apparently broke the phenomenon and again there was no one about.

Mary began to wonder who was the person in the household who made the phenomenon possible, because she knew enough about psychic phenomena to realize that someone had to be the medium. One night she received the answer. She awakened to the sound of a voice coming from her daughter Katie's room. A female voice was saying a phrase over and over and Katie was answering by repeating it. She could clearly hear "golden sand," spoken in a sweet, kindly voice and her daughter Katie repeating it in a childish voice totally different from her normal adult tone. Then she heard Katie clap her hands and say, "Now what can I do?" When Mary entered Katie's room she saw her daughter fast asleep. When questioned the next day about the incident, Katie remembered absolutely nothing. But the incidents continued.

One day Katie saw a woman in her forties, and felt someone fondling her hair. It seemed a kind gesture and Katie was not afraid. By now Mary wondered whether she herself might not be the person to whom the phenomena occurred rather than just her daughter. She had always had psychic ability so she decided to test this potential mediumship within her. Relaxing deeply in an effort to find out who the ghost was and what the ghost wanted in the house, Mary was able to hear with her inner voice the psychic message sent out from the woman. Over and over again she heard the phrase spoken within her—"I need your help to cross the stream!" Several days later she heard the same female voice whisper in her ear, "I need your help!" "Where are you?" Mary said aloud. "In the basement, in the dirt," the voice answered. Soon Mary realized there was another ghost in the house, this one male. Mary woke from an afternoon nap because she heard someone come through the front door. She sat up and yelled at the unseen presence to go away and leave her alone. But a man's gruff voice answered her. "She can see me!" But Mary did not see anyone. Still, she become more and more convinced that the man was angry at her for having paid attention to the female ghost and Mary wondered whether

the two of them had a connection. Mary called on sincere friends to form a "psychic rescue circle," that is to try to make contact with the restless ghosts and, if possible, send them away. It didn't help. Soon after, Mary heard the pleading voice again, "I need you. Come to the basement." Mary then went to the basement where she said a prayer for the departed. Whether the prayer did it, or whether the ghosts had finally realized that they were staying on in a house that belonged to another time, there were no further disturbances after that.

✳ 99

Miss Boyd of Charles Street, Manhattan

ONE OF THE OLDEST and historically most interesting sections of New York City is Greenwich Village, where many houses dating back to the early nineteenth, eighteenth, and even seventeenth century still exist. The people living in them sometimes have to share the appointments with an unseen entity or even a seen one, but ghosts and old houses seem to go together and those among the people living in this part of New York whom I have interviewed over the years because of ghostly manifestation have never thought that there was anything remarkably horrible about them. If anything they were curious about the person or persons they shared their houses with.

Some years ago I had the pleasure of meeting a certain Miss Boyd down on Charles Street and the meeting was mutually useful. Miss Boyd of course was a ghost. All of this happened because Barrie, a friend, had taken an apartment on Charles Street, and found that his ground floor apartment contained a ghost. Halloween 1964, I visited the apartment in the company of medium Sybil Leek, and I had no idea whom I might meet there apart from the flesh-and-blood people then occupying the apartment. There was a fire in the fireplace and an appropriate wind howling outside, but it was novelist Elizabeth B., Barrie's friend, who set the proper mood. She explained that the whole thing started when one of Barrie's house guests, Adriana, had been awakened in bed by a rather violent push of her arm. At the same time she felt herself compelled to burst into tears and wept profusely, although there was no reason for it. Somehow she partook of another person's feelings, involving a great deal of sorrow. This happened several nights a row. However, Adriana did not tell Barrie about it. There really was no need to because one night he arrived around 1 in the morning to find Adriana practically drowning in her tears. When his house guest left, he tried to dismiss the whole thing, but he, too, felt a "presence" watching him all the time. On one occasion, he saw a whitish mist, and was sure that someone was looking at him.

Miss Boyd used to live here on Charles Street

Sybil Leek felt that communication with the unseen entity was possible. Gradually falling deeper and deeper into a trance state, she made contact with the unhappy woman who could not leave the spot of much suffering in her own lifetime. "Her name is Boyd," Sybil explained and then the entity, the ghost herself, took over Sybil's speech mechanism and I was able to question her about her grievances. Apparently Miss Boyd was looking for a document having to do with ownership of the house; the year was 1866. The owner of the house was named Anussi. At that point we had to end the séance.

We returned a few weeks later, and again Sybil Leek made contact with the ghost. Picture my surprise when Elizabeth B. informed me that she had done some research on the house since our first meeting, and discovered that the house had indeed belonged to a family named Boyd ever since it had been bought by one Samuel Boyd in 1827!

Even the landlord named "Anussi" turned out to have some basis in fact except that the name was spelled differently, Moeslin. According to the records, this man had rented the house to Mary Boyd in 1866. But what about the paper the ghost was trying to recover, the paper that apparently caused her continued presence in the house? "Find the paper, find the paper. This is my house," the ghost said, through the medium. The paper, it appeared, was in the name of her father, Bill, and the landlord did not have any right to the house according to the ghost. That was the reason for her continued presence there.

I tried to explain that much time had gone by, and that the matter was no longer of importance. I asked Miss Boyd to let go of the house and join her equally dead relatives on the other side of life. There was no doubt that medium Sybil Leek had indeed brought through an authentic ghost, because Elizabeth B. in discussing her research had mentioned only the name Mary Boyd. But in trance, the ghost speaking through the medium had identified herself proudly as Mary Elizabeth Boyd. When the records were rechecked it was discovered that the person living in the house in 1868 was Mary E. Boyd. There was also a William Boyd, evidently the father the ghost had referred to, who had given her the paper proving her ownership and rights to the house.

I do hope that no one will encounter Miss Mary Boyd again, for it would seem a pity that she has to hang around such a long time just to prove that the house was, after all, hers.

✳ 100

The Haunted Ranch at Newbury Park, California

MRS. H. IS A remarkable lady, who had spent most of her life in the little town of Newbury Park, California, which is north of Los Angeles. Newbury Park has a population of about 15,000 people and its major claim to fame is its Stagecoach Inn, which was once used as a stopover when the stagecoach traveled between Santa Barbara and Los Angeles, discontinued, however in 1915. The inn was moved from its old location a few years ago and is now in a more convenient place, while a major highway goes through where it once stood. The land around Newbury Park is mainly ranch land and the houses, consequently, are ranch-style houses, low, spread out and usually painted white or gray. The H.s live on part of what is known locally as the Hays Ranch, which at one time consisted of hundreds of acres of farm land. They own two-and-a-half acres and a small but comfortable ranch house in the middle of it. Around 1920, it appears, there was a family living in the house that had a small girl who accidentally drowned in either a well or a cesspool on the property. Other than that, Mrs. H. was not aware of any tragedies having occurred in the immediate area of her house.

Mrs. H. had originally contacted me, explaining that she had problems with ghosts, without going too much into details. Now, I questioned her about the goings-on in the house.

"There have been three occurrences that I have not mentioned, over the past two months. The most recent was a weird 'singing' 'whistling' noise which I heard a few night ago. I am reasonably sure this was not my imagination, as my son David has told me of hearing such a noise about two months ago while he was in the bathroom. He was frightened, but no one else heard it and I could not imagine what it could be other than a little air in the pipes. But when I heard what I assume was the same noise it was while I sat up alone in our living room-kitchen.

"The other thing that happened was the day I saw the ghost. I knew from the voice that it was a boy of about ten or twelve. But this day (in late January) while I was washing the windows, I saw through the window pane clearly standing by the fence a young boy *and you could see the fence through him*! It was in the morning and that side of the house was shaded but the yard behind it was in brilliant sunlight. I wasn't sure I could believe my eyes and when I turned around he was gone.

"Another hard-to-explain event that happened was one evening at least a month ago—maybe more—when my husband and I were sitting in the living room and the room was fairly quiet. We both heard a sound that could only be called a whimpering near the door. I had heard this several months before but no one else had."

Apparently the H.'s children also had some experiences in the house. "David told me about some misty shapes he had seen, and said the other kids also saw them some time ago, in their bedroom. He said it was dark in the room and these 'things' were light. Near the ceiling he saw three misty shapes and they seemed to be looking down at the children. They were vague but he thought they were people. He called me and when I came in and opened the door they disappeared."

"The 'shapeless, horrible' thing the kids saw was on my mind for a while after that, and when I saw something in there later on, I was not sure it was not subconscious suggestion on my part and I never mentioned it to anyone, but it was about three weeks later that it happened. The children were insisting upon the door being left open and I allowed it for several weeks after they saw this thing. The night I saw something, the door was, therefore, open. I was sitting across from the door by the windows and looked up to see a *misty, whitish shape in the doorway* next to the partition and partly over it—above floor level, some six feet I would say.

"There hasn't been much else happening around here recently other than my hearing outdoors, apparently on the hill behind the clothesline, a whimpering sound, quite loud, that lasted for several minutes at a time.

"Also, yesterday afternoon, my daughter and I were sitting on the patio and we both heard distinctly two car doors slam on the other side of the house. She went to see if the truck doors had slammed shut, but they were both open and there were no cars out there."

Who the ghost or ghosts at Newbury Park are, I do not know. It may well be that the H.s are simply picking up memories from the past, at least in part. But the white shapes floating into the room are hard to explain on that basis. In an area which has been lived in for such a long time as this area, tragedies are bound to occur without being recorded. Perhaps someone from the past is still around, wondering who the newcomers are in what used to be his place.

The haunted ranch at Newbury Park

✳ 101

The Narrowsburgh Ghost

NARROWSBURGH, NEW YORK lies about four hours from New York City on the Delaware River, where Pennsylvania, New York, and New Jersey meet. This is a beautiful and somewhat remote area of the country, with large, open acreage and beautiful trees, and the houses, mainly farms, can be very isolated. The house in question is directly on the Delaware and had been owned by the parents of the lady who contacted me originally to investigate it, Mrs. M. of Long Island. Prior to the parents' acquisition of the house in 1942, it had been vacant for seven years and was in a run-down condition. However, it has since been restored and is used mainly on weekends by Mrs. M. and her family. The house itself is about two-hundred years old and much restructuring has gone on over the years. However, the foundation and the outside walls are intact and are exactly as they were when the building was first erected. On many occasions, the ghost of a woman has been seen just outside the house as though she were about to enter. This happens usually at the same hour, and with some regularity. Both Mrs. M. and her husband have actually watched for her and seen her. Also, the sound of a door closing by itself has been heard for years and Mrs. M. has been awakened during the night many times with the feeling that someone is watching her.

One night in 1971, Mrs. M., her husband and two friends attempted a séance. For a few minutes, the room seemed to change to what it once was and Mrs. M. found herself crying uncontrollably without reason. She had the feeling that she was experiencing something that happened to a woman in 1793. In addition to the woman in distress, Mrs. M. felt a male presence as well, but from a different time period.

I asked for additional information about the house and learned that it was built in 1752 by Dutch settlers. The deed itself goes back to 1861. Narrowsburgh can be reached over Route 97. In addition, Mrs. M. explained that she had the increasing feeling that a skeleton may still be buried in the basement, but has so far not tried to dig for it. The M.'s children have also seen the apparition of the man, and Mrs. M.'s mother has felt very uneasy in certain parts of the house. Since they felt that the ghost was frightening the children, they got in touch with me in the hope I would visit and exorcise either one of the presences in their house. I agreed to visit the house in the company of my psychic friend, Ingrid Beckman, who had been an excellent medium on a number of earlier occasions. We went through the house, room by room, hoping that she would pick up some of the puzzles of the past. Within moments, Ingrid picked up the impressions of a man who was staying on after death in the northeast bedroom. Ingrid felt that the house once belonged to this man, perhaps fifty or sixty years ago, and the reason for his continued presence was that he didn't realize he was dead and considered the people he saw in his house as intruders. This is a common misconception among ghosts.

We then went into the cellar, an area in which Mrs. M. had felt some of the strongest vibrations. It was then that we discovered a secret room, almost concealed by the rough stones of the basement. What was this room used for, I wondered? Today it is used as a coal bin. Ingrid felt that someone was buried in that area. Now Ingrid got the entire picture more clearly. "I feel it is a woman about twenty-five years old and she was looking for some man to come to her, but he didn't show up and somehow she left the room and went down here where she was entombed. Whether she was murdered or went in there to hide, I cannot say. I feel there was a defense of the house and I sense a man with a very long rifle. This happened a long time ago. I think the woman died in this little room, either she was hiding or she couldn't get out and died there."

The house in Narrowsburgh is privately owned, and I doubt very much that visitors would be welcome.

✳ 102

The Ghost in the Pink Bedroom

THE AREA AROUND Charlottesville, Virginia, abounds with haunted houses, which is not surprising since this was at one time the hub of the emerging young American republic. There was a time when the American government had its capital, if only briefly, in Charlottesville and prior to the Revolution, the large landowners had built many magnificent manor houses which still dot the area. Much history and much tragedy has occurred in some of them, so it is not surprising to find that the reports of strange goings-on in the area are comparatively plentiful. One such house is the property of Colonel Clark Lawrence and his family, known as Castle Hill. It is considered one of the historical landmarks of the area and while it is not open to visitors, especially those looking for the ghost, it is conceivable that prior arrangements with the owners could be made for a student of history to have a brief visit. If this is diplomatically handled, the chances of being allowed to visit are good.

The main portion of the house was built by Dr. Thomas Walker in 1765, but additions were made in 1820. The original portion was made of wood, while the additions were of brick. These later changes executed under the direction of the new owner, Senator William Cabell Rives, gave Castle Hill its majestic appearance. Senator Rives had been American ambassador to France and was much influenced in his tastes by French architecture. This is clear when one sees the entrance hall with its twelve-foot ceilings and the large garden laid out in the traditional French manner.

On the ground floor, to the rear, there is a suite of rooms which has a decidedly feminine flavor. This is not surprising since they were the private quarters of a later owner, Amelie Rives, an author and poet whose body lies buried in the family plot on the grounds.

In this suite there is a bedroom called the pink bedroom, which is the center of ghostly activities. Whenever guests have been assigned to sleep in this room, they

Castle Hill, Virginia

invariably complain of disturbances during the night. Writer Julian Green, a firm skeptic, left the next morning in great hurry. Amelie Rives herself spoke of a strange perfume in the room, which did not match any of her own scents. The ghostly manifestations go back a long time, but no one knows exactly who is attached to the room.

From the testimony of various guests, however, it appears that the ghost is a woman, not very old, rather pretty, and at times playful. Her intentions seem to be to frighten people using the room. Curiously, however, a few guests have slept in it without being aroused by uncanny noises or footsteps. Legend has it that those the lady ghost likes may sleep peacefully in "her" bedroom, while those she does not like must be frightened out of their wits.

I visited the bedroom in the company of sensitive Virginia Cloud, who had been there many times before. Curiously, I felt the vibrations of another presence, a fine, almost gentle person, but I could not see anyone. Nevertheless, I realized that I was not alone in the room, and Miss Cloud also felt that we were being observed by the unseen former owner of the place.

During the Revolutionary War, British General Banastre Tarleton and his troops occupied Castle Hill. The then owner, Dr. Walker, served them breakfast on June 4, 1781, and in the course of his hospitality delayed them as long as he could so that Jefferson, then in nearby Charlottesville, could make good his escape from the British. Whether or not one of the ladies played any significant part in this delaying action is not known, but I suspect that there is involvement of this kind connected with the appearance of the ghostly lady at Castle Hill. It was not uncommon for the women of the Revolutionary period to use their charms on the British, in order to further the cause of the revolution. Several such instances are known, and it must be said for the gallantry of the British officers, that they did not mind the intrigues of the American Colonial ladies at all.

The haunted "pink bedroom"

✳ 103

The Poughkeepsie Rectory Ghost

A FEW YEARS AGO Bishop James Pike made news by publicly declaring that he had spoken with his dead son James in a séance arranged on Canadian television with the late medium Arthur Ford. Not much later he himself became news when he died near the Dead Sea, having run out of gas and water in the desert. A controversial figure both in life and afterlife, Bishop James Pike, one-time Bishop of California, and the author of a number of remarkable books, was no stranger to psychic phenomena.

During my work with him, I got to know the Christ Church rectory at Poughkeepsie pretty well. In 1947 Pike had been offered the position of rector, and he spent several years there. Christ Church is a large, beautiful, almost modern Episcopal church. The altar with its candles indicates what are generally called "high church" attitudes, that is, closer to Roman Catholicism. The outside of the church has remained turn-of-the-century, and so has the rectory attached immediately the church itself. There is also a small library between the rectory and the church.

I asked permission of the rector of Christ Church to visit, and in July 1968 took medium Ethel Johnson Meyers there. She relived practically the entire incident Bishop Pike had reported to me privately earlier.

What had occurred during the two-and-a-half years of James Pike's residency at Poughkeepsie was not unusual as hauntings go. To him it seemed merely puzzling, and he made no attempt to follow up on it in the way I did when I brought Mrs. Meyers to the scene. Pike had taken over his position at Poughkeepsie, replacing an elderly rector with diametrically opposed views in church matters. The former rector had died shortly afterward.

Pike soon found that his candles were being blown out, that doors shut of their own volition, and that objects

The haunted rectory in Poughkeepsie

overhead would move—or seemingly move—when in fact they did not. All the noises and disturbances did not particularly upset Bishop Pike. However, on one occasion he found himself faced with a bat flying about madly in the library. Knowing that there was no way in or out of the library except by the door he had just opened, he immediately closed the door again and went to look for an instrument with which to capture the bat. When he returned and cautiously opened the door to the library, the bat had disappeared. There is no possible way by which the animal could have escaped.

Those wishing to visit Poughkeepsie can do so freely, although the rector may not be too keen to discuss psychic phenomena.

104

The Ghost at West Point

SO MUCH HISTORY has taken place at the Military Academy at West Point, which used to be a fortress guarding the approaches of the Hudson River, it is no surprising that ghostly apparitions should have also occurred from time to time.

Four military cadets at the United States Military Academy saw the apparition of a soldier dressed in eighteenth century cavalry uniform, and according to the witnesses, the apparition seemed luminous and shimmering. Apparently, the ghost materialized out of the wall and a closet in room 4714 and on one occasion also from the middle of the floor. Once it ruffled the bathrobe of a cadet, and on another occasion it turned on a shower!

As soon as the publicity drew the attention of the guiding spirits (of the military kind) to the incident, room 4714 was emptied of its inhabitants. The room itself was then declared off-limits to one and all. Ghosts, of course, do not obey military authorities. Cadet Captain Keith B., however, was willing to discuss it intelligently. "There is no doubt about it at all," he said, "the room grew unnaturally cold." Two weeks before, he and another upperclassman spent a night sleeping in the room, their beds separated by a partition. At about two in the morning Cadet B's companion began to shout. He jumped from his bed and rounded the partition, but he could not see anything special. What he did feel, however, was an icy cold for which there was no rational explanation.

However, he and his companion weren't the first ones to encounter the ghost. Two plebes who occupied room 4714 before them also saw it. The second time the apparition walked out of the bureau that stood about in the middle of the floor. He heard the plebes shout, and ran into the room. One of the cadets who actually saw the apparition was able to furnish a drawing. It is the face of a man with a drooping moustache and a high, old-fashioned cap surmounted by a feather. It is the uniform of a cavalry man of about two hundred years ago.

West Point, where an unhappy plebe still walks

West Point has a number of ghostly legends, what is now the superintendent's mansion allegedly has a one-hundred-fifty-year-old ghostly girl, a woman named Molly, who in life was a sort of camp follower.

Another cadet was taking a shower, prior to moving into the haunted room on the same floor and on leaving the shower noticed that his bathrobe was swinging back and forth on the hook. Since the door was closed and the window closed, there could be no breeze causing the robe to move. The building in which this occurred stands on old grounds; an earlier barrack stood there which has long since been demolished. Could it be that the ghostly cavalry man might have died there and been unable to adjust to his new surroundings?

If you visit West Point, try to find the building that contains room 4714. Company G-4 is quartered there, and perhaps someone will help you find the way.

105

The Stenton House, Cincinnati

IN ONE OF THE QUIETEST and most elegant sections of old Cincinnati, where ghosts and hauntings are rarely whispered about, stands a lovely Victorian mansion built around 1850 in what was then a wealthy suburb of the city.

The house was brought to my attention some years ago by John S. of Clifton, a descendant of one of the early Dutch families who settled Cincinnati, and himself a student of the paranormal. The owners at that time were the Stenton family, or rather, of one of the apartments in the mansion, for it had long been subdivided into a number of apartments lived in by various people.

Soon after they had taken up residence in the old house, the Stentons were startled by noises, as if someone were walking in the hall, and when they checked, there was never anyone about who could have caused the walking.

The haunted Stenton House—Cincinnati, Ohio

The study where footsteps were being heard

Then, two weeks after they had moved in, and always at exactly the same time, 2:10 A.M., they would hear the noise of a heavy object hitting the marble floor—of course there was nothing that could have caused it.

Shortly thereafter, while Mrs. Stenton and her father were doing some research work in the flat, someone softly called out her name, Marilyn. Both heard it. What really upset them was the sound of arguing voices coming from the area of the ceiling in their bedroom: Mrs. Stenton had the impression that there was a group of young girls up there!

But the most dramatic event was to transpire a couple of weeks later. Someone had entered the bedroom, and as she knew she was alone, her family being in other parts of the house, she was frightened, especially when she saw what appeared to be a misty figure—as soon as she had made eye contact with it, the figure shot out of the room, through the French doors leading to a studio, and whilst doing so, the misty shape managed to knock the Venetian blinds on the doors, causing them to sway back and forth!

Shortly before I visited Cincinnati to deal with this case, Mrs. Stenton had another eerie experience. It was winter and had been snowing the night before. When Mrs. Stenton stepped out onto their porch, she immediately noticed a fresh set of footprints on the porch, heading away from the house!

The house was built in 1850, originally as a large private home; later it became a girls' school and much later became an apartment house of sorts. The Stenton's apart-

ment is the largest in the house, encompassing seven rooms.

When I looked into the case I discovered some additional details. In 1880, a young man of the Henry family had committed suicide in the house by shooting himself, and after the family moved, the house could not be sold for a long time. It became known as being haunted and was boarded up. Finally, a girls' school, the Ealy School, bought it in 1900.

Other tenants had also encountered unusual phenomena, ranging from "presences," to noises of objects hitting floors, and footsteps following one around when no one was, in fact, doing so. Even the dog owned by one of the tenants would under no condition enter the area of the disturbances and would put up a fearsome howl.

But the item most likely to have an answer to the goings-on came to me by talking to some of the oldsters in the area: one of the young girls in the school was said to have hanged herself upstairs, above the Stenton's apartment. Was it her ghost or that of young Henry who could not leave well enough alone?

106

The Ghost at El Centro

WHEN MR. AND MRS. C. moved from France to Los Angeles in the 1960s, they did not figure on moving into a haunted house, but that is exactly what they did. With their daughters, they took an old one-story house built in the Spanish style, on El Centro Avenue, a quiet section of the city.

One of the daughters, Lilliane had married shortly before their arrival, and the second daughter, Nicole, decided to have her own place, so it was Mr. and Mrs. C. and their third daughter, Martine, who actually lived in the house. The dining room had been turned into a bedroom for Martine, leaving the master bedroom to the parents.

On her first night in the house, Mrs. C., who is very psychic, had the distinct impression there was someone observing her, someone she could not see. Martine, too, felt very uncomfortable but the business of settling in took precedence over their concern for the next few days.

However, strong impressions of a presence continued night after night. They were never "alone." There was a noise in the kitchen, and Mrs. C. thought her husband had gotten up in the middle of the night to get something—but there he was, fast asleep in bed. Instead, a strange man was standing between their two beds, and worse yet, she could see right through him! She gave out a startling cry and the apparition vanished instantly.

She discussed the matter with her daughters who had lived in the apartment before their arrival: it then became clear that the girls, too, had been bothered by ghostly manifestations. They had tried to deal with it by lighting a candle every night. But apparently it did not help at all.

During the following days, the hauntings continued. The girls, too, had seen a male ghost between the beds.

The ghost house on El Centro, Los Angeles

But now the mother saw a woman's apparition, and it was decided to seek the help of a competent medium. This turned out to be Brenda Crenshaw, who made contact with the entities. She reported that the "problem" consisted of the fact a young couple who had formerly occupied the apartment, had committed suicide in it.

When the family checked this out with the appropriate records, it turned out to be correct. But now what? The idea of continuing to share the place with the ghost couple was not at all appealing to them. Mrs. C. decided to pray for the release of the ghosts and did so relentlessly for several weeks. One night, there was the young man again, as if to acknowledge her efforts. Then he vanished, and the apartment has been quiet ever since.

107

The Ghostly Stagecoach Inn

NOT FAR FROM VENTURA, at Thousand Oaks, a few yards back from the main road, stands an old stagecoach inn, now run as a museum; between 1952 and 1965, while in the process of being restored to its original appearance, it also served as a gift shop under the direction of a Mr. and Mrs. M. who had sensed the presence of a female ghost in the structure.

The house has nineteen rooms and an imposing frontage with columns running from the floor to the roof.

There is a balcony in the central portion, and all windows have shutters, in the manner of the middle nineteenth century. Surrounded by trees until a few years ago, it has been moved recently to a new position to make room for the main road running through here. Nevertheless, its grandeur has not been affected by the move.

During the stagecoach days, bandits were active in this area. The inn had been erected because of the Butterfield Mail route, which was to have gone through the Conejo Valley on the way to St. Louis. The Civil War halted this plan, and the routing was changed to go through the Santa Clara Valley.

I investigated the stagecoach inn with Mrs. Gwen Hinzie and Sybil Leek. Up the stairs to the left of the staircase Sybil noticed one of the particularly haunted rooms.

Ghostly Stagecoach Inn—Thousand Oaks, California

She felt that a man named Pierre Devon was somehow connected with the building. Since the structure was still in a state of disrepair, with building activities going on all around us, the task of walking up the stairs was not only a difficult one but also somewhat dangerous, for we could not be sure that the wooden structure would not collapse from our weight. We stepped very gingerly. Sybil seemed to know just where to turn as if she had been there before. Eventually, we ended up in a little room to the left of the stairwell. It must have been one of the smaller rooms, a "single" in today's terms.

Sybil complained of being cold all over. The man, Pierre Devon, had been killed in that room, she insisted, sometime between 1882 and 1889.

She did not connect with the female ghost. However, several people living in the area have reported the presence of a tall stranger who could only be seen out of the corner of an eye, never for long. Pungent odors, perfume of a particularly heavy kind, also seem to waft in and out of the structure.

Like inns in general, this one may have more undiscovered ghosts hanging on to the spot. Life in nineteenth-century wayside inns did not compare favorably with life in today's Hilton. Some people going to these stagecoach inns for a night's rest never woke up to see another day.

✳ 108

Mrs. Dickey's Ghostly Companions

THERE ARE TWO VIENNAS I've been to: One, the better-known city, is in Austria, and I was born there; the other is in Virginia, right outside Washington, D.C., and it consists mainly of old homes, lovely gardens, shady streets, and a kind of atmosphere that makes one wonder if there really is a bustling world capital nearby. Especially in the spring, Vienna, Virginia, is a jewel of a place. You ride down broad, shady roads, look at houses—even mansions—that have been in the same hands perhaps for generations, see children playing in the streets as if there weren't any cars buzzing by.

I heard about Mrs. Dickey from a mutual friend in Washington. Nicole d'Amercourt, who is now Mrs. Bruce Jackson, had met her and heard about her disturbing experiences with ghosts. Nicole thought that perhaps I could help Mrs. Dickey either get rid of her ghosts, or at least come to terms with them, I readily agreed, and on May 11, 1968, we drove out to Vienna.

When we arrived at the Dickey house, I was immediately impressed by the comparative grandeur of its appearance. Although not a very large house, it nevertheless gave the impression of a country manor—the way it was set back from the road amid the trees, with a view towards a somewhat wild garden in the rear. A few steps led up to the front entrance. After Nicole had parked the car, we entered the house and were immediately greeted by a lively, petite young woman with sparkling eyes and the aura of determination around her.

We entered a large living room that led to a passage into a dining room and thence into the kitchen. In the center of the ground floor is a staircase to another floor, and from the second floor, on which most of the bedrooms are located, there is a narrow staircase to a garret that contains another bedroom.

The house was beautifully furnished in late colonial style, and antiques had been set out in the proper places with a display of taste not always met these days.

After I had inspected the house superficially from top to bottom, I asked Mrs. Dickey to sit down with me so we could go over the situation that had caused her to ask for my help.

We sat in comfortable chairs in the downstairs living room, and I began to question her about the house.

* * *

"Mrs. Dickey, how long have you lived here?"

"About two-and-a-half years. Myself and five children live here now. And we have two young foreign students living in with us now; they've been here about a month."

"How many rooms are there in the house?"

"There are about twenty."

"About twenty? You're not sure?"

"Well, twenty. Real *estate-wise* we don't count the bathrooms, but I do."

"Yes, and the closets. Don't forget the large closets."

"I don't count closets."

"Did you know much about the house at the time you moved in?"

"Not much. Although we were told, before we purchased it, that it was haunted."

"By whom? I mean told by whom, not haunted by whom."

"By several people. The real-estate woman mentioned it, but laughed about it, and I was intrigued. She said the house has quite a history, and there are many tales about what went on here. After we moved in, more people told us. I suspect they were trying to worry us a bit."

"What sort of tales did you hear before you moved in?"

"Just that the house was haunted."

"No details?"

"No."

"What was the first thing that made you think that there was something to these tales?"

"I was about the last member of the family to be aware that something was going on, but I had heard repeated stories from the children. I was sleeping in one of the children's rooms upstairs one night, and was awakened by heavy footsteps—not in the room but in the next room. I wondered who was up, and I heard them walking back and forth and back and forth. I finally went back to sleep, but I was kind of excited. The next morning I asked who was up during the night, and no one had been up."

"Who was in the rooms in which the footsteps were heard?"

"A six-year-old child was in one room, and my daughter, then eighteen, was in the other."

"In the room in which you thought the footsteps occurred, was there only the six-year-old child?"

"Yes, but the wall was where the old staircase went up. It's now closed off, but the staircase is still there, and I had the feeling it was either in the stairwell, or in the next room. But it felt as if it were right beside me."

"Have there been many structural changes in the house?"

"Yes."

"Did the steps sound like a man's or a woman's?"

"A man's."

"How long did it go on?"

"At least for ten minutes."

"Didn't it worry you that some burglar or a prowler might be in there?"

"No. We have dogs, and I thought it was probably a spirit."

"Do you mean you just accepted it like that without worrying about it?"

"I was a little frightened because I don't want to be touched, and I don't want to look up and *see someone looking* at me, but I don't care if they *walk around!*"

"This was the first thing you heard. What was the next thing?"

"I was sleeping in my son Douglas' room again, and I was having a very frightening dream. I don't remember what the dream was, but I was terrified. Suddenly I awoke and looked at the wall. Before I had gone off to sleep, I had noticed that the room had been sort of flooded with panels of light, and there were two shafts of light side by side, right directly at the wall. I sat right up in bed and I looked up and there was a *shadow of a head*. I don't know whether it was a man's or a woman's, because there were no features, but there was a neck, there was hair, it was the size of a head, and it was high up on the wall. It could have been a woman with short, bushy hair. It was so real that I thought it was Joyce, my daughter, who was about eighteen then. I said, 'Joyce,' and I started speaking to it. Then I realized it was waving a little bit. I became frightened. After about ten minutes of saying, 'Joyce, Joyce, who is it? Who is there?' it moved directly sideways, into the darkness and into the next panel of light, and by then I was crying out, 'Joyce, Joyce, where are you?' I wanted someone to see it with me."

"You still couldn't see any features?"

"No features at all."

"No body?"

"No body."

"Just a head?"

"Well, that's where the shaft of light ended. It was about that long, and it included the head and the neck, and nothing else showed because that was the end of the light on the wall. Then Joyce came in and I said, 'Joyce, look quickly,' and it was still there. But as I stared at this thing, it went out. It moved directly sideways and went."

"Did she see it too?"

"I don't know. You'll have to ask her when she gets here. She was quite excited. The next night we tried to get the panels of light to get back on the wall again. But we couldn't ever get the two panels of light there, and we don't know what they were."

"Do you think these panels of light had anything to do with it? Were they from the moonlight or were they part of this apparition?"

"That's what I don't know, but I would suspect that it had to have something to do with the thing that was there because we could never get the light back again."

"Was there any change in the atmosphere? Any chills?"

"I was extremely aware that there was *something* there."

"Did you feel cold?"

"Yes."

"What was the next event that happened after that?"

"In 1967 we decided to get a Ouija board. We had some friends who knew this house well, and said, 'You ought to work a board and find out what was there.' They owned this house for about ten or fifteen years; their names are Dean and Jean Vanderhoff."

"Have *they* had any experiences here?"

"Oh yes, definitely."

"When did they tell you about them"

"*After* we noticed things."

"They are not here today, so you can briefly sum up what their experiences were."

"Well, on several occasions they heard a woman talking in the kitchen when there was no other woman in the house. They heard the voice, and they also heard the heavy garage doors bang up and down at night, with great noise."

"What did the woman say to them?"

"Nothing to *them*. They were upstairs in bed, but they heard a woman talking. Also, very often they heard everything in the kitchen being banged, and thought all the china in the kitchen was being broken. A great clattering and banging,"

"Now, you decided to tell the Vanderhoffs about *your* experiences?"

"Yes. We worked the Ouija board the night after I had seen this 'thing' on the wall. We immediately got the names of people. There was a Martha and a Morgan, who communicated with us."

"What do they tell you?"

"Martha said that it was *she* who was appearing on the wall, because one child in the next room had fallen out of bed, and Martha loves children, and tried to help. And Martha said dear things about me—that I have a big job, and it's hard for me to handle the children, and she's here to help."

"Does she give you any evidence of her existence as a person?"

"I think she and Morgan are brother and sister and they're both children of Sarah. And Sarah was the first wife of Homer Leroy Salisbury who built this house in 1865."

Did you know at the time you worked the board that this was a fact, that they had children by these names?"

"No, but we had been told that Sarah is buried here in the yard somewhere with two children. I've searched the records and I can't find the names of these children. I don't know for sure whether Martha and Morgan are these two."

"But yet you do now know that there were such people connected with this house."

"There were two children and there was Sarah. But we don't know the names of the *children*."

"But you do know there was a Sarah."

"There definitely was a Sarah."

"Now, when did you find that out? That there was a Sarah?"

"Someone must have told me, and then I did find a record about it."

"Was it before or after the first Ouija board session?"

"No, we got Sarah, the name, on the board; *we didn't know*."

"You didn't know what it meant. It was afterwards, then, that you discovered there was a Sarah connected with this house. And she's buried on the grounds?"

"Yes."

"Still is?"

"Some people say they know where, but we don't."

"You haven't found it?"

"No. I've looked."

"What about the house now?"

"Homer Leroy Salisbury built it in 1865, and structural changes were made in 1939, and there were some since then. Last summer I decided that I would enlarge the terrace because a lot of stones were here. We used all the stones that were here and did it ourselves.

"It was the night after we started tearing it all out and putting new footing down and all. It was the night after, two of my children, Lelia and Doug, had an experience that we thought was because we were making this big change. We worked the board every time we had something happen. But Martha and Morgan came and said they were not unhappy with the terrace."

"What was the next visual or auditory experience, apart from the Ouija board?"

"I have had no other, except a month ago I felt, but did not see, the apparition. That night, we had a big party here. A twenty-two-year-old girl named Nancy Camp offered to work the board. We had never met before. She and I sat at the board and started working it."

"And what happened?"

"The interesting thing was that immediately a new spirit came. His name was Adam, and he gave his last name—it began with a B, something like Bullock. He said he'd been slaughtered in the 1800s by Beatrice. Beatrice had killed both him and his daughter. He needed help. We asked, 'Would you appear?' He agreed to appear to the two of us only. So we went to the back room, closed the door, and sat there."

"Did you actually see him?"

"I didn't, but Nancy did. I watched her as she saw him. She knocked me over backwards and the chair went in the air, then she knocked her chair down, threw the board in the air, and became absolutely terrified, and finally ran out the door."

"Who was this Adam?"

"I don't know."

"Was he connected with this house?"

"I don't know. But he appeared again, and she watched him for at least five minutes, and she described him."

"Since then, have you had any further disturbances?"

"Yes, I have. Since then it has been very difficult for me to sleep in my room at night. I'm very much aware that there's something there, in my bedroom. I definitely feel a presence."

"Is it a man or a woman?"

"Well, we worked the board and we were told it was Adam. I'd been *compelled* to look at the chaise lounge in the corner, and I didn't want to because I didn't want to be frightened. So I made myself not look at it, but I was terribly drawn to it, and when we worked the board the next day Sarah came and said, 'Adam was in your room, and I was in the chaise lounge, and I was there to protect you.'"

"You said earlier a lot of history happened here. You mean, on the grounds? The house is only a hundred years old, but prior to that there was something here. Do you know anything about it?"

"Many people have said there was a house, the Town Hall, standing here that was occupied during the Civil War. But it was riddled with bullets, and it was burned down during the Civil War. This was a camping ground for both the Union and the Confederate armies. Slaves are buried in the yard—ten or twelve people have told me that."

"What about prior to the Civil War period?"

"I was told that there were tunnels here. This was a dairy farm and there's a tunnel from the barn, a walking tunnel. There were said to be tunnels from the basement, but we have found nothing."

"Does this sum up your own firsthand experiences?"

"There is one more thing. This has happened to me many times in my bedroom, while I was in bed. Early in the morning I hear heavy footsteps, at least twelve of them, walking, overhead. But there is no room to walk over my bedroom!"

"You mean, on the roof?"

"No, in the attic."

"Is it a male or female footstep?"

"I would think a man."

"Are these similar to the footsteps you heard when you were in your room and didn't get up?"

"Yes."

"Have you had experiences that I would call ESP experiences before you moved to this house?"

"No, but I've got one more thing to tell you. On a very hot Summer night in June of 1967 I couldn't sleep. I woke up and went to my daughter's empty room, which is the little eleven-by-eleven top cupola. I had gone up there because I thought it would be breezy, and I tried to sleep. I was soon awakened by crying, whimpering, and moaning. I got up and walked around a couple of times, and it stopped. Then I went back to bed. About five times I had to get up because I heard moaning and crying. Finally I

said to myself, 'Well, I've got two puppy dogs, it must be a dog.' I walked all the way down and went into the kitchen, but the dogs were sound asleep. I went back to bed in my own room. I had no sooner gotten into bed, when the phone rang. My daughter, then eighteen, had been in a very serious automobile accident. My husband then slept with ear plugs, and he would never have noticed the phone. I thought, I wouldn't have even been down here, had I not been awakened by the *moaning and crying!*"

"Was it your daughter's voice you heard?"

"Yes—she said she had been left with the most severely injured girl alone on the road, while the others went for help, and that the girl was crying and they were moaning; they were all crying and whimpering."

"Who else has had experiences in this house?"

"A friend, Pat Hughes, saw a woman here one night. Pat was here with a man named Jackson McBride, and they were talking, and at 3 o'clock I left and went to bed. At about 4 o'clock in the morning, Pat heard noises the kitchen and thought that I had gotten up. She heard someone walking back and forth. Pat was over there, and said, 'Come on in, Lucy, stop being silly. Come in and talk to us.' And this apparition walked in, and then Pat said, 'It's not Lucy'—she realized that the ghost looked similar to me. It was tall and slim, had long dark hair, and had a red robe on and something like a shawl collar, and her hand was holding the collar. Pat was exited and said, 'My God, it's not Lucy! *Who is it?*' She said to this man, 'Come and look,' but he was afraid. Then Pat turned to go back and try to communicate, but it had vanished! Later, they heard a great rattle of things in the kitchen."

"How long ago did that happen?"

"About six months."

"Has anyone else seen or heard anything here?"

"One night, Joe Camp, Nancy Camp's brother, saw a shadowy woman in white. On two different occasion."

"Anything else?"

"A year ago when we came home around 11 P.M. we found two of the children still up and frightened. I've never seen Douglas and Lelia so terrified."

"And what did they tell you?"

"I'd like Lelia to tell it to you herself."

I turned to Lelia, who was ten at the time, and encouraged her to speak.

"I was sleeping in bed," she began, "when I saw something go past the window. I said, 'Oh it's nothing, it's probably just the trees.' Then my brother saw it pass his window. He came out and we just started running around the house until mother came home."

"What did it look like?"

"Sort of blurry—"

"Did you see a face?"

"No. Grayish. Sort of fuzzy. And a crinkling noise."

"And how long did it last?"

"About three or five minutes."

"We found a ring with three rubies in it, the night after this woman in red appeared," Mrs. Dickey interjected at this point. "She found it in her room. A lovely gold ring."

"Was it there before?"

"We never saw it before. Do you believe in animal ghosts?" Mrs. Dickey asked thoughtfully. "We had eleven people here once, in the living room and we were working the Ouija board one afternoon. Suddenly, and for no reason at all, we heard a big horse run *across the front porch*! We stared out the windows, but saw absolutely nothing. Still, we heard it; every one of us heard it!"

But Lelia had something more to tell. "A year-and-a-half ago we had a farewell party for my sister's fiancé—my other sister, Joyce—and on the side of the porch there was a coiled head."

"A head?"

"A head. Face. Coiled—like coiled—in a lot of wires. It had features too."

"Male or female?"

"Man."

"How long did it last?"

"Fifteen minutes."

"And how did it go away?"

"It just went—*twee*. Another time, my sister Joyce and I went down into the basement because we thought our father was there. We saw a coat hanging on the door, and all of a sudden this coat just moved. But our father wasn't down there."

"Is there any particular area of the house that is most involved in these activities? Or is it all over the house?" I asked Mrs. Dickey now.

"Under the staircase!" Lelia volunteered.

"If you were to draw a straight line from the basement to those upstairs rooms, what would you hit?"

"The basement, the stairwell, and the room upstairs, definitely; if you had to draw."

"To your knowledge, what was the upstairs' use? Who lived there in the old days? Were there small rooms up there?"

"There were small rooms, yes."

"Servants' quarters?"

"I doubt it. I know there were servants' houses around here—this was more or less the manor house. There were other slave quarters."

"So these were just small rooms on the top floor."

"Yes."

"What about the little room under the cupola?"

"That's where I had another experience," Mrs. Dickey exclaimed. "I was awakened at night, about 3 o'clock in the morning. Patty was out on a date, but I had told her to get in early. I heard *heavy* footsteps going up those old, tiny, narrow stairs to Patty's room. I called out, 'Patty, are you just getting in?' She didn't answer, and I got annoyed. I thought, why isn't she answering me and why is she making so much noise. So I went racing up the stairs and pulled down the covers, and she'd been sound asleep for hours. Another girl was with her, and they were both asleep, and I had frightened them. But the noise was so loud and so apparent, you could hear the leaning on the banister, every foot on the stair—"

"Was it like the other footsteps, the male footsteps that you heard?"

"Yes. Slow, methodical, steady, heavy footsteps."

"Did it sound as if somebody had *trouble* walking up?"

"No. Just walking up."

"As it is, we have two personalities to deal with, a woman and a man. Is there anything known about the house involving tragedy?"

"Not that I know of; I haven't been able to find it out. I had a maid about two months ago and she said, 'I haven't been in this place in years, but my uncle had been riding on a horse, and the horse reared and threw him up and hanged him in a tree.' And she pointed the tree out to me."

"Because the horse got frightened?"

"Threw him up in the air and he was hanged to death in the tree."

"What about that door in the wall? What is the history of that door?"

"A seventy-year-old woman has come here repeatedly to visit. She says she was born in this house; her name is Susan Richmond. She told me that when guests came, and the people in the house were in their aprons and wanted to get upstairs quickly and change, they would scoot up through the little door."

"This staircase was here from the beginning? Where does it lead to?"

"It's boarded over now, but it connected where the stairs are upstairs."

* * *

I finally questioned Joyce Dickey about her experiences in the house. Joyce, twenty, had been in the house with her mother from the beginning, two-and-a-half years ago.

"You've had some experiences with your sister?"

"Yes. It was in the basement."

"Have you had any spontaneous experiences?"

"I would sit in the dining room, and all of a sudden it would get really cold. I could feel a presence. One night we were listening to the record player when there was a sound like a huge waterfall—right by the back entrance. First, it sounded like water dripping down, and then it became like a big waterfall."

"You mean it sounded like it."

"Yes, sounded like it."

"Was there anything there?"

"No."

"Your sister said something about a coat in the basement."

"When we had first moved in here, I had to go down to the basement. My father's coat was hanging on the door, and it was kind of swinging. I just thought my father had gone down into the basement. I opened the door and started to go down. There was this figure, supposedly my father, in front of me; I could just barely see a man's figure, walking down in front of me. I got down and turned on the light and looked around. My father wasn't there."

"But you saw a man?"

"Well—very faint."

"Did you see his face?"

"No—it was just the back, going down in front of me."

"Anything else that I ought to know?"

"I thought the last séance we had stirred things up."

"In which way?"

"The dogs were in the basement, and they started to get upset, so I took them outside. One of them I couldn't get—she ran away, and I couldn't get her into the kennel. But I got the other two in, and came back into the house. There was a noise in the kitchen, like somebody clinking against the pots and pans, and banging around. In the basement there was the sound of a man walking. Then the sounds stopped, and then they started up again, and it was dragging something along the basement floor—sounded like a big sick of potatoes. And then the dogs started barking really furiously. This was last winter."

"Did you hear the horse, out front here?"

"Yes, I did. We were working with the Ouija board, when a huge horse just went clomping across the porch."

"On the wood, you mean?"

"On the wood! He just went clomping—! Like he was trotting. On the porch."

"And did you look to see if there was a horse?"

"Yes. It wasn't one of our horses."

"Where are your horses kept?"

"In the back."

"There wasn't any chance of one of them having gotten loose?"

"No. It was a big horse, and our little pony couldn't have made that much noise."

I thought of the man who had been "hanged" by his horse, then turned my attention to Patty Dickey. Patty was almost eighteen.

"I haven't really had any experiences," she explained and smiled somewhat embarrassed. "Only one time, when my mother saw a figure in my little brother's room. That same night I woke up from a sound sleep and I felt something was in my room."

* * *

Despite their employing Oujia boards to make contact with the spirits or alleged spirits in the house, I felt that the Dickey family had indeed undergone some genuine psychic experiences. I was more convinced of this as I realized that the apparition and the auditory phenomena preceded any attempt to make contact with what was in the house by means of a Ouija board. I have never held boards of this kind in high esteem, and have on occasion warned against their use by children or by those likely to be mediums and not aware of it. Then, too, the information gleaned from the use of these boards is not very reliable on the whole. If anything tangible comes from their usage, it generally can also be obtained by other means, such as meditation, genuine mediumship, or automatic writing. But at the time when I had arrived at the Dickey homestead, the use of the Ouija board was already a matter of record, and there was nothing I could have done about it.

"It is quite clear you have a ghost, or possibly two ghosts, in this house," I said to Mrs. Dickey as I prepared to leave. "I will arrange to come back with a competent medium sometime in the future, and we'll have a go at it."

Mrs. Dickey nodded enthusiastically. A small woman, she belies the fact that she has five children, looking more as if she were in her early twenties. Her enthusiasm was such that I tried to come back immediately, but failed due to the fact that summer had come and I was off to Europe, as I do every year.

* * *

It was therefore not until April 10, 1969 that I was able to arrange for a return visit to Mrs. Dickey's house. The house, by the way, is called Windover, and stands on Walnut Lane, appropriately called that because of the tall old walnut trees on both sides of the street. We agreed that I would come down in the company of Mrs. Ethel Johnson Meyers, and on May 11, 1969, we arrived fully prepared to encounter whatever ghosts in the house wished to be talked to.

This time the living room downstairs was filled with several other people. I had never seen them before, of course, and I was later told that they were in some way connected with the house and the hauntings in it; but I suspect that they were more friends or curious neighbors who wanted to be in on something special. At any rate, they kept in the background and allowed Mrs. Meyers and me to roam around freely so that the medium could get her psychic bearings.

Ethel ascended the front steps like a bloodhound heading for prey. Once inside, she casually greeted everyone without wishing to be introduced any further. Apparently she was already picking up something in the atmosphere. Somewhat as an afterthought I started to instruct her in the usual manner as to my desires.

"What I would like you to do is—if in walking about freely any impressions come to your mind, or if at any point you feel like sitting in a chair, do so, and we will follow you. And—if you have any feelings about the house—this is a very old house. It will be a little difficult to differentiate between what is naturally here and these fine antiques, all of which have some emanations. Apart from that, let me know if you get any response or vibrations."

"Well, there are a lot of things here, all right. But presently there is a tremendous amount of peace. Vitality and peace at the same time. But I'll have to get down lower in order to pick up other things. There is a catalyst around here, and I want to find that catalyst."

Ethel had now entered the living room and stood in the center.

"There's a woman coming close to me. There is also a man—I don't think he's old—he has all this hair. The woman is looking at me and smiling."

* * *

At this point, I had to change tapes. While I busied myself I with the recorder, Ethel kept right on talking about the spectral man she felt in the atmosphere. As soon as my tape I was in place, I asked her to repeat the last few impressions so I could record them.

* * *

"Is this name of 'Lewis,' that you get, connected with the man standing by the fireplace? Would you repeat that description again: gold-buckled shoes, and he has his elbow on the wooden mantelpiece?"

"Well, he has these tan short trousers on, tight-fitting; definitely gold-colored or mustard-colored, cummerbund around here about so wide...."

"What period would he belong to?"

"Oh, I think he has his hair tied in a queue back here. It's grayish or he's got a wig on."

"Anything else?"

"He has got a blue jacket on that seems to come down in the back."

"Are there any buttons on that jacket?"

"Yes."

"What color are they?"

"Silver."

"Why is he here?"

"He looks contemplative, and yet I feel as if he wants to grit his teeth."

"Is this a presence, or is this an imprint?"

"I think it's a presence."

"He comes with the house?"

"I would say so."

"Is there anything that is unfinished about his life?"

Ethel turned to the unseen man at the fireplace. "Tell me what's bothering you, friend. You have your eyes half-closed and I can't see the color of your eyes. Will you look around at me?"

I reinforced her offer with one of my own. "You may use this instrument to communicate if you wish. We come as friends."

Ethel reported some reaction now. "Oh! He's looking around at me. His eyes are sort of a green-hazel."

"Any idea why he is here?"

"He just disappeared. Like, went through here."

"Where did he go towards?"

"Went through here." She pointed towards the old staircase in back of the room, where most of the manifestations had occurred.

"Follow the way he went!"

"I can't go through that wall!" She started walking around it, however, and I followed her. "This room was not there. Something is different," she said suddenly and halted.

"Different in which way?"

"Is this part later?"

"I am told that it is later. What is different about that end of the house?"

Evidently she felt nothing in the more modern portion of the house.

"All right, we're going back to the older part of the house."

"You see, I couldn't hear anything there. Here is a man, with a lot of hair, sort of hangs down; has a drooping mustache and a beard."

"What period does he belong to?"

"Oh, this is much later, I would say."

I pointed towards the wall where so much had occurred: "Would you go to that wall over there. Just that area generally, which is the oldest part of the house, I believe. I would like you to see whether this impresses you in any way."

"This man I was just seeing is not around any of the people here, like those that I saw a moment ago; not that late."

"Nothing contemporary?"

"No—there's nothing contemporary about the man I just saw there."

"Another period from the first one?"

"That is right."

"Two levels, in other words."

"There is a woman's voice, very penetrating; as I am getting her, she is very slim."

"What period does she belong to?"

"Around the same as the first man I saw. Do you notice a coldness here? A difference in temperature? Something has happened right in here."

"You mean in the corridor to the next room? It leads us back to the entrance door. What do you suppose has happened here?"

"There's been an acc—I don't want to say acc—I don't want to say *anything but* accident. There's been an accident, and a woman *screaming about it.*"

"You are grabbing your neck. Why?"

"She went out of her body here."

"Is she still here?"

"I would say she is. She's the thin woman I speak of."

"Who is the person that is most dominant in this house at the moment?"

"I know that voice is terribly dominant, but the man in there was very dominant also." Ethel pointed towards the front hall again. "Can I go further in here?"

I nodded and followed.

"She cannot come through here. It is blocked. This was an opening, but there is *something hanging there.*"

"What is hanging there?"

"I'm afraid it is the man I saw at the fireplace, in there."

"How did he die?"

"By the neck."

"Is this the man you called Lewis?"

"I think it could be. It is strange—while I am in this terribly depressed mood I can hear laughter and carrying-on about something of great honor that has happened, and it is being celebrated *here.* Somebody comes into this house with the greatest feeling of triumph, as it were; that they've conquered something. At the same time I'm pulled down like mad over here."

"When you say 'conquered,' are you speaking of a military victory?"

"I don't know yet, what it is. These are all impressions. I have to get much lower."

"I would suggest you find your way to a comfortable chair, and let whatever might be here find you."

But Ethel was not quite ready for trance. She kept on getting clairvoyant impressions galore.

"So many people are trying to come in. A heavier-set man, kind of bald, here. Now there's another one. Now a girl, hair caught across and down in curls. She doesn't look more than ten, twelve."

"Is she connected with either the man or woman?"

"I would say around the earlier time, because she has a long dress on, down to here. Laced shoes, with like ribbons tied here; you might call them ballet slippers. She has a very pointed little chin, and the eyes are sort of wide, as if they were seeing things. Then there is an older woman, with her dark hair coming down and then as if it were drawn up very high."

"Does she give you any names?"

"Anne or Annette. I get a peaceful feeling around this individual, with the exception that I seem to be communing with someone that *I can't really touch.*"

"Would you mind explaining that?"

"Perhaps with a ghost that I can't touch."

"Do you feel that they have something they wish to tell us?"

"'We're not on speaking terms yet!'"

"Well, perhaps Albert can catch them and tell us what they are about. If Albert would like to be present—"

But Ethel ignored my hint to let her control come through in trance. Not just yet. She was still rattling off her psychic impressions of this apparently very overcrowded house, spiritually speaking.

"Funny—there's a strange little dog, also, yonder. It looks something like a Scotty, but isn't. It has stiff hair."

"Does it come with any of these three characters you mentioned?"

"I think he belongs to the woman I just described. I have a feeling that I am *seeing* her for the first time, and that I *heard* her in the other room."

"The voices you heard before?"

"I think so. She looks terribly sad here. I know someone runs out that way."

"Why are they running out of the house?"

"I'm so reluctant to say that someone is hanging there...."

We sat down, and Ethel closed her eyes. Patiently I waited for her spirit control, Albert, to take over the conversation. Finally, after about two or three minutes of silence, a familiar, *male* voice greeted me from Ethel's entranced lips.

"Hello."

"Albert, are you in control?"

"There's strain, but I seem to be doing it."

"Do you have any information about this house, Albert?" I asked as soon as I was sure he was in firm control.

"You have come on a day very close to an anniversary of something."

"Can you enlighten me as to details?"

"The one who relives this is Emma."

"This Emma—what is her problem?"

"She is quiet, but *he* is tight-lipped. Inadvertent deception led to destruction of moral character. One person made a quick decision, 'I would be myself if you would let me free.' Details cannot be brought into the light, even though it was inadvertent. The attitude leading up to this situation was, if you die, your secret dies with you."

"But the other one can talk?"

"I will try to see if this other one will talk too, because it is within him the secret lies. If he will talk, so much the better. Because the other one knows not the secret of the woman."

"Can you give us the names?"

"There are two Ls. Leon is one. I cannot tell you which it is now. There are two individuals, one who comes to visit the other. One who has sat in this vicinity and made his declaration. A declaration against an L., another L."

"What sort of declaration?"

"Opening up and giving publicly accounts that this one living here would keep a secret."

"What did the account deal with?"

"When one holds them quietly to themselves and desires not to give it, it is a law over here—you know this—so I would like to have *him* speak, rather than the woman, Emma, who is not completely aware of what was going on between the two Ls."

"Is he willing to speak to us?"

"We are trying to get them to speak. However, he made the decision to do away with the whole business by destroying himself and take it with him. He was alone when he did it. The other L. has departed. He will not divulge his name."

"Do you know his name?"

"I do not. When it is held a secret, and it is here, I am not allowed to penetrate it until he will divulge it himself."

"Is he connected with this house as an owner?"

"I would say so."

"A long time ago?"

"It looks to me, turn of century."

"Which century?"

"Into eighteen hundred."

"Did he build the house?"

"I believe so."

"Then he would be the one that first lived here?"

"I believe this to be true. I am looking as hard as I can, to see. There may have been transactions of another builder and his taking it over before too long. Somehow there is some unsavory business, in the past. He is a reputable individual and cannot afford to allow some past things to come into the light."

"What was the disreputable business he was worried about?"

"This is his secret."

"Would you try to let him speak?"

"I will try to force him into the *instrument*. It is done, you know, by a kind of shock treatment."

* * *

Again, I had to change tapes at the very moment when another person took over Ethel's vocal apparatus.

After some painful and emotional groans, a hoarse voice whispering "Emma!" came through her lips. I bent closer to bear better.

"Do you want Emma? We'll try to help. You may speak. You're fine."

Ethel's hand grasped at her throat now, indicating sharp pain. I continued to calm the possessing spirit's anguish.

"Emma is here. What do you want? We're your friends. The rope is no longer there, it has been removed. Put your tongue back in and speak. You have suffered, but your neck is fine again. Tell me, how did it happen?"

"They'll never know, they'll never know!"

"What will they never know? You can trust us. We have come to save you. You've been rescued. They've gone. You're safe. You're among friends."

Gradually, the voice became clearer, but still full of anxiety.

"Rope."

"No more rope. Did somebody try to hurt you? Tell me, who was it?"

"Leon."

"Who is Leon? Where would I find him?"

"I know—here—Emma."

"You're fine . . . it's only a memory . . . you're all right."

"Save me—from that—save me—"

"Tell me what has happened?"

"Poor Emma."

"Why poor Emma? Tell me about it."

"Don't call Emma, don't call Emma. I don't want to see Emma."

"All right, I'll send her away. Who is she to you?"

"Oh—I love her."

"Are you her husband? What is your name, sir? I am a stranger here. I have come to help you."

"What is the matter? Who calls on me?"

"I heard that you were suffering, and I felt I would try to help you. What can we do?"

"I—I am guilty. I am guilty. Go away. Let me say nothing."

"Guilty of what?"

"It all comes alive. Alive, alive! Oh—no."

"In telling me of your suffering, you will end it. You will free yourself of it."

"I thought it would be gone forever. Alackaday, alackaday, I cannot crush it like the weeds of the fields. It grows in my soul, and I cannot live anymore without the seed."

"What is it that you think you did that is so bad?"

"Oh—let it be, my own climate in which to live."

"But I'd like to free you from it. You want to be free."

"Oh, alack, alack, I cannot."

"Look, you cannot be free until you tell someone and purge yourself."

"But, Emma, Emma!"

"I will not tell her, if you wish me not to. You have passed over, and you have taken with you your memories."

"Over *where* have I gone?"

"You have gone."

"Where have I gone? I was here—how do you say so?"

"Yes, you are here, and you should not be. You have gone into the better side of life, where you will live forever. But you're taking with you—"

"With this, will this live forever?"

"No."

"Oh, I want Emma. She must never know—"

"There is only one way to do this. And you've got to do it the way I suggest."

"I will not go forever! I have lived, and I am living."

"Is this your house?"

"Go and seek Emma to stay away."

"All right. I will do that."

"She comes always to cry."

"Why is she crying?"

"Oh—I cannot stop her. Do not let me look on her."

"What have you done that you feel so ashamed of?"

"That is my own secret in my soul of souls. Must I look upon it forever?"

"In telling me, I will take it from you."

"Take me away from myself that I may die and be oblivious forever."

"Or be reborn into a free and happy world."

"Beyond the life lies the deep dark pool in which oblivion covers you forever. That is what I seek."

"But you are still alive..."

"I am going there, friend. They won't let us live in silence."

"You have passed over. You are now speaking to us through an instrument...."

"I am living always."

"In spirit—but not in body."

"In body, too. I am *in* a body."

"Not yours."

"Mine."

"No. Lent to you, temporarily, so you may speak to me. So we can help you."

"No one lends me anything. Not even a good name. The merciful God hates me..."

"Are these *your* hands? Touch them."

"My hands?"

"That's a watch you have on your hand—a woman's watch."

"A woman?"

"You are in the body of a woman, speaking to me, through one of the great miracles made possible for you."

"Body. My body."

"Not your body. Temporarily...."

"Mine! How can you say, when the rope is still here?"

"There's no rope. It is a memory—an unhappy memory."

"Hang."

"You're quite free now."

"I can't get free from this!"

"Because you don't wish to. If you wished, you could."

"I live! How can I get to that beyond?"

"If you leave your memories behind."

"The silence of the pool, of the blackness."

"I've helped you so far. Touch your left ear gently and I will prove it to you. You feel that there is an earring? Women wear earrings; men do not."

"Who did this to me?"

"Nobody did it to you. It isn't you."

"Makes talk so radical."

"There are things that you don't understand about yourself, and I am here to teach you. You are free to go if you wish."

"Free, free! May I go then—into the blackness where it is no longer memory?"

"Yes, I will send you there if you wish. But you've got to be calm and listen to me. It's no use being angry and desperate."

"Who shackles me so!"

"Nobody shackles you. This is a woman's body, and you are speaking through her voice."

"Woman!"

"A lady who has been kind enough to help you."

"Who does it to me—these outrageous things?"

"You have passed into another dimension, another world, from which you are now speaking to us, by means that you do not understand. We are here to help you, not to make you unhappy. Would you like me to help you out of here? It is up to you."

"Out of here?"

"Into a better world, if you wish."

"Better world? That is oblivion?"

"You've got to ask for it. It cannot be done without your approval."

"I ask for it. I ask for that. Give it to me, give it to me."

"Then do you obey the laws to lead you there? There are certain laws. You have to follow them."

"Take my Emma. Take her into the happy land."

"All right. But in order for you to go, there is something you must do. Are you listening to me?"

"I hear. I hear."

"You must leave behind your unhappy memories."

"I can't leave them. They are part of me."

"You will give them to me, and I will take them out."

"But Leon—he will not leave me in peace."

"Leon is dead. He cannot touch you."

"Dead?"

"He's gone."

"Like that? Gone?"

"Yes. Many years have passed."

"Dead?"

"Dead. You're safe. Free."

"She will not know."

"No."

"I can see light again, and happiness, forgetful that he is gone?"

"He's gone."

"Then it will not be divulged."

"You cannot be free from it until you divulge it to me—only to me, and to no one else."

"When I go into oblivion, I can give nothing to anyone. Let me live my life."

"Who is Leon? Who is he to you?"

"I must seal my lips. I must go my unhappy way."

"Then you will never be free."

"I must go into oblivion. You promised. You take away."

"I don't take away, but you promised to obey the law. The law is you must tell the story and then forget it."

"I tell it to my own soul. You are not God. And I have no obligation to anyone but my own God!"

I decided to find another approach. Evidently the discarnate spirit was a tough nut to crack.

"What year is this?"

There was only silence to the question.

"Who rules this country?"

"Thomas Jefferson."

"No, Jefferson is dead. This isn't Jefferson's day."

"Then I am dead."

"You are!"

"Let me go in peace. Good day!"

"You're dead, and yet you're alive. They all are alive, too, over there."

"Good day, my good friend. I cannot longer speak. We do not exist on the same plane."

"No, but we speak to each other through this lady. A hundred and seventy years have gone by, my friend, a hundred and seventy years. Do you understand? It is a hundred seventy years later. It's very difficult for you to understand this. You have been staying in this house for a long time for no reason, except to suffer. What happened to you, happened a long time ago. And it is all in the past. You are completely free. You needn't go into oblivion. You needn't go any place if you don't wish. You're a free person."

"Ahh—and Emma?"

"She's just as free as you are. You have nothing to fear."

"My hands are free. My mind is free. Let me go with my own."

"Not until you tell me who you are. This is part of our deal, remember? If you're a man of honor you must obey the law."

"Until I find myself a man of honor—"

"You are."

"If there is a heaven above, if there is a golden light, and I am alive—these hundred and seventy years—man, are you mad? You do not speak the truth. I cannot trust you."

"It is the truth. You'll find out for yourself."

"Let me go. I have been always free."

"Very well then, tell the one who has brought you what you want to be kept a secret, that he may take you away from here."

"Emma—where is she?"

"She's over there waiting for you. They're all over there. Leon is over there, too."

"God, no! Then I can't go! He will talk!"

"Then why don't you tell *me*? I can arrange it."

"No, you cannot. If I go into my grave with the secret, and my soul—"

"*You are in your grave.* You've been *through* the grave. You're out of it now. The secret is *known.*"

"Then it is on my soul and it remains there."

"You can't be free with it. You must get rid of it."

"I have been told by those who have spoken to me from pulpits that if I take my great burden to Him beyond, I will never—"

"You will not succeed unless you wish to."

Again, I changed my approach, since the personality seemed unyielding.

"Is your name Lewis?"

"I will take that with me, too. I have pride, have soul, and a sense of being, and it is coming back to me. I thank you friend, for opening the ropes that bound me. I am free. I feel it."

"Then go. Go in peace."

"Emma—I can look on you now."

"Albert, help him across."

"I can go with you now, Emma. I give you thanks, my friend. But I still maintain my freedom of soul."

"Albert, take him. Albert, please."

Immediately, Albert's crisp voice returned. "Yes, yes."

"Have you learned anything further?"

"I think he's right, my good friend. Confessions are not the best fate, and this is true."

"How did he die, and why?"

"He did it himself."

"It was suicide?"

"Yes it was."

"Why?"

"To keep from revealing the truth."

"What was so terrible about the truth?"

"That is his secret."

"What period was this?"

"It was the turn of the century I believe."

"Did he do anything wrong?"

"He has a guilt complex, that is quite certain."

"Did he tie his own arms and hang himself?"

"He put a rope around his neck—he put a rope around his hands in back of himself . . ."

"Who is this Leon he keeps yelling about?"

"An individual, I believe, he harmed. I would say that it was a ghost that taunted him."

"You mean the man died before him?"

"That is right."

"And Emma?"

"Emma saw the swaying body."

"Emma was his wife."

"That is right. There were three offspring."

"Is the girl one of them—the teen-age girl that the instrument saw?"

"I believe the granddaughter."

"Are any of them still here?"

"I do not see them. Emma is also listening, has gone with him."

"Is anything buried in the garden?"

"Leon."

"Did he kill Leon?"

"I would say so."

"Oh, he killed him? For some reason?"

"Yes."

"You haven't got any idea what this is?"

"That would not divulge what had happened in their youth."

"What was this man's background?"

"I think he was a man of considerable wealth."

"He built this house?"

"That is right. Earlier. It could have belonged to Leon; that is, the property."

"Was he in any official position or just a businessman?"

"Man of fortune; let's put it this way. A gentleman."

"He's a bit insane, isn't he?"

"Well—when one lives for a hundred and seventy years with a memory of guilt, plus your throat being crushed by rope and your arms torn by the ropes that are on the hands..."

"Yes, it must be uncomfortable. Well, be sure the instrument is protected, and I suggest we bring her back."

"I will release the instrument."

"Thank you for coming."

A moment later, Ethel was back as "herself," remembering *nothing* of the previous hour. I handed her the ring that had so mysteriously appeared in the house and asked her to psychometrize it.

"I would say that this belongs to an older woman. It would be mother to the younger woman."

"Do you get any additional information about this?"

"I would say an E. She's the mother of a younger woman, also with an E."

"That younger woman—what about her? How does she fit in?"

"The younger woman I think is the one I hear screaming. I feel this woman may be sometimes even seen. I want to rock, I want to rock. She says nothing, or does nothing but just rock. The younger woman, the thin woman, they seem concerned about each other."

* * *

I turned to Mrs. Dickey to check out some of the material. "Mrs. Dickey, to refresh my memory, who built the house?"

"This structure was built in 1865 by Homer Leroy Salisbury."

"But before that?"

"The records for those years are destroyed; the books are not in existence. But the basement foundation is very much older. Revolutionary, perhaps. There are windows down there, and doorways. It may have been originally the first place that people lived in."

"Is there any record of the owner of the land before the turn of the eighteenth century?"

"Not that I know of."

"Have you ever seen a person in the area in which Mrs. Meyers felt the main disturbance?"

"I have not, but a friend has."

"Who was the friend?"

"Pat Hughes."

"What did she see or feel *in that area?*"

"She heard noises and footsteps, and saw a woman walking into this room, right by this wall. Walked right in and stood in the room."

"What did the woman look like?"

"She had dark hair, fairly young, tall and slender, with a red robe or long red dress on, and she had her hand *up at her throat.*"

"What about the man Mrs. Meyers described?"

"Adam comes here, and we think he's harmful. He frightens us. Since I've seen you last, we've had something happen that we never had before. Joyce and Patty and I walked in here. It was a quiet day and we sat down on these two couches. It was evening. We were just talking quietly and had our minds on Joyce's forthcoming wedding when we heard the most enormous noise—just like the whole house was crashing down. This wall over here almost vibrated. We all jumped up and we couldn't figure it out."

"There was nothing to cause it?"

"No. Again, during the night, a shattering noise woke up everybody."

Mrs. Jean Vanderhoff, who had formerly owned the house, was among those present. Long after she had left this house, she found herself working a Ouija board. To her surprise, a personality contacted her through the board —and not too gently, either.

"He said he had been hunting for me," Mrs. Vanderboff began.

"Now this is a character that came through your Ouija board?"

"That came through the Ouija board."

"Long after you moved out of here."

"Yes, several months ago; this year. He said he had been hunting for me for a long time because *I had to take him back*—to bring him back to this house—and that I was the only one that could do it."

"What was his name?"

"Nat. And he said he was the master's servant, and that he and his daughter were buried out behind the barn. I asked him various and sundry questions, but mainly he wanted to come back because his daughter was still here, and I said, 'Well, why are you causing these people all of this trouble? You never caused *us* any.' He replied, 'Well, you have never lain at the top and tasted the unhappiness.' I said, 'Are you telling me your room was in the tower?' He said, 'Yes,' and he had to get back, because his daughter *was still here.* I said, 'I wouldn't consider taking you back as long as you misbehave.' He replied, 'I will misbehave because *I will drive them out.*"

"While you were living here, did you have any experiences?"

"Only when we remodeled. We put in this bay window across here."

"What happened when you remodeled?"

"At night there were the most tremendous noises, and it sounded as though they were throwing the furniture around, and every morning at 2 o'clock the garage doors banged up and down. We had a friend sleeping in the back room, and one morning I said, 'What were you doing with a girl in your room?' And he said, 'I had no girl in my room.'"

"Do you remember who it was who slept in that room—this friend?"

"Colonel Powell."

"Did he know about anything unusual about the house beforehand?"

"No, he said he had no one in his room. Then the next night he heard all this racket out there and rushed out to catch whatever it was, and the table had been moved in the kitchen. He fell over this table and hurt his leg."

"Interestingly," commented Mrs. Dickey now, "we got a communicator named Emma, that came through on the board."

"When? This is important."

"Since you were here the last time. We never had Emma before, but we don't play with the board much anymore because you said, leave it alone."

"When was the first time the name Emma came to you?"

"After your first visit. But we got no messages, we just kept getting this name."

"Prior to our visit today, has anybody discussed with you the name Emma?"

"No."

"Therefore, the Emma you got on the Ouija board is separate from what we got here today."

"There was a moment of silence, then Mrs. Dickey resumed talking about the past of the house.

"Indians were around here a long time ago as this was part of the Indian trail. Also, the foundations of the older house are underneath the fireplace."

"I see a door, where the man was," Ethel said and scowled. "He was standing about here, when I first saw him, and he went through right about there. I think *there were two rooms here.*"

"Is this correct?" I asked Mrs. Dickey.

"Correct," she replied. "It was divided."

Ethel suddenly seemed to be listening to something or someone. "I don't think you'll get this disturbance, but I keep hearing a sound like moaning, high moaning—ooh—ooh."

With Ethel leading us, we ascended the narrow stairs to the top room.

"What do you think of this room?" I asked the medium.

"I get a different person up here altogether. Male. High forehead, hair parted, longish face, fairly good-sized nose. Looks like an Irishman. Seems to have a beard on, and then takes it off."

"Is he connected with the other situation?"

"No, he's dressed differently, I get the name Pat. I think he went out with a heart condition."

Ethel stopped at the desk in the corner.

"Somebody sat here and wrote."

"Is a writer connected with this house?" I asked Mrs. Dickey.

"I think you're talking about Salisbury, the man who built this house. He was tall, and lean, and very erudite. He wrote a diary of his Civil War experiences."

"The noise that came when you changed things about the house, I think came from the Irishman, Pat."

* * *

It was getting late in the day and I wanted to get Ethel Meyers home in time for dinner, so we said good-by and just caught the New York flight. Once in the air, I had a chance to think over some of the things that had happened this eventful afternoon. For one thing, a whole array of characters from the past had been identified, more or less, by my medium. Most outstanding, in an evidential sense, was the fact that the name Emma had been received by those in the house prior to Ethel's coming and the trance session with her in which the name Emma was disclosed. Despite my misgivings about the use of the Ouija board, I have always held that on occasion true psychic material can come in this manner. Later, I was to learn that Lucy Dickey was indeed a budding medium, and that it was her presence in the house that made the Ouija board work. It is possible that the young people living with her might have added some psychic power to it, but the essential catalyst was Mrs. Dickey herself.

It is not remarkable but rather pleasing in a scientific way that Ethel Meyers pinpointed immediately upon arrival the area of the main disturbances. The staircase and the door leading to an area that had been rearranged structurally was indeed where the figure of the man had appeared and where most of the noises had originated. We had inspected the premises from the cellar to the top, especially around the area of the chimney, which roughly took up the center of the house. There had been no rational explanation for any loud noises in the area. Nothing was loose, nothing could have caused a loud noise, rattling, movement of objects, or anything of the kind, so eloquently and distinctively described by several witnesses.

* * *

The following day, Mrs. Dickey wrote me a note thanking us for coming out. She promised to look into the background of the house somewhat more thoroughly at the Library of Congress.

"I believe I have exhausted the usefulness of the Fairfax County Courthouse records. If I can help you in any way, let me know. I will be happy to pick you up and chauffeur you if Nicole is busy. I believe fully in your work, and I like your approach. You leave behind a string of grateful admirers. Your friend, Lucy."

I thanked Lucy Dickey and instructed her to be alert to any further manifestations, should they occur. With so large a cast of spectral characters in the house, it was just possible that we had not dislodged all of them. As a matter of fact it was highly likely that we might have overlooked one or the other.

When I returned from Europe I received another letter from her, dated September 25, 1969. Mrs. Dickey wrote: "I have noticed in the past few months a growing sensitivity and psychic development in myself. Things are happening to me I do not quite understand. Nothing further has happened with our 'friends' in the house. No news from them at all. The house remains for sale."

Mrs. Dickey had previously mentioned her intent to sell the house.

But we had not heard the last of ghostly Adam. On December 9, 1969, I had an urgent report from Lucy Dickey. There had been a party at the house for young college-age friends of her daughter. One of the young men had gone upstairs to one of the bathrooms. As he was going about his business he turned to find a man staring at him from behind. Terrified, he rushed downstairs. He had, of course, never been told about the ghost or any details of the specter's appearance. Nevertheless, he described Adam in every detail, from the white, full-sleeved shirt and black baggy knicker-type pants on to the expression in his eyes. But despite this frightening encounter, there was nothing further to disturb Lucy's peace in the house: no more uncanny noises, no spectral appearances. Only one thing— she had difficulty selling the house. The more she tried, the less it worked. It was almost as if someone, unseen perhaps, prevented the house from being sold—perhaps because they had come to like Lucy and considered her a

channel of expression. To make things worse, her husband was still in part of the house despite the fact that they had obtained a divorce. Lucy was extremely unhappy about the situation, and desired nothing more than to sell the house, although she loved every inch of it.

Time went on, and finally a buyer for the house showed up. Overjoyed, Lucy Dickey advised me of the fact that ownership was soon to pass into other hands. She had already taken an apartment in Washington and was ready to move. Naturally, she had told the new owner, a Mrs. Mary Jane Lightner, all about the ghosts in the house and what the Dickeys and their predecessors had gone through with them. Mrs. Lightner was not a believer in such things as ghostly phenomena, but her curiosity was aroused since, after all, this was now going to be her home. Together the two ladies asked me to send them a good psychic to see whether there was indeed anything left in the house or whether perhaps all was quiet.

I advised them that a medium might very well relive past impressions without this proving the continued presence of a ghost or ghosts. It is sometimes very difficult to distinguish between an imprint from the past and actual living spirit entities.

I sent them John Reeves, a teacher turned medium, with whom I have lately been much impressed. On May 10, 1970, John Reeves went to Washington and saw the two ladies at the house in Vienna. He knew nothing whatsoever about the circumstances or about the ladies, merely that he was to look at an old house and give his impressions.

Immediately upon entering the downstairs of the house, he went to the fireplace and disclosed that there had been a murder and much violence in that area. He then described a woman, thin, with straight hair in back, wearing a long dark gray dress. He felt this was in the 1860s, and that the woman was not the only spirit on the premises. "A man killed his wife's lover in this passageway," John Reeves intoned, "and then he hanged himself." While the two ladies shuddered, the medium continued describing what he felt had happened in the house. "I can see blood drop from his mouth, on both sides of his mouth."

"How was the man killed?" Lucy wanted to know.

John Reeves pointed at a heavy set of black andirons. "One of these andirons was used to kill," he explained. "Somehow these events put a curse on this house. There may also be another separate murder in one of the rooms," he added cheerfully.

Mrs. Lightner had heard quite enough. "Mrs. Dickey must have told you," she said to the medium. It seemed impossible for John Reeves to come up with practically the same story Ethel Johnson Meyers had come up with a year ago, without some sort of collusion, she thought. Lucy Dickey assured her that there was no such thing. John Reeves knew nothing of either the house or Mrs. Meyers' and my work in the house. While the ladies shook their heads, Reeves left and went back to New York.

* * *

Were Adam and Lewis one and the same person? We know that Leon was the name of the other man, whose bones presumably still rot in the garden behind the barn. The woman's name was Emma. Adam—or Lewis, whichever he was—no longer can claim that his secret is all his. Thanks to John Reeves, and of course Ethel Meyers, we know that his problem was one of the oldest problems in the world. *Cherchez la femme*. A debt of honor had apparently been paid and all was now quiet at Windover down in Vienna, Virginia.

* * *

A short time ago I wanted to visit the White House and make one more attempt to get into the Lincoln Bed-room. There was some indication that I might get permission, and I called upon Lucy Dickey to come along and serve as my medium for the occasion since she already lived in Washington.

"Me? A medium?" she replied, taken aback. "Why, I never thought of myself in that manner!"

I sensed a disturbed feeling in the way she put it. Had I frightened her? Patiently I explained that her psychic experiences at Windover made it plain that she had mediumistic abilities. She didn't have to be a professional medium to be classified as psychic.

She breathed easier after that, but I couldn't get her to go with me into the Lincoln Bedroom. Even if I had gotten permission, I am sure Lucy Dickey would have avoided meeting Mr. Lincoln. And who is to blame her? After all, she has had quite enough with Adam, Leo, Emma, Martha, and Morgan.

✳ 109

The "Presence" on the Second-Floor Landing

SOMEWHERE BETWEEN WASHINGTON and Baltimore is a small community called Sykesville. It is a little bit closer to Baltimore than in it is to Washington, and most of the people who live there work in Baltimore. Some don't work at all. It is not what you might call a poor community but, to the contrary, is one of the last remaining strongholds of the rural hunting set whose main occupation and pride were their farms and minor houses.

Howard Lodge was built there in 1774 by Edward Dorsey. Tradition has it that it was named Howard Lodge when Governor Howard of Maryland stayed in it during the period in which the United States became independent. Tax records seem to indicate that it was owned at one time by relatives of Francis Scott Key, the author of our national anthem. Key himself visited Howard Lodge and carved his name in one of the upstairs window sills, but unfortunately, the windows were later destroyed by storms.

The house consists of two stories and is made of brick imported from England. The attic and roof beams were made by hand from chestnut wood and are held fast by pegs driven their full length. Today's owners, Mr. and Mrs. Roy Emery, have made some changes, especially in the attic. At one time the attic was two stories high, but it has been divided into storage rooms above the beams and finished rooms below. At the turn of this century dormer windows were installed by a previous owner, a Mrs. Mottu of Baltimore. The oldest part of the house is the thick-walled stone kitchen downstairs. On the ample grounds there is an old smokehouse and a spring house, both dating from the original period when the house was built. Surrounded by tall trees, the estate is truly European in flavor, and one can very well imagine how previous owners must have felt sitting on their lawn looking out into the rolling hills of Maryland and dreaming of past glory.

The house has been furnished in exquisite taste by its present owners, the Emerys. Mr. Emery is an attorney in Baltimore, and his wife, a descendant of very old French nobility, saw service as a nurse in the late unlamented French-Indochina campaign. The furnishings include period pieces assembled with an eye towards fitting them into the general tone of the house, and French heirlooms brought into the house by Mrs. Emery. There isn't a piece out of key at Howard Lodge, and the house may well serve as an example to others who would live in eighteenth-century manor houses.

In 1967 I appeared on Baltimore television. Shortly after my appearance I received a letter from Mrs. Emery, in which she asked me to have a look at Howard Lodge and its resident ghosts. It would appear that she had several, and that while they were not malicious or mischievous, they nevertheless bore investigation if only to find out who they were and what they wanted.

* * *

Long before Mrs. Emery had heard of me, she had invited two men, who were aware of the existence of ghosts, to come to the house. They were not private investigators or apprentice ghost-hunters, to be sure—simply two gentlemen interested in the supernatural. Barry and Glenn Hammond of Washington, D.C., coming to the house as friends, reported seeing a gentleman outside looking towards the house. The gentleman in question was not of this world, they hastily explained. They knew all about such personalities since they were accustomed to distinguishing between the flesh-and-blood and the ethereal kind. The Emerys had other guests at the time, so the two gentlemen from Washington were not as much at liberty to speak of the resident ghosts as if they had come alone. While they were wandering about the house in search of other phantoms, Mrs. Emery busied herself with her guests. On leaving, however, the Hammonds happily informed Mrs. Emery that Howard Lodge had not just two ghosts—as the Emerys had surmised—but a total of five. They left it at that and went back to Connecticut Avenue.

Jacqueline Emery was not particularly overtaken with worry. She was born Countess de Beauregard, and as with many old aristocratic families, there had been a family specter and she was quite familiar with it while growing up. The specter, known as the White Lady, apparently can be seen only by members of the de Montrichard family, who happened to be related to Mrs. Emery. No one knows who the White Lady is, but she appears regularly when a member of the family is about to die, very much as an Irish banshee announces the coming of death. There may be a relationship there since so many old French families are also of Celtic origin.

* * *

In 1969 my wife and I met Mrs. Emery's uncle, the Baron Jean Bergier de Beauregard, who lives with his family it Chateau de Villelouet in the heartland of France. The Baron readily confirmed that many members of the Beauregard family have indeed shown the ability of second sight, and that psychic occurrences were not particularly upsetting to any of them. They took it in their stride.

Jacqueline Emery has inherited this particular talent also. She frequently knows what is in the mail or what phone calls are about to be made to her, and she is aware of the future in many small ways, but she takes it as part of her character. Nevertheless, it indicates in all the Beauregards a natural vein of psychic ability, and it is that psychic ability that made the appearances at Howard Lodge possible, in my view.

* * *

Jacqueline Emery herself has more than a casual acquaintance with ESP. When I asked her to recall any incidents of a psychic nature prior to coming to Howard Lodge, she thought for a while and then reported a startling incident that occurred to her in December of 1944, when she was living in Germany.

* * *

For some reason I had gone to a village near Munich with a woman who wanted to buy eggs and chicken and also pick up some apples in the basement of a home she owned and had rented to a family from either Düsseldorf or Köln. I believe its name was Kaiserbrunn. A Mrs. Schwarz was renting.

Mrs. Kolb, with whom I had come, wanted me to go to the village with her, but for some reason I excused myself and went in quest of Mrs. Schwarz. She was in the dining room, busily writing letters. For some unknown reason I asked her what she was writing. It was odd because, at twenty, I was very shy. She then told me that she was sending farewell letters to her husband and children. She had, I noticed then, in front of her, some pills, which she said were poison. Upon my asking her she unfolded the following story:

She feared that her husband, a university professor, had been killed and their home demolished in a recent bombing of either of the cities I mentioned above. One of her sons was on the French front and hadn't been heard of for quite a period of time. Two other sons were on the Russian front, and she had no news from them either.

Perhaps worst of all, her daughter Lütte Paschedag, her two small children and their nurse, Schwester Margarethe, had supposedly left Potsdam several days before to come and stay with her and had not been heard from. News had been on the radio of several trains from the direction of Berlin being attacked and many deaths having ensued.

For some unexplained reason, I took her in my arms (I'd never seen her before) and promised her that her daughter, the nurse and the children were very close to Kaiserbrunn, that Hänsel, the one on the French front would be home within a week and stay for Christmas, that Professor Schwarz would call her up during the week, that their home had only been partly damaged, and that the two other sons and the son-in-law would write. One, Wolfgang, would be home for Christmas; the other was a doctor and I didn't think he could be spared for the holiday. Upon hearing me out, she fainted. She came to and together we burned the pills and letters. There was a knock at the door, it was Lütte, the two children and the nurse. Hänsel came the following week, Wolfgang was home for Christmas. Professor Schwarz called up two days after my visit, and the doctor wrote before Christmas. She was kind enough to send Hänsel to Munich to tell me and invite me to be with them for Christmas, which I did.

* * *

On June 11, 1969, I finally managed to come out to Howard Lodge. Roy Emery picked me up in Baltimore and drove me to his house. Present were not only his wife but their two daughters, both college students. Ariane the elder, is an avid reader of mine and wants to devote herself to psychic studies if all goes well. Proudly, Jacqueline Emery showed me about the house and around the grounds while there was still enough light to see everything. While we were walking I learned further details about Howard Lodge. For one thing, it appeared that Jerome Bonaparte had actually been to the house while he was courting Mrs. Patterson, whom he later married. Not three miles away from Howard Lodge was the estate of the Pattersons, where Napoleon's brother lived out his life in peace and harmony. All around us was plantation country, and what little was left of the old plantations could still be seen in the area.

"We now have only two hundred acres," Mrs. Emery explained, "but when we bought the property it was part of five hundred acres, and a hundred years ago it was about seven or eight hundred acres. I imagine that in the beginning it must have been about two thousand acres. That's what the plantations around here were like."

Before I went into the matter of the hauntings properly, I wanted to learn as much as possible about the house itself, its background, its structure, and since Mrs. Emery already knew these facts I saw no reason not to discuss them.

* * *

"Was this the plantation house, actually?" I asked.

"It must have been, yes. And it is a rather formal house, which is typical of the English houses, with the hall going all the way through the house, and two rooms deep on either side. The kitchen must have been an addition later, even though it is old."

"There are four rooms downstairs?"

"There are more than that, but it is two rooms deep on either side of the hall. You see, here you have the living room and the music room, my husband's library, and the dining room. The dining room has been extended going east-west because the hall doesn't go all the way through to the door; the partition has been removed."

"And upstairs?"

"Upstairs, there are six bedrooms, and then the attic, which I will show you, was a two-story one. Now we've made it a third floor, with still a large attic on top."

"So it's actually a three-level house?"

"Well, we have the basement, we have this floor, the second floor, the third floor, and the attic; that's five stories."

"How long ago did you come here?"

"It will be ten years in December. We moved in here in 1959. The house had been lived in by hillbillies, and horribly mistreated. The kitchen, through which you came in, had pigs, with litters. This room was used—the various corners were used instead of bathrooms. It had a couch that was full of rats. The rats were so used to people that they didn't move when you came in. It was full of flies and fleas and rats and mice and smells, and chewing gum on the floors. And Roy and I spent about a month, on our knees, on this very floor, trying to remove all of this. All the walls were covered with six to seven layers of wallpaper, which were removed, and then I painted. Of course the hard part was removing the paper. Each time there had been a draft in the room, due to some hole in the masonry

or something, they had put on another layer of wallpaper, thus cutting off, or hiding, the problem, rather than doing anything about it. And so forth!"

"Were they squatters or had they bought it?"

"They had bought it because they had had a farm on what is now Friendship Airport. Needless to tell you, it was a very nice thing to have. They bought this house from a man who worked in a bank in Washington. They bought it cash."

"But they didn't know how to live."

"Oh, no! See, they used a house as you would squeeze a lemon; after there was nothing left, they left and abandoned the house—went to another one. The time had come for them to leave; they had been here seven years, and it was going to pot. The plumbing was completely shot. The heating system was so dangerous that the electrician said, 'You really must believe in God'; and everything about like that."

"And you took it over then and restored it?"

"Yes, and everybody told us we were absolutely crazy. We spent the first month, five of us, in one room. I had disinfected that room, working in it for a month."

"You have three children?"

"Yes. And Chris was only two. And—well, we are *still* working on it."

I decided to come to the point.

"When was the first time you noticed anything *unusual* anywhere?"

"It was when I became less busy with doing things in the house. You know, when you are terribly busy you don't have time to realize what's going on. Three years ago I became aware of *a man on the landing*. I know it is a man, though I have never *seen* him. I'm absolutely convinced that he's a man in either his late forties or early fifties, and in addition, he's from the eighteenth century *because in my mind's eye I can see him*."

"Was there anything for the first seven years of your occupancy here?"

"I cannot recall. Except possibly some vague sensation about steps going from the second to the third floor."

"Noises?"

"Oh yes, you always have the feeling somebody's going up the steps. Always. We've always taken it for granted it was because it was an old house, but since we have rugs I still hear steps."

"Now, what were the circumstances when you felt the man on the stairs? On the landing, I mean."

"Well, I was going to my room, on the second floor, and you have to go through the landing. This is the only way to go to that room. And then suddenly I had to stop, *because he was there*."

"Did you feel cold?"

"No, I just felt he had to move and he wasn't going to move, and eventually he did, but he wasn't aware of me as fast as I was of him."

"What time of day was that?"

"Evening. It's always dusk, for some reason. You see, the landing has a southern exposure, which may have something to do with it, and it's always very sunny during the day."

"After this first experience, did you have more?"

"Oh yes, often. For quite a while he was constantly there."

"Always on that spot?"

"Always on the landing. You see, the landing has a very good vantage point, because *nobody* can go upstairs or downstairs without going through it."

"Then would you say somebody might watch from that spot?"

"You can *see everything*—originally the lane was not what you came through, but at the front of the house. From the landing you have a perfect command of the entire lane."

"After this first experience three years ago did you ever see him, other than the way you describe?"

"No. Although I have to be very careful when I say that because after a while, as you well know, it is difficult to separate something you see in your mind from something you see physically. Because I feel that I could touch him if I tried, but I never have. Even though I'm not afraid of him, I still don't feel like it."

"Did you ever walk up the stairs and run into *something*?"

"A wall. Sometimes I feel that there is a partition or something there."

"Something that you have to displace?"

"Yes. But then I wait until it displaces itself, or I move around it. But somehow I know where it is because I can move around it."

"Have you ever seen anything?"

"Often. On the landing."

"What does it look like?"

"Fog. And I always think it's my eyes."

"How tall is it?"

"Frankly I have never thought about it, because I will blink a few times. I've always thought it was *me*. You see, it's very foggy here, outside. But then I saw it in several rooms."

"Did you ever smell anything peculiar...."

"Yes, I often do. There are some smells in this house and they often take me back to something, but don't know what."

"Do you ever hear sounds that sound like a high-pitched voice, or a bird?"

"Bird, yes. Very often."

"Where do you hear that? What part of the house?"

"Never on this floor. Upstairs."

"Have there been any structural changes in the house?"

"I think the landing."

"Only the landing? How was it affected?"

"We changed one partition, for it was much too illogically altered to have been something that existed when the house was built. The way we found it, it couldn't have been that way because it was ridiculous. Anybody with a hoop skirt, for instance, or a wide dress, could never have managed the top of the steps onto the landing with the partition the way it was there. We changed it, and I will show you because the seam is in the floor. We were told that the landing *had* been changed, and for some reason everything is around that landing."

"You mean changed back to what it was originally, or changed?"

"We don't know, because we don't know how it was."

"Did you widen it or narrow it?"

"We widened it."

"Now, since living in this house have you ever had odd dreams? Have you felt as if a person were trying to communicate with you?"

"Yes. Often."

"Will you talk about that?"

"Only that I'm rather ashamed, that I usually try to block it out."

"Well, do you ever get any feeling of the communicators?"

"Because I'm negative I don't think there is any actual communication, but I've often been *aware of someone even coming in the room where I am.*"

"How does this manifest itself?"

"I'm aware of a shadow. With my eyes open."

"This is on the second floor?"

"Yes."

"At night?"

"Yes. And then, that night while I slept on the third floor—I'm sure it's my man on the landing. He came up, and why I got scared I don't know because this man is awfully nice, and there is nothing...."

"What do you mean, he came up?"

"I heard him come up the stairs, and he came and watched me."

"Why did you sleep on the third floor that night?"

"Because Roy had turned on the air conditioner. I cannot sleep with an air conditioner."

"So you took one of the guest rooms. Does this room have any particular connection with the landing?"

"You have to go through the landing because of the steps going up and going down. Both end up on the second-floor landing."

"And he came up the stairs, and you felt him standing by your bed?"

"Yes. Watching—probably wondering what I was doing there. But originally this was not a floor used for bedrooms. We did that."

"What was it used for?"

"It was a two-story attic, and we divided it in two by putting in a ceiling, and I don't believe it could have been used except possibly, for servants."

"When was the last time you had a sense of this being?"

"In the fall."

"Is there any particular time when it's stronger?"

"Yes, in the summer."

"Any particular time of day?"

"Dusk."

"Is it always the same person?"

"Well, I always thought it was, but I never gave it too much thought."

"Is there more than one?"

"Yes."

"When did you notice the second 'presence'?"

"It was about two years ago, when Chris, my boy, was moved up to the third floor, that I heard *breathing*. It was in the master bedroom. I can show you exactly where because the breathing came from the right side of the bed, below, as if a child would have slept in a trundle bed or in a low cradle or something, and that breathing came from below me. The bed is fairly high."

"On the second floor?"

"Yes. And it was very definitely a child, and I can explain that very readily—there is not a mother in the world who will not recognize the breathing of a child, when it's sick and has a fever."

"Did your husband hear this?"

"No. He never hears anything of this."

"But was he present?"

"No. He was in his library, downstairs."

"Was this late at night?"

"No—I go to bed much earlier than Roy. It must have been around eleven, or maybe midnight."

"The first time you heard this, did you wonder what it was?"

"Well, I knew what it was, or what it had to be, since I couldn't possibly hear my children breathe from where I was. I was aware that it must be something which had occurred in that very room before."

"Did you ever hear any other noise?"

"Yes. That child cries, and there is pain."

"How often have you heard it?"

"The breathing more often than the crying. The crying only a couple of times."

"In the same spot?"

"Yes."

"Is there a woman around? Do you have a feeling of a woman when that happens?"

"Yes, and she would be on my side of the bed. And this is the part that bothers me!"

"What do you mean?"

"Because I have the feeling her bed was where mine is. I'm sure she slept on the right, because the child is on the right."

"The furniture in the bedroom is yours—you brought this in yourself?"

"Oh yes, there wasn't anything that belonged to this house."

I thought all this over for a moment, then decided to continue questioning my psychic hostess.

"Was there anything else, other than what we have just discussed?"

"Yes, the portrait of my ancestor that I brought back from France. I was born in 1923, and she was born in 1787."

"And what was her name?"

"I don't remember her maiden name, but she was an Alcazar. She married a Spaniard."

"What is special about the portrait?"

"Of course, the eyes—you will find those eyes in any well-painted portrait—they are eyes that follow you everywhere. But I wouldn't refer to that because this is very common in any museum or in any home where they have family portraits. This is not so much that, but the moods she goes through. She definitely changes her expression. When she disapproves of someone she shows it. And every once in a while, if you glance at her rapidly, she is not the woman you now see in the portrait, but somebody else."

"Does anyone other than you see this?"

"Yes, two other people—my English friend of whom I talked of before, and another English friend who is married to an American friend. They both saw it."

"Have you ever felt anything outside the house, in the grounds?"

"You think there is a branch that's going to hit your face, and yet there is no branch. I thought that people always felt like that when they walked outside, but they *don't*. Also I can't walk straight in the dark."

"What do you mean?"

"I don't know! I could walk on a straight line, painted line, on the roof without the slightest difficulty, but in the dark I never walk straight."

"You have two dogs. Have they ever behaved strangely?"

"All the time. They bark when there is absolutely nothing there." Mrs. Emery interrupted my thoughtful pause.

* * *

"There is also something about a room on this floor, Mr. Holzer."

"The one we're sitting in?"

"No—the next one, where the piano is. Every night before I go to bed I have to have a glass of orange juice. And sometimes I'll *race* downstairs—I'll feel there is somebody in that rocking chair and I'm afraid to go and check."

"Do you have a feeling of a presence in that room?"

"Yes—oh yes, yes, very strong. Almost every day, I'd say."

"It's that *room*, and the landing, then?"

"Yes."

* * *

At this point I had to change tapes. I thought again about all I had heard and tried to make the various elements fall into place. It didn't seem to add up as yet—at least not in the same time layer.

"To your knowledge," I asked Mrs. Emery, "has anything tragic ever happened here in the house?"

"We don't know. This is the thing that is so disappointing in this country, that so few records are kept. In France you have records for six hundred years. But here, past fifty years people wonder why you want to know."

"Is there any legend, rumor, or tradition attached to the house?"

"There are several legends. They also say that Governor Howard, who gave his name to Howard County, which until 1860 was part of Anne Arundel County, lived in this house. But it's extraordinary, at least to me it is, coming from France, that people cannot be sure of facts which are so recent, really."

"What about the people who lived here before? Have you ever met anybody who lived here before?"

"Yes. I met a man named Talbot Shipley, who is seventy-eight and was born here."

"Did he own the house at one time?"

"His parents did, and—he was the kind, you know, who went, 'Oh! where you have that couch, this is where Aunt Martha was laid out'; and, 'Oh, over there, this is where my mother was when she became an invalid, and this was made into a bedroom and then she died in there'; and, 'Oh, Lynn, you sleep in that room? Well, this is where I was born!' And that's the kind of story we got, but he's a farmer, and he would perhaps not have quite the same conception of a house as we do. To him, a house is where people are born and die. And perhaps to me a house is where people live."

"What about servants? Did you ever have a gardener or anyone working for you?"

"Oh, I have people work for me once in a while. I have discarded all of them because everything is below their dignity and nothing is below mine, so it's much easier to do things myself!"

"Did they ever complain about anything?"

"I had a woman once who said she wouldn't go to the third floor. There is something else," Mrs. Emery said.

"There are two niches on either side of where there must have been a triangular porch, which would go with the style of the house. They seem to be *sealed*. The man who is remodeling the smokehouse into my future antique shop, is dying to open them up and see what's inside them, because really they *don't make any sense*."

"Do you have any particular feelings about the two niches?"

"They are on each side of my desk on the landing, but on the outside. As a matter of fact, I never thought of that! It's towards the ceiling of the landing but on the outside."

"What could possibly be in them?"

"I don't know. We thought perhaps the records of the house."

"Not a treasure?"

"They say that during the Civil War people buried things, and also during the Revolution, so there could be treasures. Somebody found a coin—1743—on the lane."

"An English coin?"

"Yes."

"Who found it?"

"A young girl who came to see us. So we let her keep it. And a window sill was replaced in the dining room, and quite a few artifacts were found in that window sill. Buttons and coins."

* * *

After dinner I went with Mrs. Emery through the house from top to bottom, photographing as I went along. None of the pictures show anything unusual, even in the area of the landing upstairs—but that, of course, does not prove that there is not a presence there lurking for the right moment to be recognized. Only on rare occasions do manifestations of this kind show up on photographic film or paper. It would have taken a great deal more time and patience to come up with positive results.

I talked to the two girls, Ariane and Lynn, now in their early twenties, and to Chris, the little boy, but none of the children had had any unusual experiences as far as the specter on the landing was concerned, nor were they frightened by the prospect of having a ghost or two in the house. It was all part of living in the country. I took a good look at the portrait of the maternal ancestor, and could find only that it was a very good portrait indeed. Perhaps she didn't disapprove of me, or at any rate didn't show it if she did.

But when I stood on the landing, on the spot where most of the manifestations had taken place, I felt rather strange. Granted that I knew where I was and what had occurred in the spot I was standing. Granted also that suggestion works even with professional psychic investigators. There was still a residue of the unexplained. I can't quite put into words what I felt, but it reminded me, in retrospect, of the uneasy feeling I sometimes had when an airplane took a quick and unexpected dive. It is as if your stomach isn't quite where it ought to be. The feeling was passing, but somehow I knew that the spot I had stepped into was not like the rest of the house. I looked around very carefully. Nothing indicated anything special about this landing. The ceiling at this point was not very high, since the available room had been cut in two when the floor was created. But there was a sense of coziness in the area, almost creating an impression of a safe retreat for someone. Could it be then, I reasoned afterwards, that the spectral gentleman had found himself his own niche, his own retreat, and that he very much liked it? Could it not be that he was pleased with the arrangement; that perhaps when the Emerys created an extra floor out of part of the old attic, they had unconsciously carried out the designs of those who had lived in the house before them? Usually hauntings are due to some structural change which does not meet with the approval of those who had lived before in the house. Here we might have the reverse: a later owner doing the bidding of someone who did not have the time or inclination to carry out similar plans. For it must be recalled that a good house is never finished, but lives almost like a human being and thrives on the ministrations of those who truly love it.

It was quite dark outside by now. Nevertheless, I stepped to the nearest window and peered out onto the land below. A sense of calmness came over me, and yet a certain restlessness as if I were expecting something or someone to arrive. Was I picking up the dim vibrations left over from a past event? I don't fancy myself a medium or even remotely psychic, but when I stood on the second floor landing at Howard Lodge, there was a moment when I, too, felt something uncanny within me.

A little later, Roy Emery drove me back to Baltimore and dropped me off at my hotel. Coming back into town was almost like walking into a cold shower, but twenty-four hours later I had again grown accustomed to the rough and materialistic atmosphere of big-city life. I had promised the Emerys to come back someday with a trance medium and see whether I could perhaps let the unknown man on the landing have his say. In the meantime, however, I promised to look up the de Beauregards in France, and Mr. and Mrs. Emery promised to keep me informed of any further developments at Howard Lodge should they occur.

I had hardly returned from Europe when I received an urgent note from Mrs. Emery. On October 20, 1969, she wrote of an incident that had just happened a few weeks before my return.

A friend of mine recently lost her mother and I invited her for the weekend. She was brought here by a mutual friend who also spent the weekend. I was very tired that evening, and shortly before midnight I had to excuse myself. Barbara wanted to stay up and Don stayed with her, feeling that she wanted to talk.

The following morning they told me that they had been sitting in the living room, and that Barbara had turned off the lights because she wanted to enjoy the country peace to the utmost. They then both heard footsteps coming down the steps and assumed that I'd changed my mind and had joined them. They heard the steps cross the threshold and the loveseat creaked under the weight of someone sitting there. Barbara became aware that it was not I there with them, and she could hear someone breathing very regularly. Holding her own breath, she then asked Don if he could hear anything. He had, and had also been holding his breath, to hear better. Barbara and Don both commented on how friendly they felt this presence to be. They are both absolutely convinced that there was someone with them in that room.

It is perhaps a good thing that the unknown gentleman on the second-floor landing does not have to leave his safe retreat to go out into the countryside and search for whatever it is that keeps him on the spot. He would find his beloved countryside vastly changed beyond a few miles. As it is, he can remember it the way he loved it, the way Howard Lodge still reflects it. And the Emerys, far from being upset by the additional inhabitant in their old house, consider it a good omen that someone other than flesh and blood stands guard and peers out, the way a night watchman stands guard over precious property. It assures them of one more pair of eyes and ears should there be something dangerous approaching their house. In this day and age such thoughts are not entirely without reason.

As for the child whose breathing Mrs. Emery heard time and again, we must remember that children died far more often in bygone years than they do today. Child mortality rates were very high because medicine had not yet reached the point where many diseases could be prevented or their death toll sharply reduced. A child then was a far more fragile human being than perhaps it is today. Perhaps it was one of the children belonging to a former owner, who fell ill from a fever and died.

But the gentleman on the landing is another matter. Since it was the lady of the house primarily who felt him and got his attention, I assume that it was a woman who concerned him. Was he, then, looking out from his vantage point to see whether someone were returning home? Had someone left, perhaps, and did part of the gentleman go with her?

One can only surmise such things; there is no concrete evidence whatsoever that it is a gentleman whose lady had left him. Without wishing to romanticize the story, I feel that that may very well have been the case. It is perhaps a bit distressing not to know how to address one's unseen guest other than to call him the "presence on the second-floor landing." But Mrs. Emery knows he is friendly, and that is good enough for her.

✳ 110

The Oakton Haunt

OAKTON, VIRGINIA, IS ONE OF those very quiet suburban communities nestling fairly close to Washington, D.C., that has changed slowly but inevitably from completely rural to slightly suburban during the last few years. Many people who work in Washington have bought houses in this community. The houses are fairly far apart still, and the general character is one of uncrowded, rustic environment. When one drives through Oakton, one gets a rather placid, friendly feeling. None of the houses look particularly distinguished, nor do they look sinister or in any way outstanding. It takes all of forty-five minutes to get there when you leave the center of Washington, and you pass through several other villages before reaching Oakton. Thus, the community is well buffered from the main stream of capital life, and not given to extremes of either appearance or habit.

The house we were yet to know was owned by the Ray family. Virginia Ray and her husband, Albert, had come to friends of ours, Countess Gertrude d'Amecourt and her daughter, Nicole, now Mrs. Jackson, when they heard that I was amongst their friends. They had seen me on television in Washington and knew of my interest in hauntings. What they had seemed to fit into that category, and it occurred to the Rays to ask whether I could not have a look at their "problem." On May 11, 1968 I was finally able to do so.

* * *

Nicole Jackson drove us out to Oakton—by "us" I mean my wife Catherine and myself. As yet we were not able to bring a medium along, but then I wanted to find out firsthand what exactly had happened that had disturbed the Rays to such an extent that they needed my help. After about forty-five minutes we arrived in a pleasant-looking country lane, at the end of which the house stood. The house itself was somewhat inside the grounds, and as we drove up we noticed a large barn to the left. Later on, we were to learn how important that barn was in the goings-on at the house.

Mr. and Mrs. Ray and various children and relatives had assembled to greet us. After some hand-shaking we were led into the downstairs parlor and made comfortable with various juices. It was a warm day for May, and the refreshments were welcome. When the excitement of our arrival had died down somewhat, I asked that those who had had experiences in the house come nearer so I could question them. The others I requested to keep back, so I could get my bearings without interruptions. In a roomful of people, young and old, this is an absolute necessity.

Albert Bartow Ray is retired now, and gives the impression of a man well set in his ways, happy to live in the country, and not particularly disturbed by unusual goings-on. His pleasant tone of voice, his slow way of moving about, seemed to me indicative of an average person, not in any way an occult buff or an hysterical individual likely to manufacture phenomena that did not really exist.

Virginia Ray also gave a very solid impression, and neither of the Rays was in any way frightened by what they had experienced. It was simply a matter of knowing what one had in one's house, and if possible getting rid of it. But if I had not come, they would have lived on in the house—at least, in May they felt that way.

They had been in this house for about six years at the time of our visit. They liked it; they considered it a comfortable old house. They knew nothing about its history or background, except that the timbers holding up the house were old logs, and they had wooden pegs in them. Even the rafters of the roof were made of logs. This indicated that the house must have been built at least a hundred years ago.

* * *

When I inspected the building I found it pleasant and in no way eerie. The stairs leading to the upper story were wide and the bedrooms upstairs friendly and inviting. The land upon which the house stood was fairly substantial —perhaps two or three acres or more. About the most unusual thing outside the house was the large old barn, somewhat to the left of the house, and a stone in front of the house that looked not quite natural. Upon close inspection, I wondered whether perhaps it wasn't an Indian tombstone, or perhaps an Indian altar of sorts. It looked far too regular to be completely shaped by nature. The Rays had no idea as to how it got into their garden, nor did they know anything particular about the history of the barn. All they knew was that both barn and house were old and that a long time before this the property had indeed been Indian territory. But so was most of the land around this area, so the fact that Indians lived there before is not terribly surprising.

The Rays had bought the house in June 1962 from a family named Staton. The Statons stayed on until October of that year before the Rays could move in. After the series of events that had caused them to seek my help had happened, the Rays quite naturally made some inquiries about their house. Mrs. Ray tried to talk to neighbors about it, but it was difficult to get any concrete information. The former owner's daughter, however, allowed that certain things did happen at the house, but she would not go into details.

Even before the Rays moved into the place, however, their experiences with the uncanny began.

* * *

"I came up one day," Mr. Ray explained, "and the house was open. I locked the house up, and because the house was still vacant I would come by here two or three times a week and check it. Frank Pannell, a friend of mine who works for the county and sells real estate on the side called me one day and he says, would I meet him someplace, he had a contract he'd like for me to read over. I told him I would be here by 4:30, so he met me here. That was in the first part of November. We walked down to the lake—there's a lake back here—we walked around and got in the house just about dark. There were two lights over this mantel that worked from a switch, and we had that light on. I was reading the contract, and he was standing here with me, when we heard *something start to walk around upstairs.* It sounded like a person. So I looked at Frank and said, 'Frank, what is that?' He said, 'It's somebody up there.' I said, 'Couldn't be, the house is locked.' He said, 'Just the same, there's someone up there.' We went upstairs, but didn't see anyone and came back down again. I started to read the contract when we heard something walking around again. We went halfway up the steps, when *something* seemed to walk right by our heads there. We came down here, and Frank said he could hear voices.

"The next thing that occurred was that my son Albert, Jr., and I came by here on a Friday after that following Thanksgiving. We had had some vandalism, kids had shot some windows out with a .22-rifle. So we had decided we'd spend the night here. We brought out some camping equipment and slept in the dining room. About 8:30, he said, 'Dad, wouldn't you like a cup of coffee or something?' He took the car and drove up to Camp Washington. Well, while he was gone, I was lying here reading, with a reading light on. All of a sudden I heard something in the kitchen that sounded like somebody suffering—making all kinds of noises. I got up and walked in, turned the light on, and it stopped. We had a little fox terrier who'd bark at any noise. When the noise started again I called her and she came directly to me, but she never barked or growled as if she were afraid. I stood it is long as I could, then I got up and went into the kitchen again, but I didn't see anything. I went down to the basement. I went all over the house. I went all over the yard. I went every place. There was no one there."

"Did it sound human?" I interjected.

"Well, sir, it sounded like somebody *moaning.* I felt the hair standing up on the back of my neck."

"And when your son came back?"

"We ate and went to sleep. I didn't tell him about the noise I'd heard. He woke me about 3 o'clock in the morning telling me that he had been *hearing noises.* He had heard something moaning—the same noise, apparently, that I had heard."

"Any other experiences prior to your actually moving in?" I asked. Evidently these phenomena were not dependent on human power source to manifest.

"My married daughter, Martha, then still in college, came here one night with me to check the house. She went upstairs, while I went in this room to check the thermostat. It was extremely cold, and I wanted to make sure the furnace would cut on and cut off. Suddenly she screamed and ran down the stairs, and said, 'Daddy, *something bumped into me!*' We went up, and every time I'd take a step, she'd take a step right behind me, almost stepping on me the whole time. So we went all over the house and didn't find anything.

"A cousin named Martin was then stationed at Fort Belvoir, and he would come up over the weekend. He was having dinner with us, and we got to talking about it. He laughed and said, 'Oh I don't believe in anything like that.' So he said to my son, 'How about you and I spending the night out there? We'll show your dad he doesn't know what he's talking about.' So they came out. About 3 o'clock in the morning they called me from Camp Washington up here, and they were both talking over the phone at the same time. I couldn't understand what they were saying, and finally I quieted them down. Martin kept saying, 'I believe it, I believe it!' I said, 'You believe *what?*' And he said, 'There's *something* in that house.' They could hear 'things' walking around, and different noises. I was living down in Sleepy Hollow then, and so I said, 'I'll meet you there.' They said, 'We won't meet you at the house. We'll meet you at the driveway.' I locked the house up. Two weeks later, a group of boys—high school boys and my son—decided to come by and spend the night. But about 3 o'clock in the morning, there was a pounding on the door, and when I opened the door, in burst these five boys, all excited, all of them talking at the same time. They had meant to stay overnight, but left about 2:30 in the morning. They heard a lot of noise; they heard things walking around. There was snow on the ground at the time. But when they raised the blinds to the bay window, there was a man—a big man—with a straw hat on, standing outside looking in at them. They loosened the cord and the blind fell down. In a little while they got nerve enough to look out again. They could see a man standing *out at the barn.* They saw the white doors of that barn, and right in front they could see the outline of a man standing. That was too much. They ran out, got in the car, and drove away just as fast as they could. I had to come out here and lock the house up and turn all the lights out.

"That spring, 1964, there'd been termites in the house. I had a man working for me by the name of Omar Herrington. Mr. Herrington dug a trench all around the house and worked here for about four or five days. And we put chlordane around the foundation, the house, the barn, and garage. We removed the shrubs. I came out on a Friday to pay him, just about 11:30. As I drove up, he said, 'Mr. Ray, weren't you out here a little earlier? I heard you come in. I heard you walking around.' I said, 'I'm sorry, it wasn't me.' 'That's funny,' he replied. 'The other day I heard something moaning like somebody in misery."

"Did you ever *see* anything?" I asked Ray.

"Yes, on two occasions. One night in 1965 I stayed in this room, in the downstairs part of the house, and after watching television I went to sleep on the couch. My wife went upstairs. About 2 o'clock in the morning, *something* woke me up. I could hear some tingling noise. It sounded like glass wind chimes. I sat up on the couch, and I could see in the corner a bunch of little lights, floating in the air. It looked like they were trying to take on the shape of something. That's the first time I really got scared. I turned the light on, and it just faded away."

"And what was the second occasion that you saw something unusual?"

"That was in the bedroom upstairs, where my wife and I sleep, two or three months later. I woke up, and I thought it was my son standing by my bed. I said, 'Bartow, what are you doing here?' There was no answer. I said it again; I could see the outline and face of a person! I turned the light on, and there wasn't anyone there. Then I got up and went to my son's room, and there he was, sound asleep."

"Did your wife see the apparition?"

"I don't think so, but she kept telling me that there was something *out in the barn.* The barn is about a hundred and fifty feet away. I'm in the construction business, and one day I was drawing up a set of plans for a private school, working on the porch.

"All of a sudden, I heard a noise like tools being handled, out in the barn, as if they were being thrown all over the place! I went out and opened the door, but *everything was in place.* I came back three times that afternoon. I heard noise, went out, and everything was in place. I have three pigs, and I put them into the lower part of the barn. Mr. Herrington would come by and feed the pigs every morning. One morning he said, 'If you don't stop following me around and standing back in the shadows and not saying anything, I'm going to stop feeding those pigs.' I said, 'Well, Mr. Herrington, I have *not* been standing out here.' He said, 'I know better, you were there!'"

"In digging around the house, have you ever found anything unusual in the soil?" I asked.

Mr. Ray nodded. "Yes, I found some things—broken old pottery, and in the garden I have found something that I think may be a tombstone. It's a black rock; weather-beaten, but it was covered over with grass and the grass kept dying at that spot."

"What did you do with it?"

"I dug down to see what it was, but I left it there. I pulled the grass off, and there's a stone there, a square, cut stone."

"Did the phenomena begin after you found this stone, or was it before?"

"Oh no, it started before that. It was two or three years later that I found that stone."

"Did it make any difference, after you found the stone?"

"No, it didn't seem to. Then, when my aunt, Alberta Barber, was visiting us, she broke her ankle. I had to sleep down here on a pallet beside her couch so that if she had to go to the bathroom, I could help her. One night, about 1 o'clock, there was a knocking on the wall, and it woke me up. She said, 'What is it?' I got up and turned the lights on, and didn't see a thing. On two occasions my wife and I were dressing to go out for the evening, when there was a loud knock on the porch door. Virginia said to me, 'Go down and see who it is.' I went down, and there wasn't a soul. One time, not too long ago, I was sleeping in the front left bedroom upstairs, and I felt something was in there; I could hear someone *breathing.* I got up and turned the light on and I didn't see anybody. This was about 3 o'clock. I had some papers in the car. I went out, got the papers, and slammed the car door. At that moment *something* went up the side of the storage shed. I don't know what it was."

"It went up—which way?"

"I could hear the noise, and I saw something go up on top of that shed and then take off. That sort of scared me. I sat up and worked the rest of the night."

"Any other unusual happenings?" I asked.

"A lot of times the switch to the furnace at the head of the stairs is turned off, and the house starts to get cold. Also, often, when I step out of the car and start to walk in here, I've heard *something walking behind me.* Four or five different people have had that experience."

"Who were these other people who heard this person walking behind them?"

"My son for one. Then Bob, a friend of our nephew's. Bob would go out and work on his car when he got home, and he was late for dinner every evening. One night he came home mad and said, 'Why don't you stop coming out and walking up and down without coming in where I'm working?' We looked at him and assured him, we hadn't been doing that."

"Did he see anyone?"

"No, he never saw anyone, but he could hear them walk on the gravel, halfway between the barn and the garage where he was working."

"All right, thank you very much," I said, and turned to the Rays' daughter, who had been listening attentively.

"Mrs. Bonnie Williams, what were your experiences in this house?"

* * *

"When I was seventeen, three years ago, I was asleep one night on this same couch. It was about 1 o'clock in the morning, and I had just turned out the light, after reading for a while. My parents were asleep upstairs. I was lying there, and I wasn't asleep, when I noticed a light right in this corner. I didn't pay any attention to it, but rolled over. As I rolled over, I looked out the two windows which are right above the couch, and there was no light *outside*. It was a very dark night. So I became curious, and I rolled back over and I looked at the light, and it was still there. I sat up, turned on the light and there was nothing. So I turned out the light and pulled the covers over my head. About five minutes later, I thought, I'd look again. This light was still here. It was a strange light, not a flashlight beam but sort of translucent, shimmering, and pulsating."

"What color was it?"

"It was a bright white."

"Did it have any shape?"

"It seemed to; as it was pulsating, it would grow in size. But when it started doing that, I got scared and I turned on the light, and there was nothing."

"Anything else?"

"This was at the time when Tommy Young, my cousin, and Bob Brichard were here. Everybody was at the dinner table, and my girlfriend, Kathy Murray, and I were leaving the house as we were eating dinner over at her house. We went out the back door, and we got about half-way down the walk when we heard moaning. It seemed to be coming from the bushes near the fence. I said, 'Come on,' and we started walking along but after we had taken about four steps, it started again. Well, when she heard it the second time she took off running for the house, and I decided I wasn't going to stand there by myself, so I went running into the house too."

"Did it sound like a woman or a man?"

"A man."

"Any other visual experiences?'

"No, but I've heard something upstairs many times when I'm the only one home, sitting downstairs. There was something walking around upstairs."

"Well was there in fact someone there?"

"I went upstairs. There was nothing."

"Did you ever feel any 'presences'?" I asked.

"One night," Bonnie replied, "at 1 o'clock in the morning, we wanted to have a séance. Since you get the feeling more often upstairs, we went up into my brother's room. We were sitting on the edge of the bed, my brother was nearest to the closet, Jackie Bergin, my aunt, was next to me, and I was on the other side. We were really concentrating for 'it' to appear. Then my brother spoke up and said, 'Do you see what I see?' And there was a shimmering light in the closet. It was very faint."

I thanked Bonnie and questioned her mother, Mrs. Virginia Ray, about her own experiences here.

* * *

"First of all," she said seriously, "I believe that there is a relationship between the barn and the house. The first things I heard were the noises of tools or whatever being knocked around in the barn. I heard it from inside the house. Then I had a very peculiar experience one Sunday afternoon. An acquaintance, Mrs. Ramsier, and I were standing on the front porch talking when all of a sudden it sounded as if the whole barn were collapsing. We both ran out the door and got as far as the maple tree in the side yard, but the barn was still standing. The noise took off about at the level of the eaves, where the gable comes down, and then travelled in a straight line over into the woods, and got quieter as it went away into the woods."

"I understand your mother also had an experience here?"

"My mother, Mrs. Bonnie Young, was here last July for my daughter Martha's wedding. She didn't believe anything we had said previously about this. I got up and left my room. I saw her light on and stuck my head in the door. I had intended to say absolutely nothing to her about what I had just experienced, but she said, 'Did you hear the ghost?' I asked her what she'd heard, and she said in the bedroom immediately adjoining hers she heard all the furniture moving around. She thought, what in the world is Martha doing, moving all the furniture around in the middle of the night! Then the noise left that room and moved to the side of the house, to this chimney, and then it disappeared."

"What was it, the thing that you yourself had heard at the same time your mother experienced this?"

"I was asleep in Bonnie's room, which does seem to be a center of activities too—the barn and Bonnie's room are the centers. I became aware of a very loud noise—loud and gathering in the distance. It was coming closer together and getting louder and just moving towards the house. By the time it got to the house it seemed to be in two forms."

"What did it sound like?"

"Not like a boom; it was just a loud, *gathering* noise."

"Was it high-pitched or low-pitched?"

"I would say nearer low than high."

"Did you see any figure or any face of any kind?"

"Well, I didn't see it, but I was conscious of this noise coming into a configuration as it got to the window. All of a sudden these two noises came right through the window and up to my bed, and just went *wrrp, rrr*; hard-sounding noises. They seemed to be two separate noises. At this point I tried to get up enough courage to talk to it, but I couldn't. I was frightened by that time. I thought, I'll just go to sleep, but I couldn't. Finally, I got up, when I felt it had diminished, and left the room. Then I found out about Mother's experience."

"Have you had any *unusual* dreams in the house?"

"Yes, but not in this house. I went down to visit my mother once before she came up here. I woke up in the middle of the night, with this very loud, distinct voice that said, *there is something wrong, pack up and move away*! I didn't know whether it was *there* or *here*."

"Was it a man or a woman?"

"I would say it was a man. I got up, walked the floor, and decided to pay attention. I had not planned to leave that day, but I told Bonnie about it and we went home that day."

"But it could have applied to this house."

"Yes, even though Mother's place is eleven hundred miles away, in Florida. The first night after we moved into this house, I went to bed. I had the feeling that a mouse started at the tip of the bed and ran straight to the floor. But my thought was—well, it wasn't a mouse because it didn't go *anywhere else.* I refused to worry about it. Then, a week or ten days ago, in April [1968], my husband's brother, Gilbert Ray, was here. He came out of the bathroom with the light off. He called to me, 'Ginny, do you mind coming here for a minute? Do you see anything over there?' I said, 'Yes I do.' And written on the metal cabinet above our washing machine in fluorescent light was the word L-A-R-U, in one line. And below that was sort of a smeared G, and an O. On the side of the cabinet there was one small slash. And then, between the cabinet and the window sill, in a narrow area about eight inches, there was an abstract face—eyebrows, nose, and mouth, and the face was sort of cocked on the wall. It was definitely there. We washed it off. It seemed like fluorescent paint. Two or three days afterward, in the bathroom, I did find on the cap of a deodorant a tiny bit of fluorescent paint. We have tended to say that it was somebody who did it, some physical person. *But we have no idea who did it.*"

"Well, did anybody in the family do it?"

"They say no."

"Were there any kids in the house?"

"No."

"There is no logical reason for it?"

"We have no logical reason for it."

"You saw the fluorescent light?"

"Three people saw it."

*　*　*

So there had been something more than just noises. I tried to put some meaning into the letters L-A-R-U-G-O, assuming they were of supernormal origin for the moment. It was a pity that the fluorescent paint was no longer available for inspection or analysis. It might have been ordinary, natural fluorescent paint, of course. But then again, the ectoplastic substance often found in connection with materialization does have similar fluorescent qualities and upon exposure to light eventually dissolves. What the Rays had described was by no means new or unique. In photographs taken under test conditions in an experiment in San Francisco and published by me in *Psychic Photography—Threshold of a New Science*, I also have shown similar writings appearing upon polaroid film. In one particular instance, the word WAR, in capital letters, appears next to the portrait of the late John F. Kennedy.

The substance seems to be greenish-white, soap-like, soft material, and there is a glow to it, although it is not as strong a glow as that of commercial fluorescent material.

I questioned all members of the household again. There was no doubt that no one had been playing tricks on any of them by painting fluorescent letters or that anyone from the outside could have gotten into the house to do so without the Rays' knowledge. Of that I became sure and quite satisfied. Under the circumstances, the supernormal origin of the writing was indeed the more probable explanation.

Who, however, was *Larugo,* or did it mean *Laru* and the word *Go*? I realized that I had to return to the house with a competent medium, preferably of the trance variety, to delve further into the personality causing the various phenomena. That there was a disturbed entity in and around the Ray house I was, of course, convinced. It would appear also that there was some connection with the barn, which, in turn, indicated that the disturbed entity was not an owner but perhaps someone who just worked there. Finally, the tombstone-like stone in the ground found by the Rays indicated that perhaps someone had been buried on the grounds of the house.

We walked over to the barn, which turned out to be rather large and dark. Quite obviously it was not of recent origin, and it was filled with the usual implements, tools, and other paraphernalia found in country house barns. There was a certain clammy chill in the atmosphere inside the barn that I could not completely account for in view of the warm weather outside. Even if the barn had been closed off for several days during the day and night, the wet chill of the atmosphere inside—especially the lower portion—was far beyond that which would have been produced under such conditions.

*　*　*

Unfortunately, I could not return immediately with a medium to investigate the matter further. Towards fall of 1968, word came to me through the mutual friends of the Rays and ourselves that they would eventually move from the house. Without knowing any of the details, I felt it was imperative that I get in touch with Mrs. Ray.

I called her on October 31, apologizing for the seeming connection between Halloween and their ghostly phenomena, and inquired how matters stood in house and barn. I also was able to tell Mrs. Ray that I would be at the house on November 7 at noon with a medium, Mrs. Ethel Johnson Meyers. This was good news to her indeed for the phenomena had continued and had not been any less since my first visit.

To begin with, Mrs. Virginia Ray was forced to sleep with the hall light on and had done so for about five months because of an increasing uneasiness at night. One afternoon during the summer two small boys living in the neighbourhood came to her door inquiring about the noises that were going on in the barn. Mrs. Ray had been taking a nap and had heard nothing, but the boys insisted that something was going on in the barn. Together they investigated, only to find everything in place and quiet. "We have bats, swallows, and we were developing a colony of pigeons in the barn," Mrs. Ray explained, "the last of which we do not want. My son, who is now twenty-one, was home on vacation when he decided to use a rifle to get rid of the pigeons. When he did so, an unusual spot of light came on the walls of the barn. He took one look at it and declined to spend any time in the barn after that."

One of the most impressive experiences perhaps occurred to the Rays' new son-in-law, who had come to spend the summer in June 1968. He had heard all the stories of the phenomena and didn't believe any of them. One night, he was awakened at about quarter to four in the morning by the noise of loud knocking outside the screen. Then the noise came on into the room, and he observed that it was a high hum mixed in with what sounded like the tinkling of a wind chime. The same night Mrs. Ray herself was awakened by a sound that she at first thought was high above her outside of the house, and which she sleepily took to he the noise of an airplane. Then she realized that the noise was not moving. Independent of the son-in-law and Mrs. Ray, Mr. Ray had also heard a similar noise at the same time.

Mrs. Ray's mother came for a visit during the summer. During her stay, the hall lights were being turned off —or went off by themselves—not less than four times in one night. There was no faulty equipment to be blamed; no other explanation to be found. Lights would go on and off more frequently now, without hands touching them, and the furnace again went off. Somebody or something had turned the emergency switch.

I was all set to pay the Rays a visit on November 7, 1968. At the last moment I received a hurried telephone call from Mrs. Ray. She informed me unhappily that the new owners objected to the visit and that therefore she could not offer the hospitality of the house again. They would move from the house on December 2 and the new owner had already started to take over.

"That's nothing," I said. "Perhaps I can get permission from them to pay a short visit."

Mrs. Ray seemed even more nervous than at first. "I don't think so, but you could try," she said, and supplied me with the name and address of the new owner. And she added, cryptically, "But he is a military man and I don't think he likes what you are doing."

I wrote a polite letter requesting only that we complete what we had started earlier, both in the interests of parapsychology and the house itself. I included my credentials as a scientist and teacher, and promised not to permit any undue publicity to arise from the case. This is standard procedure with me, since it is not my intention to cause the owners of haunted houses any embarrassment or difficulty in the community. I assumed, quite rightly, that whatever it was that caused the Rays to leave would not go

out with them but would remain tied to the house. There is an overwhelming body of evidence to support this view. Only once in a while, and in special cases, is a haunting attached to one particular person in a house. Clearly this is not the case in the Oakton haunt, and I had to assume that the matter was not resolved.

I made some inquiries about the new owner, and discovered that Colonel S. is a retired army officer, who had served in nearby Washington for many years while his wife was a teacher. Since there was very little time left before my impending visit, I hoped that permission would come through prior to November 7. The day before I received a certified letter with return receipt request from Colonel S. The letter was truly the letter of a military man: curt, insulting, and full of non sequiturs. The colonel tried hard to convince me that my work wasn't worthwhile or that it made no sense whatsoever. I realized that the man was more to be pitied than scorned, so I took his letter, wrote on it that I did not accept discourteous letters because they would contaminate my files, and returned it to him. I have heard nothing further from the colonel or his wife, and if there is any phenomenon going on at his Oakton, Virginia, house, he is handling it all by himself. He is most welcome to it. Quite possibly, he is not even aware of it, for he may be gifted with a lack of sensitivity that some people have. On the other hand, one cannot be sure. It is quite possible that the noises have since continued and will continue, or that other, more stringent phenomena will follow them. I don't think that a disturbed spirit has any respect for the opinion of a military man who wishes that spirits wouldn't exist.

* * *

On November 7 we did drive by the house and Mrs. Meyers stepped out briefly and went as close to the grounds as we could without entering the house proper or without violating the colonel's newly acquired property rights. Happily, the public thoroughfares in Virginia may be walked upon by parapsychologists and mediums with no need to ask permission to do so. As Ethel faced the enclosure of the house, she received the distinct impression of a troubled entity. Without having been told anything at all about the nature of the phenomenon or the location of it, she pointed at the barn further back as the seat of all the troubles. "It's down there, whatever it is," Ethel said, and looked at me. "But I would have to be closer to do anything about it. All I can tell you is that someone is awfully mad down there." Under the circumstances, I asked her to come back with me and let the matter rest.

* * *

Nothing further was heard from either the Rays or anyone else concerning the house until April 20, 1969.

Mrs. Ray wrote us from her new address in McLean, Virginia. "I feel like we have gone off and left the 'presence.' Mr. Ray is much less tense, as we all are to a degree." But that same day at 4 o'clock in the morning she woke up with a start. Suddenly she knew what the troubled entity wanted. Even though they had left the house, the unfortunate one was able to reach out to her at the same hour at which most of the audible phenomena had taken place. Perhaps this was a last message from the haunt of Oakton. Mrs. Ray hoped that it would indeed be the final message, and that she would be troubled no more.

When she understood what the entity wanted, she immediately set about to fulfill his wish. Quietly and without fanfare she made arrangements with an Episcopal priest to have the house exorcised. This, of course, was done through prayer, in a very ancient ritual going back to the early days of the Church. Sometimes it is effective, sometimes it is not. It depends upon the one who is being exorcised, whether or not he accepts the teachings of the Church, and whether or not he is a believer in a Deity.

*　*　*

The Rays did not keep in touch any longer with the new owners of their property, but once in a while word came back to them about their former home. A friend who hadn't heard of their removal to McLean tried to visit them. When the gentleman drove up to the gate, he realized that something was different. The gates had always been wide open, as had the hospitality and heart of the Rays. Now, however, he found the gate was closed. A somber, almost forbidding air hung around the Oakton house. Sadly, the gentleman turned around and left. He knew then without asking that the Rays had moved on.

A tombstone unmarked in the garden, a haunted barn, and a scrawled message written by a desperate hand from beyond the grave—do they indicate someone's unavenged death? So often I have heard "pray for me" when a soul has passed over in anguish and, clinging steadfastly to the beliefs of the Church, wants the final benediction, even postmortem. Could it not be that the Oakton haunt was resolved not by a parapsychologist and his medium prying further into the tangled affairs of someone long dead, but by the simple prayer of an Episcopal priest doing so at a distance? If and when the house is again for sale, we will know for sure.

✳ 111

The Restless Ghost of the Sea Captain

WHEN A NEW ENGLAND SALT has a grievance, he can sometimes take it to his grave. That is, if he *were* in his grave. In this case the sea captain in question never really passed away completely. He is still in what used to be his house, pushing people around and generally frightening one and all.

Spending time in this house is not easy. But I did, and somehow survived the night.

Some of the best leads regarding a good ghost story come to me as the result of my having appeared on one of many television or radio programs, usually discussing a book dealing with the subject of psychic phenomena. So it happened that one of my many appearances on the Bob Kennedy television show in Boston drew unusually heavy mail from places as far away as other New England states and even New York.

Now if there is one thing ghosts don't really care much about it is time—to them everything is suspended in a timeless dimension where the intensity of their suffering or problem remains forever instant and alive. After all, they are unable to let go of what it is that ties them to a specific location, otherwise they would not be that we so commonly (and perhaps a little callously) call ghosts. I am mentioning this as a way of explaining why, sometimes, I cannot respond as quickly as I would like to when someone among the living reports a case of a haunting that needs to be looked into. Reasons were and are now mainly lack of time but more likely lack of funds to organize a team and go after the case. Still, by and large, I do manage to show up in time and usually manage to resolve the situation.

Thus it happened that I received a letter dated August 4, 1966 sent to me via station WBZ-TV in Boston, from the owner of Cap'n Grey's Smorgasbord, an inn located in Barnstable on Cape Cod. The owner, Lennart Svensson, had seen me on the show.

"We have experienced many unusual happenings here. The building in which our restaurant and guest house is located was built in 1716 and was formerly a sea captain's residence," Svensson wrote.

I'm a sucker for sea captains haunting their old houses so I wrote back asking for details. Svensson replied a few weeks later, pleased to have aroused my interest. Both he and his wife had seen the apparition of a young woman, and their eldest son had also felt an unseen presence; guests in their rooms also mentioned unusual happenings. It appeared that when the house was first built the foundation had been meant as a fortification against Indian attacks. Rumor has it, Svensson informed me, that the late sea captain had been a slave trader and sold slaves on the premises.

Svensson and his wife, both of Swedish origin, had lived on the Cape in the early 1930s, later moved back to Sweden, to return in 1947. After a stint working in various restaurants in New York, they acquired the inn on Cape Cod.

I decided a trip to the Cape was in order. I asked Sybil Leek to accompany me as the medium. Svensson explained that the inn would close in October for the winter, but he, and perhaps other witnesses to the phenomena, could be seen even after that date, should I wish to come up then. But it was not until June 1967, the following year, that I finally contacted Svensson to set a date for our visit. Unfortunately, he had since sold the inn and, as he put it, the new owner was not as interested in the ghost as he was, so there was no way for him to arrange for our visit now.

But Svensson did not realize how stubborn I can be when I want to do something. I never gave up on this case, and decided to wait a little and then approach the new owners. Before I could do so, however, the new owner saw fit to get in touch with me instead. He referred to the correspondence between Svensson and myself, and explained that at the time I had wanted to come up, he had been in the process of redoing the inn for its opening. That having taken place several weeks ago, it would appear that "we have experienced evidence of the spirit on several occasions, and I now feel we should look into this matter as soon as possible." He invited us to come on up whenever it was convenient, preferably yesterday.

The new owner turned out to be a very personable attorney named Jack Furman of Hyannis. When I wrote we would indeed be pleased to meet him, and the ghost or ghosts as the case might be, he sent us all sorts of information regarding flights and offered to pick us up at the airport. Furman was not shy in reporting his own experiences since he had taken over the house.

"There has been on one occasion an umbrella mysteriously stuck into the stairwell in an open position. This was observed by my employee, Thaddeus B. Ozimek. On another occasion when the inn was closed in the early evening, my manager returned to find the front door bolted from *the inside*, which appeared strange since no one was in the building. At another time, my chef observed that the heating plant went off at 2:30 A.M., and the serviceman, whom I called the next day, found that a fuse was removed from the fuse box. At 2:30 in the morning, obviously, no one that we know of was up and around to do this. In addition, noises during the night have been heard by occupants of the inn."

I suggested in my reply that our team, consisting of Sybil Leek, Catherine (my wife at the time), and myself, should spend the night at the inn as good ghost hunters do. I also requested that the former owner, Svensson, be present for further questioning, as well as any direct witnesses to phenomena. On the other hand, I delicately suggested that no one not concerned with the case should be present, keeping in mind some occasions where my investigations had been turned into entertainment by my hosts to amuse and astound neighbors and friends.

The date for our visit was scheduled for August 17, 1967—a car and two weeks after the case first came to my attention. But much of a time lag, the way it is with ghosts.

When we arrived at the inn, after a long and dusty journey by car, the sight that greeted us was well worth the trip. There, set back from a quiet country road amid tall, aged trees, sat an impeccable white colonial house, two stories high with an attic, nicely surrounded by a picket fence, and an old bronze and iron lamp at the corner. The windows all had their wooden shutters opened to the outside and the place presented such a picture of peace that it was difficult to realize we had come here to confront a disturbance. The house was empty, as we soon realized, because the new owner had not yet allowed guests to return—considering what the problems were!

Soon after we arrived at the house, Sybil Leek let go of her conscious self in order to immerse herself in the atmosphere and potential presences of the place.

"There is something in the bedroom . . . in the attic," Sybil said immediately as we climbed the winding stairs. "I thought just now someone was pushing my hair up from the back," she then added.

Mr. Furman had, of course, come along for the investigation. At this point we all saw a flash of light in the middle of the room. None of us was frightened by it, not even the lawyer who by now had taken the presence of the supernatural in his house in stride.

We then proceeded downstairs again, with Sybil Leek assuring us that whatever it was that perturbed her up in the attic did not seem to be present downstairs. With that we came to a locked door, a door that Mr. Furman assured us had not been opened in a long time. When we managed to get it open, it led us to the downstairs office or the room now used as such. Catherine, ever the alert artist and designer that she was, noticed that a door had been barred from the inside, almost as if someone had once been kept in that little room. Where did this particular door lead to, I asked Mr. Furman. It led to a narrow corridor and finally came out into the fireplace in the large main room.

"Someone told me if I ever dug up the fireplace," Furman intoned significantly, "I might find something."

What that something would be, was left to our imagination. Furman added that his informant had hinted at some sort of valuables, but Sybil immediately added, "bodies . . . you may find bodies."

She described, psychically, many people suffering in the house, and a secret way out of the house—possibly from the captain's slave trading days?

Like a doctor examining a patient, I then examined the walls both in the little room and the main room and found many hollow spots. A bookcase turned out to be a false front. Hidden passages seemed to suggest themselves. Quite obviously, Furman was not about to tear open the walls to find them. But Mrs. Leek was right: the house was honeycombed with areas not visible to the casual observer.

Sybil insisted we seat ourselves around the fireplace, and I insisted that the ghost, if any, should contact us there rather than our trying to chase the elusive phantom from room to room. "A way out of the house is very important," Mrs. Leek said, and I couldn't help visualizing the unfortunate slaves the good (or not so good) captain had held captive in this place way back.

But when nothing much happened, we went back to the office, where I discovered that the front portion of the wall seemed to block off another room beyond it, not accounted for when measuring the outside walls. When we managed to pry it open, we found a stairwell, narrow though it was, where apparently a flight of stairs had once been. Catherine shone a flashlight up the shaft, and we found ourselves below a toilet in an upstairs bathroom! No ghost here.

We sat down again, and I invited the presence, whomever it was, to manifest. Immediately Mrs. Leek remarked she felt a young boy around the place, one hundred fifty years ago. As she went more and more into a trance state, she mentioned the name Chet...someone who wanted to be safe from an enemy...Carson...

"Let him speak," I said.

"Carson...1858...," Sybil replied, now almost totally entranced as I listened carefully for words coming from her in halting fashion.

"I will fight...Charles...the child is missing...."

"Whom will you fight? Who took the child?" I asked in return.

"Chicopee...child is dead."

"Whose house is this?"

"Fort...

"Whose is it?"

"Carson...."

"Are you Carson?"

"Captain Carson."

"What regiment?"

"Belvedere...cavalry...9th...

"Where is the regiment stationed?"

There was no reply.

"Who commanded the regiment?" I insisted.

"Wainwright...Edward Wainwright...commander."

"How long have you been here?"

"Four years."

"Where were you born?"

"Montgomery...Massachusetts."

"How old are you now?"

There was no reply.

"Are you married?"

"My son...Tom...ten

"What year was he born in?"

"Forty...seven..."

"Your wife's name?"

"Gina..."

"What church do you go to?"

"I don't go."

"What church do you belong to?"

"She is...of Scottish background...Scottish kirk."

"Where is the kirk located?"

"Six miles..."

"What is the name of this village we are in now?"

"Chicopee..."

Further questioning provided more information. We learned that "the enemy" had taken his boy, and the enemy were the Iroquois. This was his fort and he was to defend it. I then began, as I usually do, when exorcism is called for, to speak of the passage of time and the need to realize that the entity communicating through the medium was aware of the true situation in this respect. Did Captain Carson realize that time had passed since the boy had disappeared?

"Oh yes," he replied. "Four years."

"No, a hundred and seven years," I replied.

Once again I established that he was Captain Carson, and there was a river nearby and Iroquois were the enemy. Was he aware that there were "others" here besides himself.

He did not understand this. Would he want me to help him find his son since they had both passed over and should be able to find each other there?

"I need permission...from Wainwright...."

As I often do in such cases, I pretended to speak for Wainwright and granted him the permission. A ghost, after all, is not a rational human being but an entity existing in a delusion where only emotions count.

"Are you now ready to look for your son?"

"I am ready."

"Then I will send a messenger to help you find him," I said, "but you must call out to your son...in a loud voice."

The need to reach out to a loved one is of cardinal importance in the release of a trapped spirit.

"John Carson is dead...but not dead forever," he said in a faint voice.

"You lived here in 1858, but this is 1967," I reminded him.

"You are mad!"

"No, I'm not mad. Touch your forehead...you will see this is not the body you are accustomed to. We have lent you a body to communicate with us. But it is not yours."

Evidently touching a woman's head did jolt the entity from his beliefs. I decided to press on.

"Go from this house and join your loved ones who await you outside...."

A moment later Captain Carson had slipped away and a sleepy Leek opened her eyes.

I now turned to Furman, who had watched the proceedings with mounting fascination. Could he corroborate any of the information that had come to us through the entranced medium?

"This house was built on the foundations of an Indian fort," he confirmed, "to defend the settlers against the Indians."

"Were there any Indians here in 1858?"

"There are Indians here even now," Furman replied. "We have an Indian reservation at Mashpee, near here, and on Martha's Vineyard there is a tribal chief and quite a large Indian population."

We later learned that Chicopee Indians were indeed in this area. Also there was an Indian uprising in Massachusetts as late as the middle of the nineteenth century, giving more credence to the date, 1858, that had come through Mrs. Leek.

He also confirmed having once seen a sign in the western part of Massachusetts that read "Montgomery"—the place Captain Carson had claimed as his birthplace. Also that a Wainwright family was known to have lived in an area not far from where we were now.

However, Furman had no idea of any military personnel by that name.

"Sybil mentioned a river in connection with this house," I noted. Furman said, "And, yes, there is a river running through the house, it is still here."

Earlier Sybil had drawn a rough map of the house as it was in the past, from her psychic viewpoint, a house surrounded by a high fence. Furman pronounced the drawing amazingly accurate—especially as Leek had not set foot on the property or known about it until our actual arrival.

"My former secretary, Carole E. Howes, and her family occupied this house," Furman explained when I turned my attention to the manifestations themselves. "They operated this house as an inn twenty years ago, and often had unusual things happen here as she grew up, but it did not seem to bother them. Then the house passed into the hands of a Mrs. Nielson; then Svensson took over. But he did not speak of the phenomena until about a year and a half ago. The winter of 1965 he was shingling the roof, and he was just coming in from the roof on the second floor balcony on a cold day—he had left the window ajar and secured—when suddenly he heard the window sash come down. He turned around on the second floor platform and he saw the young girl, her hair windswept behind her. She was wearing white. He could not see anything below the waist, and he confronted her for a short period, but could not bring himself to talk—and she went away. His wife was in the kitchen sometime later, in the afternoon, when she felt the presence of someone in the room. She turned around and saw an older man dressed in black at the other end of the kitchen. She ran out of the kitchen and never went back in again.

"The accountant John Dillon's son was working in the kitchen one evening around ten. Now some of these heavy pots were hanging there on pegs from the ceiling. Young Dillon told his father two of them lifted themselves up from the ceiling, unhooked themselves from the pegs, and came down on the floor."

Did any guests staying at the inn during Svensson's ownership complain of any unusual happenings?

"There was this young couple staying at what Svensson called the honeymoon suite," Furman replied. "At 6:30 in the morning, the couple heard three knocks at the door, three loud, distinct knocks, and when they opened the door, there was no one there. This sort of thing had happened before."

Another case involved a lone diner who complained to Svensson that "someone" was pushing him from his chair at the table in the dining room onto another chair, but since he did not see another person, how could this be? Svensson hastily explained that the floor was a bit rickety and that was probably the cause.

Was the restless spirit of the captain satisfied with our coming? Did he and his son meet up in the great beyond? Whatever came of our visit, nothing further has been heard of any disturbances at Cap'n Grey's Inn in Barnstable.

✳ **112**

The Confused Ghost of the Trailer Park

I MET RITA ATLANTA when she worked in a Frankfurt, Germany nightclub. That is when I first heard about her unsought ability to communicate with spirits.

Later that year, after my return to New York, I received what appeared to be an urgent communication from her.

Rita's initial letter merely requested that I help her get rid of her ghost. Such requests are not unusual, but this one was—and I am not referring to the lady's occupation: exotic dancing in sundry nightclubs around the more or less civilized world.

What made her case unusual was the fact that "her" ghost appeared in a 30-year-old trailer near Boston.

The haunted trailer and owner—Rita Atlanta

Psychic manifestations inside the trailer

"When I told my husband that we had a ghost," she wrote, "he laughed and said, 'Why should a respectable ghost move into a trailer? We have hardly room in it ourselves with three kids.'"

It seemed the whole business had started during the summer when the specter made its first sudden appearance. Although her husband could not see what she saw, Miss Atlanta's pet skunk evidently didn't like it and moved into another room. Three months later, her husband passed away and Miss Atlanta was kept hopping the Atlantic (hence her stage name) in quest of nightclub work.

Ever since her first encounter with the figure of a man in her Massachusetts trailer, the dancer had kept the lights burning all night long. As someone once put it, "I don't believe in ghosts, I'm scared of them."

Despite the lights, Miss Atlanta always felt a presence at the same time that her initial experience had taken place—between 3 and 3:30 in the morning. It would awaken her with such regularity that at last she decided to seek help.

In September of the previous year, she and her family had moved into a brand-new trailer in Peabody, Massachusetts. After her encounter with the ghost Rita made some inquiries about the nice grassy spot where she had chosen to park the trailer. Nothing had ever stood on the spot before. No ghost stories. Nothing. Just one little thing.

One of the neighbors in the trailer camp, which is at the outskirts of greater Boston, came to see her one evening. By this time Rita's heart was already filled with fear, fear of the unknown that had suddenly come into her

life here. She freely confided in her neighbor, a woman by the name of Birdie Gleason.

To her amazement, the neighbor nodded with understanding. She, too, had felt "something," an unseen presence in her house trailer next to Rita Atlanta's.

"Sometimes I feel someone is touching me," she added.

When I interviewed Rita, I asked her to describe exactly what she saw.

"I saw a big man, almost seven feet tall, about 350 pounds, and he wore a long coat and a big hat," she reported.

But the ghost didn't just stand there glaring at her. Sometime she made himself comfortable on her kitchen counter, with his ghostly legs dangling down from it. He was as solid as a man of flesh and blood, except that she could not see his face clearly since it was in the darkness of early morning.

Later, when I visited the house trailer with my highly sensitive camera, I took some pictures in the areas indicated by Miss Atlanta: the bedroom, the door to it, and the kitchen counter. In all three areas, strange phenomena manifested on my film. Some mirrorlike transparencies developed in normally opaque areas, which could not and cannot be explained.

When it happened the first time, she raced for the light and turned the switch, her heart beating wildly. The yellowish light of the electric lamp bathed the bedroom in a nightmarish twilight. But the spook had vanished. There was no possible way a real intruder could have come and gone so fast. No way out, no way in. Because this was during the time Boston was being terrorized by the infamous

Psychic energy in the trailer

Rita in working costume

Boston Strangler, Rita had taken special care to doublelock the doors and secure all the windows. Nobody could have entered the trailer without making a great deal of noise. I have examined the locks and the windows—not even Houdini could have done it.

The ghost, having once established himself in Rita's bedroom, returned for additional visits—always in the early morning hours. Sometimes he appeared three times a week, sometimes even more often.

"He was staring in my direction all the time," Rita said with a slight Viennese accent, and one could see that the terror had never really left her eyes. Even three thousand miles away, the spectral stranger had a hold on the woman.

Was he perhaps looking for something? No, he didn't seem to be. In the kitchen, he either stood by the table or sat down on the counter. Ghosts don't need food—so why the kitchen?

"Did he ever take his hat off?" I wondered.

"No, never," she said and smiled. Imagine a ghost doffing his hat to the lady of the trailer!

What was particularly horrifying was the noiselessness of the apparition. She never heard any footfalls or rustling of his clothes as he silently passed by. There was no clearing of the throat as if he wanted to speak. Nothing. Just silent stares. When the visitations grew more frequent, Rita decided to leave the lights on all night. After that, she did not *see* him any more. But he was still there, at the usual hour, standing behind the bed, staring at her. She knew he was. She could almost feel the sting of his gaze.

One night she decided she had been paying huge light bills long enough. She hopped out of bed, turned the light switch to the off position and, as the room was plunged back into semidarkness, she lay down in bed again. Within a few minutes her eyes had gotten accustomed to the dark. Her senses were on the alert, for she was not at all sure what she might see. Finally, she forced herself to turn her head in the direction of the door. Was her mind playing tricks on her? There, in the doorway, stood the ghost. As big and brooding as ever.

With a scream, she dove under the covers. When she came up, eternities later, the shadow was gone from the door.

The next evening, the lights were burning again in the trailer, and every night thereafter, until it was time for her to fly to Germany for her season's nightclub work. Then she closed up the trailer, sent her children to stay with friends, and left with the faint hope that on her return in the winter, the trailer might be free of its ghost. But she wasn't at all certain.

It was obvious to me that this exotic dancer was a medium, as only the psychic can "see" apparitions.

The Ghost Who Would Not Leave

HARDLY HAD I FINISHED investigating the rather colorful haunting in the New York State home of *Newsday* columnist Jack Altschul, which resulted in my name appearing in his column as a man who goes around chasing ghosts, than I heard from a gentleman, now deceased, who was the public relations director of the Sperry Company and a man not ordinarily connected with specters.

Ken Brigham wanted me to know that he had a resident ghost at his summer home in Maine, and what was I to do about it. He assured me that while the lady ghost he was reporting was not at all frightening to him and his family, he would, nevertheless, prefer she went elsewhere. This is a sentiment I have found pervasive with most owners of haunted property, and while it shows a certain lack of sentimentality, it is a sound point of view even from the ghost's perspective because being an earthbound spirit really has no future, so to speak.

All this happened in January 1967. I was keenly interested. At the time, I was working closely with the late Ethel Johnson Meyers, one of the finest trance mediums ever, and it occurred to me immediately that, if the case warranted it, I would get her involved in it.

I asked Mr. Brigham, as is my custom, to put his report in writing, so I could get a better idea as to the nature of the haunting. He did this with the precision expected from a public relations man representing a major instrument manufacturer. Here then is his initial report:

As a member of the public relations/advertising profession, I've always been considered a cynical, phlegmatic individual and so considered myself. I'm not superstitious, walk under ladders, have never thought about the "spirit world," am not a deeply religious person, etc.... but....

Eight years ago, my wife and I purchased, for a summer home, a nonworking farm in South Waterford, Maine. The ten-room farmhouse had been unoccupied for two years prior to our acquisition. Its former owners were in elderly couple who left no direct heirs and who had been virtually recluses in their later years. The house apparently was built in two stages, the front part about 1840, and the ell sometime around 1800. The ell contains the original kitchen and family bedroom; a loft overhead was used during the nineteenth century for farm help and children. The former owners for many years occupied only a sitting room, the kitchen, and a dining room; all other rooms being closed and shuttered. The so-called sitting room was the daily and nightly abode. We never met the Bells, both of whom died of old age in nursing homes in the area, several years before we purchased the farm. They left it to relatives; all the furniture was auctioned off.

The first summer my wife and I set about restoring the farmhouse. The old kitchen became our living room; the Bells' sitting room became another bedroom; the old dining room, our kitchen. One bright noontime, I was painting in the new living room. All the doors were open in the house. Aware that someone was looking at me, I turned toward the bedroom door and there, standing in bright sunlight, was an elderly woman; she was staring at me. Dressed in a matronly housedress, her arms were folded in the stance common to many housewives. I was startled, thinking she must have entered the house via the open front door and had walked through the front sitting room to the now-bedroom. Behind her eyeglasses, she maintained a passive, inquisitive expression. For a moment or two, we stared at each other. I thought, What do you say to a native who has walked through your house, without sounding unneighborly? and was about to say something like What can I do for you? when she disappeared. She was there and then she wasn't. I hurried through the bedrooms and, of course, there was no one.

Once or twice that summer I was awakened by a sudden, chill draft passing through the second-floor room we used as a master bedroom. One early evening, while I was taking a shower, my wife called me from the living room with near-panic in her voice. I hurried downstairs as quickly as possible only to have her ask if I intended to remain downstairs.

Before closing the house up for the winter, I casually described the apparition to local friends without disclosing my reasons, excusing the inquiry from a standpoint I was interested in the previous owner. Apparently my description was accurate, for our friends wanted to know where I'd seen Mrs. Bell; I had difficulty passing it off.

My wife wasn't put off, however, and later that evening we compared notes for the first time. The night she called me, she explained, she had felt a cold draft pass behind her and had looked up toward the door of the former sitting room (which was well-lighted). There, in the door, was the clear and full shadow of a small woman. My wife then cried out to me. The chill breeze went through the room and the shadow disappeared. My wife reported, however, that surprisingly enough she felt a sense of calm. No feeling of vindictiveness.

Over the years, we've both awakened spontaneously to the chill draft and on more than one occasion have watched a pinpoint light dance across the room. The house is isolated and on a private road, discounting any possible headlights, etc. After a moment or so, the chill vanishes.

A couple of times, guests have queried us on hearing the house creak or on hearing footsteps, but we pass these off.

The summer before last, however, our guests' reaction was different.

A couple with two small children stayed with us. The couple occupied the former sitting room, which now is furnished as a Victorian-style bedroom with a tremendous brass bed. Their daughter occupied another first-floor bedroom, and their son shared our son's bedroom on the second floor. A night light was left on in the latter bedroom and in the bathroom, thereby illuminating the upper hallway, and, dimly, the lower hallway.

My wife and I occupied another bedroom on the second floor that is our custom.

During the early hours of the morning, we were awakened by footsteps coming down the upper hallway.

They passed our door, went into the master bedroom, paused, continued into our room and after a few minutes, passed on and down the staircase. My wife called out, thinking it was one of the boys, possibly ill. No answer. The chill breeze was present, and my wife again saw the woman's shadow against the bedroom wall. The children were sound asleep.

In the morning, our adult guests were quiet during breakfast, and it wasn't until later that the woman asked if we'd been up during the night and had come downstairs. She'd been awakened by the footsteps and by someone touching her arm and her hair. Thinking it was her husband, she found him soundly sleeping. In the moonlight, she glanced toward a rocking chair in the bedroom and said she was certain someone had moved it and the clothes left on it. She tried to return to sleep, but again was awakened, certain someone was in the room, and felt someone move the blanket and touch her arm.

My wife and I finally acknowledged our "ghost," but our woman guest assured us that she felt no fright, to her own surprise, and ordinarily wouldn't have believed such "nonsense," except that I, her host, was too "worldly" to be a spiritualist.

At least one other guest volunteered a similar experience.

Finally I admitted my story to our local friends, asking them not to divulge the story in case people thought we were "kooks." But I asked them if they would locate a photograph of the Bell family. Needless to say, the photograph they located was identical with my apparition. An enlargement now is given a prominent place in our living room.

Although this experience hasn't frightened us from the house, it has left us puzzled. My wife and I both share the feeling that whatever [it is] is more curious than unpleasant; more interested than destructive.

I was impressed and replied we would indeed venture Down East. It so happened that Catherine, whom I was married to at the time, and I were doing some traveling in upper New Hampshire that August, and Ethel Johnson Meyers was vacationing at Lake Sebago. All that needed to be done was coordinate our travel plans and set the date.

Mr. Brigham, who then lived in Great Neck, New York, was delighted and gave us explicit instructions on how to traverse New Hampshire from Pike, New Hampshire, where I was lecturing at the Lake Tarleton Club, to our intended rendezvous with Ethel in Bridgton, Maine, at the Cumberland Hotel. The date we picked was August 14, 1967. Ken and Doris Brigham then suggested we could stay over at the haunted house, if necessary, and I assured them that I doubted the need for it, being a bit cocksure of getting through to, and rid of, the ghost all in the same day.

* * *

Crossing the almost untouched forests from New Hampshire to Maine on a road called the Kancamagus Highway was quite an experience for us: we rode for a very, very long time without ever seeing a human habitation, or, for that matter, a gas station. But then the Indians whose land this was never worried about such amenities.

Before we left, we had received a brief note from Ken Brigham about the existence of this road cutting through the White Mountains. He also informed me that some of the witnesses to the phenomena at the house would be there for our visit, and I would have a chance to meet them, including Mrs. Mildred Haynes Noyes, a neighbor who was able to identify the ghostly apparition for the Brighams. Most of the phenomena had occurred in the living room, downstairs in the house, as well as in the long central hall, and in one upper-story front bedroom as well, Mr. Brigham added.

At the time I had thought of bringing a television documentary crew along to record the investigations, but it never worked out that way, and in the end I did some filming myself and sound recorded the interviews, and, of course, Ethel Meyers's trance.

When we finally arrived at the house in question in Waterford, Maine, Ethel had no idea where she was exactly or why. She never asked questions when I called on her skills. Directly on arrival she began pacing up and down in the grounds adjacent to the house as if to gather up her bearings. She often did that, and I followed her around with my tape recorder like a dog follows its master.

"I see a woman at the window, crying," she suddenly said and pointed to an upstairs window. "She wears a yellow hat and dress. There is a dog with her. Not from this period. Looking out, staring at something."

We then proceeded to enter the house and found ourselves in a very well appointed living room downstairs; a fire in the fireplace gave it warmth, even though this was the middle of August. The house and all its furnishings were kept as much as possible in the Federal-period style, and one had the feeling of having suddenly stepped back into a living past.

When we entered the adjacent dining room, Ethel pointed at one of the tall windows and informed us that the lady was still standing there.

"Dark brown eyes, high cheekbones, smallish nose, now she has pushed back the bonnet hat, dark reddish-brown hair," Ethel intoned. I kept taking photographs, pointing the camera toward the area where Ethel said the ghost was standing. The pictures did not show anything special, but then Ethel was not a photography medium, someone who has that particular phase of mediumship. I asked Ethel to assure the woman we had come in friendship and peace, to help her resolve whatever conflict might still keep her here. I asked Ethel to try to get the woman's name. Ethel seemed to listen, then said, "I like to call her Isabelle, Isabelle...."

"How is she connected to the house?"

"Lived here."

I suggested that Ethel inform the woman we wanted to talk to her. Earnestly, Ethel then addressed the ghost, assuring her of no harm. Instead of being comforted, Ethel reported, the woman just kept on crying.

We asked the ghost to come with us as we continued the tour of the house; we would try and have her communicate through Ethel in trance somewhere in the house where she could be comfortable. Meanwhile Ethel gathered further psychic impressions as we went from room to room.

"Many layers here...three layers...men fighting and dying here...." she said. "Strong Indian influence also... then there is a small child here...later period...the men have guns, bleeding...no shoes...pretty far back...Adam ...Joseph...Balthazar...war victims...house looks different...they're lying around on the floor, in pain...some kind of skirmish has gone on here."

I decided to chase the lady ghost again. We returned to the living room. Ethel picked a comfortable chair and prepared herself for the trance that would follow.

"I get the names Hattie...and Martin...not the woman at the window...early period connected with the men fighting...not in house, outside...Golay? Go-something...it is their house. They are not disturbed but they give there energy to the other woman. Someone by the name of Luther comes around. Someone is called Marygold...Mary...someone says, the house is all different."

I decided to stop Ethel recounting what may well have been psychic impressions from the past rather than true ghosts, though one cannot always be sure of that distinction. But my experience has taught me that the kind of material she had picked up sounded more diffuse, more fractional than an earthbound spirit would be.

"Abraham...," Ethel mumbled and slowly went into deep trance as we watched. The next voice we would hear might be her guide, Albert's, who usually introduces other entities to follow, or it might be a stranger—but it certainly would not be Ethel's.

"It's a man. Abram...Ibram...," she said, breathing heavily. I requested her guide Albert's assistance in calming the atmosphere.

Ethel's normally placid face was now totally distorted as if in great pain and her hands were at her throat, indicating some sort of choking sensation; with this came unintelligible sounds of ah's and o's. I continued to try and calm the transition.

I kept asking who the communicator was, but the moaning continued, at the same time the entity now controlling Ethel indicated that the neck or throat had been injured as if by hanging or strangulation. Nevertheless, I

kept up my request for identification, as I always do in such cases, using a quiet, gentle vocal approach and reassurances that the pain was of the past and only a memory now.

Finally, the entity said his name was Abraham and that he was in much pain.

"Abraham...Eben...my tongue!" the entity said, and indeed he sounded as if he could not use his tongue properly. Clearly, his tongue had been cut out, and I kept telling him that he was using the medium's now and therefore should be able to speak clearly. But he continued in a way that all I could make out was "my house."

"Is this your house?"

"Yes...why do you want to know...who are you?"

"I am a friend come to help you. Is this your house?"

"I live here...."

"How old are you?"

No answer.

"What year is this?"

"Seventy-eight...going on...seventy-nine...."

"How old are you?"

"Old man...fifty-two...."

"Where were you born?"

"Massachusetts...Lowell...."

"Who was it who hurt you?"

Immediately he became agitated again, and the voice became unintelligible, the symptoms of a cut-out tongue returned. Once again, I calmed him down.

"What church did you go to?" I asked, changing the subject.

"Don't go to church much...," he replied.

"Where were you baptized?"

"St. Francis...Episcopal."

I suggested the entity should rest now, seeing that he was getting agitated again, and I also feared for the medium.

"I want justice...justice...," he said.

I assured him, in order to calm him down, that those who had done him wrong had been punished. But he would have none of it.

"They fight every night out there...."

Again, I began to exorcise him, but he was not quite ready.

"My daughter...Lisa...Elizabeth...."

"How old is she?"

"Thirteen...she cries for me, she cries for me, she weeps...all the blood...they take her, too...."

"Where is your wife?"

"She left us in misery. Johanna...don't mention her ...she left us in misery."

"What year was that?"

"This year. NOW...."

"Why did she leave you?"

" I don't know."

"Where did she go?"

" I don't know."

And he added, "I will go to find her...I never see her...."

"What about your father and mother? Are they alive?"

"Oh no...."

"When did they die?"

"1776."

The voice showed a definite brogue now.

"Where are they buried?"

"Over the water...Atlantic Ocean...home...."

"Where did your people come from?"

"Wales...Greenough...."

Further questioning brought out he was a captain in the 5th regiment.

"Did you serve the king or the government of the colonies?" I asked. Proudly the answer came.

"The king."

When I asked him for the name of the commanding officer of the regiment he served in, he became agitated and hissed at me..."I am an American citizen...I'll have you know!"

"Are you a patriot or a Tory?"

"I will not have you use that word," he replied, meaning he was not a Tory.

I went on to explain that time had passed, but he called me mad; then I suggested I had come as a friend, which elicited a bitter reply.

"What are friends in time of war?"

I explained that the war had long been over.

"The war is not over...I am an American...don't tempt me again...."

Once again I pressed him for the name of his commanding officer and this time we received a clear reply: Broderick. He was not infantry, but horse. We were finally getting some answers. I then asked him for the names of some of his fellow officers in the 5th regiment.

"All dead..," he intoned, and when I insisted on some names, he added, "Anthony...Murdoch...Surgeon...my head hurts!"

"Any officers you can remember?"

"Matthew...."

I asked, what battles was he involved in.

"Champlain...Saint Lawrence...it's bad, it's bad...."

He was showing signs of getting agitated again, and time was fleeting.

I decided to release the poor tortured soul, asking him whether he was ready to join his loved ones now. Once again he relived the wars.

"He won't come home again...Hatteras...fire...I'm weary."

I began to exorcise him, suggesting he leave the house where he had suffered so much.

"My house...my tongue...Indians," he kept repeating.

But finally with the help of Ethel's spirit guide (and first husband) Albert, I was able to help him across. Albert, in his crisp voice, explained that one of the female presences in the house, a daughter of the spirit we had just released, might be able to communicate now. But what I was wondering was whether a disturbed earthbound spirit was in the house also, not necessarily a relative of this man. Albert understood, and withdrew, and after a while, a faint, definitely female voice began to come from the medium's still entranced lips.

"Ella..." the voice said, faintly at first.

Then she added that she was very happy and had a baby with her. The baby's name was Lily. She was Ella, she repeated. When I asked as to who she was in relation to the house, she said, "He always came...every day...William...my house...."

"Where is he? You know where he went?"

There was anxiety in her voice now. She said he left St. Valentine's Day, this year...and she had no idea what year that was.

Who was William? Was he her husband?

This caused her to panic.

"Don't tell them!" she implored me. The story began to look ominous. Willie, Ella, the baby...and not her husband?

She began to cry uncontrollably now. "Willie isn't coming anymore...where is he?"

What was she doing in the house?

"Wait for Willie...by the window...always by the window. I wait for him and take care of Lily, she is so sweet. What I can do to find Willie?"

I began to exorcise her, seeing she could not tell me anything further about herself. Her memory was evidently limited by the ancient grief. As I did so, she began to notice spirits. "There is my Papa...he will be very angry...don't tell anyone...take me now...my Papa thinks we are married...but we have no marriage...Willie must marry me...."

She cried even harder now.

"Andrew...my husband...."

Once again I asked Albert, the guide, to lead her outside, from the house. It wasn't easy. It was noisy. But it worked.

"She is out," Albert reported immediately following this emotional outburst, "but her father did find out."

"What period are we in now?"

"The eighteen-something."

"Is there anything in the way of a disturbance from the more recent past?

"Yes, that is true. An older lady...she does not want to give up the home."

Albert then went on to explain that the woman at the window who had been seen had actually been used in her lifetime by the earlier entitles to manifest through, which created confusion in her own mind as to who she was. Albert regretted that he could not have her speak to us directly. Andrew, he explained, was that more recent woman's father. Both women died in this house, and since the earlier woman would not let go, the later woman could not go on either, Albert explained.

"We have them both on our side, but they are closer to you because their thoughts are on the earth plane, you can reach them, as you are doing."

After assuring us and the owners of the house that all was peaceful now and that the disturbed entities had been released, Albert withdrew, and Ethel returned to herself as usual, blissfully ignorant of what had come through her mediumship.

Two of the ladies mentioned earlier, who had been connected with the house and the phenomena therein, had meanwhile joined us. Mrs. Anthony Brooks, a lady who had been sleeping in one of the bedrooms with her husband two years prior to our visit had this to say.

"I had been asleep, when I was awakened by ruffling at the back of my head. I first thought it was my husband and turned over. But next thing I felt was pressure on my stomach, very annoying, and I turned and realized that my husband had been sound asleep. Next, my cover was being pulled from the bed, and there was a light, a very pale light for which there was no source. I was very frightened. I went upstairs to go to the bathroom and as I was on the stairs I felt I was being pushed and held on tightly to the banister."

I next talked to Mrs. Mildred Haynes Noyes, who had been able to identify the ghostly lady at the window as being the former resident, Mrs. Bell. Everything she had told the Brighams was being reiterated. Then Ken Brigham himself spoke, and we went over his experiences once more in greater detail.

"I was standing in front of the fireplace, painting, and at that time there was a door to that bedroom over there which has since been closed up. It was a bright morning, about 11 o'clock, the doors were open, windows were open, my wife Doris was upstairs at the time, I was alone, and as I stood there painting. I glanced out and there, standing in the doorway, *was a woman*. As I was glancing at her I thought it peculiar that the neighbors would simply walk through my house without knocking.

"She stood there simply looking at me, with her arms folded, a woman who was rather short, not too heavy, dressed in a flower-print housedress, cotton, she had on glasses and wore flat-heel Oxford shoes, all of this in plain daylight. I did not know what to say to this woman who had walked into my house. I was about to say to her, What can I do for you? thinking of nothing more to say than that, and with that—she was gone. I raced back to the hall, thinking this little old lady had moved awfully fast, but needless to say, there was no one there. I said nothing to

anyone, but several weeks later, during the summer, both my wife and I were awakened several times during the night by a very chilly breeze coming into the bedroom. That was one of the bedrooms upstairs. Neither of us said anything but we both sat up in bed and as we did so, we watched a little light dance across the wall! We are very isolated here, and there is no light from the outside whatsoever. This continued for the next year."

At this point it was decided that Mrs. Brigham would tell her part of the story.

"The first summer that we had the house," Mrs. Doris Brigham began, "I was sitting here, about five in the afternoon, my husband was upstairs, and my son was outside somewhere. I was alone and I was aware that someone was here, and on this white doorway there was a solid black shadow. It was the profile of a woman from top to bottom, I could see the sharp features, the outline of the glasses, the pug in the back of her head, the long dress and shoes—all of a sudden, the shadow disappeared, and a cold breeze came toward me, and it came around and stood in back of my chair, and all of a sudden I had this feeling of peace and contentment, and all was right with the world. Then, all of a sudden, the cold air around my chair, I could feel it moving off. Then, practically every night in the room upstairs, I was awakened for several years in the middle of the night, by a feeling of someone coming into the room. But many times there would be the dancing lights. We moved into another bedroom, but even there we would be awakened by someone running their fingers up my hair! Someone was pressing against me, and the same night, a neighbor was in the house, and she told us the same story. Footsteps of someone coming up the stairs. A feeling of movement of air. A black shadow on the ceiling, and then it disappeared. Often when the children were sick, we felt her around. It was always strong when there were children in the house.

I wondered whether she ever felt another presence in the house, apart from this woman.

Mrs. Brigham replied that one time, when she did not feel the woman around, she came into the house and felt very angry. That was someone else, she felt.

I decided it was time to verify, if possible, some of the material that had come through Mrs. Meyers in trance, and I turned to Ken Brigham for his comments.

"It has been one of the most astounding experiences I have ever had," he began. "There are several points which no one could know but my wife and myself. We did a considerable amount of research back through the deeds of the house. This only transpired a few weeks ago. I had been excavating up out front, preparing some drains, when I came across some foreign bricks, indicating that there had been an extension to the house. This is not the original house, the room we are in; there was a cottage here built for Continental soldiers, at the end of the Revolutionary War.

These cottages were given to Massachusetts soldiers, in lieu of pay, and they got some acres up here. This house has been remodeled many times, the most recent around 1870. The town here was formed around 1775; the deeds we have are around 1800. Several things about the house are lost in legend. For example, down there is a brook called Mutiny Brook. There was a mutiny here, and there was bloodshed. There were Indians, yes, this was definitely Indian territory. At one time this was a very well settled area; as recently as 1900 there were houses around here."

I realized, of course, that this was no longer the case: the house we were in was totally isolated within the countryside now.

"The original town was built on this hill, but it has disappeared," Mr. Brigham continued, and then disclosed a strange coincidence (if there be such a thing!) of an actual ancestor of his having lived here generations ago, and then moving on to Canada.

"We only just discovered that at one time two brothers with their families decided to share the house and remodel it," Brigham continued his account. "But one of them died before they could move in. Much of what Mrs. Meyers spoke of in trance is known only locally.

"What about the two women Mrs. Meyers described?" I asked. "She mentioned a short, dark-haired woman."

"She was short, but had gray hair when I saw her," Mr. Brigham said. "A perfectly solid human being—I did nor see her as something elusive. We only told our son about this recently, and he told us that he had heard footsteps of a man and a woman on the third floor."

"Anything else you care to comment on?"

"Well, we have the names of some of the owners over a period of time. There were many, and some of the names in the record match those given by Ethel Meyers, like Eben."

"When Mrs. Meyers mentioned the name Isabelle," Mrs. Brigham interjected, "I thought she meant to say Alice Bell, which of course was the former owner's name— the woman at the window."

"One thing I should tell you also, there seems to have been a link between the haunting and the presence of children. One of the former owners did have a child, although the neighbors never knew this," Ken Brigham said. "She had a miscarriage. Also, Lowell, Massachusetts, is where these Continental soldiers came from; that was the traditional origin at the time. Maine did not yet exist as a state; the area was still part of Massachusetts. One more thing: both Mr. and Mrs. Bell died without having any funerals performed. She died in a nursing home nearby, he in Florida. But neither had a funeral service."

"Well, they had one now," I remarked and they laughed. It was decided that the Brighams would search the records further regarding some of the other things that Ethel had said in trance, and then get back to me.

Mr. Brigham was as good as his word. On August 21, 1967, he sent me an accounting of what he had further discovered about the house, and the history of the area in which it stands. But it was not as exhaustive as I had hoped even though it confirmed many of the names and facts Ethel had given us in trance. I decided to wait until I myself could follow up on the material, when I had the chance.

Fortunately, as time passed, the Brighams came to visit my ex-wife Catherine and myself in August of the following year at our home in New York, and as a result Ken Brigham went back into the records with renewed vigor. Thus it was that on August 20, 1968, he sent me a lot of confirming material, which is presented here.

Ethel Meyers's mediumship had once again been proved right on target. The names she gave us, Bell, Eben, Murdoch, Blackguard, Willie, Abraham, why there they were in the historical records! Not ghostly fantasies, not guesswork . . . people from out of the past.

August 20, 1968
Dear Hans,
    It was good hearing from Cathy and we did enjoy visiting with you. I presume that about now you're again on one of your trips, but I promised to forward to you some additional information that we've gathered since last summer. Enclosed is a chronology of the history of the house as far as we've been able to trace back. Early this summer (the only time we made it up to Maine) we spent hours in the York, Maine, Registry of Deeds, but the trail is cold. Deeds are so vague that we can't be certain as to whether or not a particular deed refers to our property. We are, however, convinced by style of building, materials, etc., that the back part of our house is much older than thought originally—we suspect it goes back to the mid-1700s.
    Although I haven't included reference to it, our reading of the town history (which is extremely garbled and not too accurate) indicates that one of the Willard boys, whose father had an adjoining farm, went off to the Civil War and never returned, although he is not listed as one of the wounded, dead, or missing. If memory serves me right, he was simply listed as W. Willard ("Willie"?). Now, the "ghost" said her name was "Isabel"; unfortunately, we can find no records in the town history on the Bell family, although they owned the house from 1851 to 1959 and Eben Bell lived in the town from 1820–1900! This is peculiar in as much as nearly every other family is recounted in the Town History of 1874. Why? Could "Isabel" be a corruption of the Bell name, or perhaps there was an Isabel Bell. Checking backwards in a perpetual calendar it seems that during the mid-1800s Tuesday, St. Valentine's Day, occurred on February 14, 1865, 1860, and 1854; the first seems most logical since the others do not occur during the Civil War—which ended on [May] 26, 1865!*
    Some of my other notes are self-explanatory.
    Another question of course concerns the term "Blackguard " for our particular road and hill. An archaic term

that connotes "rude"—note also that the map of 1850 does not show a family name beside our house...this could be because the property was between owners, or it could be that the owners were "rude"—which also could account for the lack of reference in Town History to the Bell family. It's an interesting sidelight.

Now, to more interesting pieces of information for you: 1) we've finally decided to sell the house and it's just like losing a child...I'm personally heartbroken, but I'm also a realist and it is ridiculous to try to keep it when we can't get up there often enough to maintain it. We have a couple of prospective buyers now but since we're not under pressure we want to make sure that any new owners would love it like we do and care for it.

2) And, then the strangest...Doris was going through some old photographs of the place and came across a color print from a slide taken by a guest we had there from Dublin, Ireland. And, it truly looks like an image in the long view up the lane to the house. Three persons have noted this now. Then, on another slide it looks as though there were a house in the distance (also looking up the lane) which is only 1½ stories in height. We're having the company photographer blow them up to see what we will see. I'll certainly keep you posted on this!

Well, it all adds up to the fact that we did a lot more work and learned a lot more about the place...nearly all of which correlates with Ethel's comments. But as a Yankee realist, I'm just going to have to cast sentiment aside and let it go.

Drop us a line when you get a chance.
Sincerely yours,

*Willie left on Tuesday, St. Valentine's Day.

Two points should be made here regarding this story. Ethel Johnson Meyers had many phases or forms of mediumship, but despite her fervent belief that she might also possess the ability to produce so-called extras, or supernormal photographs, she never did during my investigations. What she did produce at times on her own were so-called scotographs, similar to Rorschach effects used in psychiatry; they were the result of briefly exposing sensitive photographic paper to light and then interpreting the resulting shapes.

But genuine psychic photography shows clear-cut images, faces, figures that need no special interpretation to be understood, and this, alas, did not occur in this case when I took the photographs with my camera in Mrs. Meyers's presence.

After the Brighams had sold the Maine property, they moved to Hampton, Virginia. Ken and Doris looked forward to many years of enjoying life in this gentler climate.

Unfortunately, exactly two years after our last contact, in August 1970, Ken slipped and injured an ankle, which in turn led to complications and his untimely and sudden death.

As for the restless ones up in Maine, nothing further was heard, and they are presumed to be where they rightfully belong.

The following research material, supplied by the late Mr. Ken Brigham, is presented here to give the reader a better feel for the territory and times in which this took place.

* * *

Brigham's documentation:

1. Roberts, Kenneth, *March to Quebec*, Doubleday, 1938, p. 32. Listed in the King's Service: Thomas Murdock.

2. Carpenter, Allan, *Enchantment of America—Maine*, Children's Press, 1966, p. 27—85 years of Indian warfare, more than 1,000 Maine residents killed, hundreds captured; by year 1675, there were about 6,000 European settlers in what is now Maine.

3. Smith, Bradford, *Roger's Rangers & The French and Indian War*, Random House, 1956, p. 5—Indians began to slaughter them when they marched out of Fort William Henry to surrender—women and children and men (1757); p. 6—Robert Rogers of New York raised company of rangers in 1755, by 1758 had five companies. Ebenezer Webster came from his home in New Hampshire; p. 46—mentioned Colonel Bradstreet; p. 176—Ebenezer, 1761, returned east to Albany as Captain and then to New Hampshire where he married a girl named Mehitable Smith...pushed northward with men under Colonel Stevens and settled on 225 acres at northern edge of town of Salisbury. Later fought in Revolutionary War.

Oxford County Registry of Deeds
(References: Book 14, p. 18; Bk. 25, p. 295; Bk. 49, p. 254; Bk. 67, p. 264; Bk. 92, p. 158; Bk. 110, p. 149; Bk. 117, p.268; Bk. 187, p. 197; Bk. 102, p. 135; Bk. 240, p. 477–478; Bk. 260, p. 381)

1805 Abraham (or Abram) Whitney sold to Nathan Jewell

1809 Nathan Jewell sold to William Monroe (part of land and the house) (1/9/09)

1823 Jonathan Stone bankrupt and sold to Peter Gerry (house), Thaddeus Brown and Josiah Shaw (5/19/23)

1836 Peter Gerry sold to Moses M. Mason (6/14/36)

1848 John Gerry sold to Daniel Billings (5/27/48)

1895 Semantha Bell sold to Caroline Bell (3/4/95)

1940 Edna Culhan (daughter of Caroline Bell) sold to Irving and Alice Bell (11/7/40)

1956 Alice Bell transferred to Archie and Ethel Bell (10/12/56)

1959 Archie and Ethel Bell sold to K. E. and D. M. Brigham (1/59)

Bk. 3, p. 484, Feb 7, 1799

Isaac Smith of Waterford for $800 sold to Nathaniel Geary of Harvard, Lot 2 in 6th Range (southerly half). Deed written February 7, 1799, but not recorded until September 24, 1808. (m. Unice Smith) (See notes 1 & 2)

Vol. 3, p. 99, Jan 6, 1800 (Fryeburg)
Nathaniel Geary and Betey Geary, his wife, sold to Peter Geary for $400 westerly end of southern half of Lot 2 in 6th Range. Notarized in York, January 6, 1800. On April 2, 1801 Betey Geary appeared and signed document which was registered on February 11, 1804.

Peter Gerry (or Geary) b. 1776—d. 6/16/1847
m. Mary (b. 1782—d. 3/16/1830)
m. Elizabeth (b. 1787—d. 5/1/1858)
    c. Mary (b. 1834 or 1804—d. 1844)
    (see note 3) John C. (b. 1808)
    Roland (b. 1810—d. 1842)
    m. Maria Farrar (b. 1811—d. 1842)
    Abbie (b. 1812—d. 1817)
    Elbridge (b. 1815—m. Anna Jenness)

Bk. 92, p. 158, May 27, 1848
John Gerry sold for $100 (?) to Daniel Billings
Daniel Billings (b. 1780 Temple, Massachusetts)
…m. Sarah Kimball (b. 1786)
…c. Louise (m. William Hamlin)
    Caroline (b. 1810—m. G. F. Wheeler—b. 1810)
    George C. (b. 1837—d. 1919)
    …m. Rebecca Whittcomb, private F. Co.,
        9th Reg.—3 years svc. Civil War)
    Maria (m. Calvin Houghton)
    James R. (m. Esther Clark)
    John D. (m. Esther Knowlton)
    Miranda

Bk. 102, p. 135, Oct 14, 1851
Daniel Billings sold to William F. Bell of Boston and Timothy Bell for $1,400

Bk. 117, p. 268, Dec 24, 1858
William Bell of Waterford paid his father, William F. Bell, $800 for Lot 2 in 6th Range

Bk. 187, p. 197, April 3, 1871
William Bell, "for support of self and wife," transferred to Timothy C. Bell "homestead farm" and its parts of lots.

Bk. 240, p. 24, 1894
Timothy Bell left property to his wife Semantha Bell

Bk. 240, p. 477–78, Mar 4, 1895
Semantha Hamlin Bell transferred to Caroline Bell of Boston
    Caroline Bell (b. 4/4/1848—d. 9/20/1926)
    …m. T. C. Bell (b. 10/10/1829—d. 7/13/1894)
    …m. J. B. Bennett

1905
Caroline Bell (d. 1905??) left property to her son Irving Bell, "her sole heir."

Bk. 442, p. 133, Oct 30, 1940
Edna Bell Culhan (unmarried) of Cambridge, Mass. transferred to Irving and Alice Bell

Nov. 7, 1940
Irving Bell transferred to Edna Culhan "premises described in deed from Semantha to his mother Caroline Bell and he was her sole heir."

Bk. 560, p. 381, Oct 12, 1956
Archie and Ethel Bell inherited Lots 1 & 2 in the 5th Range and Lots 1 & 2 bought the 6th Range from Alice Bell

Jan 1959
Archie and Ethel Bell sold property to K. E. and D. M. Brigham

Notes
    1. According to Bk. 2, pp. 445–46: On December 20, 1802, Nathaniel Gerry (wife Betey) for $800 sold to David Whitcomb of Boston, Mass., Lot 2 in 6th Range. Deed mentions road running thru land. Registered 1807 and notarized and signed by Justice of the Peace Eber Rice.
    2. According to Bk. 9, p. 467–68: On November 13, 1810, David Whitcomb for $150 sold to Peter Gerry Lot 2 in the 6th Range, including "Gerry Road." Apparently both these transactions (notes 1 & 2) were concerned with the westerly end of the northern half of Lot 2 in the 6th Range.
    3. John C. Gerry (b. 1808): m. Nancy Farrar (b. 1810–d. 1841), Nancy Sawin (b. 1819). He had an apothecary store in Fryeburg.

Interesting Notes
    1. Local cemetery has gravestone of Hon. Lewis Brigham, b. 1816, d. 1866 (at Amherst, Mass).
    2. Eben Bell, (b. 8/5/1820—d. 6/8/1900)
    3. Richard and Samuel Brigham, and David Whitcomb, signed petition for incorporation on December 9, 1795.
    4. Historical:
Waterford was in York Country when it applied for incorporation (January 27, 1796).
Fryeburg (Pequawkett) was settled in 1763, Inc. 1777; in 1768 Fryeburg had population 300 plus.
November 17, 1796—Isaac Smith petitioned, with others, Massachusetts for incorporation. Document stated there were fifty to sixty families in "said plantation."
History of Waterford, p. 25—"and when the Indians attacked the growing settlements on the Androscog-

gin in 1781, and carried Lt. Segar* and other into Canadian captivity, Lt. Stephen Farrington led twenty-three men over this trail in hot, although vain pursuit of the savages."
(*Lt. Nathaniel Segar had cleared a few acres in 1774. A few townships, as Waterford and New Suncook [Lovell and Sweden] had been surveyed and awaited settlers. p. 22)
Waterford, settled 1775, incorporated 1797; population 1790—150; 1800—535.
"Spirit of 76" (Commanger/Morris, p. 605)—General Burgoyne surrenders October 1777...General John Stark agreed to work with Seth Warner because Warner was from New Hampshire or the Hampshire Grants (1777).
November 15, 1745—First Massachusetts Regiment, under Sir William Pepperrell—8th company: Capt. Thomas Perkins, Lt. John Burbank, John Gerry (single).
Civil War: "Fifth Regiment commanded by Mark H. Dunnill of Portland. "Fifth was engaged in eleven pitched battles and eight skirmishes ere it entered on terrible campaign of the Wilderness which was an incessant battle. It captured 6 rebel flags and more prisoners than it had in its ranks."

5. Local Notes:
A) Androscoggin Trail was the main Indian route from the East Coast to Canada. Below our property, in the area of Lot 3 in the 4th Range, it follows a brook called "Mutiny Brook." The origin of the term used here is vague, but the natives say Indians mutinied there during the French and Indian Wars.
B) When the town was first settled, the pioneers built their homes on our hill rather than the flat land and the only road around Bear Lake was at the foot of Sweden and Blackguard roads.
C) Our road is called by the archaic word "Blackguard" which connotes villain. No one knows why.
D) The second floor of the house was constructed sometime after the first; timbers are hand hewn to the second floor and mill cut above. The house was rebuilt several times apparently; about 1890 or so two brothers and their families intended to live there but one died before taking residence. Also, foundations of an earlier building were uncovered near the back door.

✳ 114

The Ghost at Port Clyde

PORT CLYDE IS A LOVELY little fishing village on the coast of Maine where a small number of native Yankees, who live there all year round, try to cope with a few summer residents, usually from New York or the Midwest. Their worlds do not really mesh, but the oldtimers realize that a little—not too much—tourism is really quite good for business, especially the few small hotels in and around Port Clyde and St. George, so they don't mind them too much. But the Down Easterners do keep to themselves, and it isn't always easy to get them to open up about their private lives or such things as, let us say, ghosts.

Carol Olivieri Schulte lived in Council Bluffs, Iowa, when she first contacted me in November 1974. The wife of a lawyer, Mrs. Schulte is an inquisitive lady, a college graduate, and the mother of what was then a young son. Somehow Carol had gotten hold of some of my books and become intrigued by them, especially where ghosts were concerned, because she, too, had had a brush with the uncanny.

"It was the summer of 1972," she explained to me, "and I was sleeping in an upstairs bedroom," in the summer cottage her parents owned in Port Clyde, Maine.

"My girlfriend Marion and her boyfriend were sleeping in a bedroom across the hall with their animals, a Siamese cat and two dogs."

The cat had been restless and crept into Carol's room, touching her pillow and waking her. Carol sat up in bed, ready to turn on the light, when she saw standing beside her bed a female figure in a very white nightgown. The figure had small shoulders and long, flowing hair... and Carol could see right through her!

It became apparent, as she came closer, that she wanted to get Carol's attention, trying to talk with her hands.

"Her whole body suggested she was in desperate need of something. Her fingers were slender, and there was a diamond ring on her fourth finger, on the right hand. Her hands moved more desperately as I ducked under the covers."

Shortly after this, Carol had a dream contact with the same entity. This time she was abed in another room in the house, sleeping, when she saw the same young woman. She appeared to her at first in the air, smaller than life-size. Her breasts were large, and there was a maternal feeling about her. With her was a small child, a boy of perhaps three years of age, also dressed in a white gown. While the child was with Carol on her bed, in the dream, the mother hovered at some distance in the corner. Carol, in the dream, had the feeling the mother had turned the child over to her, as if to protect it, and then she vanished. Immediately there followed the appearance of another woman, a black-hooded female, seeming very old, coming toward her and the child. Carol began to realize the dark-hooded woman wanted to take the child from her, and the child was afraid and clung to her. When the woman stood close to Carol's bed, still in the dream, Carol noticed her bright green eyes and crooked, large nose, and her dark complexion. She decided to fight her off, concentrating her thoughts on the white light she knew was an expression of psychic protection, and the dark-hooded woman disappeared. Carol was left with the impression that she had been connected with a school or institution of some kind. At this, the mother in her white nightgown returned and took the child back, looking at Carol with an expression of gratitude before disappearing again along with her child.

Carol woke up, but the dream was so vivid, it stayed with her for weeks, and even when she contacted me, it was still crystal clear in her mind. One more curious event transpired at the exact time Carol had overcome the evil figure in the dream. Her grandmother, whom she described as "a very reasoning, no-nonsense lively Yankee lady," had a cottage right in back of Carol's parents'. She was tending her stove, as she had done many times before, when it blew up right into her face, singeing her eyebrows. There was nothing whatever wrong with the stove.

Carol had had psychic experiences before, and even her attorney husband was familiar with the world of spirits, so her contacting me for help with the house in Maine was by no means a family problem.

I was delighted to hear from her, not because a Maine ghost was so very different from the many other ghosts I had dealt with through the years, but because of the timing of Carol's request. It so happened that at that time I was in the middle writing, producing, and appearing in the NBC series called "In Search of . . ." and the ghost house in Maine would make a fine segment.

An agreement was arranged among all concerned, Carol, her husband, her parents, the broadcasting management, and me. I then set about to arrange a schedule for our visit. We had to fly into Rockland, Maine, and then drive down to Port Clyde. If I wanted to do it before Carol and her family were in residence, that, too, would be all right though she warned me about the cold climate up there during the winter months.

In the end we decided on May, when the weather would be acceptable, and the water in the house would be turned back on.

I had requested that all witnesses of actual phenomena in the house be present to be questioned by me.

Carol then sent along pictures of the house and statements from some of the witnesses. I made arrangements to have her join us at the house for the investigation and filming for the period May 13–15, 1976. The team—the crew, my psychic, and me—would all stay over at a local hotel. The psychic was a young woman artist named Ingrid Beckman with whom I had been working and helping develop her gift.

And so it happened that we congregated in Port Clyde from different directions, but with one purpose in mind—to contact the lady ghost at the house. As soon as we had settled in at the local hotel, the New Ocean House, we drove over to the spanking white cottage that was to be the center of our efforts for the next three days. Carol's brother Robert had driven up from Providence, and her close friend Marion Going from her home, also in Rhode Island.

I asked Ingrid to stay at a little distance from the house and wait for me to bring her inside, while I spoke to some of the witnesses, out of Ingrid's earshot. Ingrid understood and sat down on the lawn, taking in the beauty of the landscape.

Carol and I walked in the opposite direction, and once again we went over her experiences as she had reported them to me in her earlier statement. But was there anything beyond that, I wondered, and questioned Carol about it.

"Now since that encounter with the ghostly lady have you seen her again? Have you ever heard her again?"

"Well about three weeks ago before I was to come out here, I really wanted to communicate with her. I concentrated on it just before I went to sleep, you know. I was thinking about it, and I dreamed that she appeared to me the way she had in the dream that followed her apparition here in this house. And then I either dreamed that I woke up momentarily and saw her right there as I had actually seen her in this bedroom or I actually did wake up and see her. Now the sphere of consciousness I was in—I am doubtful as to where I was at that point. I mean it was nothing like the experience I experienced right here in this room. I was definitely awake, and *I definitely saw that ghost.* As to this other thing a couple of weeks ago—I wasn't quite sure."

"Was there any kind of message?"

"No, not this last time."

"Do you feel she was satisfied having made contact with you?"

"Yeah, I felt that she wanted to communicate with me in the same sense that I wanted to communicate with her. Like an old friend will want to get in touch with another old friend, and I get the feeling she was just saying, 'Yes, I'm still here.'"

I then turned to Carol's brother, Bob Olivieri, and questioned him about his own encounters with anything unusual in the house. He took me to the room he was occupying at the time of the experiences, years ago, but apparently the scene was still very fresh in his mind.

Mr. Olivieri, what exactly happened to you in this room?"

"Well, one night I was sleeping on this bed and all of a sudden I woke up and heard footsteps—what I thought were footsteps—it sounded like slippers or baby's feet in pajamas—something like that. Well, I woke up and I came over, and I stepped in this spot, and I looked in the hallway and the sound stopped. I thought maybe I was imagining it. So I came back to the bed, got into bed again, and again I heard footsteps. Well, this time I got up and as soon as I came to the same spot again and looked into the hallway it stopped. I figured it was my nephew who was still awake. So I walked down the hallway and looked into the room where my sister and nephew were sleeping, and they were both sound asleep. I checked my parents' room, and they were also asleep. I just walked back. I didn't know what to do so I got into bed again, and I kept on hearing them. I kept on walking over, and they would still be going until I stepped in this spot where they would stop. As soon as I stepped here. And this happened for an hour. I kept getting up. Heard the footsteps, stepped in this spot and they stopped. So finally I got kind of tired of it and came over to my bed and lay down in bed and as soon as I lay down I heard the steps again, exactly what happened before—and they seemed to stop at the end of the hallway. A few minutes later I felt a pressure on my sheets, starting from my feet, and going up, up, up, going up further, further, slowly but surely...and finally something pulled my hair! Naturally I was just scared for the rest of else night. I couldn't get to sleep."

I thought it was time to get back to Ingrid and bring her into the house. This I did, with the camera and sound people following us every step of the way to record for NBC what might transpire in the house now. Just before we entered the house, Ingrid turned to me and said, "You know that window up there? When we first arrived, I noticed someone standing in it."

"What exactly did you see?"

"It was a woman...and she was looking out at us."

The house turned out to be a veritable jewel of Yankee authenticity, the kind of house a sea captain might be happy in, or perhaps only a modern antiquarian. The white exterior was matched by a spanking clean, and sometimes sparse interior, with every piece of furniture of the right period—the nineteenth and early twentieth centuries—and a feeling of being lived in by many people, for many years.

After we had entered the downstairs part where there was an ample kitchen and a nice day room, I asked Ingrid, as usual, to tell me whatever psychic impression she was gathering about the house, its people and its history. Naturally, I had made sure all along that Ingrid knew nothing of the house or the quest we had come on to Maine, and there was absolutely no way she could have had access to specifics about the area, the people in the house—past and present—nor anything at all about the case.

Immediately Ingrid set to work, she seemed agitated.

"There is a story connected here with the 1820s or the 1840s," she began, and I turned on my tape recorder to catch the impressions she received as we went along. At

first, they were conscious psychic readings, later Ingrid seemed in a slight state of trance and communication with spirit entities directly. Here is what followed.

"1820s and 1840s. Do you mean both or one or the other?"

"Well, it's in that time period. And I sense a woman with a great sense of remorse."

"Do you feel this is a presence here?"

"Definitely a presence here."

"What part of the house do you feel it's strongest in?"

"Well, I'm being told to go upstairs."

"Is it a force pulling you up?"

"No, I just have a feeling to go upstairs."

"Before you go upstairs, before you came here did you have any feeling that there was something to it?"

"Yes, several weeks ago I saw a house—actually it was a much older house than this one, and it was on this site—and it was a dark house and it was shingled and it was—as I say, could have been an eighteenth century house, the house that I saw. It looked almost like a salt box, it had that particular look. And I saw that it was right on the water and I sensed a woman in it and a story concerned with a man in the sea with this house."

"A man with the sea?"

" Yes."

"Do you feel that this entity is still in the house?"

"I do, and of course I don't feel this is the original house. I feel it was on this property, and this is why I sense that she is throughout the house. The she comes here because this is her reenactment."

I asked her to continue.

"I can see in my mind's eye the house that was on this property before, and in my mind I sense a field back in this direction, and there was land that went with this!"

"Now we are upstairs. I want you to look into every room and give me your impressions of it," I said.

"Well, the upstairs is the most active. I sense a woman who is waiting. This is in the same time period. There are several other periods that go with this house, but I will continue with this one. I also see that she has looked out—not from this very same window, but windows in this direction of the house—*waiting for somebody to come back.*"

"What about this room?"

"Well, this room is like the room where she conducted a vigil, waiting for someone. And I just got an impression where she said that, 'She' meaning a schooner, 'was built on the Kennebec River'...It seems to be a double-masted schooner, and it seems to be her husband who is on this. And I have an impression of novelties that he has brought her back. Could be from a foreign country. Perhaps the Orient or something like that."

"Now go to the corridor again and try some of the other rooms. What about this one?"

"I sense a young man in this room, but this is from a different time period. It's a young boy. It seems to be 1920s."

"Is that all you sense in this room?"

"That is basically what I sense in this room. The woman of the double-masted schooner story is throughout the house because as I have said, she doesn't really belong to this house. She is basically on the *property*— mainly she still goes through this whole house looking for the man to come home. And the front of the house is where the major activity is. She is always watching. But I have an impression now of a storm that she is very upset about. A gale of some kind. It seems to be November. I also feel she is saying something about... flocking sheep. There are sheep on this property."

"Where would you think is the most active room?"

"The most active room I think is upstairs and to the front, where we just were. I feel it most strongly there."

"Do you think we might be able to make contact with her?"

"Yes, I think so. Definitely I feel that she is watching *and I knew about her before I came.*"

"What does she look like?"

"I see a tall woman, who is rather thin and frail with dark hair and it appears to be a white gown. It could be a nightgown I see her in—it looks like a nightgown to me with a little embroidery on the front. Hand done."

"Let us see if she cares to make contact with us?"

"All right."

"If the entity is present, and wishes to talk to us, we have come as friends; she is welcome to use this instrument, Ingrid, to manifest."

"She is very unhappy here, Hans. She says her family hailed from England. I get her name as Margaret."

"Margaret what?"

"Something like Hogen—it begins with an H. I don't think it is Hogan, Hayden, or something like that. I'm not getting the whole name."

"What period are you in now?"

"Now she says 1843. She is very unhappy because she wanted to settle in Kennebunk; she does not like it here. She doesn't like the responsibilities of the house. Her husband liked it in this fishing village. She is very unhappy about his choice."

"Is he from England?"

"Yes, their descendants are from England."

"You mean were they born here or in England?"

"That I'm not clear on. But they have told me that their descendants are English."

"Now is she here...?"

"She calls Kennebunk the city. That to her is a center."

"What does she want? Why is she still here?"

"She's left with all this responsibility. Her husband went on a ship, to come back in two years."

"Did he?"

"No, she's still waiting for him."

"The name of the ship?"

"I think it's St. Catherine."

"Is it his ship? Is he a captain?"

"He is second-in-command. It's not a mate, but a second something-or-other."

"What is she looking for?"

"She's looking to be relieved."

"Of what?"

"Of the duties and the responsibilities."

"For what?"

"This house."

"Is she aware of her passing?"

"No, she's very concerned over the flocks. She says it's now come April, and it's time for shearing. She is very unhappy over this. In this direction, Hans, I can see what appears to be a barn, and it's very old fashioned. She had two cows."

"Is she aware of the people in the house now?"

"She wants to communicate."

"What does she want them to do for her?"

"She wants for them to help her with the farm. She says it's too much, and the soil is all rocky and she can't get labor from the town. She's having a terrible time. It's too sandy here."

"Are there any children? Is she alone?"

"They have gone off, she says."

"And she's alone now?"

"Yes, she is."

"Can you see her?"

"Yes, I do see her."

"Can she see you?"

"Yes."

"Tell her that this is 1976, and that much time has passed. Does she understand this?"

"She just keeps complaining; she has nobody to write letters to."

"Does she understand that her husband has passed on and that she herself is a spirit and that there is no need to stay if she doesn't wish to?"

"She needs to get some women from the town to help with the spinning."

"Tell her that the new people in the house are taking care of everything, and she is relieved and may go on. She's free to go."

"She said, 'to Kennebunk?'"

"Any place she wishes—to the city or to join her husband on the other side of life."

"She said, 'Oh, what I would do for a town house.'"

"Ask her to call out to her husband to take her away. He's waiting for her."

"What does Johnsbury mean? A Johnsbury."

"It's a place."

"She asking about Johnsbury."

The Ghost at Port Clyde

523

"Does she wish to go there?"

"She feels someone may be there who could help her."

"Who?"

"It seems to be an uncle in Johnsbury."

"Then tell her to call out to her uncle in Johnsbury."

"She says he has not answered her letters."

"But if she speaks up now he will come for her. Tell her to do it now. Tell Margaret we are sending her to her uncle, with our love and compassion. That she need not stay here any longer. That she need not wait any longer for someone who cannot return. That she must go on to the greater world that awaits her outside, where she will rejoin her husband and she can see her uncle."

"She is wanting to turn on the lights. She is talking about the oil lamps. She wants them all lit."

"Tell her the people here will take good care of the house, of the lamps, and of the land."

"And she is saying, no tallow for the kitchen."

"Tell her not to worry."

"And the root cellar is empty."

"Tell her not to worry. We will take care of that for her. She is free to go—she is being awaited, she is being expected. Tell her to go on and go on from here in peace and with our love and compassion."

"She is looking for a lighthouse, or something about a lighthouse that disturbs her."

"What is the lighthouse?"

"She is very upset. She doesn't feel that it's been well kept; that this is one of the problems in this area. No one to tend things. I ought to be in Kennebunk, she says, where it is a city."

"Who lives in Kennebunk that she knows?"

"No one she knows. She wants to go there."

"What will she do there?"

"Have a town house."

"Very well, then let her go to Kennebunk."

"And go [to] the grocer," she says.

"Tell her she's free to go to Kennebunk. That we will send her there if she wishes. Does she wish to go to Kennebunk?"

"Yes, she does."

"Then tell her—tell her we are sending her now. With all our love...."

"In a carriage?"

"In a carriage."

"A black carriage with two horses."

"Very well. Is she ready to go?"

"Oh, I see her now in a fancy dress with a bonnet. But she's looking younger—she's looking much younger now. And I see a carriage out front with two dark horses and a man with a hat ready to take her."

"Did she get married in Kennebunk?"

"No."

"Where did she get married?"

"I don't get that."

"Is she ready to go?"

"Yes, she is."

"Tell her to get into the carriage and drive off."

"Yes, she's ready,"

"Then go, Margaret—go."

"She says, many miles—three-day trip."

"All right. Go with our blessings. Do you see her in the carriage now?"

"Yes, the road goes this way. She is going down a winding road."

"Is she alone in the carriage?"

"Yes, she is, but there is a man driving."

"Who is the man who is driving?"

"A hired man."

"Is she in the carriage now?"

"Yes, she is."

"Is she on her way?"

"Yes."

"All right, then wave at her and tell her we send her away with our love."

"She looks to be about twenty-two now. Much younger."

"She's not to return to this house."

"She doesn't want to. She grew old in this house, she says."

"What was the house called then?"

"It was Point something."

"Did they build the house? She and her husband?"

"No, it was there."

"Who built it?"

"Samuel."

"And who was Samuel?"

"A farmer."

"They bought it from him?"

"Yes, they did. She says the deed is in the town hall."

"Of which town? Is it in this village?"

"Next town. Down the road."

"I understand. And in whose name is the deed?"

"Her husband's."

"First name."

"James."

"James what. Full name."

"It's something like Haydon."

"James Haydon from...? What is Samuel's first name?"

"Samuels was the last name of the people who owned it."

"But the first name of the man who sold it. Does she remember that?"

"She never knew it."

"In what year was that?"

"1821."

"How much did they pay for the house?"

"Barter."

"What did they give them?"

"A sailing ship. A small sailing ship for fishing, and several horses. A year's supply of roots, and some paper— currency. Notes."

"But no money?"

"Just notes. Like promises, she says. Notes of promises."

"What was the full price of the house?"

"All in barter, all in exchange up here."

"But there was no sum mentioned for the house? No value?"

"She says, 'Ask my husband.'"

"Now did she and her husband live here alone?"

"Two children."

"What were their names?"

"Philip. But he went to sea."

"And the other one?"

"Francis."

"Did he go to sea too?"

"No."

"What happened to him?"

"I think Francis died."

"What did he die of?"

"Cholera. He was seventeen."

"Where did they get married? In what church?"

"Lutheran."

"Why Lutheran? Was she Lutheran?"

"She doesn't remember."

"Does she remember the name of the minister?"

"Thorpe."

"Thorpe?"

"Yes. Thorpe."

"What was his first name?"

"Thomas Thorpe."

"And when they were married, was that in this town?"

"No."

"What town was it in?"

"A long way away."

"What was the name of the town?"

"Something like Pickwick...a funny name like that...it's some kind of a province of a place. A Piccadilly —a province in the country she says."

"And they came right here after that? Or did they go anywhere else to live?"

"Saco. They went into Saco."

"That's the name of a place?"

"Yes."

"How long did they stay there?"

"Six months in Saco."

"And then?"

"Her husband had a commission."

"What kind of commission?"

"On a whaling ship."

"What was the name of the ship?"

"St. Catherine. I see St. Catherine or St. Catherines."

"And then where did they move to?"

"Port Clyde."

"...and they stayed here for the rest of their lives?"

"Yes, until he went to sea and didn't come back one time."

"His ship didn't come back?"

"No."

"Does she feel better for having told us this?"

"Oh yes."

"Tell her that she...."

"She says it's a long story."

"Tell her that she need not stay where so much unhappiness has transpired in her life. Tell her husband is over there...."

"Yes."

"Does she understand?"

"Yes, she does."

"Does she want to see him again?"

"Yes."

"Then she must call out to him to come to her. Does she understand that?"

"Yes."

"Then tell her to call out to her husband James right now."

"He'll take her to Surrey or something like that, he says."

"Surrey."

"Surrey. Some funny name."

"Is it a place?"

"Yes, it is."

"Does she see him?"

"Yes."

"Are they going off together?"

"Yes, I see her leaving, slowly, but she's looking back."

"Tell her to go and not to return here. Tell her to go with love and happiness and in peace. Are they gone?"

"They are going. It's a reunion."

"We wish them well and we send them from this house, with our blessings, with our love and compassion, and in peace. Go on, go on. What do you see?"

"They are gone."

And with that, we left the house, having done enough for one day, a very full day. The camera crew packed up, so that we could continue shooting in the morning. As for me, the real work was yet to come: corroborating the material Ingrid Beckman had come up with.

I turned to Carol for verification, if possible, of some of the names and data Ingrid had come up with while in the house. Carol showed us a book containing maps of the area, and we started to check it out.

"Look," Carol said and pointed at the passage in the book, "this strip of land was owned by John Barter and it was right next to Samuel Gardner...and it says John Barter died in 1820...the date mentioned by Ingrid! Ah, and there is also mention of the same Margaret Barter, and there is a date on the same page, November 23, 1882...I guess that is when she died."

"Great," I said, pleased to get all this verification so relatively easily. "What exactly is this book?"

"It's a copy of the town's early records, the old hypothogue, of the town of St. George."

"Isn't that the town right next door?"

"Yes, it is."

"What about the name Hogden or Hayden or Samuel?"

"Samuel Hatton was a sailor and his wife was named Elmira," Carol said, pointing at the book. Ingrid had joined us now as I saw no further need to keep her in the dark regarding verifications—her part of the work was done.

"We must verify that," I said. "Also, was there ever a ship named *St. Catherine* and was it built on the Kennebec River as Ingrid claimed?"

But who would be able to do that? Happily, fate was kind; there was a great expert who knew both the area and history of the towns better than anyone around, and he agreed to receive us. That turned out to be a colorful ex-sailor by the name of Commander Albert Smalley, who received us in his house in St. George—a house, I might add, which was superbly furnished to suggest the bridge of a ship. After we had stopped admiring his mementos, and made some chitchat to establish the seriousness of our mission, I turned to the Commander and put the vital questions to him directly.

"Commander Albert Smalley, you've been a resident in this town for how long?"

"I was born in this town seventy-six years ago."

"I understand you know more about the history of Port Clyde than anybody else."

"Well, that's a moot question, but I will say, possibly, yes."

"Now, to the best of your knowledge, do the names Samuel and Hatton mean anything in connection with this area?"

"Yes, I know Hatton lived at Port Clyde prior to 1850. That I'm sure about."

"What profession did he have?"

"Sailor."

"Was there a ship named the *St. Catherine* in these parts?"

"Yes, there was."

"And would it have been built at the Kennebec River? Or connected with it in some way?"

"Well, as I recall it was, and I believe it was built in the Sewell Yard at the Kennebec River."

"Was there any farming in a small way in the Port Clyde area in the nineteenth century?"

"Oh yes, primarily that's what they came here for. But fishing, of course, was a prime industry."

"Now there's a lighthouse not far from Port Clyde which I believe was built in the early part of the nineteenth century. Could it have been there in the 1840s?"

"Yes. It was built in 1833."

"Now if somebody would have been alive in 1840, would they somehow be concerned about this comparatively new lighthouse? Would it have worried them?"

"No, it would not. The residence is comparatively new. The old stone residence was destroyed by lightning. But the tower is the same one."

"Now you know the area of Port Clyde where the Leah Davis house now stands? Prior to this house, were there any houses in the immediate area?"

"I've always been told that there was a house there. The Davis that owned it told me that he built on an old cellar."

"And how far back would that go?"

"That would go back to probably 1870. The new house was built around 1870."

"And was there one before that?"

"Yes, there was one before that."

"Could that have been a farmhouse?"

"Yes, it could have been because there is a little farm in back of it. It's small."

"Now you of course have heard all kinds of stories—some of them true, some of them legendary. Have you ever heard any story of a great tragedy concerning the owners of the farmhouse on that point?"

"Whit Thompson used to tell some weird ghost stories. But everyone called him a damned liar. Whether it's true or not, I don't know, but I've heard them."

"About that area?"

"About that area."

"Was there, sir, any story about a female ghost—a woman?"

"I have heard of a female ghost. Yes, Whit used to tell that story."

"What did he tell you?"

"That was a long time ago, and I cannot recall just what he said about it—he said many things—but she used to appear, especially on foggy nights, and it was hard to distinguish her features—that was one of the things he used to tell about—and there was something about her ringing the bell at the lighthouse, when they used to ring the old fog bell there. I don't recall what it was."

"Now the story we found involved a woman wearing a kind of white gown, looking out to sea from the window as if she were expecting her sailor to return, and she apparently was quite faceless at first."

"I don't think Whitney ever told of her face being seen."

"Do you know of anybody in your recollection who has actually had an unusual experience in that particular area?"

"No, I don't."

"Commander, if you had the choice of spending the night in the house in question, would it worry you?"

"No, why should it?"

"You are not afraid of ghosts?"

"No. Why should I be?"

"They are people after all."

"Huh?"

"They are just people after all."

"Yes."

"Have you ever seen one?"

"No, I was brought up with mediums and spiritualists and as a kid I was frightened half to death, I didn't dare go our after dark, but I got over that."

"Thank you very much."

"The lighthouse and the gale...the ship in a gale...it all seems to fit...," Ingrid mumbled as we got back into our cars and left the Commander's house.

And there you have it. A woman from the big city who knows nothing about the case I am investigating, nor where she might be taken, still comes up with the names and data she could not possibly know on her own. Ingrid Beckman was (and is, I suppose) a gifted psychic. Shortly after we finished taping the Port Clyde story, I left for Europe.

While I was away, Ingrid met a former disc jockey then getting interested in the kind of work she and I had been doing so successfully for a while. Somehow he persuaded her to give a newspaper interview about this case—which, of course, upset NBC a lot since this segment would not air for six months—not to mention myself. The newspaper story was rather colorful, making it appear that Ingrid had heard of this ghost and taken care of it...but then newspaper stories sometimes distort things, or perhaps the verification and research of a ghost story is less interesting to them than the story itself. But to a professional like myself, the evidence only becomes evidence when it is carefully verified. I haven't worked with Ingrid since.

As for the ghostly lady of Port Clyde, nothing further has been heard about her, either, and since we gently persuaded her not to hang on any longer, chances are indeed that she has long been joined by her man, sailing an ocean where neither gales nor nosy television crews can intrude.

✳ 115

A Plymouth Ghost

I AM NOT TALKING ABOUT *the* Plymouth where the Pilgrims landed but another Plymouth. This one is located in New Hampshire, in a part of the state that is rather lonely and sparsely settled even today. If you really want to get away from it all—whatever it may be—this is a pretty good bet. I am mentioning this because a person living in this rural area isn't likely to have much choice in the way of entertainment, unless of course you provide it yourself. But I am getting ahead of my story.

I was first contacted about this case in August 1966 when a young lady named Judith Elliott, who lived in Bridgeport, Connecticut, at the time, informed me of the goings-on in her cousin's country house located in New Hampshire. Judith asked if I would be interested in contacting Mrs. Chester Fuller regarding these matters. What intrigued me about the report was not the usual array of footfalls, presences, and the house cat staring at someone unseen—but the fact that Mrs. Fuller apparently had seen a ghost and identified him from a book commemorating the Plymouth town bicentennial.

When I wrote back rather enthusiastically, Miss Elliot forwarded my letter to her cousin, requesting more detailed and chronological information. But it was not until well into the following year that I finally got around to making plans for a visit. Ethel Johnson Meyers, the late medium, and my ex-wife Catherine, always interested in spooky houses since she used to illustrate some of my books, accompanied me. Mrs. Fuller, true to my request, supplied me with all that she knew of the phenomena themselves, who experienced them, and such information about former owners of the house and the house itself as she could garner. Here, in her own words, is that report, which of course I kept from the medium at all times so as not to influence her or give her prior knowledge of the house and circumstances. Mrs. Fuller's report is as follows:

Location: The house is located at 38 Merrill Street in the town of Plymouth, New Hampshire. To reach the house, you leave Throughway 93 at the first exit for Plymouth. When you reach the set of lights on Main Street, turn right and proceed until you reach the blue Sunoco service station, then take a sharp left onto Merrill Street. The house is the only one with white picket snow fence out front. It has white siding with a red front door and a red window box and is on the right hand side of the street.

1. The first time was around the middle of June—about a month after moving in. It was the time of day when lights are needed inside, but it is still light outside. This instance was in the kitchen and bathroom. The bathroom and dining room are in an addition onto the kitchen. The doors to both rooms go out of the kitchen beside of each other, with just a small wall space between. At that time we had our kitchen table in that

space. I was getting supper, trying to put the food on the table and keep two small children (ages 2 and 5) off the table. As I put the potatoes on the table, I swung around from the sink toward the bathroom door. I thought I saw someone in the bathroom. I looked and saw a man. He was standing about halfway down the length of the room. He was wearing a brown plaid shirt, dark trousers with suspenders, and he [wore] glasses with the round metal frames. He was of medium height, a little on the short side, not fat and not thin but a good build, a roundish face, and he was smiling. Suddenly he was gone, no disappearing act or anything fancy, just gone, as he had come.

2. Footsteps. There are footsteps in other parts of the house. If I am upstairs, the footsteps are downstairs. If I am in the kitchen, they are in the living room, etc. These were scattered all through the year, in all seasons, and in the daytime. It was usually around 2 or 3 and always on a sunny days, as I recall.

3. Winter—late at night. Twice we (Seth and I) heard a door shutting upstairs. (Seth is an elderly man who stays with us now. When we first moved here he was not staying with us. His wife was a distant cousin to my father. I got acquainted with them when I was in high school. I spent a lot of time at their house and his wife and I became quite close. She died 11 years ago and since then Seth has stayed at his son's house, a rooming house, and now up here. He spent a lot of time visiting us before he moved in.) Only one door in the bedrooms upstairs works right, and that is the door to my bedroom. I checked the kids that night to see if they were up or awake, but they had not moved. My husband was also sound asleep. The door was already shut, as my husband had shut it tight when he went to bed to keep out the sound of the television. The sound of the door was very distinct—the sound of when it first made contact, then the latch clicking in place, and then the thud as it came in contact with the casing. Everything was checked out—anything that was or could be loose and have blown and banged, or anything that could have fallen down. Nothing had moved. The door only shut once during that night, but did it again later on in the winter.

4. The next appearance was in the fall. I was pregnant at the time. I lost the baby on the first of November, and this happened around the first of October. Becky Sue, my youngest daughter, was 3 at the time. She was asleep in her crib as it was around midnight or later. I was asleep in my bedroom across the hall. I woke up and heard her saying, "Mommy, what are you doing in my bedroom?" She kept saying that until I thought I had better answer her or she would begin to be frightened. I started to say "I'm not in your room," and as I did I started to turn over and I saw what seemed to be a woman in a long white nightgown in front of my bedroom door. In a flash it was gone out into the hall. At this time Becky had been saying, "Mommy, what are you doing in my room?" As the image disappeared out in the hall, Becky changed her question to, "Mommy, what were you doing in my bedroom?" Then I thought that if I told her I wasn't in her

room that she would really be scared. All this time I thought that it was Kimberly, my older daughter, getting up, and I kept waiting for her to speak to me. Becky was still sounding like a broken record with her questions. Finally I heard "It" take two steps down, turn a corner, and take three steps more. Then I went into Becky's room and told her that I had forgotten what I had gone into her room for and to lie down and go to sleep, which she did. All this time Kim had not moved. The next morning I was telling Seth (who was living with us now) about it, and I remembered about the footsteps going downstairs. I wondered if Becky had heard them too, so I called her out into the kitchen and asked her where I went after I left her room. She looked at me as if I had lost my mind and said, "Downstairs!"

5. This was in the winter, around 2. Seth was helping me make the beds upstairs as they had been skipped for some reason. We heard footsteps coming in from the playroom across the kitchen and a short way into the hall. We both thought it was Becky Sue who was playing outdoors. She comes in quite frequently for little odds and ends. Still no one spoke. We waited for a while expecting her to call to me. Finally, when she did not call, I went downstairs to see what she wanted, and there was no one there. I thought that maybe she had gone back out, but there was no snow on the floor or tracks of any kind. This was also on a very sunny day.

6. This was also late at night in 1965, around 11. I was putting my husband's lunch up when there was a step right behind me. That scared me, although I do not know why; up until that time I had never had any fear. Maybe it was because it was right behind my back and the others had always been at a distance or at least in front of me.

I cannot remember anything happening since then. Lately there have been noises as if someone was in the kitchen or dining room while I was in the living room, but I cannot be sure of that. It sounds as if something was swishing, but I cannot *definitely* say that it is not the sounds of an old house.

History of House and Background of Previous Owners
The history of the house and its previous owners is very hard to get. We bought the house from Mrs. Ora Jacques. Her husband had bought it from their son who had moved to Florida. The husband was going to do quite a bit of remodeling and then sell it. When he died, Mrs. Jacques rented it for a year and then sold it.

Mr. Jacques' son bought it from a man who used to have a doughnut shop and did his cooking in a back room, so I have been told. There was a fire in the back that was supposedly started from the fat. They bought the house from Mrs. Emma Thompson, who, with her husband, had received the house for caring for a Mr. Woodbury Langdon, and by also giving him a small sum of money. Mrs. Thompson always gave people the impression that she was really a countess and that she had a sister in Pennsylvania who would not have anything to do with her because of her odd ways.

Mrs. Thompson moved to Rumney where she contracted pneumonia about six months later and died.

Mr. and Mrs. Thompson moved in to take care of Mr. Woodbury Langdon after he kicked out Mr. and Mrs. Dinsmore. (Mr. Cushing gave me the following information. He lives next door, and has lived there since 1914 or 1918).

He was awakened by a bright flash very early in the morning. Soon he could see that the top room (tower room) was all fire. He got dressed, called the firemen, and ran over to help. He looked in the window of what is now our dining room but was then Mr. Langdon's bedroom. (Mr. Langdon was not able to go up and down stairs because of his age.) He pounded on the window trying to wake Mr. Langdon up. Through the window he could see Mr. and Mrs. Dinsmore standing in the doorway between the kitchen and the bedroom. They were laughing and Mr. Dinsmore had an oil can in his hand. All this time Mr. Langdon was sound asleep. Mr. Cushing got angry and began pounding harder and harder. Just as he began to open the window Mr. Langdon woke up and Mr. Cushing helped him out the window. He said that no one would believe his story, even the insurance company. Evidently Mr. Langdon did because soon after he kicked the Dinsmores out and that was when Mr. and Mrs. Thompson came to take care of him. Around 1927 he came down with pneumonia. He had that for two days and then he went outdoors without putting on any jacket or sweater. Mrs. Thompson ran out and brought him back in. She put him back in bed and warmed him up with coffee and wrapped him in wool blankets. He seemed better until around midnight. Then he began moaning. He kept it up until around 3, when he died.

Mr. Langdon was married twice. His first wife and his eighteen-year-old son died [of] typhoid fever. He had the wells examined and found that it came from them. He convinced his father to invest his money in putting in the first water works for the town of Plymouth. At that time he lived across town on Russell Street.

He later married a woman by the name of Donna. He worshipped her and did everything he could to please her. He remodeled the house. That was when he added on the bathroom and bedroom (dining room). He also built the tower room so that his wife could look out over the town. He also had a big estate over to Squam Lake that he poured out money on. All this time she was running around with anyone she could find. Mr. Cushing believes that he knew it deep down but refused to let himself believe it. She died, Mr. Cushing said, from the things she got from the thing she did! He insists that it was called leprosy. In the medical encyclopedia it reads, under leprosy, "differential diag: tuberculosis and esp. syphilis are the two diseases most likely to be considered."

She died either in this house or at the estate on the lake. She was buried in the family plot in Trinity Cemetery in Holderness. She has a small headstone with just one name on it, Donna. There is a large spire-shaped monument in the center of the lot, with the family's names on it and their relationship. The name of Woodbury Langdon's second wife is completely eliminated from the stone. There is nothing there to tell who she was or why she is buried there. This has puzzled me up to now, because, as she died around 1911, and he did not die until around 1927, he had plenty of time to have her name and relationship added to the family stone. Mr. Cushing thinks that, after her death, Mr. Langdon

began to realize more and more what she was really like. He has the impression that Mr. Langdon was quite broke at the time of his death.

I cannot trace any more of the previous owners, as I cannot trace the house back any farther than around 1860. Mr. Langdon evidently bought and sold houses like other men bought and sold horses. If this is the house I believe it to be, it was on the road to Rumney and had to be moved in a backward position to where it is now. They had something like six months later to move the barn back. Then they had to put in a street going from the house up to the main road. They also had to put a fence up around the house. This property *did* have a barn, and there was a fence here. There is a small piece of it left. The deeds from there just go around in circles.

The man who I think the ghost is, is Mr. Woodbury Langdon. I have asked people around here what Mr. Langdon looked like and they describe him VERY MUCH as the man I saw in the bathroom. The man in the bicentennial book was his father. There is something in his face that was in the face of the "ghost."

I have two children. They are: Kimberly Starr, age 9 years and Rebecca Sue, age 6 years. Kim's birthday is on April 2 and Becky's is on August 10.

I was born and brought up on a farm 4½ miles out in the country in the town of Plymouth. My father believes in spirits, sort of, but not really. My mother absolutely does not.

I carried the business course and the college preparatory course through my four years of high school. I had one year of nurses' training. I was married when I was 20, in June, and Kim was born the next April.

P.S. We have a black cat who has acted queer at times in the past.

1. He would go bounding up the stairs only to come to an abrupt halt at the head of the stairs. He would sit there staring at presumably empty space, and then take off as if he had never stopped.

2. Sometimes he stood at the bathroom door and absolutely refused to go in.

3. He had spells of sitting in the hallway and staring up the stairs, not moving a muscle. Then suddenly he would relax and go on his way.

* * *

We finally settled on August 12, a Saturday, 1967, to have a go at Mr. Langdon or whoever it was that haunted the house, because Miss Elliot was getting married in July and Mrs. Fuller wanted very much to be present.

Eleanor Fuller greeted us as we arrived, and led us into the house. As usual Ethel began to sniff around, and I just followed her, tape recorder running and camera at the ready. We followed her up the stairs to the upper floor, where Ethel stopped at the bedroom on the right, which happened to be decorated in pink.

"I get an older woman wearing glasses," Ethel said cautiously as she was beginning to pick up psychic leads, "and a man wearing a funny hat."

I pressed Ethel to be more specific about the "funny hat" and what period hat. The man seemed to her to belong to the early 1800s. She assured me it was not this century. She then complained about a cold spot, and when I stepped into it I too felt it. Since neither doors nor windows could be held responsible for the strong cold draft we felt, we knew that its origin was of a psychic nature, as it often is when there are entities present.

I asked Ethel to describe the woman she felt present. "She is lying down...and I get a pain in the chest," she said, picking up the spirit's condition. "The eyes are closed!"

We left the room and went farther on. Ethel grabbed her left shoulder as if in pain.

"She is here with me, looking at me," Ethel said. "She's been here."

"Why is she still here?" I asked.

"I get a sudden chill when you asked that," Ethel replied.

"She tells me to go left...I am having difficulty walking...I think this woman had that difficulty."

We were walking down the stairs, when Ethel suddenly became a crone and had difficulty managing them. The real Ethel was as spry and fast as the chipmunks that used to roam around her house in Connecticut.

"I think she fell down these stairs," Ethel said and began to cough. Obviously, she was being impressed by a very sick person.

We had barely got Ethel to a chair when she slipped into full trance and the transition took place. Her face became distorted as in suffering, and a feeble voice tried to manifest through her, prodded by me to be clearer.

"Lander...or something..." she mumbled.

What followed was an absolutely frightening realization by an alien entity inside Ethel's body that the illness she was familiar with no longer existed now. At the same time, the excitement of this discovery made it difficult for the spirit to speak clearly, and we were confronted with a series of grunts and sighs.

Finally, I managed to calm the entity down by insisting she needed to relax in order to be heard.

"Calm...calm..." she said and cried, "good...he knows...he did that...for fifty years...the woman!"

She had seized Mr. Fuller's hand so forcefully I felt embarrassed for her, and tried to persuade the spirit within Ethel to let go, at the same time explaining her true condition to her, gently, but firmly.

After I had explained how she was able to communicate with us and that the body of the medium was merely a temporary arrangement, the entity calmed down, asking only if he loved her, meaning the other spirit in the house. I assured her that this was so, and then called on Albert, Ethel's spirit guide, to help me ease the troubled one from

Ethel's body and thus free her at the same time from the house.

And then the man came into Ethel's body, very emotionally, calling out for Sylvia.

Again I explained how he was able to communicate.

"You see me, don't you," he finally said as he calmed down. "I loved everyone...I'll go, I won't bother you..."

I called again for Albert, and in a moment his crisp voice replaced the spirit's outcries.

"The man is a Henry MacLellan...there stood in this vicinity another house...around 1810, 1812...to 1820...a woman connected with this house lies buried here somewhere, and he is looking for her. His daughter...Macy?...Maisie? About 1798...16 or 18 years old...has been done wrong...had to do with a feud of two families...McDern..."

Albert then suggested letting the man speak to us directly, and so he did a little while. I offered my help.

"It is futile," he said. "My problem is my own."

"Who are you?"

"Henry. I lived right here. I was born here."

"What year? What year are we in now as I speak with you?"

"I speak to you in the year 1813."

"Are you a gentleman of some age?"

"I would have forty-seven years."

"Did you serve in any governmental force or agency?"

"My son...John Stuart Mc..."

"McDermont? Your son was John Stuart McDermont?"

"You have it from my own lips."

"Where did he serve?"

"Ticonderoga."

And then he added, "My daughter, missing, but I found the bones, buried not too far from here. I am satisfied. I have her with me."

He admitted he knew he was no longer "on the earth plane," but was drawn to the place from time to time.

"But if you ask me as a gentleman to go, I shall go," he added. Under these circumstances—rare ones, indeed, when dealing with hauntings—I suggested he not disturb those in the present house, especially the children. Also, would he not be happier in the world into which he had long passed.

"I shall consider that," he acknowledged, "You speak well, sir. I have no intention for frightening."

"Are you aware that much time has passed...that this is not 1813 any more?" I said.

"I am not aware of this, sir...it is always the same time here."

Again I asked if he served in any regiment, but he replied his leg was no good. Was it his land and house? Yes, he replied, he owned it and built the house. But when I pressed him as to where he might be buried, he balked.

"My bones are here with me...I am sufficient unto myself."

I then asked about his church affiliation, and he informed me his church was "northeast of here, on Beacon Road." The minister's name was Rooney, but he could not tell me the denomination. His head was not all it used to be.

"A hundred any fifty years have passed," I said, and began the ritual of exorcism." Go from this house in peace, and with our love."

And so he did.

Albert, Ethel's guide, returned briefly to assure us that all was as it should be and Mr. McDermot was gone from the house; also, that he was being reunited with his mother, Sarah Ann McDermot. And then Albert too withdrew and Ethel returned to her own self again.

I turned to Mrs. Fuller and her cousin, Miss Elliott, for possible comments and corroboration of the information received through Mrs. Meyers in trance.

* * *

It appears the house that the Fullers were able to trace back as far as about 1860 was moved to make room for a road, and then set down again not far from that road. Unfortunately going further back proved difficult. I heard again from Mrs. Fuller in December of that year. The footsteps were continuing, it seemed, and her seven-year-old daughter Becky was being frightened by them. She had not yet been able to find any record of Mr. McDermot, but vowed to continue her search.

That was twenty years ago, and nothing further turned up, and I really do not know if the footsteps continued or Mr. McDermot finally gave up his restless quest for a world of which he no longer was a part.

As for Mr. Langdon, whom Ethel Meyers had also identified by name as a presence in the house, he must by now be reunited with his wife Donna, and I hope he has forgiven her trespasses, as a good Christian might: over there, even her sins do not matter any longer.

✳ 116

The Ghosts at the Morris-Jumel Mansion

WE HAD HARDLY RETURNED to our home in New York, when my friend Elizabeth Byrd telephoned to inquire if I had gotten that grave opened yet. I hadn't, but I should really let you in at the beginning.

You see, it all started with an article in the *New York Journal-American* on January 11, 1964, by Joan Hanauer, in which the ghostly goings-on at Jumel Mansion in New York City were brought to public attention. Youngsters on a field trip from P.S. 164, Edgecombe Avenue and 164th Street, said a tall, gray-haired, elderly woman stepped out onto the balcony and told them to be quiet.

The description fit Mme. Jumel.

Could it have happened?

Mrs. Emma Bingay Campbell, curator of the Mansion at 160th Street and Edgecombe, said no.

"I don't believe in ghosts," she said, "but it was very strange. The house was locked and empty. We know that. There could not have been a woman there. But several of the children insist they saw and heard her.

"It was shortly before eleven, opening time for the house, which dates back to 1765.

"When I came over to the children to explain they must wait for John Duffy, the second gardener, to unlock the doors at eleven," Mrs. Campbell said, "one of the girls wanted to know why the tall woman who had come out on the balcony to reprimand them for boisterousness couldn't let them in. There couldn't have been any such woman—or anyone else—in the house.

"The woman the children described resembled Mme. Jumel, who some thought murdered her husband in the house in 1832, then married Aaron Burr the following year.

"But the children couldn't know that, or what she looked like.

"They also couldn't know that the balcony on which the apparition appeared separated Mme. Jumel's and Burr's bedrooms."

Elizabeth Byrd was then working on a story about Manhattan ghosts for a magazine, so we decided to follow up this case together. First we contacted the public school authorities and obtained permission to talk to the children. The teacher assembled the entire group she had originally taken to the Jumel Mansion, and we questioned them, separately and together. Their story was unchanged. The woman appeared on the balcony, suddenly, and she told them to be quiet.

"How did she disappear?" I wanted to know.

One youngster thought for a moment, then said hesitantly, "She sort of glided back into the house."

"Did you see the balcony doors open?" I asked the girl.

"No sir," she replied firmly.

"Then did she glide through the door?"

"She did."

The dress they described the ghost as wearing does exist—but it is put away carefully upstairs in the mansion and was not on display, nor is this common knowledge, especially among eleven-year-old school girls.

There was a cooking class in progress when we arrived, and the girls carefully offered us samples of their art. We declined for the moment and went on to see the

**The Morris-Jumel Mansion—
Washington Heights, New York**

curator of the mansion, Mrs. Campbell. This energetic lady takes care of the mansion for the Daughters of the American Revolution in whose charge the City of New York had placed the museum.

"Is this the first report of a haunting here?" I wanted to know.

Mrs. Campbell shook her head. "Here," she said, and took down from one of the shelves in her office a heavy book. "William Henry Shelton's work, *The Jumel Mansion*, pages 207 and 208 report earlier ghosts observed here."

"Have you ever seen or heard anything?"

"No, not yet, but others have. There was that German nurse who lived here in 1865—she heard strange noises even then. Footsteps have been heard by many visitors here when there was no one about. The ghost of Mme. Jumel appeared to a retired guard at the door of this room."

"How would you like me to investigate the matter?" I offered. A date was set immediately.

First, I thought it wise to familiarize myself with the physical layout of the historic house. I was immediately struck by its imposing appearance. Historian John Kent Tilton wrote:

Located on the highest elevation of Manhattan is one of the most famous old historic houses in the nation, the Morris-Jumel Mansion. The locality was originally called Harlem Heights by the Dutch in the days of New Amsterdam and was then changed to Mount Morris during the English ownership, before receiving the present name of Washington Heights.

The plot of land upon which the old mansion is situated was originally deeded in 1700 to a Dutch farmer

named Jan Kiersen, from part of the "half morgen of land of the common woods" of New Haarlem.

Lieutenant Colonel Roger Morris purchased the estate in 1765. The new owner was born in England in 1728 and came to America at the age of eighteen with a commission of captaincy in the British army.

It was here that the Morris family, with their four children, spent their summers, living the domestic life typical of a British squire and family until the outbreak of the Revolution.

Colonel Morris fled to England at the beginning of hostilities, where he remained for two and one-half years.

As early in the war as August 1776, Mount Morris was taken over by the American troops and General Heath and staff were quartered there. After the disastrous Battle of Long Island, General Washington retreated to Haarlem Heights and made the place his headquarters. After Washington decided to abandon this location, the British moved in and the Morris Mansion housed General Sir Henry Clinton and his officers and, at intervals, the Hessians, during the seven years the British occupied New York.

During the following quarter of a century it was sold and resold several times and witnessed many changes in its varied career. Renamed Calumet Hall, it served for a time as a Tavern and was a stopping place for the stage coaches en route to Albany. It was the home of an unknown farmer when President Washington paid a visit to his old headquarters and entertained at dinner, among others, his cabinet members, John Adams, Alexander Hamilton, Henry Knox, and their wives.

The locality was one that Stephen Jumel with his sprightly and ambitious wife delighted driving out to on a summer's day from their home on Whitehall Street. Mme. Jumel became entranced with the nearby old Morris Mansion and persuaded her husband to purchase it for their home in 1810, for the sum of $10,000 which included 35 acres of land still remaining of the original tract.

The old house was fast falling into decay when Mme. Jumel energetically went about renovating and refurnishing it, and when completed, it was one of the most beautiful homes in the country. The Jumels restored the mansion in the style of the early nineteenth century, when the Federal influence was in fashion.

Mme. Jumel first married, some say by trickery, the rich Frenchman, Stephen Jumel. He had at one time owned a large plantation in Santo Domingo from whence he was obliged to flee at the time of the insurrection. Arriving in the United States, a comparatively poor man, he soon amassed a new fortune as a wine merchant, and at his death in 1832, his wife became one of the richest women in America. A year later she married Aaron Burr, former vice president of the United States. This second marriage, however, was of short duration and ended in divorce. Mme. Jumel died at the age of 93 in 1865.

The Morris-Jumel Mansion is of the mid-Georgian period of architecture. The front facade has four columns, two stories in height, with a pediment at the top.

The exterior is painted white. One of the post-colonial features added by the Jumels is the imposing front entrance doorway, with flanking sidelights and elliptical fanlight.

In the interior, the wide central hall with arches is furnished with late eighteenth and early nineteenth century pieces. At the left of the entrance is the small parlor or tearoom where the marriage ceremony of the Widow Jumel and Aaron Burr was performed in 1833 when the bride was fifty-eight and the groom twenty years her senior.

Across the hall is the stately Georgian dining room where many persons of fame assembled for elaborated dinner parties.

At the rear of the hall is the large octagonal drawing room.

The broad stairway leads to the spacious hall on the upper floor, which is furnished with personal belongings of the Jumels. There is a group portrait of Mme. Jumel and the young son and daughter of her adopted daughter, Mary Eliza, who married Nelson Chase.

The northwest bedroom contains furniture owned by the Jumels, including a carved four-poster bed.

In the old days the rooms on the third floor were probably used as extra guest chambers since the servants' quarters were then located in the basement with the kitchen.

On January 19, 1964, a small group of people assembled in Betsy Jumel's old sitting room upstairs. Present were a few members of the New York Historical Society and the Daughters of the American Revolution, *Journal-American* writer Nat Adams, and a latecomer, Harry Altschuler of the *World-Telegram*. I was accompanied by Ethel Meyers, who had not been told where we were going that winter afternoon, and Jessyca Russell Gaver, who was serving us my secretary and doing a magazine article on our work at the same time.

We had barely arrived when Ethel went in and out of the Jumel bedroom as if someone were forcing her to do so. As she approached the room across the hall, her shoulder sagged and one arm hung loose as if her side and had been injured!

"I feel funny on my left side," Ethel finally said, and her voice had already taken on some of the coloring of someone else's voice.

We went back to the bedroom, which is normally closed to the public. One side is occupied by a huge carved four-poster, once the property of Napoleon I, and there are small chairs of the period in various spots throughout the room. In one corner, there is a large mirror.

"The issue is confused," Ethel said, and sounded confused herself. "There is more than one disturbed person here. I almost feel as though three people were involved. There has been sickness and a change of heart. Someone got a raw deal."

Suddenly, Ethel turned to one of the men who had sat down on Napoleon's bed. "Someone wants you to get

The haunted balcony

up from that bed," she said, and evinced difficulty in speaking. As if bitten by a tarantula, the young man shot put from the bed. No ghost was going to goose *him*.

Ethel again struggled to her feet, despite my restraining touch on her arm. "I've got to go back to that other room again," she mumbled, and off she went, with me trailing after her. She walked almost as if she were being taken over by an outside force. In front of the picture of Mme. Jumel, she suddenly fell to her knees.

"I never can go forward here...I fall whenever I'm near there." She pointed at the large picture above her, and almost shouted, "My name isn't on that picture. I want my name there!"

Mrs. Campbell, the curator, took me aside in agitation. "That's very strange she should say that," she remarked. "You see, her name really used to be on that picture a long time ago. But that picture wasn't in this spot when Betsy Jumel was alive."

I thanked her and led Ethel Meyers back to her chair in the other room.

"Henry...and a Johann...around her...," she mumbled as she started to go into a deep trance. Hoarse sounds emanated from her lips. At first they were unintelligible. Gradually I was able to make them out. Halfway into a trance, she moved over to the bed and lay down on it. I placed my chair next to her head. The others strained to hear. There was an eerie silence about the room, interrupted only by the soft words of the entranced medium.

"You think me dead..." a harsh, male voice now said.

"No, I've come to talk to you, to help you," I replied.

"Go away," the ghostly voice said. "Go away!"

"Are you a man or a woman?" I asked.

The Ghosts at the Morris-Jumel Mansion

Side view of the Morris-Jumel Mansion

A bitter laugh was the reply.

"Man... ha!" the voice finally said.

"What is your name?"

"Everybody knows who I am."

" I don't. What is your name?" I repeated.

"Let me sleep."

"Is anything troubling you?"

There was a moment of silence, then the voice was a bit softer. "Who are *you*?"

"I'm a friend come to help you."

"Nobody talks to me. They think I'm dead."

"What exactly happened to you?"

"They took me away," the voice said in plaintive tones. "I am not dead yet. Why did they take me away?"

Now the body of the medium shook as if in great agitation, while I spoke soothing words to calm the atmosphere. Suddenly, the ghost speaking through the medium was gone, and in his place was the crisp, matter-of-fact voice of Albert, Ethel's control. I asked Albert to tell us through the entranced medium who the ghost was.

"I don't hear a name, but I see a sturdy body and round face. He complains he was pronounced dead when he in fact wasn't. I believe he is the owner of the house and it bears his name. There are many jealousies in this house. There is an artist who is also under suspicion."

"Is there a woman here?"

"One thwarted of what she desired and who wants to throw herself out the window."

"Why?" I asked.

"Thwarted in love and under suspicion."

Later, I asked Mrs. Campbell about this. She thought for a moment, then confirmed the following facts: A young servant girl involved with one of the family tried to commit suicide by jumping out the window.

I questioned Albert further. "Is there a restless woman in this house?"

"That is right. The one in the picture. Her conscience disturbs her."

"About what?"

The medium now grabbed her side, as if in pain. "I am being threatened," Albert said now, "I feel the revelation would disturb."

"But how can I release her unless I know what is holding her here?"

"It has to do with the death of her husband. That he was strangled in his coffin."

I tried to question him further, but he cut us short. The medium had to be released now.

Soon, Ethel Meyers was back to her own self. She remembered very little of the trance, but her impressions of a clairvoyant nature continued for a while. I queried her about the person on the bed.

"I get the initial J.," she replied and rubbed her side.

I turned to Mrs. Campbell. "What about the story of Mme. Jumel's guilty conscience?"

"Well," the curator replied, "after her husband's death, she refused to live in this house for some time. She always felt guilty about it."

We were standing in a corner where the medium could not hear us. "Stephen Jumel bled to death from a wound he had gotten in a carriage accident. Mme. Jumel allegedly tore off his bandage and let him die. That much we know."

Mrs. Campbell naturally is a specialist on Betsy Jumel and her life, and she knows many intimate details unknown to the general public or even to researchers.

It was 5:30 in the afternoon when we left the house, which must be closed for the night after that hour.

* * *

The next morning two newspaper accounts appeared: One, fairly accurate, in the *Journal*, and a silly one in the *Telegram*, by a man who stood outside the room of the investigation and heard very little, if anything.

Several weeks went by and my ghost-hunting activities took me all over the country. Then I received a telephone call from Mrs. Campbell.

"Did you know that May twenty-second is the anniversary of Stephen Jumel's death?" I didn't and I wagered her nobody else did, except herself and the late Mr. Jumel. She allowed as to that and suggested we have another go at the case on that date. I have always felt that anniversaries are good times to solve murder cases so I readily agreed.

This time, the *Journal* and *Telegram* reporters weren't invited, but the *New York Times*, in the person of reporter Grace Glueck, was, and I am indebted to her for the notes she took of the proceedings that warm May afternoon.

Present also were the general manager of King Features, Frank McLearn; Clark Kinnaird, literary critic of the

Journal; John Allen and Bob O'Brien of *Reader's Digest*; Emeline Paige, the editor of *The Villager*; writers Elizabeth Byrd and Beverly Balin; Ed Joyce of CBS; and several members of the New York Historical Society, presumably there as observers ready to rewrite history as needed since the famous Aaron Burr might be involved.

Ethel Meyers was told nothing about the significance of the date, nor had I discussed with her the results of the first séance.

Again we assembled in the upstairs bedroom and Ed Joyce set up his tape recorder in front of Napoleon's bed, while Ethel sat on the bed itself and I next to her on a chair. To my left, the young lady from the *Times* took her seat. All in all there must have been twenty-five anxious people in the room, straining to hear all that was said and keeping a respectful silence when asked to. Within a few minutes, Ethel was in a deep trance, and a male voice spoke through her vocal cords.

"Who are you?" I asked as I usually do when an unknown person comes through a medium.

"*Je suis Stephen,*" the voice said.

"Do you speak English?"

In answer the medium clutched at her body and groaned, "Doctor! Doctor! Where is the doctor?"

"What is hurting you?" I asked.

The voice was firm and defiant now. "I'm alive, I'm alive...don't take me away."

"Did you have an accident? What happened to you?"

"She tricked me."

"Who tricked you?"

"I can't breathe...where is she? She tricked me. Look at her!"

"Don't worry about her," I said. "She's dead."

"But I'm alive!" the entranced voice continued.

"In a sense, you are. But you have also passed over."

"No—they put me in the grave when I was not yet dead."

"How did you get hurt?" I wanted to know.

The ghost gave a bitter snort. "What matter—I'm dead. You said so."

"I didn't say you were dead." I replied.

The voice became furious again. "She took it, she took it—that woman. She took my life. Go away."

"I'm your friend."

"I haven't any friends...that Aaron...."

"Aaron? Was he involved in your death?"

"That strumpet...hold him! They buried me alive, I tell you."

"When did this happen?"

"It was cold. She made me a fool, a fool!"

"How did she do that?"

"All the time I loved her, she tricked me."

"I want to help you."

"I'm bleeding."

"How did this happen?"

"Pitchfork...wagon...hay...."

Painting of Madame Betsy Jumel at the house. She is still there ...

"Was it an accident, yes or no?"

"I fell on it."

"You fell on the pitchfork?"

"Look at the blood bath...on Napoleon's bed."

"What about that pitchfork?" I insisted.

"There was a boy in the hay, and he pushed me off."

"Did you know this boy?"

"Yes...give me *her*. She wanted to be a lady. I saw it. I wasn't so foolish I didn't see it."

"What happened when you got home?"

"She told me I was going to die."

"Did you have a doctor?"

"Yes."

"Wasn't the wound bandaged?"

"They took me out alive. I was a live man he put in the grave. I want to be free from that grave!"

"Do you want me to set you free?"

"God bless you!"

"It is your hatred that keeps you here. You must forgive."

"She did it to me."

The Ghosts at the Morris-Jumel Mansion

Ethel Meyers making contact

I then pleaded with the ghost to join his own family and let go of his memories. "Do you realize how much time has gone on since? A hundred years!"

"Hundred years!"

The medium, still entranced, buried her head in her hands: "I'm mad!"

"Go from this house and don't return."

"Mary, Mary!"

Mary was the name of Jumel's daughter, a fact not known to the medium at the time.

"Go and join Mary!" I commanded, and asked that Albert, the control, help the unhappy one find the way.

Just as soon as Jumel's ghost had left us, someone else slipped into the medium's body, or so it seemed, for she sat up and peered at us with a suspicious expression: "Who are you?"

"I'm a friend, come to help," I replied.

"I didn't ask for you."

"My name is Holzer, and I have come to seek you out. If you have a name worth mentioning, please tell us."

"Get out or I'll call the police! This is my house."

There was real anger now on the medium's entranced face.

I kept asking for identification. Finally, the disdainful lips opened and in cold tones, the voice said, "I am the wife of the vice president of the United States! Leave my house!"

I checked with Mrs. Campbell and found that Betsy Jumel did so identify herself frequently. On one occasion, driving through crowded New York streets long after her divorce from Aaron Burr she shouted, "Make way for the wife of the vice president of the United States!"

"Didn't you marry someone else before that?" I asked. "How did your husband die?"

"Bastard!"

"You've been dead a hundred years, Madam," I said pleasantly.

"You are made like the billow in the captain's cabin," she replied, somewhat cryptically. Later I checked this out. A sea captain was one of her favorite lovers while married to Jumel.

"Did you murder your husband?" I inquired and drew back a little just in case.

"You belong in the scullery with my maids," she replied disdainfully, but I repeated the accusation, adding that her husband had claimed she had killed him.

"I will call for help," she countered.

"There is no help. The police are on your trail!" I suggested.

"I am the wife of the vice president of the United States!"

"I will help you if you tell me what you did. Did you cause his death?"

"The rats that crawl...they bit me. Where am I?"

"You're between two worlds. Do you wish to be helped?"

"Where is Joseph?"

"You must leave this house. Your husband has forgiven you."

"I adored him!"

"Go away, and you will see Stephen Jumel again."

"Only the crest on the carriage! That's all I did. He was a great man."

I had the feeling she wasn't at all keen on Monsieur Jumel. But that happens, even to ghosts.

I finally gave up trying to get her to go and join Jumel and tried another way.

"Go and join the vice president of the United States. He awaits you." To my surprise, this didn't work either.

"He is evil, evil," she said.

Perplexed, I asked, "Whom do you wish to join?"

"Mary."

"Then call out her name, and she'll join you and take you with her."

"No crime, no crime."

"You've been forgiven. Mary will take you away from here."

I asked Albert, the control, to come and help us get things moving, but evidently Madame had a change of heart: "This is my house I'll stay here."

"This is no longer your house. You must go!"

The struggle continued. She called for Christopher, but wouldn't tell me who Christopher was.

"He's the only one I ever trusted," she volunteered, finally.

"It's not too late," I repeated. "You can join your loved ones."

"Good-bye."

I called for Albert, who quickly took control. "She's no longer in the right mind," he said, as soon as he had firm control of the medium's vocal cords. "You may have to talk with her again."

"Is she guilty of Jumel's death?"

"Yes. It was arranged."

"Who was the boy who pushed him?"

"A trusty in the house. She told him to."

"What about Stephen Jumel?"

"He is in a better frame of mind."

"Is there anything else we did not bring out? Who is this Christopher she mentioned?"

"A sea captain. She buried him in Providence."

Mrs. Campbell later confirmed the important role the sea captain played in Betsy's life. There was also another man named Brown.

"Did Aaron Burr help bury Jumel?"

"That is true. Burr believed Mme. Jumel had more finances than she actually had."

"What about the doctor who buried him alive? Is his name known?"

"Couldn't stop the bleeding."

"Was Aaron Burr in on the crime?"

"He is very much aware that he is guilty. He still possesses his full mental faculties."

I then asked the control to help keep the peace in the house and to bring the medium back to her own body.

A few minutes later, Ethel Meyers was herself again, remembering nothing of the ordeal she had gone through the past hour, and none the worse for it.

Jumel died in 1832 and, as far as I could find, the first ghostly reports date back to 1865. The question was:

Could his remains disclose any clues as to the manner in which he died? If he suffocated in his coffin, would not the position of his bones so indicate?

I queried two physicians who disagreed in the matter. One thought that nothing would be left by now; the other thought it was worth looking into.

I thought so, too. However, my application to reopen the grave of Stephen Jumel, down in the old Catholic cemetery on Mott Street, got the official run-around. The District Attorney's office sent me to Dr. Halpern, the chief medical examiner, who told me it would be of no use to check. When I insisted, I was referred to the church offices of old St. Patrick's, which has nominal jurisdiction over the plot.

Have you ever tried to reopen a grave in the City of New York? It's easier to dig a new one, believe me!

As the years passed, I often returned to the mansion. I made several television documentaries there with the helpful support of the curator, who now is the affable and knowledgeable Patrick Broom. The famous blue gown is no longer on display, alas, having disintegrated shortly after I first published the story. But the legend persists, and the footfalls are still heard on lonely nights when the security guard locks up. Whether the Jumels, the remorseful Betsy and the victimized Stephen, have since made up on the other side, is a moot question, and I doubt that Aaron Burr will want anything further to do with the, ah, lady, either.

Bernstein Castle, Austria—Now a fine hotel, once was the site of a tragic misunderstanding and murder. The countess was innocent of having betrayed her husband, so he killed her in a fit of jealousy

Bernstein Castle exterior, Austria—The wealth of the area comes from the mining of semiprecious stone called "Smaragdt." It was in the noble Almássy family until recently.

A small shrine marks the spot where the countess was murdered—and also where her ghost was frequently seen

Castle Pflindsberg, now a total ruin, high up in the Alps near Bad Aussee, Austria is the site of a medieval rape and abduction, avenged by the family of the perpetrator. His wild ghost is sometimes seen on horseback on a stormy night

CHAPTER SIX: **This House is Haunted**

In the Gothic Cathedral of Basle, Switzerland a curious, luminous skeleton has been captured by Hans Holzer on film. During the strict Calvinistic era, people accused of "sins" were sometimes walled up alive in the church walls

Castle Altenburg, Syria—Now a romantic hotel, was the home of the unhappy ghost of a servant who betrayed his master in 1920. This happened when rebellious peasants wanted to kill the master. He did not die, but it is the servant who can't leave the place

This House is Haunted

CHAPTER SEVEN

Haunted Places

I T STANDS TO REASON THAT, if ghosts—people who have passed on from this life but who have not yet been able to enter the next stage—appear in people's houses, such earthbound spirits can also be found outside houses, in the open. And so they are.

In legends dark forests are often haunted, and in the Caribbean, crossroads are often considered ghostly places. In fact, in Haitian Voodoo, the gods of the crossroads are invoked for protection.

Legends abound about haunted ships, from the wraith of slain pirates who died in combat aboard their ship to the case of the worker killed in an accident aboard the Queen Mary, now a floating museum, who keeps appearing to tourists (without being prompted to do so by management) to the belief in "the Flying Dutchman," which inspired Richard Wagner to dramatize the Dutchman's fate in his opera of the same name. Was there a flying Dutchman? To begin with, he did not really "fly." Flying may refer here to the "racing across the seas" of his clipper ship, or it may be a description of the way ghosts move about—gliding, rather than walking, some of the time. Very likely, he was simply a captain who went down with his ship and never wanted to leave her even in death.

That there are ghosts reported on airplanes is hardly news. The most famous of these in recent years is the ghost of Flight 401, which crashed in the Florida Everglades, causing the loss of 101 lives. John Fuller wrote of this case in 1976, and if it were not for the stinginess of the airlines, we would never know about it. But it so happened that some sections of the crashed airliner were salvaged and used again (!) on another airliner; the ghost of the dead flight engineer appeared to a stewardess on this recycled plane, complaining that the airplane—both the one that had crashed and the one he appeared in now—was not safe to fly.

Ghosts, after all, are people. They are emotional beings. If they cannot let go of their particular tragedy, they will end up bound to the place where the event occurred and they will either appear or make themselves heard from time to time, when conditions are conducive—anniversaries of the event, for example, or the presence of a medium who makes contact possible. An emotional tie, therefore, is required to keep someone from going across to "the other side," free and clear. Here are some of those places I have personally investigated, and verified.

The Case of the Lost Head

ONE OF THE most famous ghosts of the South is railroad conductor Joe Baldwin. The story of Joe and his lantern was known to me, of course, and a few years ago *Life* magazine even dignified it with a photograph of the railroad track near Wilmington, North Carolina, very atmospherically adorned by a greenish lantern, presumably swinging in ghostly hands.

Then one fine day in early 1964, the legend became reality when a letter arrived from Bill Mitcham, Executive Secretary of the South Eastern North Carolina Beach Association, a public-relations office set up by the leading resort hotels in the area centering around Wilmington. Mr. Mitcham proposed that I have a look at the ghost of Joe Baldwin, and try to explain once and for all—scientifically —what the famous "Maco Light" was or is.

In addition, Mr. Mitcham arranged for a lecture on the subject to be held at the end of my investigation and sponsored jointly by the Beach Association and Wilmington College. He promised to roll out the red carpet for Catherine and me, and roll it out he did.

Seldom in the history of ghost hunting has a parapsychologist been received so royally and so fully covered by press, television and radio, and if the ghost of Joe Baldwin is basking in the reflected glory of all this attention directed towards his personal ghost hunter, he is most welcome to it.

If it were not for Joe Baldwin, the bend in the railroad track which is known as Maco Station (a few miles outside of Wilmington) would be a most unattractive and ordinary trestle. By the time I had investigated it and left, in May of 1964, the spot had almost risen to the prominence of a national shrine and sight-seeing groups arrived at all times, especially at night, to look for Joe Baldwin's ghostly light.

Bill Mitcham had seen to it that the world knew about Joe Baldwin's headless ghost and Hans Holzer seeking same, and not less than seventy-eight separate news stories of one kind or another appeared in print during the week we spent in Wilmington.

Before I even started to make plans for the Wilmington expedition, I received a friendly letter from a local student of psychic phenomena, William Edward Cox, Jr., and a manuscript entitled "The Maco Ghost Light." Mr. Cox had spent considerable time observing the strange light, and I quote:

A favorite "ghost story" in the vicinity of Wilmington, N.C., is that of "Joe Baldwin's Ghost Light," which is alleged to appear at night near Maco, N.C., 12 miles west of Wilmington on the Atlantic Coast Line Railroad.

On June 30-July 1, 1949, this writer spent considerable time investigating the phenomenon. The purpose was to make an accurate check on the behavior of the light under test conditions, with a view toward ascertaining its exact nature.

This light has been observed since shortly after the legend of the Joe Baldwin ghost light "was born in 1867." It is officially reported in a pamphlet entitled "The Story of the Coast Line, 1830–1948." In its general description it resembles a 25-watt electric light slowly moving along the tracks toward the observer, whose best point of observation is on the track itself at the point where the tracks, double at that point, are crossed by a branch of a connecting roadway between U.S. Highway 74-76 and U.S. Highway 19.

The popular explanation is that Conductor Baldwin, decapitated in an accident, is taking the nocturnal walks in search of his head....

After testing the various "natural" theories put forward for the origin of the nocturnal light, Mr. Cox admits:

Although the general consensus of opinion is that the lights stem from some relatively rare cause, such as the paranormal, *"ignis fatuus,"* etc., the opinions of residents of the Maco vicinity were found by this observer to be more divided. The proprietor of the Mobilgas Service Station was noncommittal, and a local customer said he had "never seen the light." A farmer in the area was quite certain that it is caused by automobile headlights, but would not express an opinion upon such lights as were customarily seen there before the advent of the automobile.

The proprietress of the Willet Service Station, Mrs. C. L. Benton, was firmly convinced that it was of "supernatural origin," and that the peculiar visibility of automobile headlights to observers at Maco must be more or less a subsequent coincidence.

She said that her father "often saw it as he loaded the wood burners near there over 60 years ago."

The basic question of the origin and nature of the "Maco Light," or the original light, remains incompletely answered. The findings here reported, due as they are to entirely normal causes, cannot accurately be construed as disproving the existence of a light of paranormal origin at any time in the distant past (or, for that matter, at the present time).

The unquestionable singularity of the phenomenon's being in a locale where it is so easily possible for automobiles to produce an identical phenomenon seems but to relegate it to the enigmatic "realm of forgotten mysteries."

So much for Mr. Cox's painstaking experiment conducted at the site in 1949.

The coming of the Ghost Hunter (and Mrs. Ghost Hunter) was amply heralded in the newspapers of the area. Typical of the veritable avalanche of features was the story in *The Charlotte Observer:*

Can Spook Hunter De-Ghost Old Joe?

The South Eastern N. C. Beach Association invited a leading parapsychologist Saturday to study the ghost of Old Joe Baldwin.

Bill Mitcham, executive director of the association, said he has arranged for Hans Holzer of New York to either prove or disprove the ghostly tales relating to Old Joe.

Holzer will begin his study May 1.

Tales of Joe Baldwin flagging down trains with false signals, waving his lantern on dark summer nights have been repeated since his death in 1867.

Baldwin, a conductor on the Wilmington, Manchester and Augusta Railroad, was riding the rear coach of a train the night of his death. The coach became uncoupled and Baldwin seized a lantern in an effort to signal a passenger train following.

But the engineer failed to see the signal. In the resulting crash, Baldwin was decapitated.

A witness to the wreck later recalled that the signal lantern was flung some distance from the tracks, but it burned brightly thereafter for some time.

Soon after the accident, there were reports of a mysterious light along the railroad tracks at Maco Station in Brunswick County.

Two lanterns, one green and one red, have been used by trainmen at Maco Station so that engineers would not be confused or deceived by Joe Baldwin's light.

Most helpful in a more serious vein was the Women's Editor of the *Wilmington Star-News*, Theresa Thomas, who has for years taken an interest in the psychic and probably is somewhat sensitive herself. On April 8, 1964, she asked her readers:

Have You Ever Seen the Maco Light?

Have you ever seen Old Joe Baldwin? Or his light, that is? As far as we know, nobody has actually seen Joe himself.

But if you have seen his lantern swinging along the railroad track at Maco, you can be of great help to Hans Holzer, Ghost Hunter, who will be in Wilmington April 29th.

Either write out your experience and send it to us, or call and tell us about it.

Then Miss Thomas' point of view added another angle:

His [Mr. Holzer's] wife is just as fascinating as he. She is a painter and great-great-great-granddaughter of Catherine The Great of Russia. Mrs. Holzer was born Countess Catherine Buxhoeveden in a haunted castle in Meran, the Tyrol, in the Italian Alps. And she paints—haven't you guessed?—haunted houses.

My visit was still three weeks away, but the wheels of publicity where already spinning fast and furiously in Wilmington.

Theresa Thomas' appeal for actual witnesses to the ghostly phenomena brought immediate results. For the first time people of standing took the matter seriously, and those who had seen the light, opened up. Miss Thomas did not disguise her enthusiasm. On April 12, she wrote:

It seems a great many people have seen Old Joe Baldwin's light at Maco and most of them are willing—even eager—to talk about it.

Among the first to call was Mrs. Larry Moore, 211 Orange Street, who said she had seen the light three or four times at different seasons of the year.

The first time it was a cloudy, misty winter night and again in summer, misty again. Her description of the light was "like a bluish yellow flame." She and her companions walked down the track and the light came closer as they approached the trestle. When they reached the center of the trestle with the light apparently about 10 feet away, it disappeared.

Mrs. Thelma Daughtry, 6 Shearwater Drive, Wrightsville Beach, says she saw it on a misty spring night. It was about 7 or 8 o'clock in the evening and the reddish light appeared to swing along at about knee height.

Mrs. Margaret Jackson, of 172 Colonial Circle, a native of Vienna, Austria, saw it about seven years ago on a hazy night. She was with several other people and they all saw the light, a "glary shine" steady and far away but always the same distance ahead of them.

Dixie Rambeau, 220 Pfeiffer Avenue, saw it about 1 A.M. Friday morning. She says it was "real dark" and the light appeared as a red pinpoint at a distance up the track, as it neared it became yellowish white, then closer still it was a mixed red and white.

She recalls that she and her companions watched it come closer to the left side of the track and that as it came close the reflection on the rail almost reached them. At about 10 feet away it reversed its process and as they walked toward it, it disappeared. Once it appeared to cross over. They watched it five or six times, she said.

Mrs. Marvin Clark, 406 Grace Street, a practical nurse, states that she and her husband saw the light 15 years ago. It was about midnight on a cloudy, rainy night. They were standing in the middle of the track and "it looked like a light on a train coming at full speed."

Mrs. Clark described the light as "the color of a train light."

"We picked up our little girl and ran. All of us have always seen reflections of automobiles but beyond a doubt it was the Maco Light."

Mrs. Lase V. Dail of Carolina Beach also has a story to tell. It seems she and her husband came home late one night from Fayetteville.

She writes: "As we left the cut off and headed into 74-76 highway, I shall never forget the experience we had...." She goes on, "All at once a bright light came down the road toward us, first I figured it was a car. But decided if so it had only one light. On it came steadily toward us.

"Then I figured it was a train, yet I heard nothing, and as suddenly as it appeared it vanished. I can say it

**The haunted railway crossing—
Wilmington, North Carolina**

was quite a weird feeling. I have often thought of it. I have heard many versions, but never one like this."

Three days later, Miss Thomas devoted still another full column to people who had witnessed the ghost light.

Mrs. Marjorie H. Rizer of Sneads Ferry writes: "I have seen the light three times. The last and most significant time was about a year and a half ago. My husband, three young sons and a corpsman from the United States Naval Hospital at Camp Lejeune were with me and we saw the same thing. It was about 10:30 P.M. and we were returning from a ball game. We decided to go to Maco since we were so near and the young man with us didn't believe there was anything to our story.

"The sky was cloudy and a light mist was falling. We parked the car beside the track and sure enough, there was the light down the track. I stayed in the car with my sons, and my husband and the corpsman walked down the track toward the light.

"The light would alternately dim and then become very bright. The two men walked perhaps a quarter of a mile down the track before they returned. They said the

light stayed ahead of them, but my sons and I saw the light between them and us.

"It looked as if the light would come almost to where we were parked and then it would wobble off down the track and disappear. In a moment it would reappear and do the same time after time.

"When we had been there for about an hour and started to leave, a train approached going toward Wilmington. The light was a short distance away from us. As the train passed the light, it rose and hovered over the train. We could clearly see the top of the train as the light became very bright.

"It stayed over the train until it had passed then disappeared back down near the track and finally it looked as if someone had thrown it off into the woods.

"As we pulled away from the track the light came back on the track and weaved backward and forward down the track as it had been doing."

And still the letters poured in. On April 22, after half a column devoted to my imminent arrival in the area, Miss Thomas printed a letter from a young man who had taken some interesting pictures:

He is J. Everett Huggins, home address 412 Market Street, Wilmington. The letter is addressed to Bill

Mitcham and reads in part: "I read with interest the articles on your 'ghost survey,' especially since I saw the Maco light less than two weeks ago and was actually able to catch Old Joe on film.

"On the nights of April 1 and 2 a schoolmate of mine and I went to Maco Station in the hopes of seeing the light. We saw nothing on Friday, April 1, but we had more success on Saturday, when it was a littler darker. Around 10:30 we saw a yellow light about 100 yards down the track from us (this distance is only a guess). It seemed to be about 10 feet above the tracks and looked as if it were moving slowly toward us for a while, then it went back and died out.

"The light appeared maybe three times in succession for periods up to what I would estimate to be about thirty seconds.

"I attempted to take two time exposures with my camera. Unfortunately I did not have a tripod, and so I had to hold the camera in my hands, which made clear results impossible. The pictures are not spectacular—just a small spot on each of the color transparencies—but they are pictures. If you are interested I will have some copies made.

"My friends had kidded me about the light, so I noted some details to try to end their skepticism. The headlights of cars traveling west on Highway 74 could be seen in the distance, and no doubt many who think they see Old Joe only see these lights. Old Joe could be distinguished in several ways, however. First, the light had a yellower tone than did the auto headlights.

"Secondly, unlike the headlights which grow brighter and brighter and then suddenly disappear, the Maco light would gradually grow brighter and then gradually fade out. Thirdly, the Maco light produced a reflection on the rails that was not characteristic of the headlights.

"More interesting was the fact that the reflection on the rails was seen only on a relatively short stretch of track. By observing the reflection, we could tell that the light moved backward and forward on the rails. It always remained directly above the tracks.

"I had seen the light once before, in 1956. It was on a cold winter night, and the light was brighter."

As the day of our arrival grew nearer, the tempo of the press became more hectic. On April 26, Arnold Kirk wrote in the *Wilmington Star-News*:

This tiny Brunswick County village, nestled in a small clearing a few miles west of Wilmington off U.S. Highway 74, is rapidly gaining acclaim as the "Ghost Capital" of North Carolina.

Its few dozen inhabitants, mostly farmers of moderate means, have suddenly found their once-peaceful nights disturbed by scores of vehicles sparring for vantage points from which to view the famous "Maco Light."

While the legend of the light and old Joe Baldwin, the "ghost" of Maco, has long been known, its popularity has become intense only in recent months.

Elaborate plans have already been made to welcome Holzer to the Port City. The mayors of all the towns in New Hanover and Brunswick counties, in addition to county commissioners from both counties, have agreed

to be at the New Hanover County Airport Wednesday at 7:43 P.M. when the "ghost hunter's" plane arrives.

Lanterns at Airport—Also on hand to greet the noted parapsychologist will be 1,000 high-school students, carrying, appropriately enough, lighted lanterns! The lanterns were purchased by the city years ago to offer warmth to trees and plants during blustery winter months.

Adding to the fanfare of the event will be the first public offering of "The Ballad of Old Joe Baldwin," written by the senior English class of New Hanover High School.

The reception was a bash that would have made Old Joe Baldwin feel honored. A little later, we tried to sneak out to Maco and have a first glance at the haunted spot. The results were disappointing.

It was not so much that the ghost did not show, but what did show up was most disturbing. *The Wilmington Star* summed it up like this:

An unwilling Old Joe Baldwin exercised his ghostly prerogative Wednesday night by refusing to perform before what may have been his largest audience.

Huddled in small clusters along the railroad tracks near the center of this tiny Brunswick County village, an estimated 250 persons stared into the gloomy darkness in hopes of catching a glimpse of the famous "Maco Light."

But the light would not offer the slightest flicker.

Holzer's announced visit to the scene of Baldwin's ghastly demise gave no comfort to the few dozen residents of Maco. By 10 o'clock, dozens of cars lined both sides of the narrow Maco road and scores of thrill-seeking teenagers had spilled onto the railroad track.

If Joe Baldwin had decided to make an appearance, his performance no doubt would have been engulfed in the dozens of flashlights and battery-powered lanterns searching through the darkness for at least a mile down the track.

Several times, the flashlights and lanterns were mistaken for the "Maco Light," giving hope that the mysterious glow would soon appear.

A large portion of the track was illuminated by the headlights of a jeep and small foreign car scurrying back and forth along both sides of the track. A young girl created an anxious moment when she mistook a firefly as the "Maco Light" and released a penetrating scream that sliced through the pitch-darkness.

Holzer's visit to Maco on Wednesday night was mostly for the benefit of photographers and reporters who met the noted parapsychologist at the New Hanover County airport earlier that night.

His second visit to the crossing will be kept a closely guarded secret in hopes the "ghost hunter" will be able to conduct his investigation of the light without being interrupted by pranksters and playful teenagers.

Soon I realized that it would impossible for us to go out to the tracks alone. Crowds followed us around and crowds were ever present at the spot, giving rise to a suspicion in my mind that these people were not in a working mood while we were visiting their area. Evidently we were the most exciting thing that had happened to them for some time.

Finally, the day of a scheduled press conference arrived, and at 10 o'clock in the morning, before a battery of kleig lights and microphones set up at the magnificent new Blockade Runner Hotel on the beach, I started to talk in person to those who had come to tell me about their encounters with Joe Baldwin's ghost.

In addition to those who had written to Miss Thomas and reaffirmed their original stories, others came forward who had not done so previously. There was William McGirt, an insurance executive, who called the light "buoyant," flicking itself on and off, as it were, and fully reflected on the iron rails. But you cannot see it looking east, he told me, only when you look towards Maco Station.

Margaret Bremer added to her previously told story by saying the light looked to her "like a kerosene lantern swaying back and forth."

Her husband, Mr. Bremer, had not planned on saying anything, but I coaxed him. He admitted finally that twelve years ago, when his car was standing straddled across the track, he saw a light coming towards him. It flickered like a lamp and when it came closer, it flared up. As an afterthought, he added, "Something strange—suddenly there seemed to be a rush of air, as if a train were coming from Wilmington."

"Was there?" I inquired cautiously.

"No, of course not. We wouldn't have had the car across the track if a train were expected."

Mrs. Laura Collins stepped forward and told me of the time she was at the trestle with a boy who did not believe in ghosts, not even Joe Baldwin's. When the light appeared, he sneered at it and tried to explain it as a reflection. Six feet away from the boy, the light suddenly disappeared and reappeared in back of him—as if to show him up! Mrs. Collins, along with others, observed that misty weather made the light appear clearer.

Next in the parade of witnesses came Mrs. Elizabeth Finch of Wilmington, who had offered her original testimony only the day before.

"It appeared to me many times," she said of the light, "looked like a lantern to me. Two years ago, we were parked across the tracks in our car—we were watching for a train of course, too—when I saw two dazzling lights from both sides. It was a winter evening, but I suddenly felt very hot. There was a red streak in front of the car, and then I saw what was a dim outline of a man walking with a lantern and swinging it. Mind you, it was a bare outline," Mrs. Finch added in emphasis, "and it did have a

head . . . just kept going, then suddenly he disappeared inside the tracks."

"Did you ever have psychic experiences before, Mrs. Finch?" I wanted to know.

"Yes, when we lived in a house in Masonborough, I used to hear noises, steps, even voices out of nowhere—later, I was told it was haunted."

I thanked Mrs. Finch, wondering if the local legend had impressed her unconscious to the point where she did see what everyone had said was there—or whether she really saw the outline of a man.

I really have no reason to doubt her story. She struck me as a calm, intelligent person who would not easily make up a story just to be sensational. No, I decided, Mrs. Finch might very well have been one of the very few who saw more than just the light.

"I tell you why it can't be anything ordinary," Mr. Trussle, my next informant, said. "Seven years ago, when I saw the light on a damp night about a mile away from where I was standing, I noticed its very rapid approach. It disappeared fast, went back and forth as if to attract attention to something. It was three foot above the track, about the height of where a man's arm might be.

"At first, it seemed yellowish white; when I came closer, it looked kind of pinkish. Now an ordinary car headlight wouldn't go back and forth like that, would it?"

I agreed it was most unlikely for an automobile headlight to behave in such an unusual manner.

Mrs. Miriam Moore saw it three times, always on misty, humid nights. "I had a funny ringing in my ears when I reached the spot," she said. She was sure what she saw was a lamp swinging in a slow motion. Suddenly, she broke into a cold sweat for no reason at all. I established that she was a psychic person, and had on occasion foretold the death of several members of her family.

E. S. Skipper is a dapper little man in the golden years of life, but peppery and very much alert. He used to be a freight shipper on the Atlantic Coast Line and grew up with the Maco Light the way Niagara kids grow up with the sight of the Falls.

"I've seen it hundreds of times," he volunteered. "I've seen it flag trains down—it moved just like a railroad lantern would. On one occasion I took my shotgun and walked towards it. As I got nearer, the light became so bright I could hardly look. Suddenly, it disappeared into the old Catholic cemetery on the right side of the tracks."

"Cemetery?" I asked, for I had not heard of a cemetery in this area.

Mr. Skipper was quite certain that there was one. I promised to look into this immediately. "Since you came so close to the light, Mr. Skipper," I said, "perhaps you can tell me what it looked like close up."

"Oh, I got even closer than that—back in 1929, I remember it well. It was 2 o'clock in the morning. I got to within six foot from it."

"What did you see?"

"I saw a flame. I mean, in the middle of the light, there was, unmistakably, a flame burning."

"Like a lantern?"

"Like a lantern."

I thanked Mr. Skipper and was ready to turn to my last witness, none other than Editor Thomas herself, when Mrs. E. R. Rich, who had already given her account in the newspaper, asked for another minute, which I gladly gave her.

"Ten years ago," Mrs. Rich said, "we were at the track one evening. My son Robert was in the car with me, and my older son went down the track to watch for the light. Suddenly not one but two lights appeared at the car. They were round and seemed to radiate, and sparkle—for a moment, they hung around, then one left, the other stayed. My feet went ice cold at this moment and I felt very strange."

"Miss Thomas," I said, "will you add your own experiences to this plethora of information?"

"Gladly," the Women's Editor of the *Star-News* replied. "There were three of us, all newspaper women, who decided a few weeks ago to go down to the trestle and not see anything."

"I beg your pardon?"

"We'd made up our minds not to be influenced by all the publicity Joe Baldwin's ghost was getting."

"What happened?"

"When we got to the track, dogs were baying as if disturbed by something in the atmosphere. We parked on the dirt road that runs parallel to the track, and waited. After a while, the light appeared. It had a yellow glow. Then, suddenly, there were two lights, one larger than the other, swaying in the night sky.

"The lights turned reddish after a while. There was no correlation with car lights at all. I thought at first it was a train bearing down on us, that's how big the lights appeared. Just as suddenly the lights disappeared. One light described an arc to the left of the track, landing in the grass."

"Just as those old tales say Joe's lantern did, eh?"

"It seems so, although it is hard to believe."

"What else did you notice?"

"I had a feeling that I was not alone."

And there you have it. Mass hysteria? Self-hypnosis? Suggestion? Could all these people make up similar stories?

Although the Maco Light is unique in its specific aspects, there are other lights that have been observed at spots where tragedies have occurred. There are reports of apparitions in Colorado taking the form of concentrated energy, or light globes. I don't doubt that the human personality is a form of energy that cannot be destroyed, only transmuted. The man who heard the sound of a train, the psychic chill several people experienced, the flame within the light, the two lights clearly distinguished by the news-paper women—possibly Joe's lantern and the headlight of the onrushing train—all these add up to a case.

That evening, at Bogden Hall, before an audience of some five hundred people of all ages, I stated my conviction that the track at Maco Station was, indeed, haunted. I explained that the shock of sudden death might have caused Joe Baldwin's etheric self to become glued to the spot of the tragedy, re-enacting the final moments over and over again.

I don't think we are dealing here with an "etheric impression" registered on the atmosphere and not possessing a life of its own. The phantom reacts differently with various people and seems to me a true ghost, capable of attempting communication with the living, but not fully aware of his own status or of the futility of his efforts.

I was, and am, convinced of the veracity of the phenomenon and, by comparing it to other "weaving lights" in other areas, can only conclude that the basic folklore is on the right track, except that Joe isn't likely to be looking for his head—he is rather trying to keep an imaginary train from running into his uncoupled car, which of course exists now only in his thought world.

And until someone tells Joe all's well on the line now, he will continue to wave his light. I tried to say the right words for such occasions, but I was somewhat hampered by the fact that I did not have Mrs. Ethel Meyers, my favorite medium, with me; then, too, the Wilmington people did not like the idea of having their town ghost go to his reward and leave the trestle just another second-rate railroad track.

The folks living alongside it, though, wouldn't have minded one bit. They can do without Joe Baldwin and his somewhat motley admirers.

Suddenly the thought struck me that we had no proof that a Joe Baldwin had ever really existed in this area. The next morning I went to the Wilmington Public Library and started to dig into the files and historical sources dealing with the area a hundred years ago. Bill Mitcham and I started to read all the newspapers from 1866 onwards, but after a while we gave up. Instead, I had a hunch which, eventually, paid off. If Joe Baldwin was physically fit to work on the railroad in so hazardous a job as that of a train man, he must have been well enough to be in the Armed Forces at one time or another.

I started to search the Regimental Records from 1867 on backwards. Finally I found in volume V, page 602, of a work called *North Carolina Regiments*, published in 1901, the following entry:

Joseph Baldwin, Company F, 26th N.C.T., badly wounded in the thigh. Battle of Gettysburg. July 1, 1863.

It was the only Joseph Baldwin listed in the area, or, for that matter, the state.

I also inquired about the old Catholic cemetery. It was, indeed, near the railroad track, but had been out of use for many years. Only oldsters still remembered its existence. Baldwin may have been Catholic, as are many residents of the area. Time did not permit me to look among the dilapidated tombstones for a grave bearing the name of Joe Baldwin.

But it would be interesting to find it and see if *all* of Joe Baldwin lies buried in sacred ground!

✴ 118

The Woman On the Train (Switzerland)

THE NIGHT TRAIN gave one more shrill whistle, then pulled out of Vienna's spanking new Western Station. By the next morning, it would be in Zurich, Switzerland. One could make the same journey in an hour by air, but then how many mountains and lakes can one look at from 10,000 feet up? So there are always enough people who prefer the night train, enough at any rate to make the train continue as it has for all these years. It is a good train, as trains go, far cleaner and better than American trains. The sleepers are comfortable and the dining cars serve good food, and the soup does not come up and meet you half way to your face the way it does on the rickety American diners these days.

Now the train was running at a faster pace, leaving Vienna's sprawling suburbs behind. After it passed *Huetteldorf-Hacking*, the so-called *Vorbahnhof*, or advance station, for Vienna proper, it became an express train and the clickety-clack of the rails turned into a smoother, faster ride. Travellers could now settle back into their cushioned seats and enjoy the ride. True, the landscape would not be interesting until after Tulln, but by then darkness would be setting in. But the early morning glory of seeing the mountains out of the train windows around 6 A.M., would amply compensate for the dark portions of the voyage. The Zurich Express wasn't as glamorous as the famed Orient Express but it was no less classy, and the railroad made every effort to keep their clientele from leaving for the airlines. Even to the extent of placing perfume containers into the washrooms and flowers in the compartments. Let the Penn-Central try that!

One of the travelers beginning to relax was a diminutive redhead with large, dark eyes and the unmistakable air of show business about her. She was well dressed, to be sure, but in a manner and style just a trifle too showy for the ordinary Vienna *hausfrau* or even the elegant lady of the world. There was nothing cheap about her clothes or manner, but she seemed rather self-assured, too much so to be just another wife or sister traveling to Zurich by herself.

Her luggage took up almost all of the available space, leaving very little for any other traveler if she had shared her compartment. As it was, she was alone, luckily, and having the sleeping compartment all to herself contributed immeasurably to her sense of comfort at this moment.

Rita Atlanta used the fading moments of the day to reflect on the weeks past. She had just ended a successful engagement in Vienna, two months of full houses in the nightclub where she was employed with her specialty act. Her specialty? Rita is a striptease dancer, one of the best in this somewhat "old-fashioned" field in this day of extremes —like topless dancers and bottomless chorines. But Rita, despite the fact she takes her clothes off in public, is a lady. She was once married to an American officer of high rank who had met her in Germany. Far from asking her to give up her occupation, he insisted she continue with it. It did not sit well with the general, but the enlisted men loved it, and her performances were always sellouts. Ultimately, her husband passed away and Rita began to divide her year between her European engagements and her comfortable trailer stationed near Boston. Her son was growing up and going to school and Rita's life was pretty orderly and peaceful. She came from a good Austrian family and grew up among people to whom the horrors of war and occupation were only too familiar.

Somehow she had forgotten about those horrible years and only now and then did something remind her about them as she traveled across Europe now.

Since childhood Rita had shown a remarkable degree of extrasensory powers. She was aware of the death of a relative long before it became known and she knew when someone would soon pass away by merely looking at him. This ability she found far from welcome, but it stayed with her, like it or not. Then, when she moved into a trailer near Boston, she soon discovered that she had also inherited a ghost. She was repeatedly awakened at three in the morning by the specter of a large man in a wide-brimmed hat, staring at her from the foot of her bed. Later, it was discovered that a man had been run over nearby by a car.

Show business people like to talk about the unknown and she often found herself regaling her friends in the dressing rooms with her experiences. Many a friendship was formed by her because of her special "gift," and though she viewed all this with mixed emotions, she knew she had to live with it all her life.

Now that her summer season had ended and she could look forward to a good engagement in the fall, she had decided to take some time off and visit a friend of many years in her home at Locarno, Switzerland. Susan West had been ill two years prior to this visit, but a successful operation for cancer had apparently halted the spread of the disease and she had been declared cured. Thus her friend welcomed the idea of Rita's visit, as she had never felt better in her life.

Outside the train window the landscape started to become more interesting even as the light faded. The hills of the Wachau Valley clearly etched themselves against the skyline and the Danube nearly gave one the feeling of a truly romantic journey. Rita turned the overhead lights low and settled back for a while. Then the monotonous sound of the rails affected her and she felt herself tiring. She undressed and got into bed, turning the overhead lights out and the bedside lamp on. But she was not quite ready for sleep. To begin with, in her profession one does not go off to sleep until very late at night, and the habit pattern had made early bedtimes very difficult for her. Then, too, the brisk October air outside made her feel alive and she decided to read a little before turning the lights off.

She had bought some magazines at the Western Station and now she went through them, always hoping to find perhaps a picture or mention of herself somewhere— an occupational habit most show business people have.

After about twenty minutes of this, she felt sleep reaching out to her, and dropped the magazines. Then she turned off the light and prepared herself for sleep. Within a few minutes, she was fast asleep.

All of a sudden, she woke up. Outside, it was quite dark now and the train was very quiet. She had no idea how long she had slept, but it must have been several hours by the way she felt. Still, she was wide awake and began to wonder why she had suddenly awakened. She turned her head and looked away from the bed into the compartment. Even though there was no moon, enough light from reflected surfaces streamed into the window to let her see the outlines of everything in the small room. There, in front of her bed, was a woman she had never seen before in her life, kneeling on the floor before her!

With a jerk, she sat up and stared at the figure. Stunned by the intrusion, all she could think of was how the woman could have gotten into her room. The woman was kneeling, with her hands raised over her head, looking upward. Rita saw her face, the face of a dark complexioned woman with dark hair, perhaps of Mexican or Latin ancestry. The woman's expression was one of sheer terror as if something horrible was about to be done to her!

Rita found herself scared out of her wits, her heart pounding to her teeth, and yet unable to move. Then she started to find her way to the light switch to turn on the lights. It took her several seconds, which seemed like hours to her, to find the switch and turn it.

When the light flooded the compartment, the apparition was gone. Quickly Rita tried the door, but it was locked securely, just as she had left it prior to retiring. There was no way in which the woman could have gotten into the compartment, if she had been of flesh and blood. But Rita knew from her previous experience in the trailer that she was not confronted with a human being: "do trains harbor ghosts too?" she wondered, and then the thought hit her that this had *something* to do with her friend Susan.

It did not seem to make sense, but she could not shake the feeling that the ghostly woman was someone connected with her friend, who had come to warn her of impending doom for Susan.

Perhaps it is a ghost, someone killed in this compartment, she tried to reason, but to no avail. Her inner voice told her it was not.

The entire incident cast a sad spell over her otherwise pleasant trip, but eventually she went back to sleep and arrived in Zurich somewhat more composed.

She changed trains and took the train to Bellinzona where her friend and prospective hostess was to meet her and take her the rest of the way to a little town outside of Locarno, where she lived. When she saw Susan in Bellinzona, Rita's fears vanished. Her friend looked radiant and quite obviously was in good health. In fact, she looked years younger than the last time she had seen her. She had changed her hair to red and it looked well on her. The two women embraced and the bright southern sun quickly made Rita forget the horrible experience on the train to Zurich.

They traveled together now to Locarno, and to while away the time, or perhaps out of an inner compulsion to be reassured somehow, Rita told Susan about the apparition on the train. But she did not mention her own inner fears that it had some foreboding concerning her friend.

"I hope it has nothing to do with me," Susan said, as if reading her thoughts, however. Rita immediately assured her that it didn't, and couldn't.

"How could a ghost on a train have any possible connection with you here in Locarno?" she reasoned, but her friend was not relaxed.

"I don't know," she said and then they changed the subject. Soon afterward they arrived at her apartment in Tenero, near Locarno, and the afternoon and evening was spent talking over old times and plans for the future. When it was time to go to sleep, Rita was given a bed in her friend's living room. Her hostess slept in the bedroom of the apartment.

The place was pretty and new and Rita immediately took a liking to it. She was looking forward to her visit now, and the experience on the train went even further into the background.

She read for a while, as was her custom, then she turned the light out and lay quietly in the dark, waiting for sleep to come and blot out her conscious thoughts.

As she was slowly drifting off to sleep, deliberately avoiding any recollections or reflections upon her experience on the train, she felt herself surrounded by an unseen presence. She blamed her unfamiliarity with her surroundings, the long journey, the excitement of the trip for her nervousness. But it did not help much, the feeling of an ominous presence in the room persisted.

After a while, it seemed to her as if someone were watching her from all over that room, someone she could not actually see but whom her keen senses felt very much present. She wasn't even sure whether it was one person or several, because the feeling seemed to drift over her from all sides.

It was a very bad night and she hardly slept at all, but she did not wish to alarm her hostess, so she said nothing of it at breakfast the next morning. Instead, at the first opportunity, she went into town and bought sleeping pills, the strongest she could get.

That night, she was drowsy almost at once, due to the drug in the pills. She still felt the presence however, just as strongly as the first night. Only, because she had taken the pills, *she did not care.*

Two days after her arrival, she met Mrs. Recalcati, a neighbor of Susan's. Somehow the conversation turned to the psychic world and ghosts in particular, and to her surprise Rita discovered that the lady was not at all hostile toward the possibility that such things did indeed exist.

Encouraged by this open-minded attitude, Rita confided in the neighbor, telling her of her ghostly encounter on the train and of the uncanny sensations in the apartment afterwards.

"I have the feeling Susan is going to die," she added, somehow unable to hold back her dreary thoughts.

The neighbor woman was at first horrified, but then she nodded. "Susan hasn't been well of late," she remarked and Rita shuddered. She had only seen the radiant joy of the reunion of two old friends after many years.

The five days allotted to her visit passed quickly. She returned to Vienna and her own apartment. It was good to spend a night in a room without an unseen presence staring at one from out of the dark.

For the first two days, she just rested—rested from a vacation. Then she confided in a close friend, Elfie Hartl, what had occurred on the train and in Locarno.

Soon after, she returned to America for her usual Christmas holiday with her son, and again discussed what had happened with the boy and some of her American friends. But after that, the matter was dropped and not discussed again. Rita was busy living her daily life and the less she had to do with psychic matters, the better from her own point of view.

This was not entirely possible, as the ghostly manifestations in her trailer never ceased. But she had taken her 3 A.M. "visitor" for granted by now and was not unduly disturbed by him any longer. After all, he was dead and she knew that it did not concern herself or anyone close to her. If he wanted to visit her trailer for some strange reason, that was all right with her. She had often thought of changing her residence or moving the trailer elsewhere, but it was a lot of trouble to go to on account of a ghost. Besides, she had made friends in the trailer camp and her boy was in school nearby.

Meanwhile the demands for her act were as great as ever. The "girl in the champagne glass," as she was known, had added an oriental act to her original routine, and as a belly dancer she was in almost greater demand than as a striptease artist. There are hundreds of small clubs in the United States using this type of talent and Rita had a busy winter season, traveling about the country.

Somehow, word of her preoccupation with the occult had gotten around, perhaps because she liked to talk about it on occasion with fellow performers. Agents and managers would proffer their palms and ask to be "read" as if Rita were some kind of carnival gypsy. Rita, of course, refused but did not bother to explain the difference between a casual psychic reader and a person genuinely possessed of ESP and a serious interest in that which she did not want, but nevertheless found present within her.

Still, inadvertently, she sometimes told friends what she felt about them only to find out later that it had all come true the way she had so casually mentioned it. It did not give her any sense of pride in her psychic accomplishment. To the contrary, she kept asking herself, what is the matter with me? I don't want to see ghosts; I don't want to tell people's fortune or misfortune—I just want to be left alone by the forces that cause all this.

She could handle the freshest of hecklers when performing her act, and quench the rudest remark, if necessary. But this was different. How can you deal with something you don't see or hear, something within you?

One day in Baltimore, she was sitting in her dressing room backstage at a local club. It was an icy February day of 1968 and business had been good despite the cold weather. Perhaps because of it, she reasoned, men wanted to see a pretty girl undress. She had some time to kill between performances, and her son had forwarded her mail to her from Boston.

As she casually went through the stack of fan mail, she noticed an unfamiliar stamp. It was a letter from Locarno. Quickly, she tore open the envelope. The letter was from Susan's son. She had died on January 7 of that year. As she put the letter down, she kept seeing her redheaded friend in her mind, how lifelike and joyous she had been during their last get-together.

Then, with a shudder, she felt herself think of the woman on the train again, and all at once Rita knew that this was someone connected with Susan's death. But why had she been chosen to receive this warning and not Susan herself? Was she the "telephone between worlds" for all her friends and should she have told her friend about the warning after all? "No," she said to herself, "no," it would have spoiled the last few happy months she had on earth.

With a sigh Rita put the letter back with the others and prepared herself for the next performance.

She is often in Vienna, but the night train to Zurich is out of bounds to her now. Perhaps there are ghosts on airplanes too, but at least the flight to Zurich only takes an hour.

✳ 119

The Lady Of the Garden (California)

GARDENING IS ONE OF the finest expressions of man's cultural heritage, for it stems back to the early Greek and Roman cultures, if not beyond that into Babylonian and Chaldean realms. The hanging gardens of Nineveh were far more elaborate than anything modern man can dream up no matter how green his thumb, and the rose gardens of Emperor Diocletian at Salonae, among which he spent his declining years, were a great deal more elaborate than the gardens we are apt to have for our own.

Gardening is also a health measure, for it serves two purposes admirably well: it provides man with physical exercise, and cleanses the air around him through the chemical process of photosynthesis, the miraculous arrangement whereby carbon dioxide is changed into oxygen naturally.

Americans in the eastern states often find gardening a hard-to-find pleasure especially if they live in the cities. But in the sunny west, it comes as a natural adjunct to one's house and is often the most desirable feature of it. Many of the citizens of the small communities of California have gone there, usually from the east or midwest, to have an easier life in their later years. To them, having a garden to putter in is perhaps one of the chief attractions of this unhurried way of life.

The western climate is very kind to most forms of flowers, to fruit trees and almost all the plants usually found in both moderate and tropical climates, so it is small wonder that some of the California gardens turn into veritable show places of color and scent for their loving owners.

Naomi S. is a widow who has lived in California most of her life. Since the passing of her second husband, she has lived quietly in the southern California community of Huntington Park, and nothing of great importance happens to her now. That is as it should be, for she has had a glimpse into a world that has at once amazed and frightened her and she prefers that the excursion into it remain a veiled memory that will eventually be indistinguishable from the faded pictures of other past experiences in her busy and full life.

* * *

At the time, in 1953, she and her husband had been house hunting in Lynwood for a suitable place. She did not care for the run-of-the-mill houses one often finds in American communities and when they both saw this strangely attractive old house on Lago Avenue, they knew at once that that was *it*.

It was almost as if the house had *invited* them to come and get it, but so eager were they to investigate its possibilities, they never thought of this until much, much later.

The house was built in Norman style, almost European in its faithful copying of such old houses, and it was covered with all kinds of greens and vines going up and down the stone walls. Since it was surrounded by shrubbery and trees in the manner of a fence, it was most secluded, and one had the feeling of complete privacy. There was sufficient land around it to make it even more remote from the surrounding community, and as the zoning laws in Lynwood were quite careful, chances of a new building going up next door to them were remote. They immediately went past the shrubbery and looked around, possibly to see if anyone could show them the house. The sign outside had read "For Sale" and given the name of a real estate firm, but it did not state whether or not the house was currently inhabited. As they approached the house across the soft lawn they came to realize immediately that it could not be. All around them were signs of neglect and apparently long periods of no care at all. What had once been a beautifully landscaped garden was now a semi-wilderness in which weeds had overgrown precious flowers and the shrubbery grew whichever way it chose.

The paths, so carefully outlined by a previous owner, were hardly recognizable now. The rains had washed them away and birds had done the rest.

"Needs lots of work," her husband mumbled apprehensively, as they observed the earmarks of destruction all around them. But they continued toward the house. They did not enter it but walked around it at first in the manner in which a wild animal stalks its prey. They wanted to take in all of the outside, the grounds, first, before venturing inside.

On the other side of the house was a fine patio that had apparently served as a breakfast and dining patio at one time. A forlorn broken cup and a rusty spoon lay on the ground, but otherwise the patio was empty and still.

"Boy, they sure let this place run downhill," Mr. S. remarked and shook his head. He was a businessman used to orderly procedures and this was anything but good sense. Why would anyone owning so lovely a place let it go to pot? It didn't make sense to him.

All over the neighborhood, down Elm Street, the houses were aristocratic and well-kept. It would seem *someone* would care enough to look after this little jewel of a house, too. Why hadn't the real estate man sent someone around to clean things up once in a while? He decided to question the man about it.

From the patio on down to the end of the property, clearly marked by the shrubbery, was almost nothing but roses. Or rather, there had been at one time. One could still see that some loving hand had planted rows upon rows of rose bushes, but only a few of them were flowering now. In between, other plants had grown up and what there was left of the roses needed careful and immediate pruning, his knowledgeable eyes told him at once. Still, there was hope for the roses if a lot of work were to be put in on them.

They entered the house through the patio door, which was ajar. Inside they found further proof of long neglect. The furniture was still there, so it was a furnished house for sale. This was a pleasant surprise for it would make things a lot easier for them, financially speaking, even if some of the things they might buy with the house had to be thrown out later.

The dust covering the inside and an occasional spider's web drove home the fact that no one could have lived here for years. But this did not disturb them, for there are lots of nice houses in California standing empty for years on end until someone wants them. They felt a strange sensation of being at home now, as if this had already been their house and they had just now re-entered it only after a long summer vacation.

Immediately they started to examine each room and the gray, almost blackened windows. No doubt about it, it would take months of cleaning before the house would be livable again. But there was nothing broken or inherently beyond repair in the house and their courage rose, especially when they realized that most of the Victorian furniture was in excellent condition, just dirty.

After a prolonged stay in the house, during which they examined every one of the rooms, every nook and cranny, and finally went out into the garden again, they never doubted for a moment that this would be their future home. It never occurred to them that perhaps the sign had been out there for months even though someone had already bought the place or that it might be available but priced beyond their means.

Somehow they knew immediately that the house was right for them, just the size they wanted—they had no children—not too big to manage, but yet spacious and above all quiet, as it sat in the midst of what might once again become a fine garden.

"Well, what do you say, Naomi?" Mr. S. inquired. It was more of rhetorical question since he, and she, knew very well what they were to do next. "Yes, it will do," she nodded and smiled at him. It is a good feeling to have found one's home.

They carefully closed the patio door and locked it as best they could—after all, it was *their* home now, practically, and not just a neglected, empty old house for sale. As they walked up the garden path towards Elm Street, they had the distinctive feeling of being followed by a pair of eyes. But they were so preoccupied with thoughts of how to make this place into a livable home, that they paid no heed. They didn't even turn around when they heard a rustling sound in the leaves that covered the path. It was the kind of sound the wind would make, had there *been* a wind.

After they left the place, they immediately drove down to the real estate office.

Yes, the place was still for sale. They sighed with relief, too noticeably to escape the glance of the real estate man. It bemused him, since he was only too glad to unload the white elephant the house on Lago Avenue represented to him. After some small talk, they agreed on a price and move-in date, and then Mrs. S. began to wonder about the people who had lived there before.

But the real estate man, either by design or ignorance, could not tell them much. The house had been there for about thirty years or so, but even that was not certain. It might have been sixty years, for all he knew. It could not be more than that, for Lynwood wasn't much older. Who had built it? He didn't know their names, but a couple had built it and lived in it originally, and after them a number of other people had either bought or rented it, but somehow nobody stayed very long. His company had just recently taken over its sale, he believed, in the name of some absentee heir, across the country somewhere, but he really could not tell them more than that.

"It's just an old house, you know," he finally said and looked at them puzzled. "Why do you want to know more?"

Why indeed? The man was right. Resolutely, they signed the contract and a few weeks later, when their affairs elsewhere had been wound up, they moved into the house.

The first few days were grim. They reminded one of the pioneering days of early Americans as the S.s worked from early to late to get their bedroom into livable condition. After that, the kitchen, and so forth until gradually, with much sweat and effort, the house changed. In the spring, they turned their attention to the garden, and since Mr. S. had meanwhile gone into semi-retirement from his business he had a little more time on his hands to help. Now and then they used the services of a local gardener, but by and large, it was their own effort that made the garden bloom again. Carefully pruning the roses, and whenever they found a gap, replanting a rose bush, they managed to bring back a new life to the beautiful place. Inside the house the old furniture had been dusted and repaired where necessary and they had augmented the pieces with some of their own, interspersing them where suitable. So the house took on a strange look of mixture of their old house and what must have been the former owner's own world, but the two did not seem to clash, and intermingled peacefully for their comfort.

They never tried to change anything in either house or garden just for change's sake: if they could find what had stood on the spot, they would faithfully restore it, almost as if driven by a zeal to turn the clock back to where it had stood when the house had first been built. They felt themselves motivated by the same loyalty a museum curator displays in restoring a priceless masterpiece to its original appearance. Their efforts paid off, and the house became a model of comfortable, if somewhat Victorian, living.

As they became acquainted with their garden, they became aware of the fact that it contained lots more than roses or ordinary flowers. Apparently the previous owners liked rare plants for there were remnants of unusual flowers and green plants, they had never seen before outside of museums or arboretums. With some of them, the original label had remained, giving the name and origin. Whenever they were able to, they fixed these labels so that much of the old flavor returned to the garden. They even went to the local florist and asked him to explain some of the rare plants, and in turn they bought some replacements for those that had died of neglect, and put them where they would have been before.

With all this work taking up most of their time, they found no opportunity to make friends in the community. For a long time, they knew no one except the real estate man and the gardener who had occasionally worked for them, neither persons of social acquaintance status.

But one morning Mrs. S. noticed a nice lady pass her as she was working in the front garden, and they exchanged smiles. After that, she stopped her in the street a day or so later and inquired about shops in the area and it turned out the lady was a neighbor living across the street from them, a certain Lillian G., who had been a longtime resident of the area. Not a young woman any longer, Mrs. G. knew a great deal about the community, it appeared, but the two women never talked about anything but current problems of the most mundane nature—on the few occasions that they did meet again. It was almost as if Naomi did not want to discuss the story of her house any longer, now that she owned it.

* * *

A year went by and the S.s were finally through with all their restorations in the house and could settle back to a comfortable and well-earned rest. They liked their home and knew that they had chosen well and wisely. What had seemed at the time a beckoning finger from the house itself to them, now appeared merely as an expression of horse sense upon seeing the place and they prided themselves on having been so wise.

* * *

It was summer again and the California sky was blue and all was well with the house and themselves. Mr. S. had gone out and would not be back until the afternoon. Mrs. S. was busy working in the rose garden, putting some fine touches on her bushes. Despite the approaching midday, it was not yet too hot to work.

Naomi had just straightened out one of the tea roses, when she looked up and realized she had a visitor. There, on the path no more than two yards away, stood a rather smallish lady. She was neatly dressed in a faded house dress of another era, but in California this is not particularly unusual. Lots of retired people like to dress in various old-fashioned ways and no one cares one way or another. The lady was quite elderly and fragile, and Naomi was startled to see her there.

Her surprise must have been obvious, for the visitor immediately apologized for the intrusion. "I didn't mean to scare you," she said in a thin, high-pitched voice that somehow went well with her general appearance and frailty.

"You didn't," Naomi bravely assured her. She was nothing if not hospitable. Why should a little old lady scare her?

"Well then," the visitor continued tentatively, "would it be all right if I looked around a bit?"

This seemed unusual, for the place was scarcely a famous show place, and Naomi did not feel like turning it into a public park. Again, her thoughts must have shown on her face, for the lady immediately raised her hand and said, "You see, my husband and I originally built this place."

Naomi was flabbergasted. So the owners had decided to have a look at their house after all these years. At the same time, a sense of accomplishment filled her heart. Now they could see how much had been done to fix up the house!

"It's a beautiful place," Naomi said and waved her visitor to come with her.

"Yes, isn't it?" the lady nodded. "We took great pride in it, really."

"Too bad it was in such bad shape when we bought it, though," Naomi said succinctly. "We had to put a lot of work into it to bring it back to its old state."

"Oh, I can see that," the lady commented and looked with loving eyes at each and every shrub.

They were on the garden path in the rear now.

"Oh, you've put pink roses where the tea roses used to be," she suddenly exclaimed. "How thoughtful."

Naomi did not know that the tea roses had been on that spot for there had been nothing left of them. But she was glad to hear about it. The visitor now hopped from flower to flower almost like a bird, inspecting here, caressing a plant there, and pointing out the various rare plants to Naomi, as if *she* were the hostess and Naomi the visitor.

"I am so glad you have brought life back into the house, so glad," she kept repeating.

It made Naomi even happier with her accomplishment. Too bad her husband couldn't be here to hear the lady's praise. Mr. S. had sometimes grumbled about all the hard work they had had to put in to make the place over.

"The begonia over there...oh, they are still missing, too bad. But you can fix that sometime, can you not?" she said and hurried to another part of the garden, as if eager to take it all in in whatever time Naomi allowed her to visit with her.

"Wouldn't you like to have a look at the inside of the house, too?" Naomi finally suggested. The lady glowed with happiness at the invitation.

"Yes, I would like that very much. May I?" Naomi pointed at the garden door and together they stepped inside the house. The cool atmosphere inside was in sharp contrast to the pleasant, but warm air in the garden.

"Over there, that's where the grandfather clock used to be. I see you've moved it to the den."

Naomi smiled. They had indeed. The lady surely must have an excellent memory to remember all that, for they had not yet entered the den. It never occurred to Naomi that the visitor knew the clock had been moved prior to seeing it in the den. So much at home was the little old lady in what used to be her house, that it seemed perfectly natural for her to know all sorts of things about it.

"The table is nice, too, and it fits in so well," she now commented. They had brought it with them from their former home, but it did indeed blend in with the furniture already in the house. The visitor now bounced gaily to the other end of the long room which they were using as a day room or parlor.

"That chair," she suddenly said, and pointed at the big, oaken chair near the fireplace, and there was a drop in her voice that seemed to indicate a change in mood.

"What about the chair?" Naomi inquired and stepped up to it. The visitor seemed to have difficulty in holding back a tear or two, but then composed herself and explained—

"My husband died in that chair."

There was a moment of silence as Naomi felt compassion for the strange lady.

"He was raking leaves one morning...it was a nice summer day just like today...just like today...he always liked to do a little work around the garden before breakfast. I was still in bed at that hour, but I was awake and I heard him come into the house when he had finished his chores in the garden."

Naomi had not said anything, but her eyes were on the lady with interest. She noticed how frail and ethereal she looked, and how old age had really rendered her thin and somehow tired. And yet, her eyes had an unusual, bright sparkle in them that belied her frail and aged appearance. No, this woman was all right, despite her advanced age. Probably lives alone somewhere in the area, too, now that her husband is dead, Naomi mused.

"My husband came into the house and a little later I got up to fix him breakfast as I always did," the visitor continued, all the while holding the back of the chair firmly with one hand.

"When I called out to him to come and get it, I received no reply. Finally I thought this odd and went into the room—this room—and there, in this chair, I found him. He was dead."

The account had given Naomi a strange chill. It suddenly occurred to her how little she knew about the former owners. But the icy hush that had settled over the two women was broken when the lady let go of the chair and turned towards the door.

"I'd like another look at the patio, if I may," she said and as if she wanted to make up for her seriousness before, now she chatted interminably and lightly about the pleasures of living in such a house as this.

They had arrived at the rose beds again and the visitor pointed at a particularly fullblown dark red bush Naomi had fancied all along more than any other rose bush in the garden.

"They were always my favorites," the lady said, almost with a whisper.

"Then let me give you some to take home with you," Naomi offered and since the visitor did not protest her offer, she turned around to reach for the scissors, which she kept at the foot of the patio.

Her back was not turned more than a second. But when she looked up at her visitor again, the little lady was gone.

"That's rude of her," Naomi thought immediately. Why had she suddenly run away? Surely, the offer of roses from her former home was no reason to be offended. But then it occurred to Naomi that perhaps the lady's emotions at being back in her old home, yet no longer mistress of it, might have gotten the upper hand with her and she simply could not face getting roses from *her* favorite bush by a stranger.

"I wonder which way she went, though," Naomi said out loud. She heard no car drive off, so the lady must have come on foot. Perhaps she could still catch her, for surely she could not have gotten far. It was plain silly of her not to take the proffered roses.

Naomi quickly went down the garden path and looked and then the driveway and looked there but the woman was not on the property any longer. She then ran out onto the street and even looked down Elm Street but the visitor was nowhere in sight.

"But this is impossible," Naomi thought. "She can't just disappear." So little time had elapsed between their last words and Naomi's pursuit that no human being could have disappeared without trace.

Naomi, still puzzled, went back into the house. The whole episode took on a certain dreamlike quality after a while and she forgot about it. Surely, there must be some explanation for the lady's quick disappearance, but Naomi had other things to do than worry about it.

For reasons of her own she felt it best not to tell her husband about the visit, for she was not at all sure herself now that she had not dreamed the whole thing. Of course, she hadn't. The lady's footprints were still visible in the soft soil of the lawn several days after the visit. Such small feet, too. But somehow she felt reluctant to discuss it further. Besides, what of it? A former tenant wants to visit the old home. Nothing special or newsworthy about that.

* * *

Several weeks later she happened to have tea with the neighbor across the street. Over tea and cookies, they talked about the neighborhood and how it changed over all the years Mrs. G. had lived there. Somehow the visitor came to mind again, and Naomi felt free to confide in Mrs. G.

"I had a visitor the other day, only person I've talked to except for you," Naomi began.

"Oh?" Mrs. G. perked up. "Anyone I might know?"

"Perhaps . . . it was the lady who built our house . . . who lived there before us."

Mrs. G. gave Naomi a strange look but said nothing.

"She was a little lady with a faded pink dress and kind of sparkling eyes, and she told me she and her husband had built the house," Naomi said, and described what the visitor had looked like in minute detail. When she had finished, Mrs. G. shook her head.

"Impossible," she finally said. "That woman has been dead for years."

Naomi laughed somewhat uncertainly.

"But how could she be? I saw her as plainly as I see you. She looked just like any little old lady does."

"Maybe it was someone else," the neighbor said, half hoping Naomi would readily agree to her suggestion.

"I don't think so," Naomi said firmly, however. "You see she also pointed out the chair her husband died in. He had been raking leaves before breakfast, and when she called out to him to come and get it, he didn't answer, and then she went into the parlor and there he was, dead in that big oaken chair."

Mrs. G. had suddenly become very pale.

"That is absolutely true, I mean, the story how he died," she finally managed to say. "But how would you know about it?"

Naomi shrugged helplessly.

"I didn't know it until the lady told me about it," she repeated.

"Incredible. But you've described her to a tee and he did die the way she said. They've both been dead for years and years, you know."

Naomi finally realized the implication.

"You mean I've been visited by a ghost?"

"Seems that way," Mrs. G. nodded gravely.

"But she seemed so very real . . . so solid. I'd never have known she was just a ghost. Why, we even shook hands and her hand felt fine to me."

The woman went over the experience once more, detail for detail. There was one thing that was odd, though. On recollection, Mrs. S. did recall that she had not *heard* the woman enter her garden. She had looked up from her chores, and there the woman stood, smiling at her from in front of the roses. No sound of footsteps on either entering or leaving. Then, too, her intimate knowledge of each and every plant in the garden.

"She even knew the Latin names of every one of them," Naomi pointed out.

"No doubt she did," Mrs. G. explained, and added, "she and her hubby were great horticulturists and took enormous pride in creating a genuine arboretum in their garden."

But why had she visited her old home?

After some thought, Naomi felt she knew the answer. They had just finished restoring the house and garden to their original appearance and probably the same flavor they had had in the years when the original owners had the place. The ghostly lady felt they should be rewarded for their efforts by an approving gesture from *them*. Or had she simply been homesick for her old home?

Naomi was quite sure, now, that she had never really left it. In her mind's eye it had never fallen into disrepair and the lovely roses never ceased to bloom even when the garden had become a wilderness.

She never discussed the matter again with her neighbor or with anyone else for that matter. Her husband, whom she later divorced, never knew of the incident, for Mrs. G. also kept the secret well.

The house may still be there amid the roses, and the little lady in the faded dress no doubt has a ball skipping along its paths and enjoying her beloved flowers.

The Lady Of the Garden (California)

✸ 120
The Ghost Car (Kansas)

MARLENE S. IS A thirty-seven-year-old housewife leading a typical American housewife's life—which is to say she is neither given to explorations into the unknown nor particularly involved in anything out of the ordinary. After two years of college, she found that her married life took up most, if not all, of her time, but she is still hoping to get her teacher's degree after which she would like to teach English literature on a secondary level. But with four youngsters—ranging in age from eleven to fifteen—and a husband around the house, time for study is limited. Her husband, Mr. S. is a district manager for a shoe company.

Marlene came from an average Nebraska family and nothing particularly shocking ever happened to her, that is, until she, her husband and children moved into a house in Kansas City that will forever be etched in her memories. The house itself was nothing special: about seven years old, inexpensive looking, with four bedrooms, built ranch-style all on one floor.

They moved into this house in 1958 when the children were still quite young. A few weeks after they had settled down in the house and gotten used to the new surroundings. Marlene was lying awake in bed, waiting to fall asleep. She never could go to sleep right away, and lying awake trying to sort things out in her mind was her way of inviting the sandman.

Because the children were still young, ranging in age from one to five, she had to be always alert for any moves or noises in case something was wrong. Perhaps this contributed to her light sleep, but at any rate, she was not yet drowsy at this point and was fully cognizant of what might transpire around her.

Suddenly, she felt pressure at the foot of the bed as if one of the children was trying to climb into bed to sleep with the parents.

Marlene sat up quickly but quietly, leaned toward the foot of the bed, made a grab, at the same time saying, "Got you!"—only to find herself grabbing thin air.

She assumed the little culprit had quickly scuttled back to his own bed, and got up and went across the hall to the boys' bedroom. After that, she inspected the girls' room, but all four were sound asleep, tucked in precisely the way she had earlier tucked them in and it was clear that none of her children had caused the pressure at the foot of her bed.

She decided she had imagined the whole thing and went back to bed. But the following night, the pressure was back again and again she grabbed nothing but a fistful of thin air.

It got to be such a common occurrence she quit checking on the children whether or not they were doing it.

She then decided that it had to be caused by her husband's moving his foot in a certain way. Somehow she reasoned that his moves gave the feeling the covers were drawn up against her foot, creating the impression of an outside pressure. Far-fetched though this explanation was, she accepted it gladly. But she kept her foot against his for several nights after this to find out what move of his caused all this to happen.

As her husband slept, she observed, but it got her nowhere: the pressure was still present, but there was no connection with her husband's foot or his movements.

She had hardly accepted the strange pressure in her bed when still another phenomenon caused her to wonder about the house. Near the doorway to the bedroom she heard someone breathe deeply and heavily when there was no one but her around. When this recurred several times she decided to tell her husband about it. He shook his head and said he had heard nothing. She did not tell him about the pressure on the bed, thinking it just too absurd to discuss. That night she heard the crackling of what sounded like someone stepping on cellophane just before she felt the pressure at the foot of the bed again.

She knew she had left a cellophane bag at the foot of the bed on the floor and she was sure one of her children had come out and stepped on it. Again she grabbed but again her hands held only air and the children were all soundly asleep in the respective rooms.

By now a little bit of fear crept into her mind when she came to realize that there wasn't really any rational explanation for the strange noises and especially the heavy breathing.

But she pulled her knees up at night and thus avoided coming in contact with whatever was causing the pressure at the foot of the bed.

For a while, nothing untoward happened, and the family was busy getting on with the problems of daily living. The strange occurrences drifted into the background for a while.

Then one night, several weeks later, Marlene was awakened from sleep by a most incredible sound. It was as if a giant vat of water was being poured on the house. The swooshing sound of water cascading down upon them reverberated for several seconds afterward. Her immediate thought, being just awakened from deep sleep, was a logical one—one of the kids had not been able to make it to the bathroom and what she was hearing was the result! But no: they were all fast asleep in their rooms.

The next morning, she examined the floor. In the boys' room she found a strange liquid spot. It was like water, except much thicker and did not ooze out as water would, but lay there on the floor, perfectly cohesive and round. It had neither odor nor color and when she removed it with tissue paper, it left no trace. Her husband explained that probably the liquid had oozed up from the ground or dropped from the ceiling but her logical mind refused to accept what was obviously not likely.

There was absolutely no rational explanation for either the swooshing noise or the presence of the thick liquid in the boys' room. Several months afterward, a similar spot appeared in the girls' room. Since they had no animals in the house, the matter remained a puzzle.

The house was so new that any thoughts of ghosts were far from Marlene's mind. But strange things began to occur. One day, a car securely parked across from the house on a slanting driveway, came downhill and crashed into the boys' bedroom. Luckily no one was hurt.

Not much later, another car from across the street did the same thing, only this time the car went into the girls' room. The owner swore he had put the car into parking position on leaving it. Just as he got out, he saw his car roll down the driveway *by itself!*

This wasn't too reassuring to Marlene. Was some unknown force trying to "get" them? Was there a connection between the spots of liquid in the childrens' bedrooms and the two car crashes?

Somehow the atmosphere in the house was different now from the time they had first moved in. It seemed heavy, as if some sort of tragic pressure was weighing upon it. Her husband did not notice anything unusual, or if he did, he did not discuss it with her. But to her there was an ominous presence in the house and she didn't like it.

One night her husband was working late. She had gone to bed and had just turned the lights out. No sooner had she lain down, than she began to hear the heavy breathing again. Next came the pressure at the foot of the bed. With the breathing so close to her, she was absolutely terrified and did not dare move. Whatever it was, it was very near and she realized now that all her reasoning had not explained a thing. *Someone other than herself shared her bed and that someone was not friendly.*

But what was she to do? The children were asleep in their beds and her husband was at work. She decided that under the circumstances the best thing was to play possum. She lay there as if asleep, barely breathing and not moving a muscle.

She did not know how much time had passed when she heard the car drive up to their door. The headlights shone through the bedroom window and she heard the motor being turned off.

"Thank God, Don is home," she managed to say under her breath.

Even though the presence was still close by, she somehow managed to get enough courage to jump out of bed and race to the window. Turning on the lights on the way to the living room as she went by, she reached the window and looked out to the driveway.

Instead of seeing her husband and the family car, she was greeted by the blackness of the night. Nothing. No car.

"This is the last straw!" she almost cried and ran back to her bed. Pulling the covers over her she lay there in terror, not knowing what to do next. When her husband finally returned after what seemed hours upon hours, she managed to sob out her story.

"There, there," he said, soothingly, taking her head in his hands. "You've been having nightmares."

"He doesn't believe a word I've said," she thought, between sobs, but she preferred being consoled by a non-believer than not being consoled at all.

The next few weeks passed somehow. They had requested a transfer to another location. When it came, she was a new person. The prospect of moving into another house where nothing would disturb her sleep was just too wonderful.

Her husband had rented a big, old mansion in Wichita, where they were transferred by the company, and it was filled with antiques and fine furniture of a bygone era.

When Marlene first saw the house, she thought, "Oh my God, if any house ought to be haunted, this looks like one!"

But it wasn't and the house in Wichita proved as peaceful and serene as a house can be, if it isn't inhabited by a restless ghost.

The house was full of memories of its past fifty years but none of them intruded upon her and she lived a happy, relaxed life now. The experiences in Kansas receded into her memory and she was sure now that it had all been the fault of the house and not something connected with her—least of all, her imagination, for she knew, no matter what her husband had said, that she had seen and heard that ghost car drive up to the house.

She sometimes wonders who the new owners of that house in Kansas are and whether they can hear the heavy breathing the way she did. But then she realizes that it was her own innate psychic ability that allowed the phenomena to manifest themselves when they did. Another person not so endowed might conceivably not feel anything at all.

What was the horrible accident that was being reenacted—from the sound of the water being poured down, to the rushing up of the ghost car? And whose heavy breathing was disturbing her nights?

Many times her curiosity almost made her inquire but then she decided to let sleeping dogs lie. But in later years while living in California, her psychic ability developed further until she was able to hear and see the dead as clearly and casually as she could commune with the living. It frightened her and she thought at first she was having waking nightmares. All through the night she would be aware of a room full of people while at the same time being able to sleep on. Her observation was on several levels at the same time, as if she had been turned into a radio receiver with several bands.

Clearly, she did not want any of this, least of all the heavy breathing she started to hear again after they had moved to California.

The Ghost Car (Kansas)

But then it could be the breathing of another restless soul, she decided, and not necessarily something or someone she had brought with her from Kansas. She read as much as she could now on the subject of ESP, and tried her hand at automatic writing. To her surprise, her late father and her grandparents wrote to her through her own hand.

She noticed that the various messages were in different hands and quite clearly differed from her own. Yet her logical mind told her this might all come from her own subconscious mind and she began to reject it. As she closed herself off from the messages, they dwindled away until she no longer received them.

This she regretted, for the presence of her father around her to continue the link of a lifetime and perhaps protect her from the incursions of unwanted entities of both worlds, was welcome and reassuring.

By now she knew of her psychic powers and had learned to live with them, but also to close the psychic door when necessary.

* * *

Meanwhile the house in Kansas still stands and very few tenants stay for long.

✳ 121

The Ghostly Monks of Aetna Springs

"IF YOU LIKE GOLF, you'll enjoy our nine-hole golf course," says the brochure put out by the Aetna Springs, California, resort people. They have a really fine self-contained vacationland going there. People live in comfortable cabins, children have their own playground, adults can play whatever games *they* please, there are tennis, swimming, fishing, riding, dancing, horseshoe pitching, hunting, shuffleboarding, mineral bathing—the springs—and last, but certainly not least, there is that lovely golf course stretching for several miles on the other side of the only road leading up to the place. With all the facilities on one side of the road, the golf course looks like a million miles from nowhere. I don't know if it pleases the guests, but it is fine with the *ghosts*. For I did not come up eighty-five miles north of San Francisco to admire the scenery, of which there is plenty to admire.

As the road from Napa gradually enters the hills, you get the feeling of being in a world that really knows little of what goes on outside. The fertile Napa Valley and its colorful vineyards soon give way to a winding road and before you know it you're deep in the woods. Winding higher and higher, the road leads past scattered human habitation into the Pope Valley. Here I found out that there was a mineral spring with health properties at the far end of the golf course.

In the old days, such a well would naturally be the center of any settlement, but today the water is no longer commercially bottled. You can get as much as you want for free at the resort, though.

Incidentally there are practically no other houses or people within miles of Aetna Springs. The nearest village is a good twenty minutes' ride away over rough roads. This is the real back country, and it is a good thing California knows no snow, for I wouldn't want to tackle those roads when they are slushy.

As I said before, we had not come up all that way for the mineral water. Bill Wynn, a young engineer from San Francisco, was driving us in my friend Lori Clerf's car. Lori is a social worker and by "us" I mean, of course, my wife Catherine and Sybil Leek. Sybil did not have the faintest idea why we were here. She honestly thought it was an excursion for the sheer joy of it, but then she knows me well and suspected an ulterior motive, which indeed was not long in coming.

My interest in this far-off spot started in 1965 when I met Dr. Andrew von Salza for the first time. He is a famous rejuvenation specialist and about as down-to-earth a man as you can find. Being a physician of course made him even more skeptical about anything smacking of the occult. It was therefore with considerable disbelief, even disdain, that he discovered a talent he had not bargained for: he was a photographic medium with rare abilities.

It began in 1963, when a friend, the widow of another doctor by the name of Benjamin Sweetland, asked him to photograph her. She knew von Salza was a camera bug and she wanted to have a portrait. Imagine their surprise when the face of the late Dr. Sweetland appeared on a lampshade in the room! There was no double exposure or accidental second picture. Dr. von Salza had used ordinary black and white film in his Leica.

The doctor's curiosity was aroused and his naturally inquiring mind was now stimulated by something he did not understand and, furthermore, did not really believe. But he came back with a color camera, also a Leica, and took some pictures of Mrs. Sweetland. One out of twenty produced an image of her late husband against the sky.

The experience with Mrs. Sweetland was soon followed by another event.

A patient and friend of the doctor's, Mrs. Pierson, had been discussing her daughter with Andrew in her San Francisco apartment. The girl had recently committed suicide.

Suddenly Andrew felt impelled to reach for his camera. There was little light in the room but he felt he wanted to finish the roll of film he had. For no logical reason, he photographed the bare wall of the room. On it, when the film was developed, there appeared the likeness of the dead girl von Salza had never met!

While he was still debating with himself what this strange talent of his might be, he started to take an interest in spiritualism. This was more out of curiosity than for any partisan reasons.

He met some of the professional mediums in the Bay area, and some who were not making their living from this pursuit but who were nevertheless of a standard the doctor could accept as respectable.

Among them was Evelyn Nielsen, with whom von Salza later shared a number of séance experiences and who apparently became a "battery" for his psychic picture taking, for a lot of so-called "extras," pictures of people known to be dead, have appeared on von Salza's pictures, especially when Miss Nielsen was with him.

I have examined these photographs and am satisfied that fraud is out of the question for a number of reasons, chiefly technical, since most of them were taken with Polaroid cameras and developed on the spot before competent witnesses, including myself.

One day in New York City, Mrs. Pierson, who had been intrigued by the psychic world for a number of years, took Andrew with her when she visited the famed clairvoyant Carolyn Chapman.

Andrew had never heard of the lady, since he had never been interested in mediums. Mrs. Pierson had with her a Polaroid color camera. Andrew offered to take some snapshots of Mrs. Chapman, the medium, as souvenirs.

Imagine everybody's surprise when Mrs. Chapman's grandfather appeared on one of the pictures. Needless to say, Dr. von Salza had no knowledge of what the old man looked like nor had he access to any of his photographs, since he did not know where he was going that afternoon in New York.

A friend of Andrew's by the name of Dr. Logan accompanied him, Mrs. Pierson, and Evelyn Nielsen to Mount Rushmore, where the group photographed the famous monument of America's greatest Presidents. To their utter amazement, there was another face in the picture—Kennedy's!

Dr. Logan remained skeptical, so it was arranged that he should come to Andrew's house in San Francisco for an experiment in which he was to bring his own film.

First, he took some pictures with von Salza's camera and nothing special happened. Then von Salza tried Logan's camera and still there were no results. But when Dr. Logan took a picture of a corner in von Salza's apartment, using Andrew's camera, the result was different: on the Polaroid photograph there appeared in front of an "empty" wall a woman with a hand stretched out toward him. As Andrew von Salza reports it, the other doctor turned white—that woman had died only that very morning on his operating table!

But the reason for our somewhat strenuous trip to Aetna Springs had its origin in another visit paid the place in 1963 by Andrew van Salza. At that time, he took two pictures with the stereo camera owned by a Mr. Heibel, manager of the resort.

As soon as the pictures were developed, they were in for a big surprise. His friend's exposures showed the magnificent golf course and nothing more. But Andrew's pictures, taken at the same time, clearly had *two rows of monks* on them. There were perhaps eight or ten monks wearing white robes, with shaven heads, carrying lighted candles in their outstretched hands. Around them, especially around their heads, were flame-like emanations.

There was no doubt about it, for I have the pictures before me—these are the photographs, in color, of monks who died in flames—unless the fiery areas represent life energy. They were brightest around the upper parts of the bodies. On one of the pictures, the monks walk to the right, on the other, to the left, but in both exposures one can clearly distinguish their ascetic hollow-eyed faces—as if they had suffered terribly.

The pictures were not only fascinating, they were upsetting, even to me, and I have often been successful in psychic photography. Here we had a scientific document of the first order.

I wanted to know more about these monks, and the only way to find out was to go up to Napa County. That is why we were winding our way through the Pope Valley that warm October afternoon.

We were still many miles away from Aetna Springs when Sybil took my hand and said: "The place you're taking me is a place where a small group of people must have gone for sanctuary, for survival, and there is some *religious element present*."

"What happened there?"

"They were completely wiped out."

"What sort of people were they, and who wiped them out?"

"I don't know why, but the word 'Anti-Popery' comes to me. Also a name, Hi. . . . "

A little later, she felt the influence more strongly.

"I have a feeling of people crossing water, not native to California. A Huguenot influence?"

We were passing a sign on the road reading "Red Silver Mines" and Sybil remarked she had been impressed with treasures of precious metals and the troubles that come with them.

We had now arrived at the resort. For fifteen minutes we walked around it until finally we encountered a surly caretaker, who directed us to the golf course. We drove as far onto it as we could, then we left the car behind and walked out onto the lawn. It was a wide open area, yet

The ghostly monks of Aetna Springs, California

Sybil instantly took on a harrowed look as if she felt closed in.

"Torture...crucifixion and fire..." she mumbled, somewhat shaken. "Why do we have to go through it?"

I insisted. There was no other way to find out if there was anything ghostly there.

"There is a French Protestant Huguenot influence here..." she added, "but it does not seem to make sense. Religion and anti-religion. The bench over there by the trees is the center of activity...some wiping out took place there, I should think...crosses...square crosses, red, blood crosses...."

"What nationality are they, these people?"

"Conquistadores..."

"Who were the victims?"

"I'm trying to get just one word fixed...H-I...I can't get the rest...it has meaning to this spot...many presences here...."

"How many?"

"Nine."

"How are they dressed?"

"Like a woman's dress on a man...skirted dress."

"Color?"

"Brown."

"Do they have anything in their hands or doing anything, any action?"

"They have a thing around their head...like the Ku Klux Klan...can't see their faces...light...fire light...fire is very important...."

When I asked her to look closer, she broke into tears.

"No, no," she begged off, her fists clenched, tears streaming down her cheeks. I had never seen her emotionally involved that much in a haunting.

"What do you feel?" I asked softly. She was almost in trance now.

"Hate..." she answered with a shaky voice choked with tears, "to be found here, secretly, *no escape*...from the Popish people...no faces...."

"Did they perish in this spot?" I asked.

Almost inaudibly Sybil's voice replied: "Yes...."

"Are the people, these nine, still here?"

"Have to be...Justice for their lives...."

"Who has hurt them?"

"Hieronymus." There was the "Hi" she had tried to bring out before.

"Who's Hieronymus?"

"The leader of the Popish people."

"What did he do to them?"

"He burned them...useless."

"Who were they?"

"They took the silver...."

"I intoned some words of compassion and asked the nine ghosts to join their brothers since the ancient wrong done them no longer mattered.

"Pray for us," Sybil muttered. "Passed through the fire, crosses in hand...their prayers...."

Sybil spoke the words of a prayer in which I joined. Her breath came heavily as if she were deeply moved. A moment later the spell broke and she came out of it. She seemed bewildered and at first had no recollection where she was.

"Must go..." she said and headed for the car without looking back.

It was some time before we could get her to talk again, a long way from the lonely golf course gradually sinking into the October night.

Sybil was herself again and she remembered nothing of the previous hour. But for us, who had stood by her when the ghostly monks told their story, as far as they were able to, not a word was forgotten. If recollection should ever dim, I had only to look at the photographs again that had captured the agony in which these monks had been frozen on the spot of their fiery deaths.

I took a motion picture film of the area but it showed nothing unusual, and my camera, which sometimes does yield ghost pictures, was unfortunately empty when I took some exposures. I thought I had film in it but later discovered I had forgotten to load it...or had the hand of fate stayed my efforts?

Nobody at Aetna Springs had ever heard of ghosts or monks on the spot. So the search for corroboration had to be started back home.

At the Hispanic Society in New York, books about California are available only for the period during which that land was Spanish, although they do have some general histories as well.

In one of these, Irving Richman's *California under Spain and Mexico*, I was referred to a passage about the relationship between Native American populations and their Spanish conquerors that seemed to hold a clue to our puzzle.

The specific passage referred to conditions in Santo Domingo, but it was part of the overall struggle then going on between two factions among the Spanish-American clergy. The conquistadores, as we all know, treated the native population only slightly less cruelly than Hitler's Nazis treated subjugated people during World War II.

Their methods of torture had not yet reached such infernal effectiveness in the sixteenth century, but their intentions were just as evil. We read of Indians being put to death at the whim of the colonists, of children thrown to the dogs, of rigid suppression of all opposition, both political and spiritual, to the ruling powers.

Northern California, especially the area above San Francisco, must have been the most remote part of the Spanish world imaginable, and yet outposts existed beyond the well-known missions and their sub-posts.

One of these might have occupied the site of that golf course near the springs. Thus, whatever transpired in the colonial empire of Spain would eventually have found its way, albeit belatedly, to the backwoods also, perhaps finding conditions there that could not be tolerated from the point of view of the government.

The main bone of contention at that time, the first half of the sixteenth century, was the treatment and status of the Native Americans. Although without political voice or even the slightest power, the Indians had some friends at court. Strangely enough, the protectors of the hapless natives turned out to be the Dominican friars—the very same Dominicans who were most efficient and active in the Spanish Inquisition at home!

Whether because of this, or for political expediency, the white-robed Dominicans opposed the brown-robed Franciscans in the matter of the Indians: to the Dominicans, the Indians were fellow human beings deserving every consideration and humane treatment. To the Franciscans, they were clearly none of these, even after they had been given the sacraments of Christianity!

And to the Spanish landowners, the Indians were cheap labor, slaves that could not possibly be allowed any human rights. Thus we had, circa 1530, a condition in some ways paralleling the conditions leading up to the War Between the States in 1861.

Here then is the passage referred to, from Sir A. Helps' *The Spanish Conquests in America*, London 1900, volume I, page 179 *et seq.*

The Fathers (*Jeronimite*) asked the opinions of the official persons and also of the Franciscans and Dominicans, touching the liberty of the Indians. It was very clear beforehand what the answers would be. The official persons and the Franciscans pronounced against the Indians, and the Dominicans in their favor.

The *Jeronimite Fathers*...and Sybil had insisted on a name, so important to this haunting: Hieronymus...Latin for Jerome!

How could any of us have known of such an obscure ecclesiastical term? It took me several days of research, and plain luck, to find it at all.

Who Landed First in America?

To many people, perhaps to the majority of my readers, the question posed in the title of this chapter may seem odd. Don't we know that it was Christopher Columbus? Can't every schoolchild tell us that it happened in 1492 and that he landed on what is today known as the island of San Salvador?

Well, he did do that, of course, and as late as 1956 an American, Ruth Wolper, put a simple white cross at Long Bay, San Salvador, to mark the spot where he stepped on American soil.

Still, the question remains: Was Columbus really the first to discover America and establish contact between the "Old" and the "New" Worlds?

If you want to be technical, there never was a time when some sort of contact between the Old World and the New World did not exist. Over the "land bridge," Siberia to Alaska, some people came as far back as the prehistoric period. The Eskimo population of North America is of Asian origin. The American Indian, if not Asian, is certainly related to the Mongol race and must have come to the Americas at an even earlier time, perhaps at a time when the land masses of Eurasia and North America were even closer than they are today. For we know that the continents have drifted apart over the centuries, and we suspect also that large chunks of land that are not now visible may have once been above water.

But what about the people of Western Europe? If Columbus was not the first to set sail for the New World, who then did?

Although any patriotic Italian-American may shudder at the consequences, especially on Columbus Day, the evidence of prior contact by Europeans with the American continent is pretty strong. It does not take an iota away from Columbus' courageous trip, but it adds to the lore of seafaring men and the lure of the riches across the ocean.

Perhaps the question as to who landed *first* on American soil is less vital than who will land last—but the thrill of discovery does have a certain attraction for most people, and so it may matter. It has been an American trait ever since to be first, or best, in everything, if possible.

Nothing in science is so well established that it cannot yield to *new* evidence. The Pilgrims are generally considered to have been the first permanent settlers in this country, landing at Plymouth Rock in 1620. But there is new evidence that the Portuguese got here earlier—in 1511, to be exact. Dighton Rock, in Berkley, Massachusetts, bears markings in Portuguese consisting of crosses, a date, 1511, and the name Miguel Cortereal. Artifacts of sixteenth-century Portuguese manufacture have been found at the site. Until a Rhode Island medical doctor by the name of Manuel da Silva, whose sideline is archaeology, put two and two together, this fact had been completely ignored by "the establishment" in science. And at nearby Newport, Rhode Island, there is a stone tower similar to Portuguese churches of the sixteenth century. Cannon and swords of Portuguese origin have been dated pretty exactly, and we know from their state of preservation approximately how long they have been in the ground. They antedate the Pilgrims and the trip of the *Mayflower* by a considerable span.

But we are dealing here not with the first settlement in America but with the discovery itself. How far back did civilized man reach America from Europe? Did the Phoenicians, those great sailors of antiquity, get this far? To date, we have not found any evidence that they did. But we do know that they reached Britain. Considering the type of boat these pre-Christian people used, the voyage from Asia Minor through the Mediterranean and the Straits of Gibraltar and then along the French coast and finally through the treacherous Straits of Dover must have called for great nautical skill and daring. Phoenician settlements certainly existed in England. Perhaps offshoots of these early Britons might have ventured across the Atlantic on a further exploration. I am not saying that they did, but if some day Phoenician relics are unearthed in North America, I can only hope that the established historians will not immediately yell "fraud" and step on the traces instead of investigating open-mindedly.

Another great race of seafaring explorers whom we must reckon with are the Norsemen who plowed the oceans some two thousand years after the Phoenicians.

From their homes on the barren shores of Scandinavia they sailed along the coasts of Western Europe to terrorize the people of France and eventually to establish a duchy of their own in that part of France which to this day is known as Normandy for the Normans or Norsemen who once ruled there and who from there went on to rule all of England—a country which the Vikings used to raid long before there was a William the Conqueror. Then they sailed on to raid Ireland and to establish Viking kingdoms in that country, and still farther on to distant Iceland.

Their consummate skill with boats and their advanced understanding of astronomy and meteorology, as well as their incredible fighting power, combined to make them the great nautical adventurers of the early Middle Ages.

These men had lots of wood, so they built ships, or better, longboats, capable of riding even the worst seas. At one point traces of their domination existed in such divers places as Scandinavia, the British Isles, France, southern Italy, and Sicily.

What concerns us here, however, is mainly their exploits at seafaring and discovery in a westerly direction beyond Iceland. It was Iceland, which has the world's oldest Parliament, the Althing, that also provided us with the earliest written accounts concerning the exploration of

America. Especially is *The Saga of Eric the Red* explicit in the account of one Eric, known as the Red from his beard, who lived in Iceland, which was then part of the Viking domain.

In the year 985, he quarreled with his kinsmen and was forced to leave Iceland. Banished for a three-year term, he explored the western coast of Greenland in search of new lands. It was he who gave the icy territory its name, hoping that it might attract immigrants. Greenland is considered part of the North American continent, but to Eric it was merely another island worth investigating. He thought that the land he had looked over held promise, and later brought his wife Thjodhild and their young son Leif over to Greenland, along with twenty-five ships of men and supplies. The majority of these Norsemen settled at the southern tip of Greenland in an area they called the Eastern Settlement. Here Eric operated a farm which he called Brattahlid or "steep slope." Some of the Norsemen, however, sailed on farther and founded another place they called the Western Settlement.

As his son Leif grew up, Eric sent him to Trondhjem to spend a year at Court. At that time Leif became a Christian, although Eric refused to accept the new religion to his dying day. But Leif impressed the King so strongly that Olaf appointed him his commissioner to preach Christianity in Greenland. To make sure he did his best, he sent along a Benedictine monk. The year was 1000 A.D. Leif Ericsson did what was expected of him, and Greenland became Christianized.

Sometime thereafter occurred the event that had such tremendous bearing on American history.

An Icelandic trader returning home from Norway was blown far off his course by a storm and finally, instead of getting to Iceland, somehow managed to make landfall at Brattahlid in Greenland. He was welcomed then by Leif, the son of Eric, and told his host that, while struggling with the sea far to the west of Greenland, he had sighted land still farther west, where no land was supposed to be—a land on which he had not dared to step ashore.

Now, this evidently has just the kind of challenge that would spur a man like Leif Ericsson to action. He rigged his ship and gathered a crew and sailed westward to see if, indeed, there was land there.

There *was* land, and Leif went ashore with his men, and found that wild grapes were growing there and so—the saga tells us—Leif named it Vinland.

The sagas report on this in quite considerable detail. They also tell us of several other expeditions from Greenland to Vinland following Leif's first discovery, which took place about the year 1000. And yet, until recently, these reports were considered legends or at least tradition open to question, for not every word of ancient sagas can be trusted as being accurate, although in my opinion a great deal more is than "establishment" scholars want to admit.

* * *

Follins Pond, Cape Cod—where the Vikings first landed

Then in 1967 a group of Eskimos living at the side of Brattahlid started to excavate for the foundations for a new school. To their surprise, and the Danish Archaeological Society's delight, they came upon a beautifully preserved graveyard, filled with the remains of dozens of people. In addition, the foundations of an eleventh-century church and a nearby farmhouse were also found, exactly as the saga had described them. *Life* magazine published a brief account of these exciting discoveries, and all at once the reputation of Leif Ericsson as a real-life personality was reestablished after long years of languishing in semi-legendary domains.

It is known now for sure that the Greenland colonies established by Eric lasted five centuries, but somehow they disappeared around 1500 and the land was left to the Eskimos. Only two hundred years later did the Scandinavians recolonize the vast island.

The most remarkable part of the sagas, however, is not the exploration of Greenland but the discovery and subsequent colonization of what the Vikings called Vinland. And, although few scholars will deny that the Vinland voyage did indeed take place, there has always been considerable discussion about its location.

There have been strange digs and even stranger findings in various parts of the United States and Canada, all of which tended to confuse the strait-laced archaeologists to the point where, until recently, the entire question of a Viking discovery of America was relegated to the "maybe" category.

Eventually, however, discoveries of importance came to light that could no longer be ignored, and once again the topic of Leif Ericsson's eleventh-century voyage to America became a popular subject for discussion, even among nonarchaeologists.

* * *

There were, until the present experiment was undertaken, only two ways to prove an event in history: written contemporary testimony, or artifacts that can be securely tied to specific places, periods, or historical processes. Even with the two "ordinary" methods, Leif Ericsson did not do badly. The saga of Eric the Red and his son Leif Ericsson is a historical document of considerable merit. It is factual and very meticulous in its account of the voyages and of the locations of the settlements. About twenty-five years ago it was fashionable to shrug off such ancient documents or stories as fictional or, at best, distorted and embroidered accounts of events. Certainly this holds true on occasion. One of the most notable examples of such transposition is the story of King Arthur, who changed from a real-life sixth-century post-Roman petty king to a glamorous twelfth-century chevalier-king. But the discovery of the Dead Sea scrolls gave scholars new food for thought. They, and the recent excavations at Masada, King Herod's fortress, proved that at least some very ancient historical accounts were correct. The thrill of rediscovering landmarks or buildings mentioned in contemporary accounts, and covered up by the centuries, is a feeling only an archaeologist can fully appreciate. The *unbiased* scholar should be able to find his way through the maze of such source material especially if he is aided by field work. By field work I mean excavations in areas suspected of harboring buildings or artifacts of the period and people involved. In addition, there are the chance finds which supplement the methodical digs. The trouble with chance finds is that they are not always reported immediately so that competent personnel can investigate the circumstances under which these objects show up. Thus it is easy for latter-day experts to denounce some pretty authentic relics as false, and only later, calm reappraisal puts these relics in a deserved position of prominence.

In the case of the Vikings, there had been a strong disposition on the part of the "establishment" scholars to look down on the Viking sagas, to begin with, partly on psychological grounds: How could the primitive Norsemen manage not only to cross the stormy Atlantic in their little boats, but even manage to penetrate the American continental wilderness in the face of hostile Indians and unfriendly natural conditions? How did the Egyptians get those heavy boulders onto their pyramids without modern machinery? We don't know—at least "officially"—but the Egyptians sure did, because the stones are up there for everybody to see.

Probability calculations are not always reliable in dealing with past events. Like the lemmings, the inveterate Norse sailors had a strong inner drive to seek new lands beyond the seas. This drive might have helped them overcome seemingly impossible obstacles. Men have crossed the Atlantic in tiny boats even in recent times, against all odds of survival, but they did it successfully. In recent years the feeling among scholars has tended to accept the Vinland crossings as genuine, and concentrate their search on the location of that elusive piece of land the Vikings called Vinland.

* * *

It is here that one must consider the physical evidence of Viking presences in America, for there is some evidence in the form of buildings, graves, stones, and artifacts of Norse origin that cannot be ignored.

* * *

In 1948 a retired engineer and navigator named Arlington Mallery discovered some ruins of a Norse settlement on the northern tip of Newfoundland, and promptly concluded that this was Vinland. In 1951, in a book called *Lost America*, Mallery reported his investigations of Norse traces not only in Newfoundland, but also in Ohio, Rhode Island, and Virginia. Because Mr. Mallery was not an "establishment" scholar with an impressive institution behind him, his discoveries, though carefully documented, drew little attention in the press and with the public at the time.

What exactly did Mallery find?

At a place called Sop's Island in northern Newfoundland, he discovered the remnants of four houses of the Viking type and period. In and around them he found many iron tools, nails, boat rivets, chisels, and axes of the typically Norse design completely alien to the native population of the island. William D. Conner, an Ohio journalist who has been interested in the subject of Vinland for a long time, detailed Mallery's struggle for evidence in an article in *Fate* magazine of November 1967. According to Conner, Mallery's main deficiency was that the radiocarbon dating process now commonly used to date artifacts could not have been used by Mallery, because it had not yet been invented at the time. Nevertheless, Mallery compared the iron implements found in Newfoundland with tools of Scandinavian origin and found them to be identical. Being primarily a metallurgical engineer and not an archaeologist, Mallery had the iron tools tested from the former point of view. These tests, made by independent laboratories, showed that the iron artifacts of Newfoundland were made in the same way and at the same time as definitely identified Norse tools discovered in Greenland and Denmark.

But Mallery was not satisfied with his Newfoundland discoveries. He had always felt that the Vikings had spread out from their initial landing sites to other areas along the coast and even farther inland. Mallery was an expert cartographer, and his reading of three ancient Icelandic maps helped him establish his theory of Viking landings in North America.

The first of these three, the Stephansson map, shows a large peninsula along the coast of Labrador, then called Skralingeland. This peninsula on the map is labeled Promontorium Winlandiae, promontory of Vinland. Mallery felt this referred to the northern peninsula of New-foundland rather than Labrador. The second map was drawn by one Christian Friseo in 1605 and is a copy of a much older map available to him at the time. The third of the maps mentioned by Mallery and Conner is the Thord-sen map, also of Icelandic origin, dating from the sixteenth century. It shows an area of Canada opposite Newfound-land, and refers to "Vinland the Good."

Additional support for Viking presences in North America came from excavations and discoveries made by Dr. Junius Bird, curator of archaeology at the American Museum of Natural History. These finds were made in northern Labrador in the Nain-Hopedale area, and con-sisted of iron nails, boat spikes, clinch rivets, and stone house remains. The stone houses, in Mallery's view, were also of Norse origin and not built by the local Eskimos, as some had thought. The construction of the twelve houses found was much too sophisticated to have been native, Mallery argued. But Labrador had been a way station to the Newfoundland site of a Viking camp, and it did not seem to be quite so outlandish to suggest that Vikings did indeed visit this region.

However, Mallery also discovered evidence of Norse penetration in Virginia and Ohio, consisting of iron spikes and other iron artifacts excavated in rural areas. After com-paring these finds with Scandinavian originals of the period in question, Mallery came to the conclusion that they were indeed of Viking origin.

But Mallery's discoveries were not generally accepted, and it remained for another investigator to rediscover much of Mallery's evidence all over again, in 1963. This was Dr. Helge Ingstad of Norway, who had spent three years exca-vating in Newfoundland. Dr. Ingstad found the remains of a Viking settlement, consisting of houses and even an entire iron smelter, and because he was able to utilize the new radiocarbon dating process, his discoveries were widely publicized. According to Ingstad, the Vikings founded their settlement about 1000 A.D., giving dear old Columbus a Chris-come-lately status. But in one important detail Ingstad differed with Mallery's findings: He placed the ini-tial Viking camp at L'Anse au Meadow, fifteen miles far-ther north than Mallery's site on Sop's Island.

Then Yale University jolted the traditionalists even more by announcing that an old pre-Columbian map of the area it had was authentic, and that it clearly showed Viking sites in Newfoundland.

Now the Viking saga refers to Leif's initial camp as having been in wooded hills on a long lake, that a river flowed into or through this lake, and that there was an island opposite the coast of the promontory they had landed on. There have been considerable geological changes in North America since the eleventh century, of course, the most important one, from our point of view, being the change in the level of the ocean. It is estimated that the water receded about four feet every hundred years, and thus what may have been water in the eleventh century would be dry land by now. This is important to keep in mind, as we shall presently see when our own investigation into the Viking sites gets under way.

While Ingstad did find Norse remains at the site he felt was Leif Ericsson's *first* American camp, Mallery did not do as well at the site *he* had picked for the encamp-ment, Pistolet Bay, fifteen miles to the south. His choice was based solely on his interpretation of the Viking sagas and on the old maps. The Yale map, discovered by a rare book dealer in Europe and studied at the university for eight long years before their decision was made, shows an island with two large inlets, which Yale thinks represent the Hudson Strait and the Belle Isle Strait. The map bears the inscription in Latin, "Island of Vinland, discovered by Bjarni and Leif in company." The map was made by a Swiss monk in 1440.

There seems to be general agreement among scholars now that the Vikings did sail across the ocean from Green-land, then down the coast of Labrador until they reached Newfoundland, where they made camp. Mallery claims that the Sop's Island site farther south from both L'Anse au Meadow and Pistolet Bay, where he had dug up the remains of houses and many iron artifacts, was inhabited by Vikings for a considerable period of time, and he dates the houses from the eleventh century to the end of the fourteenth century. The generally accepted archaeological view is that the Vikings lived in Greenland from about 1000 to 1500 A.D. The North American colonization period does seem to fall into place with this view.

Whether the iron artifacts found in North America were actually made there or whether they were brought there by the Vikings from their Scandinavian or Greenland settlements is immaterial: The iron implements do date back to the early Middle Ages, and if Mallery is correct, the Vikings may even have been the forefathers of an iron-making civilization he says existed in North America *before* Columbus.

* * *

While Mallery's claims of Norse penetrations to Vir-ginia and Ohio are supported only by isolated finds, there is much stronger evidence that a famed runic stone found at Alexandria, Minnesota in 1898 may be the real McCoy. Until very recently, this stone containing an unknown runic inscription had been considered a fantasy product, as the "establishment" scholars could not conceive of Viking invaders coming that far inland. Another such stone, how-ever, was found in 1912 at Heavener, Oklahoma, quite independently from the first one.

* * *

For over fifty years the puzzle remained just that, with occasional discussions as to the authenticity of the stones settling absolutely nothing. Then in 1967, a new approach was used to break the secret. A retired Army cryptographer named Alf Mongé got together with historian O. G. Landsverk to study the two stones anew. The result of their collaboration was a truly sensational book entitled *Norse Cryptography in Runic Carvings.* Now these men were not crackpots or Johnny-come-latelies in their fields. Mr. Mongé was the man who broke the principal Japanese codes during World War II and was highly honored by Britain for it. Dr. Landsverk is a Norwegian expert on Viking history. The two men worked together for five years before announcing the results to the world.

First, they deciphered a stone found near Byfield, Massachusetts, which apparently contained a date within the long Runic legend. The Norsemen had used code to convey their message. Since the native Eskimos and Indians could not read, this was not because of enemy intelligence, but the Vikings considered cryptography an art worth practicing, and practice it they did. They did not know Arabic numbers, but they used runes to represent figures.

The Massachusetts stone contains the date of November 24, 1009 A.D. as the date of the landing there. The stone unearthed in Oklahoma had the date of November 11, 1012 A.D. on it, and a second stone contained the dates 1015 and 1022. The traditional date of Leif Ericsson's arrival in America is 1003 A.D.

Mongé and Landsverk now reconstructed the dates of the various Norse expeditions. According to them, the Vikings definitely were in Oklahoma as early as 1012 and in Minnesota as late as 1362. It is noteworthy that these dates again coincide with Mallery's findings: He placed the period of the Sop's Island houses between the eleventh century and 1375 A.D.

That the Viking landings in North America were no brief, isolated affair had become clear to me from studying the record and its various interpretations. The press played up the cryptographer's discoveries, but even so astute a journal as *Newsweek* failed to see an important point in the new material: The two explorers were confident that the real Vinland was located in Massachusetts!

The Vikings had come to North America, then sailed along the coast—not necessarily all at once, but perhaps after a number of years initially in one area—and reached the Southwest. Sailing up the Mississippi, they could have traveled inland by way of the Arkansas and Poteau Rivers until they reached Oklahoma. Other groups might have started out from Hudson Bay and the Great Lakes region and reached Minnesota in that way.

Thus the puzzle of the runic stones had finally been solved. What had caused scholarly rejection for many years, was actually proof of their genuineness: the "misspellings" and "inconsistencies" in the runic writings of the stones found in inland America were actually cryptograms and code writing, and the dates based on the Catholic ecclesiastical calendar with which the newly Christianized Norsemen were already familiar, are repeated several times in the messages, so that any doubt as to the correctness of these dates has been dispelled forever.

Though the Mayor of Genoa and Spanish admirers of Christopher Columbus have grudgingly admitted defeat on technical grounds, they still maintain that the Vikings did nothing for history with their forays into America, while their man, Columbus, did a lot. Well, of course, when one considers how the Spaniards killed and robbed the Native Americans, or whenever they allowed them to live, treated them as slaves, one wonders if that great expedition of 1492 was really such a blessing after all. While the Vikings certainly defended themselves against native attacks, we do not seem to find any record of the kind of colonialization the Spaniards became famous—or, rather, infamous—for.

I felt that the evidence for the Newfoundland sites was far too strong to be ignored. Surely, a Viking camp had existed there, but was it *the* first camp? Admittedly, the description of the site in the sagas did not fit exactly with the layout of Newfoundland. Were the archaeologists not using their finds and ignoring the physical discrepancies of the reported sites? Certainly they had evidence for Viking *presences* there, but the case was by no means closed.

* * *

Long before the Mongé–Landsverk collaboration, a book by Frederick Pohl bearing on the matter was published. Pohl's account, published in 1952, is called *The Lost Discovery,* and it was followed in 1961 by another book, *They All Discovered America,* by Charles Michael Boland. Both books point out that Cape Cod might be the site of Leif Ericsson's landfall. According to the latter work, it was in 1940 that explorer Hjalmar Holand suggested to Pohl that the New England shoreline should be investigated carefully to find a place that fit the description given in the sagas of Ericsson's first camp: a cape, a river flowing from or through a lake into the sea, and an island that lay to the northward off the land.

Pohl did just that, and after long and careful research decided that the site was on Cape Cod. He found that the Bass River, in the east-central section of the cape, did indeed flow through a lake into the sea. The lake is called Follins Pond, and when Pohl investigated it more closely he discovered some ancient mooring holes at the shore and in the lake itself. These mooring holes were quite typical of the Viking methods in that they enabled them to secure their longboats while at the same time being able to strike the lines quickly in case of need to get away in a hurry. The most important one of the holes Pohl found in a rock skerry fifty feet from shore, in the center of Follins Pond.

What remained to pinpoint was the offshore island Leif had seen. Pohl thought that Great Point, now a part of Nantucket, was that island. He reasoned that it was frequently cut off from Nantucket after a storm or at high tide and thus appeared as an island rather than the sandspit it is today.

* * *

Boland, dissatisfied with Pohl's theory of the landing site despite the mooring holes, searched further. Digging in an area adjacent to Follins Pond in 1957, Boland found some colonial remains, but no Norse material. Very little interest could be aroused in the official body responsible for digs in this area, the Massachusetts Archaeological Society. In 1950, the Society members had dug at Follins Pond briefly, finding nothing, unless an obscure, handmade sign near one of the houses in the area referring to "Viking Sites"—presumably to lure tourists—is considered a "result." In 1960 the society returned at the invitation of Frederick Pohl and did some digging at Mills Pond, next to Follins Pond. The results were negative.

Boland carefully searched the cape further and finally concluded that the campsite had been to the north of the cape. Not Great Point, but the "fist" of the cape, the Provincetown area, was the "island" described in the ancient sagas! Boland took the Salt Meadow and Pilgrim Lake south of that area to be the lake of the landfall. He was reinforced in this belief by an opinion rendered him by expert geologist Dr. Rhodes W. Fairbridge of Columbia University: The waters of the Atlantic were two to three feet higher one thousand years ago than they are today. This, of course, is not as extreme a rising as the increase in the level calculated by Mallery, who thought the land rose as much as four feet every century, but all scholars are agreed that the ocean has indeed receded since the Viking era.

There is, however, no *river* flowing from or through a lake in this area, even if the island image is now a more fitting one. Boland's view also satisfies the requirement of position: The saga speaks of an island that lay to the north of the land. If the Bass River, which does flow through Follins Pond, were the proper site, where is the island to the north?

The same argument that Boland uses to make Provincetown his island also holds true of Great Point: The ocean was higher in the eleventh century for both of them, and consequently both could have been islands at the time. But looking from the mouth of the Bass River toward Great Point is looking south, not north—unless the navigators were confused as to their directions. But the Vikings knew their stars, and such an error is highly unlikely.

Boland's arguments in favor of the *north shore* of Cape Cod are indeed persuasive, except for the description of the river flowing through a lake. Had there perhaps been

two camps? Was the saga combining the account? If we could have some other method of testing the site Pohl thought was Leif Ericsson's first camp, perhaps we could then follow through with extensive diggings, rather than relying so much on speculation and guesswork.

Cape Cod as a Viking site is not too well known, although the Viking *presence* in America in general terms is reasonably established among the general public. I decided to try an experiment in ESP to determine if a good psychic might not pick up some significant clues at the site.

The rules would be strict: The psychic would have no access to information about the matter and would be brought to the site in such a way that she could not get any visual or sensory clues as to the connotation or connections of the site with the problems under investigation. Whatever she might "get," therefore, would be primary material obtained not in the ordinary way, but by *tuning in* on the imprint present at the site. Further, I made sure not to study the material myself to avoid having information in my subconscious mind that might conceivably be "read" by the psychic. All I did know, consciously, until *after* our visit to Cape Cod, was that a Viking connection existed between the site and the past. But I didn't even know how to get to Follins Pond, and as subsequent events proved, it took us a long time to locate it.

I asked Sybil Leek, who had been my medium in many important cases in the past years, to be ready for some work with me in the late summer of 1967. Mrs. Leek never asks questions or tries to find out what I expect of her. A professional writer herself, she does her psychic work as a kind of contribution to science and because she agrees with my aims in parapsychology. She is not a "psychic reader" in a professional sense, but the ESP work she does with me—and only with me—is of the highest caliber. When I called Sybil, I mentioned that I would need her presence at Cape Cod, and we arranged for her to meet me at the Hyannis airport on August 17, 1967. My wife Catherine and I had been doing some research in New Hampshire and would be driving our Citroën down from there. My wife is a marvelous driver, and we arrived at the airport within ten minutes of the appointed hour. It was a warm, humid afternoon, but Sybil felt in good spirits, if I may pun for the nonce.

I explained to her at this point that we had a "ghost case" to attend to in the area that evening; prior to driving to the place where we would spend the night, however, I wanted to do some sightseeing, and perhaps there was a spot or two where I'd like her to gather impressions. We drove off and I consulted my map. Follins Pond was nowhere to be found. Fortunately, I had had some correspondence with the gentleman who owned a ghost house we were to visit later that day, and he, being a resident of the area, knew very well where the pond was located.

Sybil was in the back of the car, resting, while we drove steadfastly toward the eastern part of Cape Cod. There were no signs whatever indicating either the Bass River or any ponds. Finally, we drove up to a gas station and I asked for directions. Despite this, we got lost twice more, and again I had to ask our way. At no time did Sybil take part in this, but when she heard me mention Follins Pond, she remarked, somewhat sleepily, "Do you want to go swimming?" It was hot enough for it, at that.

The neighborhood changed now; instead of the garish motels with minute swimming pools in back and huge colored neon lights in front to attract the tourist, we passed into a quiet, wooded area interspersed with private homes. I did not see it at the time, but when we drove back later on, I found, tucked away in a side street, a blue sign pointing in the general direction we had come from, and reading "Viking Rocks." I am sure Sybil did not see it either on our way down or back, and it may be the work of some enterprising local, since the Viking "attractions" on the cape do not form part of its official tourist lure or lore.

* * *

We had now been driving over twice the time it was supposed to have taken us to get to the pond; we had crossed a river marked Bass River and knew we were going in the right direction. Suddenly, the curving road gave upon a body of water quietly nestling between wooded slopes. The nearest house was not visible and the road broke into a fork at this point, one fork continuing toward the sea, the other rounding the pond. The pond, more like a small lake, really, was perhaps a mile in circumference, heavily wooded on all sides and quite empty of any sign of human interest: no boats, no landings, no cottages dotting its shores. Somewhat toward the center of the water there was a clump of rocks.

We halted the car and I got out, motioning to Sybil to follow me. Sybil was dressed rather stylishly—black dress, black, fringed feather hat, and high-heeled shoes. It was not exactly the best way to go around an area like this. The shore of the pond was wet and soft, sloping steeply toward the water. With the tape recorder at the ready, I took Sybil toward the water.

"What is your immediate impression of this place?" I inquired.

"We should go right to the opposite bank," Sybil said, "and come around that way."

I didn't feel like getting lost again, so I decided to stay, for the present at least, on this side of the pond.

"The water has gone over some building," Sybil added, trying to focus her psychic sense now. "There is something in the middle of the lake."

What sort of thing?

"Something like a spire," she said. A church here in the middle of the pond? Then were there any people here?

"Yes," she replied, "people have settled here, have been living here...."

"How far back?"

"Difficult to say at this stage, for there is another overlaying element here."

"You mean two different period levels?"

"Yes. But the main thing is something rising high like a church spire. Something very sharp in the center. It isn't necessarily a church spire, but something like it. It could be a masthead, something very sharp and triangular, at any rate. It was big and very important to the people who were here. People coming and going. And there is a lane here, one of the oldest used paths to where we are. I seem to be getting the date of 1784."

Although I did not know it at the time, we were close to the site where colonial material had been unearthed by Boland in 1957.

"Can you go back farther than that?" I inquired.

There was a moment of silence as Sybil closed her eyes. Standing delicately balanced on a low bluff directly overlooking the water, she was now swaying a little and I began to worry that she might fall into the pond, especially if she should go into trance. I therefore held my arm ready to catch her, should this happen. But somehow she maintained her equilibrium throughout the entire investigation.

"I feel a foreign invasion," she said now, slowly, searching her way step by step into the past. "Not people who live here but people who come here to destroy something...from another place...this is not pleasant, not a happy invasion...a war...taking things...."

"Where do they come from?"

"From far...I can see several longboats...."

Longboats! The term used for Viking boats. How would Sybil consciously know of the Viking connection at this spot?

"Longboats...fair men...this is very long time ago...the things they do are not related to this place at all...own ideas of metal and killing...."

* * *

One of the significant points of Viking presences in America is their use of iron for weapons, something totally unknown to the natives of the Western Hemisphere at that time and certainly until well after Columbus.

"The construction...is very important...about these boats...metal pieces on the boats...."

"Can you hear any sounds?"

"I don't understand the language."

"What type language is it?"

"It is a northern language...Germanic...Nordic... Helmut is a name that comes...."

"Why are they here?"

"Long time...not discover...they have long skeleton boats...one is definitely here, that was the pointed thing I saw...in the lake...it is big, it's in the middle...and around it are the metal pieces...the boat is a frame...

there are *round shields*...personal things...a broken boat... something peculiar about the front of the boat...strange gods...."

* * *

It is a fact that the Viking ships had peculiar, animal-shaped bows, and metal shields were hung on their sides in rows. We know this from Norwegian examples. Sybil "saw" this, however, in the middle of nowhere on Cape Cod. A ship had foundered and its remnants lay on the bottom of Follins Pond. Strange gods, she had just said. What gods?

"A man had a feeling for a different god than people knew," Sybil replied.

* * *

I later recalled how Leif had espoused the new Christian faith while his father, and probably many others of his people, clung to the old pagan beliefs.

"What happened to them?" I said.

"They were stranded here and could not get back," Sybil replied, slowly. "I don't think they really intended to come."

Blown off course on their way to Greenland, the sagas report—not intentionally trying to find Vinland!

"They arrived, however...didn't know where they were...it was like an accident...they were stranded... many of them ran away from the boat...."

"Was there water here at that point?"

"There was water. Connected with the sea. But this lake is not sea. The sea went away. The lake came later. This is a long time ago, you are not thinking how long it is!"

"Well, how long *is* it?"

"This is longer than we've ever been," Sybil explained, "fifteen hundred years...or something...long time...this was nothing, not a place where anything was made...no people...."

"What happened to them?"

"Die here...the boat was very important...boat was broken...some went away, one boat remained...the others could not go so they stayed here...longboat in the lake and those big round metal things...."

"Do you get any names?"

"Helmut...."

"Anything else?"

"This was first sea, then land, then on top of the land it was earth...as if something is hidden...."

"How did it all happen?"

"A lot of boats came here at the same time. They came from the fjords...toward the cold parts...they got here by accident...they left things behind while others went away...this one boat, or perhaps more but I see one...with the things that they used...no writing...just things...something strange about the metal...an eagle, but it is not the American eagle...big bird, like a vul-

ture...some signs on the round metal parts...the bird is very prominent...."

* * *

Was she trying to make out a rune? The raven was a prominent symbol among the Vikings. Also, she had correctly identified the invaders by origin: from the fjords, from the cold country. Norsemen. But what possible clues could she have had? She was standing at the shores of a nondescript little lake or pond in Cape Cod.

I became very excited at this point, or as excited as my basically scientific nature would permit me. Obviously, Sybil Leek had hit paydirt in identifying the spot as a Viking site—something not at all *certain* up to that point, but only a conjecture on the part of Frederick Pohl.

"Is there any other form or symbol you can recognize?" I inquired. Sybil was more and more in a trancelike state of immersion into another time stream.

"Constellation..." she murmured, and when I didn't grasp the meaning, added, "a group of stars...shield... this man came by the stars. No papers."

"Was this Helmut, was he the leader of the group?"

"No...not the leader."

"Who was the leader?"

"Ingrist...I can't understand it....Helmut and... Aabst...ssen...ssen or son...confusing...."

"Are these earthbound spirits?" I asked.

"Yes, this is a very drastic thing that happened. Not ghosts in the usual sense, but a feeling, a sadness...a remote, detached feeling that still remains around here. It is connected with something that is not known but has to be known. It is very important to know this. Because this place was *known before it was known*. But there is no writing."

* * *

How clearly she had delineated the problem at hand: known before it was known—America, of course, known to the Vikings before it was known to Columbus!

"And there is no writing?" I asked again.

"No, only symbols," Sybil replied, "birds, and a big sun...."

All these are the old pagan symbols of the Norsemen. "How many men are there?"

"Many...but one man is important...Helmut and...sson...son of someone."

"Son of whom?"

"Frederickson or something...it's two names and I can't read it....Frederickson is part of the name...a little name in front...k-s-o-n...."

"What is the relationship between Helmut and Frederickson?"

"Family relationship. Because this was the lot of one family."

"Which one is the leader?"

"Well, I think, Frederickson; but Helmut is very important."

"Which one stays and which one goes back?"

"Helmut stays."

"And Frederickson? Does he go back?"

"I don't know what happens to him. But he has influence with Helmut."

Suddenly she added, "Where would *sund* be?"

At first I thought she had said "sand"; later, it dawned on me that *sund*, which in English is "sound," was a Viking term of some importance in the saga, where the body of water near the first campsite is described.

"This is a very serious place," Sybil continued. "You must discover something and say, this is right. Someone arrived a thousand years ago without papers or maps and did not know where they were."

"How far back did this happen, Sybil?"

"Eight-eight-four . . . eight-eight-four are the figures in the water," she replied, cryptically. "The discovery of something in the lake is very important."

If 884 was the number of years into the past when the boat foundered here, we would arrive at the year 1083 A.D. That is exactly eighty years later than the accepted date for Leif Ericsson's voyage. Could Sybil have misread one of the digits? Not 884 but 804? If she could call Ericsson "Frederickson"—such a near-hit was not unthinkable in so delicate and difficult an undertaking as we were attempting. On the other hand, if 884 denotes the actual date, was the calendar used a different one from the A.D. calendar?

"Where would one look for the ship?"

"From the other side, where I wanted to go," Sybil said, more herself again than she had been for the past fifteen minutes.

"This is quite a deep lake, really," she added, "toward the middle and then come to the left. From the other side where that road is."

She was nearly pinpointing the same rock where Frederick Pohl had found Viking moorings!

"What would they find?"

"Old wood and metal stuff that nobody has seen before. Nobody knew was here. It was an accident. If you find it, it will be important to a lot of people. Some will say you tell lies."

I thought of the mayor of Genoa, and the Knights of Columbus. What would they be marching for on Columbus Day? His *rediscovery* of America? Sybil was still involved with the subject.

"The *sund* . . . ," she mumbled.

"Where is the *sund*?" I asked, beginning to understand now the meaning of the word more clearly.

"Beyond the lake," Sybil replied, as if it were obvious to anyone but me.

"On which side of it?"

"The far side . . . *Sund* . . . there are some things there."

She warmed up to this line of thought now. "There will be a line . . . of things to find once one is found. . . . When one thing is found there will be many others. . . ." She insisted the boat and the shields with the bird on them would be found in the water; if a line were drawn from there to the shore and beyond, more would come to light. "Longboat . . . big . . . Helmut. . . ." Again she seemed to be going under and swaying from side to side. "Longboats in the sun . . . shadows. . . ."

I decided to get Sybil out of her psychic state before she fell into the water. When she opened her eyes, which had been shut all this time, she blinked into the setting sun and yawned. Nothing she had said to me during the investigation had remained in her memory.

"Did I say anything interesting?" she queried me.

I nodded, but told her nothing more.

We got into our car and drove off toward Hyannis, where the ghost hunt of the evening was about to begin.

The next morning I pondered the information Sybil had brought me at Follins Pond. In particular, the term *sund*, which Sybil had pronounced closer to "sand," puzzled me. I decided to check it out through whatever maps I might have available. I discovered several startling facts. To begin with, the area south and southwest of the coast of Greenland was known by two names: Herjolfsnes, or *sand*. If the *sund* were situated "to the far side" of the lake, as Sybil had said, could it not be that this was a reference to the area whence the boats had sailed? The *sand* or *sund* is the coast where Eric the Red's eastern settlement stood in the eleventh century.

If Boland was looking for the *sund* much closer to Cape Cod, assuming it to be the bay between Princetown and the Massachusetts coast, was he not overlooking the other body of water? We don't know that the bay north of Cape Cod was ever named the *sund*, but we do know that the straits south of Greenland were thus called at the time of the Leif Ericsson adventure. Mallery's conviction that Newfoundland was the original Vinland did not find the problem of the river flowing through or from a lake insurmountable. There are a number of small bodies of water and small rivers in Newfoundland that *might* fit. None of them, however, as well as the Bass River and Follins Pond in Cape Cod.

Sybil had clearly and repeatedly identified a lesser leader named Helmut as being connected with the Follins Pond site. I discovered that one Helhild or Helhuld sailed the coast of Labrador around 1000 A.D. That this statement in the sagas is taken seriously can be seen by the fact that Helhild's voyage and name are included in some historic maps used in higher education for many years. Moreover, Helhild started his trip at the *sund*, south of Greenland.

This Helhild was the same leader who later joined Ericsson in a trip that lead to the discovery of Vinland.

Helhild's first name was Bjarni, the Bjarni mentioned on the ancient map. Evidently he was the second in command on the latter expedition. Now one might argue that Labrador is also part of North America and thus Bjarni Helhild was the original Viking discoverer of America. But we do not know of any landings on the Labrador trip, whereas we do have exact details of landings during the expedition headed by Ericsson and Helhild jointly. It may well be that the Labrador trip consisted merely of sailing down the hostile and unknown Labrador coast.

Frederickson and Helmut are common modern names, and to a person unfamiliar with Viking names they would sound reasonably close to Ericsson and Helhild or Helhuld. Sybil, as I have already stated several times, did not know she was on a spot with Viking traditions or connotations; thus there could not be any subconscious knowledge suggesting Norse names. Whatever came through her, came because *it was there*.

What are the implications of this adventure into the past? Surely, a dig in Follins Pond should be undertaken. It might very well yield Norse artifacts and perhaps even remnants of the Viking boat Sybil saw clairvoyantly. It seems to me that the question of the Vinland location misses an important point altogether: Could it not be that Vinland meant to the Vikings *all* of North America, the new land beyond the seas, rather than a specific *settlement?*

I find it difficult to reconcile the conflicting views of respectable researchers and the archaeological evidence to boot, with any one area under discussion. The Vikings were at Newfoundland, at more than one site and over an extended period of time; but they were also in evidence in Cape Cod and again in more than one locality. Over a period of several centuries enough immigrants must have come over to allow them to spread out over the newly discovered land. Some might have gone around Florida to Minnesota and Oklahoma, while others explored the Northeast and founded settlements along the way.

I think the end is not yet and that many more campsites of Norse origin will be discovered on our side of the Atlantic. Certainly, the Vikings discovered America long before Columbus did it all over again. It is a shame at that: He could have consulted the ancient maps even then in existence and seen that somebody had been there before. But of course Columbus wasn't looking for America. He was trying to find a better passage to India. The Vikings, on the other hand, *knew* where they had landed, as time went on, even though their original landfall was accidental.

Sybil Leek has shown that the Viking connotations of the Follins Pond area should be taken seriously. Hopefully, when this report appears in print, archaeological follow-ups of her psychic suggestions will have been initiated. Since neither Sybil nor my wife nor I had any previous knowledge of a Helmut or of the true meaning of the word *sund*, one cannot dismiss these revelations by our psychic as being drawn from anyone's subconscious knowledge or mind. Thus there is really no alternate explanation for the extraordinary results of our psychic experiment. No doubt, additional experiments of this kind should prove fruitful and interesting: For the present, let it be said that the Vikings *were* at Follins Pond.

Whether this was their only contact with America is a moot question. It certainly was the site of one of their landfalls in the early eleventh century. The Vikings may justly claim the distinction of having been the true discoverers of the New World!

* * *

Or were they?

There is a strong tradition among the Irish that St. Brendan and a group of navigators made crossings to the American coast in boats built of timber and skins. Similar boats, about twenty-two feet long, are still in use in western Ireland. Recently, two brave Canadians tried to repeat the feat in an identical canoe. The original crossing by St. Brendan took place in the sixth century—about five hundred years *before* the Vikings!

Allegedly, Brendan felt himself responsible for the drowning of one of his monks, and the voyage had been a kind of pilgrimage to atone for it.

But even St. Brendan was not *first*. According to my historian friend Paul Johnstone, Brendan did indeed cross all the way to the Florida coast, but the crossing by a certain Rossa O'Deshea, of the clan MacUmor, had managed it with eleven others, and gotten back safely again to Ireland, as early as the year 332 A.D.! The trip, according to Johnstone, was an accident, just as the Vikings' initial crossing had been. On a return trip from Britain to the west of Ireland, the Gaelic navigators were blown off course and wound up in North America. Jess Stearn's *Edgar Cayce* curiously also speaks of an Irish navigator named Rosa O'Deshea.

Johnstone also mentions earlier Atlantic crossings by other Irishmen, such as a certain Dechu in 500 A.D. and a Finnian in the first half of the sixth century, a little before Brendan's crossing in 551 A.D.

Unfortunately, we have as yet no concrete evidence of Irish settlements in the New World, although we may some day find such material proof, of course. But these Irish traditions are interesting and far from fictional. It stands to reason that every nation of sailors would at one time or other sail westward, and the wind being what it is, might have some of her natives blown off course.

The Romans, and before them, the Greeks and especially the Phoenicians, were great navigators. We suspect that the pre-Greek Phoenicians came to Britain from Asia in the second and first millennia before Christ. For all we know, even Rossa O'Deshea was not the first one to discover America.

But the Vikings, comparatively Eric-come-latelies when one speaks of the Irish navigators, managed at least to leave us concrete evidence not only of having been here, but of having lived here for many years. Thus, until new evidence comes along, I'd vote for the Norsemen as being the discoverers of the New World.

* * *

I never discussed the case or my findings with Sybil Leek. On December 30, 1967, I received an urgent call from her. She had just had a peculiar dream and wished to communicate it to me for what it was worth. The dream took place in her Los Angeles house at 5:30 A.M., December 29, 1967. She knew it was about Cape Cod and "the lake," as she called the pond, and that we should look for a peculiar rock in which "there are set big *holes* and it has a lot to do with the thing in the lake. I don't remember any rocks but I think they are *in the sea*, not the lake. There is a connection. When we go to Cape Cod again I must look around that bit of coast. I saw so many things clearly in my dream. I wasn't even thinking of the place when I dreamt this, but *I talked with a large man* last night, and it

was he who said, 'Look for the rock,' and showed me the holes; they are big and deep. Also, there is more than we think in that lake and not only the lake, we have to go from the lake to the sea and look around there. What would the holes in the rock mean? I have a peculiar feeling about this and *know* it is important."

Sybil, of course, had no way of knowing about the mooring holes in the rock in the middle of Follins Pond. She knew nothing about my sources, and I had not talked about it in front of her at any time. But it was clear to me from this experience of hers that she had made a real contact while we were in the area and that those whom she had contacted wished us to find the physical evidence of their presence in the waters of the pond.

Sybil had sent me a note giving all these bits of information she had obtained in her dream. At the end of her note, she drew a kind of seal, a large letter E in a circle—and said, this is important, is it a name?

I looked at the medieval form of the initial E and could *almost* feel Leif Ericsson's heavy hand.

✳ 123

The Haunted Organ at Yale

YALE UNIVERSITY IN New Haven, Connecticut, is an austere and respectable institution, which does not take such matters as ghostly manifestations very lightly. I must, therefore, keep the identity of my informant a secret, but anyone who wishes to visit Yale and admire its magnificent, historical organ is, of course, at liberty to do so, provided he or she gets clearance from the proper authorities. I would suggest, however, that the matter of ghostly goings-on not be mentioned at such a time. If you happen to experience something out of the ordinary while visiting the organ, well and good, but let it not be given as the reason to the university authorities for your intended visit.

I first heard about this unusual organ in 1969 when a gentleman who was then employed as an assistant organist at Yale had been asked to look after the condition and possible repairs of the huge organ, a very large instrument located in Woolsey Hall. This is the fifth largest organ in the world and has a most interesting history.

Woolsey Hall was built as part of a complex of three buildings for Yale's 200th anniversary in 1901 by the celebrated architects, Carere and Hastings. Shortly after its completion the then university organist, Mr. Harry B. Jepson, succeeded in getting the Newberry family, of the famous department store clan, to contribute a large sum of money for a truly noble organ to be built for the hall.

Even in 1903 it was considered to be an outstanding instrument because of its size and range. By 1915, certain advances in the technology of pipe organs made the 1903 instrument somewhat old-fashioned. Again Jepson contacted the Newberry family about the possibility of updating their gift so that the organ could be rebuilt and the hall enlarged. This new instrument was then dedicated in 1916 or thereabouts.

By 1926 musical tastes had again shifted toward romantic music, and it became necessary to make certain additions to the stops as well as the basic building blocks of the classical ensemble. Once again the Newberry family contributed toward the updating of the instrument. The alterations were undertaken by the Skinner Organ Company of Boston, in conjunction with an English expert by the name of G. Donald Harrison. Skinner and Harrison did not get on well together and much tension was present when they restored and brought the venerable old organ up-to-date.

Professor Harry Jepson was forced to retire in the 1940s, against his wishes, and though he lived down the street only two blocks from Woolsey Hall, he never again set foot into it to play the famous organ that he had caused to be built. He died a bitter and disappointed man sometime in 1952.

One of the university organists, Frank Bozyan, retired in the 1970s, with great misgivings. He confided to someone employed by the hall that he felt he was making a mistake; within six months after his retirement he was dead. As time went on, Woolsey Hall, once a temple of beauty for the fine arts, was being used for rock-and-roll

groups and mechanically amplified music. Undoubtedly, those connected with the building of the hall and the organ would have been horrified at the goings-on had they been able to witness them.

The gentleman who brought all of this to my attention, and who shall remain nameless, had occasion to be in the hall and involved with the organ itself frequently. He became aware of a menacing and melancholic sensation in the entire building, particularly in the basement and the organ chambers. While working there at odd hours late at night, he became acutely aware of some sort of unpleasant sensation just lurking around the next corner or even standing behind him! On many occasions he found it necessary to look behind him in order to make sure he was alone. The feeling of a presence became so strong he refused to be there by himself, especially in the evenings. Allegedly, the wife of one of the curators advised him to

bring a crucifix whenever he had occasion to go down to the organ chambers. She also claimed to have felt someone standing at the entrance door to the basement, as if to keep strangers out.

I visited Yale and the organ one fine summer evening in the company of my informant, who has since found employment elsewhere. I, too, felt the oppressive air in the organ chambers, the sense of a presence whenever I moved about. Whether we are dealing here with the ghost of the unhappy man who was forced to retire and who never set foot again into his beloved organ chamber, or whether we are dealing with an earlier influence, is hard to say. Not for a minute do I suggest that Yale University is haunted or that there are any evil influences concerning the university itself. But it is just possible that sensitive individuals visiting the magnificent organ at Woolsey Hall might pick up some remnant of an unresolved past.

✳ 124

The Ghost On Television

UNTIL 1965 I HAD HEARD OF two kinds of ghosts connected with television: those impersonated by actors and those caused by the interference of tall buildings. Now I was to learn of still another kind of ghost on television, this one being the real McCoy. It all started with a lecture I gave at the British College of Psychic Studies in London in 1965. After my lecture on ghosts, which was illustrated by slides of apparitions, I was approached by a tall,

intellectual-looking lady who wanted to tell me about a very strange haunted house in East Anglia. This was my first meeting with Ruth Plant, who explained that she was a writer and researcher, with a background in social science. Her beliefs lay in the Spiritualist philosophy, and she had had any number of psychic experiences herself. I asked her to drop me a note about the house in East Anglia. I expected it to be just another haunted house, probably containing the usual complement of footsteps, doors opening or closing by themselves, or possibly even an apparition of a deceased relative. By *my* standards, that constitutes a classic, conventional haunting.

The following January, Miss Plant lived up to her promise. She explained that the house in East Anglia was called Morley Old Hall, and though it was principally of the Stuart period, it stood on much earlier foundations, going back to pre-Saxon times. It was situated near Norwich in the northeast of England and apparently belonged to a friend of hers who had bought it with a view to restoring it. It had been in lamentable condition and not suitable to be lived in. Her friend, by the name of Ricky Cotterill, was essentially a pig farmer; nevertheless, he and his young wife and their baby managed to live in the sprawling mansion, or rather in that part of it which he had been able to restore on his own funds, and the excitement of living with so much history more than adequately made up for the deprivations he was subjecting himself to. Miss Plant explained that the house was way off the beaten track and was, in fact, hard to find unless one knew the countryside. There were two moats around it, and archeological digs had been undertaken all over that part of the country for many years, since that part of East Anglia is one of the oldest and most historic sections of England.

At the time of her first communication with me, in January, 1966, Miss Plant had not as yet undertaken any research into the background of the house or its surroundings. She thought the house worthy of my attention because of what had happened to her and a friend during a visit.

"I went to stay there with a Norwegian friend, Anne Wilhelmsen, whose father was a cultural attaché of Norway in London, and who was herself a university graduate," Ruth Plant explained. "This was two years ago at Easter. We had intended to stay at the local hotel, but Mr. Cotterill, the owner of the mansion, found that the hotel was entirely full."

Under the circumstances, the owner moved out of the room he had been occupying and let the two ladies use it for the night. As he knew of Miss Plant's interest in ghosts, he assured her that to the best of his knowledge there were no ghosts there, since he had lived there for three years and had seen nothing. As a matter of fact, the two ladies slept well, and in the morning Miss Plant got up and walked across the big room connecting the two wings with the kitchen, all of it being on the first floor.

"When I came back, I felt impressed to pause at the large window which looked down the front drive, in spite of the fact that it had no glass in it and the day was bitterly cold. I felt very peaceful and contemplative and I suddenly heard a Catholic prayer, the Hail Mary, and was sure that the 'presence' I felt was that of the lady of the house. After I had noted this, I went back into our bedroom and was surprised to find Anne sitting up in bed looking very worried. She said she had just heard the rustle of bedclothes and heavy breathing while she lay there. She had sat up in bed to listen more closely, and immediately the sound ceased, only to come back again when she lay down. We told our host about this over breakfast, but he could not enlighten us further. So I went into the village and in talking to people found out that several people who had lived in the house had experienced very much the same thing. One man had actually seen the lady quite clearly at the window, and others had heard her, like Anne."

The "Lady at the Window" fascinated Ruth Plant, especially as she didn't know her identity. As was her custom then, and is now, she decided to have a sitting with a reputable medium to see whether the medium might pick up something spiritual around her and possibly shed some light on the identity of the lady ghost of Morley Old Hall. This time she had a sitting with a certain Mr. Bogoran, one of the regulars sitting at the College of Psychic Studies, Queensbury Place. "I didn't mention anything about the ghost, but said I had a friend who was trying to restore a beautiful old Stuart house and I wondered if anyone on the other side could offer any helpful advice."

Instead of advice on how to restore the house, medium Bogoran described the house itself in minute detail and then added that he saw a ghostly lady standing at one of the windows. This of course came as a surprise to Miss Plant, but even more of a shock was in store for her: Mr. Bogoran volunteered two additional statements of interest. One, that the owner of the house, her friend, would be on television within a few weeks, and two, that there was another ghost in the house, a monk who was attached to the house, not because he had been happy there like the ghostly lady, but because he had been involved in a killing.

Since Mr. Cotterill, the owner of the house, had absolutely no connection with television, the first statement evoked nothing but doubt in Ruth Plant's mind. Picture her surprise when several days after her sitting with Mr. Bogoran, Ricky Cotterill telephoned to tell her that he had been approached by a local television station to have an all-night session at the house which would be filmed for television. The reason for his call was to invite her to Norwich to appear as part of the program. In the excitement of this development, Ruth Plant forgot all about the ghostly monk.

When she arrived at the Hall, she met Tony Cornell, a psychic researcher from Cambridge. Ruth and Mr. Cornell did not see things the same ways: she sensed him to be skeptical and negative and suspected his presence in the house was more to debunk the ghosts than to find them. It turned out later that Mr. Cornell was, as the program producer put it, "Our handiest accredited psychic investigator," called into the case not necessarily because of his commitment to the reality of ghosts, but because his offices were not too far away, and time was of the essence. Ruth brought along a sound tape of her sitting with Mr. Bogoran, but it was not used in the film. She gave the required interviews and thought no more about it. A few weeks later, the filmed report of Morley Old Hall went on the air. Ruth Plant saw it at a local hotel, where it was rather badly focused, and she could hardly recognize herself or anyone else. Nevertheless, something odd happened during that screening.

"During the performance, there was a loud bang on the set," Ruth Plant stated, "which seemed to have no normal cause. My basset hound, who had been fast asleep with her back to the screen, jumped up in great apprehension and stood gazing at the screen as though she saw *someone we could not see*."

A few days later Ruth Plant telephoned Mr. Cotterill, and it was only then that she heard the amazing results of the television of the film. It appeared that no fewer than twenty-three people from the general public had written into the broadcasting station and asked who the bearded monk was, standing behind Mr. Cornell while he was speaking!

Now no one had mentioned anything about a ghostly monk, but everyone connected with the venture knew that a ghostly *lady* had been observed by a number of witnesses. Consequently, she would have been on the minds of those participating in the experiment, if a mind picture could indeed find its way onto a television film.

The idea of a ghost appearing on television naturally excited me. Immediately I got in touch with Michael Robson, producer of the documentary and one of the executives of Anglia Television. Michael Robson, who had been to Morley Old Hall many times before the documentary was made, offered to let me see the actual film when I came to England. "Our film unit had an all-night vigil in the Hall," he explained in a statement dated September 2, 1966, "with the chairman of the Cambridge Psychical Research and Spontaneous Cases Committee, Mr. Tony Cornell. Various things of interest occurred during the night, in particular a moving tumbler, but what caused all the excitement was this: Mr. Cornell and I were discussing the Hall on film by a mullioned window as dawn was breaking. No sooner had the film been transmitted than a great many people wrote in asking who the figure was that appeared between Mr. Cornell and myself. All their descriptions were the same: the face and trunk of a monkish-type figure looking between us. Mr. Cornell and I examined the film closely afterwards ourselves and saw nothing: but in view of the large number of people who claimed to have seen the figure, Mr. Cornell thought it an interesting example of collective hallucination, and took away the letters for closer study."

It turned out that Mr. Cornell was not a parapsychologist with an academic connection, but merely an interested ghost-fancier. With the help of Miss Plant, and considerable patience, I managed to obtain the letters which Mr. Cornell had taken with him and examined them myself. His explanation of the phenomenon as a "mass hallucination" is, of course, an easy way out of coming to

grips with the problem itself—a genuine psychic phenomenon. But the twenty-three witnesses are far more eloquent in their description of what they experienced than any would-be scientist could possibly be in trying to explain away the phenomenon.

Mrs. Joan Buchan of Great Yarmouth wrote: "My husband and I saw a figure of a monk with a cowl over his head and with his hands clasped as though in prayer. It could be seen quite clearly, standing quietly in the window. It didn't appear to be looking at the men conversing, but behind them."

"I saw the figure of a man which appeared to me to be that of a monk; he had on a round hat, a long cloak, and his hands were together as in prayer," observed Miss A. Hewitt of Southrepps.

"I saw the figure quite distinctly, considering I only have a twelve-inch screen and the sunlight was pouring into my room. The figure appeared behind the profile of the man who was talking, as if looking through the window," stated L. M. Gowing. "I thought perhaps it was due to the light, but the man talking moved and seemed to partly cover it. When he went back to his former position, it was there clearer than before."

"Both my daughter and myself certainly saw the outline of a priest to the right of the speaker and to the left of the interviewer," wrote Mrs. G. D. Hayden of Bromham. Not only did Mr. and Mrs. Carter of Lincolnshire say, "It was very clear," but Mrs. Carter sent in a drawing of the monk she had seen on the television. From Norwich, where the broadcast originated, came a statement from a viewer named Elviera Panetta who also drew the bearded monk, showing him to have a long, haggard face. "Both my mother and I saw the monk looking through the window; he is cowled, bearded, and his hands are slightly raised." One viewer, Miss M. C. Grix, wrote to the station inquiring whether "it was a real person standing in the window just behind the man who was talking, dressed in black and looking as if he had his hands together in prayer," to which Nora Kononenko of Suffolk added, "It first looked to me like a skull with a hood, and then, as the gentlemen went on talking, it seemed to come forward and peer in. At that moment it distinctly changed into a gaunt-looking face, with a horrible leer upon it." The station decided to run the film again, as testimonies kept pouring in. After the second run, even more people saw the ghostly monk on the screen.

"Your repeat of the alleged haunted house shook me considerably," wrote Mrs. A. C. Mason, "not because of what I had seen in the original broadcast, but because your Mr. MacGregor gaily quipped, 'Well, did you see anything?' I was astonished that anyone else *couldn't* see what was so clear to me. I did see the monk both times." Some viewers sent in simple statements, unsolicited and to the point. "I saw the monk in the window just as plain as could be. It was there at the time and I can assure you I did not imagine it," wrote Mrs. Joan Collis of Suffolk.

"He didn't seem to be hooded but had long hair and was bearded," stated Mrs. Janet Halls of Norwich, and Mrs. F. Nicolaisen of Cambridge volunteered that "I had seen the figure on the previous showing but didn't mention it for fear of being laughed at. This time I traced it out for my husband, but he still couldn't see it, much to my annoyance."

If all these people were suffering from mass hallucination, it is certainly strange that they hallucinated in so many different ways, for many of the reports differed in slight but important details. "Towards the end of the showing, my sister and I distinctly saw an image of a cowled monk from head to waist," wrote Miss W. Caplen of Lowestoft. Probably Mrs. J. G. Watt of Cambridge put it best when she wrote, "I had no idea what sort of ghost I was expected to look for, and I saw nothing until the two men were discussing the house. But outside the window I then saw clearly, behind them, the figure of a monk. He wore a monk's habit and was bare-headed, with the monk's haircut associated with the monks of olden days, bald patch with fringe, either fair or gray hair. His face was that of a young man and had a very serene look on his face. His arms were hanging down in front of him, with his right hand placed lightly on top of his left. I saw this all very plainly and naturally and I thought everyone else would be able to, so I thought the television people were having a game with the viewers, and I thought it was all a hoax. Next day a friend told me of Anglia TV's purpose of rerunning the film, and I realized it was serious. The strange thing is that our television set is not what it used to be, and we don't get a good picture—and yet I saw this monk very clearly."

By now it was clear to me that twenty-three people—or at last count thirty-one—had actually seen or thought they had seen the figure of a monk where none was supposed to be. Many others, if not the majority of viewers, however, did not see the monk. Obviously, then, it was on the film, and yet visible only to those with psychic gifts. This raised interesting questions: while we know that ghosts appear only to those capable of seeing them, can apparitions also be photographed selectively, so that they can be seen only by those who are psychic, while others not so gifted will not be able to see them in the photograph or film? Also, was the case of the ghost on television unique, or are there other such instances on the record?

According to the *London Express* of December 19, 1969, five shop girls saw a ghostly figure on a closed-circuit TV set. "The girls and customers watched fascinated for forty-five minutes as the figure of a woman in a long Victorian dress stood at the top of the stairs in the boutique in High Street, Kent, occasionally waving her hand and patting her hair. Several times the figure walked halfway down the stairs and then went back up again to the upper floor of the boutique, which had been converted only a few months ago from an old house." The first one to see the ghostly apparition on the closed-circuit television setup was eighteen-year-old Sally White, who pointed her out to her colleague, Janet Abbs, saying, "You've got a customer." But Janet Abbs walked right through the figure. One of the other girls, Andree Weller, said "As the figure went upstairs it disappeared into a sort of mist and then reappeared again." The incident happened at lunchtime, and though five girls saw the woman, when they walked upstairs where they had seen her, they found the place empty. When they returned downstairs and looked at the screen, there was the ghost again. Unlike the monk of Morley Old Hall, who appeared for only a few seconds on screen, the Victorian lady of High Street, Chatham, Kent, stayed for a whole hour, apparently enjoying her performance hugely.

However, what none of the viewers who had written in had pointed out was the fact that the figure of the monk was not in proportion to the size of the two flesh-and-blood people talking on the screen at the time: the monk seemed considerably smaller than they were. Ruth Plant found the emergence of the second ghost most exciting. She decided to consult two other London mediums, to see whether they might pick up something concerning his identity. One of them was Trixie Allingham, who immediately "saw" a ghostly monk around the house and informed Ruth that he had been attacked by someone who came in while he was praying. The monk had defended himself by striking the intruder with a chalice. She felt that the priest, with the help of a soldier, had later buried the body and the chalice. George Southhal, primarily a drowsing medium, volunteered that there was a chalice buried on the premises and described a set of cups, the largest of which was reserved for a man of importance. He saw Morley as a place similar to a pilgrims' retreat. At the time of Miss Plant's sitting with George Southhal, neither of them knew as yet that it had been a little-known pre-Reformation practice to give a special chalice to a prior or bishop, since he was not supposed to use the chalice used by ordinary priests. All the mediums Ruth Plant sat with were emphatic about some buried treasure and secret passages leading from the house to a nearby church. The latter could be confirmed during later research. As for the treasure, it hasn't been found yet, but the effort continues.

I decided to arrange for a visit to Norfolk at the earliest opportunity. That opportunity presented itself in September of 1966 when a film producer offered to come with me to inspect potential sites for a documentary motion-picture. I suggested Morley Old Hall and notified Ruth Plant to get everything ready: arrange for a visit to the Hall, suggest a suitable hotel nearby, notify Anglia TV of our desire to see the controversial television documentary, and, finally, to make everybody happy, let the local press have a go at us—the American ghost-hunter and his entourage paying a call to the local ghost. Miss Plant was to serve as technical advisor to the film. (Unfortunately, the film was never made, because the producer and I could not see eye to eye on a treatment that would allow the story to be told in exciting but scientifically valid terms.)

We rode up to Norwich from London. The project's film producer, Gilbert Cates, who was a firm nonbeliever, could not see how such things as ghosts were possible, while the third member of the party, the distinguished motion picture scenarist Victor Wolfson, argued equally strongly that such things as spirits were indeed not only possible but likely. At one point the discussion got so heated that I began to worry whether we would ever arrive together in Norfolk. Finally, Victor Wolfson changed the subject. With a shrug, he commented, "I don't think I can convince Gil. He's underdeveloped." Gil, a good sport under all circumstances, smiled. As for me, I began to wonder about the wisdom of having brought my two fellow adventurers at all.

Ruth Plant had advised us to bed down for the night in Norfolk, but my producer friend was so eager to be close to the "action" that he insisted we stay at the little Abbey Hotel at Wyndmondham, which is very near to Morley. We arrived at the hotel, tired and dirty, just in time to have an evening meal.

Walking early, I looked out onto the church and cemetery below my windows. It seemed very peaceful and far removed from any ghostly encounters. I took a look at a local map supplied to me by Ruth Plant. The city of Norwich, where we would view the television film, was nine miles to the east, while Morley Old Hall was a little over twelve miles to the west.

The abbey church at Wyndmondham was an impressive edifice for a village of this small size. Early in the twelfth century, William D'Albini, who had been given the town and manor of Wyndmondham, which included Morley, for his help with the Norman invasion of England, established here a monastery consisting of a prior and twelve Benedictine monks. The Benedictines, wearing black habits, were the most aristocratic and wealthy of all the religious orders, and, because of that, frequently came into conflict with poorer, humbler religious orders. It also appeared that Richard, William's brother, was made Abbot of St. Alban's, in Hertfordshire, one of the largest Benedictine monasteries in England, and Wyndmondham was a sort of daughter house to St. Alban's.

"But the relationship between the two houses was never good, and the jealousies and rivalries between them only ceased when, in 1448, Wyndmondham became an abbey in its own right," writes the Reverend J. G. Tansley Thomas in his *History of Wyndmondham Abbey*. I had the occasion to study all this while waiting for the car to pick me up for the short journey to Morley Old Hall.

After twenty minutes or so, there appeared a clump of bushes, followed by tall trees—trees that showed their age and the fact that they had not been interfered with for many years. All sorts of trees were growing wild here, and as the road rounded a bend, they seemed to swallow us up. We rumbled over a wooden bridge crossing a deep and pungent moat. Directly behind it was a brick breastwork, overgrown by all sorts of plants. This was the second, inner moat, I was told later; the outer moat was farther back and scarcely noticeable today, although in Saxon times it was a major bulwark. The car stopped in front of the imposing mansion, built of red brick and topped off by grayish-blue shingles in the manner of the seventeenth century. Part of the surrounding wall was still standing, and there were two very tall trees inside the inner moat, which gave Morley Old Hall a particularly romantic appearance. The Hall rises three stories, and windows had been replaced in many of them, attesting to the owner's skill at restoring what he had bought as a virtual ruin. We walked up a beautifully restored staircase, to the second story, where the Cotterill family lived at the time. Much of the mansion was still uninhabitable. Some rooms consisted of bare walls, while others still had ancient fireplaces in them, staring at the visitor like toothless monsters.

Ruth Plant had managed to arrange it so that the principal witnesses to the phenomena at the Hall would be present for my interrogation, and so it was that we assembled upstairs in the library—not the magnificent Stuart library of old, but a reasonable facsimile. I first turned to Frank Warren, a man in his middle seventies who had once lived in the house, long before it passed into the present owner's hands. He had come from the nearby village to talk to me, and later I paid a courtesy call on his little cottage, adorned with beautiful flowers from one end to the other: Frank Warren was, and is, a dedicated gardener. Like so many people of the area, he is "fay," that is, psychic, and he recalls vividly how he saw and actually touched his pet dog two months after the animal had died. But the human ghost at Morley Old Hall was another matter.

"I was working in the garden," he began, "and the lady of the house said, 'I wish you'd clip around that window; those pieces annoy me.' So I started to clip. It was a beautiful day, with the sun shining. All at once, just like that, there appeared a lady in the window, as close to me as you are and she looked at me. She was tall, and I noticed every detail of her dress. She looked at me and the expression on her face never changed. Her lips never moved and I thought to myself, 'I can't stand it. I'll go and do some work in the vegetable garden.' When I returned she was gone, so I completed my job at the window. Well, I used to go and have a meal with the housekeeper. I said, 'There is something I'd like you to tell me: who is the other lady living in this house?'

"'Well,' she replied, 'there is no other lady living in this house. You know exactly who is in this house.' I replied that I didn't, because I had seen somebody here I had never seen before."

Apparently the housekeeper was frightened by the idea of having ghosts about the place, for Lady Ironside, who was then the owner of the Hall, summoned the gardener about the matter. "I can't help it," he replied to her protestations. "I saw her with my own eyes." It was wartime and Lady Ironside was hard put to keep servants about the place, so she asked the gardener please to keep quiet about the ghost.

"Did you ever see the lady ghost again?" I inquired.

"A fortnight afterwards I went past the other window, on the opposite side, and there sat the housekeeper reading a book, and beside her sat the same lady. The housekeeper didn't see her. She wore a plain black dress, which seemed a bit stiff and went right to the ground, so I couldn't see her feet. I had a quarter of an hour to examine her, and I didn't see her feet."

Gordon Armstrong had come from London to talk to us at Morley Old Hall. "This is my second visit," he began. "I was here toward the end of July last year, 1965. I was working in London at the time and hitchhiked my way through the night and arrived at Morley in the small hours of the morning. Having walked up the road, I came into the house—it must have been somewhere around 2 o'clock in the morning—and at the time I had already heard a ghost being there, or rumored to be there, so I was half expecting to see one. Of course, I had never seen a ghost before, so I was rather apprehensive. When I came up the stairs in the dark, with only a small flashlight to help me, I heard a sound that reminded me of a cat jumping from one landing to another. This was on the third-floor landing."

"Did you see a cat?" I asked.

"No, I didn't see a cat. I thought I was alone, that is, until I heard someone breathing in one of the rooms. Part of the floor was only rafters, without floorboards, so one could hear what went on on the floor below. It was one of the rooms on the second floor where the noise came from."

"What did the breathing sound like?"

"I thought I heard a man breathing rather heavily."

"What did you do next?"

"I was sitting up there on these rafters, and it was pretty dark. I didn't feel like meeting anyone, so I slept against a wall up there. I must have been asleep for a couple of hours. The wind was blowing, and I woke up once and went back to sleep again, and when I came to the second time it was just getting light. I went down and explored the house further and found the room where the noise had come from, and there was a sort of couch there, so I lay down for a bit and dozed off for another couple of hours. I looked at the room and realized that no one had slept there during the night."

Ruth Plant remarked at this point that the area where Mr. Armstrong had heard the heavy breathing was the same spot where her friend from Norway had also heard breathing, though she thought it could have been a woman, not necessarily a man.

Later on, the television people ran the controversial documentary for us. None of us saw the monk. We stopped action at the spot where thirty-one people said that they had seen the bearded monk, but all we could see were two men in conversation.

Nevertheless, the question of identifying the two ghosts at Morley intrigued me. This was one of the oldest and most fought-over spots in all of England, and the emotional imprint of many periods was undoubtedly still very strong. In antiquity the Iceni lived in this area. Their famous Queen Boadicea battled the Romans here in the first century. Later the Saxons made it a stronghold, and there is undoubtedly much undiscovered treasure in the ground. "A few years ago a ploughman turned up a wonderful collection of Saxon silver not far from Morley," Ruth Plant, ever the historian, explained. Scandinavian raiders had been there at an early stage: the word *mor* in Morley means mother in Norwegian. In 1066 a survey of all the land in England was undertaken. Known as the *Domesday Book*, it listed Morlea as belonging to one William de Warrenne. He was a wealthy Norman baron who took part in the Battle of Hastings. The *Domesday Book* also states that the land was let out to a priest and five freemen. Eventually the manor passed from the Warrenne family into the hands of the Morleys, and in 1545 it was sold to Martin Sedley, a Roman Catholic, whose family held it until 1789, when the direct line died out. It appears that the house fell into disrepair soon after, for, according to Ruth Plant, the Norfolk Directory of 1836 describes it even then as a "farmhouse encompassed by a deep moat." White's Norfolk Directory of 1864 named a certain Graber Brown as Lord of the Manor, and called Morley Old Hall "an Elizabethan house with a moat around it now used as a farmhouse." Eventually General Lord Ironside, World War I hero, bought it, but he passed on soon afterwards, and it passed into the hands of the Cotterills.

Since we could not stay on in Norfolk beyond the two days assigned to our visit, I entrusted further research to Ruth Plant. She concentrated on the monk and, whether through historical intuition or her psychic ability, shortly came up with some strange facts about one of the abbots of nearby Wyndmondham Abbey. "I unearthed the extraordinary fact that one of the abbots went completely mad and was so violent he was put into chains and died in them at Binham Priory. I believe I can find out more about this if I go to St. Alban's Abbey where the records are kept."

I encouraged Ruth to undertake that journey, and a few months later she contacted me again.

Ruth had managed to get hold of a rare book in a London library which contained a commentary on the records of St. Alban's Abbey done by an eighteenth-century vicar. It contained the story of a prior of Wyndmondham whose name was Alexander de Langley. "He went violently mad while in office at Wyndmondham and was recalled to St. Alban's," Ruth Plant informed me. "He lived around 1130 and died in chains at Binham Priory, about ten miles from Morley. I am sure Alexander de Langley, the mad prior, is the ghostly monk." In a further effort to throw light on the two ghosts at Morley, Ruth visited Lady Ironside, who resided at Hampton Court.

"I had agreed with Ricky Cotterill not to mention the ghostly side, " Ruth Plant explained to me. "But she greeted me by remarking about 'that lovely Morley and the lovely lady who is seen standing at the window looking at the view.' She then asked me if I had ever visited it, making it quite clear she knew nothing of my psychic experiences concerning it. She added that many people have claimed to have seen her, though she didn't think that any of them would still be alive in the village to talk about it now."

But who *was* the ghostly lady at the window? Ruth Plant showed Lady Ironside the letters written to Anglia TV. One of the letters describes not a monk but a ghostly woman wearing a mantilla. Lady Ironside felt that the ghost must be Anne Shelton, daughter of one of the great supporters of Mary Tudor, which would account for the impression received by Ruth Plant that the female ghost was Catholic, and for her hearing a Hail Mary.

"As regards the monk, Lady Ironside told me that when they went there, Frank Warren's brother Guy, who farmed the place, told them, 'There is an old monk about the place, but you have no need to take any notice of him.' But she knew nothing about the coffin lid mentioned by Frank Warren."

Apparently, when Frank Warren was first being interviewed by Ruth Plant, he recalled Lord Ironside's coming out of the house one day carrying the stone lid of a coffin saying, "This belonged to a monk."

"But Lady Ironside mentioned that men, while excavating, had found a square stone with the name ALBINI on it in Roman capitals. And since Wyndmondham was founded by Albini, the Norman baron who later became the Earl of Arundel and still later the Duke of Norfolk, the question is, was this the chapel of the Albinis, and was Morley a cell of Wyndmondham Abbey and of the Benedictine order?"

There you have it: a sixteenth-century Tudor lady, staying on forever in what was once her home, curiously looking out at a forever changing world; and a twelfth-century monk, gone mad, forced to die in chains ten miles from where he used to live. Perhaps he was drawn back to his house because it was there that he had committed his crime—killing a man, even if in self-defense, with a holy object as his weapon, thus compounding the crime. Was it the crime that had turned Alexander de Langley into a madman, or was it the madman in him that made him commit the crime?

✳ 125

The Gray Man of Pawley's Island (South Carolina)

SUSAN D. OF COLUMBIA, South Carolina, was born in Texas and was twenty-eight years old. Her father was in the service at first and after the war her parents moved to South Carolina, where her father's family had lived for generations. Susan is the eldest of three sisters. They grew up in a small town in the upper section of the state and the moved to Columbia, where her father became the superintendent of a state boarding school for unusual students. At that point Susan was seventeen. Later she entered a local college and stayed for two years. She is presently living with her husband, who is also in education, and they have a little boy. Because of a background of premonitions she had some interest in studying psychic phenomena, but this interest was rather on the vague side.

The first complete incident Susan can remember happened when she was just twelve years old. At that time she had spent the night with her grandmother, also named Susan. During the night the little girl dreamed her grandmother had died. She was awakened from her dream by her cousin Kenneth with the sad news that her grandmother had indeed died during the night.

There had always been a close relationship between her and her father, so when her father was taken to the hospital with a heart attack in 1967 she was naturally concerned. After a while the doctors allowed him to return to his home life, and by the time her little boy was a year old in March 1968 her father seemed completely well and there was no thought of further illness on the family's mind. Two days after they had all been together for the first birthday celebration of her little boy she awoke in the middle of the night with an overpowering anxiety about her father's well-being. She became convinced that her father would leave them soon. The next morning she telephoned her sister and started to discuss her concern for her father. At that moment her father interrupted her call by asking her sister to get her mother immediately. He died on the way to the hospital that very afternoon.

Susan's father had a very close friend by the name of Joe F. with whom he had shared a great love of college football games. Joe F. had passed on a short time before. A little later, Susan and her husband attended one of the games of the University of South Carolina. This was in the fall of 1968. On the way to their seats Susan looked up toward the rear section of the arena and quickly turned her head back to her husband. She was so upset at what she saw that it took her a moment to calm down and take her seat. There, not more than eight feet away from her, stood her late father just as he had looked in life. Moreover, she heard him speak to her clearly and in his usual tone of voice. Her husband had not noticed anything. She decided not to tell him about it. As she slowly turned her head back to where they had come from she noticed her father again. This time Joe F., his lifelong friend, was with him. The two dead men were walking down the walkway in front of the seats and she had a good opportunity to see them clearly. They seemed as much alive then as they had ever been when she knew them both in the flesh.

Susan D. has an aunt by the name of Mrs. Fred V. They had frequently discussed the possibility of life after death and psychic phenomena in general, especially after the death of the aunt's husband, which had come rather unexpectedly. It was then that the two women realized that they had shared a similar extraordinary experience. Mrs. Fred V. had also gone to a football game at the University of South Carolina, but her visit was a week later, for a different game than Susan's had been. Since the two women had not met for some time there had been no opportunity to discuss Susan's original psychic experience at the football game with her aunt. Nevertheless, Mrs. V. told her niece that something quite extraordinary had happened to her at that particular football game. She too had seen the two dead men watch the game as if they were still very much in the flesh. To Mrs. V. this was a signal that her own husband was to join them, for the three had been very good and close friends in life. As it happened she was right. He passed on soon afterwards.

Susan D. has heard the voice of her father since then on several occasions, although she hasn't seen him again. It appears that her father intercedes frequently when Susan is about to lose her temper in some matter or take a wrong step. On such occasions she hears his voice telling her to take it easy.

* * *

One of the best known ghosts of South Carolina's low country is the so-called Gray Man of Pawley's Island. A number of local people claim they have seen him gazing seaward from the dunes, especially when a hurricane is about to break. He is supposed to warn of impending disaster. Who the Gray Man of Pawley's Island is is open to question. According to A Perceptive Survey of South Car-

olina Ghosts by Worth Gatewood, published in 1962, he may be the original Percival Pawley who so loved his island that he felt impelled to watch over it even after he passed on. But Mr. Gatewood gives more credence to a beautiful and romantic account of the origin of the specter. According to this story, a young man who was to be married to a local belle left for New York to attend to some business but on his way back was shipwrecked and lost at sea. After a year's time the young woman married his best friend and settled down on Pawley's Island with her new husband. Years later the original young man returned, again shipwrecked and rescued by one of his former fiancée's servants.

When he realized that his love had married in the meantime, he drowned himself at the nearby shore. All this happened, if we believe it happened, a long time ago, because the Gray Man has been seen ever since 1822, or perhaps even earlier than that. A Mrs. Eileen Weaver, according to Mr. Gatewood's account, saw the specter on her veranda and it was indeed a dim outline of a man in gray. There had been unexplained footsteps on her veranda and doors opening and closing by themselves, untouched by human hands.

A businessman by the name of William Collins who did not believe in ghosts, not even in South Carolina ghosts, found himself on the lookout to check on the rising surf on the morning of famed Hurricane Hazel. As he was walking down the dunes he noticed the figure of a man standing on the beach looking seaward. Collins challenged him, thinking that perhaps he was a neighbor who had come out to check on the rising tide, but the stranger paid no attention. Busy with his task, Collins forgot about this and by the time he looked up the stranger had gone. According to the weather forecast, however, the hurricane had shifted directions and was not likely to hit the area, so Collins and his family went to bed that night, sure the worst was over. At 5 o'clock in the morning he was aroused from bed by heavy pounding on his door. Opening it, he could feel the house shake from the wind rising to tremendous force. On his veranda stood a stranger wearing a gray fishing cap and a common work shirt and pants, all of it in gray. He told Collins to get off the beach since the storm was coming in. Collins thanked him and ran upstairs to wake his family. After the excitement of the storm had passed Collins wondered about the man who had warned him to get off the island. Intelligently he investigated the matter, only to find that no one had seen the man, nor had any of his neighbors had a guest fitting his description. The state highway patrolman on duty also had not seen anyone come or go, and there is only one access road, the causeway over the marshes.

Haunted Westover (Virginia)

WITH ONE EXCEPTION no state in the Union is more often concerned with hauntings, in the public mind, than is Virginia. That is so because the rolling hills south of Washington, dotted as they are with magnificent manor houses, many of them dating back to colonial days, seem to be the kind of atmosphere ghosts prefer. The sole exception to this public image are the New England mansions perched perilously atop storm-swept cliffs where, usually during storms, the ghosts of sea captains still walk and the unwary traveler is frightened to death. That, at least, is the impression still rampant among the uninstructed, although it is perfectly true that there are sea captains in New England manor houses walking long after their time on earth has expired.

But Virginia, which is primarily horse country and was settled originally by people from the Anglo-Saxon countries, is very much like England in many respects. Even the ghosts, such as they are, that continue a shadowy existence in some of the estates and plantation houses are similar in their habits to those found in English stately homes. Almost "the first state in the Union" because of its early connection with the creation of the country and because it was the home of so many of the leaders of the Revolutionary War, Virginia must be considered the closest to an oligarchic state in America. Divided among a small number of illustrious families, Virginia has for a long time been a feudal barony of sorts, and to this very day the great houses attest to the way this first among the thirteen colonies developed. Even though the plantations that were once the lifeblood of these houses are no longer in existence, the houses themselves continue to flourish because the Virginians have a keen sense of history and tradition. Many of the houses, of course, have been restored because of decay. Nevertheless, there are still some which have stood the test of time and survived from their seventeenth- or eighteenth-century origins almost intact to this day.

Foremost among such manor houses is the magnificent estate of Westover on the James River. Built originally in 1730 by William Byrd II, the man who founded Richmond, it stands amid an 11,000-acre working farm. The formal gardens surrounding the house are open to the public, but the house itself is not. A magnificent eighteenth-century ceiling in the entrance hall matches the paneling of the walls. Throughout the manor house there is evidence of grandeur. This is not the home of a country squire but of a statesman of great wealth. When William Byrd was killed during the Revolutionary War, a descendant of the widow sold the original furniture in 1813. Eventually the house passed into the hands of Mrs. Bruce Crane Fisher. Her grandfather had bought the house in 1921 and became the eleventh owner since the plantation had been in existence. Mrs. Fisher has furnished the house in recent years with authentic eighteenth-century English and European furniture to restore it as closely as possible to the original appearance. The Georgian house stands amid tall old trees and consists of a central portion and two wings. The central portion has three stories of elegant brickwork and two tall chimneys. The two wings were originally not connected to the center portion of the house, but the right wing had to be restored in 1900 since it had been damaged by fire from a shelling during the Civil War. At that time the two wings were connected to the house and are now accessible directly from the main portion. The main entrance faces the James River and has the original wrought-iron entrance gate with stone eagles surmounting the gateposts. Thus, with minimal additions and restorations, the house today presents pretty much the same picture it did when it was first built in 1730.

Colonel Byrd took his beautiful daughter Evelyn, pronounced *Ee*velyn in Virginia, to London for the coronation of King George I. That was in 1717 when the great men of the colonies, when they could afford it, would come to the mother country when the occasion arose. Evelyn, at the time, was eighteen years old and her father decided to leave her in England to be educated. Soon he received disquieting news from his confidants at the London court. It appeared that Evelyn had seen with a certain Charles Mordaunt and that the two young people were hopelessly in love with each other. Normally this would be a matter for rejoicing, but not so in this case. Charles was an ardent Roman Catholic and the grandson of the Earl of Petersborough. Colonel Byrd, on the other hand was politically and personally a staunch Protestant, and the idea of his daughter marrying into the enemy camp, so to speak, was totally unacceptable to him. Immediately he ordered her to return to Westover and Evelyn had no choice but to obey. As soon as she arrived at the family plantation she went into isolation. She refused to see any other suitors her father sent her or to consider, or even to discuss, the possibility of marriage.

This went on for some time, and Evelyn quite literally "pined away" to death. Some weeks before her death, however, she had a very emotional discussion with her best friend, Anne Harrison. The two girls were walking up a hill when Evelyn, feeling faint, knew that her days were numbered. She turned to her friend and promised her that she would return after her death. Mrs. Harrison did not take this very seriously, but she knew that Evelyn was not well and her death did not come as a shock. The following spring, after Westover had somehow returned to a degree of normalcy and the tragic events of the previous year were not so strongly in evidence, Mrs. Harrison was walking in the garden sadly remembering what had transpired the year before. Suddenly she saw her old friend standing beside her in a dazzling white gown. The vision then drifted forward two steps, waved its hand at her and smiled. An instant later it had vanished. At the time of her untimely death Evelyn Byrd had been twenty-nine years of age, but in the apparition she seemed much younger and lovelier than she had appeared toward the end of her life. The specter has reappeared from time to time to a number of people, both those who live in the area and those who are guests at Westover. A lady who lives nearby who has been there for nearly three decades saw her in the mid-1960s. She had been coming out of the front door one summer and was walking down the path when she looked back toward the house and saw a woman come out behind her. At first she thought it was a friend and stopped at the gate to wait for her. When the woman came closer, however, she didn't recognize her. There was something very strange about the woman coming toward her. There seemed to be a glow all about her person, her black hair, and the white dress. When the woman had arrived close to her she stopped and seemed to sink into the ground.

On December 11, 1929, some guests from Washington were staying at Westover, and on the evening of their arrival the conversation turned to ghosts. The house was then owned by Mr. and Mrs. Richard H. Crane, who explained that they themselves had not seen the ghost during their tenancy. One of the house guests retired to the room assigned to her on the side of the house overlooking the great gates from which one has a fine view into the formal gardens. Sometime that night Mrs. Crane awoke and went to the window. There was no apparent reason for her behavior. It was quite dark outside and very quiet. As she glanced out the window she saw the figure of Evelyn Byrd. She described the apparition to her hosts as filmy, nebulous, and cloudy, so transparent that no features could be distinguished, only a gauzy texture of a woman's form. The figure seemed to be floating a little above the lawn and almost on the level of the window itself. As she looked at it almost transfixed, the apparition acknowledged her by raising her hand and motioning to her to go back into the room and away from the window. The gesture seemed so imperative that the house guest obeyed it.

When I requested permission to investigate the house I was politely denied access. Perhaps the present owners are afraid that I might induce the lovely Evelyn to leave Westover for a better life in paradise, and that would never do, for Westover is, after all, the nearest thing to paradise on earth, at least to an eighteenth-century lass whose lover has gone away. Had I had the opportunity to come into contact with her through some reputable medium, perhaps I might have reunited the two in a land and under conditions where her stern father Colonel Byrd could no longer keep them apart.

Another famous Virginia mansion is Blandfield, which has more than one ghost. In the late 1960s the Rich-mond *Times Dispatch* made a survey of some of the better ghost houses in the area. Tom Howard interviewed a number of people who owned such houses and he also journeyed up to Blandfield to interview the owner. Here is his report.

Blandfield, an eighteenth century mansion in Essex County, has been frequented by a variety of spooks for two centuries. They've come as eerie lights in the night and wispy figures of men and women stalking through the halls.

Mrs. William Nash Beverley, wife of the owner, related that about five years ago house guests reported apparitions on two occasions. The first was in a long, flowered dress walking across the upstairs hall. Everyone searched the home, but the stranger wasn't found. Two days later, a second guest saw a woman, in a long, dark skirt, cross a downstairs hall, and enter a room. Again an investigation found no one, said Mrs. Beverley.

The most recent episode came several months before, she said. Mrs. Beverley recounted the experience. She and two dogs were in the downstairs library one afternoon and the only other person in the house was an ill relative who she knew was asleep in an upstairs bedroom. Suddenly, heavy footsteps sounded in the room directly overhead. Startled, she listened. The dogs sprang to their feet, hair bristling.

"First I thought I would take a shotgun and go up," said Mrs. Beverley. "Then I thought how silly that was. But I was uneasy, so I put a leash on each dog and we rushed up the steps. As I went up the steps, the dogs became more excited, their hair stood straight up."

She went straight to the bedroom of her relative, who was lying quietly in bed, still asleep. The dogs strained at the leash and pulled toward the room where she heard the heavy footsteps. She opened the door and the dogs bounded in fiercely...but there was no one there. She explored every hiding place in the room, but found no trace of a living human being. The dogs quieted down and she decided that, at last, she had heard one of the famed Blandfield ghosts.

There is a rocking chair ghost at Shirley plantation in Chase City and another rocking chair ghost at Ash Lawn, once the home of President James Monroe, and the ghost of Governor Kemper is said to still inhabit Walnut Hill, his erstwhile home. I have reported a number of such cases in an earlier book called *Ghosts I've Met*. In fact, the area around Charlottesville, which I investigated personally in 1965, abounds with authentic hauntings.

It is just possible that someone who is psychic and who might have passed the building now housing the Health, Education and Welfare Department in Charlottesville might feel peculiar, perhaps a chill or two, perhaps only a sense of displacement in time.

✳ 127

The Case of the I.R.A. Ghosts

IT WAS A sunny, pleasantly comfortable day when the first expedition on Irish soil started out from the elegant confines of Dromoland Castle. Soon we left behind the international feeling of the main highway, and made our way towards the southern shore of the river Shannon which at this point is as wide as a lake.

We left behind us the bleak masonry of Limerick City, with its factories and wharves, and people going off to work. For it was a weekday and the non-tourist population of Ireland had other things to do than loaf around.

At Tarbert, we left the winding shore road and struck out inland, directly south for Listowel. We arrived in this sleepy old town around noon, just in time to have lunch at the local inn, its only hotel of some size, set back to the side of the old square still covered by cobblestones as in centuries gone by.

It was quite a sight we gave the townspeople, Catherine, elegant as ever, Sybil Leek in purple, and me, heavily burdened with tape recorders and cameras. It is to the eternal credit of the people of Listowel that no one ever asked us any questions, or perhaps this is part of the Irish spirit —to accept people as they are. At any rate, we had a pleasant meal and I went to the telephone to see what I could do about some local help.

Now the telephone is something of a rarity in Western Ireland. I mean one that works.

Our first encounter with this intrusion of the twentieth century into Irish life came at Kilcolgan Castle, that non-castle we never got to sleep in. There was a phone there which I at first took for a toy. It was light and the cord seemed to lead nowhere, but little did I know that this was it—the phone. It actually works at times, except that several hours each day it is off. The trouble is, they never tell you when. Consequently it is best to have emergencies only after you've checked the phone.

Here in Listowel I also discovered that you needed certain coins to operate the telephone properly. So I went into the bar to get some change, for to carry a large supply of pennies around was not my idea of light travelling.

The traditional Irish friendliness was quite evident here, and more so in the bar. There were only two guests having a drink at the counter, one of them an Irish priest originally from San Francisco, who had decided to return to Listowel and really *live*. I had been given the name of a playwright named Eamon Keane who might be in a position to help me find Mr. Maloney's haunted houses. I had heard about these haunted houses from Mr. Maloney himself in New York.

* * *

I was doing a radio program in New York in May 1965 on which I suggested that any Irishman with an authentic experience involving ghosts should contact me.

One of those who rose to the occasion was Patrick Maloney of Queens Village, about an hour from my home. Mr. Maloney had lived in New York for forty-three years, but had originally come from Listowel, Ireland. Mr. Maloney is a man in his early sixties, full of good cheer and about as factual as any man in his position would be. For Mr. Maloney is the supervisor of hospital aides in one of the larger mental institutions near New York. His work demands a great deal of common sense, dealing, as he does, with those who have lost theirs. As if his relationship with things medical were not enough to give Mr. Maloney a sense of caution, he is also an accomplished amateur magician and a student of hypnosis. He knows all about the tricks of the mind and the tricks of clever prestidigitators. He has met such famous magic craftsmen as Dunninger and Harry Blackstone, and to this day attends weekly meetings of the magicians' circle in New York, to keep up on the latest tricks and to sharpen his sense of illusion.

Now if there is one group of diehard skeptics, it is the magicians. To most magicians, all psychic manifestations must be fraudulent because they can make some of them. But the inability of most sleight-of-hand artists to accept the reality of ESP is based on a philosophical concept. To them, all is material, and if there are illusions they did not create, then their whole world is no longer secure.

To his eternal credit, Patrick Maloney is an exception to this breed. That this is so is due largely to his own psychic experiences. He is a Roman Catholic in good standing, married, and a grandfather many times over. One of his married daughters also has had psychic experiences, proving again that the talent does sometimes get handed down in a family, usually on the female side.

"I always keep an open mind; that's the way we learn," he commented in his note to me.

Born in Ireland in 1901, he went to National School and finished the eighth grade. Later he lived in England for a few years prior to settling in America. It was during his youth in Ireland that he became aware of his psychic gifts.

I met Patrick Maloney and we went over his experiences in great detail.

"It was the year 1908 when I had my first memorable experience," he began, "and I was about seven years old at the time. We were living in the town of Listowel, County Kerry, in an old house on Convent Street. The house is still standing; it is built of limestone and has a slate roof.

"That day I was home, taking care of one of my younger brothers who was still a baby in a crib. My mother had gone down to the store, so while she was out, I went upstairs to look at some picture books which were kept on the first landing of the stairs. Upstairs there were

two empty rooms, one facing the other, and they were not used by us.

"I was going over the picture books, when something made me look up.

"There, on the second landing, was a little man no more than five feet tall, beckoning me with his right hand to come to him!

"I can see him as clearly today as if it had just happened. He wore black clothes and his skin was dark, the color of copper, and on his head he had a skull cap with brass bells, and all the time he was laughing and motioning me to come up."

"Weren't you scared?" I interjected. What a strange sight this must have been in the sleepy little town of Listowel.

Mr. Maloney shook his head.

"Not at all," he said. "Maybe I was too young to be afraid properly, but I knew as young as I was that this was a strange thing, so I put my books down and went back

downstairs. I had seen the little man come from a totally empty room and walk into another equally empty room, and I knew there was something queer about all this. But I never told my mother about it until I was a grown man."

"Did your mother offer any explanation?"

"No, she didn't. She just listened quietly and never said a word. To this day I have no idea who the little man was."

I wondered about it myself and made a mental note to have a look at the house on Convent Street, Listowel.

But the encounter with the unknown that puzzled him most happened in 1918 when Patrick Maloney was 17 years of age. At that time there was a great deal of what the Irish euphemistically call "the trouble"—guerrilla warfare between the British occupation forces and the outlawed I.R.A., the Irish Republican Army. This group of citizen-soldiers contributed considerably to Irish independence later, and there is scarcely a spot in all Ireland where there isn't a grave or two of these "freedom fighters." Unfortunately, when the Irish Republic came into being and normal relations returned between the English and their erstwhile enemies, the I.R.A. decided to continue the struggle.

Principally, the six northern counties known as Ulster are the bone of contention. The Irish government in Dublin would like to have solved the problem peacefully and gradually, but the I.R.A. could not wait, so there was violence once again, frequently to the detriment of famed landmarks, until eventually the I.R.A. was outlawed by its own government.

The "Black and Tans" of 1918 engaged in battles and skirmishes all over the land. Nobody could be sure that a stray bullet would not hit an innocent bystander. About two miles outside the town of Listowel, there was a gate in the side of the road. Behind it, the British were waiting. An I.R.A. patrol, consisting of three men, was approaching the spot. In the ensuing ambush, two of the Irish irregulars were killed by the British. Years later, a large Celtic cross was erected over the graves, but the story itself, being similar to so many tragedies of like nature all over Ireland, became dimmed, and even the local people scarcely remember the spot.

That moonlight night in 1918, however, a young Paddy Maloney and a friend, Moss Barney, of Ballybunnon, Kerry, were bicycling down that road, eager to get to Listowel for the night. They had been to a place called Abbyfeale, about five miles away, to see a circus. It was the month of June, and around one in the morning, with the moon illuminating the road rather well. At that time, the monument did not exist, of course, and the shooting was still within memory. But the two travellers gave it no thought. It did not concern them; they were in a gay mood after a pleasant evening at the circus.

When they reached the spot in the road where the ambush had happened, something stopped them in their tracks. No matter how hard Patrick tried to ride on, he could not move from the spot.

"It felt as if someone were in back of us, holding on to our bicycles. I felt clammy and moist, and the sense of a presence behind me trying to prevent me from going down that road was very strong. I had the sensation that someone was trying to keep us *from running into trouble* farther down the road.

"I tried to bicycle as hard as I could, but to no avail. Yet, the road was level, with a stretch of wooded section for at least 500 feet. I felt myself weaken, and the cold sweat broke out all over me. I tried to tell Moss about my difficulties but found my tongue was paralyzed.

"With a last surge of power, I pushed on and finally broke away from the 'thing' behind me. As soon as we came out of the wooded section our bikes were free as before. We both jumped off and I started to tell Moss what I had experienced—only to find that he, too, had felt the same uncanny weight. He, too, was unable to talk for a while.

"'I'll never ride this road again at night,' he finally said, and meant it."

"Did you have other psychic experiences after that?" I asked, for it was plain to me that Patrick Maloney was mediumistic to a degree, having experienced such physical manifestations.

"Many times," he acknowledged.

"When I worked as a psychiatric aide in one of the hospitals here," Maloney added, "I had a most unusual experience. It was late at night and I was very tired. I went into a linen room there, and I lay down on a table to rest a bit, afraid I might fall asleep during the night when I was on duty. I was only down about five minutes, with a blanket underneath me, when someone came along and pulled that blanket from under me. Now I weigh over two hundred pounds, and yet it all happened so fast I had that blanket on top of me before I knew it."

"Was there anyone else in the room?" I inquired.

"Nobody in the room, nobody in the ward, just myself."

"What did you do?"

"I jumped up and looked around. The patients were all sleeping. So I went back to rest. Then it happened again, only this time it felt like a big, heavy hand feeling my back. That did it. I came out and locked the room up."

"What did you make of it?" I said.

"When I went to investigate the ward, I found a patient dead. He had died in his sleep. He was an ex-boxer. He had been under my personal care."

"I guess he wanted to let you know he was going on," I said. "Any other uncanny experiences?"

"Oh yes," Maloney said matter-of-fact like, "my son died in 1945, and a couple of months after he died, I was sitting in my home watching television. I was comfortable, with my legs stretched out, when I felt a person cross by my legs very fast. It made a swishing sound. I looked at my wife, but she had not moved at all. I knew it was my son, for he had a peculiar walk."

Maloney has had numerous true dreams, and often knows when a person is "not long for this world." Like the co-worker at the hospital whom he had dubbed the "dead man." For two years he did not realize why he felt that way about his colleague. Then the man committed suicide.

In 1946 he returned to Ireland again after a long absence. Suddenly, in his hotel room, he heard his wife Catherine's voice clear across from America. That week, her mother died.

Maloney takes his gift casually. He neither denies it nor does he brag about it. He is very Irish about it all.

* * *

When the priest from San Francisco heard I was trying to phone Eamon Keane for an appointment, he laughed.

"Nonsense," he intoned, "just go to his house and introduce yourself. We're all very friendly here."

Mr. Keane, it turned out, also had an unlisted number. Imagine, an unlisted number in *Listowel!* But playwrights will have ideas.

Lunch being done with, we proceeded to find Mr. Keane. I had also been informed that in addition to playwriting, he owned a bar. We walked up the road and found ourselves in front of a bar marked "Keane's." Had we come to the right place? We had not.

"You want my brother," the owner said, and off we went again, a block farther up the road, to another bar, also marked "Keane's." In fact, I don't recall much else on that street except bars—here called pubs.

Mr. Keane was most helpful. He knew what I was looking for, and he offered to take me to a man who had had some experiences and could tell me about them firsthand. So we left again and drove down a few blocks to a small house the ground floor of which was occupied by a store. The owner of the store, it developed, was the man to see. He dealt in fishing tackle.

John Garen had lived here for fifty-seven years and he had an accent to prove it.

I asked if he knew of any ghosts.

"Right here in this street, sir," he replied, "there is a house with a little brook beside it, and there was a family by the name of Loughneanes living in it. It's on Convent Street and called Glauna Foka."

"What does this mean?" I asked, my Gaelic being extremely weak.

"Glen of the Fairies," Mr. Garen replied. "I've never seen any, but it seems that chairs and everything that was inside the house would be thrown out the windows, and you'd hear the glass crashing, and when you'd come around there'd be nobody there. The people had to move out because of it. This was about sixty years ago."

I thanked Mr. Garen for his information, such as it was, and wished him the top of the afternoon. Then we drove on and stopped in front of the house on Convent Street where Patrick Maloney had seen the little fellow with the fool's cap.

The house had obviously been reconditioned and did not show its age at all. It was a two-story affair, with a garden in back, and Sybil Leek went across the street to have a quiet look at it. We could not get in, for the present owners were not too keen on the subject of ghosts. Mr. Garen asked us not to mention his name, in particular, for in a town the size of Listowel, *everything* gets around eventually.

"What do you sense here?" I asked Sybil, who of course knew nothing whatever of Patrick Maloney, his experiences, or even Mr. Garen's recent talk.

"There undoubtedly have been some manifestations in the upper right-hand room," Sybil said succinctly, "and I think this has an association with water. I think the pre-

vious owner was in some occupation in which water was very important. Someone associated with a mill; I think."

Sybil did not know that there was a brook beside the house, nor that there had once been a mill not far away.

"How long ago do you think this happened?"

"About two hundred years ago," she replied. "On the side of the house where there is no building at the moment, I can see, in my mind's eye, a smaller building, rather flat."

"How far back do you feel manifestations took place here?"

"About four years ago, then around 1948, and before that, about a hundred and twenty years ago. There has been some tragedy connected with water. I sense some wheels around that mill, and a name that sounds like Troon to me."

We drove on, out of Listowel now, towards where the mill once stood.

"On the right side," Sybil murmured, and Mr. Keane confirmed the location.

Since we could not get into the house itself I decided it was best to look into still another house Patrick Maloney had told me about. Mr. Keane excused himself and hurried back to his bar. We drove on into the open countryside looking for a farm house of which we knew little, if anything.

Mr. Maloney had provided me with a rough, hand-drawn map and it came in handy.

"The house in Greenville Road," he had explained, "near the mill, had some poltergeist activity when I was there. The kitchen is haunted, and the bedroom also. Clothes used to be pulled off people in bed and the room used to fill up with roaches—millions of them—and then they would vanish into thin air; faces were seen at the windows, looking in. Fights were taking place, tables pushed around and chairs also, and the cups and saucers would dance on their shelves in the closet. The Connors who lived there are all dead now, and others live there, but I don't know them. This was about forty-five years ago."

All this came to mind again as we rode down the bumpy road looking for the old Connors house.

A smallish one-story farm house was pointed out to us by an elderly man working beside the road. It turned out to be a Connors house all right, but the wrong Connors. Our Connors were farther down the road, and finally we found the house that fit Maloney's description and map.

Someone had evidently just moved in recently and was in the process of fixing it up. This activity had not yet extended to the garden around the house, which was lovely in its wild ways, totally untouched by human hands for years, evidently.

There was a broad iron gate closing off the garden from the road. The sun was not so high any more and the picture was one of utmost peace and tranquillity. Carefully —for there are more dogs in Ireland than anywhere else in the world—carefully I opened the gate and walked towards the house. My feet sank into the wet ground but I carried on. At the door I was greeted by a young woman in her late twenties who bid us welcome in the typical Irish country way of welcoming a stranger. Catherine and Sybil came along a moment later, and we had a look at what was once the haunted house of the Connors.

"Mrs. Healy," I began, "you moved in here a few days ago. This used to be the Connors house—am I right?"

"That is correct," she replied in almost brogue-free speech. "It is a pretty old house, but it has been reconditioned recently."

The house was a happy one to her; at any rate neither she nor her husband nor their small child had noticed anything unusual—yet.

Sybil stepped inside the house now. It was really nothing more than a smallish kitchen, a hall, and a bedroom, all on the same floor. Immediately she felt in another era.

"When the woman was talking to you just now," Sybil said, "I heard another voice. A man's voice. It's a strong voice, but I can't understand it."

"Is it Gaelic?" I asked.

"I should think so. It's the inflection of the voice that is peculiar to me. It is a hard, strong voice. There is water connected with this place."

"Any tragedy?"

"The man is connected with it. Turn of the century. He had some trouble with his head, probably due to a blow. The injury affected his life very drastically. Ultimately led to his death, but was not immediately responsible for it. A very angry person, I'd say."

We did not want to overstay our welcome at the farm house, so I thanked Mrs. Healy for letting us visit.

"There is just one more thing," she said pensively. "You see this gate over there?" We nodded, for I had admired it from the start.

"Well," Mrs. Healy said somewhat sheepishly, "no matter how often I close it, it just does not want to stay closed."

* * *

The afternoon was growing slowly old, and we still had two other places to visit. We drove back through Listowel and out the other end, following Patrick Maloney's crudely drawn map. Nobody in Listowel could direct us towards the monument at the crossroads we were seeking, and we wasted an hour going up and down wrong country roads. It is not easy to get directions in the Irish countryside, for few people know more than their immediate neighborhood. Finally we hit paydirt. Ahead of us there was a crossroad that seemed to fit Maloney's description, with the wooded area on one side. But no Celtic cross in sight!

I was puzzled. Leaving Sybil with Catherine in the car, I set out on foot to explore the land beyond the road. About twenty yards inside the area, I suddenly came upon the monument. Our driver, whose name was Sylvester, also was puzzled. He had never heard of such a monument in this place. But there it was, set back from prying eyes, a gray-white stone wall, about two feet high, beyond which stood a tall Celtic cross. Before the cross were three graves, inscribed only in Gaelic. Beyond the graves the hill sloped gently towards the faraway Kerry Coast.

The weather had become rainy and dark clouds were hanging overhead.

I asked Sybil to come forward now, and before she had a chance to look at the marble plaques on the ground, I asked for her impressions at this shrine.

"There is peace here, but only on the outside. On my right there seems to be an old building in the distance. I feel it is connected with this spot. It is a tragic, desperate spot, with a lot of unhappiness, helplessness—something had to happen here. There is mental torture."

"Did anyone die here?" I said. Sybil stepped forward and looked at the graves.

"Yes," she replied immediately, "as you see yourself the inscriptions are in Gaelic and I don't understand Gaelic, but I think this was forty years ago, between forty and fifty years ago—there was fighting, and it was unexpected. Coming again from the right of me, some mortal conflict involving death of several people—"

"How many people?"

"I can see two," Sybil replied, and it occurred to me at once that she had no knowledge of the fact that *two* I.R.A. men had perished at this spot.

"Are there any presences here still?"

"The two, because these are the people that I feel. Why, I don't know, but again, the building on my right seems to interest the people and myself. Two men. Perhaps they're only guarding something. Something to watch in this area, always watching the countryside. Perhaps they had to watch the countryside *and still must do so!*"

"Quite," I said, thinking of the detail the patrol had been assigned—to watch the countryside.

Sybil closed her eyes for a moment.

"Why are they still here, so long after?" I inquired.

"Yes," she replied, "it is still of importance to them in this time and place, as it was then."

"But there is peace in the country now."

"I don't think there is peace in this particular part of the country," Sybil countered, and I knew, of course, that the I.R.A. is far from dead, especially in the rural areas.

"Do you get any names for these men?"

"No, but I can describe them to you. One is a broad-set man, and he has a rough face, country man, or forced to take to the country, not well kept, must have been hiding; he has a thick neck, and very brown eyes, perhaps five feet eight. There is someone with him, not related, but they've been together for some time. The building on the right has some connection with them."

There was a small house on the hill about a hundred yards farther back from the road.

"What outfits are these men in, Sybil?"

"I don't see uniforms," she replied, "very ordinary dress, trousers."

"Are they regular soldiers?"

"No—ordinary clothes of about forty-five years ago."

That would make it 1920—pretty close to the year 1918 in which Patrick Maloney had had his ghostly experience here.

"Are they serving any kind of outfit other than military?"

"Serving something, but I don't know what. No uniforms, but they are serving."

"How are they then serving, by what means?"

"Something noisy. I think they've been shot. One in the shoulder, near the heart."

"Can we help them in any way?"

"Somehow this place is . . . as if someone must always watch from here. This watching must go on. I don't know why they have to watch. They do."

"Are they aware of the present?"

"I don't think so. The one I described is more in evidence than the other. Perhaps he was leading. There is a need for silence here."

I then asked Sybil to inform the two men that the war was long over and they should return home to their families, that in fact, they were relieved of duty.

Sybil told them this, and that the crossroads were now safe. They had done their job well.

"Any reaction?" I asked after a moment.

"The main man still stands," Sybil reported, "but the other one is gone now."

Again, I asked Sybil to send the man away.

"Patrick is his name," Sybil said, and later I checked the name in the largest panel on the ground—Padraic it was.

A moment later, Sybil added: "I think he goes to the right now—what was to the right?"

"I don't know," I said truthfully.

Half a mile up the hill, the ruined house stood silently.

"That's where they had to go back to. He is gone now. There is nothing."

And so it is that the two ghostly I.R.A. men finally went home on extended leave.

✳ 128

The Last Ride

CORONADO BEACH IS A pleasant seaside resort in southern California not far from San Diego. You get there by ferry from the mainland and the ride itself is worth the trip. It takes about fifteen minutes, then you continue by car or on foot into a town of small homes, none grand, none ugly —pleasantly bathed by the warm California sunshine, vigorously battered on the oceanside by the Pacific, and becalmed on the inside of the lagoon by a narrow body of water.

The big thing in Coronado Beach is the U.S. Navy; either you're in it and are stationed here, or you work for them in one way or another: directly, as a civilian, or indirectly by making a living through the people who are in the Navy and who make their homes here.

Mrs. Francis Jones is the wife of an advertising manager for a Sidney, Ohio, newspaper, who had returned to Coronado after many years in the Midwest. She is a young woman with a college background and above-average intelligence, and has a mixed Anglo-Saxon and Austrian background. Her father died a Navy hero while testing a dive bomber, making her mother an early widow.

Gloria Jones married fairly young, and when her husband took a job as advertising manager in Sidney, Ohio, she went right along with him. After some years, the job became less attractive, and the Joneses moved right back to Coronado where Jones took up work for the Navy.

They have a thirteen-year-old daughter, Vicki, and live a happy, well-adjusted life; Mr. Jones collects coins and Mrs. Jones likes to decorate their brick house surrounded by a garden filled with colorful flowers.

One January, Mrs. Jones sought me out to help her understand a series of most unusual events that had taken place in her otherwise placid life. Except for an occasional true dream, she had not had any contact with the psychic and evinced no interest whatever in it until the events that so disturbed her tranquility had come to pass. Even the time she saw her late father in a white misty cloud might have been a dream. She was only ten years old at the time, and preferred later to think it was a dream. But the experiences she came to see me about were not in that category. Moreover, her husband and a friend were present when some of the extraordinary happenings took place.

Kathleen Duffy was the daughter of a man working for the Convair company. He was a widower and Kathleen was the apple of his eye. Unfortunately the apple was a bit rotten in spots; Kathleen was a most difficult child. Her father had sent her away to a Catholic school for girls in Oceanside, but she ran away twice; after the second time she had to be sent to a home for "difficult" children.

Gloria Jones met Kathleen when both were in their teens. Her mother was a widow and Mr. Duffy was a widower, so the parents had certain things in common. The two girls struck up a close friendship and they both hoped they might become sisters through the marriage of their parents, but it did not happen.

When Kathleen was sent away to the Anthony Home, a reform school at San Diego, Gloria was genuinely sorry. That was when Kathleen was about sixteen years of age. Although they never met again, Kathleen phoned Gloria a few times. She wasn't happy in her new environment, of course, but there was little that either girl could do about it.

In mounting despair, Kathleen tried to get away again but did not succeed. Then one day, she and her roommate, June Robeson, decided to do something drastic to call attention to their dissatisfied state. They set fire to their room in the hope that they might escape in the confusion of the fire.

As the smoke of the burning beds started to billow heavier and heavier, they became frightened. Their room was kept locked at all times, and now they started to bang at the door, demanding to be let out.

The matron came and surveyed the scene. The girls had been trouble for her all along. She decided to teach them what she thought would be an unforgettable "lesson." It was. When Kathleen collapsed from smoke inhalation, the matron finally opened the door. The Robeson girl was saved, but Kathleen Duffy died the next day in the hospital.

When the matter became public, the local newspapers demanded an investigation of the Anthony Home. The matron and the manager of the Home didn't wait for it. They fled to Mexico and have never been heard from since.

Gradually, Gloria began to forget the tragedy. Two years went by and the image of the girlfriend receded into her memory.

One day she and another friend, a girl named Jackie Sudduth, went standing near the waterfront at Coronado, a sunny, wind-swept road from which you can look out onto the Pacific or back toward the orderly rows of houses that make up Coronado Beach.

The cars were whizzing by as the two girls stood idly gazing across the road. One of the cars coming into view was driven by a young man with a young girl next to him who seemed familiar to Gloria. She only saw her from the shoulders up, but as the car passed close by she knew it was Kathleen. Flabbergasted, she watched the car disappear.

"Did you know that girl?" her friend Jackie inquired.
"No, why?"
"She said your name," her friend reported.
Gloria nodded in silence. She had seen it too. Without uttering a sound, the girl in the passing car had spelled the syllables "Glo-ri-a" with her lips.

For weeks afterward, Gloria could not get the incident out of her mind. There wasn't any rational explanation, and yet how could it be? Kathleen had been dead for two years.

The years went by, then a strange incident brought the whole matter back into her consciousness. It was New Year's Eve, twelve years later. She was now a married woman with a daughter. As she entered her kitchen, she froze in her tracks: a bowl was spinning counterclockwise while moving through the kitchen of its own volition.

She called out to her husband and daughter to come quickly. Her daughter's girlfriend, Sheryl Konz, age thirteen, was first to arrive in the kitchen. She also saw the bowl spinning. By the time Mr. Jones arrived, it had stopped its most unusual behavior.

Over dinner, topic A was the self-propelled bowl. More to tease her family than out of conviction, Mrs. Jones found herself saying, "If there is anyone here, let the candle go out." Promptly the candle went out.

There was silence after that, for no current of air was present that could have accounted for the sudden extinguishing of the candle.

The following summer, Mrs. Jones was making chocolate pudding in her kitchen. When she poured it into one of three bowls, the bowl began to turn—by itself. This time her husband saw it too. He explained it as vibrations from a train or a washing machine next door. But why did the other two bowls not move also?

Finally wondering if her late friend Kathleen, who had always been a prankster, might not be the cause of this, she waited for the next blow.

On New Year's Day that following year, she took a Coke bottle out of her refrigerator, and set it down on the counter. Then she turned her back on it and went back to the refrigerator for some ice. This took only a few moments. When she got back to the counter, the Coke bottle had disappeared.

Chiding herself for being absent-minded, she assumed she had taken the bottle with her to refrigerator and had left it inside. She checked and there was no Coke.

"Am I going out of my mind?" she wondered, and picked up the Coke carton. It contained five bottles. The sixth bottle was never found.

Since these latter incidents took place during the three years when they lived in Sidney, Ohio, it was evident that the frisky spirit of Kathleen Duffy could visit them anywhere they went—if that is who it was.

In late May of that year, back again in Coronado, both Mr. and Mrs. Jones saw the bread jump out of the breadbox before their very eyes. They had locked the breadbox after placing a loaf of bread inside. A moment later, they returned to the breadbox and found it open. While they were still wondering how this could be, the bread jumped out.

The Last Ride

A practical man, Mr. Jones immediately wondered if they were having an earthquake. They weren't. Moreover, it appeared that their neighbors' breadboxes behaved normally.

They shook their heads once more. But this time Mrs. Jones dropped me a letter.

On June 3, I went to San Diego to see the Joneses. Sybil Leek and I braved the bus ride from Santa Ana on a hot day, but the Joneses picked us up at the bus terminal and drove us to the Anthony Home where Kathleen had died so tragically.

Naturally Sybil was mystified about all this, unless her ESP told her why we had come. Consciously, she knew nothing.

When we stopped at the Home, we found it boarded up and not a soul in sight. The day was sunny and warm, and the peaceful atmosphere belied the past that was probably filled with unhappy memories. After the unpleasant events that had occurred earlier, the place had been turned into a school for mentally challenged children and run as such for a number of years. At present, however, it stood abandoned.

Sybil walked around the grounds quietly and soaked up the mood of the place.

"I heard something, maybe a name," she suddenly said. "It sounds like Low Mass."

Beyond that, she felt nothing on the spot of Kathleen's unhappy memories. Was it Kathleen who asked for a Low Mass to be said for her? Raised a strict Catholic, such a thought would not be alien to her.

"The place we just left," Sybil said as we drove off, "has a feeling of sickness to it—like a place for sick people, but not a hospital."

Finally we arrived at the corner of Ocean Avenue and Lomar Drive in Coronado, where Gloria Jones had seen the car with Kathleen in it. All through the trip, on the ferry, and down again into Coronado Island, we avoided the subject at hand.

But now we had arrived and it was time to find out if Sybil felt anything still hanging on in this spot.

"I feel a sense of death," she said slowly, uncertainly. "Despite the sunshine, this is a place of death." It wasn't that there was a presence here, she explained, but rather that someone had come here to wait for another person. The noise around us—it was Sunday—did not help her concentration.

"It's a foreign face I see," Sybil continued. "Someone—a man, with very little hair—who is alien to this place. I see an iris next to his face."

Was the man using the symbol to convey the word Irish perhaps? Was he an ancestor of Kathleen's from over there?

I turned to Mrs. Jones.

"I think what you witnessed here was the superimposition on a pair of motorists of the spirit image of your late friend. These things are called transfigurations. I am sure if the car had stopped, you would have found a stranger in it. Kathleen used her so that you could see her familiar face, I think."

Perhaps Kathleen Duffy wanted to take one more ride, a joy ride in freedom, and, proud of her accomplishment, had wanted her best friend to see her taking it.

There have been no further disturbances or prankish happenings at the Jones house since.

✳ 129

The San Francisco Ghost Bride

NOT FAR FROM the Fairmont Hotel on Nob Hill, San Francisco, where the popular television series *Hotel* was taped, is a spot considered haunted by many. Here on California Street, in front of an average apartment house going back some years, the ghost of Flora Sommerton walks. Many have seen the girl, dressed in her bridal gown, walking right through living people and totally oblivious of them, and they, of her. Some years ago Mrs. Gwen H., a lady I worked with on a number of cases, was riding up the hill with a friend, in a cable car. Both ladies saw the strange girl in her bridal gown walking fast as if trying to get away from something—or someone.

The ghostly bride of Nob Hill where she was spotted

Which is exactly what she tried to do. Flora Sommerton, a San Francisco debutante, was eighteen when she disappeared from her family's Nob Hill mansion one night in 1876. It was a major society scandal at the time: Flora simply had refused to marry the young man her parents had picked for her to marry.

Flora never came back nor was she ever found, despite a vast search and huge reward offered for her return or information leading to her. The years went by and eventually the matter was forgotten. Flora's parents also died and it was not until 1926 when the truth finally came out. That year Flora died in a flophouse in Butte, Montana, still dressed in her bridal gown. Ever since, she has been seen walking up Nob Hill desperately trying to escape an unwanted marriage.

If you will slowly walk up California Street, late at night when there is little traffic, perhaps you too might run into the wide-eyed lass from 1876 and if you do, be sure to tell her it is time to let go, and that she is finally free.

CHAPTER EIGHT

Haunted People

T RUE CASES INVOLVING a ghost that attaches itself to a specific person are not nearly as common as haunted houses, but they do exist. These are not in any sense free spirits, because the attachment represents an emotional problem that has not been fully resolved.

But the ghost or earthbound spirit who attaches itself to a person in the physical world does have wider opportunities to manifest, or "get through," than the traditional haunted house ghost. Such phenomena may therefore occur in several places.

These ghosts, who are not nearly as rational as free spirits—can also make contact through deep trance mediums when communications between spirits and living people can be quite innocuous and friendly. When the spirit has unresolved problems, however, or makes demands, it can be upsetting and requires consultation with an expert.

Some cases I have investigated include the following.

The Strange Death of Valerie K.

SOMETIMES BEING A PSYCHIC investigator puts a heavy moral burden on one, especially where there may be a possibility of preventing someone's death. Of course, you're never sure that you can. Take the case of Valerie K., for instance. I am not using her full name because the case is far from closed. The police won't talk about it, but her friends are only too sure there is something mysterious about her death, and they *will* talk about it. They speak mainly to me, for that's about all they can do about it—now.

To start at the beginning, one April I got a phone call from Sheila M.—an English woman whom I had met through a mutual friend—inviting my wife and me to a cocktail party at her house on New York's East Side. Now if it's one thing my wife and I hate it's cocktail parties, even on the East Side, but Sheila is a nice person and we thought she was likely to have only nice friends, so I said we'd come. The party was on April 20, and when we arrived everybody was already there, drinking and chatting, while the butler passed between the guests, ever so quietly seeing after their needs.

Since I don't drink, I let my wife talk to Sheila and sauntered over to the hors d'oeuvres, hopefully searching for some cheese bits, for I am a vegetarian and don't touch meat or fish. Next to the buffet table I found not only an empty chair, unusual at a cocktail party, but also a lovely young woman in a shiny silver Oriental-style dress. In fact, the young lady was herself Chinese, a very impressive-looking woman perhaps in her middle twenties, with brown hair, dark eyes, and a very quiet, soigné air about her. It turned out that the girl's name was Valerie K., and I had been briefly introduced to her once before on the telephone when Sheila had told her of my interest in psychic research, and she had wanted to tell me some of her experiences.

We got to talking about our mutual interest in ESP. She sounded far away, as if something was troubling her, but I had the impression she was determined to be gay and not allow it to interfere with her enjoyment of the party. I knew she was Sheila's good friend and would not want to spoil anything for her. But I probed deeper, somehow sensing she needed help. I was right, and she asked me if she could talk to me sometime privately.

There were several eager young men at the party whose eyes were on her, so I thought it best not to preempt her time, since I knew she was not married. I gave her my telephone number and asked her to call me whenever she wanted to.

About an hour later we left the party, and when we got home I suppressed a desire to telephone this woman and see if she was all right. I dismissed my feeling as undue sentimentality, for the woman had seemed radiant, and surely the reason for her wanting to see me would have to be psychic rather than personal in the usual sense.

All through the weekend I could not get her out of my mind, but I was busy with other work and decided to call her first thing the following week.

Monday night, as I read the *Daily News*, my eye fell on a brief article tucked away inside the newspaper, an article telling of the death of two women a few hours before. The paper's date was Tuesday morning. The deaths had occurred early Monday morning. One of the two women was Valerie K.

With a shudder I put down the paper and closed my eyes.

Could I have prevented her death? I will let you be the judge. But first let me show you what happened in the final hours of this girl's life on earth. Every word is the truth. . . .

Valerie K. came from a well-to-do Chinese family residing in Hawaii. She was as American as anyone else in her speech, and yet there was that undefinable quality in the way she put her words together that hinted at Eastern thought. After an unhappy and brief marriage to a Hong Kong businessman, she came to New York City to try living on her own. Never particularly close to her parents, she was now entirely self-supporting and needed a job. She found a job vaguely described as a public relations assistant, but in fact was the secretary to the man who did publicity for the company. Somehow she was not quite right for the job or the job for her, and it came to a parting of the ways.

The new person hired to take her place was Sheila. Despite the fact that the English woman replaced her, they struck up a friendship that developed into a true attachment to each other, so much so that Valerie would confide in Sheila to a greater extent than she would in anyone else.

When Valerie left the office, there was no job waiting for her; fortunately, however, she had met the manager of a firm owned by the same company, and the manager, whose initial was G., took her on for somewhat selfish reasons. He had a sharp eye for beauty and Valerie was something special. Thus she found herself earning considerably more than she would have been paid in a similar job elsewhere. Soon the manager let her know that he liked her and she got to like him, too. Between August and October of the year before her death, they became close friends.

But in October of that year she called her friend Sheila to complain bitterly of the humiliation she had been put through. G. had found another woman to take her place. Innocently, the new woman, Lynn, became the pawn in the deadly game between the manager and the Chinese beauty.

G. found fault with her very appearance and everything she did, criticizing her and causing her to lose face—an important matter not easily forgotten.

Still, she cared for the man and hoped that he would resume his former attentions. He didn't, and after a miserable Christmas which she partially shared with Sheila, the axe fell. He fired her and gave her two weeks' pay, wishing her the best.

When Sheila heard about this she suggested that Valerie register at the unemployment office. Instead, the proud girl took sleeping pills. But she either did not take enough or changed her mind in time, for she was able to telephone Sheila and tell her what she had done. A doctor was called and she was saved. She had a session with a psychiatrist after that and seemed much more cheerful.

But the humiliation and rejection kept boiling within her. Nothing can be as daring as a person whose affections have been rejected, and one day Valerie wrote a personal letter to the owner of the companies she had once worked for, denouncing the manager and his work.

As if nourished by her hatred, her psychic abilities increased and she found she was able to influence people through telepathy, to read others' thoughts and to put herself into a state of excitement through a form of mediation.

All this of course was for the purpose of getting even, not only with the manager but with the world that had so often hurt her.

Nobody knew for sure if she ever got a reply to her letter. But she was a regular at a Chinese restaurant near her apartment and became friendly with the owners. There she talked about her plans and how she would show the world what sort of woman she was.

Meanwhile the manager found himself short of help and asked her back. Despite her deep hatred for the man, she went back, all the time scheming and hoping her fortunes would take a turn for the better. But she did confide in Sheila that she had taken a big gamble, and if it worked she'd be all right in more ways than one. The owner of the restaurant saw her on Friday, April 21—a day after the party at which I had met her for the first time—and she seemed unusually happy.

She would marry a prominent European, she told him; she had been asked and would say yes. She was almost obsessed at this point with the desire to tell the whole world she would marry him; her parents in Hawaii received a letter requesting them to have formal Chinese wedding attire made up for her in Paris because she would marry soon. Had the idea of getting even with G. robbed her of her senses? It is difficult to assess this, as the principals involved quite naturally would not talk, and even I prefer that they remain anonymous here.

That weekend—April 22 and 23—the pitch of her "wedding fever" rose higher and higher. A neighbor who had dropped in on her at her apartment found her clad only in a bikini and drinking heavily. She observed her running back and forth from her telephone, trying to reach the man overseas she said she would marry. But she couldn't get through to him. In the meantime, she started giving possessions away, saying she would not need them any longer now that she would marry so rich a man.

She also drew up a list of all those whom she would help once she had become the wife of the millionaire. The neighbor left rather perturbed by all this, and Valerie stayed alone in her apartment—or did she?

It was 4 A.M. when the police received a call from her telephone. It was a complaint about excessive noise. When an officer—initialed McG.—arrived on the scene at 4:20 A.M., Valerie herself opened the door in the nude.

"Go away," she said, and asked to be left alone. The officer quickly surveyed the scene. She became rude and explained she was expecting a phone call and did not wish to be disturbed. The officer reported that she had been alone and was drinking, and there the matter stood.

The minutes ticked away. It was early Monday morning, April 24.

At precisely 5 A.M., the building superintendent looked out his window and saw something heavy fall on his terrace.

Rushing to the scene, he discovered Valerie's broken body. She had been killed instantly. The woman had taken two roses with her—but one somehow remained behind on the window sill of the open window from which she had plunged to her death. The other sadly fluttered to earth even as she did.

The police officers found themselves back at the apartment sooner than they had expected, only this time there was a cause for action. After a routine inspection of the girl's tenth floor apartment, her death was put down to accidental death or suicide by falling or jumping from her window. Since she had been drinking heavily, they were not sure which was the actual cause of death.

Monday night Sheila called me frantically, wondering what she should do. There was no one to claim the girl's body. Neither her sister Ethel nor her parents in Hawaii could be reached. I told her to calm down and keep trying, meanwhile berating myself for not having called Valerie in time to prevent her death.

Eventually the parents were found and a proper funeral arranged.

But the puzzle remained. Had she committed suicide or not?

Did that call from Europe finally come and was it so humiliating that Valerie could no longer face the world? Was there not going to be a wedding after all—then at least there must be a funeral?

Valerie had been particularly fond of two things in life—flowers and jewelry. To her, losing a favorite piece of jewelry was bad luck.

Lynn, the woman who now worked at Valerie's office, is a rather matter-of-fact person not given to emotional scenes or superstitions.

Valerie owned a pair of jade earrings that G. had had made for her in the days when they were close. About a month before her death, Valerie gave those earrings to Lynn as a gift. There was a special stipulation, however. She must not wear them around the office, since people had seen Valerie wear them and presumably knew their history.

Lynn agreed not to wear them around the office, but when she wore them outside a most unusual phenomenon took place. Suddenly the earrings would not stay put. One and then the other would drop off her ears as if pulled by some unseen force. That was on April 13, and Valerie was still alive though she had seemed very distraught.

Word of Lynn's concern with the falling earrings got back to the former owner, and finally Valerie called to assure her the falling was a "good omen." Then a week later, on Saturday, April 22, she suddenly called Lynn shortly before midnight and asked her to wear "her" earrings at the office. Lynn promised she would wear them to work Monday.

That was the day Valerie died. The following day, Lynn was still wearing the earrings, which now seemed to cling properly to her ears. She found herself in the ladies' room, when she felt her right earring forced off and thrown into the toilet. It felt as if it had been snatched from her ear by an unseen hand.

Returning to her desk, she noticed that an unusual chill pervaded the area where Valerie's desk had stood. It disappeared at 4:30, which was the time Valerie usually left for home.

All this proved too much for Lynn and she went on a week's vacation.

Sheila was still very upset when a male friend dropped in to help her in this sorry matter. The gentleman, a lawyer by profession, had taken off his jacket when he suddenly felt a cufflink leave his shirt. It was a particularly intricate piece of jewelry, and no matter how they searched it was never found.

Was the dead girl trying to show her hand? Too fantastic, and yet. . . .

There was no rational explanation for the sudden disappearance, in plain light and in the presence of two people, of so definite an object as a cufflink.

On Friday of that week, after the girl had been buried, her sister, Ethel, who had finally arrived in town, went to the apartment to find out what she could about her sister's effects.

As soon as she entered the apartment, she realized that a terrific fight had taken place in it. Nothing had been touched from the moment of death until her arrival, as the apartment had been sealed. Three knives were lying on the floor and the place was a shambles. On the table she noticed two glasses, one partially filled with Scotch and one almost empty. When she called the police to report the

strange appearance of the place, she was given the cold shoulder.

Who was the person Valerie had entertained during her last hours on earth?

The superintendent reported to the sister that Valerie had received two letters since her death, but when they looked in the mailbox, it was empty.

A friend, the owner of the restaurant Valerie had frequented, notified the telephone company to cut off service and forward the final bill to her. She was told the bill could not be found.

And so it went. Was someone covering up his traces? Sheila heard these things and went to work. To her, something was terribly wrong about her friend's death and she was going to find out what. Questioning both the restaurant owner and the girl's sister again, she came upon another strange fact. The ash trays Ethel had found in the apartment had two different types of cigarettes in them— L&M and Winston. Valerie always smoked L&M, but who smoked Winston?

The police seem not particularly interested in pursuing the matter. They think it was Valerie herself who called them the first time, and that she just decided to end it all in a drunken stupor. That at least is the impression they gave Sheila.

The following day, Saturday, the window was still open. The rose Valerie had left behind was still on the sill, despite the windy weather of April.

That night when Sheila was putting on her jacket, she felt somebody helping her into it. She was alone, or so she thought.

It occurred to her then that Valerie's spirit was not at rest and that I might be able to help. The very least I could do was talk to her *now*, since fate had prevented me from getting to her in time.

I arranged with Betty Ritter to be ready for me the following weekend, without telling her where we would be going, of course. The date was May 6, the time 3 P.M., and Sheila was to meet us at the apartment that once belonged to Valerie, but now was cleaned out and ready for the next occupant. The superintendent agreed to let us in, perhaps sensing why we had come or not caring. At any rate he opened the tenth floor apartment and left us alone inside.

As we reached the elevator of the East Sixty-third Street building, Betty Ritter suddenly remarked that she felt death around her. I nodded and we went upstairs.

As soon as we had stepped through the door into Valerie's place, Betty became a psychic bloodhound. Making straight for the window—now closed—she touched it and withdrew in horror, then turned around and looked at me.

"There is a man here jumping around like mad," she said, "but there is also someone else here—I am impressed with the initial E." She then took off her coat and started to walk toward the bathroom. There she stopped and looked back at me.

"I hear a woman screaming...I saw blood...now I see the initial M...she was harmed...it is like suicide... as if she couldn't take it any more."

Betty had difficulty holding back her emotions and was breathing heavily.

"She left *two* behind," she said. "I see the initials L. and S."

Betty Ritter, not a trance medium but essentially a clairvoyant, is very strong on initials, names, letters, and other forms of identification and she would naturally work that way even in this case.

"I heard her say, 'Mama, Mama'—she is very agitated."

"I also get a man's spirit here...initial J."

"How did this girl die?" I interjected at this point.

"She couldn't take it any more. She shows the initial R. This is a living person. She gulped something, I think."

I thought that Betty was picking up past impressions now and wanted to get her away from that area into the current layer of imprints.

"How exactly did she die?" I queried the medium. Betty had no idea where she was or why I had brought her here.

"I think she tried...pills...blood...one way or the other...in the past. She was a little afraid but she did plan this. She is very disturbed now and she does not know how to get out of this apartment. I get the initial G. with her."

I asked Betty to convey our sympathies to her and ask her if there was something she wished us to do.

While Betty talked to the spirit woman in a low voice, I reflected on her evidence so far. The initials given —E. was the first initial of Valerie's sister's name, Ethel, M. was Mary, her mother, and G. the manager of the company with whom she had had a relationship—it all seemed to make sense. Betty Ritter had also correctly "gotten" the attempted suicide by pills and pointed out the window as a "hot" area.

What was to follow now?

"She is crying," Betty reported. "She wants her loved ones to know that she didn't mean it. She shows me the head of an Indian and it is a symbol of a car—a brand name I think—it's red—the initial H. comes with this and then she shows me writing, something she has left unfinished. She asks her mother to forgive her because she could not help herself."

I decided to ask Valerie some important questions through the medium. Was she alone at the time of her death?

"Not alone. Initial A. A man, I feel him walking out of the door. Agitating her, agitating her."

"Was he with her when she died or did he leave before?"

"She says, 'I slammed the door on him.' And then she says, 'And then I did it.' "

"Why?"

"I had gone completely out of my mind...could not think straight...he drove me to it...."

"This man is a living person?"

"Yes."

"Is he aware of what happened to her?"

"Yes."

"Did she know him well?"

"Yes, definitely."

"What was his connection with her?"

Betty was herself pretty agitated now; in psychic parlance, she was really hot.

"I see a bag of money," she reported, "and the letters M. or W."

I handed her some personal belongings of Valerie's, brought to the scene in a shopping bag by Sheila and now placed on the stove for Betty to touch. She first took up a pendant—costume jewelry—and immediately felt the owner's vibrations.

"How I loved this," she mumbled. "I see D. R., Doctor...this was given to her and there is much love here in connection with this...this goes way back...."

Somehow the personalities of Betty Ritter and Valerie K. melted into one now and Betty, not quite herself, seemed not to listen any more to my queries, but instead kept talking as if she were Valerie, yet with Betty's own voice and intonation.

"There's so much I wanted to say and I couldn't at the time...."

Now returning to herself again, she spoke of a man in spirit, who was very agitated and who had possessed the woman, not a ghost but someone who had died...an older man who had a link with her in the past. J.W. Dark-skinned, but not Negro—India or that part of the world."

It struck me suddenly that she might be talking of Valerie's late husband, the man she had married long ago in Hong King; he was much older than she at the time.

"I have a feeling of falling," Betty suddenly said, "I don't know why. May have something to do with her."

I decided to let her walk around the entire apartment and to try to pick up "hot" areas. She immediately went for the lefthand window.

"Something terrible happened here...this is the room...right here...stronger here...."

"Is there another woman involved in this story?" I asked.

"I see the initial M." Betty replied, "and she is with a man who is living, and there is also some jealousy regarding a woman's boyfriend...she could not take it."

I decided to start the exorcism immediately.

"It's such a short time ago that she went," Betty remarked. "She wants to greet Mary...or Marie...and an L. To tell L. she is relieved now. Just carry on as usual."

L. was the initial of Lynn, the girl at the office who had encountered the strange happenings with the earrings.

I decided to test this connection.

"Did she communicate with L. in any way?" I asked.

"Yes," Betty nodded, "I see her by L.'s bed...perhaps she frightened her...but now she knows...didn't mean to frighten her...she is leaving now, never wants to get back again...."

We were quiet for a moment.

"She's throwing us kisses now," Betty added.

"She would do that," Sheila confirmed, "that was the way she would do it."

And that was that.

Betty lit a cigarette and relaxed, still visibly shaken by the communications for which she had been the carrier.

We put Valerie's pitiful belongings back into the paper bag and left the apartment, which now looked shiny and new, having been given a hasty coat of paint to make it ready for the next occupant.

No further snatching of jewelry from anyone's ears occurred after that, and even Sheila, my friend, no longer tried to reopen the case despite her belief that there was more to it than met the eyes of the police.

We decided to allow Valerie a peaceful transition and not to stir up old wounds that would occur with a reopening of the case.

But somehow I can't quite bring myself to forget a scene, a scene I only "saw" through the eyes of a laconic police detective making a routine report: the tall, lovely Asian woman, intoxicated and nude, slamming the door on the police...and two liquor glasses on her table.

Who was that other glass for...and who smoked the second cigarette, the brand Valerie never smoked?

Who, then, was the man who left her to die?

✳ 131

The Warning Ghost

NOT ALL GHOSTS have selfish motives, so to speak, in reasserting their previous ownership of a home: some even help later occupants, although the limits of a ghost's rationality are very narrow. For one thing, if a ghost personality is aware of later inhabitants of a house and wants to communicate with them—not in order to get them out but to warn them—such a ghost is still unable to realize that the warning may be entirely unnecessary because time has passed, and the present reality no longer corresponds to the reality he or she knew when his or her own tragedy occurred.

Still, there is the strange case of Rose S., now a resident of New York State, but at one time living in Fort Worth, Texas. Miss S. is a secretary by profession, and during the mid-1960s worked for a well-known social leader. That summer, Miss S. moved into an old house in Fort Worth, renting a room at one end of the house. At the time, she wanted to be near her fiancé, an army pilot who was stationed not far away.

The old house she chanced upon was located on Bryce Avenue, in one of the older sections of Fort Worth. The owner was renting out a furnished room because the house had become too large for her. Her husband, an attorney, had passed away, and their children were all grown and living away from home.

The house seemed pleasant enough, and the room large and suitable, so Miss S. was indeed happy to have found it. Moreover, her landlady did not restrict her to the rented room, but allowed her to use the kitchen and in fact have the freedom of the house, especially as there were no other tenants. The landlady seemed a pleasant enough woman in her middle or late sixties at the time, and except for an occasional habit of talking to herself, there was nothing particularly unusual about her. Miss S. looked forward to a pleasant, if uneventful stay at the house on Bryce Avenue.

Not long after moving in, it happened that the landlady went off to visit a daughter in Houston, leaving the house entirely to Miss S. That night, Rose S. decided to read and then retire early. As soon as she switched off the lights to go to sleep, she began to hear footsteps walking around the house. At the same time, the light in the bathroom, which she had intended to leave on all night, started to grow dimmer and brighter alternately, which puzzled her. Frightened because she thought she had to face an intruder, Miss S. got up to investigate, but found not a living soul anywhere in the house. She then decided that the whole thing was simply her imagination acting up because she had been left alone in the house for the first time, and went to bed. The days passed and the incident was forgotten. A few weeks later, the landlady was again off for Houston, but this time Miss S.'s fiancé was visiting her. It was evening, and the couple was spending the time after dinner relaxing.

Miss S.'s fiancé, the pilot, had fallen asleep. Suddenly, in the quiet of the night, Miss S. heard someone whistle loudly and clearly from the next room. It was a marching song, which vaguely reminded her of the well-known melody, the Colonel Bogey March. Neither TV nor radio were playing at the time, and there was no one about. When she realized that the source of the whistling was uncanny, she decided not to tell her fiancé, not wishing to upset him.

Time went on, and another periodical trip by her landlady left Miss S. alone again in the house. This time she was in the TV den, trying to read and write. It was a warm night, and the air conditioner was on.

As she was sitting there, Miss S. gradually got the feeling that she was not alone. She had the distinct impression that someone was watching her, and then there came the faint whining voice of a woman above the sound of the air conditioner. The voice kept talking, and though Miss S. tried to ignore it, she had to listen. Whether by voice or telepathy, she received the impression that she was not to stay in the house, and that the voice was warning her to move out immediately. After another restless night with very little sleep, Miss S. decided she could take the phenomena no longer.

As soon as the landlady returned, she informed her that she was leaving, and moved in with friends temporarily. Eventually, her experiences at the house on Bryce Avenue aroused her curiosity and she made some quiet inquiries. It was then that she discovered the reasons for the haunting. On the very corner where the house stood, a woman and a girl had been murdered by a man while waiting for a bus. As if that were not enough to upset her, something happened to her fiancé from that moment on. Following the incident with the whistling ghost, of which her fiancé knew nothing, his behavior towards her changed drastically. It was as if he was not quite himself anymore, but under the influence of another personality. Shortly afterwards, Miss S. and her pilot broke off their engagement.

✳ 132

Jacqueline

JOHN K. IS TWENTY-SIX years old, lives in Hollywood and works as a freight cashier at a steamship company. "I don't quite know where to begin," he said when he contacted me in May 1971. He explained that he felt he was being harassed by reincarnation memories or by someone he thought was in some mysterious way connected with his personality. Since I am always on the lookout for "evidential" reincarnation cases, I was naturally interested. In October of the same year we met at the Continental Hotel in Hollywood. Mr. K. turned out to be a slight, quiet-spoken young man far from hysterical and not particularly involved with the occult. Gradually I pieced his amazing story together and discovered what lay at the base of his strange and terrifying experiences.

John K. was born in a small town in the Ozarks with a population of only forty-two people. The house he was born and raised in was quite old, built before the Civil War. His family lived there until he reached the age of twelve, when they moved to another small town in southwestern Arizona. There his father was employed by the government on a nearby Army base. At the age of twenty, Mr. K. dropped out of college after his junior year and headed straight for Los Angeles, where he has lived ever since.

His first twelve years in the Ozarks were spent on a farm with five brothers and two sisters. The family lived a very primitive life. There was no indoor plumbing; heat was provided by a coal stove, and each Saturday night the entire family would take turns bathing in the same tub of water. At first there was no electricity in the house. For the first three grades, Mr. K. went to a one-room schoolhouse. "Our teacher was very young and had not yet finished her college education but was permitted to teach us anyway."

Mr. K. explained, "The reason I am relating all of my earlier surroundings to you is to point out the fact that the first twelve years of my life I lived a very isolated existence." Until he reached the age of ten, Mr. K. had not seen a television set; entertainment in his family consisted mainly of playing cards and talking. He attended the local Southern Baptist Church, into which he was duly baptized; however, after the family left the farm they dropped out of organized religion.

From an early age John K. received the impression of a presence which no one else could see. None of his immediate family had ever been out of the country, yet he was aware of the presence of a French lady whose name, he came to know, as Jacqueline. When he mentioned the presence of this woman to his family he was laughed at and told that he had a fantastic imagination, so he stopped talking about it. At an early age he also developed the ability to dream of events that later happened *exactly* as seen in his dreams. These prophetic dreams did not forecast great events but concerned themselves with everyday matters. Nevertheless, they were upsetting to the boy. He never remembered his dreams, but when the event became objective reality he started to shiver and realized he had seen it all before. This, of course, is called *déjà vu* and is a fairly common ESP phenomenon. He could not discuss his dreams with his family, since psychic experiences were not the kind of thing one could talk about in the Ozarks in the early fifties. But he hated to stay in the house alone; he had a terrible fear of darkness and of the house itself.

One afternoon when he was ten years old, he happened to be in the house alone, upstairs in the back bedroom. All of a sudden he knew there was a presence there, and the most horrifying fear swept through him, as if he were being choked to death. The walls seemed to vibrate, and he heard a loud sound for which there did not seem to be any natural explanation. Eventually he was able to break out of his terror and flee down the stairs.

There was something else that seemed strange about John K. from an early age on. He could never relate to men and felt completely at ease only with women—his grandmother, his mother, and his older sister. When he was very young, he began playing with his older sister, six years his senior, and enjoyed playing girls' games tremendously. He would never join his brothers in boys' games. He loved wearing long flowing dresses, fashions of an earlier time that he had found in the attic. Whenever he wore these dresses, he felt completely at ease and seemed to have a rather sophisticated air about him. The strange thing was that he insisted on wearing only those dresses of an earlier period of history; the shorter dresses of the current era interested him not at all. At those times he felt as though he were another person.

It was during those early childhood days that he first became aware of Jacqueline. Especially when he played with his sister, he felt that he was sexually just like her. He continued to wear dresses around the house until the time he started to school. Often when he came home from school he would go upstairs and put on his dresses. Finally, his father became aware of the boy's tendency and threatened to send him to school wearing a dress if he didn't stop, so John stopped. However, the impression of a female life inside him and the desire to wear long dresses persisted.

"Needless to say," Mr. K. explained in complete frankness, "I was not the average run-of-the-mill boy, and I turned out to be very effeminate and was teased constantly by my schoolmates." Rejected by the other boys, he began to turn within himself and did not bother to explain his ideas to others. Although he had never traveled outside the four southern states surrounding his native village, he began to feel very emotional about France, particularly Paris. "I somehow seemed to have fond memories of a life of many human pleasures, a life of a woman who was very aware and felt a need to express herself totally," John K. explained, adding that he knew by that time that Jacqueline, whoever she might have been, had led the life of a prostitute. He thus had a sense of heavy religious condemnation, of being a wicked sinner with the threat of hell hanging over him.

When the family finally moved to Arizona, he thought that perhaps some of his agonies would subside. But the conflict between his present surroundings and the world of Jacqueline increased almost daily. At the age of fourteen he felt that since he could not belong to this world he might as well kill himself and return to where he really belonged. He wrote a farewell note to his mother, the only one to whom he could relate at the time, his sister having married and his grandmother having grown old and feeble. In the note he told his mother that he was going to return to where he belonged, that he felt he had come from another planet and it was time for him to go back. He then ran a rope over one of the rafters in his room, put a chair under it, and placed the noose around his neck, ready to jump. Then fate intervened in the person of one of his mother's friends who had stopped by unexpectedly. Since his mother was asleep, John had to answer the door. The visit lasted a long time, and by the time the lady had left he was no longer in the mood to take his own life.

From then on he did rather well in school, although most people thought him too shy and introverted. He never dated girls, since he felt himself female. But he did make friends with one particular boy and remained close friends with him for ten years. Later, the boy moved to Los Angeles. When John K. dropped out of school in his junior year of college, he came to Los Angeles and moved in with his friend. At the time he was twenty years old. He still felt like a female and was still continually aware of Jacqueline.

It was then that John became involved in the homosexual world and had the first sexual experience of his life. Whenever he had sexual relations, he felt strongly that he was fulfilling the part of the woman.

About six months after he came to Los Angeles, he started to have terrible dreams. One night when he was totally awake he suddenly saw a woman standing at the foot of his bed. She was wearing a long nightgown and had long hair and was smiling at him. She seemed to float just above the floor. At first John thought that it was his imagination and passed it off as a silly dream. The next night the same thing happened. He realized the apparition wanted to tell him something. Strangely enough, he wasn't particularly frightened. The third night the apparition returned, and her smile had turned into a frown of deep sorrow. She returned the following night, and this time her face showed utter terror. Deep veins stood out on her face, her eyes were bloodshot, and her mouth grinned hideously.

She returned once again the following night, and this time her entire head had been turn off, and blood was spilled all over her beautiful flowing gown. John was fully aware of the utter torment of her soul. That same night something grabbed hold of his arm and forcibly yanked him out of bed and onto the floor. He screamed for help from his roommate, who was in the next room, but the young man had no compassion for his condition and yelled out for John to shut up or he would have him committed. After this incident John thought he was going mad and wondered to whom he could turn for advice.

A few months passed. He was still living in Hollywood with the same roommate but by this time was a prostitute himself. He had gone to college and found himself a good job, but he had had a strong urge to become a prostitute, and so followed it. Whenever he engaged in these activities he felt a very deep satisfaction. Also at this time he resumed wearing female clothes, and since his roommate was a make-up artist by profession, he would do the make-up for him. John would never go into the streets in this array; he would wear these clothes only at home. His friends began to call him Jackie, for Jacqueline.

Whenever he put on the clothes, John became another person. The first time he saw himself in complete make-up and female clothing he felt that Jacqueline had won at last. He now felt that she had taken total possession of him and that he was cursed for life.

"It was not a simple case of transvestitism or going in female drag," John explained, "It was a complete soul satisfaction on my part, and when Jacqueline came out she controlled me completely. She was very strong and I was very weak."

It finally reached the point that when John came home at night he would dress up in female clothing and spend the entire evening in this manner. He even slept in evening gowns. He removed all the hair from his body and delighted in taking baths and dousing himself with perfumes. This went on for two years, until John felt that something had to be done about it. He realized something was wrong with him.

About that time another friend introduced him to Buddhism. For three years he practiced the Buddhist religion, and through it was able to find many answers for himself that had eluded him before. Because of his devotion to Buddhism, Jacqueline finally left, never to return again. A new male image began to emerge slowly but surely as a result of his Buddhist practices, and once again he was able to relate to the environment around him and find a reason for living.

Through a friend, John received my address. He contacted me in the hope I might hypnotize him and regress him to an earlier life in which he might encounter Jacqueline. John was firmly convinced that his predicament had been due to an unfulfilled reincarnation problem, and that perhaps through hypnosis I might put him further on the road to recovery.

"I never felt fulfillment during my pre-Buddhist sexual contacts while portraying Jacqueline," he told me, "but it did satisfy my Jacqueline personality completely. But she is totally gone now and a new John is emerging—one who is not afraid of the dark anymore and who can live alone and stand on his own two feet, and who will someday marry a girl and have a family. I am very optimistic about the future."

Although neither John nor his immediate family had had any interest in or knowledge of occult practices, this was not entirely true of others in his background. An Aunt Mary had been a practicing witch, had owned many books dealing with witchcraft of the fifteenth and sixteenth cen-

turies, and had been a sore subject in the family. Nobody dared talk about her. But she had died before John was born, and all knowledge John had of his Aunt Mary was necessarily secondhand. Nevertheless, there had been ESP talents in the family on his father's side, mainly messages from dead relatives, though John was never able to obtain any details. In his family the occult was something not suitable for family conversation.

After Jacqueline had left John, he kept having ESP experiences unrelated to his ordeal. They were not world-shaking experiences, but they did convince him that his ESP faculty had remained unimpaired by the hold Jacqueline had exercised upon him for so many years. A short time before our meeting there had been a steamship strike and he was laid off. He was wondering if he should get another job outside the steamship industry when he had a strange dream. In the dream he saw his boss at the steamship company coming out of his office and saying to someone, "Call John K. back to work." At the same time he saw the number 7 flash through the dream. Upon awakening he remembered every detail. On September 7 his boss came out of his office and told an aide, "Call John K. back to work," and, as foreseen in the dream, he returned to his former position.

I was rather interested in his continuing ESP experiences since I had begun to wonder whether Jacqueline was indeed a reincarnation memory or perhaps something else. We proceeded to begin hypnotic regression. I first took John K. down to age twenty, when he remembered every detail of his life. He even remembered the names of his best friends and what was on his desk at the time. I then took him back to age twelve and his life in Missouri. In each case he even knew his exact height at the time. He knew the names of the nearest neighbors, how many children they had and even the name of their dog. Satisfied that he was deeply in the third stage of hypnotic regression, I then took him back beyond the threshold of birth into an alleged earlier life. I worked very hard and very gradually to see whether we could locate some other personality that had been John K. in a previous lifetime, but he saw nothing. I then asked him to look specifically for Jacqueline.

"Do you know who she is?" I asked.
"She is someone who doesn't like me."
"Is she a real person?"
"Yes."
"Have you ever lived in France?"
"No."

I then took him as far back as the Middle Ages, fifty years at a time, in case there were other incarnations. When we got to the year 1350, he said he felt very strange and put his hands upon his chest in a gesture I interpreted as religious. But there was no recognition of another person. I then took him, step by step, back into the present, finally awakening him, and then inquiring how he felt. Since John was a good hypnotic subject, he remembered absolutely nothing of what he had said during hypnosis.

"Do you feel different from the way you felt fifteen minutes ago?" I inquired.

"Well, I had a headache before I came; I don't have a headache now."

He felt well-rested and satisfied with himself. Jacqueline had not put in an appearance, as she would have if she had been part of John K. I then explained to the young man that his ordeal had not been caused by reincarnation memories or an unfulfilled earlier lifetime. To the contrary, he had been victimized by an independent entity, not related to him in any way, who had somehow sought him out to serve as her medium of expression in the physical world. Jacqueline, the French prostitute, whose choice of clothes indicated that she had lived in the nineteenth century, wanted to live in this century through another body. For reasons of her own she had chosen a male body for her experiment.

If there was any reincarnation connection between the two, it remained obscure. There is, of course, the possibility that John K. had been in another life someone close to Jacqueline, in her time, and had since reincarnated while Jacqueline had not, and that the woman attached herself to John K. just as soon as she could after his birth into the present life. I myself tend to favor this theory. It is unfortunate that this earlier John K. could not be rediscovered either consciously or in hypnosis. But if this earlier incarnation had led a fully satisfactory life, the need to retain traces of memory would not be there.

In the case of Jacqueline, her inner conflict between what she was doing and the religious pressure exerted upon her must have been the compelling factor in keeping her in a time slot, or, rather, suspended in time, preventing her from reincarnating herself. In her predicament and frustration she needed to express herself through someone in the present, since she could not herself go on and be someone else. Deprived of her medium, Jacqueline perhaps will have found an avenue of escape into the next stage of existence and hopefully will not be heard from again.

✳ 133

The Wurmbrand Curse

ONE OF THE STRANGEST cases I have ever investigated took me from sunny California to the dank, dark recesses of an Austrian castle, a case so strange that I am still hard put to find a parallel in the annals of psychic research. And yet all this happened only yesterday, in the practical 1960s, barely two hours from a spanking new jetport.

It all began in Vienna in 1964, when my good friend Turhan Bey told me of a haunted castle belonging to a friend of his who resided in Hollywood. The friend's name was von Wurmbrand, and Turhan promised to introduce us. But somehow the matter slipped our minds at the time.

Fate, however, had meant for me to meet this man, apparently, for in November of the same year I received a letter from Count Wurmbrand, telling me he had read *Ghost Hunter*, and thought possibly I could help him solve his psychic problem. What had called me to his attention was not only my book but a silly newspaper article in the Vienna *Volksblatt*, a newspaper of very minor importance that had seen fit to ridicule my work. The article had dealt with the ghost at Forchtenstein reported by me in *Ghosts I've Met*.

Subsequently, I met the Count at the Hotel Roosevelt in Hollywood. Over lunch, we talked of his predicament and I promised to come to Steyersberg, his ancestral castle, that very summer. The Count, over six feet tall, was an imposing figure of a man, very much old world, but with a dash of the practical American intermingled with his historical background.

This was not surprising, since he had resided in California since 1927 and was an American citizen, married—a second marriage for him—to an American woman considerably his junior, with whom he lived at an impeccably decorated house in the Hollywood hills.

The house, which I only got to know after the Count's untimely death, is a far cry from the enormous expanse of the Steyersberg castle, but in its own way it was a perfect home, perfect for the two people who lived there happily for many years. For whatever the sinister aspects of the story, they had no powers under the warming rays of the California sun.

Degenhard von Wurmbrand was dressed conservatively—for California, anyway—in a gray business suit, but being Austrian, he was anything but stuffy. His conversation sparkled with wit and charm; his English of course was excellent, and we spent a pleasant hour together. Unfortunately I was under great pressure at the time from television work, so I could not come to his home on Bluebird Avenue.

He was seventy-two years old and, as a former Imperial officer, carried himself so erectly as to belie his years. Nothing about him gave a hint of illness or weakness, a point I find rather important in the light of later events.

It was his custom to visit his castle in the mountains of Austria every summer, to join his sister, the widowed Countess Kolowrat, in a few weeks of vacationing at a place that had been in their family for centuries past. The Wurmbrand family goes back to the Middle Ages, and its members held high honors in the Austrian Empire.

After 1939, Degenhard did not return to his castle in the summer because of the war, and only his American ownership of the estate prevented the Russians from sacking it toward the end of the Second World War. His younger brother actually administered it until his death in 1960, while Degenhard continued a carefree existence in Hollywood. But there was always a shadow, an ever present threat that even the warmth of California could not dispel.

Degenhard von Wurmbrand had grown up in the enormous castle, a gray building of some sixty rooms perched atop a tree-covered mountain some 49 miles south of Vienna, not terribly far from the busy Schwechat airport and yet remote in many ways—as we were to learn later that year. But as the Imperial Count—his full title was His Excellency, the Imperial Count of Wurmbrand-Stuppach—grew up in the castle, he was soon to learn that it harbored a terrible secret. He shared a room with his younger brother in the oldest wing of the castle, a wing going back well into the early seventeenth century and beyond. Although Steyersberg has been completely modernized and has a bathroom for each bedroom, no structural changes whatever have changed its original appearance.

The room the two boys occupied, back at the turn of the century, was a tower room looking out onto the moat below and the rolling hills of Styria in the distance. It is in what is now the top floor of that wing, looming considerably above the surrounding landscape. I have looked out of that window at the corner of the room where you can see both eastward and southward, and the isolation, the feeling of remoteness, is intense. The room the boys shared was connected to another tower room by a dark corridor. Their sister Huberta occupied that other room. Underneath, the castle extended well into the rock.

Degenhard was now six years old and on his own, so to speak; his younger brother still had a nurse who shared the accommodations with the two children. The younger boy was two.

It was dark early that evening and nothing but blackness could be seen outside the windows. The nearest village is miles away and no lights break the enveloping shadows. The nurse was reading a book—it was only about 7 p.m.—and the only light in the large room came from a small kerosene lamp on her night table. The younger boy was already asleep but Degenhard could not close his eyes. Somehow this night seemed different to him. Perhaps the budding sixth sense had already manifested itself at this early age, for Count Wurmbrand later became very psychic and was so to his end.

At any rate, the six-year-old was in bed, but fully awake, when his eyes happened to glance toward the corridor connecting the two rooms. Suddenly, he saw three black crows emerge from the corridor—flying into their room!

As the startled boy watched the strange birds which had seemingly come out of thin air, one of the crows alighted on the headboard of his brother's bed, while two perched on his bed. This was enough for him—instantly he pulled the blanket over his head. When he came up for air a moment later, there was no trace of the birds, and the nurse was reading quietly. She had not seen anything. Evidently the birds had meaning only for members of the Wurmbrand family!

When I visited Steyersberg Castle with my wife Catherine on September 6, 1965, Count Wurmbrand took me to that very room. Except for the soft carpeting now covering the floor wall to wall and the up-to-date bathroom fixtures, it had not changed very much. The view from the windows was still breathtaking.

Again, it was dark outside, as the air was heavy with rain which had come down continuously all day. It was now four in the afternoon but the atmosphere was forbidding and depressing. The instant I set foot into that part of the castle, I felt myself pulled down and somehow found myself speaking in hushed tones. The Count suddenly looked very, very tired and old—quite different from the athletic Lord of the Manor who had greeted us at his gates earlier that day. Was the atmosphere of the room transforming him too?

We discussed the past of the rock upon which the castle was built; originally erected in 1180, it passed into the Wurmbrand family in 1530 but it had fallen into disrepair when Degenhard's father rebuilt it. Degenhard himself added the bathrooms and other American touches, making it probably one of the best appointed old castles in the world.

Then our conversation turned to the ghostly crows.

"I have wondered all my life what it meant," the Count said. "I can see them even now!"

The specter of the crows—and other uncanny experiences, noises, footsteps where no one walked—troubled him through the years. But it was not until 1950 that he learned a little more about his predicament and what it meant.

"There was a German clairvoyant in California at the time," the Count explained, "and out of curiosity I went to see her. Immediately she drew back and asked me, 'What is this black entity I see behind you?' She thought I was *possessed*."

"Possessed?" I said. Had a ghost left the castle and travelled all the way to Hollywood? Impossible. Ghosts stay put.

The clairvoyant wondered where the Count could have "picked up" this possessing force, and he could not think of any meaningful incident—except the appearance of the ghostly crows. The clairvoyant then made an appointment for Count Wurmbrand to see a Buddhist priest specializing in exorcising the possessed.

Did it do any good?" I asked. The plot was becoming international.

"He did the ceremony three times," the count recalled, "but after the first attempt I questioned him about the whole thing."

The Buddhist priest, who knew nothing whatever about the Count or his background, evidently was also a medium. He described three ragged men around the Count, men who protested their expulsion since they had some unfinished business.

The Buddhist priest asked that they explain themselves, and the restless spirits informed him that two ancestors of the Count's had done them wrong; having accused them falsely of treason, these earlier Wurmbrands had then tortured and killed the men in their castle. Even though this had happened a long time ago, the victims wanted revenge. They wanted the Count to kill, to commit a crime. That was their way of getting even for a wrong done in 1710!

Count Wurmbrand thought all this very strange, but then he recalled with terrifying suddenness how he had often felt an almost uncontrollable desire to kill, to commit murder—he, a normally gentle, peace-loving man.

Another thought struck him as he walked out of the Hollywood priest's house. All the phenomena of an uncanny nature had taken place in the room where he had seen the three crows—and that room was in a direct line above the dungeon. His father had ordered the ancient dungeon walled up, and it is inaccessible to this day; to get into it, one would have to break down a thick wall. If anyone had been done to death at Steyersberg Castle, it was at that spot.

Count Wurmbrand examined the historical records concerning his ancestors. In 1710 the castle belonged to a different branch of the family, and, oddly enough, two men shared ownership and command, for they were also generals in the Imperial army. Thus the ghosts' reference to two men having done them wrong made sense.

Nothing much happened to the Count in the subsequent years that would have reminded him of the ancient curse. But in 1961 he returned to Austria again and there he met a lady who had been a friend of his father's and brother's. She was the only person interested in psychic matters the Count knew, outside of himself, and she therefore confided in him without reservation in such areas.

It appeared that a séance had been held at the castle in his absence, at which a then-famed Vienna medium was present along with the lady and his brother. The man went into trance in one of the rooms of the castle. Suddenly, the electric lights dimmed quite by themselves for no apparent reason. Then they clearly heard heavy footfalls where nobody was seen walking. The lady had had enough and left the room, leaving the continuance of the séance to his brother.

After a while, Count Ernst also left and went to his room. But the invisible footsteps followed him right to his room. This so unnerved him that he asked the medium for further advice. The man offered to do his best, and, without having any foreknowledge of the events that had happened so many years ago in the boys' bedroom above the dungeon, went directly to that room although he could have gone to some fifty others.

"This is where I want to sleep," he explained, and so he did. The following morning he was none the worse for it.

The ghost had indeed communicated with him the night before. He complained of having been wrongly imprisoned for treason and tortured by the two ancestor-generals. It was exactly the same story the Buddhist had told Count Wurmbrand in Hollywood—with one notable exception: here only one man claimed to have been wronged, only one ghost.

"Was that all?" I asked. It had been quite a story.

"Not entirely," Count Wurmbrand explained in a voice that grew slowly more tired as night fell outside. "The curse included a provision for happiness. No Wurmbrand should ever have a happy marriage within these walls, the ghost claimed. And no Wurmbrand ever has."

I took some photographs in the haunted room, photographs that later showed remarkable superimpositions. Although my camera, double-exposure-proof due to a lock mechanism, cannot take anything but square pictures, I came up with a triple picture of oblong shape, showing areas of the room that were actually in back of me, areas the camera could not possibly have photographed under ordinary conditions—and there was no mirror or window effect to account for it in the room. These pictures are now among my psychic photographs and I treasure them highly.

Another remarkable thing about them, however, was the way Count Wurmbrand looked in one of them. Very tired and ill, as if the shadows that were to come were already being etched on his face by supernormal means!

I did not want to strain my host, but there were some loose ends I wanted to clear up before we returned to the others. Because the Count's sister was not too keen on the subject, or so he left—wrongly, as I later discovered—he and I had gone to the haunted room alone, leaving my wife to discuss music and art with Countess Juliana Wurmbrand and Countess Kolowrat, the sister.

"Outside of yourself, your brother Ernst and of course the medium, has anyone else experienced anything out of the ordinary in this castle?" I asked.

"During the years when I was in America, the lady I mentioned before who had brought the medium here once brought here a man who was not of the best character. He was a member of the Nazi party, so intentionally she put him into the haunted room. The next morning, he complained bitterly about it. There had been terrific noises all night and people 'trying to come in all the time.' Some force had tried to force itself into the room, he claimed."

Were there any records of the treason trial referred to by the ghost? We went down into the library of the castle, which was on the first floor and even nearer to the walled-up dungeon. It was an ill-lit, long room filled with manuscripts, some in a state of disorder and all covered with dust. A cursory examination yielded nothing of help.

"When was the last time you felt uneasy here?" I asked, finally.

"I wouldn't sleep in this room, I assure you," the Count answered. Earlier he had told me that the curse was still hanging over him and he had never really felt *safe* from it.

When he was at the castle, he simply avoided the areas he considered haunted and lived only in the other portions. There were the living and dining rooms, magnificent in their splendor and appointments, furnished as only a very old family can furnish their house. His own apartments were in one of the other wings, quite a walk from the big fireplace that graced the large dining room to which we now returned.

The day had been a long one, and one fraught with strange incidents. Somehow it felt like the script of a Hollywood horror movie, only we were not reading it—we were in it!

I had accepted the invitation to come to Steyersberg and been given exact instructions on how to get there. Countless Kolowrat even sent me a picture postcard with the many-turreted castle on it, so I could not possibly miss it.

I hired a car in Vienna, only to discover on the very morning of our intended visit that the car had broken down and we could not go. I then telephoned Count Wurmbrand and he sent his own car and chauffeur to fetch us.

When we neared the Schlossberg, or castle hill, after about an hour's ride through the foothills of the Austrian Alps, we found the country more and more isolated and primitive.

As we started to climb the hill to get up to the top where the castle could be seen already from some distance, the chauffeur honked his horn to advise the castle of our coming. When we rounded the final curve of the road, an incomparable sight greeted us: just inside the gray stone castle gates, as we rolled into the yard, there stood, awaiting us at attention, the butler, dressed in white jacket and dark pants, a maid in Victorian uniform, and a third servant.

By the time we had gotten out of the car with all my camera and tape equipment, Count Wurmbrand himself was walking slowly toward us from the main entrance, giving us an old-fashioned welcome.

From that moment on, we spent a delightful day in a world one regretted to leave. Unfortunately, we had already —and foolishly—committed ourselves to leave Vienna in the morning, so we could not stay over. We promised to return the following summer with Sybil Leek and finish off the ghost and the curse.

That, at least, was our intention, and we corresponded with the Wurmbrands on and off, until we could set a date for our return.

Then, suddenly, there was silence. In December of 1965, I received a black-bordered letter bearing an Austrian postmark. Instinctively I knew what it meant before I opened it.

It was the official notification that my friend had passed away on November 17, and had been buried with all honors due him in the patron's church at nearby Kirchau, one of the villages "belonging" to the Steyersberg domain.

I was not satisfied with this formal announcement: I wanted to know more. Had not my friend been in excellent health when we last saw him?

In June of 1966 I spent some time in Hollywood, and it was then that I finally saw the California home of the Wurmbrands. Countess Juliana brought me up to date on events.

Her husband had been taken ill with a minor complaint, but one sufficiently important to be looked after in a good hospital. There was no danger, nor was he indeed suffering very deeply. Several days went by and the Count became impatient, eager to return to active life again. Juliana visited him regularly, and if anything was wrong with my friend, it was his distaste at being in the hospital at all.

Then one night he had a small blood clot. Normally, a quick treatment is possible and the outcome need not be fatal. But that night, the doctor could somehow not be found in time, and precious moments ticked off. By the time help came, it was too late. Count Wurmbrand had died of an unrelated accident, an accident that need not have happened nor been fatal to him. Had the fingers of fate, the far-reaching rays of a grim curse finally reached their last victim?

For the Count died without direct male heir bearing this illustrious name, and so it is that the Wurmbrand Castle is no longer in the hands of a Count Wurmbrand as I write this account of the strange curse that followed a man from Austria to sunny California, and back again to Austria. Who knows, if Degenhard von Wurmbrand had remained in California in 1965 he might still be alive.

I know this to be so, for I spoke to him briefly in the fall of 1964 when I passed through Hollywood. He was not sure at the time whether he could see us at his Castle in the summer of 1965 or not.

"Something tells me not to go," he said gravely.

"Then you should not," I advised. A man's intuition, especially when he is psychic and has had premonitions all his life as Wurmbrand had, should be heeded.

But the Count had business in Austria and in the end he relented and went, never to return to California. Thus it was that, before I could do anything about it, the Wurmbrand curse had found its mark.

✳ 134

Dick Turpin, My Love

DURING THE SUMMER OF 1973, I received a strangely elaborate and pleading letter from a young woman by the name of Cynthia von Rupprath-Snitily. The name itself was fascinating enough to warrant my further interest, but what the lady had to say concerning her strange experiences with the unknown would have attracted me even if her name had been Smith or Jones.

Cynthia had been born December 31, 1948 in Chicago, and lived in the same house until twenty-one years of age, leaving the area only to attend college at Northern Illinois University in De Kalb, Illinois. Immediately I recalled my own visit to Northern Illinois University, a huge college set in a very small town in the middle of the Illinois plains, a school which seemed forever to battle the narrow-mindedness of the surrounding town, while catering to a very large student body bent on exploring the further reaches of the human mind. Cynthia holds a Bachelor's degree in both history and art, and is an art historian by profession. "I have dealt with both fictitious legend and concrete fact," she stated, "and therefore I have knowledge of the fine lines that sometimes separate these two entities. I have thus carried over the cognizance to my everyday life and have incorporated it into my style of thinking. In truth, I am my own worst critic."

In 1970 she married a man she had met at the University of Notre Dame and moved to his home town of Seattle, Washington, where he was employed at Boeing Aircraft. With the termination of the SST project, her husband enlisted in the Air Force and at the time of contacting me they were stationed at the Edwards Air Force Base in California, about an hour's drive from Los Angeles.

Cynthia had always been a serious and sensitive person, perhaps because she was an only child of parents forty years older than herself. As a result she felt more at ease with older people, preferring their company to that of her own age. Due to her sensitivity, she was in the habit of becoming rather emotional in matters of impact to her. In

order to offset this strong character trait and in view of her profession, she tried very hard to develop a logical and orderly method of approach to things, and to think matters over several times before taking any specific course of action. Thus, when she realized that she had psychic experiences from childhood onward and saw them continue in her life, she decided to analyze and investigate the phenomena in which she was a central element. She soon realized that her psychic ability had been inherited on her mother's side of the family; her maternal grandparents had come to the United States from Croatia. Deeply embedded in the culture of many Croatian people is the belief in witchcraft, and the ability by some country folk to do unusual things or experience the uncanny. But Cynthia's attitude towards these phenomena remained critical. "I am not overwilling to accept such phenomena without further investigation," she explained. One case in particular impressed her, since it involved her personally.

"This case is unusual because it has occurred to three successive generations through the years. In the 1910s my grandmother was living in Chicago performing household tasks, when a neighbor dressed entirely in black came to the door. The latter woman was commonly known as a 'strega' and my grandmother naturally was not too happy to see her. The woman wanted to know what my grandmother was cooking in the pot on the stove. My grandmother refused and told the woman to leave, whereupon the latter reported that she would return that night, 'to find that which she was seeking.' That night while my grandparents, my mother, and my Uncle Bill were all sleeping in the same bed, the door suddenly blew open and my mother recalls seeing my grandmother literally struggling with some unseen force on the bed. Mother remembers quite vividly the movement of the mattress, as if something were jumping up and down on it. Certainly the sensation was stronger than a reclining figure could have inflicted. An aura of evil seemed to have invaded the room and left as quickly as did the 'force.' Years later, at the beginning of 1949, a similar event took place. My aunt was sitting in our Chicago home, feeding me a bottle, when this force again entered the scene, causing the two of us to be considerably uplifted from the couch. Again the jumping persisted and the evil presence was felt. The next performance by this "thing" occurred in the early months of 1971 in Seattle. It was around midnight and I was reading a novel, while my husband, Gary, slept. I suddenly sensed something wicked within the confines of our room. I tossed it off, but then there began that jumping motion. I became quite alarmed as I realized neither my sleeping husband nor my own reclined body could attest to such motion. I woke my husband, who is not psychic, and he, too, became aware of the jumping movement. It was now growing in intensity, but when I called out the Lord's name, the bed suddenly ceased pitching. It wasn't until April 1971, after moving from Seattle, that I learned of the two previous experiences."

On her father's side, Cynthia is descended from a noble German family, originally from Hanover. Her father had no interest or use for anything psychic. When Cynthia was only a few months old, her Aunt Doris came to live with the family as a temporary replacement for her mother, who was then quite ill and in the hospital. The aunt was sleeping on the living room couch, Cynthia's father in the front bedroom, and Cynthia herself in a crib placed in the back bedroom. Everyone was very much concerned with her mother's health, and her aunt, being Roman Catholic, had been praying almost around the clock. She had only been asleep for a short time, when a cold breeze awakened her and to her amazement, she saw a woman, fairly young and dressed in a nun's habit, walking slightly *above* the floor through the living room and turn down the hall toward Cynthia's room. Concerned for the little girl's safety, the aunt quickly followed the woman into the room. There she saw the nun place her hands on Cynthia's crib, look down at her and smile. She seemed quite unaware of the aunt and, her mission apparently accomplished, turned and walked down the hall. The aunt immediately checked the baby, and seeing that the child was alright, went after the apparition. When she arrived at the living room, the figure had vanished, yet there remained a strong scent of roses in the air which even Cynthia's father noticed the following morning. The scent remained in the house, even though it was winter, until Cynthia's mother came home from the hospital. There were no perfume sachets, fresh flowers, or air fresheners which could have accounted for the strange odor. The unusual scent has returned to the house from time to time and can never be satisfactorily explained; it usually coincides with an illness in the family, and has often served as a kind of telepathic warning to Cynthia's mother, when Cynthia was ill while at college. This particular event, of course, was told to Cynthia many years later at a family gathering, but it served to underline Cynthia's own awareness of her unusual faculty.

"Perhaps the most vivid and memorable personal experience occurred to me when I was in grade school," Cynthia explained. "I had always heard footsteps in the 1950s and '60s, starting in the aforementioned living room, coming into the front bedroom and stopping at my bed, both during the day and at night. My parents always

attributed the noises to the creaking of old floors, but the house was only built in 1947. At times, the footfalls backed away from the bed, thus disputing the "last footsteps before going to bed" theory. I occupied a twin bed which faced the hallway when the bedroom door was open. On the left side of the bed, my side, was the wall shared by both the living room and front bedroom; Mother slept in the other twin bed adjacent to the driveway wall.

"During one particular night, I had gotten up to go to the bathroom, and upon returning to my bed, snuggled under the covers and shot a quick glance at my sleeping mother. Suddenly, the room became exceptionally cold and on looking toward the door, which I had forgotten to close, I saw four figures coming from the living room *through* the hallway wall and turn into our bedroom. In order to assert that I hadn't unconsciously fallen asleep since returning to bed, I began pinching myself and looking from time to time to the familiar surrounding room and my mother. Thus I know I was fully awake and not dreaming. The first figure entering the room was dressed, as were all the others, in nineteenth century western American clothing. She was a woman in her forties of average height, very thin and dressed in a brown and white calico dress with high-button collar and long sleeves; her dark brown hair was parted in the middle and tied tightly on top of her head in a bun. There was a prim, austere air about her. She moved to the foot of the bed on my far left. Next came a very tall and lanky man, brown hair parted in the middle, wearing a brown three-piece suit, rather shabby. He took his place in the middle, at the foot of my bed. Following him was a woman whom I felt was out of place, even at the time of the vision. She was dressed in the most outlandish purple satin outfit, tucked up on one side as a barroom girl might have worn in the Old West. Her blonde hair was curled in ringlets, which were drawn up on one side of her head and cascaded down on the other. I sensed loneliness and a very gentle nature surrounding her as she took her place next to the tall gentleman to my right. Lastly came a very dapper if somewhat plump gray-haired gentleman. He carried a small three-legged stool and a black bag, telling me he was probably a medical man. Hatted and wearing a gray three-piece suit complete with gold watch chain, he seated himself on his stool on the right-hand side of my bed. They all seemed terribly concerned over my health, although I was not ill at the time. When the 'doctor' leaned over the bed and tried to take my hand into his, I decided I had experienced just about all I wanted to with these strangers. My voice quivered as I called out to my mother, who was a very light sleeper, and whose back was facing me, informing her of the unknowns who had invaded our bedroom. 'Mother, there are people in the room!' I called again and again. She reassured me sleepily and without turning over that I was only dreaming, and to go back to sleep. During these implorings on my part, the four strangers began backing away from the bed as if they were alarmed by my speaking. Whether they actually spoke or I heard them telepathically, I cannot be certain, but I did 'hear' them repeatedly say, 'No, please, we only want to help you. No, no, don't call out.' My cries increased and with that they turned and exited the same way they had entered, through the wall into the living room."

The house in which this vision took place had only been built in comparatively recent times. The land had formed part of a farm in the early nineteenth century, but the costumes of the figures, Cynthia felt sure, belonged to an earlier period. She wondered whether perhaps the land had been part of a western wagon trail, and she was reliving a child's death. On the other hand, she began to wonder whether it referred to a previous existence of her own, since she has very strong feelings about the nineteenth century West.

Cynthia has had a number of precognitive dreams concerning events that later took place. But the dream that impressed itself more than any other upon her consciousness had to do with the past. Actually, it was preceded by what she described as "an insatiable interest in England" she developed in early high school, long before the Beatles became the rage of America. This was not a single dream, easily forgotten, but a series of recurrent dreams, all related one to the other, mounting in intensity as if something within her was trying to come to the surface, informing her of a long-forgotten memory.

"At times I noticed myself speaking in a north country British accent and I caught myself using English spellings, drinking tea with cream, and the first time I heard the song, 'Greensleeves,' I felt very moved and certainly melancholy. There is another song, called 'North Country Maid' which has remained my great favorite. I even went so far as to compose a 200-page term paper on England for my sociology class. But long before this project took place, I began dreaming of a cloaked man mounting a horse in the moonlight and riding out of sight into the English countryside. I was in the dream also, dressed in a blue and tan peasant frock, laced up the front. I knew it was me because I remember looking down at the dress I was wearing. In other words, I was actually a participant, not a sleeping spectator of myself, nor recognizing myself as another person. At any rate, I seemed to be coming out of a stable or barn, in which I had been lying on a large pile of hay. I begin running towards the mounting horseman, as if to beg him not to leave. Then I would awaken, only to dream the same dream several nights later.

"One night when I was particularly tired, I managed to continue my dream state after the wench's running, but not for long. In the dream, I uttered between sobs, the name of Dick, and then awoke. The dream continued in this pattern until I, now exasperatedly curious, forced myself to remain sleeping. Finally, one night, I was able to

hear the whole phrase—'Dick Turpin, my love, wait! Don't go!' Its mission now seemingly fulfilled by giving me a name I had never heard before, the dream never returned again."

At that time, Cynthia had never heard of Dick Turpin. But the dreams had roused her curiosity and she started to research it. Her Encyclopedia Britannica was of very little help, nor did any of the high school encyclopedias contain the name. But in her parents' library she located a 1940 edition of Nelson's Encyclopedia. In it, she found a brief listing of one Richard Turpin, an English highwayman and associate of Tom King, who lived from 1706 to 1739, when he was executed by hanging.

About a year after the dreams had subsided, she was riding with a girlfriend, when she suddenly felt a strong urge to return home immediately. Still under a kind of compulsion, she immediately turned on the television set and picked a Walt Disney show, very much to her parents' surprise, since they knew her to dislike the program. At that moment, flashed on the screen were the words, "The Legend of Dick Turpin". Cynthia then proceeded to watch the program, her eyes glued to the set, interrupting the proceedings on screen with comments of her own. "No, that wasn't what happened," she would say and proceeded to correct it. What was remarkable was her ability to relate what was about to happen on-screen and to mention characters' names before this information became available to the viewers. Afterwards, she felt dazed and remembered little of what she had said during the program.

I suggested that Cynthia meet me in Los Angeles so that I could attempt to regress her hypnotically and determine whether her reincarnation memory was factual or merely a romantic fantasy. We met just before Christmas, 1973, at my Hollywood hotel, the Continental Hyatt House. We discussed Cynthia's psychic experiences and I discovered that she had had an accident in 1969 resulting in a brain concussion. Did the accident influence her psychic perceptions in any way? No, she replied, she had had them for years prior to the accident, and they continued after the accident. Had she ever been to England or was she of English background? Both questions she answered in the negative. Her interest in English history and literature at college came *after* the recurrent dream had occurred to her. Having established that neither Cynthia nor her family had any English background nor leanings, I proceeded to regress her hypnotically in the usual manner. It took only a short time before she was under, ready to answer my questions while hypnotized.

After describing life as a Victorian gentleman in New York, and giving the name of John Wainscott, and the year 1872 or 1892, she proceeded back into the eighteenth century and the year 1703, to a man who had something to do with a Delaware Street. The man's name was Dick, and evidently we had gotten to the subject of her recurrent dreams.

"He is mounting a horse, and he's throwing his cape back so he can take hold of the reins. He's got a hat on with a plume on it, I am standing by the barn."

"What is your relationship with this man? What is your name?" I asked.

"A wench…my name is Sally."

"What year is this?"

"1732."

"What happens then?"

"He rides away like he always does."

"What happens to you?"

"I cry."

And that was all I could get out of her through hypnotic regression. But somehow it must have settled this recurrent dream and the urgency connected with it within Cynthia, for I heard nothing further from her since then.

✳ 135

The Restless Dead

NOT ONLY HOUSES can be haunted, but people as well. There are literally thousands of cases where people have seen or heard the ghost of a dead person, usually a person with unfinished business on his/her mind at the time death overtook him/her.

Let me set down my criteria for such experience, so that we understand what we are dealing with. When a person dreams of a dead relative this may or may not have significance. When the dream includes specific details unknown to the dreamer at the time and later found correct, then the dreamer is getting a psychic message in the dream state when his unconscious is free from the conscious mind and thus easier to reach.

I have examined hundreds upon hundreds of recent cases and carefully eliminated the doubtful or hallucinatory. What remains is hardcore evidence.

California, land of sunshine and pleasant living, has a great many such incidents, perhaps because death here is something alien, something that does not quite fit with the warmth and serenity of climate and outlook.

Take the case of Mrs. G. A., in Santa Susana, for instance. Mrs. A. is not a person given to belief in the supernatural. In fact, her total disbelief that the events that shook her up in 1958 were in any way psychic caused her to contact me. Somehow the "rational" explanation—grief over the passing of her husband—did not satisfy her eager mind and ultimately she wanted to know.

Her husband and Mrs. A. were working on their boat in the backyard on a warm California day. Suddenly, she heard him cry out "Honey," as if in pain. He had been working with an electric sander at the time. Alarmed, Mrs. A. turned around in time to see him clutching the sander to his chest. He had been accidentally electrocuted. Quickly she pulled the electric plug out and tried to hold him up, all the while screaming for help; but it was too late.

The ironical part was that A. had had nightmares and waking fears about just such an accident—death from electrocution.

Two months went by and Mrs. A tried to adjust to her widowhood. One night she was roused from deep sleep by "something" in the room. As soon as she was fully awake she perceived an apparition of her late husband, suspended in the air of their room!

He did not make any sound or say anything. Strangely enough, the apparition wore no shirt; he was bare-chested, as he would not have been in life.

In a moment he was gone, and Mrs. A. went back to sleep. In the morning she convinced herself that it was just a case of nerves. The day wore on. It was 4:30 in the afternoon and Mrs. A. was seated on her living room couch, relaxing and waiting for a telephone call from her mother. All of a sudden, she heard her car drive up to the door. She realized at once that this could not be the case, since she was not driving it, but it struck her also that this was the precise time her husband always drove up to the door, every afternoon!

Before she could fully gather her wits, he was there in the room with her. He looked as he had always looked, not transparent or anything as ethereal as that. Mrs. A. was literally frozen with fear. Her late husband knelt before her seemingly in great emotion, exclaiming, "Honey, what's wrong?"

At this point, Mrs. A. found her tongue again and quietly, as quietly as she was able to, told her late husband what had happened to him.

"There has been an accident, and you were killed."

When she had said those words, he uttered the same sound he did at the time of the accident—"Honey!"—as if remembering it—and instantly he vanished.

Mrs. A. has never felt him around her again since. Evidently, her husband has adjusted to his new state.

Sometimes the ghostly denizens drive the living out—only to find themselves without a home in the end. Such was the strange case recently of a house in Paso Robles owned by the Adams family. I heard about their predicament when I appeared on the Art Linkletter Show.

Mrs. Adams has three children, aged eleven, ten, and nine. Their problem: the house they bought used to be a "red light house," as she put it. Before they bought it, two young women lived there with an old man as a kind of chaperone. After the police forced the women out of business, the old man remained behind until his death.

Shortly after moving in, the Adams family noticed that all was not well with their home. The husband worked nights, and at the time he went to work between the hours of midnight and 3 A.M., strange noises were heard outside the house, such as banging on the wall—only nobody human was doing it. This was in December of 1957. Gradually, the noises changed from a slight rattle to a big, loud bang on the walls. Occasionally it sounded as if someone were ripping the window screens off the house.

Mrs. Adams called the police repeatedly, but they could not find anything or anyone causing the disturbances. Her husband, who worked in a bakery, also heard the noises one night when he stayed home. Always at the same time, in the early morning hours.

Soon Mrs. Adams also distinguished footsteps and human voices when nobody was walking or talking. On one occasion she could clearly hear two men talking, one saying he would try to get into the house. Then there were knocks on the walls as if someone were trying to communicate.

It got so bad that the Adamses started to make inquiries about the past of their property, and it was then, two years after they had moved in, that they finally learned the truth about the house and its former use.

They decided to let the ghosts have the house and moved out, to another house which has always been free from any disturbances. The haunted red light house they rented out to people not particular about ghosts. But they did not do too well at that. Nobody liked to stay in the house for long.

That was in 1964. When I checked up on Mrs. Adams in 1966, things had changed quite a lot.

"They tore it up repeatedly," Mrs. Adams explained, and since it was an old house, the owners did not feel like putting a lot of money into it to fix the damage done by the nightly "party."

It got to be sub-standard and the city council stepped in. Thus it was that the ghost house of Paso Robles was torn down by official order. The Adams family now owns an empty lot on which they can't afford to build a new house. And the ghosts? They have no place to go to, either. Serves them right!

* * *

Ralph Madison is a man who lives life and has enjoyed every moment of it. He is a great-grandfather four times over and not a young man, but he was still working in 1965, when I heard his strange story, as a part-time security guard in the museum at Stanford University.

He makes his home in Palo Alto, and has been married to the same woman since 1916. Not boasting much formal education, Madison considers himself a self-made man. Perhaps the only thing unusual about him is a penchant to send people tape recordings instead of letters. But perhaps Madison is only being practical. In another ten years' time we may all correspond in that way.

I would not be interested in Mr. Madison if it weren't for one particular incident in his life, an incident that made him wonder about his sanity—and, after having reassured himself about it—about the meaning of such psychic experiences.

It happened in 1928 in Palo Alto, on Emerson Street. Ralph Madison was minding his own business, walking in the vicinity of the five-hundred block, when he noticed a man he knew slightly, by the name of Knight. Mr. Knight operated a cleaning establishment nearby. The two men stopped to talk and Madison shook hands with his acquaintance.

It struck him as peculiar, however, that the man's voice seemed unusually wispy. Moreover, Knight's hands were clammy and cold!

They exchanged some words of no particular significance, and then they parted. Madison started out again and then quickly glanced around at his friend. The man he had just shaken hands with had disappeared into thin air. At this moment it came to him with shocking suddenness that Mr. Knight had been dead and buried for five years.

In a high state of excitement, Madison ran into a real estate office operated nearby by a Mr. Vandervoort whom he knew well. Quickly relating what had happened to him, Madison was assured that Knight and indeed been dead for five years and that he, Madison, was seeing things.

But Ralph Madison knows in his heart he shook hands with a dead man on a street corner in Palo Alto, in plain daylight.

* * *

A strange case came to my attention recently, strange among strange experiences in that it involves a kind of possession against which orthodox medicine seems to be powerless.

Mrs. B. of Burlingame went to at least six doctors for help, took countless nerve tonics and calming agents—but to no avail. When she heard of my work in ESP, she contacted me with a cry for help. This was in March of 1966 and I finally talked to her in October of the same year. Her voice was firm and there was no sign of panic in it. Still, what had happened to her would cause a lot of stronger people to throw in the towel in a struggle against insanity.

A widow now, Mrs. B. originally came from the Midwest where her father had been a physician, as were his father and grandfather before him. Her mother before her marriage was a high school teacher and she herself was the daughter of a senator.

Mrs. B. taught school also and later took up nursing as a profession. She was married from 1949 to 1960 and considers her marriage a most happy one. No emotional turmoils followed her widowhood, since Mrs. B. was an avid reader and musician and had surrounded herself with congenial friends. One could safely say that her life was serene and well ordered.

But it took her three letters before she could commit to paper the shocking experiences that had suddenly entered her life. I always insist on written statements from those reporting seemingly paranormal cases, and Mrs. B. reluctantly complied. It was her feeling of shame that prompted me to omit her full name from this account.

It started with a presence in the room with her, when she knew that she was quite alone. Before long, she felt the intimacies of another person on her body—a person she could not see!

She thought she had cancer and consulted every conceivable specialist, but got a clean bill of health. Yet, the attacks continued. Was she imagining the unspeakable? She began to question her own sanity. The physicians she consulted knew no answer except to reassure her that she had no physical ailment to account for the strange sensations.

Now I have heard similar stories about "attacks" by sex-minded ghosts before and sometimes they are the imagination of a frustrated middle-aged woman. No doubt about it, a change of life can produce some pretty wild symptoms in a woman, or for that matter in a man. Thus it was with extreme caution that I accepted the testimony of this lady. I wanted to be sure the case was psychic, not psychiatric.

I questioned her along ESP lines. Had she never had psychic experiences—other than the very graphically described invasions of her privacy—in the house she lived in, or elsewhere?

Apparently, the answer was affirmative. Some months before contacting me, she was doing housework on a Sunday, when she heard a voice speak to her, apparently out of thin air, a voice she did not recognize but which sounded rather low and was speaking in a whisper.

"The G.s are coming today." Now the G.s were friends of Mrs. B.'s living at some distance. She had not seen or heard from them for months, thus was not expecting their visit in any way. Consequently, Mrs. B. refused to believe the strange "voice." But the voice insisted, repeating the sentence once more!

Mrs. B. continued with her work, when around 1 P.M. she decided to take a rest. At 2 o'clock, the doorbell rang. Since she was not expecting any visitors, she was slow in answering it. It was the G.s, just as the voice had said!

Since then, the ghostly voice has been heard by Mrs. B. many times, always announcing someone's coming. The voice has never erred. The name, day and exact hour are given and each time it comes to pass.

The presence of an unseen person continued to trouble Mrs. B., but in addition she heard a voice speak two words, "my wife," several times, and on another occasion,

"her husband," as if someone were trying to tell her something she should know.

Mrs. B., of course, rejected the idea that it might be her own late husband who was haunting her, for he never believed in anything psychic while in the flesh. Shortly after this line of thought, she clearly heard the voice say, "She just does not understand."

When I was ready to see Mrs. B. in Burlingame, which is near San Francisco, she had already moved to another house in Santa Monica. It was there that I finally talked to her.

The situation was much the same, it appeared, ruling out any possibility that the ghost or invader was somehow tied up with the house in Burlingame.

The voice, which she still did not recognize, was very insistent now.

"Her husband...she just does not understand" was followed on another occasion by a statement, "I would do anything in the world...I wonder what she would do if she knew."

Then the words "sweetheart" and "my wife" were added and repeated on many occasions. All this happened to Mrs. B. in a house in which she was quite alone at the time.

Still, Mrs. B. refused to face the possibility that her husband, skeptic though he might have been in the physical state, had learned the truth about psychic communications and was now trying to reach her—in the way *a husband might!*

Sometimes the tragedies that make people of flesh-and-blood into non-physical ghosts are less horrifying than the ghosts that continue a kind of forlorn existence in the world in between—or rather I should say the ghosts are not the comparatively benign apparitions of people as we knew them, but something far more terrible, far more sinister.

* * *

Wayne Barber is a young ambulance driver who used to run the service out of Baker, California, one of the worst stretches of road because of the many automobile accidents that have happened on it. Now it is my personal opinion that half the people driving cars should not, and, furthermore, that licenses should be renewed only after annual examinations of those who qualify for them. What happened to Mr. Barber is only one case in point.

Aged twenty-nine years, six feet tall and married, Wayne Barber is a rough-and-tough man who, as he put it, "can eat a ham sandwich in complete comfort with dead bodies all over the highway." It's part of his business and he isn't the least bit sentimental about it.

Until February 1966 he had absolutely no belief in anything resembling the human soul, anything beyond death. But then something pretty terrible happened.

On Washington's Birthday there was a wreck about five miles east of Baker, California, in which seven people died. A group of three drunks was heading down the freeway in the wrong direction and had a head-on collision with a carload of people going to Las Vegas. In this car a mother and father were taking their daughter and her fiancé to be married!

The car headed in the wrong direction burned before the bodies could be removed. The others, mother and father, were pinned in their car and the two children that were to be married were thrown clear. All seven were dead.

"Any wreck involving the living is worse than handling the dead," Barber explained, "and this was not the worst wreck my attendant and I had ever handled. I am mentioning this so you don't think we had a case of nerves."

After making certain there were no survivors, they cleared the bodies off the highway and started to check them for identification. Removing the bodies is part of an ambulance crew's work, and Barber and his aide did just that—or what was left of the bodies—in order to clear the road for traffic.

A day later a sandstorm came up, and five women travellers in the area could not proceed because of poor visibility on the road. They appealed to Barber to put them up overnight at the ambulance station, and he readily agreed. He then went to the rear of the building to put together five cots for them from his supplies of standby equipment.

It was around 10:30 P.M. and the yard lights failed to work. He could see only about five feet, but he carried a small flashlight. As he busied himself on the standby rig near the corner of the building, he suddenly felt himself *watched*. Who would be standing there watching him in the driving storm?

He spun around and faced something he had never faced before.

There at arm's length was what he later described as "a thing," a terribly mutilated figure of a human being, a male, with legs hanging crookedly, just as they had been compounded in the accident, the body twisted at the waist and the head hanging at a weird angle, indicating a broken neck. But the eyes were watching him, looking straight into his—living, human eyes!

Barber was frozen to the spot long enough to observe every detail of the horrible apparition.

"There was a sad longing in the eyes, and a gratitude," Barber said afterwards. "In those eyes there was no intention to harm me."

Suddenly, his reactions returned and he tore into the ghost with his flashlight as if it were a knife. But he was thrashing thin air, and nothing but sand hit his face!

At this point his German Shepherd, a very rugged animal, came out of the darkness howling, out of his senses

with fear. Barber continued on back to the house with the stretchers for the cots. It was then that he saw what he calls "the other thing." This one was female. He did not see as many details of this ghost as he had observed of the male apparition, but he saw her outline clearly. It was enough for him to take a day off immediately.

But the dog was not the same for weeks, becoming a complete nervous wreck until he had to be given away to a sympathetic lady. Soon after he was run over and killed.

Barber married after this experience and he had no intention of ever talking about it to his new bride. But the dog he had acquired to take the place of the shepherd soon behaved in the most extraordinary fashion also, precisely the same as the shepherd. What was the dog seeing around the place? Barber then told his wife about the two ghosts.

The second dog had to be given away, too, when he became unmanageable in the place. Now Barber has a pug dog and he seems to be able to tolerate the influences that still pervade the spot a little better than his two predecessors.

"Something here is protecting me," Wayne Barber explains, and he and his wife refer to the ghosts somewhat bravely as "the little people."

Had the spirits of those two who never lived out their normal lives attached themselves to their rescuer?

* * *

Mrs. Daphne R. lives in Malibu, California, with her husband and children. Her second husband is a Navy man and they have moved frequently. Originally English, Mrs. R. has had a number of psychic experiences and is unquestionably mediumistic. But the incident I found most fascinating had to do with a ghost her little daughter encountered. It interested me because not all the restless dead are hopeless, pathetic human beings in trouble, unable to help themselves. This ghost even helped another person. It happened in 1952.

"I was working in Heidelberg as a secretary, and I had a little three-year-old daughter from a broken marriage, who lived with my parents in England. I got awfully lonely, and increasingly sure that I ought to bring her over to Germany to live with me. So one day I flew over to England, and rode the train down to Folkestone, collected the child and her belongings and took her back to London. I had to wait a few days for her papers, so I stayed at the private home of a rather well-known photographer.

"He was most kind, and offered to put my daughter and me up for the time we had to spend in London. He was a widower. I hardly saw him, as he was out all the time on assignments. He had a small boy of around four or five, and an English nanny. They lived in a rather posh narrow house.

"One night I wanted to go to the theater, and asked the nanny if she would baby-sit for me and keep an eye on my little girl. I should add here that the child was in a terrible emotional state about leaving my parents (I was almost like a stranger to her), and she wept all the time, and seemed calmer with the nanny than with me.

"Anyway, I went out, and left the little girl in the double bed we were sharing, and the nanny promised to pop in and out of the bedroom to watch her, as the little boy had also gone to bed nearby. I wore a black suit—which is an item of importance. When I got back around 11:00 P.M., the nanny was in the kitchen, and she said Kitty had cried quite a bit (not for me, but for my parents, whom she missed), and that suddenly she had been quiet, so the nanny had run up to take a peek at her, and she was fast asleep and smiling in her sleep. The next morning I awakened, and the child was in a very happy mood, so much so that I said to her that I was so happy to see her smiling for the first time in about two days, and that perhaps she was a bit happier about going to live with Mummy in Germany. She replied that yes, she was very happy. Then she said, 'I was unhappy last night, and I cried, because I wanted my Nana (she referred to my mother), but then the LADY came over to my bed and stroked my head and told me you were out and would be back soon, and that she would stay with me until you got back.' I merely thought she was referring to the nanny in the house, and said 'Yes, nanny is a nice lady,' and my daughter said, 'Oh no, it wasn't the nanny, it was a pretty lady with long red hair, and she was beautiful.' Then she went on to prattle about how the 'Lady' had told her how much Mummy loved her, and how unhappy it made Mummy to see the child cry, and that really it was much better for her to be with her mother than with her grandparents, and the child ended up saying 'I realized she is right, Mummy.'

"Later that day, I asked the nanny if she had had a guest, and when she said no, I told her about the above incident, and she was quite aghast, and related to me that her master's late wife had long red hair, and was a beautiful woman, but had been very unhappy, and I suppose nowadays we would think she was mentally unbalanced; apparently she threw herself from the balcony of the room in which my daughter and I had been sleeping. She was so interested in this—the nanny, I mean—that she asked my daughter what the 'lovely lady' had been wearing, and Kitty, my daughter, said, 'A lovely long blue satin nightie,' and later the nanny said that the late lady of the house had committed suicide in a blue satin evening house-gown."

* * *

Some people with ghosts in their houses get to me in person. Some write. Others manage to get me on the phone although I am not listed any more. Still others tape record their plea to me.

One such instance occurred while I was doing television in Hollywood in November of 1966.

David Burkman, of Yorba Linda, is a married man with four children; he is thirty years old. He used to be a skeptic as far as ESP and psychic phenomena are concerned. But then it happened.

It was in Fullerton, California, in April 1962, when the Burkmans were occupying a house consisting of a large living room, bedroom, den, two bedrooms for their children, and a kitchen. At the time Mrs. Burkman was already the mother of two children and expecting her next, which, however, she later lost.

At the time of the incident that made Mr. Burkman wonder about ghosts, he and his wife were asleep in their bedroom at the southeast corner of the house. It was in the early hours of the morning when Mrs. Burkman woke up from the noise of "someone trying to open the door" which is situated on the other end of the house. She woke her husband and called his attention to the noise. The door in question was the gate to the yard. It was fully locked at the time and secured with a chain.

Mr. Burkman got his revolver, loaded it, and both he and his wife now clearly heard the door open and shut. There was no mistaking the characteristic noise with which they were quite familiar. He stepped out of the bedroom into the corridor now and heard footsteps coming toward him. Someone was walking through their kitchen, then had stopped at a point where the short hallway separated the kitchen and the boy's bedroom from the corridor leading toward the couple's own bedroom.

Mr. Burkman put his hand on the light switch, ready to bathe the intruder—for they were sure it was one—in the light of the ceiling fixtures. Now the footfalls continued toward the hallway, so Burkman turned the lights on and leveled his gun, ready to shoot—but to his dismay, there was no intruder to be seen!

However, the footsteps of an unseen person *continued*, despite the lights, down the hallway. Petrified, Mr. Burkman just stood there as the footsteps passed by and turned into the bedroom, where they stopped abruptly when they reached the spot where Mrs. Burkman was standing.

Nothing else happened to the Burkmans in this house, nor did they ever discover any cause for the strange occurrence on that April day in 1962.

However, David Burkman has had other psychic experiences.

Usually through dreams, he has had premonitions of deaths that later occurred as seen in his dreams.

What interested me in this case was the apparent disregard of the ghost of the lights being turned on and of the challenge by flesh-and-blood people.

In the case of the Integration Ghost reported by me in *Ghosts I've Met*, similar footsteps also went through the motions of a "movement remembered." It appears therefore that someone was so intent on repeating an urgent business, a walk to a certain spot in the house, that he did not even realize the presence of others, or of lights.

David Burkman of course was wondering if he was losing his sanity—but that, at least, I could prevent, by showing him that he was not an isolated case.

* * *

Mrs. Fanny K. lives not far from the International Airport in Los Angeles, in a small house of considerable age. Her house is built of wood and is situated three feet from a paved alley, at the rear of a 135-foot lot. She purchased it in 1947 from the two women who then owned it. They were the first wife and the daughter of a carpenter, she discovered, but nobody told her at the time that the house was haunted or that anything unusual came with the purchase.

Mrs. K. is a practical woman, somewhat impatient at times, and not easily frightened by anything. She has had a good education and has a moderate interest in ESP matters, especially after the events I am about to relate had entered her life.

The very first night after moving into the house on 96th Street, Los Angeles, Mrs. K. was awakened from sleep by the sound of deep groans in her bedroom in which she was alone. This continued night after night. Soon, the groaning was accompanied by the touch of unseen fingers riffling through her hair, and light prodding to her ribs by someone she could not see. It was evident to her that someone wanted to get her attention. Finally, three weeks after moving in, a neighbor took pity on her and filled her in on the background of her house.

It had originally belonged to a man named Winsten, a Scandinavian carpenter, who at age 54 had married for the second time, a woman 28 years old. Under the influence of a sudden jealous streak, he had shot his wife to death, and when the police were closing in on him, committed suicide three days after. Although the two crimes had not occurred directly in the house, he had spent many years there and it was then his home.

This knowledge in no way helped calm Mrs. K.'s nerves. For one thing, the disturbances did not stop just because she now knew who it was that was causing them. It got to be so bad, she finally asked a friend to stay with her one night so that she too could hear the goings-on. That was in 1948. As soon as the two women had gone to bed, they clearly heard measured footsteps walking from the bedroom door across the living room floor and to the front door. However, they did hear the front door open and close. The friend was convinced now Mrs. K. was not "hearing things."

Shortly after, Mrs. K. was awakened one night by the sound of a long, deep sigh followed by heartbreaking weeping.

It was a woman's voice and Mrs. K. felt her kneeling on the floor next to her bed! She decided to ignore it and turned to the wall. But she had not slept very long when she felt something like a man's fist wrapped in bedclothes push very hard into the back of her neck. She did not

move and waited. Eventually, the power ran out and the disturbances ceased. For that night, anyway.

"More than once I have felt an evil presence standing at the head of the bed," Mrs. K. explained, "and the most terrifying thing is that it tries to pin me down in bed, while I'm fully awake, something like throwing a plastic covering over me."

I had heard this description of possession or attempted possession several times before. On one occasion, a seemingly heavy object fell off the ceiling and hit the bed, in which Mrs. K. was already lying, with such force that it made it sag about a foot. Yet nothing *visible* had fallen! At first, she thought it was merely a local earthquake. But in the morning, when she put her hand behind the pillow, she plainly felt "something like a tissue paper ruffling away." It had been there all night, evidently.

In 1958, the ghost pushed her so violently that she woke up. As she gathered her senses, she clearly heard a whispered voice near her say the word, "Bottle!" a moment later, it repeated the demand for a bottle. Completely awake by now, she sat up in bed and challenged the ghostly intruder.

"Why are you talking about a bottle?" but she received no reply.

Soon after she saw an apparition of "her" ghost. He passed quickly from one corner of the bedroom to the other, dressed in black with a black hat with turned-down brim. However, she could not make out his features. Since then she noticed his face close to hers on several occasions, although she was never able to make it out clearly. By Christmas 1959 it had gotten so bad that she felt him holding onto her shoulder and had to struggle to rid herself of the intruder.

A rational and logical woman, Mrs. K. wanted additional proof of her observations. In 1954 she had a house guest who shared her quarters for three months, sleeping in her bedroom, while Mrs. K. took the living room to sleep in.

Her guest soon complained about lack of sleep. Someone kept watching her, she explained, someone she could not see but sensed right there in the room with her.

Another friend, strongly psychic, came to the house and instantly diagnosed the "ailment" of the place. There was great sadness in the house, she said, and went on to describe the tragedy that had created the ghostly phenomena.

From time to time Mrs. K. would hear a woman's voice, apparently talking to someone in the room, but she could not make out the words. The phenomenon occurred only in the bedroom area, and there were periods of quiet in between periods of disturbances.

I kept in touch with Mrs. K. after her initial contact with me in February 1960. At that time I could not rush to Los Angeles myself, so I suggested that a local man with some knowledge of exorcising techniques contact her for immediate relief. Unfortunately this man never followed up on my request and Mrs. K. became more and more worried about the whole matter. It was true that it was quiet in the house for most of 1960, she said, but sooner or later the dead carpenter would show up again, she was sure. Thus her own fears began to complicate the ghostly visitations.

She called on two local mediums to try to drive the carpenter and his wife away. The mediums failed. By now the ghostly carpenter had tried to get into her bed, she claimed. I did not laugh off such a claim, outlandish as it may sound on the surface—especially to someone unacquainted with the extent to which psychic disturbances can go. Mrs. K. had not impressed me as hysterical.

Whenever things got too bad, she moved out and stayed at a neighbor's house now, leaving the ghosts to roam the house at will.

In 1963 I was in Los Angeles and talked to her as soon as I landed. She was quite ill at that time, partly from a severe cold and partly from the nervous tension the ghosts had caused her.

I wish I could report a happy ending to this case, but I have been unable on subsequent visits to make contact with Mrs. K. Has she, like a ghost ship, vanished into the Los Angeles smog, or has the carpenter finally given up on his demand for the bottle?

Whatever the reasons, it is an object lesson to prospective house hunters not to buy suicide-owned homes. You never know what comes with the deal.

Sometimes the restless dead insist they are not dead at all. They want to participate in the activities of the living as of yore.

Mrs. Smith—this is her real name—lives in Los Angeles. Shortly after she got married for the first time in 1936, her mother joined her and her husband to live with them, but the household lacked harmony. Within a year, however, matters came to a head, when the mother became ill and was moved to the hospital, where her illness was diagnosed as terminal cancer.

At the same time, Mrs. Smith was expecting her second baby, so she, too, had to go to the hospital. Nobody knew how long her mother might live, but she was to stay at the hospital indefinitely.

After Mrs. Smith had given birth and was about to go home, she was moved one night to another ward not far from where her mother's bed was.

That night, her last night at the hospital, she could not sleep somehow. Her eyes fastened themselves on the wall and the six windows in it. She was fully awake. Suddenly she "saw" three figures come in through those windows. What to her seemed a Christ-like figure in a white robe was flanked by her father, who had died when she was only two, and her minister who had passed on three years before.

The trio passed Mrs. Smith's bed on their way to her mother's bed and as they did so, the dead minister told her they had come for her mother.

Mrs. Smith sat up in bed and reached out to touch them, but the three figures disappeared. Five minutes later a nurse came to tell her that her mother had just died.

Mrs. Smith returned home, but her grief for her mother was of short duration. A week later she was busy around the house discarding her late mother's belongings when she found that an unseen force pulled every object she was about to throw out from her hands! She could not manage to do it and had her husband take care of it.

But that was not all. Every night, when she and her husband were in bed, there would be a knock at the door and her late mother's voice would call out for her by name! Both Mrs. Smith and her husband saw the cupboard doors open and close by themselves, comparing notes, so to speak, on all the unearthly phenomena to make sure they were not imagining things. They were not.

They had been searching for her mother's door key for some time, not wishing to have it fall into strange hands, as, after all, it was the key to their home. They could not locate it anywhere no matter how carefully they looked. One night the ghost of Mrs. Smith's mother rapped at their bedroom door and told her daughter, clairaudiently, to look in a certain pocket in a coat that had not yet been given away. Then and there, Mrs. Smith jumped out of bed and looked. Sure enough, there was the key!

Mrs. Smith now realized that she had psychic powers and could hear the dead talking. Naturally, she tried to talk back to them, also via telepathy. Her mother, however, would not listen. She never answered her, never reacted to anything her daughter would say. Like all true ghosts, Mrs. Smith's mother was disturbed and could not recognize her true status.

They rented the mother's room to a woman. The board complained she could not sleep in the room. Someone was forever knocking at her door. Nobody had said a word to her about mother's ghost, of course. The board moved out and Mrs. Smith and husband moved in, letting the woman have their own room in exchange.

For a few days, all seemed peaceful. Then one night the boarder was alone in the house, taking a bath. Suddenly she heard the front door open and close and someone walking up the stairs to the second floor. But when she checked she found no one there. It was enough for her and she moved out for good.

At this point, mother's attention increased. Mrs. Smith thought things over carefully. They, too, moved out. Now her mother has the place all to herself.

* * *

Ruth Hayden is a retired school teacher who lived at Ojai, California, a quiet, retired life, when she made contact with me in 1963.

Her idleness had left her groping for something positive to contribute, and the new truths of psychic research had attracted her strongly. Thus she had come forward to contribute her own experiences in this field as part of the ever-increasing evidence of the survival of human personality after bodily death.

I asked Miss Hayden to explain herself to me first, so that I might understand better her interest in the psychic.

"As an orphan, in a school for the blind, I had twelve years of reverent Bible training, among all sorts and conditions of men, and grew up broadly tolerant, with a lovable respect for the higher Powers. My philosophy was to treat my friends the way I wanted God to treat me, and the rest of the world as I wanted the world in general to treat me. After teaching for 36 years in two large state hospitals (again among all sorts and conditions), I came to California to escape winter."

Her psychic experiences were many over the years. One particularly evidential case reminded me of an experience Eileen Garrett had a few years ago, when news of a friend's passing reached her by psychic means before anyone in New York had been notified of the event.

"I had come out of a shoe-repair shop and was headed down the narrow side street toward the city square, when up in the air between the buildings, over the heads of the traffic, about fifteen feet to my left, a familiar voice said: 'Sancho Pancho is with me now.'

"The voice was that of a friend who had died five months before. I had heard and recognized the voice and the words, but others nearby apparently did not hear anything unusual!

"'Sancho Pancho' was a pupil of mine who that week had undergone an operation for cancer of the throat. His real name was Tom Joyce, but my friend had nicknamed him Sancho Pancho because he was so helpful to me about the schoolroom—and nobody but my dead friend and I knew of this association.

"Without thinking about the incident I waited for my bus, rode five miles, and walked a little over half a mile up to the school. As I passed the switchboard I was told to 'phone the Pondville Hospital.' There I was informed that my pupil Tom—the Sancho Pancho of the spirit-voice—had just passed away, and they wanted to know if I could give them his home address. The address they had was that of the institution in which he was living and where I was a teacher."

* * *

I first heard of Adriana de Sola down on Charles Street, New York, when we investigated the strange occurrences at the home of Barrie Gaunt. Miss de Sola had been Barrie's house guest and one of the people who had encountered the melancholy ghost of "Miss Boyd" investi-

gated in my book *Ghosts I've Met*, with the help of Sybil Leek.

I had always wanted to meet the spunky lady in person and when I passed through Los Angeles in late January of 1965, I decided to call on her.

Originally from Mexico, Adriana de Sola had been a long-time resident of Los Angeles, her main occupation being that of a writer, although she took on odd jobs from time to time to make ends meet—a necessity not uncommon among American writers.

Her first uncanny experience was many years ago, when she was engaged to be married but had had a fight with her intended and he had left for Acapulco. Several weeks went by. Then one night as she was brushing her hair, she heard him stand next to her and tell her that he had drowned in Acapulco at nine that very morning!

Imagine her shock when she picked up the morning paper the next day and found the tragedy reported just as he had told her.

"I smelled his special perfume but I did not see him," she commented, "and I heard his voice as if he were whispering behind my left ear."

"Was that the end of it? Did he just come to say goodbye?"

"Not quite...you know how Latins are sometimes...I married another man a year later, and the ghost of my fiancé so bothered us that I had to divorce him. One of our servants was mediumistic and he managed to have her do his bidding while in trance, even dropping objects on my new husband. Like a plate of soup."

So she decided it was better to divorce the man than have him haunted out of her life!

Today, Miss de Sola is a vivacious, dark-haired woman in her middle or late forties, very self-reliant and philosophical. Her voice is firm and she exudes authority at every turn. Ghosts evidently would have a tough time getting the better of her, I concluded, as we faced each other in the comfortable confines of the Hollywood Roosevelt, where there are no specters to speak of.

When Adriana de Sola moved to a tiny village in Lower California, which is a desert-like province of Mexico, she bought a house which was such a bargain that she smelled a rat—or rather, a ghost. She was not wrong, for one night she awoke with the strong impression she should dig into a certain wall, 45 inches thick, and she followed her hunch only to discover a hidden earthenware pot, which, however, was empty. After that, all was quiet and she could enjoy the little house in peace. Evidently the former owner wanted her to find the pot.

After a brief stay in New York, where she encountered the sighing ghost of Miss Boyd on Charles Street, she came to Los Angeles and went to work at a house in Belair as a housekeeper. She had been sent there by a domestic employment agency and had no knowledge of the house or its history.

The house now belonged to a motion picture producer of some renown and she was engaged to supervise the staff, a task at which she proved very good. To her it was a means of saving some money and after a while cut loose again and do some writing on her own. The house was beautiful and seemed quiet at first glance, and Adriana felt she had made a good choice.

Shortly after her arrival she found herself awakened in the middle of the night. Someone was shaking her by the shoulder. When she was fully awake, she sat up in bed. There was nothing to be seen, but her psychic sense told her there was someone standing next to her bed, a tall, slim woman with blonde hair down her shoulders. With her inner eye she "saw" this very clearly. The specter was terribly grieved and bathed in blood!

Although Adriana was impressed by her plea, she could not get herself to accept the reality of the phenomenon and ascribed it to an upset stomach. She prayed for the restless one and then went back to sleep.

About six or seven days later, it happened again. This time Adriana was particularly impressed with the beauty of the ghost. The next morning she decided, finally, to make some inquiries about the matter.

Her employer's wife listened quietly to the description of the ghostly visitor, then nodded. Especially when Adriana mentioned her as appearing to her wearing a light suit, covered with blood.

The house had been Carole Lombard's house, where she had been very happy with Clark Gable! Carole Lombard had died tragically in an airplane accident when her plane, en route to the east where she was to join her husband, hit a mountain in a storm. She was wearing a light-colored suit at the time.

Miss de Sola decided she had had enough of the uncanny and left the house two days later. Thus it may well be that Carole Lombard's restless spirit is still clinging to her home, unless, of course, she has since found her husband Clark Gable on *her* side of the Veil.

* * *

Maureen B. is a San Francisco housewife now, but in 1959, when her first brush with the uncanny took place, she was attending college summer school and living by herself in the old house her parents, Mrs. and Mrs. John F., had bought recently on Toravel Street.

Records showed the house to date back to 1907, which is pretty old for the area. The parents had gone away on vacation and Maureen should have had the place to herself—but she didn't.

Sometimes she would stay awake all night because she had the feeling of not being alone in the house. There was *something* or *someone* staring at her—someone she could not see!

The tension made her ill, but nothing further happened until the summer of 1960 when she found herself studying late one night in the breakfast room downstairs.

Although physically tired, she was mentally quite alert. The door leading to the back porch, where the pantry was situated, was locked from the inside, and the key was in the lock. The door leading from this back porch into the yard outside was double-locked and the key was hidden away. None of the windows in the old house would open.

Nevertheless Maureen suddenly heard, in the still of the night, a swishing sound from the other side of the door, followed by footsteps and the clinking of a chain. Her heart pounded with fear as she sat there frozen, staring at the door. The key in it was turning and a voice outside the door was moaning.

For a couple of moments Maureen sat still. Then she gathered up her wits and ran up the stairs and roused her father. Quickly he came down and unlocked the door, and searched the back porch and the yard. There was nobody to be seen.

The next day the family decided that Maureen "must have heard" streetcar noises. As for the key turning in the lock, why, that was just her over-tired eyes playing tricks on her.

Maureen knew differently, for she had lived with the noises of streetcars for a long time and the moan she had heard outside the door was no streetcar. And the key moved back and forth in the lock before her yes. It did not make a clicking sound, however, as it does when it engages the lock to unlock the door. Since the rest of the family had not experienced anything out of the ordinary in the house and did not accept the possibility of the psychic, Maureen found it convenient to let the matter drop, even though she found out a few things about the house her folks had acquired back in 1957.

It had been an antique shop previously, and prior to that an old physically challenged person had lived there. His bed was near the front window giving onto the street, so that he could watch the goings-on outside in the way old people often want to—it gives them a feeling of not being shut-ins, but still part of the active world. By the time he died, the house was in deplorable condition and a real estate firm bought it and fixed it up.

For many years the old man had called this house his home, gradually becoming more and more immobile until death had taken him away from it. But had it?

* * *

When I appeared on a special television program with Regis Philbin in Los Angeles in the fall of 1966, on which we discussed ghosts and psychic experiences and illustrated them with some of the evidential photographs I had taken of such apparitions, many people wrote or called with psychic adventures of their own or houses they wanted me to investigate.

One of the most interesting cases involved a man not particularly friendly toward the possibility of personal survival or mediumship who had been forced by his experiences to re-evaluate his views.

* * *

Earle Burney is an ex-Marine who lives in San Diego. He was discharged from the Marine Corps in June 1945 and went to work for the Navy as a guard at a Navy Electronics Laboratory installed since World War II in an old mansion at Loma Portal, California. The work was highly classified, and security at the place was pretty strict as a consequence.

At first Burney's job was to guard the mansion during the night, coming in at 11:15 P.M. He knew nothing about the place, and the man he relieved, for some strange reason, never talked to him about the work—seconds after Burney got there, his predecessor was out the door, as if he could not get away fast enough to suit himself.

Burney then inspected the place from top to bottom, which was part of his routine. He locked the door he had come through and put a pot of coffee on the fire in the kitchen. The house had retained much of its ancient glory, with mahogany paneling and a big, winding stairway leading up to the second story. He was puzzled, though, by a bullet hole someone had put in one of the wall ventilators.

One morning not long after he had started his job, he was sitting at his watchman's desk drinking coffee, when he heard footsteps upstairs. It was just 2 o'clock and there was no one in the building besides himself.

Naturally, Burney jumped up immediately. The footsteps were heavy and were coming down the hallway toward the head of the stairs. Burney started up the stairs, but when he reached the top, the footsteps had stopped dead—and there was nobody within sight.

He searched every inch of the house but could not find any human being who could have caused the footsteps.

After that, he heard the steps again a few more times, but by now he was not so excited over it. He decided to ascribe it to "the house settling or cooling off," although he could not really explain how such a noise could sound like human footsteps.

Then another phenomenon puzzled him even more. He would be sitting by his desk with only a small light burning, and the rest of the house as dark as could be. Still, he would hear music. The first time this happened, he thought that perhaps someone had left a radio on somewhere. But he found no radio anywhere. Then he discovered, as he searched the dark recesses of the old mansion, that the music was heard everywhere exactly the same way —no louder, no softer. It was faint, but then it would stop, and Burney realized he had not imagined it but really heard "something."

Burney decided to take his little spaniel dog Amber with him. The dog was friendly and fun-loving, about as normal as a dog can be.

That night, he took her with him and made her lie down by his desk. No sooner had he done so than he noticed a strange change in the behavior of the animal. Suddenly very nervous, the dog would not go near the stairs, and just lay there near the desk, whining.

At 2 a.m. the ghostly footsteps came. The dog let out a blood-curdling scream and headed for the door. Burney let her out and she shot out into the dark, hitting an iron statue across the yard. Although not physically hurt, the dog was never the same after this incident. The slightest noise would frighten her and her fun-loving nature had given way to a pitiful existence full of neurotic fears.

Burney was very much puzzled by all this and decided to ask some questions at last.

He discovered that others had heard those nighttime footsteps too. In fact, there was a big turnover of guards at the mansion and the reason he, an ex-Marine, had been hired was primarily because of the strange events. They figured he would not be scared of a ghost. He wasn't, but the job was hard on him, nevertheless. Especially after he found out about the bullet hole in the wall ventilator. A frightened guard had put it there. But bullets don't stop ghosts.

* * *

The restless dead walk on, walk on. Some of them are lucky because someone *cares* and brings a medium to the house or calls me to help. But for every restless one who gets help, there are a thousand who don't. I have come to the conclusion that there are literally thousands and thousands of houses where someone died unhappily in one way or another—not necessarily violently, but not peacefully— and still walks the floors. I wish I could help them all.

The Devil in the Flesh (Kansas)

IF YOU LIVE IN KANSAS CITY you're bound to hear about the devil now and again if you are a Bible student or church-goer in a church that goes in for the hell-and-brimstone variety of preaching. To some people the devil is real and they will give you an argument filled with fervor and Bible quotations to prove that he exists.

Mrs. G. wasn't one of those who were impressed by demonic outbursts, however, and could not care less whether there was a devil or not. She had grown up in a well-to-do middle-class family and spent her adult years in the world of business. At age nineteen, she met and married Mr. G. and they have had a happy life together ever since. There are no children, no problems, no difficulties whatever. She was always active in her husband's gasoline business, and only lately had she decided to slow down a little, and perhaps do other things, leisure time things, or just plain nothing when the mood would strike her.

At age 49, that was a pretty good way to do things, she figured, and since she really did not have to work, it was just as well that she started to enjoy life a little more fully. Not that she was unhappy or frustrated in any way, but the gasoline business is not the most exciting activity in the world, and after thirty years of living by and with gas, she longed for some fresh air.

One day in the spring of 1964, a friend suggested something new and different for them to do. She had read an advertisement in the local paper that had intrigued her. A Spiritualist church was inviting the general public to its message service. Why didn't they have a look?

"Spiritualist church?" Mrs. G. asked with some doubt. She really did not go for that sort of thing. And yet, way back in her early years, she had had what are now called ESP experiences. When she talked to a person, she would frequently know what that person would answer before the words were actually spoken. It scared her, but she refused to think about it. Her parents' home was a twelve-year-old house in a good section of Kansas City. It was just a pleasant house without any history whatever of either violence or unhappiness. And yet, frequently she would hear strange raps at night, raps that did not come from the pipes or other natural sources. Whenever she heard those noises she would simply turn to the wall and pretend she did not hear them, but in her heart she knew they were there.

Then one night she was awakened from a deep sleep by the feeling of a presence in her room. She sat up in bed and looked out. There, right in front of her bed, was the kneeling figure of a man with extremely dark eyes in a pale face. Around his head he wore a black and white band, and he was dressed in a toga-like garment with a sash, something from another time and place, she thought. She rubbed her eyes and looked again, but the apparition was gone.

Before long, she had accepted the phenomenon as simply a dream, but again she knew this was not so and she was merely accommodating her sense of logic. But who had the stranger been? Surely, the house was not haunted. Besides, she did not believe in ghosts.

As a young woman, she once heard a friend in real estate talk about selling a haunted house not far from them. She thought this extremely funny and kidded her friend about it often. Little did she know at the time how real this subject was yet to become in her later years!

The haunted house across the street was sold, incidentally, but nothing further was heard about it, so Mrs. G. assumed the new owners did not care or perhaps weren't aware of whatever it was that was haunting the premises.

Her own life had no room for such matters, and when her friend suggested they attend the Spiritualist church meeting, she took it more as a lark than a serious attempt to find out anything about the hereafter.

They went that next night, and found the meeting absorbing, if not exactly startling. Perhaps they had envisioned a Spiritualist meeting more like a séance with dark windows and dim lights and a circle of hand-holding believers, but they were not disappointed in the quality of the messages. Evidently, some of those present did receive proof of survival from dear departed ones, even though the two women did not. At least not to their satisfaction. But the sincere atmosphere pleased them and they decided to come back again on another occasion.

At the meeting they managed to overhear a conversation between two members.

"He came through to me on the Ouija board," one lady said, and the other nodded in understanding.

A Ouija board? That was a toy, of course. No serious-minded individual would take such a tool at face value. Mrs. G. had more time than ever on her hands and the idea of "playing around" with the Ouija board tickled her fancy. Consequently she bought a board the following week and decided she would try it whenever she had a moment all to herself.

That moment came a few days later, when she was all by herself in the house. She placed her fingers lightly on the indicator. Mrs. G. was positive that only her own muscle power could move the indicator but she was willing to be amused that afternoon and, so to speak, game for whatever might come through the board.

Imagine her surprise when the board began to throb the moment she had placed her hands upon it. It was a distinct, intense vibration, similar to the throbbing of an idling motor. As soon as she lifted her hands off the board, it stopped. When she replaced them, it began again after about a minute or two, as if it were building up energy again. She decided there was nothing very alarming in all this and that it was probably due to some natural cause, very likely energy drawn from her body.

After a moment, her hand began to move across the board. She assured herself that she was not pushing the indicator knowingly but there was no doubt she was being compelled to operate the indicator by some force outside herself!

Now her curiosity got the upper hand over whatever doubts she might have had at the beginning of the "experiment," and she allowed the indicator to rush across the board at an ever-increasing speed.

As the letters spelled out words she tried to remember them, and stopped from time to time to write down what had been spelled out on the board.

"Hello," it said, "this is John W."

She gasped and let the pencil drop. John W. was someone she knew well. She had not thought of him for many years and if his name was still imbedded in her unconscious mind, it had been dormant for so long and so deeply, she could scarcely accuse her own unconscious of conjuring him up now.

John W. had worshipped her before she was married. Unfortunately, she had not been able to return the feeling with the same intensity. Ultimately, they lost track of each other and in thirty years never saw each other again. She learned from mutual acquaintances, however, that he had also gotten married and settled down in a nice house not far from where she and Mr. G. lived. But despite this proximity, she never met him nor did she feel any reason to.

John W. was also in the gasoline business, so they did have that in common, but there had been difficulties between them that made a marriage undesirable from her point of view. He was a good man, all right, but not her "type," somehow, and she never regretted having turned him down, although she supposed he did not take it lightly at the time. But so many years had passed that time would have healed whatever wounds there might have been then.

When John W. died of heart failure in 1964, he was in his late fifties. Over the years he had developed a morbid personality and it had overshadowed his former gay self.

"Hello," the Ouija board communicator had said, "this is John W."

Could it be? She wondered. She put the board away in haste. Enough for now, she thought.

But then her curiosity made her try it again. As if by magic, the indicator flew over the board.

"I want to be with you, always," the board spelled out now. And then an avalanche of words followed, all of them directed towards her and telling her how much he had always loved and wanted her.

Could this be something made up in her own unconscious mind? Why would she subject herself to this incursion? For an incursion it soon turned out to be. Every day, practically, she found herself drawn to the Ouija board. For hours, she would listen to the alleged John W. tell her how much he wanted to stay with her, now that he had found her again.

This was punctuated with bitter complaints that she had hurt him, that she had not understood his great devotion for her.

As the weeks went by, her own personality changed and she began to take on more and more of his characteristic moods. Whereas she had been a light-hearted, gay person, she turned moody and morbid and her husband could not fail to notice the change that had come over his wife.

But she did not feel she could tell him what had happened, partly because she did not really believe it herself yet, and partly because she felt it might harm their marriage. So she pretended to be depressed and her husband understood, blaming her middle years for it.

By the winter of 1964, her life was no longer her own. In addition to the frequent Ouija board sessions, she now began to hear the man's voice *directly*.

"I am with you," he explained, fervently, and with her he was. There was never a moment where she could be sure he was not nearby. Her privacy was gone. She kept hearing his voice, sad, but nevertheless his voice as it had been in life, talking to her from somewhere outside, and yet seemingly inside her head at the same time. She could not understand any of this and she did not know how to cope with it at first.

She threw away the accursed Ouija board that had opened the floodgates to the invasion from the beyond. But it did not help much. He was there, always present, and he could communicate with her through her own psychic sense. She found it difficult to fall asleep. About that time she noticed she was no longer alone in bed. At first she thought it was her imagination, spurred on by fear, that made her *think* the undesired one was with her. But she soon felt his physical presence close to her body.

One night she extended her hand and clearly felt *something* other than air above her own body! She let out a scream and turned on the light. But this merely woke her husband and she had to explain it as a bad dream, so that he would not be alarmed.

Night after night, she felt John W.'s ethereal body next to or on top of hers. There was no mistake about it. He was trying to make love to her from the shadowy world he was in, something he had been denied while in the flesh. She fought off his advances as best she could, but it did not deter him in the least.

At the beginning of their communication with the board's help, she had still felt a kind of compassion for the poor devil who had died so sadly and rather early in his life. But whatever positive feelings she still harbored for him soon went by the board and her attitude turned into one of pure hate.

Nothing mattered in her life but to rid herself of this nightmare and return to the placid life she had been leading prior to the incident with the Ouija board.

John W. added threats and intimidation to his arsenal of evil now. Threats as to what he would do to her and her husband, if she did not accept him willingly. Ultimately, she could not bear it any longer and decided to inform her husband of what she was going through.

At first she was fearful as to what he might say. Perhaps he would have her committed to an institution, or at best, subject her to the humiliating treatments of a private psychiatrist.

But her husband listened quietly and with compassion.

"Terrible," he finally commented, "we've got to get you out of this somehow."

She sighed with relief. He evidently believed her. She herself had moments now where she questioned her own sanity. Could such things be as the sexual invasion of a woman by a dead man? Was she not merely acting out her own suppressed desires due perhaps to middle-age change of life?

She went to seek the advice of a physician.

After a careful checkup, he found her physically sound but suggested a psychiatric examination and possibly an EEG—an electroencephalogram to determine brain damage, if any. None of these tests showed anything abnormal. After a while, she concluded that medicine men could not help her even if they should believe her story.

Meanwhile, the attacks became worse.

"You will always hear my voice," he promised her night and day, "You won't be able to get rid of me now."

She tried all sorts of things. Grabbing whatever books on the subject of possession she could find, she tried to learn whether others had suffered similar attacks. She tried her skill at automatic writing hoping that it might give the accursed ghost a chance to express himself and perhaps she might reason with him that way. But though she became a proficient automatist, it did not do any good.

The handwriting she wrote in was not hers. What she wrote down made no sense to her, but it was he who was using her in still one more way and so she stopped it.

That night, she felt him closer than ever. It was as if part of his body were entering hers, and suddenly she felt her heart being squeezed and she gasped for breath. For a few moments of agonizing fear, she felt herself dying of a heart attack. The next day she went to see her doctor again. Her heart was sound as could be. But she knew then that she had just relived the very moment of his death. He had died of just such a heart failure!

Clearly John W. was a disturbed personality in the in-between world in which he now existed after a fashion. He could not distinguish right from wrong, nor indeed recognize his true status.

His hatred and love at once kept him glued to her body, and her environment, it would appear, unwilling and unable to break what must have been his strongest desire at the time of death.

During their courtship, he had appeared as a good person, unselfish and kind. Now he seemed bitter and full of selfish desire to own her, unwilling to let her go or do anything she asked him to.

She enlisted the help of a local amateur hypnotist, but he failed to put her under hypnosis. Discouraged, she lost all desire to live if it meant living on with this monstrous person inside her.

One day she saw a television program on which hypnotic treatment in parapsychological cases was the subject of discussion. Again encouraged, she asked for help and went to New York for an attempt to dislodge the unwanted entity from her body and soul.

This time she did go under, although not very deeply. But it was enough for the personality of John W. to emerge and carry on a conversation of sorts with the hypnotist.

"I want her to go with me, she is all I have now," he said, speaking through Mrs. G.'s mouth in trance.

Later she confirmed that she had been on the brink of suicide recently, and this had not been in a moment of panic but as if someone had actually made her attempt it. Luckily, she had managed to pull out of it just in time.

"Do you believe in a God?" the hypnotist asked.

"No," the entity replied and brushed the question aside. "I told her, she made life hell for me, now I'll make her life hell for her."

"But why do that?"

"No one wants me—I want to cry—you don't know what this is like—over here—nothing but darkness—"

Tears came down Mrs. G.'s cheeks now.

"It's me crying, not *her*," the voice of John W. said, and then, somewhat quieter, "No one wanted me as a child. . . . I came from an orphanage . . . my grandparents never wanted me . . . she could have made me happy but she didn't want to. She's the only woman who would have made me happy, only her, but she doesn't want me."

"Then why force yourself on her? What is the point?"

"I force myself on her because I can make her miserable."

"You can't force love."

"I have no pride."

"Renounce her."

"I don't want to listen to you. She hates me now anyway. I'm going to take her with me. . . . I'll get her, one way or another, I'll get her all right."

The hypnotist, patiently, explained about the freedom of the other side and how to get there by wishing oneself with one's loved ones who have preceded one.

"This is all new to me," the confused entity replied, but seemed for a moment to be thinking it over.

But it was only a brief squint at the light, then darkness took over once again.

"I've made her cry...miserable...she made me miserable. I don't like the way she's lived her life...."

Suddenly, the personality seemed to squirm as if from guilt.

Was this his own private hell he was in?

"I'm not really that person....I've been lying to her...just so I can be around her, I tell her one thing and then another...."

"Then why not leave her and go on to the other side?"

"I want to but don't know how—I can't go without *her.*"

The hypnotist tried again, explaining that other souls had been equally confused and been helped "across" the great divide.

The voice of the possessing entity hesitated. He was willing to go, but could he see Mrs. G. now and again? Visiting privileges, the hypnotist thought, with a bitter sense of humor.

"Will I be able to come back and see her?" the voice asked again.

But then the demented mind emerged triumphant.

"She hates me for what I've done to her. I'm not going to leave. I can do anything with her. Never could do it when living."

Now the hypnotist dropped the polite approach.

"You are to leave this woman," he intoned, "on pain of eternal damnation."

"I won't go."

"You will be in hell."

"She will be with me then."

"I send you away, the psychic door is closed. You cannot return."

"I will."

A moment later, Mrs. G. awoke, somewhat dumbfounded and tired, but otherwise no worse off than she had been when she had been put under by the hypnotist.

After she returned to Kansas City, she had some hopes that the power of John W. had been broken. But the molesting continued unabated. True, there had been conversation and the entity now knew at least that he was committing a moral offense. But evidently it did not matter to him, for the attacks continued.

After a while, Mrs. G. realized that her anxiety and abject fear were contributing factors to John W.'s unholy powers. She learned that negative emotions can create energies that become usable by entities such as John W. and when she realized this fact, her attitude began to undergo a change.

Where she had been waiting for his attacks to occur and counting the moments when she was totally free from his possession, she now deliberately disregarded all he did and treated his presence with utter indifference. She could still feel the rage within him when he wanted to possess her, but the rage was slowly cooling. Gradually, her compassion for the bedeviled soul returned and as it did, his hold upon her weakened. He had made his point, after all, and now the point no longer mattered. When last heard from, Mrs. G. was living quietly in Kansas City.

✳ 137

The Case of the Buried Miners

IN THE SECOND HALF OF August 1963, every newspaper in the United States was filled with the day-to-day accounts of a mining cave-in at Hazleton, Pennsylvania. Two men, David Fellin and Henry Throne, survived fourteen days at the bottom of a caved-in mine shaft and were finally rescued through a specially drilled funnel.

On August 28, Fellin gave the Associated Press an interview, in which he said:

Now they're trying to tell me those things were hallucinations, that we imagined it all.

We didn't. Our minds weren't playing tricks on us. I've been a practical, hardheaded coal miner all my life.

My mind was clear down there in the mine. It's still clear.

We saw what we say. These things happened. I can't explain them. I'm almost afraid to think what might be the explanation.

For example, on the fourth or fifth day, *we saw this door,* although we had no light from above or from our helmets. *The door was covered in bright blue light. It was very clear, better than sunlight.*

Two men, ordinary-looking men, not miners, *opened the door.* We could see beautiful marble steps on the other side. We saw this for some time and then we didn't see it. We saw other things I *can't explain.*

One thing I was always sure of. I was convinced we'd get out even if I had to dig us out myself.

A funny thing occurred on that very first day. We [Henry Throne and Louis Bova] hadn't been down in the mine five minutes that morning when my stomach started feeling a little out of whack.

I said, "Let's go out for an hour or so."

But the boys persuaded me to stay and get some work done first.

So we stayed, down at the tunnel's bottom, more than 300 feet down. Louis was on one side and me and Hank on the other.

Louis reached up to press the buzzer for the buggy [a small wagon which carries coal on tracks up to the surface]. He pressed the buzzer and stepped back. Then it happened.

Suddenly everything was coming down—timber, coal, rocks. The stuff was rushing down between us and Louis. Then it was quiet for maybe half a minute. Then the rush started again. It went on like this, starting and stopping for some time.

We sat there, listening as hard as we could for more rushes in the dark. We sat there against the wall that way 14 to 16 hours in a place about 6 feet long, 5 feet wide and about 3 feet high.

Now, you asked me about the strange things Hank saw. I actually saw more of them than he did. But I find it hard to talk about that.

I'm positive we saw what we saw. We weren't imagining them. Even before we heard from the men on the top, we had some light now and then. How else can you explain all the work we did down there? We couldn't have done it entirely in darkness.

The only time I was really *scared was when we saw two men dressed like power linemen. Don't ask me what men like that were doing down on the bottom. But I saw them.*

Hank asked me two or three times to ask the men for some light. This idea scared me down to my toes. I had the feeling this was something outside of our reach, that we shouldn't talk or do anything.

But Hank did not. Hank said to the men, "Hey, buddy, how about showing us some light?"

They didn't answer, and after a while we didn't see them any more.

Well, similar descriptions have been given from time to time by people close to death; Arthur Ford was once in that position in a hospital, and described vividly the door and the men operating it, before he was able to return to this side of the veil once more.

Did David Fellin have a glimpse of the other side of life, the unseen world, the world of the psychic? Perhaps he did. Perhaps, too, he was being helped by these forces to return to the surface. In a television interview Fellin also claimed to have been given a message by the men, but he could not discuss it.

About the same time this happened, a millworker named Guy de Maggio had a vision of Fellin and his visitors from beyond, and actually heard the words spoken by Fellin. So vivid was the impression that he took pains to tell people about it. This was many miles away from the scene and could be confirmed only later, after Fellin was rescued. Did both men tune in on the same supernormal wave length?

The local psychiatrists have done their best to convince Fellin that he had a hallucination. But Fellin is convinced of his experience. And so am I.

I tried to coax the two miners to come on Pittsburgh television with me. They refused. They were afraid of being laughed at. Then a reporter from the *Philadelphia Sunday Bulletin* went to interview them on the anniversary of the event.

Yes, it was true that David Fellin had seen a door with beautiful marble steps, but there were also the people, apparently human, walking up and down the stairs. Yet somehow he and Hank Throne feared to go through the door.

"Did you see what was on the other side of the door?" the reporter asked.

"A beautiful garden, just as far as you can see. The flowers were more beautiful, the grass greener, than here on earth. I knew that was some special place."

"Did the man hold the door open?"

"No, Hank shouted for him to hold it, but the door slammed."

"What happened then?"

"Hank got mad. He said: 'Give me that hammer. I'll open that door.' The hammer was lying next to me, and I just handed it to him. He took it and ran at the door, then swung the hammer at it. That's when he broke a bone in his hand. And he bruised himself on the right cheek."

"What happened to the door?"

"It disappeared, and the light went out."

"What light? What did it look like?"

"It was a bluish light, not like daylight."

"Both you and Hank saw this door and the light?"

"Yes. Also Pope John. But Hank didn't know it was Pope John, not until we got to the hospital and the priest brought me a book with a picture of Pope John on the cover." (Pope John XXIII died June 3, 1963.)

"Let's start at the beginning."

"I was sitting here, and Hank was sitting like where you are [facing him]. He kept looking up over my shoulder. I looked up one time and saw Pope John there. He had his arms crossed and was just looking down at us. He didn't say anything."

"Did you and Hank speak to him?"

"I would say, 'Is our friend still there?' or 'How's our friend today?' Hank would grin and say he was still there."

"Didn't you tell him this was Pope John?"

"I figured Hank was a Protestant, and wouldn't know who he was anyway."

"How did he find out then?"

"When they took us to the hospital, my priest brought me a book with a picture of the Pope on it. And Hank points to the book and said, 'Hey, there's that guy we saw, Dave.'"

"Did you and Hank discuss these things while you saw them?"

"No, not too much. When we saw those people on the steps I told him we stumbled onto something. I had nicknamed the mine where we were trapped 'The Grave-yard of Souls.' And I told him that we stumbled onto the graveyard of souls."

The reporter later talked to Throne, who said that he saw the door, stairway, and Pope John.

Pope John XXIII was, of course, on the spiritual side of the veil at the time the two buried miners saw his apparition.

The London *Psychic News* also picked up the story and featured it. They headlined it:

ENTOMBED MINER
IS NOT AFRAID
TO DIE ANY MORE

Not after they saw where they'd be going.

✳ 138

The Ghostly Lover

PERHAPS THE MOST FANTASTIC case of recent vintage is a case involving Betty Ritter and the well-known psychoanalyst Dr. Nandor Fodor. Dr. Fodor had been treating a certain Edith Berger, in Long Island, for what seemed at first disturbing symptoms of split personality. But Dr. Fodor is a trained parapsychologist as well, and he did not fail to recognize the case for what it was, possession!

He suggested that the Bergers call in a good medium, and recommended Betty Ritter.

Half in tears, Edith Berger's mother told Betty on the telephone how a possessive spirit personality had been annoying her and her daughter for the past four months. It seemed that Edith, the daughter, had a gentleman friend, a medical doctor, who had died in the tropics not long before.

The very day after his death, the young woman found that her erstwhile suitor had attached himself to her, and was forcing himself on her—physically! The attacks were so violent, the mother said, that she had to sleep in the same bed with her daughter for protection, but to no avail. The mother also *felt* the physical contact experienced by her daughter!

Betty concentrated her psychic powers immediately on what can only be called a form of exorcism. Although there was some relief, the ghostly boyfriend was still around.

To Betty's horror, she woke up that same night to find the restless one standing before her bed, stark naked, in a menacing mood. Betty's contacts on "the other side," however, protected her and took the erring one away.

Telling Edith Berger of her experience the next day, she accurately described the visitor. Her efforts seemed to weaken the attacks somewhat, and several days later she saw him again, this time, however, fully clothed! He wore riding boots and carried a whip. The Bergers confirmed that the man had been a lover of horses. On April 20, 1961, Betty Ritter telephoned the Bergers to find out how things were going. The moment Edith answered the telephone, the ghost started to pull her hair in a most painful fashion, as if to prove he was still very much in evidence!

But the violent mind of the young doctor would not accept the separation from his physical body and its pleasures. The haunting continued; thus Betty Ritter asked me to accompany her to the Berger home for another go at the case.

The Bergers turned out to be very level-headed middle-class people, and completely ignorant of anything psychic. Edith seemed to be a highly nervous, but quite "normal" human being. Almost immediately, the entity got hold of the medium and yelled through her—"I shall not be pulled away from you. I won't go."

I learned that the father had at first been highly skeptical of all this, but his daughter's behavior changed so much, and became so different from her previous character, that he had to admit to himself that something uncanny was happening in his house. Edith, who had wanted to be a singer, and was far from tidy, suddenly became the very model of tidyness, started to clean up things, and behaved like a nurse—the profession her late boyfriend had wanted her to follow. At times, she assumed his ailments and "passing symptoms." At times, she would suffer from genuine malaria—just as he had done. Since Edith was mediumistic, it was easy for the dead doctor to have his will. The message he wanted her to deliver most was to tell his mother that he was "still alive." But how could she do that, and not reveal her agony?

One afternoon, while she was praying for him, she felt a clutching sensation on her arm. Later on, in bed, she clearly heard his voice, saying—"It is me, Don!" From that day on, he stayed with her constantly. On one particular amorous occasion, *her mother clearly discerned a man's outline in the empty bed.* She quickly grabbed a fly swatter and chased the earthbound spirit out of her daughter's bed!

Once, when she was about to put on her coat to go out, the coat, apparently of its own volition, came toward her—as if someone were holding it for her to slip on!

Whenever she was with other men, he kissed her, and she would hear his angry voice.

But this time the séance cracked his selfish shell. "I haven't been able to finish what I started," he sobbed, referring to his important medical experiments. He then asked forgiveness, and that he be allowed to come back to be with Edith now and then.

After we left—Dr. Fodor had come along, too—we all expressed hope that the Bergers would live in peace. But a few weeks later, Edith telephoned me in great excitement. The doctor had returned once more.

I then explained to her that she had to sacrifice—rid herself of her own *desire* to have this man around, unconscious though it may be—and in closing the door on this chapter of her life, make it impossible for the earthbound one to take control of her psychic energies. I have heard nothing further.

✳ 139

The Vineland Ghost

NANCY, AN ATTRACTIVE blonde and her handsome husband Tom moved into the old farm house near Vineland, New Jersey in the summer of 1975. Tom had been a captain in the Air Force when he and Nancy met and fell in love in her native Little Rock, Arkansas. After three years, Tom decided he wanted to leave his career as a pilot and settle down on a farm. They returned to Tom's hometown of Vineland, where Tom got a job as the supervisor of a large food processing company.

The house had been built in 1906 by a family named Hauser who had owned it for many generations until Tom's father acquired it from the last Hauser nineteen years before. Sitting back a few hundred yards from the road, the house has three stories and a delicate turn-of-the-century charm. There is a porch running the width of the front, and ample rooms for a growing family. Originally there were 32 acres to the surrounding farm but Tom and Nancy decided they needed only four acres to do their limited farming. Even though the house was very rundown and would need a lot of repair work, Tom and Nancy liked the quiet seclusion and decided to buy it from Tom's father and restore it to its former glory.

"The first time I walked into this house I felt something horrible had happened in it," Nancy explained to me.

By the time the family had moved in Nancy had forgotten her initial apprehension about the house. But about four weeks later the first mysterious incident occurred.

As Nancy explained it, "I was alone in the house with the children whom I had just put to bed. Suddenly I heard the sound of children laughing outside. I ran outside to look but didn't see anyone. I ran quickly back upstairs but my kinds were safely in their beds, sound asleep, exactly where I'd left them."

That summer Nancy heard the sound of children laughing several times, always when her own were fast asleep. Then one day Nancy discovered her daughter Leslie Ann, then aged three-and-a-half, engaged in lively conversation with an unseen friend. When asked what the

The house of the Vineland ghost

friend looked like, the child seemed amazed her mother couldn't see her playmate herself.

Convinced they had ghostly manifestations in the house, they decided to hold a séance with the help of a friend. After the séance the phenomenon of the unseen children ceased but something else happened—the gravestone incident.

"We found the gravestone when we cleared the land," Tom said. "We had to move it periodically to get it out of the way. We finally left it in the field about a hundred yards away from the house. Suddenly the day after our séance it just decided to relocate itself right outside our back door. It seemed impossible—it would have taken four strong men to move that stone."

For some time Nancy had the uncanny feeling that Ella Hauser, the woman who had built the house was "checking" on the new occupants. Tom had looked on the

The house is peaceful despite the deceased Emma still living there

Emma's tombstone—she isn't there

Ghostly manifestations on the staircase

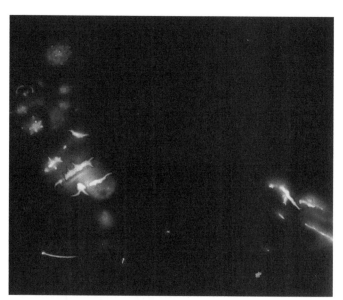

A psychic photo of Emma?

ghostly goings-on in a rather detached, clinical way, but when his tools started disappearing it was too much for even him.

Tom and Nancy were not the only ones who encountered the unknown. In August 1977, a babysitter, Nancy F., was putting the children to bed, when she heard someone going through the drawers downstairs. "She thought it was a prowler looking for something," Nancy explained, "But when she finally went downstairs nothing had been touched."

The night after the babysitter incident Nancy went downstairs to get a drink of water and found a five-foot ten inch tall man standing in her living room—3 o'clock in the morning.

"He was wearing one of those khaki farmer's shirts and a pair of brown work pants. Everything was too big for the guy. I could tell he was an old man. I took one look and ran upstairs."

When I received their telephone call I immediately asked for additional details. It became clear to me that this was a classical case of haunting where structural changes, new owners, and new routines have upset someone who lived in the house and somehow remained in the atmosphere. As is my custom, I assembled the residents and a psychic I had brought with me into an informal circle in the kitchen. Together we asked Ella and whoever else

might be "around" to please go away in peace and with our compassion—to enter those realms where they would be on their own. The atmosphere in the kitchen, which had felt rather heavy until now, seemed to lift.

When I talked to Nancy several weeks after my visit, all was well at the house.

The house is privately owned and I doubt that the Joneses are receiving visitors. But you can drive by it, and most people in Vineland, New Jersey know which one it is.

✳ 140

Amityville, America's Best Known Haunted House

THE NIGHT OF FRIDAY, November 13, 1974, six members of the DeFeo family of Amityville, Long Island, were brutally murdered in their beds—one of the most horrifying and bizarre mass murders of recent memory.

The lone survivor of the crime, Ronald DeFeo Jr., who had initially notified police, was soon after arrested and formally charged with the slayings. But there are aspects of the case that have never been satisfactorily resolved.

When Ronald DeFeo Jr. got up in the middle of the night, took this gun, and murdered his entire family, that wasn't him who did it, he says, but something...someone...who got inside his body and took over. I just couldn't stop, says DeFeo.

Was DeFeo a suitable vehicle for spirit possession? The facts of my investigation strongly suggest it. DeFeo himself doesn't believe in anything supernatural. He doesn't understand what got into him. Did he massacre his family in cold blood, or under the influence of a power from beyond this dimension?

From the outset there were strange aspects to the case: nobody seems to have heard the shots which killed six people...how was it that none of the victims resisted or ran out of the murderer's way? Did they in fact not hear the shots either?

At DeFeo's trial, two eminent psychiatrists differed sharply about the state of the murderer's sanity: Dr. Schwartz considers DeFeo psychotic at the time of the murder, while Dr. Zolan holds him fully responsible for what he did. Rumors to the effect that DeFeo had first drugged his family's food (which would have explained their seeming apathy) proved groundless. The mystery remained even though DeFeo's sentence was clear: twenty-five years to life on each of the six counts of murder in the second degree, served consecutively—as if that mattered. Over and over DeFeo repeated the same story: yes, he had

Amityville—THAT house at 114 Ocean Avenue

Side view of the house

Amityville, America's Best Known Haunted House

Ethel Meyers, the famous trance medium, getting her bearings

Ethel in deep trance. The Indian chief has made contact

Psychic manifestations in one of the rooms

what was shaping up as a case of suspected possession. Although Mrs. Meyers hadn't the slightest notion where she was or why I had brought her there, she immediately stated: "Whoever lives here is going to be the victim of all the anger...the blind fierceness...this is Indian burial ground, sacred to them." As she was gradually slipping into trance, I asked why the Indian spirits were so angry.

"A white person got to digging around and dug up a skeleton...." She described a long-jawed Indian whose influence she felt in the house.

"People get to fighting with each other and they don't know why...they're driven to it because they are taken over by him." According to Mrs. Meyers, the long-ago misdeed of a white settler is still being avenged, every white man on the spot is an enemy, and when a catalyst moves there, he becomes a perfect vehicle for possession... like Ronald DeFeo.

"I see a dark young man wandering around at night ...like in a trance...goes berserk...a whole family is involved....," the medium said and a shiver went up my spine. She had tuned right in to the terrible past of the house.

When the pictures taken by the psychic photographer were developed on the spot, some of them showed strange haloes exactly where the bullets had struck...my camera jammed even though it had been working perfectly just before and was fine again the minute we left the house on Ocean Avenue...a house totally empty of life as we know it and yet filled with the shades of those who have passed on yet linger for they know not where to go....

All sorts of charlatans had been to the house attracted by cheap publicity...until the new owners had enough. They knew all about the phenomena first-hand and eventually a best-selling book was based upon their experiences

killed his family, and felt no remorse over it...but no, he didn't know why. Something...someone had gotten inside his person and forced him to shoot...going from bedroom to bedroom at 3 A.M. and exterminating the same parents, brothers and sisters he had lovingly embraced at a birthday party in the house a scant two months before the crime... whatever had gotten into DeFeo surely knew no mercy.

On January 15, 1977 I brought reputable trance medium Ethel Johnson Meyers to the house on Ocean Avenue, along with a psychic photographer to investigate

CHAPTER EIGHT: **Haunted People**

...embellished, enlarged and elaborated upon...but that is another kind of story. The real story was clear: 112 Ocean Avenue had been a psychically active location for perhaps two centuries...the phenomena ranging from footsteps and doors opening by themselves to the apparitions of figures that dissolve into thin air are well-attested poltergeist manifestations, phenomena observed in literally thousands of similar cases all over the world...grist for the mills of the parapsychologist who knows there is no such thing as the supernatural, only facets of human personality transcending the old boundaries of conventional psychology....DeFeo had painted a little room in the basement red, because the color pleased him. The room he used as a kind of toolshed. An eighteenth century owner of the spot allegedly practiced witchcraft: add it all up, and enter the devil....DeFeo Sr. was a devoutly religious man who believed the devil was in the house, but his son left the house the minute the priest his father had called moved in.

When all the Satanic fallout had settled, I decided to investigate with the result that the real Amityville story began to emerge. What happened at Amityville could have happened anywhere in the world where passions are spent and human lives terminated by violence. The residue of the great crime lingers on even as the vehicle of possession gropes for an explanation of his true status. Young DeFeo is not a believer in things that go bump in the night, nor does he fear either God or the devil. But as he awaits still another interminable day in his cell at Dannemora prison, Ronald DeFeo cannot help wondering about the stranger within, the force that made him commit what he considers impossible crimes. He could have killed his father in an argument, perhaps, he concedes, but not his mother, not the children.

DeFeo may never get an answer he can live with, but he is young and may yet see the day when some future owner of that house has his innings with the unknown. For that day will surely come. I've tried to exorcise the angry entity in the house, and though I have frequently succeeded in such cases, so much accumulated hatred is too powerful a reservoir to simply fade away. But in the end, we all get justice, one way or another.

CHAPTER NINE

Stay-Behinds

STAY-BEHINDS IS A TERM I have invented. It refers to earthbound spirits or ghosts who owe their continued residency in what may have been their long-term home to the fact that they don't want to leave familiar surroundings. This is not simply a willful decision ("I ain't goin'"), though that can on occasion be the case; the majority are people who have never been told where to go and are expecting the kind of fanciful heaven their faith has for so long pictured for them. Naturally, when they pass out of the physical body they are disappointed, or at least surprised, not to see a reception committee of angels and cherubs showing them the way to Heaven, God, and possibly Jesus as well.

Instead, they find their loved ones who have preceded them to the "other side"; they have come to make the transition easier. If the death is due to severe illness or prolonged hospitalization (including heavy doses of drugs) the person will often be confused and need to be placed into healing facilities "over there" for a while.

But the majority of people are not prepared for what comes next: some will prefer the devil they know to the devil they don't know as yet—meaning, of course, not a literal devil (a figment of the imagination) but a figure of speech. The unknown frightens them. They cling to what they know.

The Pennsylvania lady who passed on at 90 years of age—she had spent most of them in her house—was not at all prepared for her funeral and points beyond. So when the grieving relatives returned from the cemetery, guess who was already there, in the lady's old chair, waiting to welcome them back—the lady in question, feeling no pain, naturally, having lost or gotten rid of her physical shell.

It is a bit tricky at times to differentiate between a true stay-behind (a person) and an impression from the past. Only when the apparition moves or speaks can you really judge.

Stay-behinds are different from resident ghosts in another important aspect. True ghosts will resent new tenants, or even visitors, and will consider them intruders in "their" house. But the stay-behind could not care less: it is his or her place all right, but the stay-behind's attitude is the same as it was before death. Just you leave me be and I won't bother you!

When The Dead Stay On

NOTHING IS SO EXASPERATING as a dead person in a living household. I mean a ghost has a way of disturbing things far beyond the powers held by the wraith while still among the quick. Very few people realize that a ghost is not someone out to pester you for the sake of being an annoyance, or to attract attention for the sake of being difficult. Far from it. We know by now that ghosts are unhappy beings caught between two states and unable to adjust to either one.

Most people "pass over" without difficulty and are rarely heard from again, except when a spiritualist insists on raising them, or when an emergency occurs among the family that makes intervention by the departed a desired, or even necessary, matter.

They do their bit, and then go again, looking back at their handiwork with justified pride. *The dead are always among us,* make no mistake about that. They obey their own set of laws that forbids them to approach us or let us know their presence except when conditions require it. But they can do other things to let us feel them near, and these little things can mean a great deal when they are recognized as sure signs of a loved one's nearness.

Tragedies create ghosts through shock conditions, and nothing can send them out of the place where they found a sad end except the realization of their own emotional entanglement. This can be accomplished by allowing them to communicate through trance. But there are also cases in which the tragedy is not sudden, but gradual, and the unnatural attachment to physical life creates the ghost syndrome. The person who refuses to accept peacefully the transition called death, and holds on to material surroundings, becomes a ghost when these feelings of resistance and attachment become psychotic.

Such persons will then regard the houses they lived and died in as still theirs, and will look on latter owners or tenants as merely unwanted intruders who must be forced out of the place by any means available. The natural way to accomplish this is to show themselves to the living as often as possible, to assert their continued ownership. If that won't do it, move objects, throw things, make noises— let them know whose house this is!

The reports of such happenings are many. Every week brings new cases from reliable and verified witnesses, and the pattern begins to emerge pretty clearly.

A lady from Ridgewood, New York, wrote to me about a certain house on Division Avenue in Brooklyn, where she had lived as a child. A young grandmother, Mrs. Petre had a good education and an equally good memory. She remembered the name of her landlord while she was still a youngster, and even the names of *all* her teachers at Public School 19. The house her family had rented consisted of a basement, parlor floor, and a top floor where the bedrooms were located.

On a certain warm October day, she found herself in the basement, while her mother was upstairs. She knew there was no one else in the house. When she glanced at the glass door shutting off the stairs, with the glass pane acting almost like a mirror, she saw to her amazement a man peeking around the doorway. Moments before she had heard heavy footsteps coming down the stairs, and wondered if someone had gotten into the house while she and her mother had been out shopping. She screamed and ran out of the house, but did not tell her family about the stranger.

Sometime after, she sat facing the same stairs in the company of her bother and sister-in-law, when she heard the footsteps again and the stranger appeared. Only this time she got a good look at him and was able to describe his thin, very pale face, his black hair, and the black suit and fedora hat he wore.

Nobody believed the girl, of course, and even the landlady accused her of imagining all this. But after a year, her father became alarmed at his daughter's nervousness and decided to move. Finally, the landlady asked for details of the apparition, and listened as the girl described the ghost she had seen.

"My God," the landlady, a Mrs. Grimshaw, finally said. "I knew that man—he hanged himself on the top floor!"

* * *

Sometimes the dead will only stay on until things have been straightened out to their taste. Anna Arrington was a lady with the gift of mediumship who lived in New York State. In 1944, her mother-in-law, a woman of some wealth, passed on in Wilmington, North Carolina, and was buried there. There was some question about her will. Three days after her death, Mrs. Arrington was awakened from heavy sleep at 3 A.M. by a hand touching hers.

Her first thought was that one of her two children wanted something. On awakening, however, she saw her mother-in-law in a flowing white gown standing at the foot of her bed. While her husband continued to snore, the ghost put a finger to Mrs. Arrington's lips and asked her not to awaken her son, but to remember that the missing will was in the dining room of her house on top of the dish closet under a sugar bowl. Mrs. Arrington was roundly laughed at by her husband the next morning, but several days later his sister returned from Wilmington (the Arringtons lived in New York City at the time) and confirmed that the will had indeed been found where the ghost had indicated.

* * *

Back in the 1960s, I was approached by a gentleman named Paul Herring, who was born in Germany, and who lived in a small apartment on Manhattan's East Side as well as in a country house in Westchester County, New York. He was in the restaurant business and not given to dreaming or speculation. He struck me as a simple, solid citizen. His aged mother, also German-born, lived with him, and a large German shepherd dog completed the household.

Mr. Herring was not married, and his mother was a widow. What caused them to reach me was the peculiar way in which steps were heard around the Westchester house when nobody was walking. On three separate occasions, Mrs. Herring saw an apparition in her living room.

"It was sort of blackish," she said, "but I recognized it instantly. It was my late husband."

The "black outline" of a man also appeared near light fixtures, and there were noises in the house that had no natural origins.

"The doors are forever opening and closing by themselves," the son added. "We're going crazy trying to keep up with that spook."

Their bedspreads were being pulled off at night. They were touched on the face by an unseen hand, especially after dark.

The September before, Mrs. Herring was approaching the swinging doors of the living room, when the door moved out by itself and met her! A table in the kitchen moved by its own volition in plain daylight.

Her other son, Max, who lived in Norfolk, Virginia, always left the house in a hurry because "he can't breathe" in it. Her dog, Noxy, was forever disturbed when they were out in the Westchester house.

"How long has this been going on, Mrs. Herring?" I asked.

"About four years at least," the spunky lady replied, "but my husband died ten years ago."

It then developed that he had divorced her and married another woman, and there were no surviving children from that union. Still, the "other woman" had kept all of Mr. Herring Sr.'s money—no valid will was ever found. Was the ghost protesting this injustice to his companion of so many years? Was he regretting his hasty step divorcing her and marrying another?

The Herrings weren't the only ones to hear the footsteps. A prospective tenant who came to rent the country house fled after hearing some walk *through a closed door*.

* * *

Mrs. E. F. Newbold seems to have been followed by ghosts since childhood—as if she were carrying a lamp aloft to let the denizens of the nether world know she had the sixth sense.

"I'm haunted," she said. "I've been followed by a 'what's it' since I was quite young. It simply pulls the back of my skirt. No more than that…, but when you're alone in the middle of a room, this can be awfully disconcerting."

I thought of Grandma Thurston's ghost, and how she had pulled my elbow a couple of years before while I was investigating an empty room in a pre-colonial house in Connecticut, and I couldn't agree more. Mrs. Newbold's family had psychic experiences also. Her little girl had felt a hand on her shoulder. It ran in the family.

"My husband's aunt died in Florida, while I was in New Jersey. We had been very close, and I said good-bye to her body here at the funeral at 10 A.M. At 9 P.M. I went into my kitchen and though I could not see her, I *knew* she was sitting at the table, staring at my back, and pleading with me."

"What about this skirt pulling?"

"It has followed me through a house, an apartment, a succession of rented rooms, two new houses, and two old houses. I've had a feeling of not being alone, and of sadness. I've also felt a hand on my shoulder, and heard pacing footsteps, always overhead.

"The next house we lived in was about 35 years old, had had only one owner, still alive, and no one had died there. It looked like a haunted house, but it was only from neglect. We modernized it, and *then* it started! Pulling at my skirt went on fairly often. One night when I was alone, that is, my husband was out of town and our three children were sound asleep—I checked them just before and just after—I was watching TV in the living room, when I heard the outside cellar door open. I looked out the window to see if someone was breaking in, since I had locked the door shortly before. While I was watching, I *heard* it close firmly. The door didn't move, however. This door had a distinctive sound so I couldn't have mistaken it.

"I went back to my seat and picked up my scissors, wishing for a gun. I was sure I heard a prowler. Now I heard slow footsteps come up from the cellar, through the laundry room, kitchen, into the living room, right past me, and up the stairs to the second floor. They stopped at the top of the stairs, and I never heard it again. Nor do I want to. Those steps went past me, no more than five feet away, and the room was empty. Unfortunately, I have no corroboration, but I *was* wide awake and perfectly sober!"

So much for the lady from Harrington Park, New Jersey.

* * *

Miss Margaret C. and her family lived in what surely was a haunted house, so that I won't give her full name. But here is her report.

In December of 1955, just two days before Christmas, I traveled to Pennsylvania to spend the holidays with my sister and her husband. They lived on the second floor (the apartment I am now renting) of a spacious mid-Victorian-style home built around a hundred years ago.

Due to the death of my sister's mother-in-law, who had resided on the first floor of the house, the occasion was not an entirely joyous one, but we came for the sake of my brother-in-law.

Having come all the was from Schenectady, New York, we retired between ten-thirty and eleven o'clock. The room I slept in was closest to the passage leading to the downstairs, and the two were separated only by a door.

Once in bed, I found it rather difficult to sleep. As I lay there, I heard a piano playing. It sounded like a very old piano and it played church music. I thought it quite strange that my brother-in-law's father would be listening to his radio at that hour, but felt more annoyed than curious.

The next morning, as we were having coffee, I mentioned this to my sister. She assured me that her father-in-law would *not* be listening to the radio at that hour and I assured *her* that I *had* heard piano music. It was then she mentioned the old piano her husband's mother had owned for many years and which sat in the downstairs front room.

We decided to go and have a look at it. The dust that had settled on the keyboard was quite thick, and as definite as they could possibly be were the imprints of someone's fingers. Not normal fingers, but apparently quite thin and bony fingers. My sister's mother-in-law had been terribly thin and she loved to play her piano, especially church music. There was positively no one else in the house who even knew how to play the piano, except my mother, who lived with my sister and her husband.

* * *

Another New Jersey lady named Louise B., whose full name and address I have in my files, told me of an experience she will never forget.

I cannot explain why I am sending this on to you, merely that I feel compelled to do so, and after many years of following my compulsions, as I call them, must do so.

My mother had a bachelor cousin who died and was buried around Valentine's Day, 1932. He had lived with two maiden aunts in Ridgewood, New Jersey, for most of his lifetime. He was a well-known architect in this area. He designed local monuments, one of which is standing in the Park in Ridgewood today. He was short of statute, with piercing eyes and a bushy gray full beard, and he smoked too many cigars. I was not quite 14 years old when he passed away.

My parents decided to spare me the burial detail, and they left me at home on the way to the cemetery with instructions to stay at home until they returned. They planned on attending the burial, going back to the house with my great-aunts and then coming home before dinner, which in our house was 6 P.M.

I have no recollection of what I did with my time in the afternoon, but remember that just before dusk I had gone indoors and at the time I was in our dining room, probably setting the table for dinner, as this was one of my chores.

We had three rooms downstairs: the living room faced north and ran the full length of the house, while the kitchen and dining room faced southeast and southwest respectively, and a T-shaped partition divided the rooms. There was a large archway separating the dining and living rooms.

I don't recall when I became aware of a "presence." I didn't see anything with my eyes, rather I *felt* what I "saw," or somehow sensed it and my sense "saw." This is not a good explanation, but about the closest I can come to what I felt.

This presence was not in any one spot in the room, but something that was gradually surrounding me, like the air that I was breathing, and it was frightening and menacing and very evil and stronger, and somehow he word *denser* seemed to apply and I knew that it was "Uncle" Oscar. I could feel him coming at me from every direction (like music that gets louder and louder), and my senses "saw" him as he had been dressed in the casket, with a red ribbon draped across his chest, only he was alive and I was aware of some terrible determination on his part and suddenly I knew that somehow he was trying to "get inside me" and I began to back away. I don't recall speaking, nor his speaking to me. I just knew what his intention was and who he was. I last remember screaming helplessly and uselessly at him to go away. I do not know how long this lasted. I only know that suddenly he was gone, and my parents came into the room. I was hysterical, they tell me, and it took some doing to quiet me.

Many years later Mrs. B. discovered that "Uncle" Oscar had died a raving maniac to the last.

* * *

Grace Rivers was a secretary by profession, a lady of good background, and not given to hallucinations or emotional outbursts. I had spoken with her several times and always found her most reluctant to discuss what to her seemed incredible.

It seemed that on weekends, Miss Rivers and another secretary, by the name of Juliet, were the house guests of their employer, John Bergner, in Westbrook, Connecticut. Miss Rivers was also a good friend of this furniture manufacturer, a man in his middle fifties. She had joined the Bergner firm in 1948, six years after John Bergner had become the owner of a country house built in 1865.

Bergner liked to spend his weekends among his favorite employees, and sometimes asked some of the office boys as well as his two secretaries to come up to Connecticut with him. All was most idyllic until the early 1950s, when John Bergner met an advertising man by the name of Philip Mervin. This business relationship soon broadened into a social friendship, and before long Mr. Mervin was a steady and often self-invited house guest in Westbrook.

At first, this did not disturb anyone very much, but when Mervin noticed the deep and growing friendship between Bergner and his right-hand assistant, something akin to jealousy prompted him to interfere with this relationship at every turn. What made this triangle even more difficult for Mervin to bear was the apparent innocence with which Bergner treated Mervin's approaches. Naturally, a feeling of dislike grew into hatred between Miss Rivers and the intruder, but before it came to any open argument, the advertising man suddenly died of a heart attack at age 51.

But that did not seem to be the end of it by a long shot.

Soon after his demise, the Connecticut weekends were again interrupted, this time by strange noises no natural cause could account for. Most of the uncanny experiences were witnessed by both women as well as by some of the office men, who seemed frightened by it all. With the detachment of a good executive secretary, Miss Rivers lists the phenomena:

Objects moving in space.
Stones hurled at us inside and outside the house.
Clanging of tools in the garage at night (when nobody was there).
Washing machine starting up at 1 A.M., *by itself*.
Heavy footsteps, banging of doors, in the middle of the night.
Television sets turning themselves on and off at will.
A spoon constantly leaping out of a cutlery tray.
The feeling of a cold wind being swept over one.

And there was more, much more.

When a priest was brought to the house to exorcise the ghost, things only got worse. Evidently the deceased had little regard for holy men.

Juliet, the other secretary, brought her husband along. One night in 1962, when Juliet's husband slept in what was once the advertising man's favorite guest room, he heard clearly a series of knocks, as if someone were hitting the top of the bureau. Needless to say, her husband had been alone in the room, and he did not do the knocking.

It became so bad that Grace Rivers no longer looked forward to those weekend invitations at her employer's country home. She feared them. It was then that she remembered, with terrifying suddenness, a remark the late Mr. Mervin had made to her fellow-workers.

"If anything *ever* happens to me and I die, I'm going to walk after those two girls the rest of their lives!" he had said.

Miss Rivers realized that he was keeping his word.

Her only hope was that the ghost of Mr. Mervin would someday be distracted by an earlier specter that was sharing the house with him. On several occasions, an old woman in black had been seen emerging from a side door of the house. A local man, sitting in front of the house during the weekdays when it was unoccupied—Bergner came up only on weekends—was wondering aloud to Miss Rivers about the "old lady who claimed she occupied the back part of the house." He had encountered her on many occasions, always seeing her disappear into the house by that same, seldom-used, side door. One of the office workers invited by John Bergner also saw her around 1:30 A.M. on a Sunday morning, when he stood outside the house, unable to get to sleep. When she saw him she said hello, and mentioned something about money, then disappeared into a field.

Grace Rivers looked into the background of the house and discovered that it had previously belonged to a very aged man who lived there with his mother. When she died, he found money buried in the house, but he claimed his mother had hidden more money that he had never been able to locate. Evidently the ghost of his mother felt the same way about it, and was still searching. For that's how it is with ghosts sometimes—they become forgetful about material things.

* * *

The Peter Hofmann family consisted of husband, wife Pennie, and baby—then about three or four years old. The parents were articulate, well-educated people making their home in Harvard. Not Harvard University, but Harvard near Ayer, Massachusetts, about an hour's ride from the university.

An automobile accident in 1956 had left Mrs. Hofmann partially paralyzed, but her keen gift of observation was not impaired. She had always had a peculiar liking for graveyards, and her first psychic experience, in 1951, consisted of a vision of a horse-drawn hearse that had passed near a cemetery. One could argue that lots of such hearses used to pull into cemeteries, but the fact remains that Mrs. Hofmann's was not a real one.

Their house stands next to a house built by Mrs. Hofmann's father, a well-known physician, and it seemed that both houses were haunted. The larger house, owned by Mrs. Hofmann's father, was built in 1721 "on the bounty received from an Indian scalp."

From the first moment she saw it, Pennie Hofmann had odd sensations about it. In 1960 or 1961, she and her husband were spending the night there, when at about two in the morning they both woke up for no apparent reason.

"I spoke to what I thought was Pete," she said, "as I could see someone by the front window, but it turned out that Pete was *behind* me. Needless to say, we left right away."

Peter Hofmann nodded and added: "I myself have been in the house at night a few times alone, and I've always had the feeling I was being watched."

Then in late October 1963, Pennie Hofmann phoned me in New York. Could I please come to Boston and tell her if she was *seeing things*?

What sort of things, I asked.

"Well," she replied, somewhat upset, "we'd been staying over in my father's house again a week ago. I saw a soldier in the bedroom. He was dark and had a noose around the neck; the rope was cut and his face seemed almost luminous. I swear I saw him."

I hurried to Boston and they met me at radio station WBZ.

What about the ghostly soldier? Any clues?

Both Hofmanns nodded.

"We've checked in Nourse's *History of the Town of Harvard*," Mrs. Hoffman said gravely, "and there was a colonial drummer named Hill who was hanged in this area . . . for some misdeeds."

I remembered her telling me of a ghost in their own house on Poor Farm Road, and Mrs. Hofmann filled me in on this far gentler wraith.

"During the summer months," she explained, "there is what appears to be a Quaker lady that walks across our front lawn, usually during the afternoon. This person often appears many times a day."

Her husband added that she had given him many details of the ghost's dress, which he checked for authenticity. He found that they were indeed worn by the Quaker women of the eighteenth century.

Why a member of so gentle a persuasion as the Quakers would turn into a ghost we may never know, but perhaps someday the Quaker lady will walk again for me.

* * *

There is said to be the ghost of a pirate near the water's edge in old Boston, where so many secret passages existed in the days when Massachusetts was British. The *Black Lady of Warren Island,* out in the bay, has been seen by a number of people. She was executed during the Civil War for helping her husband, a Yankee prisoner, break out of prison.

Boston's emotional climate is fine for special activities. There may not be any medieval castles, but Beacon Hill can look pretty forbidding, too—especially on a chilly November night when the fog drifts in from the sea.

In September 1963 I appeared on WBZ-TV on Mike Douglas' television show, discussing my ever-present interest in haunted houses. As a consequence, there was an avalanche of letters, many of which contained leads to new cases.

One came from a Mrs. Anne Valukis, of South Natick, near Boston, Massachusetts. She wrote me of an old house she lived in where the stairs creaked unaccountably at odd times, as if someone were walking up and down them; of the strange behavior her little boy showed whenever he was in a certain room of the house; and of an overall atmosphere of the uncanny prevailing throughout the house, as if an unseen force were always present.

I wrote for additional data about herself and the background of the house. Meanwhile, the public television station in Boston, Channel 2, took an interest in my work, and the station and I decided to join forces for an expedition to the haunted house in South Natick. Fred Barzyk, the director, undertook the preliminary task of additional research. My visit was scheduled for the last week of October. Mrs. Valukis wasn't long in answering me.

"The stairs haven't creaked for over a week, but my four-year-old woke Saturday night four times, and was really scared, so much so he would not go back upstairs to his room. . . . Years ago this house was kind of a speakeasy, connected to a dance hall that was on the Charles River. Probably anything could have happened here. Who knows?"

Not because of the spooky stairs, but for other reasons, the Valukis family decided to move to Anne's parents' house. This made our visit problematical, until Fred Barzyk discovered that the house belonging to Mrs. Valukis' parents was even more haunted than Anne Valukis' place.

Mrs. Rose Josselyn, Anne's mother, was a Canadian Indian, and, like many of her people, had had psychic experiences all her life.

About 39 years before I met her, Mrs. Josselyn was living in Annapolis Royal, Canada, in what was purported to be a haunted house. Frequently she awoke in the middle of the night and found it difficult to breathe. Her arms seemed to be pinned down by an unseen force and she was unable to move even so much as finger!

"It felt as if someone were choking me," she said to me later. "I tried to scream, but could not move my lips."

This had gone on for about a year. Finally Rose told her mother, who was mediumistic herself, and Rose was forbidden ever to sleep again in "that room." Twenty years alter, Mrs. Josselyn still remembered the stark terror of those nights in Canada, but nothing like it had happened to her since—nothing, that is, until she moved into this house.

The house itself was a gray-white, medium-sized early American house, built in the stately manner of early Georgian architecture and very well preserved. It was set back from the road a bit, framed by tall, shady trees, and one had the feeling of being far from the bustle of the big city. Built about 150 years before, the house had an upper story and total of eight rooms. Bordering on the lawn of the house was a cemetery, separated from the Josselyn house by an iron gate and fence.

When the Josselyns moved in with their family, Mrs. Josselyn had no thoughts of anything psychic or uncanny. She soon learned differently.

Upstairs, there were two bedrooms separated only by a thin wall. The larger one belonged to Mrs. Josselyn; the smaller one, to the rear of the house, to her husband Roy. It was in her bedroom that Mrs. Josselyn had another attack of the terrible feeling she had experienced in her

Canadian youth. Pinned down on her bed, it was as if someone were upon her, holding her.

"Whose bedroom was this before you took it?" I inquired.

"Well, my daughter-in-law slept here for a while," Mrs. Josselyn confided, "that is, before she died."

I asked further questions about this girl. At the age of 21, she had fallen ill and suffered her last agonies in this very room, before being taken off to a hospital, never to return. Her only child, to whom she was naturally very attached, was reared by Mrs. Josselyn and Mrs. Valukis.

I walked across the floor to a small room belonging to David Josselyn, 17, the brother of Mrs. Valukis. Here I was shown a hand-made wooden chair that was said to creak at odd moments, as if someone were sitting in it. David himself had been awakened many times by this unearthly behavior of his chair, and Anne had also observed the noise. I tried the chair. It was sturdy enough, and only strong efforts on my part produced any kind of noise. It could not have creaked by itself.

"Who gave you this chair?" I asked.

"The same man who made our clock downstairs," David said. I recalled seeing a beautiful wooden grandfather clock in the corner of the downstairs room. The odd thing about that clock was it sometimes ticked and the hands moved, even though it no longer had any works or pendulum!

The clock, chair, and a desk in David's room were the work of a skilled craftsman named Thomas Council, who was a well-liked house guest of the Josselyns and gave them these things to show his gratitude for their hospitality. He was a lonely bachelor and the Josselyns were his only close friends. David in particular was the apple of his eye. Thomas Council's body rested comfortably, it is hoped, across the way in the cemetery, and the Josselyns made sure there were always fresh flowers on his grave.

I decided to return to Mrs. Josselyn's room.

"Outside of your nightmarish experiences here and in Canada," I said, "have you had any other psychic incidents?"

Mrs. Josselyn, a serious, quiet woman of about 59, thought for a moment.

"Yes, frequently. Whenever my children are in some sort of trouble, I just know it. No matter how trifling. You might say we have telepathic contact."

"Did you also hear those stairs creak at your daughter's house across the road?"

"Yes, many times."

"Was that after or before your daughter-in-law passed away?"

"After."

"I clearly heard those steps upstairs, and there wasn't anyone but me and the baby in the house," added Anne Valukis for corroboration.

They all had been visited, it seemed to me, except the father, Roy Josselyn. It was time I turned my attention in his direction.

Mr. Josselyn sat on the bed in his room, quietly smoking a pipe. I had been warned by Fred Barzyk that the man of the house was no particular believer in the supernatural. To my relief, I discovered Mr. Josselyn at least had an open mind. I also discovered that a great-aunt of his in Vermont had been a spiritualistic medium.

I asked if he had seen or heard anything unusual.

"Well," he said, "about a year ago I started to hear some moans and groans around here . . . ," he pointed toward the wall adjoining the bedroom occupied by his wife. "At first I thought it was my wife, but there was no one in her room at the time. I looked."

"This moaning . . . was it a human voice?"

"Oh yes, very human. Couldn't sleep a wink while it lasted."

"When did you last hear it?"

"Yesterday," he said laconically.

"How did you and your daughter-in-law get along?" I suddenly felt compelled to ask.

"Very well," he said. "As a matter of fact, she took more to me than to anyone else. You know how women are —a bit jealous. She was a little on the possessive side as far her baby was concerned. I mean, she was very much worried abut the child."

"But she wasn't jealous of you?"

"No, not of me. We were very close."

I thought of the 21-year-old girl taken by death without being ready for it, and the thoughts of fear for her child that must have gone through her mind those dreadful last hours when her moaning filled the air of the room next to Roy Josselyn's.

I also thought about Mrs. Roy Josselyn's background —the fact that she was Princess of the Micmac Indian tribe. I remembered how frequent psychic experiences were among Indians, who are so much closer to nature than we city-dwellers.

Perhaps the restless spirit of the 21-year-old girl wanted some attention. Perhaps her final moments had only impressed themselves on the atmosphere of the upstairs room and were relived by the psychically sensitive members of the family. Perhaps, too, Thomas Council, the family friend, roamed the house now and then to make sure everything was all right with his favorite family.

When we drove back to Boston late that night, I felt sure I had met a haunted family, for better or worse.

✴ 142

Alabama Stay-Behinds

WARREN F. GODFREY is an educated man who works for the NASA Center in Houston. He and his wife Gwen had no particular interest in the occult and were always careful not to let their imagination run away with them. They lived in a house in Huntsville, Alabama, which was, at the time they moved into it, only three years old. At first they had only a feeling that *the house didn't want them.* There was nothing definite about this, but as time went on they would look over their shoulders to see if they were being followed, and felt silly doing so. Then, gradually, peculiar noises started. Ordinarily such noises would not disturb them, and they tried very hard to blame the settling of the house. There were cracks in the ceiling, the popping and cracking of corners, then the walls would join in, and after a while there would be silence again. Faucets would start to drip for no apparent reason. Doors would swing open and/or shut by themselves, and a dish would shift in the cupboard. All these things could perhaps have been caused by a house's settling, but the noises seemed to become organized. Warren noticed that the house had a definite atmosphere. There seemed to be a feeling that the house objected to the young couple's happiness. It seemed to want to disturb their togetherness in whatever way it could, and it managed to depress them.

Then there were knockings. At first these were regularly spaced single sharp raps proceeding from one part of the house to another. Warren ran out and checked the outside of the house, under it, and everywhere and could discover no reason for the knocks. As all this continued, they became even more depressed and neither liked to stay alone in the house. About Thanksgiving 1968 they went to visit Warren's mother in Illinois for a few days. After they returned to the empty house it seemed quieter, even happier. Shortly before Christmas, Warren had to go to Houston on business. While he was gone Gwen took a photograph of their daughter Leah. When the picture was developed there was an additional head on the film, with the face in profile and wearing some sort of hat. Warren, a scientist, made sure that there was no natural reason for this extra face on the film. Using a Kodak Instamatic camera with a mechanism that excludes any double exposure, he duplicated the picture and also made sure that a reflection could not have caused the second image. Satisfied that he had obtained sufficient proof to preclude a natural origin for the second face on the film, he accepted the psychic origin of the picture.

About that time they began hearing voices. One night Warren woke up to hear two men arguing in a nearby room. At first he dismissed it as bad dream and went back to sleep, but several nights later the same thing happened. After listening to them for a while he shrugged his shoulders and went back to sleep. He could not understand a word they were saying but was sure that there were two men arguing. After several weeks of this his wife also heard the voices. To Warren this was gratifying, since he was no longer alone in hearing them. The time when both of them heard the voices was generally around 1 A.M. In addition to the two men arguing, Gwen has also heard a woman crying and Warren has heard people laughing. The noises are not particularly directed toward them, nor do they feel that there is anything evil about them. Gradually they have learned to ignore them. As a trained scientist, Warren tried a rational approach to explain the phenomena but could not find any cause. Turning on the lights did not help either. The phenomena occurred only in the master bedroom. There are no television stations on the air at that time of the morning, and there is no house close enough for human voices to carry that far. In trying to reach for a natural explanation, Warren considered the fact that caves extended underneath the area, but what they were hearing was not the noise of rushing waters. Those were human voices and they were right there in the room with them. They decided to learn to live with their unseen boarders and perhaps the ghosts might eventually let them in on their "problem." Not that Warren and Gwen could do much about them, but it is always nice to know what your friends are talking about, especially when you share your bedroom with them.

*   *   *

Mary Carol Henry is in her early thirties, lives in Montgomery and is married to a medical technician in the USAF. She is the mother of seven children and has had psychic experiences from early childhood. When Mary was twelve years old one of her older brothers moved to Pittsburgh. She lent a helping hand with the furniture and other belongings and decided to stay overnight so she could help them finish up the work early in the morning. The house was an old four-story one in the Hazelwood section of Pittsburgh. Mary and the children slept up on the third floor, but she felt very uneasy about staying. Somehow the house bothered her. Since she had promised to stay overnight, however, she went to bed around 10 P.M. and lay in bed for a while thinking about why the house had troubled her. Her brother's baby slept in the same room with her and after a while her brother came up to check on the child. She then heard him go back downstairs. Mary wasn't sure how much time had elapsed when she thought she heard him come up again. There was the rustling of newspapers or something that sounded like it, and she assumed it was her brother, since he was in the habit of taking a newspaper with him when he went to the bathroom. She turned over, and instead of her brother, to her amazement she saw a young girl come out of a closet. Immediately she recognized her as her little sister Patsy who had been killed in a gas explosion in August 1945 at the age of five. The ghost wore the same gown she had been buried in and she looked exactly as she had when she was alive but somehow larger in build. Her apparition was enveloped by a green light. As Mary stared in disbelief the ghost came over to the bed and sat on the side of it. Mary saw the bed actually sink in where Patsy sat on it. Her sister than put her hands on Mary's and kissed her on the cheek. Mary felt the kiss as if it were the kiss of a living person. Then the apparition vanished. Still dazed with fear, Mary sprang out of bed and spent the rest of the night on the stairs. When she told her experience to her mother later, her mother assured her that her late sister had only come back to comfort her in what must have been unfamiliar surroundings, for if Mary was to see a ghost that night it might just as well be someone in the family, not a stranger.

✳ 143

Arkansas Stay-Behinds

HOLLYGROVE IS ONLY a small town in eastern Arkansas, but to Sharon Inebnit it is the center of her world. She lives there with her farmer husband in quiet, rural Arkansas far from metropolitan centers. Little Rock is a long way off and not a place one is likely to visit often. Her mother lives in Helena close to the Mississippi state line. Traveling east on Highway 86 and then on 49 Sharon has gone back and forth a few times in her young life. She knows the area well. It is not an area of particular merit but it has one advantage; it's very quiet. About halfway between Hollygrove and Helena stands an old house that attracted Sharon every time she passed it. There was no reason for it, and yet whenever she passed the old house something within her wondered what the house's secret was.

Sharon is now in her early twenties. She lived with an extraordinary gift of ESP since infancy. That is a subject one doesn't discuss freely in her part of the world. People either ridicule you or, worse, think you're in league with the devil. So Sharon managed to keep her powers to herself even though at times she couldn't help surprising people. She would often hear voices of people who weren't even within sight. If she wanted someone to call her, all she had to do was visualize the person and, presto, the person would ring her. Whenever the telephone rings she knows exactly who is calling. Frequently she has heard her neighbors talking 500 yards from her house, yet she is so sensitive she cannot stand the television when it is turned on too loud.

Her husband, a farmer of Swiss extraction, is somewhat skeptical of her powers. He is less skeptical now than he was when he first met her. Back in the summer of 1963 when she and her present husband first kept company, she was already somewhat of a puzzle to him. One day, the fifteen-year-old girl insisted they drive into Helena, which was about five miles from where they were then. Her boyfriend wanted to know why. She insisted that there was a baseball game going on and that a private swimming party was in progress at the municipal pool. She had no reason to make this statement, however, nor any proof that it was correct, but they were both very much interested in baseball games, so her boyfriend humored her and decided to drive on to Helena. When they arrived at Helena they found that a baseball game was indeed going on and that a private swimming party was in progress at the municipal pool just as Sharon had said. Helena has a population of over 10,000 people. Sharon lives 25 miles away. How could she have known this?

In March of 1964 her maternal grandmother passed away. She had been close to her but for some reason was unable to see her in her last moments. Thus the death hit her hard and she felt great remorse at not having seen her grandmother prior to her passing. On the day of the funeral she was compelled to look up, and there before her appeared her late grandmother. Smiling at her, she nodded and then vanished. But in the brief moment when she had become visible to Sharon the girl understood what her grandmother wanted her to know. The message was brief. Her grandmother understood why she had not been able to see her in her last hours and wanted to forgive her.

In April 1964 when she was just sixteen years old she married her present husband. They went to Memphis, Tennessee, for four days. All during their honeymoon Sharon insisted on returning home. She felt something was wrong at home, even though she couldn't pinpoint it. Though it wasn't a hot period of the year she felt extremely warm and very uncomfortable. Eventually her husband gave in to her urgings and returned home with her. Assuming that her psychic feelings concerned an accident they might have on the road, she insisted that they drive very carefully and slowly. There was no accident. However, when they entered the driveway of her home she found out what it was she felt all that distance away. A large fertilizer truck had hit a gasoline truck in front of her mother's house. A tremendous fire had ensued, almost setting her mother's house on fire. The blaze could be seen clearly in towns over five miles away. Both trucks burned up completely. It was the heat from the fire she had felt all the way to Memphis, Tennessee.

The house outside of Hollygrove, however, kept on calling her and somehow she didn't forget. Whenever she had a chance to drive by it she took it, looking at the house and wondering what its secret was. On one such occasion it seemed to her that she heard *someone play a piano inside the vacant house.* But that couldn't very well be; she knew that there was no one living inside. Perhaps there were mice jumping up and down the keyboard, if indeed there was a piano inside the house. She shook her head, dismissing the matter. Perhaps she had only imagined it. But somehow the sound of songs being played on an old piano kept on reverberating in her mind. She decided to do some research on the house.

Tom Kameron runs an antique shop in Hollygrove, and since the old house was likely to be filled with antiques he would be the man to question about it. That at least was Sharon's opinion. She entered the shop pretending to browse around for antiques. A lady clerk came over and pointed at an old lamp. "I want to show you something that you'll be interested in," she said. "This came from the old Mulls house here." Sharon was thunderstruck. The Mulls house was the house she was interested in. She began to question the clerk about the antiques in the Mulls house. Apparently a lot of them had been stolen or had disappeared during the last few years. Since then a caretaker had been appointed who guarded the house. At this point the owner of the shop, Tom Kameron, joined the conversation. From him Sharon learned that the house had belonged to Tom Mulls, who had passed away, but Mrs. Mulls, although very aged, was still alive and living in a sanitarium in Little Rock. Kameron himself had been a friend of the late owners for many years.

The house had been built by a Captain Mulls who had passed away around 1935. It was originally built in St. Augustine, Florida, and was later moved to Hollygrove.

The captain wasn't married, yet there was a woman with him in the house when it stood in Hollygrove. This was a Native American woman he had befriended and who lived with him until her death. The man who later inherited the house, Tom Mulls, was an adopted son. Apparently Captain Mulls was very much in love with his Native American lady. After her death he had her body embalmed and placed in a glass casket, which he kept in a room in the house. It stayed there until he died, and when Tom took over the house he buried the casket in the cemetery not far away. Her grave still exists in that cemetery. There were many Indian relics and papers dealing with Indian folklore in the house during her lifetime, but they have all disappeared since. The woman played the piano very well indeed, and it was for her that the captain had bought a very fine piano. Many time he would sit listening to her as she played song after song for his entertainment.

The house has been vacant for many years but people can't help visiting it even though it is locked. They go up to the front steps and peer in the windows. Sharon was relieved to hear that she was not the only one strangely attracted to the old house. Others have also been "called" by the house as if someone inside were beckoning to them. Over the years strangers who have passed by the house have come to Mr. Kameron with strange tales of music emanating from the empty house. What people have heard wasn't the rustling of mice scurrying over a ruined piano keyboard but definite tunes, song after song played by skilled hands. Eventually the house will pass into the hands of the state since Mrs. Mulls has no heirs. But Sharon doubts that the ghost will move out just because the house changes hands again. She feels her presence, very much alive and wholly content to live on in the old house. True, she now plays to a different kind of audience than she did when Captain Mulls was still alive, but then is it just possible that the captain has decided to stay behind also if only to listen to the songs she continues to play for his entertainment.

Georgia Stay-Behinds

THE STATE OF GEORGIA, especially the area around Atlanta, is full of people interested in psychic research. Whether this has something to do with the fact that many cases exist in the area, or whether this is simply because Georgia has some fine universities and metropolitan centers where the interest in ESP has been high for many years, is hard to tell. But the fact is that I get far more cases of interest from the area of Atlanta and of Georgia in general than, for instance, Mississippi or Louisiana. The caliber of the people who have most of the experiences or are possessed of ESP talents is also quite high. A. W. C., a science teacher from rural Georgia, says he does not believe in ghosts such as such; however, he is quick to admit that the experiences he has had will admit of no explanation other than a psychic one. When he was a teenager he was very close to his grandmother even though she lived 150 miles away. One night, while he was in bed, he awoke and saw his grandmother standing in the corner of his room. At first he thought he was imagining things. He closed his eyes and looked once again but she was still there. Now he covered his head and after a while looked back; grandmother was still standing there. At that point he heard footsteps in the kitchen and got up to see if anybody had entered the kitchen, but to his surprise he found no one there. When he returned to his bedroom he decided, in his logical mind, that what he had seen had been a dress or some other piece of material hanging on the wall and not his grandmother. In the morning he would make sure that that was so. Came the morning and he checked and there was nothing in the corner of that room. However, a few days later the family received a telegram advising them that grandmother had had a stroke and was at the point of death. Evidently the young man had seen a projected image of his dear relative at a time when partial dissolution had taken place. Shortly thereafter the grandmother died.

But Mr. C. not only has been the recipient of psychic impressions, he has also been able to send them, although not at will. During World War II he was with the Army in France. His family frequently discussed his fate abroad. One evening his wife, sister, and an aunt who had reared him and who was particularly close to the young man were sitting in front of a wooden stove in their home. Suddenly the aunt started to scream. Terror-stricken, the woman explained that she just seen Mr. C.'s face appear to her in the flames of the stove. At that very moment Mr. C. was wounded in France.

* * *

Robert Mullinax of Atlanta, Georgia, is in his early twenties. When he was seventeen years old, in 1967, he had an experience he will never forget. His mother had often had premonitions of things to come and perhaps some of this talent had come down to him also. On that particular day in April, Mrs. Mullinax had been very restless all day long as if something were about to happen. She had the feeling she should telephone her sister-in-law, but somehow she never not around to it. They were not particularly close; in fact, they had visited each other only about three times in twenty-five years. That evening she knew why she had had the strange feeling of urgency to call he sister-in-law. The woman had committed suicide by shooting herself.

It was two days after her death when young Robert found himself standing in his home in front of a large mirror. This was in their living room and he was about to comb his hair when he saw his aunt in the mirror behind him. He turned around and, sure enough, there she was standing about six feet away. As he got a closer look at her she vanished. In this fleeting moment young Robert had the impression that his aunt wanted to tell him something —perhaps express regret at what she had done and to send a message to her youngest son whom she loved very much, but she was gone before Robert could really make out the message. What is interesting about this case is the fact that the ghost was solid enough to be seen in a mirror, not merely a hallucination or a subjective vision.

* * *

Mrs. W. is a housewife living in Athens, Georgia. She is also a certified nursery school teacher, the mother of six children, and she has had ESP experiences for many years past. She is living proof that ESP messages can be very precise at times in giving the recipient an indication of what the message is all about and to prepare the recipient for any shock that might come his or her way. In 1946 Mrs. W. was living in another city in Georgia. At that time she had one son age two-and-a-half years and another six months old. She was also pregnant with another child. During that period she had many vivid dreams of a psychic nature. But after the third child was born she was particularly disturbed one night by a dream which became so powerful that it awoke her. She found herself crying uncontrollably, so much so that her husband was genuinely concerned. When she became calmer she told her husband she had dreamed she saw her brothers and sisters and her mother looking at her through the glass of their front door, saying, "Call an ambulance." The dream had no meaning for her, so after a while she went back to sleep and didn't think about it again. Three months later the dream became a reality. Her brother appeared at her front door and standing outside the glass said, "Call an ambulance." He then explained that their father, who lived on the next street and who had no telephone, had suffered a heart attack while preparing for bed. The father died three days later. It was only after her grief ceased that Mrs. W. realized that in her dream she had seen all members of her family except one —her father was not in it. Had she understood this properly perhaps she would have been more prepared for the shock that was to come her way shortly.

The relationship with her father had been a close one, so she was not surprised that after his passing there were times when she felt him standing near her. She did not see him, yet she knew of his presence. She hesitated to discuss this with her husband out of fear of being ridiculed or worse. During that time she awakened her husband five or six separate times and asked him to get up and shut the door since Daddy had come in. Her husband didn't like it, but when she insisted, he did get up in order to please his wife. They never discussed it until many years later when her husband admitted that each time she had asked him to close the door it was indeed open and there had been no reason for it to be open.

Mrs. W.'s husband is the editor of a county newspaper and a very logical man. He learned to accept his wife's special talent as the years rolled by, but there were times when he wished that she weren't as psychic as she was. One night she dreamed that a plane crash had taken place somewhere in back of their house and she saw some Army men drive up in a jeep and take away the bodies of those killed. In the morning she told her husband of this dream. He didn't say anything. Two weeks later, however, he told his wife to quit having "those crazy dreams." It appeared that Mr. W. had been traveling away from home in the direction one might properly call "back of the house" when he saw that an Army plane had crashed and Army personnel in a jeep had driven up to the site and removed some bodies, just as his wife had told him. Mrs. W. realized that she had a very special talent and perhaps had been chosen by some superior intelligence as a communicator.

A month after her daughter Karen was born in 1952 she happened to be lying down for an afternoon nap. She was facing the wall when she felt compelled to turn over in the opposite direction. There she saw the figure of a man in a white robe standing by her bed. Her first thought was that she still had in her system some of the drug that had been given her during the birth and that she was indeed hallucinating. She thought it best to turn back to the wall. Immediately, however, she felt a strong compulsion to turn back, and this time she saw the man pointing his finger at her with a stern look on his face. She got the impression she was to get up immediately and follow him. She did just that and walked straight into the next room. As if acting in a daze she saw herself dial her husband at his office. As soon as her husband came to the phone she told him not to ask questions but if he ever intended to do something that she had asked him for, this was the time to do it. She told him to go at once to a place called Curry's Creek to see if their son Joe was there. Her husband objected. He knew, he said, that the five-year-old was not there. Nevertheless Mrs. W. insisted. Her plea was so urgent she impressed her husband sufficiently that he did indeed go down to the creek. Ten minutes later he telephoned her asking her how she knew that the boy was indeed at the creek. It appeared that he found the little boy at the edge of the water looking down into it. The creek furnished the town's water supply and is next to a busy highway a mile outside of town. The child had never been there before. Had Mr. W. not arrived in time the child might very well have drowned. Mrs. W. then realized that the man in the white robe had come to save their child.

* * *

The warning of impending disaster is a recurrent theme in ghost lore. It appears that on occasion the departed are given the task of warning the living of impending difficulties or disaster but are not permitted to be specific. Evidently that would interfere with the exercise of free will under test conditions. A similar case involves a lady from Decatur by the name of Mrs. L. E., who when a child, was staying with her Aunt Mary in her house. Twenty years before that visit Mary's Great-Aunt Rev had passed on. With her cousins Mrs. E. then proceeded to one of the bedrooms in the house to fetch some of the tricycles they had stored in it to go outside and play. When they got to the door of the room they saw Great-Aunt Rev standing in the middle of the room right where the tricycles were. She was looking at the children rather sternly. She wore her long white nightgown and her nightcap, the clothing she was wearing when she died. The children stood there transfixed by shock. They spoke her name more in fear than in reverence. Then they ran out. When they described the apparition to the owner of the house, Mrs. E.'s Aunt Mary was very solemn. "She came back," she said and began to move all the furniture from the house, taking it out into the yard away from the house. This seemed like strange behavior, but the children were young and did not understand many things. Then Aunt Mary took the children and walked with them up the road to a neighbor's house. There she left them. Several hours later when they returned they found the house had burned down to ashes. No one had seen the ghost of Aunt Rev since.

✳ 145

A Tucker Ghost

TUCKER, GEORGIA, IS ABOUT an hour's ride due north of Atlanta, a pleasant, almost suburban community populated by pleasant, average people. The Stevens house, a landmark as early as 1854, was built of huge hand-hewn chestnut pine logs originally. The older part was added to by a Baptist minister around 1910. Finally another addition was made to the house in the late 1940s. When the Stevenses bought the house they were told that it was originally built by Indian settlers in the area around 1800, or even before. This is Cherokee Territory and according to the local tradition the Indians brought their sick to this house. They would stay with them overnight on their way to Decatur. Decatur was the town where the famed Dr. Chapman Powell lived. The Powell cabin has been restored and is now located in Stone Mountain Park, but originally it was in Decatur and was moved to the park to better preserve it as a landmark. The Stevens house stands about a mile off the High Tower Trail, which is the old Cherokee Indian trail, and four miles from Stone Mountain Park. Since Mrs. Stevens is herself about one thirty-second Cherokee, she has a vivid sympathy for all Indian lore and has always been interested in the Indian background of the house. Whey they first bought the house in May 1960 the Stevenses lived in it for only a year. Then, for business reasons, they moved down to Florida and sold their house to their in-laws. However, two years later they returned from Florida and bought the house back. During that first year in the house they do not recall anything strange except for a recurrent dream Mrs. Stevens had right from the start when they took up residence at the house. In that dream she saw herself looking up through an opening in the ceiling into the darkness of a loft. She could clearly make out the rafters, wooden beams, and the chimneys. Somehow this dream seemed all very familiar. As soon as she had moved to the house she realized that her dream visions concerned the attic of their house. It looked exactly like the visions she had seen so many years prior to coming to the house. Evidently it was predestined that the Stevenses should take up residence in Tucker. On recollection Mrs. Stevens remembers that her in-laws had no special experiences in the house out of the ordinary during the two years in which they resided there. But then neither of her in-laws professed any particular interest in the occult or was possessed of psychic sensitivities.

As soon as the Stevenses had returned to their original home they noticed a strange feeling, perhaps more of a current all around the house. It affected the children as well. They would not want to take a nap or go to bed because they said someone kept touching them. Soon Mrs. Stevens experienced that too. Their smallest children reported seeing a man on the porch when there was no man about. Both Mr. and Mrs. Stevens have seen a man going across the porch. This has happened a number of times. Sometimes it is only a kind of quick flash and sometimes they can clearly make out a human form. Whenever they have seen something and their children have not, they try their best to keep it from them so as not to alarm them. Nevertheless the children on their own report similar occurrences. Gradually it has become clear to the Stevenses that the oldest part of the house, the log part, is the center of the psychic phenomena. In the living room-dining room area they have seen a form when there was certainly no one else but themselves in the house. On another occasion Mrs. Stevens has seen a hand materialize by her bed. In August 1968 Mr. Stevens awoke from sound sleep because he had the feeling that there was someone in the house who should not be there. He sat up and looked into the room where their sons were sleeping across from the parents' bedroom. There he saw a gray form standing by their bunkbeds looking at the oldest boy. Fully awake now, Mr. Stevens looked closely at the form and realized it was female. The woman appeared to be wearing a cowl-type hood. When he made a move the form dissolved into thin air. Stevens discussed the appearance with his wife. She had seen a similar form in the boys' room reclining on the lower bunk beside

the youngest boy. Moreover, the apparition was not alone. Mrs. Stevens could make out additional figures in the room. Footsteps up and down the stairs when there was no one around to make them had become a common occurrence in the house. The Stevenses thought that the repair work going on in the house might have offended one or the other of its former inhabitants. They were doing their level best to save the old part of the house, repairing what could be repaired and replacing what could not.

It was soon clear to them that they had more than one unearthly visitor in their house. The woman so concerned with the well-being of the children might have been someone left behind from the Indian days or perhaps the shade of a former owner of the house. None of them ever saw her clearly enough to make sure, but there someone else. In 1966 Mr. Stevens had a strange dream. The dream was followed by similar dreams, continuing, as it were, the narrative of the first one. In these dreams his brother Bill communicated with him. Bill had been killed in a plane crash in North Carolina during World War II. However, in the dreams Bill explained that he was not dead and that he had returned home. In another dream he wanted his brother to accompany him on a trip. In all of these dreams Bill appeared to have aged. He was balding and wearing a tattered officer's khaki uniform. His overcoat in particular was tattered and faded. While the Stevenses discussed these dreams with each other, they made a special point of never talking about them with their children. So the children had no idea that dreams about Uncle Bill had indeed taken place.

About three weeks after the last of this series of dreams involving Bill, all the boys came into the kitchen very much alarmed and white as sheets. They insisted that they had seen a ghost. When questioned about the apparition they said they had seen a man walk across the front room, which is part of the 1910 addition of the house. Immediately the parents checked to see whether a trespasser had perhaps entered the house. There was no one to be seen. Skeptical, and at the same time alarmed, the parents demanded that the boys describe what they had seen. Without a moment's hesitation they described the ghost as being a thin man, sort of crouched down and bald, with clothes rather torn and sort of a faded khaki. They did in effect describe exactly what Uncle Bill looked like in the series of dreams their father had had for so long. Only what they had seen was not in the dream state. Uncle Bill evidently had returned from the grave not as a resident ghost, for ghosts do not travel, but to look after the affairs of his brother's family.

The Howard Mansion Ghost

THE OLD HOWARD HOME on South Main Street in Henderson, Texas, is a southern mansion of the kind that is so numerous throughout the South. In 1851 the mansion was erected by a certain James L. Howard on land he paid $100 for. It is the oldest brick home in town. Today it belongs to the Heritage Association and is being maintained as a museum, with visitors coming not only from other parts of Texas but even from abroad. The house has three stories and six rooms. Four columns adorn the front of it. Perhaps the most remarkable thing about the house is the fact that every room has a fireplace, some of them very large, old-fashioned fireplaces of the kind you rarely see any more. The stairs have banisters made of the highest grade walnut.

When the Howards built this home they stated proudly, to anyone who would hear it, "God Almighty Himself could not tear it down because it was well built." Even the worst storm seemingly could not touch the house. There is the account of a particularly horrifying electrical storm when a streak of lightning hit one of the corner columns, causing only slight damage. One of the Howard brothers ran out into the yard, looked up into the sky and shook his fist and said, "See. I told you that you couldn't tear down my house." With so large and outstanding a mansion in a small town, it is only natural that legends would crop up around it, some of which are true and some are not. One of them making the rounds concerns a murder in the house. The present owners, the Rusk County Heritage Association, have checked into it and found that an accident and not a murder had occurred. The accident concerns a member of the Howards name Pat Howard who lost his life in an accident in the home. In fact the descendants of the Howards went to great length to explain again and again that Pat Howard died of an accident and that the shooting that took his life was not murder in any sense of the word. Of course, where there is smoke there is sometimes fire. Was the family merely trying to kill the story, or were they correcting the facts? I have never been to the Henderson mansion but have talked with people who have been there, so my account must of necessity be second-hand.

In 1905 Mrs. M. A. Howard and Dore Howard, being alone, decided to sell the house to a certain Mrs. M. A. Dickinson. Mrs. Howard was then in ill health. The sale did not go down well with her children and the rest of the family, who would have preferred to have the house stay family property. It seems incredible today that such an imposing house could be sold for $1,500, but, of course,

that was a lot more money in 1905 than it is today. Still, even for 1905, $1,500 was very little money for a house of this kind. It seems strange therefore that the sale was made in this manner. The sale of the house from the Howard family to an outsider took the town by surprise. No one had surmised that it could be for sale, especially not for such a low price. The house had a reputation as an historical landmark. Sam Houston himself slept there many times, since he was a cousin of the Howards. In 1950 the house passed from the Dickinson family to Hobart Bryce, who in 1961 deeded the property to the Historical Association. One of the townspeople who had spent much effort in restoring the old house and who had been active on behalf of the fund-raising committee was a certain Carl Jaggers. Partly due to his efforts and those of others, the house is now in excellent condition again and open to visitors as a museum. My attention was drawn to it when I appeared on a television program in nearby Tyler, Texas. The lady who interviewed me, Jane Lassiter, provided me with much of the material about the Henderson house.

While the controversy among the townspeople concerning the restoration of the house was going on and there was some doubt whether the house could be saved or had to be torn down, no one had the time or inclination to look into any possible ghostly manifestations at the house. But as soon as the matter had quieted down and the house was safe from the wrecker's tools and perhaps because of the renewed quiet in the atmosphere, something did occur that had not been observed before. Maia Jaggers was one of those who served as honorary guides around the house, particularly during the weekends, when there were more visitors than during the week. She would act as hostess to those who came to look at the house. One Sunday afternoon in the winter of 1968, she had just finished showing the house to a group of visitors and was quite alone in it for the moment. She found herself downstairs looking toward the stairway leading to the upper stories. At that precise moment she saw a woman materialize before her eyes. Seemingly solid, or almost so, it was clearly a woman of a past age. As she looked closely at the apparition, she realized that it was the ghost of Mrs. Howard herself. As soon as Maia Jaggers and the ghost had come face to face the apparition floated up the stairway and disappeared. She has not been seen since that time. Could it be that a grateful Mrs. Howard wanted the one person directly connected with the salvage of her home made aware of her continued existence in it? Was her presence in what was once her home caused by a belated regret at having sold out to others against the wishes of her family? If you are ever in Henderson, Texas, be sure and drop in on Mrs. Howard's house. Sale or no sale, she seems to be quite at home in it still.

✳ 147

The Stay-Behinds: Not Ready to Go

THE AVERAGE PERSON THINKS that there is just one kind of ghost, and that spirits are all one and the same. Nothing could be further from the truth; ghosts are not spirits, and psychic impressions are not the same as ghosts. Basically, there are three phenomena involved when a person dies under traumatic, tragic circumstances and is unable to adjust to the passing from one state of existence to the next. The most common form of passing is of course the transition from physical human being to spirit being, without difficulty and without the need to stay in the denser physical atmosphere of the Earth. The majority of tragic passings do not present any problems, because the individual accepts the change and becomes a free spirit, capable of communicating freely with those on the Earth plane, and advancing according to his abilities, likes and dislikes, and the help he or she may receive from others already on the other side of life. A small fraction of those who die tragically are unable to recognize the change in their status and become so-called ghosts: that is, parts of human personality hung up in the physical world, but no longer part of it or able to function in it. These are the only *true* ghosts in the literal sense of the term.

However a large number of sightings of so-called ghosts are not of this nature, but represent imprints left behind in the atmosphere by the individual's actual passing. Anyone possessed of psychic ability will sense the event from the past and, in his or her mind's eye, reconstruct it. The difficulty is that one frequently does not know the difference between a psychic imprint having no life of its own and a true ghost. Both seem very real, subjectively speaking. The only way one can differentiate between the two phenomena is when several sightings are compared for minute details. True ghosts move about somewhat, although not outside the immediate area of their passing. Imprints are always identical, regardless of the observers involved, and the details do not alter at any time. Psychic imprints, then, are very much like photographs or films of an actual event, while true ghosts are events themselves, which are capable of some measure of reaction to the environment. Whenever there are slight differences in detail concerning an apparition, we are dealing with a true ghost-personality; but whenever the description of an apparition or scene from the past appears to be identical from source to source, we are most likely dealing only with a lifeless imprint reflecting the event but in no way suggesting an actual presence at the time of the observation.

However, there is a subdivision of true ghosts that I have called "the stay-behinds." The need for such a subdivision came to me several years ago when I looked through numerous cases of reported hauntings that did not fall into the category of tragic, traumatic passings, nor cases of death involving neither violence nor great suffering—the earmarks of true ghosts. To the contrary, many of these sightings involved the peaceful passings of people who had lived in their respective homes for many years and had grown to love them. I realized, by comparing these cases one with the other, that they had certain things in common, the most outstanding of which was this: they were greatly attached to their homes, had lived in them for considerable periods prior to their death, and were strong-willed individuals who had managed to develop a life routine of their own. It appears, therefore, that the stay-behinds are spirits who are unable to let go of their former homes, are more or less aware of their passing into the next dimension, but are unwilling to go on. To them, their earthly home is preferable, and the fact that they no longer possess a physical body is no deterrent to their continuing to live in it.

Some of these stay-behinds adjust to their limitations with marvelous ingenuity. They are still capable of causing physical phenomena, especially if they can draw on people living in the house. At times, however, they become annoyed at changes undertaken by the residents in their house, and when these changes evoke anger in them they are capable of some mischievous activities, like poltergeist phenomena, although of a somewhat different nature. Sometimes they are quite satisfied to continue living their former lives, staying out of the way of flesh-and-blood inhabitants of the house, and remaining undiscovered until someone with psychic ability notices them by accident. Sometimes, however, they *want* the flesh-and-blood people to know they are still very much in residence and, in asserting their continuing rights, may come into conflict with the living beings in the house. Some of these manifestations seem frightening or even threatening to people living in houses of this kind, but they should not be, since the stay-behinds are, after all, human beings like all others, who have developed a continuing and very strong attachment to their former homes. Of course, not everyone can come to terms with them.

* * *

For instance, take the case of Margaret C. A few years ago when she lived in New York state, she decided to spend Christmas with her sister and brother-in-law in Pennsylvania. The husband's mother had recently passed away, so it was going to be a sad Christmas holiday for them. Mrs. C. was given a room on the second floor of the old house, close to a passage which led to the downstairs part of the house. Being tired from her long journey, she went to bed around eleven, but found it difficult to fall asleep. Suddenly she clearly heard the sound of a piano being played in the house. It sound like a very old piano, and the music on it reminded her of music played in church. At first Mrs. C. thought someone had left a radio on, so she checked but found that this was not the case.

Somehow she managed to fall asleep, despite the tinkling sound of the piano downstairs. At breakfast, Mrs. C. mentioned her experience to her sister. Her sister gave her an odd look, then took her by the hand and led her down the stairs where she pointed to an old piano. It had been the property of the dead mother who had recently passed away, but it had not been played in many years, since no one else in the house knew how to play it. With mounting excitement, the two women pried the rusty lid open. This took some effort, but eventually they succeeded in opening the keyboard.

Picture their surprise when they found that thick dust had settled on the keys, but etched in the dust were unmistakable human fingerprints. They were thin, bony fingers, like the fingers of a very old woman. Prior to her passing, the deceased had been very thin indeed, and church music had been her favorite. Was the lady of the house still around, playing her beloved piano?

* * *

The house on South Sixth Street in Hudson, New York, is one of the many fine old town houses dotting this old town on the Hudson River. It was built between 1829 and 1849, and succession of owners lived in it to the present day. In 1904 it passed into the hands of the Parker family, who had a daughter, first-named Mabel, a very happy person with a zest for life. In her sixties, she had contracted a tragic illness and suffered very much, until she finally passed away in a nearby hospital. She had been truly house-proud, and hated to leave for the cold and ominous surroundings of the hospital. After she died, the house passed into the hands of Mr. and Mrs. Jay Dietz, who still owned it when I visited them. Mrs. Dietz had been employed by Mabel Parker's father at one time.

The psychic did not particularly interest Mrs. Dietz, although she had had one notable experience the night her step-grandfather died, a man she had loved very much. She had been at home taking care of him throughout the daytime and finally returned to her own house to spend the night. Everybody had gone to bed, and as she lay in hers with her face to the wall, she became aware of an unusual glow in the room. She turned over the opened her eyes, and noticed that on the little nightstand at the head of the bed was a large ball of light, glowing, with a soft golden color. As she was still staring at the phenomenon, the telephone rang, and she was told that her step-grandfather had passed away.

Eleven years before, the Dietzes moved into the houses on South Sixth Street. At first the house seemed peaceful enough. Previous tenants included a German war bride and her mother. The old lady had refused to sleep upstairs in the room that later became Mrs. Dietz's mother's. There was something uncanny about that room, she explained. So she slept down on the ground floor on a couch instead. The Dietzes paid no attention to these stories, until they began to notice some strange things about their house. There were footsteps heard going up and down the stairs and into the hall, where they stopped. The three of them, Mr. and Mrs. Dietz and her mother, all heard them many times.

One year, just before Christmas, Mrs. Dietz was attending to some sewing in the hall downstairs while her husband was in the bathroom. Suddenly she thought he came down the hall which was odd, since she hadn't heard the toilet being flushed. But as she turned around, no one was there. A few nights later she went upstairs and had the distinct impression that she was not alone in the room. Without knowing what she was doing, she called out to the unseen presence, "Mabel?" There was no reply then, but one night not much later, she was awakened by someone yanking at her blanket from the foot of the bed. She broke out into goose pimples, because the pull was very distinct and there was no mistaking it.

She sat up in her upstairs bedroom, very frightened by now, but there was no one to be seen. As she did this, the pulling ceased abruptly. She went back to sleep with some relief, but several nights later the visitor turned. Mrs. Dietz likes to sleep on her left side with her ear covered up by the blanket. Suddenly she felt the covers being pulled off her ear, but being already half-asleep, she simply yanked them back. There was no further movement after that.

The upstairs bedroom occupied by Mrs. Dietz's mother seemed to be the center of activities, however. More than once after the older lady had turned out the lights to go to sleep, she became aware of someone standing beside her bed, and looking down at her.

Sometimes nothing was heard for several weeks or months, only to resume in full force without warning. In February of the year I visited the Dietzes, Mrs. Dietz happened to wake up at 5 o'clock one morning. It so happened that her mother was awake too, for Mrs. Dietz heard her stir. A moment later, her mother went back to bed. At that moment, Mrs. Dietz heard, starting at the foot of the stairs, the sound of heavy footsteps coming up very slowly, going down the hall and stopping, but they were different from the footsteps she had heard many times before.

It sounded as if a very sick person were dragging herself up the stairs, trying not to fall, but determined to get there nevertheless. It sounded as if someone very tired was coming home. Was her friend finding a measure of rest, after all, by returning to the house where she had been so happy? Mrs. Dietz does not believe in ghosts, however, but only in memories left behind.

* * *

Thanks to a local group of psychic researchers, a bizarre case was brought to my attention not long ago. In the small town of Lafayette, Louisiana, there stands an old bungalow that had been the property of an elderly couple for many years. They were both retired people, and of late the wife had become an invalid confined to a wheelchair. One day a short time ago, she suffered a heart attack and died in that chair. Partially because of her demise, or perhaps because of his own fragile state, the husband also died a month later. Rather, he was found dead and declared to have died of a heart attack.

Under the circumstances the house remained vacant awhile, since there were no direct heirs. After about nine months, it was rented to four female students from the nearby university. Strangely, however, they stayed only two months—and again the house was rented out. This time it was taken by two women, one a professional microbiologist and the other a medical technician. Both were extremely rational individuals and not the least bit interested in anything supernatural. They moved into the bungalow, using it as it was, furnished with the furniture of the dead couple.

Picture their dismay, however, when they found out that all wasn't as it should be with their house. Shortly after moving in, they were awakened late at night by what appeared to be mumbled conversations and footsteps about the house. At first neither woman wanted to say anything about it to the other, out of fear that they might have dreamt the whole thing or of being ridiculed. Finally, when they talked to each other about their experiences, they realized that they had shared them, detail for detail. They discovered, for instance, that the phenomena always took place between 1 A.M. and sunrise. A man and a woman were talking, and the subject of their conversation was the new tenants!

"She has her eyes open—I can see her eyes are open now," the invisible voice said, clearly and distinctly. The voices seemed to emanate from the attic area. The two ladies realized the ghosts were talking about *them;* but what were they to do about it? They didn't see the ghostly couple, but felt themselves being watched at all times by invisible presences. What were they to do with their ghosts, the two ladies wondered.

I advised them to talk to them, plain and simple, for a ghost who can tell whether a living person's eyes are open or not is capable of knowing the difference between living in one's own house, and trespassing on someone else's, even if it *was* their former abode.

* * *

Mrs. Carolyn K. lives in Chicago, Illinois, with her husband and four children, who are between the ages of eight and thirteen. She has for years been interested in ESP experiences, unlike her husband who held no belief of this kind. The family moved into its present home some years ago. Mrs. K. does not recall any unusual experiences for the first six years, but toward the end of April, six years after they moved in, something odd happened. She and her husband had just gone to bed and her husband, being very tired, fell asleep almost immediately. Mrs. K., however, felt ill at ease and was unable to fall asleep, since she felt a presence in the bedroom.

Within a few minutes she saw, in great detail, a female figure standing beside the bed. The woman seemed about thirty years old, had fair skin and hair, a trim figure, and was rather attractive. Her dress indicated good taste and a degree of wealth, and belonged to the 1870s or 1880s. The young woman just stood there and looked at Mrs. K. and vice versa. She seemed animated enough, but made no sound. Despite this, Mrs. K. had the distinct impression that the ghost wanted her to know something specific. The encounter lasted for ten or fifteen minutes, then the figure slowly disintegrated.

The experience left Mrs. K. frightened and worried. Immediately she reported it to her husband, but he brushed the incident aside with a good deal of skepticism. In the following two weeks, Mrs. K. felt an unseen presence all about the house, without, however, seeing her mysterious visitor again. It seemed that the woman was watching her as she did her daily chores. Mrs. K. had no idea who the ghost might be, but she knew that their house was no more than fifty years old and that there had been swamp land on the spot before that. Could the ghost have some connection with the land itself, or perhaps with some of the antiques Mrs. K. treasured?

About two weeks after the initial experience, Mr. K. was studying in the kitchen, which is located at the far eastern end of the house, while Mrs. K. was watching television in the living room at the other end of the house. Twice she felt the need to go into the kitchen and warn her husband that she felt the ghost moving about the living room, but he insisted it was merely her imagination. So she returned to the living room and curled up in an easy chair to continue watching television. Fifteen minutes later, she heard a loud noise reverberating throughout the house. It made her freeze with fright in the chair, when her husband ran into the living room to ask what the noise had been.

Upon investigation, he noticed a broken string on an antique zither hanging on the dining room wall. It was unlikely that the string could have broken by itself, and if it had, how could it have reverberated so strongly? To test such a possibility, they broke several other strings of the same zither in an effort to duplicate the sound, but without success. A few weeks went by, and the ghost's presence persisted. By now Mrs. K. had the distinct impression that the ghost was annoyed at being ignored. Suddenly, a hurricane lamp which hung from a nail on the wall fell to the floor and shattered. It could not have moved of its own volition. Again some time passed, and the ghost was almost forgotten. Mrs. K.'s older daughter, then six years old, asked her mother early one morning who the company was the previous evening. Informed that there had been no guests at the house, she insisted that a lady had entered her bedroom, sat on her bed and looked at her, and then departed. In order to calm the child, Mrs. K. told her she had probably dreamt the whole thing. But the little girl insisted that she had not, and furthermore, she described the visitor in every detail including the "funny" clothes she had worn. Appalled, Mrs. K. realized that her daughter had seen the same ghostly woman. Apparently, the ghost felt greater urgency to communicate now, for a few days later, after going to bed, the apparition returned to Mrs. K.'s bedroom. This time she wore a different dress than on the first meeting, but it was still from the 1880s. She was wiping her hands on an apron, stayed only for a little while, then slowly disintegrated again. During the following year, her presence was felt only occasionally, but gradually Mrs. K. managed to snatch a few fleeting impressions about her. From this she put together the story of her ghost. She was quite unhappy about a child, and one evening the following winter, when Mrs. K. felt the ghost wandering about their basement, she actually heard her crying pitifully for two hours. Obviously, the distraught ghost wanted attention, and was determined to get it at all costs.

One day the following summer, when Mrs. K. was alone with the children after her husband had left for work, one of the children complained that the door to the bathroom was locked. Since the door can be locked only from the inside, and since all four children were accounted for, Mrs. K. assumed that her ghost lady was at it again. When the bathroom door remained locked for half an hour and the children's needs became more urgent, Mrs. K. went to the door and demanded in a loud tone of voice that the ghost open the door. There was anger in her voice and it brought quick results. Clearly the click of a *lock being turned* was heard inside the bathroom and, after a moment, Mrs. K. opened the bathroom door easily. There was no one inside the bathroom, of course. Who, then, had turned the lock—the only way the door could be opened?

For a while things went smoothly. A few weeks later, Mrs. K. again felt the ghost near her. One of her daughters was sitting at the kitchen table with her, while she was cutting out a dress pattern on the counter. Mrs. K. stepped back to search for something in the refrigerator a few feet away, when all of a sudden she and her daughter saw her box of dressmaking pins rise slightly off the counter and fall to the floor. Neither one of them had been near it, and it took them almost an hour to retrieve all the pins scattered on the floor.

A little later, they clearly heard the basement door connecting the dining room and kitchen fly open and slam shut by itself, as if someone in great anger was trying to call attention to her presence. Immediately they closed the door, and made sure there was no draft from any windows.

An instant later, it flew open again by itself. Now they attached the chain to the latch—but that didn't seem to stop the ghost from fooling around with the door. With enormous force, it flew open again as far as the chain allowed, as if someone were straining at it. Quickly Mrs. K. called a neighbor to come over and watch the strange behavior of the door but the minute the neighbor arrived, the door behaved normally, just as before. The ghost was not about to perform for strangers.

One evening in the summer some years later, Mr. K. was driving some dinner guests home and Mrs. K. was alone in the house with the children. All of a sudden, she felt her ghost following her as she went through her chores of emptying ashtrays and taking empty glasses into the kitchen. Mrs. K. tried bravely to ignore her, although she was frightened by her, and she knew that her ghost knew it, which made it all the more difficult to carry on.

Not much later, the K. family had guests again. One of the arriving guests pointed out to Mrs. K. that their basement light was on. Mrs. K. explained that it was unlikely, since the bulb had burned out the day before. She even recalled being slightly annoyed with her husband for having neglected to replace the bulb. But the guest insisted, and so the K.s opened the basement door only to find the light off. A moment later another guest arrived. He wanted to know who was working in the basement at such a late hour, since he had seen the basement light on. Moreover, he saw a figure standing at the basement window looking out. Once more, the entire party went downstairs with a flashlight, only to find the light off and no one about.

That was the last the K.s saw or heard of their ghost. Why had she so suddenly left them? Perhaps it had to do with a Chicago newspaperwoman's call. Having heard of the disturbances, she had telephoned the K.s to offer her services and that of celebrated psychic Irene Hughes to investigate the house. Although the K.s did not want any attention because of the children, Mrs. K. told the reporter what had transpired at the house. To her surprise, the reporter informed her that parallel experiences had been reported at another house not more than seven miles away. In the other case, the mother and one of her children had observed a ghostly figure, and an investigation had taken place with the help of Irene Hughes and various equipment, the result of which was that a presence named Lizzy was ascertained.

From this Mrs. K. concluded that they were sharing a ghost with a neighbor seven miles away, and she, too, began to call the ghostly visitor Lizzy. Now if Lizzy had two homes and was shuttling back and forth between them, it might account for the long stretches of no activity at the K. home. On the other hand, if the ghost at the K.s was not named Lizzy, she would naturally not want to be confused with some other unknown ghost seven miles away. Be this as it may, Mrs. K. wishes her well, wherever she is.

* * *

Mrs. J. P. lives in central Illinois, in an old three-story house with a basement. Prior to her acquiring it, it had stood empty for six months. As soon as she had moved in, she heard some neighborhood gossip that the house was presumed haunted. Although Mrs. P. is not a skeptic, she is level-headed enough to not to take rumors at face value.

She looked the house over carefully. It seemed about eighty years old, and was badly in need of repair. Since they had bought it at a bargain price, they did not mind, but as time went on, they wondered how cheap the house had really been. It became obvious to her and her husband that the price had been low for other reasons. Nevertheless, the house was theirs, and together they set out to repaint and remodel it as best they could. For the first two weeks, they were too busy to notice anything out of the ordinary. About three weeks after moving in, however, Mr. and Mrs. P. began hearing things such as doors shutting by themselves, cupboards opening, and particularly, a little girl persistently calling for "Mama, Mama" with a great deal of alarm. As yet, Mr. and Mrs. P. tried to ignore the phenomena.

One evening, however, they were having a family spat over something of little consequence. All of a sudden a frying pan standing on the stove lifted off by itself, hung suspended in mid-air for a moment, and then was flung back on the stove with full force. Their twelve-year-old son who witnessed it flew into hysterics; Mr. P. turned white, and Mrs. P. was just plain angry. How dare someone invade their privacy? The following week, the ten-year-old daughter was watching television downstairs in what had been turned into Mrs. P's office, while Mr. P. and their son were upstairs also watching television. Suddenly, a glass of milk standing on the desk in the office rose up by itself and dashed itself to the floor with full force. The child ran screaming from the room, and it took a long time for her father to calm her down.

As a result of these happenings, the children implored their mother to move from the house, but Mrs. P. would have none of it. She liked the house fine, and was not about to let some unknown ghost displace her. The more she thought about it, the angrier she got. She decided to go from floor to floor, cursing the unknown ghost and telling him or her to get out of the house, even if they used to own it.

But that is how it is with stay-behinds: they don't care if you paid for the house. After all, they can't use the money where they are, and would rather stay on in a place they are familiar with.

* * *

Strange places can have stay-behind ghosts. Take Maryknoll College of Glen Ellyn, Illinois, a Roman Catholic seminary that closed its doors in June 1972, due to a dwindling interest in what it had to offer. In the fall a few years before, a seminarian named Gary M. was working in the darkroom of the college. This was part of his regular assignments, and photography had been a regular

activity for some years, participated in by both faculty and students.

On this particular occasion, Mr. M. felt as though he were being watched while in the darkroom. Chalking it up to an active imagination, he dismissed the matter from his mind. But in the spring a few years later, Mr. M. was going through some old chemicals belonging to a former priest, when he received the strongest impression of a psychic presence. He was loading some film at the time, and as he did so, he had the uncanny feeling that he was not alone in the room. The chemicals he had just handled were once the property of a priest who had died three years before. The following day, while developing film in an open tank, he suddenly felt as though a cold hand had gone down in his back. He realized also that the chemicals felt colder than before. After he had turned the lights back on, he took the temperature of the developer. At the start it had been 70° F., while at the end it was down to 64° F. Since the room temperature was 68° F., there was a truly unaccountable decrease in temperature.

The phenomena made him wonder, and he discussed his experience with other seminarians. It was then learned that a colleague of his had also had experiences in the same place. Someone, a man, had appeared to him, and he had felt the warm touch of a hand at his cheek. Since he was not alone at the time, but in a group of five students, he immediately reported the incident to them. The description of the apparition was detailed and definite. Mr. M. quickly went into past files, and came up with several pictures, so that his fellow student, who had a similar experience, could pick out that of the fellow student, who had a similar experience, could pick out that of the ghostly apparition he had seen. Without the slightest hesitation, he identified the dead priest as the man he had seen. This was not too surprising; the students were using what was once the priest's own equipment and chemicals, and perhaps he still felt obliged to teach them their proper use.

* * *

Mr. and Mrs. E. live in an average home in Florida that was built about thirteen years ago. They moved into this house in August. Neither of them had any particular interest in the occult, and Mr. E. could be classified as a complete skeptic, if anything. For the first few months of their residence, they were much too busy to notice anything out of the ordinary, even if there were such occurrences.

It was just before Christmas when they got their first inkling that something was not as it should be with their house. Mrs. E. was sitting up late one night, busy with last-minute preparations for the holiday. All of a sudden the front door, which was secured and locked, flew open with a violent force, and immediately shut itself again, with the handle turning by itself and the latch falling into place.

Since Mrs. E. didn't expect any visitors, she was naturally surprised. Quickly walking over to the door to find out what had happened, she discovered that the door was locked. It is the kind of lock that can only be unlocked by turning a knob. Shaking her head in disbelief, she returned to her chair, but before she could sit down again and resume her chores, the door to the utility room began to rattle as though a wind were blowing. Yet there were no open windows that could have caused it. Suddenly, as she was staring at it, the knob turned and the door opened. Somehow nonplussed, Mrs. E. thought, rather sarcastically, "While you're at it, why don't you shake the Christmas tree too?" Before she had completed the thought, the tree began to shake. For a moment, Mrs. E. stood still and thought all of this over in her mind. Then she decided that she was just overtired and had contracted a case of the holiday jitters. It was probably all due to imagination. She went to bed and didn't say anything about the incident.

Two weeks later, her fourteen-year-old daughter and Mrs. E. were up late talking, when all of a sudden every cupboard in the kitchen opened by itself, one by one. Mrs. E.'s daughter stared at the phenomenon in disbelief. But Mrs. E. simply said, "Now close them." Sure enough, one by one, they shut with a hard slam by themselves, almost like a little child whose prank had not succeeded. At this point Mrs. E. thought it best to tell her daughter of her first encounter with the unseen, and implored her not to be scared of it, or tell the younger children or anyone else outside the house. She didn't want to be known as a weird individual in the neighborhood into which they had just moved. However, she decided to inform her husband about what had happened. He didn't say much, but it was clear that he was not convinced. However, as with so many cases of this kind where the man in the house takes a lot longer to be convinced than a woman, Mr. E.'s time came about two weeks later.

He was watching television when one of the stereo speakers began to tilt back all of a sudden, rocking back and forth without falling over, on its own, as if held by unseen hands. Being of a practical bent, Mr. E. got up to find an explanation, but there was no wind that would have been strong enough to tilt a 20-pound speaker. At this point, Mr. E. agreed that there was something peculiar about the house. This was the more likely as their dog, an otherwise calm and peaceful animal, went absolutely wild at the moment the speakers tilted, and ran about the house for half an hour afterwards, barking, sniffing, and generally raising Cain.

However, the ghost was out of the bag, so to speak. The two younger children, then nine and ten years old, noticed him—it was assumed to be a man all along. A house guest remarked how strange it was that the door was opening seemingly by itself. Mrs. E. explained this with a remark that the latch was not working properly. "But how did the knob turn, then?" the house guest wanted to know.

Under the circumstances, Mrs. E. owned up to their guest. The ghost doesn't scare Mrs. E., but he makes it somewhat unpleasant for her at times, such as when she is taking a shower and the doors fly open. After all, one doesn't want to be watched by a man while showering, even if he *is* a ghost. The stay-behind isn't noticeable all the time, to be sure, but frequently enough to count as an extra inhabitant of the house. Whenever she feels him near, there is a chill in the hall and an echo. This happens at various times of day or night, early or late. To the children he is a source of some concern, and they will not stay home alone.

But to Mrs. E. he is merely an unfortunate human being, caught up in the entanglement of his own emotions from the past, desperately trying to break through the time barrier to communicate with her, but unable to do so because conditions aren't just right. Sometimes she wishes she were more psychic than she is, but in the meantime she has settled down to share the her home with someone she cannot see, but who, it appears, considers himself part of the family.

* * *

One of the most amazing stories of recent origin concerns a family of farmers in central Connecticut. Some people have a ghost in the house, a stay-behind who likes the place so much he or she doesn't want to leave. But this family had entire *groups* of ghosts staying on, simply because they liked the sprawling farmhouse, and simply because it happened to be their home too. The fact that they had passed across the threshold of death did not deter them in the least. To the contrary, it seemed a natural thing to stay behind and watch what the young ones were doing with the house, to possibly help them here and there, and, at the very least, to have some fun with them by causing so-called "inexplicable" phenomena to happen.

After all, life can be pretty dull in central Connecticut, especially in the winter. It isn't any more fun being a ghost in central Connecticut, so one cannot really hold it against these stay-behinds if they amuse themselves as best they can in the afterlife. Today the house shows its age; it isn't in good condition, and needs lots of repairs. The family isn't as large as it was before some of the younger generation moved out to start lives of their own, but it's still a busy house and a friendly one, ghosts or no ghosts. It stands on a quiet country road off the main route, and on a clear day you can see the Massachusetts border in the distance; that is, if you are looking for it. It is hardly noticeable, for in this part of the country, all New England looks the same.

Because of the incredible nature of the many incidents, the family wants no publicity, no curious tourists, no reporters. To defer to their wishes, I changed the family name to help them retain that anonymity, and the peace and quiet of their country house. The house in question was already old when a map of the town, drawn in 1761, showed it. The present owners, the Harveys, have lived in it all their lives, with interruption. Mrs. Harvey's great-great-grandparents bought it from the original builder, and when her great-great-grandfather died in 1858, it happened at the old homestead. Likewise, her great-great-grandmother passed on in 1871, at the age of eighty, and again it happened at home. One of their children died in 1921, at age ninety-one, also at home.

This is important, you see, because it accounts for the events that transpired later in the lives of their descendants. A daughter named Julia married an outsider and moved to another state, but considers herself part of the family just the same, so much so that her second home was still the old homestead in central Connecticut. Another daughter, Martha, was Mrs. Harvey's great-grandmother. Great-grandmother Martha died at age ninety-one, also in the house. Then there was an aunt, a sister of her great-great-grandfather's by the name of Nancy, who came to live with them when she was a widow; she lived to be ninety and died in the house. They still have some of her furniture there. Mrs. Harvey's grandparents had only one child, Viola, who became her mother, but they took in boarders, mostly men working in the nearby sawmills. One of these boarders died in the house too, but his name is unknown. Possibly several others died there too.

Of course the house doesn't look today the way it originally did; additions were built onto the main part, stairs were moved, a well in the cellar was filled in because members of the family going down for cider used to fall into it, and many of the rooms that later became bedrooms originally had other purposes. For instance, daughter Marjorie's bedroom was once called the harness room because horses' harnesses were once made in it, and the room of one of the sons used to be called the cheese room for obvious reasons. What became a sewing room was originally used as a pantry, with shelves running across the south wall.

The fact that stairs were changed throughout the house is important, because in the mind of those who lived in the past, the original stairs would naturally take precedence over later additions or changes. Thus phantoms may appear out of the wall, seemingly without reason, except that they would be walking up staircases that no longer exist.

Mrs. Harvey was born in the house, but at age four her parents moved away from it, and did not return until much later. But even then, Mrs. Harvey recalls an incident which she was never to forget. When she was only four years old, she remembers very clearly an old lady she had never seen before appear at her crib. She cried, but when she told her parents about it, they assured her it was just a dream. But Mrs. Harvey knew she had not dreamt the incident; she remembered every detail of the old lady's dress.

When she was twelve years old, at a time when the family had returned to live in the house, she was in one of the upstairs bedrooms and again the old lady appeared to her. But when she talked about it to their parents, the matter was immediately dropped. As Frances Harvey grew up in the house, she couldn't help but notice some strange goings-on. A lamp moved by itself, without anyone being near it. Many times she could feel a presence walking close behind her in the upstairs part of the house, but when she turned around, she was alone. Nor was she the only one to notice the strange goings-on. Her brothers heard footsteps around their beds, and complained about someone bending over them, yet no one was to be seen. The doors to the bedrooms would open by themselves at night, so much so that the boys tied the door latches together so that they could not open by themselves. Just the same, when morning came, the doors were wide open with the knot still in place.

It was at that time that her father got into the habit of taking an after-dinner walk around the house before retiring. Many times he told the family of seeing a strange light going through the upstairs rooms, a glowing luminosity for which there was no rational explanation. Whenever Frances Harvey had to be alone upstairs she felt uncomfortable, but when she mentioned this to her parents she was told that all old houses made one feel like that and to nevermind. One evening, Frances was playing a game with her grandfather when both of them clearly heard footsteps coming up the back stairs. But her grandfather didn't budge. When Frances asked him who this could possibly be, he merely shrugged and said there was plenty of room for *everyone*.

As the years passed, the Harveys would come back to the house from time to time to visit. On these occasions, Frances would wake up in the night because someone was bending over her. At other times there was a heavy depression on the bed as if someone were sitting there! Too terrified to tell anyone about it, she kept her experiences to herself for the time being.

Then, in the early 1940s, Frances married, and with her husband and two children, eventually returned to the house to live there permanently with her grandparents. No sooner had they moved in when the awful feeling came back in the night. Finally she told her husband, who of course scoffed at the idea of ghosts.

The most active area in the house seemed to be upstairs, roughly from her son Don's closet, through her daughter Lolita's room, and especially the front hall and stairs. It felt as if someone were standing on the landing of the front stairs, just watching.

This goes back a long time. Mrs. Harvey's mother frequently complained, when working in the attic, that all of a sudden she would feel someone standing next to her, someone she could not see.

One day Mrs. Harvey and her youngest daughter went grocery shopping. After putting the groceries away, Mrs. Harvey reclined on the living room couch while the girl sat in the dining room reading. Suddenly they heard a noise like thunder, even though the sky outside was clear. It came again, only this time it sounded closer, as if it were upstairs! When it happened the third time, it was accompanied by a sound as if someone were making up the bed in Mrs. Harvey's son's room upstairs.

Now, they had left the bed in disorder because they had been in a hurry to go shopping. No one else could have gone upstairs, and yet when they entered the son's room, the bed was made up as smoothly as possible. As yet, part of the family still scoffed at the idea of having ghosts in the house, and considered the mother's ideas as dreams or hallucinations. They were soon to change their minds, however, when it happened to them as well.

The oldest daughter felt very brave and called up the stairs, "Little ghosties, where are you?" Her mother told her she had better not challenge them, but the others found it amusing. That night she came downstairs a short time after she had gone to bed, complaining that she felt funny in her room, but thought it was just her imagination. The following night, she awoke to the feeling that someone was bending over her. One side of her pillow was pulled away from her head as though a hand had pushed it down. She called out and heard footsteps receding from her room, followed by heavy rumblings in the attic above. Quickly she ran into her sister's room, where both of them lay awake the rest of the night listening to the rumbling and footsteps walking around overhead. The next day she noticed a dusty black footprint on the light-colored scatter rug next to her bed. It was in the exact location where she had felt someone standing and bending over her. Nobody's footprint in the house matched the black footprint, for it was long and very narrow. At this point the girls purchased special night lights and left them on in the hope of sleeping peacefully.

One day Mrs. Harvey felt brave, and started up the stairs in response to footsteps coming from her mother's bedroom. She stopped, and as the footsteps approached the top of the stairs, a loud ticking noise came with them, like a huge pocket watch. Quickly she ran down the stairs and outside to get her son to be a witness to it. Sure enough, he too could hear the ticking noise. This was followed by doors opening and closing by themselves. Finally, they dared go upstairs, and when they entered the front bedroom, they noticed a very strong, sweet smell of perfume. When two of the daughters came home from work that evening, the family compared notes and it was discovered that they, too, had smelled the strange perfume and heard the ticking noise upstairs. They concluded that one of their ghosts, at least, was a man.

About that time, the youngest daughter reported seeing an old woman in her room, standing at a bureau with something shiny in her hand. The ghost handed it to her but she was too frightened to receive it. Since her description of the woman had been very detailed, Mrs. Harvey took out the family album and asked her daughter to look through it in the hope that she might identify the ghostly visitor. When they came to one particular picture, the girl let out a small cry: that was the woman she had seen! It turned out to be Julia, a great-great-aunt of Mrs. Harvey's, the same woman whom Mrs. Harvey herself had seen when she was twelve years old. Evidently, the lady was staying around.

Mrs. Harvey's attention was deflected from the phenomena in the house by her mother's illness. Like a dutiful daughter, she attended her to the very last, but in March of that year her mother passed away. Whether there is any connection with her mother's death or not, the phenomena started to increase greatly, both in volume and intensity, in July of that same year. To be exact, the date was July 20. Mrs. Harvey was hurrying one morning to get ready to take her daughter Lolita to the center of town so she could get a ride to work. Her mind was preoccupied with domestic chores, when a car came down the road, with brakes squealing. Out of habit, she hurried to the living room window to make sure that none of their cats had been hit by the car. This had been a habit of her mother's and hers, whenever there was the sound of sudden brakes outside.

As she did so, for just a fleeting glance, she saw her late mother looking out of her favorite window. It didn't register at first, then Mrs. Harvey realized her mother couldn't possibly have been there. However, since time was of the essence, Mrs. Harvey and her daughter Lolita left for town without saying anything to any of the others in the house. When they returned, her daughter Marjorie was standing outside waiting for them. She complained of hearing someone moving around in the living room just after they had left, and it sounded just like Grandma when she straightened out the couch and chair covers.

It frightened her, so she decided to wait in the dining room for her mother's return. But while there, she heard footsteps coming from the living room and going into the den, then the sound of clothes being folded. This was something Mrs. Harvey's mother was also in the habit of doing there. It was enough for Marjorie to run outside the house and wait there. Together with her sister and mother, she returned to the living room, only to find the chair cover straightened. The sight of the straightened cover made the blood freeze in Mrs. Harvey's veins; she recalled vividly how she had asked her late mother not to bother straightening the chair covers during her illness, because it hurt her back. In reply, her mother had said, "Too bad I can't come back and do it after I die."

Daughter Jane was married to a Navy man, who used to spend his leaves at the old house. Even during his courtship days, he and Mrs. Harvey's mother got along real fine, and they used to do crossword puzzles together. He was sleeping at the house sometime after the old lady's death, when he awoke to see her standing by his bed with her puzzle book and pencil in hand. It was clear to Mrs. Harvey by now that her late mother had joined the circle of dead relatives to keep a watch on her and the family. Even while she was ill, Mrs. Harvey's mother wanted to help in the house. One day after her death, Mrs. Harvey was baking a custard pie and lay down on the couch for a few minutes while it was baking.

She must have fallen asleep, for she awoke to the voice of her mother saying, "Your pie won't burn, will it?" Mrs. Harvey hurriedly got up and checked; the pie was just right and would have burned if it had been left in any longer. That very evening, something else happened. Mrs. Harvey wanted to watch a certain program that came on television at 7:30 P.M., but she was tired and fell asleep on the couch in the late afternoon. Suddenly she heard her mother's voice say to her, "It's time for your program, dear." Mrs. Harvey looked at the clock, and it was exactly 7:30 P.M. Of course, her mother did exactly the same type of thing when she was living, so it wasn't too surprising that she should continue with her concerned habits after she passed on into the next dimension.

But if Mrs. Harvey's mother had joined the ghostly crew in the house, she was by no means furnishing the bulk of the phenomena—not by a long shot. Lolita's room upstairs seemed to be the center of many activities, with her brother Don's room next to hers also very much involved. Someone was walking from her bureau to her closet, and her brother heard the footsteps too. Lolita looked up and saw a man in a uniform with gold buttons, standing in the back of her closet. At other times she smelled perfume and heard the sound of someone dressing near her bureau. All the time she heard people going up the front stairs mumbling, then going into her closet where the sound stopped abruptly. Yet, they could not see anyone on such occasions.

Daughter Jane wasn't left out of any of this either. Many nights she would feel someone standing next to her bed, between the bed and the wall. She saw three different people, and felt hands trying to lift her out of bed. To be sure, she could not see their faces; their shapes were like dark shadows. Marjorie, sleeping in the room next to Jane's, also experienced an attempt by some unseen forces to get her out of bed. She grabbed the headboard to stop herself from falling when she noticed the apparition of the same old woman whom Mrs. Harvey had seen the time she heard several people leave her room for the front hall.

One night she awoke to catch a glimpse of someone in a long black coat hurrying through the hall. Mumbling was heard in that direction, so she put her ear against the door to see if she could hear any words, but she couldn't make out any. Marjorie, too, saw the old woman standing at the foot of her bed—the same old woman whom Mrs. Harvey had seen when she was twelve years old. Of course,

that isn't too surprising; the room Marjorie slept in used to be Julia's a long time ago. Lolita also had her share of experiences: sound coming up from the cellar bothering her, footsteps, voices, even the sound of chains. It seemed to her that they came right out of the wall by her head, where there used to be stairs. Finally, it got so bad that Lolita asked her mother to sleep with her. When Mrs. Harvey complied, the two women clearly saw a glow come in from the living room and go to where the shelves used to be. Then there was the sound of dishes, and even the smell of food.

Obviously, the ghostly presences were still keeping house in their own fashion, reliving some happy or at least busy moments from their own past. By now Mr. Harvey was firmly convinced that he shared the house with a number of dead relatives, if not friends. Several times he woke to the sound of bottles being placed on the bureau. One night he awoke because the bottom of the bed was shaking hard; as soon as he was fully awake, it stopped. This was followed by a night in which Mrs. Harvey could see a glow pass through the room at the bottom of the bed. When "they" got to the hall door, which was shut, she could hear it open, but it actually did not move. Yet the sound was that of a door opening. Next she heard several individuals walk up the stairs, mumbling as they went.

The following night a light stopped by their fireplace, and as she looked closely it resembled a figure bending down. It got so that they compared notes almost every morning to see what had happened next in their very busy home. One moonlit night Mrs. Harvey woke to see the covers of her bed folded in half, down the entire length of the bed. Her husband was fully covered, but she was totally uncovered. At the same time, she saw some dark shadows by the side of the bed. She felt someone's hand holding her own, pulling her gently. Terrified, she couldn't move, and just lay there wondering what would happen next. Then the blankets were replaced as before, she felt something cold touch her forehead, and the ghosts left. But the stay-behinds were benign, and meant no harm. Some nights, Mrs. Harvey would wake up because of the cold air, and notice that the blankets were standing up straight from the bed as if held by someone. Even after she pushed them back hard, they would not stay in place.

On the other hand, there were times when she accidentally uncovered herself at night and felt someone putting the covers back on her, as if to protect her from the night chills. This was more important, as the house has no central heating. Of course it wasn't always clear what the ghosts wanted from her. On the other hand, they were clearly concerned with her well-being and that of the family; on the other, they seemed to crave attention for themselves also.

Twice they tried to lift Mrs. Harvey out of her bed. She felt herself raised several inches above it by unseen hands, and tried to call out to her husband but somehow couldn't utter a single word. This was followed by a strange, dreamlike state, in which she remembered being taken to the attic and shown something. Unfortunately she could not remember it afterwards, except that she had been to the attic and how the floorboards looked there; she also recalled that the attic was covered with black dust. When morning came, she took a look at her feet: they were dusty, and the bottom of her bed was grayish as if from dust. Just as she was contemplating these undeniable facts, her husband asked her what had been the matter with her during the night. Evidently he had awakened to find her gone from the bed.

One night daughter Marjorie was out on a date. Mrs. Harvey awoke to the sound of a car pulling into the driveway, bringing Marjorie home. From her bed she could clearly see four steps of the back stairs. As she lay there, she saw the shape of a woman coming down without any sound, sort of floating down the stairs. She was dressed in a white chiffon dress. At the same moment, her daughter Marjorie entered the living room. She too saw the girl in the chiffon dress come down the stairs into the living room and disappear through a door to the other bedroom. Even though the door was open wide and there was plenty of room to go through the opening, evidently the ghostly lady preferred to walk through the door.

The miscellaneous stay-behinds tried hard to take part in the daily lives of the flesh-and-blood people in the house. Many times the plants in the living room would be rearranged and attended to by unseen hands. The Harveys could clearly see the plants move, yet no one was near them; no one, that is, visible to the human eye. There was a lot of mumbling about now, and eventually they could make out some words. One day daughter Marjorie heard her late grandmother say to her that "they" would be back in three weeks. Sure enough, not a single incident of a ghostly nature occurred for three weeks. To the day, after the three weeks were up, the phenomena began again. Where had the ghosts gone in the meantime? On another occasion, Marjorie heard someone say, "That is Jane on that side of the bed, but who is that on the other side? The bed looks so smooth." The remark made sense to Mrs. Harvey. Her late mother sometimes slept with Jane, when she was still in good health. On the other hand, daughter Marjorie likes to sleep perfectly flat, so her bed does look rather smooth.

Average people believe ghosts only walk at night. Nothing could be further from the truth, as Mrs. Harvey will testify. Frequently, when she was alone in the house during the daytime, she would hear doors upstairs bang shut and open again. One particular day, she heard the sound of someone putting things on Jane's bureau, so she tried to go up and see what it was. Carefully tiptoeing up the stairs to peek into her door to see if she could actually

trap a ghost, she found herself halfway along the hall when she heard footsteps coming along the foot of son Don's bed, in her direction. Quickly, she hurried back down the stairs and stopped halfway down. The footsteps sounded like a woman's, and suddenly there was the rustle of a taffeta gown. With a *whooshing* sound, the ghost passed Mrs. Harvey and went into Jane's room. Mrs. Harvey waited, rooted to the spot on the stairs.

A moment later the woman's footsteps came back, only this time someone walked with her, someone heavier. They went back through Don's room, and ended up in Lolita's closet—the place where Lolita had seen the man in the uniform with the shining gold buttons. Mrs. Harvey did not follow immediately, but that night she decided to go up to Lolita's room and have another look at the closet. As she approached the door to the room it opened, which wasn't unusual since it was in the habit of opening at the slightest vibration. But before Mrs. Harvey could close it, it shut itself tight and the latch moved into place of its own accord. Mrs. Harvey didn't wait around for anything further that night.

For a while there was peace. But in October the phenomena resumed. One night Mrs. Harvey woke up when she saw a shadow blocking the light coming from the dining room. She looked towards the door and saw a lady dressed all in black come into her bedroom and stand close to her side of the bed. This time she clearly heard her speak.

"Are you ready? It is almost time to go."

With that, the apparition turned and started up the stairs. The stairs looked unusually light, as if moonlight were illuminating them. When the woman in black got to the top step, all was quiet and the stairs were dark again, as before. Mrs. Harvey could see her clothes plainly enough, but not her face. She noticed that the apparition had carried a pouch-style pocketbook, which she had put over her arm so that her hands would be free to lift up her skirts as she went up the stairs. The next morning, Mrs. Harvey told her husband of the visitation. He assured her she must have dreamt it all. But before she could answer, her daughter Marjorie came in and said that she had heard someone talking in the night, something about coming, and it being almost time. She saw a figure at the foot of her bed, which she described as similar to what Mrs. Harvey had seen.

The night before that Thanksgiving, Marjorie heard footsteps come down the stairs. She was in bed and tried to get up to see who it was, but somehow couldn't move at all, except to open her eyes to see five people standing at the foot of her bed! Two of them were women, the others seemed just outlines or shadows. One of the two women wore an old-fashioned shaped hat, and she looked very stern. As Marjorie was watching the group, she managed to roll over a little in her bed and felt someone next to her. She felt relieved at the thought that it was her mother, but then whoever it was got up and left with the others in the group. All the time they kept talking among themselves, but Marjorie could not understand what was being said. Still talking, the ghostly visitors went back up the stairs.

Nothing much happened until Christmas time. Again the footsteps running up and down the stairs resumed, yet no one was seen. Christmas night, Jane and her mother heard walking in the room above the living room, where Mrs. Harvey's mother used to sleep. At that time, Mr. Harvey was quite ill and was sleeping in what used to be the sewing room so as not to awaken when his wife got up early.

On two different occasions Mrs. Harvey had "visitors." The first time someone lifted her a few inches off the bed. Evidently someone else was next to her in bed, for when she extended her hand that person got up and left. Next she heard footsteps going up the stairs and someone laughing, then all was quiet again. About a week later, she woke one night to feel someone pulling hard on her elbow and ankle. She hung onto the top of her bed with her other hand. But the unseen entities pushed, forcing her to brace herself against the wall.

Suddenly it all stopped, yet there were no sounds of anyone leaving. Mrs. Harvey jumped out of bed and tried to turn the light on. It wouldn't go on. She went back to bed when she heard a voice telling her not to worry, that her husband would be all right. She felt relieved at the thought, when the voice added, "But you won't be." Then the unseen voice calmly informed her that she would die in an accident caused by a piece of bark from some sort of tree. That was all the voice chose to tell her, but it was enough to start her worrying. Under the circumstances, and in order not to upset her family, she kept quiet about it, eventually thinking that she had dreamed the whole incident. After all, if it were just a dream, there was no point in telling anyone, and if it were true, there was nothing she could do anyway, so there was no point in worrying her family. She had almost forgotten the incident when she did have an accident about a week later. She hurt her head rather badly in the woodshed, requiring medical attention. While she was still wondering whether that was the incident referred to by the ghostly voice, she had a second accident: a heavy fork fell on her and knocked her unconscious.

But the voice had said that she would die in an accident, so Mrs. Harvey wasn't at all sure that the two incidents, painful though they had been, were what the voice had referred to. Evidently, ghosts get a vicarious thrill out of making people worry, because Mrs. Harvey is alive and well, years after the unseen voice had told her she would die in an accident.

But if it were not enough to cope with ghost people, Mrs. Harvey also had the company of a ghost dog. Their favorite pet, Lucy, passed into eternal dogdom the previous March. Having been treated as a member of the family, she had been permitted to sleep in the master bedroom,

but as she became older she started wetting the rug, so eventually she had to be kept out.

After the dog's death, Marjorie offered her mother another dog, but Mrs. Harvey didn't want a replacement for Lucy; no other dog could take her place. Shortly after the offer and its refusal, Lolita heard a familiar scratch at the bathroom door. It sounded exactly as Lucy had always sounded when Lolita came home late at night. At first, Mrs. Harvey thought her daughter had just imagined it, but then the familiar wet spot reappeared on the bedroom rug. They tried to look for a possible leak in the ceiling, but could find no rational cause for the rug to be wet. The wet spot remained for about a month. During that time, several of the girls heard a noise that reminded them of Lucy walking about. Finally the rug dried out and Lucy's ghost stopped walking.

For several years the house has been quiet now. Have the ghosts gone on to their just rewards, been reincarnated, or have they simply tired of living with flesh-and-blood relatives? Stay-behinds generally stay indefinitely; unless, of course, they feel they are really not wanted. Or perhaps they just got bored with it all.

* * *

Several years ago, a tragic event took place at a major university campus in Kansas. A member of one of the smaller fraternities, TKE, was killed in a head-on automobile accident on September 21. His sudden death at so young an age—he was an undergraduate—brought home a sense of tragedy to other members of the fraternity, and it was decided that they would attend his funeral in New York *en masse*.

Not quite a year after the tragic accident, several members of the fraternity were at their headquarters. Eventually, one of the brothers and his date were left behind alone, studying in the basement of the house. Upon completion of their schoolwork, they left. When they had reached the outside, the woman remembered she had left her purse in the basement and returned to get it. When she entered the basement, she noticed a man sitting at the poker table, playing with chips. She said something to him, explaining herself, then grabbed her purse and returned upstairs. There she asked her date who the man in the basement was, since she hadn't noticed him before. He laughed and said that no one had been down there but the two of them. At that point, one of the other brothers went into the basement and was surprised to see a man get up from his chair and walk away. That man was none other than the young man who had been killed in the automobile crash a year before.

One of the other members of the fraternity had also been in the same accident, but had only been injured, and survived. Several days after the incident in the fraternity house basement, this young man saw the dead man walking up the steps to the second floor of the house. By now the fraternity realized that their dead brother was still very much with them, drawn back to what was to him his true home—and so they accepted him as one of the crowd, even if he was invisible at times.

* * *

On January 7, Mr. and Mrs. S. moved into an older house on South Fourth Street, a rented, fully-furnished two-bedroom house in a medium-sized city in Oklahoma. Mrs. S.'s husband was a career service man in the Army, stationed at a nearby Army camp. They have a small boy, and looked forward to a pleasant stay in which the boy could play with neighborhood kids, while Mrs. S. tried to make friends in what to her was a new environment.

She is a determined lady, not easily frightened off by anything she cannot explain, and the occult was the last thing on her mind. They had lived in the house for about two weeks, when she noticed light footsteps walking in the hall at night. When she checked on them, there was no one there. Her ten-year-old son was sleeping across the hall, and she wondered if perhaps he was walking in his sleep. But each time she heard the footsteps and would check on her son, she found him sound asleep. The footsteps continued on and off, for a period of four months.

Then, one Sunday afternoon at about 2 o'clock, when her husband was at his post and her son in the backyard playing, she found herself in the kitchen. Suddenly she heard a child crying very softly and mutedly, as if the child were afraid to cry aloud. At once she ran into the backyard to see if her son was hurt. There was nothing wrong with him, and she found him playing happily with a neighborhood boy. It then dawned on her that she could not hear the child crying outside the house, but immediately upon re-entering the house, the faint sobs were clearly audible again.

She traced the sound to her bedroom, and when she entered the room, it ceased to be noticeable. This puzzled her to no end, since she had no idea what could cause the sounds. Added to this were strange thumping sounds, which frequently awakened her in the middle of the night. It sounded as if someone had fallen out of bed.

On these occasions, she would get out of bed quickly and rush into her son's room, only to find him fast asleep. A thorough check of the entire house revealed no source for the strange noises. But Mrs. S. noticed that their Siamese cat, who slept at the foot of her bed when these things happened, also reacted to them: his hair would bristle, his ears would fly back, and he would growl and stare into space at something or someone she could not see.

About that time, her mother decided to visit them. Since her mother was physically challenged, Mrs. S. decided not to tell her about the strange phenomena in order to avoid upsetting her. She stayed at the house for three days, when one morning she wanted to know why Mrs. S. was up at two o'clock in the morning making coffee. Since the house had only two bedrooms, they had put a half-bed into the kitchen for her mother, especially as the kitchen was very large and she could see the television from where she was sleeping. Her mother insisted she had heard footsteps coming down the hall into the kitchen. She called out to what she assumed was her daughter, and when there was no answer, she assumed that her daughter and her son-in-law had had some sort of disagreement and she had gotten up to make some coffee.

From her bed she could not reach the light switch, but she could see the time by the illuminated clock and realized it was 2 o'clock in the morning. Someone came down the hall, entered the kitchen, put water into the coffee pot, plugged it in, and then walked out of the kitchen and down the hall. She could hear the sound of coffee perking and could actually smell it. However, when she didn't hear anyone coming back, she assumed that her daughter and son-in-law had made up and gone back to sleep.

She did likewise, and decided to question her daughter about it in the morning. Mrs. S. immediately checked the kitchen, but there was no trace of the coffee to be found, which did not help her state of mind. A little later she heard some commotion outside the house, and on stepping outside noticed that the dogcatcher was trying to take a neighbor's dog with him. She decided to try and talk him out of it, and the conversation led to her husband being in the service, a statement which seemed to provoke a negative reaction on the part of the dogcatcher. He informed Mrs. S. that the last GI to live in the house was a murderer. When she wanted to know more about it, he clammed up immediately. But Mrs. S. became highly agitated. She called the local newspaper and asked for any and all information concerning her house. It was then that she learned the bitter truth.

In October two years before, a soldier stationed at the same base as her husband had beaten his two-year-old daughter to death. The murder took place in what had now become Mrs. S.'s bedroom. Mrs. S., shocked by the news, sent up a silent prayer, hoping that the restless soul of the child might find peace and not to have to haunt a house where she had suffered nothing but unhappiness in her short life. . . .

Rose Hall, Home of the "White Witch" of Jamaica

SOMETIMES REFERRED TO AS the most haunted house in the Western Hemisphere, Rose Hall is the great house on Rose Hall Plantation, one of the largest estates of Colonial Jamaica. It has recently been purchased by an American hotelman and meticulously restored to its former glory for use as a hotel for affluent tourists.

The plantation is not far from the Montage Bay airport, and a good road leads up to it. To this day, however, some natives will not go near the house, referring to it as filled with "goopies", a local term for ghosts. They are indeed right. The earthbound spirit of Annie Porter, once mistress of Rose Hall, has never been laid to rest.

I have been to Rose Hall on two occasions, but without a proper trance medium. It is particularly in the corridors beneath the house that stark terror dwells, and I caution anyone visiting Rose Hall to beware of those areas, especially at night.

Annie Porter was a sadistic woman, who first made lovers of some of her more handsome slaves, and then tortured them to death. Eventually, fate caught up with her, and she too was put to death by one of those she had first tormented. Much violence and hatred cling to the old masonry, and are not likely to have disappeared just because the building had some of its holes filled in and painted over.

The house has three stories and a magnificent staircase out front, by which one gains access to the main floor. It is surrounded by trees and some of the most beautiful landscape in Jamaica. Prior to its restoration, it looked the way a haunted house is always described in fiction or film, with empty windows and broken walls. Now, however, it presents a clean and majestic appearance.

Annie Porter is also referred to as the "White Witch of Rose Hall." There are actually two Annie Porters recorded in history and buried in a nearby cemetery. In the popular legend, the two figures have become amalgamated, but it is the Annie Porter of the late British colonial period who committed the atrocities which force her to remain tied to what was once her mansion. I do not doubt that she is still there.

I base this assumption on solid evidence. About ten years ago the late great medium Eileen Garrett paid Rose Hall a visit in the company of distinguished researchers. Her mission was to seek out and, if possible, appease the restless spirit of Annie Porter. Within a matter of moments after her arrival at the Hall, Mrs. Garrett went into a deep trance. The personality of the terror-stricken ghost took over her body, vocal cords, facial expression, and all, and tried to express the pent-up emotions that had so long been dormant.

The Haunted Rose Hall in Jamaica, now a luxury hotel—this is how it used to look

A little later, work has begun

The researchers were hard-pressed to follow the entranced Mrs. Garrett from the terrace, where their quest had begun, through half-dilapidated corridors, underground passages, and dangerously undermined rooms. But

Entrance to the underground corridors where the slaves were tortured

This remains the most haunted area at the Hall

Annie Porter wanted them to see the places where she had been the Mistress of Rose Hall, reliving through the medium some of her moments of glory.

Eventually, these revived memories led to the point where Annie met her doom at the hand of a young slave with whom she had earlier had an affair.

Crying uncontrollably, writhing on all fours, the medium was by now completely under the control of the restless ghost. No matter how soothingly the researchers spoke to her, asking Annie to let go of the dreadful past, the violent behavior continued. Annie would not leave. In one of the few rare cases on record where a ghost is so tormented and tied to the place of its tragedy that it cannot break away, Annie refused to leave. Instead, the research team left, with a very shaken medium in tow.

✳ 149

There Is Nothing Like a Scottish Ghost

WHEN IT COMES to flavor and personality, there's nothing quite like a Scottish ghost, or for that matter, like the people who see 'em. Our visit to the country of Burns was short this time, but long enough to know how much we wanted to return.

We landed on a misty morning at Prestwick Airport and immediately set out for the town of Ayr, where we bedded down in the Station Hotel, one of the lesser delights of western Scotland. Immediately upon our arrival, Jack Weir of the BBC came to interview us, and I knew I was in a land where ghost hunting was a respected pursuit. Jamison Clarke, the television commentator, came along with him and we talked at length about a television show I would do from Edinburgh; Mr. Clarke would be in Glasgow at the same time. Nothing like a little magic via split-screen and other twentieth-century miracles!

But we had not come to Ayr just to be miserable at the Station Hotel or talk to these delightful Scots. Our aim that afternoon was Culzean Castle, pronounced Coleen, unless you are a Sassanach or, worse, a Yankee. We rented a chauffeur-driven car, for they drive on the left side here, and set out for Culzean along the coastal hills of western Scotland.

Shortly afterwards we entered the formal gardens and rode along a gently descending road towards the cliff on which Culzean Castle rises sheer from the sea on the Ayrshire coast.

Built by Robert Adam in the latter part of the eighteenth century, the castle has been associated with the Kennedy family, the Earls of Cassillis and the Marquises of Ailsa, whose portraits are seen all over the house. Today it is administered by the National Trust of Scotland as a museum. Its main tower rises majestically four stories from the cliff, and one of the top floors contains an apartment given to General Eisenhower as a gesture of gratitude from Britain. He stays there with his family from time to time.

We were cordially welcomed by the administrator of Culzean, Commander John Hickley.

"I'm afraid we don't keep a tame ghost in this castle," he said apologetically, as Mrs. Hickley served us tea.

I assured him that we enjoyed the visit just the same. Neither the Commander nor Mrs. Hickley had seen a ghost in this comparatively modern castle, nor had any of the help complained about any unusual visitors. But a British visitor to Culzean by the same of Margaret Penney was somewhat luckier—if seeing a ghost is luck.

According to an Associated Press report of August 9, 1962, Mrs. Penney was going through the castle just like any other tourist when she encountered the ghost.

"She came down a corridor when I was visiting Culzean Castle recently," said Mrs. Penney, "and said to me—'It rains today.'"

Mrs. Penney said the ghost was dark-haired and very beautiful.

"She appeared to be in evening dress though it was only about five o'clock in the afternoon when I encountered her.

"Anyway, I squeezed myself against the corridor to let her pass and told her, 'Not much room for passing when you're as plump as me.'"

Mrs. Penney said the girl looked at her very sadly and answered, "I do not require any room nowadays."

Mrs. Penney said her entire right side then went cold.

"Suddenly I realized that she had walked through my side."

Was she one of the Kennedy ladies who had come to a sad end in the lonely house on the Fyrth of Clyde? Until I bring a medium to Culzean at some future date, we can only guess.

* * *

Another nearby haunted castle drew my interest because its current occupants are British nobility from Baltimore, Maryland. Sir Adrian and Lady Naomi Dunbar inherited the ramshackle estate and castle of Mochrum Park by virtue of being the nearest cousin to the last British baronet, who died in 1953.

The Americans found the house a shambles and the income of the estate far from grand. Nevertheless, they still live in it, having restored some of it, and they are making a go of their newly found position in life.

When the new owners arrived late in 1953 to take over their new home, the villagers at Kirkcowan, Wigtownshire, were wondering how the Americans would take to the ghost. This is the "white lady" of Mochrum Park, allegedly the shade of Lady Jacobina Dunbar, who married the sixth baronet back in 1789, and whose portrait was found in the debris of the old house a few years before 1953.

The National Gallery of Scotland in Edinburgh now owns this valuable painting by Raeburn. Servants of the tenth baronet, Sir James Dunbar, who died in early 1953, always complained that the ghost portrait would always be found askew, no matter how often by straightened it out, as if someone were trying to call attention to something!

Elgin Fraser, chauffeur of the Dunbars for many years, twice saw the "white lady" standing at the foot of his bed.

Perhaps the saving of the valuable painting, which was in danger of being destroyed by the customary dry rot, has assuaged the fury of the ghost. No further disturbances have been reported, and when the I asked the American-born Lady Dunbar about the ghost, she said, with a broad Baltimore accent, "Nonsense. It's all just imagination."

A fine thing for a ghost to be called—imaginary! Especially by an American.

When we reached Edinburgh, the *Weekly Scotsman's* Donald MacDonald was already waiting for us to tell our story to the Scottish people. Then, too, the Kenneth MacRaes came to tell us of their experiences with Highland ghosts—hauntings we shall follow up on next time we're in Scotland. And a fellow author, MacDonald Robertson, offered us his index-card file on ghosts of Scotland. Unfortunately, only a few of these cases were of sufficiently recent origin to be looked into with any reasonable degree of verification, but Mr. Robertson's enthusiasm for the good cause made up for it.

That evening, we drove out to Roslin, a suburb of Edinburgh, to visit a famed Scottish medium, Anne Donaldson. She gave us a pretty good sitting, although most of the material obtained was of a private or personal nature.

The next day we set out early for the border country between Scotland and England, traditionally a wild area with a long association of war and strife. Hours of driving over sometimes unlit, unmarked roads, with only sheep populating the rolling hills, finally brought us to Hermitage Castle, an ancient medieval fortress associated with the de Soulis family, and dating back to the thirteenth century. It was here also that the Earl of Bothwell, wounded in a border raid, was visited by Mary Queen of Scots, his lover, in 1566.

Rising squarely in a commanding position on the border, this fortress boasts of a dungeon into which numerous enemies were thrust to starve to death. Their remains were never removed. This barbaric custom was general usage in the Middle Ages, and Hermitage is by no means unique in this respect.

Our reasons for visiting this famous ruin were not entirely sight-seeing. One of the early owners of the castle, Lord Soulis, was a black magician and committed a number of documented atrocities until he was caught by his enemies and dispatched in a most frightful manner. Ever since his ghost has been said to return on the anniversary of this deed to haunt the walls and ruined chambers, especially the ancient kitchen downstairs.

J. R. Wilson, now the custodian of the castle, readily played the bagpipes for us to set the mood, but he had never seen or heard a ghost.

"The only thing I know," he said, "is that some dogs will not go into the castle. A lady was here a while ago, and her dog just absolutely refused to go near it, set up a howl and refused to budge."

But there were other dogs which did, in fact, go inside the castle walls. Those, presumably, were the dogs which didn't believe in ghosts.

Back of Holyrood Palace, Edinburgh, residence of Mary Queen of Scots and other Scottish monarchs, stands a little house of modest appearance going by the quaint name of Croft-en-Reigh. This house was once owned by James, Earl of Moray, half brother of Mary, and Regent of Scotland in her absence. Today, the house is subdivided into three apartments, one of which belongs to a Mrs. Clyne. But several years ago this was the official residence of the warden of Holyrood Palace. The warden is the chief guide who has charge of all tourist traffic. David Graham, the onetime warden, has now retired to his nearby house in Portobello, but fourteen years ago he had a most unusual experience in this little house.

"There were twelve of us assembled for a séance, I recall," he said, "and we had Helen Duncan, who is now dead, as our medium. There we were, seated quietly in the top floor of Croft-en-Reigh, waiting for developments."

They did not have to wait long. A figure materialized before their astonished eyes and was recognized instantly: Mary Queen of Scots herself, who had been to this house many times in moments of great emotional turmoil. Within a moment, she was gone.

On several occasions, Mr. Graham recalls, he saw the ghost of a short man in sixteenth century clothes. "I am French," the man insisted. Graham thought nothing of it until he accidentally discovered that the house was built by an architect named French!

✳ 150

The Strange Case of Mrs. C's Late but Lively Husband

DEATH IS NOT THE END, no, definitely not. At least not for Mr. C. who lived the good life in a fair-sized city in Rhode Island. But then he died, or so it would appear on the record. But Mrs. C. came to consult me about the very unusual complaint of her late husband's continuing attentions.

When someone dies unexpectedly, or in the prime of his physical life, and finds that he can no longer express his sexual appetite physically in the world into which he has been suddenly catapulted, he may indeed look around for someone through whom he can express this appetite on the earth plane. It is then merely a matter of searching out opportunities, regardless of personalities involved. It is quite conceivable that a large percentage of the unexplained or inexplicable sexual attacks by otherwise meek, timid, sexually defensive individuals upon members of the opposite sex—or even the same sex—may be due to sudden possession by an entity of this kind. This is even harder to prove objectively than are some of the murder cases involving individuals who do not recall what they have done and are for all practical purposes normal human beings before and after the crime. But I am convinced that the influence of discarnates can indeed be exercised upon susceptible individuals—that it to say, appropriately mediumistic individuals. It also appears from my studies that the most likely recipients of this doubtful honor are those who are sexually weak or inactive. Evidently the unused sexual energies are particularly useful to the discarnate entities for their own gains. There really doesn't seem to be any way in which one can foretell such attacks or prevent them, except, perhaps, by leading a sexually healthy and balanced life. *Those who are fulfilled in their natural drives on the earth plane are least likely to suffer from such invasions.*

On the other hand, there exist cases of sexual possession involving two partners who knew each other before on the earth plane. One partner was cut short by death, either violently or prematurely, and would now seek to continue a pleasurable relationship of the flesh from the new dimension. Deprived of a physical body to express such desires, however, the deceased partner would then find it rather difficult to express the physical desires to the partner remaining on the earth plane. With sex it certainly takes two, and if the remaining partner is not willing, then difficulties will have to be reckoned with. An interesting case came to my attention a few months ago. Mrs. Anna C. lives with her several children in a comparatively new house in the northeastern United States. She bought the house eighteen months after her husband had passed away. Thus there was no connection between the late husband and the new house. Nevertheless, her husband's passing was by no means the end of their relationship.

"My husband died five years ago this past September. Ever since then he has not let me have a peaceful day," she explained in desperation, seeking my help.

Two months after her husband had died, she saw him coming to her in a dream complaining that she had buried him alive. He explained that he wasn't really dead, and that it was all her fault and her family's fault that he died in the first place.

Mr. C. had lived a rather controversial life, drinking regularly and frequently staying away from home. Thus the relationship between himself and his wife was far from ideal. Nevertheless, there was a strong bond between them.

"In other dreams he would tell me that *he was going to have sex relations with me whether I wanted him to or not.* He would try to grab me and I would run all through the house with him chasing after me. I never let him get hold of me. He was like that when he was alive, too. The most important thing in life to him was sex, and he didn't care how or where he got it. Nothing else mattered to him," she complained, describing vividly how the supposedly dead husband had apparently still a great deal of life in him.

"He then started climbing on the bed and walking up and down on it and scaring me half to death. I didn't know what it was or what to do about," she said, shaking like a leaf.

When Mr. C. could not get his wife to cooperate willingly, he apparently got mad. To express his displeasure, he caused all sorts of havoc around the household. He would tear a pair of stockings every day for a week, knock things over, and even go to the place where his mother-in-law worked as a cook, causing seemingly inexplicable phenomena to occur there as well. He appeared to an aunt in Indiana and told her to mind her own business and stay out of his personal relationship with Mrs. C. (It was the aunt who tried to get rid of him and his influences by performing a spiritualist ritual at the house.) Meanwhile, Mr. C. amused himself by setting alarm clocks to go off at the wrong times or stopping them altogether, moving objects from their accustomed places or making them disappear altogether, only to return them several days later to everyone's surprise. In general, he behaved like a good poltergeist should. But it didn't endear him any more to his erstwhile wife.

When Mrs. C. rejected his attentions, he started to try to possess his ten-year-old daughter. He came to her in dreams and told her that her mother wasn't really knowledgeable about anything. He tried everything in his power to drive a wedge between the little girl and her mother. As a result of this, the little girl turned more and more away from her mother, and no matter how Mrs. C. tried to explain things to her, she found the little girl's mind made up under the influence of her late father.

In a fit of destructiveness, the late Mr. C. then started to work on the other children, creating such a state of havoc in the household that Mrs. C. did not know where to turn any longer. Then the psychic aunt from Indiana came to New England to try to help matters. Sure enough, Mr. C. appeared to her and the two had a cozy talk. He explained that he was very unhappy where he was and was having trouble getting along with the people over there. To this, the aunt replied she would be very happy to help him get to a higher plane if that was what he wanted. But that wasn't it, he replied. He just wanted to stay where he was. The aunt left for home. Now the children, one by one, became unmanageable, and Mrs. C. assumed that her late husband was interfering with their proper education and discipline. "I am fighting an unseen force and cannot get through to the children," she explained.

Her late husband did everything to embarrass her. She was working as a clerk at St. Francis' rectory in her town, doing some typing. It happened to be December 24, 1971, Christmas Eve. All of a sudden she heard a thud in her immediate vicinity and looked down to the floor. A heavy dictionary was lying at her feet. The book had been on the shelf only a fraction of a second before. A co-worker wondered what was up. She was hard-pressed to explain the presence of the dictionary on the floor since it had been on the shelf in back of them only a moment before. But she knew very well how the dictionary came to land at her feet.

Mr. C. prepared special Christmas surprises for his wife. She went to her parents' house to spend the holiday. During that time her nephew George was late for work since his alarm had not worked properly. On inspection it turned out that someone had stuck a pencil right through the clock. As soon as the pencil was removed, the clock started to work again. On investigation it turned out that no one had been near the clock, and when the family tried to place the pencil into the clock, as they had found it, no one could do it. The excitement made Mrs. C. so ill she went to bed. That was no way to escape Mr. C.'s attentions, however. The day before New Year's Eve, her late husband got to her, walking up and down on the bed itself. Finally she told him to leave her and the children alone, to go where he belonged. She didn't get an answer. But phenomena continued in the house, so she asked her aunt to come back once again. This time the aunt from Indiana brought oil with her and put it on each of the children and Mrs. C. herself. Apparently it worked, or so it seemed to

Mrs. C. But her late husband was merely changing his tactics. A few days later she was sure that he was trying to get into one of the children to express himself further since he could no longer get at her. She felt she would be close to a nervous breakdown if someone would not help her get rid of the phenomenon and, above all, break her husband's hold on her. "I am anxious to have him sent on up where he can't bother anyone anymore," she explained.

Since I could not go immediately, and the voice on the telephone sounded as if its owner could not hold out a single day more, I asked Ethel Johnson Meyers, my mediumistic friend, to go out and see what she could do. Mrs. C. had to go to Mrs. Meyers' house for a personal sitting first. A week later Ethel came down to Mrs. C.'s house to continue her work. What Mrs. Meyers discovered was somewhat of a surprise to Mrs. C. and to myself. It was Ethel's contention that the late husband, while still in the flesh,

had himself been the victim of possession and had done the many unpleasant things (of which he was justly accused) during his lifetime, not of his own volition but under the direction of another entity. That the possessor was himself possessed seemed like a novel idea to me, one neither Mrs. Meyers nor I could prove. Far more important was the fact that Mrs. Meyers' prayers and commands to the unseen entity seemed to have worked, for he walks up and down Mrs. C's bed no more, and all is quiet. I believe that hold Mr. C. had upon his wife after his death was so strong because of an unconscious desire on her part to continue their relationship. Even though she abhorred him—and the idea of being sexually possessed by a man who had lost his physical body in the usual way—something within her, perhaps deeply buried within her, may have wanted the continuous sexual attention he had bestowed upon her while still in the body.

✳ 151

The Ghost of the Little White Flower

MRS. D. AND HER SON Bucky lived in a comfortable house on a hilltop in suburban Kentucky, not far from Cincinnati, Ohio, a pleasant, white house, not much different from other houses in the area. The surroundings are lovely and peaceful, and there's a little man-made pond right in front of the house. Nothing about the house or the area looks the least bit ghostly or unusual. Nevertheless Mrs. D. needed my help in a very vexing situation.

Six months after Mrs. D. had moved into the house, she began to hear footsteps upstairs when there was no one about, and the sound of a marble being rolled across the hall. Anything supernatural was totally alien to Mrs. D.

Nevertheless, Mrs. D. had a questioning and alert mind, and was not about to accept these phenomena without finding out what caused them. When the manifestations persisted, she walked up to the foot of the stairs and yelled, "Why don't you just come out and show yourself or say something instead of making all those noises?"

As if in answer, an upstairs door slammed shut and then there was utter silence. After a moment's hesitation, Mrs. D. dashed upstairs and made a complete search. There was no one about and the marble, which seemingly had rolled across the floor, was nowhere to be seen.

When the second Christmas in the new house rolled around, the D.s were expecting Bucky home from the Army. He was going to bring his sergeant and the sergeant's wife with him, since they had become very friendly. They celebrated New Year's Eve in style and high

spirits (not the ethereal kind, but the bottled type). Nevertheless, they were far from inebriated when the sergeant suggested that New Year's Eve was a particularly suitable night for a séance. Mrs. D. would have no part of it at first. She had read all about phony séances and such, and remembered what her Bible said about such matters. Her husband had long gone to bed. The four of them decided to have a go at it. They joined hands and sat quietly in front of the fireplace. Nothing much happened for a while. Then Bucky, who had read some books on psychic phenomena, suggested that they needed a guide or control from the other side of life to help them, but no one had any suggestions concerning to whom they might turn. More in jest than as a serious proposal, Mrs. D. heard herself say, "Why don't you call your Indian ancestor Little White Flower!" Mr. D. is part Cherokee, and Bucky, the son would, of course, consider this part of his inheritance too. Mrs. D. protested that all this was nonsense, and that they should go to bed. She assured them that nothing was likely to happen. But the other three were too busy to reply, staring behind her into the fireplace. When she followed the direction of their eyes she saw what appeared to be some kind of light similar to that made by a flashlight. It stayed on for a short time and then disappeared altogether.

From that day on Mrs. D. started to find strange objects around the house that had not been there a moment before. They were little stones in the shape of Indian arrows. She threw them out as fast as she found them. Several weeks later, when she was changing the sheets on her bed, she noticed a huge red arrow had been painted on the bottom sheet—by unseen hands.

It was in the winter of 1963. One afternoon she was lying down on the couch with a book trying to rest. Before long she was asleep. Suddenly she awoke with a feeling of horror which seemed to start at her feet and gradually work its way up throughout her entire body and mind. The room seemed to be permeated with something terribly evil. She could neither see nor hear anything, but she had the feeling that there was a presence there and that it was very strong and about to overcome her.

For a few weeks she felt quite alone in the house, but then things started up again. The little stone arrowheads appeared out of nowhere again all over the house. Hysterical with fear, Mrs. D. called upon a friend who had dabbled in metaphysics and asked for advice. The friend advised a séance in order to ask Little White Flower to leave.

Although Little White Flower was not in evidence continuously and seemed to come and go, Mrs. D. felt the woman's influence upon her at all times. Later the same week, Little White Flower put in another appearance, this time visual. It was toward 4 o'clock in the morning when Mrs. D. woke up with the firm impression that her tormentor was in the room. As she looked out into the hall, she saw on the wall a little red object resembling a human eye, and directly below it what seemed like half a mouth. Looking closer, she discerned two red eyes and a white mouth below. It reminded her of some clowns she had seen in the circus. The vision remained on the wall for two or three minutes, and then vanished completely.

After several postponements I was finally able to come to Kentucky and meet with Mrs. D. in person. On June 20, 1964, I sat opposite the slightly portly, middle-aged lady who had corresponded with me for several months so voluminously.

As I intoned my solemn exorcism and demanded Little White Flower's withdrawal from the spot, I could hear Mrs. D. crying hysterically. It was almost as if some part of her was being torn out and for a while it seemed that *she* was being sent away, not Little White Flower.

The house has been quite ever since; Little White Flower has presumably gone back to her own people and Mrs. D. continues living in the house without further disturbances.

✴ 152

Raynham Hall

THREE-HUNDRED-YEAR-OLD Raynham Hall is a rambling structure of some size within a 20,000-acre estate, where American servicemen were stationed during World War II. Since then the house has been closed to outsiders and, since the Townshends are not exactly afflicted with poverty, the widely practiced custom of admitting tourists for half a crown never invaded the august portals of the Hall.

As reported in the January 4, 1937 issue of *Life* magazine, it all started innocently enough with an order to photograph the interior of the stately mansion. Indre Shira, Ltd., a London firm of Court photographers was hired to perform the task. In September 1936 the company sent Captain Hubert C. Provand and an assistant to Raynham Hall to do the job.

Immediately after his arrival, Captain Provand set out to work. He had no use for the supernatural, and if he had heard of the ghostly legends he put no stock in them. But one of his cameras was smashed by seemingly unseen hands. Still he refused to accept the possibility of a ghost being the culprit. At one point during their meticulous work of photographing the interior of the Hall, the two men found themselves facing the famous grand staircase in the Great Hall downstairs. "Look!" the assistant suddenly said, and pointed toward the staircase, terror etched on his

The famous Brown Lady of Raynham Hill

face. The captain looked but saw nothing. The young man insisted he saw a white figure slowly descending the stairs. "Well," the skeptical captain replied, "if you're so sure of it, let's photograph it." Quickly they pointed their camera toward the staircase and made an exposure. This was done with flash, but one must remember that in 1936 flash photography was not what it is today, and the intensity of the flash light very much weaker than with modern flashbulbs. At this the figure dissolved—at least the assistant reported it was no longer visible to him. The two photographers then sealed the plate and took it to the chemists' firm of Blake, Sanford & Blake, where the negative was developed. The chemists attested to the fact that nothing had been wrong with either negative or developing, and that the figure on the staircase was not due to slipshod handling of any kind.

The striking figure is that of a woman in flowing dress, descending the staircase. It is white and smoke-like, and the stairs can be seen through it. When the results were shown to the Townshends, there was a moment of embarrassed silence. Then the photograph was compared with a portrait of Lady Dorothy Walpole which hung in one of the upstairs passages. It was also pretty much the same as the reported apparition of the lady seen by a number of Townshend house guests over the years.

What made Dorothy Walpole a ghost, way back in the 1780s, was a little inconvenience called mental depressions, but in those days this was considered a disease not fit to be discussed in polite society. Being of gentle birth, the lady was therefore "contained" in a room upstairs and spent her last years in it, finally passing across the threshold of death no longer in her right mind. Perhaps she was not aware of this change and considers Raynham Hall still her rightful home, and herself free now to range it at will, and to smash intruding photographers' cameras if she so desires.

Life published the picture with all the facts and left it to the readers to make up their own minds. I have shown this picture on national television and before many college audiences and have never failed to get gasps from the audience, for it is indeed the very model of what a ghost picture should look like.

✳ 153

The Ghost of the Pennsylvania Boatsman

WHEN I DECIDED to spend a quiet weekend to celebrate my birthday at the picturesque Logan Inn in New Hope, Pennsylvania, I had no idea that I was not just going to sleep in a haunted bedroom, but actually get two ghosts for the "price" of one!

The lady who communicated with my companion and myself in the darkness of the silent January night via a flickering candle in room #6, provided a heart-warming experience and one I can only hope helped the restless one get a better sense of still "belonging" to the house. Mrs. Gwen Davis the proprietor, assured me that the ghost is the mother of a former owner, who simply liked the place so much she never left.

Mrs. Davis pointed me toward the Black Bass Inn in nearby Lumberville, an 18th-century pub and now hotel right on the Delaware Canal. The place is filled with English antiques of the period and portraits of Kings Charles I, II and James II, providing that this was indeed a Loyalist stronghold at one time.

I went around the place with my camera, taking any number of photographs with fast color film in existing light. The story here concerned the ghost of a young man who made his living as a canal boatsman. Today, the canal

The Black Bass Inn—Pennsylvania

is merely a curiosity for tourists, but in the nineteenth century it was an active waterway for trade, bringing goods on barges down river. The canal, which winds around New Hope and some of the nearby towns gives the area a charm all its own.

In the stone basement of the Black Bass, where the apparition had been seen by a number of people over the years, according to the current owner, Herbie Ward, I took some pictures and then asked my companion to take one of me. Picture my surprise when here appeared a white shape in the picture which cannot be reasonably explained as anything but the boatsman putting in a kind of appearance for me. The boatsman died in a violent argument with another boatsman. By the way, the name of the boatsman was Hans. Maybe he felt the two Hanses ought to get in touch?

CHAPTER TEN

Poltergeists

THE TERM *Poltergeist* is German. German researchers in the paranormal were the first ones to concentrate their efforts toward a better understanding of the phenomena associated with poltergeist activities. The word simply means "noisy ghost" and refers to events that parapsychology nowadays prefers to call physical phenomena, which are invariably three-dimensional, whether moving objects or visual or auditory effects produced by means that are other than ordinary or explicable.

The German scientists also decided that these events were connected with, and caused by, a young person at the threshold of puberty; the energies that make the sometimes very violent phenomena possible were actually the unreleased sexual energies of the young people in the household. They went so far as to accuse some of these young persons of unwittingly *causing* the phenomena, often to "attract attention."

This is a half-truth. Young people at the border of their sexual awakening can be the *source* of the energy allowing the phenomena to occur, but so can mentally handicapped people of any age and sexually frustrated individuals of any age, consciously or unconsciously. A poltergeist, then, is nothing more than that stage of a haunting when manifestations occur that are clearly of a physical nature, such as the movement or the throwing of objects. The originator, however, is not the youngster or mentally handicapped older person: they are merely the source, tapped against their will and usually without their knowledge, by a ghostly entity desperately trying to get attention for their plight from people in *this* world. Not to harm anyone, but to get people to notice their presence.

Years ago I pointed out that psychic phenomena use the same energies as does sexual activity, and often the repression of those energies can lead to unwanted psychical phenomena. In the 1930s, the British Society of Psychical Research undertook some tests with the help of a deep trans medium. Ectoplasm derived from the body of the trans medium turned out to be an albumin substance secreted through the glandular system. This ectoplasm was identical with seminal fluids.

Poltergeists are not what the popular movies show them to be. As a matter of fact, these films are pure hokum in every respect, from the phenomena shown to the so-called researchers and their "instruments." As so often happens, the indiscriminate exploitation of the paranormal reality by films and television paints a false picture, only to frighten people into fearing something that is simply not true.

* * *

How, then, does one deal with a poltergeist? No differently than the way one relates to an earthbound spirit, a ghost who is unable to realize her or his true condition. Contact can usually be established through a deep trance medium. This way the entity is calmed or released. Remember that the majority of ghosts are not able to obtain the kind of energies necessary to manifest physically or move objects. Only when there is a powerful source close at hand can they draw on the larger energies necessary for such a feat.

Of course it can be frightening to see objects move seemingly of their own volition. But they don't—the electromagnetic force manipulated by the ghost is responsible for this even if the ghost itself is not visible.

Even as startling an event as the movement of a knife through the air (as in the case in Rye, New York) is not an attack on anyone but an attempt to get attention, and, if possible, help.

True poltergeist cases are much rarer than "ordinary" hauntings, but they do occur. In every case I have investigated, a power source exists, either among the living or even among the discarnate, who have passed on in a state of mental distress or even insanity. Some of my cases follow.

✳ 154

The Devil in Texas

I AM FREQUENTLY ASKED to comment on poltergeists, or noisy ghosts, a term derived from the German and somehow conjuring up the image of violent physical activity beyond the pale of ordinary understanding. Poltergeists have been generally considered the work of youngsters in a house—youngsters below the age of puberty, when their physical energies have not yet been channeled either sexually or occupationally and are therefore free to play pranks on others in the household. The majority of parapsychologists consider poltergeists the unconscious expression of such repressed feelings, attention getters on the part of young people, and do not connect them to supernormal beings such as spirit entities or any other form of outside influence. I, however, have investigated dozens of cases involving poltergeists where physical objects have been moved or moved seemingly by their own volition and found that another explanation might be the true one. In each case, to be sure, there were young people in the household, or sometimes mentally handicapped adults. I discovered, for instance, that a mentally handicapped adult has the same kind of suppressed kinetic energy that is capable of being tapped by outside forces to perform the physical phenomena as the unused energy of youngsters. I also discovered that in each and every case with which I came in contact personally there had been some form of unfinished business in the house or on the grounds on which the house stood. Sometimes this involved a previous building on the same spot. At other times it involved the same building in which the activities took place. But in each instance there was some form of psychic entity present, and it is my conviction that the entity from beyond the physical world was responsible for the happenings, using, of course, the psychical energy in the young people or in the retarded adult. Thus, to me, poltergeists are the physical activities of ghosts expressed through the psychic powers within young people or mentally handicapped older people, but directed solely by outside entities no longer in the flesh. This link between the physical energies of living persons and the usually demented minds of dead persons produces the physical phenomena known as poltergeist activities, which can be very destructive, sometimes threatening, sometimes baffling to those who do not understand the underlying causes.

The purpose these physical activities is always to get the attention of living persons or perhaps to annoy them for personal reasons. The mentality behind this phenomenon is somewhere between the psychotic and the infantile, but at all times far from emotionally and mentally normal. But it can still be dealt with on the same basis as I deal with ordinary hauntings. That is to say, the cause of the activities must be understood before a cure for them can be found. Making contact with the troubled entity in the non-physical world is, of course, the best way. When that is not possible, a shielding device has to be created for the living to protect them from the unwanted poltergeist activities. In the well-publicized Seaford, Long Island, case a few years ago, a young boy in the household was held responsible for the movement of objects in plain daylight. Even so astute an investigator as Dr. Karlis Osis of the American Society of Psychical Research, who was then working for Parapsychology Foundation of New York City, could not discern the link between the boy's unconscious thought and the unseen, but very real, psychic entities beyond the world of the flesh. In his report he intimates that the activities were due to the unconscious desires of the youngster to be noticed and to get the sort of attention his unconscious self craved. I was not involved in the Seaford case personally although I was familiar with it, having discussed the matter with Mr. Herman, the boy's father. I did not enter the case because certain aspects of it suggested publicity-seeking on the part of the family, and at any rate others in my field had already entered the case. I saw no reason to crowd the scene, but I did go into the background of the house with the help of medium Ethel Johnson Meyers independently of the investigation conducted by Dr. Osis. For what it may be worth at this late date, my sitting with Mrs. Meyers disclosed that a burial ground had existed on the very site of the Seaford house and that the disturbances were due to the fact that the house had been erected on the spot. They had not occurred earlier since no physical medium lived in the house. When the young man reached the age of puberty, or nearly so, his energies were available to those wishing to manifest, and it was then that the well-publicized movement of objects occurred.

Similarly, two years ago a case attracted public attention in the city of Rosenheim, Bavaria. A young lady working for an attorney in that city was somehow able to move solid objects by her very presence. A long list of paranormal phenomena was recorded by reputable witnesses, including the attorney himself. Eventually Dr. Hans Bender of the University of Freiburg entered the case and after investigation pronounced it a classical poltergeist situation. He too did not link the activity with any outside entity that might have been present on the premises from either this house or a previous one standing on the spot. It seems to me that at the time great haste was taken to make sure that a physical or temporal solution could be put forward, making it unnecessary to link the phenomena with any kind of spirit activity.

But perhaps the most famous of all poltergeist cases, the classical American case, is the so-called Bell Witch of Tennessee. This case goes back to the 1820s and even so illustrious a witness as Andrew Jackson figures in the proceedings. Much has been written and published about the Bell Witch of Tennessee. Suffice it to say here that it involved the hatred of a certain woman for a farmer named

John Bell. This relationship resulted in a post-mortem campaign of hatred and destructiveness ultimately costing the lives of two people. In the Bell Witch of Tennessee case the entire range of physical phenomena usually associated with poltergeistic activities was observed.

Included were such astounding happening as the appearance or disappearance of solid objects into and out of thin air; strange smells and fires of unknown origin; slow deliberate movement of objects in plain sight without seeming physical source; and voices being heard out of the air when no one present was speaking. Anyone studying the proceedings of this case would notice that the phenomena were clearly the work of a demented individual. Even though a certain degree of cunning and cleverness is necessary to produce them, the reasoning behind or, rather, the lack of reasoning, clearly indicates a disturbed mind. All poltergeist activities must therefore be related to the psychotic, or, at the very least, schizophrenic state of mind of the one causing them. As yet we do not clearly understand the relationship between insanity and free energies capable of performing acts seemingly in contradiction of physical laws, but there seems to be a very close relationship between these two aspects of the human personality. When insanity exists certain energies become free and are capable of roaming at will at times and of performing feats in contradiction to physical laws. When the state of insanity in the mind under discussion is reduced to normalcy these powers cease abruptly.

I have, on occasion, reported cases of hauntings and ghostly activities bordering upon or including some poltergeist activities. Generally we speak of them as physical phenomena. A case in point is the haunted house belonging to Mr. and Mrs. John Smythe of Rye, New York. The phenomena in this house included such physical activities as doors opening by themselves, footsteps, the sound of chains rattling, ashtrays flying off the table by themselves, and, most frightening of all, a carving knife taking off by itself on a Sunday morning in full view of two adult, sane people and flinging itself at their feet, not to hurt them but to call attention to an existing unseen entity in the house. These are, of course, the kind of activities present in poltergeist cases, but they are merely a fringe activity underlining the need for communication. They are not the entire case, nor are they as disorganized and wanton as the true poltergeist cases. In the case of Rye, New York, the physical activities followed long-time mental activities such as apparitions and impressions of a presence. The physical phenomena were primarily used here to make the message more urgent. Not so with the true poltergeist case, where there is no possibility of mental communication simply because the causing person in incapable of actual thinking. In such a case all energies are channeled toward destructive physical activity and there is neither the will nor the ability to give mental impressions to those capable of receiving

them, since the prime mover of these activities is so filled with hatred and the desire to manifest in the physical world that he or she will not bother with so rational an activity as a thought message.

It is therefore difficult to cope with cases of this kind since there is no access to reasoning, as there is in true ghost cases when a trance medium can frequently make contact with the disturbed and disturbing entity in the house and slowly, but surely, bring it back to the realm of reason. With the true poltergeist case nothing of the sort can be established and other means to solve it have to be found. It is therefore quite natural that anyone who becomes the victim of such activities and is not familiar with them or with what causes them will be in a state of panic, even to the point of wanting to abandon his property and run for his life.

On September 1, 1968, I was contacted by a gentleman by the name of L. H. Beaird. He wrote to me from Tyler, Texas, requesting that I help him understand some of the extraordinary happenings that had made his life hell on earth during the period of three years between 1965 and 1968. Through his daughter who was married in Austin he learned of my work with ghosts and finally concluded that only someone as familiar with the subject as I could shed light on the mysterious happenings in his home. He had purchased their home in 1964, but after three years of living with a poltergeist and fighting a losing battle for survival he decided that his sanity and survival were more important, and in 1968 he sold it again, losing everything he had put into it. The move, however, was a fortuitous one, for the new home turned out to be quiet and peaceful. Once Mr. Beaird got his bearings again and learned to relax once more he decided to investigate what had occurred during the previous three years and find some sort of answer to this extraordinary problem.

I had never heard of Tyler before and decided to look it up on the map. It turned out to be a city of about 60,000 inhabitants also known as the "rose capital" because of the large number of horticultural activities in the area. Tyler is connected with Dallas and Houston by a local airline and lies about halfway between Dallas and Shreveport, Louisiana. It has one television station, one newspaper and some pleasant ordinary citizens going about their various businesses. The people of Tyler whom I got to know a little after my visit later on are not concerned with such things as the occult. In fact, anyone trying to lecture on the subject would do so in empty halls.

Howard Beaird works in a nearby hospital and also runs a rubber stamp shop in which he has the company of his wife and more orders than he can possibly fill. Their son, Andy, was enrolled in barber school at the time of my visit and presumably is now cutting people's hair to everyone's satisfaction somewhere in Texas. The big local hotel is called the Blackstone and it is about the same as other big hotels in small towns. Everything is very quiet in Tyler, Texas, and you can really sleep at night. There is a spirit of not wanting to change things, of letting sleeping dogs lie as much as possible, pervading the town, and I have the distinct impression that cases such as the poltergeist case were not exactly welcome subjects for discussion over a drink at the local bar.

It must be held to Mr. Beaird's credit that despite the indications of small-town life he felt compelled to make inquiries into the extraordinary happenings in his life, to look into them without fear and with great compassion for those involved—his wife and son. Others in his position might have buried the matter and tried to forget it. This is particularly important since Mr. Beaird is reasonably prosperous, does business with his neighbors and has no intention of leaving Tyler. To ask me for an investigation was tantamount to stirring things up, but Beaird took this calculated risk because he could not live with the knowledge of what he had observed and not know what caused it.

At the time of our correspondence in September 1968 the phenomena had already ended, as abruptly as they had come. This too is typical of genuine poltergeist activities, since they depend solely on the available free energies of living people. As will be seen in the course of my investigation, that energy became no longer available when the principals were removed from the house. There are other factors involved, of course. It is not as simple as plugging in on a power line, but in essence poltergeist activities depend not only the desire of the disturbing entity to manifest but also on the physical condition of the unconscious part of those whom they wish to use as power supplies.

The house which the Beairds had to leave under pressure from their poltergeists is on Elizabeth Street. It is a one-story ranch-type dwelling, pleasant enough to look at and about fourteen or fifteen years old. The new owners are not particularly keen on the history of their house, and it is for that reason that I am keeping confidential the actual location, but the house has not been altered in any way since it has been sold to Mr. M. and his family. One enters the house through a porch that is located somewhat above the road. There is a garage and a steep driveway to the right of the porch. Once one is inside the house one is in the living room with a den to the left and a dining area to the right. Beyond the living room are the kitchen and a rather long room leading directly to a breakfast room. On the extreme left are two bedrooms. To the right of the house behind the garage is the workshop, which, in the period when Mr. Beaird owned the house, was used as such. There is also a concrete slab separating the shop from the garage proper, and the garage contains a ladder leading up to the attic.

Howard Beaird, sixty-five years of age, is a pleasant man with a soft Texas accent, polite, firm, and obliging in his manner. He was overjoyed when I expressed an interest in his case and promised to cooperate in every way. In order to get a better understanding of the extraordinary happenings at Tyler I asked that he dictate in his own words the story of those three years in the house that had

come to be three years of unrelenting terror. The principals in this true account besides Howard Beaird are his wife, Johnnie, whom he has always called John; a daughter named Amy who lives in another city and was in no way involved in the strange experiences at Tyler; and a son, Andy, now nineteen, who shared all of the unspeakable horror of the experiences between 1965 and the early part of 1968 with his parents. Most of the others mentioned in his account have been dead for several years. A few are still alive, and there are some names in this account Mr. Beaird has never heard of. Here then is his own account of what occurred in the little house on Elizabeth Street in Tyler, Texas:

My story begins late in 1962, which marked the end of nearly thirty-nine years of employment with the same company. During the last twenty years of that time John worked in the same office with me; in fact her desk was only a few feet from mine. We were both retired during September of 1962.

John had always been an excellent employee, but devoted much more time to her work than the company required for any one person. She would never take a vacation, and was rarely away from her job for more than an occasional half-day at a time, mainly, I think, because she would trust no one with her work. I cannot say when her mind began to show signs of being disturbed, although as I think back on it today, she had acted a little strangely for several years prior to the time of our retirement. This, however, did not affect her work in any way; in fact she was even more precise in it than ever, and I suppose I just could not bring myself to admit that there was anything wrong with her mind. At any rate, during the next twelve months she began to act more abnormally than ever, especially when at home, until finally it was necessary that she enter a mental institution. Although the doctors there were reluctant to release her, they did not seem to be having any success in whatever treatment they were giving her, so I asked for her release after about three months. Being of very modest means I naturally had to obtain employment as soon as possible, but after working about three months in another city I felt that it was most urgent that I move my family from Grand Saline, Texas, to some other place, believing that the mere change of environment would play a big part in helping John to get well. So about the middle of 1964 we moved to Tyler, Texas, a place where John had always said she would like to live. We bought a house, and after about a month I obtained employment which, in addition to a sideline business I had begun a few years before, gave us a satisfactory, if not affluent, living. For almost a year John did seem to be better; she would go places with Andy and me, to the Little League baseball games in which Andy played, to the movies occasionally, sometimes to bowling alleys and a miniature golf course, but all of a sudden she stopped.

She had not actually kept house since we made the move and had not cooked a single meal for Andy or me.

About this time she started walking to a drugstore in a nearby shopping center for breakfast, and then in the late afternoon just before I would get home she would walk to a restaurant a few blocks away for the evening meal, usually by herself. A little later she began calling a taxi nearly every morning to go to a different place for breakfast: once to a downtown hotel; once way out on the other side of town to a roadside restaurant on the Mineola Highway, and to many other places within the course of a few weeks. Always in the evenings though she would go to the restaurant near our home. She would come home usually just after I arrived, and would change clothes and stay in her room from then on. She would get up very early in the morning, about 5 o'clock, something *she had never done* during our entire married life. For the past few years she insisted that people were spying on her, and finally, when I did not agree with her, she accused me of being at the head of this group set out to torment her, and even said that I had television cameras set up in the house to spy on her.

John smoked almost incessantly, every kind of cigarette made, but later began to smoke little cigars the size of a cigarette, and still later started on the big regular ones that men smoke. Once she bought a small can of snuff. She had never used snuff before. This was a little while after she had begun to lay cigarettes down just anywhere, although there were plenty of ashtrays throughout the house. She also began putting lighted cigarettes on table tops, the arms of a divan, or even on the bed, and if Andy or I had not been there to put them out, no doubt the house would have eventually been burned down. She did burn holes in several sheets and in the mattress on her bed. When that happened I told her that she simply could not smoke any more. She did not protest. Andy and I searched the house and found cigarettes and matches everywhere. John had hidden them everywhere, inside a little table radio by removing the back, inside a flashlight where the batteries are supposed to be, in those little shoe pockets she had hanging in her closet, in a little opening at the end of the bathtub where a trap door in the closet exposes the pipes for repairs, under the mattress, inside pillow covers, and even in the dog house outdoors. We gathered up cigarettes, matches, and cigarette lighters every day when I got home and there is no telling how many we finally found and destroyed. Of course she would get more every day at the shopping center, and once we even found one of those little automatic rollers that a person can use to make his own cigarettes.

Exactly what part John played in the frightening events that took place at our house I cannot say. I am convinced though, as is Amy, that there was some connection. The three years from late 1962 to the summer of 1965 preceded the most awesome, fantastic chain of events that the human mind can imagine. In fact, as these unbelievable episodes began to unfold before us I was beginning to doubt my own sanity. Andy, who was 13 at the time this began, shared with me every one of the horrible experiences, which started in midsummer 1965 and lasted without interruption until near the end of 1966, when we were "told" that they were over with,

only to find that during the next fifteen months we were in for even worse things. If Andy had not been with me to substantiate these awful experiences I would have indeed considered myself hopelessly insane.

The frightening events began to take place near the middle of 1965, about the time John quit going places with Andy and me. When at home she would stay in her bedroom and close the door and leave it closed after she went to bed. Andy and I slept in the same bed in another room.

During our first year at this house we were not bothered by the usual summertime insects, so I did not bother to repair the screens needing fixing at that time. However, during July of 1965, Andy and I would go to bed, and as soon as we turned out the light we were plagued by hordes of June bugs of all sizes, which would hit us on our heads and faces, some glancing off on the floor, others landing on the bed, and some missing us entirely and smashing themselves against the metal window blinds. Night after night we fought these bugs in the dark, grabbing those that landed on the bed and throwing them against the blinds as hard as we could.

Then we discovered that at least half of the bugs that hit us were *already dead*, in fact had been dead so long that they were crisp and would crumble between our fingers when we picked them up! I would get up and turn on the lights, and the raids would cease immediately; we could see no sign of them in the air...only those hundreds that littered the floor and bed. The instant I turned off the light, though, the air would be filled with bugs again, just as if someone were standing there ready to throw handfuls at us *as soon as it was dark*. One night I got up and swept and vacuumed the entire room, moved every piece of furniture away from the walls, dusted the backs of the dresser, chest and tables, and vacuumed the floor again. When I was through I could swear that there was not a living creature in that room other than Andy and me. I got some rags and stuffed them in the cracks beneath the closet door and the one leading from the room into the hall. The windows were closed. The room was *absolutely clean*. Andy was in bed, awake. I turned off the light. At that exact instant hundreds of bugs hit us!

About this time John began to act more strangely than ever, doing things she would not dream of doing under ordinary circumstances. For example, I might look in my closet to get a shirt or a pair of trousers, and there would not be any there. I do not know what prompted me to do it, but I would go to John's closet, and there would be my clothes hanging alongside some of hers.

At this time I had a rubber stamp shop in a room behind the garage, which was a part of the house, and I worked out there every night. There was no direct connection from the house. One had to go out the kitchen door into the garage and then through another door into the shop. On many occasions I would hear the kitchen door being opened, and would rush to the shop door to see who it was. No matter how hard I tried, though, I could never get there fast enough to see *anybody*...only my clothes, suits, shirts, etc., on hangers *just as they landed in the middle of the garage floor*.

It was during the hottest part of summer while we had the air-conditioners running that other strange things took place for which we assumed John was responsible. Andy or I would suddenly find the bathroom wall heater lighted and the flames running out the top, with the door closed. The room would be hot enough to burst into flames. John insisted that she had not lit the heater...that one of *us* had. After this had happened several times, I removed the handle that turns on the gas. A short time later, while I was out in the shop, Andy came running out and called me in. There was a bunch of paper towels stuffed into the heater where the burners are and they were on fire, some of them on the floor, burning. I then decided to turn off all the pilot lights in the house. This was on the weekend before Labor Day, and I did not know how I could possibly go to work on Tuesday following the holiday and leave John at home alone, since Andy would be in school. I had talked with Dr. —— until I could determine what I would eventually be able to do with her, but the psychiatric wards were already running over, and he did not want to admit her as a patient. I decided to tell John that if she did "any of those things" again I would have to put her in jail. Monday night she started waving a pistol around, so I called the police station and told them the predicament I was in. They said they would keep her until things could be settled and told me to bring her on down. She went without protest. When my lawyer returned he made appointments for her to be examined by two psychiatrists, after which I thought there would be no further question about the need for commitment, and she stayed at home that week. However, on the Monday following Labor Day she called her sister-in-law Mack in Daingerfield, Texas, about a hundred miles from Tyler, and asked if she could visit her at once. I was at work and knew nothing of this until Mack got to Tyler and asked it if would be all right for John to go with her. I objected, but my lawyer advised me that I should let her go, as she could be brought back for the commitment hearing, so they left that day for Daingerfield.

A few days later John's lawyer had her examined by a psychiatrist again, and he finally said that she might benefit somewhat from getting a job, although she would have to undergo psychiatric treatment at various times in the future. It would be almost impossible to have her committed voluntarily, so we decided to just let things stand as they were. For the record, John's attorney insisted that I be examined by the same doctors who had examined her. The reports on me were favorable.

Shortly after John had gone off to stay with Mack, Andy and I were lying in bed with the lights off, talking about the terrible things we had gone through. *Suddenly I heard a voice calling my name*...a high-pitched, falsetto voice that seemed to be coming from out in space. The voice said it was John, and although it sounded nothing at all like her, I am convinced it was, since she talked about several things that only she and I knew of.... One was about some disagreeable words she had had with one of my sisters at the time of my father's death in 1950. She said that although my other sister had insulted her, she was good, and that she had forgiven her. Andy did not hear any part of this conversation.

Apparently John, or the voice, could talk to either of us without the other listening to the voice. I even suspected that Andy was doing the talking, and I held my fingers to his lips while listening to the voice. I knew then it could not have been coming from his lips.

One night while I was lying in bed and Andy was in the bathroom I heard his voice say "good-bye," though, just before he came to bed, and *he told me he had been talking with his mother.* During the following weeks we heard six other voices *from right out of nowhere,* all from people *who had been dead for some time.* I knew all but one of them while they were living. Two of them had always been friendly toward me, and both were old enough to be my mother. Andy also knew these who women and one of the men named George Swinney. This latter person was killed in an accident some time *after* he visited us "by voice." The other two women were mothers of friends of mine and both had died some time before we moved to Tyler. One was Mrs. Snow and the other was Mrs. Elliott, and theirs were the next two voices we heard after John had left, and they came to us about the time the visits by Henry Anglin started. He was the only one of the lot who gave us trouble to start with; in fact I am convinced that he is the one responsible for the bug raids and other awful things that happened to us.

One of the work benches in my shop was against the wall dividing the shop and the kitchen, and at the bottom of the wall was an opening with a grill over it to handle the return air from the central heating system. For some reason the grill on the shop side had been removed, and by stooping down near the floor under the bench I could see much of what was going on in the kitchen. I worked in the shop every night, and when these "ghosts" first began visiting us they would call my name, the voices seeming to come from the opening into the kitchen. I would stoop down and answer. At that time I would carry on lengthy conversations with all of them. Mrs. Snow and Mrs. Elliott were very friendly and seemed to want to give me all kinds of good advice. Henry Anglin was just the opposite. He was extremely mean and demanded that I do all sorts of things I would not do. When I refused, he would be very nasty. Once he got a can of insect spray we kept on the kitchen cabinet top and held it down at the opening to my shop. He would start spraying through the hole. He used a whole can of spray and in that little room I nearly suffocated. One cannot imagine what a feeling it is *to see a can of insect spray suspended in midair with apparently nothing holding it and to have it sprayed right in one's face!* When I went inside I could see the dents made by the edge of the can where he had banged it against the wall.

About the middle of September 1965 the nightly bug raids began to taper off. We thought that we were going to get a few nights' sleep without fear. However, when we went to bed we would feel something moving on an arm or in our hair—*after* we had turned off the lights. We jumped up and found one or several *slugs* somewhere on us or on the bed. They are the ugliest, slimiest wormlike creatures that can be imagined, big at the head and tapering to a point toward their rear end. They have whiskers on each side of the head, and although they have eyes, they are not supposed to see very well, according to Andy, who, strangely enough, was studying them at school at that time. The large ones are as big as a Vienna sausage, about three inches long, and leave a silvery looking trail wherever they crawl. When the first few of these creatures appeared Andy thought they had clung to his shoes while he was playing in the yard and had gotten into the house that way. However, night after night the number of slugs increased, and we went through the same torture as with the bugs, only much worse. One cannot imagine how awful it is to wake up in the middle of the night and find oneself surrounded by a horde of slimy, ugly worms! Andy said that salt would dissolve the slugs. So we sprinkled salt all around the baseboard, around the bed legs, but still the slugs came *as soon as the lights were out.* A few nights later we were again bombarded with bugs...not June bugs this time, but the wood louse, the little bug about the size of a blackeyed pea. They have lots of tiny legs, will roll up into a round ball when touched, and are generally called pill bugs. I knew they could not fly, yet there they came, *hitting us just as if they were shot out of a gun,* at the exact moment we turned out the lights! Mixed in with these were some bugs I had never seen anywhere before, like a doodle bug but brown in color. I knew doodle bugs couldn't fly, and these things no more had wings than I did. Yet there they came, shooting through the air, and, just as the June bugs had done, they started out one or two at a time, until finally dozens began hitting us at once the moment the lights were out. I also found little pieces of clear material which looked like pieces of broken glass. I finally discovered that these pieces were making the loud noise against the blinds... some of them landed on the bed along with the peculiar bugs. I then washed off a piece about the size of a pea and tasted it; it was pure rock salt! I had not the slightest idea where it came from, as we certainly had had no use for any here. As baffling as the idea of bugs flying without wings was, it was no more so than rock salt sailing through the air with apparently nothing to propel it. There was absolutely no human being in the house except Andy and me.

A day or two after John had left, I cleaned up her room thoroughly, moved every piece of furniture, swept, vacuumed, dusted, and made up the bed, putting on a spread that came nearly to the floor. A few days after the second series of bug raids, Andy called me into John's room. He raised up the spread, and there under the bed was a conglomeration of objects, among which was a ten-pound sack of rock salt, most of which had been poured in a pile on the carpet under the bed. There was an old hair net mixed with it, some burned matches, an unwrapped cake of "hotel" soap, and on top of the pile was a note, printed the way a six-year-old child would do it, "Evil spirit go away."

In the next few days we began looking through things in John's room and found lots of notes written in longhand, most of which were like those of a child just learning to write, although a few words were unmistakably John's handwriting. They were mainly of people's names, a date which might be the birthdate, and then another date some time in the future...some up past 1977. There were many names contained in the notes. One name was of a man I am sure John could not have known. He was Henry Anglin, a pitifully ignorant old man who used to farm just west of Grand Saline, and, like all farmers in the adjoining territory back in 1918, would come to town each Saturday to buy groceries and other supplies for the following week. When I was about fourteen years old I worked in a department store that also handled groceries. My job was to keep track of the farmers' stacks of groceries so that when they were ready to leave in the evening I could show them where their purchases were and help load their wagons. Henry Anglin was among the people I regularly waited on. He seemed old to me then and that was about fifty years ago. I have no doubt that he has long since died. I cannot imagine how his name entered John's mind. There were also some typewritten sheets in John's room which contained the same items as the notes we had found. One mentioned a certain "Tink" Byford. There was a date that was probably his birthdate, then a date in 1964. We had moved to Tyler in July 1964, and it was several months after that when I read in the paper that "Tink" Byford had been killed in an auto accident while returning to Grand Saline from Dallas. Another name was "Bill" Robertson, a friend of both of us. There was an early date, then "Hosp. 1965, death 1967." There were many other names, some now dead, but most still living, *always with two dates!* One day when I got home from work Andy and I found in the living room between the divan and table a new bar of soap which had been crumbled up and scattered over a two-or three-foot area. Andy found a potato masher in John's room with soap on it, so we assumed it was used in the living room where the soap was scattered. We did not clean it up right away. That night, after we went to bed, several pieces of soap about the size of a quarter hit our blinds like bullets, although the door to the living room was closed and the den and hallway are between the living room and our bedroom.

I had to wash some clothes that night and it was after dark when I hung them on the line. While I was doing that, Andy came to the door and advised me that bugs and slugs were *flying* all over the house. I told him I thought I had heard something thud against the dog house near the clothesline. He checked and picked up a little leather wallet about the size of a billfold, which we had seen earlier in John's room, filled with loose tobacco. I told him to put it into the garbage can at the end of the house. The can had a lid on it. When I got through, it was time to take a bath and go to bed. While I was in the tub and Andy in the den, I heard something that sounded like a shotgun just outside the bathroom window. I called Andy to run out and see what he could find; he had heard the noise too. Just beneath the window he picked up the *same leather purse* he had put into the garbage can *an hour earlier!* It had hit the house flat, I suppose, near the bathroom window, to cause such a loud noise.

During the preceding days we had found several other notes, all written or printed in the same peculiar way, as a little child might write. I had no idea what they meant, if anything, but some examples are:

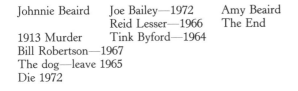

Johnnie Beaird   Joe Bailey—1972   Amy Beaird
                  Reid Lesser—1966   The End

1913 Murder   Tink Byford—1964

Bill Robertson—1967

The dog—leave 1965

Die 1972

In a little notebook we found:

Allie L. Lewis (This woman worked for the same
company we did, and probably still does).
Luther Anderson (He owns a truck line that hauls
salt).
Die 1980
Jeraldine Fail (This woman used to be a good friend
of John's).
Die 1977
Louise Beaird (This is my sister, who would be 118
years of age in 2018).
Die 2018

One day we found an old wooden box where John had kept her canceled checks. She had burned something in it, as the ashes were still in the box. The only thing left was one half of a calling card saying, "burn spirit burn." On just a scratch of paper were the words, "Johnnie Beaird—Death 1991."

There were many more. Note the peculiar use of capital letters. All of these notes were printed:

JoHN is
goIN to Die

Be NIce
FROnt
      OF
OLD
FOOLish
MacK

There IS A
Hertz in Mt
PleaSant
SnEak
AWAY
From There
*(I checked,
and there is
not a Hertz
in Mt. Pleas-
ant).*

I pOisOned
little
FOOLS
white kittEn
ShALL i
poisOn The
Jap Cat
*(Andy did
have a white
kitten which
had died for
some reason,
and at this
time still had
a Siamese
cat).*

On a Canton bank blank check was written in the "pay to" line: Johnnie B. Walker $1,000,000; in the "for" line: Bill is NUTTY, and on the "signature" line; ha ha.

The ghastly events continued through October and into November, when they seemed to be letting up a little. One day early in the month when I got home from work Andy took me into John's room. Lined up under the edge of her bed but behind the spread were some pictures in little frames of various kinds. There was one of Amy, of John and Andy, of me, of Thelma Lowrie, who had been John's best friend and who had died in 1951, and several others. I don't know what significance they were supposed to have, but I left them right there. I assumed that John had been to the house that day. Bugs, dead and alive, continued to bombard us every night; even the slugs started flying through the air,

smashing against the blinds and walls, making an awful mess wherever they hit.

I decided to clean up both bedrooms as soon as I could, and to start taking up the carpets. While I was doing that Andy found a note in John's room saying: "Bugs will end for ThursDay Dec. 29." I think the 23rd was the day I cleaned up our room, and the bugs were worse than ever that night, so we decided that maybe it was meant that the 23rd would be the last night. The next night, strangely enough, was pretty quiet.

On the 24th I took up the carpet in John's room. While doing that I was hit by hundreds of bugs, slugs, and even some of the *nails I pulled out of the floor simply flew through the air and hit against the blinds.* Finally I was able to completely clean the room, paint the walls and woodwork, put up curtains, and the room looked very nice when I was finished.

On November 26 I cleaned the house thoroughly, and no unusual activity took place that night. On the 27th bugs were everywhere. Just before dark I was taking a bath, and when I was through, standing up in the tub, I saw something hit the screen but could not tell what it was. I called Andy from the den and told him to go out to see what it was. It turned out to be one of John's rubber gloves I had put out beside the garbage can to be hauled off.

On Thanksgiving day I took all of our outside locks and had Andy take them to a locksmith in town the next morning to have them changed and get new keys, as I was convinced that John had been somehow coming from Daingerfield and using her keys to get in. I put the locks in place on Saturday. On Wednesday, December 1, 1965, somebody (I supposed it was John) punched a hole in the back screen door near the hook and unhooked the door. If it was John, though, her key would not fit.

December 4 was the worst. It was Saturday, and we went to bed about 10:30. Something that sounded exactly like fingers drummed lightly on the bed. Although we were under the covers we could feel *whatever it was tugging at the sheets,* actually trying to jerk the covers off us! We would turn on the light and the tugging would stop. There were no bugs that night, but when the lights were off both Andy and I could feel something on our arms that seemed like small flying bugs bouncing up and down, sort of like gnats might do. We would slap at them, but there was absolutely nothing there. We would turn the lights on and see nothing. We sprayed the air everywhere with insect spray but it did no good. It felt exactly like someone lightly grabbing the hair on your arms with the thumb and forefinger, not actually pulling very hard at first, but later jerking the hair hard enough to hurt.

While we were lying in bed with the light on, my shoes, weighing possibly two pounds each, *flew right over our heads* and landed on the other side of the bed. Andy's house shoes got up from the floor and flung themselves against the blinds. My clothes, which were hanging in the closet *with the door closed,* got out of there somehow *without the door being opened and landed* across the room. Finally we turned off the lights and heard a strange sound we could not identify. It was under the bed, and sounded like bed rollers being turned rapidly with the fingers; but the bed was not even on rollers! Suddenly something hit the blind like a bullet. We turned on the light and found that the handle from the gas jet *under the bed had unscrewed itself, and both the bolt and the handle had flung themselves against the blind.* Then the bed started moving away from the wall. We would roll it back again only to have it do the same thing over and over. That was about all we could stand, and as it was 2 A.M. Sunday, I told Andy to put on his clothes. *We went to a motel to spend the rest of the night.*

As we were walking down the driveway, after closing and locking the door, *a handkerchief still folded hit me on the back of the neck.* Just as we got in the car another handkerchief I had left on the bedside table hit me on the back after I had closed the car doors.

We were so weary that we were asleep almost by the time we were in bed at the motel, and nothing happened to us while we were there. We came home about 9:30 the next morning. Some of John's clothes were in my closet, and most of mine were in hers. All sorts of weird notes were flying all about the house. I cleaned the house, and just as I was through, *a big cigar hit the back of my neck from out of nowhere.* I put it in the kitchen waste basket. Andy wanted some soup, so I started to a Cabell grocery store a few blocks away. Just as I left the house Andy saw the cigar jump up out of the waste basket and land on the floor. He put it back in the basket. When he came to the door to tell me about it I was getting into the car parked at the foot of the driveway, and when I turned toward him *I saw the cigar come sailing over his head and land at the side of the car,* about 60 feet from the house. When I came back and stepped in the door from the garage to the kitchen *I saw a clean shirt of mine coming flying from the den* and land near the back door of the kitchen.

By this time I had decided that it did absolutely no good to change the locks on the doors, although John had not broken in, if, indeed, this was John. Apparently whoever it was did not *need* a door, nor did he need to break in. Andy and I were standing in the kitchen watching things fly through the air, when all of a sudden his cap, which had been resting on the refrigerator, hit me in the back of the head. A roll of paper towels flew through the air; a can of soup on the cabinet top jumped off onto the floor several times after Andy picked it up and put it back.

All of a sudden we heard a click. The toaster had been turned on, and the click meant it had turned itself off. *There was a piece of soap in it, melted!* A note nearby read "clean toaster." I felt something like a slight brush on my shoulder and heard Andy shout, "Look out!" He saw the faint *outline of a hand which looked like his mother's* vanish near my head.

Later, while in the den, I began to ask questions aloud, such as: "John, tell me where we stayed last night?" A few seconds later a note came floating down in front of us, reading: "Motel on T. B. Road. Couldn't get in." "Got to go, you've ruined me." We did spend

the night before at a motel on the road to the Tuberculosis Hospital where I work. I then said aloud, trying to sound funny in a totally unfunny situation: "With all that power, why don't you just drop $5,000 on us?" Almost immediately a check with nothing but $5,000 written on the face dropped from out of nowhere. I said, "John, why don't you appear here before us right this minute?" In about five seconds a note came down saying, "Can't come ToDay haPPy YuLeTide." I then asked, "Are we going to be able to sleep tonight?" This answer came down to us: "CaN't maKE aNyTHing haPPen tONighT you BROKE MY POWER Call HOUsTon."

Previously she told me to call Houston police and ask them about a witch who had solved the murder of a man named Gonzales. I felt like a fool, but I did call the Houston police department. I told them they could think I was drunk, crazy, or anything they wished to, but I just wanted a yes or no answer, and asked if they had any record of a witch ever helping the Houston police solve a murder of a man named Gonzales. The man I talked to did not appear surprised and simply asked me to wait a moment, and a few seconds later said that he could find no record of any such event.

John had also given us directions for breaking her power. It was to "break an egg, mix with a little water and a dash of salt and then throw it out in the back yard."

I have never been superstitious before, and this sounded awfully silly to me, but I think I would have done absolutely anything I was told if it meant a chance to put an end to these uncanny events, so I told Andy to go ahead and follow the directions. That night we had a few bugs and a note came floating down reading, "power will end at 10 o'clock give or take an hour."

For several days we received what seemed like hundreds of *notes from right out of nowhere, simply materializing in midair, some folding themselves as they came toward us.* Some time after he had seen the hand vanish near my head, Andy was sitting in the den facing the outside windows. For a few fleeting seconds he saw the outline of John in front of the windows. Her back was to him as she looked out the windows, and Andy heard a faint "goodbye" just as the figure melted in the air.

We heard other voices after talking with John. All seemed very strained, especially the female speakers, and they would often say that they had a "mist" in their throat and could not continue talking to me, although they could always talk to Andy and he would hear them. I have dozens of notes that fell down to us from somewhere above, and most of them are from the same two people who stayed with us for the longest period of time. One of these was Mrs. Elliott, who had been dead for three or four years when all this began to happen. The other was from Mr. Gree, of whom I had never heard, but who seemed eager to help Andy and me with advice especially concerning the care of Andy's cats and dogs. We were "visited" by a great variety of "people," some long since dead, some still living, most of whom we know, or knew, but also some well-known public figures whose names were often in the news. I dated the notes from then on, but at times so many descended on us at once that I did not try to record the exact order in which we received them.

It was Henry Anglin who tormented us from the very beginning, and who caused us to move out of the house. One night Anglin came to our room after we had gone to bed and his voice asked if he could cook himself an egg. We heard nothing else from him that night, but the next morning when I went to the kitchen to prepare breakfast, there in a teflon-lined skillet on the stove burner which was turned down low was an egg burned to a crisp!

Another night Anglin came to our room and insisted that I call Houston. This was about the time he was beginning to be so terribly mean. I told him that I had already made one silly call to the Houston police, and that I had no intention of doing it again. He countered that I had not questioned them enough, and for me to phone them again. I refused, and he tormented us relentlessly. Finally he said he would leave us alone if we would drive around the loop, which was a distance of a little over twenty miles around the city of Tyler. Andy and I put on our clothes and did just that. We drove completely around the town, and sure enough, when we got home we were able to sleep the rest of the night without further trouble.

A few nights after this, both Mrs. Elliott and Mrs. Snow told me verbally, while I was working in my shop, that they had taken Henry Anglin "back to his grave," and had driven a stake, prepared by Mr. Gree, through Anglin's heart. They promised that he would not bother us again.

About this time we received notes allegedly from people who were still living, and also some from persons other than those previously mentioned who had been dead for several years. Among those still living were Mrs. W. H. Jarvis, and Odell Young, who lives in Grand Saline at this time. I also had one note from Mr. W. H. Quinn, *who had been dead for several years.* He used to be a railroad agent in Grand Saline. For a number of years I had occasion to have him sign numerous shipping papers, so I had become familiar with his handwriting. The note I got from him *was written in the same backhand fashion.* I believe that this note was written by him:

Dear Howard and Andy,

I pay tribute to you. You have put up with a lot from old man Anglin. It is all over now. Friday I am going to my grave to join my wife, whom I love. I am going to Marion's house to see him once more. He is my favorite child. I have always like you, John and the boy and hope someday you will be together again.

Hiram Quinn

P.S. I enjoyed hearing about John going with Marion to get new teeth.

The P.S. about his son's false teeth refers to the time about thirty years ago when John and I went to see Marion just after he had received his first set of dentures. At that time we lived just across the street from Marion and his wife and were friendly with them.

We also got notes allegedly from Marilyn Monroe, Dorothy Kilgallen, and former Governor Jim Allred, who sympathized with us for what Henry Anglin was

doing to us and about John's condition. Mrs. Snow and Mrs. Elliot had previously told us that Anglin had caused many deaths, some by auto accident, and some by switching a person's pills, *as they said he had done in the case of Dorothy Kilgallen.* The note we received with her name also said that was the cause of her death. I am not certain, but I believe they also said Anglin caused Marilyn Monroe's death.

None of the people still living, except John, ever spoke to me; they just dropped their notes from the air. Mrs. Jarvis actually spoke to Andy, though, and had him tell me to answer aloud each of the questions she put in her note to me. Mr. Quinn's note was struck in the grate between the kitchen and my shop.

For the first few weeks in January 1966 only Mrs. Elliott and Mr. Jack Gree "visited" us. She and I had lots of conversations, but she gradually got so she could barely talk to me, although Andy could still hear her. The notes were written either on some note paper Andy kept in the kitchen or on some Canton, Texas, bank deposit slips in John's room. If I was working in the shop she would stick the notes in the grill and bang on the wall to attract my attention, and then I would stoop down under the work bench and retrieve the note. Mr. Gree, who told us we had never heard of him, had a very low, deep, gruff voice. Most of his communications to me were in the form of notes, however, but he and Andy carried on lengthy conversations nearly every day. He also used the grill "post office" for depositing his notes, then banged on the wall to let me know they were there.

At times, when Andy and I were in the car, Mrs. Elliott or Mr. Gree would be with us. They would ride along for a while and then suddenly say they were going to Canada, Russia, Minnesota, or some other far-off place, saying it took only two or three minutes for them to travel those distances, and then we might not hear anything else from them until the next day or night. Early in January of 1966 Andy came out to my shop and said Mr. Gree wanted to know if it was OK for him to use the telephone, and of course I told him it was. I did not know what control I would have had over the situation anyway. That first time he said it was something personal and asked Andy if he would mind leaving the room. *I could hear the phone being dialed,* and stooped down near the floor so I could look through the grilled opening, but of course I could not see anyone there and could not quite see the phone itself. After that he used the phone many times, while I was working and while Andy was studying at the kitchen table in full view of the telephone. *It was really spooky to see the receiver stand up on end by itself, and then after a while put itself back down where it belonged,* but always upside down. Some nights he would dial many times after we had gone to bed, and we could hear the sound plainly in our bedroom. The next morning I would find the receiver on the phone upside down. One night while Andy was taking a bath Mr. Gree called somebody *and I heard him say* in a low, deep voice, "I'm weird...I'm unusual." I thought to myself, "You can say that again." He repeated it several times and then all I could hear would be a series of low grunts, from which I could not make out any real words. One evening while we were in the car coming home from the post office I asked Andy whom he supposed Mr. Gree called on the phone. Without a moment's hesitation Mrs. Elliott, who we did not know was with us, spoke up and said he was calling her. We did not ask her where she was when she received the call!

Both Mr. Gree and Mrs. Elliott certainly had Andy's welfare in mind. Practically every day for the whole month of January there was a note from one of them stuck in the screen door. It appeared to be Mrs. Elliott's job to help get John home and to take care of Andy. She said if she could do that she would probably go back to her grave early.

After John had left home I felt sorry for Andy. He was lonely being at home alone so much of the time. He indicated a desire for a cat, and a little later for a dog. At the insistence and complete direction of Mrs. Elliott I spent quite a sum of money for such pets. Mr. Gree then took over completely the direction for our taking care of these dogs and cats.

On January 29, 1966, while I was writing a letter, there was a pounding on the kitchen wall, indicating that there was a note in our "post office." It was from Mrs. Elliott. "I love that beagle. Sorry the dogs have been sick. I feel responsible. Andy worries. He loves them so much. If something does happen I only hope it isn't the beagle. The beagle will be a better companion. Andy would give up one if you asked him to. Not that he wants to. But he would understand. He loves dogs. He understands. El. Reply to this note. Reply to every line I wrote."

The other dog she referred to was a brown dachshund, which did not look very healthy when we bought it. It never did gain any weight and after we had given away the black dachshund the brown one continued to get worse. During the next few days and nights some of the most unbelievable things happened in connection with this brown dachshund. I would be working in my shop and suddenly hear a slight noise on the roof of the house. It would be utterly impossible for the dog to jump up there from the ground, and there was nothing else around for him to get on in order to jump up on the house. Yet *there he was clear up on the peak walking from one end to the other!* We would get a ladder and finally coax him down into the eave where we could get hold of him and put him on the ground. This happened time after time. We finally decided to leave him up there and go on to bed. The next night Mrs. Elliott told us she knew about the dog. We asked her how it was possible and said we would like to see how the dog got up there. She said we could not see it...that it was just a case of "now he's down here...now he's up there." She said that even if we were watching him, he would just simply vanish from his spot on the ground and at the same instant be on the roof. Later that night Mrs. Elliott called Andy and me and said the dog was trying to commit suicide and for us to go to the back door and look in the flower bed on the south side of the back steps. Sure enough we looked, and the ground had been

freshly dug and looked as if it had been loosely put back in place. We could see the dirt moving, and I told Andy to go and get the shovel from the garage. Mrs. Elliott said it was not in the garage, but for us to wait just a few seconds and we would find it out in the front yard under the tree, where it would be when it got back from "Heaven." Andy did go and found the shovel just where she said it would be and brought it to me. I dug down beside where the dirt was moving and pulled the dog out by the tail. He was barely breathing and looked very pitiful, but after a few seconds was able to feebly walk a little. Mrs. Elliott told us that we had better put it out of its misery that night. I told her I did not have anything to put it to sleep with, but she finally told me to just go ahead and kill it, using a hammer, a brick or anything that would put it to death. It was a sickening experience, but I did kill the dog with a brick, as I was certain that it was in pain and would be better off dead. *We buried the dog where it had apparently dug its own grave!* I cannot say that the dog actually dug this hole, crawled into it and covered itself up with dirt, as I find it hard to see how it could possibly have dragged the dirt in on top of it...I have only Mrs. Elliott's word for that. I am merely starting what she told us, although I did find the dog in the hole, covered with loose dirt, and barely breathing when I pulled it out.

While John was away in Daingerfield, I had bought a little plastic toilet bowl cleaner on which a disposable pad is used. The handle had come apart the first time I tried to use it. It cost only a few cents, and ordinarily I would have just bought another and forgotten about it. However, I decided to write the manufacturer, and some time later I received a letter from them, advising me that they were sending me another handle. Eventually I received a notice that there was a package at the post office. I would have had to drive about ten miles from the place were I work to the post office and back during the noon hour to pick it up, and since it was of no importance I intended to just wait until Saturday to call for the package. That evening, though, when I went to my shop to start work there was a package on my work bench. The shop had been locked all day and was still locked when I started to work. I asked Andy if he knew anything about it and he assured me that he did not even know about the package being in the post office. At that moment Mrs. Elliott spoke up and admitted she had gotten it out of the post office and brought it home to me!

Not long after John had gone to Daingerfield another mystifying thing happened. In one of the kitchen drawers where we kept some silverware in one of those little compartments made for that purpose, there was a space five or six inches behind that section clear across the drawer. In there I kept a few tools such as screwdriver, pliers, tack hammer, where they would be conveniently available when I needed them. I had not had occasion to look in there for some time, and when I finally did I noticed a pistol. It was .22 cal. and looked very real, and only when I picked it up did I discover it was just a blank pistol. I asked Andy where it came from, but he knew nothing whatever about it. Mrs. Elliott spoke and said *she* had brought it from Daingerfield. She told us that John had ordered it from some magazine ad and had paid $12 for it. She said it was awfully hard for her to bring it to our house and that it had taken her several hours to do so. She did not say why she did it but intimated that she just wanted us to know about it. Later, when we were moving away from that house, the pistol was gone, and I have not seen it since.

For many years I had owned a .25 cal. Colt automatic pistol. I always kept it in good condition but it had not been fired in thirty years at the time we moved to Tyler. John's mother also had had pistol exactly like mine except for the handles, as I bought a pair of white, carved bone handles for mine. When she died we brought that pistol to our house, although we never had occasion to shoot it either. We still had them both when we moved to Tyler. With so many mysterious events taking place, I decided to keep a pistol out in my shop, so I brought the one that had belonged to John's mother and left it on top of my work bench. It stayed there for several weeks. One night it was missing. My shop was always locked and I had the only key. I had wrapped my own gun in a polyethylene bag after cleaning it thoroughly, and put it in a little compartment between the two drawers in a chest in my room. One of the drawers had to be removed completely to get the gun, and even then one had to look closely to find it. I had told no one about the hiding place. When the gun in my shop suddenly disappeared I decided to get mine that I had hidden in the chest. However, when I looked in the hiding place my pistol was not there, *but in its place was that one which had been in the shop!* I did not take it to my shop then, but some time later when I did decide to, that gun too was gone, and we have seen neither of them since that time.

Occasionally during all this time I would write to John, saying that I wished she would come home so that we might be able to get her well and be happy together again. She never replied to any of my letters, although she wrote Andy a note now and then when he would write her first. I talked to her on the phone a short while later. I do not remember whether I called her on the phone or whether she was the one who called, but she finally said she would be home on a given date in February 1967, and that Mack would bring her. When she got to Tyler she called me at work. She had taken a room in a private home for a few days before coming back to our house. Andy and I talked her into coming home that night, though, and during the remainder of 1967 things seemed to be more normal for us than they had been in many years.

During March of 1967 I moved my shop to a building downtown. I was getting too crowded in the little room I had been using at the house, and when I got things all set up at the new location I thought that it would be good for John to run the shop during the day, or at least part of each day, which she agreed to do. Things went along very well throughout the rest of the year. Our daughter Amy came for a few days' visit at Christmas time. A little while before this, though, John had begun to throw cigarettes all over the house again, and there were burned places everywhere. John, of course, insisted that she had *not* thrown them there.

Some time in late 1967 Mrs. Elliott reappeared and began giving us more advice about how to handle John. By this time I believe Andy was about to go to pieces. One of the officials of the school Andy attended called

me and asked why Andy had not been to school. Mrs. Elliott had said for him not to go to school anymore, that he could take a correspondence course and get his high school diploma that way. I tried to convince him to return to school.

I received all sorts of notes from Mrs. Elliott, telling me that Andy was becoming a nervous wreck, and that if I tried to make him go back to school she would take him with her. Andy also told me he would rather go with *her* than to return to school. Finally I asked her why she did not get away from us and never return. The last note I received from her read as follows:

Howard,
    You might wish I wouldn't come back but I did. You can do whatever you want to with John. I won't ask Jr. if he wants to come with me, though he might kill himself. Taking John away will only make him worry more. You don't care. THERE IS ONE THING YOU CARE ABOUT AND THAT IS YOU. I wish you would leave Jr. alone. He can get a course to finish school and get a diploma and leave you. If you cause any trouble I'll take him or he'll kill himself. I could help him go to California but that wouldn't be good he be better off dead, which he probably will be. There's not going to be a world in 15 years so he doesn't care. He just wants to have some enjoyment. You are real silly. John's going to get violent. That's the silliest thing I ever heard. Now you are really going to hurt things when you send John away. All I asked was 1 week. You don't want John well you just want rid of her, so you cause trouble and get her mad. John doesn't cost you all that money you selfish fool. I can't make John love you but I could get her to clean house and if you had any sense (which you don't) you would leave her at Trumark. Now when you send her away and start giving Jr. trouble you are going to be sorrier than you have been or will ever be. I don't know Jr. is good at music and would be excellent and be able to make 3 times your money. Maybe he will be better off gone. You silly old selfish idiot.
    You can holler and anything else but it will be of no avail. When you see the nut doctor, tell him about me, maybe they'll put you away.

During the last part of March and early February the most ghastly things yet began to happen at the house. Henry Anglin came back. I could not hear him, but Andy said he talked very little and what few words he did speak were barely understandable. Andy could hear his evil laughter. He began by putting an egg under the mattress about where my head would be. We would not have known at the time, of course, but he would tell Andy to have me look in certain places. There was an egg, broken, in one of my house shoes, one in a pocket of my robe, one in the shade of the ceiling light, one broken in the corner of the room where it was running down the wall, and one broken against the chest of drawers. There was even one inside my pillow case. Andy said that Anglin would just give a sort of insane-sounding laugh each time we would find another egg.

We cleaned up the mess, and that was the end of the egg episode.

A few days later when I got home from work, Andy called me into our room and there *in the middle of the bed was our dresser.* It was not very heavy, and I was able to lift it down by myself. The next day the chest of drawers was on the bed. This was very heavy, and it took both Andy and me to set it on the floor again. The following day, when I got home, Andy was not there. I noticed that the door to the room he and I shared was closed. That was not unusual, though, as we often kept it closed during the day. However, when I started to open it, *it simply came off the hinges in my hands.* I could see that the pins had been removed from the hinges, so I just leaned the door against the wall. The next day I found the closet door wrenched from the opening, bringing most of the door facing with it. These were hollow doors and both of them had holes knocked in them about the size of a fist. The next night, about nine o'clock, while I was working at the shop, Andy telephoned me and said *the refrigerator was in our room.* He had heard a noise while he and John were watching television, and got up to see what it was. To reach the bedroom the refrigerator had had to go through the length of the breakfast room, the den, and a hallway before reaching our room. I knew we could not move it back that night so I told Andy to just leave it alone and we would decide what to do the next day. However, a little later he called and said the washing machine, which was located in the kitchen, had been pulled away from the wall and the faucets behind it were leaking and water was running all over the floor.

I told him to cut off the hydrants, which he did. I then called the police and asked them to meet me at the house. When we got there the holes in the two doors in the bedroom had *increased to about fifteen or twenty* and some of them were through both sides of the doors and big enough to put one's head through.

Pretty soon, the house was swarming with policemen and detectives. That is when I decided to tell them as briefly as I could what we had been going through. Some of them, I am certain, thought the whole thing was a hoax, and came right out and said they thought I was being hoodwinked by John, who had enlisted Andy's help. That was absolutely ridiculous though, *as practically all of the strange happenings occurred when Andy and I were together, and while John was staying with Mack about a hundred miles away.* One of the chief detectives talked a long time with John, and later told me that she talked sensibly, but that he was amazed *at her lack of concern about the strange things* that had happened. I too had noticed that she was wholly indifferent to the entire "show."

About the middle of February 1968 things got so bad that I made John give me her key to the shop, and told her that I was going to have to do one of three things. I was going to try and have her committed to a state hospital as I was not financially able to have her take psychiatric treatments, or she could take them and pay for them herself, or I was going to get a divorce. A divorce at my age I thought was ridiculous, but I felt as if I

could not stand to go on as things were. Andy was going to move with me as soon as I found a suitable place. John did not seem perturbed one way or the other, and probably did not believe I would really do any of those things. However, on February 24, I did move out of the house, and had my attorney begin divorce proceedings, since he again stated that he did not think I would have a chance in trying to have her committed. I think that when the papers were served on John it was the first time she actually realized what was happening. I got an apartment only a few blocks from my shop. I told Andy to call me every night to let me know how things were at home. I met him at a nearby shopping center each Saturday and gave him enough money to buy food for himself and John during the following week.

For several weeks we went on this way. One night Andy called me and said *that the dining table was up in the attic.* The only opening to the attic was a rectangular hole in the garage ceiling about 16 by 24 inches, through which *it was absolutely impossible for the table to go.* The next night the table was back in the house again. This happened several times. Other things also "went" to the attic, such as a small table, an ottoman, and another kidney-shaped end table. Finally, the dining table came down and Andy found it in the garage, and after considerable work was able to get it inside the house, where it belonged.

Eventually, John was beginning to believe that the strange things we had been talking about were really happening. Previously she had just made fun of us whenever we would mention them. Several weeks after I had left, Andy was sitting in the den, playing his guitar, when the lights went out. At first he thought that a bulb had burned out, but when he looked at the switch he could see that it had *been turned off.* This happened several times. Once when John was going through the den the light went out and she too saw that the switch had been turned; Andy was not anywhere near it, and there was nobody else who could have done it.

It was well into the second month after I left home. I had just finished work in the shop. The telephone rang. It was John and she sounded hysterical. She said she was very sick and begged me to come home. I got there a few minutes later, and she could hardly talk. She continued to beg me to come home, but I told her I could never spend another night in that house. Finally I got her calmed down enough to talk seriously. I finally told her that I would come back, but that first we would have to find another place to live. I demanded that she never smoke again. Finally, on April 15, 1968, we moved out of the house of horrors, and I have nor been there since.

John has not smoked since that time. It has now been over three months since we left the house, and John does the normal things about the house except cook. She is again at my rubber stamp shop and seems to enjoy it.

* * *

In retrospect, as I read over these words, I realized how difficult it must have been for Mr. Beaird to report on his experiences, especially to a stranger. What had appeared completely impossible to him would, of course, have been even more unbelievable to someone who was not present when it happened, and he doubted his own sanity at times, which was not surprising.

Having met Howard Beaird I am sure that he is completely sane, in fact, so sane he could not even be called neurotic. Had I not heard of parallel cases before, perhaps I too would have wondered about it. None of the phenomena reported by Mr. Beaird are, however, impossible in the light of parapsychological research. We are dealing here with forces that seem to be in contradiction of ordinary or orthodox physical laws, but the more we learn of the nature of matter and the structure of the atom, the more it seems likely that poltergeist activities connect with physics in such a way as to make seeming de-materialization and re-materialization of solid objects possible practically without time loss. But the case was a question of studying not so much the techniques involved in the phenomena as the reasons behind them and those causing them.

I informed Mr. Beaird that I was eager to enter the case, especially as I wanted to make sure that the poltergeist activities had really ceased once and for all and would never recur at his new location. In cases of this kind there is always the possibility that the phenomena are attached to one or the other person in the household rather than to a location. Moving to another house seems to have stopped the activities, but as there had been pauses before that culminated in renewed and even stronger physical activities, I wanted to be sure that this would not be the case in this new location. I explained that I would have to interview all those concerned, even the police detectives who had come to the house on that fateful night. Mr. Beaird assured me that he would make all the necessary arrangements, and, after discussing my plans with his wife and son, they too agreed to talk to me. Mack, her sister-in-law, who had been hostess to Mrs. Beaird while most of the phenomena took place at the house, was unable to meet me in Tyler, but I was assured that Mrs. Beaird had never left her care during all that time. For a while Howard Beaird had thought that his wife had returned without his knowledge and done some of the things about the house that had startled him. This, of course, turned out to be a false impression. At no time did Mrs. Beaird leave her sister-in-law's house in Daingerfield, 75 miles away. Whether or not her astral self visited the home is another matter and would be subject to my investigation and verification as far as possible.

Mr. Beaird also went back to his former home to talk to the present owners. Somewhat suspicious of him, for no apparent reason, they were willing to see me if I came to Tyler. Mr. M. works for a local bakery and returns home at 5:30 P.M., and since his wife would not entertain strange visitors in the absence of her husband, my visit would have to be at such an hour as was convenient to the M.s. Perhaps the somewhat battered condition of the house when the M.s had bought it from Mr. Beaird might be the reason for their reluctance to discuss my visit. At any rate it

was agreed that I could call briefly on them and talk to them about the matter at hand. Howard Beaird's daughter, who is now Mrs. Howard Wilson, lives in Austin, Texas. She has had some interest in the occult and mind development and had suggested that someone from the Silva Mind Center in Laredo should come up to Tyler to investigate the case. That was prior to my entering the situation, however, and now Mrs. Wilson wanted very much to come up to Tyler herself and be present during my investigation. Unfortunately it turned out later that she was unable to keep the date due to prior commitments. Thorough man that he is, Howard Beaird also talked to Detective Weaver at the police station to make sure I could see him and question him about his own investigation of the house. I was assured of the welcome mat at the police station, so I decided to set the time when I could go down to Tyler and look for myself into what appeared to be one of the most unusual cases of psychic phenomena.

On February 5, 1969, I arrived at the Tyler airport. It was 5:42 in the afternoon and Howard Beaird was there to welcome me. We had made exact plans beforehand so he whisked me away to the Blackstone Hotel, allowed me to check in quickly, then went with me to see Detective Weaver at the police situation.

As we passed through town I had the opportunity to observe what Tyler, Texas, was all about. Clean shops, quiet streets, a few tree-lined avenues, small houses, many of them very old—well, old anyway in terms of the United States—and people quietly going about their business seem to be characteristic of this small town. We passed by Howard Beaird's shop, a neat, tidy shop, the company name Trumark plainly written on the window pane. As in many small towns, the telephone wires were all above ground, strung in a lazy haphazard fashion from street to street. The police station turned out to be a modern concrete building set back a little from the street. Detective Weaver readily agreed to talk to me. Howard Beaird left us for the moment in a fine sense of propriety just in case the detective wanted to say something not destined for his ears. As it turned out, there wasn't anything he could not have said in front of him. Was there anything in the detective's opinion indicating participation by either the boy or Mrs. Beaird in the strange phenomena? The detective shrugged. There was nothing he could pinpoint along those lines. He then went to the files and extricated a manila envelope inscribed "pictures and letter, reference mysterious call at ——Elizabeth, February 19, 1968, 11:00 P.M., case number 67273. Officer B. Rosenstein and officer M. Garrett." Inside the envelope there were two pictures, photographs taken at the time by a police photographer named George Bain. One picture was of the door, clearly showing the extreme violence with which a hole had been punched into it. The entire rim of the hole was splintered as if extremely strong methods had been employed to punch this hole through the door.

The other picture showed a heavy chest of drawers of dark wood sitting squarely upon a bed. Quite clearly the description given to me by Howard Beaird had been correct. What exactly did the two police officers find when they arrived at the house on Elizabeth Street? The house was in disorder, the detective explained, and furniture in places where it wasn't supposed to be. On the whole he bore out the description of events given by Howard Beaird.

Somehow he made me understand that the police did not accept the supernatural origin of the phenomena even though they could not come up with anything better in the way of a solution. Almost reluctantly, the officer wondered whether perhaps Andy wasn't in some way responsible for the phenomena although he did not say so in direct words. I decided to discuss the practical theories concerning poltergeists with him and found him amazingly interested. "Would you like to have the photographs?" the detective asked and handed me the folder. Surprised by his generosity, I took the folder and I still have it in my files. It isn't very often that a researcher such as I is given the original folder from the files of a police department. But then the mystery on Elizabeth Street is no longer on active situation —or is it?

After we had thanked Detective Weaver for his courtesies we decided to pay a visit to the house itself. After a moment of hesitation, the officer suggested that he come along since it might make things easier for us. How right he was. When we arrived at the house on Elizabeth Street and cautiously approached the entrance, with me staying behind at first, there was something less than a cordial reception awaiting us. Mr. M. was fully aware of my purpose, of course, so that we were hardly surprising him with all this.

After a moment of low-key discussion at the door between Howard Beaird and Detective Weaver on one hand and Mr. M. on the other, I was permitted to enter the house and look around for myself. The M. family had come to see me, if not to greet, and looked at me with curious eyes. I explained politely and briefly that I wanted to take some photographs for the record and I was permitted to do so. I took black and white pictures with a high sensitivity film in various areas of the house, especially the kitchen area where it connects with the garage and the living room, both places where many of the phenomena have been reported in Mr. Beaird's testimony.

On developing these, under laboratory conditions, we found there was nothing unusual except perhaps certain bright light formations in the kitchen area where there should be none since no reflective surfaces existed. Then I returned to the living room to talk briefly with Mr. M. and his family.

Was there anything unusual about the house that he had noticed since he had moved in? Almost too fast he replied, "Nothing whatsoever. Everything was just fine." When Mr. M. explained how splendid things were with the house he shot an anxious look at his wife, and I had the distinct impression they were trying to be as pleasant and superficial as possible and to get rid of me as fast as possible. Did they have any interest in occult phenomena such as ghosts? I finally asked. Mr. M. shook his head. Their religion did not allow them such considerations, he explained somewhat sternly. Then I knew the time had come to make my departure.

I made inquiries with real estate people in the area and discovered a few things about the house neither Mr. Beard nor Mr. M. had told me. The house was thirteen years old and had been built by a certain Terry Graham. There had been two tenants before the Beairds. Prior to 1835 the area had been Indian territory and was used as a cow pasture by the Cherokee Indians.

I also discovered that Mrs. M. had complained to the authorities about footsteps in the house when there was no one walking, of doors opening by themselves, and the uncanny feeling of being watched by someone she could not see. That was shortly after the M.s had moved into the house. The M.s also have young children. It is conceivable that the entities who caused such problems to the Beaird family might have been able to manifest through them also. Be that as it may, the matter was not followed up. Perhaps their religious upbringing and beliefs did not permit them to discuss such matters and they preferred to ignore them, or perhaps the activities died of their own volition. At any rate, it seemed pretty certain to me that the poltergeist activities did not entirely cease with the removal of the Beairds from the house. But did these activities continue in the new house the Beairds had chosen for their own? That was a far more important question.

I asked Howard Beaird to send me a report of further activities if and when they occurred at the new house. On February 23 he communicated with me by letter. I had asked him to send me samples of John's and Andy's handwriting so that I could compare them with the notes he had let me have for further study. In order to arrive at a satisfactory explanation of the phenomena it was, of course, necessary to consider all ordinary sources for them. Amongst the explanations one would have to take into account was the possibility of either conscious or unconscious fraud, that is to say, the writing of the notes by either John or Andy and their somehow manipulating them so that they would seem to appear out of nowhere in front of Mr. Beaird. For that purpose I needed examples of the two handwritings to compare them with some of the handwritings on the notes.

There were a number of noises in the new home that could be attributed to natural causes. But there were two separate incidents which, in the opinion of Howard Beaird, could not be so explained. Shortly before I arrived in Tyler a minor incident occurred which makes Howard wonder whether the entities from beyond the veil are still with him in the new house. One evening he had peeled two hard-boiled eggs in order to have them for lunch the following day. He had placed them in the refrigerator on a paper towel. The following morning he discovered that both eggs were frozen solid even though they were still on the lower shelf of the refrigerator. This could only have been accomplished if they had spent considerable time in the freezer compartment during the night. Questioning his wife and son as to whether they had put the eggs in the freezer, he discovered that neither of them had done so. He decided to test the occurrence by repeating the process. He found that the two new eggs which he had placed in the refrigerator that night were still only chilled but not frozen the next day. What had made the first pair of eggs as hard as stone he is unable to understand, but he is satisfied that the occurrence may be of non-psychic origin.

Then there was the matter of a clock playing a certain tune as part of its alarm clock device. Through no apparent reason this clock went off several times, even though no one had been near it. Even though it had not been wound for a long time and had only a 24-hour movement, it played this tune several times from deep inside a chest of drawers. Eventually the clock was removed, and in retrospect Mr. Beaird does not think that a supernatural situation could have been responsible for it. But the two separate incidents did frighten the Beairds somewhat. They were afraid that the change of address had not been sufficient to free them from the influences of the past. As it turned out, the move was successful and the separation complete.

I had to work with two kind of evidence. There was, first of all, the massive evidence of mysterious notes which had fallen out of the sky and which showed handwriting of various kinds. Perhaps I could make something out of that by comparing them with the handwritings of living people. Then there was the question of talking personally and in depth with the main participants, the Beairds, and, finally, to see what others who knew them had to say about them. Howard Beaird's daughter, Amy, now Mrs. Howard C. Wilson, thought that the real victim of what she thought "a circus of horrors" was her brother Andy. "If you had known Andy when he was small, up to the time mother began to show real signs of her illness, it would be impossible for you to recognize him as the same person now. He was typically, for a little boy, simply brimming over with mischievous humor. He would do anything to make people laugh and would run simply hooting with joy through the house when he had done something devilish." That was not the Andy I met when I came to Tyler. The boy I talked to was quiet, withdrawn, painfully shy, and showed definite signs of being disturbed.

The following morning I went to see the Beairds at their new home. The home itself is pleasant and small and stands in a quiet, tree-lined street. As prearranged, Mr.

Beaird left me alone with each of the two other members of his family so that I could speak to them in complete confidence. Andy, a lanky boy, seemed ill at ease at first when we sat down. In order to gain his confidence, I talked about songs and the records popular at the time, since I had seen a number of record albums in his room. Somehow this helped open him up; he spoke more freely after that. Now sixteen, he was studying at a local barber college. When I wondered how a young man, in this day and age, would choose this somewhat unusual profession, he assured me that the money was good in this line of work and that he really liked it. He felt he could put his heart and soul into it. After some discussion of the future as far as Andy was concerned, I brought the conversation around the matter at hand.

"When these peculiar events took place you and your father lived alone in the other house. Did you ever see anyone?" "Well, I had seen a vision of my mother this one time. It looked like her but nobody was there really...kind of like a shadow, or a form." "Have you seen the notes?" "Yes." "Did you ever actually see anyone writing them?" "No." "Did you ever hear any voices?" "Yeh. I talked to them." "How did they sound?" "Well, the women that were here all sounded alike...real high voices. The men were dead, you know...the spirits, or whatever you want to call them. They had real deep voices. They were hard to understand." "Did they talk to you in the room?" "From out of nowhere. No matter where I might be." "You didn't see them anywhere?" "Never saw them." "Was your father with you at the time you heard the voices or were you alone?" "He was with me at times and not at others." "These voices...are they mostly in the daytime or are the at night?" "At night...mostly at night, or afternoon, when I'd get home from school." "Did it start right after you moved in?" "No...it was two or three months after...." "Did you see the insects?" "Oh yes." "Where did they come from?" "It seemed like just out of the ceiling." "Could they have come in any other way?" "They couldn't have come in...not that many." "Whose voices did you hear?" "First of all my mother's." "The time she was away at Daingerfield?" "Yes." "What did the voice sound like?" "The same high voice. It sounded a little like her." "What did she say?" "She started to talk about my grandfather's funeral and about someone being mean to her."

Clearly the boy was not at his best. Whether it was my presence and the pressure the questioning was putting on him or whether he genuinely did not remember, he was somewhat uncertain about a lot of the things his father had told me about. But he was quite sure that he had heard his mother's voice at a time when she was away at Daingerfield. He was equally sure that none of the insects could have gotten into the house by ordinary means and that the notes came down, somehow of their own volition, from the ceiling. I did not wish to frighten him and thanked him for his testimony, short though it was. I then asked that John, Mrs. Beaird that is, be asked to join me in the front room so we could talk quietly. Mrs. Beaird seemed quite at ease with me and belied the rather turbulent history I knew she had had. Evidently the stay at her sister-in-law's house and the prior psychiatric treatment had done some good. Her behavior was not at all unusual; in fact, it was deceivingly normal. Having seen one of her earlier photographs I realized that she had aged tremendously. Of course I realized that her husband would have discussed many of the things with her so that she would have gained secondhand knowledge of the phenomena. Nevertheless, I felt it important to probe into them because sometimes a person thinks she is covering up while, in fact, she is giving evidence.

"Now we are going to discuss the other house," I said pleasantly. "Do you remember some of the events that happened in the other house?" "Well, I wasn't there when they took place. They told me about it ... and actually, you will learn more from my son than from me because I don't know anything." "You were away all that time?" "Yes." "Before you went, did anything unusual happen?" "Nothing." "After you came back did anything happen?" "Well, I don't know ... I don't remember anything." "Before you bought the house, did you have any unusual experience involving extrasensory perception at any time?" "Never. I know nothing whatever about it." "You were living somewhere else for a while." "I was with my sister-in-law." "How would you describe that period of your life? Was it an unhappy one? A confusing one? What would you say that period was?" "I have never been unhappy. I have never been confused." "Why did you go?" "I felt I needed to for personal reasons." "During that time did you have contact with your husband and son? Did you telephone or did you come back from time to time?" "I did not come back, but I had some letters from them and I believe that I talked some...." "Did your husband ever tell you some of the things that had happened in your absence?" "Yes. He told me." "What did you make of it?" "I didn't understand it. If I had seen it, I'd have gotten to the bottom of it somehow." "The people who are mentioned in some of these notes, are you familiar with them? Were there any of them that you had a personal difficulty with or grudge against?" "None whatever. They were friends." "Now, you are familiar with this lady, Mrs. Elliott, who has, apparently, sent some notes." "Oh yes. She was a very good friend of mine. Of course, she is much older. She had a daughter my age and we were very good friends." "Did you have any difficulties?" "I have no difficulties," she replied and her eyes filled with tears. "No? You had at the time you left here." "Not real difficulties. For several reasons, I needed a change. I didn't intend to stay so long. She was living alone and she worked during the day. And we sort of got into a most enjoyable relationship whereby I took care of certain household chores while she was

gone..." "What made you stay so long?" "I just really can't tell you what it was." "You still have no answer to the puzzle as to what happened?" "None. I have no idea." "Do you remember having any treatments?" "I'm just getting old. That is the difficulty."

It was clear that her mind had blocked out all memory of the unpleasant occurrences in her life. As often happens with people who have undergone psychiatric treatment, there remains a void afterwards, even if electric shock therapy has not been used. Partially this is, of course, due to the treatment, but sometimes it is self-induced deliberately by the patient in order to avoid discussing the unpleasant. Mrs. Beaird had returned to her husband and son to resume life and try to make the best of it. To go back over the past would have served no purpose from her point of view. This was not a matter of refusing to discuss these things with me. She did not remember them quite consciously and no amount of probing would have helped, except perhaps in-depth hypnosis, and I was not prepared to undertake this with a former mental patient. Clearly then I could not get any additional material from the principal. I decided to re-examine the evidence and talk again with the one man who seemed, after all, the most reliable witness in the entire case, Mr. Beaird himself.

In particular, I wanted to re-examine his own personal observations of certain phenomena, for it is one thing to make a report alone, quietly, filled with the memory of what one has experienced, and another to report on phenomena while being interrogated by a knowledgeable, experienced investigator. Quite possibly some new aspects might be unearthed in this fashion. At the very least it would solidify some of the incredible things that had happened in the Beaird household.

On the morning of February 6, 1969, I met with Howard Beaird at my hotel and we sat down, quietly, to go over the fantastic events of the past three years. In order to arrive at some sort of conclusion, which I wanted very much to do, I had to be sure that Mr. Beaird's powers of observation had been completely reliable. In going over some of his statements once again I wasn't trying to be repetitive but rather to observe his reaction to my questions and to better determine in my own mind whether or not he had observed correctly. In retrospect I can only say that Howard Beaird was completely unshaken and repeated, in essence, exactly what he had reported to me earlier. I feel that he has been telling the truth all along, neither embellishing it nor diminishing it. Our conversation started on a calm emotional note which was now much more possible than at the time he first made his report to me, when he was still under the influence of recent events. Things had been quiet at the house and seemed to continue to remain quiet, so he was able to gather his thoughts more clearly and speak of the past without the emotional involvement which would have made it somewhat more difficult for me to judge his veracity.

"Now we had better start at the beginning. I am interested in discussing whatever *you yourself* observed. Your wife was still in the house when the first thing happened?" "Yes." "Were those *real* bugs?" "Yes." "When you turned the light on?" "You could see thousands of bugs on the floor." "How did you get rid of them?" "We had a vacuum cleaner." "Did they come from the direction of the windows or the door?" "The door." "Now, after the bugs, what was the next thing that you personally observed?" "I heard my wife's voice. After my son and I had gone to bed we were lying there talking about these things that had happened. That was after she had left Tyler." "Did it sound like her voice?" "No. It didn't sound like her voice to me but it was *her....*" "Well, how did you know it was her?" "She told me it was and was talking about my sister having insulted her. Nobody else knew that except my wife and I." "Where did the voice seem to come from? Was it in the room?" "Yes." "What happened after that?" "Several nights after that, she appeared to Andy. I heard him talking in the bathroom. He talked for two or three minutes, and then I heard him say, well, goodbye." "Didn't it make you feel peculiar? His mother was obviously not there and he was talking to her?" "Well, I had already had my encounter with her." "Did you call your wife in Daingerfield?" "No." "Why not?" "Well, she wouldn't have believed me. I had thought about writing her sister-in-law and telling her that you've got to keep my wife in Daingerfield. I don't want her here. Yet, I thought, that's a foolish thing to do, because all she'll say is, *she wasn't here.* She wasn't in person. Her body wasn't here." "After the voice, what came next?" "Well, it was shortly after that we started hearing these other voices." "Did you hear those voices?" "All of them, yes. All four." "Did they sound alike or did they sound different?" "The men had deep rough voices, but I could tell them apart. And the ladies were all subtle voices and I couldn't tell them apart, except when they told me." "Did you ever hear two voices at the same time?" "I don't believe so. However, Mrs. Snow and Mrs. Elliott were there at the same time. That is, *they said* they were. That was when Henry Anglin was giving us so much trouble and they had to carry him back to his grave." "Let's talk about anything that you have actually seen move." "I saw these notes that were folded. Sometimes as many as ten or fifteen notes a day." "From an enclosed room?" "Well, the doors weren't closed between the rooms, but I'd be sitting at the table eating something, and all of a sudden I'd see one fall. I'd look up toward the ceiling and there'd be one up there." "Most of these notes were signed 'Mrs. Elliott'?" "Yes. Later she signed them. At first, Elie and then El. Now after my wife came back from Daingerfield she, too, would send me notes through Andy. I was working in my shop and Andy would bring me a note written with numbers, in code. 1 was A, 2 was B, and so forth. I hated to take the time to decipher those things, but I would sit down and find out what they said. In one note she asked me if I didn't 'lose'

some weight?" "Did your wife ever write you a note in longhand or in block letters?" "No." "Was there any similarity in the writing of your wife's note and those that later came down from the ceiling?" "I can't say, but Mrs. Elliott had been after me to lose weight. I thought it was peculiar—that my wife came from Daingerfield and asked about my losing weight also." "Mrs. Elliott was a contemporary of your wife?" "She died in 1963. About a year before we moved here." "Were those two women very close in life?" "Not particularly. They were neighbors." "What about Mrs. Snow?" "She was peculiar." "What objects did you see move in person?" "I saw a heavy pair of shoes lift themselves off the floor and fly right over my bed and land on the opposite side of the bed." "Did they land fast or did they land slowly?" "It was just as if I'd picked them up and thrown them. Andy's house shoes came the same way. I've watched the cat being lifted up about a foot from where he was sitting and just be suspended for several seconds and it didn't fall on the floor. I saw a can of insect spray which was sitting on the cabinet come over and suspend itself right over that opening, and spray into that little room, and I was nearly suffocated. I had to open the doors or the insect spray would have got me." "You weren't holding the can?" "No." "I am particularly interested in anything where you were *actually* present when movement occurred, or voices were heard." "I've seen my clothes fly through the air as I was coming home." "Did these things occur whether your wife was physically in the house or not?" "Yes." "Did anything ever happen while neither your son nor your wife was at home but you were alone?" "I believe so." "Your wife had some personal shock in 1951, I believe. When her best friend died suddenly. Do you feel her mental state changed as a result?" "Very gradually, yes. She was very happy, though, when she found out she was going to have another child, because she thought this would make up for the loss of her friend. She was just crazy about him." "Now, when was the first time you noticed there was something wrong with her mentally?" "In 1960 my wife took over her daughter's room. She stopped up all the windows with newspapers scotch-taped against the wall and hung a blanket in each window of the bedroom." "Why did she do that?" "She felt someone was spying on her. At the office, she took the telephone apart, and adding machines and typewriters, looking for microphones to see who was spying on her." "But the phenomena themselves did not start until you moved into this house?" "That's right."

I thanked Mr. Beaird for his honest testimony, for he had not claimed anything beyond or different from his original report to me. I took the voluminous handwritten notes and the letters pertaining to the case and went back to New York to study them. This would take some time since I planned to compare the handwriting by both Mrs. Beaird and Andy. I didn't, for a moment, think that the notes had been written consciously by either one of them and simply thrown at Mr. Beaird in the ordinary way. Quite obviously Mr. Beaird was no fool, and any such clumsy attempt at fake phenomena would not have gone unnoticed, but there are other possibilities that could account for the presence of either Mr. Beaird's or Andy's handwriting in the notes, if indeed there was that similarity.

There were already, clearly visible to me, certain parallels between this case and the Bell Witch case of Tennessee. Vengeance was being wrought on Howard Beaird by some entity or entities for alleged wrongs, in this case his failure to execute minor orders given him. But there were other elements differing greatly from the classic case. In the Bell Witch situation there was not present, in the household, anyone who could be classed as psychotic. In Tyler we have two individuals capable of supplying unused psychic energies. One definitely psychotic, the other on the borderline, or at least psychoneurotic.

I then decided to examine the notes written in this peculiar style longhand, almost always in block letters but upper case letters in the middle of words where they do not belong. It became immediately clear to me that this was a crude way of disguising his handwriting and was not used for any other reason. It is of course a fact that no one can effectively disguise his handwriting to fool the expert. He may think so, but an expert graphologist can always trace the peculiarities of a person's handwriting back to the original writer provided samples are available to compare the two handwritings letter by letter, word for word. Some of the notes were downright infantile. For instance, on December 6, 1965, a note read "My power is decreasing. I'm going back to Mack. I must hurry. I would like to come home but I don't guess I will. I love you. Please give me a Yule gift. I can't restore my power. I am allowed only three a year. Phone police." What the cryptic remark, "I am allowed only three a year," is supposed to mean is not explained.

Sometimes Howard Beaird played right into the hands of the unknown writer. The Sunday morning after he and Andy has spent the night at a motel because of the goings on in the house, he received the notice of a package at the post office. He knew that he couldn't get it except by noon on a weekday, so he asked aloud, "Is this notice about anything important, as I don't want to come in from the hospital if it doesn't amount to anything?" A few seconds later a note fluttered down from the ceiling reading only "something." That of course was not a satisfactory answer such as an adult or reasonable person would give. It sounded more like a petulant child having a game. On December 6, 1965, a note materialized equally mysteriously, reading, "I don't want to admit to Mack that I'm nutty." Another note dated December 6, 1965, simply read, "Howard got jilted." Another note read "My powers

were restored by the Houston witch. Call the police and ask about her." There doesn't seem to be any great difference between the notes signed by Henry Anglin or by Mrs. Elliott or not signed at all by someone intimating that they were the work of Mrs. Beaird. The letters and the formation of the words are similar. A note dated December 8, 1965, read: "Dear Howard, I love you. I have been wrong. I want to come home but I don't want stupid Mack to know I am unusual. I am really two people. If things end I won't remember nothin'. I can be in three places at one. I love you and Junior. Please dear."

The note signed "Dorothy Kilgallen," mentioned previously and received by Howard Beaird December 22, 1965, reads, "Dear Mr. Beaird: Mrs. Elliott told me about what all has happened to your family and what Henry Anglin is responsible for. It is very tragic. He is the reason I am dead because he changed my pills. Good night and good luck." Having been personally acquainted with the late Hearst columnist Dorothy Kilgallen, I am quite certain that she would not have expressed herself in this manner, dead or alive.

A note signed Pont Thornton dated December 23, 1965, reads, "Dear Howard P.S. an Andy: I no yu well. I no yu good. I don't drinck much do yu haf had hardships. Anglin is a mean man. I am smarter than Henry Lee. I am distant kin of Abe Lincoln and Lewis Armstrong and Sam Davis Junior and Jon F. Kenede." Not only was the note atrociously misspelled but it lists several quite improbable relationships. When writing as Mrs. Elliott the personality is much more concise and logical than when the writer is supposed to be Henry Anglin or Mrs. Beaird. But despite the difference in style the letters are very similar. Of course since the notes came down for almost three years it is to be expected that there are some differences in both style and appearance between them.

On September 17, 1 967, Howard Beaird observed, "About 9 or 10 P.M. Andy heard Mrs. Elliott call. She told him he could talk to her and that mother could not hear so he did and apparently mother knew nothing of it. Just as I was getting ready for bed I heard Mrs. Elliott calling me. *The sound seemed to come toward the kitchen and as Andy and Johnny were watching* TV *in her bedroom I went to the kitchen.* Mrs. Elliott called me several more times and the sound then seemed to be coming from my room. She said that Johnny couldn't hear me so I tried to talk to her but Andy said she told him she never could hear me. Anyway before going to bed I found a very small piece of paper folded so small on the floor in the hall and also a South Side Bank deposit slip folded near it. The small note said 'Be very generous. Say hi to me. Mrs. Snow.' The larger note said, 'Don't be stingy Sam be a generous Joe. George Swiney.' After I had gone to bed I heard Mrs. Elliott calling me several times but could never make her hear me answer. Just as I was about to go to sleep, Andy came in and said Mrs. Elliott told him she had left me a note on the floor. Just as I got up to look for it a note dropped in the chair next to my bed. *I took it to the kitchen to get my glasses and it said, 'Howard, I hope there won't be any slugs. Try to be generous, you have a lot of money. There's so much you could get you, John and Andy.'* This was followed by a list of objects, clothing primarily, which he could get for his family on her suggestion. Howard Beaird tried to talk to Mrs. Elliott to ask her where all that alleged money was but he could never get an answer to that.

On September 29, 1967, Howard Beaird noticed that Mrs. Elliott came to visit him around 7:30 P.M. He can't understand how she can make him hear her when she calls him by name and then make it impossible for him to hear the rest of her. Apparently the rest of the conversation has to be relayed through Andy. On the other hand, if he speaks loudly enough she can hear him. That night Mrs. Elliott informed him that a Mr. Quinn had been by earlier. A little later Mr. Quinn himself came back and Howard Beaird actually heard him call, but he could hear nothing else, and again Andy had to be the interpreter. Andy said that Mr. Quinn sounded like a robot talking, and that, of course, made sense to Mr. Beaird, since he knew that Quinn, who had lost his voice due to cancer prior to his death, used an instrument held to his throat to enable him to talk. The late Mr. Quinn apparently wanted to know how some of the people back in Grand Saline were, including a Mrs. Drake, Mr. And Mrs. Watkins, and the McMullens. This information, of course, could not have been known to Andy, who had been much too young at the time the Beairds knew these people in the town where they formerly lived.

Mrs. Elliott also explained the reason she and the other spirits were able to be with Mr. Beaird that evening was that they had been given time off for the holidays—because of Halloween, although that was a little early for All Hallow's Eve. Mr. Beaird thought it peculiar that spirits get furloughs from whatever place they are in.

On September 30, 1967, Beaird had heard nothing at all from Mrs. Elliott during the day. Andy had been out pretty late that night and Mr. Beaird was asleep when he came in. Sometime after, Andy woke him and said that Mrs. Elliott had left him a note. They found it on his bed. It read, "Howard, think about what I said. Are you going to do it Monday. Elliott." Just below it was a note reading, "John wants a vacuum cleaner and a purse. Junior wants a coat for school and some banjo strings. Hiram." Now the remarkable thing about this note is that the first part was definitely in the handwriting of Mrs. Beaird, while the second part was a crude note put together with a lot of capital letters where they did not belong and generally disorganized. Hiram Quinn, the alleged writer, was of course a very sick man for some time prior to his passing. When Howard Beaird confronted the alleged Mrs. Elliott with the fact that her note was written in the handwriting of his wife, she shrugged it off by explaining that she could write like anybody she wished.

On October 2, 1967, Mr. Beaird noted, "About 7:30 P.M. Mrs. Snow called my name. I was in the kitchen and the voice seemed to come from the back part of the house where Andy and John were. The voice sounded exactly like Mrs. Elliott's and although I could hear it plainly enough and answered aloud immediately I could hear nothing else and Andy had to tell me what she had said. She just wanted to tell me about my stamp business and how John had been. She barely could hear me and told Andy to turn off the attic fan and for me to go into my room and close the door so she could hear. She couldn't explain how I could hear her call my name and then hear nothing more and said it was some kind of 'law.'"

The notes signed by Mrs. Elliott from that period onward frequently looked as if they had been written by Mrs. Beaird. The handwriting is unquestionably hers. That is to say it looks like hers. Howard Beaird does not doubt that the notes were genuinely materialized in a psychic sense. On October 23 he had dozed off to sleep several times and on one occasion was awakened by the rustling of papers on the floor beside his bed. He was alone in the room at the time. He turned the light on and found a sort of pornographic magazine folded up on the floor. Andy came in at this point and explained that Mrs. Elliott had told him she had found this magazine in Mrs. Beaird's room. She said that Mrs. Beaird had gotten it at the beauty shop and the piece of paper was torn from it. On the note was printed "Somebody loves you," signed underneath, El.

On November 12, 1967, a Sunday, Howard Beaird heard Mrs. Elliott talk to him. She advised him that he should go to Mrs. Beaird's room and look for some nudist pictures and also some hand-drawn pictures of naked men and women. Mr. Beaird found all these things but his wife denied any knowledge of them. The following night, November 13, 1967, was particularly remarkable in the kind of phenomena experienced by Howard Beaird. "Mrs. Elliott came by before I left for the shop and told me to look for some more lewd pictures. I found some and destroyed them. Mrs. Elliott told me to be sure and tear them up in front of John and maybe she would quit drawing them, and also quit buying the nudist magazine pictures. Later that night, about 9:15, Mrs. Elliott called me on the telephone. *That's the first time I ever talked to a ghost on the telephone.* I could understand what she said on the phone, yet I could never hear anything except her calling my name when I was at home. Of course all she said on the phone was to come home. I then talked to Andy and he said she wanted me to come home right then and get some more drawings and nudist magazines from John's hiding places. I did go home and got the pictures and went back to the shop after I had destroyed them."

Some of the notes showed the underlying conflict, imagined or real, between the young boy and his father which was of much concern to "guardian angel" Mrs.

Elliott. On January 11, 1968, a note read, "Howard, I need to write you notes. Junior has had to worry so much. Why do you mind him coming with me? He would be happy. It would be right for him not to worry. I agree he must get an education but at seventeen he could get a course and then to college. In the meantime I will help John and him. He could play music and he would be great at seventeen. He would also like to take care of the house. John would get so much better. You would be better financially and Junior could get better. This is the only thing I will allow or I will take him with me if he wants to . . . He said he would tell me to go and wouldn't go but that wouldn't change him from wanting to. You had better pay attention cause he wants to come. I have all the divine right to take him. El." This threat by the spirit of Mrs. Elliott to take the young boy with her into the spirit world did not sit lightly with his father, of course. Analyzed on its face value, it has the ring of a petulant threat a mentally handicapped youngster would make against his parents if he didn't get his way. If Mrs. Elliott was the spirit of a mature and rational person then this kind of threat didn't seem, to me, to be in character with the personality of the alleged Mrs. Elliott.

The following night, January 12, 1968, the communicator wrote, "Howard, I have the divine right. I will prove it by taking Junior and I take him tonight. You don't love him at all. You don't care about anyone." Mrs. Elliott had not taken Andy by January 15, but she let Howard know that she might do so anyway any time now. In fact, her notes sounded more and more like a spokesman for Andy if he wanted to complain about life at home but didn't have the courage to say so consciously and openly. On January 18, Mrs. Elliott decided she wasn't going to take the boy after all. She had promised several times before that she would not come back any longer and that her appearance was the last one. But she always broke this pledge.

By now any orthodox psychologist or even parapsychologist would assume that the young man was materially involved not only in the composition of the notes but in actually writing them. I don't like to jump to conclusions needlessly, especially not when a prejudice concerning the method of communication would clearly be involved in assuming that the young man did the actual writing. But I decided to continue examining each and every word and to see whether the letters or the words themselves gave me any clue as to what human hand had actually written them, if any. It appeared clear to me by now that some if not all of the notes purporting to be the work of Mrs. Elliott were in the hand of Mrs. Beaird. But it was not a very good copy of her handwriting. Rather did it seem to me that someone had attempted to write in Mrs. Beaird's hand who wasn't actually Mrs. Beaird. As for the other notes, those signed by Henry Anglin, Hiram Quinn and those unsigned but seemingly the work of Mrs. Beaird herself, they had

certain common denominators amongst them. I had asked Mr. Beaird to supply me with adequate examples of the handwriting of both Andy and Mrs. Beaird. That is to say, handwritten notes not connected in any way with the psychic phenomena at the house. I then studied these examples and compared them with the notes which allegedly came from nowhere or which materialized by falling from the ceiling in front of a very astonished Mr. Beaird.

I singled out the following letters as being characteristic of the writer, whoever he or she may be. The capital letter T, the lower case e, lower case p, g, y, r, and capital B, C, L, and the figure 9. All of these appeared in a number of notes. They also appear in the sample of Andy's handwriting, in this case a list of song titles which he liked and which he was apparently going to learn on his guitar. There is no doubt in my mind that the letters in the psychic note and the letters on Andy's song list are identical. *That is to say that they were written by the same hand.* By that I do not mean to say, necessarily, that Andy wrote the notes. I do say, however, that the hand used to create the psychic notes is the same hand used consciously by Andy Beaird when writing notes of his own. I am less sure, but suspect, that even the notes seemingly in the handwriting of his mother are also done in the same fashion and also traceable to Andy Beaird.

On December 7, 1965, one of the few drawings in the stack of notes appeared. It showed a man in a barber chair and read, among other annotations, "Aren't the barbers sweet, ha ha." It should be remembered that Andy's great ambition in life was to be a barber. In fact, when I met and interviewed him he was going to barber school.

What then is the meaning of all this? Let us not jump to conclusions and say Andy Beaird wrote the notes somehow unobserved, smuggled them into Mr. Beaird's room somehow unnoticed, and made them fall from the ceiling seemingly by their own volition, somehow without Mr. Beaird noticing this. In a number of reported instances this is a possibility, but in the majority of cases it simply couldn't have happened in this manner, not unless Howard Beaird was not a rational individual and was, in fact, telling me lies. I have no doubt that Mr. Beaird is telling me the truth and that he is a keen and rational observer. Consequently the burden of truth for the validity of the phenomena does not rest on his gift of observation, but on the possibility of producing such paranormal occurrences despite their seeming improbability yet reconciling this with the ominous fact that they show strong indications of being Andy Beaird's handwriting.

We must recognize the tension existing for many years in the Beaird household, the unhappy condition in which young Andy found himself as he grew up, and the fact that for a number of years he was an introspected and suppressed human being unable to relate properly to the outside world and forced to find stimulation where he could. Under such conditions certain forces within a young person can be exteriorized and become almost independent of the person himself. Since these forces are part of the unconscious in the person and therefore not subject to the logical controls of the conscious mind, they are, in fact, childish and frequently irrational. They are easily angered and easily appeased and, in general, behave in an infantile fashion. By the same token these split-off parts of personality are capable of performing physical feats, moving objects, materializing things out of nowhere and, in general, contravening the ordinary laws of science. This we know already because cases of poltergeists have occurred with reasonable frequency in many parts of the world. In the case of the Beaird family, however, we have two other circumstances which must be taken into account. The first is the presence in the house of not one but two emotionally unstable individuals. Mrs. Beaird's increasing divorce from reality, leading to a state of schizophrenia, must have freed some powerful forces within her. Her seemingly unconscious preoccupation with some aspects of sex indicates a degree of frustration on her part yet an inability to do anything about it at the conscious level. We have recognized that the power supply used to perform psychic phenomena is the same power inherent in the life force or the sexual drive in humans, and when this force is not used in the ordinary way it can be diverted to the supernormal expression, which in this case took the form of poltergeist phenomena. We have, therefore, in the Beaird case, a tremendous reservoir of untapped psychic energy subject to very little conscious control on the part of the two individuals in whose bodies these energies were stored and developed.

Were the entities purporting to use these facilities to express themselves beyond the grave actually the people who had once lived and died in the community? Were they, in fact, who they claimed to be, or were they simply being re-enacted unconsciously perhaps by the split-off part of the personalities of both Andy and Mrs. Beaird? Since Howard Beaird has examined the signature of one of those entities, at least, and found it to be closely similar, if not identical, with the signature of the person while alive, and since, in that particular case, access to the signature was not possible to either Andy or Mrs. Beaird, I'm inclined to believe that actual non-physical entities were, in fact, using the untapped energies of these two unfortunate individuals to express themselves in the physical world. Additional evidence, I think, would be the fact that in several cases the names and certain details concerning the personalities of several individuals whom Howard Beaird knew in their former residence in Grand Saline were not known or accessible to either his wife or the young man. I am not fully satisfied that there could not have been some form of collusion between Andy and these so-called spirit entities in creating the phenomena, but if there was such collusion it was on the unconscious level. It is my view that Andy's unexpressed frustrations and desires were picked up by some of these discarnate entities and mingled with their own desire to continue involving themselves in earth conditions and thus became the driving force in making the manifestations possible.

What about the fact that Andy Beaird's handwriting appears in the majority of the notes? If Andy did not write these notes physically himself, could they have been produced in some other manner? There is no doubt in my mind that in at least a large percentage of the notes Andy could not have written them physically and dropped them in front of his father without Mr. Beaird noticing it. Yet, these very same notes also bear unmistakable signs that they are the work of Andy Beaird's hand. Therefore the only plausible solution is to assume that a spiritual part of Andy's body was used to create the notes in the same way in which seemingly solid objects have, at times, been materialized and dematerialized. This is known as a "physical" phenomenon and it is not entirely restricted to poltergeist cases but has, on occasion, been observed with solid objects which were moved from one place to another, or which appeared at a place seemingly out of nowhere, or disappeared from a place without leaving any trace. The phenomenon is not unique nor particularly new. What is unique, or nearly so in the case of the Beaird family of Tyler, Texas, is the fact that here the obvious is not the most likely explanation. I do not think Andy Beaird wrote those notes consciously. I do believe that his writing ability was used by the entities expressing themselves through him. I believe that Andy was telling the truth when he said he was surprised by the appearance of the notes and at no time did he have knowledge of their contents except when one of the other spirit entities informed him about them. The same applies, of course, to Mrs. Beaird. In the phenomenon known as a automatic writing, the hand of a living person, normally a fully rational and conscious individual, is used to express the views, memories and frequently the style of writing of a dead individual. The notes which fluttered down from the ceiling at the Beaird home are not of the same kind. Here the paper had first to be taken from one place and impressed with pencil writing in the hand of another person before the note itself could be materialized in plain view of witnesses. This is far more complex than merely impressing the muscular apparatus of a human being to write certain words in a certain way.

Why then did the phenomena cease when the Beairds moved from one house to another if the entities expressing themselves through Andy and Mrs. Beaird had not found satisfaction? There was no need for them to simply leave off just because the Beairds moved from one house to the other. There must have been something in the atmosphere of the first house that in combination with the untapped psychic energies of Andy and Mrs. Beaird provided a fertile ground for the phenomena.

Apparently some disturbances have continued in the former Beaird home, while none have been reported by them in their new house. The current owners of the old

Beaird home, however, refused to discuss such matters as psychic phenomena in the house. They are fully convinced that their fundamentalist religion will allow them to take care of these occurrences. To them psychic phenomena *are all the work of the devil.*

And so the devil in Tyler, Texas, may yet erupt once again to engulf a family, if not an entire community, with the strange and frightening goings on which, for three years, plagued the Beaird family to the point of emotional and physical exhaustion. The Beairds themselves are out of danger. Andy has grown up and his untapped powers will unquestionably be used in more constructive channels as the years go by. Mrs. Beaird has assumed her rightful position in her husband's house and has closed the door on her unhappy past. Howard Beaird, the main victim of all the terrible goings on between 1965 and 1968, is satisfied that they are nothing now but memories. He has no desire to bring them back. His sole interest in my publishing an account of these incredible happenings was to inform the public and to help those who might have similar experiences.

✳ 155

Diary of a Poltergeist

PAUL LEUTHOLD IS A MAN in his late forties with a pleasant personality and reasonably good educational background, perhaps better read than most farmers in other countries but, certainly, far from sophistication or knowledgeability in areas of philosophy or the occult. He has a wife and two children—a son, now in his seventeenth year, and a daughter, a few years younger.

Life on the Leuthold farm—a modest-sized establishment consisting of a house, stables, acreage, and perhaps two dozen cattle housed in stables directly across from the farmhouse on a narrow street in the little village of Maschwanden—was normal and routine year after year. That is, until the year 1960 rolled around. In the cold, moist fall of 1960, the Leuthold family and their homestead became the center of a poltergeist case unique in the annals of Swiss psychic research.

The "cast of characters" at the time consisted of Paul Leuthold, forty-eight; Mrs. Leuthold, forty-seven; daughter Elizabeth, ten; son Paul, thirteen; and a maid named Elfi, age eighteen, who was somewhat mentally handicapped, a factor not to be overlooked in cases of this kind. There was also an Italian handyman named Angelo, who was at the farm only a part of the time during which the uncanny happenings took place.

Next door to the Leuthold homestead stands the house of the Eichenberger family. Mr. Eichenberger, fifty, was an active spiritualist, a rarity in Switzerland. His wife, forty-five, is a simple woman without any interest in the subject, and there were four children ranging in age from three to nine years at the time.

At first, the strange events only puzzled the Leuthold family, and they did not suspect that anything unusual was happening. But when no human agency could be found responsible for the moving of objects, disappearances and reappearances and other obviously mischievous actions in and around the house and stables, it dawned on Leuthold that he was the victim of a poltergeist and he began to take notes.

Between November 12, 1960, and August 20, 1961, no less than 104 separate entries were made by him in his "diary of a poltergeist." They were brief, to the point, and without any attempt at a rational explanation. That he left for others to ponder over. His first entry dates from November 12, 1960:

> *November 12, 6 p.m.* The large metal milk can has moved 3 yards to the west. At the same time, stones are thrown against the window—no one there.
> *November 13, 6 p.m.* The milk container with 18 liter milk in it has disappeared. We find it again at a far corner of the stables.
> *November 14, 6 p.m.* Neighbor Eichenberger's umbrella stand disappears and the scraper, usually at the staircase, is found outside against the wall.
> *Same day, half an hour later.* Two boots disappear from the stables and are later found in the feeding area behind the potato rack. Mrs. Eichenberger, the neighbor, brings our pig bucket which she found in the cellar next to their umbrella stand! My wife had fed the pigs barely ten minutes before and left the pig bucket in the stables. How did it get to the cellar?

Every day now, something disappears, moves from its accustomed spot and reappears at a strange place. Such things as milking accessories, very necessary in the daily work of a farmer, are not where they should be and this interrupts the normal life on the farm.

Two bicycles are suddenly without air in their tires. Another inconvenience, since the Swiss use bikes extensively. Most of these events take place around 6 or 7 P.M. Leuthold examined all possibilities of pranksters. His own family and household were always accounted for at the critical times. The village is small and strangers lurking about could not escape attention, certainly not that often.

As I carefully examined the written notes of poltergeistic or other uncanny activities in the Leuthold house, I realized that it was certainly worth looking into. Consequently, I telephoned the farmer and we arranged for a visit the following afternoon. The Swiss television network had evinced great interest in my work, although they had never heard of the Maschwanden case, or, for that matter of any other psychic investigation. It took an American to bring the entire area to their attention and reluctantly Jacob Fischer, the production head, agreed to send a crew with me.

"But we won't pay for this, you understand," he added with careful Swiss frugality.

The next afternoon, my wife and I joined two newsreel reporters, one handling the camera and the other the sound equipment, in a station wagon. We rode along the outskirts of Zurich, over a couple of hills and out into the open country to the west of the city. It took us more than an hour to get to Maschwanden, a village very few people, especially Americans, ever visit. When we reached the Leuthold farmhouse, we were expected. While the television people started to set up their equipment, I lost no time asking Paul Leuthold about the most memorable incident in the haunting of his house.

"My wife and I were inside the house. Suddenly, there was a knock at the door which sounded as if it was made by a hard object. My wife was in the kitchen. She left her work and went to look outside. There was no one outside. Shortly after, there was another knock. The maid was downstairs in her room and she didn't see anyone either. My wife went back to her work. Soon there was a third set of knocks. This time, she was alerted and kept close to the door. As soon as she heard the knocking, she jumped outside."

"Did she see anything or anyone?" I asked.

"She saw a piece of wood, about a yard in length, hitting the ground from a height of about a foot."

"You mean a piece of wood moving through the air by itself?"

"Yes. The wooden stick was there in the air, all by itself. Nobody could have thrown it and run away. It was plain daylight, too."

I examined the wooden stick. It was a heavy piece of wood, weighing perhaps half a pound.

"How did the whole thing get started, Mr. Leuthold?" I asked, and he brought his diary and showed me an entry:

November 18, 5:15 p.m. The cover of the milk can is found inside the barn, on the grassy floor. Fifteen minutes earlier I had left it in place in the stable.

"The next day," he added, "the cover was again found in the ash can."

"Charming," I said. "May I see the book?"

The entries followed each other in the orderly, clinical manner of a medical history. Only, the patient was invisible.

November 19, 5 a.m. I plug in the motor of the cider press and leave it to do my milking chores. Suddenly, there is a singe boot in the middle of the barn. The milking pail floats in the water trough. I decide to check on the cider press. I hear the motor sputtering as I reach the cellar. I find the plug pulled out and the cable pulled back about four yards.

That day was a particularly busy one for the ghost. At 7:30 A.M. Leuthold finished his first meal and returned to the stables.

I turn the light on and fetch a container full of unthrashed corn, which I place inside the barn, in front of the door leading to the stables. Elfi, the maid, is busy washing milking equipment at a considerable distance in the feed kitchen. I leave for a moment to go to the bathroom, when I return, I find the light turned out and the container of unthrashed corn gone. I find it upside down, in the middle of the barn, and next to it, a broom, which had not been there before either.

But that wasn't the end of it by a long shot, that busy morning. Half an hour later Mrs. Leuthold appeared in the barn and asked where his watch was.

"Where it always is," Leuthold replied, somewhat cross, "on the window latch where I always hang it when I clean the cattle."

Not so, his wife replied, and dangled the watch and chain before his eyes. She had just found them in front of the stables on top of a milk can.

That very evening one of their cows was due to give birth. Consequently it was necessary to have all the help available present for the occasion. But the poltergeist was among them.

9 p.m. The following are present to help with the birth: schoolteacher Strickler, Max Studer junior, Werner Siedler, my wife, Elfi the maid, my son Paul and myself are in the stables. The spout of the milking machine disappears under our eyes! We search and finally find it tucked away in the aluminum shelf that holds the rubber nipples. My wife sends Elfi to lock the house while we are all over here. The maid returns, the key is gone. Later we find it on the window sill outside. We had left it in the lock on the *inside*.

By midnight it was all over. The calf had come and the Leutholds went to bed. But the uncanny phenomena did not cease. From the direction of the pigsty there was a loud whistling sound. It changed direction from time to time. There are people in front of the house still up, who hear it too. Elfi, the maid, complains about the noises. The moment she is out of the house, the whistling stops. By 2 A.M., all is finally quiet.

I asked Mr. Leuthold to show me the ash can in which the milk bottle cover was found and the potato bin where it showed up next. The lid of the potato bin weighs perhaps twenty pounds. Anyone placing the aluminum cover of the milk can inside it must have had considerable strength. Two people had to pull it to open it.

All was quiet now for a few days. Then the mysterious events started up again.

December 1, 6:30 p.m. I open the door to the stables to do my milking chores. Everything is normal. My wife arrives a few moments later and opens the same door. This time a hay fork is leaning against it from the outside. "Where is the plate for the cat?" my wife wants to know. "Next to the milk can, as always," I reply. It isn't. My wife finds the plate on top of the refuse. The light goes on and off by itself.

Flickering lights going on and off by their own volition are old stuff with hauntings. In the Rockland County Ghost case in *Ghost Hunter* I reported similar happenings which drove to distraction a certain Broadway composer then guesting at the Danton Walker home.

Evidently, the Swiss ghost had discovered the usefulness of the lights in the stables, for a series of incidents involving the electric installations now followed.

December 2, 5:15 a.m. The light goes out by itself for a short time. The plate for the cat disappears again and is discovered on top of the refuse, like yesterday. I put it back on the refuse. Suddenly, the light goes on by itself in the barn. There is no one there who could have turned it on.

That day turned out rather significantly for the Leutholds, since it brought the first visual phenomena to their tranquil midst. The incident with the knocks at the door and the subsequent discovery by Mrs. Leuthold of the stick of wood suspended in the air, described earlier, took place that day around 10:15 A.M.

Saturdays are usually quiet periods in the small towns and villages of Switzerland. But not this time. Leuthold's diary continues:

December 3, 7:35 a.m. Suddenly the light in the barn goes on. I go to check on it and notice that the light is also on in the hayloft. I turn out both lights and go to the stables. Just then, I clearly hear knocking in the hayloft. I go up to look, but there is nobody there. Since it is getting lighter outside, I turn off the light in the stables, but suddenly it is on again. I am busy distributing the fertilizer. I go inside, turn the light off again. Shortly afterwards it is burning once more. Werner Frei, a tractor driver, was passing by at that time. He saw the light. There was, of course, nobody about who could have done it.
December 4, 8 a.m. The lights go on by themselves in the barn. Elfi is in front of the stables and asks if everything is quiet. It is now 8:30. I reply, in jest, "The

ghost is gone." Within seconds, the light is on again in the stables, although no one could have gotten in to do it.

At one time, four lights were burning simultaneously although no human agency could be held accountable for it. For weeks on end the Leutholds were harassed by the poltergeist's game of turning the lights on.

"Finally I said one day," Leuthold explained, "it is strange that the lights should only go on, but never off by themselves. I had hardly finished when I stood in total darkness in the stables—the light had been turned off."

"As if the ghost were listening?" I said.

Leuthold nodded and smiled somewhat sheepishly. "But it really got worse later in the week," he said, and showed me the entry for the eighth of December.

December 8, 7:40 a.m. Elfi goes to feed the chickens, but the pot containing the chicken feed is gone. She finally finds it in front of the barn door. Six pumpkins, used for decorative purposes, are scattered around the yard. The rabbit hutch is open and two rabbits are running around outside. The feed tray for the rabbits has disappeared. It is later discovered by my wife on a cart in the carriage house.

Evidently, the ghost had it in for the domestic animals as well as the people. The following day, matters got even worse.

December 9, 7:30 a.m. The pot with the chicken feed is gone again. The plate for the cat is again on top of the refuse heap. Elfi prepares new chicken feed in another pot, puts it down for a moment on the stairs and goes into the kitchen. When she gets back just seconds later, the new chicken feed is also gone. She comes to tell me about it. I go back with her and find the chicken feed hidden behind the stairs, covered with a burlap bag.

The Leutholds were beginning to get furious. Mrs. Leuthold decided to trap the furtive ghost. She put the chicken-feed pot onto the window sill near the house door, and tied a nylon string to it, with a small bell at the other end, putting it down in the corridor leading away from the entrance door. That way they thought they would hear any movements the pot might make.

By 9:30 A.M. the pot had moved twice in both directions, yet no human agency could be discovered!

That very afternoon the poltergeist played a new kind of trick on them. When Mrs. Leuthold entered the barn around 2 P.M., she found all sorts of boots scattered around, and in one of them four receipts for cattle, which Mr. Leuthold distinctly remembered to have placed high on a shelf that very morning. The ghost stepped up its activities in the following days, it seems. Not content with moving objects when nobody was looking, it now moved them in the presence of people.

December 10, 9:30 a.m. The light goes on by itself in the hayloft. The missing pot for chicken feed is finally found near the door of the old stables. 6:30 P.M. the light goes on in the barn, nobody is there. I put it out just as Elfi enters and tells me the milking brush is gone. We look everywhere, without success. Just then I notice the umbrella which is usually found in front of the house door hanging from the window sill of the pigsty! Elfi takes it down and replaces it next to the entrance door of the house, and we continue our search for the milking brush. Suddenly, the umbrella lies in front of us on the ground near the old stables! Three times the lights in the barn go on and I have to put them out. There is, of course, nobody in there at the time.

Whatever happened to the missing milking brush, you'll wonder. The next morning, a Sunday too, Mrs. Leuthold was doing her chore of feeding the pigs. In one of the feed bags she felt something hard and firm that did not feel like pig's feed. You guessed it. It was the milking brush. The Leutholds were glad to have their brush back, but their joy was marred by the disappearance of the chicken-feed pot. If it wasn't the pigs, it was the chickens the ghost had it in for!

"I remember that morning well," Mr. Leuthold said grimly. "I was standing in the stables around quarter to eight, when the light went out and on again and a moment later something knocked loudly in the hayloft, while at the same moment the light went on in the barn! I didn't know where to run first to check."

Those who suspected the somewhat simple maid, Elfi, to be causing these pranks did not realize that she was certainly not consciously contributing to them. She herself was the victim along with others in the house.

On the 12th of December, for instance, she put the milk cart into a corner of the barn where it usually stood. A few minutes later, however, she found it in front of the chicken house.

That same day, Paul Leuthold again came to grips with the ghost. "It was 9:15 in the morning and I walked up the stairs. Suddenly the window banged shut in the fruit-storage room ahead of me. There was no draft, no movement of air whatsoever."

"Your wife mentioned something about the disappearing applesauce," I said. "This sounds intriguing. What happened?"

"On December 13th," Leuthold replied, refreshing his memory from his diary, "my wife put a dish of hot applesauce on the window sill next to the house door, to cool it off. I came home from the fields around 4:30 in the afternoon and to my amazement saw a dish of applesauce on the sill of the old stable, across the yard from the house. I went to the kitchen and asked Elfi where they had put the applesauce. 'Why, on the kitchen window, of course.' Silently I showed her where it now was. Shaking her head, she took it and put it back on the kitchen window sill. A few minutes later, we checked to see if it was still there. It

was, but had moved about a foot away from the spot where we had placed it."

That, however, was only the beginning. All day long "things" kept happening. Parts of the milking machine disappeared and reappeared in odd places. Lights went on and off seemingly without human hands touching the switches. These switches incidentally are large, black porcelain light switches mounted at shoulder height on the walls of the buildings, and there is no other way of turning lights on or off individually.

At 7:45 P.M., dinner time, the entire family and servants were in the main room of the house. The barns and other buildings were securely locked. Suddenly, the lights in the barn and chicken house went on by themselves. The following morning, auditory phenomena joined the long list of uncanny happenings.

December 14, 6:50 a.m. As I leave the chicken house I clearly hear a bell, striking and lingering on for about half a minute, coming from the direction of the other barn. But, of course, there was no bell there.

"This is going too far," Mrs. Leuthold remarked to her husband. "We've got to do something about this."

She took the chicken-feed pot and placed it again on the stairs from where it had disappeared some days before. Then she tied a nylon string to the pot, with a small bell on the other end; the string she placed inside the corridor leading to the door and almost but not quite closed the door. In this manner the string could be moved freely should anyone pull on it.

The family then ate their breakfast. After ten minutes, they checked on the string. It had been pulled outside by at least a foot and was cut or torn about two inches from the pot. The pot itself stood one step below the one on which Mrs. Leuthold had placed it!

Once in a while the ghost was obliging: that same day, around 8 A.M., Elfi, the maid, took a lumber bucket to fetch some wood. As she crossed by the rabbit hutch, lights went on in the cellar, the hayloft and the chicken house. Quickly Elfi put the bucket down to investigate. When she returned to pick it up again, it was gone. It was standing in front of the wood pile, some distance away— where it was needed!

Daughter Elizabeth also had her share of experiences, Leuthold reports:

December 14, 5:30 p.m. Elizabeth is busy upstairs in the house. She hears something hit the ground outside. Immediately she runs downstairs to find the six ornamental pumpkins scattered around the yard, all the way to the pigsty. When she left the house again an hour later, she found that somehow the carpet beater and brush had found their way from inside the house to be hung on the outside of the door!

And so it went. Every day something else moved about. The chicken-feed pot, or the boots, or the milk can. The lights kept going on and off merrily. Something or someone knocks at the door, yet there is never anyone outside. Nobody can knock and run out of sight—the yard between house and barn and the village street can easily be checked for human visitors. The milk cart disappears and reappears. The washroom window is taken off its hinges and thrown on the floor. The manure rake moves from the front of the barn to the inside of the washroom. The pigsty gate is opened by unseen hands and the pigs promenade around the chicken house. Lights keep going on and off. Even Christmas did not halt the goings on.

December 24, 3 p.m. My cousin Ernest Gautschi and I are talking in the stables, when suddenly the light goes on—in the middle of the afternoon. 5:30 P.M. I enter the barn to give the cows their hay, when I notice the lights go on by themselves in the old barn. I go back immediately and find the dog howling pitifully at the light switch! I went on to the house to see if anyone was outside, but nobody left even for a moment. My son, Paul, returns with me to the barn. It was he who had left the dog tied up outside half an hour earlier. Now he is tied up inside the barn, and the barn door is locked tight. How did the dog get inside?

Evidently, the poltergeist had now begun to turn his attentions towards the dog.

December 25, 7:30 a.m. The dog is found locked into the stables. Yet, half an hour ago Elfi left him roaming freely outside after giving him his food.
February 2, 5 a.m. I went to the stables and the dog, which slept in the barn, followed me into the stables. He became noisy and one of the calves seemed to get frightened, so I said to the dog, "Go outside at once!" As I am turning around to open the door back into the barn for him to let him out, I see him already outside the barn. Who opened the door for him? I didn't.

The children also got their attention from the obnoxious spirit. That same day, February 2, Leuthold reported in his diary:

February 2, 6:15 p.m. The three sleds, which normally are stacked in the corner of the barn, are found across the manure trough.

The Leutholds took their unseen "visitor" in stride, always hoping it would go away as it had come. Their spiritualist neighbor insisted that "Leo the Ghost," as they had dubbed it, was somehow connected with Elfi, a notion the Leutholds rejected instantly, since they were in an excellent position to vouch for the maid's honesty and non-involvement. The phenomena continued unabated.

March 14, 6 a.m. The window in the dining room is taken from its hinges and found in a flower pot in front of the house. 7:30 A.M. My slipper disappears from the barn and reappears in another part of the stables beneath a shoe shelf.
March 29, 7:30 a.m. The dog lies in the yard. A few minutes later he is locked into the old stables. Everybody in the house is questioned and accounted for. Nobody could have done it. 7 P.M. Elfi and I empty the skimmed milk into four pails which we then place next to the door to the pigsty. At 9 P.M. we find the four pails directly in front of the door.

Elfi got married in April and presumably her "uncommitted" vital energies were no longer free to be used in poltergeist activities. But the Maschwanden ghost did not obey the standard rules laid down by psychic researchers. The disturbances went on, Elfi or no Elfi.

August 9, morning. As I clean my boots, I find below the inner sole a small tie pin which I had missed for three months.
August 10, 5:30 p.m. A pitchfork is left stuck in a bag of mineral salt. It took two men to pull it out. Half an hour before the same fork was still in the barn.
August 19, 4:45 a.m. Angelo, the Italian working for us, misses one of his boots. He finds it 3 yards distant inside the barn and a heavy pitchfork on top of it.

Similar events took place for another few weeks, then it gradually became quiet again around the Leuthold farm.

I looked around the house, the stables, the barn. I talked to all members of the family, except the Italian, who had only shared their lives briefly, and Elfi, who had left long ago for wedded bliss.

I asked, "Did anyone die violently in the house?"

Paul Leuthold Sr., thought for a moment. "About ten years ago we had an Italian working for us. His pride was a motorcycle, but he could not afford insurance. One day he decided to return to Italy with some friends for a vacation. To get an early start, they would leave around three in the morning. The night before my mother warned him, 'Be careful, and don't get home with your head under your arm.' He replied, shrugging, 'If I am dead, it doesn't matter either.'

"He started an hour late the next morning. When he got to the St. Gotthard, his motorcycle started to kick up. The other fellows went on ahead and promised to wait for him at the height of the mountain. He went to a garage and had his machine fixed, determined not to miss his colleagues. He would have been better off had he stayed behind, for a short time later a piece of rock fell down onto the road and killed him instantly."

"And you think it may be his ghost that is causing all this?" I asked.

"No, I don't," Leuthold assured me. "I'm only wondering who is doing it."

I gathered that Leuthold had some suspicions about his neighbors. Could an active spiritualist "cause" such phenomena to happen? Not a spiritualist, I assured him, but maybe a black magician.

Nobody had died violently in the house or farm. But then, an older house of which we know nothing may have stood on the spot. The Leuthold children are now beyond the age of puberty where their untapped energies might have contributed the power to make the phenomena occur.

My guess is that both Elfi and the children supplied that energy. When Elfi left, and only the children were available, the phenomena gradually faded away. They have not returned since. They are not likely to, unless, of course, another unwitting supplier of such energy moves into the house. The discarnate personality behind the disturbances may still be lurking about, untamed, waiting for another chance. If this happens, Mr. Leuthold can bet that the Ghost Hunter will be on hand, too!

✳ 156

The Millbrae Poltergeist Case

One wouldn't think a spanking, modern home perched on a hill at Millbrae, a sunny little town outside San Francisco, could harbor a poltergeist case, one of those sinister disturbances, usually Germanic, involving a teenager or otherwise emotionally unabsorbed person in the household of the living. The youngster is not playing any pranks; the youngster is being used to play them with, by a disturbed person no longer in possession of a physical body.

I heard of the Millbrae case from a young girl who used to live in that house before she decided she was old enough to have a place of her own and consequently moved out to a nearby town called Burlingame. Now twenty, Jean Grasso has a high school education and a big curiosity about things she cannot explain. Such as ESP.

In 1964, she had an experience that particularly upset her because it did not fit in with the usual experiences of life she had been taught in school.

She was in bed at the time, just before falling asleep, or, as she puts it so poetically, "just before the void of sleep engulfs you." Miss Grasso is not at a loss for words. Her world is very real to her and has little or no room for fantasies.

Still, there it was. Something prevented her from giving in to sleep. Before she knew what she was doing, she saw her own bare feet moving across the floor of her bedroom; she grabbed the telephone receiver and blurted into it—"Jeannie, what's wrong? Did you get hurt?" The telephone had *not* rung. Yet her best friend, who was almost like a sister to her, was on the line. She had been in an automobile accident in which she had been run off the road and collided with a steel pole, but except for being shook up, she was all right.

What made Jean Grasso jump out of a warm bed to answer a phone that had not yet rung, to speak by name to someone who had not yet said "hello," and to inquire about an accident that no one had told her about as yet?

The dark-haired woman is of Italian and Greek background and works as the local representative of a milk company. She is neither brooding nor particularly emotional, it seemed to me, and far from hysterical. The uncanny things that happened in her life intrigued her more in an intellectual way than in an emotional, fearful way.

When she was sixteen, she and five other girls were playing the popular parlor game of the Ouija board in one of the bedrooms. Jean and Michele di Giovanni, one of the girls, were working the board when it started to move as if pushed by some force stronger than themselves.

Still very skeptical about Ouija boards, Jean demanded some sign or proof of a spiritual presence. She got a quick reply: four loud knocks on the wall. There was nobody in back of the walls who could have caused them. Suddenly, the room got very cold, and they panicked and called the "séance" off then and there.

Ever since, she has heard uncanny noises in her parents' house. These have ranged from footsteps to crashing sounds as if someone or something were thrown against a wall or onto the floor. There never was a rational explanation for these sounds.

After Jean moved out to her own place in Burlingame, she returned home for occasional weekends to be with her mother. Her mother sleeps in the living-dining room area upstairs, to save her the trouble of walking up and down the stairs to the bedroom level, since she has a heart condition.

On the occasions when Jean spent a weekend at home, she would sleep in her mother's former bedroom, situated directly underneath the one fixed for her on the upper level.

One night, as Jean lay awake in bed, she heard footsteps overhead. They walked across the ceiling, "as if they had no place to go."

Thinking that her mother had breathing difficulties, she raced upstairs, but found her mother fast asleep in bed. Moreover, when questioned about the footsteps the next morning, she assured her daughter she had heard nothing.

The Millbrae Poltergeist Case—The owner's daughter surrounded by psychic mist

"Were they a man's footsteps or a woman's?" I asked Jean Grasso when we discussed this after the investigation was over.

"A man's," she replied without hesitation.

Once in a while when she is in the dining area upstairs, she will see something out of the corner of an eye —a flash—something or somebody moving about—and as soon as she concentrates on it, it is not there. She has chalked all that up to her imagination, of course.

"When I'm coming down the steps, in the hall, I get a chill up my spine," the girl said, "as if I didn't want to continue on. My mother gets the same feelings there, too, I recently discovered."

That was the spot where my psychic photograph was taken, I later realized. Did these two psychic people, mother and daughter, act like living cameras?

"Do you ever have a feeling of a presence with you when you are all alone?"

"Yes, in my mother's bedroom, I feel someone is watching me and I turn but there's no one there."

I questioned her about the garden and the area around the basement. Jean confessed she did not go there often since the garden gave her an uneasy feeling. She avoided it whenever she could for no reason she could logically explain.

One night when she spent the weekend at her parents' house and was just falling asleep a little after midnight, she was awakened by the sound of distant voices. The murmur of the voices was clear enough but when she sat up to listen further, they went away. She went back to

sleep, blaming her imagination for the incident. But a week later, to the day, her incipient sleep was again interrupted by the sound of a human voice. This time it was a little girl's or a woman's voice crying out, *"Help . . . help me!"*

She jumped up so fast she could hear her heartbeat in her ears. Surely, her mother had called her. Then she remembered that her mother had gone to Santa Cruz. There was nobody in the house who could have called for help. She looked outside. It was way after midnight and the surrounding houses were all dark. But the voice she had just heard had not come from the outside. It was there, right in the haunted room with her!

I decided to interview Jean's mother, Mrs. Adriana Grasso, a calm pleasant woman whose skepticism in psychic matters has always been pretty strong.

"We've had this house since 1957," she explained, "but it was already five years old when we bought it. The previous owners were named Stovell and they were about to lose it when we bought it. I know nothing about them beyond that."

The very first night she went to bed in the house, something tried to prevent her from doing so. Something kept pushing her back up. On the first landing of the stairs leading down to the bedroom level, something kept her from continuing on down. She decided to fight it out. Every time after that first experience she had the same impression—that she really *shouldn't* be coming downstairs!

"I hear footsteps upstairs when I'm downstairs and I hear footsteps downstairs when I'm upstairs, and there never is anyone there causing them," she complained.

On several occasions, she awoke screaming, which brought her daughter running in anxiously. To calm her, she assured her she had had a nightmare. But it was not true. On several different occasions, she felt something grabbing her and trying to crush her bones. Something held her arms pinned down. Finally, she had to sleep with the lights on, and it seemed to help.

A big crash also made the family wonder what was wrong with their house. Mrs. Grasso heard it *upstairs* and her son Allen, upstairs at the same time, thought it was *downstairs*—only to discover that it was neither here nor there!

"Many times the doorbell would ring and there was no one outside," Mrs. Grasso added, "but I always assumed it was the children of the neighborhood, playing tricks on us."

Loud noises as if a heavy object had fallen brought her into the garage to investigate, but nothing had fallen, nothing was out of place. The garage was locked and so was the front door. Nobody had gotten in. And yet the noises continued; only three days before our arrival, Mrs. Grasso awoke around one in the morning to the sound of "someone opening a can in the bathroom," a metal container. In addition, there was thumping. She thought, why is my son working on his movies at this hour of the night? She assumed the can-opening noises referred to motion picture film cans, of which her son has many. But he had done nothing of the sort.

Soon even Allen and Mr. Grasso heard the loud crashes, although they were unwilling to concede that it represented anything uncanny. But the family that hears ghosts together, also finds solutions together—and the Grassos were not particularly panicky about the whole thing. Just curious.

It was at this point that I decided to investigate the case and I so advised Jean Grasso, who greeted us at the door of her parents' house on a very warm day in October 1966. In addition to Sybil and my wife Catherine, two friends, Lori Clerf and Bill Wynn, were with us. We had Lori's car and Bill was doing the driving.

We entered the house and immediately I asked Sybil for her psychic impressions. She had not had a chance to orient herself nor did I allow her to meet the Grassos officially. Whatever she might "get" now would therefore not be colored by any rational impressions of the people she met or the house she was in.

"There is something peculiar about the lower portion of the house." Sybil began, referring to the bedroom floor. The house *was* built in a most peculiar manner. Because the lot was sloping toward a ravine, the top floor reached to street level on the front side of the house only. It was here that the house had its living room and entrance hall. On the floor below were the bedrooms, and finally, a garage and adjoining work room. Underneath was a basement, which, however, led to ground level in the rear, where it touched the bottom of the ravine.

At this point, however, Sybil and I did not even know if there was a lower portion to the house, but Jean Grasso assured us there was. We immediately descended the stairs into the section Sybil had felt invaded by psychic influences.

We stopped at the northeast corner of the bedroom floor where a rear entrance to the house was also situated, leading to a closed-in porch whence one could descend to the ground level outside by wooden stairs.

"What do you feel here, Sybil?" I asked, for I noticed she was getting on to something.

"Whatever I feel is below this spot," she commented. "It must have come from the old foundations, from the land."

Never let it be said that a ghost hunter shies away from dusty basements. Down we went, with Catherine carrying the tape recorder and one of the cameras. In the basement we could not stand entirely upright—at least I couldn't.

"That goes underneath the corridor, doesn't it?" Sybil said as if she knew.

"That's right," Jean Grasso confirmed.

"Somebody was chased here," Sybil commented now, "two men...an accident that should never have happened...someone died here... *a case of mistaken identity.*"

"Can you get more?" I urged her.

The staircase and psychic mist

"There is a lingering feeling of a man," Sybil intoned. "He is the victim. He was not the person concerned. He was running from the water's edge to a higher part of land. He was a fugitive."

Anyone coming from the San Francisco waterfront would be coming up here to higher ground.

"Whom was he running from?"

"The Law...I feel uniforms. There is an element of supposed justice in it, but...."

"How long ago was he killed?"

"1884."

"His name?"

"Wasserman...that's how I get it. I feel the influence of his last moments here, but not his body. He wants us to know he was Wasserman but not the Wasserman wanted by the man."

"What does he look like to you?"

"Ruddy face, peculiarly deep eyes...he's here but not particularly cooperative."

"Does he know he is *dead?*" I asked.

"I don't think he knows that. But he notices *me.*"

I asked Sybil to convey the message that we knew he was innocent.

"Two names I have to get," Sybil insisted and started to spell, "Pottrene...P-o-t-t-r-e-n-e...Wasserman tells me these names...P-o-v-e-y...Povey...he says to find them ...these people are the men who killed him."

"How was he killed?"

"They *had* to kill him. They thought that he was someone else."

"What was the other one wanted for?"

"He doesn't know. He was unfortunate to have been here."

"What is his first name?"

"Jan. J-a-n."

Upon my prodding, Sybil elicited also the information that this Jan Wasserman was a native of San Francisco, that his father's name was Johan or John, and he lived at 324 Emil Street.

I proceeded then to exorcise the ghost in my usual manner, speaking gently of the "other side" and what awaited him there.

Sybil conveyed my wishes to the restless one and reported that he understood his situation now.

"He's no trouble," Sybil murmured. She's very sympathetic to ghosts.

With that we left the basement and went back up the stairs into the haunted bedroom, where I took some photographs; then I moved into the living room area upstairs and took some more—all in all about a dozen black-and-white photographs, including some of the garage and stairs.

Imagine my pleased reaction when I discovered a week later, when the film came back from the laboratory, that two of the photographs had psychic material on them. One, taken of the stairs leading from the bedroom floor to the top floor, shows a whitish substance like a dense fog filling the front right half of my picture. The other remarkable photograph taken of Mrs. Grasso leaning against the wall in the adjoining room shows a similar substance with mirror effect, covering the front third of the area of the picture.

There is a reflection of a head and shoulders of a figure which at first glance I took to be Mrs. Grasso's. On close inspection, however, it is quite dissimilar and shows rather a heavy head of hair whereas Mrs. Grasso's hairdo is close to the head. Mrs. Grasso wears a dark housecoat over a light dress but the image shows a woman or girl wearing a dark dress or sweater over a white blouse.

I asked Jean Grasso to report to me any changes in the house after our visit.

On November 21, 1966, I heard from her again. The footsteps were gone all right, but there was still something strange going on in the house. Could there have been *two* ghosts?

Loud crashing noises, the slamming of doors, noises similar to the thumping of ash cans when no sensible reason exists for the noises have been observed not only by Jean Grasso and her mother since we were there, but also by her brother and his fiancée and even the non-believing father. No part of the house seems to be immune from the disturbance.

To test things, Jean Grasso slept at her mother's house soon after we left. At 11 P.M., the thumping started. About the same time Mrs. Grasso was awakened by three knocks under her pillow. These were followed almost

immediately by the sound of thumping downstairs and movements of a heavy metallic can.

Before I could answer Jean, I had another report from her. Things were far from quiet at the house in Millbrae. Her brother's fiancée, Ellen, was washing clothes in the washing machine. She had closed and secured the door so that the noise would not disturb her intended, who was asleep in the bedroom situated next to the laundry room.

Suddenly she distinctly heard someone trying to get into the room by force, and then she felt a "presence" with her which caused her to run upstairs in panic.

About the same time, Jean and her mother had heard a strange noise from the bathroom below the floor they were then on. Jean went downstairs and found a brush on the tile floor of the bathroom. Nobody had been downstairs at the time. The brush had fallen by itself...into the middle of the floor.

When a picture in brother Allen's room lost its customary place on the wall, the thumb tack holding it up disappeared, and the picture itself somehow got to the other side of his bookcase. The frame is pretty heavy, and had the picture just fallen off it would have landed on the floor behind the bookcase; instead it was neatly leaning against the wall on top of it. This unnerved the young man somewhat, as he had not really accepted the possibility of the uncanny up to this point, even though he had witnessed some pretty unusual things himself.

Meanwhile, Jean Grasso managed to plow through the microfilm files at the San Mateo county library in Belmont. There was nothing of interest in the newspapers for 1884, but the files were far from complete.

However, in another newspaper of the area, the *Redwood City Gazette*, there was an entry that Jean Grasso thought worth passing on for my opinion. A captain Watterman is mentioned in a brief piece, and the fact the townspeople are glad that his bill had died and they could be well rid of it.

The possibility that Sybil heard Wasserman when the name was actually Watterman was not to be dismissed—at least not until a Jan Wasserman could be identified from the records somewhere.

Since the year 1884 had been mentioned by the ghost, I looked up that year in H.H. Bancroft's *History of California*, an imposing record of that state's history published in 1890 in San Francisco.

In Volume VII, on pages 434 and 435, I learned that there had been great irregularities during the election of 1884 and political conditions bordered on anarchy. The man who had been first Lieutenant Governor and later Governor of the state was named R.W. Waterman!

This, of course, may only be conjecture and not correct. Perhaps she really did mean Wasserman with two "S's." But my search in the San Francisco Directory (Langley's) for 1882 and 1884 did not yield any Jan Wasserman. The 1881 Langley did, however, list an Ernst Wassermann, a partner in Wassermann brothers. He was located at 24th Street and *Potrero Avenue*.

Sybil reported that Wasserman had been killed by a certain Pottrene and a certain Povey. Pottrene as a name does not appear anywhere. Could she have meant Potrero? The name Povey, equally unusual, does, however, appear in the 1902 Langley on page 1416.

A Francis J. Povey was a foreman at Kast & Company and lived at 1 Beideman Street. It seems rather amazing that Sybil Leek would come up with such an unusual name as Povey, even if this is not the right Povey in our case. Wasserman claimed to have lived on Emil Street. There was no such street in San Francisco. There was, however, an Emma Street, listed by Langley in 1884 (page 118).

The city directories available to me are in shambles and plowing through them is a costly and difficult task. There are other works that might yield clues to the identity of our man. It is perhaps unfortunate that my setup does not allow for capable research assistants to help with so monumental a task, and that the occasional exact corroboration of ghostly statements is due more to good luck than to complete coverage of all cases brought to me.

Fortunately, the liberated ghosts do not really care. They know the truth already.

But I was destined to hear further from the Grasso residence.

On January 24, 1967, all was well. Except for one thing, and that really happened back on Christmas Eve.

Jean's sister-in-law was sleeping on the couch upstairs in the living room. It was around two in the morning, and she could not drop off to sleep, because she had taken too much coffee. While she was lying there, wide awake, she suddenly noticed the tall, muscular figure of a man, somewhat shadowy, coming over from the top of the stairs to the Christmas tree as if to inspect the gifts placed near it. At first she thought it was Jean's brother, but as she focused on the figure, she began to realize it was nobody of flesh-and-blood. She noticed his face now, and that it was bearded. When it dawned on her what she was seeing, and she began to react, the stranger just vanished from the spot where he had been standing a moment before. Had he come to say good-bye and had the Christmas tree evoked a long-ago Christmas holiday of his own?

Before the sister-in-law, Ellen, could tell Jean Grasso about her uncanny experience, Jean herself asked if she had heard the footsteps that kept *her* awake overhead that night. They compared the time, and it appeared that the footsteps and the apparition occurred in about the same time period.

For a few days all was quiet, as if the ghost were thinking it over. But then the pacing resumed, more furiously now, perhaps because something within him had been aroused and he was beginning to understand his position.

At this point everybody in the family heard the attention-getting noises. Mrs. Grasso decided to address the intruder and to tell him that I would correct the record of his death—that I would tell the world that he was not, after all, a bad fellow, but a case of mistaken identity.

It must have pleased the unseen visitor, for things began to quiet down again, and as of February 6, at least, the house had settled down to an ordinary suburban existence on the outskirts of bustling San Francisco.

But until this book is in print, the Grassos won't breathe with complete ease. There is always that chance that the ghost decides I am not telling the world fast enough. But that would seem patently unreasonable. After all, he had to wait an awfully long time before we took notice of him. And I've jumped several ghosts to get him into print as an emergency case. So be it: Mr. Wasserman of Millbrae is not *the* Mr. Wasserman they were looking for, whoever they were. They just had themselves a wild ghost chase for nothing.

✳ 157

The Ghosts of Barbery Lane

"I KNOW A HOUSE IN RYE, New York, with a ghost," painter Mary Melikian said to me, and there was pleasure in her voice at being the harbinger of good news. Mary knew how eager I was to find a haunted house, preferably one that was still haunted.

"A ghost," Mary repeated and added, tantalizingly, "a ghost that *likes to slam doors*."

I pumped Mary for details. One of her friends was the celebrated portrait painter Molly Guion, known in Rye as Mrs. John Smythe. Molly and her husband, an architect, lived in a sprawling mid-nineteenth-century house atop a bluff overlooking the old New Haven Railroad bed, surrounded by houses built in later years. The Smythes house was the first one on the tract, the original Manor House, built there around 1860 by one Jared B. Peck.

I arranged with Mrs. Smythe to visit the house the following week, in August 1963. My wife Catherine and I were met at the train by Mrs. Smythe, whose husband also came along to welcome us. The drive to the house (originally called "The Cedars" but now only known as a number on Barbery Lane) took less than five minutes, yet you might well have entered another world—so serene and rural was the atmosphere that greeted us that moonlit evening, when the station wagon pulled up to the gleaming-white 100-year-old house the Smythes had called home since the summer of 1957.

Rising to four floors, the structure reminded me of the stylized paintings of Victorian houses associated with another world. A wide porch went around it at the ground level, and shady trees protected it from view and intrusion.

The huge living room was tastefully furnished with fine antiques and all over the house we encountered the marvelously alive portraits painted by Molly Guion, which blended naturally into the decor of the house. This was a stately mansion, only an hour from New York but as quiet and removed from the city of subways as if it stood in the Deep South or Down East. We seated ourselves comfortably. Then I came right to the point.

"This ghost," I began. "What exactly does it do and when did you first notice anything unusual in the house?"

This is my standard opener. Molly Guion was more than happy to tell us everything. Her husband left for a while to tend to some chores.

"We arrived in this house on a hot summer day in 1957—in July," she recalled. "About a week later—I remember it was a particularly hot night—we heard a door slam. Both my husband and I heard it."

"Well?"

"But there was absolutely nobody in the house at the time except us," Molly said, significantly. "We heard it many times after that. Maybe six or seven separate instances. Once around 10 o'clock at night I heard the front door open and close again with a characteristic squeak. Mother was living with us then and I was not feeling well, so that a nurse was staying with me. I called out 'Mother,' thinking she had come home a bit early, but there was no reply. Since then I've heard the front door open many times, but there is never anyone there."

"Is it the front door then?"

"No, not always. Sometimes it is the front door and sometimes it is this door on the second floor. Come, I'll show you."

Molly led us up the winding stairs to a second floor containing many small rooms, all exquisitely furnished with the solid furniture of the Victorian period. There was a tiny room on one side of the corridor leading to the rear of the house, and across from it, the door that was heard to slam. It was a heavy wooden door, leading to a narrow winding staircase which in turn led up another flight of stairs to the third floor. Here Molly Guion had built herself a magnificent studio, taking up most of the floor space.

"One day in January of 1962," she volunteered, "I was downstairs in the kitchen talking to an exterminator, when I heard a door slam hard—it seemed to me. Yet, there was no one in the house at the time, only we two downstairs."

"Outside of yourself and your husband, has anyone else heard these uncanny noises?"

Molly nodded quickly.

"There was this man that worked for me. He said, 'Mrs. Smythe, ever time I'm alone in the house, I hear a door slam!'"

"Anyone else?"

"A Scottish cleaning woman, name of Roberta Gillan. She lives in Harrison, New York. She once came to me and said, 'Did you just slam a door?' Of course, I hadn't."

We were now seated in a small room off the second-floor corridor. The light was moody and the air dank. There was a quietness around the house so heavy I almost *wished* I could hear a door slam. Molly had more to reveal.

"Once, a little girl named Andree, age eleven, came to visit us and within seconds exclaimed—'Mamma, there is a ghost in this house!'"

Our hostess admitted to being somewhat psychic, with sometimes comical results. Years ago, when a boyfriend had failed to keep their date, she saw him clearly in a dream-vision with a certain blonde girl. He later explained his absence in a casual way, but she nailed him with a description of his blonde—and he confessed the truth.

Two years after she moved into the house, Molly developed a case of asthma, the kind very old people sometimes suffer from. Strangely, it bothered her only in certain rooms and not at all in others. It started like a kind of allergy, and gradually worsened until it became a fully grown asthmatic condition. Although two rooms were side by side, sleeping in one would aggravate the condition, but sleeping in the other made her completely free of it!

"Did you hear any other noises—I mean, outside of the door slamming?" I asked.

"Yes. Not so long ago we had a dinner party here, and among the guests was a John Gardner, a vice president of the Bankers Trust Company."

Suddenly she had heard someone rap at the window of the big room downstairs. They tried to ignore the noise, but Gardner heard it too.

"Is someone rapping at your window?" he inquired.

He was assured it was nothing. Later he took Molly aside and remonstrated with her. "I distinctly heard the raps," he said. Molly just smiled.

Finally the Smythes called on the American Society for Psychic Research to find an explanation for all these goings-on. But the Society was in no hurry to do anything about the case. They suggested Molly write them a letter, which she did, but they still took no action.

I thoroughly inspected the premises—walked up the narrow staircase into Molly Guion's studio where some of the best portrait oils hung. Her paintings of famous Britons had just toured as an exhibition and the house was full of those she owned (the greater part of her work was commissioned and scattered in collections, museums, and private homes).

There was a tiny bedroom next to the landing in back of the studio, evidently a servant's room, since the entire floor had originally been servants' quarters. The house had sixteen rooms in all.

By now Mr. Smythe had joined us and I explained my mission. Had he ever noticed anything unusual about the house?

"Oh yes," he volunteered, speaking slowly and deliberately. "There are all sorts of noises in this house and they're not ordinary noises—I mean, the kind you can *explain*."

"For instance?"

"I was sleeping up here one night in the little bedroom here," he said, pointing to the servant's room in back of the landing, "when I heard footsteps. They were the steps of an older person."

But there was no one about, he asserted.

Jared Peck, who built the house in 1860, died in 1895, and the house passed into the hands of his estate to be rented to various tenants. In 1910, Stuyvesant Wainwright bought the property. In the following year, his ex-wife, now Mrs. Catlin, bought it from him and lived in it until her death in the 1920s.

The former Mrs. Wainwright turned out to be a colorful person. Born wealthy, she had a very short temper and the servants never stayed long in her house.

"She certainly liked to slam doors," Mr. Smythe observed. "I mean she was the kind of person who would do that sort of thing."

"One day she became very ill and everybody thought she would die," Molly related. "There she was stretched out on this very couch and the doctor felt free to talk about her condition. 'She won't last much longer,' he said, and shrugged. Mrs. Wainwright sat up with a angry jolt and barked, 'I intend to!' And she did, for many more years of hot-tempered shenanigans."

In her later years Mrs. Wainwright moved to the former servants' quarters on the second floor—whether out of economy or for reasons of privacy no one knows for sure. The *slamming door* was right in the heart of her rooms and no doubt she traveled up those narrow stairs to the floor above many times.

The plumber, painter, and carpenter who worked for Mrs. Wainwright were still living in Rye and they all remembered her as a willful and headstrong woman who liked to have her own way. Her granddaughter, Mrs. Condit, recalled her vividly. The Smythes were pretty sure that Mrs. Wainwright slept up there on the second floor—they found a screen marked "My bedroom window" that fit no other window in any of the rooms.

The Smythes acquired the handsome house from the next owner, one Arthur Flemming, who used Mrs. Wainwright's old room. But he didn't experience anything unusual, or at any rate said nothing about it.

There was a big theft once in the house and Mrs. Wainwright may have been worried about it. Strongly

attached to worldly possessions, she kept valuables in various trunks on the third floor, and ran up to look at them from time to time to make sure everything was still there.

Could the slamming of the door be a re-enactment of these frequent nervous expeditions up the stairs? Could the opening and closing of the entrance door be a fearful examination of the door to see if the lock was secure, or if there was anyone strange lurking about outside?

The very day after our visit to this haunted house, a young painter friend of Molly's named Helen Charleton, of Bronxville, New York, was alone in the studio that Molly let her use occasionally to do some painting of her own. She was quite alone in the big house when she clearly heard the front door open. Calling out, she received no answer. Thinking that the gardener might have a key, and that she might be in danger, she took hold of what heavy objects she could put her hands on and waited anxiously for the steps that were sure to resound any moment. No steps came. An hour later, the doorbell rang and she finally dashed down to the entrance door. *The door was tightly shut*, and no one was about. Yet she *had* heard the characteristic noise of the opening of the old-fashioned door!

The mailman's truck was just pulling away, so she assumed it was he who had rung the bell. Just then Molly returned.

"I've heard the door slam many times," Helen Charleton said to me, "and it always sounds so far away. I think it's on the first floor, but I can't be sure."

Was Mrs. Wainwright still walking the Victorian corridors of "The Cedars," guarding her treasures upstairs?

When Catherine and I returned from Europe in the fall of 1964, Molly Guion had news for us. All was far from quiet in Rye. In the upstairs room where Molly's physically challenged mother was bedridden, a knob had flown off a table while Mrs. Guion stood next to it. In the presence of a nurse, the bathroom lights had gone on and off by themselves. More sinister, a heavy ashtray had taken off on its own to sail clear across the room. A door had opened by itself, and footsteps had been heard again.

A new nurse had come, and the number of witnesses who had heard or seen uncanny goings-on was now eight.

I decided it was time for a séance, and on January 6, 1965, medium Ethel Meyers, Mary Melikian, Catherine and I took a New Haven train for Rye, where John Smythe picked us up in his station wagon.

While Ethel Meyers waited in the large sitting room downstairs, I checked on the house and got the latest word on the hauntings. Molly Guion took me to the kitchen to show me the spot where one of the most frightening incidents had taken place.

"Last Christmas, my mother, my husband, and I were here in the kitchen having lunch, and right near us on a small table next to the wall was a great big bread knife. Suddenly, to our amazement, *the knife took off into the air,* performed an arc in the air and landed about a yard away from the table. This was about noon, in good light."

"Was that the only time something like this happened?"

"The other day the same thing happened. We were down in the kitchen again at nighttime. My husband and I heard a terrific crash upstairs. It was in the area of the servants' quarters on the second floor, which is in the area where that door keeps slamming. I went up to investigate and found a heavy ashtray lying on the floor about a yard away from the table in my husband's den."

"And there was no one upstairs—flesh-and-blood, that is?"

"No. The object could not have just slipped off the table. It landed some distance away."

"Amazing," I conceded. "Was there more?"

"Last week I was standing in the upstairs sitting room with one of the nurses, when a piece of a chair that was lying in the center of a table took off and landed in the middle of the floor."

"Before your eyes?"

"Before our eyes."

"What would you say is the most frequent phenomenon here?" I asked.

"The opening of the front door downstairs. We and others have heard this characteristic noise any number of times, and there is never anyone there."

I turned to Mrs. Witty, the nurse currently on duty with Molly Guion's mother.

"How long have you been in this house?"

"Since October, 1964."

"Have you noticed anything unusual in these four months?"

"Well, Mrs. Smythe and I were in the patient's bedroom upstairs, when we heard the front door downstairs open. I remarked to Mrs. Smythe that she had a visitor, and went down to the front door, and looked. *The heavy chain was swinging loose, and the front door was slightly ajar!*"

"Did you see any visitor?"

"No. I opened the door, looked all around, but there was no one there."

"Anything else?"

"A couple of weeks later, the same thing happened. I was alone in the house with the patient, and the door was locked securely. An hour after I had myself locked it, I heard the door shut tightly, but the chain was again swinging by itself."

I next turned to Mr. Smythe to check up on his own experiences since we had last talked. Mr. Smythe was a naval architect and very cautious in his appraisal of the uncanny. He was still hearing the "measured steps" in the attic room where he sometimes slept, even when he was all alone in the house.

I returned to Ethel Meyers, the medium, who had seated herself in a large chair in the front sitting room downstairs.

"Anything happening?" I asked, for I noticed a peculiar expression on Ethel's face, as if she were observing something or someone.

"I picture a woman clairvoyantly," Ethel said. "She looks at me with a great deal of defiance."

"Why are you pointing across the room at that sofa?" I asked my wife.

"I saw a light from the corner of my eye and I thought it was a car, but no car has passed by," Catherine said.

If a car *had* passed by, no reflection could have been seen at that spot, since no window faced in that direction.

While Ethel prepared for the trance sitting, I went outside the room to talk to Georgia Anne Warren, a young dancer who had modeled for some of Molly Guion's paintings. Her full-length nude study graced the studio upstairs, and there amid the Churchill portraits and faces of the famous or near-famous, it was like a shining beacon of beauty. But Miss Warren wasn't only posing for a painter, we discovered—she was also modeling for a ghost.

"I heard a thumping noise, as if someone were going upstairs. I was in the kitchen. The steps sounded as if they were coming from the dining room. There was no one coming in. The only people in the house at the time were Molly Guion and myself. No doubt about it."

I thanked the redheaded model and followed Ethel Meyers up the stairs, to which she seemed propelled by a sudden impulse. There, on the winding Victorian steps, Ethel made her first contact with the ghost.

"Make the body very cold. Don't put it in the ground when it's warm. Let it get very cold!" she mumbled, as if not quite herself.

"Let her speak through you," I suggested.

"She is," Ethel replied, and continued in a somewhat strange voice. "Ring around the rosies, a pocketful of posies...."

I turned toward the stairwell and asked the ghost to communicate with us, tell her tale, and find help through us. There was no further answer.

I led Mrs. Meyers back to her chair, and asked Molly Guion to dim the lights a little so we could all relax. Meanwhile, other witnesses had arrived. They included *New York Times* reporter N. Berkowitz, Benton & Bowles vice-president Gordon Webber, publicist Bill Ryan, and book critic John K. Hutchins. We formed a long oval around Ethel Meyers and waited for the ghost to make her appearance.

We did not have to wait long. With a sudden shriek, Ethel, deep in trance, leapt to her feet, and in the awkward posture of an old crone, walked toward the front door. Nothing I could do would hold her back. I followed her quickly, as the medium, now possessed by the ghost, made her way through the long room to the door.

As if a strong wind had swept into the sitting room, the rest of the guests were thrown back by the sheer drive of Ethel's advance. She flung herself against the heavy wooden door and started to alternately gnaw at it and pound against it in an unmistakable desire to open it and go through. Then she seized the brass chain—the one Mrs. Witty had twice seen swinging by itself—and pulled it with astonishing force. I had all I could do to keep the medium from falling as she threw her body against the door.

In one hand I held a microphone, which I pressed close to her lips to catch as much of the dialogue as possible. I kept the other hand ready to prevent Ethel's fall to the floor.

"Rotten," the entranced medium now mumbled, still clutching the chain.

I tried to coax her back to the chair, but the ghost evidently would have none of it.

"It stinks...Where is it?"

"Is this your house?" I asked.

Heavy breathing.

"Yes. Get out!"

"I've come to help you. What is your name?"

"Get out!" the microphone picked up.

"What is it that you want?" I asked.

"My body."

"You've passed on, don't you understand?"

"No...I want my body. Where is it?"

I explained again that this was no longer her house, but she kept calling for the return of "her body" in such anger and despair that I began to wonder if it had not been buried on the premises.

"They took it, my body. I saw them, I saw them!"

"You must let go of this house. It is no longer yours," I said.

"No, my house, my house. They took it. My body. I have nothing. Get it. I feel I have one."

I explained that we had lent her a body to speak through for the moment.

"Who are you?" It sounded quieter.

"A friend," I replied, "come to help you."

Instead of replying, the entranced medium grabbed the door again.

"Why do you want to open the door?" I asked. It took a moment for the answer to come through trembling lips.

"Go out," she finally said. "I don't know you. Let me go, let me go."

I continued to question the ghost.

"Who are you? Did you live in this house?"

"My house. They took it out. My body is out there!"

I explained about the passage of time.

"You were not well. You've died."

"No, no...I wasn't cold."

"You are free to go from this door. Your loved ones, your family, await you outside."

"They hate me."

"No, they have made up with you. Why should they hate you?"

"They took me out the door."

Then, suddenly the medium's expression changed. Had someone come to fetch her?

"Oh, Baba, darling...Oh, he loved me."

There was hysterical crying now.

"He's gone...My beloved...."

"What is his name?"

"*Wain*...Where is he...Let me go!"

The crying was now almost uncontrollable, so I sent the ghost on her way. At the same time I asked that Albert, Ethel's control on the etheric side of the veil, take over her physical body for the moment to speak to us.

It took a moment or two until Albert was in command. The medium's body visibly straightened out and all traces of a bent old crone vanished. Albert's crisp voice was heard.

"She's a former tenant here, who has not been too well beloved. She also seems to have been carried out before complete death. This has brought her back to try and rectify it and make contact with the physical body. But here is always unhappiness. I believe there was no love toward her as she was older."

"Can you get a name?" I asked.

"If she refused, I cannot."

"How long ago was this?"

"During the Nineties. Between 1890 and 1900."

"Is this a woman?"

"Yes."

"Anything peculiar about her appearance?"

"Large eyes, and almost a harelip."

"Why is she concerned about her body?"

"There was no great funeral for her. She was put in a box and a few words were said over her grave. That is part of her problem, that she was thus rejected and neglected."

"Why does she run up to the attic?"

"This was her house, and it was denied to her later in life."

"By whom?"

"By those living here. Relatives to her."

"Her heirs?"

"Those who took it over when she could no longer function. She was still alive."

"Anything else we should know?"

"There is a great deal of hate for anyone in this house. Her last days were full of hate. Should she return, if she is spoken to kindly, she will leave. We will help her."

"Why is she so full of hate?"

"Her grief, her oppressions. She never left her tongue quiet when she was disrupted in her desire to go from her quarters to the rest of the house."

"What was her character?"

"As a young person she was indeed a lady. Later in life, a strong personality, going slightly toward dual personality. She was an autocrat. At the very end, not beloved."

"And her relationship with the servants?"

"Not too friendly. Tyrannical."

"What troubled her about her servants?"

"They knew too much."

"Of what?"

"Her downfall. Her pride was hurt."

"Before that, how was she?"

"A suspicious woman. She could not help but take things from others which she believed were hers by right."

"What did she think her servants were doing?"

"They pried on her secret life. She trusted no one toward the end of life."

"Before she was prevented, as you say, from freely going about the house—did she have any belongings in the attic?"

"Yes, hidden. She trusted no one."

I then suggested that the "instrument" be brought back to herself. A very surprised Ethel Meyers awakened to find herself leaning against the entrance door.

"What's the matter with my lip?" she asked when she was able to speak. After a moment, Ethel Meyers was her old self, and the excursion into Mrs. Wainwright's world had come to an end.

The following morning Molly Smythe called me on the phone. "Remember about Albert's remarks that Mrs. Wainwright was restrained within her own rooms?"

Of course I remembered.

"Well," Molly continued, "we've just made a thorough investigation of all the doors upstairs in the servants' quarters where she spent her last years. They all show evidence of locks having been on them, later removed. *Someone was locked up there for sure.*"

Ironically, death had not released Mrs. Wainwright from confinement. To her, freedom still lay beyond the heavy wooden door with its brass chain.

Now that her spirit self had been taken in hand, perhaps she would find her way out of the maze of her delusions to rejoin her first husband, for whom she had called.

The next time Molly Smythe hears the front door opening, it'll be just her husband coming home from the office. *Or so I thought.*

But the last week of April 1965, Molly called me again. Footsteps had been heard *upstairs* this time, and the sound of a door somewhere being opened and closed, and of course, on inspection, there was no one *visible* about.

Before I could make arrangements to come out to Rye once again, something else happened. Mr. Smythe was in the bathtub, when a large tube of toothpaste, safely resting well back on a shelf, flew off the shelf by its own volition. No vibration or other *natural* cause could account for

it. Also, a hypodermic needle belonging to one of the nurses attending Molly's mother had somehow disappeared.

I promised to bring Sybil Leek to the house. The British medium knew nothing whatever of the earlier history of the case, and I was curious to see if she would make contact with the same or different conditions, as sometimes happens when two mediums are used in the same house. It's like tuning in on different radio wavelengths.

It was a cool, wet day in May when we seated ourselves in a circle upstairs in the "haunted room." Present in addition to the hosts, Sybil Leek, and myself, were Mrs. Betty Salter (Molly's sister); David Ellingson, a reporter from the Port Chester, N.Y., *Item*; Mr. And Mrs. Robert Bendick, neighbors and friends of the Smythes; and Mary Melikian. Mr. Bendick was a television producer specializing in news programs.

Sybil went into hypnotic trance. It took several minutes before anything audible could be recorded.

"Who are you?" I asked.

A feeble voice answered:

"Marion . . . Marion Gernt. . . ."

Before going into trance, Sybil had volunteered the information that the name "Grant," or something like it, had been on her mind ever since she set foot into the house.

"What year is this?" I asked.

"1706."

"Who built the house?"

"My father . . . Walden."

She then complained that people in the house were disturbing *her*, and that therefore she was *pulling it down.*

"My face is swollen," she added. "I'm sick . . . Blood."

Suddenly, something went wrong with my reliable tape recorder. In all my previous investigations it had worked perfectly. Now it wouldn't, and some parts of the conversation were not recorded. The wheels would turn and then stop, and then start again, as if someone were sticking their fingers into them at will!

I tried my camera, and to my amazement, I couldn't take any pictures. All of a sudden, the mechanism wouldn't function properly, and the shutter could not be uncocked. I did not get any photographs. Bob Bendick, after the séance, took a good look at the camera. In a moment it was working fine again. After the séance, too, we tried to make the tape recorder work. It started and then stopped completely.

"The batteries have run out," I explained, confident that there was nothing more than that to it. So we put the machine on house current. Nothing happened. It wasn't the batteries. It was something else.

After we left the "haunted room" and went downstairs, I put the tape recorder into my traveling case. About ten minutes later, I heard a ghostly voice coming from my case. *My voice.* The tape recorder that I had left in a secure turn-off position had started up by itself...or...so it seemed.

But one can't be sure in haunted houses. *Item* reporter David Ellingson and Mary Melikian were standing next to me when it happened. John Smythe was wondering if someone had turned on the radio or TV. So much for the instruments that didn't work—temporarily.

But, let us get back to Sybil and the ghost speaking through her. She claimed to have been burned all over in a fire. John Smythe confirmed later that there were traces of a fire in the house that have never been satisfactorily explained.

The ghost seemed confused about it. She was burned, on this spot, in what was then a little house. The place was called Rocher. Her named was spelled M-a-r-i-o-n G-e-r-n-t. She was born at Rodey, eight miles distant. She was not sure about her age. At first she said 29, then it was 57. The house was built by one Dion, of Rocher.

I then tried to explain, as I always do, that the house belonged to someone else and that she must not stay.

"Go away," the ghost mumbled, not at all pleased with the idea of moving. But I insisted. I told her of her husband who wanted her to join him "over there."

"I hate him!" she volunteered, then added—"I start moving things...I break things up...I want my chair."

"You must not stay here," I pleaded. "You're not wanted here."

"*He* said that," she replied in a sullen voice. "Alfred did. My husband."

"You must join him and your children."

"I'll stay."

I repeated the incantation for her to leave.

"I can't go. I'm burned. I can't move," she countered.

I explained that these were only memories.

Finally she relented, and said—"I'll need a lot of rags...to cover myself."

Gently now, she started to fade.

"I need my chair," she pleaded, and I told her she could have it.

Then she was gone.

Sybil came back now. Still in trance, she responded quickly to my questions about what she saw and felt on the other side of the veil. This is a technique I find particularly effective when used prior to bringing the medium out of trance or from under hypnosis.

"An old lady," Sybil said. "She is quite small. I think she is Dutch. Shriveled. She is very difficult. Can't move.

Very unpleasant. Throws things because she can't walk. This is her house. She lived here about three hundred years ago. She wants everything *as it was*. She has marks on her face. She was in a fire."

"Did she die in it?" I asked.

"No. She died near here. Doesn't communicate well."

"There is a box with two hearts, two shields," Sybil said. "It means something to this woman."

"Were there any others around?" I asked.

"Lots, like shadows," Sybil explained, "but this little woman was the one causing the commotion."

"She likes to throw things," Sybil added, and I couldn't help thinking that she had never been briefed on all the objects the ghost had been throwing.

"She doesn't know where any doors are, so she just goes on. The door worries her a lot, because she doesn't know where it is. The front and rear have been changed around."

Sybil, of course, knew nothing of the noises centering around the main door, nor the fact that the rear of the house was once the front.

I told Sybil to send her away, and in a quiet voice, Sybil did so.

The séance was over, at least for the time being.

A little later, we went up to the top floor, where both Molly and Sybil suddenly senses a strong odor of perfume. I joined them, and I smelled it, too. It was as if *someone were following us about the house!*

But it was time to return to New York. Our hosts offered to drive us to the city.

"Too bad," I said in parting, "that nobody has *seen* an apparition here. Only sounds seem to have been noticed."

Betty Salter, Mrs. Smythe's perky sister, shook her head.

"Not true," she said. "I was here not so long ago when I saw a black figure downstairs in the dining room. I thought it was Molly, but on checking found that I was quite alone downstairs...That is, except for *her*."

Mrs. Wainwright, of course, was of Dutch ancestry, and the description of the character, appearance, and general impression of the ghost Sybil gave did rather fit Mrs. Wainwright.

Was the 1706 lady an ancestor or just someone who happened to be on the spot when only a small farm house occupied the site?

The Smythes really didn't care whether they have two ghosts or one ghost. They preferred to have none.

The Garrick's Head Inn, Bath

THREE HOURS BY CAR from London is the elegant resort city of Bath. Here, in a Regency architectural wonderland, there is an eighteenth century inn called Garrick's Head Inn. At one time there was a connection between the inn and the theater next door, but the theater no longer exists. In the eighteenth century, the famous gambler Beau Nash owned this inn which was then a gambling casino as well.

The downstairs bar looks like any other bar, divided as it is between a large, rather dark room where the customers sip their drinks, and a heavy wooden bar behind which the owner dispenses liquor and small talk. There is an upstairs, however, with a window that, tradition says, is impossible to keep closed for some reason. The rooms upstairs are no longer used for guests, but are mainly storage rooms or private rooms of the owners. At the time of my first visit to the Garrick's Head Inn it was owned by Bill Loud, who was a firm skeptic when he had arrived in Bath. Within two months, however, his skepticism was shattered by the phenomena he was able to witness. The heavy till once took off by itself and smashed a chair. The noises of people walking were heard at night at a time when the place was entirely empty. He once walked into what he described as "cobwebs" and felt his head stroked by a gentle hand. He also smelled perfume when he was entirely alone in the cellar.

A reporter from a Bristol newspaper, who spent the night at the inn, also vouched for the authenticity of the footsteps and strange noises.

Finally, the owner decided to dig into the past of the building, and he discovered that there have been incidents which could very well be the basis for the haunting. During the ownership of gambling king Beau Nash, there had been an argument one night, and two men had words over a woman. A duel followed. The winner was to take possession of the woman. One man was killed and the survivor rushed up the stairs to claim his prize. The woman, who had started to flee when she saw him win, was not agreeable, and when she heard him coming barricaded herself in the upstairs room and hanged herself.

Whether you will see or hear the lady ghost at the Garrick's Head Inn in Bath is a matter of individual ability to communicate with the psychic world. It also depends upon the hours of the night you are there, for the Garrick's Head Inn is pretty noisy in the early part of the evening when it is filled with people looking for spirits in the bottle rather than the more ethereal kind.

Garrick's Head Inn—Bath, England: Extremely haunted

Bill Loud, who saw the till fly through the air

CHAPTER ELEVEN

Ghosts That Aren't

W HEN YOU SEE SOMEONE who has passed on, you are not necessarily seeing a ghost. Especially if the person is a relative or friend and the communication—either verbal or telepathic—is clearly reasonable. In these cases, you are dealing with a spirit visit.

These visits occur, whenever there is a *need* for them, because of two kinds of situations. Either the departed loved one wants you to know she or he is well and is now living in another world, or the spirit has come because you need help in your own life *here*. This help can have to do with your job, your family, or your personal life, or it may be a warning of things to come, some of which you can avert, and some of which are inevitable. The spirit person has gotten *permission* from the folks "over there" who run the contact very much according to their laws, and the visits are never haphazard or without meaning.

I have often said that of all ghostly manifestations only perhaps ten percent are true ghosts— human beings trapped by their unfinished business on earth in the spot where their traumatic death occurred. The rest may be simply impressions left behind by an emotional event in the past, and a sensitive person will feel and relive it.

Finally, rare cases do exist of "ghosts of the living," in which a perfectly fine person is seen at a distance by someone with a psychic gift. The Germans used to call this the "doppelgänger," or the etheric double, but it is really only a projection of the inner body. This occurs sometimes when the person at a distance is in a state of great relaxation or, conversely, great anxiety, and it is rare. Usually, if not always, the traveler returns quickly to the physical body.

If anything, these cases prove that we do have an inner body, because the physical outer body keeps right on going. Some astral travel (or out-of-body experiences) happen during sleep, but some occur while the person is simply deep in thought or emotionally detached. None of them are harmful or dangerous, despite a warning issued by Madame Helen Blavatzky, the founder of theosophy, many years ago, that "strangers" can get into your body while the real you is out there traveling.

Here are some true examples from my files of these kinds of "non-ghosts," which are often confused with real ghosts.

CONTACTS AND VISITS BY SPIRITS

When the Dead Reach Out to the Living

The annals of psychic research are full of verified cases in which the dead come to bid the living a last good-bye. But the thought of separation is often overshadowed by the desire to announce the continuance of life. This, of course, is implied in the very fact of an appearance after death: only a person who survives can come to say good-bye. Orthodox psychiatry has labored hard and long to explain most of these appearances as "hallucinations," but the fact is that the majority of cases show total ignorance on the part of the recipient that the person who communicates after death is no longer alive. You cannot hallucinate something you don't know.

This type of communication occurs frequently with professional psychics. Eileen Garrett once reported to me that she was riding in a taxi down New York's Fifth Avenue when a long-dead friend spoke to her clairvoyantly and advised her that Marie H., whom both knew, had just passed on and was over there with him. Mrs. Garrett looked at her watch and registered the time. Shortly after, when she reached her offices, she put in a call to California, where Miss H. lived. The message was correct, and when she compared the time of passing as recorded in California with the time she had received her message, she found that, allowing for the time differential, it had been given her a moment after Miss H.'s death! But laypeople, that is, people not at all concerned with the psychic or even interested in it, who are often skeptics and firm nonbelievers in an afterlife—are frequently the recipients of such messages and experience communications from the dead.

Once, when I lecturing at Waynesburg College in Waynesburg, Pennsylvania, I was approached by a young lady who had had a most interesting experience along such lines in April 1963.

Sandra R. lived with her family in a house in a small town south of Pittsburgh. Her brother Neal R., then aged twenty-two, had been working as a bank teller for the past three years. Young Neal had often expressed a dislike of going into the Army; he had a feeling he would be killed. As a consequence, his mother and sister, to whom the young man was quite close, persuaded him to join the National Guard for a six-month tour of duty. Since he would be drafted anyway, he might thus shorten the period of his service.

Neal finally agreed that this was the best thing to do under the circumstances, and he joined the National Guard. He resigned his position at the bank and seemed reconciled to making the best of the situation.

In April he got his orders and tickets and was to report for basic training a week from the following Monday. Several times during those final days at home, he mentioned the fact that he was to leave at 5 A.M. Sunday, as if this were indeed something important and final. On the Monday preceding his departure, he visited friends to say good-bye. Leaving home as usual with a kiss on the cheek for his mother, he gaily said, "I'll see you," and went out.

He never returned. The following morning the family was notified that he had been found dead in his car parked along a lonely country road about two miles from his home. He had committed suicide by inhaling carbon monoxide.

The news created a state of shock in his family. At first they would not believe the news, for they were sure he would have left some sort of note for his family. But nothing was ever found, even though the family searched the house from top to bottom. He had put all his things in order, leaving no debts or commitments, but there was no message of any kind for anyone.

He was buried in his hometown, and the family tried to adjust to their great loss. Sandra, his sister, was three years his junior, but the two had been close enough to have many telepathic experiences in which they would read each other's thoughts. She could not understand why her brother had not confided in her before taking this drastic step.

In the house, both Sandra's room and Neal's had been upstairs. After Neal's death, Sandra could not bear the thought of sleeping so near to her late brother's room, so she slept on a rollout divan placed in the living room downstairs. The day of the funeral was a Friday, and it seemed to Sandra that it would never pass. Finally, after a restless, almost sleepless night, Saturday dawned. All day long she felt uneasy, and there was an atmosphere of tension in the air that she found almost unbearable. When night came, Sandra asked that her mother share the couch with her. Neither woman had taken any tranquilizers or sleeping pills. They discussed the suicide again from all angles but failed to arrive at any clues. Finally they fell asleep from exhaustion.

Suddenly Sandra was awakened from deep slumber by a clicking sound. It sounded exactly as if someone had snapped his fingers just above her head. As Sandra became fully awake, she heard her mother stir next to her.

"Did you hear that?" her mother asked. She too had heard the strange snapping sound. Both women were now fully awake.

They felt a tingling sensation pervading them from head to toe, as if they were plugged into an electric socket! Some sort of current was running through them, and they were quite unable to move a limb.

The living room is situated in the front part of the house. The blinds were all closed, and no light whatever shone through them. The only light coming into the room came from a doorway behind them, a doorway that led into the hall. All of a sudden, they noticed a bright light to their left, moving toward them. It had the brightness of an electric bulb when they first saw it approach. It appeared about two feet from the couch on the mother's side and was getting brighter and brighter. "What is it, what is it?" they cried to each other, and then Sandra noticed that the light had a form. There was a head and shoulders encased in light!

Frightened, her heart pounding, Sandra heard herself cry out: "It's Neal!" At the moment she called out her late brother's name, the light blew up to its brightest glare. With that, a feeling of great peace and relief came over the two women.

Mrs. R., still unable to move her body, asked: "What do you want? Why did you do it?"

With that, she started to cry. At that moment waves of light in the form of fingers appeared inside the bright light *as if someone were waving good-bye.* Then the light gradually dimmed until it vanished completely.

At that instant a rush of cold air moved across the room. A moment later they clearly heard someone walking up the stairs. They were alone in the house, so they knew it could not be a flesh-and-blood person. Now the steps approached Neal's room upstairs. When they reached the top step, the step squeaked as it had always done when Sandra's brother had walked up the stairs. Over the years, Sandra had heard this particular noise time and again. Neal's room was directly over their heads, and there wasn't a sound in the house. Except those footsteps overhead. The two women were lying quite still on the couch, unable to move even if they had wanted to. The steps continued through the hallway and then went into Neal's room. Next they heard the sound of someone sitting down on his bed, and they clearly heard the bed springs give from the weight of a person! Since the bed stood almost directly over their heads down in the living room, there was no mistaking these sounds. At this moment, their bodies suddenly returned to normal. The tension was broken, and Sandra jumped up, turned on the lights, and looked at the clock next to the couch. The time was 5 o'clock Sunday morning —the exact moment Neal had been scheduled to leave, had he not committed suicide!

With this, all was quiet again in the house. But Sandra and her mother no longer grieved for Neal. They accepted the inevitable and began to realize that life did continue in another dimension. The bond between their Neal and themselves was reestablished, and they felt a certain relief to know he was all right wherever he now was.

At different times after that initial good-bye visit, they experienced the strong smell of Neal's favorite after-shave lotion in the house. At the time of his death, he had a bottle of it in the glove compartment of his car. As no one else in the house was using any aftershave lotion, an alternative explanation would be hard to come by.

Neither Mrs. R. nor her daughter is given to hysterics. They accepted these events as perfectly natural, always carefully making sure no ordinary explanation would fit. But when all was said and done, they knew that their Neal had not let them down, after all. The bond was still unbroken.

Mrs. G. B., a housewife living in a Pittsburgh suburb, and her brother, Frank G., had been close in their childhood, which may be of some importance in the event I am about to relate. Whenever there exists an emotional bond between people, the communication between the world of the dead and that of the living seems to be easier. But this is by no means always the case, as even strangers have communicated in this way with each other.

Frank G. and forty-one others were aboard a Navy transport flying over the ocean. On the nights of October 26, 27, and 28, 1954, Mrs. B. had a vivid dream in which she felt someone was drowning. This recurrent dream puzzled her, but she did not connect it with her brother as she had no idea where he was or what he was doing at the time. On October 30, 1954, she was awakened from sleep by the feeling of a presence in her room. This was not at her own home but at the house of her in-laws. Her husband was sleeping in an adjoining room. As she looked up, fully awake now, she saw at the foot of her bed a figure all in white. A feeling of great sorrow came over her at this moment. Frightened, she jumped out of bed and ran to her husband.

The following evening, the telephone rang. Her brother, Frank, crewman on an ill-fated air transport, had been lost at sea.

Mrs. William F. of Salem, Massachusetts, no witch but rather a well-adjusted housewife, had what she calls a "spiritual experience," which was enough to assure her that life did indeed exist beyond the grave.

In 1957, her aged grandmother had passed on, leaving the care of her grandfather to her parents. The old man was lost without his companion of so many years, and eventually he deteriorated to the point where he had to be placed in a hospital. He died in 1961, and the family went jointly to the local funeral parlor for a last good-bye.

Mrs. F. and her older sister were sitting in the room where the body lay, when suddenly both of them—as they later realized—had the same strange feeling of a presence with them.

The feeling became so strong that Mrs. F. eventually lifted her head, which had been lowered in mourning. It may be mentioned that she did not like funeral parlors and had never been inside one before.

As she looked up beyond the coffin, she saw her grandfather and her grandmother with smiles on their faces. Although their lips did not move, the woman got

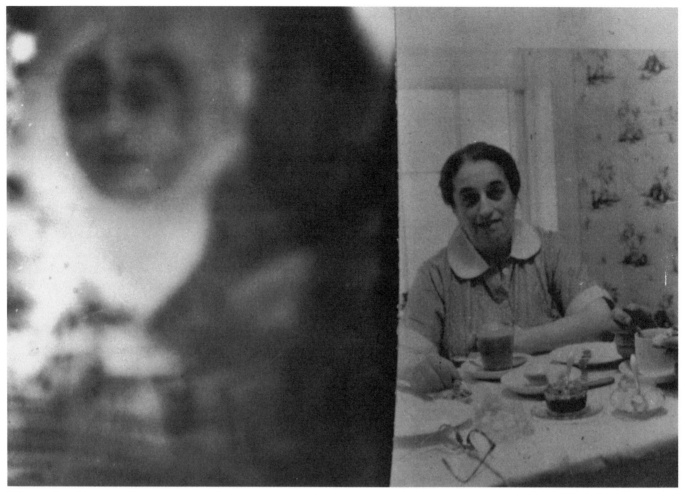

When the dead reach out to the living—A portrait of Mrs. Martha Holzer, Hans Holzer's mother. This was obtained through photographic mediumship of the late Dr. John Myers, with Mike Wallace as the monitor. Life time photo on the right

the impression her "Nana" was saying to her: "It's all right now. I am taking care of him now. Don't be sad. We're together again."

The parents did not see this vision, but the older sister did.

The apparitions of the dead wish to be recognized as the people they were and are. Thus the majority of them appear looking as they did in physical life—that is, wearing the clothes they had on when they died or clothes they liked to wear ordinarily. But there are also cases where the dead have appeared dressed in a simple white robe instead of their customary clothing. I myself saw my mother several years after her passing, wearing what I then called "a long nightshirt." The moment was brief but long enough for me to realize I was fully awake and that she cast a shadow on the opposite wall.

I think that this white robe is perhaps the "ordinary" dress over there, with the earth-type clothing optional when and if needed. No doubt the white robe is behind

many legends of white-robed angels appearing to mortals and the generally accepted description of ghost being "white." It is also true that ectoplasm, the material of which materializations of the dead are created, is white. It is an albumen substance that has been analyzed in laboratories and that is drawn from the living during physical séances.

The white color has some bearing on the need for darkness whenever such manifestations are induced in the séance room. Evidently strong white light destroys the material, perhaps because light and psychic energies are traveling on collision courses and might cancel each other out. But the ectoplastic substance is tangible and real and is by no means a figment of the imagination.

Mrs. C. M. R., a widow living in eastern New England, was married more than forty years to her husband, John, who passed away in 1966. John R. had worked as a machinist for a leather factory. When he complained of pain in his chest, his ailment was diagnosed as pleurisy, and he was told to stay in bed. There was no indication of imminent death on that March day in 1966. The doctor left after a routine inspection, and John R. went back to bed.

Between 2 and 3 A.M., he suddenly complained of pain. He was sitting on the bed when his wife rushed to his side. She made him comfortable, and he went back to sleep—never to wake up again. Because of the complaint, Mrs. R. kept a vigil close to the bed. Suddenly she saw a white-robed figure rise up from the bed and sit on it for a moment, as if to get its bearings. There was a rustling sound of sheets moving. Since the figure's back was turned toward her, Mrs. R. could not make out its features. But it was a large person, and so was her husband. At the same time, she had a peculiar sensation inside her head. Suddenly, as if a balloon inside had burst, the sensation stopped and all was silent. The white-robed figure had disappeared. She stepped to the bed and realized that her husband was gone.

Mrs. R.'s brother, Robert C., was a lieutenant in the army during the Second World War and later worked for the C.N.R. railroad in Canada. Mrs. R. had not been in constant touch with him, since she lived a thousand miles away. But on April 11, 1948, she and her daughter were in their bedroom when both women saw the figure of Robert C., dressed in black, looking into the room, his hand on the doorknob. He smiled at them and Mrs. R. spoke to her brother, but he vanished into thin air. That was between midnight and 1 A.M. Hospital records at the Halifax Victoria General Hospital show that Lieutenant C. passed away officially at 7 A.M., April 12, 1948. Evidently he had already been out of the body and on his last journey several hours before. Stopping in at his sister's house on the way, he had come to say good-bye.

Diane S., a high school graduate and as level-headed as you would want to meet, did not show the slightest interest in psychic matters until age seventeen. She lived with her parents in a medium-sized town in Michigan. Her friend Kerm was the apple of her eye, and vice versa. No doubt, if things had preceded normally, they would have married.

But one night, after he had driven her home, Kerm was killed in a car accident on the way to his own place. The shock hit Diane very strongly, and she missed him. She wondered whether there was anything in the belief that one survived death.

One week after the funeral of her friend, she smelled the scent of funeral flowers on arising. For five days this phenomenon took place. There were no such flowers in the house at that time. Then other things followed. Diane was on her way home from a girlfriend's house. It was around midnight. As she drove home, she gradually felt another presence with her in the car. She laughed it off as being due to an overactive imagination, but the sensation persisted. She looked around for a moment, but the back seat was empty. Again she focused her eyes on the road. Suddenly she felt something touch first her left hand, then her right. There was no mistaking it; the touch was very real.

At another time she awoke in the middle of a sound sleep. She felt the presence of something or someone in the room with her. Finally, she opened her eyes and looked in all directions. She saw nothing unusual, but she was sure there was another person sitting on the second bed, watching her. The feeling became so intense that she broke out in a cold sweat. But she did not dare get up, and finally she managed to get back to sleep. The next morning, when she awoke, her first act was to have a look at the other bed. There, at the foot of the bed, was an imprint on the bedspread, as if someone had been sitting on it!

After that there was a period of quiet, and Diane thought with great relief that the psychic manifestations had finally come to an end.

But in late July 1965, something happened that caused her to reconsider that opinion. A young man named Jerry had been a steady companion of hers since the unfortunate accident in which Kerm had been killed. There was a party at Diane's house one evening. After the company left, Jerry stayed on.

Together they sat and talked for several hours. It grew late, and dawn began to show itself. The two young people were sitting on the couch downstairs when suddenly Jerry looked up and asked if her mother was standing at the top of the stairs! Diane knew that her mother would be asleep in her room, yet she followed Jerry's eyes to the top landing of the stairs.

There was a figure standing there, rather vaguely outlined and seemingly composed of a white filmy substance. At its base there was a luminous sparkle. As the two young people stared at the figure, without daring to move, it gradually faded away.

Jerry then left for home, and Diane went to bed. As he drove down the road, he was about to pass the spot where Kerm had been killed a couple of months before. He stopped for a moment and got out to stretch his legs. When he walked back to his car, he noticed that it was enveloped by a thick fog. He got into the car, which felt strangely cold and clammy. He glanced to his right, and to his horror he saw a white, cloudlike object cross the road toward the car. As it approached the car, Jerry could make it out clearly enough: it was a blurred image of a human body, but the face was as plain as day. It was Kerm. He got into the front seat with Jerry, who shook with terror. Jerry's eyes were watering, and he dared not move.

"Take care of Di," a strangely broken voice said next to him. It sounded as though it were coming from far away, like an echo.

Then a hand reached out for his, and Jerry passed out. When he came to, he found himself parked in front of the local cemetery. How he had got there he did not know. It is some distance from the spot of Kerm's accident to the cemetery. But there he was, barely able to start his car and drive home.

When he told his story to his parents, they thought he had dreamed it. Jerry was sure he had not. The events that followed bore him out. It would seem that Kerm wanted to make sure Jerry took good care of his former girlfriend. At various times, Jerry would feel a hand at his shoulder.

At this point Diane got in touch with me. As I could not then rush out to Michigan, I sent her explicit instructions about what to do. On the next occasion when the restless form was in evidence, she was to address him calmly and ask that he cease worrying over her. Jerry would indeed look out for her, and they would rather not have him, Kerm, around also. Three does make a crowd, even if one is a ghost.

Apparently Kerm took the hint and left for good. But to Diane it was an indication that there is another world where we all may meet again.

Although many visits of departing loved ones take place while the recipients of the message are fully awake or as they are being awakened to receive the news, there are many more such incidents on record where the events seemingly occur in the dream state. I devoted an entire chapter to the many-sided nature of dreams in my book *ESP and You.* Many dreams are physically caused or are psychoanalytical material. But there are such things as true dreams and psychic dreams, in which precise messages are received that later come true.

Mrs. Madeline M. lives in a large Eastern city. She is a "true dreamer" and has accepted her ESP abilities calmly and without fears.

"True dreams I can't forget on awakening, even if I try," she explained to me, "while the ordinary kind fade away quickly and I couldn't recall them no matter how hard I try to."

When Madeline was fourteen, her mother was taken to the hospital with a fatal illness. The girl was not aware of its seriousness, however, and only later found out that her mother knew she would soon die and was worried about leaving her daughter at so tender an age.

At the time, Madeline had accepted the invitation of a friend and former neighbor to stay overnight with her. That night she had a vivid dream. She saw her mother standing at the foot of the bed, stroking her feet and smiling at her with a sweet yet sad smile. What puzzled Madeline, however, was the way her mother looked in the vision. To begin with, she wore a strange dress with tiny buttons. Her hair was done in a way she had never worn it before. Both dress and strange hairdo impressed themselves upon the young woman, along with a feeling of emptiness at the sight of her mother.

"I have to leave now, Madeline," the mother said in the dream.

"But where are you going?" Madeline heard herself ask in the dream.

"Never mind, Madeline, it's just that I *must* go!"

And with that remark, her mother eased herself toward the door, gently closing it behind her and looking back once more, saying: "Good-bye, Madeline."

With that, the door was shut.

The next thing Madeline knew, she found herself sitting on the bed, sobbing hysterically, "Mother, don't go, please don't go!" Her hostess was next to her trying to get her out of the state she was in.

"It's only a dream," the friend explained, "and look, it's late—*five minutes past two!* We must both get some sleep now!"

With that, Madeline and her friend went back to sleep, but not until after Madeline had reported her vision to her friend in every detail.

She was roused from deep sleep by her friend early the next morning.

"Your brother is here to have breakfast with us," her friend explained. Hurriedly Madeline got dressed to meet her brother.

"Tell him about your dream," the friend nudged her.

There was a pause, then the brother remarked: "I'm jealous, Madeline; why didn't she come to *me?*"

He then informed her that their mother had passed away at *five minutes past two* the previous night.

Too stunned to cry, Madeline realized that her mother had come to say good-bye. In the dream state the connection can be made a lot easier, because there is no conscious thought wall to penetrate and that interferes with the flow of communication.

They went to the viewing of the body. When Madeline caught sight of her mother's body, she grabbed her brother's hand and dug her nails deeply into it.

"What is it?" he asked with surprise. She could only point to her mother's appearance: the dress with the tiny buttons she had never worn before and the strange hairdo —exactly as Madeline had seen it in her "dream."

Evidently Madeline M. was and is a good recipient of messages from the departing and departed. Many years later, in 1957, she had another true dream. This time she saw herself walk into a house, go straight to the back of the house, and stop in a doorway that opened into a large dining room. As she stood in this doorway, in the dream, she noticed her dead father seated at the head of the table. Her dead mother walked in just as Madeline arrived at her observation point. Her mother now stood next to her father, whose face was aglow with joy. Both father and mother appeared very much younger than they were at the time of their deaths, and both seemed very excited. But it was not the dreamer's presence that caused all this commotion; in fact they paid no attention to her at all. In her dream Madeline felt left out and wondered why she had not been asked to sit down at the dinner table, since there was an extra place set at the table.

"Isn't it wonderful that we are all here together again?" she heard herself ask. "Where is my brother?"

Finally her mother spoke up, pointing to the empty chair. "Oh, he will be here; we're expecting him—in fact, he is on his way now!"

The next morning Mrs. M. recalled her dream vision only too clearly. But it was not until nine months later that the events alluded to in the dream became reality. Her brother had the same fatal illness that had taken her mother, and after a brief hospital stay he too passed into the world of the spirit, where a place had already been set for him at Thanksgiving the year before.

There are instances when the dead wish to let someone living know that they are across the veil and not merely somewhere on earth and out of touch. Especially in the United States, where the movement of people is unchecked by police registration, people can easily drop out of one another's sight and may be hard to trace or track down. One case involved a young lady who had moved in with a married sister in coastal Virginia.

Mrs. Doris S., the married sister, has a husband in the Army, and consequently they move around a lot. But at that time she had a house, and her sister was welcome in it. The sister was engaged to a young man with whom she had kept company for several years. Her weakness was cigarettes, and even her young man frowned on her excessive smoking.

"I'll be back in one month to take you with me," he had promised before he left, "and if you've cut down on cigarettes to ten a day, I'll marry you!"

Soon after he had left, strange occurrences began to puzzle the two women. The sister's clothes would be moved around in her closet without any reason. Cigarette butts would be found all over the house like markers, although neither sister had put them there. One of the dresses disappeared completely, only to show up a week later, neatly folded, in another drawer. There was walking upstairs at times when there was no human being in that part of the house. Then one day a shoe of the sister's walked down the steps by itself—as if someone were moving it!

Mrs. S.'s husband was impressed with the unaccountable events she wrote him about, and it was decided that they would look for another house. Then, when he had some leave coming to him, the family decided to go home to Pennsylvania. There they found out something they had not known before: the sister's friend had been killed in a car accident several weeks earlier. As he didn't have any family, nobody had let them know of his death.

"It must have been he," Mrs. S. remarked, "trying to keep his word. After all, he did promise to get sister in a month."

After that there were no unusual happenings in the house.

Mrs. Darlene V., a housewife in suburban New York City, has had numerous premonitory experiences. But the incident that convinced her that she had a special gift happened when she was sixteen years old and a junior in high school in Beaver Dam, Wisconsin. Mrs. V., a Catholic, attended a religious study course at the time. It was held at the local church, and the group consisted of youngsters of both sexes. During her study sessions she noticed a certain young man who sat all by himself on the side; his sad and lonely expression attracted her interest. She inquired about him and learned that his name was Roger but that his friends called him Rocky. He had been studying for the priesthood but had had to stop recently because of illness. He was then in his early twenties. A bond of friendship grew between Darlene and this unhappy young man, although her mother did not approve of it.

Around the end of October, he failed to show up at the study evenings, and it wasn't until the week before Christmas that Darlene found out why. Her parish priest informed her that Rocky was very ill and in the hospital. She asked her mother for permission to visit her sick friend, but her mother refused. The following day she had the strongest feeling that Rocky needed her, so she went anyway, after school. The young man was overjoyed and confirmed that he had indeed wanted to see her very much.

During the next two months, she went to visit him as often as she could. In February she had an accident in her gym class that forced her to remain in bed for two weeks. But she continued her interest in Rocky through telephone calls to his mother, whom she had never met. The young man had cancer and had been operated upon, and the mother gave Darlene daily reports of his progress.

On a Friday in February she was able to return to school, and it was her intention to visit her friend Rocky at the hospital that Friday afternoon. But before she could do so, her brother showed her the morning paper: Rocky had died the night before. The shock sent Darlene back to bed.

Very late that night she awoke from deep sleep with the feeling that she was not alone. She sat up in bed and looked round. There, at the foot of her bed, stood her friend Rocky. His features were plain, and he was surrounded by a soft glow. As soon as he noticed that she saw him, he held out his hands toward her and said: "Please help my mother; she wants and needs you." Then he was gone.

Darlene called the man's mother the next morning. Before she could relay her message, the mother broke into tears, saying that she had been trying to locate Darlene, whose family name she did not know.

Darlene was at Rocky's mother's side from then until after the funeral. It was only then that she finally told the man's mother what had happened the night after Rocky's passing. It was a great comfort to the mother, but the parish priest, whom Darlene also told of her experience, tried to convince her that it was all "a young girl's emotional imagination."

Visual phenomena are not the only way by which the dead seemingly assert themselves to the living. Sometimes the phenomena are only auditory but no less evidential. It is somewhat like playing an instrument: some people gravitate toward the piano, others to the violin—but both make music. So it is with psychic communication, which, more than any ordinary communication, depends on the makeup of both individuals, the receiver as well as the sender.

Mrs. William S. is a housewife in Pennsylvania. A friend of her husband's by the name of Paul F., who was employed by a large mail-order house, died in his early fifties of a heart attack. A few weeks after his death Mrs. S. was in her bedroom making the bed when she suddenly heard him call out to her. There was no mistaking his voice, for she knew it well. He had called her by name, as if he wanted her attention. The voice sounded as if it came from the adjoining room, so she entered that room and responded by calling Paul's name. There was no answer. A religious person, Mrs. S. then knelt on the floor and prayed for the man. She has not heard his voice since.

For many years, Elizabeth S. had been friendly with a young woman named Dorothy B. This was in Pittsburgh, and they were almost next-door neighbors. Dorothy had a sister named Leona, who was a housewife also. She passed away suddenly, only twenty-eight years of age. The shock was very great for Dorothy, who could not reconcile herself to this passing. Despite attempts by Mrs. S. and others to bring her out of this state of grief, Dorothy refused to listen and even cried in her sleep at night.

One night Dorothy was awakened by something or someone shaking her bed. She got up and looked but found no explanation for this. Everybody in her house was fast asleep. As she stood in front of her bed, puzzled about the strange occurrence, she clearly heard footsteps on the stairs. Frightened, she woke her husband, and together they searched the whole house. They found no one who could have caused the steps. The following night, the same phenomena occurred. Again there was no natural explanation.

But during that second night, a strange thing also happened to Mrs. S., five doors away. She was in bed, reading a book, when all of a sudden the printed page seemed to disappear in front of her eyes, and different words appeared instead. Mrs. S. shook her head, assuming her eyes were tired, but it happened again. At this point she closed her eyes and lay back in bed, when she heard a voice beside her pillow calling her name, "Betty!" It was a very sharp voice, full of despair. Although Mrs. S. had never met Dorothy's sister Leona in life, she knew it was she, calling out for recognition.

The two women got together the next day and compared experiences. It was then that they decided Leona wanted them to know that she continued to enjoy a kind of life in another world, and to stop grieving for her. It was the push that Dorothy had needed to get out of her grief, and the two women became like sisters after this common experience. Leona never called on either of them again.

I have often doubted the reliability of Ouija boards as a means of communication between the two worlds, but once in a while something genuine can come through them. The proof must rest with the individuals operating the board, of course, and depends upon the presence or absence of the information in their unconscious minds. But Mrs. S. had an experience that to me rings true.

At the time, she was nineteen, as yet unmarried, and lived with her parents. She did not really believe there was anything supernatural in a Ouija board. More to amuse themselves than for any serious reason, she and a neighbor sat down to try their luck with a board. Hardly had they started to operate the indicator when it moved with great rapidity to spell out a name. That name was Parker. It surprised Elizabeth, for she had not thought of this person in a long time. Now one might argue that his name would always be present in her subconscious mind, but so would many other names of people who had gone on before.

"Do you want anything?" Elizabeth cried out.

The board spelled "yes," and at the very same moment she clearly felt a kiss on her right cheek. It was not her imagination. The sensation was quite physical.

Parker S. was a young man she had dated two years before, and the two young people had been very much in love. At the time he worked at a service station. One day, on his way to see her, he was killed in a car accident. Mrs. S. feels he had finally delivered his good-bye kiss to her, albeit a little late.

Lastly, there are phenomena of letting the living know that death has taken a loved one. The thought going out from the dying person at the moment of separation is not strong enough or not organized sufficiently to send a full image to a loved one remaining behind. But there is enough psychic or psychokinetic energy to move an object or cause some other telltale sign so that the loved ones may look up and wonder. In German these phenomena are called *gaenger*, or goers, and they are quite common.

A typical case is the experience Mrs. Maria P. of California shared with her husband a few days before Christmas 1955. The couple were in bed asleep in their Toronto home, when suddenly they were awakened by the noise of a knickknack falling off a bookshelf. The object could not possibly have fallen off accidentally or by itself. At the same moment, the woman was impressed with the idea that her father had just died. A few days later she learned that her father had indeed passed on at that identical moment in his native Germany, across the ocean.

This was not the first time Maria had experienced anything along these lines. When she was only five years old and her mother left for the hospital, the little girl said, "You will not come back, Mother." It was nine days later that the entire family heard a loud, snapping noise in the main bedroom. All the clocks in the house stopped at that instant. The time was 1:10 P.M. A few hours later, word came that her mother had died at that hour.

There are other cases involving the falling of paintings, or the moving of shutters at windows, or the closing of doors in a gust of wind when no wind was blowing. All of these supernormal phenomena are, in my estimation, different ways of saying the same thing: I am going, folks, but I'm not finished.

Sometimes the message needs no words: the very presence of the "deceased" is enough to bring home the facts of afterlife. Once, my friend Gail B., public relations director for many leading hotels, called me to ask my help for a friend who was extremely upset because of a visit from the beyond. Would I please go and talk to her? I would and I did.

Carina L., a onetime professional singer who later went into business in New York City, was originally from Romania and a firm "nonbeliever" in anything she could not touch, smell, hear, or count. Thus it was with considerable apprehension that she reported two seemingly impossible experiences.

When she was a young girl in the old country, Carina had a favorite grandmother by the name of Minta M. Grandmother M. lived to be a hale and healthy eighty-six; then she left this vale of tears as the result of a heart attack. To be sure, the old lady was no longer so spry as she had been in her youth. One could see her around the neighborhood in her faded brown coat and her little bonnet and special shoes made for her swollen feet, as she suffered from foot trouble.

She had a shuffling walk, not too fast, not too slow; her gait was well known in her neighborhood in Bucharest. When Grandmother M. had called it a day on earth, her daughters inherited her various belongings. The famed brown coat went to Carina's Aunt Rosa, who promptly cut it apart in order to remodel it for herself.

Grandmother was gone, and the three daughters—Carina's mother and her two aunts, Rosa and Ita—lived together at the house. Two months after Grandmother's death, Ita and her little son went to the grocer's for some shopping. On their way they had to pass a neighbor's house and stopped for a chat. As they were standing there with the neighbor, who should come around the corner but Grandmother, the way she had done so often in life. Ita saw her first and stared, mouth wide open. Then the little boy noticed Grandmother and said so.

Meanwhile the figure came closer, shuffling on her bad feet as she had always done. But she didn't pay any attention to the little group staring at her. As she came within an arm's length, she merely kept going, looking straight ahead. She wore the same faded brown coat that had been her favorite in life. Ita was dumbfounded. By the time she came to her senses, the figure had simply disappeared.

"Did you see Mrs. M.?" the neighbor asked in awe. Ita could only nod. What was there to say? It was something she never forgot. On getting home she rushed to her sister's room. There, cut apart as it had been for several weeks, lay the brown coat!

Many things changed over the years, and finally Carina found herself living in New York City. Her Aunt Ita, now living in Toronto, decided to pay her a visit and stayed with Carina at her apartment. About two weeks after the aunt's arrival, she accompanied her niece on a routine shopping errand in the neighborhood. It was a breezy March afternoon as the two ladies went along Broadway, looking at the windows. Between West Eighty-first and Eighty-second Streets, they suddenly saw a familiar figure. There, coming toward them, was Grandmother M. again, dressed exactly as she had been twenty-five years before, with her faded brown coat, the little bonnet, and the peculiar shoes.

The two ladies were flabbergasted. What does one do under such conditions? They decided to wait and see. And see they did, for they stopped and let Grandmother M. pass them by. When she was only inches away from them, they could clearly see her face. She was as solid as anyone in the street, but she did not look at them. Instead, she kept staring ahead as if she were not aware of them or anyone else around. As she passed them, they could clearly hear the sound of her shuffling feet. There was no mistaking it: this was Grandmother M. dead twenty-five years but looking as good as new.

When the figure reached the next corner and disappeared around it, Carina sprang to life again. Within a few seconds she was at the corner. Before her, the side street was almost empty. No Grandmother. Again she had disappeared into thin air. What had the old lady wanted? Why did she appear to them? I could only guess that it was her way of saying, "Don't you forget your Granny. I'm still going strong!"

Unfinished Business

The second category of "spirit returns," as the spiritualists like to call it, is unfinished business. While the first thought of a newly dead person might be to let the grieving family know there is no reason to cry and that life does continue, the second thought might well be how to attend to whatever was left unfinished on earth and should be taken care of.

The evidence pointing to a continuance of personality after dissolution of the body shows that mundane worries and desires go right along with the newly liberated soul. Just because one is now in another, finer dimension does not mean one can entirely neglect one's obligations in the physical world. This will vary according to the individual and his or her attitudes toward responsibilities in general while in the body. A coward does not become a hero after death, and a slob does not turn into a paragon of orderliness. There is, it appears, really nothing ennobling in dying per se. It would seem that there is an opportunity to grasp the overall scheme of the universe a lot better from over there, but this comprehension is by no means compulsory, nor is the newly arrived soul brainwashed in any way. Freedom to advance or stand still exists on both sides of the veil.

However, if a person dies suddenly and manages to move on without staying in the earth's atmosphere and becoming a so-called ghost, then that person may also take along all unresolved problems. These problems may range from such major matters as insurance and sustenance for the family, guidance for the young, lack of a legal will, unfinished works of one kind or another, incomplete manuscripts or compositions, disorderly states of affairs leaving the heirs in a quandary as to where "everything" is, to such minor matters as leaving the desk in disorder, not having answered a couple of letters, or having spoken rashly to a loved one. To various individuals such frustrations may mean either a little or a lot, depending again on the makeup of the person's personality. There are no objective standards as to what constitutes a major problem and what is minor. What appears to one person a major problem may seem quite unimportant when viewed through another individual's eyes.

Generally speaking, the need to communicate with living people arises from a compulsion to set matters right. Once the contact has been made and the problem understood by the living, the deceased's need to reappear is no longer present, unless the living *fail* to act on the deceased communicator's request. Then that person will return again and again until he gets his way.

All communications are by no means as crystal clear as a Western Union message. Some come in symbolic language or can only be understood if one knows the communicator's habit patterns. But the grasping of the request is generally enough to relieve the very real anxieties of the deceased. There are cases where the request cannot possibly be granted, because conditions have changed or much time has gone on. Some of these communications stem from very old grievances.

A communicator appearing in what was once her home in the 1880s insisted that the papers confirming her ownership of the house be found and the property be turned back to her from the current owners. To her the ancient wrong was a current problem, of course, but we could not very well oblige her eighty-five years later and throw out an owner who had bought the property in good faith many years after her passing. We finally persuaded the restless personality that we would *try* to do what she wanted, at the same time assuring her that things had changed. It calmed her anxiety, and because we had at least listened to her with a sympathetic ear, she did not insist on actual performance of the promise.

An extreme case of this kind concerns a Mrs. Sally V. of Chicago. This lady was married to a plasterer who gave her ten children, but in 1943 she nevertheless divorced her active spouse. She then married a distant relative of her husband's, also called V. But divorce did not stop the plasterer from molesting her. He allegedly threatened her over the years until she could stand it no longer. It was then that the woman, in her despair, decided to get rid of her ex-husband in a most dramatic and, she thought, final way by murdering him.

The opportunity came when a nineteen-year-old cousin of hers stopped in on leave from his outfit, which was stationed at Fort Benning, Georgia.

"Would you kill my ex-husband for me? I'd give a month's pay for it."

"You've got yourself a deal," the cousin is quoted as saying obligingly, according to the United Press, and when she offered him $90 for the job, he thought $50 was quite enough. To a soldier conditioned to war, human life is sometimes cheap.

Soon afterward Mr. Charles V. was found dead in his basement apartment, his head bashed in by a hammer.

The story might have remained a secret between the willing widow and her obliging cousin had it not been for the unwilling spirit of the late Mr. V.

The murder took place on a Tuesday night, right after she made the deal. On Wednesday morning, August 5, 1953, Mrs. V. was startled to see her late husband standing before her in a menacing attitude. She was terrified and called the police. The detectives took a dim view of her ghost story, but in the questioning her own guilt was brought out and the soldier was arrested. One certainly cannot blame the late Mr. V. for wanting the unfinished business of his murder cleared up.

The psychic experience of Clarence T. of California is particularly interesting, because Mr. T. has been blind all his life. In 1946 he was married in San Francisco to a lady who is still his wife. They went to New York shortly afterward, and he did not know any of his wife's friends or family at the time.

Mr. T. remembers the day of his arrival in New York: it was the day famed baseball player Babe Ruth was to be buried. Mr. T. and his wife were to stay with his new mother-in-law on the lower East Side.

The mother-in-law worked as a janitor and usually came home around 1 A.M. The apartment itself was on the ground floor, the last apartment on the floor, about seventy feet from the front door of the house. It was a warm night, and the newly married couple decided to sit up and await the mother's return. The radio was playing a rebroadcast of the solemn mass given at Babe Ruth's funeral, and the time was just 11 o'clock.

At the moment when the music started, both Mr. and Mrs. T. heard the front door open and someone walk down the hall toward them. With Mr. T.'s extrasensive hearing—many blind people have this—he could distinguish the fact that the person coming toward them wore no shoes. Then this person came through the door, and Mr. T. felt a hand go over his eyes. He thought it was the mother-in-law and said, "Mother?"

Mrs. T. assured him he was mistaken; there was no one to be seen, although she, too, had heard footsteps. Now the invisible person walked past T. and turned around, facing him. All at once both T. and his wife noticed the strong smell of garlic, and each asked the other if he or she was cleaning garlic! But even stranger, T., who is totally blind, could suddenly *see* a woman standing before him—a short woman with long hair, wearing a loose dress and no shoes. Over the dress she wore an apron, and she had one hand in the apron pocket. There was a noise coming from the pocket as if paper were being crumpled. Her eyes were droopy almost to the point of being shut. T. stared at the apparition for what seemed like a long time to him. Finally the woman spoke: "Tell Julia to throw away those stones!"

She repeated it twice. When the religious music on the radio had ended, she turned and walked from the room, although neither of them could hear any footsteps this time. But T. *saw* her walk away. All the time the visitor had been with them, they had felt very strange, as if they were paralyzed. They could not move and just sat there in a daze. The moment the figure disappeared, the spell was broken, and they discovered to their surprise that it had lasted a full hour.

Since Mrs. T. had not seen the figure, T. told her what the woman had said. Mrs. T.'s first name is Julia, but the message made no sense to her. While they were trying to figure out what had happened to them, the mother-in-law returned, and they reported the incident to her.

"My God," the mother-in-law exclaimed, "what does she want?" There was *another* Julia whom she knew, and the message might apply to her. It seemed that this Julia had been in the apartment the night before and was due to return the next morning for another visit. Why not question her about the apparition? Next morning, the T.s met the other Julia and described their experience to her in every detail. The young woman nodded with understanding.

"That was my mother," she cried. "She's been dead for two years."

Then she explained that her late mother had been in the habit of carrying garlic on her person, in her apron pocket to be exact. She had collected small stones wherever she went and would put them into small containers to keep. These containers with the stones her mother had collected were still cluttering up her home. Under the circumstances, the young woman decided to take the stones and scatter them over her mother's grave. The apparition has not returned since.

The N.s lived in a large brick house on Delaware Avenue, Buffalo, in one of the better residential districts. They shared the house with the actual owner, Mr. N.'s

uncle by marriage. After Mr. N's aunt died, strange knockings began to disturb the inhabitants of the house. There never was any rational explanation for these raps. Then, several months later, Mr. N. happened to be cleaning out a closet in what had been the aunt's storeroom. There she had put away personal souvenirs and other belongings. In the cleanup, he came across a wrapped package in a drawer. He picked it up, and as he did so he distinctly heard a voice—a human voice—talking to him, although he knew he was quite alone in the room. It was not clear enough for him to make out the words. It was late at night; no one else was stirring in the house, and there was no radio or TV playing.

Mr. N. took the package with him and walked down a long hall to the bedroom where his wife was reading in bed. For a distance of seventy-five feet, all along the way, the voice kept talking to him!

As he entered the bedroom, Mrs. N. looked up from her book and said: "Who was that talking to you?"

Mr. N. became very agitated and somehow found himself taking the strange package to the basement. As if he had been led there he then opened the furnace and threw the package into it. He had the strong feeling that his aunt did not wish to have that package opened or found. As soon as the flames had destroyed the contents of the package, Mr. N.'s mood returned to normal. There were no further psychic occurrences in the house after that. Evidently the aunt did not wish to have her private correspondence or other papers made public, and once that possibility was obviated, her need to communicate ended.

Sometimes the "unfinished business" is monkey business. A person who dies but is unable to accept the change in status, unable to let go of earthly appetites, will be drawn back to the people he or she was close to, and sometimes this return may express itself rather physically. Wild as it sounds, it is entirely possible for a dead man to express love to a living woman, and vice versa. It is not proper, of course, not because of moral reasons but simply because it is very impractical and truly "out of its element." But it does happen.

Mrs. Audrey L. of Baltimore, Maryland, has been a widow for four years. As soon as her husband died, her troubles started. She would hear him "still around." He would call her by name. He would move around in his usual manner in what used to be his house. Mrs. L. did not see this, but she heard it clearly. At night she would hear him snore. Finally she decided to sell their house and move to an apartment.

For a while Mr. L. was not in evidence. But not for long. The nocturnal disturbances began again. This time the phenomena were also visual. Her husband's figure appeared next to her bed, grabbed her by the wrists, and tried to pull her out of bed. She looked at him closely, despite her terror, and noticed that the familiar figure was somewhat transparent. Nevertheless, he was real, and the touch of his hands was the touch of two strong hands.

There is no easy solution for this type of "unfinished business." Exorcism will yield results only if the other part is willing to accept it. But if the dead husband's moral level is not attuned to that approach, the service will not work. Only the woman herself can reject him, if she is strong enough in her determination to close this psychic door. For it is true that there may be a deep-seated desire present in the unconscious that permits the transgression to take place.

Sometimes the business the departing person wishes to complete cannot be finished until many years later. Yet there are cases where the dead communicator somehow knows this beforehand, indicating that the threshold of death removes also the limitations of time.

An interesting case in point concerns a prominent midwestern physician's wife, herself an educator. A number of years ago Mrs. B. was married to a professional gentleman. They had two children. Their marriage was happy, there were no financial or professional problems, and yet the husband was given to unaccountable depressions. One evening the husband went out, never to return. Hours went by. Mrs. B. anxiously awaited his return, although she had no suspicion that anything drastic had happened. Her husband had been in excellent spirits when he left. Finally she became too tired to sit up and wait for his return. She went to bed, assuming her husband would be coming in very late.

Her sleep was interrupted in the middle of the night by the feeling of a presence in the room. As she opened her eyes and looked, she discerned at the foot of her bed the form of her husband, and all at once she realized that he had gone across to the hereafter.

"You are not to worry," the husband spoke; "everything will be all right. Wally will take care of you and the children." The apparition vanished.

Early the next morning she was notified that he had fatally shot himself, evidently overcome by a fit of depression. In her great grief she tried to pass the visitation off as a dream, although she knew in her heart that she had been quite awake at the time she saw her husband standing at the foot of her bed.

Two years passed, and the matter sank into the deepest recesses of her subconscious mind. At the time of the message, she had not been able to make much of it. Wally was a dear friend of her late husband and herself but nothing more. Out of a clear blue sky the telephone rang one day, and before she picked up the receiver Mrs. B. *knew* it was Wally! The friendship was resumed and ultimately led to marriage, and Wally has indeed taken care of her and the children ever since!

Bernhard M., sixty-four, happily married, and a largely self-taught scholar, makes his home in Southern California. His literary criticism and philosophical essays have appeared largely in such scholarly publications as *Books Abroad*. A disability pension augments his income from writing. His mother, Frances M., was a gifted musician who has always shown an interest in psychic research. When Mr. M. Sr., who had been with the San Francisco Symphony Orchestra, had passed on, the family went through difficult times, and young Bernhard had to work hard to keep the family in groceries. At the age of forty-two, Mrs. M. died of a stroke at her place of work, the Conservatory of Music and Drama in Point Loma, California.

A few days after her passing, Bernhard attended the funeral. At the time, he was told that the ashes would be placed in a niche in Greenwood Cemetery. With that reassurance, he left town. Returning to Point Loma from his business trip a month later, he had a strange dream. His late mother appeared to him in what seemed to be a small room, quite dark, and she seemed in great distress.

"Everything went wrong," she complained. "Even my ashes are mislaid!"

Her son remonstrated with her in his dream, assuring her that this could not be the case. But in reply she showed him a little table on which there was a wire basket containing a small copper box.

When he awoke the next morning, Bernhard M. rejected what he thought was an absurd dream brought on, no doubt, by his grief and recent upset over the death of his beloved brother. But it so happened he had planned on going into town to see if his mother's name had been properly inscribed on the door to the niche at the cemetery.

On the way he ran into a friend, May L., a singer, who informed him that she had just been to the cemetery to pay her respects to Mrs. M.—and his mother's ashes were not there!

On hearing this, Mr. M. asked Mrs. L. to return to the cemetery with him to make inquiry. Sure enough, his father's ashes were there, but his mother's were not. He questioned the caretaker, who checked the entries in his books.

"No record of a Mrs. M.," the caretaker informed him.

With mounting agony and anger, Bernhard M. went to the funeral parlor.

After some embarrassing investigations, it developed that the box of ashes had never left the building. Bernhard then took them personally out to the cemetery, to make sure everything would be as it should. By a strange quirk of fate, he traveled the identical route he had often taken with his mother when they had gone together to Point Loma.

When Mr. M. related this experience to me, he suddenly felt his mother's presence again, as if she were pleased at his having told me, so that others might know that the dead *can* return.

Florine McC.'s solid stone house, built on one of San Francisco's many hills in the year 1895, has withstood earthquakes and the big fire and is likely to withstand the next catastrophe, if one comes. Mrs. McC.'s brush with the uncanny started in 1929, when she was a newlywed living in Tampa, Florida. To everyone's surprise—including her own—she suffered an unexpected heart attack. A doctor was summoned to the home and, after examining her, pronounced her dead. A towel was then placed over her face and the doctor started to console the young husband.

"I'll have to pass the undertaker on the way, and I'll leave the death certificate there," the doctor said to her husband.

"But she's so young," the husband sighed, for Mrs. McC. was only nineteen at the time.

The strange part of it was that Mrs. McC. could hear the conversation, although she could not move. Despite the fact that her eyes were covered, she could *see* the entire scene. Moreover, she had the strangest sensation that she was about two inches high!

Then, it seemed to her, through her mouth came a replica of her own body, very small and without clothing. She went up to the corner of the ceiling and stayed there, looking down. She had left her body down below. The landlady had joined the mourners now, and young Mrs. McC. thought what fun it would be to wiggle her hands and frighten the woman. The thought of seeing the landlady scurry from the room in haste amused her. But then she became serious and suddenly dived down and reentered her own body through the nostrils, or so it seemed. Her physical body then became warm again, and she broke into an uncontrollable burst of laughter. Immediately the doctor proceeded to give her an injection to revive her. As soon as she was conscious she explained what had happened to her.

The doctor shook his head. But he listened with widening eyes when Mrs. McC. repeated every word that had been said during the time she had been "legally dead."

She had noticed, during her temporary stay at the ceiling, that the doctor had squeezed her arms, perhaps to bring her back to life, and she wondered if she would feel sore when she returned into her body. But the arms did not feel painful. A curious thought, though, kept intruding: "He forgot something. . . . Whoever was in charge forgot some duty I had to do, . . . but I don't understand it."

Perhaps that was why she was still alive. Someone forgot to pull a switch?

Throughout the years, Florine McC. displayed extrasensory abilities. These ranged from such simple things as foreknowledge of events or places where she had not been, to the more disturbing forebodings of trouble affecting her loved ones, and her subsequent ability to come to the aid of her troubled family.

Her father, Olaus S., born in Norway and brought to the United States at age two, was in the hotel business until his retirement many years later. He passed away in 1946 at age seventy-nine, after a full and satisfactory life.

About a month after his death, Mrs. McC. was in bed in her room on the fourth floor of the house on Grove Street, which had been her father's. She had not been asleep long when she was awakened by a knock at the door. She woke up, and to her amazement she saw her late father stick his head into the opened door, calling out in a cheery voice: "Hi there, Florence!"

Mrs. McC.'s baptismal name is Florence, but she has never liked it, preferring the form "Florine" instead. However, her father liked to tease her about it, and on such occasions he would call her Florence.

It was about 2 o'clock in the morning. Mr. S. entered the room of his daughter and stood near the bed, looking at her.

"You can't find it," he said.

Mrs. McC., fully awake now, observed her father's apparition. She noticed that he wore a tweed overcoat, his customary shirt and tie, and his hat. He removed the hat and put his hands into his pockets. The strange thing was that she could see *through* him, and he was surrounded by the most beautiful blue rays, lighting up the entire room.

"Dad, come over and sit down," she said, and pointed to the chaise longue. There was no fear, even though she was aware that he was dead. It seemed somehow perfectly natural to her now. Although she had heard of psychic matters, she had been raised in a house where such matters were neither discussed or believed.

The apparition walked over and sat on the chaise longue, putting his feet on a stool, as he had often done in life. This was his chair.

"You're looking for a paper, Florine," her father said.

"Yes, Dad," she nodded, "and I can't find it."

"You go down to my bedroom and take the top drawer out," her father instructed her, "and underneath the drawer you will find it pasted on. Also, honey, you will find a letter!" The voice sounded as normal and steady as her father's voice had always sounded.

"Dad, I'm going to cover you up," the daughter said, and she took a robe to place over his feet, as she had often done in his life.

The moment the robe touched her father's legs, the apparition disappeared—gone like a puff of smoke!

"Did I dream it?" she asked herself, wondering if it had really happened. She felt awake, but she was still not sure whether she was in the midst of a dream. She decided then and there, with the curious logic of dreamers who see themselves within the dream, not to touch anything and to go straight back to bed. This she did and quickly went off to sleep.

In the morning, she arose and inspected the room. The door, which she had closed firmly on retiring, was still ajar. Her robe was lying on the chaise longue. She looked closer and discovered that the material was still folded in a way that indicated that it had been supported by a pair of legs! She then knew she had not dreamed the visitation.

She ran downstairs and looked for the drawer her father had indicated. There, underneath, were the papers that had been missing. These papers proved her father's birth and nationality and were of great importance in the settling of the estate. There was also the letter he had mentioned, and it was a beautiful farewell letter from a father to his daughter. Throughout his long life, Olaus S. had never scoffed at the possibility of personal survival. The family took a dim view of Florine's experience, but the close communion father and daughter had always enjoyed during his lifetime was the reason she had been singled out for the visit—plus the fact that there was a real need, unfinished business, that only a visit from the deceased could bring to a close.

When the Dead Help the Living

We have seen how the departed manifest to the living to let them know that their lives continue in another world or because they have some unfinished business in the mundane sphere that needs completing. Having thus manifested, they will not communicate again unless a crisis comes up in the lives of their loved ones or friends and their services are perhaps "required." This is another category of communication, and it is one that also occurs frequently.

In many recorded instances, people who have died will nevertheless retain an interest in the affairs of those they have left behind. It is moot what drives them to do this. Is there a law over there that rewards them for shepherding or watching over their people? Are they doing it because virtue has its own rewards? Are they compelled to continue the bond from a motivation of ego importance? Do they want not to be left out of the continuing lives of their families? Or is it because the living so strongly need their help that they are drawn back to intercede by the very need for their intercession? I am rather inclined to think that there are set rules as to when there may be this kind of communication and how far they may go in warning the living of impending dangers or other future developments.

What this law is in detail is not easy to fathom, and even more difficult is the question of who originated the law and who created the originator. Suffice it to establish rationally and methodically that the law exists and that there are bona fide instances of an interest taken in the affairs of the living by their dead.

This interest can take many forms, but the common denominator is always the fact that the communication results in some benefit to the living from the knowledge obtained through the communication. This may be a warning of disaster or a foretelling of events to come that cannot be changed, but if one knows what is in store ahead of time, the blow is softened for him.

The interest in the living may be less striking and merely gently supervisory, a part of seeing how things are going or of encouraging a depressed person. It is not at all like a Big Brother feeling, with the invisibles watching you, but it gives a warm, comfortable impression that one is not alone and that forces greater than oneself *care*.

Thus this interest is an expression of love, and as such it is certainly a positive force, far from frightening or dangerous.

The living who are fortunate enough to have a deceased relative take an interest in their lives should accept this as natural and live with it. They should not defer decisions to the spiritual watchdog, of course, but make their own mundane decisions as they feel best. Nevertheless, sometimes the greater knowledge of the ones beyond the veil can help the living understand their own problems better and thus provide them with ammunition for a better judgment.

Mrs. Harry C. lives near a large city in Pennsylvania. Of Irish-English ancestry, she was born in North Carolina and came from an old family that was given a land grant there by George III. The psychic gift was not unknown in her family, mainly on her mother's side. After a year in college, Mrs. C. became a trained practical nurse. She married a soldier from Pennsylvania in 1945 and over the years bore five sons.

Although she had had clairvoyant experiences from time to time, it was not until she was eleven years old that she received a visit from the beyond. At that time an aunt was living with her family to look after the children while their mother worked. Thus it happened that in her childhood Mrs. C. spent many hours with her aunt; they read and sewed together, and there was a strong bond between them. Until the aunt died, Mrs. C. had shared a room with her mother, but after the death of the aunt she was given her aunt's bedroom. A few weeks after the funeral, Mrs. C., then eleven, was sitting on the porch of the house when she heard her name being called. She glanced up and saw her late aunt standing in the door, holding it ajar.

"Gretchen, will you please come in here for a moment. I have something to tell you," the aunt said in the same tone of voice Mrs. C. had heard her use while alive. Obediently and not at all frightened, the eleven-year-old girl put down her sewing and followed her beckoning aunt into the house. But as she started to go in, the apparition slowly faded away! What did the aunt want to tell her little companion? That life continued and that she still cared how the family was?

A few weeks after this incident, a girlfriend of Gretchen's by the name of Maxine F. stopped in so that they might attend a movie together. Just as the two girls were about to leave, Mrs. C. heard her name being called. All set to go to the movie, she decided to ignore this. But the voice called again: "Gretchen! Gretchen!"

"Your mother's calling you," Maxine said, and waited.

So the two children went back to the kitchen, where Gretchen's mother was washing dishes. The mother had not called her. Other than the three of them, the house was empty at the time. But Gretchen knew her late aunt was calling her.

As the days went on, the aunt continued to make her presence felt in the house. She was not about to be abandoned at the cemetery but insisted on continuing with her duties—and rights—in the household. At night, Gretchen would hear someone drumming fingernails on the table. This was a lifelong habit of her aunt's. Often she would awaken to see the aunt standing at the foot of her bed, looking at her. Gretchen was by no means alone in observing these phenomena. A friend of her mother's by the name of Mary L. once occupied the same room. She too heard the drumming of the invisible fingernails.

It also fell to Gretchen to go through her late aunt's effects. This was a very difficult task. On certain days she felt her aunt's overpowering presence hovering over her, taking a keen interest in what she was doing. When the pressure became too great, Gretchen threw her aunt's old letters down and ran out of the house for a breath of fresh air. Somehow she knew her aunt would not follow her there.

Many years later, when Gretchen had become Mrs. Harry C., she and her husband occupied a house in Pennsylvania. At first Mrs. C. thought they had acquired a "resident ghost," something left over from the past of one of the earlier owners of the house. The house itself had been built in 1904 as part of a "company town" for the Westinghouse Corporation. The houses then were occupied by workers of that corporation, but in the 1920s the company decided to get out of the real estate business, and the houses reverted to individual ownership. A number of tenants then occupied the house in succession. Several ladies had died on the third floor of the house, center of the psychic manifestations during the time Mr. and Mrs. C. occupied the dwelling. But none of these people had died violently or were part of a tragic situation of the kind that may sometimes create a ghostly phenomenon. Of course, the early history of the house when it was company property could not be checked out as there were no records kept of the tenants during that time. Mrs. C. thought that perhaps one of the early owners of the house had been the victim of a tragedy and that it was the restless shade of that person that was staying on. Her belief was reinforced by the fact that since her childhood and the encounters with her late aunt, she had not experienced anything so strong in the other houses they had lived in. But her clairvoyance had been active elsewhere, and she has never been entirely without some form of ESP experience.

The phenomena were mainly footsteps on the third floor of the house and someone walking down the stairs when the occupants knew no one was up there. In 1961 Mrs. C. learned that their unseen guest was a woman. One of her boys was in delicate health and had major surgery when only seven weeks old. One night Mrs. C. woke up to hear the baby crying. At the same time, however, she became aware of another voice, someone singing softly as if to quiet the baby. Wondering who it might be, Mrs. C. rose and went into the baby's room.

There, near the crib, stood a lady. She was a small woman with a lovely face, dressed in what seemed World War I clothes and hairstyle. The dress was pale lavender trimmed with black braid and filigree buttons. It had a lace bodice and jabot and a hobble skirt in the manner of the turn-of-the-century clothes.

Far from being terrified by the stranger, Mrs. C. stepped closer. When she approached the crib, the lady smiled and stepped to one side to let her pass so that she might tend the baby. When she looked up again, the lady was gone. The visitor's presence was no longer required; the mother had come to look after her own.

After that first time, she saw the lady several times—sometimes in the baby's room, sometimes going up and down the third-floor stairs. Later Mrs. C. had another baby, and the stranger also occupied herself with the new arrival, as if tending babies were something very natural and dear to her. But who could she possibly be?

When Mrs. C.'s five-year-old son was sick in the fall of 1967, he once asked his mother who the strange lady was who had come and sung to him, and he proceeded to describe her. Mrs. C. had never discussed her own experiences with the boy, but she knew at once that he too had seen the lady upstairs.

By this time it began to dawn on her that perhaps this lady was not a "resident ghost" but a deceased relative continuing an interest in her family. But she could not be sure one way or the other, and there the matter stood when her oldest son Lonnie and his wife Sally came to spend their Christmas weekend with her in 1967. Sally is a registered nurse by profession and scientifically minded. For that reason Mrs. C. had not seen fit to discuss psychic experiences with her or to tell her of the unusual goings-on on the third floor of the house.

It so happened that the young couple were put into the third-floor bedroom for the weekend. Because they were both tired from the trip, Mrs. C. thought it best to put them up there, as far removed from street noises as possible. The room is rather large, with one bed on each side and a dormer window between the two beds. The daughter-in-law took one bed, the son the other. They were soon fast asleep.

On Saturday morning Lonnie, the son, came down first for breakfast. He and his mother were having coffee in the kitchen when Sally arrived. She looked rather pale and haggard. After Mrs. C. had poured her a cup of coffee, Sally looked at her mother-in-law.

"Mom, did you come up to the room for any reason during the night?"

"Of course not," Mrs. C. replied.

"Did *you* get up during the night, Lonnie?" Sally turned to her husband. He assured her that he had not budged all night.

"Well," the girl said, swallowing hard, "then I have something strange to tell you."

She had been awakened in the middle of the night by a voice calling her name. Fully awake, she saw a lady standing beside her bed. She was not sure how the apparition disappeared, but eventually she went back to sleep, being very tired. Nothing further happened. What she had seen, she was sure of. That it was not a dream—that, too, she knew for a fact. But who was the stranger? The two young people left a couple of days later, and nothing further was said about the incident.

About three weeks after Christmas, Mrs. C. went to North Carolina to spend a week at her mother's home. During a conversation, Mrs. C.'s mother mentioned that she had recently been going through some things in an old trunk in the attic. Among many other items, she had found a small photograph of her grandmother that she did not know she had. If Mrs. C. wanted it she would be happy to give it to her, especially as Grandmother L. had always shown a special interest in her family.

Mrs. C. thanked her mother and took the little photograph home with her to Pennsylvania. In her own home she propped it up on the dresser in her room, until she could find a proper frame for it. But after it had stood there for a couple of days, Mrs. C. thought that the old photograph might become soiled and decided to put it away in the top dresser drawer.

That night Mrs. C. was almost asleep when she became aware of a humming sound in the room. She opened her eyes and noticed that the air in her room was as thick as fog and she could scarcely see the opposite side of the room. In a moment, her grandmother walked in from the hall and stood beside her bed. Mrs. C., now fully awake, raised herself up on one elbow so that the apparition would know she was awake and observing her. Immediately the figure turned and put one hand on Mrs. C.'s dresser, on exactly the spot where the picture had been until two days ago. Then she turned her head and looked directly at Mrs. C. Somehow Mrs. C. understood what her grandmother wanted. She got out of bed and took the picture from the drawer and put it back on top of the dresser again. With that the apparition smiled and walked out of the room. The air cleared, and the humming stopped.

Mrs. C. had been "aware" of her grandmother's presence in the house for some time but never in so definite a way. She knew that Grandmother L. still considered herself one of the family and took a keen interest in the living. That is why she had appeared to Mrs. C.'s daughter-in-law

Sally, not to frighten her or even to ask for anything or because of any unfinished business, but merely to let her know she *cared*.

As a member of the household, Grandmother L. had naturally felt a bit hemmed in when her picture was relegated to a stuffy drawer. Especially as she had probably instigated its rediscovery to begin with! Until the picture turned up, Mrs. C. could not have been sure who the lady was. But now that she realized she had her own grandmother to protect her family, Mrs. C. did not mind at all. With help being scarce these days, and expensive and unreliable, it was rather comforting to know that an unpaid relative was around to look for the well-being of the family.

But the lady did not show up after the incident with the photograph. Could it be that, like Lohengrin, once she was recognized her usefulness to the C.s had come to an end?

Mrs. Betty S., a California housewife, has not the slightest interest in the psychic. When her father passed away in 1957 she mourned him, but since he left his wife well provided for, she did not worry unduly about her mother, even though they lived in different cities. Shortly after, she had a vision of her late father so real that she felt it could not have been a dream. Dream or vision, there stood her father wearing a white shirt and blue pants. He looked radiant and alive.

"Is mother all right?" he asked.

Mrs. S. assured her father everything was just fine. The apparition went away. But a few days later Mrs. S.'s mother was on the telephone. She was in great distress. Someone had been in her bank deposit box, and two valuable deeds had disappeared without a trace! In addition, money and bonds had also been taken, making her position anything but financially secure.

All at once Mrs. S. realized why her late father had been concerned. Evidently he knew or sensed something she had not yet become aware of.

Her father never reappeared to her. But the missing two deeds mysteriously returned to the deposit box about three months later. To this day this is a puzzle Mrs. S. has not been able to solve. But it was comforting to know that her late father had continued to care for her mother.

It is well known that often grandparents get very attached to the offspring of their children. When death separates a grandparent from the third generation, a desire to look in on them can be very strong. Consider the case of Mrs. Carol S. of Massachusetts.

In 1963 her first son was born. On one of the first nights after her return from the hospital, she awoke in the night to see a misty light near the ceiling of her room. It hovered between the baby's bassinet and the foot of the bed. A moment later the light took the form of her late grandfather's face and continued to glow. At the same time, Mrs. S. had the impression her grandfather had come to see his first great-grandchild.

She herself had been a first grandchild, and her mother had been the grandfather's firstborn; the interest would have been understandable. For a moment the face remained, then it drifted into a fog and soon disappeared altogether.

In 1969, Mrs. S.'s other grandfather—on her father's side of the family—also passed away. A little later her grandmother gave his bed to Mrs. S. The first night her six-year-old son slept in it, he reported a strange "dream."

His great-grandfather had come to him and told him he lived in heaven and was happy and could look down and see him. This "dream" was strange because the boy had no knowledge that the bed he slept in had any connection with the great-grandfather.

Mrs. Joseph B., a housewife living in a medium-sized eastern city, a member of the Girl Scout council, a Sunday school teacher, and a busy, average person with a good, healthy mind, has no time for fantasies or daydreaming. Of Pennsylvania Dutch background, she is married to a steelworker of Italian antecedents. Her hobbies are bowling and reading, not psychic research.

She and her husband and son shared a house, while her mother lived across town by herself. But every ten days or so her mother would visit them. The mother was familiar with the house and would always let herself in by the front door. These visits became a normal routine, and the years went by peacefully until the mother died. She was not forgotten, but neither did the B. family go into deep mourning. Her death was simply accepted as a natural occurrence, and life went on.

One year after her passing, Mr. and Mrs. B. were getting ready for bed upstairs in their house. Their son was fast asleep in his room. The time was 1 A.M. Mr. B. was in the bathroom, and Mrs. B. had just gotten into bed, looking forward to a good night's sleep. Tomorrow was Saturday, and they could sleep longer.

At this moment she heard the downstairs front door of the house open. Her husband, who had evidently heard it also, came to the bathroom door and said: "I thought I heard someone come in."

"So did I," replied Mrs. B., and she called downstairs: "Who's down there?"

Her mother's voice came back. "It's only me; don't come down—I'm not staying!" Then they heard her familiar steps resounding through the house as she walked about and finally left by the back door.

As if it were the most ordinary thing in the world for her mother to visit them at 1 A.M., the husband returned to the bathroom, and Mrs. B. went back to bed. The power of the routine they had grown accustomed to over the years had left them immune to Mother's visits as being anything but routine. They were both tired and fell asleep soon afterward. In the morning, Mr. B. looked at the doors, both the front and the rear doors. They were locked *from the inside*, just as he had left them the previous night before retiring! As Mrs. B. came down for breakfast he

silently pointed at the door. It was then that it hit them with sudden impact that the mother had been dead for just a year.

They talked it over. Both agreed that the voice they had heard had been the mother's voice and that it had sounded the same as it used to. Evidently this was Mother's way of saying she was still visiting them. Nothing more was heard from her for a long time. Perhaps she had other things to do or found her new world more intriguing.

But on January 9, 1967, Mrs. B.'s older sister woke up to hear her mother calling her urgently. She immediately got out of bed to answer her mother, completely forgetting for the moment that her mother had been dead for all those years. Three times the voice called, and the tone was one of great distress. Was she trying to tell her something, and if so, what? The following night, Mrs. B.'s sister found out. Her husband died quite suddenly. Perhaps her mother had tried to soften the blow by forewarning her.

Not every communication from the dead is welcomed by the living. A certain percentage of superstitious people might even consider such contacts evil or devil-inspired or dangerous. Otherwise rational people refuse the proffered hand from beyond the grave. They don't doubt that their loved ones continue to exist in another world. They just don't want those loved ones around in *theirs*.

A Mrs. Marge C. in New Jersey has had trouble with her grandfather for years. It all started when he was dying in the local hospital and asked to see her. Although she had not been really close to him, it was his dying wish; yet her mother did not grant it. Soon after, she felt a strange chill. Later she realized that it had occurred at the very moment of his passing, but she did not know it at the time.

Still a little girl, Marge was present when her uncle and aunt brought their new baby home with them. She happened to look up, and there at the back door stood her grandfather, watching. As he noticed her look, he reached out to her. But instead of compassion for the old man, she only felt terror at the thought.

A little later, one evening as she was getting ready for bed she heard someone calling her. This was peculiar because she was home *alone*. But she went downstairs to the kitchen. There was her grandfather, gazing at her. She yelled in fright, and he vanished.

The next time the unwelcome visitor made an appearance she was sixteen. This time she was at a girlfriend's house and happened to glance out the window at a quiet moment. There was grandfather again, looking at her from outside. She still did not want any part of the manifestations.

Just before she met her husband in 1965 she saw her grandfather again. He reached for her and tried to speak, but she yelled and fainted. Perhaps the grandfather got the message that appearing in all his celestial glory was frightening to his granddaughter; at any rate he did not come back again. But the problem was by no means solved. Frequently Marge could sense him around and hear him call out to her. Even her husband heard the voice and of course could understand it. Finally, Marge took her problem to her mother to find out why her grandfather was so insistent. Her mother had been his favorite child, it seems, and Marge, ever since she was born, had grown into the image of her mother. Was that the reason her grandfather wanted to communicate with her?

I explained the possible reasons to Mrs. C. and asked her to be understanding toward her grandfather. I never heard anything further from her, so perhaps grandfather has given up.

Dr. Lucia B., a medical doctor specializing in cancer research and a graduate of a leading European university, has had a distinguished medical career as a chest specialist. A vivacious lady, she speaks several languages. Her parents moved from her native Vienna to Prague, where her father was editor and published a group of magazines. Later her father lived in Berlin, where he ran a successful publishing house.

Dr. B. is married to a retired Italian army general and lives in an apartment on New York's West Side. She has lived in the United States on and off since 1932. Prior to that, she was a physician with the Health Department of Puerto Rico. Her major contribution to medicine, she feels, was the discovery of the enzyme that inhibits the cancer cells of the respiratory system. Unfortunately the New York climate did not agree with her, and when I met her she was ready to pull up stakes again and return to Italy.

Dr. B. came to my study in New York to talk about some unusual psychic experiences she wanted explained. As a medical doctor, she had a certain reluctance to accept these events at face value, and yet, as an observant and brilliantly logical individual, she knew that what had happened to her was perfectly real and not the result of an overactive hallucinatory imagination.

In 1940, when the first of these astounding events took place, Lucia B. lived at the famous Villa Horace in Tivoli, Italy. World War II was on, and her husband was on active duty as a major in the Italian army. They had just been transferred to Tivoli and lived at the villa, which was then the property of an Englishwoman whom the Fascists did not touch because she had lived among the Italians for a very long time. Dr. B. was and is a U.S. citizen, and there was some concern felt for her status. But for the moment no overt move had been made against her, and as the wife of an Italian officer she seemed safe for the time being, especially since the United States had not yet entered the war.

In May of that year, the Englishwoman left for two days to visit friends. Major B. had gone off to Civitavecchia to get some briefings at the military academy, leaving Dr. B. all alone for a day. She decided to make good use of her "freedom" to go to nearby Rome the next morning for a full day's visit. It was a beautiful, warm evening, and there was one of those marvelous early summer sunsets Italy is famous for. Dr. B. stood by her windows and looked out into the landscape, unusually happy despite the heavy clouds of war all around her.

They had a pet turkey, which she went to visit in the downstairs portion of the villa. The house, built upon the original Roman foundations and incorporating much of the ancient house, is one of the great historical attractions of the area and is listed in most guidebooks. After a brief visit with the bird, she returned to her quarters and went to bed in a serene frame of mind.

She had left word to be awakened at 7 A.M. This was to be the duty of Gino, her husband's young aide-de-camp. But she was aroused from deep sleep at 6 A.M. not by Gino but by Oscar, Gino's orderly.

"Wake up—it's 6 o'clock," he said, and shook her.

Dr. Barrett was upset at this unusual treatment. "But it's supposed to be at seven," she countered, "and not you, but Gino's supposed to wake me. What are you doing in here? Get out!"

With that, the orderly fled, and Dr. B. tried to go back to sleep. But she could not. She got up and opened the shutters that let in the light of the already bright day. Then she opened the door that led to a long, spacious room called the mensa that was used as a mess hall. There was a chapel within the walls of the villa, and a row of benches formerly in the chapel had been placed along the walls of this long room so that people might sit there and pray, or just rest. Dr. B. stepped into the mess hall. On one of the first bench seats she saw a man sitting. It was her father, and then she realized why the orderly had awakened her out of turn: to let her know that her father had arrived.

"So you're not dead after all," she said, and went over to greet him.

Her father had left New York in October 1938 and gone back to Prague. In February of the following year she received a telegram from her father's mistress advising her briefly that her father had died and had been buried. There were some suspicious circumstances surrounding his death, Dr. B. learned later when she went to Prague to investigate. It was not a natural death, and there were witnesses who said he was afraid that he was being poisoned. But there was nothing she could do. Prague was already German-occupied, and it was difficult to open old wounds. She could not locate the ashes, but she did find the man who had signed her late father's death certificate. He freely admitted that he had not examined the body, but the death had occurred on the day the Nazis took over Czechoslovakia, so he took it for granted that it was suicide as he had "been told." Dr. B. has always suspected her father was "done in" through a plot involving a mistress, but she cannot prove it. She left Prague again, sure only that her father was indeed no longer alive.

But there he was, exactly as he used to look in the happy days when they went hiking into the mountains together. He was dressed in a brown tweed suit, a suit her mother had loathed because it was so old. His head was bent down, and at first she did not see his face. He wore a wide-brimmed hat.

"You're here," Dr. B. exclaimed. "I knew you weren't dead!"

For the moment she had forgotten all about her trip to Prague and the certainty of his demise. But she was otherwise awake and alert, and the day was already very bright.

She knelt down to look into his face and noticed how worn his suit was. He was as solid a man as ever, nothing transparent or vague about him. She started to talk to him in a voice filled with joy. He lifted his head somewhat, and the hat moved back up on his head a little. Now she could see his forehead and face more clearly, and she noticed that his skin was *greenish*.

"You must have been ill," she said, puzzled by this strange color. "Or have you been a prisoner?"

He answered her in a voice that came from his lips with great difficulty. "Yes," he said, "they let me sit in the sun so you would not get so scared."

(A materialization in full daylight requires a great deal of power and preparation, I thought, and is not at all common. But evidently the people arranging this strange encounter had seen a way to bring it off successfully.)

Dr. B. did not grasp the meaning of his remark. "You've been sick," she repeated. "Who brought you?"

Her father pointed to the rear of the huge room. Dr. B. looked in that direction. There were six other benches behind the one her father sat on, and then there was a buffet where the soldiers quartered in the house would eat, and beyond that, next to a wide open door, she saw standing Dr. K., a friend of both her father and herself. At the time she saw this man, he was living in New York, but as it dawned upon her that her father was a visitor from the other side, she asked him whether Dr. K. was also dead.

His reply came in a faltering voice. "No. *They* brought me."

Dr. B. looked again and saw behind the erect figure of Dr. K. five yellow-skinned people of small stature, apparently East Indians. They stood at a short distance from the doctor in a respectful position and were dressed in dark clothes.

"Who are these men?" she asked.

"They are from Java," her father replied. "They brought me here."

This did not make any sense whatever. She took her father's hand into her own now. It felt like ice. Now she realized that her intuitive feeling a moment before had been right.

"You are ——?"

He nodded.

"Why did you come? There must be a reason for it."

"Yes, there is."

"Am I in danger?"

"Yes," he replied, "you are. You must join the mountaineers."

"I must *what*?"

"Go over the mountains," her father admonished. "You must get guides."

This made very little sense, but before she could question her dead father further, he added: "When you're on the ship, these Javanese will look after you."

"But I don't need to be looked after."

"They'll watch you during the sea voyage," he repeated in a tired, faraway tone of voice.

At this moment, Gino the aide-de-camp who was supposed to wake her at 7 A.M., burst through the door. Seeing her already up and about, he became agitated.

"Who are all these people?" he demanded. Evidently he too could see them! "Who opened the gates for them?"

As Gino thundered into the mess hall, Dr. B.'s attention was momentarily distracted by him. When she looked back to her father, he had vanished! She glanced toward the other end of the room and found the Javanese and Dr. K. had also disappeared.

She explained that Oscar had awakened her an hour earlier. Gino swore he would punish the orderly for doing this and left immediately. Fifteen minutes later Gino returned rather sheepishly. It seemed that Oscar was supposed to get up at 5 A.M. but did not. No matter how the soldiers tried to rouse him, he would not wake up but seemed to be in a strange stupor. He was still asleep when Gino saw him, and there was no question that he had never set foot into the mensa room that morning!

Evidently Oscar was a physical medium, and it was his "substance" those in charge of "arrangements" had borrowed to make the materialization of Dr. B.'s father possible.

An additional proof that it was not the real Oscar but only a projection or simulation of the orderly that had awakened her at 6 A.M. could be seen in the fact that the keys to the outer gates were still in Gino's possession. No one else had a set of keys, and yet the doors were open when Gino arrived! They could not be opened from the inside; only with a key put into the lock from outside the gates could they be opened.

A long succession of soldiers testified that Oscar had never left his bed. At 7:10 A.M. he was still unconscious, and awoke only much later in the day.

When questioned by his superiors and Dr. B., Oscar was as mystified as they were. He recalled absolutely nothing and had never had a similar experience before.

"I should have known something was odd when he touched me and shook me violently to awaken me," Dr. B.

said as an afterthought. "In Italy that sort of thing just isn't done—you don't touch the *Signora*."

The real Oscar, of course, would never have dared to, but apparently the astrally-projected Oscar, perhaps under the control of another will, *had* to awaken her in order for her to receive the message her father had brought. It seemed to me like a wonderfully well-organized psychic plot.

With all the commotion, Dr. B. had completely forgotten she had to catch the 8 o'clock train to Rome. Getting hold of her emotions, she made the train just in time. When her husband returned two days later, she did not tell him about the incident. It wasn't the sort of thing an Italian officer would accept, she felt, and she thought it best to put it aside. Time would tell if there was something to all this.

Two months later her husband left for the war in earnest. This left her alone at the villa, and as the Germans took over more and more in Italy she was advised by the U.S. consul to leave the country. But just as she was ready to leave for Switzerland, the Italian government confiscated her passport. Marriages between Italian officers and foreigners were dissolved, leaving her in even greater difficulties.

All this time her husband was fighting somewhere in Greece, and she had very little news of him. There was a hint she might wind up in a detention camp. She decided to leave while she could.

"Go over the mountains," a friend suggested, and suddenly it hit her what her father had meant.

Twice she was unsuccessful. The third time she succeeded and wound up in a French prison for two months. As she was a good skier, she had crossed the Little St. Bernard pass on skis. However, in order not to get caught and sent back again she had taken a guide. Just as her dead father had predicted she would!

Her mother in New York arranged for her to come back and got her to Lisbon, where she was to take a boat. Through a highly placed acquaintance in Washington her mother arranged for passage aboard a tiny vessel never meant for the Atlantic passage. The boat belonged to a Portuguese industrialist, and there were just twelve cabins aboard.

The yacht was named the *Cavalho Arrujo*, or Red Horse, and it took twenty-one days to cross the ocean. When the ship reached the Azores, a Dutch radioman and five Javanese crewmen from a torpedoed Dutch ship were taken aboard. Evidently they had been torpedoed by the Germans and taken blindfolded to the Azores, then neutral. In a rare gesture of humanitarianism the Germans left them there to be rescued and sent home.

From the very first, the five Javanese attached themselves to Dr. B., watching over her just as her father had told her they would. They looked exactly as they had

appeared to her in the glimpse into the future her father had given at the villa in Tivoli!

After she landed in New York and joined her mother, she never saw the Javanese crewmen again. They vanished as quickly and quietly as they had entered her life.

Just as soon as she could, she looked up Dr. K. She was sure he would not believe her, but she was determined to tell him what she had seen.

To her amazement Dr. K., a celebrated biochemist, did not scoff. They compared the time differential to determine where he had been at the time she had seen him in Tivoli. He had been at work in his New York lab and had felt nothing special at the time.

Since there was no close connection between Dr. B. and Dr. K., she was puzzled as to why her father had "shown" him to her at the time of his visit. But Dr. K. represented New York to her father, and perhaps this was his way of saying: "You'll get to New York."

Since Dr. K. did not project his image to Italy, I can only assume that what Dr. B. saw was a simulation—that is, a materialization created by the same powers that arranged for her father's temporary return. Ectoplasm can be molded in many ways, and as Dr. B. did not actually speak to the Javanese and to the Dr. K. she saw in Tivoli., they might also have been merely projections or visions. Whatever the technique of their amazing appearances, the purpose was clear: to give her a glimpse into the future.

Her father never contacted her again after her safe return to the United States.

Dr. B.'s encounters with the supernormal have been rare and far between, but whatever experiences she has had were unusually vivid. Shortly after her marriage she was spending some time alone in a summer resort not far from Venice, where she and her husband were living at the time. Two days before she was to rejoin her husband in the city, she was dressing for dinner. It was the last Sunday, and she was putting on her fanciest evening gown for the occasion. It was a warm June evening. She was sitting in front of the dresser, and as she bent forward to put on her lipstick, she suddenly saw in the mirror that *two candles* were burning behind her. She turned around, but there were no candles in back of her. She looked back into the mirror, and there were the two candles again! Back and forth her head went, and the candles were still there—but only in the mirror.

"It must be some kind of reflection," she said to herself aloud and rose to look for the original candles. She examined first the windows, then the doors and walls, but there was no possible way in which two burning candles could appear in her mirror. Disquieted, she sat down again and looked. Perhaps it was only her imagination. But the two candles were back again! Only this time one of the candles flickered, and the flame moved a little.

It was 7 o'clock. She was hungry and thought: "I've got to go down. I don't care, candles or no candles."

No sooner had she thought this than she heard a voice behind her—a woman's voice, speaking in Italian.

"Promise me never to abandon him!"

"Of course not," she replied, without thinking how a disembodied voice could suddenly sound in her room. She turned around. There was no one there!

She wondered: Who was she never to abandon? It could only be her husband, Alberto.

She decided she had had enough unusual experiences for one day and left the room. Coming down the stairs, she was met on the second floor by her husband, racing up to meet her. He seemed upset.

"What is it?" she asked.

"Mother died. I've just come from her funeral." Tears streamed down his face. He had not wished to alarm her or to allow his grief to interfere with their vacation. His mother had been buried the day before, and he thought it best to come and tell her personally rather than to telephone.

The voice Dr. B. had heard had been her mother-in-law's.

Years later the request made strange sense to her. Between 1941 and 1945, when she was in New York, her husband was a prisoner of the Germans. She had no contact with him and knew nothing about his fate. The Red Cross told her that he had died, so legally she could remarry after five years. But the voice of a mother from beyond the grave stuck in her mind, and she realized what the voice had meant; she never abandoned her husband, and eventually she was reunited with him.

Loved ones or known members of one's family are not the only ones who communicate with the living. Sometimes a total stranger may do so.

Before the war, Dr. B. spent some time vacationing in Arosa, Switzerland. She stayed at a modest pension at the time, as it was toward the end of her vacation and she was beginning to run low on funds. Her room was on one of the upper floors.

She had just rung for her breakfast, which the maid would very shortly bring her. But before this happened, the door was flung open, and a woman burst into her room. She wore a kind of negligee, and her black hair was flying behind her in disorder. Out of breath, the woman demanded: "You must tell him. It is very important! Please tell him!"

Her hands moved with great agitation. Dr. B. was annoyed by the intrusion. She eyed the woman coolly and asked her to leave the room, assuming the woman had stepped into her room in error. The woman had spoken German.

"*Raus!*" Dr. B. said, and the girl tried once again to implore her to "tell him." Then she *backed out* of the room by sliding backward.

The next moment the maid came into the room carrying the breakfast tray. "Who was that crazy woman who just came in?" Dr. B. demanded.

"What woman? There is no one else on this floor."

"But she was just here this minute."

"Impossible. You're the only one on this floor. There is no one left. After all, this is the end of the season." The maid shook her head and left, wondering about the good doctor.

It was late, so Dr. B. did not bother to make inquiries at the desk downstairs about the strange visitor. She took her skis and went out to the slope. She had a favorite spot on the mountain where she could enjoy a marvelous view of the surrounding countryside. She could not get up there fast enough this morning. As she approached the spot, she suddenly saw a man coming toward her from behind some trees.

"May I join you?" he said. He looked like a nice young man and she was not afraid, but she told the young man as gracefully as she could that she was a married woman.

"No, no, it's nothing like that," he assured her. "I just want to talk to you for moment."

He was a physician from Zurich whose first practice had been here in Arosa. At that time he had treated a young woman for advanced tuberculosis. When he first saw the patient, she was a great beauty. They were almost instantly in love, but to his horror he realized that she had only a short time to live. The woman was only eighteen at the time, and he was a young doctor just starting out. But he would not accept this verdict and decided he could somehow change her fate.

"I'm going to die," the girl said. But the young doctor asked for her hand in marriage and, despite her parents' objection, insisted on marrying her. Since both the doctor's family and the girl's people were well off financially, he gladly signed the waiver as to her fortune and promised in addition to take care of her, no matter what.

Dr. B. listened to the story with keen interest. He asked her to accompany him a bit farther and showed her a small chalet where he and his bride had spent their honeymoon. Everything had been brand-new. He had bought the chalet for her, and it looked for a while as though the dire predictions about her death would not come true. Months went by, and her condition, far from worsening, gradually improved.

The doctor spent every moment of his time with her, completely putting aside his career and never leaving her. But when she seemed to be improving so much, he decided he should see a few of his patients again. He thought it safe and did not think she would die now.

One day there was an emergency in the village. An accident occurred, and he was called. While he was gone, something strange must have happened to the woman. Suddenly she left the chalet and came running down the winding road to the village in sheer terror. Whether it was a sudden realization that her protector was not by her side for a few hours or because of some inexplicable worsening of her condition, no one knew. She came running down the hill after him. When she got to the little pension, her physical strength gave out. Her disease-ridden lungs could not stand the great strain of running. Collapsing in the pension, she was carried to one of the rooms upstairs, where she died without ever seeing her husband again.

"One of the rooms?" Dr. B. asked. "On the third floor?"

The young man nodded.

She then described her experience of that morning to him.

"That's she, all right," the young man acknowledged sadly. "Wasn't she beautiful?"

Every year the young physician would come to Arosa on the anniversary of her death, always hoping to find out why she had run out of their chalet.

Today was that day.

After a moment of reflection, Dr. B. told the young man that she too was a physician. It pleased him to know

this, and he asked her whether she had read anything in the wraith's face that might have indicated the nature of her fears. Had she seen death approaching, and did she not want to go without her husband by her side? Or was it something else, something they might never know, that drove her to undertake her fatal dash?

Dr. B. conjectured that perhaps the girl discovered she was pregnant and wanted her husband to know right away. But there was a telephone in the chalet, and the doctor had told his wife where he was going. She could have reached him at the scene of the accident, or she might have waited for his return.

Two days later, Dr. B. left Arosa and never returned to the little pension. But the young man probably continues to come back on the anniversary of the day when his loved one was taken from him. And on the third floor of the pension a tragedy will be enacted once a year, a tragedy involving a beautiful girl with flying black hair, until the two lovers meet for good in the land beyond the veil.

✳ 159

Vivien Leigh's Post-Mortem Photograph

ALTHOUGH SYBIL LEEK, the British author, trance medium, and psychic, had done extraordinary things in my presence, notably fine trance work and clairvoyance, she never considered herself a photographic medium. On one or two occasions strange objects did appear on photographs taken of her or in her presence, but she had never pursued the matter.

On a Friday morning in July 1967, Sybil telephoned me in great agitation. She had just had a very vivid dream, or at any rate fallen into a state similar to the dream state. Someone named Vivien had communicated with her and remarked that she was now going on a holiday. Did I know any Vivien? Why me, I asked. Because this communicator wanted Sybil Leek to call me and tell me. Was there anything more? No, just that much. I pondered the matter. The only Vivien I ever knew personally was a young woman not likely to be on the other side as yet. But, of course, one never knows. I was still pondering the matter when the Saturday newspaper headlines proclaimed the death of Vivien Leigh. It appeared that she had just been discovered dead in her London apartment, but death might have come to her any time before Saturday, most likely on Friday. Suddenly I saw the connection and called Sybil. Did she know Vivien Leigh at all? She did indeed,

Psychic photo of Sybil Leek with the just-passed Vivian Leigh

although she had not seen her for some time. Years ago Vivien Leigh would consult Sybil Leek in personal matters, for Sybil was pretty good at sorting things out for her friends.

There was definitely a relationship. Nobody in the world knew that Vivien Leigh had died *on Friday*. The discovery was made on Saturday. And yet Sybil had her communication during Thursday night. The date? June 30, 1967. I felt it was the actress' way of saying goodbye and at the same time letting the world know that life continued. That was on Saturday. On Monday Sybil had a visitor at the Stewart Studios, where she usually stays when in New York. Her visitor, Edmond Hanrahan, was so impressed with the unusual decor of the studio that he decided to take some color pictures with his camera, which he happened to have with him at the time. The date was July 3, 1967. Several pictures were of Sybil Leek. There was nothing remarkable about any of them, except one. Partially obstructing Sybil is the face of a dark-haired woman with an unmistakable profile—that of Vivien Leigh!

Both Sybil and the photographer remember clearly that there was nobody else with them at the time, nor was there anything wrong with either film or camera. The psychic extra seems soft and out of focus, as if the figure had stepped between the camera and Sybil, but too close to be fully in focus.

I questioned Mr. Hanrahan about the incident. He admitted that this was not the first time something or someone other than the person he was photographing showed up on a negative. On one particularly chilling occasion he had been photographing the widow of a man who had been murdered. On the negative the murdered man appeared next to his widow! Hanrahan used a Honeywell Pentax 35mm camera and Ektachrome film when he caught Vivien Leigh on film. He did not employ a flashgun but used all the available room light. He was relieved to hear that there was nothing wrong with his ability as a photographer or his camera, and he could not very well be held accountable for unseen models.

✳ 160

How the Dead Teacher Said Good-bye

EVELYN ENGLAND, A BUSY professional portrait photographer in Los Angeles, California, had always known of her psychic gift but paid no attention to it. To her, this was simply part of life, and the supernatural was farthest from her mind.

Even as a youngster, England had ESP experiences, especially of the gift of finding lost objects under strange circumstances, as if driven by some inner voice. But despite these leanings she had no particular interest in the subject itself and merely took it for granted that others also had ESP.

One of England's jobs was photographing high-school yearbook pictures. So it was merely a routine assignment when she was called on to take the picture of Mr. G., a mathematics teacher. The date was Saturday, April 3, 1965. He was the last of the faculty to come in for his portrait. Her studio was closed on Sunday. On Monday England developed and retouched the print, and Tuesday morning she mailed it to the school. A few hours later she received a phone call from the school principal. Had Mr. G. come in for his sitting? Yes, Miss England answered, and informed the principal that the print was already in the mail. At this there was a slight pause. Then the principal explained that Mr. G. had died unexpectedly on Sunday.

In May a Mr. H. came into her studio who remarked that he felt she had a good deal of ESP, being himself interested in such matters. Miss England took his portrait. He then came in to pick his choice from the proofs. When she placed the print into the developer, to her amazement, it was not Mr. H.'s face that came up — but Mr. G.'s, the dead mathematics teacher's face. A moment later, while she was still staring in disbelief, the portrait of her client Mr. H. came upon the same print, stronger than the first portrait and facing the opposite way from it.

Miss England was a very meticulous photographer. She never left an undeveloped print around. She always developed each print fully, never leaving half-finished prints behind. No one but she used the studio. There was no "rational" explanation for what had happened. The smiling face of the late mathematics teacher was there to remind her that life was not over for him—or perhaps a token of gratitude for having been the last person to have seen him "alive." Hastily, Miss England printed another picture of Mr. H., and it was just a normal photograph.

Other "dead" persons later used her skills to manifest themselves, but this incident was the most remarkable one in her psychic life.

BILOCATION OR THE ETHERIC DOUBLE OF A LIVING PERSON

Bilocation is a phenomenon closely allied with astral travel, but it is a manifestation of its own with certain distinct features that set it apart from astral travel or out-of-body experiences per se. In bilocation a living person is projected to another site and observed there by one or more witnesses while at the same time continuing to function fully and normally in the physical body at the original place. In this respect it differs greatly from astral projection since the astral traveler cannot be seen in two places at once, especially as the physical body of the astral traveler usually rests in bed, or, if it concerns a daytime projection, is continuing to do whatever the person is doing rather automatically and without consciousness. With bilocation there is full consciousness and unawareness that one is in fact being seen at a distance as well.

Bilocation occurs mostly in mentally active people, people whose minds are filled with a variety of ideas, perhaps to the point of distraction. They may be doing one thing while thinking of another. That is not to say that people without imagination cannot be seen in two places at once, but the majority of cases known to me do indeed fall into the first category. A good case in point is a close friend of mine by the name of Mina Lauterer of California. I have written of her previously in ESP and You. Miss Lauterer has pronounced ESP talents. In addition, however, she is a well-balanced and very keen observer, since she is a professional writer. She has had several experiences of being seen in a distant place while not actually being there in the flesh.

In one such case she was walking down the street in Greenwich Village, New York, when she saw a gentleman whom she knew from Chicago. Surprised to find this person out of his usual element, she crossed the street in order to greet him. She tried to reach out toward him and he evaporated before her eyes. The incident so disturbed her that she wrote to the man in Chicago and found out that he had been in Chicago at the time she had observed him in New York. However, he had just then been thinking of her. Whether his thought projection was seen by Mina Lauterer or whether a part of himself was actually projected to appear is a moot question. What is even more interesting is the fact that he, too, saw Miss Lauterer at the same time he was thinking about her in Chicago. This, of course, is a case of double bilocation, something that does not happen very often.

In another instance, Miss Lauterer reported a case to me that had overtones of precognition in addition to bilocation. "One night not long ago, in New York, as I was in bed, halfway between sleep and being fully awake," she said, "I saw a face as clearly as one sees a picture projected on a screen. I saw it with the mind's eye, for my eyes were closed. This was the first experience that I can recall, where I saw, in my mind, a face I had never seen before.

"About six weeks later, I received an invitation to go to Colombia, South America. I stayed on a banana plantation in Turbo, which is a primitive little town on the Gulf of Urabá. Most of the people who live there are the descendants of runaway slaves and Indian tribes. Transportation is by launch or canoe from the mainland to the tiny cluster of nearby islands. The plantation was located near the airport on the mainland, as was the customs office. The village of Turbo is on a peninsula.

"One Sunday afternoon I went into town with my host, an American, and my Colombian friend. As we walked through the dirty streets bordered with sewage drains and looked around at the tin-roofed hovels and the populace of the place, I thought, this is the edge of the world.

"Sunday seemed to be the market day; the streets were crowded with people mostly of two hues, black and red-skinned. As we passed a drugstore, walking single file, a tall, handsome, well-dressed young man caught my attention. He seemed as out of place as I and my companions did. He did not look at me, even as I passed directly in front of him. It struck me as strange. South American men always look at women in the most frank manner. Also, he looked familiar, and I realized that this was the face that I had seen in my mind, weeks before in New York!

"The following day we were invited to cocktails by our neighbor, the Captain of Customs. He told us that a young flyer arrived every month around the same time, stopped in Turbo overnight, and then continued on his regular route to other villages. He always bunked in with his soldiers, instead of staying at the filthy hotel in the village. He mentioned that the young man was the son of the governor of one of the Colombian states, and that he had just arrived from Cartagena, the main office of his small airline.

"He brought the young man out and introduced him to us. It was the young man that I had seen in the village! I asked him if he had really arrived Monday morning and he later proved beyond all doubt that he had not been in Turbo on Sunday afternoon when I saw him. He was dressed in the same clothes on Monday as those that I had seen him wearing on Sunday in my vision.

"I do not know why I saw him when he wasn't there. Later he asked me to marry him, but I did not.

"When I and my companions went to Cartagena later on we checked and again confirmed the facts—he was miles away when I had seen him!"

* * *

I am indebted to Herbert Schaefer of Savannah, Georgia, for the account of a case of bilocation that occurred some time ago to two elderly friends of his.

Carl Pfau was awakened one night by the feeling that he was not alone. Turning over in bed, he saw his good friend Morton Deutsch standing by his bedside. "How did you get in here?" he asked, since the door had been securely locked. Deutsch made no reply but merely smiled, then, turning, walked to the door, where he disappeared. On checking the matter, it was discovered that Mr. Deutsch had been sitting in a large comfortable chair at the time of his appearance at this friend's bedside and had just wondered how his friend Carl was doing. Suddenly he had felt himself lifted from the chair and to Carl's bedside. There was a distance of about two miles between their houses.

* * *

Bilocation cannot be artificially induced the way astral projection can, but if you are bent on being seen in two places at once, you may encourage the condition through certain steps. For one thing, being in a relaxed and comfortable position in a quiet place, whether indoors or outdoors, and allowing your thoughts to drift might induce the condition. The more you concentrate, the less likely it is to happen. It is very difficult to produce that certain state of dissociation that is conducive to bilocation experiences. The only thing I can suggest is that such a condition may occur if you set up the favorable conditions often enough. It should be remembered that the majority of bilocation incidents is not known to the projected individual until after it has occurred and been confirmed on the other end.

ASTRAL PROJECTIONS OR OUT-OF-BODY EXPERIENCES

One of the terms frequently met with in the discussions of paranormal phenomena is the word "astral." Although vaguely reminiscent of stars and celestial conditions, it actually means the same as etheric, at least to me it does. By astral or etheric dimension, I mean that world outside the physical world which contains all spiritual phenomena and ESP manifestations. This dimension is made up of very fine particles and is certainly not intangible. The inner body, which in my opinion represents the true personality in humans, is made up of the same type of substance; consequently, it is able to exist freely in the astral or etheric dimension upon dissolution of the physical body at physical death. According to theosophy and, to a lesser degree, the ancient Egyptian religion, a human being has five bodies of which the astral body is but one, the astral world being the second lowest of seven worlds, characterized by emotions, desires, and passions. This, of course, is a philosophical concept. It is as valid or invalid as one chooses it to be. By relating to the astral world as merely the "other side of life," I may be simplifying things and perhaps run counter to certain philosophical assumptions, but it appears to me that to prove one nonphysical sphere is enough at this stage of the game in parapsychology. If there be other, finer layers—and I do not doubt in the least that there are —let that be the task at a time when the existence of the nonphysical world is no longer being doubted by the majority of scientists.

* * *

In speaking of "astral projection," we are in fact speaking of projection into the astral world; what is projected seems to be the inner layer of the body, referred to as the astral or etheric body. By projecting it outward into the world outside the physical body, it is capable of a degree of freedom that it does not enjoy while encased in the physical body. As long as the person is alive in the physical world, however, the astral body remains attached to the physical counterpart by a thin connecting link called the "silver cord." If the cord is severed, death results. At the time of physical death, the cord is indeed severed and the astral body freely floats upward into the next dimension. Nowadays we tend to call such projections "out-of-body experiences." Robert Monroe, a communications engineer by profession and a medium by accident, has written a knowledgeable book about his own experiences with out-of-body sensations, and a few years before him, Dr. Hereward Carrington, together with Sylvan Muldoon, authored a book, considered a classic nowadays, on the subject of astral projection. The reason that out-of-body experience is a more accurate term to describe the phenomena is to be found in the fact that projection, that is to say a willful outward movement out of the physical body, is rarely the method by which the phenomena occur. Rather it is a sensation of dissociation between physical and etheric body, a floating sensation during which the inner self seems to be leaving its physical counterpart and traveling away from it. The movement toward the outside is by no means rapid or projectionlike; it is a slow gradual disengagement most of the time and with most witnesses. Occasionally there are dramatic instances where astral projection occurs spontaneously and rather suddenly. But in such cases some form of shock or artificial trauma is usually present such as during surgery and the use of an anesthetizing agent or in cases of sudden grief, sudden joy, or states of great fatigue.

Out-of-the-body experiences can be classified roughly into two main categories: the spontaneous cases, where it occurs without being induced in any way and is usually as a surprise, and experimental cases, where the state of dissociation is deliberately induced by various means. In the latter category certain controlled experiments are of course possible, and I will go into this toward the end of this chapter.

* * *

The crux of all astral projection, whether involuntary or voluntary, is the question whether the traveler makes an impact on the other end of the line, so to speak. If the travel is observed, preferably in some detail, by the recipient of the projection, and if that information is obtained after the event itself, it constitutes a valuable piece of evidence for the reality of this particular ESP phenomenon.

There is the case of a Japanese-American lady, Mrs. Y., who lived in New York and had a sister in California. One day she found herself projected through space from her New York home to her sister's place on the West Coast. She had not been there for many years and had no idea what it looked like inasmuch as her sister had informed her that considerable alterations had taken place about the house. As she swooped down onto her sister's home, Mrs. Y. noticed the changes in the house and saw her sister, wearing a green dress, standing on the front lawn. She tried to attract her sister's attention but was unable to do so. Worried about her unusual state of being, that is, floating above the ground and seemingly being unable to be observed, Mrs. Y. became anxious. That moment she found herself yanked back to her New York home and bed. As she returned to her own body, she experienced a sensation of falling from great heights. This sensation accompanies most, if not all, incidents of astral travel. The feeling of spinning down from great heights is, however, a reverse reaction to the slowing down in speed of the etheric body as it reaches the physical body and prepares to return into it. Many people complain of dreams in which they fall from great heights only to awaken to a sensation of a dizzying fall and resulting anxiety. The majority of such experiences are due to astral travel, with most of it not remembered. In the case of Mrs. Y., however, all of it was remembered. The following day she wrote her sister a letter, setting down what she had seen and asking her to confirm or deny the details on the house and of herself. To Mrs. Y.'s surprise, a letter arrived from her sister a few days later confirming everything she had seen during her astral flight.

* * *

Ruth E. Knuths, a former schoolteacher who currently works as a legal secretary in California, has had many ESP experiences, and like many others, she filed a report in conformity with a suggestion made by me in an earlier book concerning any ESP experiences people wished to register with me.

In the spring of 1941 when I lived in San Diego, where I had moved from Del Rio, Texas, I was riding to work on a streetcar. I had nothing on my mind in particular; I was not thinking of my friends in Texas and the time was 8 A.M. Suddenly I found myself standing on the front porch of Jo Comstock's house in Del Rio. Jo and I have been friends for many years. The same dusty green mesquite and cat claw covered the vacant lot across the road, which we called Caliche Flat. People were driving up and parking their cars at the edge of the unfenced yard. They were coming to express sympathy to Jo because of the death of her mother. Jo was inside the house. I knew this although I did not see her. I was greeting the friends for her. The funeral was to be that afternoon. Then as suddenly as I had gone to Del Rio, I was back in the streetcar, still two or three blocks away from my stop.

Two weeks later Joe wrote, telling me that on a certain date, which was the same date I had this vision on, her mother had been found by neighbors unconscious from a stroke, which they estimated had occurred about 10 o'clock in the morning. Jo was notified at 10:30. She said that she badly wished me to be there with her. Allowing for the difference in time, two hours, I had had this experience at the time of the stroke, but the vision itself was projected ahead of that two days, to the day of the funeral.

On May 28, 1955, she had another experience of astral projection, which she was able to note in detail and report to me:

My husband and I had dinner with Velva and Jess McDougle and I had seen Jess one time downtown, afterward, and we spoke and passed. I had not seen Velva. Then on June 11, a Saturday, I was cleaning house, monotonously pushing the vacuum sweeper brush under the dresser in the bedroom, when suddenly I was standing at the door of a hospital room, looking in. To the left, white curtains blew gently from a breeze coming from a window. The room was bright with sunlight; directly opposite the door and in front of me was a bed with a man propped up on pillows; on the left side of the bed stood Velva. The man was Jess. No word was spoken, but I knew that Jess was dead, although as I saw him he was alive though ill. I "came back" and was still cleaning under the dresser. I didn't contact Velva, nor did I hear from her. However, about a week later my sister, Mary Hatfield, told me that she was shocked to hear of Mr. McDougle's death. That was the first confirmation I had. I immediately went to see Velva, and she told me that he had suffered a heart attack on Thursday before the Saturday of my vision, and had died the following Sunday, the day after the vision occurred.

* * *

Richard Smith is a self-employed landscape service contractor, in his thirties, married and living in Georgia. He has had many ESP experiences involving both living people and the dead. Sometimes he is not sure whether he has visions of events at a distance or is actually traveling to them. In his report to me he states:

On one very unusual occasion, just before sleep came, I found myself floating through the air across the country to my wife's parents' home in Michigan where I moved about the house. I saw Karen's father as he read the newspaper, his movements through the rooms, and drinking a cup of coffee. I could not find her mother in the house. She was apparently working at the hospital. I was floating at a point near the ceiling and looking down. Mr. Voelker, her father, happened to look up from his coffee and seemed to be frightened. He looked all around the room in a state of great uneasiness as if he could sense me in the room. He would look up toward me but his eyes would pass by as though I were invisible. I left him, as I did not wish to frighten him by my presence.

This latter experience I seem almost able to do at will when the conditions are right, and travel anywheres. Sometimes, involuntarily, I find myself looking upon a scene that is taking place miles away and of which I have no personal knowledge. These experiences have taken place since my childhood, although I have kept them to myself with the exception of my wife.

* * *

From a scientific control point of view, astral projection is mainly a subjective experience and only the large volume of parallel testimony can give clues to its operational setup. However, there are a number of verified cases on record where the astral traveler was actually seen, heard, or felt by those at the other end of the trip, thus corroborating a subjective experience by objective observation.

That time is truly a convention and not an independent dimension at all can be seen from the fact that differences in regional observation times in such cases are always adjusted to coincide with the proper local time: if an astrally projected person is seen in his etheric or non-physical state at 3 P.M. in Los Angeles, and the traveler himself recalls his experience in New York to have taken place at exactly 6 P.M., we know that the time differential between California and the Eastern Seaboard is three hours and thus practically no measurable time seems to have elapsed between the commencement and the completion of the astral trip.

That a tiny amount of what we call time does elapse I am sure, for the speed of astral travel cannot be greater than the speed of thought, the ultimate according to Einstein (and not the speed of light, as formerly thought). Even thought takes time to travel, although it can cover huge distances in fractions of a second. But thought—and astral projection—are electric impulses and cannot travel entirely without some loss of the time element, no matter how tiny this loss is. Some day, when we have built apparatus to measure these occurrences, it will no doubt be found that a tiny delay factor does exist between the two ends of the astral road.

The duration of astral flight varies according to the relaxed state of the projected person. A very nervous, fearful individual need only panic and desire to be in his own bed—and pronto, he is pulled back, nay, snapped back, into his body with rubber-band-like impact and some subsequent unpleasantness.

The sensation, according to many who have experienced this, is like falling from great heights or spinning down in a mad spiral and waking up suddenly in one's bed as if from a bad dream, which in a way it is.

I am convinced that the falling sensation is not due to any actual physical fall at all, but merely represents the sudden deceleration of the vibratory speed of the person. Astral travel, like all psychic life, is at a much higher rate of speed than is physical life. Thus when the personality is suddenly yanked off the road, so to speak, and forcibly slowed down very quickly, a shock-like condition results. The denser atmosphere in which our physical bodies move requires a slower rate of pulsation. Normally, in astral projection, the person returns gradually to his body and the process is orderly and gradual, so no ill effects result. But when the return is too sudden there is no time for this, and the screeching coming to a stop of the bodily vehicle is the result.

Psychiatrists have tried to explain the very common sensation of falling from great heights in one's dream as an expression of fear. The trouble with this explanation is that the experience is so common that it could not possibly cover all the people who have had it; many of them do not have unexpressed fears or fear complexes. Also, some astral travelers have had this while partially or fully awake.

I think it is a purely mechanical symptom in which the etheric body is forced to snap back into the physical body at too fast a rate of speed. No permanent injury results, to be sure. The moments of confusion that follow are no worse than the mental fogginess that one often feels on awaking after a vivid dream, without astral projection involved. However, many travelers find themselves strangely tired, as if physical energies had been used up, which indeed they have!

One such person, perhaps a typical case, is Dorothy W., who is a young grandmother in her fifties. She is a mentally and physically alert and well-adjusted person who works as an executive secretary for a large community center. Dorothy has had many psychic experiences involving premonitions of impending death, and has been visited by the shades of the departed on several occasions. She takes these things in her stride and is neither alarmed nor unduly concerned over them.

Frequently she finds that her dream-state is a very tiring one. She visits places known and unknown, and meets people she knows and others she does not know. Those that she recognizes she knows are dead in the conventional sense. She cannot prevent these nocturnal excursions and she has learned to live with them. What is annoying to her, however, is that on awakening she finds her feet physically tired, as if she had been walking for miles and miles!

A typical case where corroboration is available from the other end of the trip is in the files of the American Society for Psychic Research, which made it available to *True* magazine for a report on ESP published two years ago. The case involves a young lady whom the Society calls Betsy, who traveled astrally to her mother's house over a thousand miles away. In what the report described as a kind of vivid dream state, Betsy saw herself projected to her mother's house.

> After I entered, I leaned against the dish cupboard with folded arms, a post I often assume. I looked at my mother, who was bending over something white and doing something with her hands. She did not appear to see me at first, but she finally looked up. I had a sort of pleased feeling, and then after standing a second more, I turned and walked about four steps.

At this point, Betsy awoke. The clock of her bedside showed the time as 2:10 A.M. The impression that she had actually just seen (and been seen by) her mother a thousand miles away was so overwhelming that the next morning Betsy wrote her parent asking whether she had experienced anything unusual that night.

The mother's reply in part follows: "Why don't you stay home and not go gallivanting so far from home when you sleep? Did you know you were here for a few seconds?" The mother said it was 1:10 A.M. on the night in question. Her letter continued: "It would have been 10 after 2 your time. I was pressing a blouse here in the kitchen—I couldn't sleep either. I looked up and there you were by the cupboard, just standing smiling at me. I started to speak and saw you were gone." The woman, according to the mother (who saw her only from the waist up), wore the light blouse of her dream.

Finally, there is a kind of semi-voluntary astral projection, where a person wills himself or herself to visit a distant place, without, however, knowing anything about the place itself or its appearance. When such a visit yields verified details, no matter how seemingly small or insignificant, we can judge the verity of the experiment so much more accurately.

Some researchers refer to this particular phase also as "traveling clairvoyance." Others maintain that really only a part of the personality doing the projecting is visiting distant places and that the essential portion of oneself does not move. To me, this is harder to believe than the more natural explanation of duality—the physical body stays behind and the etheric body travels. Not a part of the etheric body, but all of it.

What about thought projections, then? There are known cases where an apparition of a *living* person has suddenly and momentarily appeared to others in the flesh great distances away. Usually, there are emotional situations involved in this type of phenomenon. Either the apparition of the living is to warn of impending disaster or danger, or the sender himself is in trouble and seeks help. But the projection is sudden and momentary in all cases and does not compare to the lingering qualities of a true ghost or an apparition of a person who is deceased.

I am inclined to think that these thought projections in which a living person appears to another living person are extremely fast astral projections, so fast, in fact, that the etheric body is back home again before the traveler realizes it, and that, therefore, there is no need to be in a prone position in bed—a sudden sense of absence, of being not all there, at the most.

✳ 161

The Monks of Winchester Cathedral

MY WIFE AND I were on a journey to Southampton to appear there on television and then go on to Beaulieu, where I wanted to investigate hauntings at the ancient abbey. Winchester Cathedral is in direct line with this destination, and so I decided to stop over briefly at the famed cathedral. I had heard that a number of witnesses had observed ghostly monks walking in the aisles of this church, where no monks have actually walked since the 1500s. During the dissolution of the monasteries upon orders of Henry VIII, monks and abbots were abused and occasionally executed or murdered, especially when they resisted the orders driving them from their customary places. Here at Winchester, so close to the capital, the order was strictly enforced and the ghostly monks seen by a number of witnesses may indeed have had some unfinished "business"! On researching the matter, I discovered that I was not the first man to obtain psychic photographs in this place. According to a dispatch of the *Newark Evening News* of September 9, 1958, an amateur photographer by the name of T. L. Taylor was visiting the ancient cathedral with his family. Taylor, who was then forty-two years old, an electrical engineer by profession, was on a

The Monks of Winchester: still walking?

sightseeing trip as a tourist without the slightest interest in or knowledge of the supernormal. He took a number of pictures in the choir area—the same area where my ghostly monks appeared—in late 1957. With him at the time was Mrs. Taylor and his then sixteen-year-old daughter

The haunted pews

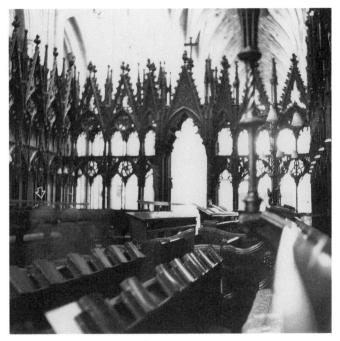

The monks in the aisle

Close-up of the monks who were driven out by Henry VIII

Valerie. Incidentally, none of them observed any ghostly goings-on whatever.

The first exposure turned out to be a normal view of the choir chairs, but on the following picture—perhaps taken from a slightly different angle—there appeared in these same *empty* chairs thirteen human figures dressed in what appeared to be medieval costumes. When the film and prints came back from the lab, Taylor was aghast. As

a technician he knew that his camera could not take double exposures accidentally—just as mine can't—because of a locking mechanism, and the manufacturer of the film confirmed to him upon inquiry that the film was in no way faulty and the "ghosts" could not be explained through some form of error in manufacture of film or developing. Satisfied that he had somehow obtained some supernormal material, Taylor turned the results over to the Lewisham Psychic Research Society, where they presumably still are.

As soon as we had dashed from the car through the heavy rainfall into the cathedral, Catherine and I walked up to the choir chair area and I began to take black-and-white photographs, exposing two seconds for each picture. The high content of moisture in the atmosphere may have had some bearing on the supernormal results. On other occasions I have found that moist air is a better psychic conductor than dry air. After I had exposed the entire roll of eleven pictures in various directions, but from the same area, we returned to our car, still of course totally ignorant as to whether anything unusual would show on the negatives. Since all of my psychic photography is unexpected and purely accidental, no thoughts of what might turn up filled my mind at the time. I was merely taking photographs of the cathedral because people had observed ghosts in it. Only later did I discover that someone else had also obtained photographs of ghosts there.

Upon developing and printing it became immediately clear that I had caught the cowled, hooded figures of three monks walking in the aisle. On close inspection it is clear that we are dealing here not with one identical picture of a monk exposed somehow three times as he moved about but

The Monks of Winchester Cathedral

with three slightly different figures, one of which looks sideways, while the other two are caught from the rear. I was puzzled by the apparent lack of height on the part of these figures and wondered if sixteenth-century men were that much smaller than we are. But on examination of the records I discovered that the stone floor of the cathedral was raised a hundred years after the last monks had been driven out from Winchester. Thus the figures caught here are walking on what to them must be the original floor!

✳ 162

The Secret of Ballinguile

"YOU MAY LIKE TO follow up the enclosed," wrote Patrick Byrne of the *Dublin Herald*, who had been running pieces about our impending return to Ireland in search of haunted houses. The enclosure turned out to be a letter written in longhand, dated April 2, 1966, from a Mrs. O'Ferrall, who had a sister living near Dartry, a suburb of Dublin, said sister having but recently removed there from a haunted house on Eglington Road, Donnybrook.

After a consultation about the matter—talking about ghosts is not taken lightly by the Irish—Mrs. O'Ferrall got her sister's approval, and, more important, address. Thus it was that I addressed myself to Mrs. Mary Healy of Temple Road, so that I might learn of her adventures in the house firsthand.

The house in question, it turned out, was still standing, but had lately been falling into disrepair, since the new owners were bent on eventual demolition. Mrs. Healy had sold it in 1963. Part of the sprawling gray stone house is eighteenth century and part is nineteenth, but the site has been inhabited continuously since at least the fifteenth century. A high wall that surrounds the property gives it the appearance of a country house rather than a city residence, which it is, for Donnybrook is really a part of Dublin. The word Donnybrook, incidentally, is derived from St. Broc, a local patron, and there is on the grounds of this house, called *Ballinguile*, a natural well of great antiquity, dedicated to St. Broc.

Thus it is that the house may have given the whole district its name. The well, situated towards the rear wall of the garden, is greatly overgrown with lush vegetation, for everything grows well in moist Ireland. The house itself is set back a bit from the road—a busy road it is—thus affording a degree of privacy. In back of the main house are a now totally rundown flower and vegetable garden, and the extensive stables, long fallen into disuse or partially used as garages. There is farther back a small, compact gatehouse, still occupied by a tenant who also vaguely looks after the empty house itself.

There are large sitting rooms downstairs fore and aft, attesting to the somewhat haphazard fashion in which the house was altered and added to over the years. The house consists of three portions, with the middle portion the highest; there is a second story, and above it an attic to which one gains access only by a metal ladder. Set down in front of the sidewall of Ballinguile is a greenhouse which a previous owner had made into a kind of verandah. Now it lay in shambles, just as most of the ground-floor windows had long been shattered by neighborhood youngsters in a peculiar spirit of defiance common to all young people wherever unbroken—and unattended—windows stare!

"The principal unusual happenings," Mrs. Healy explained, "were the sound of footsteps, mostly on the stairs. They were so natural that one did not at once realize that all the household were present. They occurred during the daytime and most frequently during July and August. In fact, August was the time the two strangest things happened. The year I moved there, my youngest son was living with me and he was still a student and a bit lively. When he had friends in I usually retired and went to bed.

"One night he had just one friend downstairs, and about 9 P.M. came to me and said they were going out for a while, and so they went. Shortly after I woke from a doze to hear a lot of people downstairs; they were laughing and joking, and talking, and I could hear them moving about. They seemed very happy and really enjoying themselves. I was very angry and thought to get up and tell them that was no time to be having an unprepared party, but I didn't.

"After quite a while there was silence, and shortly after, the hall door opened and my son came in. He had gone to see his friend home and stayed with him a while. *There had been no party!*

"Two years later, also in August, my daughter, who lived with her husband and little girl in half the house, and I were standing in my dining room, an old converted kitchen. Suddenly we saw the little girl of three and a half talking to someone in the enclosed yard. She would say something and wait for the answer. There was no one that we could see anywhere, but we distinctly heard her say, 'but you are my friend!' We asked her who she was speaking to and she said casually, 'the tall dark man,' and gave us the impression she knew him well.

"Just before we left, one evening after we had all retired to bed about 11 P.M., we were aroused by the doorbell. My son-in-law went down to find two policemen inquiring if all was well. Passing, they had heard a lot of

violent noise in the house, and seeing all dark, came to investigate.

"We had heard nothing!

"To me the strangest thing was that one did not feel frightened, everything seemed so completely natural. It was only afterwards one realized it was strange. At no time was there any 'creepy' feeling.

"The only person who was frightened at night was the little girl, who would not stay in bed at night saying something frightened her. But children often do that. We did not tell her anything about our own experiences, for children are quick to elaborate."

So much for Mrs. Healy's experiences. I reported none of this to Sybil, of course, and as we were on the lookout for a house to buy in Ireland, it was simply still another house to inspect for that reason.

On arrival in Dublin I arranged a date to meet Mrs. Healy at her new home, after we had been to the former Healy home in Donnybrook. To get permission and keys, I telephoned the present owner, Arthur Lurie, who was most cooperative although I never told him about any potential ghost. But then I doubt it would have impressed him. Mr. Lurie sounded to me like a man who was all business. The price he asked for the house was unfortunately too high for us, but we did like the house and might have bought it otherwise.

Keys in pocket, we set out for Ballinguile on a very warm July afternoon. The driver obligingly opened the rusty gates for us and the car drove into the grounds. At that moment, a little lady practically flew past us in pursuit of two small dogs, explaining on the run—"They used to play in here, you know. Mind if I give them a run?"

Before we could answer she was past us and inside. Five minutes later I had her out again, dogs and all.

Now we started our exploration, carefully avoiding the many broken windows that had let in a veritable avalanche of birds, to whom some rooms had become home, judging from their evidences.

We were still standing outside, while the driver was napping in the sun. I was busy putting my tape recording equipment and cameras into operating condition, while Catherine explored the wider reaches of the lush garden. Sybil and I found ourselves directly outside the rear sitting room.

Suddenly, *I heard muffled voices* coming from the room and my first thought was, oh, there are some other people here also; how inconsiderate of the landlord to send them at the same time! Sybil turned her head to me and there was one big question mark written all over her face. She, too had heard the voices. It was over in a matter of perhaps two or three seconds, and the voices, one of which was male and deep, sounded as if coming from under water, but they certainly were human voices in conversation...*such as at a party!* We entered the room immediately, but of course there wasn't a soul in it.

I decided it was time to enter the house and see what Sybil's psychic sense would "get" us.

"Funny thing," Sybil remarked as we started up the path towards the house, "I feel as if I'd been here before.

I've 'seen' this house many times over the years. This house had a lot of unwarranted hatred directed towards it. When we got out of the car, I thought I saw a man...in one of the upper rooms...I thought I heard a voice... something beginning with S, like Sure, or Sean...the central portion, upper window, there seemed to be a man reading a paper...."

Since Sybil did not get any strong impressions in the downstairs part of the house, we ascended the stairs and soon found ourselves on the second floor, in the very room in which most of the psychic occurrences had taken place.

"There is plotting here...in this particular room I have the feeling of somebody very sick, worried, very excitable, a man—not too far back, the grounds seem to have an older influence but not this room. About 300 years on the grounds, but in the house, perhaps fifty years. There is a foreign influence here. Another language."

"Can you get any names?" I asked as Sybil leaned against the wall of the empty room. There was no chair to sit down in, so we had to do our trance work in this awkward fashion.

"Wyman," Sybil mumbled now, and gradually she became more and more entranced, although at no time was she in full trance.

"French influence...Wyban, Vyvern...don't know what it means," she added, "he is here now. Not too long ago. He's the one who brought us here."

"What does he want us to do?"

I too had felt that this case was more than routine, that we were drawn to this house in some mysterious way. *What was the secret of Ballinguile?*

"It seems ridiculous, but the man looks like Abraham Lincoln," Sybil finally stated, "thin, gaunt, stooping shoulders...it's his house, fifty years ago...Whibern...he has papers...something to be careful about...the land...the deed, there is trouble...the house and the land are not completely together."

I discovered later that the house was built on ground that belonged to different owners and that there were great legal problems involved in this. Sybil had no knowledge of this fact.

"Another man knows this," Sybil continued. "There is some trouble about the land. That's the conflict of two families. He wants us to settle the land. Samly, Seamly... that was the name that was spelled when I came into the house. It's a family name."

"Did he die here?"

There was a moment of silence as Sybil queried the ghost.

"Reading the papers carefully," she finally mumbled instead, "check the papers, Miss Seamly...check the papers carefully...the money was wrong...Simmely (Seamly) made a mistake about the ground...sort it out..."

Sybil was almost in trance now and her voice became weak and irregular. "Twenty-four," she whispered under the influence of the ghost, "1924...year...."

"Is there any other problem?" I inquired matter-of-factly. Might as well clean out the lot.

"The woman," Sybil said, "where did she go? He says the woman left!"

I assured him there was nobody here now but us ghost hunters. Did he want us to buy the house perhaps? Not that it would help with the landlord.

"Good people," he mumbled, "people from overseas live here...now...not for the Irish...traitors...stolen the land...the land to the Institute...Institute for sick people...."

"Did you leave the land to the Institute?" I asked.

"Took it...the Institute...."

"And who should have gotten it instead?"

"Wyman...Wynan." The name still was not quite clear, but I promised we would try and look into the matter of the land if we could.

"He knows..." Sybil murmured, and a moment or two later she came out of the state bordering on trance. We were still upstairs.

Sybil remembered absolutely nothing, but "her eyes did not feel right" for a moment.

We went downstairs and closed the house, got into the car and drove to the nearby house where Mrs. Healy and her married daughter now reside.

Suddenly it struck me that Sybil had talked about a man named White ever since we had met again in Dublin. Did I know any Mr. White? I did not. Would we be meeting such a person in one of our investigations? No, I said, we would not as far as I could tell.

But then Mary Healy cleared up the mystery for us.

A Mr. Bantry White used to live in the house we had just left. Since this name was unknown to me prior to that moment, Sybil of course could not have gotten it from my unconscious mind prior to visiting the Donnybrook house. Were Wynan and White the same person, I wondered.

Another thing that struck me as peculiar was Sybil's insistence on going to a house *with an iron gate*. No such house was on my list but Sybil kept asking for it. When we arrived at Ballinguile, however, there was no iron gate within view; still, Sybil demanded to see it, sure it was part of this house.

I then learned from Mrs. Healy that she had had such an iron gate removed when she bought the house, and moved the entrance to where it is now, away from where the old iron gate once stood. Sybil again could not have known this consciously.

The new home of the Healy family was neat and functional, and Mrs. Healy a charming lady gifted with elaborate speech and a sense of proportion.

"There lived a Mr. Kerrigan there, a lawyer also," she said. "I think he is dead. We bought it from a Dr.

Graham who died quite recently. But nobody has ever lived in that house *very long*. We left it for purely personal reasons, not because of any ghost, however."

"What about the cottage?"

"That was built by Dr. Graham for his gardener. That is of no age at all. A Mr. Barron is living in it now."

"Which staircase did you hear the footsteps on?" I asked.

"There are two, as there are two of everything in the house. My son-in-law and I bought it together, you see, and it was on the little staircase that I heard the footsteps. In the back of the house. The party sounds I heard, that was in the older house, too, in the back."

Where Sybil and I had heard the voices, I thought! Same spot, actually, and I did not realize it until now.

"Did you find any traces of older buildings on the spot?" I asked Mrs. Healy.

"There is supposed to have been a monastery on these grounds at one time," she explained; "only the well in the garden is left now. We still used the clear water from it, incidentally."

Later, Mrs. Healy's brother came and joined us. He listened quietly as I explained about the land business and the complaint of the ghost.

Both tenants prior to the Doctor had been lawyers, it turned out, and the difficulty about the land ownership underneath the house was quite real. If there had been some mistake, however, nothing could be done about it *now*. At least not without costly and extended search and litigation. And that, you will admit, even a ghost wouldn't want. Especially not a lawyer-ghost who is getting no fee out of it! I am sure that my explanation, that time had gone on, must have given the ghostly owner a chance to let go of it all, and since Mr. Lurie, the present owner, foresees that an apartment structure will soon replace the old house, there really is no point in worrying about a bit of land. *Caveat emptor!*

CHAPTER TWELVE

Psychic Photography— the Visual Proof

COMMUNICATIONS FROM BEYOND THROUGH PHOTOGRAPHY:
TRACK RECORD AND TEST CONDITIONS

For the past 100 years, psychic research has painstakingly assembled proof for the continuance of life and has gradually emerged from a metaphysical mantle into the full glare of scientific inquiry. Although various researchers interpret the results of these investigations according to their own attitudes toward survival of human personality, it is no longer possible to bury the evidence itself, as some materialistically inclined scientists in other fields have attempted to do over the years. The challenge is always present: does man have a soul, scientifically speaking, and if so, how can we prove it?

Material on communications with the so-called dead is very large and, to me, often convincing, though not necessarily all of it in the way it is sometimes presented by partisans of the spiritualist religion. But additional proof that man does continue an existence in what Dr. Joseph Rhine, then of Duke University, has called "the world of the mind" was always wanted, especially the kind of proof that could be viewed objectively without the need for subjective observation through psychic experiences, either spontaneous or induced in the laboratory. One of the greatest potential tools was given to us when photography was invented: for if we could photograph the dead under conditions that carefully exclude trickery, we would surely be so much the wiser—and the argument for survival would indeed be stronger.

Photography itself goes back to the 1840s, when the technique evolved gradually from very crude light-and-shadow pictures, through daguerreotypes and tintypes to photography as we now know it.

Major Tom Patterson, a British psychic researcher, in a booklet entitled *Spirit Photography*, has dealt with the beginnings of photographic mediumship in Britain, where it has produced the largest amount of experimental material in the century since.

But the initial experiment took place in 1862, in Boston, not Britain; 23 years after photography itself came into being. William H. Mumler, an engraver, who was neither interested in nor a believer in spiritualism or any other form of psychic research, had been busy in his off-hours experimenting with a camera. At that time the photographic camera was still a novelty. The engraver liked to take snapshots of his family and friends to learn more about his camera. Imagine Mumler's surprise and dismay when some of his negatives showed faces that were not supposed to be on them. In addition to the living people he had so carefully posed and photographed, Mumler discovered the portraits of dead relatives alongside the "normal" portraits.

This was the beginning of psychic photography. It happened accidentally—if there is such a thing as an accident in our well-organized universe—and the news of Mumler's unsought achievements spread across the world. Other photographers, both professionals and amateurs, discovered talents similar to Mumler's, and the psychic research societies in Britain and America began to take notice of this amazing development.

Since then a great many changes have taken place in the technology and we have greater knowledge of its pitfalls. But the basic principle of photography is still the same: film covered with silver salts is exposed to the radiation called light and reacts to it. This reaction results in certain areas of the emulsion being eaten away, leaving an exact replica of the image seen by the camera lens on the photographic film. Depending on the intensity with which light hits the various portions of the film, the eating away of silver salts will vary, thus rendering the tones and shadings of the resulting negative on light-sensitive photographic paper and hence the positive print, which is a mechanical reproduction of the negative's light and shadow areas, but in reverse.

To make a print, the operator merely inserts the finished negative into a printer, places the light-sensitive paper underneath the negative and exposes it through the negative with an electric light. Nothing new can be added in this manner, nor can anything already on the negative be taken away, but the skill of the craftsman operating the printer will determine how well balanced the resulting positive print will be, depending on the duration and intensity of the printing lamp.

Most people who are photographers know these simple facts, but there are many who are not, and for whom this information might be useful.

The obtaining of any sort of images on photographic paper, especially recognizable pictures such as faces or figures, without having first made a negative in the usual manner is, of course, a scientific impossibility—*except* in psychic photography.

Until the arrival on the scene of Polaroid cameras and Polaroid film, this was certainly 100% true. The Polaroid method, with its instant result and development of film within a matter of a few seconds after exposure, adds the

valuable element of close supervision to an experiment. It also allows an even more direct contact between psychic radiation and sensitive surface. The disadvantage of Polaroid photography is its ephemeral character. Even the improved film does not promise to stay unspoiled forever, and it is wise to protect unusual Polaroid photographs by obtaining slide copies. Actually, Polaroid photography uses a combination of both film and sensitive paper simultaneously, one being peeled off the other after the instant development process inside the camera.

Fakery with the ordinary type of photography would depend on double exposure or double printing by unscrupulous operators, in which case no authentic negative could be produced that would stand up to *experienced* scrutiny. Fakery with Polaroid equipment is impossible if camera, film, and operator are closely watched. Because of the great light sensitivity of Polaroid film, double exposure, if intended, is not a simple matter, as one exposure would severely cancel out the other and certainly leave traces of double exposure. And the film, of course, would have to be switched in the presence of the observer, something not even a trained conjurer is likely to do to an experienced psychic investigator. A psychic researcher must also be familiar with magic and sleight-of-hand tricks, in order to qualify for that title.

The important thing to remember about psychic photography is that the bulk of it occurred unexpectedly and often embarrassingly to amateur photographers not the least bit interested in parapsychology or any form of occultism. The extras on the negatives were not placed there by these people to confuse themselves. They were the portraits of dead relatives or friends that could be recognized. The literature on this phase of psychic photography, notably in Britain, is impressive; and I particularly recommended the scholarly work by F. W. Warrick, the celebrated British parapsychologist, called *Experiments in Psychics*, in which hundreds of experimental photographs are reproduced. Warrick's work published in 1939 by E. P. Dutton, deals primarily with the photographic mediumship of Emma Deane, although other examples are included. Warrick points out that he and his colleagues, having spent some 30 years working with and closely supervising their subjects, knew their personal habits and quirks. Any kind of trickery was therefore out of the question, unless one wanted to call a researcher who propounded unusual ideas self-deluded or incompetent, as some latter-day critics have done to Harry Price and Sir William Crookes, respected British psychic researchers now dead.

Any person who is not present when the original experiments or investigations take place and who does not possess firsthand knowledge of the conditions and processes of that investigation is no more qualified to judge its results than an armchair strategist trying to rewrite history. Although Patterson's booklet frankly uses the scientific evidence at hand to support the spiritualistic view, it also serves as a useful source of factual information. Mumler's record as the "first" spirit photographer is upheld by U.S. Court of Appeals Judge John Edmond, who investigated Mumler personally and obtained photographs under test conditions of people known only to him who were dead. Originally, Judge Edmond had gone into the investigation thinking it was all a deception. In a letter published by the *New York Herald* on August 6, 1853, however, the judge spoke not only of Mumler's experiments but also of his subsequent sittings with well-known mediums of his day. These investigations convinced him that spiritualism had a valid base, and he became a confirmed believer from then on, displaying some psychic abilities of his own as time went by.

In England, the craft of psychic photography developed slowly from the 1870s onward. The first person in Britain to show successful results in this field was Frederick Hudson, who in 1872 produced a number of authentic likenesses of the dead under conditions excluding fraud. Several experiments were undertaken under the careful scrutiny of Dr. Alfred Russel Wallace, a famed naturalist in his day. Wallace attested to the genuineness of the observed phenomena. Since then several dozen talented psychic photographers have appeared on the scene, producing for a few pennies genuine likenesses of persons known to have died previously, in the presence of "sitters" (or portrait subjects) they had never before met in their lives.

As the craft became better known and men of science wondered about it, researchers devised more and more rigid test conditions for this type of experimental psychic photography. Film, paper, cameras, developing fluid—in short, all implements necessary to produce photographs of any kind—were furnished, controlled, and held by uncommitted researchers. The medium was not allowed to touch anything and was kept at a distance from the camera and film. In many cases he was not even present in the room itself. Nevertheless psychic "extras" kept appearing on the properly exposed film and were duly recognized as the portraits of dead persons, often of obscure identity, but traceable as relatives or friends of someone present. Occasionally, as with John Myers, America's leading psychic photographer, in his early days the portraits thus obtained by the photographic medium were strangers to all concerned until the pictures were first published in *Psychic News*, a leading spiritualist newspaper of the day. Only then did the "owners" of the psychic "extras" write in to the editor to claim their dead relatives!

Despite the overwhelming evidence that these photographs were genuine—in almost all cases even the motive for fraud was totally absent—some researchers kept rejecting then—and indeed they do now—the possibility that the results were nothing but fraudulently manufactured double exposures. Even so brilliant a person as Eileen Garrett, president of Parapsychology Foundation, insisted for many years that all psychic photographs *had* to be fraudulent, having been so informed by a pair of self-styled experts. It was only when I myself produced the pho-

tographs of ghosts, and acquainted Mrs. Garrett with the camera, film, and other details of how the pictures were obtained, that she reluctantly agreed that we had indeed "made a breakthrough" in the field of psychic photography. Prejudice against anything involving a major shift in one's thinking, philosophy of life, and general training is much stronger than we dare admit to ourselves sometimes.

Often psychic photography also occurs at so-called home circles where neither money nor notoriety is involved and where certainly no need exists for self-delusion by those taking the pictures. They are, presumably, already convinced of survival of personality after death, otherwise they would not be members of the circle.

Photographs of ghosts or haunted areas are much rarer because of the great element of chance in obtaining any results at all. Whereas psychic photography in the experimental sense is subject to schedules and human plans, the taking of ghost pictures is not. Even I had neither advance knowledge nor control over the ones I managed to obtain, and I could not do it again that way if I tried.

We still don't know *all* of the conditions that make these extraordinary photographs possible and, until we do, obtaining them will be a hit-and-miss affair at best. But the fact that genuine photographs of what are commonly called ghosts have been taken by a number of people, under conditions excluding fraud or faulty equipment, of course, is food for serious thought.

An example in recent years is the photograph of a Danish sailor fighting for his life at Ballyheigue Castle, Ireland, taken by a vacationing army officer named Captain P. D. O'Donnell, on June 4, 1962. Unbeknownst to O'Donnell, that was the anniversary of the sailor's death during the so-called silver raid, in which the silver stored at the castle was stolen by local bandits and fighting ensued. O'Donnell took this snapshot without thought or knowledge of ghosts, while inspecting the ruins of the once-proud castle. The picture was later lost in transit and could not be located by the post office.

Many newspapers the world over, including *The People* of July 3, 1966, reported and published a ghost photograph taken by 18-year-old Gordon Carroll in St. Mary the Virgin Church, Woodford, Northhamptonshire, England. The picture clearly shows a monk kneeling before the altar, but at the time he took it Carroll was the only person inside the church. Fortunately, he found an understanding ear in the person of Canon John Pearce-Higgins, Provost of Southwark Cathedral and a member of the Church's Fellowship of Psychical and Physical Research. Pearce-Higgins, after inspecting camera and film and questioning the young man, was satisfied that the phenomenon was authentic. Carroll used a tripod and a brand-new Ilford Sportsman Rangefinder camera. He loaded it with Agfa C.T. 18 film, which he often used to photograph stained-glass windows in churches, a hobby of his. The Agfa Company, on examining the film, confirmed that trick photography had not been used and that neither film nor developing showed any faults. As for the ghost, no one seems to have bothered to find out who he was. The church itself is a very ancient place, mentioned in the *Domesday Book*, a list of important properties compiled under William the Conqueror. A church stood on that spot even before the Norman conquest of Britain, so it is quite possible that at one time or other a monk died there, tragically becoming the ghost that Carroll's camera accidentally saw and recorded.

Joe Hyams, writer-husband of actress Elke Sommer, shared a haunted house with her for some time in Hollywood, only to give up to the ghost in the end. During the last stages of their occupancy, photographer Allan Grant, strictly a nonbeliever, took some pictures in the aftermath of a fire of mysterious origin. The pictures, published in *The Saturday Evening Post* of June 3, 1967, clearly show manifestations not compatible with ordinary photographic results.

The very latest development in the area of psychic photography, although not concerned with images of ghosts, is still germane to the entire question. Thought forms registering on photographic film or other light-sensitive surfaces are the result of years of hard work by Colorado University Professor Jule Eisenbud, a well-known psychiatrist interested in parapsychology as well, with Chicago photographic medium Ted Serios. These amazing pictures were published in 1989 by Eisenbud in an impressive volume called *The World of Ted Serios*. In addition, more material has become available as the experiments continued, thanks to the efforts of a number of universities and study groups who have belatedly recognized the importance of this type of experiment.

Serios has the ability of projecting images of objects and scenes often at great distances in space, or even *time* onto film or a TV tube. This includes places he has never visited or seen before. Eisenbud does not suggest that there are spirit forces at work here. He merely points out, quite rightly, that we do not as yet realize some of the areas in which the human mind can operate. Without having been present at the many sessions in which Eisenbud and a host of other scientists subjected Serios to every conceivable test, I cannot judge the results. But it appears to me from what I have read in the book, and from other Serios photographs shown to me privately, that Serios is capable of astral projection. In these out-of-body states he does visit distant places in a flash, then almost instantly returns to his physical body and records the impressions received by his etheric eyes onto Polaroid film. Above all, I feel that Serios is one of an impressive line of photography mediums.

There may be differences of opinion concerning the implications of psychic photography, with some quarters taking the attitude that it merely represents a record of past events that somehow got left behind in the atmosphere during the event itself. This is undoubtedly possible in a number of cases. But there are also an impressive number of other instances where this view does not fit and where only the unpopular theory (scientifically speaking) of survival of human personality in a thought world will satisfy as an explanation. Either way, psychic photography, like it or not, is the very threshold of a new science.

THE MEDIUMSHIP OF JOHN MYERS

The *possibility* of fraud is always present when planned experiments take place. But the possibility of an explosion is also always present when munitions are being manufactured, and nobody stops making them. One simply proceeds with great care in both cases. Magicians and other conjurers have assaulted psychic photography as patently fake, since *they* could fake it. This, of course, is a neat trick. By suggesting the possibility as the probability, these limited individuals (spiritually speaking) miss the point of scientifically controlled experiments in psychic photography: it is not what *could* be that matters, but what actually *does* happen.

I have no valid reason to doubt the majority of the older psychic photographs I have examined but, since I was not present when they were taken and have no way of knowing how rigid the controls were at the time, I will not personally vouch for them. This does not mean that they are not genuine. It does mean that anything I vouch for has occurred in my presence and/or under my control and with persons known to me under conditions generally considered appropriate by professional parapsychologists. When I studied the literature on this subject, notably Warrick's work on *Experiments in Psychics*, I was impressed by the sincerity of Warrick's approach and by his sensible controls through which he made sure that his subjects could not obtain their amazing results by trickery of any kind. Warrick's work deals to a large extent with the mediumship of Emma Deane, a British psychic famed for her ability to produce photographs of the dead under conditions excluding fraud. It was the same Mrs. Deane, who was once visited by John Myers, then a novice in the field. He came merely to have a "sitting," like everybody else who sought out the elderly lady, and, for a few pennies, was photographed in her presence. Frequently Myers was to discover afterward the portrait of a dead loved one near him on the plate! To his surprise Mrs. Deane told him that some day soon he would be taking her place. Myers smiled incredulously and walked out. But when Mrs. Deane's health failed some time later, Myers, who had since discovered his own psychic and photographic powers, did indeed take over her studio.

In these pictures, Hans Holzer is supervising the experiment of John Meyers' psychic photography

I met John Myers in New York in 1959 because I had heard of his special psychic talents and was anxious to test him. Myers, at that point, was a man of independent means, a successful industrialist and well-known philanthropist who could not possibly gain anything from exposing himself to psychic research. But he also felt he owed something to his benefactors on "the other side of life," as the spiritualists call it, and for that reason he agreed to meet me. This indebtedness went back many years to when he was a dental surgeon in London, already aware of his psychic abilities and practicing two of his special crafts as sidelines. These were psychic photography—later a full-time occupation—and psychic healing. As a healer, he managed to help Laurence Parish, a wealthy American businessman, regain his eyesight where orthodox doctors had failed. In gratitude Parish offered Myers a position in his company in New York. At the time Myers was not making too much money, since he charged only a few pennies for each psychic photograph he took, and nothing for his healing work. He felt that the opportunity to go to America was being sent his way so that he might be useful in his new career *and* as a psychic, so he accepted.

In New York Myers proved himself a good asset to the company and eventually he rose to become its vice president, second only to the head of the company. Because of his new duties Myers now pursued his psychic work on only a sporadic basis, but behind the scenes he often backed other psychics or sponsored spiritualistic meetings that could not have found a hall were it not for Myers' financial support. He himself continued his activities as a psychic healer, however. Occasionally Myers agreed to tests, but only when important scientists or newspaper reporters were to be present. What Myers could no longer do in amount of work he made up for by the sheer power of observers' rosters.

I tested Myers' abilities as a psychic photographer on several occasions. At no time did he try to influence me in any way, or suggest anything, except that he was a sensitive man who resents being insulted. On one occasion I managed to persuade him to give a second public demonstration of his psychic photography on television. Since the first TV test in 1961 was, to my mind, very impressive, I felt another such test might prove valuable also. The program that had requested this test was the American Broadcasting Company's late night show emceed by Les Crane. This brash young man had on a previous occasion proved himself to me to be without sympathy toward psychic research, but I was there to protect Myers from any unpleasant remarks. We had brought the usual chemicals, all open to examination, and the program's producer had provided the photographic paper to be exposed; that is, they had it ready. But the moment never came. They had booked too many "acts" on this particular occasion, and

Pans for developer and fixative

Hans Holzer opening a bag of chemicals

Psychic Photography—the Visual Proof

time ran out before Myers and I could undertake the test. For over two hours Myers sat waiting quietly in the wings. But the little people who were in charge failed to understand the significance of Myers' willingness to do this experiment, and so he went home.

My first meeting with Myers in 1959 was followed by a sitting which was arranged for the purpose of demonstrating his abilities as a psychic photographer. This was in late July, and I set up the following test conditions: Myers was to accompany me on the afternoon of the planned sitting to a photographic supply store of my choice, where I would select and purchase the light-sensitive paper he required. Myers asked the clerk for ordinary developing paper. There are many types, of varying light-sensitivity, and Myers picked a medium-fast paper. The clerk brought the package of paper and I satisfied myself that it was from a fresh batch of materials, properly sealed and in no way damaged or tampered with. I then placed my signature across all corners of the outer envelope, and Myers did the same. The reason for Myers' insistence that he too should be allowed to place his own safeguards on the package goes back many years. When still a young man in England gaining a reputation as a psychic photographer, Myers was challenged to a test by a journalist named Lord Donegal. Not content to look for possible fraud by Myers, Donegal wanted to make sure he *would* be able to find some. Rather than take his chance that Myers might be honest, Donegal switched plates on him and thus produced a foolproof "fraud"—marked plates he himself had supplied. Naturally, Myers was accused publicly, and it took years of hard work to undo the damage. In the end, tiring of the joke, Donegal admitted his deeds. But the incident had turned Myers from a friendly, openhearted man into a cautious, suspicious person, who never quite trusted any experimenter fully.

For this reason, Myers wanted his signature on the package next to mine, so that he too could be sure I had not been tampering with the package. As soon as the bill for the paper was paid, I took the package and put it safely into my pocket. At no time did Myers hold it in his hands. We parted company and I went home, the package still in my possession. After dinner I went to Myers' apartment, where he and five other witnesses were already present. One of these was a photographer named Charles Hagedorn, a skeptic, and one was Myers' legal advisor, Jacob Gerstein, an attorney well known in business circles for his integrity and keen observation. Also present was the late Danton Walker, Broadway columnist of the *Daily News*, himself psychic and keenly interested in the subject, but by no means sure of its implications. None of the observers were "believers" as the term is usually used, but rather all were enlightened witnesses who were willing to accept unusual facts if they could be proven to them.

CHAPTER TWELVE: **Psychic Photography— the Visual Proof**

We entered a medium-sized room in which there was a table surrounded by four chairs, with additional chairs in the four corners. The only illumination came from a yellow overhead bulb, but the light was strong enough to read by without difficulty. The corners of the room were somewhat darker. Myers sat down on a chair in the left-hand corner, placed his hands over his eyes and went into a trance. I took the photographic paper out of my pocket, where it had been all this time, and placed it on the table in plain view of everyone present. At no time had Myers or anyone else among the guests "brushed past" me, or jostled me—a typical means of switching packages. Whenever I have the misfortune of sharing a microphone with a professional conjurer, this is one of his "explanations" of how the psychic phenomena must have been accomplished. I am, of course, familiar with many tricks of magic and always look out for them, but nothing of the sort was attempted. The package was still sealed, exactly as it had been all afternoon. After about five minutes Myers breathed deeply and opened his eyes, saying with a somewhat tired voice, "The paper is now exposed. You can open the package." With that, Walker and I proceeded to tear open the outer envelope, then the package of light-sensitive paper itself, and quickly threw the 20 sheets contained in it into the developing liquid we had also brought along. As soon as the sheets hit the liquid, various things happened to them that really should not have, if this had not been a psychic experiment.

Unexposed photographic paper should show uniform results when exposed to a 60-watt yellow light and then developed. But here different things happened with each and every sheet! Some were totally blank. Others had forms on them, and some showed human faces. A few showed symbols, such as a tombstone, a tablet, a cross. As rapidly as we could we worked over the whole pack. Walker pulled out the sheets and threw them into the developer. I pulled them from the latter and into the fixative solution and out into clear water. Myers was still on his chair in the corner. We then put all the papers on a big towel to dry, and turned on all the lights in the room. Without touching any of the prints, we started to examine the results of Myers' psychic mediumship.

Clearly, if faces or figures appeared on these papers, fraud could not be the cause. One of the intriguing aspects of such an experiment is to hope for a likeness of someone one knew in physical life. Of course you never know *who* might turn up. Those who experiment or investigate psychic channels of various kinds, and anxiously hope for a specific loved one to make an entrance, are almost invariably disappointed. The genuine result of these experiments is quite unpredictable, as well it should be. So it was with considerable glee that I discovered among the faces a familiar one. As soon as the paper was completely dry I took it over to a strong light to make sure I was not guilty of wishful thinking. No, there was no mistake about it. Before me was a portrait of an aunt of mine, not particularly close,

but someone I once knew well. Her name was Irma D. She had lived in Czechoslovakia and had fallen victim to the war. Exactly where or when she died we still do not know, for she, along with thousands of others, just disappeared under the Nazi occupation of her homeland. I found out about her sad end in 1945, when communications were restored with Europe. But this was 1959, and I really had not thought of her for many years. So it was with surprise that I found this sign of life, if you will, from a relative. Of course I went to my family album on returning home, to make sure it was she. I did not have the identical picture, but I had a group photograph taken more or less about the same period of her life. In this group shot, Irma is the girl on the right. The one on the left is my later mother, and the one in the middle a mutual school friend of both girls. This was taken when both sisters were still single; the psychic face, however, dates to her early years of marriage, a period one might think she would have considered her best and happiest years.

I took the psychic likeness and presented it to my father, a total skeptic at that time, without telling him anything about it. Instantly he recognized his late sister-in-law. I tested various other relatives, and the results were the same. I was so intrigued with all this that I implored Myers to give us another sitting immediately. He acceded to my request and on August 6, 1959, we met again at Myers' apartment. This time photographic film rather than paper was to be used, and a camera was brought into the room. The camera itself was a bellows type using 120-size film, and there was nothing unusual about its appearance. Myers used cut film rather than roll film, and the bellows

seemed to be in perfect condition when I examined the camera. But there is romance connected with the history of this old camera. It used to belong to the celebrated British psychic photographers William Hope and, later, Mrs. Deane, and passed into Myers' hands in 1930, coming with him to America five years later.

Again present were the photographer Hagedorn and attorney Gerstein, along with two ladies, Gail Benedict, a publicist, and Mrs. Riccardi, an astrologer and artist. Hagedorn and Gerstein had bought the film at Kodak in New York, and the materials were in Hagedorn's possession until the moment when he and Gerstein loaded the camera in full view of the two ladies and myself. Farther back in the apartment, a group of about ten other persons watched the entire experiment, without taking part in it. It took somewhat longer to develop the exposed film than the paper of the first experiment, but again strange "extras" appeared on the film. In addition, the paper experiment was repeated and several faces appeared on the sheets, none of them, however, known to me or identified. This is not surprising, as psychic photography mediums are rare and the number of persons wishing to communicate from "over there" is presumably very great. For what is more vital than to let those left behind know that life does go on? I kept in touch with Myers after this experiment, but we did not try our hands again at it for some time.

One day in 1960 I visited his office and he told me of some pictures he had recently taken by himself. I realized that these were not as valid as those taken under my eyes,

Hans Holzer's Aunt Irma in the psychic photograph

but it seemed to me rather ludicrous to assume that Myers would spend an evening trying to defraud himself! So I asked to be shown the pictures. Strangely, Myers felt compelled to show me but one of the pictures. I blanched when I looked at it. Though not as sharp as an "ordinary" photograph, the portrait was clearly that of a dear young friend of mine who had died unhappily not long before. At no time had I discussed her with Myers, nor had Myers ever met her in life. To be doubly sure I showed the picture to the young lady's mother and found her agreeing with me. At various séances and sittings this girl had made her presence known to me, often through strange mediums who did not even know my name or who had never met me until then. So it did not exactly come as a shock to see this further proof of continued desire to communicate.

It was not until the summer of 1961 that Myers and I again discussed a major experiment. PM East, produced then by channel 5 New York, came to me with a request to put together a "package" of psychic experiments. I decided to include Myers and his psychic photography prominently. It was not easy to convince him to step into this kind of limelight, with all its limitations and pressures, but in the end he agreed to come. We made our conditions known, and Mike Wallace accepted them on behalf of the show. Wallace, a total skeptic, was to purchase ordinary photographic paper in a shop of his own choice and keep it on his person until air time. This he did, and the sealed, untampered-with paper was produced by him when the three of us went on camera. The developing and fixation liquids as well as the bowls were also supplied by the studio. Myers waited patiently in the wings while other segments of the program were telecast. All this time Wallace had the paper and liquids under his control. Finally we proceeded to take our seats onstage, with Myers on my left and Wallace on my right, perched on wooden stools without backs. The sole source of light now was an overhead yellow bulb, 60 watts in strength, and all the studio lights were turned off.

Immediately upon being on camera, the experiment began. When Wallace opened the package of sealed papers, and threw them one by one into the first liquid, immediately forms started to appear where no forms should appear, as we were dealing with totally virgin photographic paper. If by some freak condition these papers could have been exposed, then they should at the very least have appeared identical. This, however, was not the case. Several were totally blank, while others showed amorphous shapes and figures, one a human arm, one a head and one an as yet indistinct face. At this point a commercial made continuation of the experiment impossible, and the results were less than conclusive as far as the television audience was concerned. Something had, of course, appeared on the unexposed papers, but what? After the show I examined the dried prints carefully. One of them clearly showed a very fine portrait of my late mother, who had died exactly four years before the experiment took place. Now I had not thought of having my late mother put in an appearance, so to speak, to convince the skeptics of survival, nor had Myers any access to my family album. In fact Myers did not know that my mother had passed away.

Certainly Wallace did not manufacture this picture, for he was a firm nonbeliever in the possibility of personal survival. And I, as the researcher, certainly would know better than to produce a fake picture of my own mother if I intended to put over a trick. If anyone's mother, then Wallace's or Myers', certainly not my own, when I was the one person who did have access to a likeness of my mother! The fact that the portrait which thus appeared is that of my late mother is less important than the fact that *any* face appeared at all, for even *that* is paranormal. Even if Myers had wanted to forge this psychic photograph, he would not have been able to do so. The picture of my mother in the family album is not accessible and had to be searched out from storage by me in order to match it up with the psychic image. I also had the negative stored away. The similarity is striking, notably the form of the nose and the parting of the hair; but there is a certain *glow* about the psychic photograph that is not present in the portrait made during her lifetime. The white, cottonlike substance surrounding the face is what I call a "matrix," made up from substance drawn from Myers' body in some fashion and, in my opinion, superimposed on the light-sensitive paper, thus making it, in addition, *physically* sensitive. On this "film upon a film," then a thought form of my later mother was imbedded, very much like a wire photo, except that the machine that made this possible was Myers' *body*.

Controlled experiments of this kind have established that communications from the so-called dead can indeed be received under conditions excluding any form of fraud, delusion, or self-delusion. Needless, perhaps, to add that no financial rewards whatever were involved for Myers in this experiment.

My next session with Myers came about as a result of United Press reporter Pat Davis' interest in the subject. I asked Myers that we try another experiment, and he agreed to do so on April 25, 1964. On this occasion the photographic paper was purchased by a trio of outsiders, Dr. S. A. Bell, a dentist, a female associate of the doctor's, and Miss Lee Perkins of New York City. They accompanied Myers to a store of their own selection, where the paper was bought and initialed by them in the usual manner. Myers never touched the package. Three packages had been bought from a batch of photographic paper, presumed to be identical in all respects. The initialed three packages were then placed in a large envelope and the envelope sealed and stapled in the presence of attorney Gerstein. Gerstein then took charge of the paper and kept it with him until that evening when he brought it to the Myers apartment for the experiment.

In full view of all those present—about a dozen observers unfamiliar with the subject matter, plus Miss Davis and myself—Gerstein placed the three packages on the table and brought out three basins filled with developing and fixation liquids and water. Pat Davis, who had never met Myers until then, now stepped forward and, on Myers' suggestion, picked one of the three packages, which again was examined by Gerstein and me carefully as to possible violations. There were none. Miss Davis then opened the package and, one by one, placed the photographic paper sheets contained in it onto the first pan. All this was in full electric light, with the observers standing close by around the table.

As soon as the sheets touched the first liquid, forms and faces began to appear on them, varying from sheet to sheet. Among them was a clear likeness of the late Frank Navroth, immediately identified by Gerstein, who knew this man before his death. Another photograph was that of a young girl who had passed on five or six years ago and was identified by one of the observers present, Dan Kriger, an oil executive. Several people recognized the likeness of the late Congressman Adolph Sabath also. Pat Davis then requested that Myers leave the room so that we could determine whether his bodily nearness had any influence on the outcome of the experiment. Myers agreed and went to another part of the apartment. Pat Davis then took the second of the packages and opened it and again submerged the sheets in it exactly as she had done with the first package. Nothing happened. All sheets were blank and exactly alike, a little fogged from the exposure to the strong room light, but without any distinguishing marks whatever. She then opened the third and last package and did the same. Again nothing appeared on the sheets. Finally we used a few sheets still remaining in the first package, and again the results were negative as long as Myers was not within the same room.

AUTHENTIC "SPIRIT PICTURES" TAKEN AT SÉANCES

Myers was not the only reputable psychic photography medium. For many years I worked with New Yorker Betty Ritter in cases involving her major talents as a clairvoyant. She is a medium who supplies valid information from the so-called dead and predicts events before they become objective reality. In this area Betty Ritter was excellent. She also developed her psychic photography to a point where it deserves to be taken very seriously.

Miss Ritter was a middle-aged woman of Italian descent, a pensioner who lived quietly and occasionally saw friends of friends who wanted professional "readings" or psychic consultations. She was a sincere spiritualist and also a devoted Catholic. Any thought of fraud or commercialism was completely alien to her character, and she remained a person of very modest circumstances. On the occasions when I requested photographic prints of her negatives she would not even ask for her own expenses.

From about 1955 on, Betty Ritter obtained unusual photographs with her old-fashioned bellows camera, results that came as much as a surprise to her as to the people she photographed. She was guided by an intuitive feeling that she should photograph the audiences where psychic energies might be present, perhaps as a result of large-scale production of thought forms, prayers, and other man-made force fields. She took her camera with her whenever going to a spiritualist church or meeting, or when sitting privately with people whom she knew well enough to be relaxed with. I often examined her camera and found it in perfect working order. She used standard film and average developing laboratories. Many years later, she finally learned to print from her negatives, although she did not develop them herself. By no means was Betty Ritter a photographic technician. Some of the many pictures I have in my files that were taken by her, were snapped in my presence, others under conditions I consider satisfactory. I have selected four outstanding photographs from them, although each photograph is merely one of several similar ones obtained on the same roll of film and under similar conditions.

Both the medium and I considered the white lines to the left and the round ball to be concentrations of psychic energy. They cannot be explained by any kind of faulty equipment or materials. Pictures of this type are not too rare, and there seems to be a connection between the number of persons present in the room and the intensity of the phenomena. If ectoplasm is a substance drawn from the bodies of emotionally stimulated sitters, and I think it is, then this substance must assemble in some form or shape before it can be utilized via thought direction to perform some intelligent task. I think these streaks, known as "rods," are the raw materials that are used also in material-

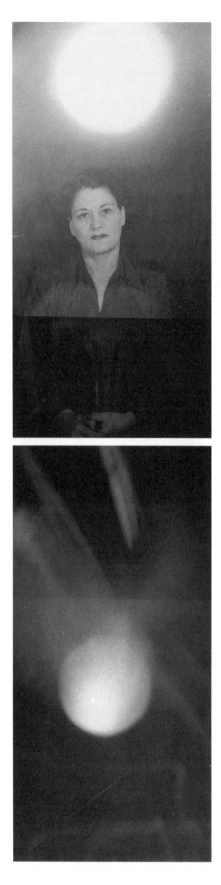

izations of the dead, when these are genuine phenomena, and in poltergeist cases, when objects seemingly move of their own volition. This material, isolated some years ago in London and found to be a moist, smelly whitish substance related to albumen, undoubtedly comes from the body glands of the medium and her sitters or helpers. It is later returned to the sources, or that portion of it not used up at the end of the séance. It can be molded like wax into any form or shape. Strange as this may sound, it is thought direction that does the molding.

In the case of the spiritualist séance picture, no such molding took place, and what we see on the picture is merely the free ectoplasm as it is manufactured and assembled. The naked eye does not normally see this, of course. But then the human eye does not register much of the spectrum, either. The combination of sensitive camera and sensitive photographer or operator seems to be the catalyst to put this material onto photographic film. Just how this works we do not know fully, but it happens frequently under similar conditions and in all such cases faulty materials or cameras have been ruled out.

One of those present at this small gathering in Reverend Boyd's church was Helen M., whose father had died seven years before. He had lost a leg in his physical life. The communicator, through the medium, wanted to prove his identity in some form and proposed to show his severed leg as a kind of signature, while at the same time making a point of his having two good legs once more in *his* world.

On the print (which matches the negative which I have seen) the white substance of the "new" leg is superimposed on the leg of the sitter. There appear to be two extra hands in the picture, while the rest of the photograph is sharp, pointing to supernormal origin of the extras rather than conventional double exposure—the rest of the picture is sharply defined. It is my opinion that ectoplasm was molded through thought into the desired shapes and the latter then made capable of being photographed.

As the psychic photographer develops his or her skill, the extras become more sophisticated until they eventually are faces or entire figures. With Betty Ritter it started with concentrations of power or ectoplasm, and later included such higher forms of imagery as hands, a cross symbol and, eventually, writing. In 1965 I had recommended a young lady named Trudy S. to Betty. I had unsuccessfully tried to break the hold a dead person evidently had on her. This was probably due to the fact that Trudy herself is psychic and therefore supplies the desired entrance way. The attentions of this young man, who died in a car accident and had been a friend of the young woman's during his lifetime, were not welcomed by Miss S. after his death. I thought that perhaps Betty Ritter, being a strong medium (which I decidedly am not), might be able to "outdraw"

the unwelcome intruder and, as it turned out, I was right in my suggestion.

During the time when Trudy S. went to see Betty Ritter to break the hold of the dead man, she also had a boyfriend in her physical world. But the intruder from beyond the veil kept interfering until the couple broke up, largely because of the situation. On March 3, 1965, Trudy S. had a sitting with Betty during which Betty took some photographs. On one of them, imbedded in the well-known "cotton wool" of psychic photography, there appears the word ROME in black letters. Nothing in the negative, the camera, the film or the paper can account for this writing. Why ROME? At the time of the sitting Trudy's boyfriend was in Italy and on his way to Rome.

SPIRIT PHOTOGRAPHY AT A CAMP

Spiritualist camps have been the subject of much controversy and investigation as to their honesty, and are at best a mixed bag of evidence. Years ago the late Eileen Garrett commissioned me to look into fake materializations at some of the camps. I found many of the resident psychic readers at these camps to be honest and the number of fraudulent cases small. Nevertheless, they do happen and one must guard against being too trusting when visiting these places.

Maggy Conn was a well-known newspaper columnist for a string of Eastern newspapers. In February 1982 she asked me to examine a picture taken in 1947 at Camp Silverbelle, in Ephrata, Pennsylvania.

While neither Maggy nor I know who the manifesting spirit in the photograph is, it does appear to match in texture and general appearance the kind of spirit pictures taken under test conditions, so I have no reason to doubt it.

SOME UNEXPECTED SPIRIT FACES

Mary Krauss of Boston, Massachusetts, contacted me in late September 1972 because of an odd spirit picture she had taken.

The little boy holding the cat in this picture, taken in October 1965 in Pearl River, New York, is apparently quite unaware of any "presence," but the cat evidently is not, as she stares, not into the camera or at the photographer, but at "something" she can see to the left of the boy, which neither he nor the photographer could see.

The swirling white mass on the lower right of the picture contains two faintly visible faces, which Mrs. Krauss circled. At the time, only the little boy, Krauss' brother, and Mrs. Krauss herself were in the room with the cat. But whose face or faces is it?

Shortly after Mrs. Krauss' family moved into the house, it became clear that they were not alone though they could not actually see a presence. On cleaning out the attic, however, they noticed that objects had been moved about, and sensed a strong presence in the area. It was in the attic that the picture was taken. Could it be the previous occupant wanted to manifest his or her continued presence in the house?

PHOTOGRAPHING MATERIALIZATIONS

Born in Westphalia in 1911, Hanna Hamilton was always "unusual" to her family. She had an uncanny (but uncontrollable) ability to produce psychic photographs.

In early August 1977 Miss Hamilton attempted to take a photograph of her living room toward her outdoor garden (see the following page). Only Hanna and her cats were in the room at the time. Picture her surprise when a whitish female body (Hamilton called her "the streaker")

Hanna Hamilton's materialization picture

Hanna Hamilton—psychic photographer

appeared in the picture. But what appears to be a nude is really a white materialization made of ectoplasm.

Hamilton had no idea who the visitor was, but with so many "spirit friends" in her earthly life, it might have been anyone's guess.

Dixie Tomkins, a very religious lady in Troy, Michigan, contacted me regarding a series of unusual photographs taken in December 1968 during the christening of one of her children (opposite page). Mrs. Tomkins had been psychic all her life, and the picture did not surprise her, but she turned to me for an explanation.

A materialized male figure appears in the picture, close to the baby, evidently watching the ceremony.

This also seems to show that such ectoplastic figures can be invisible to the naked eye but not to the camera. That is, if and when a psychic catalyst is present in close vicinity.

THE PHYSICIAN, CATHERINE THE GREAT, AND POLAROID SPIRIT PHOTOGRAPHY

Dr. Andrew von Salza, a West Coast physician originally without any interest in psychic matters, began to realize that he had a strange gift for psychic photography. He was a jolly and successful man with medical degrees from the Universities of Berlin and Tartu (Estonia). A leading rejuvenation specialist in California, he was nothing more than an amateur shutterbug without the slightest interest in anything supernormal or psychic. Unexpected and totally unwarranted "extras" have appeared on his photographs, both those taken with regular cameras and with the speedy Polaroid type. He had known of my interest in psychic research through a mutual friend, Gail Benedict, the public-relations director of the Savoy-Hilton, where he usually stayed. Although I had heard about his strange encounters with this subject, my only previous meeting with the doctor was on a social occasion, where others were present and when the chance to discuss the matter deeply did not present itself. At that time, too, von Salza met my ex-wife, Catherine, and was told that she was of Russian descent, to which he remarked that he was a Balt himself. But neither the doctor nor my wife went into any detailed history of her background.

Finally, in March 1966, von Salza arrived in New York on business and unexpectedly telephoned me, offering to experiment in my presence, as I had so long desired him to do. We arranged for a get-together at our house on Sunday, March 13, and I asked Gail Benedict to bring the doctor over. In addition, a friend of Miss Benedict's, Mrs. Marsha Slansky, a designer and not particularly experienced in matters of psychic research, joined us as an additional observer. Shortly after their arrival, the doctor suddenly requested that my wife seat herself in an armchair at the far end of the living room, because he felt the urge to take a picture of her. It was at this point that I examined the camera and film and satisfied myself that no fraud could have taken place.

The first picture taken showed a clear superimposition, next to my wife, of a female figure, made up of a white, semitransparent substance (see page 754). As a trained historian I immediately recognized that as an attempted portrait of Catherine the Great. The sash of her

Materialization photographs by Dixie Tomkins of Troy, Michigan

order, which she liked to wear in many of her official portraits, stood out quite clearly on this print. We continued to expose the rest of the pack, and still another pack which I purchased at a corner drugstore a little later that evening, but the results were negative except for some strange light streaks which could not be accounted for normally. The doctor handed me the original picture, and the following day I had a laboratory try to make me a duplicate which I was to send him for the record. Unfortunately the results were poor, the sash did not show at all in the reproduction, and I was told that this was the best they could do because the original was a Polaroid picture and not as easily copied as an ordinary print. At any rate I mailed this poor copy to Andrew von Salza in San Francisco with my explanation and regrets. To my surprise we received a letter from him, dated March 25, 1966, in which he enclosed two pictures of the same subject. Only this time the figure of Catherine the Great was sharp and detailed, much more so than in the original picture and, in fact, superimposed on the whitish outline of the first photograph. The whole thing looked so patently fraudulent at first glance that I requested exact data on how this second "round" was taken. Not that I suspected the doctor of malpractice, but I am a researcher and cannot afford to be noble.

Von Salza obliged. When he had received my poor copy of his fine psychic picture, he had tacked it to a blank wall in a corner of his San Francisco apartment in order to rephotograph it. Why he did this he cannot explain, except that he felt "an urge" to do so. He used a Crown Graphic camera with Polaroid back, size 4 x 5, an enlarging lens opening of F/32, with the camera mounted on a tropod about a yard or less away from the subject. His exposure for the rephotographing experiment was one second by daylight plus one 150-watt lamp.

Furthermore, Dr. von Salza offered to repeat the experiment in my presence whenever I came to San Francisco. What struck me as remarkable about the whole business was of course the fact, unknown to the doctor, that my ex-wife Catherine is a direct sixth-generation descendant of Catherine the Great. This was not discussed with him until after the first picture was obtained. Nevertheless Gail Benedict reported that on the way over to our apartment, von Salza suddenly and cryptically asked, "Why do I keep thinking of Catherine the Great?" Now had he wanted to defraud us, surely he would not have tipped his hand in this manner. The two rephotographed pictures sent to me by the doctor are not identical; on one of them a crown appears over my ex-wife's head! Several psychics with whom my ex-wife and I have "sat," who knew nothing whatever about my ex-wife or her background, have remarked that they "saw" a royal personality protecting my

wife. New York medium Betty Ritter even described her by name as Catherine. It is true also that my ex-wife has a strong interest in the historical Catherine, and finds herself drawn frequently to books dealing with the life of the Empress. Although her sisters and brothers are equally close in descent to the Russian ruler, they do not show any particular affinity toward her.

The whole matter of these pictures was so outlandish that I felt either they were clever frauds and that I was being duped (although I did not see how this was possible under my stringent conditions) or that the material had to be factual, appearances to the contrary. Circumstantial evidence can be very misleading in so controversial a subject as psychic photography and I was determined not to allow opinions, pro or con, to influence my findings in this case.

Psychic photograph of Catherine the Great appearing with her descendant

Contemporary print of Catherine the Great

Clearer psychic picture of Catherine the Great

Consequently, I went to San Francisco in May 1966, to test the good doctor. In my presence he took the original picture and mounted it on the wall, then placed film into his Crown Graphic camera with a Polaroid back. I inspected camera and film and nothing had been tampered with. The first two pictures yielded results; again a clear imprint of Catherine the Great was superimposed on the whitish outline of the original. But this time Catherine extended an arm toward her descendant! In her extended right hand the Empress tendered a crown to my ex-wife, but the two pictures are otherwise somewhat different in detail and intensity, although taken one after the other

under identical light and exposure conditions *in my presence*. At this point I confess I became somewhat impatient and said aloud, "I wish Catherine would give us a message. What is she trying to tell us?" As if I had committed *lèse majestè*, the psychic camera fell silent; the next picture showed nothing further than the whitish outline. We discontinued the experiment at this point. I inspected the camera once more and then left the doctor.

Before we parted I once more inspected the camera. It looked just like any ordinary Crown Graphic does, except for the Polaroid back. The enlarging lens was still set at F/32; the exposure, I knew, had been just one second, using ordinary daylight reinforced by one 150-watt lamp. Dr. von Salza later sent me a cheerful note in which he said, "Seeing is believing, but even seeing, so many cannot believe, including myself." He found the whole situation very amusing and made no serious effort to do much about it scientifically, except that he did cooperate with me whenever I asked him to.

Von Salza's first encounter with the uncanny was in 1963, when the widow of a colleague of his, Dr. Benjamin Sweetland, asked him to do a photo portrait of her. Von Salza obliged, but imagine their surprise when the face of the late husband appeared superimposed on a lampshade in the room. No double exposure, no fraud, no rational explanation for this phenomenon could be found, although von Salza, with his worldly training, insisted that "there had to be some other explanation!" To test this situation, he decided to photograph the widow Sweetland again, but with another camera and outdoors. Using a Leica and color film, and making sure that all was in order he found to his

amazement that one of the 20 exposures showed the late doctor's face against the sky.

Dismissing the whole incident for want of an explanation and trying his best to forget it, he was again surprised when another incident took place. This time he was merely using up the last picture in his roll, shooting at random against the wall of his own room. When the roll was developed, there appeared on the wall the face of a young girl that had not been there when he took the picture. He was upset by this and found himself discussing the matter with a friend and patient of his by the name of Mrs. Pierson. She asked to be shown the picture. On inspection, she blanched. Andrew von Salza had somehow photographed the face of her "dead" young daughter. Although the doctor knew of the girl's untimely death, he had never seen her in life.

Several more incidents of this nature convinced the doctor that he had somehow stumbled onto a very special talent, like it or not. He began to investigate the subject to find out if others also had his kind of "problems." Among the people interested in psychic phenomena in the San Francisco area was Evelyn Nielsen, with whom von Salza later shared a number of experiments. He soon discovered that her presence increased the incidence rate of psychic "extras" on his exposures, although Miss Nielsen herself never took a psychic photograph without von Salza's presence, proving that it was he who was the mainspring of the phenomenon.

I have examined these photographs and am satisfied that fraud is out of the question for a number of reasons, chiefly technical, since most of them were taken with Polaroid cameras and developed on the spot before competent witnesses, including myself.

In early May 1965 I went to San Francisco to observe Dr. von Salza at work—psychic photography work, that is, not his regular occupation, which is never open to anyone but the subjects! I fortified myself with the company of two "outsiders," my sister-in-law, Countess Marie Rose Buxhoeveden, and a friend, social worker Lori Wyn, who came with me to von Salza's apartment. There we met the doctor, Evelyn Nielsen, and Mrs. Sweetland, as well as two other ladies, friends of the doctor's, who had been sympathetic to the subject at hand. It was late afternoon, and we all had dinner engagements, so we decided to get started right away.

With a sweeping gesture the doctor invited me to inspect the camera, already on its tripod facing the wall, or, as he called it, his "ghost corner," for he had always had best results by shooting away from the bright windows toward the darker portion of his big living room. The walls were bare except for an Indian wall decoration and a portrait of the doctor. In a way, they reminded me of motion-picture screens in their smoothness and blue-gray texture. But there was absolutely nothing on those walls that could be blamed for what eventually appeared "on" them.

I stepped up to the camera and looked inside, satisfying myself that nothing had been pasted in the bellows or gizmo, or on the lens. Then I looked at the film, which was an ordinary Polaroid film pack, black-and-white, and there was no evidence of its having been tampered with. The only way to do this, by the way, would have been to slit open the pack and insert extraneous matter into the individual pieces of film, something requiring great skill, total darkness and time. Even then traces of the cuttings would

Psychic photograph taken by Mae Burrows

Cecilia Hoods' psychic photograph

have to appear. The pack Dr. von Salza used was fresh and untouched.

The room was bright enough, as light streamed in from the windows opposite the L-shaped couch which lined the walls. The seven of us now sat down on the couch. Von Salza set the camera and exposed the first piece of film. Within sight of all of us, he developed the film in the usual fast Polaroid manner and then showed it to me. Over our heads there appear clearly four extra portraits, and the wall can be seen through them. I did not recognize any of the four in this instance. The doctor continued, this time including himself in the picture by presetting the camera and then taking his place next to Evelyn Nielsen on the couch.

The second picture, when developed, evoked some gasps of recognition from the audience. Four faces of various sizes appeared and a light-shaft (of psychic energy?) also was now evident on the left side of the photograph. But the gasp of recognition was due to the likeness of the late John D. Rockefeller, Sr. I might add here that this gentleman must have an avid interest in communicating with the world he left in 1937 at age 90. His face has appeared in other instances of psychic photography, especially in Britain with John Myers.

MAE BURROWS' GHOSTLY FAMILY PICTURE

Mae Burrows has long since joined her family on "the other side of life." But for many years she was the undis-

puted premier medium in Cincinnati, Ohio, and her reputation as such, and a devout spiritualist, was similar to the celebrated mediums of turn-of-the-century England.

In 1930 a photographer friend visited Mrs. Burrows, and asked to photograph her with a plate camera, then the best way of taking photographs. She readily agreed to sit for him, and the result was indeed startling, though not so much to the medium as to the photographer.

Instead of getting just a nice portrait of his friend, the photographer captured images of a lot of "extras."

First of all, there is the picture of Mrs. Burrow's Indian guide, and while investigators may have differing opinions about the prevalence of Indians among spirit guides (controls), the fact is, most professional mediums do have them, perhaps because Indian shamans were so close to being spiritualist mediums.

I saw Mrs. Burrows in 1970 and again in 1971, when she described the others in the remarkable photograph. There are three women in the picture, which she identified as her great-grandmother who died seventy-five years prior, her aunt who had been gone for seventy-three years, and her sister, who died sixty-four years before our meeting. As for the men, they were two medical doctors named Crowley and Ramey, and the man who turns his head sideways in the picture was a friend of the family who had taken his own life seventy-six years before.

Group spirit pictures like this are not so rare and
have been obtained under strictest test conditions. There is
no question as to the authenticity of this one.

A GHOSTLY APPARITION IN THE SKY

Reports of miraculous apparitions of the Virgin Mary, even
of Jesus, and of various angels and saints, come to public
attention from time to time. Invariably, the believers
immediately flock to such sites mainly to obtain miraculous
cures, or at least be spiritually enriched.

Since ancient times, people have reported these
events, usually interpreting them as the spirit visitations of
heavenly personalities. Rarely has anyone who actually
observed such an apparition considered the visions to be
spiritual beings of lesser stature, such as relatives or friends
of worshippers, or simply people who have passed on to
the next stage of existence, and for one or the other reason,
decided to manifest in this manner and place.

An interesting and unsought photograph was taken
by Cecilia Hood, a very spiritual lady from upstate New
York. Rev. Hood is an ordained spiritual minister and has
practiced as such for many years. On October 14, 1975,
she shared with me an extraordinary original photograph
which falls into this category. The picture was actually
taken in 1971 during a terrible storm in rural Pennsylvania
by Rev. Hood's friend and associate Margie Brooks. There
was a terrible flood and the sky was very dark. Suddenly
Miss Brooks observed a figure in white in the sky and took
this picture. Was it a way those from the other side wanted
to reassure her of her safety?

THE PARISH HOUSE GHOSTS

Ron and Nancy Stallings head the Maryland Committee
for Psychical Research, a body of researchers I helped create some years ago. The Stallings are dedicated, scientifi-
cally-oriented people. When I first met this couple, they
lived with their children in a haunted house near Baltimore, which I investigated and we eventually put down as
a solved case.

Since then, the Stallings have taken their camera to
many haunted places and come up with positive results of
photographs taken under test conditions. Nancy is
undoubtedly the catalyst as she is a strong medium.

Three pictures taken by Ron and Nancy at a haunted
parish house in Baltimore County, are presented here for
the first time in print.

Photo A shows Nancy, the dark woman on the right.
There appear to be three figures in the doorway, one of
which is indeed very clear. When the photo was taken,
there wasn't anyone in that doorway.

A

B

C

Hans Holzer with ghost of Pennsylvania Boatsman at the Black Bass Inn—photographed by Rosemary Khalil

Photo B shows three people standing in an empty doorway—it appeared empty when Ron took this picture!

Photo C shows Nancy standing on the right, being hugged by what she described as a little girl, and two standing figures again in the same doorway. Nancy reported that they recorded a child's voice at the same time, calling out for "Mommy" and literally following the investigators around as they made their way about the premises of the old parish house.

Books Previously Published by Hans Holzer

CURRENT

The Secret of Healing: The power of the healer Ze'ev Kolman

Healing Beyond Medicine: Alternative paths to wellness

Prophecies: Truth, Possibilities, or Fallacies?

The Directory of Psychics

Life Beyond

Hans Holzer's Haunted America

Great American Ghost Stories

Real Hauntings

The Power of Hypnosis

Tales at Midnight

The Psychic Side of Dreams

The Ghosts of Old Europe

Hans Holzer's Haunted House Album

Where the Ghosts Are

True Ghost Stories

Yankee Ghosts

Dixie Ghosts

Ghosts of New England

The Lively Ghosts of Ireland

Are You Psychic? ESP and you and the truth about ESP

Window to the Past

In Quest of Ghosts

Ghost Hunter

Ghosts I've Met

Gothic Ghosts

The Ghosts that Walk in Washinton

Westghosts

The Spirits of '76

In Search of Ghosts

some of My Best Friends are Ghosts

The Truth About Witchcraft

The New Pagans

The Witchcraft Report

Star in the East

The UFOnauts: New Facts on Extraterrestrial landings

The Habsburg Curse

Word Play

Murder in Amityville: Amityville II The Possession

America's Mysterious Places

America's Haunted Houses

America's Restless Ghosts: Psychic photography

Elvis Speaks From Beyond

Ghostly Lovers: True cases of love beyond the grave

Born Again

Life After Death: The challenge and the evidence

The Handbook of Parapsychology

The Great British Ghost Hunt

Patterns of Destiny

The Truth About ESP

ESP and You

Predictions — Fact or Fallacy?

The Prophets Speak

Psychic Investigator

Best True Ghost Stories

The Powers of the New Age

Possessed

The Psychic World of Bishop Pike

The Directory of the Occult

The Psydhic World of Plants

The Human Dynamo

Charismatics: How to make things happen for you

How to Cope with Problems
Speed Thinking
How to Win at Life
Astrology: What it can do for you
The Vegetarian Way of Life
The Aquarian Age
Psycho-Ecstasy

FICTION

The Alchemist
Heather, Confessions of a Witch
The Clairvoyant
The Entry
The Amityville Curse
The Secret Amityville
The Zodiac Affairs
Circle of Love
The Randy Knowles Adventure Series:
    The Red Chindvit Conspiracy
    The Alchemy Deception
    The Unicorn